SEVENTH EDITION

Educational Psychology

Developing Learners

Jeanne Ellis Ormrod

Professor Emerita, University of Northern Colorado

University of New Hampshire

PEARSON

Bost[illegible]olumbus • Indianapolis • New York • San Francisco • Upper Saddle River

Amsterdam • [illegible] Town • Dubai • London • Madrid • Milan • Munich • Paris • Montreal • Toronto

Delhi • Me[illegible]ity • Sao Paula • Sydney • Hong Kong • Seoul • Singapore • Taipei • Tokyo

Editor-in-Chief: Paul A. Smith
Development Editor: Christina Robb
Editorial Assistant: Matthew Buchholz
Vice President, Director of Marketing: Quinn Perkson
Marketing Manager: Jared Brueckner
Production Editor: Annette Joseph
Editorial Production Service: Marty Tenney, Modern Graphics, Inc.
Manufacturing Buyer: Megan Cochran
Electronic Composition: Modern Graphics, Inc.
Interior Design: Denise Hoffman, Glenview Studios
Photo Researcher: Annie Pickert
Cover Designer: Studio Montage

For related titles and support materials, visit our online catalog at www.pearsonhighered.com.

Library of Congress Cataloging-in-Publication Data
Ormrod, Jeanne Ellis.
Educational psychology : developing learners / Jeanne Ellis Ormrod. -- 7td.
p. cm.
Includes bibliographical references and index.
ISBN-13: 978-0-13-700114-9
ISBN-10: 0-13-700114-2
1. Educational psychology. 2. Teaching. 3. Learning. 4. Classroom management. I. Title.
LB1051.O66 2011
370.15--dc22

2009034081

Printed in the United States of America

10 9 8 7 6 5 4 3 CIN 13 12 11 10

Photo credits appear on p. P–1, which constitutes an extension of thpyright page.

PEARSON

www.pearsonhighered.com

3N-10: 0-13-700114-2
3N-13: 978-0-13-700114-9

About the Author

Jeanne Ellis Ormrod received her A.B. in psychology from Brown University and her M.S. and Ph.D. in educational psychology from The Pennsylvania State University. She earned licensure in school psychology through postdoctoral work at Temple University and the University of Colorado at Boulder and has worked as a middle school geography teacher and school psychologist. She was Professor of Educational Psychology at the University of Northern Colorado until 1998, when she moved east to return to her native New England. She is currently affiliated with the University of New Hampshire, where she occasionally teaches courses in educational psychology and research methods. She has published numerous research articles on cognition and memory, cognitive development, and giftedness, but she is probably best known for this textbook and four others: *Human Learning* (currently in its fifth edition); *Essentials of Educational Psychology* (currently in its second edition); *Child Development and Education* (co-authored with Teresa McDevitt, currently in its fourth edition); and *Practical Research* (co-authored with Paul Leedy, currently in its ninth edition). With her three children now grown and out on their own, she lives in New Hampshire with her husband Richard.

Brief Contents

Contents

Preface

New to This Edition

The seventh edition of *Educational Psychology: Developing Learners* expands on the strengths found in previous editions that make this book one of the most popular educational psychology textbooks for both instructors and students. The seventh edition includes:

- **A sharpened focus on the core principles of educational psychology**
  - Specific instructional objectives have been added to each chapter to keep students' reading on target.
  - The book has been significantly streamlined in this edition to ensure that information is presented efficiently and accessibly. The book is now 15 chapters long, making the contents easier to cover in a single academic term.
- **Additional opportunities for readers to see those principles in action**
  - Video examples allow students to explore the principles of educational psychology through the actions and words of children from various age-groups.
- **Additional opportunities to apply the principles**
  - Classroom applications are not limited to the text. Accompanying the book is an exciting new online resource, MyEducationLab, which provides readers with opportunities to apply the core principles and build their teaching skills.

Many details throughout the book have changed as well. As always, I've updated every chapter with recent research findings and citations. The "Big Picture" sections at the end of each chapter have been revised to better emphasize key principles of their respective chapters. Other noteworthy additions and changes to this edition include the following:

- **Every chapter:** Specific instructional objectives that students should strive to accomplish as they read the chapter; many features within MyEducationLab are closely aligned with these objectives.
- **Chapter 1:** Discussion of teaching as evidence-based practice; new section on qualitative research; expanded discussion of action research.
- **Chapter 2:** New opening case study called "Apple Tarts" (in the previous edition, this case appeared in the middle of Chapter 7); new sections on Bronfenbrenner's ecological systems perspective, neo-Piagetian theories, sociocognitive conflict, and dynamic assessment (the last of these moved from one of the assessment chapters to accommodate the wishes of several reviewers); new section on diversity in language development, including specific language impairments and a more in-depth discussion of English language learners.
- **Chapter 3:** Expanded discussion of personality, including the "big five" personality characteristics and goodness of fit; new section on technology and peer relationships, including discussion of cyberbullying.
- **Chapter 4:** Discussions of acculturation and culturally responsive teaching; new section on cultural diversity in emotional expressiveness.
- **Chapter 5:** New section on the Cattell-Horn-Carroll theory of cognitive abilities; discussion of Section 504 of the Rehabilitation Act of 1973 as a means of providing services for students who do not meet the criteria for the Individuals with Disabilities Education Act; discussion of response to intervention as an alternative approach to identifying students with disabilities, especially those with learning disabilities; switch to the term *intellectual disabilities* for students who have mental retardation, in accordance with current trends in special education.
- **Chapter 6:** New opening case study called "Bones" (in the previous edition, this case appeared in the middle of the chapter); broader usage of the term *meaningful learning* to encompass such processes

as elaboration, organization, and visual imagery; new sections on distinctiveness, emotional overtones of cognition (including a discussion of hot cognition), and consolidation as factors affecting long-term memory retrieval and forgetting (in the previous edition, hot cognition appeared only in the discussion of affect in a later chapter).

- **Chapter 7:** Discussion of service learning, problem-based learning, and project-based learning within the context of authentic activities (in the previous edition, these concepts were discussed only in Chapters 3 and 8).
- **Chapter 8:** Significantly updated section on computer technology as a vehicle for promoting problem-solving skills; discussion of the importance of critical thinking in online research.
- **Chapter 9:** Significant reorganization of chapter content; switch to the term *instrumental conditioning* (replacing *operant conditioning*) to accommodate a more integrated discussion of the effects of reinforcement and punishment.
- **Chapter 10:** Discussion of effortful control as a temperamental factor affecting self-regulation.
- **Chapter 11:** Integration of the previous edition's two chapters on motivation and affect into a single chapter; expanded discussion of affect and its interrelationships with motivation, learning, and cognition.
- **Chapter 12:** Discussion of backward design in instructional planning; closer links among state standards, classroom objectives, and instructional strategies (including a substantially revised table that now links state standards, instructional goals, and instructional strategies); significantly updated discussions of technology (e.g., new sections on setting up a class website and making use of instructional websites, expanded discussion of technology-based collaborative learning); expanded discussion of discovery learning to include inquiry learning.
- **Chapter 13:** Significant reorganization to more closely connect the section on preventive strategies with the section on coordinating efforts with others; discussion of I-messages.
- **Chapter 14:** New section on assessment as a means of evaluating the quality of instruction; substantially revised table that now links classroom assessment practices with state standards, instructional goals, and instructional strategies; expanded discussion of rubrics in performance assessment.
- **Chapter 15:** Expanded discussion of portfolios; expanded discussion of cultural and linguistic differences (including English language learners) and their implications for standardized and high-stakes tests.

My Rationale for the Book

As teachers, we play critical roles in the lives of children and adolescents. Some of us help them learn to read and write. Some of us help them understand their physical and social worlds through explorations of science, mathematics, geography, history, or literature. Some of us help them express themselves through physical movement, the visual arts, or music. But regardless of the subject matter we teach, we help the generation that follows us to become knowledgeable, self-confident, and productive citizens.

In my mind, teaching is the most rewarding profession we could possibly choose. Yet it is often a challenging profession as well. Students don't always come to us ready or eager to learn classroom subject matter. How can we help them develop the knowledge and skills they need to become productive adults? What strategies can we use to motivate them? What tasks and instructional materials are appropriate for children at different developmental levels? Over the years, researchers and practitioners have worked together to answer such questions. We are in the fortunate position of being able to benefit from the many insights that such experts offer.

I have been teaching educational psychology since 1974, and I've loved every minute of it. How children and adolescents learn and think, how they change as they grow and develop, why they do the things they do, how they are often very different from one another—our understanding of all of these things has innumerable implications for classroom practice and, ultimately, for the lives of young people.

I have written this textbook in much the same way that I teach my college classes. Because I want the field of educational psychology to captivate you the way it has captivated me, I have tried to make the book interesting, meaningful, and thought-provoking as well as informative. I have a definite philosophy about how future teachers can best learn and apply educational psychology, and this philosophy has guided me as I have written all seven editions of the book. In particular, I believe that human learners of all ages actively construct their own understandings of what they read in textbooks—an idea reflected in the puzzle-piece motif you will see throughout the book.

Helping My Readers Learn and Apply Educational Psychology

You can gain much more from your study of educational psychology when you:

- Focus on core concepts and principles of the discipline
- See these concepts and principles in action in your own learning and behavior
- Use the concepts and principles to understand the learning and behavior of children and adolescents
- Consistently apply the concepts and principles to classroom practice

I have incorporated numerous features into the book to help you do all of these things. I hope that you will learn a great deal from what educational psychology has to offer, not only about the students you will be teaching but also about yourself—a human being who continues to learn and develop even as an adult.

Focusing on Core Concepts and Principles

Rather than superficially explore every aspect of educational psychology, this book zeroes in on fundamental concepts and principles that have broad applicability to classroom practice. Throughout the book, core concepts appear in boldfaced purple font. Core principles are clearly identified in sections labeled "Basic Principles" or "Basic Assumptions" and then often summarized in Principles/Assumptions tables. Each table includes educational implications and concrete examples.

Principles/Assumptions

TABLE 6.2
Basic Assumptions of Cognitive Psychology and Their Educational Implications

Assumption	Educational Implication	Example
Influence of cognitive processes	• Encourage students to think about classroom subject matter in ways that will help them remember it.	• When introducing the concept *mammal*, ask students to identify numerous examples.
Behavior as a reflection of cognitive processes	• Ask students to explain their reasoning, and look closely at what they do and say to make educated guesses about how they are thinking about classroom topics.	• When a student says that 16+19=25 and that 27+27=44, suspect that the student is forgetting to carry when solving two-digit addition problems.
Selectivity about what is learned	• Help students to identify the most important things for them to learn and to understand why these things are important.	• Give students questions they should try to answer as they read their textbooks. Include questions that ask them to apply what they read to their own lives.
Construction of meanings and understandings	• Provide experiences that will help students make sense of the topics they are studying, and regularly	• When studying Nathaniel Hawthorne's *The Scarlet Letter*, have students convene in small

Seeing Concepts and Principles in Action in Your Own Learning

A central goal of this book has always been to help my readers discover more about themselves as thinkers and learners. Thus, I include Experiencing Firsthand exercises throughout the book—exercises that illustrate such diverse concepts as constructive processes, working memory, sense of self, social cognition, ethnic stereotyping, and confidentiality in assessment. All of these exercises are designed to do exactly what their name implies: help my readers observe concepts and principles of educational psychology in themselves.

Remembering 12 Words

Read through the 12 words below *one time only*. Then cover up the page, and write down the words in the order they come to mind.

shirt	table	hat
carrot	bed	squash
pants	potatoes	stool
chair	shoe	bean

Understanding Children's and Adolescents' Learning and Behavior

Throughout the book I continually urge my readers to look closely at and try to make sense of what children and adolescents do and say. Each chapter begins with a Case Study that situates chapter content in a real-life scenario. I also make frequent use of real artifacts from children's journals and school assignments to illustrate concepts and principles in action.

FIGURE 7.4 In this picture 9-year-old Trisha integrates what she has learned about the water cycle.

Examining Developmental Trends Unique to this book is a focus on children's development in every chapter. For example, Chapters 2 through 15 all have one or more Developmental Trends tables that summarize age-typical characteristics at four grade levels (K–2, 3–5, 6–8, and 9–12) and offer suggested classroom strategies for each level.

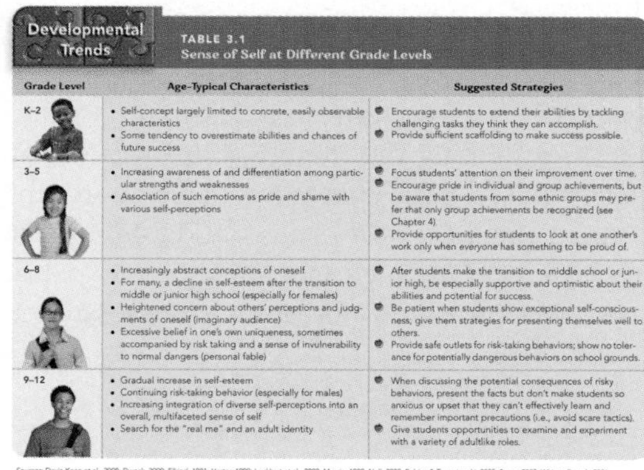

Developmental Trends

TABLE 3.1
Sense of Self at Different Grade Levels

Grade Level	Age-Typical Characteristics	Suggested Strategies
K–2	• Self-concept largely limited to concrete, easily observable characteristics • Some tendency to overestimate abilities and chances of future success	• Encourage students to extend their abilities by tackling challenging tasks they think they can accomplish. • Provide sufficient scaffolding to make success possible.
3–5	• Increasing awareness of and differentiation among particular strengths and weaknesses • Association of such emotions as pride and shame with various self-perceptions	• Focus students' attention on their improvement over time. • Encourage pride in individual and group achievements, but be aware that students from some ethnic groups may prefer that only group achievements be recognized (see Chapter 4). • Provide opportunities for students to look at one another's work only when *everyone* has something to be proud of.
6–8	• Increasingly abstract conceptions of oneself • For many, a decline in self-esteem after the transition to middle or junior high school (especially for females) • Heightened concern about others' perceptions and judgments of oneself (imaginary audience) • Excessive belief in one's own uniqueness, sometimes accompanied by risk taking and a sense of invulnerability to normal dangers (personal fable)	• After students make the transition to middle school or junior high, be especially supportive and optimistic about their abilities and potential for success. • Be patient when students show exceptional self-consciousness; give them strategies for presenting themselves well to others. • Provide safe outlets for risk-taking behaviors; show no tolerance for potentially dangerous behaviors on school grounds.
9–12	• Gradual increase in self-esteem • Continuing risk-taking behavior (especially for males) • Increasing integration of diverse self-perceptions into an overall, multifaceted sense of self • Search for the "real me" and an adult identity	• When discussing the potential consequences of risky behaviors, present the facts but don't make students so anxious or upset that they can't effectively learn and remember important precautions (i.e., avoid scare tactics). • Give students opportunities to examine and experiment with a variety of adultlike roles.

Sources: Davis-Kean et al., 2008; Dweck, 2000; Elkind, 1981; Harter, 1999; Lockhart et al., 2002; Marcia, 1980; Nell, 2002; Robins & Trzesniewski, 2005; Spear, 2007; Whitesell et al., 2006.

Applying Core Ideas of Educational Psychology to Classroom Practice

Throughout this text, psychological concepts and principles are consistently applied to classroom practice. I also provide Into the Classroom and Creating a Productive Classroom Environment boxes that suggest and illustrate strategies related to particular areas of concern for teachers.

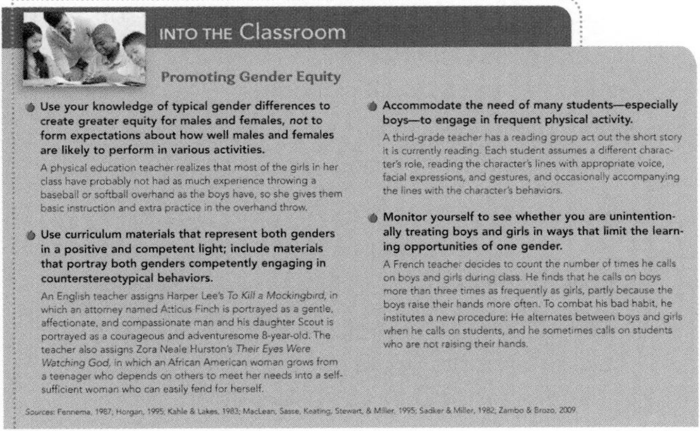

INTO THE Classroom

Promoting Gender Equity

- **Use your knowledge of typical gender differences to create greater equity for males and females, *not* to form expectations about how well males and females are likely to perform in various activities.**
  A physical education teacher realizes that most of the girls in her class have probably not had as much experience throwing a baseball or softball overhand as the boys have, so she gives them basic instruction and extra practice in the overhand throw.
- **Use curriculum materials that represent both genders in a positive and competent light; include materials that portray both genders competently engaging in counterstereotypical behaviors.**
  An English teacher assigns Harper Lee's *To Kill a Mockingbird*, in which an attorney named Atticus Finch is portrayed as a gentle, affectionate, and compassionate man and his daughter Scout is portrayed as a courageous and adventuresome 8-year-old. The teacher also assigns Zora Neale Hurston's *Their Eyes Were Watching God*, in which an African American woman grows from a teenager who depends on others to meet her needs into a self-sufficient woman who can easily fend for herself.
- **Accommodate the need of many students—especially boys—to engage in frequent physical activity.**
  A third-grade teacher has a reading group act out the short story it is currently reading. Each student assumes a different character's role, reading the character's lines with appropriate voice, facial expressions, and gestures, and occasionally accompanying the lines with the character's behaviors.
- **Monitor yourself to see whether you are unintentionally treating boys and girls in ways that limit the learning opportunities of one gender.**
  A French teacher decides to count the number of times he calls on boys and girls during class. He finds that he calls on boys more than three times as frequently as girls, partly because the boys raise their hands more often. To combat his bad habit, he institutes a new procedure: He alternates between boys and girls when he calls on students, and he sometimes calls on students who are not raising their hands.

Sources: Fennema, 1987; Horgan, 1995; Kahle & Lakes, 1983; MacLean, Sasse, Keating, Stewart, & Miller, 1995; Sadker & Miller, 1982; Zambo & Brozo, 2009

This book is consistently praised for its emphasis on application, application, application. Throughout the book I identify suggested strategies—within the text, in tables, and in the margins—with apple icons that look like this:

Helping You Prepare for Licensure All chapters end with Practice for Your Licensure Exam exercises designed to resemble the kinds of case-study questions that appear on many teacher licensure tests.

Practice for Your Licensure Exam

The Good Buddy

Mr. Schulak has wanted to be a teacher for as long as he can remember. In his many volunteer activities over the years—coaching a girls' basketball team, assisting with a Boy Scout troop, teaching Sunday school—he has discovered how much he enjoys working with children. Children obviously enjoy working with him as well: Many occasionally call or stop by his home to shoot baskets, talk over old times, or just say hello. Some of them even call him by his first name.

Now that Mr. Schulak has completed his college degree and obtained his teaching certificate, he has accepted a teaching position at his hometown's junior high school. He's delighted to find that he already knows many of his students, and he spends the first few days of class renewing his friendships with them. But by the end of the week, he realizes that his classes have accomplished little of an academic nature.

The following Monday, Mr. Schulak vows to get down to business. He begins each of his six class sessions by describing his instructional goals for the weeks to come and then introduces the first lesson. Unfortunately, many of his students are resistant to settling down and getting to work. They want to move from one seat to another, talk with friends, toss wadded-up paper

Building Your Teaching Skills Throughout the book, margin notes alert readers to opportunities to apply chapter content and build their teaching skills by going to the new MyEducationLab to complete scaffolded learning units.

> **myeducationlab**
>
> Gain practice in applying Vygotsky's theory by completing the Building Teaching Skills and Dispositions exercise "Using Cognitive Tools and Instructional Strategies to Scaffold Learning" in MyEducationLab. (To find this exercise go to the topic Cognitive and Linguistic Development in MyEducationLab, and click on *Building Teaching Skills and Dispositions.*)

New! 

Classroom applications are by no means limited to the book itself! Accompanying the book is an exciting new online resource, MyEducationLab at www.myeducationlab.com, that provides my readers with many interactive, multimedia learning experiences. An access code for MyEducationLab is packaged with every new copy of this seventh edition of the book. I alert you to many of its resources with margin notes—again with apple icons to stress its value in helping my readers apply what they're learning to real children and classrooms.

"Teacher educators who are developing pedagogies for the analysis of teaching and learning contend that analyzing teaching artifacts has three advantages: it enables new teachers time for reflection while still using the real materials of practice; it provides new teachers with experience thinking about and approaching the complexity of the classroom; and in some cases, it can help new teachers and teacher educators develop a shared understanding and common language about teaching. . . ."[1]

Grounding teacher education in real classrooms—among real teachers and students and among actual examples of students' and teachers' work—is an important, and perhaps even an essential, part of training teachers for the complexities of teaching in today's classrooms. For this reason, the valuable, time-saving website—MyEducationLab—provides readers with the context of real classrooms and artifacts that research on teacher education tells us is so important. The authentic in-class video footage, interactive skill-building exercises, and other resources available on MyEducationLab offers a uniquely valuable teacher education tool.

As an educational psychologist, I am truly excited by the many resources that MyEducationLab can offer my readers—resources that can help them understand and apply the concepts and principles I describe in this book.

MyEducationLab is easy to use and integrate into both assignments and courses. Wherever you see the apple icon in the margins or elsewhere in the text, follow the simple instructions to access the videos, supplementary readings, and activities on MyEducationLab. MyEducationLab is organized topically to enhance the coverage of the core concepts discussed in the chapters of this book. For each topic covered in the course readers will find most or all of the following resources:

Connection to National Standards Now it is easier than ever for readers to see how course work is connected to national standards. In each topic of

[1]Darling-Hammond, L., & Bransford, J., Eds. (2005). *Preparing Teachers for a Changing World.* San Francisco: John Wiley & Sons.

MyEducationLab readers will find intended learning outcomes connected to the appropriate national standards. All of the Assignments and Activities and all of the Building Teaching Skills and Dispositions exercises in MyEducationLab are mapped to the appropriate national standards and learning outcomes as well.

Assignments and Activities Designed to save instructors preparation time and enhance student understanding, these assignable exercises show concepts in action (through videos, case studies, or student and teacher artifacts). They help readers synthesize and apply concepts and strategies they read about in the book. (Feedback for these assignments is available to the instructor.) Assignments and Activities include:

- Understanding Research exercises related to particular topics that help readers enhance their research interpretation skills and
- Student and Teacher Artifact Analysis and Video Analysis exercises that provide additional opportunities to practice applying chapter content to interpretations of actual students' work and teachers' classroom practices.

Building Teaching Skills and Dispositions These exercises help readers practice and strengthen skills that are essential to quality teaching. First the reader is presented with core concepts and ideas and then given an opportunity to practice their understanding of these concepts and ideas multiple times by watching video footage (or interacting with other media) and then critically analyzing the behaviors and strategies.

IRIS Center Resources The IRIS Center at Vanderbilt University (http://iris.peabody.vanderbilt.edu—funded by the U.S. Department of Education's Office of Special Education Programs, or OSEP)—develops training enhancement materials for pre-service and in-service teachers. The Center works with experts from across the country to create challenge-based interactive modules, case study units, and podcasts that provide research-validated information about working with students in inclusive settings. MyEducationLab has included this content in appropriate topic areas to enhance the content coverage in the book.

Teacher Talk This feature links to videos of teachers of the year across the country discussing their personal stories of why they teach. This National Teacher of the Year Program is sponsored by the Council of Chief State School Officers (CCSSO) and focuses public attention on teaching excellence. MyEducationLab includes motivational and inspiring Teacher Talk videos in topic areas to which they are relevant.

General Resources on Your MyEducationLab Course The Resources section on MyEducationLab is designed to help teacher candidates pass their licensure exam, put together effective portfolios and lesson plans, prepare for and navigate the first year of teaching, and understand key educational standards, policies, and laws. This section includes:

- Licensure Exams: Access guidelines for passing the Praxis exam. The Practice Test Exam includes multiple choice questions, case history questions, and video case studies with sample questions.
- Lesson Plan Builder: Create and share lesson plans.
- Licensure and Standards: Link to state licensure standards and national standards.
- Beginning Your Career: Access tips, advice, and valuable information on:
    - Resume Writing and Interviewing: Expert advice on how to write impressive resumes and prepare for job interviews.
    - Your First Year of Teaching: Practical tips to set up a classroom, manage student behavior, and plan for instruction and assessment.
    - Law and Public Policies: Specific directives and requirements teachers need to understand under the No Child Left Behind Act and the Individuals with Disabilities Education Improvement Act of 2004.
- Special Education Interactive Timeline: Build detailed time lines based on different facets of the history and evolution of special education.

Book-Specific Resources The Book-Specific Resources section of MyEducationLab contains useful material organized by chapter rather than by topic. Readers can go to this section to check their comprehension of chapter content. The Book-Specific Resources section offers the following resources:

Study Plan A MyEducationLab Study Plan is a multiple-choice assessment tied to chapter objectives, supported by study material. A well-designed Study Plan offers multiple opportunities to fully master required course content as identified by the objectives in each chapter:

- Chapter Objectives identify the learning outcomes for the chapter and give readers targets to shoot for as they read and study.
- Focus Questions help guide the reading of chapter content.
- Self-Check Quizzes assess mastery of the content. These assessments are mapped to chapter objectives. Readers can take the multiple-choice quizzes as many times as needed. Not only do these quizzes provide overall scores for each objective, but they also explain why responses to particular items are correct or incorrect.

- Study Material: Review, Practice and Enrichment gives readers a deeper understanding of what they do and do not know related to chapter content. This material includes text excerpts, activities that include hints and feedback, and interactive multimedia exercises built around videos, simulations, cases, or classroom artifacts.
- Flashcards help readers review the core concepts and principles within each chapter.
- Common Beliefs and Misconceptions about Educational Psychology help alert readers to typical misunderstandings in educational psychology classes.

Video Examples Video examples, referenced by margin notes in every chapter, provide concrete illustrations of various concepts and principles illustrated in each chapter.

Supplementary Readings Supplementary readings related to chapter concepts provide an opportunity to explore certain topics in more depth.

A Practice for Your Licensure Exam Exercise Each chapter ends with a Practice for Your Licensure Exam exercise that resembles the kinds of questions that appear on many teacher licensure tests. The same chapter-ending exercise is also located on MyEducationLab. Once on MyEducationLab, readers can complete the exercise while receiving hints that help scaffold the reader toward a correct response. The reader can also compare their responses to the expert feedback provided.

Visit www.myeducationlab.com for a demonstration of this exciting new online teaching resource.

Customizing Your Textbook

It is now possible for instructors to customize textbooks by selecting portions of this book and perhaps combining them with portions of other Pearson Education books. In addition to creating a standard seventh edition of my book, I have divided most of the book's content into a number of stand-alone modules that instructors can order singly or in combination. Instructors should contact their local Pearson sales representative for information on how to customize their textbook.

Ancillary Materials

Support Materials for Instructors

Videotapes The videotapes that accompany this textbook portray a wide variety of teachers, students, and classrooms in action. Many of the videos present numerous case studies in many content domains and at a variety of grade levels. Two additional videos are: *A Private Universe* (which examines learner misconceptions in science) and Constance Kamii's *Double-Column Addition: A Teacher Uses Piaget's Theory* (which depicts a constructivist approach to teaching mathematics). Opportunities to react to these videos in class discussions can further enhance students' ability to think analytically and identify good teaching practices.

- *Double-Column Addition: A Teacher Uses Piaget's Theory* (0-13-751413-1)
- *Windows on Classrooms Video Case Studies* (0-13-579948-1)
- *Educational Psychology: Video Package, Video 1* (0-02-389496-2)
- *A Private Universe* (0-13-859646-8)
- *Elementary Video Case Studies* (0-13-118642-6)
- *Secondary Video Case Studies* (0-13-118641-8)
- *Video Workshop for Educational Psychology:* Student Learning Guide with CD-ROM, Second Edition (0-205-45834-3).

Instructors should contact their local Pearson sales representative to order copies of these videos.

The following resources are available for instructors to download on www.pearsonhighered.com/educators. Instructors can enter the author or title of this book, select this edition, and then click on the "Resources" tab to log in and download textbook supplements or request premium content for a course management system.

Instructor's Manual (0-13-700118-5) An Instructor's Manual includes suggestions for learning activities, supplementary lectures, case study analyses, discussion topics, group activities, and additional media resources.

PowerPoint Slides (0-13-700117-7) The PowerPoint slides include key concept summarizations, diagrams and other graphic aids to enhance learning. They are designed to help students understand, organize, and remember core concepts and theories.

Test Bank (0-13-700078-2) and TestGen (0-13-700115-0) I've personally written all of the test questions in the Test Bank that accompanies the book. Some items (lower-level questions) simply ask students to identify or explain concepts and principles they have learned. But many others (higher-level questions) ask students to apply those same concepts and principles to specific classroom situations—that is, to actual student behaviors and teaching strategies. Ultimately, it is these higher-level questions that assess students' ability to use principles of educational psychology in their own teaching practice. The test bank is also available electronically in computerized test bank software known as TestGen, which enables instructors to create and customize exams. TestGen is available in both Macintosh and PC/Windows versions.

Web CT (0-13-700160-6) and BlackBoard (0-13-700159-2) Course Content Cartridges The course content cartridges contain the content of the Test Bank, available for use on either course management system.

Supplementary Materials for Students

***Case Studies: Applying Educational Psychology* (2nd ed.)** Many instructors use Ormrod and McGuire's *Case Studies* book (0-13-198046-7) as a supplement to this book. It includes 48 real cases involving students and classrooms ranging from preschool to high school. It illustrates concepts and principles in many areas of educational psychology, including child and adolescent development, learning and cognition, motivation, classroom management, instructional practices, and assessment.

Artifact Case Studies: Interpreting Children's Work and Teachers' Classroom Strategies Another possible supplement to the book is my Artifact Case Studies book (0-13-114671-8). The artifact cases in this supplement offer work samples and instructional materials that cover a broad range of topics, including literacy, mathematics, science, social studies, and art. Every artifact case includes background information and questions to consider as readers examine the artifact. Instructors should contact their local Pearson sales representative to order a copy of this book.

***Simulations in Educational Psychology and Research* (version 2.1)** This CD-ROM (0-13-113717-4) features five interactive psychological/educational experiments, along with exercises and readings that can help students explore the research components and procedures connected to the experiments. Qualitative and quantitative designs are included. Instructors should contact their local Pearson sales representative to order a copy of these simulations.

Observing Children and Adolescents CD-ROMs: Guided Interactive Practice in Understanding Development This unique set of three CDs (0-13-094379-7) guides students through activities that help them develop a discerning "eye" for the developmental nuances of children's behavior. In more than 50 activities, students view video clips of real children from infancy through adolescence, reflect on their observations, and record their interpretations. Students can explore 14 topics, including Memory, Intrinsic Motivation, Cognitive Development, Emotional Development, Families, Friendship, and Intelligence. Viewing these clips and responding to a series of questions across five age groups will familiarize students with the abilities and concerns of children at every development level—and enhance their understanding of many key concepts. Instructors should contact their local Pearson sales representative to order a copy of these CDs.

Acknowledgments

Although I am listed as the sole author of this textbook, I have been fortunate to have had a great deal of help in writing it. First and foremost, this book would not be what it is today without a long-term partnership with my former editor, Kevin Davis. Kevin first came on board as developmental editor for the book in 1989 and continued to stand by my side through several promotions. Kevin has not penned the words, but his influence permeates every page, and with each new edition he has insisted that I stretch my knowledge and skills in ways I never imagined and didn't think were possible. I thank Kevin for his inspiration, guidance, friendship, and undying dedication to the quality of teacher education.

Taking over Kevin's role as editor in the fall of 2008 was Paul Smith, of whom I am also most appreciative. As I've worked with Paul in the last few months, I've found him to be a continuing source of advice and support in my ongoing efforts to make this book the very best that it can be. To quote Rick Blaine in one of my favorite movies, *Casablanca,* "I think this is the beginning of a beautiful friendship."

I am equally indebted to Christie Robb, developmental editor for the seventh edition. Christie has always "been there" for me, generously dropping what she's doing at a moment's notice to provide counsel or assistance. She's kept me on course—no doubt about it—whenever I've gone astray from my mission. And on numerous occasions, she's helped me to take a deep breath and calm down when new, unanticipated, do-it-yesterday tasks have appeared at my doorstep.

Four previous developmental editors have left footprints on the book as well. Linda Peterson helped shape many of the book's pedagogical features in the first and second editions. Linda Bishop and Julie Peters brought fresh perspectives and creative ideas to the third and fourth editions, respectively, as did Autumn Benson for the fifth and sixth editions. All of these women continued to keep me upbeat and on-task throughout my arduous, yearlong writing efforts. I am thrilled that I can continue to work with Autumn in her new role as Media Producer.

Three additional individuals played key roles in transforming the book's manuscript into the finished product you see before you now. Annette Joseph at Pearson Education oversaw the entire production process and, in doing so, responded to my gazillion questions and requests without complaint. Marty Tenney of Modern Graphics served as the day-to-day project manager, expertly coordinating the many seemingly "little things" that turn a simple word-processing document into several hundred pages of text, complete with complex layouts requiring both an aesthetic eye and a meticulous attention to detail. As copy editor, Susan Freese looked at my every word and punctuation mark for places where I hadn't expressed myself as well as I might have. I thank Annette, Marty, and Susan for their patience and forbearance regarding my never-ending obsessive-compulsiveness regarding the book.

In addition to the folks at Pearson Education and Modern Graphics, several colleagues across the country have provided assistance with various ancillary materials. Gail Gottfried at Developmental Science and several people at the University of Nebraska's Center for Instructional Innovation—especially Roger Bruning, Christy A. Horn, Katherine Smith, and Jeremy J. Sydik—have created many of the interactive features now on MyEducationLab. Gail Gottfried also created an Instructor's Manual and PowerPoint slides that can give both novice and seasoned instructors assistance in using the book and teaching educational psychology more effectively.

Many other colleagues have strengthened the book itself by reviewing one or more of its previous versions. Reviewers for the first six editions were Joyce Alexander, Indiana University; Eric Anderman, University of Kentucky; Linda M. Anderson, Michigan State University; Margaret D. Anderson, SUNY–Cortland; J. C. Barton, Tennessee Technical University; Timothy A. Bender, Southwest Missouri State University; Phyllis Blumenfeld, University of Michigan; Kathy Brown, University of Central Oklahoma; Randy L. Brown, University of Central Oklahoma; Stephen L. Benton, Kansas State University; Karen L. Block, University of Pittsburgh; Kathryn J. Biacindo, California State University–Fresno; Barbara Bishop, Eastern New Mexico University; Robert Braswell, Winthrop College; Kay S. Bull, Oklahoma State University; Margaret W. Cohen, University of Missouri–St. Louis; Theodore Coladarci, University of Maine; Sharon Cordell, Roane State Community College; Roberta Corrigan, University of Wisconsin–Milwaukee; Richard D. Craig, Towson State University; José Cruz, Jr., The Ohio State University; Peggy Dettmer, Kansas State University; Joan Dixon, Gonzaga University; Leland K. Doebler, University of Montevallo; Catherine Emilhovich, SUNY–Buffalo; Joanne B. Engel, Oregon State University; Kathy Farber, Bowling Green State University; William R. Fisk, Clemson University; Victoria Fleming, Miami University of Ohio; M. Arthur Garmon, Western Michigan University; Roberta J. Garza, Pan American University–Brownsville; Mary Gauvain, University of California–Riverside; Cheryl Greenberg, University of North Carolina–Greensboro; Richard Hamilton, University of Houston; Jennifer Mistretta Hampston, Youngstown State University; Arthur Hernandez, University of Texas–San Antonio; Heather Higgins, University of North Carolina–Greensboro; Frederick C. Howe, Buffalo State College; Dinah Jackson, University of Northern Colorado; Janina M. Jolley, Clarion University of Pennsylvania; Caroline Kaczala, Cleveland State University; CarolAnne M. Kardash, University of Missouri–Columbia; Pamela Kidder-Ashley, Appalachian State University; Nancy F. Knapp, University of Georgia; Mary Lou Koran, University of Florida; Randy Lennon, University of Northern Colorado; Susan C. Losh, Florida State University; Pamela Manners, Troy State University; Hermine H. Marshall, San Francisco State University; Teresa McDevitt, University of Northern Colorado; Sharon McNeely, Northeastern Illinois University; Michael Meloth, University of Colorado–Boulder; Kelly S. Mix, Michigan State University; Bruce P. Mortenson, Louisiana State University; Janet Moursund, University of Oregon; P. Karen Murphy, The Pennsylvania State University; Gary A. Negin, California State University; Joe Olmi, The University of Southern Mississippi; Helena Osana, Concordia University; Judy Pierce, Western Kentucky University; James R. Pullen, Central Missouri State University; Gary F. Render, University of Wyoming; Robert S. Ristow, Western Illinois University; Jeff Sandoz, University of Louisiana–Lafayette; Rolando Santos, California State University–Los Angeles; Gregg Schraw, University of Nebraska–Lincoln; Dale H. Schunk, University of North Carolina–Greensboro; Mark Seng, University of Texas; Glenn E. Snelbecker, Temple University; Johnna Shapiro, University of California–Davis; Harry L. Steger, Boise State University; Bruce Torff, Hofstra University; Ann Turnbull, University of Kansas; Julianne C. Turner, University of Notre Dame; Enedina Vazquez, New Mexico State University; Alice A. Walker, SUNY–Cortland; Mary Wellman, Rhode Island College; Jane A. Wolfle, Bowling Green State University; and Karen Zabrucky, Georgia State University.

Coming on board for the seventh edition were these reviewers: Jane Abraham, Virginia Tech University; Joyce Alexander, Indiana University; Peggy Hsieh, University of Texas–San Antonio; Pamela Kidder-Ashley, Appalachian State University; Kenneth Kiewra, University of Nebraska–Lincoln; James Persinger, Emporia State University; and Kenneth Springer, Southern Methodist University.

Some of my own students and teacher interns—especially Jenny Bressler, Kathryn Broadhead, Ryan Francoeur, Gerry Holly, Michele Minichiello, Shelly Lamb, Kim Sandman, Melissa Tillman, Nick Valente, and Brian Zottoli—have agreed to let me use their interviews, essays, and experiences as examples. Teachers and administrators at schools both home and abroad (including two of my own children, now teachers themselves) have allowed me to share their strategies with my readers; I thank Liz Birnam, Berneen Bratt, Don Burger, Tom Carroll, Barbara Dee, Jackie Filion, Tina Ormrod Fox, Sarah Gagnon, Dinah Jackson, Sheila Johnson, Don Lafferty, Carol Lincoln, Gary MacDonald, Sharon McManus, Linda Mengers, Mark Nichols, Susan O'Byrne, Jeff Ormrod, Ann Reilly, and Gwen Ross.

Many young people, too, deserve thanks for letting me use their work. In particular, I want to acknowledge the contributions of the following present and former students: Andrew and Katie Belcher; Noah and Shea Davis; Zachary Derr; Amaryth, Andrew, and Anthony Gass; Ben and Darcy Geraud; Dana Gogolin; Colin Hedges; Erin Islo; Charlotte Jeppsen; Laura Linton; Michael McShane; Frederik Meissner; Meghan Milligan; Alex, Jeff, and Tina Ormrod; Patrick Paddock; Isabelle Peters; Ian Rhoads; Corey and Trisha Ross; Ashton and Haley Russo; Alex and Connor Sheehan; Matt and Melinda Shump; Andrew Teplitz; Emma Thompson; Grace Tober; Grant Valentine; and Geoff Wuehrmann.

Last but certainly not least, I must thank my husband and children, who have for many years forgiven my countless hours spent either buried in my books and journals or else glued to my computer. Without their continuing support and understanding of what has, for me, become a passion, this book would never have seen the light of day.

J. E. O.

Special Topics

Child and Adolescent Development

Classroom Management and Teacher–Student Relationships

Cultural and Ethnic Differences

Low Socioeconomic Status and Students at Risk

CHAPTER OUTLINE

- CASE STUDY: PICTURE YOURSELF
- TEACHING AS EVIDENCE-BASED PRACTICE
- UNDERSTANDING RESEARCH
  Quantitative Research • Qualitative Research • Interpreting Research Results: A Cautionary Note • From Research to Practice: The Importance of Theories
- COLLECTING DATA AND DRAWING CONCLUSIONS ABOUT YOUR OWN STUDENTS
  Assessing Students' Achievements and Behaviors • Conducting Action Research
- DEVELOPING AS A TEACHER
- STRATEGIES FOR STUDYING AND LEARNING EFFECTIVELY
- THE BIG PICTURE
- PRACTICE FOR YOUR LICENSURE EXAM: NEW SOFTWARE

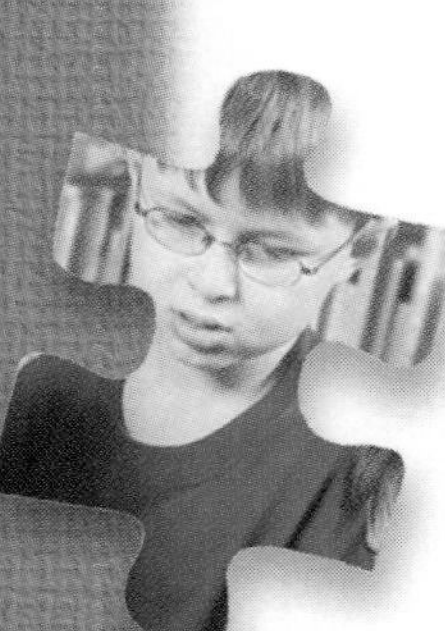

CHAPTER OBJECTIVES

- **Objective 1.1:** Explain the importance of research in classroom decision making.
- **Objective 1.2:** Draw appropriate conclusions from different types of research studies.
- **Objective 1.3:** Describe several strategies for collecting information about your own students.
- **Objective 1.4:** Plan long-term strategies for gaining expertise as a teacher.
- **Objective 1.5:** Use effective strategies when you read and study.

Chapter 1

Teaching and Educational Psychology

CASE STUDY: Picture Yourself

Picture yourself standing in front of a class of twenty-five children or adolescents. Your goal is for your students to *learn* something—perhaps how to distinguish between nouns and pronouns, interpret bar graphs, dribble a basketball, or diagnose the problem in a malfunctioning automobile engine. Some of your students are clearly engaged in your lesson, but others appear to have different priorities. Sarah and Marta, the best of friends, are whispering and giggling. Clifton and Lenesa seem lost in their thoughts. Danny, Joe, and Friedrich are shoving one another, and their behavior seems to be escalating into a major conflict. At the back of the room, Nicole is slumped deep in her chair with her arms crossed and a "you-can't-make-me-do-it" expression on her face.

- **As the teacher in this situation, what things might you immediately do to increase the likelihood that your students will benefit from your lesson? What things might you also do over the next few days and weeks to increase your students' ability and desire to learn the things you want to teach them?**

TEACHING OTHER PEOPLE—especially teaching the generation that will follow you into the adult world—can be one of the most rewarding professions on the planet. It can also be a very complex, challenging profession. Certainly, effective teaching involves presenting a topic or skill in such a way that students can understand and master it. Yet it involves many other things as well. For instance, teachers must get students' attention (consider Clifton and Lenesa), motivate students to *want* to learn the subject matter (consider Nicole), and transform existing interpersonal relationships—some friendly, some not—into a cohesive, respectful, and productive learning community. Furthermore, effective teaching requires determining where students are currently "at" in their learning and development—what they know and don't know, what they can and can't do, what cognitive and social skills they have and have not acquired, and so on. And it requires accommodating students' diverse backgrounds, beliefs, and family circumstances, as well as the physical, cognitive, and behavioral disabilities that some students may have.

Mastering the multifaceted nature of teaching takes time and practice, of course. But it also takes knowledge about human learning and motivation, developmental trends, individual and group differences, and effective instruction and assessment practices. Such topics are the domain of **educational psychology**. This book will help you understand children and adolescents—how they learn and develop, how they are likely to be similar to but also different from one another, what topics and activities are apt to "turn them on" in the classroom, and so on. It will also give you a toolbox of strategies for planning and carrying out instruction, creating an environment that keeps students motivated and on task, and assessing students' progress and achievement.

Teaching as Evidence-Based Practice

You have been a student for many years now, and in the process you have undoubtedly learned a great deal about how children learn and change over time and about how teachers can foster their learning and development. But exactly how much *do* you know? To help you find out, I've developed a short pretest, Ormrod's Own Psychological Survey (OOPS).

EXPERIENCING FIRSTHAND

Ormrod's Own Psychological Survey

Decide whether each of the following statements is *true* or *false*.

True/False

______ 1. Some children are predominantly left-brain thinkers, whereas others are predominantly right-brain thinkers.

______ 2. When we compare boys and girls, we find that the two groups are, on average, similar in their mathematical and verbal abilities.

______ 3. The best way to learn and remember a new fact is to repeat it over and over.

______ 4. Although students initially have many misconceptions about the world, they quickly revise their thinking once their teacher presents information that contradicts their existing beliefs.

______ 5. Taking notes during a lecture usually interferes with learning more than it helps.

______ 6. Students often misjudge how much they know about a topic.

______ 7. When a teacher rewards one student for appropriate behavior, the behavior of other students may also improve.

______ 8. Anxiety sometimes helps students learn and perform more successfully in the classroom.

______ 9. When teachers have children tutor their peers in academic subjects, the tutors gain very little from the process.

______ 10. The ways in which teachers assess students' learning influence what and how students actually learn.

educational psychology Academic discipline that (a) systematically studies the nature of learning, child development, motivation, and related topics and (b) applies its research findings to the identification and development of effective instructional practices.

Now let's see how well you did on the OOPS. Here are the answers, along with an explanation for each one:

1. *Some children are predominantly left-brain thinkers, whereas others are predominantly right-brain thinkers. FALSE.* With the development of new medical technologies in recent years, researchers have learned a great deal about how the human

brain works and which parts of it specialize in which aspects of human thinking. The two halves, or *hemispheres*, of the brain do seem to have somewhat different specialties, but they continually communicate and collaborate in tackling even the simplest of daily tasks. Practically speaking, there is no such thing as exclusively left-brain or right-brain thinking. We'll look at the brain and its development in Chapter 2.

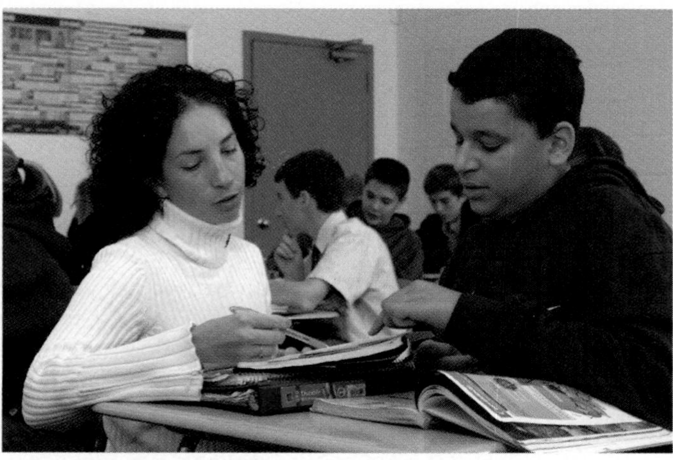

Effective teachers consider their students' diverse backgrounds, abilities, and needs when planning and delivering instruction.

2. *When we compare boys and girls, we find that the two groups are, on average, similar in their mathematical and verbal abilities. TRUE.* Despite widespread beliefs to the contrary, boys and girls tend to be similar in their abilities to perform mathematical and verbal tasks. Any differences in the average performance of boys and girls in these areas are usually too small for teachers to worry about. We'll explore gender differences—and similarities as well—in Chapter 4.

3. *The best way to learn and remember a new fact is to repeat it over and over. FALSE.* Although repeating information numerous times is better than doing nothing at all, repetition of specific facts is a relatively *in*effective way to learn. Students learn information more easily and remember it longer when they relate it to things they already know. One especially effective strategy is **elaboration**: using prior knowledge to expand or embellish on a new idea in some way, perhaps by critiquing it, thinking of an example of it, or generating potential applications of it. We'll revisit elaboration later in the chapter and examine it in more depth in Chapter 6.

4. *Although students initially have many misconceptions about the world, they quickly revise their thinking once their teacher presents information that contradicts their existing beliefs. FALSE.* As you will discover in Chapter 7, students typically have many misconceptions about the world. For instance, they may believe that the earth is round only in the sense that a pancake is round or that people would fall into space if they traveled to the South Pole. Students often hold strongly to these misconceptions, even in the face of contradictory evidence or instruction. As teachers, one of our biggest challenges is to help students discard their erroneous beliefs in favor of more accurate and useful perspectives. We'll identify strategies for promoting such *conceptual change* in Chapter 7.

5. *Taking notes during a lecture usually interferes with learning more than it helps. FALSE.* In general, students who take notes learn more material from a lecture than students who don't take notes. Note taking appears to facilitate learning in at least two ways: It helps students put, or *store*, information into memory more effectively, and it enables them to review the information at a later time. We'll look at research concerning the effectiveness of note taking and other study strategies in Chapter 8.

6. *Students often misjudge how much they know about a topic. TRUE.* Contrary to popular opinion, students are usually *not* the best judges of what they do and don't know. For example, many students think that if they have spent a long time studying a textbook chapter, they must know its contents very well. Yet if they have spent most of their study time inefficiently (perhaps by "reading" while thinking about something else altogether or by mindlessly copying definitions), they may know far less than they think they do. We'll consider this *illusion of knowing* further in Chapter 8.

7. *When a teacher rewards one student for appropriate behavior, the behavior of other students may also improve. TRUE.* When a teacher rewards one student for behaving in a particular way, others who have observed the student being rewarded sometimes begin to behave similarly. We'll identify numerous roles that observation plays in learning as we explore social cognitive theory in Chapter 10.

elaboration Cognitive process in which learners embellish on new information based on what they already know.

8. *Anxiety sometimes helps students learn and perform more successfully in the classroom. TRUE.* Many people think that anxiety is always a bad thing. Yet for some classroom tasks, and especially for relatively easy tasks, a moderate level of anxiety actually *improves* learning and performance. In Chapter 11, we'll discover that the specific effects of anxiety, whether helpful or counterproductive, depend on the situation.

9. *When teachers have children tutor their peers in academic subjects, the tutors gain very little from the process. FALSE.* When students teach one another, the tutors often benefit as much as the students being tutored. For instance, in one research study, fourth graders who were doing relatively poorly in mathematics served as arithmetic tutors for first and second graders; the tutors themselves showed a substantial improvement in arithmetic skills (Inglis & Biemiller, 1997). We'll look more closely at the effects of student-to-student tutoring in Chapter 12.

10. *The ways in which teachers assess students' learning influence what and how students actually learn. TRUE.* What and how students learn depend, in part, on how they expect their learning to be assessed. For example, students typically spend more time studying the things they think will be on a test than the things they think the test won't cover. And they are more likely to organize and integrate class material as they study if they expect assessment activities to require such organization and integration. In Chapter 14, we'll identify a variety of ways in which classroom assessment practices can influence students' learning.

How many of the OOPS items did you answer correctly? Did some of the false items seem convincing enough that you marked them true? Did some of the true items contradict certain beliefs you had? If either of these was the case, you are hardly alone. College students often agree with statements that seem obvious but are, in fact, completely wrong (Gage, 1991; Lennon, Ormrod, Burger, & Warren, 1990). Furthermore, many students in teacher education classes reject research findings that appear to contradict their personal beliefs and experiences (Gregoire, 2003; Holt-Reynolds, 1992; Wideen, Mayer-Smith, & Moon, 1998).

It's easy to be persuaded by common sense and assume that what seems logical must be reality. Yet common sense and logic don't always tell us the true story about how people actually learn and develop, nor do they always give us accurate information about how best to help students succeed in the classroom. Instead, our knowledge about learning and instruction must come from a more objective source of information—that is, from systematic research. Increasingly, educators and policy makers alike are calling for **evidence-based practice**—the use of instructional methods and other classroom strategies that research has consistently shown to bring about significant gains in students' development and academic achievement (e.g., Darling-Hammond & Bransford, 2005; Waterhouse, 2006).

Understanding Research

evidence-based practice Instructional method or other classroom strategy that research has consistently shown to bring about significant gains in students' development and/or academic achievement.

quantitative research Research yielding information that is inherently numerical in nature or can easily be reduced to numbers.

qualitative research Research yielding information that cannot be easily reduced to numbers; typically involves an in-depth examination of a complex phenomenon.

Historically, most research related to learning, development, and educational practice has been **quantitative research**; that is, it has involved collecting data that either take the form of numbers or can easily be converted into numbers. These numbers are tabulated and usually statistically analyzed to determine underlying trends and other patterns in the data. For example, we are apt to get quantitative information from students' performance on achievement tests, students' responses to rating-scale questionnaires, and school district records of students' attendance and dropout rates.

In recent years, educational researchers have also made considerable use of **qualitative research**, in which they examine complex phenomena that cannot be easily reduced to numerical values. For example, a qualitative research study might involve lengthy interviews in which students describe their hopes for the future, a detailed case study of interpersonal relationships within a tight-knit clique of adolescent girls, or in-depth observations of several teachers who create distinctly different psychological "climates" in their classrooms.

Ultimately, teachers gain a better understanding of students and effective classroom practices when they consider findings from *both* quantitative and qualitative research. It is important, then, that you understand what these two different kinds of research can—and also what they *cannot*—do for you.

descriptive study Research study that enables researchers to draw conclusions about the current state of affairs but not about correlational or cause-and-effect relationships.

Quantitative Research

Most quantitative research studies fall into one of three general categories: descriptive, correlational, or experimental. These three categories yield different kinds of information and warrant different kinds of conclusions.

Descriptive Studies A **descriptive study** does exactly what its name implies: It *describes* a situation. Descriptive studies might give us information about the characteristics of students, teachers, or schools. They might also provide information about how often certain events or behaviors occur. In general, descriptive studies enable us to draw conclusions about the way things are—the current state of affairs. The second column of Table 1.1 presents examples of questions we could answer with descriptive studies.

Compare/ Contrast

TABLE 1.1
Questions We Might Answer with Quantitative and Qualitative Research Studies

Topic	Quantitative Research			
	Descriptive Studies	*Correlational Studies*	*Experimental Studies*	*Qualitative Research*
Reading	How pervasive are gender stereotypes in books commonly used to teach reading in the elementary grades?	Are better readers also better spellers?	Which of two reading programs produces greater gains in reading comprehension?	What things do high-achieving students say they do "in their heads" when they read and study their textbooks?
Abstract Thinking	What percentage of high school students can think abstractly about academic topics?	Are older students more capable of abstract thought than younger students?	Can abstract thinking skills be improved through specially designed educational programs?	What misconceptions are often seen in high school students' explanations of abstract concepts?
Aggression	What kinds of aggressive behaviors occur in schools, and with what frequencies?	Are students more likely to be aggressive at school if they often see violence at home or in their neighborhoods?	Which method is most effective in reducing aggressive behavior: reinforcing appropriate behavior, punishing aggressive behavior, or a combination of both?	What distinct qualities characterize high schools in which members of violence-prone adolescent gangs interact congenially and respectfully?
Achievement Tests	How well have students performed on a recent national achievement test?	Do students who get the highest scores on multiple-choice tests also get the highest scores on essay tests dealing with the same content domain?	Do different kinds of tests (e.g., multiple choice vs. essay tests) encourage students to study in different ways and therefore affect what students actually learn?	In what ways do teachers' instructional practices change when their jobs and salaries depend on their students' scores on statewide or national achievement tests?

Correlational Studies A **correlational study** explores possible associations among two or more variables. For instance, it might tell us how closely two human characteristics are associated with each other, or it might give us information about the consistency with which certain human behaviors occur in conjunction with certain environmental conditions. In general, correlational studies enable us to draw conclusions about **correlation**: the extent to which two characteristics or phenomena tend to be found together or to change together. Two variables are correlated when one tends to increase as the other increases (a *positive correlation*) or when one tends to *de*crease as the other increases (a *negative correlation*). Such correlations are often described numerically with a statistic known as a *correlation coefficient* (see Appendix A).

The middle column of Table 1.1 presents examples of questions we might answer with correlational studies. Notice that each of these questions asks about an association between two variables—between reading ability and spelling ability, between age and abstract thought, between students' aggression levels and the violence they're exposed to at home, or between multiple-choice and essay test scores.

Correlations between two variables allow us to make *predictions* about one variable if we know the status of the other. For example, if we find that older students are more capable of abstract thought than younger students, we can predict that tenth graders will benefit more from an abstract discussion of democratic government than fourth graders will. If we find a positive correlation between multiple-choice and essay test scores, we can predict that students who have done well on an essay test in a biology class will probably also do well on a biology test covering the same topics in a multiple-choice format.

In general, although correlational studies demonstrate that an association exists, they can never tell us for certain *why* it exists. They don't tell us what factors—previous learning experiences, personality, motivation, or perhaps other things we haven't thought of—are the cause of the association we see. In other words, *correlation does not necessarily indicate causation.*

Experimental Studies Descriptive and correlational studies describe things as they exist naturally in the environment. In contrast, an **experimental study** is a study in which the researcher somehow changes, or *manipulates*, one or more aspects of the environment (often called *independent variables*) and then measures the effects of such changes on something else. In educational research the "something else" being affected (often called the *dependent variable*) is usually some aspect of student behavior—perhaps end-of-semester grades, skill in executing a complex physical movement, persistence in trying to solve difficult math problems, or ability to interact appropriately with peers. In a good experiment, a researcher *separates and controls variables*, testing the possible effects of one independent variable while holding all other potentially influential variables constant.

Experimental studies often involve two or more groups that are treated differently. The following are examples:

- A researcher uses two different instructional methods to teach reading comprehension skills to two different groups of students. (Instructional method is the independent variable.) The researcher then assesses students' reading ability (the dependent variable) and compares the average performances of the two groups.
- A researcher gives three different groups of students varying amounts of practice with woodworking skills. (Amount of practice is the independent variable.) The researcher subsequently scores the quality of each student's woodworking project (the dependent variable) and compares the average quality scores of the three groups.
- A researcher gives one group of students an intensive training program designed to improve their study habits. The researcher gives another group either no training at all or, better still, training in subject matter unrelated to study habits. (Presence or absence of training in study habits is the independent variable.) The researcher later assesses students' study habits and obtains their

correlational study Research study that explores associations among variables.

correlation Extent to which two variables are associated, such that when one variable increases, the other either increases or decreases somewhat predictably.

experimental study Research study that involves the manipulation of one variable to determine its possible effect on another variable, allowing conclusions to be drawn about cause-and-effect relationships.

grade point averages (two dependent variables) to see whether the training program had an effect.

Each of these examples includes one or more **treatment groups**, which are the recipients of a planned intervention. The third example also includes a **control group**, which receives either no intervention or a *placebo* intervention that is unlikely to affect the dependent variable(s) in question. In many experimental studies, participants are assigned to groups *randomly*—for instance, by drawing names out of a hat. Such random assignment is apt to yield groups that are roughly equivalent on other variables (e.g., ability levels, personality characteristics, motivation) that might affect the dependent variable.

When carefully designed and conducted, experimental studies enable us to draw conclusions about *causation*—about *why* behaviors occur. The fourth column of Table 1.1 presents examples of questions that might be answered through experimental studies. Notice that each question addresses a cause-and-effect relationship—the effect of a reading program on the development of reading comprehension, the effect of educational programs on abstract thinking, the effect of rewards and punishment on aggressive behavior, or the effect of test-item format on students' learning.

As you can see from the examples in the table, the difference between correlational and experimental research is an important one: Whereas correlational studies let us draw conclusions about associations, only experimental studies enable us to draw conclusions about cause and effect. Ultimately, we can be most effective as teachers when we are confident that certain things that we do in the classroom will, in a cause-and-effect manner, have a positive impact on students' learning and behavior.

Yet for practical or ethical reasons, many important questions in education do not easily lend themselves to carefully controlled experimental studies. For instance, although we might reasonably hypothesize that children can better master difficult math concepts if they receive individual tutoring, most public school systems cannot afford such a luxury, and it would be unfair to provide tutoring for some students and deny it to a control group of other, equally needy students. And, of course, it would be highly unethical to study the effects of aggression by intentionally placing some children in a violent environment. Some important educational questions, then, can be addressed only with descriptive or correlational studies, even though such studies cannot help us pin down precise cause-and-effect relationships.

Qualitative Research

Rather than address questions related to quantity—questions regarding *how much*, *how many*, or *how frequently*—researchers sometimes want to look in depth at certain characteristics or behaviors. Imagine, for example, that a researcher wants to find out what kinds of study strategies high-achieving students tend to use. One logical approach would be simply to ask the students questions such as "What things do you do to help you remember what you read in your textbooks?" and "How do you prepare for tests in your classes?" Students' responses to such open-ended questions are apt to go in many different directions, sometimes focusing on various behaviors (e.g., taking notes, working on practice problems) and at other times focusing on various mental processes (e.g., trying to make sense of a passage, generating new examples of concepts). Although it might be possible to categorize students' responses and count those falling into each category (thereby obtaining some quantitative data), the researcher may also want to preserve the multifaceted qualities of students' responses by reporting lengthy excerpts from the interviews.

Qualitative research is often used to explore the complex nature of human behavior in social settings—perhaps in particular social groups, classrooms, schools, or cultures. For instance, in-depth qualitative studies have contributed in important ways to our knowledge of school characteristics that affect the academic and social success of students from diverse backgrounds (e.g., Hemmings, 2004; Ladson-Billings, 1995b; Ogbu, 2003). The rightmost column of Table 1.1 presents several examples of questions that might best be answered by qualitative research.

treatment group Group of people in a research study who are given a particular experimental intervention (e.g., a particular method of instruction).

control group Group of people in a research study who are given either no intervention or one that is unlikely to have an effect on the dependent variable (i.e., a *placebo* treatment).

Ultimately, you shouldn't think of quantitative and qualitative research as an either-or situation. Many educational researchers effectively combine elements of both quantitative and qualitative research in a single study. For example, in a study described in the *American Educational Research Journal* in 1999, researchers Melissa Roderick and Eric Camburn tracked more than 27,000 students' academic progress as they made the transition from small elementary or middle schools to much larger high schools in the Chicago public school system. Many students showed a sharp decline in academic achievement in ninth grade, their first year of high school. More than 40% of first-semester ninth graders (males especially) failed at least one course, and students who achieved at low levels early in their high school career were more likely to drop out before graduation.

Such troubling findings are examples of quantitative data, but the researchers also provided qualitative information that might help us understand them. For instance, Roderick and Camburn described a student named Anna, who had done well in her neighborhood K–8 school and seemingly had the basic skills she needed to successfully tackle a high school curriculum. Unfortunately, Anna seemed overwhelmed by the new demands that her ninth-grade classes placed on her, and her first-semester final grades included several Ds and an F. She gave the following explanation in an interview with one of the researchers:

> In geography, "he said the reason why I got a lower grade is 'cause I missed one assignment and I had to do a report, and I forgot that one." In English, "I got a C . . . 'cause we were supposed to keep a journal, and I keep on forgetting it 'cause I don't have a locker. Well I do, but my locker partner she lets her cousins use it, and I lost my two books there. . . . I would forget to buy a notebook, and then I would have them on separate pieces of paper, and I would lose them." And, in biology, "the reason I failed was because I lost my folder . . . it had everything I needed, and I had to do it again, and, by the time I had to turn in the new folder, I did, but he said it was too late . . . 'cause I didn't have the folder, and the folder has everything, all the work." (Roderick & Camburn, 1999, p. 305)

Although Anna's math teacher offered to find tutors for students who were having difficulty, Anna perceived most of her teachers as being uncaring, inattentive to students' difficulties, and inflexible in evaluating students' achievement. Twice, she went to the school counselor's office—visits that got her in trouble for being late to her next class—but on neither occasion was the counselor available to meet with her.

If Anna's behaviors, experiences, and perceptions are typical—and apparently they are—they point to the need for greater faculty support as students make the transition from a close-knit elementary or K–8 school to a more impersonal high school environment. This support might not only be emotional but also *academic*—for instance, including instruction and guidance in organizational skills and effective study habits. We must be careful in drawing such inferences, however. Qualitative research is essentially *descriptive* in nature. Just as is true for a descriptive quantitative study, a qualitative study tells us *how things are*, rather than *what causes what.* Any hypotheses about cause-and-effect relationships are only that—hypotheses—that ideally should be tested with experimental, quantitative studies (e.g., Bransford, Darling-Hammond, & LePage, 2005).

Interpreting Research Results: A Cautionary Note

Whenever we look at the results of a research study, we can determine that a particular condition or intervention has led to a particular outcome—that is, there is a cause-and-effect relationship between the two—only when we've eliminated all other possible explanations for the results we've observed. As an example, imagine that Hometown School District wants to find out which of two reading programs, Reading Is Great (RIG) or Reading and You (RAY), leads to better reading in third grade. The district asks each of its third-grade teachers to choose one of these two reading programs and use it throughout the school year. The district then compares the end-of-year achievement test scores of students in the RIG and RAY classrooms and finds that RIG students have substantially higher reading comprehension scores than RAY students. We might quickly jump to the conclusion that RIG promotes better reading comprehension than RAY—in other words, that a cause-and-effect relationship exists between the instructional method and reading comprehension. But is this really so?

We can be confident that one reading program is superior to another only if a carefully controlled experimental study has eliminated alternative explanations for differences in students' learning.

Not necessarily. The fact is, the school district hasn't eliminated all other possible explanations for the difference in students' reading comprehension scores. Remember, the third-grade teachers personally *selected* the instructional program they used. Why did some teachers choose RIG and others choose RAY? Were the teachers who chose RIG different in some way from the teachers who chose RAY? Had RIG teachers taken more graduate courses in reading instruction, were they more open minded and enthusiastic about using innovative methods, did they have higher expectations for their students, or did they devote more class time to reading instruction? Or, perhaps, did the RIG teachers have students who were, on average, better readers to begin with?

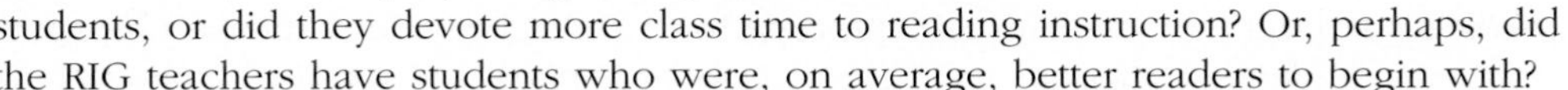

If the RIG and RAY classrooms were different from each other in any of these ways—or perhaps different in some other way we haven't thought of—then the district hasn't eliminated alternative explanations for why the RIG students have acquired better reading skills than the RAY students. A better way to study the causal influence of a reading program on reading comprehension would be to *randomly assign* third-grade classes to the RIG and RAY programs, thereby making the two groups similar (on average) in terms of students' reading abilities and teachers' backgrounds, motives, expectations, dedication to reading instruction, and so on.

Be careful that you don't jump too quickly to conclusions about what factors are affecting students' learning, development, and behavior in particular situations. Scrutinize descriptions of research carefully, always with these questions in mind: *Have the researchers separated and controlled variables that might have an influence on the outcome? Have they ruled out other possible explanations for their results?* Only when the answers to these questions are undeniably *yes* and *yes* should you draw a conclusion about a cause-and-effect relationship.

Draw conclusions about cause-and-effect relationships only when you have an experimental study—one in which other possibly influential factors have been controlled.

MyEducationLab, the online resource that accompanies this book, includes numerous Understanding Research exercises. Every exercise presents a synopsis of a research study, including the method used, the results obtained, and the conclusions drawn. Questions that follow the synopsis can help you think about and interpret the study in appropriate ways, reaching valid conclusions but steering clear of unwarranted ones.

myeducationlab

Gain practice in understanding and critiquing a variety of research methods by completing the Understanding Research exercises in the Assignments and Activities sections in each topic area of MyEducationLab **(www.myeducationlab.com)**.

From Research to Practice: The Importance of Theories

Some research studies have obvious, direct implications for educational practice. Other studies contribute to educational practice indirectly through the **theories** that researchers develop to integrate and explain their findings. In these theories, researchers typically speculate about the underlying (and often unobservable) mechanisms involved in thinking, learning, development, motivation, or some other aspect of human functioning. By giving us ideas about such underlying mechanisms, theories can ultimately help us create learning environments that facilitate students' learning and achievement to the greatest extent possible.

theory Integrated set of concepts and principles developed to explain a particular phenomenon.

Let's take an example. In Chapter 6, we'll discover that a particular theory of how people learn—information processing theory—proposes that attention is an essential ingredient in the learning process. More specifically, if a learner pays attention to new information, the information moves from the first component of the human memory system (the sensory register) to the second component (working memory). If the learner *does not* pay attention, the information disappears from the memory system; as a common expression puts it, it "goes in one ear and out the other." The importance of attention in information processing theory suggests that strategies that capture and maintain students' attention—perhaps providing interesting reading materials, presenting intriguing problems, or praising good performance—are apt to enhance students' learning and achievement.

Psychological theories are rarely, if ever, set in stone. Instead, they are continually expanded and modified as additional data come to light, and in some cases, one theory may be abandoned in favor of another that better explains the phenomena researchers have observed. Furthermore, different theories focus on different aspects of human functioning, and psychologists have not yet pulled them together into a single mega-theory that adequately accounts for all the diverse phenomena and experiences that comprise human existence.

Throughout the book, we'll examine theories related to thinking, learning, development, motivation, and behavior. Although these theories will inevitably change in the future, they can be quite useful even in their present, unfinished forms. They can help us integrate thousands of research studies into concise understandings of how children typically learn and develop, and they enable us to draw inferences and make predictions about how students are apt to perform and achieve in particular classroom situations. In general, theories can help us to both *explain* and *predict* human behavior, thereby giving us numerous ideas about how best to help children and adolescents achieve academic and social success at school.

Collecting Data and Drawing Conclusions About Your Own Students

Collecting and interpreting data are hardly activities conducted only by highly trained researchers in faraway settings. Quite the contrary is true: Teachers continually collect data about their own students through their formal and informal assessments of students' written work and classroom behaviors. Furthermore, many teachers plan and conduct their own research to help them better understand their students and schools—a process known as *action research*.

Assessing Students' Achievements and Behaviors

Most teachers regularly assess what their students know and can do, perhaps in the form of assignments, projects, presentations, and quizzes. But effective teachers don't limit themselves only to such formal, planned evaluations. They continually observe their students in a variety of contexts—in the classroom, in the cafeteria, on the playground, on field trips, during extracurricular activities, with family members at parent–teacher conferences and school open houses—for clues about what students might be thinking, believing, feeling, and learning. Students' comments, questions, facial expressions, body language, work habits, and interactions with friends and classmates can provide valuable insights into their learning, development, and motivation.

We'll explore the topic of assessment in depth in Chapters 14 and 15, but you'll find implications for assessment in virtually every chapter. To get your feet wet in the process of assessment, read 7-year-old Justin's short story "The Pet Who Came to Dinner," presented in Figure 1.1. As you read it, consider what you might conclude about Justin's progress in writing. Consider, too, what inferences you might make about Justin's family and home life.

As you can see, Justin has learned how to spell some words (e.g., *dinner, came*) but has not yet learned many others (e.g., he spells *once* as "owans" and *started* as "stor did"). Overall, he knows which alphabet letters represent which sounds in speech, but he sometimes reverses the letter *d* so that it looks like a *b*, and he occasionally leaves out a sound when he spells a word (e.g., his spelling of *drink* begins with *b* and omits the *n* sound). Justin has also made some progress in common spelling patterns (e.g., the *-ing* suffix for verbs) and in the use of periods and apostrophes. He has learned to tell a simple story, but he does so merely by listing a series of seemingly unrelated events, and he has not yet learned that the title of a story should appear in a line by itself, centered at the top of the page.

Justin's story also gives us a few insights into his family and home life. It appears that he lives with both his mother and father. The family gives some attention to nutrition (it serves "melk" at dinner) and has sufficient financial resources to provide dessert ("dasrt") after the main course. Justin also talks about the pet reading the newspaper ("nuwspapr"), suggesting that reading is a familiar activity in the home.

Are such inferences about Justin accurate? Not necessarily. The conclusions we reach about our students are, like theories of development and learning, only reasonable guesses based on the evidence at hand. We must think of such conclusions as tentative *hypotheses* to be tested further, rather than as indisputable *facts*.

FIGURE 1.1 Seven-year-old Justin's story "The Pet Who Came to Dinner"

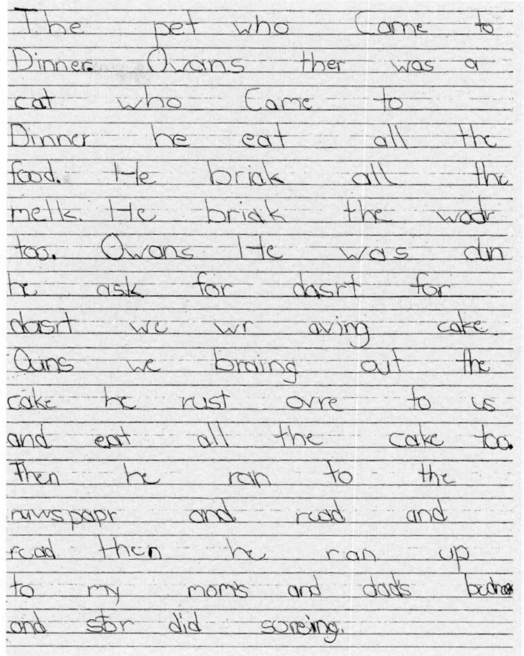

The pet who Came to
Dinner Owans ther was a
cat who Came to
Dinner he eat all the
food. He brink all the
melk. He brink the wodr
too. Owans He was dun
he ask for dasrt for
dasrt we wr aving cake.
Ouns we braing out the
cake he rust ovre to us
and eat all the cake too.
Then he ran to the
nuwspapr and read and
read then he ran up
to my moms and dads bedroom
and stor did soreing.

Conducting Action Research

Teachers sometimes encounter problems that existing research findings do not address. In **action research**, teachers conduct systematic studies of issues in their own schools, with the goal of seeking more effective strategies in working with students (Cochran-Smith & Lytle, 1993; Mills, 2007). For instance, an action research project might involve examining the effectiveness of a new teaching technique, seeking students' opinions on a controversial school policy, or ascertaining reasons why many students rarely complete homework assignments.

Use assessment results to form hypotheses—but *not* to draw hard-and-fast conclusions—about students' current characteristics and abilities and about effective instructional strategies.

Any action research study typically involves the following steps (Mills, 2007):

1. *Identify an area of focus.* The teacher–researcher begins with a problem and gathers preliminary information that might shed light on the problem—usually by reading books or journal articles related to the problem and perhaps also by surfing the Internet or conducting informal interviews of colleagues or students. The teacher–researcher then identifies one or more specific questions to address and develops a research plan (data collection techniques, necessary resources, schedule, etc.) for answering those questions. At this point, the teacher also seeks permission to conduct the study from school administrators and any other appropriate authorities. Depending on the nature of the study, parents' permission may be necessary as well.

2. *Collect data.* The teacher–researcher collects data relevant to the research questions. Such data might, for example, be obtained from questionnaires, interviews, achievement tests, students' journals or portfolios, existing school records (e.g., attendance patterns, rates of referral for discipline problems), or observations. Many times, the teacher–researcher uses two or more of these sources in order to approach the research questions from various angles.

3. *Analyze and interpret the data.* The teacher–researcher looks for patterns in the data. Sometimes the analysis involves computing particular statistics (e.g., percentages, means, correlation coefficients)—this would be a quantitative study. At other times, the analysis involves an in-depth, nonnumerical inspection of the data—this would be a qualitative study. In either case, the teacher–researcher relates the patterns observed to the original research questions.

action research Research conducted by teachers and other school personnel to address issues and problems in their own schools or classrooms.

4. *Develop an action plan.* The final step distinguishes action research from the more traditional research studies we've previously considered: The teacher–researcher uses the information collected to *take action*—for instance, to change instructional strategies, school policies, or the classroom environment.

Many colleges and universities now offer courses in action research. You can also find inexpensive paperback books on the topic (e.g., Craig, 2009; Mills, 2007; Stringer, 2008).

Developing as a Teacher

As a beginning teacher, you may initially find your role a bit overwhelming. Virtually any classroom will be one of nonstop action, requiring you to be consistently attentive and on your toes, and there will always be a great deal to think about.

If you are currently enrolled in a teacher education program, you should think of your program as a very good start on the road to becoming a skillful teacher (Bransford, Darling-Hammond, et al., 2005; Brouwer & Korthagen, 2005). However, it is *only* a start. Developing true expertise in any profession, including teaching, takes many years and a great deal of experience to acquire (P. A. Alexander, 2003; Berliner, 2001). So be patient with yourself, and recognize that occasionally feeling a bit unsure and making mistakes is par for the course. But as you gain experience, you will gradually become able to make decisions about routine situations and problems quickly and efficiently, giving you the time and energy to think creatively and flexibly about how best to teach classroom subject matter (Borko & Putnam, 1996; Bransford, Derry, Berliner, & Hammerness, 2005; Feldon, 2007).

Throughout the book, I'll describe many ways in which you can help your students learn and develop. But it is equally important that *you* learn and develop, especially in your role as a teacher. Drawing from research on teacher effectiveness, I offer the following strategies:

Keep up to date on research findings and new innovations in education. Additional university course work and in-service training sessions at your school are two good ways to increase your teaching effectiveness (Bransford, Darling-Hammond, et al., 2005; Guskey & Sparks, 2002). In addition, effective teachers typically subscribe to one or more professional journals, and as time allows, they occasionally attend professional conferences in their region.

Learn as much as you can about the subject matter you teach. When we look at effective teachers—for example, those who are flexible in their approaches to instruction, help students develop a thorough understanding of classroom topics, and convey obvious enthusiasm for whatever they are teaching—we typically find teachers who know their subject matter extremely well (Borko & Putnam, 1996; Cochran & Jones, 1998; H. C. Hill et al., 2008; Windschitl, 2002).

Learn as much as you can about specific strategies for teaching your particular subject matter. In addition to knowing general teaching strategies, it is helpful to acquire strategies specific to the topic you are teaching—strategies that are collectively known as **pedagogical content knowledge**. Effective teachers typically have a large number of strategies for teaching particular topics and skills (Cochran & Jones, 1998; Krauss et al., 2008; L. S. Shulman, 1986). Furthermore, they can usually anticipate—and so can also address—the difficulties students will have and the kinds of errors students will make in the process of mastering a skill or body of knowledge (Borko & Putnam, 1996; D. C. Smith & Neale, 1991). Some teachers keep journals or other records of the strategies they develop and use in particular situations and then reuse these strategies as needed (Berliner, 1988).

pedagogical content knowledge Knowledge about effective methods of teaching a specific topic or content area.

Learn as much as you can about the culture(s) of the community in which you are working. In the following chapters (especially in Chapter 4), we'll identify numerous ways in which children from diverse cultural groups may think and behave differently than *you* did as a child. But a textbook can offer only a sampling of the many possible differences. You can become more informed about students' cultural beliefs and practices if you participate in local community activities and converse regularly with community members (Castagno & Brayboy, 2008; National Research Council, 2000; Rogoff, 2003).

Continually reflect on and critically examine your assumptions, inferences, and teaching practices. In Chapter 8, we'll address **critical thinking**, the process of evaluating the accuracy, credibility, and worth of information and lines of reasoning. Our focus in that chapter will be on encouraging students to think critically about classroom subject matter. Yet it is essential that *we teachers* think critically as well, both about why our students might be behaving in particular ways and achieving at particular levels and also about how our own classroom practices may be influencing their behavior and achievement. Effective teachers engage in **reflective teaching**: They continually examine and critique their assumptions, inferences, and instructional practices, and they regularly adjust their beliefs and strategies in the face of new evidence (Hammerness, Darling-Hammond, & Bransford, 2005; T. Hogan, Rabinowitz, & Craven, 2003; Larrivee, 2006).

Communicate and collaborate with colleagues. Effective teachers rarely work in isolation. Instead, they frequently communicate with colleagues in their own school district and across the nation—perhaps with colleagues in other countries as well—and effective teachers at any single school regularly coordinate their efforts to enhance students' learning and personal well-being (Bransford, Darling-Hammond, et al., 2005). Thanks to both teacher lounges and e-mail, interpersonal communication is often quick and easy. And innumerable Internet websites offer ideas for lesson plans and instructional activities on a wide range of topics. One helpful resource is www.tappedin.org, an online community of educators from around the world. You should also look at the websites of professional organizations related to your field; the websites for the National Council of Teachers of Mathematics (www.nctm.org) and the National Council for Geographic Education (ww.ncge.org) are just two of the many possibilities.

Keep in mind, too, that even the most masterful of teachers had to begin their teaching careers as novices, and they probably entered their first classroom with the same concerns and uncertainties that you may initially have. Most experienced teachers are apt to be quite willing to offer you advice and support during challenging times. In fact, they are apt to be quite flattered that you've asked them!

Believe that you can make a difference in students' lives. In Chapter 10, we'll consider the nature of **self-efficacy**: the extent to which people believe they are capable of executing certain behaviors or reaching certain goals. Students are more likely to try to learn something if they believe they *can* learn it—in other words, if they have high self-efficacy. But you, too, must have high self-efficacy. Believing that you can be a good teacher will help you persist in the face of occasional setbacks and ultimately be effective in the classroom (Ashton, 1985). Students who achieve at high levels are apt to be those whose teachers have confidence in what *they* can do for their students (Brophy, 2006; J. A. Langer, 2000; Tschannen-Moran, Woolfolk Hoy, & Hoy, 1998).

critical thinking Process of evaluating the accuracy, credibility, and worth of information and lines of reasoning.

reflective teaching Regular, ongoing examination and critique of one's assumptions and instructional strategies and revision of them as necessary to enhance students' learning and development.

self-efficacy Belief that one is capable of executing certain behaviors or reaching certain goals.

Strategies for Studying and Learning Effectively

As you read this book, you'll gain many insights into how you can help students more effectively learn classroom subject matter. I hope you will also gain insights into how *you* can better learn and remember course material. But rather than wait until we begin our discussion of learning in Chapter 6, let's look briefly at four strategies you can use as you read and study this book:

myeducationlab

Go to the Book-Specific Resources located in MyEducationLab to access Focus Questions in every chapter's Study Plan that can help you relate what you read to things you already know. Use the Video Examples within the Book-Specific Resources to help you tie the concepts and theories of educational psychology to real children, adolescents, and classroom lessons.

Relate what you read to things you already know. Try to connect the ideas in the book with things you already know and believe. For example, connect new concepts and principles with your own past experiences, your previous course work, and your general knowledge about people and their behavior. Be careful, however. As my earlier OOPS test may have already shown you, some of what you currently "know" and believe may be sort-of-but-not-quite accurate or even out-and-out *in*accurate. As you read the book, then, think about how some ideas and research findings may actually contradict your prior "knowledge." In such instances, I hope you'll revise your understanding of whatever topic we're discussing.

Tie abstract concepts and principles to concrete examples. As we'll discover in Chapter 2, children become increasingly able to think about abstract ideas as they get older, but people of *all* ages can more readily understand and remember abstract information when they tie it to concrete objects and events. Thus, I will often illustrate new concepts and principles with opening case studies or brief vignettes that describe specific children's behaviors. In addition, I will occasionally ask you to watch video clips located in the Book-Specific Resources section in MyEducationLab. Seeing psychological concepts and principles in action in case studies and video clips can enhance your memory of them and help you recognize them when you see them in your own work with children and adolescents.

myeducationlab

Find additional strategies in a supplementary reading "Study Tips." (To find this reading, go to Chapter 1 of the Book-Specific Resources in MyEducationLab, and then select "*Supplementary Readings.*"

Sometimes it's even better to see a concept or principle in action in *oneself.* Thus, I will occasionally give you experiences that illustrate key ideas in the form of Experiencing Firsthand exercises. You have already completed one of these exercises—the OOPS test—and will encounter many additional ones throughout the book.

Elaborate on what you read, going beyond it and adding to it. Earlier in the chapter, I mentioned that the process of *elaboration*—using prior knowledge to expand on new information—enhances learning and memory of the information. So, try to think *beyond* the information you read. Draw inferences from the ideas presented. Generate new examples of concepts. Identify your own educational applications of various principles of learning, development, and motivation.

Periodically check yourself to make sure you remember and understand what you've read. There are times when even the most diligent students don't concentrate on what they're reading—when they're actually thinking about something else as their eyes go down the page. So stop once in a while (perhaps once every two or three pages) to make sure you have really learned and understood the things you've been reading. Try to summarize the material. Ask yourself questions about it. Make sure everything makes sense to you. Tackle the Practice for Your Licensure Exam exercise that appears at the end of each chapter. Check your mastery of various concepts by taking the Self-Check Quizzes in each chapter of the Book-Specific Resources section in MyEducationLab. Further enhance your understanding by applying what you've learned in the Building Teaching Skills and Dispositions exercises located in various topic-area sections in MyEducationLab.

myeducationlab

Check your mastery of various concepts by taking the Self-Check Quizzes in each chapter of the Book-Specific Resources section in MyEducationLab. Further enhance your understanding by applying what you've learned in the Building Teaching Skills and Dispositions exercises located in various topic-area sections in MyEducationLab.

The Big Picture

A consistent feature of every chapter of this book is *The Big Picture*, a section that highlights key ideas in the chapter. In the following four bulleted paragraphs, I suggest the most important points to take with you from Chapter 1:

- ***Teacher decision making must be based, at least in part, on research findings related to human learning processes, children's development, and effective classroom practices.*** As teachers, we must make innumerable daily decisions about how to teach, interact with, and respond to the students in our classrooms. Although we can sometimes use simple common sense in making these decisions, such "sense" may occasionally lead us to draw unwarranted, even inaccurate conclusions. We are most likely to make good decisions—those that maximize students' learning and development over the long run—when we base them on contemporary research findings and on theoretical syntheses of those findings.

- ***Different kinds of research studies lead to different kinds of conclusions.*** Both quantitative and qualitative research can greatly enhance our understandings of the diverse students we are apt to have and the classroom practices that are apt to be most effective in working with each of them. Ideally, we would like research studies to yield insights about the specific classroom practices that can have a significant impact on our students' academic achievement and personal well-being. Findings from many research studies—say, from qualitative research or from correlational quantitative studies—can suggest hypotheses about potentially effective classroom strategies. However, only carefully controlled *experimental* studies yield dependable conclusions about cause-and-effect relationships.

- ***In one way or another, teachers are researchers themselves.*** To be effective teachers, we must regularly collect data about our students, sometimes by giving them preplanned assignments and quizzes and sometimes by observing them "on the fly" as they act and interact in class, on the playground, and elsewhere. In addition, we may often find it helpful to conduct action research in order to address questions about our own particular students or about local issues and concerns.

- ***Teachers are also learners.*** To maximize our own development as teachers, we must think critically and reflectively about our assumptions, beliefs, and classroom strategies. We must also continue to modify what we think and do as we acquire new information related to our profession. Such information can come from a variety of sources, including formal course work, in-service training sessions, professional journals and conferences, Internet websites, consultation with colleagues and community members, and, of course, our own research studies.

As you look forward to your entry into the teaching profession, I urge you to be confident that with time, practice, a solid understanding of how children and adolescents learn and develop, a large toolkit of instructional strategies, and every student's best interests at heart, you can truly make a significant difference in young people's lives.

Practice for Your Licensure Exam

New Software

High school math teacher Mr. Gualtieri begins his class one Monday with an important announcement: "Our school has just purchased a new instructional software program for the school's computer lab. This program, called Problem-Excel, will give you practice in applying the mathematical concepts and procedures we'll be studying this year. I strongly encourage you to stay after school once or twice a week to get extra practice with the software whenever you're having trouble with the assignments I give you."

Mr. Gualtieri is firmly convinced that the new instructional software will help his students better understand and apply mathematics. To test his hypothesis, he keeps a record of which students report to the computer lab after school and which students do not. He then looks at how well the two groups of students perform on his next classroom test. Much to his surprise, he discovers that, on average, the students who have stayed after school to use the computer software have earned *lower* scores than those who have not used the software. "How can this be?" he puzzles. "Is the computer software actually doing more harm than good?"

1. **Constructed-response question:**

   Mr. Gualtieri wonders whether the computer software is actually hurting, rather than helping, his students. Assume that the software has been carefully designed by an experienced educator. Assume, too, that Mr. Gualtieri's classroom test is a good measure of how well his students have learned the material they've been studying.

   A. Explain why Mr. Gualtieri cannot draw a conclusion about a cause-and-effect relationship from the evidence he has. Base your response on principles of educational research.

   B. Identify another plausible explanation for the results Mr. Gualtieri has obtained.

2. **Multiple-choice question:**

   Which one of the following results would provide the most convincing evidence that the Problem-Excel software enhances students' mathematics achievement?

a. Ten high schools in New York City purchase Problem-Excel and make it available to their students. Students at these high schools get higher mathematics achievement test scores than students at ten other high schools that have *not* purchased the software.
b. A high school purchases Problem-Excel, but only four of the eight math teachers at the school decide to have their students use it. The students of these four teachers score at higher levels on a mathematics achievement test than the students of the other four teachers.
c. All tenth graders at a large high school take a mathematics achievement test in September. At some point during the next two months, each student spends 20 hours working with Problem-Excel. The students all take the same math achievement test again in December and, on average, get substantially higher scores than they did in September.
d. Students at a high school are randomly assigned to two groups. One group works with Problem-Excel, and the other group works with a software program called Write-Away, designed to teach better writing skills. The Problem-Excel group scores higher than the Write-Away group on a subsequent mathematics achievement test.

Go to Chapter 1 of the Book-Specific Resources section in **MyEducationLab**, and click on "Practice for Your Licensure Exam" to answer these questions. Compare your responses with the feedback provided.

PRAXIS

Turn to Appendix C, "Matching Book and MyEducationLab to the Praxis Principles of Learning and Teaching Tests," to discover sections of this chapter that may be especially applicable to the Praxis tests.

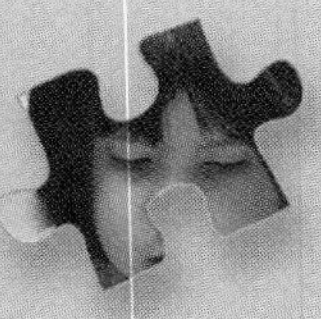

PEARSON **myeducationlab**

Now go to MyEducationLab (**www.myeducationlab.com**), where you can:

- Find learning outcomes for Research Methods and Teacher Reflection, along with the national standards that connect to these outcomes.
- Complete Assignments and Activities that can help you more deeply understand the chapter content.
- Engage in Building Teaching Skills and Dispositions exercises in which you can apply and practice core teaching skills identified in the chapter.
- Access Book-Specific Resources:
  - Check your comprehension of chapter content by going to the Study Plan, where you can find (a) Chapter Objectives; (b) Focus Questions that can guide your reading; (c) a Self-Check Quiz that can help you monitor your progress in mastering chapter content; (d) Review, Practice, and Enrichment exercises with detailed feedback that will deepen your understanding of various concepts and principles; (e) Flashcards that can give you practice in understanding and defining key terms; and (f) Common Beliefs and Misconceptions about Educational Psychology that will alert you to typical misunderstandings in educational psychology classes.
  - Supplementary Readings that enable you to pursue certain topics in greater depth.
  - A Practice for Your Licensure Exam exercise that resembles the kinds of questions appearing on many teacher licensure tests.

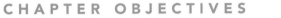

CHAPTER OUTLINE

- **CASE STUDY: APPLE TARTS**
- **GENERAL PRINCIPLES OF HUMAN DEVELOPMENT**
  The Multiple Layers of Environmental Influence: Bronfenbrenner's Theory
- **ROLE OF THE BRAIN IN LEARNING AND DEVELOPMENT**
- **PIAGET'S THEORY OF COGNITIVE DEVELOPMENT**
  Piaget's Basic Assumptions • Piaget's Stages of Cognitive Development • Critiquing Piaget's Theory • Considering Diversity from the Perspective of Piaget's Theory • Contemporary Extensions and Applications of Piaget's Theory
- **VYGOTSKY'S THEORY OF COGNITIVE DEVELOPMENT**
  Vygotsky's Basic Assumptions • Critiquing Vygotsky's Theory • Considering Diversity from the Perspective of Vygotsky's Theory • Contemporary Extensions and Applications of Vygotsky's Theory
- **LANGUAGE DEVELOPMENT**
  Theoretical Issues Regarding Language Development • Trends in Language Development • Diversity in Language Development • Second-Language Learning and English Language Learners
- **THE BIG PICTURE**
- **PRACTICE FOR YOUR LICENSURE EXAM: STONES LESSON**

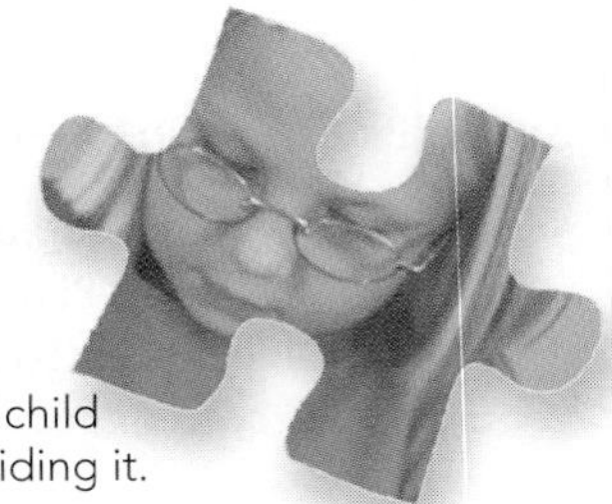

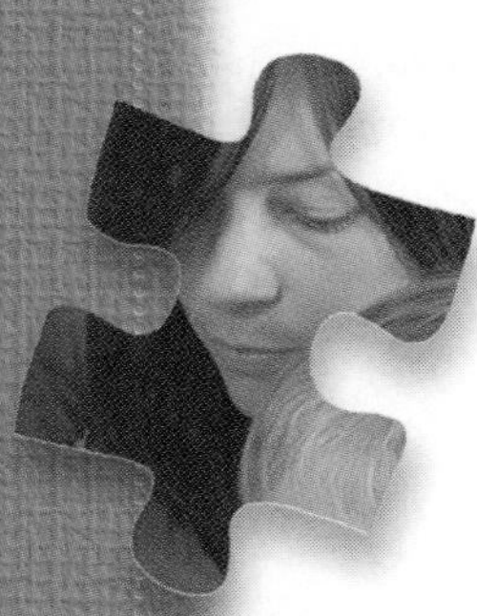

CHAPTER OBJECTIVES

- **Objective 2.1:** Describe four principles portraying the general nature of child development and the importance of both heredity and environment in guiding it.
- **Objective 2.2:** Explain how the brain and its development influence children's learning and thinking.
- **Objective 2.3:** Apply Piaget's theory of cognitive development to classroom practice.
- **Objective 2.4:** Apply Vygotsky's theory of cognitive development to classroom practice.
- **Objective 2.5:** Describe the typical course of language development over childhood and adolescence, and explain how you might adapt instruction to children with diverse language abilities and needs.

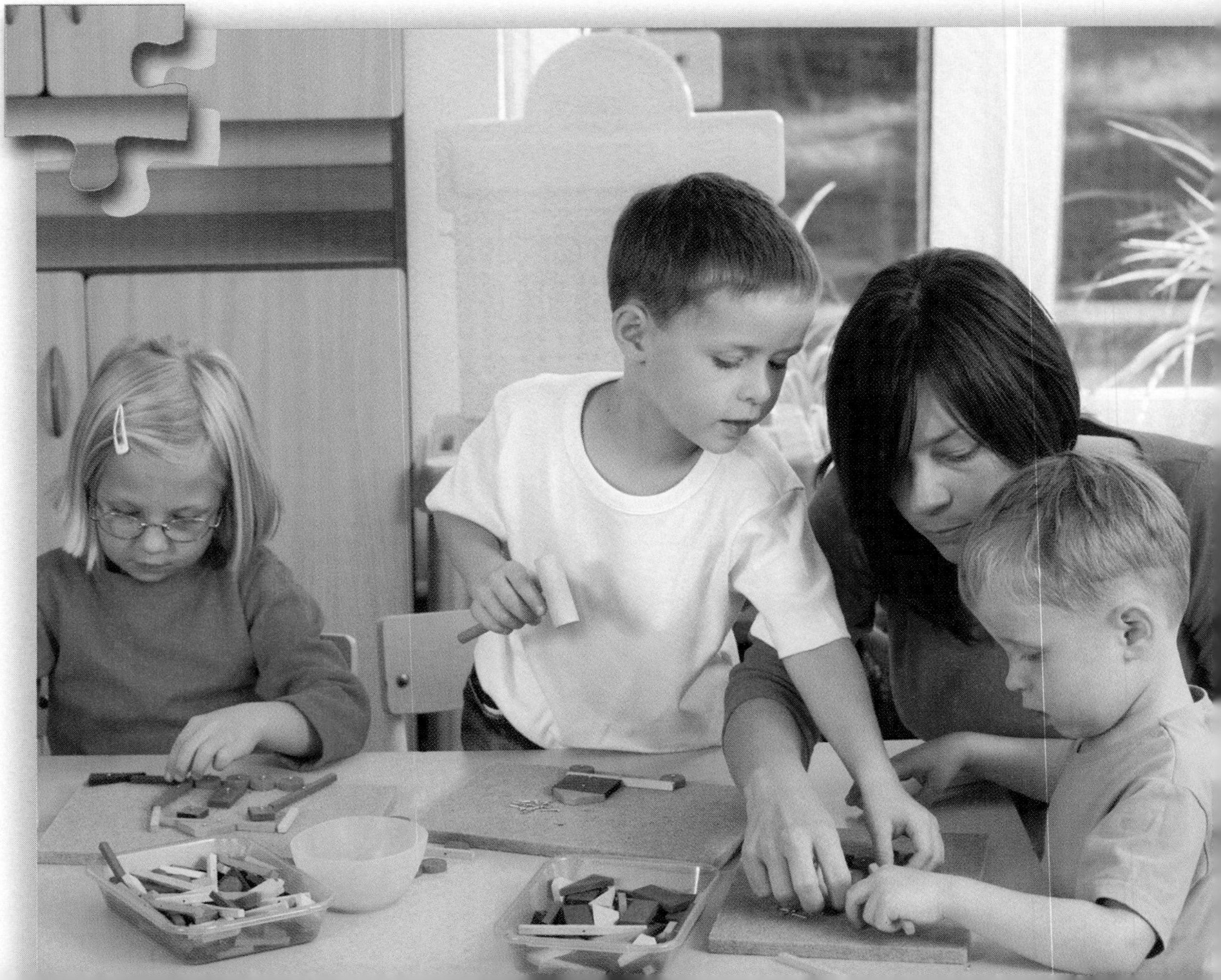

Chapter 2

Cognitive and Linguistic Development

CASE STUDY: Apple Tarts

Ms. Lombard's fourth-grade class has been studying fractions. The students have learned how to add and subtract fractions, but Ms. Lombard has not yet taught them how to *divide* by fractions. Nevertheless, she gives her students the following problem, which can be solved by dividing 20 by ¾:

> Mom makes small apple tarts, using three-quarters of an apple for each small tart. She has 20 apples. How many small apple tarts can she make? (J. Hiebert et al., 1997, p. 118)

Ms. Lombard asks her students to work in small groups to figure out how they might solve the problem. One group of four girls—Jeanette, Liz, Kerri, and Nina—has been working on the problem for some time and so far has arrived at such answers as 15, 38, and 23. We join them midway through their discussion, when they've already agreed that they can use three-fourths of each apple to make a total of 20 tarts, with one-fourth of each apple being left over.

Jeanette: In each apple there is a quarter left. In each apple there is a quarter left, so you've used, you've made twenty tarts already and you've got a quarter of twenty see—

Liz: So you've got twenty quarters *left.*

Jeanette: Yes, . . . and twenty quarters is equal to five apples, . . . so five apples divided by—

Liz: Six, seven, eight.

Jeanette: But three-quarters equals three.

Kerri: But she can't make only three apple tarts!

Jeanette: No, you've still got twenty.

Liz: But you've got twenty quarters, if you've got twenty quarters you might be right.

Jeanette: I'll show you.

Liz: No, I've drawn them all here.

Kerri: How many quarters have you got? Twenty?

Liz: Yes, one quarter makes five apples and out of five apples she can make five tarts which will make that twenty-five tarts and then she will have, wait, one, two, three, four, five quarters, she'll have one, two, three, four, five quarters. . . .

Nina: I've got a better . . .

Kerri: Yes?

Liz: Twenty-six quarters and a remainder of one quarter left. (J. Hiebert et al., 1997, p. 121)

The discussion and occasional disagreements continue, and the girls eventually arrive at the correct answer: Mom can make 26 tarts and then will have half an apple left over.

- **Why do the girls find this problem so difficult?**

ONE REASON THAT THE STUDENTS ARE STRUGGLING, of course, is that Ms. Lombard has never taught them how to divide by fractions. But in addition, fractions are inherently more complex and abstract than whole numbers are. If you think back to your own elementary school years, you may possibly recall fractions being a source of confusion for you, especially once you had to begin using them in multiplication

and division problems. Perhaps you gained a greater understanding of fractions—and a greater comfort level with using them—as you got older and used them more frequently in your math classes and elsewhere. Even so, some of my readers are apt to have difficulty with the apple tarts problem even now, as adults.[1]

As children get older, they change in many obvious physical ways. For instance, they grow taller and stronger, can run faster, and can write and draw with more dexterity and precision. But just as important are their many *internal* changes. For example, they become increasingly able to think about complex topics, greatly expand their understandings of who they are as individuals, and gradually develop a set of personal standards that guide their day-to-day behaviors and moral decision making.

Classroom instruction must be *developmentally appropriate*: It must take into account the physical, cognitive, social, and emotional characteristics and abilities that a particular age-group is likely to have. To some extent, we'll look at developmental differences in children's thinking and behavior in every chapter of this book. But the nature of child and adolescent development will be our particular focus in Chapters 2 and 3. In this chapter, we'll look at general principles of development and then zero in on children's **cognitive development**—that is, developmental changes in their thinking, reasoning, and language. As we look at these topics in the pages ahead, we'll gain additional insights into the opening case study.

General Principles of Human Development

Regardless of whether we're talking about children's physical development, cognitive development, or some other developmental domain, four general principles seem to hold true:

- *The sequence of development is somewhat predictable.* Researchers have observed many **universals** in development; that is, they've seen similar patterns in how children change over time despite considerable differences in the environments in which the children grow up. Some of this universality is marked by the acquisition of **developmental milestones**—new, developmentally more advanced behaviors—in predictable sequences. For example, children usually learn to walk only after they have already learned to sit up and crawl. They become capable of using fractions in mathematical problem solving only after they have mastered counting and the use of whole numbers. And they become concerned about what other people think of them only after they realize that other people *do* think about them.

- *Children develop at different rates.* Not all children reach particular milestones at the same age: Some reach them earlier, some later. Accordingly, we are apt to see considerable *diversity* in students' developmental accomplishments at any single grade level. Accordingly, we should never jump to conclusions about what individual students can and cannot do based on age alone.

Keep in mind that students of any single age show considerable diversity in what they can and cannot do.

- *Development is often marked by periods of relatively rapid growth (spurts) between periods of slower growth (plateaus).* Development does not necessarily proceed at a constant rate. For example, toddlers may speak with a limited vocabulary and one-word "sentences" for several months, yet sometime around their second birthday their vocabulary expands rapidly and their sentences become longer and longer within just a few weeks. As another example, children gain an average of two or three inches in height per year during the early elementary school grades

cognitive development Development of increasingly sophisticated thinking, reasoning, and language with age.

universals Similar patterns in how children change and progress over time regardless of their specific environment.

developmental milestone Appearance of a new, more advanced behavior that indicates significant progress in a child's development.

[1]In case your memory of how to divide by a fraction is rusty, you can approach the problem $20 \div \frac{3}{4}$ by inverting the fraction and multiplying, as in $20 \times \frac{4}{3} = \frac{80}{3} = 26\frac{2}{3}$. Thus, Mom can make 26 tarts and have enough apple left to make two-thirds of another tart. If she needs three-fourths of an apple and she has two-thirds of what she needs to make another whole tart, then she has $\frac{2}{3} \times \frac{3}{4} = \frac{6}{12} = \frac{1}{2}$. Thus, half an apple is left over.

but may gain as much as five inches per year during their adolescent growth spurt (A. C. Harris, 1986). Occasionally children even take a temporary step *backward*, apparently because they are in the process of overhauling a particular skill or way of thinking and are about to make a major leap forward (Gershkoff-Stowe & Thelen, 2004; Nucci, 2009). Some developmental theorists use such patterns of uneven growth and change as evidence of qualitatively distinct periods, or *stages*, in development.

Some descriptive research studies tell us the *average* age at which children reach various developmental milestones. But we must remember that individual children develop at different rates.

- *Heredity and environment interact in their effects on development.* Virtually all aspects of development are influenced either directly or indirectly by a child's genetic makeup. For example, soon after birth children begin to show genetic predispositions to respond to physical and social events in certain ways—perhaps to be calm or irritable, outgoing or shy, cheerful or fearful (more on such *temperaments* in Chapter 3). Not all inherited characteristics appear so early, however. Heredity continues to guide a child's growth through the process of **maturation**, a gradual, genetically controlled progression of physical advancements as the child develops. For example, motor skills such as walking, running, and jumping develop primarily as a result of neurological development, increased strength, and increased muscular control—changes that are largely determined by inherited biological "instructions."

myeducationlab

Learn more about children's physical development in a supplementary reading, "Physical Development Across Childhood and Adolescence." (To find this reading, go to Chapter 2 of the Book-Specific Resources in MyEducationLab, and then select Supplementary Readings.)

Yet environmental factors also make substantial contributions to development. For example, although height and body build are primarily inherited characteristics, the nutritional value of a child's food affects the specific height and body build the child ultimately acquires. And although children's behaviors are partly the result of inherited temperaments, the ways in which their environment encourages them to behave are just as influential—sometimes even more so.

Historically, many researchers have sought to determine the degree to which certain human characteristics (intelligence, personality, etc.) are the result of heredity versus environment—a question often referred to as *nature versus nurture*. But increasingly, psychologists have come to realize that heredity and environment interact in ways we can probably never disentangle (e.g., Belsky, Bakermans-Kranenburg, & van IJzendoorn, 2007; Gottlieb, 2000; Kolb, Gibb, & Robinson, 2003). First and foremost, genes need environmental support in order to do their work. For instance, a child with "tall" genes can become tall only if good nutrition supports such growth. Furthermore, some genetically driven maturational processes seem to be characterized by **sensitive periods**, limited time periods during which certain environmental conditions seem to be especially important for normal development (we'll see examples in our upcoming discussions of brain development and language development). In addition, children's inherited characteristics may lead other people to treat them in particular ways (Scarr & McCartney, 1983). For instance, a physically attractive child will be accepted more readily by peers than a less attractive one, and a temperamentally hyperactive child may be disciplined more harshly than a quieter one. Finally, children can *choose* their environments to some extent, especially as they get older, and they are apt to seek out situations that match their inherited temperaments and abilities (Scarr & McCartney, 1983).

The last point in the preceding paragraph is important enough that it bears repeating: *Children can choose their environments to some extent.* As we will see frequently throughout the book, children are hardly passive recipients of their environmental legacies. Instead, they actively and intentionally *think about* and *act on* their environments, and in doing so, they alter their environments—and the effects of those environments—in significant ways (e.g., Kağitçibaşi, 2007; Mareschal et al., 2007; Nettles, Caughy, & O'Campo, 2008).

maturation Occurrence of genetically controlled physical advancements as a child develops.

sensitive period Age range during which a certain aspect of a child's development is especially susceptible to environmental conditions (you may sometimes see the term *critical period*).

myeducationlab

Learn more about Bronfenbrenner's ecological systems perspectives in a supplementary reading, "Ecological Systems Perspectives of Child Development." (To find this reading, go to Chapter 2 of the Book-Specific Resources in MyEducationLab and then select Supplementary Readings.)

The Multiple Layers of Environmental Influence: Bronfenbrenner's Theory

As we consider the various ways in which environment might influence children's development, we must be careful that we don't limit our thinking only to children's immediate surroundings. In fact, as the late developmental theorist Urie Bronfenbrenner pointed out, any large society (e.g., a state, province, or country) encompasses various "layers" of environment that affect children's development in one way or another (Bronfenbrenner, 1989, 2005; Bronfenbrenner & Morris, 1998).

The most basic level for most children is the *family*, which can potentially support development in a number of ways—for instance, by providing good nutrition, helping with homework assignments, working cooperatively with teachers to address learning and behavior problems, and so on. Surrounding the family is another layer, the neighborhood and community, which can offer additional support, definitely through its schools (in industrialized societies, at least) and perhaps also through preschools, after-school homework assistance programs, libraries, museums, zoos, and internships in local businesses. At a still broader level, the state (or province) and country in which children reside influence development through legislation that governs school policy, tax dollars that flow back to local schools, agencies and professional groups that offer information and training in new teaching strategies, and so on. Figure 2.1 illustrates the kinds of environmental influences that the different layers might involve.

FIGURE 2.1 Examples of various layers of environmental influences

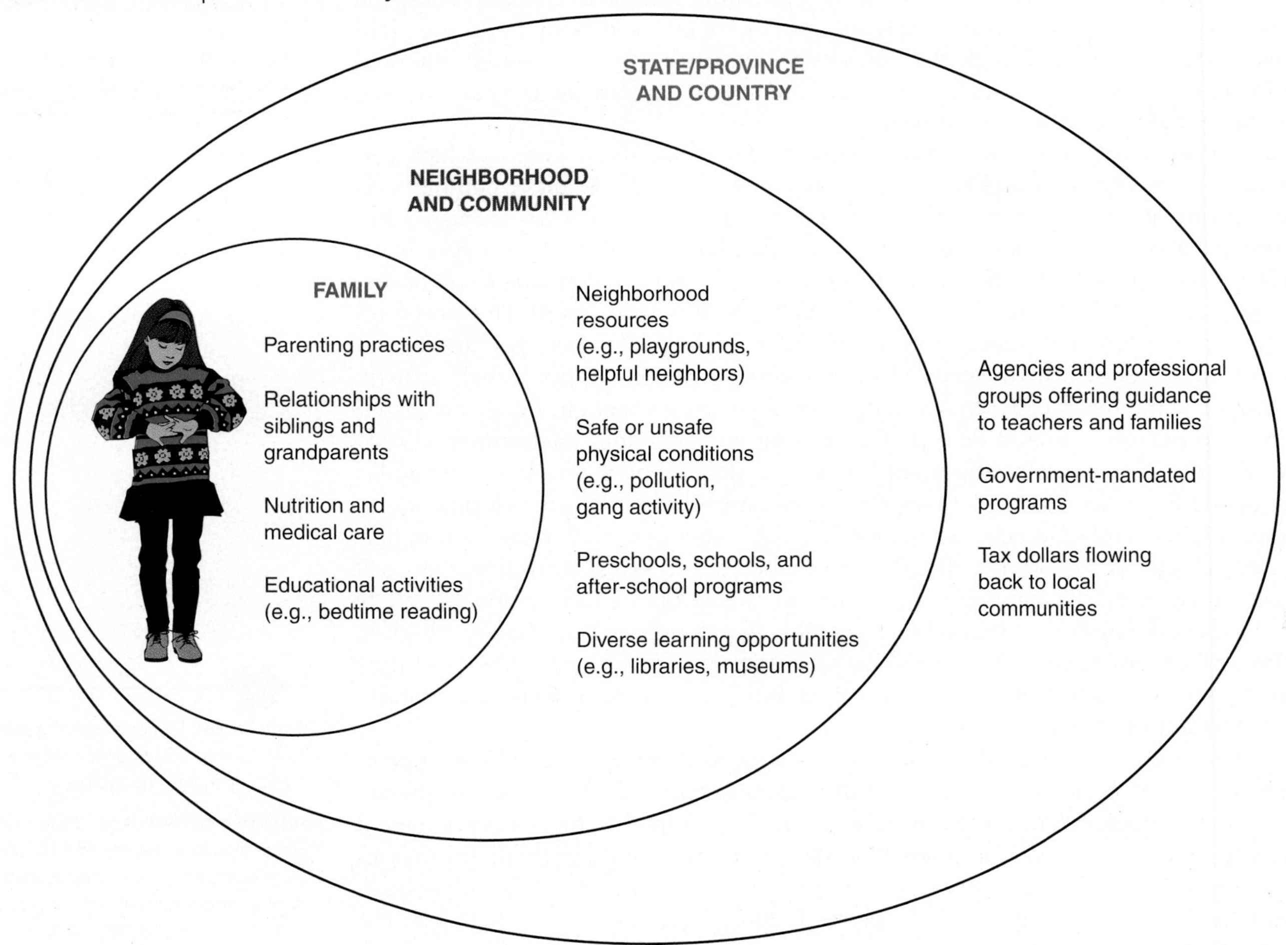

Permeating all of these layers is a child's **culture**—the behaviors and belief systems that characterize the long-standing social group of which the child is a member. Culture is pervasive in many aspects of a child's environment—for instance, in the behaviors family members encourage, the disciplinary practices parents use, the books children have access to, the television shows they watch, and so on. But culture is an inside-the-head thing as well as an out-there-in-the-world thing: It provides an overall framework by which a child comes to determine what things are normal and abnormal, true and not true, rational and irrational, good and bad (M. Cole, 2006; Shweder et al., 1998).

FIGURE 2.2 Neurons and their interconnections

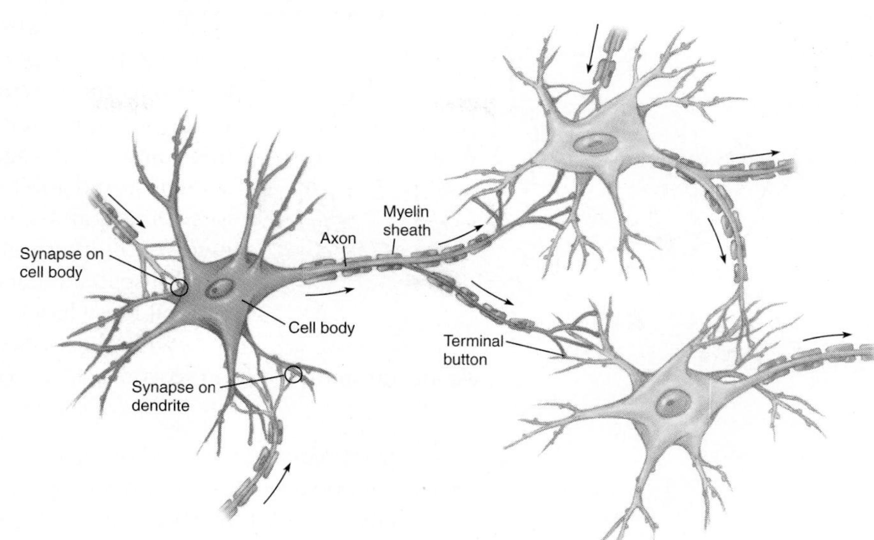

Role of the Brain in Learning and Development

One key player in children's development is, of course, the brain. The human brain is an incredibly complicated organ that includes roughly 100 billion nerve cells (Goodman & Tessier-Lavigne, 1997; Siegel, 1999). These nerve cells, known as **neurons**, are microscopic in size and interconnected in innumerable ways. Some neurons receive information from the rest of the body, others synthesize and interpret that information, and still others send messages that tell the body how to respond to its present circumstances.

Neurons vary in shape and size, but all of them have several features in common (see Figure 2.2). First, like other cells in living creatures, a neuron has a *cell body*, which contains its nucleus and is responsible for its health and well-being. Furthermore, it has a number of branchlike structures called *dendrites*, which receive messages from other neurons. A neuron also has an *axon*, a long, armlike structure that transmits information to other neurons. The axon may branch out many times, and the ends of its tiny branches have *terminal buttons* that contain certain chemical substances (more about these substances in a moment). For some (but not all) neurons, much of the axon has a white, fatty coating called a *myelin sheath*.

When a neuron's dendrites are stimulated by other neurons (either those in the brain or those extending from other parts of the body), the dendrites become electrically charged. If the total charge reaches a certain level, the neuron fires, sending an electrical impulse along its axon to the terminal buttons. If the axon has a myelin sheath, the impulse travels quite rapidly, because it leaps from one gap in the myelin to the next, almost as if it were playing leap frog. If the axon does not have a myelin sheath, the impulse travels more slowly.

Curiously, neurons don't actually touch one another. Instead, they send chemical messages to their neighbors across tiny spaces known as **synapses**. When an electrical impulse moves along a neuron's axon, it signals the terminal buttons to release chemicals known as **neurotransmitters**. These chemicals travel across the synapses and stimulate the dendrites or cell bodies of neighboring neurons. Any single neuron may have synaptic connections with hundreds or even thousands of other neurons (Goodman & Tessier-Lavigne, 1997; Lichtman, 2001).

Groups of neurons in different parts of the brain seem to specialize in different things. Structures in the lower and middle parts of the brain specialize in essential physiological processes (e.g., breathing, heart rate), bodily movements (e.g., walking, riding a bicycle), and basic perceptual skills (e.g., coordinating eye movements, diverting

culture Behaviors and belief systems of a long-standing social group.

neuron Cell in the brain or another part of the nervous system that transmits information to other cells.

synapse Junction between two neurons that allows transmission of messages from one to the other.

neurotransmitter Chemical substance through which one neuron sends a message to another.

FIGURE 2.3 Cortex of the human brain

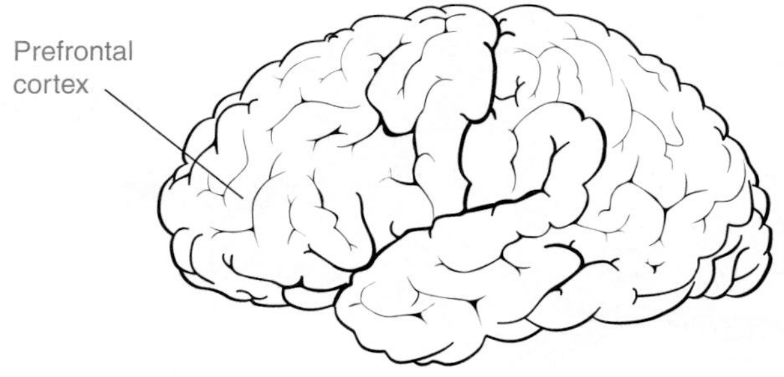

attention to potentially life-threatening stimuli). Complex, conscious thinking takes place primarily in the **cortex**, which rests on the top and sides of the brain like a thick, bumpy toupee (see Figure 2.3). The portion of the cortex located near the forehead, known as the *prefrontal cortex*, is largely responsible for a wide variety of very human activities, including sustained attention, reasoning, planning, decision making, coordination of complex activities, and inhibition of nonproductive thoughts and behaviors. Other parts of the cortex are important as well, being actively involved in interpreting visual and auditory information, identifying the spatial characteristics of objects and events, and retaining general knowledge about the world.

With these basics in mind, let's consider four key points about the brain's role in learning and cognitive development:

• *Most learning probably involves changes in neurons and synapses.* Many researchers believe that the physiological basis for learning (and thus for a good deal of cognitive development) lies in changes in the interconnections among neurons. In particular, learning often involves strengthening existing synapses or forming new ones. In some instances, however, making progress actually involves *eliminating* synapses. Effective learning requires not only that people think and do certain things but also that they *not* think and do other things—in other words, that they inhibit tendencies to think or behave in particular ways (Bruer & Greenough, 2001; Lichtman, 2001; Merzenich, 2001).

Another phenomenon may be involved in learning as well. Until recently, most experts believed that all the neurons a person would ever have are produced in the first few weeks after conception—that is, many months before a child is born. Researchers are finding, however, that some new neurons continue to form throughout life in certain parts of the brain (Gould, Beylin, Tanapat, Reeves, & Shors, 1999; C. A. Nelson, Thomas, & de Haan, 2006; R. A. Thompson & Nelson, 2001). Neuron formation appears to be stimulated by new learning experiences, although its exact role in the learning process is still unknown.

• *Developmental changes in the brain enable increasingly complex and efficient thought.* Neurons begin to form synapses long before a child is born. But shortly after birth, the rate of synapse formation increases dramatically. Neurons sprout new dendrites in many directions, and so they come into contact with many of their neighbors, especially in the first two or three years of life. Much of this early **synaptogenesis** appears to be driven primarily by genetic programming, rather than by learning experiences. Thanks to synaptogenesis, children in the elementary grades have many more synapses than adults do (Bruer, 1999; C. A. Nelson et al., 2006).

Theorists speculate that by generating a large number of synapses in the early years, children have the potential to adapt to a wide variety of conditions and circumstances. As they encounter different stimuli and experiences in their daily lives, some of their synapses come in quite handy and are used repeatedly. Other synapses are largely useless, and these gradually fade away through a process known as **synaptic pruning**. Synaptic pruning is a good thing, not a bad one, as it eliminates nuisance synapses that are inconsistent with typical environmental events and behavioral patterns (Bruer & Greenough, 2001; Spear, 2007). In some parts of the brain, intensive synaptic pruning occurs fairly early (e.g., in the preschool or early elementary years). In other parts, it begins later and extends into adolescence and beyond (Bruer, 1999; Huttenlocher & Dabholkar, 1997; M. H. Johnson & de Haan, 2001; Silveri et al., 2006). But even as synaptic pruning is occurring, children and adolescents—in fact, people of all ages—continue to form new synapses in response to their experiences (R. D. Brown & Bjorklund, 1998; Fischer & Rose, 1996; O'Boyle & Gill, 1998).

Another important developmental process in the brain is **myelination**. When neurons first develop, their axons have no myelin sheath. As they acquire this myelin over

cortex Upper part of the brain; site of complex, conscious thinking processes.

synaptogenesis Universal process in early brain development in which many new synapses form spontaneously.

synaptic pruning Universal process in brain development in which many previously formed synapses wither away.

myelination Growth of a fatty sheath (myelin) around the axons of neurons, enabling faster transmission of messages.

time, they fire much more quickly, greatly enhancing the brain's overall efficiency. Myelination continues throughout childhood, adolescence, and early adulthood, especially in the cortex (Lenroot & Giedd, 2007; Merzenich, 2001; Paus et al., 1999).

In addition, the onset of puberty is marked by significant changes in hormone levels, which affect the continuing maturation of brain structures and possibly also affect the production and effectiveness of neurotransmitters (Eisenberg, Martin, & Fabes, 1996; Kolb et al., 2003; E. F. Walker, 2002). Theorists have speculated that such changes may have an impact on adolescents' functioning in a variety of areas, including attention, planning, and impulse control.

Keep in mind that adolescents' brains have not yet fully matured. In particular, they may have trouble with maintaining attention, planning, and controlling impulses.

• *Many parts of the brain work in harmony to enable complex thinking and behavior.* To some degree, the left and right halves, or *hemispheres*, of the cortex have different specialties. For most people (perhaps 80%), the left hemisphere takes primary responsibility for language and logical thinking, whereas the right hemisphere is more dominant in visual and spatial tasks (Byrnes, 2001; Ornstein, 1997; Siegel, 1999). Yet contrary to popular belief, people rarely, if ever, think exclusively in one part of the brain or even in one hemisphere. There is no such thing as "left-brain" or "right-brain" thinking: The two hemispheres constantly collaborate in day-to-day tasks. In fact, learning or thinking about virtually anything, even a fairly simple idea, tends to be *distributed* across many parts of the brain (Bressler, 2002; Posner & Rothbart, 2007). As an illustration, Figure 2.4 shows a computer-generated average of brain activation patterns measured in six adults who were asked to look at various photographs of single objects (Haxby et al., 2001). The figure shows two horizontal slices of the brain from the perspective of someone looking at the brain from above. Although the specific activation patterns differed somewhat depending on the kind of object being viewed (e.g., faces, cats, or houses), multiple parts of both the left and right hemispheres were activated for each of the objects.

FIGURE 2.4 Computer-generated pattern of typical brain activation in two different cross-sections of the brain when people look at photographs of single objects. Areas in red, orange, and yellow indicate higher-than-normal activation, and areas in blue indicate lower-than-normal activation (as compared to a "nonlooking" baseline).

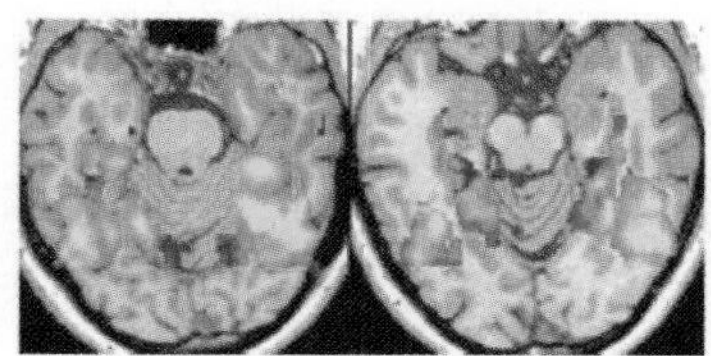

Source: From "Distributed and Overlapping Representations of Faces and Objects in Ventral Temporal Cortex" by J. V. Haxby, M. I. Gobbini, M. L. Furey, A. Ishai, J. L. Schouten, & P. Pietrini, 2001, *Science, 293*, p. 2427. Reprinted by permission of the American Association for the Advancement of Science.

• *The brain remains adaptable throughout life.* Some well-meaning educators have proposed that the proliferation of new synapses in the preschool and early elementary years points to a sensitive period in brain development. Accordingly, they urge us to maximize children's educational experiences—providing reading instruction, violin lessons, art classes, and so on—during this time period. But before you, too, jump to such a conclusion, consider this point: Although adequate nutrition and everyday forms of stimulation are critical for normal brain development, there is no evidence that jam-packed, information- and skill-intensive experiences in the early years enhance brain power over the long run (Bruer, 1999; R. A. Thompson & Nelson, 2001). If infants don't have normal exposure to patterns of light (e.g., if they are born with cataracts), they may soon lose the ability to see normally, and if children don't hear spoken language until age 5, they may never acquire the language's subtle grammatical complexities (Bruer, 1999; M. S. C. Thomas & Johnson, 2008). But seeing patterned light and hearing spoken language are *normal* experiences, not exceptional ones. There is *no* evidence to indicate that sensitive periods exist for traditional academic subjects such as reading and mathematics (Bruer, 1999; Geary, 1998; Greenough, Black, & Wallace, 1987).

From a physiological standpoint, the brain's ability to adapt to changing circumstances—that is, its ability to *learn*—continues throughout the life span (Kolb et al., 2003; C. A. Nelson et al., 2006). The early years are important for development, to be sure, but so are the later years. For most topics and skills, there is *not* a single "best" or "only" time to learn (R. D. Brown & Bjorklund, 1998; Bruer, 1999; Byrnes & Fox, 1998).

Be optimistic that students of all ages can acquire a wide variety of new topics and skills.

Even as researchers gradually pin down how the brain works and develops, current knowledge of brain physiology doesn't give us many specifics about how best to foster students' learning and cognitive development (Byrnes, 2001, 2007; Mayer, 1998; Varma, McCandliss, & Schwartz, 2008). In fact, educators who talk about "using brain research" or "brain-based learning" are, in most instances, actually talking about what psychologists have learned from studies of human *behavior*, rather than from studies of brain anatomy and physiology. By and large, if we want to understand the nature of human learning and cognitive development, we must look primarily at what psychologists, rather than neurologists, have discovered.

Over the years, psychologists have offered numerous explanations of how and why children's thinking processes develop and change with time. Two early theories—those of Jean Piaget and Lev Vygotsky—have been especially influential in guiding contemporary theorists' views of how children develop and learn.

Piaget's Theory of Cognitive Development

Do you think of yourself as a logical individual? Just how logical *are* you? Try your logical reasoning abilities in the following exercise.

EXPERIENCING FIRSTHAND
Beads, Beings, and Basketballs

Take a moment to solve the following three problems:

1. In the margin are 12 wooden beads. Ten are brown and 2 are white. Are there more brown beads or more wooden beads?
2. If all children are human beings,
   and if all human beings are living creatures,
   then must all children be living creatures?
3. If all children are basketballs,
   and if all basketballs are jellybeans,
   then must all children be jellybeans?

You undoubtedly found the first problem ridiculously easy; there are, of course, more wooden beads than brown beads. You may have found the second problem more difficult but were probably able to conclude fairly quickly that, yes, all children must be living creatures. The third problem is a bit tricky: It follows the same line of reasoning as the second, but the conclusion it leads to—that all children must be jellybeans—contradicts what is true in reality.

In the early 1920s, the Swiss biologist Jean Piaget began studying children's responses to problems of this nature. He used an approach he called the **clinical method**, in which an adult presents a task or problem and asks a child a series of questions about it, tailoring later questions to the child's responses to previous ones. As an example, let's look at what happened when a researcher in Piaget's laboratory presented the wooden beads problem to a 6-year-old, whom we'll call Brian:[2]

Adult: Are there more wooden beads or more brown beads?

Brian: More brown ones, because there are two white ones.

Adult: Are the white ones made of wood?

Brian: Yes.

Adult: And the brown ones?

Brian: Yes.

clinical method Procedure in which an adult presents a task or problem and asks a child a series of questions about it, tailoring later questions to the child's responses to previous ones.

[2]Piaget used abbreviations to identify specific children in his studies. In this case, he used the letters *BRI,* but I've given the child a name to allow for easier discussion.

Adult: Then are there more brown ones or more wooden ones?

Brian: More brown ones.

Adult: What color would a necklace made of the wooden beads be?

Brian: Brown and white. (Here Brian shows that he understands that all the beads are wooden.)

Adult: And what color would a necklace made with the brown beads be?

Brian: Brown.

Adult: Then which would be longer, the one made with the wooden beads or the one made with the brown beads?

Brian: The one with the brown beads.

Adult: Draw the necklaces for me.

Brian draws a series of black rings for the necklace of brown beads; he then draws a series of black rings plus two white rings for the necklace of wooden beads.

Adult: Good. Now which will be longer, the one with the brown beads or the one with the wooden beads?

Brian: The one with the brown beads. (Piaget, 1952a, pp. 163–164)

Notice how the adult continues to probe Brian's reasoning to be sure he realizes that all of the beads are wooden but only some are brown. Even so, Brian holds steadfastly to his conclusion that there are more brown beads than wooden ones. Piaget suggested that young children such as Brian have trouble with **class inclusion** tasks, in which they must think of an object as simultaneously belonging to a category and one of its subcategories—in this case, thinking of a bead as being both *wooden* and *brown* at the same time.

In his research, Piaget found that many 4- and 5-year-olds have difficulty with class inclusion tasks such as the beads problem but that 7- and 8-year-olds almost always respond to such tasks correctly. He found, too, that 10-year-olds have an easier time with logic problems that involve real-world phenomena (such as categories and subcategories of living creatures) than with problems involving hypothetical and contrary-to-fact ideas (such as jellybean children). Only adolescents can effectively deal with the latter kinds of problems. Through a variety of thought-provoking questions and tasks, Piaget and his research colleagues discovered a great deal about how children think and learn about the world around them (e.g., Inhelder & Piaget, 1958; Piaget, 1928, 1952b, 1959, 1970, 1980).

myeducationlab

Observe 2-year-old Maddie's experimentation with a new object in the video "Cognitive Development: Early Childhood." (To find this video, go to Chapter 2 of the Book-Specific Resources in MyEducationLab, select *Video Examples*, and then click on the title.)

Piaget's Basic Assumptions

Piaget introduced a number of ideas and concepts to describe and explain the changes in logical thinking he observed in children and adolescents:

- *Children are active and motivated learners.* Piaget believed that children are naturally motivated to learn how to live in and adapt to their environment. Accordingly, they are curious about their world and actively seek out information to help them understand and make sense of it. They continually experiment with the objects they encounter, manipulating them and observing the effects of their actions.

- *Children construct rather than absorb knowledge.* In their day-to-day experiences, children don't just passively soak up a collection of isolated facts. Instead, they pull their experiences together into an integrated view of how the world operates. For example, by observing that food, toys, and other objects always fall down (never up) when released, children begin to construct a rudimentary understanding of gravity. As they interact with family pets, visit zoos, look at picture books, and so on, they develop more complex understandings of animals. Because Piaget

class inclusion Recognition that an object simultaneously belongs to a particular category and to one of its subcategories.

proposed that children construct their own beliefs and understandings from their experiences, his theory is sometimes called a *constructivist* theory or, more generally, **constructivism**.

In Piaget's terminology, the things that children do and know are organized as **schemes**—groups of similar actions or thoughts that are used repeatedly in response to the environment. Initially, schemes are largely behavioral in nature, but over time, they become increasingly mental and, eventually, abstract. For example, an infant may have a putting-things-in-mouth scheme that she calls on when dealing with a variety of objects, including her thumb, cookies, and toys. A 7-year-old may have a scheme for identifying snakes that includes their long, thin bodies, their lack of legs, and their slithery nature. A 13-year-old may have a scheme for what constitutes *fashion*, allowing her to classify her peers as being either very cool or "total losers."

Over time, children's schemes are modified with experience and become integrated with one another. For instance, children begin to take hierarchical interrelationships into account: They learn that poodles and cocker spaniels are both dogs, that dogs and cats are both animals, and so on. A progressively more organized body of knowledge and thought processes allows children to think in increasingly complex and logical ways.

• *Children learn through a combination of assimilation and accommodation.* Although children's schemes change over time, the processes by which children develop them remain the same. Piaget proposed that learning and cognitive development occur as a result of two complementary processes: assimilation and accommodation. **Assimilation** entails dealing with an object or event in a way that is consistent with an existing scheme. For example, an infant may assimilate a new teddy bear into her putting-things-in-mouth scheme. A 7-year-old may quickly identify a new slithery object in the backyard as a snake. A 13-year-old may readily label a classmate's clothing as being either quite fashionable or "soooo yesterday."

But sometimes children cannot easily relate to a new object or event with existing schemes. In these situations one of two forms of **accommodation** occurs: Children either modify an existing scheme to account for the new object or event or else form an entirely new scheme to deal with it. For example, an infant may have to open her mouth wider than usual to accommodate a teddy bear's fat paw. A 13-year-old may have to revise her existing scheme of fashion according to changes in what's hot and what's not. A 7-year-old may find a long, thin, slithery thing that can't possibly be a snake because it has four legs. After some research, he may develop a new scheme—*salamander*—for this creature.

When introducing a new concept or procedure, show students how it relates to something they already know.

Assimilation and accommodation typically work hand in hand as children develop their knowledge and understanding of the world. Children interpret each new event within the context of their existing knowledge (assimilation) but at the same time may modify their knowledge as a result of the new event (accommodation). Accommodation rarely happens without assimilation: Children can benefit from, or accommodate to, new experiences only when they can relate those experiences to their current knowledge and beliefs.

constructivism Theoretical perspective proposing that learners construct, rather than absorb, knowledge from their experiences.

scheme Organized group of similar actions or thoughts that are used repeatedly in response to the environment.

assimilation Process of dealing with a new event in a way that is consistent with an existing scheme.

accommodation Process of dealing with a new event by either modifying an existing scheme or forming a new one.

• *Interactions with one's physical and social environments are essential for cognitive development.* According to Piaget, active experimentation with the physical world is critical for cognitive growth. By exploring and manipulating physical objects—fiddling with sand and water, playing games with balls and bats, and so on—children learn the nature of such characteristics as volume and weight, discover principles related to force and gravity, and so on.

In Piaget's view, social interaction is equally important for cognitive development. Through interactions with other people—both pleasant (e.g., conversations) and unpleasant (e.g., conflicts about sharing and fair play)—young children gradually come to realize that different individuals see things differently and that their own view of the world is not necessarily a completely accurate or logical one. And as was evident in the case study at the beginning of the chapter, older children and adolescents may begin to recognize logical inconsistencies in what they say and do when someone else points out those inconsistencies.

• *The process of equilibration promotes progression toward increasingly complex thought.* Piaget suggested that children are often in a state of **equilibrium**: They can comfortably interpret and respond to new events using existing schemes. But as children grow older and expand their horizons, they sometimes encounter situations for which their current knowledge and skills are inadequate. Such situations create **disequilibrium**, a sort of mental discomfort that spurs them to try to make sense of what they are observing. By replacing, reorganizing, or better integrating certain schemes (i.e., through accommodation), children can better understand and address previously puzzling events. The process of moving from equilibrium to disequilibrium and back to equilibrium again is known as **equilibration**. In Piaget's view, equilibration and children's intrinsic desire to achieve equilibrium promote the development of more complex levels of thought and knowledge.

Present puzzling phenomena that students cannot easily explain using their existing understandings.

As an example, let's return to 6-year-old Brian's responses to the wooden beads problem. Recall that the adult asks Brian to draw two necklaces, one made with the wooden beads and one made with the brown beads. The adult hopes that after Brian draws a brown-and-white necklace that is longer than an all-brown necklace, he will notice that his drawings are inconsistent with his statement that there are more brown beads. The inconsistency might lead Brian to experience disequilibrium, perhaps to the point where he would reevaluate his conclusion and realize that the number of all the brown beads plus two white ones *must* be greater than the number of brown beads alone. In this case, however, Brian is apparently oblivious to the inconsistency, remains in equilibrium, and thus has no need to revise his thinking.

• *In part as a result of maturational changes in the brain, children think in qualitatively different ways at different ages.* Long before we knew much about how the brain changes with age, Piaget speculated that it *does* change in significant ways and that such changes enable more complex thought processes. He suggested that major neurological changes take place when children are about 2 years old, again when they are 6 or 7, and yet again around puberty. Changes at each of these times allow new abilities to emerge, such that children progress through a sequence of stages that reflect increasingly sophisticated thought. As we've seen, the brain does, in fact, continue to develop in childhood and adolescence, but whether such changes are specifically related to the cognitive changes Piaget described is still an open question.

Piaget's Stages of Cognitive Development

Piaget proposed that as a result of brain maturation, innumerable environmental experiences, and children's natural desire to make sense of and adapt to their world, cognitive development proceeds through four distinct stages (e.g., Piaget, 1971). Abilities at any one stage are constructed out of the accomplishments of any preceding stages. Thus, the four stages are *hierarchical*—each one provides a foundation for any subsequent stages—and so children progress through them in a particular order.

Table 2.1 summarizes these stages and presents examples of abilities acquired during each one. As you look at the table, keep in mind that many children are apt to be in *transition* from one stage to the next, displaying characteristics of two adjacent stages at the same time. Furthermore, as children gain abilities associated with more advanced stages, they don't necessarily leave behind the characteristics they acquired in previous stages.

As you can see from the age ranges in the table, the preoperational, concrete operations, and formal operations stages all occur during the school years, and so we will look at these three stages more closely.

equilibrium State of being able to address new events with existing schemes.

disequilibrium State of being unable to address new events with existing schemes; typically accompanied by some mental discomfort.

equilibration Movement from equilibrium to disequilibrium and back to equilibrium, a process that promotes development of more complex thought and understandings.

preoperational stage Piaget's second stage of cognitive development, in which children can think about objects and events beyond their immediate view but do not yet reason in logical, adultlike ways.

Preoperational Stage (age 2 until age 6 or 7) In the early part of the **preoperational stage**, children's language skills virtually explode, and the many words in their rapidly increasing vocabularies serve as *symbols* that enable them to

Compare/Contrast

TABLE 2.1
Piaget's Four Stages of Cognitive Development

Stage	Age of Onset	General Description	Examples of Abilities Acquired
Sensorimotor	Begins at birth	Schemes are based largely on behaviors and perceptions. Especially in the early part of this stage, children can't think about things that aren't immediately in front of them, and so they focus on what they are doing and seeing at the moment.	• *Trial-and-error experimentation with physical objects:* Exploration and manipulation of objects to determine their properties • *Object permanence:* Realization that objects continue to exist even when removed from view • *Symbolic thought:* Representation of physical objects and events as mental entities *(symbols)*
Preoperational	Emerges at about age 2	Thanks, in part, to their rapidly developing symbolic thinking abilities, children can now think and talk about things beyond their immediate experience. However, they don't yet reason in logical, adultlike ways.	• *Language:* Rapid expansion of vocabulary and grammatical structures • *Extensive pretend play:* Enactment of imaginary scenarios with plots and assigned roles (e.g., Mommy, doctor, Superman) • *Intuitive thought:* Some logical thinking (especially after age 4) but based primarily on hunches and intuition, rather than on conscious awareness of logical principles
Concrete Operations	Emerges at about age 6 or 7	Adultlike logic appears but is limited to reasoning about concrete, real-life situations.	• *Distinction between one's own and others' perspectives:* Recognition that one's own thoughts and feelings may be different from those of others and do not necessarily reflect reality • *Class inclusion:* Ability to classify objects as belonging to two or more categories simultaneously • *Conservation:* Realization that the amount stays the same if nothing is added or taken away, regardless of alterations in shape or arrangement
Formal Operations	Emerges at about age 11 or 12	Logical reasoning processes are applied to abstract ideas as well as to concrete objects and situations. Many capabilities appear that are essential for advanced reasoning in science and mathematics.	• *Logical reasoning about abstract, hypothetical, and contrary-to-fact ideas:* Ability to draw logical deductions about situations that have no basis in physical reality • *Proportional reasoning:* Conceptual understanding of fractions, percentages, decimals, and ratios • *Formulation of multiple hypotheses:* Ability to identify two or more competing hypotheses about possible cause-and-effect relationships • *Separation and control of variables:* Ability to test hypotheses by manipulating one variable while holding other relevant variables constant • *Idealism:* Ability to envision alternatives to current social and political practices, sometimes with little regard for what is realistically possible under existing circumstances

mentally represent and think about a wide variety of objects and events. However, preoperational thought has some definite limitations, especially when compared to the concrete operational thinking that emerges later. For example, Piaget described young children as exhibiting **preoperational egocentrism**, an inability to view situations from another person's perspective. As illustrations, preschoolers may play games together without checking to be sure that they are playing by the same rules, and they may tell stories in which they leave out details that are critical for their listeners' understanding.

sensorimotor stage Piaget's first stage of cognitive development, in which schemes are based largely on behaviors and perceptions.

preoperational egocentrism Inability of children in Piaget's preoperational stage to view situations from another person's perspective.

Young children's thinking also tends to be somewhat illogical at times, at least from an adult's point of view. We've already seen how young children have difficulty with class inclusion problems (recall 6-year-old Brian's insistence that the brown beads outnumber the wooden ones). In addition, they are apt to have trouble with

conservation: They fail to realize that if nothing is added or taken away, the amount must stay the same, regardless of changes in the shape or arrangement of items. As illustrations, consider what happens when we present two conservation tasks to 5-year-old Nathan:

Conservation of liquid: We show Nathan the three glasses in Figure 2.5. We ask him whether Glasses A and B contain the same amount of water, and he replies confidently that they do. We then pour the water from Glass B into Glass C and ask him whether A and C have the same amount. Nathan replies, "No, that glass [pointing to Glass A] has more because it's taller."

Conservation of number: We next show Nathan two rows of seven pennies each, like so:

Nathan counts the pennies in each row and agrees that the two rows have the same amount. We spread the second row out, and the pennies now look like this:

When we ask Nathan whether the two rows still have the same number, he replies, "No, this one [pointing to the bottom row] has more because it's longer."

Young children such as Nathan often confuse changes in appearance with changes in amount.

As children approach the later part of the preoperational stage, perhaps at around age 4 or 5, they show early signs of adultlike logic. For example, they sometimes draw correct conclusions about class inclusion and conservation problems. But they base their reasoning on hunches and intuition, rather than on any conscious awareness of underlying logical principles, and thus they cannot yet explain *why* their conclusions are correct.

Concrete Operations Stage (age 6 or 7 until age 11 or 12) Piaget proposed that as children enter the **concrete operations stage**, their thought processes become organized into larger systems of mental processes—*operations*—that allow them to think more logically than they have previously. They now realize that their own perspectives and feelings are not necessarily shared by others and may reflect personal opinion rather than reality. They also exhibit such logical reasoning abilities as class inclusion and conservation. For example, consider how an 8-year-old, whom we'll call "Natalie," responded to the same wooden beads problem that Brian tackled:

Adult: Are there more wooden beads or more brown beads?

Natalie: More wooden ones.

Adult: Why?

Natalie: Because the two white ones are made of wood as well.

Adult: Suppose we made two necklaces, one with all the wooden beads and one with all the brown ones. Which one would be longer?

Natalie: Well, the wooden ones and the brown ones are the same, and it would be longer with the wooden ones because there are two white ones as well. (Piaget, 1952a, p. 176)

FIGURE 2.5 Do Glasses A and C contain the same amount of water?

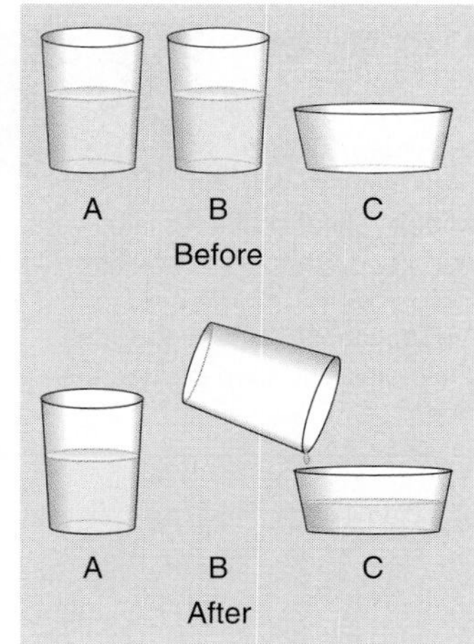

conservation Recognition that if nothing is added or taken away, amount stays the same regardless of alterations in shape or arrangement.

concrete operations stage Piaget's third stage of cognitive development, in which adultlike logic appears but is limited to concrete reality.

Notice how easily Natalie reaches her conclusion: Because the wooden beads include white ones as well as brown ones, there obviously must be more wooden ones.

Children continue to refine their newly acquired logical thinking capabilities for several years. For instance, some forms of conservation, such as conservation of liquid and conservation of number, appear at age 6 or 7. Other forms don't emerge until later. Consider the problem in Figure 2.6. Using a balance scale, an adult shows a child that two balls of clay have the same weight. One ball is removed from the scale and smashed into a pancake shape. Does the pancake weigh the same as the unsmashed ball, or are the weights different? Children typically do not achieve conservation of weight—they don't realize that the flattened pancake weighs the same as the round ball it was earlier—until sometime between ages 8 and 11 (Sroufe, Cooper, DeHart, & Bronfenbrenner, 1992; Sund, 1976).

myeducationlab

Observe 10-year-old Kent's conservation of number in the video "Cognitive Development: Middle Childhood." (To find this video, go to the Book-Specific Resources in Chapter 2 of MyEducationLab, select *Video Examples*, and then click on the title.)

Although students displaying concrete operational thought show many signs of logical thinking, their cognitive development is not yet complete. For instance, they have trouble understanding abstract ideas, and they may struggle with problems involving proportions (recall the difficulty the fourth graders had with the apple tarts problem in the opening case study). Such capabilities emerge in the final stage, formal operations.

Formal Operations Stage (age 11 or 12 through adulthood) Once children acquire abilities characterizing the **formal operations stage**, they can think about concepts that have little or no basis in concrete reality (e.g., see Figure 2.7). Furthermore, they recognize that what is logically valid is different from what is true in the real world. For example, recall the earlier children-basketballs-jellybeans problem: *If* all children are basketballs and *if* all basketballs are jellybeans, then formal operational thinkers can logically conclude that all children must be jellybeans, even though in the real world children *aren't* jellybeans. Several abilities essential for sophisticated mathematical and scientific reasoning—proportional reasoning, formulation of multiple hypotheses, and separation and control of variables—also emerge in the formal operations stage (see Table 2.1).

From Piaget's perspective, students' capabilities in mathematics are likely to improve once formal operational thinking develops. Abstract problems, such as mathematical word problems, should become easier to solve. And students should become capable of understanding such concepts as *negative number*, *pi* (π), and *infinity*. For instance, they should now comprehend how the temperature can be below zero and how two parallel lines will never touch even if they go on forever. In addition, because students can now understand proportions, they can more easily use fractions, decimals, and ratios when solving problems.

Scientific reasoning is also likely to improve once students are capable of formal operational thought. Three formal operational abilities—reasoning logically about hypothetical ideas, formulating multiple hypotheses, and separating and controlling variables—together allow many adolescents to use the *scientific method*, in which they

formal operations stage Piaget's fourth and final stage of cognitive development, in which logical reasoning processes are applied to abstract ideas as well as to concrete objects.

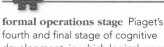

FIGURE 2.6 Conservation of weight: Ball A and Ball B initially weigh the same. When Ball B is flattened into a pancake shape, how does its weight now compare with that of Ball A?

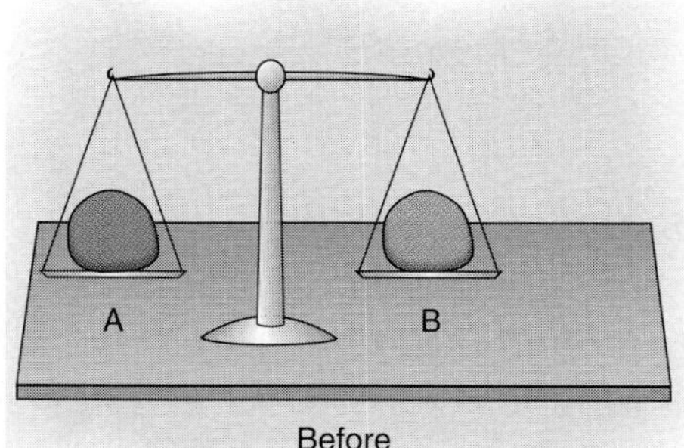

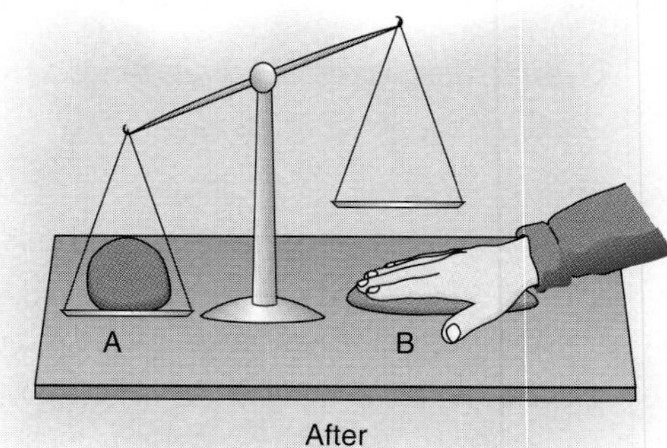

FIGURE 2.7 In this excerpt from a comic book he has created, 12-year-old Zach depicts an army of noses (led by Napoleon Nose), a time warp trap, and villain Dark Fang's evil new weapon. In doing so, Zach shows an ability to think about contrary-to-fact ideas.

test several possible explanations for an observed phenomenon in a systematic manner. As an example, consider the pendulum problem in the following exercise.

EXPERIENCING FIRSTHAND

Pendulum Problem

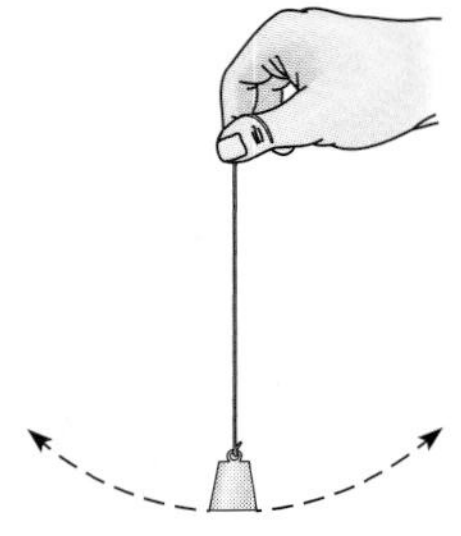

In the absence of other forces, an object suspended by a rope or string—a pendulum—swings at a constant rate. (A yo-yo and a playground swing are two everyday examples.) Some pendulums swing back and forth rather slowly, others more quickly. What characteristics of a pendulum determine how quickly it swings? Write down at least three hypotheses about the variable(s) that might affect a pendulum's oscillation rate.

Now gather several small, heavy objects (an eraser, a metal bolt, and a fishing sinker are three possibilities) and a piece of string. Tie one of the objects to one end of the string, and set your pendulum in motion. Conduct one or more experiments to test each of your hypotheses.

What can you conclude? What variable or variables affect the rate with which a pendulum swings?

What hypotheses did you generate? Four common hypotheses are the weight of the object, the length of the string, the force with which the pendulum is pushed, and the height from which the object is first released.

myeducationlab

Observe seventh graders' difficulty in separating and controlling variables in the video "Designing Experiments." (To find this video, go to the Book-Specific Resources in Chapter 2 of MyEducationLab, select *Video Examples*, and then click on the title.)

Did you test each of your hypotheses in a systematic fashion? That is, did you *separate and control variables*, testing one at a time while holding all others constant? For example, if you were testing the hypothesis that weight makes a difference, you might have tried objects of different weights while keeping constant the length of the string, the force with which you pushed each object, and the height from which you released or pushed each one. Similarly, if you hypothesized that the length of the string was a critical factor, you might have varied the length while continuing to use the same object and setting the pendulum in motion in a consistent manner. If you carefully separated and controlled each variable, then you would have come to the correct conclusion: Only length affects a pendulum's oscillation rate.

An additional outcome of abstract and hypothetical thinking is the ability to envision how the world might be different from the way it actually is. In some cases, adolescents envision a world that is much *better* than the one they live in, and they exhibit considerable concern and idealism about social and political issues. Some secondary school students devote a great deal of energy to local or global problems, such as water pollution and animal rights. However, they may offer recommendations for change that seem logical but aren't practical in today's world. For example, a teenager might argue that racism could disappear overnight if people would just begin to "love one another" or that a nation should eliminate its armed forces and weaponry as a way of moving toward world peace. Piaget proposed that adolescent idealism reflects **formal operational egocentrism**, an inability to separate one's own logical abstractions from the perspectives of others and from practical considerations. Only through experience do adolescents eventually begin to temper their optimism with some realism about what is possible in a given time frame and with limited resources.

Encourage adolescents to discuss their visions for a better world, but point out instances when their ideals are unrealistic.

Critiquing Piaget's Theory

Perhaps Piaget's greatest contribution to our understanding of cognitive development was the nature of the *questions* he asked and tried to answer about how children think and reason. In addition, some of his key ideas—for instance, that children construct their own knowledge about the world, that they must relate new experiences to what they already know, and that encountering puzzling phenomena can sometimes spur them to revise their understandings—have stood the test of time.

Piaget's descriptions of processes that *propel* development—especially assimilation, accommodation, and equilibration—can be frustratingly vague, however (Chapman, 1988; diSessa, 2006; Klahr, 2001). And interaction with one's physical environment, while certainly valuable, may be less critical than Piaget believed. For instance, children with significant physical disabilities, who cannot actively experiment with physical objects, learn a great deal about the world simply by observing what happens around them (Bebko, Burke, Craven, & Sarlo, 1992; Brainerd, 2003). In contrast, social interaction—not only with peers but also with adults—is clearly very important, as we'll see in upcoming sections of the chapter.

A Second Look at Piaget's Stages Piaget's proposal that cognitive development progresses in stages has sparked a great deal of follow-up research. In general, this research supports Piaget's proposed *sequence* in which—but not necessarily the *ages* at which—different abilities emerge. Piaget probably underestimated the thinking capabilities of preschoolers and elementary school students. For example, under some circumstances, preschoolers are capable of class inclusion and conservation, and they can occasionally imagine things that are contrary to fact (S. R. Beck, Robinson, Carroll, & Apperly, 2006; R. Gelman & Baillargeon, 1983; Rosser, 1994). Many first and second graders have some ability to understand and use simple proportions (e.g., fractions such as ½, ⅓, and ¼), if they can relate the proportions to everyday objects and situations (Empson, 1999; Van Dooren, De Bock, Hessels, Janssens, & Verschaffel, 2005). And some older elementary school children can separate and control variables if a task is simplified in some way (Barchfeld, Sodian, Thoermer, & Bullock, 2005; Metz, 1995; Ruffman, Perner, Olson, & Doherty, 1993).

formal operational egocentrism Inability of adolescents in Piaget's formal operations stage to separate their own abstract logic from the perspectives of others and from practical considerations.

In contrast, Piaget probably overestimated what adolescents can do. Formal operational thinking processes emerge more gradually than Piaget suggested, and even high school students don't use them as regularly as Piaget would have us believe (Flieller, 1999; Kuhn & Franklin, 2006; Schauble, 1996; Tourniaire & Pulos, 1985). Furthermore, students may demonstrate formal operational thought in one content domain while thinking concretely in another. Evidence of formal operational reasoning typically appears in the physical sciences earlier than in subjects such as history and geography (Lovell, 1979; Tamburrini, 1982).

Expect that even high school students will sometimes have difficulty with abstract subject matter.

Explicit training and other structured experiences can sometimes help children acquire reasoning abilities sooner than Piaget thought was possible (Brainerd, 2003; Kuhn, 2006). For instance, children as young as age 4 or 5 begin to show conservation after having experience with conservation tasks, especially if they can actively manipulate the task materials and discuss their reasoning with someone who already exhibits conservation (Field, 1987; Halford & Andrews, 2006; Mayer, 1992). Experience helps children acquire formal operational reasoning abilities as well. For instance, children ages 10 and 11 can more easily solve logical problems involving hypothetical ideas if they are taught relevant problem-solving strategies, and they become increasingly able to separate and control variables with appropriate guidance and practice (Kuhn & Franklin, 2006; Kuhn & Pease, 2008; S. Lee, 1985; Schauble, 1990).

PEARSON myeducationlab

Discover how certain kinds of experiences can help 5-year-olds grasp class inclusion by completing the Understanding Research exercise "Class Inclusion" in MyEducationLab. (To find this activity, go to the topic Cognitiive and Linguistic Development in MyEducationLab, click on Assignments and *Activities*, and then select *Understanding Research*.)

In light of all the evidence, does it still make sense to talk about discrete stages of cognitive development? As we'll see shortly, a few theorists have offered stage-based theories that may more adequately account for current findings about children's logical thinking in specific skill areas or content domains. But most theorists now believe that cognitive development can more accurately be described in terms of gradual *trends*, rather than discrete stages. They also suggest—and Piaget himself acknowledged—that the four stages better describe how children and adolescents *can* think, rather than how they always *do* think, at any particular age (Flavell, 1994; Halford & Andrews, 2006; Klaczynski, 2001; Tanner & Inhelder, 1960).

Considering Diversity from the Perspective of Piaget's Theory

As a researcher working in Switzerland, Piaget conducted his research with a particular population: Swiss children. However, some research indicates that the course of cognitive development differs somewhat from one cultural group to another. For example, Mexican children whose families make pottery for a living acquire conservation skills much earlier than Piaget proposed (Price-Williams, Gordon, & Ramirez, 1969). Apparently, making pottery requires children to make frequent judgments about needed quantities of clay and water—judgments that must be fairly accurate regardless of the specific shape or form of the clay or water container. In other cultures, especially in some in which children don't attend school, conservation and other concrete operational abilities may appear several years later than they do in Western societies (Artman & Cahan, 1993; Fahrmeier, 1978).

Formal operational reasoning skills—reasoning about abstract or hypothetical ideas, separating and controlling variables, and so on—vary from culture to culture as well (Flieller, 1999; Norenzayan, Choi, & Peng, 2007; Rogoff, 2003). Mainstream Western culture actively nurtures these skills through formal instruction in such academic content domains as science, mathematics, literature, and social studies. In some other cultures, however, such skills may have little relevance to people's daily lives and activities (M. Cole, 1990; J. G. Miller, 1997; Norenzayan et al., 2007).

Even within a single cultural group, logical reasoning abilities vary considerably from one individual to another. Some of this diversity is the result of differences in background knowledge about a particular topic. For instance, adolescents (adults, too) often apply formal operational thought to topics about which they know a great deal yet think concretely about topics with which they are unfamiliar (Girotto & Light, 1993; M. C. Linn, Clement, Pulos, & Sullivan, 1989; Schliemann & Carraher, 1993). As an

Use familiar topics when asking students to engage in formal operational reasoning processes.

FIGURE 2.8 What are some possible reasons that Herb is catching more fish than the others?

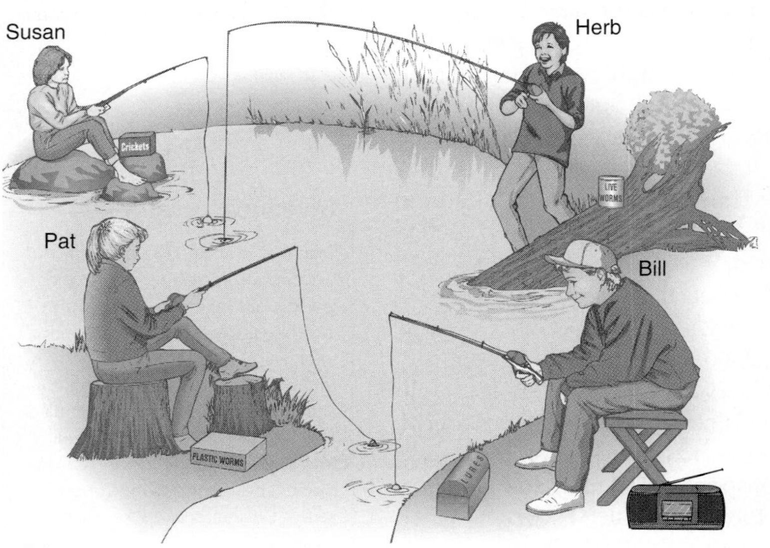

Source: Based on Pulos & Linn, 1981.

illustration, consider the fishing pond in Figure 2.8. In a study by Pulos and Linn (1981), 13-year-olds were shown a similar picture and told, "These four children go fishing every week, and one child, Herb, always catches the most fish. The other children wonder why." If you look at the picture, it is obvious that Herb differs from the other children in several ways, including the kind of bait he uses, the length of his fishing rod, and his location by the pond. Students who had fished a lot more effectively separated and controlled variables for this situation than they did for the pendulum problem presented earlier, whereas the reverse was true for students with little or no experience fishing.

myeducationlab

Observe how knowledge about fishing affects students' ability to identify relevant variables in the video "Cognitive Development." Ten-year-old Kent, an experienced fisherman, considers several relevant variables. In contrast, 14-year-old Alicia, who has never fished, considers only two and almost immediately concludes that one of them—type of bait—is the deciding factor. (To find this video, go to Chapter 2 of the Book-Specific Resources in MyEducationLab, select *Video Examples*, and then click on the title.)

Contemporary Extensions and Applications of Piaget's Theory

Despite its shortcomings, Piaget's theory has had considerable influence on present-day thinking about cognitive development and classroom practice. A few contemporary theories, known as **neo-Piagetian theories**, have combined elements of Piaget's theory with recent research findings and theoretical concepts about human cognition to describe how children's learning and reasoning capabilities in specific content domains may change with age. And educators have found many of Piaget's ideas quite useful in instructional settings. We'll discuss three of his contributions—his clinical method, his emphasis on the importance of hands-on interactions with the physical environment, and his concept of disequilibrium—in upcoming sections. The Into the Classroom feature "Applying Piaget's Theory" offers additional suggestions for translating Piaget's ideas into classroom practice.

Neo-Piagetian Theories Neo-Piagetian theorists echo Piaget's belief that cognitive development depends somewhat on brain maturation. One prominent neo-Piagetian, Robbie Case, has suggested that a component of the human memory system known as *working memory* is especially important for cognitive development (e.g., Case, 1985, 1991). In particular, working memory is a brain-based mechanism that enables people to temporarily hold and think about a small amount of new information. As you'll discover in Chapter 6, children's working memory capacity increases with age, and so their ability to think about several things simultaneously increases as well (Case & Okamoto, 1996; Fischer & Bidell, 1991; Lautrey, 1993).

Neo-Piagetian theorists reject Piaget's notion that a single series of stages characterizes children's overall cognitive development. However, they speculate that cognitive development in specific content domains—for instance, in understanding numbers or spatial relationships—often has a stagelike nature (e.g., Case, 1985; Case & Okamoto, 1996; Fischer & Immordino-Yang, 2006). Children's entry into a particular stage is marked by the acquisition of new abilities, which children practice and gradually master over time. Eventually they integrate these abilities into more complex structures that mark their transition into a subsequent stage. Thus, as is true in Piaget's theory, the stages are *hierarchical*, with each one being constructed out of abilities acquired in the preceding stage.

neo-Piagetian theory Theoretical perspective that combines elements of Piaget's theory with more contemporary research findings and theoretical concepts and that suggests that development in specific content domains is often stagelike in nature.

Even in a particular subject area, however, cognitive development is not necessarily a single series of stages through which children progress as if they were climbing rungs on a ladder. In some cases, development might be better characterized as progression along "multiple strands" of skills that occasionally interconnect, consolidate, or separate in a weblike fashion (Fischer & Daley, 2007; Fischer & Immordino-

INTO THE Classroom

Applying Piaget's Theory

- **Use Piaget's stages as a rough guide to what students at different grade levels can do, but don't take them too literally.**

  Knowing from both research and her own experience that 6- and 7-year-olds are capable of understanding simple proportions in familiar situations, a first-grade teacher asks her students to tackle this problem: "Two children want to share five cupcakes so that each child gets the same amount. Show how much each child can have." When some of the students decide that each child can have two cupcakes, she points to the fifth cupcake and says, "They want to share this one too. How can they do that?"

- **When young children show signs of egocentric thinking, express confusion or explain that others think differently.**

  A kindergartner asks, "What's this?" about an object that is out of the teacher's view. The teacher responds, "What's *what?* I can't see the object you're looking at."

- **Relate abstract and hypothetical ideas to concrete objects and observable events.**

  To help students understand that even seemingly weightless substances such as air have mass and weight, an eighth-grade teacher blows up a balloon and places it on one side of a balance scale. She then places an uninflated balloon on the other side of the scale. The inflated balloon tips the scale downward, showing that it weighs more than the uninflated one.

- **Ask students to explain their reasoning about physical phenomena, and challenge illogical explanations.**

  When learning about pendulums, cooperative groups in a middle school science class conduct experiments with three variables (weight, length, and height from which the pendulum is first dropped) to see which variable or variables determine the rate at which a pendulum swings. After a student in one group asserts that weight affects the oscillation rate, her teacher asks a series of questions that eventually lead the student's group to realize it has simultaneously varied both weight and length in its experiments. (This example is depicted in the "Designing Experiments" Video Example in Chapter 2 of the Book-Specific Resources in MyEducationLab.)

- **Draw on adolescents' idealism to engage them in public service projects and other charitable endeavors.**

  In a unit on Africa, several students in a ninth-grade social studies class express their horror about the extremely impoverished conditions in which some African people live. The teacher mentions that a friend of his is traveling to Rwanda the following month and wants to take several large suitcases full of used children's clothing to give to an especially poor Rwandan village. Over the next few days, the students ask their parents and neighbors for donations and gather many usable items for the teacher's friend to take.

Sources: Empson, 1999, p. 295 (cupcake example); C. L. Smith, 2007 (balloon example).

Yang, 2006; Fischer, Knight, & Van Parys, 1993). From this perspective, children may acquire more advanced levels of competence in a particular area through any one of several pathways. For instance, as they become increasingly proficient in reading, children may gradually develop their word decoding skills, their comprehension skills, and so on—and they draw on all of these skills when reading a book. However, the rate at which each of the skills is mastered varies from one child to the next.

Piaget's Clinical Method as an Assessment Tool Earlier in the chapter I described Piaget's clinical method, in which an adult probes children's thoughts about a particular task or problem through a sequence of individually tailored questions (e.g., recall the discussions with Brian and Natalie about the wooden beads problem). By presenting a variety of Piagetian tasks involving either concrete or formal operational thinking skills—tasks involving class inclusion, conservation, separation and control of variables, and so on—and asking students to explain their thinking while tackling the tasks, we can gain valuable insights into their logical reasoning abilities (e.g., diSessa, 2007). We need not stick to traditional Piagetian reasoning tasks, however. To illustrate, a teacher might present various kinds of maps (e.g., a road map of Pennsylvania, an aerial map of Chicago, a three-dimensional relief map of a mountainous area) and ask students to interpret what they see. Children in the early elementary grades are apt to interpret the maps very concretely, perhaps thinking that lines

Probe students' reasoning about various logical thinking tasks and problems.

separating states and countries are actually painted on the earth or that an airport denoted by a picture of an airplane has only one plane. They might also have difficulty with the scale of a map, perhaps thinking that a line can't be a road because "it's not fat enough for two cars to go on" or that a mountain depicted by a bump on a relief map isn't really a mountain because "it's not high enough" (Liben & Downs, 1989; Liben & Myers, 2007, p. 202). Understanding the concept of *scale* in a map requires proportional reasoning—an ability that doesn't fully emerge until after puberty—and thus it is hardly surprising that young children will be confused by it.

Hands-On Experiences Piaget suggested that exploration of the physical environment should be largely a child-initiated and child-directed effort. Young children can certainly learn a great deal from their informal interactions with sand, water, and other natural substances (Hutt, Tyler, Hutt, & Christopherson, 1989). Researchers are finding, however, that hands-on experiences with concrete objects and events are typically more effective *when combined with instruction* that helps students draw appropriate conclusions from what they observe (Fujimura, 2001; Hardy, Jonen, Möller, & Stern, 2006; Lorch et al., 2008; Mayer, 2004). In the absence of teacher guidance and directive questions, students may draw inferences based solely on what they see and feel—for instance, concluding that a very small piece of Styrofoam must have no weight whatsoever (C. L. Smith, 2007). And, of course, they may fail to separate and control variables in their experimentation (Lorch et al., 2008).

Combine hands-on experiences with age-appropriate instruction that enables students to draw appropriate conclusions from their observations.

Creating Disequilibrium: The Value of Sociocognitive Conflict In the opening case study, four girls argue about various ways to solve a problem involving the use of a fraction (3/4) in making apple tarts. When one girl offers a seemingly nonproductive idea ("But three-quarters equals three"), another points out her illogical thinking ("But she can't make only three apple tarts!"). As noted earlier, Piaget proposed that interaction with peers helps children realize that others often view the world very differently than they do and that their own ideas are not always completely logical or accurate. Furthermore, interactions with age-mates that involve wrestling with contradictory viewpoints—interactions that involve **sociocognitive conflict**—create disequilibrium that may spur children to reevaluate and possibly revise their current understandings.

Many contemporary psychologists share Piaget's belief in the importance of sociocognitive conflict among age-mates (e.g., N. Bell, Grossen, and Perret-Clermont, 1985; De Lisi & Golbeck, 1999; C. L. Smith, 2007; Webb & Palincsar, 1996). They have offered several reasons that interactions with peers may help promote cognitive growth:

- Peers speak at a level that children can understand.
- Whereas children may accept an adult's ideas without argument, they are more willing to disagree with and challenge the ideas of their peers.
- When children hear competing views held by peers—individuals who presumably have knowledge and abilities similar to their own—they may be motivated to reconcile the contradictions. (Champagne & Bunce, 1991; Damon, 1984; Hatano & Inagaki, 1991; C. L. Smith, 2007)

Have students wrestle with complex issues and problems in small groups, where they can hear opinions and arguments that might conflict with their own ways of thinking. Monitor such interactions to be sure that they are mutually respectful and socially appropriate.

Ultimately, social interaction—not only with peers but also with adults—is probably more important for children's cognitive development than Piaget realized (Callanan & Oakes, 1992; Gauvain, 2001). Lev Vygotsky's theory, which we turn to now, describes additional ways in which interactions with fellow human beings promote cognitive growth.

Vygotsky's Theory of Cognitive Development

sociocognitive conflict Situation in which one encounters and has to wrestle with ideas and viewpoints inconsistent with one's own.

As you should recall, Piaget proposed that children develop increasingly advanced and integrated schemes through two processes, assimilation and accommodation. In Piaget's view, then, children are largely in control of their own cognitive development.

In contrast, an early Russian developmentalist, Lev Vygotsky, believed that the adults in any society foster children's cognitive development in an intentional and somewhat systematic manner. Because Vygotsky emphasized the importance of adult instruction and guidance for promoting cognitive development—and, more generally, because he emphasized the influence of social and cultural factors in children's cognitive growth—his perspective is known as a **sociocultural theory**.

Vygotsky and his students conducted numerous studies of children's thinking from the 1920s until Vygotsky's early death from tuberculosis in 1934. Rather than determine the kinds of tasks children could successfully perform *on their own* (as Piaget did), Vygotsky often examined the kinds of tasks children could complete *only with adult assistance*. For example, he described two hypothetical children who could, without help, do things that a typical 8-year-old might be able to do. He would give each of the children progressively more difficult tasks and offer some help, perhaps asking a leading question or suggesting a reasonable first step. With such assistance, both children could almost invariably tackle more difficult tasks than they could handle on their own. However, the *range* of tasks that the two children could complete with assistance might be quite different, with one child stretching his or her abilities to succeed at typical 12-year-old-level tasks and the other succeeding only with typical 9-year-old-level tasks (Vygotsky, 1934/1986, p. 187).

Western psychologists were largely unfamiliar with Vygotsky's work until the last few decades of the twentieth century, when his major writings were translated from Russian into English (e.g., Vygotsky, 1978, 1934/1986, 1997). Although Vygotsky never had the chance to develop his theory fully, his views are clearly evident in many contemporary theorists' discussions of learning and development today. In fact, whereas Piaget's influence has been on the wane in recent years (Bjorklund, 1997), Vygotsky's influence has become increasingly prominent.

Vygotsky's Basic Assumptions

Vygotsky acknowledged that biological factors (e.g., brain maturation) play a role in development. Children bring certain characteristics and dispositions to the situations they encounter, and their responses to those situations vary accordingly. Furthermore, children's behaviors, which are influenced in part by inherited traits, affect the particular experiences that they have (Vygotsky, 1997). However, Vygotsky's primary focus was on the role of nurture, and especially on the ways in which a child's social and cultural environments foster cognitive growth. Following are central ideas and concepts in Vygotsky's theory:

- *Through both informal conversations and formal schooling, adults convey to children the ways in which their culture interprets the world.* Vygotsky proposed that as adults interact with children, they share the *meanings* they attach to objects, events, and, more generally, human experience. In the process they transform, or *mediate,* the situations that children encounter. Meanings are conveyed through a variety of mechanisms, including language (spoken words, writing, etc.), mathematical symbols, art, music, and so on.

Informal conversations are one common mechanism through which adults pass along culturally relevant ways of interpreting situations. But even more important is formal education, through which teachers systematically impart the ideas, concepts, and terminology used in various academic disciplines (Vygotsky, 1934/1986). Although Vygotsky, like Piaget, saw value in allowing children to make some discoveries themselves, he also saw value in having adults describe the discoveries of previous generations (Vygotsky, 1934/1986).

Show students how various academic disciplines conceptualize the world.

- *Every culture passes along physical and cognitive tools that make daily living more productive and efficient.* Not only do adults teach children specific ways of interpreting experience, but they also pass along specific tools that can help children tackle the various tasks and problems they are apt to face. Some tools, such as scissors, sewing machines, and computers, are physical objects. Others, such as writing

sociocultural theory Theoretical perspective emphasizing the importance of society and culture in promoting cognitive development.

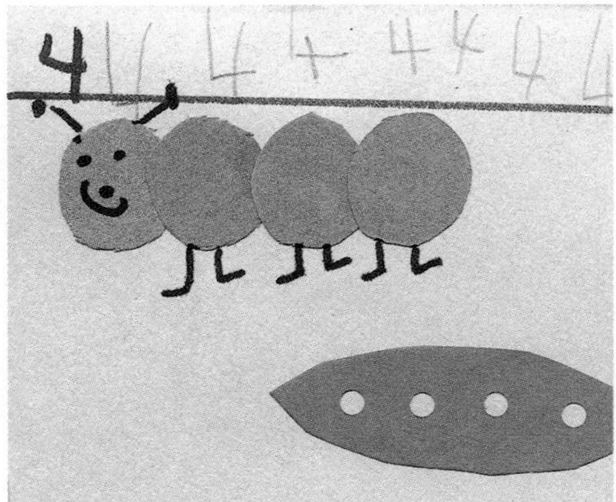

These excerpts from 5-year-old Luisa's "Caterpillar Number Book" show how one kindergarten teacher had her students practice using two important cognitive tools in industrialized societies: a writing system and a number system.

systems, maps, and spreadsheets, are partly physical and partly symbolic. Still others, such as the concept of *fraction* and the process of division (recall the opening case study involving apple tarts), may have little physical basis at all. In Vygotsky's view, acquiring tools that are at least partly symbolic or mental in nature—**cognitive tools**—greatly enhances children's thinking abilities.

• *Thought and language become increasingly interdependent in the first few years of life.* One very important cognitive tool is language. For us as adults, thought and language are closely interconnected. We often think by using specific words that our language provides. For example, when we think about household pets, our thoughts contain such words as *dog* and *cat*. In addition, we usually express our thoughts when we converse with others. In other words, we literally "speak our minds."

Vygotsky proposed that thought and language are separate functions for infants and young toddlers. In these early years, thinking occurs independently of language, and when language appears, it is first used primarily as a means of communication, rather than as a mechanism of thought. Sometime around age 2, thought and language become intertwined: Children begin to express their thoughts when they speak, and they begin to think in words.

When thought and language first merge, children often talk to themselves, a phenomenon known as **self-talk**. (You may also see the term *private speech*.) Vygotsky suggested that self-talk serves an important function in cognitive development. By talking to themselves, children learn to guide and direct their own behaviors through difficult tasks and complex maneuvers in much the same way that adults have previously guided them. Self-talk eventually evolves into **inner speech**, in which children talk to themselves mentally rather than aloud. They continue to direct themselves verbally through tasks and activities, but others can no longer see and hear them do it (Vygotsky, 1934/1986).

• *Complex mental processes begin as social activities and gradually evolve into internal mental activities that children can use independently.* Vygotsky proposed that many complex thought processes have their roots in social interactions. As children discuss objects, events, tasks, and problems with adults and other knowledgeable individuals, they gradually incorporate into their own thinking the ways in which the people around them talk about and interpret the world, and they begin to use the words, concepts, symbols, and strategies—in essence, the cognitive tools—that are commonly used in their culture.

The process through which social activities evolve into internal mental activities is called **internalization**. The progression from self-talk to inner speech just described illustrates this process: Over time, children gradually internalize adults' directions so that they are eventually giving *themselves* the directions. Children do not necessarily internalize *exactly* what they see and hear in a social context. Rather, internalization often involves transforming ideas and processes to make them uniquely one's own.

Not all mental processes emerge as children interact with adults; some instead develop as children interact with peers. For example, children frequently argue with one another about a variety of matters—how best to carry out an activity, what games to play, who did what to whom, and so on. According to Vygotsky, having arguments helps children discover that there are often several ways to view the same situation. Eventually, he suggested, children internalize the arguing process, developing the ability to look at a situation from several different angles *on their own*.

• *Children can perform more challenging tasks when assisted by more advanced and competent individuals.* Vygotsky distinguished between two kinds of abilities that characterize children's skills at any particular point in development. A child's **actual developmental level** is the upper limit of tasks that he or she can perform indepen-

cognitive tool Concept, symbol, strategy, procedure, or other culturally constructed mechanism that helps people think about and respond to situations more effectively.

self-talk Process of talking to oneself as a way of guiding oneself through a task.

inner speech Process of talking to and guiding oneself mentally, rather than aloud.

internalization Process through which a learner gradually incorporates socially based activities into his or her internal cognitive processes.

actual developmental level Upper limit of tasks that a learner can successfully perform independently.

dently, without help from anyone else. A child's **level of potential development** is the upper limit of tasks that he or she can perform with the assistance of a more competent individual. To get a true sense of children's cognitive development, Vygotsky suggested, we should assess their capabilities both when performing alone *and* when performing with assistance.

level of potential development Upper limit of tasks that a learner can successfully perform with the assistance of a more competent individual.

zone of proximal development (ZPD) Range of tasks that a learner can perform with the help and guidance of others but cannot yet perform independently.

As mentioned earlier, Vygotsky found that children can typically do more difficult things in collaboration with adults than they can do on their own. For example, with the assistance of a parent or teacher, they may be able to read more complex prose than they are likely to read independently. And notice how a student who cannot independently solve division problems with remainders begins to learn the correct procedure through an interaction with her teacher:

> *Teacher:* [writes 6)44 on the board] 44 divided by 6. What number times 6 is close to 44?
>
> *Child:* 6.
>
> *Teacher:* What's 6 times 6? [writes 6]
>
> *Child:* 36.
>
> *Teacher:* 36. Can you get one that's any closer? [erasing the 6]
>
> *Child:* 8.
>
> *Teacher:* What's 6 times 8?
>
> *Child:* 64 . . . 48.
>
> *Teacher:* 48. Too big. Can you think of something . . .
>
> *Child:* 6 times 7 is 42. (Pettito, 1985, p. 251)

Occasionally perform difficult tasks in partnership with students.

• *Challenging tasks promote maximum cognitive growth.* The range of tasks that children cannot yet perform independently but can perform with the help and guidance of others is, in Vygotsky's terminology, the **zone of proximal development (ZPD)** (see Figure 2.9). A child's zone of proximal development includes learning and problem-solving abilities that are just beginning to emerge and develop.

Vygotsky proposed that children learn very little from performing tasks they can already do independently. Instead, they develop primarily by attempting tasks they can accomplish only with assistance and support—that is, when they attempt tasks within their zone of proximal development. In a nutshell, it is the challenges in life, not the easy successes, that promote cognitive development. But whereas challenging

FIGURE 2.9 In Vygotsky's view, tasks in a child's zone of proximal development promote maximum cognitive growth.

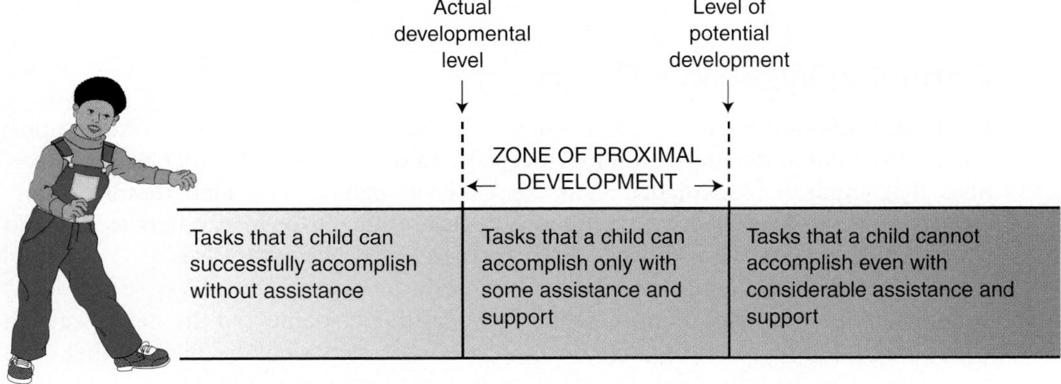

tasks are beneficial, impossible tasks, which children cannot do even with considerable structure and guidance, are of no benefit whatsoever (Vygotsky, 1987). A child's ZPD therefore sets an upper limit on what he or she is cognitively capable of learning.

As teachers, then, we should assign some tasks that students can accomplish successfully *only* with other people's support. In some instances, this support must come from more skilled individuals, such as adults or older students. In other situations, students of equal ability can work together to jointly accomplish difficult assignments (e.g., the apple tart problem in the opening case study), with each student bringing unique strengths to contribute to the overall effort.

myeducationlab

Observe examples of children working within their zones of proximal development in the two "Zone of Proximal Development" videos. (To find these videos, go to Chapter 2 of the Book-Specific Resources in MyEducationLab, select *Video Examples*, and then click on the titles.)

Regardless of the nature of the support we provide, we must remember that every student's ZPD will change over time. As some tasks are mastered, other, more complex ones will appear on the horizon to take their place. In addition, students' ZPDs may vary considerably in "width." Whereas some students may, with assistance, be able to stretch several years above their actual (independent) developmental level, others may be able to handle tasks that are only slightly more difficult than what they can currently do on their own. In some instances, students with different zones of proximal development will need individualized tasks and assignments so that they all have challenges that can optimally promote their personal cognitive growth.

- *Play allows children to stretch themselves cognitively.* As a young child, my son Jeff often played restaurant with his friend Scott. In a corner of our basement, the boys created a restaurant "kitchen" with a toy sink and stove and stocked it with plastic dishes, cooking utensils, and "food" items. They created a separate dining area with child-sized tables and chairs and made menus for their customers. On one occasion they invited both sets of parents to "dine" at the restaurant, taking our orders, serving us our food, and eventually giving us our bills. (Fortunately, they seemed quite happy with the few pennies we paid them for our meals.)

In their restaurant play, the two boys took on several adult roles (restaurant manager, waiter, cook) and practiced a variety of adultlike behaviors. In real life, such a scenario would, of course, be impossible: Very few 5-year-old children have the cooking, reading, writing, mathematical, and organizational skills necessary to run a restaurant. Yet the element of make-believe brought these tasks within the boys' reach. In Vygotsky's words, "In play a child always behaves beyond his average age, above his daily behavior; in play it is as though he were a head taller than himself" (Vygotsky, 1978, p. 102).

Furthermore, as children play, their behaviors must conform to certain standards or expectations. In the early elementary school years, children often act in accordance with how a father, teacher, or waiter would behave. In the organized group games and sports that come later, children must follow specific sets of rules. By adhering to such restrictions on their behavior, children learn to plan ahead, to think before they act, and to engage in self-restraint—skills critical for successful participation in the adult world.

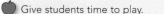

Give students time to play.

Play, then, is hardly a waste of time. Instead, it provides a valuable training ground for the adult world. Perhaps for this reason, it is seen in virtually all cultures worldwide.

Critiquing Vygotsky's Theory

Vygotsky's descriptions of developmental processes were, like Piaget's, often imprecise and lacking in detail. In addition, Vygotsky said little about the specific characteristics that children of particular ages are likely to exhibit. For such reasons, many aspects of Vygotsky's theory have been especially difficult for researchers to test and either verify or disprove (Gauvain, 2001; Haenan, 1996; Wertsch, 1984).

Nevertheless, contemporary theorists and educators have found Vygotsky's ideas quite insightful and helpful. Most significantly, his theory points out the many ways in which *culture* influences cognitive development. A society's culture ensures that each new generation benefits from the wisdom that preceding generations have accumulated. Any culture guides children in certain directions by encouraging them to pay

Many contemporary theorists agree with Vygotsky's proposal that challenges spur children to acquire new skills and abilities.

attention to particular stimuli (and not to others) and to engage in particular activities (and not in others). In addition, it provides a lens through which children come to view and interpret their experiences in culturally appropriate ways. We see obvious effects of culture in many of children's everyday activities—in the books they read, the roles they enact in pretend play, the extracurricular activities they pursue—but we must remember that culture permeates their unobservable thinking processes as well.

Furthermore, some research has supported Vygotsky's views regarding the progression and role of self-talk and inner speech. The frequency of children's audible self-talk decreases during the preschool and early elementary years, but this decrease is at first accompanied by an increase in whispered mumbling and silent lip movements, presumably reflecting a transition to inner speech (Bivens & Berk, 1990; Winsler & Naglieri, 2003). Self-talk increases when children are performing more challenging tasks, at which they must exert considerable effort to be successful (Berk, 1994; Schimmoeller, 1998). As you undoubtedly know from your own experience, even adults occasionally talk to themselves when they face new challenges!

Considering Diversity from the Perspective of Vygotsky's Theory

Vygotsky's theory leads us to expect greater diversity among children, at least in cognitive development, than Piaget's theory does. As we have seen, children in any single age-group are likely to have different zones of proximal development: Tasks that are easy for some children may be quite challenging or virtually impossible for others. In addition, to the extent that specific cultural groups pass along unique concepts, ideas, and beliefs, children from different cultural backgrounds will acquire somewhat different knowledge, skills, and ways of thinking. For instance, children are more likely to acquire map-reading skills if they regularly encounter maps (e.g., of roads, subway systems, and shopping malls) in their community and family life (Liben &

mediated learning experience Discussion between an adult and a child in which the adult helps the child make sense of an event they have mutually experienced.

Myers, 2007). And children are more apt to have a keen sense of time if cultural activities are tightly regulated by clocks and calendars (K. Nelson, 1996).

Contemporary Extensions and Applications of Vygotsky's Theory

The Into the Classroom feature "Applying Vygotsky's Theory" presents concrete examples of how teachers might make use of Vygotsky's ideas. In the upcoming sections, we'll consider several ways in which contemporary theorists and educators have built on the foundation that Vygotsky laid. We'll also continue to apply Vygotsky's ideas in the chapters ahead.

Social Construction of Meaning Contemporary psychologists have elaborated on Vygotsky's proposal that adults help children attach meaning to the objects and events around them. They point out that an adult often helps a child make sense of the world through joint discussion of a phenomenon or event they have mutually experienced (Crowley & Jacobs, 2002; Eacott, 1999; Feuerstein, 1990). Such an interaction, sometimes called a **mediated learning experience**, encourages the child to

INTO THE Classroom

Applying Vygotsky's Theory

- **Provide cognitive tools that students can use in thinking about and tackling difficult tasks.**

  A high school chemistry teacher places two equal-size inflated balloons into two beakers of water, one heated to 25°C and the other heated to 50°C. The students all agree that the balloon placed in the warmer water expands more. "How much more did the 50° balloon expand?" the teacher asks. "Let's use Charles's law to figure it out."

- **Encourage students to talk themselves through difficult tasks.**

  As his students work on complex mathematical equations such as this one,

  $$x = \frac{2(4 \times 9)^2}{6} + 3$$

  a junior high school mathematics teacher gives students a mnemonic (**P**lease **e**xcuse **m**y **d**ear **A**unt **S**ally) they might repeat to themselves to help them remember the order in which they should perform various operations (**p**arentheses, **e**xponents, **m**ultiplication and **d**ivision, **a**ddition and **s**ubtraction).

- **Present some tasks that students can perform successfully only with assistance.**

  A fifth-grade teacher assigns students their first research paper, knowing that he will have to give them a great deal of guidance as they work on it.

- **Provide sufficient support, or scaffolding, to enable students to perform challenging tasks successfully; gradually withdraw the support as they become more proficient.**

  An elementary physical education teacher begins a lesson on tumbling by demonstrating forward and backward rolls in slow motion and physically guiding her students through the correct movements. As the students become more skillful, the teacher stands back from the mat and gives verbal feedback about how to improve.

- **Have students work in small groups to accomplish complex, multifaceted tasks.**

  A middle school art teacher asks his students to work in groups of four or five to design large murals that depict various ecosystems—rainforest, desert, grassland, tundra, and so on—and the kinds of plant and animal species that live in each one. The groups then paint their murals on the walls of the school corridors.

- **Engage students in adult activities that are common in their culture.**

  A high school publishes a monthly school newspaper with news articles, editorials, cartoons, announcements of upcoming events, advertisements for local businesses, and classified ads. Students assume various roles, including reporters, cartoonists, editors, proofreaders, photocopiers, marketers, and distributors.

- **Give young children time to practice adult roles and behaviors through play.**

  A kindergarten teacher equips his classroom with many household items (dress-up clothes, cooking utensils, a toy telephone, etc.) so that students can play "house" during free-play time.

think about the phenomenon or event in particular ways—to attach labels to it, recognize principles that underlie it, draw certain conclusions from it, and so on.

As an example, consider the following exchange, in which a 5-year-old boy and his mother are talking about a prehistoric animal exhibit at a natural history museum:

> ***Boy:*** Cool. Wow, look. Look giant teeth. Mom, look at his giant teeth.
>
> ***Mom:*** He looks like a saber tooth. Do you think he eats meat or plants?
>
> ***Boy:*** Mom, look at his giant little tooth, look at his teeth in his mouth, so big.
>
> ***Mom:*** He looks like a saber tooth, doesn't he. Do you think he eats plants or meat?
>
> ***Boy:*** Ouch, ouch, ouch, ouch. (referring to sharp tooth)
>
> ***Mom:*** Do you think he eats plants or meat?
>
> ***Boy:*** Meat.
>
> ***Mom:*** How come?
>
> ***Boy:*** Because he has sharp teeth. (growling noises) (Ash, 2002, p. 378)

Even without his mother's assistance, the boy would almost certainly have learned something about the characteristics of saber tooth tigers from his museum visit. Yet Mom has helped her son make better sense of the experience than he might have done on his own—for instance, by using the label *saber tooth* and helping him connect tooth characteristics to eating preferences. Notice how persistent Mom is in asking her son to make the tooth–food connection. She continues to ask her question about meat versus plants until the boy finally infers, correctly, that saber tooth tigers must have been meat eaters.

In addition to co-constructing meanings with adults, children and adolescents often talk among themselves to make sense of their experiences. School provides an ideal setting in which young people can toss around ideas and perhaps reach consensus about how best to interpret and understand a complex issue or problem, as the four girls do in the opening case study.

Contemporary sociocultural theorists suggest that interacting with adults and interacting with peers play somewhat different roles in development. Adults usually have more experience and expertise than age-mates do, and they tend to be more skillful teachers. Accordingly, adults are often the partners of choice when children are trying to master complex new tasks and procedures (Gauvain, 2001; Radziszewska & Rogoff, 1988). Working with peers has a different set of advantages. First, as was mentioned in the earlier discussion of Piaget's theory, children who mutually discuss a topic can often construct a more sophisticated understanding of it, especially when they experience some sociocognitive conflict that motivates them to overhaul their understandings (J. Hiebert et al., 1997; Lampert, Rittenhouse, & Crumbaugh, 1996). Second, as Vygotsky suggested, peer interactions provide a social context in which children practice and eventually internalize complex cognitive processes, such as effective reading comprehension and argumentation skills (Andriessen, 2006; Chinn, Anderson, & Waggoner, 2001; Palincsar & Herrenkohl, 1999). A third benefit is that children learn valuable social behaviors—how to plan a joint enterprise, how to coordinate differing roles, and so on—when they work on cognitive tasks with their peers (Gauvain, 2001).

Scaffolding Contemporary theorists have given considerable thought to the kinds of assistance that can help children successfully accomplish challenging tasks and activities. The term **scaffolding** is often used to describe the guidance or structure provided by more competent individuals to help children perform tasks in their zone of proximal development. To understand this concept, think of the scaffolding used in the construction of a new building. A *scaffold* is an external structure that provides support for the workers (e.g., a place where they can stand) until the building itself is strong enough to support them. As the building gains stability, the scaffold becomes less necessary and is gradually removed.

scaffolding Support mechanism that helps a learner successfully perform a task within his or her zone of proximal development.

In much the same way, an adult guiding a child through a new task may initially provide a scaffold to support the child's efforts. For example, as we saw earlier in the teacher–student dialogue about how to divide 44 by 6, a teacher might suggest effective strategies, such as searching for the multiple of 6 closest to but still less than 44. Following are other forms that scaffolding can take:

- Help students develop a plan for dealing with a new task.
- Demonstrate the proper performance of a task in a way that students can easily imitate.
- Divide a complex task into several smaller, simpler tasks.
- Give specific guidelines for accomplishing the task (e.g., see Figure 2.10).
- Provide a calculator, computer software (word processing program, spreadsheet, etc.), or other technology that makes some aspects of the task easier.
- Keep students' attention focused on the relevant aspects of the task.
- Ask questions that get students thinking about the task in productive ways.
- Keep students motivated to complete the task.
- Remind students of what their goals are in performing the task (e.g., what a problem's solution should look like).
- Give frequent feedback about how students are progressing. (A. Collins, 2006; Hmelo-Silver, 2006; Lajoie & Derry, 1993; Lodewyk & Winne, 2005; P. F. Merrill et al., 1996; Rogoff, 1990; Rosenshine & Meister, 1992; D. Wood, Bruner, & Ross, 1976)

Depending on their particular knowledge and ability levels, different students in any single grade may need different kinds of scaffolding to support their success in a task

FIGURE 2.10 High school language arts teacher Jeff Ormrod uses this checklist to scaffold ninth graders' efforts to write a five-paragraph essay.

Essay Checklist

Use the following checklist each time you write an essay to make sure that you have completed the steps and included every part you need.

Introduction

____ My first sentence is a Hook sentence.

____ I have a clear Thesis sentence that answers the question of the assignment.

____ I have a List sentence that introduces my three main body paragraphs.

____ I have a Transition sentence at the end.

Main Body Paragraphs

____ Each of my main body paragraphs talks about one main idea or point.

____ Each of my main body paragraphs gives information that supports this point.

Conclusion

____ My conclusion paragraph restates my List sentence in a different way.

____ My conclusion paragraph restates my Thesis sentence.

____ My conclusion paragraph connects my essay to me or to the world.

Length

____ My Introduction has at least four sentences.

____ My Main Body Paragraph 1 has at least four sentences.

____ My Main Body Paragraph 2 has at least four sentences.

____ My Main Body Paragraph 3 has at least four sentences.

____ My Conclusion has at least four sentences.

Source: Used courtesy of Jeff Ormrod.

(Lodewyk & Winne, 2005; Puntambekar & Hübscher, 2005; Rittle-Johnson & Koedinger, 2005). As students become more adept at performing a task, scaffolding is ideally modified to nurture newly emerging skills. And over time, the scaffolding is gradually phased out—a process known as *fading*—until students can complete the task entirely on their own.

myeducationlab

Gain practice in applying Vygotsky's theory by completing the Building Teaching Skills and Dispositions exercise "Using Cognitive Tools and Instructional Strategies to Scaffold Learning" in MyEducationLab. (To find this exercise go to the topic Cognitive and Linguistic Development in MyEducationLab and click on *Building Teaching Skills and Dispositions*.)

Guided Participation in Adult Activities When you were a young child, did you sometimes help a parent or older sibling bake pastries in the kitchen? Did the cook let you pour, measure, and mix ingredients when you were old enough to do so? Did the cook also give you directions or suggestions as you performed these tasks?

Virtually all cultures allow—and, in fact, usually require—children to be involved in adult activities to some degree (Rogoff, 2003). Children's early experiences often occur at the fringe of an activity, and their involvement is mediated, scaffolded, and supervised through what is sometimes known as **guided participation**. From a Vygotskian perspective, gradual entry into adult activities enables children to engage in behaviors and thinking skills within their zones of proximal development. It also helps children tie newly acquired skills and thinking abilities to the specific contexts in which they are apt to be useful later on (more on this point in Chapter 8). As children acquire greater competence, they gradually take a more central role in a particular activity until, eventually, they are full-fledged participants (R. Gaskins, 1999; Lave & Wenger, 1991; Rogoff et al., 2007).

Adultlike activities can take many forms in the classroom. For instance, we might ask students to conduct laboratory experiments, write letters to government officials, or search the Internet for specific information, while always providing the support the students need to accomplish such tasks successfully. As we engage students in these activities, we might also use some of the language that adults frequently use in such contexts. For example, when students conduct scientific experiments, we should use words such as *hypothesis*, *evidence*, and *theory* as we help them evaluate their procedures and results (Perkins, 1992).

Have students apply new skills in adultlike activities.

Apprenticeships An especially intensive form of guided participation is an **apprenticeship**, a one-on-one relationship in which a novice works with an expert for a lengthy period to learn how to perform complex tasks within a particular domain. The expert provides considerable structure and guidance throughout the process, gradually removing scaffolding and giving the novice more independence and responsibility as competence increases (A. Collins, 2006; Rogoff, 1990, 1991). Many cultures use apprenticeships as a means of gradually introducing children to particular skills and trades in the adult community—perhaps weaving, tailoring, or playing a musical instrument (D. J. Elliott, 1995; Lave & Wenger, 1991; Rogoff, 1990).

Through an apprenticeship, a student often learns not only how to perform a task but also how to *think about* the task—a situation known as a **cognitive apprenticeship** (J. S. Brown, Collins, & Duguid, 1989; A. Collins, 2006; Roth & Bowen, 1995). For instance, a student and a teacher might work together to accomplish a challenging task or solve a difficult problem—perhaps collecting data samples in biology fieldwork, solving a mathematical brainteaser, or translating a difficult passage from German to English. In the process of talking about various aspects of the task or problem, the teacher and the student together analyze the situation and develop the best approach to take, and the teacher models effective ways of thinking about and mentally processing the situation.

Although apprenticeships can differ widely from one context to another, they typically have some or all of these features (A. Collins, 2006; A. Collins, Brown, & Newman, 1989):

- *Modeling.* The teacher demonstrates the task while simultaneously thinking aloud about the process, and the student observes and listens.
- *Coaching.* As the student performs the task, the teacher gives frequent suggestions, hints, and feedback.

guided participation A child's performance, with guidance and support, of an activity in the adult world.

apprenticeship Mentorship in which a novice works intensively with an expert to learn how to perform complex new skills.

cognitive apprenticeship Mentorship in which a teacher and a student work together on a challenging task and the teacher provides guidance in how to think about the task.

- *Scaffolding.* The teacher provides various forms of support for the student, perhaps by simplifying the task, breaking it into smaller and more manageable components, or providing less complicated equipment.
- *Articulation.* The student explains what he or she is doing and why, allowing the teacher to examine the student's knowledge, reasoning, and problem-solving strategies.
- *Reflection.* The teacher asks the student to compare his or her performance with that of experts or perhaps with an ideal model of how the task should be done.
- *Increasing complexity and diversity of tasks.* As the student gains greater proficiency, the teacher presents more complex, challenging, and varied tasks to be completed.
- *Exploration.* The teacher encourages the student to frame questions and problems on his or her own and thereby to expand and refine acquired skills.

Because apprenticeships are clearly labor intensive, their use in the classroom is not always practical or logistically feasible (De Corte, Greer, & Verschaffel, 1996). Even so, we can certainly use elements of an apprenticeship to help students develop more complex skills. For example, prompts such as the following help students think about writing tasks in the same ways that expert writers do:

- My main point is . . .
- An example of this is . . .
- To liven this up, I'll . . .
- I'm not being very clear about what I just said, so . . .
- This isn't very convincing because . . .
- I can tie this together by . . . (Scardamalia & Bereiter, 1985)

Give prompts that get students thinking about a complex task like an expert might.

Such prompts provide the same sort of scaffolding that an expert writer might provide, and they help students develop more sophisticated writing strategies (Scardamalia & Bereiter, 1985).

Dynamic Assessment Recall Vygotsky's proposal that we can get a more complete picture of children's cognitive development when we assess both their *actual developmental level* (the upper limit of tasks they can successfully accomplish on their own) and their *level of potential development* (the upper limit of tasks they can accomplish when they have the assistance of more competent individuals). When teachers assess students' abilities in the classroom, they typically focus on students' *actual* developmental level, asking students to complete assignments and tests without help from anyone else. In recent years, some theorists have suggested an alternative approach known as **dynamic assessment** (e.g., Lidz & Gindis, 2003; L. A. Shepard, 2000; H. L. Swanson & Lussier, 2001). In this approach, rather than find out what students have already learned, a teacher assesses students' ability to learn something new, perhaps with adult assistance or some other form of scaffolding. In particular, dynamic assessment involves the following:

1. Identifying tasks that students cannot initially do independently.
2. Providing in-depth instruction and practice in behaviors and thinking processes related to the tasks.
3. Determining the extent to which each student has benefited from the instruction. (Feuerstein, 1980; Kozulin & Falik, 1995; Lidz & Gindis, 2003; Tzuriel, 2000)

dynamic assessment Systematic examination of how readily and in what ways a student can acquire new knowledge or skills, usually with adult assistance or some other form of scaffolding.

Such an approach can provide a wealth of information about children's thinking processes and approaches to learning and therefore may be helpful in guiding future instruction. It may be especially useful in assessing the abilities of children from diverse cultural backgrounds (Feuerstein, 1979; Sternberg, 2004; Tzuriel, 2000).

Piaget and Vygotsky have each given us groundbreaking insights into the nature of children's learning and thinking, and each of their theories has had a profound influence on contemporary views of learning, thinking, and cognitive development. Piaget's and Vygotsky's theories complement each other to some extent, with the former helping us understand how children often reason on their own and the latter providing ideas about how adults can help children reason more effectively.

Language Development

Both Piaget and Vygotsky argued that language plays key roles in cognitive development. Piaget suggested that words help children mentally represent and think about external objects and events and that language is necessary for the social exchange of ideas that enables children to think less egocentrically and more logically. In Vygotsky's view, language is even more critical for cognitive growth. Children's thought processes are internalized versions of social interactions that are largely verbal in nature. Furthermore, in their conversations with adults, children learn the meanings that their culture ascribes to particular events and gradually begin to interpret the world in culture-specific ways. In addition, through two language-based phenomena—self-talk and inner speech—children begin to guide their own behaviors in ways that others have previously guided them.

Many contemporary theorists share Piaget's and Vygotsky's belief that acquiring language is an important—perhaps the *most* important—factor in cognitive development (e.g., K. Nelson, 1996; Premack, 2004; Spelke, 2003). We can better understand cognitive development, then, when we also know something about language development.

To communicate effectively, children must master many aspects of language, including the meanings of thousands of words, a complex set of rules for putting words together, and social conventions for interacting with others in culturally appropriate ways. Such knowledge and skills continue to develop throughout the school years, usually with some guidance from teachers.

Theoretical Issues Regarding Language Development

Without question, a child's environment plays a significant role in language development. Obviously, children can learn a language only if the people around them regularly converse in it. The richer the language that young children hear—that is, the greater the variety of words and the greater the complexity of syntactic structures that the people around them use—the faster their vocabulary develops (B. Hart & Risley, 1995; Hoff, 2003; Pan, Rowe, Singer, & Snow, 2005). Yet children do not simply absorb the language spoken around them. Instead, they appear to use what they hear to construct their own understanding of the language, including knowledge about what words mean, rules governing how words can be combined into meaningful sentences, and so on (Cairns, 1996; Cromer, 1993; Karmiloff-Smith, 1993). Thus, we see in language development some of the knowledge *construction* of which Piaget spoke.

Most developmental theorists agree that heredity is also involved in language development to some degree. Human beings have the capacity to acquire a far more complex language than any other species on the planet. Exactly *what* human beings inherit that enables them to learn language is a matter of considerable controversy, however. At a minimum, human infants appear to inherit a few key predispositions—for instance, a preference for human voices over other sounds and an ability to hear very subtle differences among speech sounds—that make language learning possible

(DeCasper & Fifer, 1980; Jusczyk, 1995; P. K. Kuhl, 2004; J. L. Locke, 1993). In addition, some theorists believe that part of our genetic heritage is a *language acquisition device*, a language-specific learning mechanism that enables infants and toddlers to acquire many intricacies of language in an amazingly short amount of time (Chomsky, 1972, 2006; M. Gopnik, 1997; Karmiloff-Smith, 1993). Other theorists believe instead that children learn language in much the same way they learn other things about their environment and culture: through detecting and making use of regular patterns of input from their social environment (Gentner & Namy, 2006; Saffran, 2003; Saffran, Aslin, & Newport, 1996).

Research evidence does point to a language-specific developmental mechanism for at least *some* aspects of language learning (Flavell, Miller, & Miller, 2002; Maratsos, 1998; Siegler & Alibali, 2005; Trout, 2003). Children of all cultures learn language very quickly and acquire complex syntactic structures even when those structures are unnecessary for effective communication. In addition, children who show significant delays in their overall cognitive development (i.e., children with mental retardation) show marked differences in language development, depending on their particular disability (N. G. S. Harris, Bellugi, Bates, Jones, & Rossen, 1997; Tager-Flusberg & Skwerer, 2007).

Additional evidence for the influence of heredity comes from research findings suggesting that there may be *sensitive periods* in certain aspects of language development (Bortfeld & Whitehurst, 2001; Bruer, 1999; J. L. Locke, 1993). Children who have little or no exposure to *any* language in the early years often have trouble acquiring language later on, even with intensive language instruction (Curtiss, 1977; Newport, 1990). Furthermore, when learning a *second* language, people have an easier time mastering pronunciation and various verb tenses if they are immersed in the language during childhood or early adolescence (Bialystok, 1994; Bortfeld & Whitehurst, 2001; Bruer, 1999; M. S. C. Thomas & Johnson, 2008). Such sensitive periods may reflect biologically built-in time frames for learning language. Alternatively, perhaps what appear to be predetermined "best" times for learning particular aspects of language are simply the result of the brain's tendency to adapt fairly quickly to whatever form its early auditory environment takes (P. K. Kuhl, 2004; P. K. Kuhl, Conboy, Padden, Nelson, & Pruitt, 2005).

Trends in Language Development

The vast majority of children are consistently immersed in a language-rich environment beginning in infancy. In such an environment, most children begin using recognizable words sometime around their first birthday and are putting these words together by their second birthday. During the preschool years, they become capable of forming longer and more complex sentences. By the time they begin school at age 5 or 6, they use language that seems adultlike in many respects. Yet their language capabilities continue to develop and mature throughout childhood and adolescence. Examples of linguistic characteristics at different grade levels are shown in Table 2.2.

Development of Vocabulary One obvious change in students' language during the school years is the increase in their vocabulary (see Table 2.2). Children learn some words through direct vocabulary instruction at school, but they probably learn many more by inferring meaning from the contexts in which they hear or read the words (Nippold, 1988; Pinker, 1987; Thelen & Smith, 1998).

Children's initial understandings of words are sometimes vague or only partially correct. For instance, I once asked my son Jeff, then age 6, to tell me what an *animal* is. He replied, "It has a head, tail, feet, paws, eyes, noses, ears, lots of hair." Like Jeff, young elementary school children often restrict the meaning of *animal* primarily to mammals, such as dogs and horses, and insist that fish, birds, and insects are *not* animals (S. Carey, 1985; Saltz, 1971). With age, experience, and instruction, students continue to refine their understandings of words, and many initially concrete definitions become more abstract. For example, when Jeff was 4, he defined *summer* as the time of year when school is out and it's hot outside, but later, after he had studied the seasons in his middle school science class, he was able to define summer in terms of the earth's tilt relative to the sun—a far more abstract notion.

TABLE 2.2
Examples of Linguistic Characteristics and Abilities at Different Grade Levels

Grade Level	Age-Typical Characteristics	Suggested Strategies
K–2	• Knowledge of 8,000 to 14,000 words by age 6 • Difficulty understanding complex sentences (e.g., those with multiple clauses) • Overdependence on word order and context (instead of syntax) when interpreting messages • Superficial understanding of being a good listener (e.g., just sitting quietly) • Literal interpretations of messages and requests (e.g., not realizing that "Goodness, this class is noisy" means "Be quiet") • Increasing ability to tell a story • Mastery of most sounds; some difficulty pronouncing *r*, *th*, *dr*, *sl*, and *str* • Occasional use of regular word endings (*-s*, *-ed*, *-er*) with irregular words (*sheeps*, *goed*, *gooder*) • Basic etiquette in conversations (e.g., taking turns, answering questions) • Reluctance to initiate conversations with adults (for many students from Asian and Mexican American backgrounds)	• Read age-appropriate storybooks as a way of enhancing vocabulary. • Give corrective feedback when students' use of words indicates inaccurate understanding. • Work on listening skills (e.g., sitting quietly, paying attention, trying to understand and remember). • Ask follow-up questions to make sure students accurately understand important messages. • Ask students to construct narratives about recent events (e.g., "Tell me about your camping trip last weekend.").
3–5	• Increasing understanding of temporal words (e.g., *before*, *after*) and comparatives (e.g., *bigger*, *as big as*) • Occasional confusion about when to use *the* versus *a* • Incomplete knowledge of irregular word forms • Increasing awareness of when sentences are and are not grammatically correct • Correct pronunciation of all sounds in one's language (by age 9) • Sustained conversations about concrete topics • Increasing ability to take listeners' prior knowledge into account during explanations • Construction of stories with plots and cause-and-effect relationships • Linguistic creativity and word play (e.g., rhymes, word games)	• Teach irregular word forms (e.g., the past tense of *ring* is *rang*, the past tense of *bring* is *brought*). • Begin instruction about parts of speech (e.g., nouns, verbs). • Use group discussion as a way to explore academic subject matter. • Have students create short stories that they present orally or in writing. • When articulation problems are evident in the upper elementary grades, consult with a speech–language pathologist. • Encourage telling jokes and reciting rhymes that capitalize on double meanings and homonyms (i.e., sound-alike words).
6–8	• Knowledge of about 50,000 words at age 12 • Increasing awareness of the terminology used in various academic disciplines • Some confusion about when to use various connectives (e.g., *but*, *although*, *unless*) • Ability to understand complex, multiclause sentences • Emerging ability to look beyond literal interpretations; comprehension of simple proverbs and increasing ability to detect sarcasm • Emerging ability to carry on lengthy conversations about abstract topics • Significant growth in knowledge about the nature of language (i.e., increased metalinguistic awareness)	• Assign reading materials that introduce new vocabulary. • Introduce some of the terminology used by experts in various academic disciplines (e.g., *simile* in language arts, *molecule* in science). • Conduct structured debates to explore controversial issues. • Ask students to consider the underlying meanings of common proverbs. • Explore the nature of words and language as entities in and of themselves.
9–12	• Knowledge of about 80,000 words • Acquisition of many vocabulary words related to particular academic disciplines • Subtle refinements in syntax, mostly as a result of formal instruction • Mastery of a wide variety of connectives (e.g., *although*, *however*, *nevertheless*) • General ability to understand figurative language (e.g., metaphors, proverbs, hyperbole)	• Consistently use the terminology associated with various academic disciplines. • Distinguish between similar abstract words (e.g., *weather* vs. *climate*, *velocity* vs. *acceleration*). • Explore complex syntactic structures (e.g., multiple embedded clauses). • Consider the underlying meanings and messages in poetry and fiction. • When students have a native dialect other than Standard English, encourage them to use it in informal conversations and creative writing; encourage the use of Standard English for more formal situations.

Sources: Bowey, 1986; L. Bradley & Bryant, 1991; Capelli, Nakagawa, & Madden, 1990; S. Carey, 1978; Delgado-Gaitan, 1994; Karmiloff-Smith, 1979; Maratsos, 1998; McDevitt et al., 1990; McDevitt & Ford, 1987; Nippold, 1988; O'Grady, 1997; Owens, 2008; Reich, 1986; Sheldon, 1974; Stanovich, 2000; Swanborn & de Glopper, 1999; Thelen & Smith, 1998.

Consider students' existing vocabularies when conducting lessons and choosing reading materials, but also teach new words on an ongoing basis.

To some extent, we must, of course, tailor lessons and reading materials to students' current vocabularies. Yet we should regularly introduce new words into lessons, providing definitions and encouraging students to use the words in a variety of contexts. We should also correct any misconceptions about word meanings that reveal themselves in students' speech and written work. And we must encourage students to *read, read, read*: Children and adolescents learn many new words through their reading activities (Stanovich, 2000; Swanborn & de Glopper, 1999).

Development of Syntax As children grow older, they gain increasing competence in the various rules of **syntax** that underlie correct sentence constructions. Their understanding and use of complex constructions (e.g., passive sentences, sentences with multiple clauses) continue to evolve throughout the elementary years, and even more subtle aspects of syntax appear in the middle school and high school grades (see Table 2.2).

Provide formal instruction in grammar and composition at all grade levels.

In the later grades, most syntactical development probably occurs as the result of formal language instruction—perhaps courses in language arts, English composition, and foreign language (Maratsos, 1998). Students are more likely to improve their speech and writing when they have ample opportunities to express their ideas orally and on paper and when they receive direct feedback about ambiguities and grammatical errors in their speech and writing.

Development of Listening Comprehension Students' ability to comprehend what they hear is obviously influenced by their knowledge of vocabulary and syntax, but other factors contribute as well. For instance, children's conception of what listening comprehension *is* seems to change during the elementary school years. Children in the early elementary grades believe they are good listeners if they simply sit quietly without interrupting the teacher. Not until about age 11 do they realize that good listening also requires *understanding* what is said (Imhof, 2001; McDevitt, Spivey, Sheehan, Lennon, & Story, 1990). And when they don't understand, many children believe it is inappropriate to ask an adult for clarification (McDevitt, 1990; McDevitt et al., 1990). Such a belief is especially common when children's cultures have taught them that initiating conversation with an adult is disrespectful, as is true in many Asian and Mexican American communities (Delgado-Gaitan, 1994; Grant & Gomez, 2001).

Check young children's understanding of important information or instructions by asking them to restate your messages in their own words.

In the early elementary grades, children tend to take the words they hear at face value—for instance, interpreting the expression "Your eyes are bigger than your stomach" quite literally (e.g., see Figure 2.11). And they have little success drawing generalizations from such proverbs as "A rolling stone gathers no moss" and "Don't put the cart before the horse." As children get older and gain an increasing capacity for abstract thought, they become better able to look beyond the literal meanings of messages (Owens, 2008; Pexman, 2008; Winner, 1988).

myeducationlab

Observe developmental differences in interpreting proverbs in the video "Cognitive Development." (To find this video, go to Chapter 2 of the Book-Specific Resources in MyEducationLab, select *Video Examples*, and then click on the title.)

Development of Oral Communication Skills Most children master the sounds of spoken English (including such difficult ones as *th* and *sl*) by age 8 or 9 (see Table 2.2). Yet in order to communicate effectively, children must also consider the characteristics of the people receiving their messages (e.g., age, prior knowledge, perspectives). Even in the upper elementary grades, children sometimes neglect to take into account what prior information their listeners are apt to have, making their messages difficult to understand (Glucksberg & Krauss, 1967; McDevitt & Ford, 1987).

Give students a lot of practice speaking in class, and let them know when you don't fully understand what they mean.

Another component of effective oral communication is **pragmatics**, the social conventions governing appropriate verbal interactions with others. Pragmatics include not only rules of etiquette—taking turns when talking with others, saying goodbye when leaving, and so on—but also strategies for beginning and ending conversations, changing the subject, telling stories, and arguing effectively. Children continue to refine their knowledge of pragmatics throughout the elementary grades (Owens, 2008). My own observations indicate that this process continues into the middle and high school years, often even longer. When students haven't mastered certain social conventions—for instance, when they interrupt frequently or change the subject with-

syntax Set of rules that one uses, often unconsciously, to put words together into sentences.

pragmatics Use of socially effective and culturally appropriate behaviors in verbal interactions with others.

out warning—others may find their behavior irritating or strange. A lack of pragmatic skills, then, can seriously interfere with students' relationships with peers.

Explicitly teach any social conventions of everyday speech that certain students have not yet mastered.

Development of Metalinguistic Awareness Children's **metalinguistic awareness** is their conscious understanding of the nature and functions of language (Owens, 2008; Yaden & Templeton, 1986). For instance, it includes awareness that speech is comprised of smaller units (e.g., words and their component sounds), that some words and phrases have multiple meanings, and that some messages aren't intended to be taken literally.

Encourage students to reflect on the underlying nature of words and language.

Metalinguistic awareness emerges slowly over time. During the elementary years, students gradually become capable of determining when sentences are grammatically acceptable and when they are not (Bowey, 1986). As students move into the upper elementary and middle school grades, they become increasingly aware of the various functions of words in a sentence (nouns, verbs, adjectives, etc.), in large part as a result of formal instruction about parts of speech. High school students enhance their metalinguistic awareness still further as they consciously consider the figurative nature of words—the nonliteral meanings of proverbs, the symbolism in poems and literature, and so on. Studying a second language also promotes metalinguistic awareness, as we will see shortly.

FIGURE 2.11 Adults typically use this common expression figuratively, perhaps to describe a situation in which someone has ordered more food than he or she can possibly eat. Here, however, 8-year-old Jeff interprets the expression quite literally.

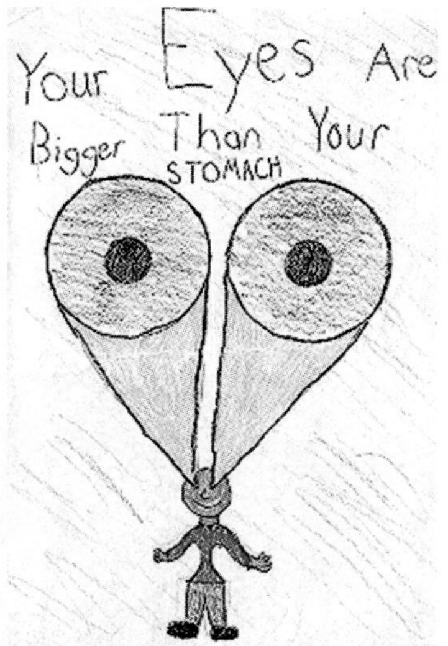

Diversity in Language Development

Some diversity in language development appears to be the result of biology. For instance, children with a **specific language impairment** develop normally in all respects except for language. These children have difficulty perceiving and mentally processing particular aspects of spoken language—perhaps the quality, pitch, duration, or intensity of specific sounds in speech (Corriveau, Pasquini, & Goswami, 2007; P. R. Hill, Hogben, & Bishop, 2005; J. W. Montgomery & Windsor, 2007). Often, although not always, the source of the impairment can be traced to heredity or a specific brain abnormality (Bishop, 2006; J. L. Locke, 1993; Spinath, Price, Dale, & Plomin, 2004).

Environmental factors play a role in linguistic diversity as well. For example, the size of children's vocabularies is partly the result of their prior exposure to various words through storybook reading, trips to museums, and so on (e.g., Hoff, 2003; Raikes et al., 2006). Furthermore, as we'll discover in Chapter 4, different cultural groups may nurture different *dialects*—distinct forms of English that characterize particular ethnicities or geographic regions—and different social conventions for human conversation (i.e., different pragmatic skills).

Occasionally, a cultural or ethnic group specifically nurtures certain aspects of language development. For example, many inner-city African American communities make heavy use of figurative language—such as similes, metaphors, and hyperbole (intentional exaggeration)—in their day-to-day conversations, jokes, and stories (Hale-Benson, 1986; H. L. Smith, 1998; Smitherman, 2007). The following anecdote illustrates this point:

> I once asked my mother, upon her arrival from church, "Mom, was it a good sermon?" To which she replied, "Son, by the time the minister finished preaching, the men were crying and the women had passed out on the floor." (H. L. Smith, 1998, p. 202)

With such a rich oral tradition, it is not surprising that many inner-city African American youth are especially advanced in their use and understanding of figurative language (Ortony, Turner, & Larson-Shapiro, 1985; H. L. Smith, 1998; Smitherman, 2007).

metalinguistic awareness Ability to think consciously about the nature and functions of language.

specific language impairment Disability characterized by abnormalities in the production or comprehension of spoken language, to the point that special educational services are required.

Second-Language Learning and English Language Learners

As mentioned earlier, exposure to a second language in childhood or early adolescence may be especially important for acquiring flawless pronunciation and certain aspects of syntax. Early exposure to a second language seems to be most advantageous if the second language is very different from the first. For example, a native English speaker benefits more from an early start in Japanese or Arabic than from an early start in, say, Spanish or German (Bialystok, 1994; Strozer, 1994). Aside from such caveats, there appears to be no definitive "best" time to begin studying a second language (e.g., P. K. Kuhl et al., 2005; Stevens, 2004).

Encourage students of all ages to learn one or more foreign languages.

Although there may be no hard-and-fast sensitive period for learning a second language, beginning second-language instruction in the early years has definite advantages. For one thing, it appears that learning a second language facilitates achievement in other academic areas, such as reading, vocabulary, and grammar (Diaz, 1983; Reich, 1986). Instruction in a foreign language also sensitizes young children to the international and multicultural nature of the world. Students who learn a second language during the elementary school years express more positive attitudes toward people who speak that language and are more likely to enroll in foreign language classes in high school (Reich, 1986).

Bilingualism At least half of the world's children are *bilingual*; that is, they speak two (sometimes three or more) languages fluently (Hoff-Ginsberg, 1997). In most instances, bilingualism involves two *spoken* languages, but in some cases, it involves knowing one spoken language and one manual language (e.g., American Sign Language).

myeducationlab

Observe a bilingual teacher simultaneously talking and signing in the video "Teacher Use of Sign Language." (To find this video, go to Chapter 2 of the Book-Specific Resources in MyEducationLab, select *Video Examples*, and then click on the title.)

Research reveals clear advantages to being bilingual. Bilingual children appear to have a head start in their development of metalinguistic awareness (Bialystok, 2001; Diaz & Klingler, 1991; E. E. García, 1994; C. E. Moran & Hakuta, 1995). For instance, in the early elementary grades, bilingual children have greater **phonological awareness**—awareness of the individual sounds, or *phonemes*, that make up spoken words—and this awareness may get them off to an especially good start in learning to read (X. Chen et al., 2004; Rayner, Foorman, Perfetti, Pesetsky, & Seidenberg, 2001). Furthermore, when children are truly fluent in both languages, they tend to perform better on tasks requiring advanced cognitive functioning—for instance, on intelligence tests and on tasks requiring creativity (Diaz & Klingler, 1991; E. E. García, 1994; Leung, Maddux, Galinsky, & Chiu, 2008; C. E. Moran & Hakuta, 1995). Their superior performance in such areas may be partly the result of enhanced development in certain areas of the brain (Espinosa, 2008; Mechelli et al., 2004).

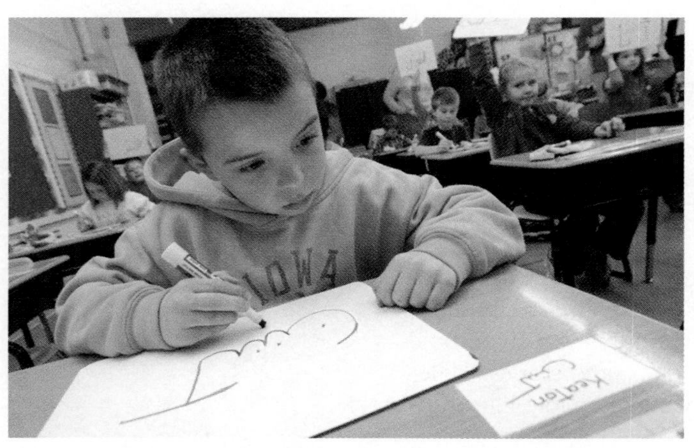

Students gain both cognitive and social benefits from learning a second language.

Being bilingual can have cultural and personal advantages as well. In any English-speaking country, mastery of spoken and written English is, of course, essential for long-term educational and professional success. But when a resident of that country belongs to a cultural group that speaks a different language, maintaining social relationships within the culture requires knowledge of its language (McBrien, 2005b). For instance, in many Native American groups, the ancestral language is important for communicating oral history and cultural heritage and for conducting local business (McCarty & Watahomigie, 1998). And Puerto Rican children in the United States often speak Spanish at home as a way of showing respect to their elders (Torres-Guzmán, 1998).

Bilingualism has additional social benefits at school. In classrooms where different students speak only one of two different languages (perhaps some speaking only English and others speaking only Spanish), teaching students both languages increases student interaction and cross-cultural understanding (A. Doyle, 1982; Padilla, 2006).

phonological awareness Ability to hear the distinct sounds that comprise spoken words.

Teaching a Second Language Most children in Western, English-speaking countries are exposed to only one language before they reach school age. That single language may or may not be English. For instance, in the United States, several million children are members of families who speak a language other than English at home (D.

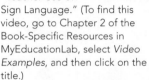

Meyer, Madden, & McGrath, 2005; National Association of Bilingual Education, 1993; Pérez, 1998). Many of these children have little exposure to English before they begin school.

School-age children who are fluent in their native language but not in English are often referred to as **English language learners (ELLs)**. More than 5% of the public school population in the United States has limited proficiency in English, and the number increases every year (Federal Interagency Forum on Child and Family Statistics, 2007; D. Meyer et al., 2005; U.S. Department of Education, 1993). To the extent that elementary and secondary school students have limited knowledge of English, they are apt to have trouble with schoolwork in an English-based classroom (Kieffer, 2008; Padilla, 2006; Slavin & Cheung, 2005; Valdés, Bunch, Snow, & Lee, 2005).

myeducationlab

Discover some of the challenges that many English language learners and their teachers face by completing the Building Teaching Skills and Dispositions exercise "Working with English Language Learners" in MyEducationLab. (To find this activity, go to the topic Student Diversity in MyEducationLab and click on *Building Teaching Skills and Dispositions.*)

Just as very young children typically learn their native language through informal daily exposure, so, too, can they learn two languages simultaneously if they have frequent, ongoing exposure to both languages. However, when children begin to learn a second language at an older age, perhaps in the elementary grades or even later, they often learn it more quickly if their language-learning experiences are fairly structured (Strozer, 1994).

Yet teaching a foreign language for one 45-minute period a day (as is typically done in high schools) hardly promotes mastery. Two more intensive approaches, immersion and bilingual education, can be quite effective, with each being useful in somewhat different situations. To keep our discussion simple, let's assume that students are living in an English-speaking country. If these students are native English speakers, total **immersion** in the second language—hearing and speaking it almost exclusively in the classroom during the school day—appears to be the more effective approach. A variation of this approach is a *dual-immersion program*, in which some topics are taught exclusively in English and others are taught exclusively in the second language. For native English speakers living in an English-speaking country, immersion in the second language for part or all of the school day helps students acquire proficiency in the language fairly quickly, and any adverse effects on achievement in other academic areas appear to be short lived (Collier, 1992; T. H. Cunningham & Graham, 2000; Genesee, 1985; Padilla, 2006).

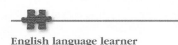

To maximize second-language learning for native English speakers who live in an English-speaking country, completely immerse them in the second language for part or all of the school day.

In contrast, English language learners living in an English-speaking country typically fare better in **bilingual education**, in which they receive intensive instruction in English while studying other academic subject areas in their native language. Not only is their academic achievement at least as good or better in bilingual education, but they also have greater self-esteem and better attitudes toward school (Marsh, Hau, & Kong, 2002; McBrien, 2005b; Snow, 1990; Tong, Lara-Alecio, Irby, Mathes, & Kwok, 2008; Wright, Taylor, & Macarthur, 2000). The optimal bilingual education program proceeds through a gradual phase-in of English in instruction, perhaps in a sequence such as the following:

Remember that English language learners fare better when they study other school subjects in their native language.

1. Students join native English speakers for classes in subject areas that do not depend too heavily on language skills (e.g., art, music, physical education). They study other subject areas in their native language and also begin classes in English as a second language (ESL).
2. Once students have acquired some English proficiency, instruction in English begins for one or two additional subject areas (perhaps for math and science).
3. When it is clear that students can learn successfully in English in the subject areas identified in step 2, they join their English-speaking classmates in regular classes in these subjects.
4. Eventually students are sufficiently proficient in English to join the mainstream in all subject areas, and they may no longer require their ESL classes (Krashen, 1996; Padilla, 2006; Valdés et al., 2005).

English language learner (ELL) School-age child who is not fully fluent in English because of limited exposure to English prior to enrollment in an English-speaking school.

immersion Second-language instruction in which students hear and speak that language almost exclusively in the classroom.

bilingual education Second-language instruction in which students are instructed in academic subject areas in their native language while simultaneously being taught to speak and write in the second language.

Ideally, the transition from instruction in a student's native language to instruction in English occurs very gradually over a period of several years. Simple knowledge of basic conversational English—knowledge collectively known as **basic interpersonal**

INTO THE Classroom

Working with English Language Learners

- **Teach early reading skills in students' native languages.**

  When working with students whose families recently immigrated to the United States from Mexico, a first-grade teacher teaches basic letter–sound relationships and word decoding skills in Spanish (e.g., showing how the printed word *dos,* meaning "two," can be broken up into the sounds "duh," "oh," and "sss").

- **If you don't speak a student's native language yourself, recruit and train parents, community volunteers, or other students to assist in providing instruction in that language.**

  A boy in a kindergarten class has grown up speaking Hmong, a language spoken in some Asian immigrant communities in the United States. His teacher recruits a fourth grader who can read an English picture book to the boy and translate it into Hmong. At one point, the teacher points to a lily pad on a page of the book and asks the fourth grader to describe a lily pad in Hmong, as the boy has never seen lily pads in his own neighborhood. (You can see this example in action in the "Reading a Picture Book to a Hmong Student" video in Chapter 2 of the Book-Specific Resources in **MyEducationLab**.)

- **Make use of bilingual software.**

  Conducting a quick Google search using the key terms *bilingual, educational,* and *software,* a teacher finds many educational software programs with both English and Spanish options, including some free programs that he can easily download to his classroom computers.

- **When using English to communicate, speak more slowly than you might otherwise, and clearly enunciate each word.**

  A third-grade teacher is careful that he always says "going to" rather than "gonna" and "want to" rather than "wanna."

- **Use visual aids to supplement verbal explanations.**

  A high school history teacher uses photographs that she downloaded from the Internet to illustrate her verbal description of ancient Egypt. She also gives students a one-page outline that identifies the main ideas in her lesson.

- **During small-group learning activities, encourage same-language students to communicate with one another in their native language.**

  When a high school science teacher breaks students into cooperative groups to study the effects of weight, length, and amount of push on a pendulum's oscillation rate, she puts three native Chinese speakers in a single group. She suggests that they can talk in either English or Chinese as they do their experiments.

- **Encourage, but don't force, students to contribute to class discussions in English; be understanding of students who are initially reluctant to participate.**

  A high school social studies teacher often breaks his class into small groups to discuss controversial social and political issues. He intentionally places recent immigrants with peers who are likely to be supportive as these English language learners struggle in their efforts to communicate.

- **Have students work in pairs to make sense of textbook material.**

  As two middle school students read a section of their geography textbook, one reads aloud while the other listens and takes notes. They frequently stop to talk about what's been read, and then they switch roles.

- **Have students read, write, and report about their native countries; also have them create art that depicts aspects of their countries and cultures.**

  A middle school social studies teacher has students conduct research on a country from which they or their ancestors emigrated. The students create posters to display what they've learned, and they proudly talk about their posters at a class-sponsored International Day that students from other classes attend.

Sources: Strategies are based on research and recommendations by Carhill et al., 2008; Comeau, Cormier, Grandmaison, & Lacroix, 1999; Duff, 2001; Egbert, 2009; Espinosa, 2007; E. E. García, 1995; Herrell & Jordan, 2004; Igoa, 1995, 2007; Janzen, 2008; Krashen, 1996; McClelland, 2001; McClelland, Fiez, & McCandliss, 2002; Padilla, 2006; Slavin & Cheung, 2005; Solórzano, 2008; Tong et al., 2008; Valdés et al., 2005; Walshaw & Anthony, 2008.

communication skills (BICS)—is not enough for academic success in an English-only curriculum. Ultimately, students must have sufficient mastery of English vocabulary and syntax that they can easily understand and learn from English-based textbooks and lectures; in other words, they must have **cognitive academic language proficiency (CALP)**. Such mastery of English takes considerable time to achieve—often, five to seven years (Carhill, Suárez-Orozco, & Páez, 2008; Cummins, 1981, 1984, 2000, 2008; Padilla, 2006).

Why is immersion better for some students whereas bilingual education is better for others? As we've learned, language is an important foundation for cognitive development: It provides symbols for mentally representing the world, enables children to exchange ideas with others, helps them internalize sophisticated cognitive strategies, and so on. Students in an English-speaking country who are immersed in a different language at school still have many opportunities—at home, with their friends, and in the local community—to continue using and developing their English. In contrast, nonnative English speakers may have few opportunities outside their homes to use their native language. If they are taught exclusively in English, they may very well lose proficiency in their native language before developing adequate proficiency in English—a phenomenon known as **subtractive bilingualism**—and their cognitive development will suffer in the process. Because bilingual education is designed to foster growth in *both* English and a child's native language, it is apt to promote cognitive development as well as English proficiency (Pérez, 1998; Tse, 2001; Winsler, Díaz, Espinosa, & Rodriguez, 1999).

We must remember that students' native languages are very much a part of their sense of identity—their sense of who they are as people (Nieto, 1995; Tatum, 1997). A high school student named Marisol made the point this way:

> I'm proud of [being Puerto Rican]. I guess I speak Spanish whenever I can. . . . I used to have a lot of problems with one of my teachers 'cause she didn't want us to talk Spanish in class and I thought that was like an insult to us, you know? (Nieto, 1995, p. 127)

Incorporating children's *culture* as well as their native language into the classroom curriculum can further promote their academic success (Igoa, 1995, 2007; U.S. Department of Education, 1993). The strategies in the Into the Classroom Feature "Working with English Language Learners" take language, sense of identity, and culture into account.

basic interpersonal communication skills (BICS) Proficiency in English sufficient for day-to-day conversation with English speakers but *not* sufficient for academic success in an English-only curriculum.

cognitive academic language proficiency (CALP) Mastery of English vocabulary and syntax sufficient for English language learners to achieve academic success in an English-only curriculum.

subtractive bilingualism Phenomenon in which immersion in a new-language environment leads to deficits in a child's native language.

The Big Picture

Our explorations of general developmental principles, brain development, Piaget's and Vygotsky's theories, and language development have taken us in a variety of directions. Nevertheless, several common themes have repeatedly appeared in one form or another:

- ***Children's development is guided by both heredity and environment.*** To some degree, children's physical, cognitive, and social abilities depend on maturation—that is, on a genetically driven unfolding of physiological advancements. But environmental factors are equally critical: Children must have appropriate experiences and social support to acquire the knowledge and skills they will need to be successful in their physical and social worlds.

- ***Children actively construct, rather than passively absorb, their knowledge.*** Piaget described cognitive development as a process of constructing one's own unique understandings of the world. Vygotsky and his followers have suggested that children and adults often work together to make sense of and find meaning in events. Constructive processes appear to be important in language development as well—for instance, in acquiring word meanings and syntactical rules. We'll pursue the process of knowledge construction further in Chapter 7.

- ***With age, children become capable of increasingly complex thought.*** Both Piaget and Vygotsky suggested that children acquire many new cognitive abilities as they grow older. Piaget described such development in terms of four qualitatively distinct stages, whereas Vygotsky theorized that children gradually internalize many of the processes they initially use in social interactions. Regardless of which theorist's perspective we take, we may reasonably speculate that developmental changes in the brain—synaptic pruning, increasing myelination of neurons, hormonal changes after puberty, and so on—provide increasingly sophisticated mental "hardware" that enables many new cognitive acquisitions over time.

- ***Language provides a foundation for many cognitive advancements.*** Words provide the basis for much of the symbolic thought about which Piaget spoke. And many words and phrases specific to various academic disciplines—for example, *square root, atom, supply-and-demand*—become cognitive tools that, in Vygotsky's view, help children take advantage of and build on the accumulating wisdom of previous generations.

  Language propels cognitive development in a second important way as well: It enables children to exchange ideas with adults and peers. In Piaget's view, the people in a child's life can present information and arguments that create disequilibrium and foster greater perspective taking. In Vygotsky's view, internalization of complex thought processes comes only after children first use such processes in their verbal interactions with others.

- ***Challenging situations and tasks promote development.*** The importance of challenge is most evident in Vygotsky's concept of the *zone of proximal development*: Children benefit most from tasks they can perform only with the assistance of more competent individuals. However, challenge, albeit of a somewhat different sort, also lies at the heart of Piaget's theory: Children develop more sophisticated knowledge and thought processes only when they encounter phenomena they cannot adequately understand using their existing schemes—in other words, phenomena that create disequilibrium.

Yet we must not take this idea of challenge too far. As noted in our earlier discussion of brain development, bombarding children with a great deal of information every day is unlikely to nurture their cognitive development any more than a reasonably stimulating but otherwise normal learning environment would. Furthermore, asking children to tackle one challenge after another throughout the school day can be unsettling and, especially if children meet with frequent frustration and failure, can adversely affect their self-esteem. We'll look at self-esteem and more generally at the development of children's *sense of self* in the next chapter.

Practice for Your Licensure Exam

Stones Lesson

Ms. Hennessey is conducting a demonstration in her first-grade class. She shows the children a large glass tank filled with water. She also shows them two stones. One stone, a piece of granite, is fairly small (about 2 cm in diameter). The other stone, a piece of pumice (i.e., cooled volcanic lava), is much larger (about 10 cm in diameter). Because Ms. Hennessey does not allow the children to touch or hold the stones, they have no way of knowing that the piece of pumice, which has many small air pockets in it, is much lighter than the piece of granite. The demonstration proceeds as follows:

> *Ms. H.:* Would anyone like to predict what he or she thinks will happen to these stones? Yes, Brianna.
> *Brianna:* I think the . . . both stones will sink because I know stones sink. I've seen lots of stones sink and every time I throw a rock into the water, like it always sinks, yeah, it always does.
> *Ms. H.:* You look like you want to say something else.
> *Brianna:* Yeah the water can't hold up rocks like it holds up boats and I know they'll sink.
> *Ms. H.:* You sound so sure, let me try another object.
> *Brianna:* No you gotta throw it in, you gotta test my idea first. [Ms. H. places the smaller stone in the tank; it sinks.] See, I told you I knew it would sink. [Ms. H. puts the larger, pumice stone down and picks up another object.] No you've gotta test the big one too because if the little one sunk the big one's gotta sunk. [Ms. H. places the pumice stone in the tank; it floats.] No! No! That's not right! That doesn't go with my mind [Brianna grabs hold of her head], it just doesn't go with my mind. (M. G. Hennessey, 2003, pp. 120–121)

1. Constructed-response question:

Brianna is noticeably surprised, maybe even a little upset, when she sees the pumice stone float.

A. Use one or more concepts from Jean Piaget's theory of cognitive development to explain why Brianna reacts as strongly as she does to the floating pumice.

B. Again drawing on Piaget's theory, explain why Ms. Hennessey intentionally presents a phenomenon that will surprise the children.

2. Multiple-choice question:

Imagine that you perform the same demonstration with high school students, rather than first graders. If you were to follow Vygotsky's theory of cognitive development, which one of the following approaches would you take in helping the students understand the floating pumice?

a. Before performing the demonstration, ask students to draw a picture of the tank and two stones.
b. Drop several light objects (e.g., a feather, a piece of paper, a small sponge) into the tank before dropping either stone into it.
c. Teach the concept of *density*, and explain that an object's average density relative to water determines whether it floats or sinks.
d. Praise students who correctly predict that the larger stone will float, even if they initially give an incorrect explanation about why it will float.

Go to Chapter 2 of the Book-Specific Resources in **MyEducationLab**, and click on "Practice for Your Licensure Exam" to answer these questions. Compare your responses with the feedback provided.

PRAXIS

Turn to Appendix C, "Matching Book and MyEducationLab Content to the Praxis Principles of Learning and Teaching Tests," to discover sections of this chapter that may be especially applicable to the Praxis tests.

PEARSON myeducationlab

Now go to MyEducationLab (**www.myeducationlab.com**), where you can:

- Find learning outcomes for Cognitive and Linguistic Development, along with the national standards that connect to these outcomes.
- Complete Assignments and Activities that can help you more deeply understand the chapter content.
- Engage in Building Teaching Skills and Dispositions exercises in which you can apply and practice core teaching skills identified in the chapter.
- Access Book-Specific Resources:
  - Check your comprehension of chapter content by going to the Study Plan, where you can find (a) Chapter Objectives; (b) Focus Questions that can guide your reading; (c) a Self-Check Quiz that can help you monitor your progress in mastering chapter content; (d) Review, Practice, and Enrichment exercises with detailed feedback that will deepen your understanding of various concepts and principles; (e) Flashcards that can give you practice in understanding and defining key terms; and (f) Common Beliefs and Misconceptions about Educational Psychology that will alert you to typical misunderstandings in educational psychology classes.
  - Video Examples of various concepts and principles presented in the chapter.
  - Supplementary Readings that enable you to pursue certain topics in greater depth.
  - A Practice for Your Licensure Exam exercise that resembles the kinds of questions appearing on many teacher licensure tests.

CHAPTER OUTLINE

- **CASE STUDY: HIDDEN TREASURE**
- **PERSONALITY DEVELOPMENT**
  Temperament • Environmental Influences on Personality Development • The "Big Five" Personality Traits • Temperament, Personality, and Goodness of Fit
- **DEVELOPMENT OF A SENSE OF SELF**
  Factors Influencing Sense of Self • Developmental Changes in Sense of Self • Diversity in Sense of Self
- **DEVELOPMENT OF PEER RELATIONSHIPS AND INTERPERSONAL UNDERSTANDINGS**
  Roles of Peers in Children's Development • Characteristics of Peer Relationships • Social Cognition • Aggression • Technology and Peer Relationships • Diversity in Peer Relationships and Social Cognition • Promoting Healthy Peer Relationships
- **MORAL AND PROSOCIAL DEVELOPMENT**
  Developmental Trends in Morality and Prosocial Behavior • Factors Influencing Moral and Prosocial Development • Diversity in Moral and Prosocial Development • Encouraging Moral and Prosocial Development in the Classroom
- **THE BIG PICTURE**
- **PRACTICE FOR YOUR LICENSURE EXAM: *THE SCARLET LETTER***

CHAPTER OBJECTIVES

- **Objective 3.1:** Describe the nature and origins of children's temperaments and personality characteristics, and explain how you might adapt your classroom practices to students' diverse personalities.
- **Objective 3.2:** Explain how students' sense of self is apt to influence their behavior and how you can help students develop healthy self-perceptions.

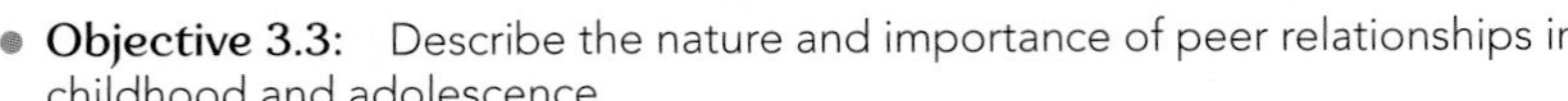

- **Objective 3.3:** Describe the nature and importance of peer relationships in childhood and adolescence.
- **Objective 3.4:** Apply your knowledge of peer relationships and social cognition in promoting productive social skills and addressing student aggression.
- **Objective 3.5:** Describe typical advancements in moral and prosocial development over the course of childhood and adolescence, and identify strategies for promoting moral and prosocial development in the classroom.

Chapter 3

Personal and Social Development

CASE STUDY: Hidden Treasure

Six-year-old Lupita has spent most of her life in Mexico with her grandmother, a woman with limited financial means and no knowledge of English. But Lupita has recently joined her migrant-worker parents in the United States, and she is now a quiet, well-behaved student in Ms. Padilla's kindergarten class. Ms. Padilla rarely calls on her because of her apparent lack of academic skills and is thinking about holding her back for a second year of kindergarten.

Yet a researcher's videocamera captures a side of Lupita that her teacher hasn't noticed. On one occasion, Lupita is quick to finish her Spanish assignment and starts to work on a puzzle during her free time. A classmate approaches, and he and Lupita begin playing with a box of toys. A teacher aide asks the boy whether he has finished his Spanish assignment, implying that he should return to complete it, but the boy doesn't understand the aide's subtle message. Lupita gently persuades the boy to go back and finish his work and then returns to her puzzle and successfully fits most of it together. Two classmates having difficulty with their own puzzles request Lupita's assistance, and she competently and patiently shows them how to work cooperatively to assemble the puzzles.

Ms. Padilla is amazed when she views the videotape, which shows Lupita to be a competent girl with strong teaching and leadership skills. Ms. Padilla readily admits, "I had written her off . . . her and three others. They had met my expectations, and I just wasn't looking for anything else."

Ms. Padilla and her aides begin working closely with Lupita on academic skills and often allow her to take a leadership role in group activities. At the end of the school year, Lupita obtains achievement test scores indicating exceptional competence in language skills and mathematics, and she is promoted to first grade. (Case described by Carrasco, 1981)

- **Why might Ms. Padilla have initially underestimated Lupita's academic potential? What might have happened to Lupita if her many strengths had gone unnoticed?**
- **What distinctive personality characteristics and social skills does Lupita exhibit? Which of them are likely to enhance her classroom success? Which might potentially interfere with her classroom success?**

OVER THE YEARS, Ms. Padilla has almost certainly had kindergartners who lacked some of the basic knowledge and skills on which early academic success depends—color and shape names, the alphabet, counting, and so on. And in Ms. Padilla's experience, children who can answer questions and contribute to class discussions usually speak up or raise their hands, but Lupita is quiet and restrained. With such

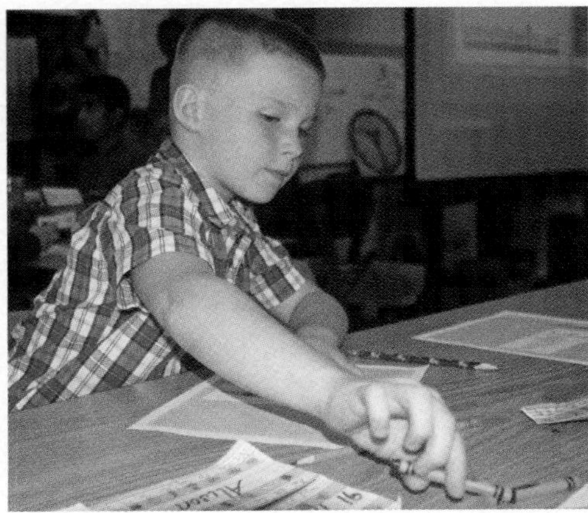

Children's ability to work on sedentary tasks for extended periods depends partly on biologically built-in temperaments. By nature, some children tend to be quiet and attentive, whereas others are more energetic and distractible.

data in hand, Ms. Padilla initially concludes that Lupita has not mastered the knowledge and skills she will need in first grade. If the researcher's videotape had not captured Lupita's social skills and proficiency with puzzles, Lupita might very well have remained on the sidelines throughout much of the school year, getting little assistance on academic skills and having few opportunities to capitalize on her many positive personal attributes. Thus, Ms. Padilla's low expectations for Lupita may have ensured that Lupita *wouldn't* gain the knowledge and skills she would need in first grade—a self-fulfilling prophecy.

School is not just a place for acquiring cognitive and linguistic skills. It is also a place for **personal development**, whereby children and adolescents build on and possibly modify their distinctive patterns of behavior (i.e., their *personalities*) and gain an increasing understanding of who they are as individuals. Furthermore, the very social nature of school makes it an ideal context for **social development**, in which young people come to better understand their fellow human beings, develop productive social skills and interpersonal relationships, and gradually internalize their society's standards for behavior.

Personality Development

Long before children begin school, they show noticeable differences in **personality**. That is, they show some consistency in their behaviors and patterns of thought in a wide variety of situations. For instance, Lupita tends to be quiet and well behaved, whereas some of her peers are probably noisy and rambunctious. Lupita is also conscientious about completing her work, whereas at least one of her classmates must be reminded to complete his Spanish assignment. And she is socially astute, quickly tuning in to the nuances of others' behavior and responding appropriately, whereas some of her age-mates may have trouble interpreting other people's verbal and nonverbal messages.

Children's personalities are the result of both heredity—especially in the form of inherited temperaments—and environmental factors. As you will see, heredity and environment often interact in their influences.

Temperament

A child's **temperament** is his or her general tendency to respond to and deal with environmental stimuli and events in particular ways. Children seem to have distinct temperaments almost from birth. For instance, some (like Lupita) are quiet and subdued, whereas others are more active and energetic. Researchers have identified many temperamental styles that emerge early in life and are relatively enduring, including general activity level, adaptability, persistence, adventurousness, outgoingness, shyness, fearfulness, inhibitedness, irritability, and distractibility. Most psychologists agree that such temperamental differences are biologically based and have genetic origins (Keogh, 2003; Rothbart, 2007; A. Thomas & Chess, 1977). To some degree, these differences persist into adolescence and adulthood (Caspi & Silva, 1995; Kagan & Snidman, 2007).

By influencing children's behaviors, inherited temperaments also influence the specific environmental circumstances they experience and so indirectly affect other aspects of personal and social development (N. A. Fox, Henderson, Rubin, Calkins, & Schmidt, 2001; Keogh, 2003). For example, children who are energetic and adventuresome seek out a wider variety of experiences than those who are quiet and restrained. Children who are naturally vivacious and outgoing have more opportunities to learn social skills and establish rewarding interpersonal relationships.

personal development Development, with age, of distinctive behavioral styles and increasingly complex self-understandings.

social development Development, with age, of increasingly sophisticated understandings of other people and of society as a whole, as well as increasingly effective interpersonal skills and more internalized standards for behavior.

personality Characteristic ways in which an individual behaves and thinks in a wide range of circumstances.

temperament Genetic predisposition to respond in particular ways to one's physical and social environments.

Furthermore, many temperamental characteristics affect how students engage in and respond to classroom activities and thus indirectly affect their academic achievement (Keogh, 2003; Rothbart, 2007; Saudino & Plomin, 2007). For instance, students are more likely to achieve at high levels if they are persistent, reasonably (but not overly) energetic, and able to ignore minor distractions. They can also achieve greater academic success if their behaviors lead to friendly, productive relationships with teachers and peers—people who can bolster their self-confidence and support their efforts to learn.

attachment Strong, affectionate bond formed between a child and a caregiver.

authoritative parenting Parenting style characterized by emotional warmth, high standards for behavior, explanation and consistent enforcement of rules, and inclusion of children in decision making.

authoritarian parenting Parenting style characterized by rigid rules and expectations for behavior that children are asked to obey without question.

Environmental Influences on Personality Development

Genetic differences in temperament are only *predispositions* to behave in certain ways, and environmental conditions may point different children with the same predisposition in somewhat different directions (Keogh, 2003; R. A. Thompson, 1998). Two key environmental factors influencing personality development are parents' behaviors toward their children and cultural expectations regarding appropriate behavior.

Parents' Behaviors Many parents and other important family members (e.g., grandparents, older siblings) lovingly interact with a new infant and consistently and dependably provide for the infant's physical and psychological needs. When they do such things, a strong, affectionate caregiver–child bond known as **attachment** typically forms (Ainsworth, Blehar, Waters, & Wall, 1978). Infants who become closely attached to parents or other caregivers early in life are apt to develop into amiable, independent, self-confident children and adolescents who adjust easily to the classroom environment, establish productive relationships with teachers and peers, and have an inner conscience that guides their behavior. In contrast, children who do not become closely attached to a parent or some other individual early in life can be immature, dependent, unpopular, and prone to disruptive and aggressive behaviors later on (J. P. Allen, Porter, McFarland, McElhaney, & Marsh, 2007; Hartup, 1989; Kochanska, Aksan, Knaack, & Rhines, 2004; Mikulincer & Shaver, 2005; S. Shulman, Elicker, & Sroufe, 1994; Sroufe, Carlson, & Shulman, 1993).

In addition to forming emotional attachments with children, parents and other primary caregivers adopt certain *parenting styles* that they use in raising the children. In mainstream Western culture, the ideal situation seems to be **authoritative parenting**, which combines affection and respect for children with reasonable restrictions on behavior. Authoritative parents provide a loving and supportive home, hold high expectations and standards for performance, explain why behaviors are or are not acceptable, enforce household rules consistently, include children in decision making, and provide age-appropriate opportunities for autonomy. Children from authoritative homes tend to be happy, energetic, self-confident, and likeable. They make friends easily and show self-control and concern for the rights and needs of others. Children of authoritative parents appear well adjusted, in part, because their behavior fits well with the values espoused by mainstream Western culture. They listen respectfully to others, can follow rules by the time they reach school age, work well independently, and strive for academic achievement (Barber, Stolz, & Olsen, 2005; Baumrind, 1989, 1991; M. R. Gray & Steinberg, 1999; Stright, Gallagher, & Kelley, 2008; J. M. T. Walker & Hoover-Dempsey, 2006). As we'll discover in Chapter 13, authoritative parenting provides a good model for how we, as teachers, should generally conduct our classrooms.

Adopt a generally authoritative style in the classroom.

Authoritative parenting is not universally best, however. Certain other parenting styles may be better suited to particular cultures and environments. For instance, in **authoritarian parenting**, parents expect complete and immediate compliance; they neither negotiate expectations nor provide reasons for their requests. In many Asian American and Hispanic families, high demands for obedience are made within the context of close, supportive parent–child relationships. Underlying the message of control is a more important message: "I love you and want you to do well, but it is equally important that you act for the good of the family and community" (Halgunseth, Ispa, & Rudy, 2006; Kağitçibaşi, 2007; Rothbaum & Trommsdorff, 2007). Authoritarian parenting is also more common in impoverished economic environments. When families live in low-income, inner-city neighborhoods where danger potentially lurks around every corner, parents may better serve their children by being very strict and directive about activities (Hale-Benson, 1986; McLoyd, 1998).

child maltreatment Consistent neglect or abuse of a child that jeopardizes the child's physical and psychological well-being.

Some degree of parental guidance and discipline seems to be important for optimal personal and social development. Parents who are overly permissive—for instance, those who let their children come and go as they please and impose few consequences for inappropriate actions—tend to have children who are immature and impulsive, do poorly in school, and act aggressively with peers (Aunola & Nurmi, 2005; Joussemet et al., 2008; Lamborn, Mounts, Steinberg, & Dornbusch, 1991). Yet as teachers, we must take care not to point an accusatory finger or in any other way be judgmental about how parents are bringing up their children. Some parents may have learned ineffective parenting strategies from their own parents. Others may have challenges in their lives—perhaps mental illness, marital conflict, or serious financial problems—that hamper their ability to nurture and support their children. Although we can certainly serve as valuable sources of information about effective disciplinary techniques, we must be careful that we don't give total credit to or place total blame on parents for how they interact with their children.

Serve as a resource regarding effective parenting strategies, perhaps through newsletters or parent discussion groups.

It is important to note, too, that most research on parenting involves correlational studies that reveal associations between parents' behaviors and children's characteristics but do not necessarily demonstrate cause-and-effect relationships. A few experimental studies have documented that specific parenting styles probably *do* influence children's personalities to some degree (W. A. Collins et al., 2000). In other cases, however, parents' disciplinary strategies seem to be the *result*, rather than the cause, of how children behave. For instance, temperamentally lively or adventuresome children typically require more parental control than quieter, restrained ones (J. R. Harris, 1998; Jaffee et al., 2004; Stice & Barrera, 1995).

In any case, keep in mind that parenting styles have, at most, only a *moderate* influence on children's personalities (W. A. Collins, Maccoby, Steinberg, Hetherington, & Bornstein, 2000; Weiss & Schwarz, 1996). Many children and adolescents thrive despite their caregivers' diverse parenting styles, provided that those caregivers aren't severely neglectful or abusive (J. R. Harris, 1995, 1998; Lykken, 1997; Scarr, 1992). Children with certain temperaments—for instance, those who tend to be adaptable, persistent, and outgoing—seem to be especially resilient in the face of difficult family circumstances (Bates & Pettit, 2007; D. Hart, Atkins, & Fegley, 2003; Keogh, 2003).

Child Maltreatment In a few unfortunate instances, parents' behaviors toward their children constitute **child maltreatment**. In some cases, parents neglect children: They fail to provide nutritious meals, adequate clothing, and other basic necessities of life. In other cases, parents (or possibly other family members) abuse children physically, sexually, or emotionally. Possible indicators of neglect or abuse are chronic hunger, lack of warm clothing in cold weather, untreated medical needs, frequent or serious physical injuries (e.g., bruises, burns, broken bones), and exceptional knowledge about sexual matters.

Parental neglect and abuse can have significant adverse effects on children's personal and social development. On average, children who have been routinely neglected or abused have low self-esteem, poorly developed social skills, and low school achievement. Many are angry, aggressive, and defiant. Others can be depressed, anxious, socially withdrawn, and possibly suicidal (Dodge, Pettit, Bates, & Valente, 1995; J. Kim & Cicchetti, 2006; Maughan & Cicchetti, 2002; Nix et al., 1999; R. A. Thompson & Wyatt, 1999).

Report suspected cases of child maltreatment *immediately*.

Teachers are both morally and legally obligated to report any cases of suspected child abuse or neglect to the proper authorities (e.g., the school principal or child protective services). Two helpful resources are the National Child Abuse Hotline at 1-800-4-A-CHILD (1-800-422-4453) and the website for Childhelp at www.childhelp.org.

socialization Process of molding a child's behavior and beliefs to be appropriate for his or her cultural group.

culture shock Sense of confusion when a student encounters a new environment with behavioral expectations very different from those previously learned.

Cultural Expectations and Socialization As we've seen, cultural groups can influence children's personalities indirectly through the parenting styles they encourage. Culture also has a more direct influence on children's personal and social development through a process known as **socialization**. That is, members of a cultural group work hard to help growing children adopt the behaviors and beliefs that the group holds dear. Children typically learn their earliest lessons about their culture's standards and expectations for behavior from parents and other family members, who teach them rudimentary manners (e.g., saying please and thank-you), encourage them to do well in school, and so on (W.-B. Chen & Gregory, 2008; Eccles, 2007). Once children reach school age, teachers become equally important socialization agents. For example, in mainstream Western society, teachers typically expect and encourage a variety of specific behaviors: showing respect for authority figures, following rules and directions, controlling impulses, working independently, asking for help when it's needed, cooperating with peers, and so on (Helton & Oakland, 1977; Hess & Holloway, 1984; Wentzel & Looney, 2007). Cultures around the globe encourage many of these behaviors, but they don't necessarily endorse *all* of them. As an example, in the opening case study, Lupita sits quietly in class, apparently even in situations where she might need help with an assigned task. Many children of Mexican heritage are more accustomed to observing events quietly and unobtrusively than to asking adults for explanations (more on this point in Chapter 4).

Schools socialize children to engage in many behaviors that they haven't necessarily learned at home.

Researchers have observed other cultural differences in socialization practices as well. For instance, European American families often encourage assertiveness and independence, but families from many other countries (e.g., Mexico, China, Japan, India) are more likely to encourage restraint, obedience, and deference to elders (Goodnow, 1992; Joshi & MacLean, 1994; Morelli & Rothbaum, 2007; Rothbaum, Weisz, Pott, Miyake, & Morelli, 2000). And whereas many American children are encouraged to be outgoing and emotionally expressive, children in many Asian cultures are encouraged to be shy and emotionally reserved (P. M. Cole & Tan, 2007; Huntsinger & Jose, 2006; Morelli & Rothbaum, 2007). However, considerable diversity exists *within* any culture, with different parents, teachers, and other adults encouraging somewhat different behaviors and beliefs.

When behaviors expected of students at school differ from those expected at home, or when belief systems presented by teachers are inconsistent with those of children's parents, children may initially experience some **culture shock**. At a minimum, children are apt to be confused and less productive than they might be otherwise, at least in the first few days or weeks of school. Some children with less adaptable or more irritable temperaments may even become angry or resistant (Hess & Holloway, 1984; Kumar, Gheen, & Kaplan, 2002).

As teachers, we must especially encourage our students to exhibit those behaviors essential for long-term school success, such as obeying school rules, following instructions, and working independently. For example, when we expect students to work independently, even those students who have not had this expectation placed on them at home show improved work habits (J. L. Epstein, 1983). At the same time, students will need our guidance, support, and patience when our expectations differ from those of their family or cultural group.

Teach students behaviors they will need for long-term success in Western society, but be patient when such behaviors are very different from those learned at home.

The "Big Five" Personality Traits

As children grow older, the many interactions among their inherited temperaments and environmental circumstances lead to unique and relatively stable personality profiles. Research with both children and adults has yielded five general personality traits that are relatively independent of one another. You can remember them using the mnemonic *OCEAN:*

- *Openness.* The extent to which one is imaginative, curious about the world, and receptive to new experiences and ideas
- *Conscientiousness.* The extent to which one is careful, organized, self-disciplined, and likely to follow through on plans and commitments
- *Extraversion.* The extent to which one is socially outgoing and seeks excitement
- *Agreeableness.* The extent to which one is pleasant, kind, and cooperative in social situations
- *Neuroticism.* The extent to which one is prone to negative emotions (e.g., anxiety, anger, depression) (Caspi, 1998; Matthews, Zeidner, & Roberts, 2006; Saarni, Campos, Camras, & Witherington, 2006)

Remember that despite some consistency in students' personalities, their behaviors are likely to vary somewhat as when circumstances change.

Such traits lead to some consistency—but not *total* consistency—in children's behaviors across situations (Hampson, 2008; Mendoza-Denton & Mischel, 2007). Variability is particularly common when circumstances change considerably. For instance, a student might be very outgoing and sociable with his close friends but shy and withdrawn with people he doesn't know very well. And a student is more likely to be conscientious about completing homework if she's given some guidance about how to organize her assignments in a "to-do" list (Belfiore & Hornyak, 1998).

Temperament, Personality, and Goodness of Fit

There is no single best temperament or personality that maximizes students' adjustment and achievement in the classroom. Instead, children are more likely to succeed at school when there is a **goodness of fit**, rather than a mismatch, between their natural inclinations and typical behaviors, on the one hand, and classroom expectations, on the other (Thomas & Chess, 1977). For instance, when teachers want students to participate actively in whole-class discussions, highly energetic, outgoing children are apt to shine, but quieter students (like Lupita) might feel anxious or intimidated. When teachers require a lot of independent seatwork, quieter children often do well, but some energetic children may be viewed as disruptive (Keogh, 2003).

As teachers, we must recognize that, to a considerable degree, students' ways of behaving in the classroom—their energy levels, their sociability, their impulse control, and so on—reflect temperamental differences that are not entirely within their control. If we keep this fact in mind, we will be more apt to accept students' behavioral idiosyncrasies and more willing to adapt our instruction and classroom management strategies to accommodate their individual behavioral styles (Keogh, 2003). The Creating a Productive Classroom Environment feature "Accommodating Students' Diverse Temperaments and Personality Traits" presents several examples of strategies we might use.

goodness of fit Situation in which classroom conditions and expectations are compatible with students' temperaments and personality characteristics.

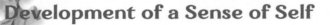

Development of a Sense of Self

With their capacity for symbolic thinking and (eventually) abstract reasoning, human beings often draw conclusions about who they are as people. As an example, try the Experiencing Firsthand exercise on the following page.

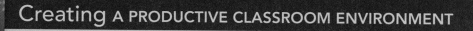

Creating A PRODUCTIVE CLASSROOM ENVIRONMENT

Accommodating Students' Diverse Temperaments and Personality Traits

- **Minimize down time for students with high energy levels.**

  A third grader seems unable to sit still for more than a couple of minutes. As a way of letting him release pent-up energy throughout the school day, his teacher gives him small chores to do (e.g., erasing the board, sharpening pencils, cleaning art supplies) and shows him how to complete the chores quietly so as not to disturb his classmates.

- **Provide numerous opportunities for highly sociable students to interact with classmates.**

  In a unit on colonial America, a fifth-grade teacher assigns a project in which students must depict a typical colonial village in some way (e.g., by writing a research paper, drawing a map on poster board, or creating a miniature three-dimensional model). The students can choose to work on the project alone or with one or two classmates, with the stipulation that students who work with peers must undertake more complex projects than students who work alone.

- **Be especially warm and attentive with very shy students.**

  Midway through the school year, a ninth-grade teacher has a new student join one of his classes—a girl who's just moved to town from a distant state. He notices that during the girl's first week at school, she comes to class alone each day and doesn't join in conversations with peers before or after class. One day, the teacher also sees her eating lunch by herself in the cafeteria. He sits down beside her with his own lunch and engages her in conversation about her previous school and community. The following day in class, he assigns a small-group, cooperative learning project that students will work on periodically over the next two weeks. He forms cooperative groups of three or four students each, making sure to place the new girl with two students whom he knows will be friendly and helpful to her.

- **When students have trouble adapting to new circumstances, give them advance notice of unusual activities and provide extra structure and reassurance.**

  A kindergarten teacher has discovered that two children in his class do well when the school day is orderly and predictable but often become anxious or upset when the class departs from its usual routine. To prepare the children for a field trip to the fire station on Friday, the teacher begins to talk about the trip at the beginning of the week, explaining what the class will do and see during the visit. He also recruits the father of one of the two anxiety-prone children to serve as a parent assistant that day.

- **If students seem overwhelmed by noisy or chaotic situations, find or create a more calm and peaceful environment for them.**

  Several middle school students find the school cafeteria loud and unsettling. Their math teacher offers her classroom as a place where they can occasionally eat instead. On some days, she eats with them. At other times, she sits at her desk and grades papers, but the students know that she will gladly stop to talk if they have a question or concern.

- **Teach self-control strategies to students who act impulsively.**

  A high school student often shouts out comments and opinions in her history class. The student's teacher takes her aside after school one day and gently explains that her lack of restraint is interfering with her classmates' ability to participate in discussions. To sensitize the student to the extent of the problem, the teacher asks her to keep a daily tally of how many times she talks without first raising her hand. A week later, the two meet again, and the teacher suggests a self-talk strategy that can help the student participate actively without dominating a discussion.

Source: Some strategies based on suggestions by Keogh (2003).

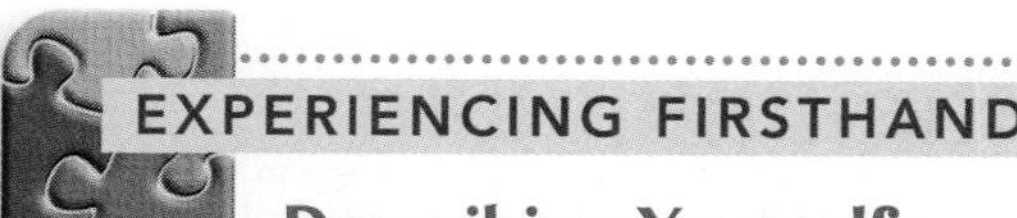

EXPERIENCING FIRSTHAND

Describing Yourself

On a sheet of paper, list at least 10 adjectives or phrases that describe the kind of person you are.

How did you describe yourself? Are you a good student? Are you friendly? smart? open minded? physically attractive? moody? uncoordinated? Some of your answers probably reflect certain personality traits. But *all* of your answers provide a window into your **sense of self**—your perceptions, beliefs, judgments, and feelings about who you are as a person. Many psychologists distinguish between two aspects

sense of self Perceptions, beliefs, judgments, and feelings about oneself as a person; includes *self-concept* and *self-esteem*.

of the sense of self: *self-concept*—assessments of one's own characteristics, strengths, and weaknesses—and *self-esteem*—judgments and feelings about one's own value and worth. In everyday usage, however, the two terms overlap considerably and are often used interchangeably (Byrne, 2002; Harter, 1999; O'Mara, Marsh, Craven, & Debus, 2006).

In overall self-assessments, children in the early elementary grades tend to make distinctions between two general domains: how competent they are at day-to-day tasks and how well they are liked by family and friends. As they grow older, children make finer and finer distinctions. In the upper elementary grades, they realize that they may be more or less competent or "good" in their academic work, athletic activities, classroom behavior, acceptance by peers, and physical attractiveness. By adolescence, they also make general self-assessments about their ability to make friends, their competence at adultlike work tasks, and their romantic appeal (Davis-Kean & Sandler, 2001; Harter, 1999). Each of these domains may have a greater or lesser influence on students' overall sense of self. For some, academic achievement may be the overriding factor, whereas for others, physical attractiveness or popularity with peers may be more important (Crocker & Knight, 2005; D. Hart, 1988; Harter, 1999).

Children and adolescents tend to behave in ways that mirror their beliefs about themselves. In general, students who have positive self-perceptions are more likely to succeed academically, socially, and physically (M. S. Caldwell, Rudolph, Troop-Gordon, & Kim, 2004; Marsh & Craven, 2006; Marsh, Gerlach, Trautwein, Lüdtke, & Brettschneider, 2007; Valentine, DuBois, & Cooper, 2004). For instance, if they see themselves as good students, they are more apt to pay attention, follow directions, persist at difficult problems, and enroll in challenging courses. If they see themselves as friendly and socially desirable, they are more likely to seek the company of their classmates and perhaps run for student council. If they see themselves as physically competent, they will more eagerly pursue extracurricular athletics.

Students' beliefs about themselves are, like their beliefs about the world around them, largely self-constructed. Accordingly, their self-assessments may or may not be accurate (Dunning, Heath, & Suls, 2004; Harter, 1999). When students evaluate themselves fairly accurately, they are in a good position to choose age-appropriate tasks and activities (R. F. Baumeister, Campbell, Krueger, & Vohs, 2003; Harter, 1999). A slightly inflated self-assessment can be beneficial as well, because it encourages students to work toward challenging yet potentially reachable goals (Bjorklund & Green, 1992; Schunk & Pajares, 2004). However, a sense of self that is *too* inflated may give some students an unwarranted sense of superiority over classmates and lead them to bully or in other ways act aggressively toward peers (Baumeister et al., 2003; Baumeister, Smart, & Boden, 1996; Menon et al., 2007). And as you might guess, students who significantly *under*estimate their abilities are apt to avoid the many challenges that would enhance their cognitive and social growth (Assor & Connell, 1992; Schunk & Pajares, 2004).

Factors Influencing Sense of Self

Simply telling students that they are good or smart or popular is unlikely to make much of a dent in low self-esteem (Crocker & Knight, 2005; Marsh et al., 2007; Swann, Chang-Schneider, & McClarty, 2007). Furthermore, vague, abstract statements such as "You're special" have little meaning in the concrete realities of young children (McMillan, Singh, & Simonetta, 1994).

However, at least three factors definitely *do* influence the kinds of self-concepts that students form. Often, students gain initial insights about their general competence in a certain domain from their *own successes and failures* in that domain (Damon, 1991; Marsh & Craven, 2006; Marsh et al., 2007). For instance, they may discover that they can easily solve—or consistently struggle with—simple addition and subtraction word problems. Or they may find that they can run faster—or more slowly—than most of their peers. Through such experiences, students acquire a sense of **self-efficacy** about the degree to which they can succeed in certain activities and accomplish cer-

self-efficacy Belief that one is capable of executing certain behaviors or achieving certain goals.

tain goals. Over time, students' specific self-efficacies for various tasks and activities contribute to their more general sense of self (Bong & Skaalvik, 2003; Schunk & Pajares, 2004).

Unfortunately, the interplay between students' self-perceptions and behaviors can create a vicious cycle: A poor sense of self leads to less productive behaviors, which leads to fewer successes, which perpetuates the poor sense of self. To break the cycle, we must make sure that students have numerous opportunities to succeed at academic, social, and physical tasks—or at least to show significant improvement in those tasks (Damon, 1991; Leary, 1999; Marsh & Craven, 1997). But success in very *easy* activities is unlikely to have much of an impact, as Figure 3.1 humorously illustrates. Instead, we should assign challenging tasks, making sure that students have the prerequisite knowledge and skills to tackle those tasks successfully and providing age-appropriate scaffolding to facilitate success (Bouchey & Harter, 2005; Dunning et al., 2004). In fact, the occasional failures that challenging activities bring—provided that students eventually do achieve success—will ultimately lead to a more realistic and resilient sense of self that can take failure in stride (Bandura, 1989; Dweck, 2000).

Enhance students' sense of self by supporting their efforts to meet new challenges.

Students' history of successes and failures is not the only thing affecting sense of self, however. A second important factor is *other people's behaviors*, which influence students' self-perceptions in at least two ways. For one thing, how students evaluate themselves depends to some extent on how their own performance compares to that of other individuals, especially peers (Dijkstra, Kuyper, van der Werf, Buunk, & van der Zee, 2008; Trautwein, Gerlach, & Lüdtke, 2008; Wheeler & Suls, 2005). Adolescents in particular tend to judge themselves in comparison with classmates. Those who see themselves achieving at higher levels than others are apt to develop a more positive sense of self than those who consistently find themselves falling short.

Minimize competitive situations in which students might judge themselves unfavorably in comparison with peers.

In addition, students' self-perceptions are affected by how others behave *toward* them (Dweck, 2000; Harter, 1996). For example, peers often communicate information about children's social and athletic competence, perhaps by seeking out a child's companionship or ridiculing a child in front of others (M. S. Caldwell et al., 2004; Harter, 1999; Rudolph, Caldwell, & Conley, 2005). Meanwhile, adults influence children's sense of self both by the kinds of expectations they hold for children's performance and by drawing attention to the various things that children do well or poorly (Eccles, Jacobs, Harold-Goldsmith, Jayaratne, & Yee, 1989; M. J. Harris & Rosenthal, 1985). As teachers, we should, of course, communicate realistically high expectations for achievement (more about this point in Chapter 11) and give positive feedback about the specific things students do well (O'Mara et al., 2006). And when we find that we must give students negative feedback—and occasionally we must—we should do so while also communicating respect and affection for them as human beings. For instance, we might point out that mistakes are a

Point out the things students do well, and present any negative feedback within the context of overall positive regard.

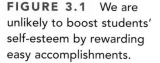

FIGURE 3.1 We are unlikely to boost students' self-esteem by rewarding easy accomplishments.

natural part of the learning process, and we should offer concrete suggestions about how to improve (Clifford, 1990; Dweck, 2000).

Get students actively involved in successful group activities.

A third general factor that can impact students' sense of self is *membership in a successful group* (Harter, 1999; Wigfield, Eccles, & Pintrich, 1996). If you think back to your own school years, perhaps you can recall taking pride in something your entire class accomplished, feeling good about a community service project completed through an extracurricular club, or reveling in the state championship earned by one of your school's athletic teams. School groups are not the only groups affecting students' sense of self. For instance, some cultures encourage children to take pride in the accomplishments of their families, as well as or perhaps even *instead of* their own accomplishments (Banks & Banks, 1995; P. M. Cole & Tan, 2007). And as we'll see a bit later in the chapter, students' membership in certain ethnic groups can also be a source of pride.

Developmental Changes in Sense of Self

We have already seen one way in which self-perceptions change with age: Children increasingly differentiate among the many aspects of who they are as people—the academic aspect, the social aspect, the physical appearance aspect, and so on. But developmental theorists have long recognized that children's and adolescents' beliefs and feelings about themselves change in other ways as well. One early developmentalist, Erik Erikson, proposed that people's views of both themselves and others change significantly not only in childhood and adolescence but throughout the life span. Figure 3.2 on pages 72–73 summarizes and critiques Erikson's classic theory of eight psychosocial stages. In the following sections, we'll look at what more contemporary researchers have learned about developmental changes in children's and adolescents' sense of self.

FIGURE 3.3 As early as the primary grades, students in racially diverse communities have some awareness of their membership in a particular racial group. Notice how 7-year-old Tina portrays herself as having darker hair and skin than the classmates behind her.

Childhood Elementary school children tend to think of themselves in terms of concrete, easily observable characteristics and behaviors (D. Hart, 1988; Harter, 1983). For example, when my son Alex was 9, he described himself this way:

> I have brown hair, brown eyes. I like wearing short-sleeved shirts. My hair is curly. I was adopted. I was born in Denver. I like all sorts of critters. The major sport I like is baseball. I do fairly well in school. I have a lizard, and I'm going to get a second one.

In racially and culturally diverse communities, where different skin colors, languages, customs, and so on are obvious, children may also classify themselves as belonging to one or another racial or ethnic group (Phinney, 1990; Sheets, 1999). For instance, although my daughter Tina was raised in a European American family, her genetic heritage is Native American and Hispanic. In a self-portrait she drew in second grade (see Figure 3.3), she was clearly aware that her hair and skin tone were darker than those of most of her classmates.

In the preschool and primary grades, most children have a generally positive sense of self (Robins & Trzesniewski, 2005). Sometimes they believe they are more capable than they really *are* and that they can easily overcome initial failures (Harter, 1999; Lockhart, Chang, & Story, 2002; Paris & Cunningham, 1996). As children have more opportunities to compare themselves with peers during the elementary grades and as they become cognitively more able to *make* such comparisons, their self-assessments become increasingly realistic (Chapman, Tunmer, & Prochnow, 2000; Davis-Kean et al., 2008; Harter, 1999). They also begin to pull together their many self-observations into generalizations about the kinds of people they are—perhaps friendly, good at sports, smart, or dumb—and such generalizations lead to the development of increasingly stable self-concepts (D. A. Cole et al., 2001; Harter, 1999).

Remember that a student's sense of self becomes increasingly stable with age. In the upper elementary and secondary grades, then, enhancing students' self-esteem may take time and persistence.

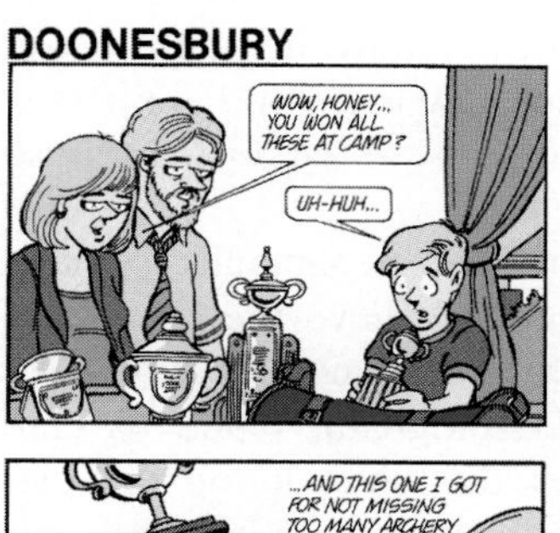

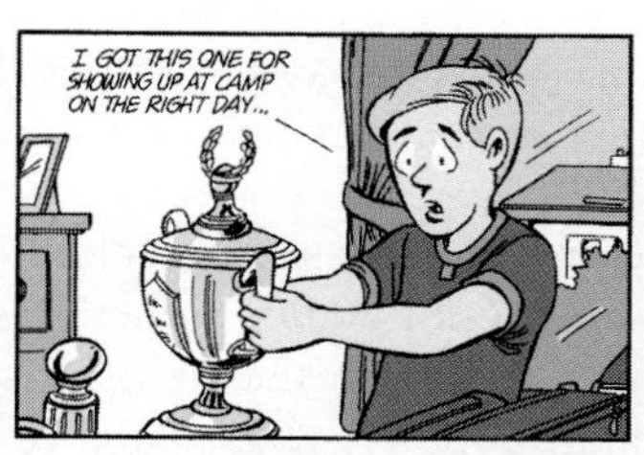

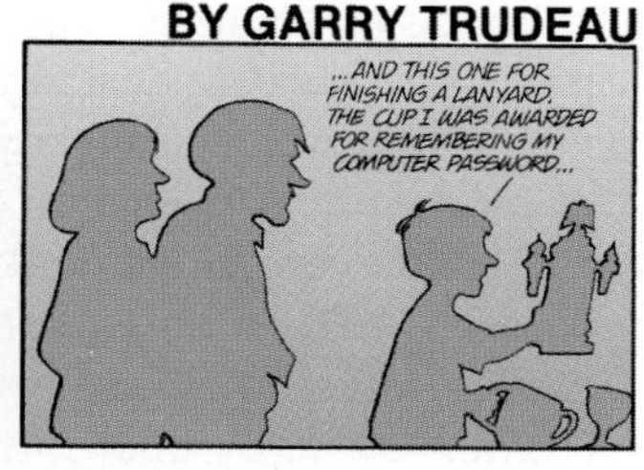

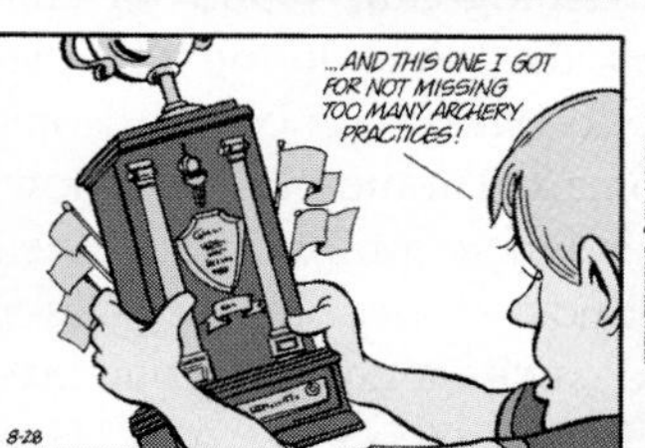

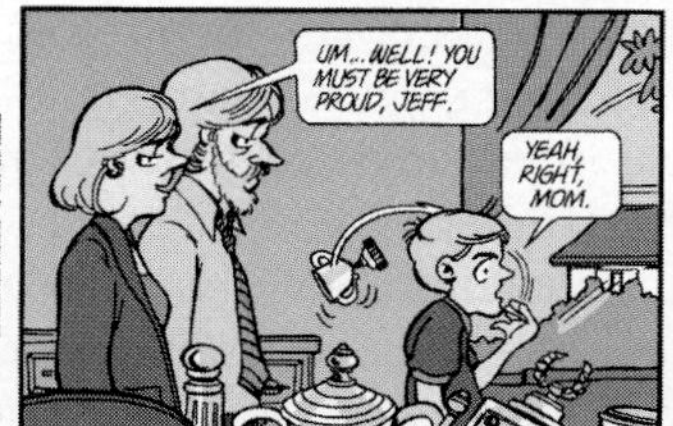

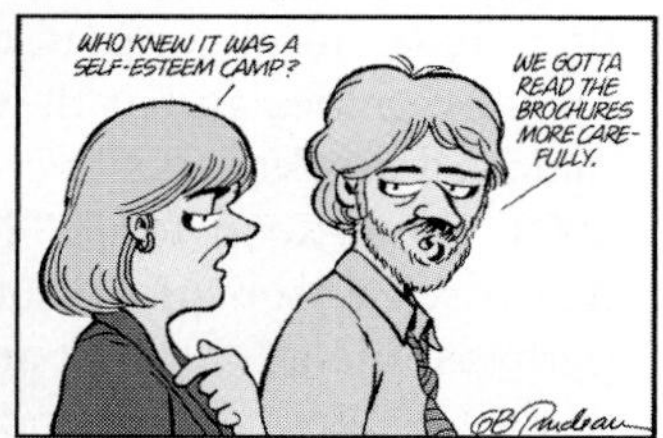

Early Adolescence As students reach adolescence and gain greater capability for abstract thought, they increasingly think of themselves in terms of general, fairly stable traits. Consider my daughter Tina's self-description when she was in sixth grade:

> I'm cool. I'm awesome. I'm way cool. I'm 12. I'm boy crazy. I go to Brentwood Middle School. I'm popular with my fans. I play viola. My best friend is Lindsay. I have a gerbil named Taj. I'm adopted. I'm beautiful.

Although Tina listed a few concrete features, she had clearly developed a fairly abstract self-perception. Her focus on coolness, popularity, and beauty, rather than on intelligence or academic achievement (or, I might add, modesty), is fairly typical: Social acceptance and physical appearance are far more important to most young adolescents than academic competence (D. Hart, 1988; Harter, 1999).

Students' self-concepts and self-esteem often drop as they make the transition from elementary school to middle school or junior high, with the drop being more pronounced for girls (D. A. Cole et al., 2001; Harter, 1999; Robins & Trzesniewski, 2005). The physiological changes accompanying puberty may be a factor: Many boys and girls think of themselves as being somewhat less attractive once they reach adolescence (Cornell et al., 1990; Harter, Whitesell, & Junkin, 1998; Stice, 2003). Changes in the school environment—disrupted friendships, more superficial teacher–student relationships, more rigorous academic standards, and so on—probably also have a negative impact (more on this point in Chapter 11).

imaginary audience Belief that one is the center of attention in any social situation.

personal fable Belief that one is completely unlike anyone else and so cannot be understood by others.

Also with early adolescence come two new phenomena with implications for sense of self. First, students become more cognitively able to reflect on how others might see them (Harter, 1999). They may initially go to extremes, thinking that in any social situation everyone else's attention is focused squarely on them—a phenomenon known as the **imaginary audience** (Elkind, 1981; Lapsley, 1993; R. M. Ryan & Kuczkowski, 1994). A statement by one eighth grader (a female) illustrates this phenomenon:

> In algebra I had to cough but I knew if I did everyone would stare at me and think I was stupid, hacking away. So I held my breath until I turned red and tears ran down my face and finally I coughed anyway and everyone *really* noticed then. It was horrible. (Orenstein, 1994, p. 47)

Because they believe themselves to be the center of attention, young teenagers (especially girls) are often preoccupied with their physical appearance and can be quite self-critical.

A second noteworthy phenomenon in early adolescence is emergence of the **personal fable**: Young teenagers often believe they are completely unlike anyone else (Elkind, 1981; Lapsley, 1993). For instance, they may think that no one else—and certainly not parents and teachers—has ever experienced the intensity of emotions they feel about thwarted goals or unhappy love affairs. Furthermore, some have a sense of invulnerability and immortality, believing themselves immune to the normal dangers of life. Thus, they may take foolish risks, such as experimenting with drugs and alcohol, having unprotected sexual intercourse, and driving at high speeds (DeRidder, 1993; Jacobs & Klaczynski, 2002; Nell, 2002; S. P. Thomas, Groër, & Droppleman, 1993).

It's important to note, however, that adolescents are apt to take risks even when they *don't* believe themselves to be invulnerable. Thanks, in part, to brains that have not yet fully matured, adolescents often have trouble planning ahead and controlling their impulses (Silveri et al., 2006; Spear, 2007; also see Chapter 2). In addition, they tend to make choices based on emotions ("This will be fun") rather than on logic ("There is a high probability of a bad outcome") (Cleveland, Gibbons, Gerrard, Pomery, & Brody, 2005; V. F. Reyna & Farley, 2006; Steinberg, 2007). Thus, adolescent risk taking is most common in social contexts, where having fun is typically a high priority and it's easy to get swept away by what peers are doing or suggesting.

Channel adolescents' risk-taking tendencies into safe activities—climbing walls, after-prom parties, and so on.

identity Self-constructed definition of who one is and what things are important to accomplish in life.

Late Adolescence The majority of older adolescents recover sufficiently from the double whammy of puberty and a less warm-and-fuzzy school environment to enjoy positive self-concepts and overall mental health (Harter, 1999; S. I. Powers, Hauser, & Kilner, 1989). The imaginary audience and personal fable phenomena slowly decline, although remnants remain throughout the high school years. For instance, some teens (especially boys) persist in risky behaviors, leading to early deaths through automobile accidents or drug overdoses (Frankenberger, 2000; Lapsley, 1993; Nell, 2002).

Older teenagers increasingly reflect on their own characteristics and abilities and begin to struggle with seeming inconsistencies in their self-perceptions. One ninth grader explained it this way:

> I really don't understand how I can switch so fast from being cheerful with my friends, then coming home and feeling anxious, and then getting frustrated and sarcastic with my parents. Which one is the *real* me? (Harter, 1999, p. 67)

Eventually, perhaps around eleventh grade, most students integrate their various self-perceptions into a complex, multifaceted sense of self that reconciles apparent contradictions—for instance, recognizing that their inconsistent behaviors on different occasions mean they are "flexible" (Harter, 1999).

As older adolescents pull the numerous parts of themselves together, many of them begin to form a general sense of **identity**: a self-constructed definition of who they are, what things they find important, and what goals they want to accomplish in

FIGURE 3.2 Erikson's eight stages of psychosocial development

Overview of Erikson's Stages

Erik Erikson (1963, 1972) described eight stages through which people proceed over the course of development. Each stage presents a unique developmental task, and how an individual addresses it influences the person's general mental health and progress through later stages.

Trust versus mistrust (infancy). According to Erikson, the major developmental task in infancy is to learn whether other people, especially primary caregivers, regularly satisfy basic needs. If caregivers are consistent sources of food, comfort, and affection, an infant learns *trust*—that others are dependable and reliable. If caregivers are neglectful or perhaps even abusive, the infant instead learns *mistrust*—that the world is an undependable, unpredictable, and possibly dangerous place.

Autonomy versus shame and doubt (toddler years). As toddlers gain increasing muscle coordination and mobility, they become capable of satisfying some of their own needs. They begin to feed themselves, wash and dress themselves, and use the toilet. If caregivers encourage self-sufficient behavior, toddlers develop a sense of *autonomy*—a sense of being able to handle many problems on their own. But if caregivers demand too much too soon, refuse to let children perform tasks of which they are capable, or ridicule early attempts at self-sufficiency, children may instead develop *shame and doubt* about their ability to handle problems.

Initiative versus guilt (preschool years). Preschoolers are increasingly able to accomplish tasks on their own, and with this growing independence come many choices about activities to be pursued. Sometimes children take on projects they can readily accomplish, but at other times they undertake projects that are beyond their capabilities or that interfere with other people's plans and activities. If parents and preschool teachers encourage and support children's efforts, while also helping them make realistic and appropriate choices, children develop *initiative*—independence in planning and undertaking activities. But if, instead, adults discourage the pursuit of independent activities or dismiss them as silly and bothersome, children develop *guilt* about their needs and desires.

Industry versus inferiority (elementary school years). Erikson viewed the elementary school years as critical for the development of self-confidence. Ideally, elementary school provides many opportunities for children to achieve the recognition of teachers, parents, and peers by producing things—drawing pictures, solving addition problems, writing poetry, and so on. If children are encouraged to make and do things and are then praised for their accomplishments, they begin to demonstrate *industry* by being diligent, persevering at tasks until completed, and putting work before pleasure. If children are instead ridiculed or punished for their efforts or if they find they are incapable of meeting their teachers' and parents' expectations, they develop feelings of *inferiority* about their capabilities.

Identity versus role confusion (adolescence). As adolescents make the transition from childhood to adulthood, they ponder the roles they will play in the adult world. Initially, they are apt to experience some *role confusion*—mixed ideas and feelings about the specific ways in which they will fit into society—and may experiment with a variety of behaviors and activities (e.g., tinkering with cars, baby-sitting for neighbors, affiliating with certain political or religious groups). Erikson proposed that eventually most adolescents achieve a sense of *identity* regarding who they are and where their lives are headed.

life (Erikson, 1963, 1972; Wigfield et al., 1996). In their ongoing search for a long-term identity, adolescents may initially take on temporary identities, aligning themselves strongly with a particular peer group, adhering rigidly to a single brand of clothing, or insisting on a certain hairstyle (Hemmings, 2004; Seaton, Scottham, & Sellers, 2006). For example, as a 15-year-old, my son Alex described himself as a "skater"—someone for whom skateboarding becomes a way of life as well as a form of transportation—and insisted on wearing the oversized shirts and hip-hugging, baggy pants that came with the territory.

Erik Erikson proposed that most people achieve an overall sense of identity by the end of adolescence (see Figure 3.2). Many current developmental theorists disagree and suggest that identity may continue to be a work in progress for some time. Some adolescents have considerable difficulty integrating their various self-perceptions and often struggle with the question, Who am I *really?* Even by the end of high school, only a small minority of teenagers in Western cultures have begun to think seriously about the eventual role they will play in society and to identify lifelong goals (Archer, 1982; Durkin, 1995; Marcia, 1980, 1988).

Most young people need considerable time to explore various options related to careers, political beliefs, religious affiliations, and so on before they achieve a true sense of their adult identity. Marcia (1980, 1991) has described four distinct patterns of behavior that may characterize the status of an adolescent's search for identity:

1. *Identity diffusion.* The adolescent has made no commitment to a particular career path or ideological belief system. Some haphazard experimentation with

Intimacy versus isolation (young adulthood). Once young people have established their identities, they are ready to make long-term commitments to others. They become capable of forming *intimate*, reciprocal relationships (e.g., through close friendships or marriage) and willingly make the sacrifices and compromises that such relationships require. If people cannot form these intimate relationships—perhaps because of their reluctance or inability to forego the satisfaction of their own needs—then a sense of *isolation* may result.

Generativity versus stagnation (middle age). During middle age, the primary developmental task is one of contributing to society and helping to guide future generations. When a person makes a contribution during this period, perhaps by raising a family or working toward the betterment of society, he or she feels a sense of *generativity*—a sense of productivity and accomplishment. In contrast, a person who is self-centered and unable or unwilling to help society move forward develops a feeling of *stagnation*—a dissatisfaction with his or her relative lack of productivity.

Integrity versus despair (retirement years). The final developmental task is retrospection: People look back on their lives and accomplishments. They develop feelings of contentment and *integrity* if they believe that they have led a happy, productive life. Conversely, they may develop a sense of *despair* if they look back on a life of disappointments and unachieved goals.

Critiquing Erikson's Theory

Erikson's theory was groundbreaking in one very important respect: It portrayed development as a lifelong process. Even as adults, human beings have new things to learn and new challenges to meet. At the same time, Erikson's theory has its shortcomings. Erikson drew his ideas largely from personal anecdotes, rather than systematic research (Crain, 2005). Furthermore, he based his stages primarily on work with men; for many women, a focus on intimacy occurs simultaneously with, and in some cases may even precede, a focus on identity (Josselson, 1988). An additional weakness is that Erikson did not take into account the important role that culture plays in development. Many cultures intentionally discourage autonomy, initiative, and self-assertiveness in young children, sometimes as a way of protecting children from the very real dangers of their environments (Dennis, Cole, Zahn-Waxler, & Mizuta, 2002; Harwood, Miller, & Irizarry, 1995; Kağitçibaşi, 2007; G. J. Powell, 1983).

As teachers, we should keep in mind that the age ranges for accomplishing Erikson's eight developmental tasks are probably broader than Erikson proposed. For instance, most people probably do not achieve a sense of identity as early or as easily as Erikson suggested. Nevertheless, the first five stages have implications for us as teachers, who must work hard to do the following:

- Help students overcome early difficulties with trust, autonomy, or initiative—in particular, by being reliable sources of affection and support (trust) and by giving students age-appropriate opportunities to work independently (autonomy) and undertake self-chosen activities (initiative).
- Promote a sense of industry by engaging students in meaningful tasks and completing worthwhile projects.
- Help adolescents in their search for identity by providing opportunities to explore various roles they might play in adult society.

particular roles or beliefs may have taken place, but the individual has not yet embarked on a serious exploration of issues related to self-definition.

2. *Foreclosure.* The adolescent has made a firm commitment to an occupation, a particular set of beliefs, or both. The choices have been based largely on what others (especially parents), have prescribed, without an earnest exploration of other possibilities.
3. *Moratorium.* The adolescent has no strong commitment to a particular career or set of beliefs but is actively exploring and considering a variety of professions and ideologies. In essence, the individual is undergoing an identity crisis.
4. *Identity achievement.* After going through a period of moratorium, the adolescent has emerged with a clear choice of occupation, a commitment to particular political or religious beliefs, or both.

Of these four possible identity statuses, diffusion is probably the most problematic, as it leaves the young person without a clear sense of direction in life. For some teenagers, firmly settling on a life path without some exploration first (foreclosure) can be comforting but comes at the cost of ruling out potentially more satisfying alternatives. For most adolescents, the ideal situation seems to be to proceed through a period of moratorium—an exploration that may continue into early adulthood—and to eventually settle on a clear identity (Berzonsky, 1988; Marcia, 1988; Seaton et al., 2006).

Table 3.1 presents developmental changes in children's and adolescents' sense of self and offers suggestions for how we, as teachers, can enhance their self-perceptions at different grade levels.

Diversity in Sense of Self

As you undoubtedly know from your own experience, students differ considerably in their self-esteem and overall sense of self. Sometimes such differences are indirectly the result of biology. For instance, students who are physically attractive tend to have more positive self-concepts than students with less appealing physical features (Harter et al., 1998). And many students with cognitive, social, or physical disabilities have lower self-esteem than their classmates (Brown-Mizuno, 1990; T. Bryan, 1991; Marsh & Craven, 1997).

Gender Differences Some researchers find gender differences in overall self-esteem, with boys rating themselves more highly than girls, especially in adolescence. Many students' self-perceptions tend to be consistent with stereotypes about what males and females are "good at." For instance, even when actual ability levels are the same, boys tend to rate themselves more highly in mathematics and sports and girls tend to rate themselves more highly in reading and literature (D. A. Cole et al., 2001; Eccles, Wigfield, & Schiefele, 1998; Harter, 1999; Herbert & Stipek, 2005).

Cultural and Ethnic Differences Cultural and ethnic-group differences in sense of self have also been observed. For example, in many Native American communities and many Middle Eastern and Far Eastern countries, children and adolescents see their group membership and connections with other individuals as central parts of who they are as human beings (Kağitçibaşi, 2007; Q. Wang, 2006; Whitesell, Mitchell, Kaufman, Spicer, & the Voices of Indian Teens Project Team, 2006). In addition, many young people have a strong **ethnic identity**: They are both aware and proud of their ethnic group and willingly adopt some of the group's behaviors (L. Allen & Aber, 2006; Phinney, 1993; Sheets & Hollins, 1999). Occasionally, students' ethnic identities can lead them to reject mainstream Western values. In some ethnic minority groups, peers may accuse high-achieving students of "acting white," a label that essentially means "You're not one of us" (Bergin & Cooks, 2008; Cross, Strauss, & Fhagen-Smith, 1999; Ogbu, 2008a). For the most part, however, students with a strong and positive ethnic identity do *well* in school, both academically and socially (Altschul, Oyserman, & Bybee, 2006; Chavous et al., 2003; M. B. Spencer, Noll, Stoltzfus, & Harpalani, 2001). Furthermore, pride in one's ethnic heritage and high academic achievement can serve as an emotional buffer against the insults and discrimination that children and adolescents from

ethnic identity Awareness of one's membership in a particular ethnic or cultural group and willingness to adopt behaviors characteristic of the group.

TABLE 3.1
Sense of Self at Different Grade Levels

Grade Level	Age-Typical Characteristics	Suggested Strategies
K–2	• Self-concept largely limited to concrete, easily observable characteristics • Some tendency to overestimate abilities and chances of future success	• Encourage students to extend their abilities by tackling challenging tasks they think they can accomplish. • Provide sufficient scaffolding to make success possible.
3–5	• Increasing awareness of and differentiation among particular strengths and weaknesses • Association of such emotions as pride and shame with various self-perceptions	• Focus students' attention on their improvement over time. • Encourage pride in individual and group achievements, but be aware that students from some ethnic groups may prefer that only group achievements be recognized (see Chapter 4). • Provide opportunities for students to look at one another's work only when *everyone* has something to be proud of.
6–8	• Increasingly abstract conceptions of oneself • For many, a decline in self-esteem after the transition to middle or junior high school (especially for females) • Heightened concern about others' perceptions and judgments of oneself (imaginary audience) • Excessive belief in one's own uniqueness, sometimes accompanied by risk taking and a sense of invulnerability to normal dangers (personal fable)	• After students make the transition to middle school or junior high, be especially supportive and optimistic about their abilities and potential for success. • Be patient when students show exceptional self-consciousness; give them strategies for presenting themselves well to others. • Provide safe outlets for risk-taking behaviors; show no tolerance for potentially dangerous behaviors on school grounds.
9–12	• Gradual increase in self-esteem • Continuing risk-taking behavior (especially for males) • Increasing integration of diverse self-perceptions into an overall, multifaceted sense of self • Search for the "real me" and an adult identity	• When discussing the potential consequences of risky behaviors, present the facts but don't make students so anxious or upset that they can't effectively learn and remember important precautions (i.e., avoid scare tactics). • Give students opportunities to examine and experiment with a variety of adultlike roles.

Sources: Davis-Kean et al., 2008; Dweck, 2000; Elkind, 1981; Harter, 1999; Lockhart et al., 2002; Marcia, 1980; Nell, 2002; Robins & Trzesniewski, 2005; Spear, 2007; Whitesell et al., 2006.

minority groups sometimes encounter (L. Allen & Aber, 2006; C. H. Caldwell, Zimmerman, Bernat, Sellers, & Notaro, 2002; P. J. Cook & Ludwig, 2008; DuBois, Burk-Braxton, Swenson, Tevendale, & Hardesty, 2002). Consider this statement by Eva, an African American high school student, as an example:

Encourage students to take pride in their cultural heritage.

> I'm proud to be black and everything. But, um, I'm aware of, you know, racist acts and racist things that are happening in the world, but I use that as no excuse, you know. I feel as though I can succeed. . . . I just know that I'm not gonna let [racism] stop me. (Way, 1998, p. 257)

Not all students from minority groups affiliate strongly with their cultural and ethnic groups. Some students (especially those with multiple racial or cultural heritages) fluctuate in the strength of their ethnic identity, depending on the context and situation (Hitlin, Brown, & Elder, 2006; Y.-Y. Hong, Wan, No, & Chiu, 2007; Yip & Fuligni, 2002). In addition, older adolescents may experiment with varying forms of an ethnic identity. Some teens, for instance, may initially adopt a fairly intense, inflexible, and perhaps hostile ethnic identify before eventually retreating to a more relaxed, open-minded, and productive one (Cross et al., 1999; Seaton et al., 2006).

Observe Greg's preference for the social aspects of school in the video "Motivation." (To find this video, go to Chapter 3 of the Book-Specific Resources in MyEducationLab, select *Video Examples*, and then click on the title.)

Development of Peer Relationships and Interpersonal Understandings

School is very much a social place. For many students, interacting with and gaining the acceptance of peers are more important than classroom learning and achievement

(B. B. Brown, 1993; Dowson & McInerney, 2001; W. Doyle, 1986a). Yet social success and academic success are not an either-or situation. In fact, students who enjoy good relationships with their peers at school are *more*, rather than less, likely to achieve at high levels (Gest, Domitrovich, & Welsh, 2005; Guay, Boivin, & Hodges, 1999; Patrick, Anderman, & Ryan, 2002; Pellegrini & Bohn, 2005).

Roles of Peers in Children's Development

Peer relationships, especially friendships, serve at least three unique functions in children's and adolescents' personal and social development. For one thing, they provide an arena for learning and practicing a variety of social skills, including cooperation, negotiation, emotional control, and conflict resolution (Erwin, 1993; Gauvain, 2001; Larson & Brown, 2007). In addition, peers provide companionship, safety, and emotional support. They become a group with whom to eat lunch, a safe haven from playground bullies, and shoulders to cry on in times of confusion or trouble (Jordan, 2006; Laursen, Bukowski, Aunola, & Nurmi, 2007; Wentzel, Barry, & Caldwell, 2004). In the writing sample in Figure 3.4, 7-year-old Andrew shows his awareness of the many benefits of friends.

FIGURE 3.4 In this writing sample, 7-year-old Andrew sees friends primarily as companions and sources of entertainment (they're for "when you are lonley," "they play with you," "they tell stories"). Yet he also recognizes that friends can occasionally be a source of support ("they walk you to the nursce").

frends our for you when
youare lonley and sad.
they play with you,
theyare nice; theyare
mean; they tell stores
And the thingsthey Do.
they waik youto the
nursce,

Many adolescents (especially girls) reveal their innermost thoughts and feelings to their friends (Levitt, Guacci-Franco, & Levitt, 1993; Patrick et al., 2002; A. J. Rose, 2002). Friends often comprehend a teenager's perspectives—the preoccupation with physical appearance, the concerns about the opposite sex, and so on—when no one else seems to understand. By sharing their thoughts and feelings with one another, teens may discover that they aren't as unique as they once thought and thus may gradually abandon the personal fable mentioned earlier (Elkind, 1981).

Peers play a third important role in personal and social development as well: They serve as socialization agents that help to mold children's behaviors and beliefs (J. R. Harris, 1998; Laursen et al., 2007; A. M. Ryan, 2000). For example, they define options for leisure time, perhaps getting together in a study group or smoking cigarettes on the corner. They serve as role models and provide standards for acceptable behavior, showing what is possible, what is admirable, what is cool. And they sanction one another for stepping beyond acceptable bounds, perhaps through ridicule, gossip, or ostracism. Such **peer pressure** has its greatest effects during early adolescence, with teenagers who have weak emotional bonds to their families being especially susceptible (Berndt, Laychak, & Park, 1990; Erwin, 1993; Urdan & Maehr, 1995).

myeducationlab

Learn more about such conflicting peer messages by completing the Understanding Research exercise "Navigating Adolescence" in MyEducationLab. (To find this activity, go to the topic Personal, Social, and Moral Development in MyEducationLab, click on Assignments and *Activities*, and then select Understanding Research.)

The Real Scoop on Peer Pressure A common misconception is that peer pressure is invariably a bad thing. In fact, it's a mixed bag. Many peers encourage such desirable qualities as honesty, cooperation, and abstinence from drugs and alcohol (Berndt & Keefe, 1996; Damon, 1988; McCallum & Bracken, 1993; Wentzel & Looney, 2007). Others, however, encourage aggression, criminal activity, and other antisocial behaviors (X. Chen, Chang, He, & Liu, 2005; Espelage, Holt, & Henkel, 2003; D. C. Gottfredson, 2001). Some peers encourage academic achievement, whereas others convey the message that academic achievement is undesirable, perhaps by making fun of "brainy" students or by encouraging friends to cut class or skip school (Altermatt & Pomerantz, 2003; Ogbu, 2008b; E. N. Walker, 2006).

Although peer pressure certainly is a factor affecting development, its overall influence on children's behaviors has probably been overrated (Berndt & Keefe, 1996; Kindermann, 2007). Most children acquire a strong set of values and behavioral standards from their families, and they don't necessarily abandon these values and standards in the company of peers (B. B. Brown, 1990; W. A. Collins et al., 2000; Galambos, Barker, & Almeida, 2003). Furthermore, they tend to choose friends who are similar to themselves in academic achievement, leisure-time activities, and long-term goals (Card & Ramos, 2005; W. A. Collins et al., 2000; Kindermann, McCollam, & Gibson, 1996; A. M. Ryan, 2001).

peer pressure Phenomenon whereby age-mates strongly encourage some behaviors and discourage others.

self-socialization Self-motivated tendency to conform to what one believes are other people's expectations for behavior.

Curiously, much of the pressure to conform to others' standards and expectations comes from within rather than from outside. In particular, most children and adolescents engage in **self-socialization**, putting pressure on *themselves* to adopt the behaviors they think others will find acceptable (B. B. Brown, 1990; Durkin, 1995; Juvonen, 2006). Concerned about how others may evaluate them (recall our earlier discussion of the imaginary audience), young adolescents can be very conforming, rigidly imitating peers' choices in dress, music, slang, and behavior (Hacker & Bol, 2004; Hartup, 1983; Owens, 2008).

In some cases, students lead double lives that enable them to attain academic success while maintaining peer acceptance (B. B. Brown, 1993; Hemmings, 2004; Juvonen, 2006; Mac Iver, Reuman, & Main, 1995). For example, although they attend class and do their homework faithfully, they may feign disinterest in scholarly activities, disrupt class with jokes or goofy behaviors, and express surprise at receiving high grades. In addition, they may act tough when they're in public, saving their softer sides for more private circumstances, as one sixth grader's reflection reveals:

Young adolescents often work hard to look cool in the eyes of their peers, as this drawing by 11-year-old Marci illustrates.

> You'd still have to have your bad attitude. You have to act—it's just like a movie. You have to act. And then at home you're a regular kind of guy, you don't act mean or nothing. But when you're around your friends you have to be sharp and stuff like that, like push everybody around. (Juvonen & Cadigan, 2002, p. 282)

As teachers, we can help students maintain a good public image in a variety of ways. For instance, we can help them acquire skills for presenting themselves in a favorable light—public-speaking techniques, personal hygiene strategies, and so on. We can assign small-group projects in which every student has a unique talent to contribute. And when valued classmates ridicule academic achievement, we can allow students to demonstrate their accomplishments to us privately (e.g., through written assignments or one-on-one conversations) instead of in front of classmates.

Help students look good in the eyes of their peers.

Characteristics of Peer Relationships

Some peers are, of course, more influential than others. In this section, we look at a variety of peer relationships and then consider the effects of popularity and social isolation.

Friendships Close friends tend to be similar in age and are usually (but not always) of the same sex (Gottman, 1986; Hartup, 1992; Kovacs, Parker, & Hoffman, 1996; Maccoby, 2002). Friends find activities that are mutually meaningful and enjoyable, and over time they acquire a common set of experiences that enable them to share certain perspectives on life (Gottman, 1986; Suttles, 1970). Because friends typically have an emotional investment in their relationship, they work hard to look at situations from one another's points of view and to resolve disputes that threaten to separate them. As a result, they develop increased perspective-taking and conflict resolution skills (Basinger, Gibbs, & Fuller, 1995; DeVries, 1997; Newcomb & Bagwell, 1995). Close friendships also foster self-esteem and, especially in the secondary grades, provide a sense of identity for students, a sense that they *belong* to a particular group (Berndt, 1992; Knapp & Woolverton, 1995).

PEARSON myeducationlab

Observe developmental trends in the importance of friends in the video "Friendships." (To find this video, go to Chapter 3 of the Book-Specific Resources in MyEducationLab, select *Video Examples*, and then click on the title.)

Larger Social Groups With age and experience, many students form larger social groups that get together on a regular basis. As students reach puberty, moderately sized peer groups become an especially prominent feature of their social worlds. In early adolescence, **cliques**, which are moderately stable friendship groups of perhaps three to ten individuals, provide the setting for most voluntary social interactions (Crockett, Losoff, & Peterson, 1984; J. L. Epstein, 1986; Kindermann et al., 1996).

clique Moderately stable friendship group of perhaps three to ten members.

crowd Large, loose-knit social group that shares certain common interests and behaviors.

subculture Group that resists the ways of the dominant culture and adopts its own norms for behavior.

gang Cohesive social group characterized by initiation rites, distinctive colors and symbols, territorial orientation, and feuds with rival groups.

Clique boundaries tend to be fairly rigid and exclusive—some people are "in," others are "out"—and memberships in various cliques often affect students' social status (Goodwin, 2006; Wigfield et al., 1996).

Crowds are considerably larger than cliques and may not have the tight-knit cohesiveness and carefully drawn boundaries of cliques. Their members tend to share certain characteristics and behaviors (e.g., "brains" study a lot, "jocks" are active in sports), attitudes about academic achievement, and (occasionally) ethnic background (B. B. Brown, Herman, Hamm, & Heck, 2008; Steinberg, 1996). Crowd membership may or may not be a voluntary thing; for instance, membership in a so-called "popular" crowd is apt to be based as much on a student's reputation as on his or her actual efforts to affiliate with certain peers (B. B. Brown et al., 2008).

Sometimes, a crowd takes the form of a **subculture**, a group that resists a powerful dominant culture by adopting a significantly different way of life (J. S. Epstein, 1998). Some subcultures are relatively benign; for example, the baggy-pants skaters with whom my son Alex affiliated spent much of their free time riding their skateboards and addressing almost everyone as "dude." Other subcultures are more worrisome, such as those that endorse racist and anti-Semitic behaviors (e.g., skinheads) and those that practice Satanic worship and rituals. Adolescents are more likely to affiliate with troublesome subcultures when they feel alienated from the dominant culture—perhaps that of their school or that of society more generally—and want to distinguish themselves from it in some way (C. C. Clark, 1992; J. R. Harris, 1998).

In the upper high school grades, a greater capacity for abstract thought allows many adolescents to think of other people more as unique individuals and less as members of specific categories. They also gain new awareness of the characteristics they share with people from diverse backgrounds. Perhaps as a result of such changes, ties to specific peer groups tend to dissipate, hostilities between groups soften, and young people become more flexible about the people with whom they associate (B. B. Brown, Eicher, & Petrie, 1986; Gavin & Fuhrman, 1989; Larkin, 1979; Shrum & Cheek, 1987).

Gangs A **gang** is a cohesive social group characterized by initiation rites, distinctive colors and symbols, "ownership" of a specific territory, and feuds with one or more rival groups. Typically, gangs are governed by strict rules for behavior and stiff penalties for violations. Adolescents (and sometimes younger children as well) affiliate with gangs for a variety of reasons (C. C. Clark, 1992; Kodluboy, 2004; Parks, 1995; Simons, Whitbeck, Conger, & Conger, 1991). Some do so as a way of demonstrating loyalty to their family, friends, or neighborhood. Some seek the status and prestige that gang membership brings. Some have poor academic records and perceive the gang as an alternative arena in which they might gain recognition for their accomplishments. Many members of gangs have troubled relationships with their families or have been consistently rejected by peers, and so they turn to gangs to get the emotional support they can find nowhere else.

As teachers, we can definitely make a difference in the lives of any gang members in our classes (S. G. Freedman, 1990; Parks, 1995). We must, first and foremost, show these students that we truly care about them and their well-being. For instance, we can be willing listeners in times of trouble and can provide the support that gang members need to achieve both academic and social success. We must also have some knowledge of students' backgrounds—their cultural values, economic circumstances, and so on—so that we can better understand the issues with which they may be dealing. And we must certainly work cooperatively and proactively with our colleagues to minimize violent gang activity at school (more about this point in Chapter 13).

Provide the academic, social, and emotional support that gang members need to be successful at school.

Romantic Relationships Even in the primary grades, many children talk of having boyfriends or girlfriends, and the opposite sex is a subject of interest throughout the elementary school years. With the onset of adolescence, the biological changes of puberty are accompanied by new and sometimes unsettling feelings and sexual desires. Not surprisingly, then, romance is often on adolescents' minds and is a frequent topic of conversation at school (B. B. Brown, Feiring, & Furman, 1999).

From a developmental standpoint, romantic relationships have definite benefits: They can address young people's needs for companionship, affection, and security, and they provide an opportunity to experiment with new social skills and interpersonal behaviors (Davila, 2008; Furman & Simon, 1999; B. C. Miller & Benson, 1999). At the same time, romance can wreak havoc with adolescents' emotions. Adolescents have more extreme mood swings than younger children or adults, and for many, this instability may be partly due to the excitement and frustration of being romantically involved or *not* involved (Arnett, 1999; Davila, 2008; Larson, Clore, & Wood, 1999).

For many students, thoughts of romance emerge early. Here is just one of many notes 5-year-old Isabelle wrote about a classmate named Will.

Initially, romances often exist more in students' minds than in reality (Gottman & Mettetal, 1986). Consider Sandy's recollection of her first foray into couplehood:

> In about fifth and sixth grade, all our little group that we had . . . was like, "OK," you know, "we're getting ready for junior high," you know, "it's time we all have to get a boyfriend." So I remember, it was funny, Carol, like, there were two guys who were just the heartthrobs of our class, you know . . . so, um, I guess it was Carol and Cindy really, they were, like, sort of the leaders of our group, you know, they were the, yeah, they were just the leaders, and they got Tim and Joe, each of those you know. Carol had Tim and Cindy had Joe. And then, you know, everyone else, then it kind of went down the line, everyone else found someone. I remember thinking, "Well, who am I gonna get? I don't even like anybody," you know. I remember, you know, all sitting around, we were saying, "OK, who can we find for Sandy?" you know, looking, so finally we decided, you know, we were trying to decide between Al and Dave and so finally I took Dave. (Eckert, 1989, p. 84)

Middle school students' romantic thoughts may also involve crushes on people who are out of reach—perhaps favorite teachers, movie idols, or rock stars (B. B. Brown, 1999; B. C. Miller & Benson, 1999).

Eventually, many adolescents begin to date, especially if their friends are also dating. Their early choices in dating partners are often based on physical attractiveness or social status, and dates may involve only limited and superficial interaction (Furman, Brown, & Feiring, 1999; Pellegrini, 2002). As adolescents move into the high school grades, some form more intense, affectionate, and long-term relationships with members of the opposite sex, and these relationships often (but by no means always) lead to some degree of sexual intimacy (B. B. Brown, 1999; J. Connolly & Goldberg, 1999). The age of first sexual intercourse has decreased steadily over the last few decades, perhaps in part because the media often communicate that sexual activity among unmarried partners is acceptable (Brooks-Gunn & Paikoff, 1993; Larson et al., 1999). In the United States the average age of first sexual intercourse is now around age 16, and the majority of adolescents are sexually active by 18. However, the age varies considerably as a function of gender (boys begin earlier) and cultural background (Hofferth, 1990; Katchadourian, 1990; Lippa, 2002; Moore & Erickson, 1985).

As students reach high school (sometimes earlier), some of them find themselves attracted to their own sex either instead of or in addition to the opposite sex. Adolescence can be a particularly confusing time for gay, lesbian, and bisexual individuals. Some actively try to ignore or stifle what they perceive to be deviant urges. Others accept their sexual yearnings yet struggle to form an identity while feeling different and isolated from peers. Many describe feelings of anger and depression, some entertain thoughts of suicide, and a higher-than-average proportion drop out of school (Elia, 1994; Morrow, 1997; S. L. Nichols, 1999; Patterson, 1995).

Be on the lookout for gay or lesbian teens who seem especially depressed and socially isolated.

Teenagers often have mixed feelings about their early sexual experiences, and those around them—parents, teachers, peers—are often uncertain about how to handle the topic (Alapack, 1991; Katchadourian, 1990). When parents and teachers do broach the topic of sexuality, they often raise it in conjunction with *problems*, such as irresponsible behavior, substance abuse, disease, and unwanted pregnancy. And they rarely raise the topic of gay, lesbian, and bisexual orientations except within the context of acquired immune deficiency syndrome (AIDS) and other risks (M. B. Harris, 1997).

Offer emotional support when valued romantic relationships fizzle.

The extent to which we, as teachers, talk about sexuality with our students must be dictated, in part, by the policies of the school and the values of the community in which we work. At the same time, especially if we are teaching at the middle school or high school level, we must be aware that romantic and sexual relationships, whether real or imagined, are a considerable source of excitement, frustration, confusion, and distraction for students, and we must lend a sympathetic ear and an open mind to those students who seek our counsel and support.

Popularity and Social Isolation When my daughter Tina was in junior high school, she sometimes told me, "No one likes the popular kids." As self-contradictory as Tina's remark might seem, it's consistent with research findings. When students are asked to identify their most "popular" classmates, they identify peers who have dominant social status at school (perhaps those who belong to a prestigious social group) but in many cases are aggressive or snobby (Cillessen & Mayeux, 2007; W. E. Ellis & Zarbatany, 2007).

Truly **popular students**—those whom many classmates select as people they'd like to do things with—may or may not hold high-status positions, but they are kind and trustworthy (Cillessen & Rose, 2005; Parkhurst & Hopmeyer, 1998). Students who are popular in this way typically have good social skills, as Lupita does in the opening case study. They know how to initiate and sustain conversations, are sensitive to the subtle social and emotional cues that other people give them, and adjust their behavior to changing circumstances. They also tend to show genuine concern for others—for instance, by sharing, cooperating, and empathizing with peers (Crick & Dodge, 1994; Mostow, Izard, Fine, & Trantacosta, 2002; A. J. Rose & Asher, 2004; Wentzel & Asher, 1995).

In contrast to popular students, **rejected students** are those whom classmates select as being the *least* preferred social companions. Students with few social skills—for example, those who are impulsive or aggressive, as well as those who continually try to draw attention to themselves—typically experience peer rejection (Bukowski, Brendgen, & Vitaro, 2007; Pellegrini, Bartini, & Brooks, 1999; S. Pedersen, Vitaro, Barker, & Borge, 2007). In addition, students from racial and ethnic minority groups often find themselves the targets of derogatory remarks and other forms of racism and discrimination, as do students from low-income families (Banks & Banks, 1995; Phelan, Yu, & Davidson, 1994). Students who experience consistent peer rejection over a lengthy period tend to withdraw either physically or mentally from classroom activities, or they may engage in inappropriate attention-getting behaviors, and their classroom learning typically suffers as a result (Buhs, Ladd, & Herald, 2006; Ladd, 2006; Ladd, Herald-Brown, & Reiser, 2008; Snyder et al., 2008).

A third group, **controversial students**, are a mixed bag, in that some peers really like them and others really *dis*like them. These students can, like rejected students, be quite aggressive, but they also have good social skills that make them popular with at least some of their peers (Bukowski et al., 2007; Espelage & Swearer, 2004; Newcomb, Bukowski, & Pattee, 1993).

Researchers have described a fourth category as well. **Neglected students** are those whom peers rarely choose as someone they would either most like or least like to do something with (Asher & Renshaw, 1981). Neglected students tend to be quiet and keep to themselves. Some prefer to be alone, others may be very shy or don't know how to go about initiating interaction, and still others may be content with having only one or two close friends (Gazelle & Ladd, 2003; Guay et al. 1999; McElhaney, Antonishak, & Allen, 2008). For some students, neglected status is a relatively temporary situation. Others are totally friendless for extended periods—for instance, this is often the case for recent immigrants and for students with disabilities—and these students are at greater than normal risk for depression (Gazelle & Ladd, 2003; Igoa, 2007; Yuker, 1988).

popular student Student whom many peers like and perceive to be kind and trustworthy.

rejected student Student whom many peers identify as being an undesirable social partner.

controversial student Student whom some peers strongly like and other peers strongly dislike.

neglected student Student about whom most peers have no strong feelings, either positive or negative.

As teachers, we can help offset the hard feelings that peer rejection or neglect may engender by being particularly warm and attentive to socially isolated students (Wentzel, 1999). In fact, when *we* show that we like particular students, their classmates are more likely to accept and act positively toward them as well (Chang, 2003; Chang et al., 2004). We can also assist with interpersonal skills. Because of their social isolation, rejected and neglected students have fewer opportunities to develop the social skills that many of them desperately need (Coie & Cillessen, 1993; McElhaney et al., 2008).

Model positive fe behaviors toward r neglected student these students ac social skills.

Social Cognition

To be effective in interpersonal relationships, students must engage in **social cognition**—that is, they must consider how people around them are likely to think about, behave in, and react to various situations. At any single grade level, students vary considerably in their interest in and awareness of other people's thoughts and feelings. Those who think regularly about such matters tend to be socially skillful and make friends easily (Bosacki, 2000; P. L. Harris, 2006; Izard et al., 2001).

Perspective Taking One important element of social cognition is **perspective taking**, or looking at the world from other people's viewpoints—stepping into other people's shoes, so to speak. The following situation provides an example.

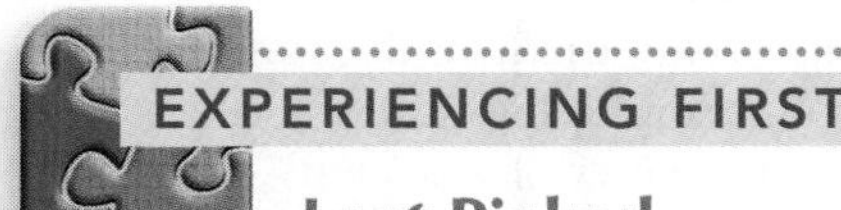

EXPERIENCING FIRSTHAND

Last Picked

Consider the following scenario:

> Kenny and Mark are co-captains of the soccer team. They have one person left to choose for the team. Without saying anything, Mark winks at Kenny and looks at Tom, who is one of the remaining children left to be chosen for the team. Mark looks back at Kenny and smiles. Kenny nods and chooses Tom to be on their team. Tom sees Mark and Kenny winking and smiling at each other. Tom, who is usually one of the last to be picked for team sports, wonders why Kenny wants him to be on his team. . . .
>
> - Why did Mark smile at Kenny?
> - Why did Kenny nod?
> - Why did Kenny choose Tom to be on the team? How do you know this?
> - Do you think that Tom has any idea of why Kenny chose him to be on the team? How do you know this? . . .
> - How do you think Tom feels? (Bosacki, 2000, p. 711)

To answer these questions, you must look at the situation from the perspectives of the three children involved. For instance, if you put yourself in Tom's shoes, you might suspect that he has mixed feelings. If he enjoys soccer, he may be happy to have a chance to play. But he may also feel embarrassed or demoralized at being one of the last children picked for a team. (For this reason, asking one or two students to choose peers for sports teams is generally *not* recommended.) And he may wonder what Mark's smile means. Perhaps it means that Mark is delighted to find a capable player still available to be picked, or perhaps it signals a malicious intention to make Tom look foolish on the soccer field.

Underlying children's perspective-taking abilities is a **theory of mind**, a general, self-constructed understanding of human beings' mental and psychological states—thoughts, beliefs, feelings, motives, and so on. As children grow older, they gain an increasingly complex understanding of human thought processes and feelings, enabling them to become increasingly effective in interacting with others (Flavell, 2000; A. Gopnik

social cognition Process of thinking about how other people are likely to think, act, and react.

perspective taking Ability to look at a situation from someone else's viewpoint.

theory of mind General understanding of one's own and other people's mental and psychological states (thoughts, feelings, etc.).

& Meltzoff, 1997; Wellman & Gelman, 1998). Table 3.2 describes ways in which perspective taking and theory of mind tend to change over the course of childhood and adolescence. In the following sections, we'll look at some of these changes more closely.

Childhood Consistent with what we've learned about cognitive development, young children tend to focus on other people's concrete, observable characteristics and behaviors (e.g., look once again at Andrew's essay in Figure 3.4). However, they do have some awareness of other people's inner worlds. As early as age 4 or 5, they realize that what *they* know may be different from what *other people* know (Wellman, Cross, & Watson, 2001; Wimmer & Perner, 1983). In addition, they have some ability to make inferences about other people's mental and emotional states—for instance, to deduce that people who behave in certain ways have certain intentions or feelings (P. L. Harris, 2006; Schult, 2002; Wellman, Phillips, & Rodriguez, 2000). As children progress through the elementary grades, they also begin to understand that people's actions do not always reflect their thoughts and feelings (e.g., someone who appears happy may actually feel sad) (Gnepp, 1989; Selman, 1980).

When students seem focused only on their own points of view, encourage them to consider why others might reasonably think and behave as they do.

Early Adolescence Most young adolescents realize that people can have mixed feelings about events and other individuals (Donaldson & Westerman, 1986; Flavell & Miller, 1998; Harter & Whitesell, 1989). And courtesy of their expanding cognitive abilities, memory capacity, and social awareness, young adolescents become capable of **recursive thinking** (Oppenheimer, 1986; Perner & Wimmer, 1985). That is, they can think about what other people might be thinking about them and eventually can reflect on other people's thoughts about them through multiple iterations (e.g., "You think that I think that you think . . ."). This is not to say that adolescents (or adults, for that matter) always use this capacity. In fact, consistent with our earlier discussion of the *imaginary audience*, thinking primarily about one's *own* perspective is a common phenomenon in the early adolescent years (Tsethlikai & Greenhoot, 2006; Tsethlikai, Guthrie-Fulbright, & Loera, 2007).

myeducationlab

See examples of social cognition at different age levels in the video "Emotions." (To find this video, go to Chapter 3 of the Book-Specific Resources in MyEducationLab, select *Video Examples*, and then click on the title.)

Late Adolescence In the high school years, teenagers can draw on a rich knowledge base derived from numerous social experiences. Consequently, they become ever more skillful at drawing inferences about people's psychological characteristics, intentions, and needs (Eisenberg, Carlo, Murphy, & Van Court, 1995; Paget, Kritt, & Bergemann, 1984). In addition, they are more attuned to the complex dynamics that influence behavior—not only thoughts, feelings, and present circumstances but also past experiences (C. A. Flanagan & Tucker, 1999; Selman, 1980). What we see emerging in the high school years, then, is a budding psychologist: an individual who can be quite astute in deciphering and explaining the motives and actions of others.

Promoting Perspective Taking In any classroom, day-to-day events offer many opportunities for perspective taking. One strategy is to create opportunities for students to encounter multiple—and perhaps equally legitimate—perspectives and beliefs. Another is to talk frequently about people's thoughts, feelings, and motives (Ruffman, Slade, & Crowe, 2002; Woolfe, Want, & Siegal, 2002). In the process, we must, of course, use age-appropriate language (J. Chalmers & Townsend, 1990; Wittmer & Honig, 1994). With first graders, such words might be *think*, *want*, and *sadness*. With fifth graders, we might use the words *misunderstand*, *frustration*, and *mixed feelings*. High school students have the cognitive and social reasoning capabilities to understand descriptions that use fairly abstract and complex psychological terms, such as *being passive-aggressive* and *having an inner moral compass*. These and other strategies are presented in the right-hand column of Table 3.2.

Frequently ask students to reflect on other people's thoughts, feelings, and motives.

The following anecdote shows how one teacher effectively used a perspective-taking assignment to improve students' classroom behavior:

> During gym lesson five of the boys misbehaved and were dismissed from class. They acted out their anger by insulting the gym teacher and the other staff greatly by answering back, shouting and even swearing, and throwing eggs at the school buildings. . . . When the boys came to my class they were very upset. . . . I told them I was not going to blame them at this point but I wanted them to write an essay at home

recursive thinking Thinking about what other people may be thinking about oneself, possibly through multiple iterations.

TABLE 3.2
Perspective Taking and Theory of Mind at Different Grade Levels

Grade Level	Age-Typical Characteristics	Suggested Strategies
K–2	• Awareness that mental events are not physical entities • Awareness that others' knowledge and thoughts may be different from one's own • Ability to draw inferences about people's thoughts, feelings, and intentions from their behaviors, albeit in a simplistic manner (e.g., "She's sad"); nature of inferences depends on one's own past experiences in social interactions	• Talk frequently about people's thoughts, feelings, and motives; use words such as *think, remember, feel,* and *want.* • Ask questions about thoughts, feelings, and motives during storybook readings; encourage students to share and compare diverse perspectives and inferences.
3–5	• Growing recognition that others interpret (rather than simply absorb) experiences and so may misconstrue events • Realization that people's actions may hide their true feelings • Preoccupation with own feelings, rather than others' feelings, in conflict situations	• As students read literature, ask them to consider why various characters might behave as they do. • As students study historical events, have them speculate about what people at the time might have been thinking and feeling. • Help students resolve interpersonal conflicts by asking them to consider one another's perspectives and to develop a solution that addresses everyone's needs. (See the discussion of *peer mediation* in Chapter 10.)
6–8	• Increasing interest in other people's thoughts and feelings • Recognition that people may have multiple and possibly conflicting motives and emotions • Ability to think recursively about one's own and others' thoughts	• Encourage students to look at historical and current events from the perspectives of various historical figures and cultural groups; use role-playing activities to enhance perspective taking. • In discussions of literature, talk about other people's complex (and sometimes conflicting) motives.
9–12	• Recognition that people are products of their environments and that past events and present circumstances influence personality and behavior • Realization that people are not always aware of why they act as they do	• Explore the possible origins of people's perspectives and motives in discussions of real and fictional events. • Schedule debates in which students must present convincing arguments for perspectives opposite to their own. • Offer units or courses in psychology, with a focus on such internal phenomena as cognition, motivation, and emotion.

Sources: Astington & Pelletier, 1996; Bosacki, 2000; Brophy & Alleman, 1996; Brophy & VanSledright, 1997; Chandler, 1987; Eisenberg, Carlo, Murphy, & Van Court, 1995; C. A. Flanagan & Tucker, 1999; Flavell, 2000; Flavell, Green, & Flavell, 1995; Flavell & Miller, 1998; Flavell et al., 2002; Greenhoot, Tsethlikai, & Wagoner, 2006; Harter & Whitesell, 1989; Mar & Oatley, 2008; Perner & Wimmer, 1985; Ruffman, Slade, & Crowe, 2002; Schult, 2002; Selman, 1980; Tsethlikai, Guthrie-Fulbright, & Loera, 2007; Wainryb, Brehl, & Matwin, 2005; Wellman, 1990; Wellman et al., 2001; Wellman, Phillips, & Rodriguez, 2000; Woolfe, Want, & Siegal, 2002; Woolley, 1995.

> about what had happened. . . . [The essays] were written sincerely in the sense that they described clearly what they had done but to my surprise without any regret or tendency to see the staff members' point of view. Having read the essays I decided to discuss the event in class. . . . The children defined the problem and thought about the feelings of those involved. I spent a considerable time asking them to consider the staff members' feelings, whether they knew of somebody who worked in a place similar to the gym, which in fact they did, how that person felt, etc. Gradually, the boys' vehemence subsided. I never blamed them so that they wouldn't become defensive, because then I thought I might lose them. Instead, I tried to improve their understanding of the opinions and feelings of other people, which might differ from their own. . . . The boys improved their behavior in gym class, and this never happened again. (Adalbjarnardottir & Selman, 1997, pp. 423–424)

Social Information Processing Children and adolescents have a lot to think about when they consider what other people are thinking, feeling, and doing. The mental processes involved in understanding and responding to social events are collectively known as **social information processing**, a socially oriented version of the information processing theory we'll examine in Chapter 6 (e.g., Burgess, Wojslawowicz, Rubin, Rose-Krasnor, & Booth-LaForce, 2006; Fontaine, Yang, Dodge, Bates, & Pettit, 2008; E. R. Smith & Semin, 2007). Among other things, social information

social information processing Mental processes involved in making sense of and responding to social events.

processing involves paying *attention* to certain behaviors in a social situation and trying to *interpret* and make sense of those behaviors. For example, when students interact with classmates, they might focus on certain remarks, facial expressions, and body language and try to figure out what a classmate really means by, say, a thoughtless comment or sheepish grin. Students also consider one or more *goals* they hope to achieve during an interaction—perhaps preserving a friendship or teaching somebody a "lesson." Taking into account both their interpretations and their goals, students draw on their previous knowledge and experiences to identify a number of possible responses and choose what is, in their eyes, a productive course of action. As we will see in the next section, an understanding of social information processing is especially helpful in explaining why some students are unusually aggressive toward their peers.

Aggression

Aggressive behavior is an action intentionally taken to hurt another person either physically or psychologically. Aggressive behavior sometimes involves **physical aggression**, an action that can potentially cause bodily injury (e.g., hitting, shoving). In other cases, it involves **relational aggression**, an action that can adversely affect friendships and other interpersonal relationships (e.g., ostracizing a peer, spreading unkind rumors). As a general rule, aggression declines over the course of childhood and adolescence, but it increases for a short time after students make the transition from elementary school to middle school or junior high (Pellegrini, 2002).

Researchers have identified two distinct groups of aggressive students (Crick & Dodge, 1996; Poulin & Boivin, 1999; Vitaro, Gendreau, Tremblay, & Oligny, 1998). Those who engage in **proactive aggression** deliberately initiate aggressive behaviors as a means of obtaining desired goals. Those who engage in **reactive aggression** act aggressively primarily in response to frustration or provocation. Of the two groups, students who exhibit proactive aggression are more likely to have difficulty maintaining friendships with others (Hanish, Kochenderfer-Ladd, Fabes, Martin, & Denning, 2004; Poulin & Boivin, 1999). Those who direct considerable aggression toward particular peers—whether it be physical aggression or relational aggression—are known as **bullies**. Their hapless victims often are children who are immature, anxious, friendless, and lacking in self-esteem—some also have disabilities—and so are relatively defenseless (Espelage & Swearer, 2004; Rosen, Milich, & Harris, 2007; M. W. Watson, Andreas, Fischer, & Smith, 2005).

Some children and adolescents are genetically more predisposed to aggression than their peers, and others may exhibit heightened aggression as a result of neurological abnormalities (Brendgen et al., 2008; Raine, 2008; van Goozen, Fairchild, & Harold, 2008). But environmental factors can foster aggressive behavior as well. Many aggressive students live in dysfunctional conditions at home, perhaps including frequent conflicts and displays of anger, harsh punishment or child maltreatment, and a general lack of affection and appropriate social behavior (Christenson, 2004; Maikovich, Jaffee, Odgers, & Gallop, 2008; Pettit, 2004). In addition, regular exposure to violence in the community or through various media (e.g., television, video games) seems to increase aggressive behavior in young people (C. A. Anderson et al., 2003; Guerra, Huesmann, & Spindler, 2003; Huesmann, Moise-Titus, Podolski, & Eron, 2003).

It is important to note that many children and adolescents who are routinely exposed to violence at home or elsewhere are *not* especially aggressive (Margolin & Gordis, 2004; Pearce, Jones, Schwab-Stone, & Ruchkin, 2003). Certain cognitive and motivational factors seem to underlie aggressive behavior, including the following:

- *Poor perspective-taking ability.* Students who are highly aggressive tend to have limited ability to look at situations from other people's perspectives or to empathize with their victims (Coie & Dodge, 1998; Damon & Hart, 1988; Marcus, 1980).
- *Misinterpretation of social cues.* Students who are either physically or relationally aggressive toward peers tend to interpret others' behaviors as reflecting hostile intentions, especially when such behaviors have ambiguous meanings. This **hostile attributional bias** is especially prevalent in children who are prone to

aggressive behavior Action intentionally taken to hurt another either physically or psychologically.

physical aggression Action that can potentially cause bodily injury.

relational aggression Action that can adversely affect interpersonal relationships.

proactive aggression Deliberate aggression against another as a means of obtaining a desired goal.

reactive aggression Aggressive response to frustration or provocation.

bully Child or adolescent who frequently threatens, harasses, or causes injury to particular peers.

hostile attributional bias Tendency to interpret others' behaviors as reflecting hostile or aggressive intentions.

reactive aggression (Bukowski et al., 2007; Crick, Grotpeter, & Bigbee, 2002; Dodge et al., 2003).

- *Prevalence of self-serving goals.* For most students, establishing and maintaining interpersonal relationships is a high priority. For aggressive students, however, achieving more self-serving goals—perhaps maintaining an inflated self-image, seeking revenge, or gaining power and dominance—often takes precedence (Baumeister et al., 1996; Menon et al., 2007; Cillessen & Rose, 2005; Pellegrini & Long, 2004).
- *Ineffective social problem-solving strategies.* Aggressive students often have little knowledge of how to persuade, negotiate, or compromise. Instead, they are apt to resort to hitting, shoving, barging into play activities, and other ineffective strategies (Neel, Jenkins, & Meadows, 1990; D. Schwartz et al., 1998; Troop-Gordon & Asher, 2005).
- *Belief in the appropriateness and effectiveness of aggression.* Many aggressive students believe that violence and other forms of aggression are acceptable ways of resolving conflicts and retaliating against others' misdeeds (Paciello, Fida, Tramontano, Lupinetti, & Caprara, 2008; M. W. Watson et al., 2005; Zelli, Dodge, Lochman, & Laird, 1999). Those who display high rates of *proactive* aggression are also apt to believe that aggressive action will yield positive results—for instance, that it will enhance social status (Dodge, Lochman, Harnish, Bates, & Pettit, 1997; Espelage & Swearer, 2004; Pellegrini & Bartini, 2000). Not surprisingly, aggressive children tend to associate with one another, thereby confirming one another's beliefs that aggression is appropriate (Espelage & Swearer, 2004).

Both initiators and recipients of aggression often have problems later on. Unless adults actively intervene, many aggressive students (especially those who exhibit proactive aggression) show a continuing pattern of aggression and violence as they grow older, and such a pattern almost guarantees long-term maladjustment and difficulties with peers (Dodge et al., 2003; Kupersmidt & Coie, 1990; Ladd & Troop-Gordon, 2003). Meanwhile, children who are frequent targets of bullying can become anxious, depressed, possibly even suicidal, and their classroom performance may deteriorate as a result (Hoglund, 2007; Hyman et al., 2006; D. Schwartz, Gorman, Nakamoto, & Toblin, 2005). Over time, their self-esteem declines, and some begin to believe that they are responsible for the harassment they endure (Troop-Gordon & Ladd, 2005). An entry in one high school student's journal illustrates just how devastating bullying can be:

> One day in junior high, I was getting off the school bus from a seat in the back. . . . I heard people shouting, "Hey, Fatso!" "You big buffalo!" . . . I knew I had to face them before getting off. In order to leave the bus I had to walk through a long crowded aisle and face the obnoxious girls. As I stood up, the girls followed. They crowded together, and approached me as if they were ready to strike at me. . . . All of [a] sudden, the girls began to kick and sock me repeatedly. . . . They continued to hurt me as if there was nothing more important to them than to see me in pain. The last few kicks were the hardest; all I wanted to do was get off the bus alive. My friends were staring at me, hoping that I would do something to make the girls stop. . . . Finally, after what seemed like an eternity, I was able to release myself from their torture. I got off the bus alive. Imagining that the worst had already passed, I began to walk away from the bus and the girls stuck their heads out the window and spit on me. I could not believe it! They spit on my face! . . . While I was cleaning my face with a napkin, I could still hear the girls laughing. (Freedom Writers, 1999, pp. 37–38)

Chapter 1
The Bully

"Mom, do I have to go to school?"
"Yes, you do Kevin."
"But what if there are bullies?"
"There will not be bullies."
"Fine, I'll go to school."
I got on the bus.
"Hey you, come here."
"No."
"Ill give you my bike if you come here!"
"No!"
"Why?"
"'Cause I have my own."
"Yeah, right. Why should I believe you?"
"I do not know."
"Because you are a liar."
"No, I am not."
"Yes, you are."
"No, I am not."
"Yes, you are."
"Fine, I am."

Many children and adolescents encounter bullies at school and elsewhere. This excerpt is from the first chapter in "The Biggest Bully Ever," a story in which 7-year-old Michael describes an encounter with a bully on the school bus. In a second chapter, Michael describes how he and his friends defended themselves against the bully.

cyberbullying Engaging in relational aggression via wireless technologies or the Internet.

Often, the relational aggression involved in bullying—taunts, name-calling, blatant exclusion from social activities, and so on—is even more harmful than any physical aggression that accompanies it (Doll, Song, & Siemers, 2004; Goodwin, 2006).

As teachers, we *must* intervene when some students victimize others, and we must keep a watchful eye for additional incidents of bullying down the road. Regular victims of bullies need social and emotional support from us and from their classmates. Some may also need one or more sessions with a school counselor, perhaps to address feelings of vulnerability and depression or perhaps to learn skills that will minimize future bullying incidents (Espelage & Swearer, 2004; R. S. Newman, 2008; Yeung & Leadbeater, 2007).

Be on the lookout for bullying, and take appropriate actions with both the victims and the perpetrators.

The perpetrators of aggression require intervention as well. They must be given appropriate consequences for their actions, of course, but they should also be helped to behave more appropriately. Specific strategies should be tailored to the thoughts and motives that underlie their aggression (Crick & Dodge, 1996). Such strategies as encouraging perspective taking, helping students interpret social situations more accurately, and teaching effective social problem-solving skills are potentially useful in reducing aggression and other disruptive behaviors (Cunningham & Cunningham, 2006; Guerra & Slaby, 1990; Horne, Orpinas, Newman-Carlson, & Bartolomucci, 2004; Hudley & Graham, 1993). Putting students in situations where they must explicitly *help*, rather than harm, others—for instance, asking them to tutor younger children—can also be effective (J. R. Sullivan & Conoley, 2004).

Interventions with aggressive students will most likely be effective if schools communicate the importance of acting kindly and respectfully toward all members of the school community—teachers and students alike (Espelage & Swearer, 2004). At some schools, however, violence and aggression are commonplace, and students may believe that acting aggressively is the only way to ensure that they don't become victims of *someone else's* aggression. Unfortunately, they may be right: Putting on a tough, seemingly invulnerable appearance (sometimes known as "frontin' it") can be critical for their survival (K. M. Williams, 2001a). We'll look at strategies for addressing schoolwide aggression and violence in Chapter 13.

Technology and Peer Relationships

With the advent of cellular telephone technology and text-messaging software, many students now communicate quite frequently—daily, sometimes almost hourly—with some of their peers (Gross, 2004; Valkenburg & Peter, 2007). And for students who have easy access to computers, the Internet provides a variety of mechanisms for interacting with peers, both those in town and those in distant places. For instance, e-mail and instant messaging ("IMing") allow quick and easy ways of asking classmates about homework assignments, making plans for weekend social activities, and seeking friends' advice and emotional support. Networking sites (e.g., facebook.com, myspace.com) provide a means of sharing personal information (e.g., news, interests, photos) and potentially finding like-minded age-mates. Internet-based chat rooms allow group discussions about virtually any topic. Judicious use of such mechanisms can enhance students' self-esteem, connectedness with peers, and general psychological well-being (Ellison, Steinfield, & Lampe, 2007; Gross, Juvonen, & Gable, 2002; Valkenburg & Peter, 2009).

Unfortunately, wireless technologies and the Internet also provide vehicles through which students can send demeaning messages or spread vicious rumors that adversely affect a peer's sense of self and social reputation (Valkenburg & Peter, 2009; Willard, 2007). Furthermore, unscrupulous individuals (usually adults) can misrepresent themselves in attempts (sometimes successful) to prey on unsuspecting children and adolescents (K. J. Mitchell, Wolak, & Finkelhor, 2005; Schofield, 2006). To the extent that we have opportunities, then, we should talk with students about wise and socially appropriate uses of modern technology, and we must explain in no uncertain terms that taunts, threats, and unkind rumors sent via wireless technologies or the Internet—**cyberbullying**—can cause great harm to others and is totally unacceptable (Juvonen & Graham, 2004; Willard, 2007). And, of course, we must monitor students' in-class use of the Internet.

Explain what cyberbullying is and why it is unacceptable.

Diversity in Peer Relationships and Social Cognition

Some students with disabilities have delays in the development of social cognition and, as a result, often have trouble in interpersonal relationships. For example, students with significant delays in their overall cognitive development (i.e., children with mental retardation) typically have limited understanding of appropriate behaviors in social situations (S. Greenspan & Granfield, 1992; Leffert, Siperstein, & Millikan, 2000). Also, some students with seemingly normal cognitive abilities have specific deficits in social cognition. In a mild form of autism known as *Asperger syndrome*, students may show average or above-average academic achievement but have great difficulty drawing accurate inferences from others' behaviors and body language, apparently as a result of a brain abnormality (Dawson & Bernier, 2007; Hobson, 2004; Tager-Flusberg, 2007). In addition, many students with chronic emotional and behavioral disabilities may have poor perspective-taking and social problem-solving abilities and thus may have few, if any, friends (Harter et al., 1998; Lind, 1994).

Gender Differences Gender differences have been observed in interpersonal behaviors. Boys tend to hang out in large groups, whereas girls tend to favor smaller, more intimate gatherings with close friends (Maccoby, 2002). Also, girls seem to be more astute at reading other people's body language, and they work hard to maintain group harmony (see Chapter 4). Furthermore, aggression tends to take different forms in boys (who are prone to physical aggression) and in girls (who are more apt to engage in relational aggression, disrupting friendships and tarnishing others' reputations) (Card, Stucky, Sawalani, & Little, 2008; Crick et al., 2002; French, Jansen, & Pidada, 2002; Pellegrini & Archer, 2005).

Cultural and Ethnic Differences Interpersonal behaviors vary from culture to culture as well. For instance, some cultural groups (e.g., some groups in northern Canada and in the South Pacific) regularly use seemingly antisocial behaviors—especially teasing and ridicule—to teach children to remain calm and handle criticism (Rogoff, 2003). In contrast, many Native Americans, many people of Hispanic heritage, and certain African American communities place particular emphasis on maintaining group harmony and resolving interpersonal conflicts peacefully. Children from these groups may be especially adept at negotiation and peace making (Gardiner & Kosmitzki, 2008; Guthrie, 2001; Halgunseth et al., 2006; Witmer, 1996).

Promoting Healthy Peer Relationships

As teachers, we are in an excellent position to assess how students think about and behave in social situations and to help them interact more effectively with others. Following are several strategies that research has shown to be effective:

Provide numerous opportunities for social interaction and cooperation. For instance, students' play activities—whether the fantasy play of preschoolers and kindergartners or the rule-based games of older children and adolescents—can promote cooperation, sharing, perspective taking, and conflict resolution skills (Creasey, Jarvis, & Berk, 1998; Gottman, 1986; K. H. Rubin, 1982). Assignments and activities that require students to cooperate with one another to achieve a common goal can foster leadership skills and a willingness to both help and get help from peers (Certo, Miller, Reffitt, Moxley, & Sportsman, 2008; Y. Li et al., 2007; N. M. Webb & Farivar, 1994). Extracurricular activities provide additional opportunities for students to interact and work cooperatively with a wide range of peers (Feldman & Matjasko, 2005; Genova & Walberg, 1984; Mahoney, Cairns, & Farmer, 2003). Furthermore, participation in extracurricular activities can help students find common grounds for communication, as one high school student explained:

> If you feel like you have something to do after school, it's really neat. You get to talk to people in the hall, like, "Oh, is that meeting today?" Or, "What are we doing next week?" It gives you a feeling of, I have people who are in the same club as me. (Certo, Cauley, & Chafin, 2002, p. 20)

Extracurricular activities not only provide a means through which students can interact with peers, but they can also be a source of success for students who struggle with academic tasks. Here, 7-year-old Daniel, who has attention and cognitive-processing deficits that make reading and writing quite difficult, expresses his love of baseball.

Help students interpret social situations accurately and productively. When students consistently have trouble getting along with others, explicit training in social cognition can make a difference. For example, in one research study (Hudley & Graham, 1993), boys in two low-income, inner-city neighborhoods attended a series of training sessions in which they used role playing, discussions of personal experiences, brainstorming, and similar activities to practice making inferences about other people's intentions and identifying appropriate courses of action. They also learned several strategies for reminding themselves of how to behave in various situations. For example, they might think to themselves, "When I don't have the information to tell what he meant, I should act as if it were an accident" (p. 128). Following the training, the students were less likely to presume hostile intent or endorse aggressive retaliation in interpersonal situations than control-group students who did not receive the training, and their teachers rated the trained students as less aggressive.

Teach specific social skills, provide opportunities for students to practice them, and give feedback. We can teach students appropriate ways of behaving both through explicit verbal instructions and through modeling desired behaviors. Such instruction is especially effective when we also ask students to practice their newly learned social skills (perhaps through role playing) and give them concrete feedback about how they are doing (S. N. Elliott & Busse, 1991; Themann & Goldstein, 2001; S. Vaughn, 1991; Zirpoli & Melloy, 2001). In addition, we must actively *dis*courage such inappropriate behaviors as inconsiderateness, aggression, and prejudicial remarks. When we establish and enforce firm rules about aggression and other antisocial behaviors while simultaneously teaching appropriate social skills, we will often see noticeable improvements in behavior (e.g., Bierman, Miller, & Stabb, 1987; Braukmann, Kirigin, & Wolf, 1981; Schofield, 1995).

Close cross-ethnicity friendships are more common when the number of available peers is relatively small, as is apt to be the case in small classes and rural communities (Hallinan & Teixeria, 1987; Roopnarine, Lasker, Sacks, & Stores, 1998).

Promote understanding, communication, and interaction among diverse groups. Even when students have good social skills, many of them interact almost exclusively within small, close-knit groups, and a few others remain socially isolated. For example, students often divide themselves along ethnic lines when they eat lunch and interact in the school yard. In fact, ethnic segregation *increases* once students reach the middle school grades. As young adolescents from ethnic minority groups begin to look closely and introspectively at issues of racism and ethnic identity, they often find it helpful to compare experiences and perspectives with other group members (B. B. Brown et al., 2008; Tatum, 1997).

Frequently change students' assigned seats as a way of broadening their friendships.

Yet students have much of value to learn from classmates very different from themselves. One simple way of expanding students' friendship networks is to give students assigned seats in class and frequently change the seating chart (Schofield, 1995). Other strategies are presented in the Creating a Productive Classroom Environment box "Encouraging Positive Interactions Among Diverse Individuals and Groups." When students from diverse groups interact regularly—and especially when they come together as equals, work toward a common goal, and see themselves as members of the same team—they are more apt to accept and possibly even *value* one another's differences (Dovidio & Gaertner, 1999; Oskamp, 2000; Pfeifer, Brown, & Juvonen, 2007; Ramsey, 1995).

Explain what bullying is and why it cannot be tolerated. Students often have misconceptions about bullying. For instance, they may think it involves only physical aggression, even though significant relational aggression constitutes bullying as well. Another common student misconception is that the victims of bullies somehow deserve what they get, perhaps because they display immature behaviors or need to "toughen up" and learn to defend themselves. Thus, many students condone bullying and act as a supportive audience for the perpetrators (Doll, et al., 2004; Hyman et al., 2004).

Creating A PRODUCTIVE CLASSROOM ENVIRONMENT

Encouraging Positive Interactions Among Diverse Individuals and Groups

- **Set up situations in which students can form cross-group friendships.**

  A junior high school science teacher decides how students will be paired for weekly lab activities. She changes the pairings every month and frequently pairs students from different ethnic backgrounds.

- **Minimize or eliminate barriers to social interaction.**

  Students in a third-grade class learn basic words and phrases in American Sign Language so that they can work and play with a classmate who is deaf.

- **Encourage and facilitate participation in extracurricular activities, and take steps to ensure that no single group dominates in membership or leadership in any particular activity.**

  When recruiting members for the scenery committee for the eighth grade's annual class play, the committee's teacher–adviser encourages both popular and unpopular eighth graders to participate. Later, he divides the workload in such a way that students who don't know one another very well must work closely and cooperatively.

- **As a class, discuss the negative consequences of intergroup hostilities.**

  A high school English teacher in a low-income, inner-city school district uses a lesson on Shakespeare's *Romeo and Juliet* to initiate a discussion about an ongoing conflict between two rival ethnic-group gangs in the community. "Don't you think this family feud is stupid?" she asks her students, referring to Shakespeare's play. When they agree, she continues, "The Capulets are like the Latino gang, and the Montagues are like the Asian gang. . . .
  Don't you think it's stupid that the Latino gang and the Asian gang are killing each other?" The students immediately protest, but when she presses them to justify their thinking, they gradually begin to acknowledge the pointlessness of a long-standing rivalry whose origins they can't even recall.

- **Develop nondisabled students' understanding of students with disabilities, provided that the students and their parents give permission to share what might otherwise be confidential information.**

  In a widely publicized case, Ryan White, a boy who had contracted AIDS from a blood transfusion, met considerable resistance against his return to his neighborhood school because parents and students thought he might infect others. After Ryan's family moved to a different school district, school personnel actively educated the community about the fact that AIDS does not spread through typical day-to-day contact. Ryan's reception at his new school was overwhelmingly positive. Later, Ryan described his first day at school: "When I walked into classrooms or the cafeteria, several kids called out at once, 'Hey, Ryan! Sit with me!' "

Sources: Feldman & Matjasko, 2005; Freedom Writers, 1999, p. 33 (Shakespeare example); Genova & Walberg, 1984; Mahoney et al., 2003; Schofield, 1995; Schultz, Buck, & Niesz, 2000; Sleeter & Grant, 1999; Tatum, 1997; M. Thompson & Grace, 2001 (school play example); R. White & Cunningham, 1991, p. 149 (Ryan White example).

Earlier I urged you to be on the lookout for incidents of bullying. This is easier said than done, because many incidents of bullying occur beyond the watchful eyes of school faculty members (Carter & Doyle, 2006; Hyman et al., 2004). Furthermore, the victims may fear retaliation if they alert adults to their plight (R. S. Newman & Murray, 2005). It is important, then, that we encourage other students to report (perhaps anonymously) any incidents of bullying they witness. One effective strategy is to use the mnemonic *PIC* to describe what bullying involves:

- **P**urposeful behavior—"He meant to do it."
- **I**mbalanced—"That's not fair, he's bigger."
- **C**ontinual—"I'm afraid to enter the classroom because she's always picking on me." (Horne et al., 2004, pp. 298–299)

> **myeducationlab**
>
> Gain practice in assessing students' social cognition and social skills by completing the Building Teaching Skills and Dispositions exercise "Fostering Perspective Taking and Social Skills" in MyEducationLab. (To find this activity, go to the topic Personal, Social, and Moral Development in MyEducationLab and click on *Building Teaching Skills and Dispositions.*)

Help change the reputations of formerly antisocial students. Unfortunately, students' bad reputations often live on long after their behavior has changed for the better, and thus their classmates may continue to dislike and reject them (Bierman et al., 1987; Caprara, Dodge, Pastorelli, & Zelli, 2007; Juvonen & Weiner, 1993). So when we work to improve the behaviors of aggressive and other antisocial students, we must work to improve their reputations as well. For example, we might encourage their active involvement in extracurricular activities or place them in structured cooperative learning groups where they can use their newly developed social skills. We should also demonstrate through our words and actions that *we* like and appreciate them, as our attitudes are apt to be contagious (Chang, 2003; Chang et al., 2004). In one way or another, we must help students discover that formerly antisocial classmates have changed and are worth getting to know better.

Create a general climate of respect for others. Teachers who effectively cultivate friendships among diverse groups of students are often those who communicate a consistent message over and over: We must all respect one another as human beings. Fernando Arias, a high school vocational education teacher, has put it this way:

> In our school, our philosophy is that we treat everybody the way we'd like to be treated. . . . Our school is a unique situation where we have pregnant young ladies who go to our school. We have special education children. We have the regular kids, and we have the drop-out recovery program . . . we're all equal. We all have an equal chance. And we have members of every gang at our school, and we hardly have any fights, and there are close to about 300 gangs in our city. We all get along. It's one big family unit it seems like. (Turnbull, Pereira, & Blue-Banning, 2000, p. 67)

Truly productive interpersonal relationships depend on students' ability to respect one another's rights and needs and to support classmates who are going through hard times. Such capabilities are aspects of students' moral and prosocial development, a domain we turn to now.

On a page in her "Happiness Book," 6-year-old Jaquita expresses her pleasure in behaving prosocially.

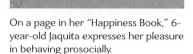

Moral and Prosocial Development

In the opening case study, Lupita helps a classmate interpret a teacher aide's subtle message and assists two others with their puzzles. Such actions are examples of **prosocial behavior**, behavior aimed at benefiting others more than oneself. Prosocial behaviors—plus such traits as honesty, fairness, and concern about other people's rights and welfare—fall into the domain of **morality**. By and large, students who think and behave in moral and prosocial ways gain more support from their teachers and peers and, as a result, achieve greater academic and social success over the long run (Caprara, Barbaranelli, Pastorelli, Bandura, & Zimbardo, 2000).

Developmental Trends in Morality and Prosocial Behavior

Most children behave more morally and prosocially as they grow older. Table 3.3 describes the forms that morality and prosocial behavior are apt to take at various grade levels. Some of the entries in the table reflect the following developmental trends:

- *Children begin using internal standards to evaluate behavior at an early age.* Even preschoolers have some understanding that behaviors causing physical or psychological harm are inappropriate (Helwig, Zelazo, & Wilson, 2001; J. M. Kim & Turiel, 1996). By age 4, most children understand that causing harm to another person is wrong regardless of what authority figures might tell them and regardless of what consequences certain behaviors may or may not bring (Laupa & Turiel, 1995; Smetana, 1981; Tisak, 1993).

- *Children increasingly distinguish between moral and conventional transgressions.* Virtually every culture discourages some behaviors—**moral transgressions**—because they cause damage or harm, violate human rights, or run counter to basic principles of equality, freedom, or justice, and it discourages other behaviors—**conventional transgressions**—that, although not unethical, violate widely held understandings about how one should act (e.g., children shouldn't talk back to adults or burp at meals). Conventional transgressions are usually specific to a particular cul-

prosocial behavior Behavior directed toward promoting the well-being of people other than oneself.

morality One's general standards about right and wrong behavior.

moral transgression Action that causes harm or infringes on the needs or rights of others.

conventional transgression Action that violates a culture's general expectations regarding socially appropriate behavior.

TABLE 3.3
Moral Reasoning and Prosocial Behavior at Different Grade Levels

Grade Level	Age-Typical Characteristics	Suggested Strategies
K–2	• Ability to distinguish between behaviors that violate human rights and dignity and those that violate social conventions • Some awareness that behaviors that cause physical or psychological harm are morally wrong • Guilt and shame about misbehaviors that cause obvious harm or damage • Some empathy for and attempts to comfort people in distress, especially people whom one knows well • Greater concern for one's own needs than for those of others • Appreciation for the need to be fair; fairness seen as strict equality in how a desired commodity is divided	• Make standards for behavior very clear. • When students misbehave, give reasons that such behaviors are not acceptable, focusing on the harm and distress they have caused others (i.e., use *induction*; see discussion on p. 95). • Encourage students to comfort others in times of distress. • Model sympathetic responses; explain what you are doing and why you are doing it. • Recognize that some selfish behavior is typical for the age-group; when it occurs, encourage perspective taking and prosocial behavior (e.g., "Hmm, we have three children who all want to read *Green Eggs and Ham*. We have only one copy. How can we solve this problem?").
3–5	• Knowledge of social conventions for appropriate behavior • Increasing empathy for unknown individuals who are suffering or needy • Recognition that one should strive to meet others' needs as well as one's own; growing appreciation of cooperation and compromise • Growing realization that fairness does not necessarily mean equality—that some people (e.g., peers with disabilities) may need more of a desired commodity than others • Increased desire to help others as an objective in and of itself	• Talk about how having rules enables classrooms and other groups to run more smoothly. • Explain how students can often meet their own needs while helping others (e.g., when asking students to be "reading buddies" for younger children, explain that doing so will help them become better readers themselves). • Use prosocial adjectives (e.g., *kind, helpful*) when praising altruistic behavior.
6–8	• Growing awareness that some rules and conventions are arbitrary; in some cases, accompanied by resistance to these rules and conventions • Interest in pleasing and helping others but with a tendency to oversimplify what helping requires • Tendency to believe that people in dire circumstances (e.g., homeless people) are entirely responsible for their own fate	• Make prosocial behavior (e.g., giving, sharing, caring for others) a high priority in the classroom. • Involve students in group projects that will benefit their school or community. • When imposing discipline for moral transgressions, accompany it with explanations about the harm that has been caused (i.e., use *induction*), especially when working with students who have deficits in empathy and moral reasoning.
9–12	• Understanding that having rules and conventions helps society run more smoothly • Increasing concern about doing one's duty and abiding by the rules of society as a whole, rather than simply pleasing certain authority figures • Genuine empathy for those in distress • Belief that society has an obligation to help people in need	• Explore moral issues in social studies, science, and literature. • Encourage performing community service to engender feelings of commitment to helping others. Ask students to reflect on their experiences through group discussions or written essays. • Have students read autobiographies and other literature that depict heroic figures who have actively worked to help others.

Sources: Eisenberg, 1982; Eisenberg & Fabes, 1998; Eisenberg, Lennon, & Pasternack, 1986; Farver & Branstetter, 1994; C. A. Flanagan & Faison, 2001; Gibbs, 1995; Gummerum, Keller, Takezawa, & Mata, 2008; D. Hart & Fegley, 1995; Hastings, Utendale, & Sullivan, 2007; Helwig & Jasiobedzka, 2001; Helwig et al., 2001; M. L. Hoffman, 1975, 1991; Kohlberg, 1984; Krebs & Van Hesteren, 1994; Kurtines, Berman, Ittel, & Williamson, 1995; Laupa & Turiel, 1995; M. Lewis & Sullivan, 2005; Nucci, 2009; Nucci & Weber, 1995; Rushton, 1980; Smetana & Braeges, 1990; Turiel, 1983, 1998; Yates & Youniss, 1996; Yau & Smetana, 2003; Youniss & Yates, 1999; Zahn-Waxler, Radke-Yarrow, Wagner, & Chapman, 1992.

ture; in contrast, many moral transgressions are universal across cultures (Nucci, 2009; Smetana, 2006; Turiel, 2002).

Children's awareness of social conventions increases throughout the elementary school years (Helwig & Jasiobedzka, 2001; Laupa & Turiel, 1995; Nucci & Nucci, 1982). But especially as children reach adolescence, they do not always agree with adults about which behaviors constitute moral transgressions, which ones fall into the

hopes
goals
dreams
happiness
broken
destroyed
eliminated
exterminated
no steps forward
no evolution
no prosperity
no hope
But
maybe
perhaps
except
if we
help
together
we stand
a chance.

In this poem, Matt, a middle school student, shows empathy for victims of the Holocaust.

conventional domain, and which ones are simply a matter of personal choice (Nucci, 2009; Smetana, 2005). Hence, many adolescents resist rules they think are infringements on their personal freedoms—rules about clothing, hair style, talking in class, and so on (Nucci, 2009).

• *Children's capacity to respond emotionally to others' harm and distress increases over the school years.* Within the first two or three years of life, two emotions important for moral development emerge (Kochanska, Gross, Lin, & Nichols, 2002; M. Lewis & Sullivan, 2005). First, children occasionally show **guilt**: a feeling of discomfort when they know they have inflicted damage or caused someone else pain or distress. They also experience **shame**: a feeling of embarrassment or humiliation when they fail to meet the standards for moral behavior that either they or others have established. Both guilt and shame, although unpleasant emotions, are good signs that children are developing a sense of right and wrong and will work hard to correct their misdeeds (Eisenberg, 1995; Harter, 1999; Narváez & Rest, 1995).

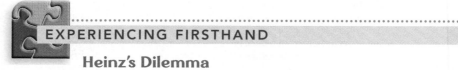

Guilt and shame emerge when children believe they have done something wrong. In contrast, **empathy**—experiencing the same feelings as someone in unfortunate circumstances—appears in the absence of wrongdoing. The ability to empathize emerges in the preschool years and continues to develop throughout childhood and adolescence (Eisenberg, 1982; Eisenberg et al., 1986, 1995). Truly prosocial children—those who help others even in the absence of their own wrongdoing—typically have a considerable capacity for perspective taking and empathy (Damon, 1988; Eisenberg, Zhou, & Koller, 2001; M. L. Hoffman, 1991). Empathy is especially likely to spur prosocial behavior when it leads to **sympathy**, whereby children not only assume another person's feelings but also have concerns for the individual's well-being (Batson, 1991; Eisenberg & Fabes, 1998; Turiel, 1998).

• *With age, reasoning about moral issues becomes increasingly abstract and flexible.* To probe children's thinking about moral issues, researchers sometimes present **moral dilemmas**, situations in which two or more people's rights or needs may be at odds and for which there are no clear-cut right or wrong responses. The following exercise presents an example.

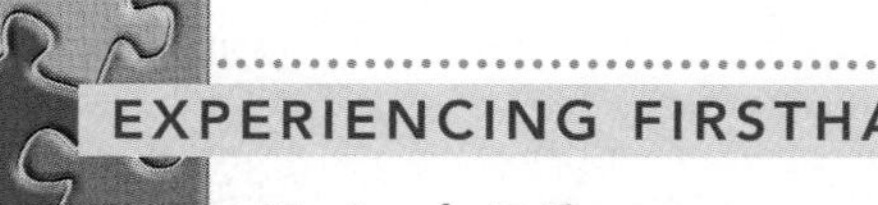

Heinz's Dilemma

Consider this scenario:

> In Europe, a woman was near death from a rare form of cancer. There was one drug that the doctors thought might save her, a form of radium that a druggist in the same town had recently discovered. The druggist was charging $2,000, ten times what the drug cost him to make. The sick woman's husband, Heinz, went to everyone he knew to borrow the money, but he could only get together about half of what the drug cost. He told the druggist that his wife was dying and asked him to sell it cheaper or let him pay later. But the druggist said no. So Heinz got desperate and broke into the man's store to steal the drug for his wife. (Kohlberg, 1984, p. 186)

- Should Heinz have stolen the drug?
- What would *you* have done if you were Heinz?
- Which is worse: stealing something that belongs to someone else or letting another person die a preventable death? Why?

After obtaining hundreds of responses to moral dilemmas such as this one, groundbreaking researcher Lawrence Kohlberg proposed that as children grow older, they construct increasingly complex views of morality. In Kohlberg's view, the development of moral reasoning is characterized by a sequence of six stages grouped into three

guilt Feeling of discomfort about having caused someone else pain or distress.

shame Feeling of embarrassment or humiliation after failing to meet certain standards for moral behavior.

empathy Experience of sharing the same feelings as someone in unfortunate circumstances.

sympathy Feeling of sorrow for another person's distress, accompanied by concern for the person's well-being.

moral dilemma Situation in which two or more people's rights or needs may be at odds and the morally correct action is not clear cut.

general *levels* of morality: preconventional, conventional, and postconventional (see Table 3.4). A child with **preconventional morality** has not yet adopted or internalized society's conventions regarding what is right or wrong but instead focuses largely on external consequences that certain actions may bring. We see an example of preconventional reasoning in one fifth grader's response to the Heinz dilemma:

> Maybe his wife is an important person and runs a store, and the man buys stuff from her and can't get it any other place. The police would blame the owner that he didn't save the wife. He didn't save an important person, and that's just like killing with a gun or a knife. You can get the electric chair for that. (Kohlberg, 1981, pp. 265–266)

Kohlberg's second level—**conventional morality**—is characterized by general, often unquestioning obedience either to an authority figure's dictates or to the rules and norms of society in general, even when there are no consequences for disobedience. In contrast, people at Kohlberg's third level—**postconventional morality**—view rules as useful but changeable mechanisms that ideally can maintain the general social order and protect human rights; rules are not absolute dictates that must be obeyed without question. These people live by their own abstract principles about right and wrong and may disobey rules inconsistent with these principles, as we see in one high school student's response to the Heinz dilemma:

> In that particular situation Heinz was right to do it. In the eyes of the law he would not be doing the right thing, but in the eyes of the moral law he would. If he had exhausted every other alternative I think it would be worth it to save a life. (Kohlberg, 1984, pp. 446–447)

A great deal of research on the development of moral reasoning has followed on the heels of Kohlberg's work. Some of it supports Kohlberg's proposed sequence: Generally speaking, people seem to make advancements in the order that Kohlberg proposed (Boom, Brugman, & van der Heijden, 2001; Colby & Kohlberg, 1984; Snarey, 1995; Stewart & Pascual-Leone, 1992). Nevertheless, contemporary psychologists have identified several weaknesses in Kohlberg's theory. For one thing, Kohlberg included both moral issues (e.g., causing harm) and social conventions (e.g., having rules to help society run smoothly) in his views of morality, but as we have seen, children distinguish between these two domains, and their views about each domain may change differently over time (Nucci, 2001, 2009). Furthermore, Kohlberg paid little attention to one very important aspect of morality: *helping and showing compassion for* other people (we'll return to this point in our later discussion of diversity). Kohlberg also underestimated young children, who, as we discovered earlier, acquire some internal standards of right and wrong long before they begin kindergarten or first grade. Finally, Kohlberg largely overlooked situational factors that youngsters take into account when deciding what's morally right and wrong in specific contexts (more about these factors in a moment).

Many contemporary developmental psychologists believe that moral reasoning involves general *trends*, rather than distinct stages. It appears that children and adolescents gradually construct several different standards that guide their moral reasoning, including the need to address one's own personal interests, consideration of other people's needs and motives, a desire to abide by society's rules and conventions, and, eventually, an appreciation of abstract ideals regarding human rights and society's overall needs (Killen & Smetana, 2008; Krebs, 2008; Rest, Narvaez, Bebeau, & Thoma, 1999). With age students increasingly apply more advanced standards, but even a fairly primitive one—satisfying one's own needs without regard for others—may occasionally take priority (Rest et al., 1999; Turiel, 1998).

• *As children get older, they increasingly behave in accordance with their self-constructed moral standards, but other factors come into play as well.* To some degree, students with more advanced moral reasoning behave in more moral and prosocial ways (e.g., Blasi, 1980; P. A. Miller, Eisenberg, Fabes, & Shell, 1996; Paciello et al., 2008). However, the correlation between moral reasoning and moral behavior is not

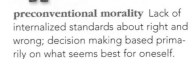

myeducationlab

Observe preconventional and conventional responses to a moral dilemma in the video "Moral Reasoning." (To find this video, go to Chapter 3 of the Book-Specific Resources in MyEducationLab, select *Video Examples*, and then click on the title.)

preconventional morality Lack of internalized standards about right and wrong; decision making based primarily on what seems best for oneself.

conventional morality Uncritical acceptance of society's conventions regarding right and wrong.

postconventional morality Thinking in accordance with self-developed, abstract principles regarding right and wrong.

Compare/ Contrast

TABLE 3.4
Kohlberg's Three Levels and Six Stages of Moral Reasoning

Level	Age Range	Stage	Nature of Moral Reasoning
Level I: Preconventional morality	Seen in preschool children, most elementary school students, some junior high school students, and a few high school students	Stage 1: Punishment–avoidance and obedience	People make decisions based on what is best for themselves, without regard for others' needs or feelings. They obey rules only if established by more powerful individuals; they may disobey if they aren't likely to get caught. "Wrong" behaviors are those that will be punished.
		Stage 2: Exchange of favors	People recognize that others also have needs. They may try to satisfy others' needs if their own needs are met simultaneously (e.g., "You scratch my back; I'll scratch yours"). They continue to define right and wrong primarily in terms of consequences to themselves.
Level II: Conventional morality	Seen in a few older elementary school students, some junior high school students, and many high school students (Stage 4 typically does not appear before high school)	Stage 3: Good boy/good girl	People make decisions based on what actions will please others, especially authority figures (e.g., teachers, popular peers). They are concerned about maintaining relationships through sharing, trust, and loyalty, and they consider other people's perspectives and intentions when making decisions.
		Stage 4: Law and order	People look to society as a whole for guidelines about right or wrong. They know that having rules is necessary for keeping society running smoothly and believe it is their duty to obey them. However, they perceive rules to be inflexible; they don't necessarily recognize that as society's needs change, its rules should change as well.
Level III: Postconventional morality	Rarely seen before college	Stage 5: Social contract	People recognize that rules represent agreements among many individuals about what is appropriate behavior. Rules are seen as useful mechanisms that maintain the general social order and protect individual rights, rather than as absolute dictates that must be obeyed simply because they are the law. People also recognize the flexibility of rules; rules that no longer serve society's best interests can and should be changed.
		Stage 6: Universal ethical principle	Stage 6 is a hypothetical, ideal stage that few people ever reach. People in this stage adhere to a few abstract, universal principles (e.g., equality of all people, respect for human dignity, commitment to justice) that transcend specific norms and rules. They answer to a strong inner conscience and willingly disobey laws that violate their own ethical principles.

Sources: Colby & Kohlberg, 1984; Colby, Kohlberg, Gibbs, & Lieberman, 1983; Kohlberg, 1976, 1984, 1986; Reimer, Paolitto, & Hersh, 1983; Snarey, 1995.

an especially strong one. Students' perspective-taking ability and emotions (shame, guilt, empathy, sympathy) also influence their decisions to behave morally or otherwise (Batson, 1991; Damon, 1988; Eisenberg et al., 2001). Influential, too, are students' personal needs and goals. For instance, students who are especially eager to maintain good relationships with others are more likely to act prosocially than their less socially inclined peers (Lawlor & Schonert-Reichl, 2008; Wentzel, Filisetti, & Looney, 2007).

And although students may truly want to do the right thing, they may also be concerned about what positive or negative consequences might result. Students are more apt to behave in moral and prosocial ways if the benefits are high (e.g., they gain others' approval or respect) and the personal costs are low (e.g., the action involves little personal sacrifice) (Batson & Thompson, 2001; Narváez & Rest, 1995).

Finally, students' sense of self seems to be an important factor affecting their inclinations to act morally and prosocially. For one thing, students must believe they are actually capable of helping other people; in other words, they must have high self-efficacy about their ability to make a difference (Narváez & Rest, 1995). Furthermore, in adolescence, some young people begin to integrate a commitment to moral values into their overall sense of identity (Arnold, 2000; Blasi, 1995; Hastings, Utendale, & Sullivan, 2007; Nucci, 2001). They think of themselves as moral, caring individuals who are concerned about the rights and well-being of others. In one study (D. Hart & Fegley, 1995), researchers conducted in-depth interviews with inner-city Hispanic and African American teenagers who showed an exceptional commitment to helping others—by volunteering many hours at Special Olympics, a neighborhood political organization, a nursing home, and so on. These teens did not necessarily display more advanced moral reasoning than their peers, but they were more likely to describe themselves in terms of moral traits and goals (e.g., helping others) and to mention certain ideals toward which they were striving.

Factors Influencing Moral and Prosocial Development

Developmental researchers have identified several factors associated with the development of moral reasoning and prosocial behavior. To some degree, advanced moral reasoning depends on *cognitive development.* In particular, it depends on the ability to think simultaneously about multiple issues (e.g., about various people's motives and intentions in a situation) and also on the ability to comprehend such abstract ideals as justice and basic human rights (Kohlberg, 1976; Nucci, 2006, 2009; Turiel, 2002). However, cognitive development does not *guarantee* moral development. For instance, it is quite possible to think abstractly about academic subject matter and yet reason in a self-centered, preconventional manner (Kohlberg, 1976; Silverman, 1994).

In addition, children are more likely to make gains in moral and prosocial development when adults consistently use **induction**, asking children to think about the harm and distress that some of their behaviors have caused others (M. L. Hoffman, 1970, 1975). Induction is victim centered: It helps students focus on others' distress and recognize that they themselves have been the cause (M. L. Hoffman, 1970). Consistent use of induction in disciplining children, especially when accompanied by *mild* punishment for misbehavior—for instance, insisting that children make amends for their wrongdoings—appears to promote compliance with rules and foster the development of empathy, compassion, and altruism (G. H. Brody & Shaffer, 1982; M. L. Hoffman, 1975; Nucci, 2001; Rushton, 1980).

A third factor that appears to promote moral and prosocial advancements is *disequilibrium*—in particular, encountering moral dilemmas and arguments that children cannot adequately address with their current moral standards and viewpoints. For instance, classroom discussions of controversial topics and moral issues can promote increased perspective taking and a gradual transition to more advanced reasoning (DeVries & Zan, 1996; Power, Higgins, & Kohlberg, 1989; Schlaefli, Rest, & Thoma, 1985). Implicit in this finding is a very important point: Children's moral reasoning does *not* result simply from adults handing down particular moral values and preachings (Damon, 1988; Higgins, 1995; Turiel, 1998). Instead, it emerges out of children's own, personally constructed beliefs—beliefs that they often revisit, revise, and ultimately improve on over time.

Diversity in Moral and Prosocial Development

induction Explanation of why a certain behavior is unacceptable, often with a focus on the pain or distress that someone has caused another.

As we've just seen, some diversity in moral and prosocial development is the result of environmental factors. But biology seems to be involved as well. For example, other things being equal, children who have a somewhat fearful, anxious temperament in infancy tend to show more guilt and empathy in the early elementary grades than their less anxious classmates (Rothbart, 2007). Also, certain human genes seem to give rise to the development of minor brain abnormalities that, in turn, predispose their owners to antisocial behavior (Raine, 2008).

Gender Differences Researchers have observed minor gender differences in moral and prosocial development. For instance, on average, girls are more likely than boys to feel guilt and shame—in part, because they're more willing to take personal responsibility for their misdeeds. Girls are also more likely to feel empathy for people in distress (Alessandri & Lewis, 1993; Lippa, 2002; A. J. Rose, 2002; Zahn-Waxler & Robinson, 1995).

Yet historically, researchers have disagreed about the extent to which girls and boys *reason* differently about situations involving moral issues. In his work with college students and moral dilemmas, Kohlberg found that males reasoned at a slightly more advanced level than females (Kohlberg & Kramer, 1969). However, psychologist Carol Gilligan argued that Kohlberg's stages do not adequately describe female moral development (Gilligan, 1982, 1987; Gilligan & Attanucci, 1988). In particular, she suggested that Kohlberg's stages reflect a *justice orientation*—an emphasis on fairness and equal rights—which characterizes males' moral reasoning. In contrast, females are socialized to take a *care orientation* toward moral issues—that is, to focus on interpersonal relationships and take responsibility for others' well-being. To see how these two orientations might play out differently, try the following exercise.

The Porcupine Dilemma

Consider the following scenario:

> A group of industrious, prudent moles have spent the summer digging a burrow where they will spend the winter. A lazy, improvident porcupine who has not prepared a winter shelter approaches the moles and pleads to share their burrow. The moles take pity on the porcupine and agree to let him in. Unfortunately, the moles did not anticipate the problem the porcupine's sharp quills would pose in close quarters. Once the porcupine has moved in, the moles are constantly being stabbed. (Meyers, 1987, p. 141, adapted from Gilligan, 1985)

- What do you think the moles should do? Why?

According to Gilligan, males are apt to view the problem as involving a violation of someone's rights. They might point out that the burrow belongs to the moles, who can legitimately throw the porcupine out, using physical force if necessary. In contrast, females are more likely to show compassion and caring when addressing the dilemma, perhaps suggesting that the moles cover the porcupine with a blanket so that his quills won't annoy anyone (Meyers, 1987).

Gilligan raised a good point: Males and females are often socialized quite differently, as you'll discover in Chapter 4. Furthermore, by including compassion for other human beings, as well as consideration for their rights, Gilligan broadened our conception of what morality *is* (L. J. Walker, 1995). But in fact, most research studies do *not* find major gender differences in moral reasoning (Eisenberg, Martin, & Fabes, 1996; Nunner-Winkler, 1984; L. J. Walker, 1991). And as Gilligan herself has acknowledged, males and females alike typically reveal concern for both justice and compassion in their moral reasoning (L. M. Brown, Tappan, & Gilligan, 1995; Gilligan & Attanucci, 1988; Turiel, 1998).

Cultural and Ethnic Differences Virtually all cultures worldwide acknowledge the importance of both individual rights and fairness (reflecting a justice orientation) and compassion for others (reflecting a care orientation). However, different cultural groups tend to place greater emphasis on one than on the other (J. G. Miller, 2007; Snarey, 1995; Turiel, 2002). For instance, in the United States, helping others (or not) is often considered to be a voluntary choice, but in some societies (e.g., in India and in many Muslim countries), it is one's *duty* to help people in need. Such a sense of duty, which is often coupled with strong ties to family and community, can lead to considerable prosocial behavior (J. G. Miller, 2007; Greenfield, 1994; Markus & Kitayama, 1991; Triandis, 1995).

Some diversity is also seen in the behaviors that cultural groups view as moral transgressions versus those they see as conventional transgressions (Nucci, 2001, 2009). For instance, in mainstream Western culture, how one dresses is largely a matter of convention and personal choice. In some deeply religious groups, however, certain forms of dress (e.g., head coverings) are seen as moral imperatives that must be adhered to. As another example, in mainstream Western culture, lying to avoid punishment for inappropriate behavior is considered morally wrong, but it is a legitimate way of saving face in certain other cultures (Triandis, 1995). As teachers, then, we must remember that our students' notions of morally appropriate and inappropriate behaviors may sometimes be quite different from our own. At the same time, of course, we should never accept behavior that violates such basic principles as equality and respect for other people's rights and well-being.

Keep in mind that students from diverse cultures may have different ideas about behaviors that are morally desirable (and, in some cases, mandatory) versus behaviors that are morally wrong. If necessary, explain to a student in private that some behaviors considered appropriate in his or her culture are unacceptable in your classroom because they infringe on other people's rights and well-being.

Encouraging Moral and Prosocial Development in the Classroom

In recent years, some prominent, well-meaning individuals have suggested that Western society is in a sharp moral decline; accordingly, they have urged parents and teachers to lecture students about desirable moral traits (honesty, responsibility, etc.) and to firmly discipline students for seemingly immoral behaviors. In fact, there is *no* evidence that the present generation of young people is in any way less moral or prosocial than previous generations (Turiel, 1998, 2002). Furthermore, lecturing students about morally appropriate behavior and imposing firm control on their actions do little to instill a particular set of moral values (Damon, 1988; Higgins, 1995; Turiel, 1998).

As teachers, we play an important role in helping children and adolescents acquire the beliefs, values, and behaviors critical to their effective participation in a democratic and compassionate society—a society in which everyone's rights are respected and everyone's needs are taken into consideration. Following are several general suggestions based on research findings:

Encourage perspective taking, empathy, and prosocial behaviors. Systematic efforts to promote perspective taking, empathy, and such skills as cooperation and helping others do seem to enhance students' moral and prosocial development (J. M. Hughes, Bigler, & Levy, 2007; Nucci, 2009; N. M. Webb & Palincsar, 1996). For instance, when students have interpersonal conflicts, we can encourage them to look at situations from classmates' perspectives and work cooperatively toward an equitable solution (Nucci, 2009; see also the discussion of *peer mediation* in Chapter 10). Perspective taking and empathy can and should be encouraged in the study of academic subject matter as well (e.g., Kahne & Sporte, 2008).

Figure 3.5 shows two writing samples created during history lessons about slavery in the pre–Civil War United States. The reaction paper on the left was written by 10-year-old Charmaine, whose fifth-grade class had been watching *Roots*, a miniseries about a young African man (Kunta Kinte) who is captured and brought to America to be a slave. Charmaine acknowledges that she cannot fully grasp Kunta Kinte's physical pain (her own experience with pain has been limited to having a paper cut in saltwater). Even so, she talks about his "pain" and "fright" and about his parents' "hurt" at losing their firstborn son, and she is incensed by some colonists' view of African women as little more than "beeby [baby] warmers." The diary on the right was written by 14-year-old Craig, whose ninth-grade history teacher asked his class to write journal entries that might capture the life of a Southern plantation owner. Notice that

FIGURE 3.5 Two examples of perspective taking related to slavery

Roots II ON THE BOAT TO AMERICA

I could feel the pain Kunta-Kinte was having. Once I had a paper cut and when in the ocean it hurt more than a wasp sting, and that was just paper cut! I can't even imagine the pain or fright that Kunta-Kinte had being taken from his family and home. Or his parents hurt finding out that their first son was being taken to be a slave, their son that had just become a man. I also am horrified about how they treated women. Bedy-warmers! The makes angre!

My Diary

July 1, 1700
Dear Diary - Today was a scorcher. I could not stand it and I was not even working. The slaves looked so hot. I even felt for them. and it is affecting my tobacco. It's too hot too early in the season. The tobacco plants are not growing quickly enough. I can only hope that it rains. Also today Robert Smith invited me to a ball at his house in two days. In 5 days I am going to have my masked ball. We mailed out the invitations two days ago. My wife, Beth, and I thought of a great idea of a masked ball. We will hire our own band.

July 2, 1700
Dear Diary - It was another scorcher. I wish it would cool down. I don't think the salves can handle it. It looked like some of them would faint. I had them drink more water. Later in the day a nice breeze came up. Then I gave them the rest of the day off. Also today we planned a trip to Richmond. . . .

July 5, 1700
Dear Diary - Today we had to wake up before the sun had risen. After a breakfast of hot cakes, eggs, and sausage, we headed back home. We got there at the end of the morning. When I got back it was very, very hot. One of the slaves fainted so I gave him the rest of the day off, fearing revolt. I also gave them extra food and water. It makes me think that they are only people too. I know that this is unheard of but it really makes me think.

Craig tries to imagine someone else (a plantation owner) taking *other people's* perspectives (those of slaves). Such two-tiered perspective taking is, in a way, similar to recursive thinking, but in this case it is a matter of thinking "I think that you think that someone else thinks . . ." Notice, too, that Craig has the plantation owner engage in some minimal prosocial behavior: giving the slaves time off on hot summer days and providing extra food and water. It may not surprise you to learn that Charmaine and Craig, now young adults, are both actively involved in public service.

Give reasons that some behaviors are unacceptable. Although it is important to impose consequences for immoral and antisocial behaviors, punishment by itself often focuses children's attention primarily on their own hurt and distress (M. L. Hoffman, 1975). To promote moral and prosocial development, we must accompany punishment with induction, focusing students' attention on the hurt and distress their behaviors have caused *others* (Nucci, 2009; M. Watson, 2008). For example, we might describe how a behavior harms someone else either physically ("Having your hair pulled the way you just pulled Mai's can really be painful") or emotionally ("You hurt John's feelings when you call him names like that"). We might also show students how they have caused someone else inconvenience ("Because you ruined Marie's jacket, her parents are making her work around the house to earn the money for a new one"). Still another approach is to explain someone else's perspective, intention, or motive ("This science project you've just ridiculed may not be as fancy as yours, but I know that Jacob spent many hours working on it and is quite proud of what he's done").

Expose students to numerous models of moral and prosocial behavior. Children and adolescents are more likely to exhibit moral and prosocial behavior when they see others (including their teachers!) behaving in moral rather than immoral ways. For instance, when youngsters see adults or peers being generous and showing concern for others, they tend to do likewise (Rushton, 1980; C. C. Wilson, Piazza, & Nagle, 1990). When they watch television shows that emphasize perspective taking and prosocial actions (e.g., *Sesame Street, Saved by the Bell*), they are more inclined to exhibit such behaviors themselves (Dubow, Huesmann, & Greenwood, 2007; Hearold, 1986; Rushton, 1980; Singer & Singer, 1994). Powerful models of moral behavior can be found in literature as well—for instance, in Harper Lee's *To Kill a Mockingbird* and in John Gunther's *Death Be Not Proud* (Ellenwood & Ryan, 1991; Nucci, 2001).

Engage students in discussions of moral issues related to academic subject matter. Social and moral dilemmas often arise within the school curriculum. Consider the following questions that might emerge in discussions about academic topics:

- Is military retaliation for acts of terrorism justified if it involves killing innocent people?
- Should laboratory rats be used to study the effects of cancer-producing agents?
- Was Hamlet justified in killing Claudius to avenge the murder of his father?

Such dilemmas do not always have clear-cut right or wrong answers. As teachers, we can encourage student discussions of such issues in a variety of ways (Reimer et al., 1983):

- Create a trusting and nonthreatening classroom atmosphere, in which students can express their beliefs without fear of censure or embarrassment.
- Help students identify all aspects of a dilemma, including the needs and perspectives of the various individuals involved.
- Encourage students to explore their reasons for thinking as they do—that is, to clarify and reflect on the moral principles on which they are basing their judgments.

service learning Activity that promotes learning and development through contributing to the betterment of others and the outside community.

Get students actively involved in community service. As we've seen, students are more likely to adhere to strong moral principles when they have high self-efficacy for helping others and when they have integrated a commitment to moral ideals into their overall sense of identity. Such self-perceptions don't appear out of the blue, of course. Children are more likely to have high self-efficacy for prosocial activities when they have the guidance and support they need to carry out the activities successfully. And they are more likely to integrate moral and prosocial values into their overall sense of self when they become actively involved in service to others even before they reach puberty (Hastings et al., 2007; Nucci, 2001; Youniss & Yates, 1999). Through ongoing community service activities—sometimes collectively referred to as **service learning**—elementary and secondary students alike learn that they have the skills and the responsibility for helping people in dire straits and in other ways making the world a better place in which to live. In the process, they also begin to think of themselves as concerned, compassionate, and moral citizens who have an obligation to help those less fortunate than themselves (Celio, Durlak, Pachan, & Berger, 2007; D. Hart, Donnelly, Youniss, & Atkins, 2007; Kahne & Sporte, 2008).

Engaging in community service projects encourages students to integrate a commitment to helping others into their overall sense of identity.

The Big Picture

Despite the diversity of topics we've addressed in this chapter, several general themes have been evident throughout:

- ***Students' personal, social, and moral understandings are self-constructed.*** Just as children and adolescents construct their own knowledge and beliefs about the physical world (see Chapter 2), so, too, do they construct their beliefs about themselves (e.g., their self-concepts and identities), the nature of other people (e.g., their interpretations of peers' motives and intentions), and morality (e.g., their definitions of right and wrong).

- ***Social and moral development involves changes not only in behavior but also in social cognition and emotional reactions.*** Underlying effective social and prosocial behaviors are productive ways of thinking about fellow human beings—looking at situations from other people's perspectives, accurately interpreting other people's body language, and so on. Important, too, are feeling empathy and sympathy for people in distress and feeling guilty and ashamed when one has been the cause of that distress.

• ***Interactions with other people provide the impetus for many personal and social advancements.*** Social interaction is critical not only for children's cognitive development (again see Chapter 2) but also for their personal and social development. For example, students learn a great deal about their own strengths and weaknesses by observing and interacting with others. Relationships with peers provide an arena in which to practice existing social skills and experiment with new ones. And conversations about controversial issues encourage greater perspective taking and more advanced moral reasoning.

• ***Development is best fostered within the context of a warm, supportive environment that also provides structure and support for productive behaviors.*** Well-adjusted children are often those who grow up in an authoritative environment that combines affection and respect with rules for appropriate behavior, rationales for those rules, and reasonable negative consequences for rule infractions. Furthermore, a healthy sense of self and good social skills are best fostered by positive feedback for things well done *and* by scaffolded opportunities to tackle new personal and social challenges.

Practice for Your Licensure Exam

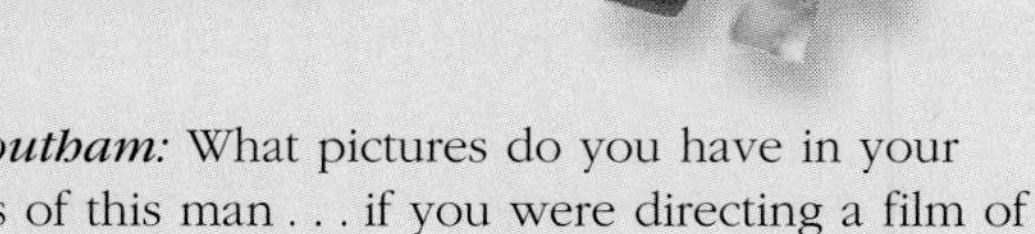

The Scarlet Letter

Ms. Southam's eleventh-grade English class has been reading Nathaniel Hawthorne's *The Scarlet Letter.* Set in seventeenth-century Boston, the novel focuses largely on two characters who have been carrying on an illicit love affair: Hester Prynne, a young woman who has not seen or heard from her husband for the past two years, and the Reverend Arthur Dimmesdale, a pious and well-respected local preacher. When Hester becomes pregnant, she is imprisoned for adultery and soon bears a child. The class is currently discussing Chapter 3, in which the governor and town leaders, including Dimmesdale, are urging Hester to name the baby's father:

> **myeducationlab**
> Observe this lesson firsthand in the video "Scarlet Letter." (To find this video, go to Chapter 3 of the Book-Specific Resources in MyEducationLab, select *Video Examples*, and then click on the title.)

> ***Ms. Southam:*** The father of the baby . . . How do you know it's Dimmesdale—the Reverend Arthur Dimmesdale? . . . What are the clues in the text in Chapter 3? . . . Nicole?
> ***Nicole:*** He acts very withdrawn. He doesn't even want to be involved with the situation. He wants the other guy to question her, because he doesn't want to look her in the face and ask her to name *him.*
> ***Ms. Southam:*** OK. Anything else? . . .
> ***Student:*** The baby.
> ***Ms. Southam:*** What about the baby?
> ***Student:*** She starts to cry, and her eyes follow him.
> ***Ms. Southam:*** That is one of my absolutely favorite little Hawthornisms.

Ms. Southam reads a paragraph about Dimmesdale and then asks students to jot down their thoughts about him. She then walks around the room, monitoring what students are doing until they appear to have finished writing.

> ***Ms. Southam:*** What pictures do you have in your minds of this man . . . if you were directing a film of *The Scarlet Letter?*
> ***Mike:*** I don't have a person in mind, just characteristics. About five-foot-ten, short, well-groomed hair, well dressed. He looks really nervous and inexperienced. Guilty look on his face. Always nervous, shaking a lot.
> ***Ms. Southam:*** He's got a guilty look on his face. His lips always trembling, always shaking.
> ***Mike:*** He's very unsure about himself.
> ***Matt:*** Sweating really bad. Always going like this. [He shows how Dimmesdale might be wiping his forehead.] He does . . . he has his hanky . . .
> ***Ms. Southam:*** Actually, we don't see him mopping his brow, but we do see him doing what? What's the action? Do you remember? If you go to the text, he's holding his hand over his heart, as though he's somehow suffering some pain.
> ***Student:*** Wire-framed glasses . . . I don't know why. He's like . . .
> ***Mike:*** He's kind of like a nerd-type guy . . . short pants. Michael J. Fox's dad . . . [Mike is referring to a nerdish character in the film *Back to the Future.*]
> ***Ms. Southam:*** With the short pants and everything.
> ***Student:*** Yeah, George McFly. [Student identifies the nerdish character's name in the film.]
> ***Ms. Southam:*** George McFly in his younger years. But at the same time . . . I don't know if it was somebody in this class or somebody in another class . . . He said, "Well, she was sure *worth* it." Worth risking your immortal soul for, you know? . . . Obviously she's sinned, but so has he, right? And if she was worth it, don't we also have to see him as somehow having been worthy of her risking *her* soul for this?
> ***Student:*** Maybe he's got a good personality . . .

Ms. Southam: He apparently is, you know, a spell-binding preacher. He really can grab the crowd.
Student: It's his eyes. Yeah, the eyes.
Ms. Southam: Those brown, melancholy eyes. Yeah, those brown, melancholy eyes. Absolutely.

1. Constructed-response question:

In this classroom dialogue, Ms. Southam and her students speculate about what the characters in the novel, especially Arthur Dimmesdale, might be thinking and feeling. In other words, they are engaging in social cognition.

A. Identify two examples of student statements that show social cognition.

B. For each example you identify, explain what it reveals about the speaker's social cognition.

2. Multiple-choice question:

Ms. Southam does several things that are apt to enhance students' perspective-taking ability. Which one of the following is the best example?

a. She models enthusiasm for the novel ("That is one of my absolutely favorite little Hawthornisms").

b. She walks around the room as the students write down their thoughts about Dimmesdale.

c. She points out that Dimmesdale is "holding his hand over his heart, as though he's somehow suffering some pain."

d. She agrees with Mike's comparison of Dimmesdale to a character in the film *Back to the Future.*

Go to Chapter 3 of the Book-Specific Resources in **MyEducationLab** and click on "Practice for Your Licensure Exam" to answer these questions. Compare your responses with the feedback provided.

PRAXIS

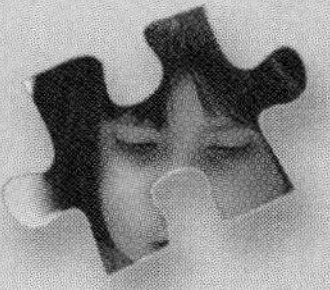

Turn to Appendix C, "Matching Book and MyEducationLab Content to the Praxis Principles of Learning and Teaching Tests," to discover sections of this chapter that may be especially applicable to the Praxis tests.

PEARSON myeducationlab

Now go to MyEducationLab (**www.myeducationlab.com**), where you can:

- Find learning outcomes for Personal, Social, and Moral Development, along with the national standards that connect to these outcomes.
- Complete Assignments and Activities that can help you more deeply understand the chapter content.
- Engage in Building Teaching Skills and Dispositions exercises in which you can apply and practice core teaching skills identified in the chapter.
- Access Book-Specific Resources:
    - Check your comprehension of chapter content by going to the Study Plan, where you can find (a) Chapter Objectives; (b) Focus Questions that can guide your reading; (c) a Self-Check Quiz that can help you monitor your progress in mastering chapter content; (d) Review, Practice, and Enrichment exercises with detailed feedback that will deepen your understanding of various concepts and principles; (e) Flashcards that can give you practice in understanding and defining key terms; and (f) Common Beliefs and Misconceptions about Educational Psychology that will alert you to typical misunderstandings in educational psychology classes.
    - Video Examples of various concepts and principles presented in the chapter.
    - A Practice for Your Licensure Exam exercise that resembles the kinds of questions appearing on many teacher licensure tests.

CHAPTER OUTLINE

CHAPTER OBJECTIVES

- **Objective 4.1:** Describe frequently observed between-group differences and within-group variability for various cultural and ethnic groups; also describe the teacher attitudes and teaching strategies that underlie culturally responsive teaching.
- **Objective 4.2:** Describe the nature and origins of typical gender differences in school-age children and adolescents, and explain how you can accommodate such differences in your classroom.
- **Objective 4.3:** Identify challenges that students from low-income families often face, along with several strategies through which you can foster their resilience and help them be successful at school.
- **Objective 4.4:** Explain how you might identify students who are at risk for academic failure and dropping out of school, and identify strategies for helping these students get on the path to academic and social success.

Chapter 4

Group Differences

CASE STUDY: Why Jack Wasn't in School

Jack was a Native American seventh grader who lived in the Navajo Nation in the American Southwest. Although he enjoyed school, worked hard in his studies, and got along well with his classmates, he had been absent from school all week. In fact, he had been absent from home as well, and his family (which didn't have a telephone) wasn't sure exactly where he was.

Jack's English teacher described the situation to Donna Deyhle, an educator who had known Jack for many years:

> That seventh grader was away from home for 5 days, and his parents don't care! . . . Almost one-third of my Navajo students were absent this week. Their parents just don't support their education. How can I teach when they are not in my classes? (Deyhle & LeCompte, 1999, p. 127)

A few days later, Jack's sister explained why her parents had eventually begun to look for Jack:

> He went to see [the film] Rambo II with friends and never came home. If he was in trouble we would know. But now the family needs him to herd sheep tomorrow. (Deyhle & LeCompte, 1999, p. 127)

It was spring—time for the family to plant crops and shear the sheep—and all family members needed to help out. Jack's whereabouts were soon discovered, and the family stopped by Donna's house to share the news:

> As they unfolded from the car, Jack's dad said, "We found him." His mother turned in his direction and said teasingly, "Now maybe school will look easy!" Jack stayed at home for several days, helping with the irrigation of the corn field, before he decided to return to school. (Deyhle & LeCompte, 1999, p. 128)

- **Jack's parents didn't insist that he attend school every day. Did you interpret Jack's absence from school in the same way his English teacher did, concluding that "his parents don't care" about his education?**
- **On the surface, Jack's parents appeared unconcerned that he had not come home. But most parents care deeply about their children's safety and welfare. What alternative explanations might account for the parents' delay in looking for Jack?**

IF YOU ARE A PRODUCT OF MAINSTREAM WESTERN CULTURE, you may have concluded that neither Jack nor his parents cared much about Jack's education. But in reality, most Navajo people—Jack and his parents included—fully recognize the importance of a good education. To truly understand what transpired in Jack's family, we need to know a couple of things about Navajo culture. First, Navajo people place high value on individual autonomy: People must respect others' right (even children's right) to make their own decisions (Deyhle & LeCompte, 1999). From this perspective, good parenting doesn't mean demanding that children do certain things or behave in certain ways; thus, Jack's parents didn't insist that Jack come home after the movie. Instead, Navajo parents offer suggestions and guidance, perhaps in the form of gentle teasing ("Now maybe school will look easy!"), that nudge children toward productive choices. If children make poor choices despite their parents' guidance, they often learn a great deal from the consequences.

But in addition to individual autonomy, Navajos value cooperation and interdependence, believing that community members should work together for the common good. Even though Jack enjoyed school, when he returned home, his highest priority was helping his family. In the Navajo view, people must cooperate of their own free will; being forced to help others is not true cooperation at all (Chisholm, 1996). Such respect for both individual decision making and cooperative interdependence is seen in many other Native American communities as well (Rogoff, 2003; Tyler et al., 2008).

FIGURE 4.1 Typical difference between boys and girls on tests of verbal ability

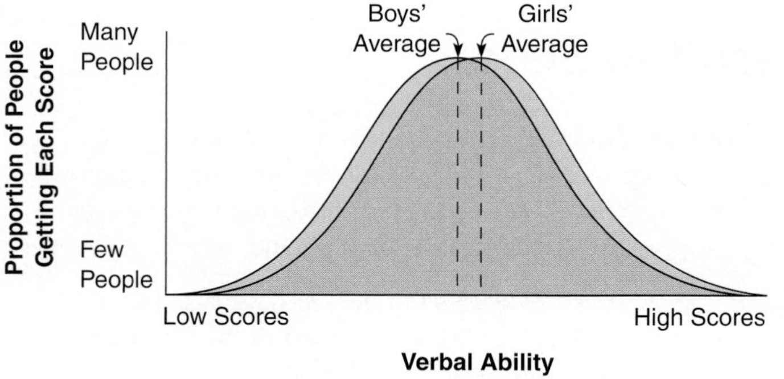

In Chapters 2 and 3, we occasionally looked at how children might develop somewhat differently depending on their cultural background, gender, or family income level. In this chapter, we'll look in depth at such **group differences**—in particular, differences we are apt to see *on average* among students of diverse cultural and ethnic groups, different genders, or different socioeconomic backgrounds. As we do so, we must keep in mind two very important points. First, *a great deal of individual variability exists within any group.* We'll be examining research regarding how students of different groups behave *on average*, even though some students may be very different from that average description. Second, *a great deal of overlap typically exists between two groups.*

Consider gender differences in verbal ability as an example. Many research studies have found girls to have slightly higher verbal ability than boys (Halpern & LaMay, 2000). The difference is often statistically significant—that is, it probably wasn't a one-time-in-a-hundred fluke that happened simply by chance. Yet the average difference between girls and boys in overall verbal ability is quite small, with a great deal of overlap between the sexes. Figure 4.1 shows the typical overlap between girls and boys on general measures of verbal ability. Notice that some boys (those whose scores fall in the rightmost part of their curve) have higher verbal ability than most of their female peers despite the average advantage for girls.

Remember that, despite average group differences, there is considerable variability within any group and considerable overlap between any two groups.

If we are to maximize the learning and development of all of our students, we must be aware of group differences that may influence their learning and classroom performance. Our challenge is to keep these differences in mind without assuming that all members of a particular group fit typical group patterns.[1]

Cultural and Ethnic Differences

The concept of **culture** encompasses the behaviors and belief systems that characterize a long-standing social group. The culture in which we live influences the perspectives and values we acquire, the skills we master and find important, and the adult roles to which we aspire. It also guides the development of our language and communication skills, our expression and regulation of emotions, and our formation of a sense of self.

Sometimes we use the word *culture* to refer to behaviors and beliefs that are widely shared over a large geographic area. As an example, *mainstream Western cul-*

group differences Consistently observed differences (on average) among diverse groups of students (e.g., students of different genders or ethnic backgrounds).

culture Behaviors and belief systems of a long-standing social group.

[1]Teachers' preconceived notions about how students will behave may actually *increase* differences among those students—a phenomenon we'll look at more closely in Chapter 11.

ture encompasses behaviors, beliefs, and values shared by many people in North America and Western Europe. Members of this culture generally value self-reliance, academic achievement, democratic decision making, and respect for other individuals' rights and possessions, among other things. However, any single country in North America or Western Europe—in fact, almost every country on the planet—encompasses considerable cultural diversity within its borders. Some of this within-country diversity is the result of growing up in particular geographic regions, religious groups, or socioeconomic circumstances (e.g., Payne, 2005). In addition, most countries include citizens from a variety of ethnic groups. In general, an **ethnic group** is a group of individuals with a common culture and the following characteristics:

- Its roots either precede the creation of or are external to the country in which it resides. It may be comprised of people of the same race, national origin, or religious background.
- Its members share a sense of interdependence—a sense that their lives are intertwined. (NCSS Task Force on Ethnic Studies Curriculum Guidelines, 1992)

Holiday Family Traditions
Ever year I do
a grinnger bread makeing
party with all of
my friends at and
with my cousins too.

Considerable diversity exists even within a single culture. For example, different families may celebrate the same religious holiday quite differently. Making a gingerbread house is an annual holiday tradition at 7-year-old Emma's house.

Cultures are not static entities. Instead, they continue to change over time as they incorporate new ideas, innovations, and ways of thinking, particularly as they interact with other cultures (Kitayama, Duffy, & Uchida, 2007; O. Lee, 1999; Rogoff, 2003). Furthermore, there is considerable variation in attitudes and behaviors within a particular culture; individual members may adopt some cultural values and societal practices but reject others (Markus & Hamedani, 2007; Tudge et al., 1999).

When people come into contact with a culture very different from their own (e.g., through immigration to a new country), many of them—especially children—gradually undergo **acculturation**, adopting some of the values and customs of that new culture. Some degree of acculturation is critical for success in the new cultural environment, but *rapid* acculturation can be detrimental to children's social and emotional well-being. In most instances, children's own cultural groups give them a support network and stable set of values that enable them to do well in school and maintain their self-esteem in the face of discrimination and other challenges (P. M. Cole & Tan, 2007; Deyhle, 2008; Matute-Bianchi, 2008).

In general, we can get the best sense of students' cultural backgrounds and ethnic-group memberships by learning the extent to which they have participated and continue to participate in various cultural and ethnic-group activities (Gutiérrez & Rogoff, 2003). For example, some Mexican American students live in small, close-knit communities where Spanish is spoken and traditional Mexican practices and beliefs permeate everyday life, but others live in more culturally heterogeneous communities in which Mexican traditions may be cast aside to make time for mainstream American activities. And in some instances, students may participate actively in two or more cultures, perhaps because they have immigrated from one country to another or perhaps because their parents come from distinctly different ethnic or racial backgrounds (Herman, 2004; A. M. Lopez, 2003; Root, 1999).

In general, membership in a particular cultural or ethnic group is a more-or-less phenomenon rather than an either-or situation. As teachers, we must acknowledge—both to ourselves and to our students—that in this age of increasing cross-cultural interaction, many people cannot easily be pigeonholed.

Keep in mind that some students may have multiple cultural affiliations.

ethnic group People who have common historical roots, values, beliefs, and behaviors and who share a sense of interdependence.

acculturation Gradual process of adopting the values and customs of a new culture.

Navigating Different Cultures at Home and at School

You may recall from Chapter 3 that many children entering school for the first time experience some culture shock. This culture shock is more intense for some students than for others. Because most schools in North America and western Europe are based largely on mainstream Western culture, students with this cultural upbringing often

myeducationlab

Hear an expert discuss the issue of cultural mismatch in the video "Incorporating the Home Experiences of Culturally Diverse Students into the Classroom—Part 3." (To find this video, go to Chapter 4 of the Book-Specific Resources in MyEducationLab, select *Video Examples*, and then click on the title.)

adjust quickly to the classroom environment. But students who come from cultural backgrounds with very different norms for acceptable behavior may experience a **cultural mismatch** between home and school (A. S. Cole & Ibarra, 2005; Igoa, 1995; Payne, 2005; Tyler et al., 2008). In particular, they may find school a confusing place where they don't know what to expect from others or what behaviors others expect of them. Significant differences between home and school cultures can interfere with students' adjustment to the school setting and ultimately with their academic achievement as well (García, 1995; Phalet, Andriessen, & Lens, 2004; Phelan et al., 1994).

Cultural mismatch is compounded when teachers misinterpret the behaviors of students from cultural and ethnic minority groups. The following exercise provides an example.

EXPERIENCING FIRSTHAND

Ruckus in the Lunchroom

In the following passage, a young adolescent named Sam describes an incident in the school cafeteria to his friend Joe:

> I got in line behind Bubba. As usual the line was moving pretty slow and we were all getting pretty restless. For a little action Bubba turned around and said, "Hey Sam! What you doin' man? You so ugly that when the doctor delivered you he slapped your face!" Everyone laughed, but they laughed even harder when I shot back, "Oh yeah? Well, you so ugly the doctor turned around and slapped your momma!" It got even wilder when Bubba said, "Well, man, at least my daddy ain't no girl scout!" We really got into it then. After a while more people got involved—4, 5, then 6. It was a riot! People helping out anyone who seemed to be getting the worst of the deal. All of a sudden Mr. Reynolds the gym teacher came over to try to quiet things down. The next thing we knew we were all in the office. The principal made us stay after school for a week; he's so straight! On top of that, he sent word home that he wanted to talk to our folks in his office Monday afternoon. Boy! Did I get it when I got home. That's the third notice I've gotten this semester. As we were leaving the principal's office, I ran into Bubba again. We decided we'd finish where we left off, but this time we would wait until we were off the school grounds. (R. E. Reynolds, Taylor, Steffensen, Shirey, & Anderson, 1982, p. 358)

- Exactly what happened in the school cafeteria? Were the boys fighting? Or were they simply having a good time?

The story you just read depicts "playing the dozens," a friendly exchange of insults common among male youth in some African American communities. Some boys engage in such exchanges to achieve status among their peers—those who concoct the biggest insults are the winners—whereas others do it simply for amusement. If you interpreted the cafeteria incident as a knock-down, drag-out fight, you're hardly alone; many eighth graders in a research study did likewise (R. E. Reynolds et al., 1982). But put yourself in the place of Sam, the child who narrates the story. If you were punished simply for what was, in your mind, an enjoyable game of verbal one-upmanship, you might understandably feel angry and alienated.

As students gain experience with the culture of their school, they become increasingly aware of their teachers' and peers' expectations for behavior and ways of thinking, and many eventually become adept at switching their cultural vantage point as they move from home to school and back again (Y. Hong, Morris, Chiu, & Benet-Martínez, 2000; LaFromboise, Coleman, & Gerton, 1993; Matute-Bianchi, 2008). One Mexican American student's recollection provides an example:

cultural mismatch Situation in which a child's home culture and the school culture hold conflicting expectations for behavior.

> At home with my parents and grandparents the only acceptable language was Spanish; actually that's all they really understood. Everything was really Mexican, but at the same

> time they wanted me to speak good English. . . . But at school, I felt really different because everyone was American, including me. Then I would go home in the afternoon and be Mexican again. (Padilla, 1994, p. 30)

Not all students make an easy adjustment, however. Some students actively resist adapting to the school culture, perhaps because they view it as being inconsistent with—even contradictory to—their own cultural background and identity (Cross et al., 1999; Irving & Hudley, 2008; Phelan et al., 1994). Still others try desperately to fit in at school yet find the inconsistencies between home and school difficult to resolve, as you'll see in this report from a teacher who worked with immigrant Muslim children from Pakistan and Afghanistan:

> During the days of preparation for Ramadan Feast, the children fasted with the adults. . . . They had breakfast [before dawn] and then went back to sleep until it was time to get themselves ready for school. In school they refrained from food or drink—even a drop of water—until sunset. By noon, especially on warm days, they were a bit listless. . . . They spoke about their obligation to pray five times daily. In their writing they expressed the conflict within: "*I always think about my country. I think about going there one day, seeing it and practicing my religion with no problems. . . . Before sunrise, I can pray with my family. But at school we can't say to my teacher, "Please, teacher, I need to pray.*" (Igoa, 1995, p. 135)

When we don't understand students' cultural traditions, our relationships with them—and thus their classroom success—are likely to suffer as a result (Banks et al., 2005; Gay, 2006). As teachers, we must do our part by learning as much as we can about the ways in which students from various cultural and ethnic backgrounds are apt to be different from one another and from ourselves. Equipped with such knowledge, we can make reasonable accommodations to help students from all walks of life adjust to and thrive in our classrooms.

Examples of Cultural and Ethnic Diversity

Tremendous cultural variation exists within African American, Hispanic, Asian American, Native American, and European American groups. Thus, we must be careful not to form stereotypes about *any* group. At the same time, knowledge of frequently observed cultural differences can sometimes help us better understand why students behave as they do. Psychologists and educators have identified many ways in which students from diverse backgrounds may, on average, think and act differently.

Language and Dialect One obvious cultural difference is language. As we noted in our discussion of English language learners (ELLs) in Chapter 2, several million students in American schools speak a language other than English at home. But even when children do speak English at home, they may use a form of English different from the **Standard English** typically considered acceptable at school. More specifically, they may speak in a different **dialect**, a form of a particular language that includes some unique pronunciations and grammatical structures. Dialects tend to be associated either with particular geographical regions or with particular ethnic and cultural groups (e.g., see Wolfram & Schilling-Estes, 2006).

Perhaps the most widely studied ethnic dialect is **African American English** (also known as *Black English Vernacular* or *Ebonics*). This dialect, which is actually a group of similar dialects, is used in many African American communities throughout the United States and is characterized by certain unique pronunciations, idioms, and grammatical constructions, such as the following:

- The *th* sound at the beginning of a word is often pronounced as *d* (e.g., *that* is pronounced "dat").
- The *-ed* ending on past-tense verbs is often dropped (e.g., "We walk to the park last night").

Standard English Form of English generally considered acceptable at school, as reflected in textbooks and grammar instruction.

dialect Form of a language that has certain unique pronunciations and grammatical structures and is characteristic of a particular region or ethnic group.

African American English Dialect of some African American communities that includes some pronunciations, idioms, and grammatical constructions different from those of Standard English.

- The present- and past-tense forms of the verb *to be* are consistently *is* and *was*, even if the subject of the sentence is the pronoun *I* or a plural noun or pronoun (e.g., "I is runnin'," "They was runnin'").
- The verb *is* is often dropped in simple descriptive sentences (e.g., "He a handsome man").
- The word *be* is used to indicate a constant or frequently occurring characteristic (e.g., "He be talking" describes someone who talks much of the time) (Hulit & Howard, 2006, pp. 345–346).

At one time, many researchers believed that an African American dialect represented a less complex form of speech than Standard English and urged educators to teach students to speak "properly" as quickly as possible. But most researchers now realize that African American dialects are, in fact, very complex languages that promote communication and sophisticated thought processes as readily as Standard English (Alim & Baugh, 2007; Fairchild & Edwards-Evans, 1990; Hulit & Howard, 2006).

When a local dialect is the language preferred by residents of a community, it is often the means through which people can most effectively connect with one another in day-to-day interactions. Furthermore, many children and adolescents view their native dialect as an integral part of their ethnic identity (McAlpine, 1992; Ogbu, 2003; Tatum, 1997). The following incident, which took place among rural Native American students at a public boarding school in Alaska, illustrates this point:

> Many of the students at the school spoke English with a native dialect and seemed unable to utter certain essential sounds in the English language. . . . The teachers worked consistently with the students in an attempt to improve speech patterns and intonation, but found that their efforts were in vain.
>
> One night, the boys in the dormitory were seeming to have too much fun, and peals of laughter were rolling out from under the door. An investigating counselor approached cautiously, and listened quietly outside the door to see if he could discover the source of the laughter. From behind the door he heard a voice, speaking in perfect English, giving instructions to the rest of the crowd. The others were finding the situation very amusing. When the counselor entered the room he found that one of the students was speaking. "Joseph," he said, "you've been cured! Your English is perfect." "No," said Joseph returning to his familiar dialect, "I was just doing an imitation of you." "But if you can speak in standard English, why don't you do it all of the time?" the counselor queried. "I can," responded Joseph, "but it sounds funny, and I feel dumb doing it." (Garrison, 1989, p. 121)

Many people in mainstream Western culture associate higher social status with people who speak Standard English and perceive speakers of other dialects in a less favorable light (DeBose, 2007; Purcell-Gates, 1995; H. L. Smith, 1998). In addition, children who are familiar with Standard English have an easier time learning to read than those who are not (Charity, Scarborough, & Griffin, 2004; T. A. Roberts, 2005). For such reasons, most experts recommend that all students in English-speaking countries develop proficiency in Standard English (e.g., Craft, 1984; DeBose, 2007; Ogbu, 1999). Ultimately, children and adolescents function most effectively when they can use both their local dialect and Standard English in appropriate settings. For example, although we may wish to encourage Standard English in most written work or in formal oral presentations, we might find other dialects quite appropriate in creative writing or informal classroom discussions (DeBose, 2007; Ogbu, 1999, 2003; Smitherman, 1994).

Encourage students to use both Standard English and their local dialect, each in appropriate settings.

Talking versus Remaining Silent Relatively speaking, mainstream Western culture is a chatty one. People often say things to one another even when they have very little to communicate, making small talk as a way of maintaining interpersonal relationships and filling awkward silences (Irujo, 1988; Trawick-Smith, 2003). In some

African American communities as well, people speak frequently and often with a great deal of energy and enthusiasm (Gay, 2006; Tyler et al., 2008). In certain other cultures, however, silence is golden (Norenzayan, Choi, & Peng, 2007; Trawick-Smith, 2003). For example, many people from Southeast Asian countries believe that effective learning is best accomplished through attentive listening, rather than through speaking (J. Li, 2005; J. Li & Fischer, 2004; Volet, 1999).

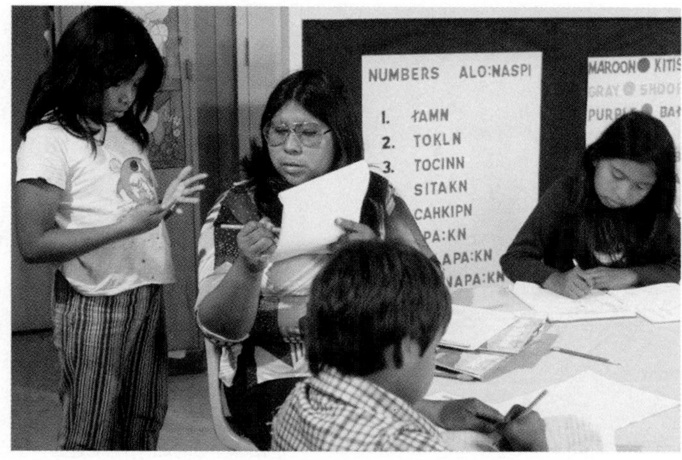

In some cultures, including many Native American communities, children are taught to look down as a sign of respect to an adult who speaks to them.

Different cultural and ethnic groups also have diverse views about when it is appropriate for children to speak to adults. In mainstream Western culture, a common expectation is that children will speak up whenever they have comments or questions. Yet in many parts of the world, children are expected to learn primarily by close, quiet observation of adults, rather than by asking questions or otherwise interrupting what adults are doing (Correa-Chávez, Rogoff, & Mejía Arauz, 2005; Gutiérrez & Rogoff, 2003; Kağitçibaşi, 2007). And in some cultures—for instance, in many Mexican American and Southeast Asian communities and in some African American communities—children learn very early that they should engage in conversation with adults only when their participation has been directly solicited (Delgado-Gaitan, 1994; C. A. Grant & Gomez, 2001; Ochs, 1982). In fact, children from some backgrounds—including many Puerto Ricans, Mexican Americans, and Native Americans—have been taught that speaking directly and assertively to adults is rude, perhaps even rebellious (Banks & Banks, 1995; Delgado-Gaitan, 1994).

Keep in mind that some students have been taught that initiating a conversation with an adult is rude or disrespectful.

Emotional Expressiveness On average, cultural groups differ in the degree to which they reveal their feelings in their behaviors and facial expressions. For example, whereas Americans and Mexicans are often quite expressive, children from East Asian cultures are encouraged to be more reserved (P. M. Cole & Tan, 2007; Morelli & Rothbaum, 2007). Considerable variability exists in any large society, of course. For instance, in one study with Americans, people of Irish ancestry were more apt to reveal their feelings in their facial expressions than were people of Scandinavian ancestry (Tsai & Chentsova-Dutton, 2003).

Also keep in mind that some students may have been socialized to hide their emotions.

The emotion for which cultural differences are most prevalent is anger. Mainstream Western culture encourages children to act and speak up if someone infringes on their rights and needs, and expressing anger in a nonviolent way is considered quite acceptable. In many Southeast Asian cultures, however, any expression of anger is viewed as potentially undermining adults' authority or disrupting social harmony (Mesquita & Leu, 2007; Morelli & Rothbaum, 2007; Zahn-Waxler, Friedman, Cole, Mizuta, & Hiruma, 1996).

Eye Contact For many of us, looking someone in the eye is a way to show that we are trying to communicate or are listening intently to what the person is saying. But in many Native American, African American, Mexican American, and Puerto Rican communities, a child who looks an adult in the eye is showing disrespect. In these communities, children are taught to look down in the presence of adults (Irujo, 1988; Torres-Guzmán, 1998; Tyler et al., 2008). The following anecdote shows how a teacher's recognition of children's beliefs about eye contact can make a difference:

Don't rely on eye contact as the only indicator that students are paying attention.

> A teacher [described a Native American] student who would never say a word, nor even answer when she greeted him. Then one day when he came in she looked in the other direction and said, "Hello, Jimmy." He answered enthusiastically, "Why hello Miss Jacobs." She found that he would always talk if she looked at a book or at the wall, but when she looked at him, he appeared frightened. (Gilliland, 1988, p. 26)

Personal Space In some cultures, such as those in some African American and Hispanic communities, people stand close together when they talk, and they may touch one another frequently (Hale-Benson, 1986; Slonim, 1991; D. W. Sue, 1990). In contrast, European Americans and Japanese Americans tend to keep a fair distance from one another, maintaining some **personal space**, especially if they don't know each other very well (Irujo, 1988; Trawick-Smith, 2003). As teachers, we must be sensitive to the personal space that students from various cultural backgrounds need in order to feel comfortable in interactions with us and with classmates.

Responding to Questions A common interaction pattern in many Western classrooms is the **IRE cycle**: A teacher *initiates* an interaction by asking a question, a student *responds* to the question, and the teacher *evaluates* the response (Mehan, 1979). Similar interactions are often found in parent–child interactions in middle-income European American homes. For instance, when my own children were toddlers and preschoolers, I often asked them questions such as "How old are you?" and "What does a cow say?" and praised them when they answered correctly. But children reared in other environments—for example, in many lower-income homes, as well as in some Central American, Native American, and Hawaiian communities—are unfamiliar with such question-and-answer sessions when they first come to school (Losey, 1995; Rogoff, 2003, 2007). Furthermore, some children may be quite puzzled when a teacher asks questions to which he or she already knows the answers (Crago, Annahatak, & Ningiuruvik, 1993; Heath, 1989; Rogoff, 2003).

Be aware that some children are unaccustomed to answering certain kinds of questions.

The issue is not that children are unaccustomed to questions; it's that they have little experience with certain *kinds* of questions. For example, parents in African American communities in parts of the southeastern United States are more likely to ask questions involving comparisons and analogies. Rather than ask "What's that?" they may instead ask "What's that *like*?" (Heath, 1980, 1989). In addition, children in these communities are specifically taught *not* to answer questions from strangers about personal and home life—questions such as "What's your name?" and "Where do you live?" The complaints of parents in these communities illustrate how much of a cultural mismatch there can be between students and their European American teachers:

> "My kid, he too scared to talk, 'cause nobody play by the rules he know. At home I can't shut him up."
>
> "Miss Davis, she complain 'bout Ned not answerin' back. He says she asks dumb questions she already know about." (Heath, 1980, p. 107)

Teachers' comments about these children reflect their own lack of understanding about the culture from which the children come:

> "I would almost think some of them have a hearing problem; it is as though they don't hear me ask a question. I get blank stares to my questions. Yet when I am making statements or telling stories which interest them, they always seem to hear me."
>
> "The simplest questions are the ones they can't answer in the classroom; yet on the playground, they can explain a rule for a ballgame or describe a particular kind of bait with no problem. Therefore, I know they can't be as dumb as they seem in my class." (Heath, 1980, pp. 107–108)

personal space Personally or culturally preferred distance between two people during social interaction.

IRE cycle Adult–child interaction marked by adult initiation (usually involving a question), child response, and adult evaluation.

wait time Length of time a teacher pauses, either after asking a question or hearing a student's comment, before saying something else.

Waiting versus Interrupting Teachers frequently ask their students a question and then wait for an answer. But exactly how long do they wait? The typical **wait time** for many teachers is a second or even less; at that point, they either answer a question themselves or call on another student (M. B. Rowe, 1974, 1987). Yet people from some cultures use lengthy pauses before responding as a way of indicating respect, as this statement by a Northern Cheyenne individual illustrates:

> Even if I had a quick answer to your question, I would never answer immediately. That would be saying that your question was not worth thinking about. (Gilliland, 1988, p. 27)

Students from such cultures are more likely to participate in class and answer questions when given several seconds to respond (Castagno & Brayboy, 2008; Mohatt & Erickson, 1981; Tharp, 1989). Not only does such an extended wait time allow students to show respect, but it also gives those with limited English proficiency some mental translation time (Gilliland, 1988). Furthermore, increasing wait time enhances thinking and learning, as we'll discover in Chapter 6.

Increase the wait time as a means of encouraging students from diverse backgrounds to participate in discussions.

In contrast, children from certain other backgrounds may interrupt adults or peers who haven't finished speaking—behavior that many from mainstream Western culture might interpret as rudeness. For instance, in some African American, Hawaiian, and Jewish cultures, adults and children alike may speak spontaneously and simultaneously, perhaps to show personal involvement in a conversation or perhaps to avoid being excluded from the conversation altogether (Farber, Mindel, & Lazerwitz, 1988; Hale-Benson, 1986; Tharp, 1989; Tyler et al., 2008).

Public versus Private Performance In many classrooms, learning is a very public enterprise. Individual students are often expected to answer questions or demonstrate skills in full view of their classmates, and they are encouraged to ask questions themselves when they don't understand. Such practices, which many teachers take for granted, may confuse or even alienate the students of some ethnic groups (Eriks-Brophy & Crago, 1994; García, 1994; Lomawaima, 1995). For example, many Native American children are accustomed to practicing a skill privately at first, performing in front of a group only after they have attained a reasonable level of mastery (Castagno & Brayboy, 2008; Suina & Smolkin, 1994). And children in some Native American and Hawaiian communities may feel more comfortable responding to adults' questions as a group, rather than interacting with adults one on one (K. H. Au, 1980; L. S. Miller, 1995).

Accommodate students who prefer to practice new skills in private.

Views About Teasing Although some people think of teasing as mean spirited and inappropriate, it is a common form of social interaction in some cultures. For example, in the "Ruckus in the Lunchroom" exercise presented earlier, two African American boys engaged in one-upmanship, flinging increasingly outlandish insults at each other. And in the opening case study, Jack's mother teased him by suggesting that "Now maybe school will look easy!" When taken in the right spirit, teasing serves a variety of functions for particular cultural groups—perhaps providing a source of amusement and an outlet for verbal creativity, exerting gentle pressure to engage in more productive behavior, or helping children learn how to take criticism in stride (P. M. Cole, Tamang, & Shrestha, 2006; Rogoff, 2003).

Cooperation versus Competition In a traditional Western classroom, learning is often a solitary, individual endeavor: Students receive praise, stickers, and good grades when they perform at high levels, regardless of how their classmates perform. Sometimes individual school achievement is even quite competitive, such that students' performance is evaluated by comparing it with that of classmates (e.g., teachers grade on a curve or post "best" papers on the bulletin board).

Yet in some cultures—including many Native American, Mexican American, African, Southeast Asian, and Pacific Island communities—it is *group* achievement, rather than individual achievement, that is recognized: The success of the village or community is valued over personal success. Students from these cultures are often more accustomed to working cooperatively and for the benefit of the community, rather than for themselves (Lomawaima, 1995; Mejía-Arauz, Rogoff, Dexter, & Najafi, 2007; Tharp, 1994; Tyler et al., 2008). We saw this situation in the opening case study when Jack stayed home from school to help the family irrigate the cornfield. Such a cooperative spirit is epitomized by the Zulu word *ubuntu*, which reflects the belief that people attain their humanness largely through caring relationships with others and regular contributions to the common good.

In many Mexican American and Native American communities, group achievement is valued over individual or competitive achievement, and cooperation is commonplace.

Students from cooperative cultures may resist when asked to compete against their classmates, as 16-year-old Maria explains:

> I love sports, but not competitive sports. [My brother is] the same way. I think we learned that from our folks. They both try to set things up so that everyone wins in our family and no one is competing for anything. (Pipher, 1994, p. 280)

Make frequent use of cooperative activities when students' cultures place a high priority on cooperation.

Students may also be confused when teachers scold them for helping one another on assignments or for sharing answers, and they may feel uncomfortable when their individual achievements are publicly acknowledged (Deyhle & Margonis, 1995; Lipka, 1998; Rogoff, 2003). Group work, with an emphasis on cooperation rather than competition, often facilitates the school achievement of these students (García, 1995; Losey, 1995; McAlpine & Taylor, 1993; L. S. Miller, 1995).

Family Relationships and Expectations In some groups—for example, in many Hispanic, Native American, and Asian communities, as well as in some rural European American communities—family bonds and relationships are especially important, and extended family members often live nearby. Students growing up in these cultures are likely to feel responsibility for their family's well-being and to have a strong sense of loyalty to other family members. They may exhibit considerable respect for, and also go to great efforts to please, their parents. It is not unusual for students in such communities to leave school when their help is needed at home (Banks & Banks, 1995; Fuligni, 1998; Kağitçibaşi, 2007; Timm & Borman, 1997).

In most cultures, school achievement is valued highly, and parents encourage their children to do well in school (Goldenberg, Gallimore, Reese, & Garnier, 2001; R. R. Pearce, 2006; Spera, 2005). But some cultural groups place even higher priority on other accomplishments. For example, when preparing young children for school, many Hispanic families place particular emphasis on instilling appropriate social behaviors—for instance, showing respect for adults and cooperating with peers (Greenfield et al., 2006; Tyler et al., 2008). And in some African American and Native American families, an early pregnancy is a cause for joy, even if the mother-to-be has not yet completed high school (Deyhle & Margonis, 1995; Stack & Burton, 1993).

Relate the school curriculum to students' home environments and cultures. Establish and maintain open lines of communication with parents, and work with them to identify ways in which home and school can collaborate in helping students be successful in the classroom.

We must certainly be sensitive to situations in which the achievements that *we* think are important are seemingly not valued by students' families. Whenever possible, we must show our students how the school curriculum and classroom activities relate to their cultural environments and their own life goals (Brayboy & Searle, 2007; Lipman, 1995; Moje & Hinchman, 2004). We must also maintain open lines of communication with students' parents. Because some parents, especially parents of minority-group children, may be intimidated by school personnel, teachers often need to take the first step in establishing productive parent–teacher relationships. When teachers and parents realize that both groups want students to succeed in the classroom, they are more apt to work cooperatively to promote student achievement (Banks & Banks, 1995; Salend & Taylor, 1993; R. L. Warren, 1988). Chapter 13 identifies many strategies for working effectively with parents.

Conceptions of Time Many people regulate their lives by the clock: Being on time to appointments, social engagements, and the dinner table is important. This emphasis on punctuality is not characteristic of all cultures, however. For example, many Hispanic and Native American communities don't observe strict schedules and time lines (H. G. Burger, 1973; Garrison, 1989; Gilliland, 1988; Tyler et al., 2008). Not surprisingly, children from these communities may sometimes be late for school and may have trouble understanding the need to complete school tasks within a certain time frame.

To succeed in mainstream Western society, students eventually need to learn punctuality. At the same time, we must recognize that not all of our students will be especially concerned about clock time when they first enter our classrooms. Certainly, we should expect students to arrive in class on time and to turn in assignments when they are due. But we must be patient and understanding when, for cultural reasons, students do not develop such habits immediately.

Encourage punctuality, but be patient if students' cultural backgrounds have placed little emphasis on clock time.

Worldviews The cultural and ethnic differences we have identified so far reveal themselves, in one way or another, in students' behaviors. Yet the definition of culture presented earlier includes the behaviors and *belief systems* that characterize a social group. Our general beliefs and assumptions about the world—collectively known as our **worldview**—are often so integral to our everyday thinking that we take them for granted and aren't consciously aware of them (Koltko-Rivera, 2004; Losh, 2003). Some beliefs that permeate the curriculum in traditional Western schools are not universally shared, however. Consider the following examples:

- After a major hurricane ripped through southern Florida in the summer of 1992, many fourth and fifth graders attributed the hurricane to natural causes, but some children from minority-group backgrounds had heard explanations elsewhere that led them to believe that people's actions or supernatural forces also played a role in the hurricane's origins and destructiveness (O. Lee, 1999).
- Fourth graders from the Menominee culture (a Native American group that resides primarily in Wisconsin and Michigan) often show exceptionally high achievement scores in science, but by eighth grade, their scores may decline considerably. The Menominee culture encourages children to think about the many ways in which they are a *part* of nature, rather than taking care of or dominating it, and children increasingly find the school science curriculum at odds with this view (Atran, Medin, & Ross, 2005; Medin, 2005).
- When American high school students read newspaper articles about the appropriateness or inappropriateness of prayer in public schools, some view the trend away from prayer as a sign of progress toward greater religious freedom. But others—those from deeply religious Christian families, for instance—view the same trend as a decline that reflects abandonment of the country's religious heritage (Mosborg, 2002).

Consider how students' diverse worldviews might influence their interpretations of classroom subject matter.

As you can see, then, students' worldviews are likely to influence their interpretations of current events and classroom subject matter (Kağitçibaşi, 2007; Nelson-Barber & Estrin, 1995).

Creating a Culturally Inclusive Classroom Environment

Clearly, we must be aware of and responsive to the different ways in which students of various cultural and ethnic groups are likely to think and act. It is equally important that we help our *students* develop such awareness and responsiveness, enabling them to become productive members both of the school community and of our increasingly multicultural society. Following are several suggestions:

Identify your own cultural lens and biases. In the opening case study, Jack's English teacher complained that "his parents don't care" and that, in general, the parents of Navajo students "just don't support their [children's] education" (Deyhle & LeCompte, 1999, p. 127). This teacher was looking at the behaviors of her students and their parents from the perspective of a non-Navajo. The assumptions and worldviews we have acquired in our own culture—for instance, the assumption that good parents actively direct and control their children's behaviors—are often so pervasive in our lives that we tend to treat them as common sense or even facts, rather than as the beliefs they really are. These beliefs become a *cultural lens* through which we view events—a lens that may lead us to perceive other cultures' practices as somehow irrational and inferior to our own.

Teachers who work effectively with students from diverse backgrounds are keenly aware that their own cultural beliefs are just that—beliefs. And they make a concerted effort *not* to pass judgment on cultural practices and beliefs very different

worldview General, culturally based set of assumptions about reality that influence understandings of a wide variety of phenomena.

from their own but rather to try to understand *why* people of other cultural groups think and act as they do (Banks et al., 2005; Rogoff, 2003).

Educate yourself about your students' cultural backgrounds. One way to do this, of course, is to read as much as you can about various cultural groups (e.g., see Kitayama & Cohen, 2007). But in addition, effective teachers immerse themselves in the daily lives and cultures of their students—talking with students about their outside interests and activities, getting to know students' families, patronizing local businesses, and so on (Castagno & Brayboy, 2008; Ladson-Billings, 1995a; Moje & Hinchman, 2004). Only when you immerse yourself in a very different cultural environment can you truly begin to understand how you, too, are a product of your own culture and to appreciate the potential benefits of growing up in a culture very different from your own (Banks et al., 2005; Rogoff, 2003).

myeducationlab

Hear an expert speak about what it's like for a Native American to study a strictly European American version of American history in the videos "Self-Concept Challenge" and "Genocide Impact." (To find these videos, go to Chapter 4 of the Book-Specific Resources in MyEducationLab, select *Video Examples*, and then click on the titles.)

Incorporate the perspectives and traditions of many cultures into the curriculum. True **multicultural education** is not limited to cooking ethnic foods, celebrating Cinco de Mayo, or studying famous African Americans during Black History Month. Rather, it integrates throughout the curriculum the perspectives and experiences of numerous cultural groups and gives all students reason for pride in their own cultural heritages (Banks & Banks, 1995; Hollins, 1996; Tatum, 1997). Students from diverse backgrounds are more likely to be motivated to do well in school—and to *actually* do well there—when they perceive the school curriculum to be relevant to their own cultures (Brayboy & Searle, 2007; Moje & Hinchman, 2004; Tyler et al., 2008).

As teachers, we can incorporate content from diverse cultures into many aspects of the school curriculum:

- In language arts, study the work of authors and poets from a variety of ethnic groups (e.g., study the lyrics of popular rap and hip-hop songs).
- In mathematics, use mathematical principles to address multicultural tasks and problems (e.g., use geometry and graph paper to design a Navajo rug).
- In science, draw on students' experiences with the natural environment (e.g., relate biological concepts to their community's farming and hunting practices).
- In social studies, look at different religious beliefs and their effects on people's behaviors (e.g., see Figure 4.2).
- In history, look at wars and other major events from diverse perspectives (e.g., the Native American perspective on the pioneers' westward migration in North America, the Spanish perspective on the Spanish–American War, the Japanese perspective on World War II).
- In both history and current events, consider such issues as discrimination and oppression. (Alim, 2007; J. M. Hughes, Bigler, & Levy, 2007; NCSS Task Force on Ethnic Studies Curriculum Guidelines, 1992; Nelson-Barber & Estrin, 1995; K. Schultz, Buck, & Niesz, 2000)

Look for both commonalities and differences among people from different cultural backgrounds.

In our exploration of diverse cultures, we should look for commonalities as well as differences. For example, we might study how various cultural groups celebrate the beginning of a new year, discovering that "Out with the old and in with the new" is a common theme among many such celebrations (Ramsey, 1987). In the secondary grades, it can be beneficial to explore issues that adolescents of all cultures face: gaining the respect of elders, forming trusting relationships with peers, and finding a meaningful place in society (Ulichny, 1996). One important goal of multicultural education should be to communicate that, underneath it all, people are more alike than different.

multicultural education Instruction that integrates throughout the curriculum the perspectives and experiences of numerous cultural groups.

Ultimately, we should help students realize that diverse cultural groups have much to learn from one another. As an example, students might be surprised to discover that several key practices underlying many democratic governments in Western nations—such as sending delegates to represent particular groups, allowing only one person in a governing council to speak at a time, keeping government and military bodies separate—were adopted from Native American governing practices (specifically those of the Iroquois League) in the 1700s (Rogoff, 2003; Weatherford, 1988).

Adapt instructional strategies to students' preferred ways of learning and behaving. Using strategies consistent with students' accustomed ways of learning and behaving is known as **culturally responsive teaching**. For example, if students are accustomed to working collaboratively with others, we should make frequent use of cooperative learning activities (Castagno & Brayboy, 2008; Ladson-Billings, 1995a). If, in their informal interactions with peers, students are accustomed to talking simultaneously and building on one another's ideas, we might ask them to answer questions in chorus, rather than as individuals (K. H. Au, 1980). And if students' home environments are high-energy ones, in which several activities may take place simultaneously—as is sometimes true in African American and Hispanic families—we might create a similarly high-energy, multiactivity classroom environment (Tyler et al., 2008).

FIGURE 4.2 Thirteen-year-old Melinda wrote about the Shinto religion of Japan for her language arts and social studies classes. Students were required to go beyond the facts to draw their own conclusions and relate what they learned to their personal lives. These excerpts from Melinda's paper show her efforts to do so.

Shinto gods are called Kami. It is believed that these spirits are found in the basic forces of fire, wind, and water. Most influence agriculture and this of course was how the earliest people survived. They relied on what they grew to live. So the gods had to help them grow their crops or they died. It seems natural for people to worship things that will help them survive, and worshiping forces that affect what you grow was the common practice in early history. These basic forces even affect the survival of modern people. We all still need agriculture to live and forces of nature really determine whether crops grow or not.

Shintoists never developed strong doctrines, such as the belief in life after death that many other religions have. However they have developed some moral standards such as devotion, sincerity, and purity. . . .

All Shintoists have a very good and simple set of rules or practice. They want to be honorable, have feelings for others, support the government, and keep their families safe and healthy. I think these are good principles for all people, whether they practice a religion or not. . . .

Work hard to break down students' stereotypes of particular ethnic groups. Although we and our students should certainly be aware of real differences among various ethnic groups, it is counterproductive to hold a **stereotype**—a rigid, simplistic, and inevitably inaccurate caricature—of any particular group. Even the most open minded of us are sometimes prone to holding ethnic stereotypes, as you may discover in the following exercise.

Stress that people from diverse cultures can all benefit from considering one another's perspectives.

EXPERIENCING FIRSTHAND

Picture This #1

Form a picture in your mind of someone from each of the following three places. Focus on the *first* image that comes to mind in each case:

The Netherlands (Holland) **Mexico** **Hawaii**

Now answer yes or no to each of these questions:

- Was the person from the Netherlands wearing wooden shoes?
- Was the person from Mexico wearing a sombrero?
- Was the person from Hawaii wearing a hula skirt or flower lei?

If you answered yes to any of the three questions, then one or more of your images reflected an ethnic stereotype. Most people in the Netherlands, Mexico, and Hawaii do *not* routinely wear such stereotypical attire.

culturally responsive teaching Intentional use of instructional strategies consistent with students' culturally preferred ways of learning and behaving.

stereotype Rigid, simplistic, and erroneous view of a particular group of people.

In the preceding exercise, your stereotypes involved only superficial qualities. Yet people's stereotypes can also include notions about typical personality characteristics and behaviors. Some stereotypes—for instance, perceptions of a certain group as being "stupid," "lazy," or "aggressive"—are derogatory and certainly *not* conducive to productive cross-group interactions.

Researchers have identified several possible origins of counterproductive stereotypes. In some instances, family members or friends communicate stereotypes through prejudicial remarks and practices (Nesdale, Maass, Durkin, & Griffiths, 2005; Branch, 1999). In other cases, a history of conflict and animosity between two groups may lead children to conclude that people in the opposing group have undesirable qualities (Pitner, Astor, Benbenishty, Haj-Yahia, & Zeira, 2003). Occasionally, stereotypes appear in curriculum materials and classroom instruction—as happens, for instance, when American children role-play the first Thanksgiving by dressing up in paper-bag "leather" vests, painting their faces, and wearing feathers on their heads (Bigler & Liben, 2007; Brayboy & Searle, 2007). And sometimes, students simply have little or no knowledge about a cultural group very different from their own. For example, thoughtless classmates might taunt a Muslim girl with a name such as "Osama bin Laden's sister." Or, if she wears a head scarf to school, they might ask, "Are you bald? Is there something wrong with your hair?" (McBrien, 2005a, p. 86).

myeducationlab

Hear 13-year-old Crystal's concerns about racism in the video "Emotions." (To find this video, go to Chapter 4 of the Book-Specific Resources in MyEducationLab, select *Video Examples,* and then click on the title.)

At a minimum, unflattering stereotypes are likely to lead to misunderstanding among members of diverse cultural groups. When left uncorrected, stereotypes can also lead to overtly discriminatory and malicious behaviors against others—ethnic jokes, racial taunts, social exclusion, and so on (Killen, 2007; Pfeifer, Brown, & Juvonen, 2007). Students who are frequent victims of others' misunderstandings and prejudices are more likely than their peers to become chronically ill or depressed (Allison, 1998; G. H. Brody et al., 2006; Tatum, 1997).

As teachers, we must work hard to correct students' inaccurate and demeaning stereotypes of groups different from themselves, and we must vigorously address any acts of prejudice and discrimination we witness in the classroom and elsewhere. The Into the Classroom feature "Addressing Students' Stereotypes and Prejudices" suggests several concrete strategies. In addition, we can promote friendship among students of diverse ethnic backgrounds by using some of the strategies identified in Chapter 3: using cooperative learning activities, teaching simple words and phrases in one another's native languages, encouraging schoolwide participation in extracurricular activities, and so on. By learning to appreciate multicultural differences within a single classroom, students take an important step toward appreciating the multicultural nature of the world at large.

Bring cultural diversity to culturally homogeneous classrooms. Not all schools have a culturally diverse population, of course. For example, in the United States, the vast majority of European American students attend schools in which students of color are very much in the minority (Berliner, 2005). Children in culturally homogeneous communities sometimes hold naive and potentially counterproductive stereotypes about other cultural and ethnic groups (McGlothlin & Killen, 2006; Pfeifer et al., 2007). In such situations, we may have to take students, either physically or vicariously, beyond school boundaries. For instance, we might engage students in community action projects that provide services to particular ethnic groups—perhaps in preschools, nursing homes, or city cultural centers (Sleeter & Grant, 1999). Alternatively, we might initiate a sister schools program, in which students from two ethnically different communities regularly communicate, exchanging letters, photographs, stories, local news items, and the like (Koeppel & Mulrooney, 1992).

myeducationlab

Gain insights into appropriate accommodations for children from diverse cultural backgrounds by completing the Building Teaching Skills and Dispositions exercise "Accommodating Cultural Differences" in MyEducationLab. (To find this activity, go to the topic Student Diversity in MyEducationLab and click on *Building Teaching Skills and Dispositions.*)

Foster democratic ideals, and empower students to bring about meaningful change. Any multicultural education program must include such democratic ideals as human dignity, equality, justice, and appreciation of diverse viewpoints (NCSS Task

INTO THE Classroom

Addressing Students' Stereotypes and Prejudices

Use curriculum materials that represent all cultures and ethnic groups as competent, legitimate participants in mainstream society, rather than as exotic curiosities who live in a separate world.

A history teacher peruses a history textbook to make sure that it portrays members of all ethnic groups in a nonstereotypical manner. He supplements the text with readings that highlight the important roles that members of various ethnic groups have played in history.

Assign literature depicting peers from diverse cultural backgrounds.

As part of a research project in England, several elementary school teachers read to their students a series of stories depicting close friendships between English children and refugees from other countries. Following this experimental intervention, the students express more positive attitudes toward refugee children than do control-group students who have not heard the stories.

Conduct class discussions about prejudice and racism that exist in the school and local community.

A middle school in a suburban community creates a number of mixed-race focus groups in which students regularly convene to share their views about interracial relations at the school. Although some students of European American ancestry initially feel uncomfortable talking about this topic with their minority-group peers, once the ice has been broken, greater cross-cultural understanding and communication result.

Expose students to successful role models from various ethnic backgrounds.

A teacher invites several successful professionals from minority groups to speak with her class about their careers. When some students seem especially interested in one or more of these careers, she arranges for the students to spend time with the professionals in their workplaces.

Assign small-group cooperative projects in which students from diverse backgrounds must combine their unique talents to achieve a common goal.

A fourth-grade teacher has small cooperative learning groups design and conduct schoolwide surveys soliciting other students' opinions on various topics (e.g., ideas for school fundraisers, preferences for cafeteria menu items, etc.). The teacher intentionally creates groups that are heterogeneous in cultural background, knowing that the group members can draw on diverse friendship networks in seeking volunteers to take the surveys. In addition, he makes sure that every member of a group has something unique to offer in survey design or results tabulation—perhaps knowledge of word processing software, artistic talent, or math skills.

Emphasize that individual members of any single group are often very different from one another in their behaviors, beliefs, and values.

In a geography unit on major world religions, a middle school teacher regularly points out that members of any single religion often have very different customs. "For example," he says, "some Muslim women dress in much the same way that women in this country do; others wear head scarves in addition to regular, modern clothes; and still others dress in a burqa that covers everything except their hands. Usually the women wear a scarf or burqa to show modesty about their bodies. In fact, some Jewish women also wear head scarves to show that they are modest, but many others do not."

Sources: Banks, 1994; Boutte & McCormick, 1992; L. Cameron, Rutland, Brown, & Douch, 2006 (refugee stories example); Dovidio & Gaertner, 1999; Gutiérrez & Rogoff, 2003; Ladson-Billings, 1994b; O. Lee, 1999; Oskamp, 2000; Pang, 1995; Pfeifer et al., 2007; Ramsey, 1995; K. Schultz et al., 2000 (focus groups example); Tatum, 1997.

Force on Ethnic Studies Curriculum Guidelines, 1992; Sleeter & Grant, 1999). We better prepare students to function effectively in a democratic society when we help them understand that virtually every nation includes numerous cultures and that such diversity provides a richness of ideas and perspectives that will inevitably yield a more creative, productive society overall. The student writing sample presented in Figure 4.3 illustrates such understanding.

Teaching respect for diverse perspectives does not necessarily mean that we treat all beliefs as equally acceptable. For instance, we should certainly not embrace a culture that blatantly violates some people's basic human rights. Respect does mean, however, that we and our students should try to understand another cultural group's behaviors within the context of that culture's beliefs and assumptions.

Ideally, a democracy also provides a context in which students can bring about meaningful change. Students should be encouraged to challenge the status quo—

FIGURE 4.3 In an essay for his American history class, 16-year-old Randy reveals his appreciation of cultural differences.

> To me, diversity is not only a fact of life, but it is life. To be different and unique is what allows people to live a fulfilling life. To learn and admire other people's differences is perhaps one of the keys to life and without that key, there will be too many doors that will be locked, keeping you out and not allowing you to succeed. To learn that a majority of one kind in one place may be a minority of another kind in another place can help to initiate an outlook on life that promotes perspective and reason of any situation.

perhaps substandard housing, poor voter turnout in certain neighborhoods, or misuse of natural resources (Ladson-Billings, 1995a; Lipman, 1995). For example, in some high schools in the Navajo Nation of the American Southwest, students take on controversial commercial practices (e.g., excessive tree cutting in local forests, mining practices that scar the landscape) that threaten the long-term well-being of their local community. Students conduct library research on their chosen topics, conduct interviews with community leaders, prepare a written report, and possibly also give a presentation to the community (Nelson-Barber & Estrin, 1995). Service learning projects such as these seem to instill a "can-do" spirit and optimism that all citizens can have a significant impact on the quality of their own and other people's lives (Eccles, 2007; Kahne & Sporte, 2008; Tate, 1995).

Gender Differences

In their academic abilities, boys and girls are probably more similar than you think. But in other respects, they may be more different than you realize.

Research Findings Regarding Gender Differences

Researchers have identified a number of differences in the physical, cognitive, personal, and social domains.

Physical Activity and Motor Skills Boys are temperamentally predisposed to be more active than girls. Thus, they have more trouble sitting still for long periods and are less likely to enjoy reading, a decidedly sedentary activity (W. O. Eaton & Enns, 1986; Newkirk, 2002). Before puberty, boys and girls seem to have similar *potential* for physical and psychomotor growth, although girls have a slight edge in fine motor skills (e.g., writing numbers and letters). But overall, boys develop their physical and motor skills more, perhaps through participation in organized sports (Eccles, 2005; J. R. Thomas & French, 1985). After puberty, boys have a biological advantage in height and muscular strength—that is, they're taller and, because of increased levels of the male sex hormone testosterone, they're stronger (Halpern, 2006; Hyde, 2005; J. R. Thomas & French, 1985).

Make sure that students, especially boys, have frequent opportunities to release pent-up energy.

Such differences are hardly justification for favoring either gender when enhancing students' physical fitness, of course. Physical education curricula and sports programs should provide equal opportunities for boys and girls to maximize their physical well-being and athletic skills. Furthermore, participation in school sports is one way through which boys and girls alike can gain the admiration of their peers (Leaper & Friedman, 2007).

Cognitive and Academic Abilities On average, boys and girls perform similarly on tests of general intelligence, in part because experts who construct the tests eliminate items that favor one group or the other (Halpern & LaMay, 2000). Researchers sometimes do find differences in more specific cognitive abilities, however. The most consistently observed gender difference is in **visual–spatial ability**, the ability to imagine and mentally manipulate two- and three-dimensional figures (see Figure 4.4). On average, males do better at such visual–spatial tasks than females (Gallagher & Kaufman, 2005). In contrast, females seem to have the advantage in some but not all verbal skills; for instance, girls have, on average, larger vocabularies and can more

visual–spatial ability Ability to imagine and mentally manipulate two- and three-dimensional figures.

FIGURE 4.4 Two examples of visual–spatial thinking

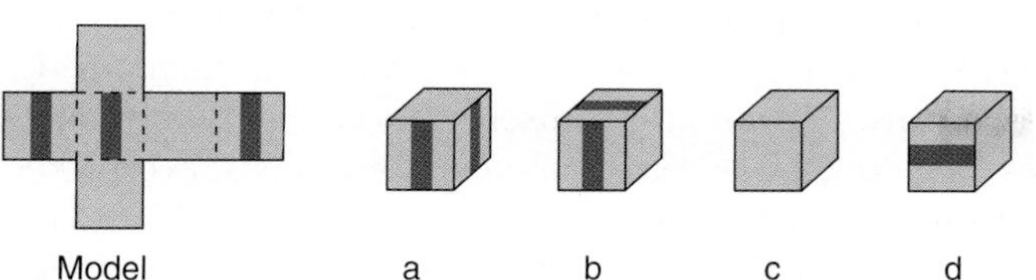

When the figure on the left is folded along the dotted lines, it becomes a three-dimensional object. Which one or more of the four figures on the right represent(s) how this object might appear from a particular perspective?

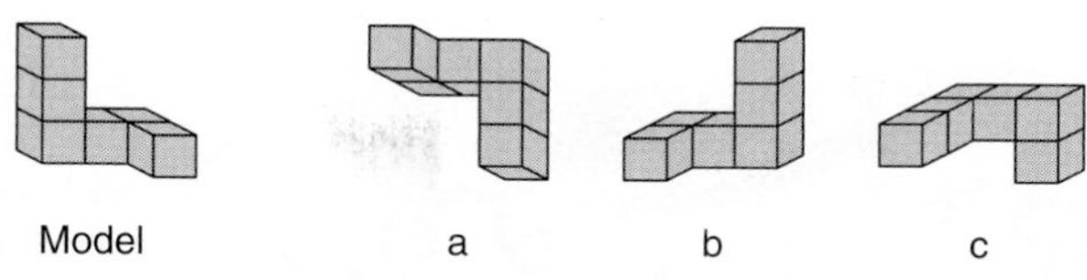

When the object on the left is rotated in three-dimensional space, it can look like one or more of the objects on the right. Which one(s)?

Answer key: Depending on the direction from which it is viewed, the first model might look like either *a* or *d*. The second model can be rotated to look like either *a* or *c*.

Source: Examples modeled after G. K. Bennett, Seashore, & Wesman, 1982; R. N. Shepard & Metzler, 1971.

quickly think of the words they need to express their thoughts (Halpern, 2004, 2006; Halpern & LaMay, 2000; Lippa, 2002).

However, most gender differences in specific cognitive abilities tend to be quite small, with considerable overlap between the two groups (e.g., return to Figure 4.1). In addition, boys sometimes show greater variability in cognitive abilities than girls do, causing more boys than girls to demonstrate extremely high or low ability levels relative to their age-group (Halpern et al., 2007; Halpern & LaMay, 2000; Hedges & Nowell, 1995).

Even though girls' and boys' ability levels may be similar, girls consistently earn higher grades in school (Halpern et al., 2007; Halpern & LaMay, 2000). But if achievement is measured by achievement tests, rather than grades, research findings are inconsistent. When differences are found, girls typically have an advantage in reading and writing, and after puberty, boys tend to have the advantage in mathematical problem solving (Halpern, 2006; Halpern & LaMay, 2000; Hedges & Nowell, 1995; Penner, 2003).

Not only are gender differences in visual–spatial, verbal, and mathematical performance quite small, but some researchers have found them to be getting *smaller* in recent years. In other words, boys and girls are becoming increasingly similar in their academic performance (Hyde, Lindberg, Linn, Ellis, & Williams, 2008; Leaper & Friedman, 2007; Spelke, 2005). Thus, in general, we should expect boys and girls to have similar academic aptitudes for different subject areas.

Expect boys and girls to have similar aptitudes for all academic subject areas.

Motivation in Academic Activities On average, girls are more concerned about doing well in school: They are more engaged in classroom activities, more diligent in working on school assignments, and more likely to graduate from high school (Duckworth & Seligman, 2006; H. M. Marks, 2000; Marsh, Martin, & Cheng, 2008; McCall, 1994). Furthermore, girls are more interested in getting a college education than boys are, and in many countries, more females than males earn college degrees (Halpern et al., 2007; National Science Foundation, 2007). However, this eagerness to achieve academically leads girls to prefer tasks at which they know they can succeed, and some find academic failure devastating. Boys are more willing to take on academic challenges and risks and more likely to take their failures in stride (Dweck, 2000; Yu, Elder, & Urdan, 1995).

Make a special effort to motivate boys—for instance, by incorporating their personal interests into classroom activities.

Help girls understand that taking risks and making mistakes are signs that they are willing to take on challenges and stretch their abilities in new directions.

Sense of Self Beginning in the upper elementary or middle school grades, boys appear to have a slightly more positive overall sense of self than girls do. This gender difference appears to be partly due to boys' tendency to *over*estimate their abilities and possibly also to girls' tendency to *under*estimate theirs (Harter, 1999; Hyde, 2007;

Boys' more aggressive nature often shows up in their fantasy play and fiction, as shown in this story by 7-year-old Grant. (His teacher has corrected some of his misspellings.)

Pajares, 2005). Boys' and girls' self-perceptions also tend to be consistent with stereotypes about what males and females are good at, especially in adolescence. Boys tend to rate themselves more highly in mathematics and sports, whereas girls tend to rate themselves more highly in reading and social studies. Such differences in self-perceptions persist even when boys' and girls' actual ability levels are *equal* (D. A. Cole et al., 2001; Herbert & Stipek, 2005; Leaper & Friedman, 2007; Wigfield, Byrnes, & Eccles, 2006).

Interpersonal Behaviors and Relationships Boys and girls interact with peers in distinctly different ways. One of the most consistently observed gender differences involves aggression. In early childhood and throughout the elementary and secondary school years, boys are more physically aggressive than girls (Card, Stucky, Sawalani, & Little, 2008; Hyde, 2007). This gender difference is especially large for *unprovoked* aggression. For example, boys are more likely than girls to bully peers for no apparent reason (Lippa, 2002; Pellegrini, 2002). However, girls can be equally aggressive in a nonphysical way. As noted in Chapter 3, girls are more apt to engage in *relational* aggression, behavior that adversely affects interpersonal relationships—for instance, spreading rumors or snubbing peers (Crick et al., 2002; French et al., 2002; Pellegrini & Archer, 2005). Female age-mates are often quite hurt—sometimes devastated—by such unkind remarks and actions (Rudolph et al., 2005).

Consistent differences are also seen in boys' and girls' interpersonal activities and relationships. Boys tend to congregate in relatively large groups that engage in rough-and-tumble play, organized group games, and physical risk-taking activities (Maccoby, 2002; Pellegrini, Kato, Blatchford, & Baines, 2002). They enjoy competition and can be fairly assertive in their efforts to achieve individual and group goals (Benenson et al., 2002; Eisenberg et al., 1996; Maccoby, 2002). They may often try to hide their true emotions in social situations, putting up a tough, "nothing-can-bother-me" front (Lippa, 2002; Pollack, 2006). A high school student named Jason put it this way:

Communicate to students that showing emotion is a natural human trait that is appropriate for males as well as females.

> If something happens to you, you have to say, "Yeah, no big deal," even when you're really hurting. . . . I've punched so many lockers in my life, it's not even funny. When I get home, I'll cry about it. (Pollack, 2006, p. 72)

myeducationlab

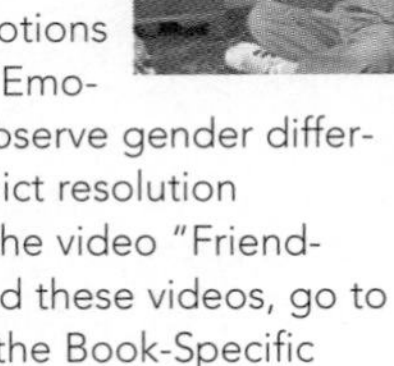

Listen to 15-year-old Greg talk about how boys try to hide their emotions in the video "Emotions," and observe gender differences in conflict resolution strategies in the video "Friendships." (To find these videos, go to Chapter 4 of the Book-Specific Resources in MyEducationLab, select *Video Examples*, and then click on the titles.)

Whereas boys are apt to be competitive, girls are more likely to be affiliative and cooperative. Thus, they tend to form closer relationships with their teachers and to achieve at higher levels when classroom activities involve cooperation rather than competition (Inglehart, Brown, & Vida, 1994; Pianta, 2006). Girls also seem to be more attuned to others' mental states and more sensitive to the subtle, nonverbal messages—the body language—that others communicate (Bosacki, 2000; Deaux, 1984). Girls spend much of their leisure time with one or two close friends, with whom they may share their innermost thoughts and feelings (Eisenberg et al., 1996; Leaper & Friedman, 2007; A. J. Rose, 2002). Although girls can be quite assertive in making their wishes known, they are also concerned about resolving conflicts and maintaining group harmony, and they may sometimes subordinate their own needs to those of others (Benenson et al., 2002; Leaper & Friedman, 2007; Rudolph et al., 2005).

Classroom Behaviors In part because boys tend to be physically more active than girls, they are more likely to misbehave in class (Altermatt, Jovanovic, & Perry, 1998; Gay, 2006; Sadker & Sadker, 1994). Boys talk more and ask more questions, sometimes without waiting to be called on. They also tend to dominate small-group discussions and work sessions. Girls are more reticent classroom participants. They are less likely to publicly volunteer ideas and ask questions, perhaps for fear of looking stupid or perhaps because they worry that looking too smart will reduce their popularity with the opposite sex (Harter, 1999; Jovanovic & King, 1998; Sadker & Sadker, 1994; Théberge, 1994). Occasionally, then, it may be beneficial to group girls with girls and boys with boys in order to ensure that girls participate actively in classroom activities (Kahle & Lakes, 1983; MacLean, Sasse, Keating, Stewart, & Miller, 1995). Girls are more likely to express their opinions in small-group rather than large-group discussions, and they are more apt to assume the role of leader (thereby developing valuable leadership skills) in same-sex groups (Fennema, 1987; Théberge, 1994).

Accommodate girls' affiliative nature by providing numerous opportunities for cooperative group work. Occasionally have students work in same-sex pairs or groups.

Career Aspirations Historically, boys have had more ambitious career aspirations than girls have (Deaux, 1984; Lueptow, 1984). In recent years, however, many girls—especially those in Western countries—have also begun to set their sights on challenging professions (Bandura, Barbaranelli, Caprara, & Pastorelli, 2001; Lapan, Tucker, Kim, & Kosciulek, 2003). Often, boys and girls alike focus on careers that are stereotypically appropriate for their gender, in part because they have greater self-confidence about their ability to succeed in such careers (Bandura et al., 2001; Liben, Bigler, & Krogh, 2002; Weisgram & Bigler, 2007).

Some gender differences are especially prevalent for particular age-groups. Table 4.1 identifies differences you are apt to see at various grade levels and offers relevant classroom strategies for accommodating them.

Origins of Gender Differences

Obviously, heredity determines basic physical differences (some present at birth, some emerging at puberty) between males and females. And because of heredity, girls reach puberty earlier, and boys eventually become taller and stronger. Underlying such differences are different levels of sex-related hormones, especially estrogen for girls and testosterone for boys.

Hormones may also account for some nonphysiological gender differences. The gender difference in physical aggression almost certainly has a biological basis: It is seen across cultures and appears to be related to testosterone levels (Lippa, 2002). Furthermore, hormones may play a role in the small differences observed in visual–spatial and verbal abilities, possibly by affecting neurological development in different areas of the brain (Halpern et al., 2007; Lippa, 2002; O'Boyle & Gill, 1998). Hormones even seem to influence children's preferences for male-stereotypical versus female-stereotypical behaviors (Hines et al., 2002; Lippa, 2002).

Yet environmental factors clearly play a role as well, often by interacting with and amplifying any existing biology-based gender differences (Lippa, 2002; Nuttall, Casey, & Pezaris, 2005). Virtually every culture teaches children that some behaviors are more appropriate for males and others more appropriate for females, as the following exercise may show you.

EXPERIENCING FIRSTHAND

Picture This #2

Form a picture in your mind of each of the following individuals. Focus on the *first* image that comes to mind in each case:

Secretary	Scientist
Bank president	Fashion model
Elementary school teacher	Building contractor

Which individuals did you picture as male, and which did you picture as female?

TABLE 4.1
Gender-Related Characteristics at Different Grade Levels

	Age-Typical Characteristics	Suggested Strategies
K–2 	• Physical abilities, general intelligence, and more specific cognitive abilities roughly equivalent for boys and girls • Recognition that gender remains constant despite changes in dress, hairstyle, and so on • Rigid stereotypes about gender-appropriate behavior; eagerness to conform to these stereotypes • Play groups largely segregated by gender • Different themes in fantasy play (e.g., boys depict heroism, girls depict romance) • Play activities more active and forceful for boys than for girls; less awareness in boys that some activities are potentially dangerous	• Foster athletic skills equally in boys and girls. • Expect and encourage equal achievement in all areas of the academic curriculum. • Provide materials for a wide range of play activities (e.g., household items, dress-up clothes, toy trucks, building blocks, balls). • Monitor students' play activities for potentially dangerous behaviors; provide guidance about which actions are and are not safe.
3–5 	• Gender differences in self-evaluations of math ability, with boys rating themselves more highly than girls despite equal math achievement • Play groups largely segregated by gender • Organized large-group games more common for boys than for girls • More competition, aggression, and risk taking in boys than in girls • Onset of puberty earlier for girls (average age 10) • Tendency for some early maturing girls to feel out of sync with peers, putting them at greater risk for low self-confidence and depression	• Assure students that boys and girls have equal potential in all areas of the academic curriculum. • Provide materials for group games (e.g., balls, bats, soccer goal nets, etc.). • Set and enforce reasonable limits on play behaviors so that students' physical safety is ensured. • Be especially sensitive and supportive as girls show signs of puberty (e.g., allow trips to the restroom as needed).
6–8 	• Onset of puberty later for boys (average age 11½) • Greater physical ability, as well as more participation in sports, for boys than for girls; participation in sports more prestigious for boys • Emergence of gender differences in visual–spatial ability, with boys having higher ability (on average) • Emergence of gender differences in overall self-esteem and assessments of physical attractiveness and athletic competence, with self-ratings being higher for boys and preoccupation with physical appearance being greater for girls • Increasing flexibility about which behaviors are gender appropriate, especially for girls • Tendency for boys' social groups to be larger and less intimate than girls' • More emotional distress for girls than for boys when interpersonal relationships go badly; tendency for boys to try to hide feelings of sadness and distress	• Respect students' modesty and need for privacy when they must change clothes or take a shower in physical education or after-school sports. • Encourage both boys and girls to pursue extracurricular sports activities; encourage attendance at both boys' and girls' sports events. • Use concrete objects to facilitate visual–spatial understandings in math and science. • In appropriate contexts, teach good grooming habits and other skills for presenting oneself well to others.
9–12 	• Gradual improvement in girls' self-assessments of physical attractiveness • Greater interest in a college education among girls than among boys • Tendency for boys to aspire more to hands-on professions (e.g., working with tools and machines) and for girls to aspire more to social or artistic occupations (e.g., teaching, counseling, writing) • Prosocial behavior seen more frequently in girls than in boys, despite equal ability to act prosocially • More positive attitudes about casual sexual intercourse, as well as earlier sexual experiences, among boys than among girls • More substance abuse (alcohol, drugs) among boys than among girls • Depression and eating disorders more common in girls than in boys	• Encourage students to cross stereotypical boundaries in course selection (e.g., girls taking advanced math, boys taking creative writing). • Provide information about the benefits of a college education (e.g., invite recent high school graduates to come and share their college experiences). • Expose students to diverse occupations and professions through guest lectures, trips to community businesses and agencies, and the like. • Encourage and acknowledge prosocial behavior in both boys and girls. • Work with colleagues and parents to vigorously address unhealthful and risky out-of-school behaviors. • Alert the school counselor when you suspect substance abuse, serious depression, an eating disorder, or some other potentially life-threatening condition.

Sources: Benenson & Christakos, 2003; Binns et al., 1997; Bussey & Bandura, 1992; Card, Stucky, Sawalani, & Little, 2008; D. A. Cole et al., 2001; Crouter, Whiteman, McHale, & Osgood, 2007; Davenport et al., 1998; Davila, 2008; Eisenberg et al., 1996; Fabes, Martin, & Hanish, 2003; M. E. Ford, 1996; Grusec & Hastings, 2007; Halpern, 2004, 2006; Halpern et al., 2007; Hankin, Mermelstein, & Roesch, 2007; Hardy, 2002; J. R. Harris, 1995; Harter, 1999; Hayward, 2003; Hegarty & Kozhevnikov, 1999; Herbert & Stipek, 2005; Hyde, 2005; Hyde & Durik, 2005; Leaper & Friedman, 2007; Liben & Bigler, 2002; Lippa, 2002; Maccoby, 2002; McDevitt & Ormrod, 2010; Pollack, 2006; M. Rhodes & Gelman, 2008; Rogoff, 2003; Rudolph et al., 2005; R. M. Ryan & Kuczkowski, 1994; Sadker & Sadker, 1994; D. M. Stein & Reichert, 1990; J. R. Thomas & French, 1985; Trautner, 1992; Wigfield, Byrnes, & Eccles, 2006; Wigfield et al., 1996.

If you are like most people, your secretary, teacher, and fashion model were females, and your bank president, scientist, and building contractor were males. Gender stereotypes—rigid ideas about how males and females typically behave—persist throughout our society, and even preschool children are aware of them (Bornholt, Goodnow, & Cooney, 1994; Eisenberg et al., 1996).

Students of both genders should be encouraged to master a wide variety of skills, including those that are stereotypically associated with the opposite gender.

Many aspects of society conspire to socialize growing children to conform to gender stereotypes. For example, many parents believe—and communicate their beliefs—that boys are naturally better in some domains (e.g., math) and that girls are naturally better in others (e.g., reading), even in cases where no gender differences in achievement exist (Bleeker & Jacobs, 2004; Herbert & Stipek, 2005; Jacobs, Davis-Kean, Bleeker, Eccles, & Malanchuk, 2005). Many parents also encourage gender-typical play activities, which may foster some skills over others (Frost, Shin, & Jacobs, 1998; Liss, 1983; Lytton & Romney, 1991). Girls are apt to get dolls and stuffed animals and to play house and board games—toys and activities that foster the development of verbal and social skills. In contrast, boys get blocks, model airplanes, and science equipment, and they play football, basketball, and video games—toys and activities that foster greater development of visual–spatial skills. Furthermore, boys are often reinforced for aggressive behavior and athletic accomplishments, whereas girls are reinforced for being nurturing and ladylike (Block, 1983; Fagot, Hagan, Leinbach, & Kronsberg, 1985; Jacobs et al., 2005; Leaper & Friedman, 2007; J. R. Thomas & French, 1985).

Children's playmates and classmates, too, frequently encourage adherence to traditional gender stereotypes. Peers tend to respond more positively to children who act in traditionally gender-appropriate ways and more negatively to those who do not; such peer pressure is especially common for boys (Bussey & Bandura, 1992; Eisenberg et al., 1996; Leaper & Friedman, 2007). Boys and girls may also acquire different behaviors as a result of the types of groups in which they typically interact and play (Benenson et al., 2002; Hyde & Durik, 2005; Maccoby, 2002). In the large-group activities so common for boys, children must be fairly assertive and possibly competitive (i.e., "boy" traits) to satisfy their goals and desires. In the pairs and threesomes more common for girls, children can often meet their own needs through collaboration and compromise (i.e., "girl" traits).

Keep students' exceptional achievement levels private, especially in counterstereotypical domains that some classmates might find inappropriate for a particular gender.

Society at large, including the popular media, also influences the development of gender stereotypes, in part by providing adult models who demonstrate very different behaviors for males and females. For instance, children more often see women, rather than men, reading (B. A. Freedman, 2003). In addition, movies, television programs, and books often portray males and females in gender-stereotypical ways: Males are aggressive leaders and successful problem solvers, whereas females are domestic, demure, and obedient followers (Furnham & Mak, 1999; Leaper & Friedman, 2007; Sadker & Sadker, 1994; T. L. Thompson & Zerbinos, 1995).

As young children become increasingly aware of the typical characteristics and behaviors of boys, girls, men, and women, they gradually pull their knowledge together into self-constructed understandings, or **gender schemas**, of what males are like and what females are like. These gender schemas, in turn, become part of their sense of self and provide guidance in how they themselves should behave—an example of the *self-socialization* phenomenon described in Chapter 3. By the time children reach school age, much of the pressure to act "appropriately" for their gender comes from within, rather than from others (Bem, 1981; Leaper & Friedman, 2007; C. L. Martin & Ruble, 2004). For instance, when teachers actively encourage children to engage in non-gender-stereotypical activities, the children may do so for a short time, but most soon revert to their former, gender-typical ways (Lippa, 2002).

gender schema Self-constructed, organized body of beliefs about the traits and behaviors of males or females.

Because gender schemas are self-constructed, their contents may vary considerably from one individual to another (Liben & Bigler, 2002). For example, in adolescence, some girls incorporate into their "female" schema the unrealistic standards of beauty presented in popular media (films, fashion magazines, etc.). As girls compare themselves to these standards, they almost invariably come up short, and their self-assessments of physical attractiveness decline. In an effort to achieve the super-thin bodies they believe to be ideal, they may fall victim to eating disorders (Attie, Brooks-Gunn, & Petersen, 1990; Weichold, Silbereisen, & Schmitt-Rodermund, 2003). Likewise, some teenage boys go out of their way to meet self-constructed macho standards of male behavior by putting on a tough-guy act at school and bragging (perhaps accurately, but more often not) about their many sexual conquests (Pollack, 2006; K. M. Williams, 2001a).

Not all students have rigid or unrealistic stereotypes of what their gender should be like, of course. In fact, as students get older, many become increasingly flexible about what males and females can and should do (C. L. Martin & Ruble, 2004). Those with more flexible gender schemas are more likely to pursue counterstereotypical interests and career paths (Liben & Bigler, 2002).

Making Appropriate Accommodations for Gender Differences

In recent years, a greater awareness of gender differences has led many teachers to be especially careful about treating their male and female students equitably. Even so, subtle differences in the treatment of boys and girls continue. For instance, teachers tend to give more attention to boys, partly because boys ask more questions and present more discipline problems. Teachers also give boys more feedback—praise and criticism alike—than they give girls (Altermatt et al., 1998; Eisenberg et al., 1996; Gay, 2006; Halpern et al., 2007; S. M. Jones & Dindia, 2004).

In most cases, teachers are probably unaware that they discriminate between boys and girls as much as they do. The first step toward ensuring more equitable treatment of males and females is to become aware of existing inequities. Once we have such awareness, we can try to correct the inequities—for example, by interacting regularly with *all* of our students, accommodating their varying activity levels, and having equivalent expectations for achievement in stereotypically male and female subject areas. The Into the Classroom feature "Promoting Gender Equity" offers several concrete suggestions.

Ultimately, we must help all of our students recognize that gender stereotypes are just that—*stereotypes*—and don't necessarily limit what males and females can or should be. We can encourage students to overcome restrictive gender stereotypes in several ways:

- Expose students to same-gender adults and peers who excel in domains commonly associated with the opposite gender.
- Talk about the importance of all academic content areas for students' future success.
- Help students understand that knowledge of stereotypes does *not* require endorsement of them.
- Explain the historical roots of stereotypes—for instance, that differing expectations for males and females are a holdover from an era when many jobs outside the home required considerable strength (and thus were more appropriate for men) and jobs inside the home could easily be combined with breastfeeding and other aspects of child care (and thus were more appropriate for women).
- Engage students in discussions about the negative consequences of rigid stereotypes for society as a whole—noting, for instance, that adhering to such roles causes a great deal of talent to go to waste. (Bem, 1983, 1984; Fennema, 1987; Huguet & Régner, 2007; A. Kelly & Smail, 1986; Pollack, 2006)

INTO THE Classroom

Promoting Gender Equity

- **Use your knowledge of typical gender differences to create greater equity for males and females, *not* to form expectations about how well males and females are likely to perform in various activities.**

  A physical education teacher realizes that most of the girls in her class have probably not had as much experience throwing a baseball or softball overhand as the boys have, so she gives them basic instruction and extra practice in the overhand throw.

- **Use curriculum materials that represent both genders in a positive and competent light; include materials that portray both genders competently engaging in counterstereotypical behaviors.**

  An English teacher assigns Harper Lee's *To Kill a Mockingbird*, in which an attorney named Atticus Finch is portrayed as a gentle, affectionate, and compassionate man and his daughter Scout is portrayed as a courageous and adventuresome 8-year-old. The teacher also assigns Zora Neale Hurston's *Their Eyes Were Watching God*, in which an African American woman grows from a teenager who depends on others to meet her needs into a self-sufficient woman who can easily fend for herself.

- **Accommodate the need of many students—especially boys—to engage in frequent physical activity.**

  A third-grade teacher has a reading group act out the short story it is currently reading. Each student assumes a different character's role, reading the character's lines with appropriate voice, facial expressions, and gestures, and occasionally accompanying the lines with the character's behaviors.

- **Monitor yourself to see whether you are unintentionally treating boys and girls in ways that limit the learning opportunities of one gender.**

  A French teacher decides to count the number of times he calls on boys and girls during class. He finds that he calls on boys more than three times as frequently as girls, partly because the boys raise their hands more often. To combat his bad habit, he institutes a new procedure: He alternates between boys and girls when he calls on students, and he sometimes calls on students who are not raising their hands.

Sources: Fennema, 1987; Horgan, 1995; Kahle & Lakes, 1983; MacLean, Sasse, Keating, Stewart, & Miller, 1995; Sadker & Miller, 1982; Zambo & Brozo, 2009.

At the same time, we must recognize that gender differences sometimes *do* warrant differential treatment of girls and boys. For example, girls are likely to improve their visual–spatial ability if we give them frequent opportunities to engage in activities requiring visual–spatial thinking (B. M. Casey et al., 2008; Gallagher & Kaufman, 2005). And we can increase girls' interest in science by regularly including hands-on activities in science classes (Burkam, Lee, & Smerdon, 1997). Meanwhile, boys are more likely to improve their literacy skills if we allow them to pursue typical "boy" interests, such as sports and adventure, while reading and writing (Newkirk, 2002). And we must regularly communicate to them that occasionally showing emotion and vulnerability is both manly and healthy (Pollack, 2006).

Recognize that some differential treatment of girls and boys is appropriate, especially if it helps to reduce gender gaps in particular abilities and predispositions.

Socioeconomic Differences

The concept of **socioeconomic status (SES)** encompasses a number of variables, including family income, parents' education levels, and parents' occupations. A family's socioeconomic status—whether high-SES, middle-SES, or low-SES—gives us a sense of the family's standing in the community: what type of neighborhood they live in, how much influence they have on political decision making, what educational opportunities they can offer their children, and so on.

Students' school performance is correlated with their socioeconomic status: Higher-SES students tend to have higher academic achievement, and lower-SES students tend to be at greater risk for dropping out of school (J.-S. Lee & Bowen, 2006; McLoyd, 1998; Sirin, 2005). As students from lower-SES families move through the grade levels, they tend to fall further and further behind their higher-SES peers (Farkas,

socioeconomic status (SES) One's general social and economic standing in society; encompasses family income, occupation, and educational level.

2008; Jimerson, Egeland, & Teo, 1999). When researchers find achievement differences among students from different ethnic groups, the differences in the students' socio-economic status, *not* their cultural differences per se, seem largely to blame (Byrnes, 2003; N. E. Hill, Bush, & Roosa, 2003; Murdock, 2000).

Life certainly isn't perfect for students from high-SES homes (Luthar, 2006; Luthar & Latendresse, 2005). For instance, some parents in high-income families put so much pressure on their children to achieve at high levels that the children suffer from significant anxiety and depression. In addition, some high-income parents have demanding jobs that keep them both physically and emotionally distant from their children, thereby limiting the guidance and support they can provide. But ultimately, it is children who live in poverty—especially *chronic* poverty—who face the most significant obstacles to academic success and personal well-being.

Challenges Associated with Poverty

Poverty is more common than you might think. In 2007, 12.5% of the U.S. population—more than 37 million people—were categorized as living in poverty (U.S. Census Bureau, 2008). Children and adolescents who live in poverty are a diverse group (Sidel, 1996). Many live in inner-city neighborhoods, others live in rural areas, and some live in modest apartments or homes in wealthy suburbs. Some come from families that can meet life's basic necessities (e.g., food, warm clothes, and adequate shelter) but have little money left over for luxuries. Many others live in extreme poverty; these students are the ones most at risk for academic failure and thus most in need of our attention and support.

Several factors tend to contribute to the generally lower school achievement of low-SES students. Students who face only one or two of these challenges often do quite well in school, but those who face many or all of them are at high risk for academic failure and other negative outcomes (Becker & Luthar, 2002; Gerard & Buehler, 2004; Grissmer, Williamson, Kirby, & Berends, 1998).

Poor Nutrition and Health Low-income families have few financial resources to ensure that their children have adequate nutrition and health care. Poor nutrition in the early years of life (including the nine months before birth) can lead to impairments in children's attention, memory, and learning ability (D'Amato, Chitooran, & Whitten, 1992; Noble, Tottenham, & Casey, 2005). Poor nutrition seems to influence school achievement both directly—for instance, by hampering early brain development—and indirectly—for example, by leaving children listless and inattentive in class (Ashiabi & O'Neal, 2008; Sigman & Whaley, 1998). And inadequate health care means that some conditions that interfere with school attendance and performance, such as asthma and hearing problems, go unaddressed (Berliner, 2005).

Help families apply for free and reduced-cost meal programs. Refer students with chronic health problems to the school nurse.

Inadequate Housing and Frequent Moves Many poor children live in tight quarters, perhaps sharing one or two rooms with several other family members (Hawkins, 1997; Hernandez, Denton, & Macartney, 2008). Furthermore, children who move frequently from one rental apartment to another must often change schools as well. In the process, they lose existing social support networks and may miss lessons on important academic skills (Gruman, Harachi, Abbott, Catalano, & Fleming, 2008; Mantzicopoulos & Knutson, 2000).

Exposure to Toxic Substances Especially when children live in poor, inner-city neighborhoods, their surroundings may expose them to excessive levels of environmental toxins that can seriously jeopardize their health and long-term cognitive development (Hubbs-Tait, Nation, Krebs, & Bellinger, 2005; Koger, Schettler, & Weiss, 2005). For instance, in old, badly maintained apartment buildings, children may be exposed to lead in the dust from deteriorating paint. In addition, the city water supply may contain pesticides or small amounts of industrial waste, and the local air may be polluted by power plants and industrial incinerators.

Unhealthy Social Environments On average, low-SES neighborhoods and communities have more street gangs and organized crime, higher frequencies of violence and vandalism, greater prevalence of alcoholism and drug abuse, and greater numbers of antisocial peers. Furthermore, there are fewer productive outlets for leisure time—libraries, recreation centers, sports leagues, and so on—and fewer positive adult role models. Such factors appear to be partly responsible for the lower academic achievement of students who live in poverty (Aikens & Barbarin, 2008; T. D. Cook, Herman, Phillips, & Settersten, 2002; Duncan & Magnuson, 2005; Leventhal & Brooks-Gunn, 2000; Nettles, Caughy, & O'Campo, 2008).

Emotional Stress Although students at all income levels experience stressful conditions at various points in their lives, students from low-income families have more than their share (Brooks-Gunn, Linver, & Fauth, 2005; G. W. Evans & Kim, 2007; Gershoff, Aber, Raver, & Lennon, 2007). On average, low-SES homes are more chaotic and unpredictable than affluent ones (G. W. Evans, Gonnella, Marcynyszyn, Gentile, & Salpekar, 2005; Payne, 2005). Children may wonder where their next meal is coming from or how long it will be before the landlord evicts them for not paying the rent. The preponderance of single-parent homes among low-SES families is another source of anxiety. A single parent may be too distracted by personal problems to offer much affection or consistent discipline (Dodge, Greenberg, Malone, & Conduct Problems Prevention Research Group, 2008; Parke et al., 2004). As a result, students from low-SES families show higher than average rates of depression and other emotional problems (Ashiabi & O'Neal, 2008; Caspi, Taylor, Moffitt, & Plomin, 2000; G. W. Evans & English, 2002; Morales & Guerra, 2006).

Not all children from low-income homes live in chronically stressful conditions, and those whose families provide consistent support, guidance, and discipline generally enjoy good mental health (N. E. Hill et al., 2003; M. O. Wright & Masten, 2006). Nevertheless, we should continually be on the lookout for signs that our students are undergoing unusual stress at home and then provide whatever support we can. In some instances, effective support may involve nothing more than being a willing listener. In other cases, we may want to consult with a school counselor or social worker about possible support systems at school and resources in the local community.

Provide emotional support and appropriate referrals when students seem to be undergoing exceptional stress at home.

Gaps in Background Knowledge Some students from low-SES families lack the basic knowledge and skills (e.g., familiarity with letters and numbers) on which successful school learning so often depends (Aikens & Barbarin, 2008; Brooks-Gunn et al., 2005; Hauser-Cram, Sirin, & Stipek, 2003). Access to early educational opportunities that might develop such skills—books, educational toys, trips to zoos and museums, and so on—is always somewhat dependent on a family's financial resources. In addition, some parents have few basic academic skills to share with their children (Hernandez, 2004; Portes, 1996). However, as always, we must be careful not to overgeneralize. Some low-income parents have considerable education (perhaps a college degree) and may be well equipped to read to their children and provide other enriching educational experiences (Goldenberg, 2001; Raikes et al., 2006; Sidel, 1996).

Identify and address any missing basic skills.

Lower-Quality Schools Unfortunately, the students who most need a good education are often least likely to have access to it. Schools in low-income neighborhoods and communities tend to receive less funding and, as a result, are often poorly equipped and maintained. Teacher turnover rates are high in these schools, and disciplinary tactics tend to be more harsh and less effective. Furthermore, some teachers at these schools have low expectations for students, offering a less-challenging curriculum, assigning less homework, and providing fewer opportunities to develop advanced thinking skills than do teachers in wealthier school districts (Eccles et al., 1998; G. W. Evans, 2004; McLoyd, 1998; Skiba & Knesting, 2001).

Of course, schools in low-income school districts don't *have* to be this way. In fact, we teachers can make a *huge* difference in the quality of children's educational experiences at even the poorest of schools. Consider a teacher whom researchers called Miss A:

resilient student Student who succeeds in school and in life despite exceptional hardships at home.

Miss A was a teacher at Ray School, an elementary school in a large, North American city. The school building—constructed like a fortress, with iron bars on its windows—was hardly appealing or welcoming. Its neighbors included old tenement buildings, a junkyard, an auto repair shop, and a brothel. Fewer than 10% of its students eventually completed high school.

Nonetheless, Miss A worked wonders with the students in her first-grade classes. She showed obvious affection for them, insisted on appropriate behavior without ever losing her temper, and shared her lunch with those who hadn't brought one. She continually hammered home the importance of learning and education and had high expectations for achievement. She made sure her students learned to read, and she stayed after school with them whenever they needed extra help.

Be optimistic that you *can* make a difference in students' lives.

Miss A's students got higher grades than students in other classes not only in their first-grade year but also for several years after that. On average, their IQ scores went *up* between third and sixth grade (one girl's score changed from 93 to 126), whereas the IQs of most students at Ray School went down. When researchers tracked down some of Miss A's students many years later, they found that these students were far more financially and professionally successful than the typical Ray graduate. And every single one of them remembered her name (E. Pedersen, Faucher, & Eaton, 1978).

Fostering Resilience

Thanks, in part, to teachers like Miss A, many students of low-income families succeed in school despite exceptional hardships. Some are **resilient students** who acquire characteristics and coping skills that help them rise above their adverse circumstances. As a group, resilient students have likable personalities, a positive sense of self, and high yet realistic goals. They believe that success comes with hard work, and their bad experiences serve as constant reminders of the importance of getting a good education (S. Goldstein & Brooks, 2006; Schoon, 2006; Werner & Smith, 2001).

Remember that many bright, capable students come from low-income families.

Researchers have learned a great deal about factors that can foster resilience in students from challenging backgrounds. With their findings in mind, I offer the following suggestions:

Be a dependable source of academic and emotional support. Resilient students usually have one or more individuals in their lives whom they trust and can turn to in difficult times (Masten, 2001; McLoyd, 1998; Werner, 1995, 2006). For example, resilient students often mention teachers who have taken a personal interest in them and have been instrumental in their school success (R. M. Clark, 1983; McMillan & Reed, 1994; D. A. O'Donnell, Schwab-Stone, & Muyeed, 2002). As teachers, we are most likely to promote resilience in low-SES students when we show that we like and respect them, are available and willing to listen to their concerns, hold high expectations for their performance, and provide the encouragement and support they need to succeed both inside and outside the classroom (Masten & Coatsworth, 1998; Milner, 2006; Schoon, 2006; Werner, 1995).

myeducationlab

Listen to a discussion of strengths that children from low-income homes are likely to have in the video "Incorporating the Home Experiences of Culturally Diverse Students into the Classroom—Part 1." (To find this video, go to Chapter 4 of the Book-Specific Resources in MyEducationLab, select *Video Examples*, and then click on the title.)

Build on students' strengths. Although some students from lower-SES backgrounds may lag behind their classmates in such basic academic skills as reading, writing, and arithmetic, they may bring other strengths to the classroom. For example, these students are often more clever at improvising with everyday objects (Torrance, 1995). If they work part time to help their families make ends meet, they may have a good understanding of the working world. If they are children of single, working parents, they may know far more than their classmates about cooking, cleaning house, and taking care of younger siblings. If financial resources have been particularly scarce, they may have a special appreciation for basic human needs and true empathy for victims of war or famine around the world. And many of these students are apt to be quite knowledgeable about certain aspects of popular culture—characters and plot lines in television shows, lyrics from current rap songs, and so on (Freedom Writers, 1999).

As teachers, then, we must remember that students who have grown up in poverty may, in some respects, have more knowledge and skills than their economically advantaged peers. Such knowledge and skills can often provide a basis for teaching classroom subject matter (Schoon, 2006; Varelas & Pappas, 2006). Furthermore, students who are willing to talk about the challenges they have faced can sensitize their classmates to the serious inequities that currently exist in our society.

Visits to museums, zoos, farms, and other information-rich locations can be especially beneficial for students from low-income families, who often don't have the resources to make such visits on their own.

Identify and provide missing resources and experiences important for successful learning. Some students from very poor families lack basic essentials—such as nutritious meals, warm clothing, adequate health care, and school supplies—that will be important for their school success. Many government programs and community agencies can help to provide such essentials. School districts offer free and reduced-cost meal programs for children from low-income families. Charitable organizations often distribute warm winter jackets gathered from annual clothing drives. Many communities have low-cost health clinics. And some office supply stores and large discount chains donate notebooks, pens, and other school supplies to children who need them. Indeed, most communities provide a variety of resources for children and adolescents with limited financial means.

Beyond connecting low-income students and families with community resources, we should identify any basic experiences that students may not have had. Field trips to zoos, aquariums, natural history museums, farms, the mountains, or the ocean may be in order. And of course, we should identify and teach any basic skills that, for whatever reason, students have not yet acquired. When we do so, we are likely to see significant improvements in students' classroom performance (S. A. Griffin, Case, & Capodilupo, 1995; McLoyd, 1998; G. Phillips, McNaughton, & MacDonald, 2004). However, we must be careful not to focus *exclusively* on basic skills, especially when doing so means a fair amount of drill and practice. Students' academic progress will suffer over the long run if they don't also have frequent opportunities to engage in complex academic tasks—reading for understanding, solving real-world problems, and so on (Cazden, 2001; B. Williams & Woods, 1997).

Balance any needed instruction in basic skills with more interesting and challenging real-world activities.

Working with Homeless Students

Children of homeless families typically face far greater challenges than other students from low-SES families. Many have health problems, low self-esteem, a short attention span, poor language skills, and inappropriate behaviors. Some may be reluctant to come to school because they lack bathing facilities and appropriate clothing. And some may have moved so frequently from one school to another that there are large gaps in their academic skills (Coe, Salamon, & Molnar, 1991; Gollnick & Chinn, 2002; McLoyd, 1998; Pawlas, 1994; Polakow, 2007).

As teachers, we, too, face more challenges when teaching students who live in homeless shelters. The following are several suggestions for giving these students the extra support they may need to achieve both academic and social success at school (Pawlas, 1994):

- Pair new students with classmates who can provide assistance and support—for example, by explaining school procedures and making introductions to other students.
- Provide a notebook, clipboard, or other portable "desk" on which students can do their homework at the shelter.
- Find adult or teenage volunteers to serve as tutors at the shelter.

- Meet with students' parents at the shelter, rather than at school.
- Share copies of homework assignments, school calendars, and newsletters with shelter officials.

When we use such strategies, however, we must keep in mind that students and their families are apt to feel embarrassed about their homeless status (Polakow, 2007). Accordingly, showing respect for their privacy and self-esteem must be a high priority.

Students at Risk

Students at risk are those with a high probability of failing to acquire the minimum academic skills necessary for success in the adult world. Many students at risk drop out before high school graduation, and many others graduate without mastery of basic skills in reading or mathematics (e.g., Boling & Evans, 2008; Laird, Kienzl, DeBell, & Chapman, 2007). In the United States, estimates of current high school graduation rates range from 65% to 75%, depending on the particular data sources used in the calculations (J. R. Warren & Halpern-Manners, 2007). Thus, although many students are currently achieving at high levels in American schools, a great many others—somewhere between 25% and 35%—are falling by the wayside.

A common assumption is that the reasons for dropping out lie primarily in the students themselves (V. E. Lee & Burkam, 2003; U.S. Department of Education, 1992). But as we shall see, school characteristics also play a significant role.

Characteristics of Students at Risk

Students at risk come from all socioeconomic levels, but children of poor, single-parent families are especially likely to leave school before high school graduation. Boys are more likely than girls to drop out, and African Americans, Hispanics, and Native Americans are more likely than European American and Asian American students to drop out. Also, students in large cities and rural areas are more likely to drop out than students in the suburbs are; graduation rates in some big cities are less than 40%. Students at greatest risk for dropping out are those whose families speak little or no English and whose own knowledge of English is also quite limited (Farkas, 2008; Hardré & Reeve, 2003; L. S. Miller, 1995; National Research Council, 2004; Roderick & Camburn, 1999; U.S. Department of Education, 1997).

Students at risk, especially those who eventually drop out, typically have some or all of the following characteristics:

- *A history of academic failure.* On average, students who drop out have less effective reading and study skills, achieve at lower levels, and are more likely to have repeated a grade than their classmates who graduate. Consistent patterns of low achievement are sometimes seen as early as third grade (K. L. Alexander, Entwisle, & Dauber, 1995; Battin-Pearson et al., 2000; Belfiore & Hornyak, 1998; Brophy, 2002; Garnier, Stein, & Jacobs, 1997; Suh, Suh, & Houston, 2007).
- *Emotional and behavioral problems.* Potential dropouts tend to have lower self-esteem than their more successful classmates. They are also more likely to exhibit serious behavioral problems (e.g., fighting, substance abuse) both in and out of school. Often, their close friends are low achieving and, in some cases, antisocial peers (Battin-Pearson et al., 2000; Garnier et al., 1997; Jozefowicz, Arbreton, Eccles, Barber, & Colarossi, 1994; Suh et al., 2007).
- *Lack of psychological attachment to school.* Students at risk for academic failure are less likely to identify with their school or to perceive themselves as a vital part of the school community. For example, they engage in few extracurricular activities and are apt to express dissatisfaction with school in general (Christenson & Thurlow, 2004; Hymel, Comfort, Schonert-Reichl, & McDougall, 1996; Rumberger, 1995).

student at risk Student with a high probability of failing to acquire minimal academic skills necessary for success in the adult world.

- *Increasing disinvolvement with school.* Dropping out is not necessarily an all-or-nothing event. In fact, many high school dropouts show lesser forms of dropping out many years before they officially leave school. Future dropouts are absent from school more frequently than their peers, even in the early elementary grades. In addition, they are more likely to have been suspended from school and to show a long-term pattern of dropping out, returning to school, and dropping out again (Christenson & Thurlow, 2004; Finn, 1989; Raber, 1990; Suh et al., 2007).

Many students who drop out find the school curriculum boring and irrelevant to their needs.

These characteristics are by no means surefire indicators of which students will drop out, however. For instance, some dropouts come from two-parent, middle-income homes, and some are actively involved in school activities almost until the time they drop out (Hymel et al., 1996; Janosz, Le Blanc, Boulerice, & Tremblay, 2000).

Why Students Drop Out

Students drop out for a variety of reasons. Some have little family and peer encouragement and support for school success. Others have extenuating life circumstances; for example, they may have medical problems, take an outside job to help support the family, or get pregnant. Many simply become dissatisfied with school: They don't do well in their classes, have trouble getting along with classmates, find the school environment too dangerous or restrictive, or perceive the curriculum to be boring and irrelevant to their needs (Brayboy & Searle, 2007; Hardré & Reeve, 2003; Portes, 1996; Rumberger, 1995; L. Steinberg, Blinde, & Chan, 1984). And some students are pessimistic that they can pass the achievement tests on which high school graduation may depend (Hursh, 2007; more on this point in our discussion of *high-stakes tests* in Chapter 15).

Sadly, teacher behaviors can enter into the picture as well, as illustrated in the following dialogue between an interviewer (Ron) and two at-risk high school students (George and Rasheed):

> *Ron:* Why do you think someone drops out of school?
>
> *George:* I think people drop out of school cuz of the pressure that school brings them. Like, sometimes the teacher might get on the back of a student so much that the student doesn't want to do the work. . . . And then that passes and he says, "I'm gonna start doing good. . . ." Then he's not doing as good as he's supposed to and when he sees his grade, he's, "you mean I'm doin' all that for nothin'? I'd rather not come to school." . . .
>
> *Rasheed:* I think kids drop out of school because they gettin' too old to be in high school. And I think they got, like, they think it's time to get a responsibility and to get a job and stuff. And, like George says, sometimes the teachers, you know, tell you to drop out, knowing that you might not graduate anyway.
>
> *Ron:* How does a teacher tell you to drop out?
>
> *Rasheed:* No, they recommend you take the GED program[2] sometimes. Like, some kids just say, "Why don't you just take the GED. Just get it over with." Then, job or something.
>
> *Ron:* You talked about a kid being too old. Why is a kid too old?
>
> *Rasheed:* Cuz he got left back too many times. (Farrell, 1990, p. 91)

---

[2]Rasheed is referring to a general equivalency diploma, obtained by taking a series of achievement tests rather than by completing the requirements for high school graduation.

Students are more likely to stay in school when they feel as if they truly belong there.

Supporting Students at Risk

Because students who are at risk for academic failure are a diverse group of individuals with a diverse set of needs, there is no single strategy that can keep all of them in school until high school graduation (Christenson & Thurlow, 2004; Janosz et al., 2000). Nevertheless, effective school and classroom practices will go a long way in helping these students stay on the road to academic success and high school graduation. Following are several suggestions based on research findings:

Identify students at risk as early as possible. We begin to see indicators of dropping out, such as low school achievement and high absenteeism, as early as elementary school. And other signs—such as low self-esteem, disruptive behavior, and lack of involvement in school activities—often appear years before students officially withdraw from school. Therefore, it is quite possible to identify at-risk students early in their school careers and take steps to prevent or remediate academic difficulties before they become insurmountable. Research indicates clearly that for students at risk, prevention, early intervention, and long-term support are more effective than later, short-term efforts (Brooks-Gunn, 2003; Christenson & Thurlow, 2004; McCall & Plemons, 2001; Ramey & Ramey, 1998).

myeducationlab

Discover the importance of teacher–student relationships for students at risk by completing the Understanding Research exercise "Supporting Children at Risk" in MyEducationLab. (To find this activity, go to the topic Student Diversity in MyEducationLab, click on *Assignments and Activities,* and then select Understanding Research.)

Create a warm, supportive school and classroom atmosphere. Teachers and schools that have high success rates with students at risk tend to be those that communicate a sense of caring, concern, and high regard for students (Christenson & Thurlow, 2004; Hamre & Pianta, 2005; Pianta, 1999). We'll look at many specific strategies for creating warm, supportive schools and classrooms in Chapter 13.

Make long-term, systematic efforts to engage students in the academic curriculum. Students are more likely to stay in school and more likely to learn and achieve at high levels if they believe that their classes are worth their time and effort (e.g., L. W. Anderson & Pellicer, 1998; S. M. Miller, 2003; Ramey & Ramey, 1998; Suh et al., 2007). The Into the Classroom feature "Engaging Students at Risk in the Academic Curriculum" offers several concrete examples of what we might do.

Encourage and facilitate identification with school. Students are far more likely to stay in school if they have an emotional attachment to their school and believe that they are important members of the school community (Christenson & Thurlow, 2004; Fredricks, Blumenfeld, & Paris, 2004). The following strategies illustrate how we might help them become more involved in and feel more psychologically attached to the school community:

- Encourage participation in athletic programs, extracurricular activities, and student government. This strategy is especially important when students are having academic difficulties because it provides an alternative way of experiencing school success.
- Involve students in school policy and management decisions.
- Give students positions of responsibility in managing school activities.
- Provide rewards (e.g., a trip to a local amusement park) for good attendance records. (Eccles, 2007; Finn, 1989; Garibaldi, 1992; Newmann, 1981; M. G. Sanders, 1996)

As you may have noticed, the recommendations I've just offered would be helpful for *any* student. In general, the most effective programs for students at risk are those that incorporate common, educationally sound teaching practices (Slavin, Karweit, & Madden, 1989).

INTO THE Classroom

Engaging Students at Risk in the Academic Curriculum

Engage students' interest with stimulating activities.

In a unit on the physics of sound, a junior high school science teacher shows students how basic principles of sound reveal themselves in rock music. On one occasion, the teacher brings in a guitar and explains why holding down a string at different points along the neck of the guitar creates different frequencies and thus different notes.

Make the curriculum relevant to students' lives and needs—for example, through service-learning activities.

A math teacher at an inner-city middle school consistently encourages her students to identify and work to solve problems in their community. One of her classes expresses concern about the many liquor stores located near the school and the questionable customers and drug dealers the stores attract. The students use yardsticks and maps to calculate the distance of each store from the school, gather information about zoning restrictions and other city government regulations, identify potential violations, meet with a local newspaper editor (who publishes an editorial describing the situation), and eventually meet with state legislators and the city council. As a result of the students' efforts, city police begin to monitor the liquor stores more closely, major violations are identified (leading to the closing of two stores), and the city council makes it illegal to consume alcohol within 600 feet of the school.

Use students' strengths to promote a positive sense of self.

A low-income, inner-city elementary school forms a singing group (the Jazz Cats), for which students must try out. The group performs at a variety of community events, and the students enjoy considerable visibility for their talent. Group members exhibit increased self-esteem, improvement in other school subjects, and greater teamwork and leadership skills.

Communicate high expectations for short-term and long-term academic success.

A math teacher at a low-income, inner-city high school recruits students to participate in an intensive math program. The teacher and students work on evenings, Saturdays, and vacations, and all of them later pass the Advanced Placement calculus exam. (This real-life example is depicted in the 1988 film *Stand and Deliver,* currently available on DVD.)

Provide extra support for academic success.

A middle school homework program meets every day after school in Room 103, where students find their homework assignments on a shelf. Students follow a particular sequence of steps to do each assignment (assembling materials, having someone check their work, etc.) and use a checklist to make sure they don't skip any steps. Initially, a supervising teacher closely monitors what they do, but with time and practice, the students are able to complete their homework with only minimal help and guidance.

Show students that they are personally responsible for their successes.

A teacher says to a student, "Your essay about recent hate crimes in the community is very powerful. You've given the topic considerable thought, and you've clearly mastered some of the techniques of persuasive writing that we've talked about this semester. I'd like you to think seriously about submitting your essay to the local paper for its editorial page. Can we spend some time during lunch tomorrow fine-tuning the grammar and spelling?"

Sources: Alderman, 1990; L. W. Anderson & Pellicer, 1998; Belfiore & Hornyak, 1998 (homework program example); Christenson & Thurlow, 2004; Cosden, Morrison, Albanese, & Macias, 2001; Eccles, 2007; L. S. Fuchs, D. Fuchs, et al., 2008; Jenlink, 1994 (Jazz Cats example); Ladson-Billings, 1994a; Mathews, 1988 (inner-city math program example); Suh et al., 2007; Tate, 1995 (liquor store example).

The Big Picture

As teachers, we can work more effectively with students from different cultures, genders, and socioeconomic groups if we keep the following general principles in mind:

- ***For better or for worse, all people's cultural backgrounds influence their interpretations of events.*** We all use our own cultural lenses when we interact with others. That is, we interpret others' behaviors according to what such behaviors typically mean in *our* culture and ethnic group. Yet specific behaviors and activities can mean different things for different cultural and ethnic groups and sometimes for different genders and socioeconomic groups as well. Consider the following examples:
  - When children ask questions of adults who are demonstrating new skills, adults in some communities might see those children as intelligent and interested, whereas adults in other communities might view them as inappropriate and out of line.
  - When students are asked to compete with one another, many boys may delight in the challenge, but

many girls may wilt at the possibility of alienating peers.
- For most students from middle-income homes, a homework assignment is, at worst, a chore they would rather not do, but for some students from low-income homes, even finding a time and quiet place to complete it may be a challenge.

As teachers, we must remember, too, that there are often many effective ways of doing things. The people in our own culture don't always know what's best, and in many cases, there *is* no "best." For example, consider the following:

- Asking questions of a teacher is one good way to learn a new skill, but watching quietly and reflectively can be equally valuable.
- Competitive activities might prepare students for working as adults in a capitalistic society, but cooperative activities offer a very different set of advantages: fostering social skills, enabling students to build on one another's strengths, and ultimately enabling students to accomplish more complex tasks than they could complete on their own.
- Growing up in a wealthy family increases the odds that children will have good health care and enriching educational opportunities, yet many children who grow up in poverty do quite well in school and in life despite—and, in some cases, probably because of—the challenges they have faced.

• ***All students have strengths and talents on which they can build, and all students have considerable potential to develop new skills and abilities.*** The unique characteristics and backgrounds that different students bring to class—for instance, the preference of many minority-group students to be cooperative rather than competitive, the concern of many girls to maintain group harmony, and some students' first-hand knowledge about such social issues as poverty and homelessness—together create a situation in which we and our students all have much to learn from one another.

• ***A great deal of variability exists within any group, and a great deal of overlap exists between any two groups.*** I made these two points at the beginning of the chapter, but they're both so important that I repeat them here. We must never—and I do mean *never*—form expectations for individual students on the basis of group averages alone. As we tailor our curriculum and instructional strategies for each of our students, what we know about them as *individuals* should be our primary guide. At the same time, what we know about their group membership—their cultural and ethnic heritage, their gender, their socioeconomic background—can help us immeasurably in understanding why they behave as they do and how we can better foster their cognitive and social development.

Practice for Your Licensure Exam

The Active and the Passive

Ms. Stewart has noticed that only a few students actively participate in her junior high school science classes. When she asks a question, especially one that requires students to draw inferences from information presented in class, the same hands always shoot up. She gives the matter some thought and realizes that all of the active participants are of European American descent and most of them are boys.

Ms. Stewart sees the same pattern in students' involvement in lab activities. When she forms small groups for particular lab assignments, the same students (notably, the European American males) always take charge. The females and minority-group males take more passive roles, either providing assistance to the group leaders or else just sitting back and watching.

Ms. Stewart is a firm believer that students learn much more about science when they participate in class and when they engage in hands-on activities. Consequently, she is concerned about the lack of involvement of many of her students. She wonders whether they really even care about science.

1. **Constructed-response question:**

   Effective teachers place a high priority on *equity;* that is, they ensure that their classroom practices are not biased in ways that enhance some students' achievement more than others'. In this situation, the European American boys appear to be benefiting more from instruction than their classmates are. Using what you know about group differences, identify at least three possible reasons that minority-group students are not actively participating in classroom lessons.

2. **Multiple-choice question:**

   Three of the following explanations are possible reasons that the boys in Ms. Stewart's class are participating more than the girls. Which alternative *contradicts* research findings on gender differences?

   a. On average, boys are more motivated to get good grades.
   b. On average, boys are more physically active in their classes.

c. On average, boys tend to be more confident about their abilities.
d. On average, boys are more likely to speak up without waiting to be called on.

3. **Constructed-response question:**

Describe three different strategies you might use to increase the participation of both girls and minority-group students in Ms. Stewart's class.

Go to Chapter 4 of the Book-Specific Resources in **MyEducationLab** and click on "Practice for Your Licensure Exam" to answer these questions. Compare your responses with the feedback provided.

PRAXIS

Turn to Appendix C, "Matching Book and MyEducationLab Content to the Praxis Principles of Learning and Teaching Tests," to discover sections of this chapter that may be especially applicable to the Praxis tests.

PEARSON myeducationlab

Now go to MyEducationLab (**www.myeducationlab.com**), where you can:

- Find learning outcomes for Student Diversity, along with the national standards that connect to these outcomes.
- Complete Assignments and Activities that can help you more deeply understand the chapter content.
- Engage in Building Teaching Skills and Dispositions exercises in which you can apply and practice core teaching skills identified in the chapter.
- Access Book-Specific Resources:
  - Check your comprehension of chapter content by going to the Study Plan, where you can find (a) Chapter Objectives; (b) Focus Questions that can guide your reading; (c) a Self-Check Quiz that can help you monitor your progress in mastering chapter content; (d) Review, Practice, and Enrichment exercises with detailed feedback that will deepen your understanding of various concepts and principles; (e) Flashcards that can give you practice in understanding and defining key terms; and (f) Common Beliefs and Misconceptions about Educational Psychology that will alert you to typical misunderstandings in educational psychology classes.
  - Supplementary Readings that enable you to pursue certain topics in greater depth.
  - A Practice for Your Licensure Exam exercise that resembles the kinds of questions appearing on many teacher licensure tests.

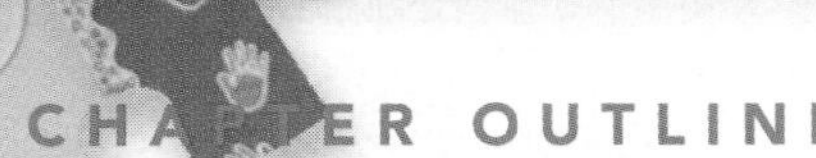

CHAPTER OUTLINE

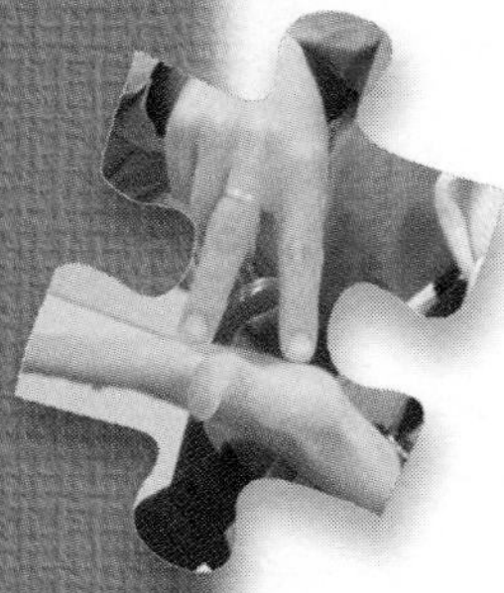

CHAPTER OBJECTIVES

- **Objective 5.1:** Describe various perspectives on the nature of intelligence, and identify several ways in which you can nurture intelligence in your own students.
- **Objective 5.2:** Explain how students' various cognitive styles and dispositions may influence their classroom performance.
- **Objective 5.3:** Identify implications of the U.S. Individuals with Disabilities Education Act (IDEA) for your own work as a teacher.
- **Objective 5.4:** Explain how you might adapt your instruction and classroom practices to the unique strengths and limitations of students with various disabilities.
- **Objective 5.5:** Explain how you might nurture the development of students who show exceptional gifts and talents.

Chapter 5

Individual Differences and Special Educational Needs

CASE STUDY: Tim

In elementary school, Tim earned reasonable grades, despite having poor reading comprehension skills. And although he often appeared to be in a daze during classroom activities, he was generally well behaved in class. A diagnostic evaluation in the third grade found no cognitive or physical disability that would make him eligible for special educational services.

In middle school, Tim's grades began to decline, and teachers complained of his "spaciness" and tendency to daydream. He had trouble completing in-class assignments and was so disorganized that he seldom finished his work at home. As assignments demanded increasing independence in later years, Tim's school performance continued to drop. He failed several classes in the ninth and tenth grades and had to retake them in summer school.

Now, midway through Tim's eleventh-grade year, his mother has taken him for an in-depth psychological evaluation at a university diagnostic clinic. An IQ test yields a score of 96, reflecting average intelligence, and measures of social and emotional adjustment are within an average range, but measures of attention consistently show this to be an area of weakness. Tim explains to clinic staff that he has trouble ignoring distractions and must find a very quiet place to do his schoolwork. Even then, he says, he often has to reread something several times to grasp its meaning (based on Hathaway, Dooling-Litfin, & Edwards, 2006, pp. 410–412).

- **As a teacher, what strategies might you use to accommodate Tim's unique needs?**

THE CLINIC EVALUATION TEAM'S FINAL DIAGNOSIS is that Tim has attention-deficit hyperactivity disorder, or ADHD. (Like Tim, some children identified as having ADHD exhibit attention problems *without* hyperactivity.) The team suspects that a subtle learning disability might be at the root of the problem but does not have sufficiently precise diagnostic techniques to determine this with certainty. Researchers and practitioners have identified many effective strategies for students with ADHD and learning disabilities—locating a quiet place to read and study, developing organizational skills, breaking complex tasks into several shorter, simpler ones—and such strategies are apt to help 17-year-old Tim stay on task and complete assignments (Barkley, 2006; Meltzer, 2007).

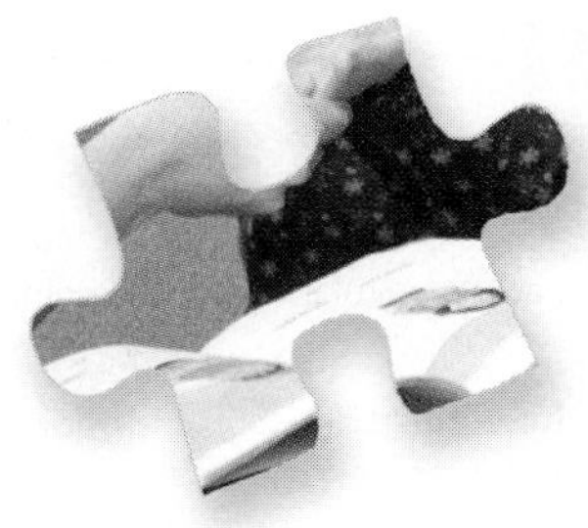

In Chapter 4, we considered *group differences*—the many ways in which students of different ethnic groups, genders, and socioeconomic backgrounds tend to be different from one another. Yet significant **individual differences** exist within any group—differences in cognitive abilities, personalities, physical skills, and so on. In this chapter, we'll look at individual differences in intelligence, cognitive styles, and dispositions. We'll then consider *students with special needs*—students who, like Tim, are different enough from their peers that they require specially adapted curriculum materials, instructional practices, or both.

Intelligence

Theorists define and conceptualize intelligence in a variety of ways, but most agree that it has several distinctive qualities:

One component of intelligence is the ability to use prior knowledge to analyze new situations. This student is trying to calculate the volume of the large pyramid by applying geometric principles he's learned in his math class.

- It is *adaptive:* It can be used flexibly to respond to a variety of situations and problems.
- It is related to *learning ability:* People who are intelligent in particular domains learn new information and behaviors in those domains more quickly and easily than people who are less intelligent in those domains.
- It involves the *use of prior knowledge* to analyze and understand new situations effectively.
- It involves the complex interaction and coordination of *many different mental processes.*
- It is *culture specific:* What is intelligent behavior in one culture is not necessarily intelligent behavior in another culture. (Greenfield, 1998; Laboratory of Human Cognition, 1982; J. Li, 2004; Neisser et al., 1996; Sternberg, 1997, 2004, 2007; Sternberg & Detterman, 1986)

With these qualities in mind, I offer an intentionally broad definition of **intelligence**: the ability to apply prior knowledge and experiences flexibly to accomplish challenging new tasks.

For most theorists, intelligence is somewhat different from what a person has actually learned—for example, as reflected in school achievement. At the same time, intelligent thinking and intelligent behavior *depend* on prior learning. The more students know about the world in general and about the specific tasks they need to perform, the more intelligently they can behave. Intelligence, then, is not necessarily a permanent, unchanging characteristic; it can be modified through experience and learning.

Theoretical Perspectives of Intelligence

Some psychologists have suggested that intelligence is a single, general ability that people have to varying degrees and apply in a wide range of activities. Others have disagreed, citing evidence that people can be more or less intelligent on different kinds of tasks. Here we'll look at several theoretical perspectives on the single-entity versus multiple-abilities nature of intelligence.

Spearman's Concept of *g* Imagine that you give a large group of students a wide variety of tests—some measuring verbal skills, others measuring visual–spatial thinking, still others measuring mathematical problem solving, and so on. Chances are that all of the test scores would correlate with one another: Students who score high on one test would tend to score high on the other tests as well. The correlations would be especially strong among tests of very similar abilities. For example, a student who scored very high on a vocabulary test would probably score very high on other meas-

individual differences Diversity in abilities and characteristics (intelligence, personality, etc.) among students at a particular age and within any given group.

intelligence Ability to apply prior knowledge and experiences flexibly to accomplish challenging new tasks.

ures of verbal ability. The correlations between measures of distinctly different abilities would be weaker. For example, a student with an exceptionally large vocabulary might have only modest success in solving math problems (N. Brody, 1999; McGrew, Flanagan, Zeith, & Vanderwood, 1997; Neisser et al., 1996; Spearman, 1904).

In the early 1900s, Charles Spearman (1904, 1927) drew on such findings to propose that intelligence comprises both (a) a single, pervasive reasoning ability (a *general factor*) that is used across the board and (b) a number of narrow abilities (*specific factors*) involved in executing particular tasks. For example, measures of various language skills (vocabulary, reading comprehension, spelling, etc.) are all highly correlated, presumably because they all reflect both general intelligence and the same specific factor: verbal ability. A measure of language skills will correlate less with a measure of mathematical problem solving because the two measures are apt to tap into somewhat different specific abilities.

Many contemporary psychologists believe that sufficient evidence supports Spearman's concept of a general factor in intelligence—often known simply as Spearman's **g**. Underlying it, they suspect, may be a general ability to process information quickly and efficiently (Bornstein et al., 2006; Demetriou, Christou, Spanoudis, & Platsidou, 2002; Haier, 2003).

Cattell's Fluid and Crystallized Intelligences Several decades after Spearman's groundbreaking work, Raymond Cattell (1963, 1987) found evidence for two distinctly different components of general intelligence (*g*). First, children differ in **fluid intelligence**, their ability to acquire knowledge quickly and adapt to new situations effectively. Second, they differ in **crystallized intelligence**, the knowledge and skills they have accumulated from their experiences, schooling, and culture. Fluid intelligence is more important for new, unfamiliar tasks, especially those that require rapid decision making and involve nonverbal content. Crystallized intelligence is more important for familiar tasks, especially those that depend heavily on language and prior knowledge. Cattell suggested that fluid intelligence is largely the result of inherited biological factors, whereas crystallized intelligence depends on both fluid intelligence and experience and thus is influenced by both heredity and environment.

Cattell–Horn–Carroll Theory of Cognitive Abilities In recent years, other theorists have built on Cattell's distinction to suggest that intelligence may have three layers, or *strata* (Ackerman & Lohman, 2006; Carroll, 1993, 2003; Flanagan & Ortiz, 2001; Horn, 2008). In this *Cattell–Horn–Carroll theory of cognitive abilities*, the top stratum is general intelligence, or *g*. Underlying it, in the middle stratum, are 9 or 10 more specific abilities—processing speed, general reasoning ability, general world knowledge, ability to process visual input, and so on—that encompass fluid and/or crystallized intelligence to varying degrees. And underlying *these* abilities, in the bottom stratum, are more than 70 very specific abilities, such as reading speed, mechanical knowledge, and number and richness of associations in memory. With its large number of specific abilities, the Cattell–Horn–Carroll theory is too complex to describe in detail here, but you should be aware that psychologists are increasingly finding it useful in predicting and understanding students' achievement in various content domains (e.g., J. J. Evans, Floyd, McGrew, & Leforgee, 2001; Phelps, McGrew, Knopik, & Ford, 2005; B. E. Proctor, Floyd, & Shaver, 2005).

Keep in mind that different students are likely to be intelligent in different ways.

Gardner's Multiple Intelligences Howard Gardner (1983, 1998, 1999; Gardner & Hatch, 1990) suggests that people have at least eight distinctly different abilities, or *multiple intelligences*, that are relatively independent of one another (see Table 5.1). In his view, there may also be a ninth (existential) intelligence dedicated to philosophical and spiritual issues (e.g., Who are we? Why do we die?). However, because evidence for it is weaker than that for the other intelligences (Gardner, 1999, 2000a, 2003), I have omitted it from the table.

Gardner presents some evidence to support the existence of these distinctly different intelligences. For instance, he describes people who are quite skilled in one area, perhaps in composing music, yet have seemingly average abilities in other areas. He

g Theoretical general factor in intelligence that influences one's ability to learn and perform in a wide variety of contexts.

fluid intelligence Ability to acquire knowledge quickly and adapt effectively to new situations.

crystallized intelligence Knowledge and skills accumulated from prior experience, schooling, and culture.

TABLE 5.1
Gardner's Multiple Intelligences

Type of Intelligence	Examples of Relevant Behaviors
Linguistic intelligence: Ability to use language effectively	• Making persuasive arguments • Writing poetry • Noticing subtle nuances in meanings of words
Logical–mathematical intelligence: Ability to reason logically, especially in mathematics and science	• Solving mathematical problems quickly • Generating mathematical proofs • Formulating and testing hypotheses about observed phenomena*
Spatial intelligence: Ability to notice details of what one sees and to imagine and manipulate visual objects in one's mind	• Conjuring up mental images • Drawing a visual likeness of an object • Seeing subtle differences among visually similar objects
Musical intelligence: Ability to create, comprehend, and appreciate music	• Playing a musical instrument • Composing a musical work • Identifying the underlying structure of music
Bodily–kinesthetic intelligence: Ability to use one's body skillfully	• Dancing • Playing basketball • Performing pantomime
Interpersonal intelligence: Ability to notice subtle aspects of other people's behaviors	• Reading other people's moods • Detecting other people's underlying intentions and desires • Using knowledge of others to influence their thoughts and behaviors
Intrapersonal intelligence: Awareness of one's own feelings,motives, and desires	• Discriminating among such similar emotions as sadness and regret • Identifying the motives guiding one's own behavior • Using self-knowledge to relate more effectively with others
Naturalist intelligence: Ability to recognize patterns in nature and differences among various life-forms and natural objects	• Identifying members of particular plant or animal species • Classifying natural forms (e.g., rocks, types of mountains) • Applying one's knowledge of nature in activities such as farming, landscaping, or animal training

*This example may remind you of Piaget's theory of cognitive development. Many of the stage-specific characteristics that Piaget described reflect logical–mathematical intelligence.
Sources: Gardner, 1983, 1999.

Attention to detail in 10-year-old Luther's drawing of a plant suggests some talent in what Gardner calls *naturalist* intelligence.

also points out that people who suffer brain damage sometimes lose abilities that are restricted primarily to one intelligence. One person might show deficits primarily in language, whereas another might have difficulty with tasks that require spatial reasoning.

Among psychologists, reviews of Gardner's theory are mixed. Some theorists don't believe that Gardner's evidence is sufficiently compelling to support the notion of eight or nine distinctly different abilities (N. Brody, 1992; Corno et al., 2002; Sternberg, 2003; Waterhouse, 2006). Others agree that people may have a variety of relatively independent abilities but argue for different distinctions than those Gardner makes. For instance, such abilities might take the form of the second-stratum abilities in the Cattell–Horn–Carroll theory just described. Still others reject the idea that abilities in certain domains, such as in music or bodily movement, are really "intelligences" per se (Bracken, McCallum, & Shaughnessy, 1999; Sattler, 2001).

Despite psychologists' lukewarm reception to Gardner's theory of multiple intelligences, many educators have wholeheartedly embraced it because of its optimistic view of human potential. Gardner's perspective encourages us to use many different teaching methods, so that we can capitalize on students' diverse talents to help them learn and understand classroom subject matter (L. Campbell, Campbell, & Dickinson, 1998; Gardner, 2000b; Kornhaber, Fierros, & Veenema, 2004). Consider how one eighth-grade teacher took advantage of two girls' musical talent to teach spelling, something with which both girls were having difficulty:

> [I] asked the girls to label the piano keys with the letters of the alphabet, so that the girls could "play" the words on their keyboards. Later, on spelling tests, the students were asked to recall the tones and sounds of each word and write its corresponding letters. Not only did spelling scores improve, but the two pianists began thinking of other "sound" texts to set to music. Soon, they performed each classmate's name and transcribed entire sentences. (L. Campbell et al., 1998, p. 142)

Whether or not human beings have eight or more distinctly different intelligences, they certainly benefit when they are encouraged to think about a particular topic in several ways—perhaps with words, pictures, bodily movements, and so on (more on this point in the discussion of *encoding* in Chapter 6). We won't always want to teach to students' strengths, however. In some instances, we should present tasks that encourage students to address, and thereby strengthen, their areas of weakness (Sternberg, 2002).

Present classroom subject matter using a variety of approaches to capitalize on students' diverse abilities, but also give them tasks that require them to work on areas of weakness.

Sternberg's Triarchic Theory Robert Sternberg (1998, 2004; Sternberg et al., 2000) has speculated that people may be more or less intelligent in three different domains—hence, the term *triarchic. Analytical intelligence* involves making sense of, analyzing, contrasting, and evaluating the kinds of information and problems often seen in academic settings and on intelligence tests. *Creative intelligence* involves imagination, invention, and synthesis of ideas within the context of new situations. *Practical intelligence* involves applying knowledge and skills effectively to manage and respond to everyday problems and social situations.

In addition, Sternberg proposes that intelligent behavior involves an interplay of three factors, all of which vary from one occasion to the next (Sternberg, 1985, 1997, 2003):

1. *The environmental context in which the behavior occurs.* Different behaviors may be more or less adaptive and effective in different cultures. For example, learning to read is an adaptive response in industrialized societies yet largely irrelevant to certain other cultures.
2. *The relevance of prior experiences to a particular task.* Prior experiences can enhance intelligence in either of two ways. In some cases, extensive practice with a particular kind of task enables students to perform that task with increasing speed and efficiency (more about such *automaticity* in Chapter 6). In other instances, students are able to draw on what they have learned in previous situations to help them with *new* tasks.
3. *The cognitive processes required by the task.* Numerous cognitive processes are involved in intelligent behavior: interpreting new situations in adaptive ways, separating important information from irrelevant details, identifying possible problem-solving strategies, finding relationships among seemingly different ideas, making effective use of feedback, and so on. Different cognitive processes may be more or less important in different contexts, and an individual may behave more or less intelligently depending on the specific cognitive processes needed at the time.

To date, research neither supports nor refutes the notion that intelligence has the various triarchic components that Sternberg describes. Certain aspects of Sternberg's theory (e.g., how various factors work together) are described in such general terms that they are difficult to either confirm or disconfirm through research (Sattler, 2001; Siegler & Alibali, 2005). Moreover, Sternberg acknowledges that most of the data supporting his theory have been collected by his own research team, rather than by

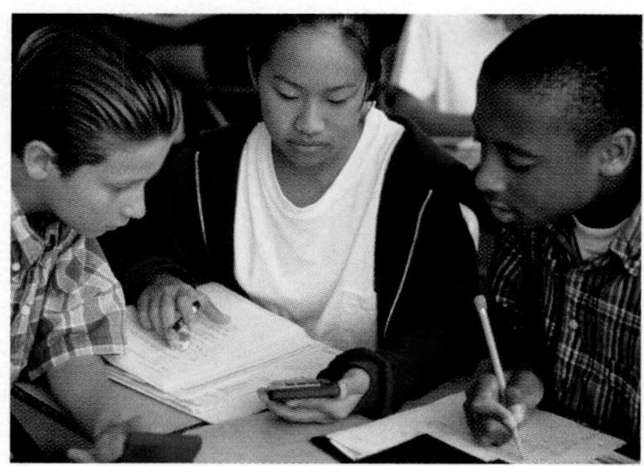

The concept of *distributed intelligence* suggests that learners can often think more intelligently by using technology to manipulate large bodies of data, using culturally based symbolic systems to simplify complex ideas and processes, and brainstorming possible problem solutions with peers.

outsiders who might be more objective or critical (Sternberg, 2003). Nevertheless, the theory reminds us that students' ability to behave intelligently may vary considerably depending on the context, previously learned knowledge and skills, and cognitive processes that a task involves.

Distributed Intelligence Implicit in our discussion so far has been the assumption that intelligent behavior is something people engage in with little or no help from the objects or people around them. Yet people are far more likely to think and behave intelligently when they have assistance from their physical, cultural, and social environments—an idea that is sometimes referred to as **distributed intelligence** (e.g., Barab & Plucker, 2002; Pea, 1993; Perkins, 1992, 1995).

Students can "distribute" a challenging task—that is, they can pass some of the cognitive burden onto something or someone else—in at least three ways. First, they can use physical objects, especially technology (e.g., calculators, computers), to handle and manipulate large amounts of information. Second, they can represent and think about the situations they encounter by using their culture's various symbolic systems—words, charts, diagrams, mathematical equations, and so on—and other cognitive tools. And third, they can work with other people to explore ideas and solve problems—as we've often heard, two heads are (usually) better than one. In fact, when students work together on complex, challenging tasks and problems, they teach one another strategies and ways of thinking that can help each of them think even *more* intelligently on future occasions (Salomon, 1993; also see Chapter 7).

Identify physical, symbolic, and social supports that can help students think more intelligently.

From this theoretical perspective, intelligence is not a characteristic that resides inside a person, nor is it something that can be easily measured and then summarized with one or more test scores. Instead, it is a highly variable and context-specific ability that increases when appropriate environmental supports are available.

Measuring Intelligence

When a student consistently struggles with certain aspects of the school curriculum, as Tim does in the opening case study, psychologists sometimes find it helpful to get a measure of the student's general level of cognitive functioning. Such measures are commonly known as **intelligence tests**. To get a sense of what intelligence tests are like, try the following exercise.

myeducationlab

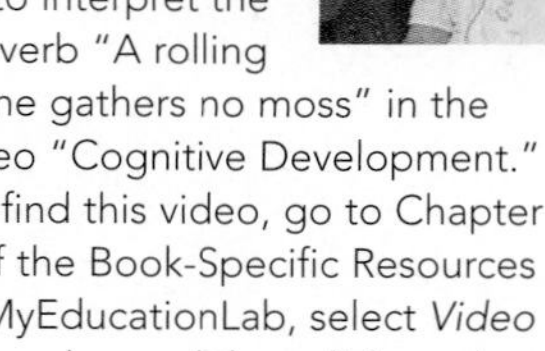

Observe developmental differences in adolescents' ability to interpret the proverb "A rolling stone gathers no moss" in the video "Cognitive Development." (To find this video, go to Chapter 5 of the Book-Specific Resources in MyEducationLab, select *Video Examples*, and then click on the title.)

EXPERIENCING FIRSTHAND

Mock Intelligence Test

Answer each of these questions:

1. What does the word *penitence* mean?
2. How are a goat and a beetle alike?
3. What should you do if you get separated from your family in a large department store?
4. What do people mean when they say "A rolling stone gathers no moss"?
5. Complete the following analogy: ⧗ is to ⧗ as ○● is to:

   a. ●●   b. ●○   c. ● ○   d. ▷◀

These test items are modeled after items on many contemporary intelligence tests. Often, the tests include a mixture of verbal tasks (such as Items 1 through 4) and less verbal, more visual tasks (such as Item 5).

distributed intelligence Thinking facilitated by physical objects and technology, concepts and symbols of one's culture, and/or social collaboration and support.

intelligence test General measure of current level of cognitive functioning; often used to predict academic achievement in the short run.

Scores on intelligence tests were originally calculated using a formula that involves division. Hence, they were called intelligence quotient scores, or **IQ scores**. Although we still use the term IQ, intelligence test scores are no longer based on the old formula. Instead, they are determined by comparing a student's performance on a given test with the performance of others in the same age-group. A score of 100 indicates average performance on the test: Students with this score have performed better than half of their age-mates but not as well as the other half. Scores well below 100 indicate below-average performance on the test; scores well above 100 indicate above-average performance.

FIGURE 5.1 Percentages of IQ scores in different ranges

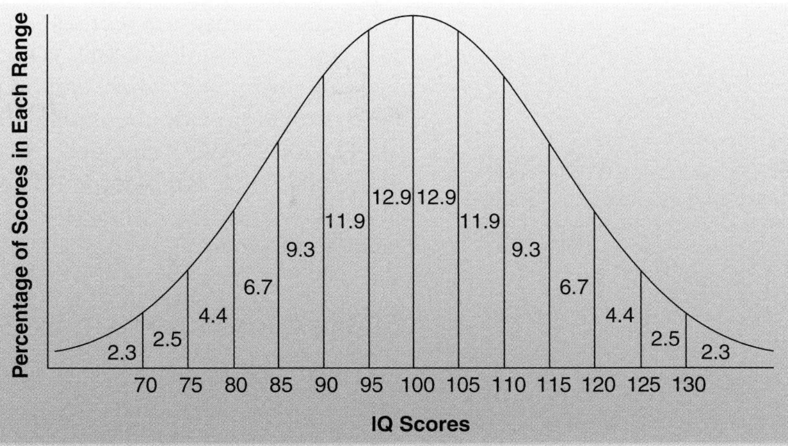

Figure 5.1 shows the percentages of students getting scores at different points along the scale (e.g., 12.9% get scores between 100 and 105). Notice that the curve is high in the middle and low at both ends, indicating that many more students obtain scores close to 100 than much higher or lower than 100. For example, if we add up the percentages in different parts of Figure 5.1, we find that approximately two-thirds (68%) of students score within 15 points of 100 (i.e., between 85 and 115). In contrast, only 2% of students score as low as 70, and only 2% score as high as 130. Such a many-in-the-middle-and-few-at-the-extremes distribution of scores seems to characterize a wide variety of human characteristics. Hence, psychologists have created a method of scoring intelligence test performance that intentionally yields this distribution.[1]

In the opening case study, Tim's performance on an intelligence test yields an IQ score of 96, which we are now in a better position to interpret. As you can see in Figure 5.1, a score of 96 is so close to 100 that we should consider it to be well within an average range.

IQ Scores and School Achievement Studies repeatedly show that performance on intelligence tests is correlated with school achievement (N. Brody, 1997; Gustafsson & Undheim, 1996; Sattler, 2001). On average, children with higher IQ scores earn higher course grades, do better on standardized achievement tests, and complete more years of education. However, three points about the relationship between intelligence test scores and school achievement are important to note:

- ***Intelligence does not necessarily cause achievement; it is simply correlated with it.*** Although students with high IQs typically perform well in school, we cannot say conclusively that their high achievement is the *result* of their intelligence. Intelligence probably does play an important role in school achievement, but many other factors—motivation, quality of instruction, family resources, peer group norms, and so on—are also involved.

- ***The relationship between IQ scores and achievement is an imperfect one, with many exceptions to the rule.*** For a variety of reasons, some students with high IQ scores don't perform well in the classroom, and other students achieve at higher levels than we would predict from their IQ scores alone. Furthermore, IQ tests seem to predict performance on traditional academic tasks better than they predict performance on everyday, real-world tasks or on unusual, multifaceted problems (J. E. Davidson, 2003; Sternberg, Grigorenko, & Kidd, 2005; Wenke & Frensch, 2003).

IQ score Score on an intelligence test, determined by comparing a person's performance with that of others in the same age-group.

[1]If you have taken a course in descriptive statistics, you may recognize IQ scores as being *standard scores,* which are based on the *normal distribution.* We'll look more closely at these concepts in Chapter 15.

• ***IQ scores can and often do change over time.*** The longer the time interval between two measures of intelligence, the greater the fluctuation in IQ, especially when the first measure was taken early in the individual's life (Bracken & Walker, 1997; Hayslip, 1994; Sattler, 2001). IQ scores and other measures of cognitive ability often increase over time when children are highly motivated, independent learners and when adults provide them with stimulating activities and a variety of reading materials (Echols, West, Stanovich, & Kehr, 1996; Kyllonen, Stankov, & Roberts, 2008; Sameroff, Seifer, Baldwin, & Baldwin, 1993; Stanovich, West, & Harrison, 1995). As a general rule, then, we should *not* use IQ scores to predict students' achievement many years in advance.

Don't use students' IQ scores to make long-term predictions about their school achievement.

Nature and Nurture in the Development of Intelligence

Research tells us that heredity probably plays some role in intelligence. For instance, identical twins (who have the same genetic makeup) tend to have more similar IQ scores than nonidentical (fraternal) twins do, even when the twins are adopted at birth by different parents and grow up in different homes (Bouchard, 1997; Plomin, 1994). This is not to say, however, that children inherit a single IQ gene that determines their intellectual ability. Rather, they probably inherit a variety of characteristics that, in one way or another, affect particular cognitive abilities and talents (Horn, 2008; Kovas & Plomin, 2007; Simonton, 2001).

Environmental factors influence intelligence as well, sometimes for the better and sometimes for the worse. Poor nutrition in the early years of development (including the nine months before birth) leads to lower IQ scores, as does a mother's excessive use of alcohol during pregnancy (D'Amato et al., 1992; Neisser et al., 1996; Ricciuti, 1993). Moving a child from a neglectful, impoverished home environment to a more nurturing, stimulating one (e.g., through adoption) can result in IQ gains of 15 points or more (Beckett et al., 2006; Capron & Duyme, 1989; van IJzendoorn & Juffer, 2005). Effective, too, are long-term intervention programs designed to help children acquire basic cognitive and academic skills (e.g., F. A. Campbell & Burchinal, 2008; Kağitçibaşi, 2007). Even simply *going to school* has a positive effect on IQ scores (Ceci, 2003; Ramey, 1992). Furthermore, researchers are finding that, worldwide, there is a slow but steady increase in people's IQ scores—a trend that is probably due to better nutrition, smaller family sizes, better schooling, increasing cognitive stimulation (through increased access to television, reading materials, etc.), and other improvements in people's environments (Flynn, 2007; E. Hunt, 2008; Neisser, 1998b).

The question of how *much* nature and nurture each play a role in influencing intelligence has been a source of considerable controversy over the years. But in fact, genetic and environmental factors interact in their influences on cognitive development and intelligence in ways that can probably never be disentangled (e.g., W. A. Collins et al., 2000; Flynn, 2008; Rogoff, 2003; Turkheimer, 2000). First of all, genes require reasonable environmental support to do their work. In an extremely impoverished environment—one with a lack of adequate nutrition and very limited stimulation—heredity may have little to say about children's intellectual growth, but under better circumstances, it can have a significant influence (Ceci, 2003; D. C. Rowe, Jacobson, & Van den Oord, 1999; Turkheimer, Haley, Waldron, D'Onofrio, & Gottesman, 2003). Second, heredity seems to affect how susceptible or impervious a child is to particular environmental conditions (Rutter, 1997). For instance, some students—such as those with certain inherited disabilities, like Tim in the opening case study—may need a quiet, well-structured learning environment in which to acquire good reading comprehension skills, but other students might pick up good reading skills regardless of the quality of the environment. And third, children tend to seek out environmental conditions that match their inherited abilities (Flynn, 2003; Halpern & LaMay, 2000; Scarr & McCartney, 1983). For example, children who inherit exceptional quantitative reasoning ability may enroll in advanced math courses and in other ways nurture their inherited talents. Children with average quantitative ability are less likely to take on such challenges and thus have fewer opportunities to develop their mathematical skills.

Cultural and Ethnic Diversity in Intelligence

Historically, some ethnic groups in the United States have, *on average*, performed better than other ethnic groups on intelligence tests (McLoyd, 1998; Neisser, 1998a). Most experts agree that such group differences in IQ are probably due to differences in environment and, more specifically, to economic circumstances that affect the quality of prenatal and postnatal nutrition, availability of stimulating books and toys, access to educational opportunities, and so on (Brooks-Gunn, Klebanov, & Duncan, 1996; Byrnes, 2003; McLoyd, 1998). Furthermore, various groups have become increasingly *similar* in average IQ score in recent years—a trend that can be attributed only to more equitable environmental conditions (Dickens & Flynn, 2006; Neisser et al., 1996).

Assume that when children from diverse ethnic groups all have reasonably stimulating environments, they have equal potential to develop their intellectual abilities.

Yet it is important to note that different cultural groups have somewhat different views about what intelligence *is* and may therefore nurture somewhat different abilities in their children. Many people of European descent think of intelligence primarily as an ability that influences children's academic achievement and adults' professional success. In contrast, people in many African, Asian, Hispanic, and Native American cultures think of intelligence as involving social as well as academic skills—maintaining harmonious interpersonal relationships, working effectively together to accomplish challenging tasks, and so on (Greenfield et al., 2006; J. Li & Fischer, 2004; Sternberg, 2004, 2007). And in Buddhist and Confucian societies in the Far East (e.g., China, Taiwan), intelligence also involves acquiring strong moral values and making meaningful contributions to society (J. Li, 2004; Sternberg, 2003).

Cultural groups differ, too, in the behaviors that they believe reflect intelligence. For instance, many traditional measures of intelligence take speed into account on certain test items: Children score higher if they respond quickly as well as correctly. Yet people in some cultures tend to value thoroughness over speed and may even be suspicious of accomplishments that are completed very quickly (Sternberg, 2007). As another example, in mainstream Western culture, strong verbal skills are considered to be a sign of high intelligence. Not all cultures value chattiness, however. Among many Japanese and among the Inuit people of northern Quebec, talking a lot can be interpreted as a sign of immaturity or low intelligence (Crago, 1988; Minami & McCabe, 1996; Sternberg, 2003). One researcher working at an Inuit school in northern Quebec asked a teacher about a boy whose language seemed unusually advanced for his age-group. The teacher gave this reply:

> Do you think he might have a learning problem? Some of these children who don't have such high intelligence have trouble stopping themselves. They don't know when to stop talking. (Crago, 1988, p. 219)

As teachers, then, we must be careful not to assume that our own views of intelligence are shared by the students and families of cultures very different from our own.

Being Smart About Intelligence and IQ Scores

Whatever its nature and origins, intelligence appears to be an important factor in students' ability to learn and achieve in the classroom. Accordingly, we must have a good grasp of how we can best nurture students' intellectual growth and how we can reasonably interpret their performance on intelligence tests. Following are several recommendations:

Place higher priority on developing—rather than on determining—intelligence. As we have seen, intelligence is hardly a fixed, unchangeable characteristic: Environmental factors, including schooling, can lead to increases in children's measured intelligence. And the notion of distributed intelligence suggests that virtually all students can act more intelligently when they have tools, symbolic systems, and social groups to assist them in their efforts (B. Rhodes, 2008; Salomon, 1993; Sfard, 1998). As teachers, we should think more about *enhancing and supporting* students' intelligence than about measuring it (P. D. Nichols & Mittelholtz, 1997; Posner & Rothbart, 2007; B. Rhodes, 2008). Rather than ask, How intelligent are our students? we should instead ask, How can we help our students think as intelligently as possible? What tools and social networks can we give them? What useful concepts and procedures can we teach them?

Think of intelligence tests as useful but imperfect measures. As we've seen, intelligence tests are hardly magical instruments that mysteriously determine a learner's true intelligence—if, in fact, such a thing as "true" intelligence exists. Instead, these tests are simply collections of questions and tasks that psychologists have developed and continue to revise in order to get a handle on how well students can think, reason, and learn at a particular point in time.

Used in conjunction with other information, IQ scores can often give us a general idea of a student's current cognitive functioning. To interpret IQ scores appropriately, however, we must be aware of the limitations of intelligence tests:

- Different kinds of tests may yield somewhat different scores.
- A student's performance on any test will inevitably be affected by many temporary factors—general health, mood, time of day, distracting circumstances, and so on. Such factors are especially influential for young children, who are apt to have high energy levels, short attention spans, and little interest in sitting still for more than a few minutes. (As you'll discover in Chapters 14 and 15, this is an issue of test *reliability*.)
- Test items typically focus on skills that are important in mainstream Western culture, especially in school settings. They don't necessarily tap skills that might be more highly valued and nurtured in other contexts or cultures.
- Some students may be unfamiliar with the content or types of tasks involved in particular test items and may perform poorly on those items as a result.
- **English language learners (ELLs)**—students who have only limited proficiency in English as a result of growing up in a non-English-speaking environment—are at an obvious disadvantage when an intelligence test is administered in English. Thus, their IQ scores will typically be poor indicators of what they will be able to do once their English improves. (Dirks, 1982; Heath, 1989; Neisser et al., 1996; Perkins, 1995; Sternberg, 2007; Sternberg et al., 2005; Zigler & Finn-Stevenson, 1992)

Be skeptical of any IQ scores obtained for recent immigrants and other students who were not fluent in English when tested. And in general, never base expectations for students' achievement *solely* on IQ scores.

Obviously, then, we should never think of IQ scores as precise measures of intellectual functioning for *all* students. IQs give us a rough estimate of intelligence for many students, but we must be skeptical of the scores' accuracy when students come from diverse cultural backgrounds, know little English, or were fairly young when the scores were obtained.

Use the results of more focused measures when you want to assess specific abilities. Whenever we obtain and use IQ scores, we are buying into the idea that a general factor, or *g*, underlies students' school performance. But as Spearman, Cattell, Gardner, Sternberg, and many others have suggested, intelligence has many facets. Hence, scores from any single IQ test cannot possibly give us a complete picture of a student's intelligence. If we want to estimate a student's potential for success in a particular domain—say, in mathematics or mechanical reasoning—we are probably better off using measures of more specific abilities (Ackerman & Lohman, 2006; Horn, 2008; McGrew et al., 1997). However, I urge you to rely *only* on instruments available from well-respected test publishers. Tests that you might find on the Internet—for instance, tests that claim to be measures of Gardner's multiple intelligences—have typ-

English language learner (ELL) School-age child who is not fully fluent in English because of limited exposure to English prior to enrollment in an English-speaking school.

ically undergone little or no research scrutiny, which makes their results questionable at best. Keep in mind, too, that intelligence tests should be administered only by school psychologists and other professionals who have been specifically trained in their use.

Don't use so-called "intelligence tests" you find on the Internet.

Look for behaviors that reveal exceptional talents within the context of a student's culture. To the extent that intelligence is culture dependent, intelligent behavior is apt to take different forms in children from different backgrounds (Neisser et al., 1996; Perkins, 1995; Sternberg, 2007). For instance, among students who have grown up in predominantly African American communities, intelligence might be reflected in oral language, such as colorful speech, creative storytelling, or humor (Torrance, 1989). For students from Native American cultures, intelligence might be reflected in interpersonal skills, highly skilled craftsmanship, or an exceptional ability to notice and remember subtle landmarks in one's physical environment (Maker & Schiever, 1989; Sternberg, 2005).

As teachers, then, we must be careful not to limit our conception of intelligence only to students' ability to succeed at traditional academic tasks and to perform well on traditional intelligence tests. One alternative is *dynamic assessment*, an approach introduced in Chapter 2: Rather than assess what students already know and can do, teach them something new and see how quickly and easily they master it (Haywood & Lidz, 2007; Sternberg, 2007).

Remember that many other factors also affect students' classroom achievement. Most measures of intelligence focus on specific things that a student *can* do, with little consideration of what a student is *likely* to do. For instance, intelligence tests don't evaluate the extent to which students are willing to view a situation from multiple perspectives, examine data with a critical eye, or actively take charge of their own learning. Yet such traits are often just as important as intellectual ability in determining success on academic and real-world tasks (Duckworth & Seligman, 2005; Kuhn, 2001a; Perkins, Tishman, Ritchhart, Donis, & Andrade, 2000). In the next section, we'll examine forms that these *cognitive styles* and *dispositions* might take.

myeducationlab

Examine research evidence regarding the importance of one such trait—self-discipline—by completing the Understanding Research exercise "Self-Discipline and Academic Achievement" in MyEducationLab. (To find this activity, go to the topic Student Diversity in MyEducationLab, click on *Assignments and Activities*, and then select *Understanding Research*.)

Cognitive Styles and Dispositions

Students with the same general level of intelligence often approach classroom tasks and think about classroom topics differently. Some of these individual differences reflect **cognitive styles**, over which students don't necessarily have much conscious control. Others reflect **dispositions**, which students voluntarily and intentionally bring to bear on their efforts to master school subject matter. Don't agonize over the distinction between these two concepts, because their meanings overlap considerably. Both involve not only specific cognitive tendencies but also personality characteristics (Messick, 1994b; Zhang & Sternberg, 2006). Disposition also has a motivational component—an I-*want*-to-do-it-this-way quality (Kuhn, 2001a; Perkins & Ritchhart, 2004; Stanovich, 1999).[2]

Over the years, psychologists and educators have examined a wide variety of cognitive styles (some have used the term *learning styles*) and dispositions. The traits they

cognitive style Characteristic way in which a learner tends to think about a task and process new information; typically comes into play automatically, rather than by choice.

disposition General inclination and desire to approach and think about learning and problem-solving tasks in a particular way; typically has a motivational component in addition to cognitive components.

[2]The bodies of research on cognitive styles and on dispositions have evolved independently of each other, and to my knowledge, theorists have not contrasted the two concepts. The cognitive-style-as-involuntary and disposition-as-intentional ideas seem to underlie most theoretical discussions in the two areas.

Don't plan instruction based on results you might get from easily available and aggressively marketed "learning style" inventories.

have identified and the instruments they have developed to assess these traits don't always hold up under the scrutiny of other researchers (Irvine & York, 1995; Krätzig & Arbuthnott, 2006; Messick, 1994b). And tailoring particular instructional strategies to students' self-reported styles—which, in some cases, are nothing more than students' *preferences*—doesn't necessarily enhance academic achievement (Curry, 1990; Kavale & Forness, 1987; Snider, 1990).

Nonetheless, some cognitive styles and dispositions *do* seem to influence how and what students learn. For instance, at least two dimensions of cognitive style appear to be influential:

- *Analytic versus holistic processing.* Some students tend to break new stimuli and tasks into their subordinate parts (an *analytic* approach), whereas others tend to perceive stimuli primarily as integrated, indivisible wholes (a *holistic* approach) (A. Miller, 1987; Norenzayan, Choi, & Peng, 2007; Riding & Cheema, 1991).[3] Overall, an analytic approach appears to be more beneficial in school learning, although research is not entirely consistent on this point (e.g., Bagley & Mallick, 1998; Irvine & York, 1995; Jonassen & Grabowski, 1993; Norenzayan et al., 2007). On average, students become increasingly analytical as they grow older (Shipman & Shipman, 1985).
- *Verbal versus visual learning.* Some students seem to learn better when information is presented through words (*verbal* learners), whereas others seem to learn better when it's presented through pictures (*visual* learners) (Mayer & Massa, 2003; Riding & Cheema, 1991). There isn't necessarily a good or bad style here. Rather, learning success probably depends on which modality is used more extensively in classroom activities and instructional materials. Using *both* verbal and visual material to present important ideas is one easy way to accommodate these differing styles.

Although psychologists have often been reluctant to identify some cognitive styles as being more adaptive than others, certain kinds of dispositions are clearly beneficial in the classroom:

- *Stimulation seeking:* Eagerly interacting with one's physical and social environment
- *Need for cognition:* Regularly seeking and engaging in challenging cognitive tasks
- *Critical thinking:* Consistently evaluating information or arguments in terms of their accuracy, credibility, and worth, rather than accepting them at face value (more on critical thinking in Chapter 8)
- *Open-mindedness:* Being willing to consider alternative perspectives and multiple sources of evidence and to suspend judgment rather than leap to an immediate conclusion (Bransford & Schwartz, 1999; Cacioppo, Petty, Feinstein, & Jarvis, 1996; DeBacker & Crowson, 2008; Halpern, 1997, 2008; Kardash & Scholes, 1996; P. M. King & Kitchener, 2002; Raine, Reynolds, & Venables, 2002; Southerland & Sinatra, 2003; Stanovich, 1999; West, Toplak, & Stanovich, 2008)

Such dispositions are often positively correlated with students' learning and achievement, and many theorists have suggested that they play a causal role in what and how much students learn. In fact, dispositions sometimes overrule intelligence in their influence on long-term achievement (Dai & Sternberg, 2004; Kuhn & Franklin, 2006; Perkins & Ritchhart, 2004). For instance, children who eagerly seek out physical and social stimulation as preschoolers later become better readers and earn higher grades in school (Raine et al., 2002). Students with a high need for cognition learn more from

[3]In the research literature, you might see distinctions between *field independence* and *field dependence* or between *reflectivity* and *impulsivity*. Both of these distinctions fall along a continuum of analytic versus holistic processing (A. Miller, 1987; Riding & Cheema, 1991).

what they read and are more likely to base conclusions on sound evidence and logical reasoning (Cacioppo et al., 1996; Dai, 2002; P. K. Murphy & Mason, 2006). And students who critically evaluate new evidence and are receptive to and open minded about diverse perspectives show more advanced reasoning capabilities and achieve at higher levels (Matthews, Zeidner, & Roberts, 2006; Stanovich, 1999).

Researchers do not yet have a good understanding of the origins of various cognitive styles and dispositions. Perhaps inherited characteristics play a role; for instance, a student may have an energetic, inquisitive temperament or a biologically based strength in visual processing. Perhaps parents or cultural groups encourage certain ways of looking at and dealing with the world (Irvine & York, 1995; Kuhn, Daniels, & Krishnan, 2003; Norenzayan et al., 2007). For instance, if oral histories have been a significant part of students' cultural heritage, students might be accustomed to learning from information presented auditorially rather than visually (Kirk, 1972; Trawick-Smith, 2003). And quite possibly, teachers' actions in the classroom make a difference—for instance, whether teachers encourage exploration, risk taking, and critical thinking with respect to classroom topics (Flum & Kaplan, 2006; Kuhn, 2001b, 2006). In the following explanation of the metric system, the teacher actually seems to *discourage* any disposition to think analytically and critically about classroom material:

> ***Teacher:*** Write this on your paper . . . it's simply memorizing this pattern. We have meters, centimeters, and millimeters. Let's say . . . write millimeters, centimeters, and meters. We want to make sure that our metric measurement is the same. If I gave you this decimal, let's say .234 m (yes, write that). In order to come up with .234 m in centimeters, the only thing that is necessary is that you move the decimal. How do we move the decimal? You move it to the right two places. (Jason, sit up please.) If I move it to the right two places, what should .234 m look like, Daniel, in centimeters? What does it look like, Ashley?
>
> ***Ashley:*** 23.4 cm.
>
> ***Teacher:*** Twenty-three point four. Simple stuff. In order to find [millimeters], we're still moving that decimal to the right, but this time, boys and girls, we're only going to move it one place. So, if I move this decimal one place, what is my answer for millimeters? (Turner, Meyer, et al., 1998, p. 741)

Undoubtedly, this teacher means well: She wants her students to understand how to convert from one unit of measurement to another. But notice the attitude she engenders by suggesting that the task is "simply memorizing this pattern."

Although researchers have not yet determined how best to promote productive styles and dispositions, we can reasonably assume that modeling and encouraging effective ways of thinking about classroom subject matter will get students off to a good start. For instance, as teachers, we should consistently demonstrate open-mindedness about diverse perspectives, and we might regularly ask students to evaluate the quality of scientific evidence (Halpern, 1998; Kuhn, 2001b; Messer, 1976; Perkins & Ritchhart, 2004). The Into the Classroom feature "Promoting Productive Styles and Dispositions" presents examples of what we might do.

Most of the time, we can accommodate individual differences in intelligence and dispositions within the context of general education practices and activities. Occasionally, however, students are different enough from their peers—perhaps in cognitive ability, physical ability, or classroom behavior—that they require special adaptations. We turn to such students now.

Educating Students with Special Needs in General Education Classrooms

Students with special needs are those who are different enough from their peers that they require specially adapted instructional materials and practices to help them maximize their learning and achievement. Many of these students have cognitive,

students with special needs Students different enough from their peers that they require specially adapted instructional materials and practices to maximize their learning and achievement.

INTO THE Classroom

Promoting Productive Styles and Dispositions

- **When students consistently approach tasks in an impulsive, nonanalytical manner, focus their attention on accuracy, rather than speed, and teach them to talk themselves through detailed tasks.**

  To help an impulsive third grader subtract two-digit numbers with regrouping (i.e., borrowing), his teacher instructs him to say these three phrases to himself as he solves each problem: (a) "Compare top and bottom numbers," (b) "If top number is smaller, borrow," and (c) "Subtract."

- **Present important ideas both verbally and visually, with each modality offering unique insights into the subject matter.**

  As a high school history teacher describes key World War II battles, he presents maps and photographs of each battlefield and describes specific strategies that one side or the other used to outsmart its opponent. To get his students to think analytically about both the visual and verbal information, the teacher asks them questions such as "What challenges did the local topography present for the troops?" and "Why did the commanders choose the strategies they did?"

- **Communicate your own eagerness to learn about new topics.**

  A middle school science teacher asks her students "Have you ever wondered why so many people are concerned about global climate change? I certainly have! I've brought in some magazine articles that can help us understand why they're worried."

- **Model open-mindedness about diverse viewpoints and a willingness to suspend judgment until all the facts are in.**

  In a lesson about the properties of air—especially the fact that it takes up space—a first-grade teacher asks her students to predict whether the inside of a glass will get wet or stay dry when it is pushed upside down into a bowl of water. After the glass has been immersed, students come to different conclusions about the wetness or dryness of its inside. The teacher responds, "Uh-oh. Now we have two different opinions. We are going to have to figure out how to solve this problem." She devises a simple strategy—stuffing a crumpled paper towel into the glass and then reimmersing it in the water—to get more conclusive evidence. (This example is depicted in the "Properties of Air" video in Chapter 5 of the Book-Specific Resources in **MyEducationLab**.)

personal, social, or physical disabilities that adversely affect their performance in a typical classroom. Others, instead, are so advanced in a particular domain—that is, they are *gifted*—that they gain little from the activities and assignments suitable for most of their age-mates.

In the United States, more than 90% of students with special educational needs are in general education classrooms for part or all of the school day—a practice known as **inclusion** (U.S. Department of Education, National Center for Education Statistics, 2007). In fact, federal legislation mandates that students with disabilities be educated in neighborhood schools and, ideally, in regular classrooms to the greatest extent possible.

Public Law 94-142: Individuals with Disabilities Education Act (IDEA)

In 1975, the U.S. Congress passed Public Law 94-142, which is now known as the **Individuals with Disabilities Education Act (IDEA)**. IDEA has been amended and reauthorized several times since then, most recently in 2004 under the name *Individuals with Disabilities Education Improvement Act.* It currently grants educational rights from birth until age 21 for people with cognitive, emotional, and physical disabilities. It guarantees several rights for students with disabilities:

- *A free and appropriate education.* All students with disabilities are entitled to a free educational program designed specifically to meet their unique educational needs. For example, to acquire adequate reading skills, a student with a reading disability might require tailor-made reading materials and some one-on-one instruction.

inclusion Practice of educating all students, including those with severe and multiple disabilities, in neighborhood schools and general education classrooms.

Individuals with Disabilities Education Act (IDEA) U.S. federal legislation granting educational rights from birth until age 21 for people with cognitive, emotional, or physical disabilities.

FIGURE 5.2 Typical components of an individualized education plan (IEP)

The IEP is a written statement for an individual aged 3 to 21 who has been identified as having a special educational need. Any IEP that is developed or revised should contain the following:

- Present levels of educational performance, including
  - How the disability affects involvement and progress in the general education curriculum (for students 6–21 years old), *or*
  - How the disability affects participation in appropriate activities (for children 3–5 years old)
- Short-term objectives or benchmarks (for a student who will work toward achievement standards different from those of classmates)
- Measurable annual goals related to
  - Meeting needs resulting from the disability, to ensure that the student is involved in and can progress through a general education curriculum
  - Meeting each of the student's other disability-related educational needs
- How the student's progress toward annual goals will be assessed and when reports on the student's progress will be provided
- The special education, related services, supplementary aids, program modifications, and supports that will be provided so that the student can
  - Advance appropriately toward annual goals
  - Be involved in and progress through the general curriculum
  - Participate in extracurricular and other nonacademic activities
  - Participate in general education with other students with disabilities and with students who do not have disabilities
- Explanation of the extent, if any, to which the student will *not* participate with nondisabled students in general education classes and in extracurricular and other nonacademic activities of the general curriculum
- Any modifications in the administration of state- or district-wide assessments of achievement so that the student can participate in those assessments, or, if the IEP determines that the student will not participate in part or all of an assessment, why the assessment is inappropriate and how the student will alternatively be assessed
- Projected date for beginning services and program modifications and the anticipated frequency, location, and duration of each
- Transition plans, including
  - Beginning no later than age 16 and each year thereafter, a statement of goals and the student's needs related to transition services, including those related to training, education, employment, and (if appropriate) independent living skills
  - Beginning at least one year before the student reaches the age of majority under state law (usually age 18), a statement that the student has been informed of those rights under IDEA that will transfer from parents to student when the student becomes of age

Source: Adapted from *Exceptional Lives* 5/E by Turnbull et al., 2007, Upper Saddle River, NJ: Merrill/Prentice Hall. Adapted by permission of Pearson Education, Inc., Upper Saddle River, NJ.

- *Fair and nondiscriminatory evaluation.* A multidisciplinary team conducts an in-depth evaluation of any student who may be eligible for special services. The team's makeup depends on the student's needs but typically consists of two or more teachers, any appropriate specialists, and the student's parent(s) or guardian(s). Using a variety of tests and other evaluation tools, school personnel conduct a complete assessment of potential disabling conditions. Evaluation procedures must take a student's background and any suspected physical or communication difficulties into account. For example, tests must be administered in a student's primary language.
- *Education in the least restrictive environment.* To the greatest extent possible, students with disabilities should be included in the same academic environment, extracurricular activities, and social interactions as their nondisabled peers. That is, they must have the **least restrictive environment**: the most typical and standard educational environment that, with sufficient supplementary aids and support services, can reasonably meet their needs. Exclusion from general education is warranted only when others' safety would be jeopardized or when, even with proper support and assistance, a student cannot make appreciable progress in a general education setting.
- *Individualized education program (IEP).* When an individual aged 3 to 21 is identified as having a disability, the multidisciplinary team collaboratively develops an instructional program, called an **individualized education program**

Provide as typical an educational experience as possible for *all* students in your classes.

least restrictive environment Most typical and standard educational environment that can reasonably meet the needs of a student with a disability.

individualized education program (IEP) Written description of an appropriate instructional program for a student with special needs.

(IEP), tailored to the individual's strengths and weaknesses (see Figure 5.2). The IEP is a written statement that the team continues to review and, if appropriate, to revise at least once a year—more frequently if conditions warrant.

- *Due process.* IDEA mandates several practices that ensure that students' and parents' rights are preserved throughout the decision-making process. For instance, parents can give or withhold permission to have their child evaluated for special education services, and they must be notified in writing before the school takes any action that might change their child's educational program. Upon request, parents can see all school records about their child. And if the parents and school system disagree on the most appropriate placement for a child, mediation or a hearing before an impartial individual (i.e., someone who is not employed by the school district) can be used to resolve the differences.

myeducationlab

Gain practice in inclusive education by completing the Building Teaching Skills and Dispositions exercise "Participating in an IEP Meeting" in MyEducationLab. (To find this activity, go to the topic Students with Special Needs in MyEducationLab and click on *Building Teaching Skills and Dispositions.*)

IDEA has now been in effect for more than 30 years, and in that time it has had a significant impact on the nature of special education. More and more, teachers are realizing that truly inclusive practices require individualization of instruction for *all* students, not just those with formally identified needs. And rather than provide specialized instruction in a separate classroom, many special education teachers now partner with regular classroom teachers to jointly teach all students—both those with disabilities and those without—during part or all of the school day.

Potential Benefits and Drawbacks of Inclusion

Despite the mandates of IDEA, the common practice of inclusion for students with disabilities has been controversial among both theorists and practitioners. Some argue that students are most likely to develop normal peer relationships and social skills when they participate as fully as possible in the overall social life of their school (e.g., Hahn, 1989; Will, 1986). But other experts worry that when students with special needs are in a regular classroom for the entire school day, they cannot possibly get the intense specialized instruction that many need to achieve essential basic skills in reading, mathematics, and so on (Manset & Semmel, 1997; Zigmond et al., 1995). Furthermore, nondisabled classmates may stigmatize, avoid, or bully students who appear to be odd or incompetent in some way (Hamovitch, 2007; also see Chapter 3).

Many research studies indicate that placing students with disabilities in general education classrooms can have several benefits over educating them in self-contained special education classrooms. In particular, inclusion can lead to the following benefits:

- Better social skills
- More appropriate classroom behavior
- More frequent interaction with nondisabled peers
- Academic achievement equivalent to (and sometimes higher than) that in a self-contained classroom
- More positive sense of self *if* the school environment is one in which all students accept and respect individual differences in their classmates (Halvorsen & Sailor, 1990; Hamovitch, 2007; P. Hunt & Goetz, 1997; MacMaster, Donovan, & MacIntyre, 2002; Scruggs & Mastropieri, 1994; Slavin, 1987; Soodak & McCarthy, 2006; Stainback & Stainback, 1992)

We are especially likely to see such benefits when students understand the nature of their disabilities and when instruction and materials are tailored to students' specific educational needs. For instance, it is *not* helpful to pretend that a student with a learning disability is simply having a "bad day" whenever he or she struggles with an assignment.

Nondisabled students often benefit from inclusive practices as well: They develop an increasing awareness of the heterogeneous nature of the human race and discover that individuals with special needs are, in many respects, very much like themselves (P. Hunt & Goetz, 1997; D. Staub, 1998). I think of my son Jeff's friendship with Evan, a classmate with severe physical and cognitive disabilities, during their third-grade year. The boys' teacher had asked Jeff to be a special friend to Evan, interacting with him at lunch and whenever else the class schedule allowed. Although largely unable to speak, Evan always made it clear through gestures and facial expressions that he was delighted to spend time with his friend, giving Jeff—who was quite shy—a considerable boost in social self-confidence. Several years later, Jeff reflected on his friendship with Evan:

> It made me realize that Evan was a person too. It made me realize that I could have a friendship with a boy with disabilities. Doing things that made Evan happy made me happy as well. I knew that *Evan* knew that we were friends.

It is essential, of course, that nondisabled students treat classmates who have disabilities in respectful and supportive ways and, better still, forge friendships with these classmates. To nurture positive relationships between students with and without disabilities, we can do several things:

- Explicitly point out the strengths of a student with a disability.
- Ask students with and without disabilities to assist others in their particular areas of strength.
- Plan academic and recreational activities that require cooperation.
- Encourage students with disabilities to participate in extracurricular activities and community events. (Bassett et al., 1996; DuPaul, Ervin, Hook, & McGoey, 1998; Hamovitch, 2007; Madden & Slavin, 1983; Turnbull, Pereira, & Blue-Banning, 2000)

Identifying Students' Particular Special Needs: Response to Intervention and People-First Language

Historically, experts have not always agreed about how to define various categories of special needs—especially those not involving obvious physical conditions—or about how best to identify the students that fit into each category. In the United States, IDEA provides specific criteria to be used in identifying particular disabling conditions. Students with disabilities who do not meet IDEA's criteria are often eligible for special educational services under Section 504 of the Rehabilitation Act of 1973 (sometimes referred to simply as *Section 504*). This act stipulates that institutions that benefit from federal funding (including public schools) cannot discriminate against individuals on the basis of a disability. Procedures for assessing and accommodating students' disabilities are less prescriptive in Section 504 than they are in IDEA—a situation that can be either advantageous or disadvantageous, depending on the circumstances. (For more details on the differences between IDEA and Section 504, see deBettencourt, 2002.)

One approach to identification that is gaining increasing support (and that is endorsed in the 2004 reauthorization of IDEA) involves determining **response to intervention (RTI)**. In this approach, a teacher keeps an eye out for any student who has exceptional difficulty with basic skills in a certain domain (e.g., reading or math) despite normal whole-class instruction *and* intensive follow-up small-group instruction that have both been shown *by research* to be effective for most children. Such a student is referred for in-depth assessment of various characteristics and abilities. If the assessment rules out obvious disabling conditions (e.g., significant genetic abnormalities, sensory impairments), the student is assumed to have a specific cognitive impairment—usually falling in the general category of learning disabilities—and is therefore eligible for special services (e.g., Division for Learning Disabilities, 2007; L. S. Fuchs & Fuchs, 2007; Mellard & Johnson, 2008).

response to intervention (RTI) Approach to diagnosing a cognitive impairment in which students are identified for in-depth assessment after failing to master certain basic skills despite both whole-class and remedial small-group instruction that research has shown to be effective for most students.

Whenever we identify a student as having a particular disability, however, we run the risk of focusing other people's attention on weaknesses, rather than the student's many strengths and age-typical characteristics. To minimize such an effect, special

FIGURE 5.3 Examples of cognitive processing deficiencies in students with learning disabilities

Perceptual difficulty. Students have trouble understanding or remembering information they receive through a particular modality, such as vision or hearing.

Memory difficulty. Students have less capacity for remembering information over either the short or long run (i.e., they may have problems with either *working memory* or *long-term memory*; see Chapter 6).

Metacognitive difficulty. Students have difficulty using effective learning strategies, monitoring progress toward learning goals, and in other ways directing their own learning. (Chapter 8 looks at the nature of metacognition.)

Oral language processing difficulty. Students have trouble understanding spoken language or remembering what they have been told.

Reading difficulty. Students have trouble recognizing printed words or comprehending what they read; an extreme form is known as *dyslexia*.

Written language difficulty. Students have problems in handwriting, spelling, or expressing themselves coherently on paper; an extreme form is known as *dysgraphia*.

Mathematical difficulty. Students have trouble thinking about or remembering information involving numbers; an extreme form is known as *dyscalculia*.

Social perception difficulty. Students have trouble interpreting others' social cues and signals and so respond inappropriately in social situations.

Music processing difficulty. Students have little sensitivity to differences in pitch and are unable to recognize familiar tunes; an extreme form is known as *amusia*.

Sources: Coch, Dawson, & Fischer, 2007; Conte, 1991; Eden, Stein, & Wood, 1995; Fletcher, Lyon, Fuchs, & Barnes, 2007; L. S. Fuchs et al., 2005; Hanich, Jordan, Kaplan, & Dick, 2001; Meltzer, 2007; Peretz, 2008; H. L. Swanson, 1993; H. L. Swanson, Cooney, & O'Shaughnessy, 1998; H. L. Swanson & Jerman, 2006; Turnbull et al., 2007; Wong, 1991a, 1991b.

Use people-first language when talking about students with disabilities.

educators urge us all to use **people-first language** when referring to students with disabilities—in other words, to mention the person *before* the disability. For instance, we might say *student with a learning disability*, rather than *learning-disabled student*, or *student who is blind*, rather than *blind student*.

In upcoming sections of this chapter, as well as in the Students in Inclusive Settings tables that appear in later chapters of the book, I group students with special needs into five general categories. Table 5.2 lists the specific kinds of special needs that fall within each category. Disabilities covered by IDEA appear in red type in the table.

Students with Specific Cognitive or Academic Difficulties

Some students with special educational needs show no outward signs of physical disability yet have cognitive difficulties that interfere with their ability to learn academic material or perform typical classroom tasks. Such students include those with learning disabilities, attention-deficit hyperactivity disorder, and speech and communication disorders.

Learning Disabilities

Students with **learning disabilities** comprise the largest single category of students with special needs (U.S. Department of Education, 2006). These students have significant difficulties in one or more specific cognitive processes that cannot be attributed to mental retardation, emotional problems, sensory impairment, or environmental deprivation. Such difficulties often appear to result from specific and possibly inherited brain dysfunctions (Coch, Dawson, & Fischer, 2007; Kovas & Plomin, 2007; Yeo, Gangestad, & Thoma, 2007). Figure 5.3 lists several forms that a learning disability might take.

people-first language Language usage in which a student's disability is identified *after* the student is named.

learning disabilities Deficiencies in one or more specific cognitive processes but not in overall cognitive functioning.

Students in Inclusive Settings

TABLE 5.2
General and Specific Categories of Students with Special Needs (specific categories listed in red covered by IDEA)

General Category	Specific Categories	Description
Students with specific cognitive or academic difficulties: These students exhibit an uneven pattern of academic performance; they may have unusual difficulty with certain tasks yet perform quite successfully on other tasks.	Learning disabilities	Difficulties in specific cognitive processes (e.g., in perception, language, or memory) that cannot be attributed to other disabilities, such as mental retardation, emotional or behavioral disorders, or sensory impairments
	Attention-deficit hyperactivity disorder (ADHD) (not specifically covered by IDEA, but students are often eligible for special services under the IDEA category Other Health Impairments)	Disorder marked by either or both of these characteristics: (a) difficulty focusing and maintaining attention and (b) frequent hyperactive and impulsive behavior
	Speech and communication disorders	Impairments in spoken language (e.g., mispronunciations of certain sounds, stuttering, or abnormal syntactical patterns) or in language comprehension that significantly interfere with classroom performance
Students with social or behavioral problems: These students exhibit social, emotional, or behavioral difficulties serious enough to interfere significantly with their academic performance.	Emotional and behavioral disorders	Emotional states and behaviors that are present over a substantial period of time and significantly disrupt academic learning and performance
	Autism spectrum disorders	Disorders marked by impaired social cognition, social skills, and social interaction, as well as repetition of certain idiosyncratic behaviors; milder forms (e.g., Asperger syndrome) associated with normal development in other domains; extreme forms associated with delayed cognitive and linguistic development and highly unusual behaviors
Students with general delays in cognitive and social functioning: These students exhibit low achievement in virtually all academic areas and have social skills typical of much younger children.	Intellectual disabilities (mental retardation)	Significantly below-average general intelligence and deficits in adaptive behavior (i.e., in practical and social intelligence); deficits are evident in childhood and typically appear at an early age
Students with physical or sensory challenges: These students have disabilities caused by diagnosed physical or medical problems.	Physical and health impairments	Physical or medical conditions (usually long term) that interfere with school performance as a result of limited energy and strength, reduced mental alertness, or little muscle control
	Visual impairments	Malfunctions of the eyes or optic nerves that prevent normal vision even with corrective lenses
	Hearing loss	Malfunctions of the ear or associated nerves that interfere with the perception of sounds within the frequency range of normal speech
Students with advanced cognitive development: These students have unusually high ability in one or more areas.	Giftedness (not covered by IDEA unless a disability is also present)	Unusually high ability or aptitude in one or more domains within the academic curriculum, requiring special educational services to help students meet their full potential

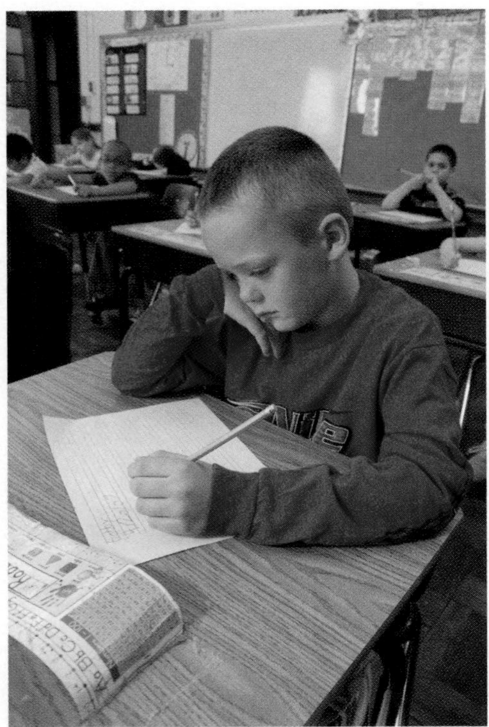

Students with learning disabilities often have less effective learning and memory skills, lower self-esteem, and less motivation to succeed at academic tasks.

Common Characteristics In general, students with learning disabilities are different in many more ways than they are similar (Bassett et al., 1996; Fletcher, Lyon, Fuchs, & Barnes, 2007). They typically have many strengths but may face challenges such as these:

- Difficulty sustaining attention in the face of distractions
- Poor reading skills
- Ineffective learning and memory strategies
- Difficulty with tasks involving abstract reasoning
- Poor sense of self and low motivation for academic tasks (especially if they receive no special assistance in areas of difficulty)
- Poor motor skills
- Poor social skills (Chapman, 1988; Fletcher et al., 2007; Gresham & MacMillan, 1997; Mastropieri & Scruggs, 2007; Meltzer & Krishnan, 2007; Mercer & Pullen, 2005; H. L. Swanson, 1993; Wong, 1991b)

By no means do such characteristics describe *all* students with learning disabilities, however. For instance, some are attentive in class and work diligently on assignments, and some are socially skillful and popular with peers (Heward, 2009).

Learning disabilities can manifest themselves somewhat differently in elementary and secondary school students. At the elementary level, students with learning disabilities are apt to exhibit poor attention and motor skills, and as they reach the upper elementary grades, they may also begin to show emotional problems, due at least partly to frustration with their repeated academic failures (Fletcher et al., 2007; Lerner, 1985). By middle school or high school, difficulties with attention and motor skills often diminish, but students may be especially susceptible to emotional problems. In addition to dealing with the usual emotional issues of adolescence (e.g., dating and peer pressure), students must also deal with more stringent academic demands. Learning in the secondary grades often depends on reading and learning from relatively sophisticated textbooks, yet the average high school student with a learning disability reads at a fourth- to fifth-grade level and has few, if any, effective study strategies (Deshler et al., 2001; Meltzer & Krishnan, 2007). The following exercise can give you a sense of how these students might feel under such circumstances.

EXPERIENCING FIRSTHAND

A Reading Assignment

Read the following passage carefully. I will test you on its content later in the chapter.

> Personality research needs to refocus on global traits because such traits are an important part of everyday social discourse, because they embody a good deal of folk wisdom and common sense, because understanding and evaluating trait judgments can provide an important route toward the improvement of social judgment, and because global traits offer legitimate, if necessarily incomplete, explanations of behavior. A substantial body of evidence supporting the existence of global traits includes personality correlates of behavior, interjudge agreement in personality ratings, and the longitudinal stability of personality over time. Future research should clarify the origins of global traits, the dynamic mechanisms through which they influence behavior, and the behavioral cues through which they can most accurately be judged. (Funder, 1991, p. 31)

How well do you think you will perform on the upcoming test about this passage?

The passage you just read is a fairly typical one from *Psychological Science*, a professional journal written for people with advanced education (e.g., doctoral degrees) in psychology. Hence, it was written well above a typical college student's reading level. I won't *really* test you on the passage's content, but I hope that the exercise gave you a feel for the frustration that high school students with learning disabilities might experience every day. For many students with learning disabilities, completing school work may constantly seem like fighting an uphill battle. Perhaps for this reason, students with learning disabilities are often at risk for dropping out of school (U.S. Department of Education, 2006).

Adapting Instruction Instructional strategies for students with learning disabilities must be tailored to students' specific strengths and weaknesses. Nevertheless, several strategies should benefit many of these students:

Minimize distractions. Because many students with learning disabilities are easily distracted, we should minimize the presence of other stimuli that might compete for their attention. For example, we might pull down window shades if other classes are working or playing outside, and we might ask students to keep their desks clear of objects and materials they don't immediately need (Buchoff, 1990).

Present new information in an explicit and well-organized manner. Most students with learning disabilities learn more successfully when instruction directly communicates what they need to learn, rather than requiring them to draw inferences and synthesize ideas on their own. Frequent and carefully structured practice of important skills is also critical (Fletcher et al., 2007; Hallenbeck, 1996; J. A. Stein & Krishnan, 2007).

Use multiple modalities to present information. Because some students with learning disabilities have trouble learning through a particular sensory modality, we need to think broadly about the modalities we use to communicate information. For example, when teaching students to recognize alphabet letters, we might have them not only look at the letters but also trace large, textured letter shapes with their fingers (Florence, Gentaz, Pascale, & Sprenger-Charolles, 2004). And in lectures to secondary students, we might incorporate videos, graphics, and other visual materials, and we might encourage students to audiotape the lectures (J. A. Stein & Krishnan, 2007; J. W. Wood & Rosbe, 1985).

Analyze students' errors for clues about processing difficulties. As an example of this strategy, look at 7-year-old Daniel's attempt to write "I trust a policeman" in Figure 5.4. Daniel captured several sounds correctly, including the "s" and final "t" sounds in *trust* and all of the consonant sounds in *policeman*. However, he misrepresented the first two consonant sounds in *trust*, replacing the *t* and *r* with an *N*. He also neglected to represent most of the vowel sounds in both *trust* and *policeman*, and two of the three vowels that he did include (*I* for the article *a* and the *E* near the end of *policeman*) are incorrect. We might suspect that Daniel has difficulty hearing all of the distinct sounds in spoken words and matching them with the letters he sees in written words. Such difficulties are quite common in elementary school students who have significant reading disabilities (Goswami, 2007; H. L. Swanson, Mink, & Bocian, 1999).

Teach study skills and learning strategies. Many students with learning disabilities benefit from being taught specific strategies for completing assignments and remembering classroom subject matter (Fletcher et al., 2007; Meltzer, 2007; Wilder & Williams, 2001). For example, we might teach them concrete strategies for taking notes and organizing homework assignments. And we might teach them specific *mnemonics*, or memory tricks, to help them remember particular facts (e.g., see Figure 5.5). (In Chapters 6 and 8, we'll look more closely at how to help students study and learn.)

FIGURE 5.4 Seven-year-old Daniel's attempt to write "I trust a policeman"

FIGURE 5.5 A mnemonic for remembering the letters *b* and *d*

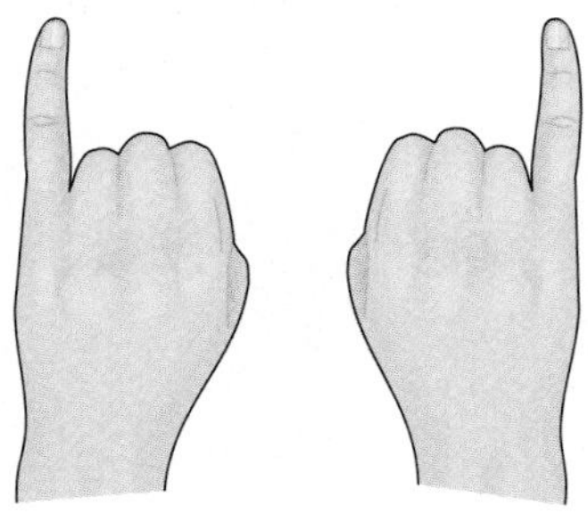

Young children with learning disabilities often confuse lowercase *b* and *d*. By clenching their fists, as shown here, and "reading" their hands in the normal left-to-right direction, they can more easily remember the difference: *b* comes first in both the alphabet and the fists.

Provide study aids. Students with learning disabilities often study more effectively when they are given scaffolding to guide their efforts (Brigham & Scruggs, 1995; Mastropieri & Scruggs, 1992; Meltzer, 2007). For instance, we might provide study guides, outlines, or graphics that help students identify and interconnect important concepts and ideas. We might also let students copy (or receive a photocopy of) the class notes of high-achieving classmates.

Attention-Deficit Hyperactivity Disorder (ADHD)

Almost all students are apt to be inattentive, hyperactive, and impulsive at one time or another. But those with **attention-deficit hyperactivity disorder (ADHD)** typically have significant and chronic deficits in these areas, as reflected in the following identification criteria:

- *Inattention.* Students may have considerable difficulty focusing and maintaining attention on assigned tasks. They may have trouble listening to and following directions, make frequent and careless mistakes, or be easily distracted by appealing alternative activities.
- *Hyperactivity.* Students may seem to have an excess amount of energy. They are apt to be fidgety, move around the classroom at inappropriate times, or have trouble working or playing quietly.
- *Impulsivity.* Students almost invariably have trouble inhibiting inappropriate behaviors. They may blurt out answers, begin assignments prematurely, or engage in risky or destructive behaviors without thinking about potential consequences. (American Psychiatric Association, 2000; Barkley, 2006; Gatzke-Kopp & Beauchaine, 2007)

Students with ADHD do not necessarily show all three of these characteristics. For instance, some are inattentive without also being hyperactive, as is true for Tim in the opening case study. But all students with ADHD appear to have one characteristic in common: *an inability to inhibit inappropriate thoughts, inappropriate actions, or both* (Barkley, 2006; B. J. Casey, 2001; Fischer & Daley, 2007). Tim, for example, is easily distracted by his thoughts and daydreams when he should be focusing on a classroom lesson.

ADHD is assumed to have a biological and sometimes genetic origin (Faraone & Doyle, 2001; Gatzke-Kopp & Beauchaine, 2007; Shaw et al., 2007). But once identified as having ADHD, many students can be helped through behaviorist techniques (see Chapter 9) and remediation of cognitive difficulties. For some students with ADHD—but by no means *all* of them—medication is also helpful (Gulley et al., 2003; Hallahan, Kauffman, & Pullen, 2009; Purdie, Hattie, & Carroll, 2002).

Common Characteristics In addition to inattentiveness, hyperactivity, and impulsivity, students identified as having ADHD may have characteristics such as these:

- Exceptional imagination and creativity
- Exceptionally detailed memories of past events
- Certain specific cognitive processing difficulties (e.g., see Figure 5.6) and low school achievement
- Poor sense of self
- Classroom behavior problems (e.g., disruptiveness, noncompliance with rules)
- Poor social skills; sometimes outright rejection by peers
- Increased probability of substance abuse in adolescence (Barkley, 2006; Denckla, 2007; Gatzke-Kopp & Beauchaine, 2007; S. Goldstein & Rider, 2006; Hallowell, 1996; Skowronek, Leichtman, & Pillemer, 2008)

attention-deficit hyperactivity disorder (ADHD) Disorder marked by inattention, hyperactivity, impulsive behavior, or some combination of these characteristics.

Some students with ADHD may also have a learning disability or an emotional or behavioral disorder, whereas others may be gifted (Barkley, 2006; Conte, 1991; Denckla, 2007).

The symptoms associated with ADHD may diminish in adolescence, but to some degree they persist throughout the school years, making it difficult for students to handle the increasing demands for independence and responsible behavior that come in high school. Accordingly, students with ADHD are at greater than average risk for dropping out of school (Barkley, 2006; S. Goldstein & Rider, 2006; E. L. Hart, Lahey, Loeber, Applegate, & Frick, 1995).

FIGURE 5.6 Like many students with ADHD, 10-year-old Joshua has specific cognitive processing difficulties. Although he has the math skills of a typical fifth grader, he has delayed reading comprehension and writing skills, as reflected in the book report shown here. Josh can more easily express his thoughts orally.

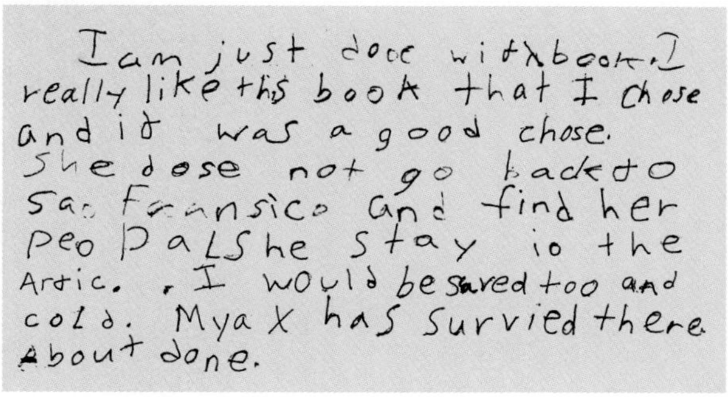

I am just doce witx book. I
really like this book that I chose
and it was a good chose.
She dose not go back to
San Fransico and find her
peo pal. She stay in the
Artic. . I would be scared too and
cold. Mya X has survied there
About done.

Adapting Instruction The strategies previously listed for students with learning disabilities can be helpful for students with ADHD as well. Researchers and practitioners have offered several additional suggestions:

Modify students' schedules and work environments. The symptoms of ADHD tend to get progressively worse as the day goes on. Ideally, then, students should have most academic subjects and challenging tasks in the morning rather than in the afternoon. Furthermore, moving students' desks away from distractions (e.g., away from the door and window but not too close to classmates) and close to the teacher, where behavior can be monitored, can enhance their attention and achievement (Barkley, 2006).

Teach attention-maintaining strategies. Students with ADHD often benefit from learning concrete strategies for keeping their attention on an assigned task (Buchoff, 1990). For instance, we can ask them to keep their eyes on us when we're giving directions or providing new information. And we can encourage them to move to a new location if their current one presents too many distracting sights or sounds.

Provide outlets for excess energy. To help students control excess energy, we should intersperse quiet academic work with frequent opportunities for physical exercise (Pellegrini & Bohn, 2005; Pfiffner, Barkley, & DuPaul, 2006). We might also give students a settling-in time after recess or lunch—perhaps reading an excerpt from a high-interest storybook or magazine article—before asking them to engage in an activity that involves quiet concentration (Pellegrini & Horvat, 1995).

Help students organize and use their time effectively. Because of their inattentiveness and hyperactivity, students with ADHD often have difficulty completing daily classroom tasks. Several strategies can help these students organize themselves and use class time more effectively. We can show them how to create to-do lists and establish a daily routine that they post on their desks. We can also break large tasks into smaller ones and set a short time limit for each subtask. And we can provide a folder in which students transport homework assignments to and from school (Buchoff, 1990; Pfiffner et al., 2006).

Speech and Communication Disorders

Speech and communication disorders are impairments in spoken language or language comprehension that significantly interfere with students' classroom performance. Examples include persistent articulation problems (e.g., see Figure 5.7), stuttering, abnormal syntactical patterns, and difficulty understanding other people's speech. Sometimes, but not always, these children have difficulty perceiving and mentally processing particular aspects of spoken language (see the discussion of *specific*

speech and communication disorders Impairments in spoken language or language comprehension that significantly interfere with classroom performance.

FIGURE 5.7 Seven-year-old Isaac receives speech therapy at school to address his consistent mispronunciation of certain sounds (such as pronouncing "th" as "v"). In his writing, he sometimes spells words as he says them, rather than as he hears them (for instance, he writes *ven* for *then*).

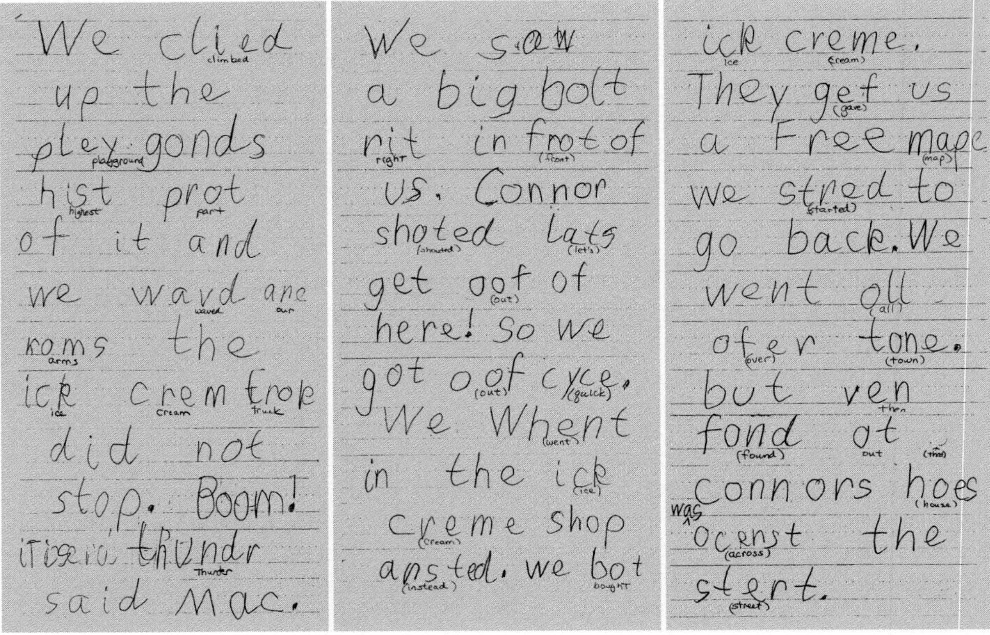

language impairments in Chapter 2). And often—but again, not always—the source of the disorders can be traced to heredity or specific brain abnormalities (Bishop, 2006; J. L. Locke, 1993; Spinath, Price, Dale, & Plomin, 2004).

The great majority of students with speech and communication disorders are in general education classrooms for most or all of the school day (U.S. Department of Education, 2006). Some of these students have other disabilities as well, but many are, in all other respects, just typical students (Turnbull, Turnbull, & Wehmeyer, 2007).

Common Characteristics Several characteristics are sometimes, although not always, observed in students with speech and communication disorders:

- Reluctance to speak
- Embarrassment and self-consciousness when speaking
- Difficulties in reading and writing (Fey, Catts, & Larrivee, 1995; Heward, 2009; LaBlance, Steckol, & Smith, 1994; Rice, Hadley, & Alexander, 1993)

Adapting Instruction Typically, a trained specialist will work with students to help them improve or overcome their speech and communication difficulties. Nevertheless, general education teachers can assist in several ways:

Encourage regular oral communication. Students with speech and communication disorders need as much practice in classroom-based public speaking as their classmates do. Thus, we should encourage them to talk in class, provided that doing so does not create exceptional stress (Hallahan et al., 2009; Patton, Blackbourn, & Fad, 1996).

Listen patiently. When students have trouble expressing themselves, we might be tempted to assist them—for instance, by finishing their sentences for them. But we better help them when we allow them to complete their own thoughts. We must learn to listen politely and attentively to students with speech problems, and we must encourage their peers to do likewise (Heward, 2009; Patton et al., 1996).

Ask for clarification when a message is unclear. When we haven't entirely understood what a student is saying, we should explain what we *did* understand and ask for clarification of the rest. Providing honest feedback helps students learn how well they are communicating (Patton et al., 1996).

General Recommendations

In addition to the strategies described in the preceding pages, several general strategies apply to many students with specific cognitive or academic difficulties:

Get an early start on appropriate interventions. When students lack basic concepts and skills on which their future learning will depend, providing intensive instruction to fill in the gaps—and the earlier, the better—can often make a significant difference in their long-term achievement (Fletcher et al., 2007; L. S. Fuchs et al., 2005; Pitoniak & Royer, 2001).

Take skill levels into account when assigning reading materials. Despite receiving intensive reading instruction, many students with specific cognitive or academic difficulties will continue to have poor reading skills. Thus, we may sometimes need to identify alternatives to standard grade-level textbooks for presenting academic content. For instance, we might reduce the amount of required reading, substitute materials written on a simpler (yet not babyish) level, or present information through some medium other than written text (Mastropieri & Scruggs, 2007).

Clearly describe expectations for academic performance. Students will have an easier time accomplishing classroom tasks if they are told, in concrete and precise terms, what is expected of them (Meltzer & Krishnan, 2007). For example, before students begin a science lab activity, we might first remind them to carefully follow the steps described on the lab sheet, then review safety precautions, and finally provide a written list of components they should be sure to include in their lab reports.

Take steps to enhance self-confidence and motivation. Students with a long history of failure at academic tasks need to see that they are making progress and that they do some things very well. For instance, we can give them daily or weekly goals we know they can attain. We can also have them keep journals in which they describe the successes they have achieved each day. And we can give them opportunities to do tasks they enjoy and usually perform well (Buchoff, 1990; J. A. Stein & Krishnan, 2007).

Students with Social or Behavioral Problems

Many students have minor social, emotional, or behavioral difficulties at one time or another, particularly during times of unusual stress or major life changes. Often, these problems are temporary, especially when students have the support of caring adults. At other times, problems are more enduring but do *not* reflect a disability. Perhaps a student's temperament is a poor fit with a teacher's instructional strategies (see Chapter 3), or perhaps a teacher has simply not made clear the expectations and rules for classroom behavior (Keogh, 2003; Mehan, 1979). In such situations, students' problems may decrease or disappear with a change in instructional practices or classroom management strategies.

However, some students show a pattern of behavior problems that consistently interfere with their learning and performance *regardless* of the teacher and the classroom environment. In this section, we'll look at two groups of students who fit into this category: those with emotional and behavioral disorders and those with autism spectrum disorders.

Emotional and Behavioral Disorders

Students with **emotional and behavioral disorders** become identified as students with special needs—and therefore qualify for special educational services—when their problems have a substantial negative impact on classroom learning. Symptoms of emotional and behavioral disorders typically fall into one of two broad categories. **Externalizing behaviors** have direct or indirect effects on other people; examples include aggression, defiance, lying, stealing, and general lack of self-control. **Internalizing behaviors** primarily affect the student with the disorder; examples include severe anxiety or depression, exaggerated mood swings, withdrawal from social interaction, and eating disorders. Students with externalizing behaviors—who are more apt to be boys than girls—are more likely to be referred for evaluation and possible special services. However, students with internalizing behaviors—who are more likely to be girls than boys—can be just as much at risk for school failure (Angold, Worthman, & Costello, 2003; Gay, 2006; Hayward, 2003).

Report suspicions about child maltreatment *immediately* (see Chapter 3 for details).

Some emotional and behavioral disorders result from environmental factors, such as stressful living conditions, child maltreatment, or family alcohol or drug abuse (Davies & Woitach, 2008; D. Glaser, 2000; Maughan & Cicchetti, 2002). But biological causes—such as inherited predispositions, chemical imbalances, and brain injuries—may also be involved (H. C. Johnson & Friesen, 1993; Raine, 2008; Yeo et al., 2007). Some students with a genetic predisposition for an emotional or behavioral disorder exhibit few, if any, signs of a problem until adolescence, as the following case illustrates:

> As a ninth grader, Kirk was a well-behaved, likable student who earned As and Bs and showed particular promise in science and math. But in tenth grade, his grades began to slip, and he occasionally exhibited mildly hostile or defiant behaviors. Despite his parents' and teachers' efforts to keep him in line, Kirk began hanging out with high school dropouts who engaged in minor criminal activities, and his grades fell to Cs and Ds.
>
> When Kirk failed three classes during the fall of his senior year, the school principal convened a meeting with him, his parents, and his faculty advisor to discuss how to help Kirk get back on track. At the meeting, the principal described several occasions on which Kirk had acted disoriented, belligerent, and seemingly "high" on drugs. At this point, an appropriate and constructive response would have been for Kirk to appear contrite and willing to change his behavior so that he could graduate—an essential goal, given his strong desire to attend college the following year. Instead, Kirk sat at the meeting smirking (seemingly gleeful about his predicament) and focusing his attention on sorting pieces of trail mix in a bowl on the conference room table. By the end of the meeting, the principal was so infuriated that she expelled him from school.
>
> A few days later, Kirk was arrested for carrying an illegal weapon (a knife) on school property. Over the next two weeks, as he waited in the juvenile detention facility for his court hearing, his mental condition deteriorated rapidly, and a judge ordered his hospitalization in the state mental institution.

emotional and behavioral disorders Emotional states and behaviors that consistently and significantly disrupt academic learning and performance.

externalizing behavior Symptom of an emotional or behavioral disorder that has a direct effect on other people (e.g., aggression, lack of self-control).

internalizing behavior Symptom of an emotional or behavioral disorder that significantly affects the student with the disorder but has little or no direct effect on other people (e.g., depression, social withdrawal).

Kirk was eventually diagnosed with *bipolar disorder*, a condition that is usually inherited and is characterized by excessive mood swings (hence, the disorder is sometimes called *manic depression*) and, in cases such as Kirk's, by distorted thought processes. Bipolar disorder often doesn't appear until adolescence, even though its biological underpinnings have been present since birth (Griswold & Pessar, 2000).

Factors at school may exacerbate the challenges that students with emotional and behavioral problems face. Their inappropriate behaviors interfere not only with academic achievement but also with peer relationships, leading to social as well as academic failure. Many students, especially those with externalizing behaviors, eventually seek the companionship of the few peers who will accept them—peers who typically behave in similarly inappropriate ways and may introduce one another to drugs, alcohol, or criminal activity (J. Snyder et al., 2008; Webber & Plotts, 2008).

Common Characteristics Students with emotional and behavioral disorders differ considerably in their abilities and personalities. However, in addition to the difficulty in maintaining healthy peer relationships just mentioned, you may observe one or more of the following characteristics:

- Frequent absences from school
- Deteriorating academic performance with increasing age
- Low self-esteem
- Little, if any, empathy for others' distress
- Significant substance abuse
- Lack of awareness of the severity of existing problems (Espelage, Mebane, & Adams, 2004; Grinberg & McLean-Heywood, 1999; Harter, 1999; Leiter & Johnsen, 1997; McGlynn, 1998; C. M. Richards, Symons, Greene, & Szuszkiewicz, 1995; Turnbull et al., 2007; Webber & Plotts, 2008)

Some students with emotional and behavioral disorders have other special needs as well, including learning disabilities, ADHD, or giftedness (Fessler, Rosenberg, & Rosenberg, 1991; Gatzke-Kopp & Beauchaine, 2007; Webber & Plotts, 2008).

Adapting Instruction Effective interventions must be tailored to each student's unique needs, but several strategies can benefit many of these students:

Show an interest in students' well-being and personal growth. A good first step in helping students with emotional and behavioral disorders is simply showing that we care about them (Clarke et al., 1995; Diamond, 1991; Heward, 2009). For instance, we can greet them warmly when we see them, express concern when they seem upset or overly stressed, and lend a supportive ear when they want to share their opinions or frustrations. Also, when appropriate, we can reveal aspects of our own lives, thereby communicating that self-disclosure can sometimes be cathartic and therapeutic. And we can take students' personal interests into account when planning instruction and assignments.

Give students a sense that they have some control over their circumstances. Some students, especially those who are frequently defiant, often respond to efforts to control them by behaving even *less* appropriately. With such students, it's important to avoid power struggles, situations in which only one person wins and the other inevitably loses. Instead, we must create situations in which we ensure that students conform to classroom expectations yet feel as if they have some control over what happens to them. For example, we can teach them techniques for observing and monitoring their own actions, with the goal of developing more productive classroom behavior (Kern, Dunlap, Childs, & Clark, 1994). We can also give them choices, within reasonable limits, about what they want to do in particular situations (Knowlton, 1995; Lane, Falk, & Wehby, 2006). (Such strategies enhance *self-regulation* and *self-determination*, discussed in Chapters 10 and 11, respectively.)

To create win–win situations with students who misbehave frequently, teach them strategies for controlling their own behavior and give them choices when appropriate.

Be alert for signs that a student may be contemplating suicide. In the United States, suicide is the third-leading cause of death for adolescents (Goldston et al., 2008). Warning signs include the following:

- Sudden withdrawal from social relationships
- Increasing disregard for personal appearance
- Dramatic personality change (e.g., sudden elevation in mood)
- Preoccupation with death and morbid themes
- Overt or veiled threats (e.g., "I won't be around much longer")
- Actions that indicate putting one's affairs in order (e.g., giving away prized possessions) (Kerns & Lieberman, 1993; Wiles & Bondi, 2001)

As teachers, we must take these warning signs seriously and seek help *immediately* from a trained professional, such as a school psychologist or counselor.

It is also essential, of course, that we help students with emotional and behavioral disorders acquire more appropriate behaviors, but I will postpone describing effective strategies until after we have examined autism spectrum disorders in the next section.

Autism Spectrum Disorders

The vast majority of **autism spectrum disorders** are probably caused by abnormalities in the brain (I. L. Cohen, 2007; Dapretto et al., 2006; Théoret et al., 2005). Common to all of these disorders are marked impairments in social cognition (e.g., perspective taking), social skills, and social interaction (Hobson, 2004; Pelphrey & Carter, 2007; Tager-Flusberg, 2007). In fact, many students with these disorders prefer to be alone and form weak, if any, emotional attachments to other people. Common, too, are repetitive behaviors (often very odd ones rarely seen in age-mates) and inflexible adherence to certain routines or rituals (American Psychiatric Association, 2000; I. L. Cohen, 2007).

Aside from similarities in social impairments and repetitive behaviors, individuals with autism spectrum disorders differ considerably in the severity of their condition (hence the term *spectrum*). For instance, in **Asperger syndrome**, a fairly mild form, students have normal language skills and average or above-average intelligence. In severe cases, which are often referred to simply as *autism*, children have major delays in cognitive development and language and may exhibit certain bizarre behaviors—perhaps constantly rocking or waving fingers, continually repeating what someone else has said, or showing unusual fascination with a very narrow category of objects (American Psychiatric Association, 2000; Koegel, 1995). Underlying some of these behaviors may be an undersensitivity or oversensitivity to sensory stimulation (R. C. Sullivan, 1994; D. Williams, 1996). Temple Grandin, a woman who has gained international prominence as a designer of livestock facilities, recalls what it was like to be a child with autism:

> From as far back as I can remember, I always hated to be hugged. I wanted to experience the good feeling of being hugged, but it was just too overwhelming. It was like a great, all-engulfing tidal wave of stimulation, and I reacted like a wild animal. . . . When I was little, loud noises were also a problem, often feeling like a dentist's drill hitting a nerve. They actually caused pain. I was scared to death of balloons popping, because the sound was like an explosion in my ear. (Grandin, 1995, pp. 63, 67)

autism spectrum disorders Disorders marked by impaired social cognition, social skills, and social interaction, as well as by repetitive behaviors; extreme forms are often associated with significant cognitive and linguistic delays and highly unusual behaviors.

Asperger syndrome Mild form of autism in which students have normal intelligence and language skills but show significant deficits in social cognition and social skills.

Most children with Asperger syndrome are placed in general education classes (Little, 2002). Some students with more severe forms of autism also participate in general education classes for part or all of the school day (U.S. Department of Education, 2006).

Common Characteristics In addition to the traits already described, students with autism spectrum disorders may have characteristics such as these:

- Strong visual–spatial thinking skills and exceptional awareness of visual details
- Unusual ability to maintain attention or focus during distractions
- Good memory for a set of unrelated facts
- Difficulty planning and organizing a future course of action
- Abnormal posture and movements (e.g., awkward gait)
- Strong need for a consistent, predictable environment (I. L. Cohen, 2007; M. Dawson, Soulières, Gernsbacher, & Mottron, 2007; Gernsbacher, Stevenson, Khandakar, & Goldsmith, 2008; Grandin & Johnson, 2005; Leary & Hill, 1996; Meltzer, 2007; Pelphrey & Carter, 2007; Tager-Flusberg, 2007)

Occasionally, students with autism exhibit *savant syndrome,* possessing an extraordinary ability (e.g., exceptional artistic or musical talent) that is quite remarkable in contrast to other aspects of their mental functioning (I. L. Cohen, 2007; Treffert & Wallace, 2002).

Adapting Instruction Many of the classroom strategies described throughout this chapter are applicable for students with autism spectrum disorders. Two additional strategies are also helpful:

Maximize consistency in the classroom layout and weekly schedule. Many students with autism spectrum disorders feel more comfortable when their physical environment remains the same and they can follow a predictable routine. At the beginning of the school year, then, we should arrange furniture and equipment in ways that will be serviceable throughout the year, making adjustments later only if absolutely necessary. And to the greatest extent possible, we should schedule recurring activities at the same times each day or on particular days of the week. If the schedule must change for some reason, we should alert students well in advance (Dalrymple, 1995).

Use visual approaches to instruction. Because students with autism spectrum disorders often have strong visual–spatial skills but may have impaired language skills, a heavy emphasis on visual materials may be in order (Ozonoff & Schetter, 2007; C. C. Peterson, 2002; Quill, 1995). We might use objects, pictures, and photographs to convey ideas about academic topics, or we might use some sort of visual cue to signal the start of a new activity.

General Recommendations

Although the causes of emotional and behavioral disorders and those of autism spectrum disorders are usually quite different, students with these disabilities may benefit from some of the same classroom interventions. Certainly, we want to promote success on academic tasks, perhaps by using instructional strategies presented earlier for students with specific cognitive or academic difficulties. Researchers and experienced educators also offer the following suggestions:

Insist on appropriate classroom behavior. Although certain students with disabilities may be more prone to counterproductive classroom behaviors than many of their peers are, teachers clearly *can* help them behave in productive ways—for instance, by putting reasonable limits on their behavior and imposing consequences when they go beyond those limits (Evertson & Weinstein, 2006; Webber & Plotts, 2008). The Creating a Productive Classroom Environment feature "Encouraging Appropriate Behavior in Students with Social or Behavioral Problems" offers several useful strategies.

Foster social cognition and effective interpersonal skills. Students with social or behavioral problems often benefit from training in social cognition and perspective taking (Hudley & Graham, 1993; LeBlanc et al., 2003; Myles & Simpson, 2001). Explicit instruction in and reinforcement of social skills can also be quite powerful (E. G. Carr et al., 1994; Koegel, Koegel, & Dunlap, 1996; Nikopoulos & Keenan, 2004). And of

myeducationlab

Observe a child with autism interact appropriately with classmates in the video "Allyson Practices her Social Skills." (To find this video, go to Chapter 5 of the Book-Specific Resources in MyEducationLab, select *Video Examples,* and then click on the title.)

Creating A PRODUCTIVE CLASSROOM ENVIRONMENT

Encouraging Appropriate Behavior in Students with Social or Behavioral Problems

Make expectations for behavior clear and specific.

A teacher reminds a student, "You cannot borrow Mary's bottle of glue without getting her permission. Check with Mary first to make sure it's all right for you to use her things. If Mary says no, ask someone else."

Specify and follow through on consequences for appropriate and inappropriate behaviors.

A teacher tells a student, "Sam, you know that certain four-letter words, such as the two you just used, are unacceptable in this classroom. You also know the consequence for such behavior, so please go to the time-out corner for 10 minutes."

Give feedback about specific behaviors, rather than general areas of performance.

A teacher tells a student, "You did a good job in study hall today. You focused your attention on your homework, and you didn't retaliate when Jerome accidentally brushed past you on his way to my desk."

Try to anticipate problems and nip them in the bud.

A student has occasional temper tantrums that disrupt the entire class. Although the tantrums usually seem to occur at random, his teacher eventually realizes that his ears always turn red just before an outburst. This knowledge allows the teacher to divert the student's tantrums to a punching bag, where he can unleash his feelings with only minimal distraction to others.

Sources: Hallahan et al., 2009; Heward, 2009; Myles & Simpson, 2001; Ormrod & McGuire, 2007 (temper tantrum example); Webber & Plotts, 2008.

course, students need numerous opportunities to *practice* their new skills (Chan & O'Reilly, 2008; Themann & Goldstein, 2001).

Be persistent, and look for gradual improvement, rather than overnight success. Many students with social or behavioral problems will, at first, resist our efforts to help them. They may begin to recognize the value of our guidance and support only when they see the natural consequences of their changing behavior—for example, when they start to make new friends or get along better with their teachers. Their progress may be slow, but by focusing on small improvements, we and our students alike can be encouraged by the changes we *do* see, rather than being discouraged by problems that persist (Gearheart, Weishahn, & Gearheart, 1992; Patton et al., 1996).

Students with General Delays in Cognitive and Social Functioning

One category you will see in the Students in Inclusive Settings tables in subsequent chapters of the book is *students with general delays in cognitive and social functioning*. I have intentionally used this term to include any student with a consistent pattern of developmental delays, regardless of whether the student has been specifically identified as having a disability. Educators sometimes use the term *slow learner* to describe a student who obtains intelligence test scores in the 70s and has noticeable difficulties in most or all parts of the academic curriculum. A student with especially pronounced difficulties may be identified as having an *intellectual disability*.

Intellectual Disabilities

Up to this point, I have been using a term you're undoubtedly familiar with—*mental retardation*—when referring to students who show consistent developmental delays across most domains. In recent years, however, many special educators have instead advocated for the term **intellectual disability** (e.g., Luckasson et al., 2002; also see www.aamr.org). Students with intellectual disabilities show pronounced delays in most aspects of cognitive and social development. More specifically, they exhibit *both* of the following characteristics (Luckasson et al., 2002):

- *Significantly below-average general intelligence.* These students have intelligence test scores that are quite low—usually no higher than 70, reflecting performance in the bottom 2% of their age-group. In addition, these students learn slowly and show consistently poor achievement in virtually all academic subject areas.
- *Deficits in adaptive behavior.* These students behave in ways that we would expect of much younger children. Their deficits in **adaptive behavior** include limitations in *practical intelligence*—that is, managing the ordinary activities of daily living—and *social intelligence*—that is, conducting themselves appropriately in social situations.

These characteristics must be evident in childhood. Thus, a person who showed them beginning at age 18, perhaps as the result of a serious head injury, would *not* be classified as having an intellectual disability.

Intellectual disabilities are often caused by genetic conditions. For example, most children with Down syndrome have delayed cognitive and social development. Other cases of intellectual disabilities are due to biological but noninherited causes, such as severe malnutrition or excessive alcohol consumption during the mother's pregnancy or oxygen deprivation during a difficult birth. In still other situations, environmental factors, such as parental neglect or an extremely impoverished and unstimulating home environment, may be at fault (Beirne-Smith, Patton, & Kim, 2006).

PEARSON myeducationlab

Learn more about these adaptive behaviors in a supplementary reading, "Adaptive Behaviors and Intellectual Disabilities." (To find this reading, go to Chapter 5 of the Book-Specific Resources in MyEducationLab and then select *Supplementary Readings*.)

Common Characteristics Most students with intellectual disabilities attend general education classes for part or all of the school day (U.S. Department of Education, 2006). Like students in any category of special needs, these students have differing personalities, strengths, and needs. Nevertheless, many of them are apt to exhibit characteristics such as the following:

- Sociability and a genuine desire to belong and fit in at school
- Less general knowledge about the world
- Poor reading and language skills
- Short attention span
- Poor memory; few or no effective learning and memory strategies
- Difficulty drawing inferences and understanding abstract ideas
- Difficulty generalizing something learned in one situation to a new situation
- Immature play behaviors and interpersonal skills
- Delayed motor skills; conditions that adversely affect performance in physical activities (e.g., heart defects, poor muscle tone) (Beirne-Smith et al., 2006; Bergeron & Floyd, 2006; Carlin et al., 2003; Heward, 2009; F. P. Hughes, 1998; Tager-Flusberg & Skwerer, 2007)

Adapting Instruction With proper support, many students with mild intellectual disabilities can learn basic skills in reading, writing, and mathematics, perhaps even mastering components of a typical fifth- or sixth-grade curriculum (Hallahan et al., 2009; Heward, 2009). Many of the strategies previously described in this chapter can be useful for these students. Here are several additional strategies to keep in mind:

intellectual disability Disability characterized by significantly below-average general intelligence and deficits in adaptive behavior, both of which first appear in infancy or childhood (also known as *mental retardation*).

adaptive behavior Behavior related to daily living skills and appropriate conduct in social situations; used as a criterion for identifying students with intellectual disabilities.

Pace instruction slowly enough to ensure success. When working with students who have intellectual disabilities, we should move through new topics and tasks

When instruction proceeds at an appropriate pace and provides sufficient scaffolding, students with intellectual disabilities can succeed in a wide variety of activities.

slowly enough—and with enough repetition—that students can eventually master them. Students with intellectual disabilities typically have a long history of failure at academic tasks. Thus, they need frequent successful experiences to learn that, with hard work, they *can* succeed at many tasks (Fidler, Hepburn, Mankin, & Rogers, 2005; Heward, 2009).

Provide considerable scaffolding to promote effective cognitive processing and desired behaviors. Because students with intellectual disabilities often have little awareness of how best to learn and remember new information, it can be helpful to provide detailed suggestions about what they can do to remember things—repeating instructions to themselves, practicing a new spelling word several times every day, and so on. We can provide simple study guides that tell students specifically what to focus on as they study. And we can be quite explicit in our directions to perform various tasks. For instance, we might say "John, go to the principal's office, give Mrs. Smith the absentee sheet, and come back here" (Beirne-Smith et al., 2006; Mastropieri & Scruggs, 1992; Patton et al., 1996, p. 105).

Include vocational and general life skills in the curriculum. For most students with intellectual disabilities, training in general life and work skills is an important part of the high school curriculum. Such training is most likely to be effective when it takes place in realistic settings that closely resemble those in which students will find themselves once they leave school (Beirne-Smith et al., 2006; Turnbull et al., 2007).

myeducationlab

Observe teachers providing considerable scaffolding for students with intellectual disabilities in the video "Teaching Cooking Skills." (To find this video, go to Chapter 5 of the Book-Specific Resources in MyEducationLab, select *Video Examples*, and then click on the title.)

Students with Physical or Sensory Challenges

Some students with special needs have obvious physical disabilities caused by medically detectable physiological conditions. These include physical and health impairments, visual impairments, and hearing loss. The great majority of these students attend general education classrooms for part or all of the school day (U.S. Department of Education, 2006). A small subset have **severe and multiple disabilities** that require significant adaptations and highly specialized services; such students are typically accompanied by child-specific teacher aides or other specialists when they are in general education classrooms.

Physical and Health Impairments

Physical and health impairments are general physical or medical conditions (usually long term) that interfere with school performance to such a degree that special instruction, curricular materials, equipment, or facilities are necessary. Students in this category may have limited energy and strength, reduced mental alertness, or little muscle control. Examples of conditions that might qualify students for special services are traumatic brain injury, spinal cord injury, cerebral palsy, epilepsy, cystic fibrosis, cancer, and acquired immune deficiency disorder (AIDS).

severe and multiple disabilities Combination of two or more disabilities that, taken together, require significant classroom adaptations and highly specialized educational services.

physical and health impairments General physical or medical conditions that interfere so significantly with school performance that special accommodations are required.

Common Characteristics It's hard to generalize about students with physical and health impairments because their conditions are so very different from one another. Nevertheless, several common characteristics are noteworthy:

- Low stamina and a tendency to tire easily
- Varying degrees of intellectual functioning (many of these students have learning ability similar to that of nondisabled peers)
- Lower levels of academic achievement as a result of frequent school absences

- Fewer opportunities to experience and interact with the outside world in educationally important ways (e.g., less use of public transportation, fewer visits to museums and zoos)
- Possible low self-esteem, insecurity, or heavy dependence on adults, depending partly on how parents and others have responded to their impairments (Heward, 2009; Patton et al., 1996; J. W. Wood, 1998)

Adapting Instruction Although we won't necessarily need to modify the academic curriculum for students with physical and health impairments, we will definitely want to make certain accommodations:

Be sensitive to specific limitations, and accommodate them flexibly. One student may require extra time with a writing assignment and perhaps should not be held to the same standards of neatness and legibility. Another may need to respond to test questions orally, rather than on paper. Still another may tire easily and need to take frequent breaks.

Know what to do in emergencies. A student with acute asthma may have trouble breathing. A student with diabetes may go into insulin shock. A student with epilepsy may have a grand mal seizure. We should consult with school medical personnel ahead of time so that we are prepared to respond appropriately in such life- and health-threatening situations.

If students and parents give permission, educate classmates about the nature of students' disabilities. Many children treat peers with physical disabilities kindly and respectfully, but some others do not. Sometimes, peers are simply ignorant about the nature of a disability, and giving them accurate information can help them become more tolerant and accepting. In one widely publicized case, Ryan White, a student with AIDS, was initially barred from his neighborhood school because of classmates' and parents' unwarranted fear that other children would be infected (R. White & Cunningham, 1991). Ryan returned to school only after the public was convinced that AIDS could not be contracted through breathing or normal bodily contact. Even so, his reception was hardly a warm one, as Ryan himself revealed: "Kids backed up against their lockers when they saw me coming, or they threw themselves against the hallway walls, shouting, 'Watch out! Watch out! There he is!' " (R. White & Cunningham, 1991, p. 118). Only when Ryan's family moved to a different school district—one that went to great lengths to inform parents and students about the true nature of AIDS—did he find teachers and peers who were happy to have him at their school.

Visual Impairments

Students with **visual impairments** have malfunctions of their eyes or optic nerves that prevent normal vision even with corrective lenses, adversely affecting classroom performance. Some students are totally blind, others see only fuzzy patterns of light and dark, and still others have a restricted visual field (*tunnel vision*) that allows them to see only a very small area at a time. Visual impairments are caused by congenital abnormalities in or later damage to either the eye or the visual pathway to the brain.

Common Characteristics Students with visual impairments are apt to have many or all of these characteristics:

- Normal functioning of other senses (hearing, touch, etc.)
- General learning ability similar to that of nondisabled students
- More limited vocabulary and general world knowledge, in part, because of fewer opportunities to experience the outside world in educationally important ways (e.g., less exposure to maps, films, and other visual materials)
- Delayed motor development; reduced capability to imitate others' behaviors
- Inability to observe other people's body language and other nonverbal cues, leading to occasional misunderstanding of others' messages

visual impairments Malfunctions of the eyes or optic nerves that prevent normal vision even with corrective lenses.

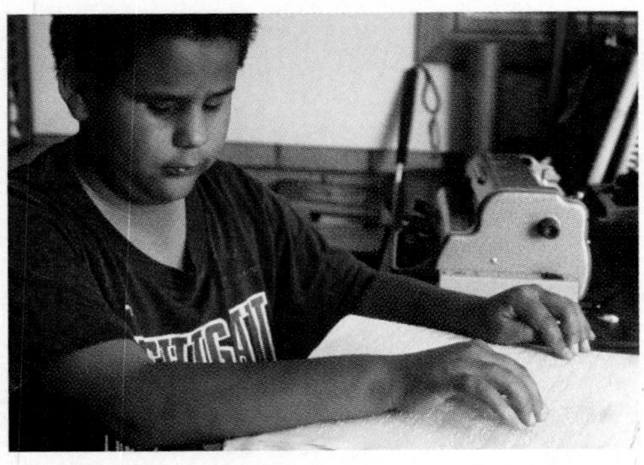

Students with visual impairments can often keep pace with their sighted classmates if instructional materials are adapted to meet their individual needs.

- Uncertainty and anxiety (especially in chaotic environments, such as the lunchroom or playground) as a result of having no visual knowledge of ongoing events
- In the primary grades, less knowledge about the conventions of written language (direction of print, punctuation, etc.) (M. Harris, 1992; Heward, 2009; Hobson, 2004; Patton et al., 1996; Tompkins & McGee, 1986; Turnbull et al., 2007; Tuttle & Tuttle, 1996)

Adapting Instruction Specialists typically give students training in Braille, orientation and mobility, and specially adapted computer technology. In addition, several strategies can help students with visual impairments succeed in a general education classroom:

Orient students ahead of time to the physical layout of the classroom. Students should have a chance to explore the classroom before other students arrive—ideally, before the first day of class. At that time, we can help students locate important objects (e.g., wastebasket and pencil sharpener) and point out special sounds (e.g., the buzzing of a wall clock) to help students get their bearings (J. W. Wood, 1998).

Use visual materials with sharp contrast. Some students with partial sight can use visual materials with clearly distinguishable features, such as enlarged documents on computer screens and large-print books available at most public libraries. Students' eyes may tire quickly, however, so we should limit use of visual materials to short time periods (Heward, 2009; Patton et al., 1996).

Depend heavily on other modalities. Print-reading computer software and portable print-reading devices easily translate most printed language into speech to which students can listen. Many novels, school textbooks, and published curriculum materials are available in Braille, and school district employees or parent volunteers can sometimes be enlisted to convert other written materials into Braille. We can also conduct hands-on activities involving objects that students can feel and manipulate. For example, we might use plastic relief maps that portray mountains, valleys, and coastlines in three dimensions, perhaps embellishing them with pin pricks to indicate country borders and small dabs of nail polish to indicate major cities.

Allow extra time for learning and performance. Learning by hearing often takes more time than learning by seeing. When students *look* at something, they can perceive a great deal of information all at once and can easily see how certain things are connected (e.g., a cat and the sound it makes). When they must *listen* to it, however, they receive it sequentially—only one piece at a time—and often without obvious interconnections (Ferrell, 1996; Heward, 2009; M. B. Rowe, 1978).

Hearing Loss

Students with **hearing loss** have a malfunction of the ears or associated nerves that interferes with the perception of sounds within the frequency range of normal human speech. Students who are completely *deaf* have insufficient sensation to understand any spoken language, even with the help of a hearing aid. Students who are *hard of hearing* understand some speech but experience exceptional difficulty in doing so.

hearing loss Malfunction of the ears or associated nerves that interferes with perception of sounds within the frequency range of normal human speech.

Common Characteristics Most students with hearing loss have normal intellectual abilities (Braden, 1992; Schirmer, 1994). However, they may have characteristics such as these:

- Delayed language development because of reduced exposure to spoken language, especially if the impairment was present at birth or occurred early in life

- Proficiency in sign language, such as American Sign Language (ASL) or finger spelling
- Some ability to read lips (*speechreading*)
- Less oral language than hearing classmates have; perhaps a monotonous, hollow quality to speech
- Less developed reading skills, especially if language development has been delayed
- Less general world knowledge because of reduced exposure to spoken language
- Some social isolation, more limited social skills, and reduced perspective-taking ability as a result of a reduced ability to communicate (Bassett et al., 1996; Chall, 1996; P. L. Harris, 2006; Heward, 2009; C. C. Peterson, 2002; M. B. Rowe, 1978; Schick, de Villiers, de Villiers, & Hoffmeister, 2007; Turnbull et al., 2007)

myeducationlab

Hear the speech of a child with hearing loss in the video "Teacher Use of Sign Language"; listen to the boy with the green shirt two minutes into the video. (To find this video, go to Chapter 5 of the Book-Specific Resources in MyEducationLab, select *Video Examples*, and then click on the title.)

Adapting Instruction Specialists typically provide training in such communication skills as American Sign Language, finger spelling, and speechreading. With these additions (and possibly some remedial instruction in reading and vocabulary), the regular school curriculum is appropriate for most students with hearing loss. However, several accommodations can facilitate students' success in general education classrooms:

Minimize irrelevant noise. Even when students can benefit from the use of hearing aids, what they hear is often diminished or distorted; consequently, it's helpful to minimize potentially distracting sounds. For example, carpeting and bulletin boards can absorb some extraneous noise, and fans and pencil sharpeners should be located as far away as possible.

Supplement auditory presentations with visual information and hands-on experiences. We can write important points on the chalkboard, illustrate key ideas with pictures, provide reading materials that duplicate lectures, and ask an aide or student volunteer to take notes on in-class discussions. We can also provide speech-to-text software, which enables students to translate spoken words into written language with reasonable accuracy. And we can use concrete activities (e.g., role playing) to make abstract ideas more understandable.

Communicate in ways that help students hear and speechread. Students who are hard of hearing are most likely to understand us when we speak in a normal tone of voice (not overly loud) and pronounce words distinctly but otherwise normally. To help students speechread, we should speak only while facing them and never while sitting in a dark corner or standing in front of a window or bright light (Gearheart et al., 1992; J. W. Wood, 1998).

Teach American Sign Language and finger spelling to other class members. To facilitate communication with students who have hearing loss, other class members (students and teachers alike) should gain some competence in American Sign Language and finger spelling. I once taught at a school where *every* student—those with hearing loss and those without—received instruction in signing. One girl in my class was totally deaf yet quite popular with her classmates. She and her friends communicated easily both before and after class—and, much to my dismay, sometimes at inappropriate times *during* class.

General Recommendations

In addition to the strategies we have identified for specific physical disabilities, several more general strategies are useful with all students who have physical or sensory challenges:

Ensure that all students have access to important educational resources and opportunities. Such access may involve modifying instructional materials (e.g., obtaining large-print copies of textbooks), modifying a classroom's physical arrangement (e.g., widening aisles and placing bulletin board displays at eye level to accommodate students in wheelchairs), or making special arrangements that enable students to participate in field trips or sports activities.

Provide assistance only when students really need it. Out of eagerness to help students with physical and sensory challenges, many adults inadvertently perform tasks and solve problems that these students are perfectly capable of handling on their own. Yet one of our goals for these students should be to promote their independence, not their dependence on others (Wehmeyer et al., 2007).

Use technology to facilitate learning and performance. I've already mentioned the value of print-reading software and speech-to-text software for students with sensory challenges. In addition, some computer printers can create Braille documents, enabling students with visual impairments to read their own class notes and compositions. Specially adapted joysticks and voice recognition systems can supplement or replace computer keyboards for students with limited muscle control. And machines known as *augmentative communication devices* provide synthesized speech for students incapable of producing normal speech.

Students with Advanced Cognitive Development

Many students are apt to have advanced abilities, either in specific subject areas or across the curriculum, that warrant our attention and encouragement. Some students—those who are *gifted*—are so far above the norm that special educational services are often appropriate.

Giftedness

In general, **giftedness** is unusually high ability or aptitude in one or more areas (e.g., in math, science, creative writing, art, or music) to such a degree that special educational services are necessary to help the student meet his or her full potential. In most instances, giftedness is probably the result of both a genetic predisposition and environmental nurturing (Shavinina & Ferrari, 2004; Simonton, 2001; Winner, 2000b). In some cases, however, special gifts and talents are largely the result of intensive practice and mentoring (Ericsson, 2003; Gladwell, 2006).

In the United States, the Jacob K. Javits Gifted and Talented Student Education Act of 1987 (reauthorized in 1994 and 2001) encourages but does not necessarily mandate special educational services for students who are gifted. Many state governments also either encourage or mandate such services. School districts often use multiple criteria—sometimes including intelligence test scores, sometimes not—to identify students who show exceptional promise in general academic ability, specific academic fields, creativity, or the arts.

Common Characteristics Students who are gifted vary considerably in their unique strengths and talents, and those who show exceptional talent in one area may have only average ability in another (Winner, 2000b). Nevertheless, many students who are gifted have characteristics such as these:

- Advanced vocabulary, language, and reading skills
- Extensive general knowledge about the world
- Ability to learn more quickly, easily, and independently than peers

giftedness Unusually high ability or aptitude in one or more areas, to such a degree that students require special educational services to help them meet their full potential.

- Advanced and efficient cognitive processes and learning strategies
- Considerable flexibility in ideas and approaches to tasks
- High standards for performance (sometimes to the point of unhealthy perfectionism)
- High motivation to accomplish challenging tasks; boredom during easy tasks
- Positive self-concept, especially with regard to academic endeavors
- Above-average social development and emotional adjustment (although a few extremely gifted students may have difficulties because they are so *very* different from their peers) (B. Clark, 1997; Cornell et al., 1990; A. W. Gottfried, Gottfried, Bathurst, & Guerin, 1994; Lupart, 1995; Parker, 1997; Shavinina & Ferrari, 2004; Silverman, 1994; Steiner & Carr, 2003; Winner, 2000a, 2000b)

Students identified as gifted show exceptional achievement or promise in general intellectual ability, specific academic fields, creativity, or the visual and performing arts.

Students can be gifted yet also have one or more disabilities—for instance, a learning disability or an emotional or behavioral disorder—that warrant special services under IDEA (S. Dole, 2000; Hettinger & Knapp, 2001). In planning instruction for such students, we must address their disabilities as well as their unique gifts.

Adapting Instruction Recalling Lev Vygotsky's view of cognitive development from Chapter 2, we could say that gifted students are unlikely to be working within their *zone of proximal development*—the range of challenging tasks most likely to promote their cognitive development—if we limit them to the assignments we give other students. In fact, many students with special gifts and talents become bored or frustrated when their school experiences don't provide tasks and assignments that challenge them and help them develop their unique abilities (Feldhusen, Van Winkel, & Ehle, 1996; Lubinski & Bleske-Rechek, 2008; Winner, 2000b). Following are several suggestions for teaching students with unique gifts and talents:

Provide individualized tasks and assignments. Different students are apt to need special services in very different areas—for example, in math, creative writing, or studio art. Some students who are gifted, especially those with only a limited background in English, may even need training in certain basic skills (C. R. Harris, 1991; Udall, 1989).

Form study groups of students with similar interests and abilities. In some cases, a study group might explore a topic with greater depth and more sophisticated analysis than other students (an *enrichment* approach). In other instances, a study group might simply move through the standard school curriculum at a more rapid pace (an *acceleration* approach). Students benefit both academically and socially from increased contact with peers who have similar interests and talents (Fiedler, Lange, & Winebrenner, 1993; J. A. Kulik & Kulik, 1997; McGinn, Viernstein, & Hogan, 1980).

Teach complex cognitive skills within the context of specific subject areas. Programs that teach complex thinking processes (e.g., creativity, critical thinking) separately from school subject matter tend to have minimal impact on students' cognitive development. A more effective approach is to teach complex thinking skills within the context of specific topics—for example, creativity in writing or reasoning and problem-solving skills in science (M. C. Linn, Clement, Pulos, & Sullivan, 1989; Moon, Feldhusen, & Dillon, 1994; Pulos & Linn, 1981; Stanley, 1980).

Provide opportunities for independent study. Because many students who are gifted are highly motivated and learn effectively on their own, independent study or service-learning projects in areas of interest may be quite appropriate (Candler-Lotven, Tallent-Runnels, Olivárez, & Hildreth, 1994; Lupart, 1995; Terry, 2008). If we provide such opportunities, we must be sure students have the work habits, study strategies, and research skills they need to use their time and resources effectively.

Seek outside resources. When students have high abilities in domains outside our own areas of expertise, it is often helpful to identify suitable mentors elsewhere in the school district or in the community at large—perhaps at a local university, government office, private business, or volunteer community group (Ambrose, Allen, & Huntley, 1994; Piirto, 1999; Seeley, 1989). In such instances, *cognitive apprenticeships*—teaching students how to think about complex tasks in sophisticated ways—can be quite effective (see Chapter 2).

Considering Diversity When Identifying and Addressing Special Needs

Sadly, a disproportionately large number of students identified as having disabilities—especially learning disabilities, intellectual disabilities, and emotional and behavioral disorders—are members of certain ethnic minority groups (McLoyd, 1998; U.S. Department of Education, 2006; VanTassel-Baska, 2008). Most theorists attribute the differing identification rates to environmental conditions that often accompany low socioeconomic status—higher than normal exposure to environmental toxins, inadequate medical care, limited access to enriching educational resources, and so on (e.g., Dyson, 2008; Jacoby & Glauberman, 1995; McLoyd, 1998; H. W. Stevenson, Chen, & Uttal, 1990). English language learners are also identified as having learning disabilities or intellectual abilities more often than native English speakers, a finding that probably reflects students' difficulty in understanding and responding to items on language-based diagnostic tests (A. L. Sullivan, 2008).

The inequitable representation of particular groups in various disability categories poses a dilemma for educators. On the one hand, we don't want to assign a label such as *intellectual disability* or *emotional disorder* to students whose classroom performance and behavior may be due largely to the adverse conditions in which they have grown up. On the other hand, we don't want to deprive these students of special educational services that might help them learn and achieve more successfully over the long run. In such situations, we must conduct fair and nondiscriminatory evaluations of students' needs, and if students qualify under a special-needs category, we must create IEPs to meet those needs. We should consider these categories of special needs as *temporary* classifications that may no longer be applicable as students' classroom performance improves. *All* students, with and without disability classifications, have changing needs that evolve over time.

Especially when working with students identified as having cognitive, emotional, or behavioral difficulties, think of their disability labels as *temporary* classifications that may no longer be applicable as students' classroom performance improves.

In addition to being overrepresented in programs for students with disabilities, members of some minority groups—especially African Americans, Hispanic Americans, and Native Americans—are *under*represented in programs for gifted students (D. Y. Ford, Moore, & Whiting, 2006; VanTassel-Baska, 2008). On average, students from ethnic minority groups are at a disadvantage when traditional measures of ability (e.g., IQ tests) are used to identify giftedness—in some cases, because they have had little experience with the kinds of tasks that appear on those tests (Rogoff, 2003). It is critical, then, that we be on the lookout for other signs of giftedness, including the following:

- Ability to learn quickly from experiences
- Exceptional communication skills (e.g., articulateness, richness of language)
- Originality and resourcefulness in thinking and problem solving
- Ability to generalize concepts and ideas to new, seemingly unrelated situations (Haywood & Lidz, 2007; Maker & Schiever, 1989; Winner, 1996)

Look beyond IQ scores in identifying students who may be gifted; for instance, look for richness of language, an ability to learn new things quickly, and exceptional resourcefulness in solving problems.

For the growth of our society over the long run, it is imperative that we nurture the many gifted students that we find in *all* cultural and ethnic groups.

General Recommendations for Working with Students Who Have Special Needs

Although students with special educational needs vary widely in their abilities and disabilities, several recommendations apply across the board:

Be flexible in approaches to instruction. Even when students clearly fall within a particular category of special needs, we can't always predict which instructional methods will be most effective for each of them. If we don't succeed with a particular approach, we should try again, but we might also want to try *differently*.

Unless there is reason to do otherwise, hold the same expectations for students with disabilities as for other students. Sometimes, having a disability may make it difficult or impossible for students to accomplish certain school tasks, and we will have to modify our expectations and assessment practices accordingly. Aside from such situations, however, we should generally have the same expectations for students with special needs that we have for other students. Rather than think of reasons that a student *can't* do something, we should think about how we can help the student *do* it.

Identify and teach the prerequisite knowledge and skills students may not have acquired because of their disabilities. As either a direct or indirect result of certain disabilities, some students lack the knowledge and skills essential for their school success. For instance, students with visual impairments have not been able to observe many of the cause-and-effect relationships that form a foundation for learning science—such as the changes in the appearance of wood when it's burned (Ferrell, 1996; M. B. Rowe, 1978). And students whose medical conditions have limited their contact with other children may have poorly developed interpersonal skills.

Consult and collaborate with specialists. School districts usually employ a variety of specialists, including special educators, counselors, school psychologists, nurses, speech pathologists, and physical and occupational therapists. Some students leave the classroom for part of the day to work with these individuals. However, in today's inclusive schools, many special services are provided within the regular classroom context by teachers and specialists working in close collaboration.

Communicate regularly with parents. In accordance with IDEA, parents are part of the multidisciplinary team that determines the most appropriate program for a student with special needs. Parents can often tell us what works and what does not, and they can alert us to certain conditions or events at home that may trigger problem behaviors in class. Furthermore, we can bring about desired behavioral changes more effectively if the same expectations for behavior exist both at school and at home.

Include students in planning and decision making. Educational programs for most students with special needs—especially those with disabilities—are so highly structured that students have little say regarding what and how they learn. But increasingly, educators are recognizing the importance of letting *all* students make some choices about their academic goals and curriculum (Algozzine, Browder, Karvonen, Test, & Wood, 2001; Mithaug & Mithaug, 2003; Wehmeyer et al., 2007). Students' decision making can ultimately promote greater self-regulation and a greater sense of self-determination (topics we'll discuss in Chapters 10 and 11, respectively).

Keep your eyes open for students who may qualify for special services. The more we work with a particular age-group of students, the more we learn about their age-typical abilities and behaviors. Hence, we teachers are in an excellent position to identify children who are in one way or another *not* typical. Although specialists usually conduct the in-depth assessments necessary to identify particular special needs, the job of referring students for such assessments—and thereby gaining them access to the specialized services they may need—is ultimately up to teachers in general education classrooms.

The Big Picture

In this chapter, we've discovered many ways in which students in any single classroom are likely to be different from one another, often as a result of heredity and environment working in concert to create distinctly unique human beings. As a beginning teacher, you may initially find students' individual differences a bit overwhelming, but with time and experience, you'll begin to take them in stride and grow increasingly appreciative of the many benefits that students' diverse abilities bring to a classroom community. Following are three general principles to keep in mind:

- ***All students have unique profiles of characteristics and needs.*** Regardless of whether students have been identified as having special educational needs, they are *individuals* first, each with a particular set of strengths and weaknesses. The more we know about students' specific characteristics and needs—academic, social, behavioral, and physical—the more effectively we can help every one of them succeed at classroom tasks and activities. And the more we individualize instruction for all students—both those who have and those who have *not* been identified as having certain disabilities—the less stigmatized and "special" students with special needs are likely to seem and the more easily they can become full participants in an inclusive setting.

- ***Intelligence and IQ scores go only so far in accounting for students' classroom learning and achievement.*** On average, students with higher IQ scores achieve at higher levels than do students with lower scores, but the correlation is not an especially strong one. One likely reason is that intelligence encompasses many specific abilities that are each more or less useful for different tasks and in different cultures. Also, many other factors—for example, cognitive styles, dispositions, motives, and, most importantly, *quality of instruction*—are just as influential, sometimes even more so, in determining how much students learn and achieve both inside and outside the classroom.

- ***Students' abilities and disabilities are dynamic, rather than static, entities.*** Numerous factors affect students' ability to think and act intelligently in different contexts, and some of these factors (schooling, for instance) can help students become *increasingly* intelligent with age. Students' cognitive styles and dispositions, too, can probably change in productive directions if teachers model and encourage inclinations to think analytically, critically, and with an open mind. And with appropriate interventions, many students with cognitive, social, emotional, and behavioral disabilities become increasingly proficient and productive—that is, they become less *dis*abled—over time.

Practice for Your Licensure Exam

Quiet Amy

As a veteran kindergarten teacher, Mr. Mahoney knows that many kindergarteners initially have difficulty adjusting to the school environment, especially if they haven't previously attended daycare or preschool. But Amy is giving him cause for concern. Amy never speaks, either to him or to the other children, even when she is directly spoken to. On the infrequent occasions when she wants to communicate, she does so primarily by looking and pointing at something or someone in the room. Amy also has trouble following simple directions, almost as if she hasn't heard what she's been asked to do. And she seems distracted during daily storybook readings and science lessons. The only activities that give her pleasure are arts and crafts. She may spend hours at a time working with construction paper, crayons, scissors, and glue, and her creations are often the most inventive and detailed in the class.

Mr. Mahoney suspects that Amy may have a disability that qualifies her for special services. To get permission for an in-depth evaluation of her abilities and needs, he and the school psychologist visit Amy's mother, a single woman raising five other children as well. "Amy doesn't talk at home either," the mother admits. "I work two jobs to make ends meet, and I haven't been able to spend as much time with her as I'd like. Her brothers and sisters take good care of her, though. They always seem to know what she wants, and they make sure she gets it."

1. **Multiple-choice question:**

   Mr. Mahoney suspects that Amy may qualify for special educational services. If she does, in which of the following categories of special needs is she *least* likely to fall?

a. Hearing loss
b. Autism spectrum disorders
c. Speech and communication disorders
d. Attention-deficit hyperactivity disorder

2. **Constructed-response question:**

Amy's evaluation will undoubtedly take several weeks to complete. In the meantime, what strategies might Mr. Mahoney use to improve Amy's classroom behavior and performance? Describe at least three different things he might do. Be specific and concrete in your descriptions.

Go to Chapter 5 of the Book-Specific Resources in **MyEducationLab**, and click on "Practice for Your Licensure Exam" to answer these questions. Compare your responses with the feedback provided.

PRAXIS

Turn to Appendix C, "Matching Book and MyEducationLab Content to the Praxis Principles of Learning and Teaching Tests," to discover sections of this chapter that may be especially applicable to the Praxis tests.

PEARSON myeducationlab

Now go to MyEducationLab (**www.myeducationlab.com**), where you can:

- Find learning outcomes for two topics relevant to this chapter—Student Diversity and Students with Special Needs—along with the national standards that connect to these outcomes.
- Complete Assignments and Activities that can help you more deeply understand the chapter content.
- Engage in Building Teaching Skills and Dispositions exercises in which you can apply and practice core teaching skills identified in the chapter.
- Access Book-Specific Resources:
  - Check your comprehension of chapter content by going to the Study Plan, where you can find (a) Chapter Objectives; (b) Focus Questions that can guide your reading; (c) a Self-Check Quiz that can help you monitor your progress in mastering chapter content; (d) Review, Practice, and Enrichment exercises with detailed feedback that will deepen your understanding of various concepts and principles; (e) Flashcards that can give you practice in understanding and defining key terms; and (f) Common Beliefs and Misconceptions about Educational Psychology that will alert you to typical misunderstandings in educational psychology classes
  - Video Examples of various concepts and principles presented in the chapter.
  - Supplementary Readings that enable you to pursue certain topics in greater depth.
  - A Practice for Your Licensure Exam exercise that resembles the kinds of questions appearing on many teacher licensure tests.

CHAPTER OUTLINE

CHAPTER OBJECTIVES

- **Objective 6.1:** Describe five basic assumptions underlying cognitive psychology's views of learning, and apply these assumptions to classroom practice.
- **Objective 6.2:** Describe and illustrate the key components that many researchers believe may characterize the human memory system.
- **Objective 6.3:** Apply your knowledge of long-term memory storage processes in identifying effective strategies for teaching children and adolescents.
- **Objective 6.4:** Describe several factors that influence people's ability to remember what they have learned, and identify several reasons why students sometimes forget classroom material.
- **Objective 6.5:** Give examples of the diversity in cognitive processes you might see in students as a result of their gender, socioeconomic and cultural background, and special educational needs.

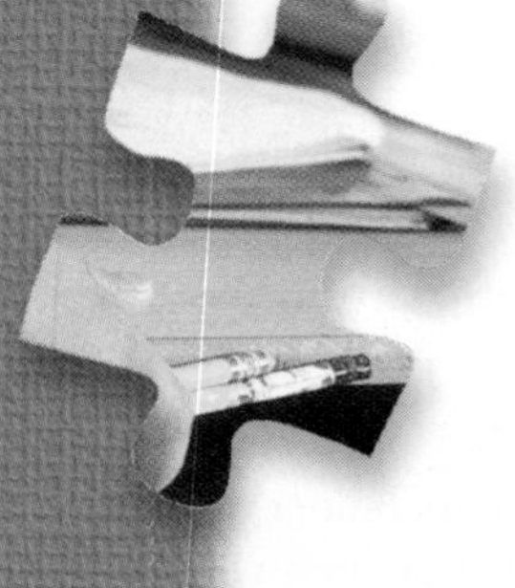

Chapter 6

Learning and Cognitive Processes

CASE STUDY: Bones

In biology class, Kanesha has been struggling to learn the names of the bones in the human body, from head (cranium) to toe (metatarsus). She has learned a few bones quickly and easily. For example, she realizes that, logically, the *nasal bone* should form part of the nose, and she remembers the *humerus* (upper arm bone) by thinking of it as being just above one's funny ("humorous") bone. But she is still confused about some of the other bones. For example, the *tibia* and *fibula* have similar-sounding names and are both located in the lower leg. And she keeps thinking that the *sternum* (at the front of the chest) is actually in the back of the body, just as the stern of a boat is at its rear. She also has trouble remembering bones whose names don't provide any kind of clue for her—the coccyx, ulna, sacrum, clavicle, patella, and so on.

To prepare for an upcoming biology quiz, Kanesha looks at a diagram of the human skeleton and whispers the name of each bone to herself several times. She also writes each name on a sheet of paper. "These terms will certainly sink in if I repeat them enough times," she tells herself. But Kanesha scores only 70% on the biology quiz. As she looks over her incorrect answers, she sees that she confused the tibia and the fibula, labeled the ulna as "clavicle," put the sternum in the wrong place, and completely forgot about the coccyx, sacrum, and patella.

- **Why are some bones easier for Kanesha to remember than others?**
- **Which ones would be easiest for *you* to remember?**

KANESHA SEEMS TO HAVE AN EASIER TIME learning bone names that she can relate to things she already knows. In particular, she relates *nasal bone* to *nose* and *humerus* to *funny bone*. She applies her existing knowledge in trying to learn *sternum*, as well, but her strategy backfires; a boat's *stern* is at its rear, whereas the sternum is in front of the chest cavity. She also has trouble with bone names she can't connect to anything in her previous experience.

Over the course of a lifetime, human beings learn many millions of new pieces of information and many millions of new behaviors and skills. For our discussion in this book, we'll define **learning** as a long-term change in mental representations or associations as a result of experience. Let's divide this definition into its three parts. First, learning is a *long-term change* in that it isn't just a brief, transitory use of information—such as remembering a phone number only long enough to dial it—but it doesn't necessarily last forever. Second, learning involves *mental representations or associations* and so presumably has its basis in the brain (see Chapter 2). Third, learning is a change *due to experience*, rather than the result of physiological maturation, fatigue, use of alcohol or drugs, or onset of mental illness.

Psychologists have been studying the nature of learning for more than a century and, in the process, have taken a variety of theoretical perspectives. Several especially influential perspectives are summarized in Table 6.1. If you've read Chapter 2, you've already encountered the first two. The other four are listed more or less in the order in which they've appeared on the scene.

myeducationlab

Track changes in psychological perspectives of learning in a supplementary reading, "How Learning Theories Have Evolved Over Time." (To find this reading, go to Chapter 6 of the Book-Specific Resources in MyEducationLab and then select *Supplementary Readings*.)

In this chapter, we'll look primarily at what goes on *inside* the learner. In doing so, we'll draw from **cognitive psychology**, a large body of research that addresses a variety of mental phenomena that underlie human behavior—perception, memory, reasoning, and so on. As you'll discover shortly, cognitive psychology encompasses two of the perspectives listed in the table: information processing theory and constructivism. Keep in mind, however, that diverse perspectives of learning often complement, rather than contradict, one another, and together they give us a richer, more multifaceted picture of human learning than any single perspective can give us alone. As we continue to explore the nature of learning in upcoming chapters, then, we will draw useful ideas from all of the perspectives listed in Table 6.1.

Basic Assumptions of Cognitive Psychology

At the core of cognitive psychology are several basic assumptions about how people learn:

- *Cognitive processes influence what is learned.* **Cognitive processes**—the specific things people do mentally as they try to interpret and remember what people see, hear, and study—can have a profound effect on what they specifically learn and remember. For example, in the opening case study, Kanesha thinks about the nasal bone and the humerus in ways that should help her remember them. However, she thinks about the sternum in a way that interferes with her ability to remember that bone correctly, and she gives little or no thought about why the other bones have particular names. The extent to which Kanesha thinks about the material she needs to learn—and also *how* she thinks about it—affects her performance on the biology quiz.

Cognitive psychologists have offered numerous explanations of how people mentally process information. Many of these explanations are collectively known as **information processing theory**. Some early information processing explanations portrayed human thinking and learning as being similar to the ways computers operate. It has since become clear, however, that the computer analogy is too simple—that people often think about and interpret information in ways that are difficult to explain in the relatively simplistic, one-thing-always-leads-to-another ways that characterize computers (Munakata, 2006; Reisberg, 1997; D. C. Rubin, 2006).

- *People's cognitive processes can sometimes be inferred from their behaviors.* Historically, some psychologists—especially behaviorists—have argued that we cannot directly observe people's thinking and therefore cannot study it objectively and scientifically. Cognitive psychologists disagree, suggesting that by observing people's responses to various objects and events, it is possible to draw reasonable *inferences*—to make educated guesses—about the cognitive processes that probably underlie the responses. As an example of how we might learn about people's cognitive processes by observing their behaviors, try the following exercise.

learning Long-term change in mental representations or associations as a result of experience.

cognitive psychology General theoretical perspective that focuses on the mental processes underlying learning and behavior.

cognitive process Particular way of thinking about and mentally responding to a certain event or piece of information.

information processing theory Theoretical perspective that focuses on the specific ways in which learners mentally think about, or process, new information and events.

Compare/Contrast

TABLE 6.1
General Theoretical Approaches to the Study of Learning

Theoretical Perspective	General Description
Piaget's theory of cognitive development	Piaget suggested that children *construct*, rather than absorb, knowledge about the world, often organizing what they learn as *schemes*: groups of similar actions or thoughts that they use repeatedly in response to the environment. Children's learning and cognitive development occur as a result of two complementary processes: *assimilation* (physically or mentally responding to a new object or event in a way that's consistent with an existing scheme) and *accommodation* (either modifying an existing scheme to account for the new object or event or forming an entirely new scheme to deal with it). Piaget's theory is described in Chapter 2.
Vygotsky's theory of cognitive development	Vygotsky emphasized that social, cultural, and historical contexts have profound influences on children's thinking and learning. In social interactions within their communities, children encounter culturally appropriate ways of thinking about and interpreting objects and events. With time and practice, these ways of thinking—which are first used in a social context—are gradually *internalized* into nonspoken, mental processes that learners use independently and adapt for their own purposes. Because of varying environments, historical circumstances, and needs, different cultures have developed somewhat different ways of thinking, learning, and teaching. Vygotsky's theory and the *sociocultural theory* it has inspired are described in Chapter 2.
Behaviorism	Behaviorists argue that because thought processes cannot be directly observed and measured, it is difficult to study thinking objectively and scientifically. Instead, they focus on two things that researchers *can* observe and measure: people's behaviors (*responses*) and the environmental events (*stimuli*) that precede and follow those responses. Learning is viewed as a process of acquiring and modifying associations among stimuli and responses, largely through a learner's direct interactions with the environment. Behaviorism has much to offer us in the way of helping students acquire more productive classroom behaviors (see Chapters 9 and 13).
Social cognitive theory	Social cognitive theorists focus largely on what and how people learn from observing one another. Environmental stimuli certainly affect behavior, but cognitive processes (e.g., awareness of stimulus–response relationships, expectations about future events) also play a significant role. Often, people learn through *modeling*—that is, watching and imitating what others do. Whether people learn and perform effectively is also a function of their *self-efficacy*, the extent to which they believe they can successfully accomplish a particular task or activity. Over time, most people increasingly engage in *self-regulation*, taking charge of and directing their own actions. Social cognitive theory has been influential in our understanding of motivation as well as learning (see Chapters 10 and 11).
Information processing theory	While not denying that the environment plays a critical role in learning, information processing theorists investigate what goes on *inside* learners, focusing on the cognitive processes involved in learning, memory, and performance. From observations of how people execute various tasks and behave in various situations, these theorists make inferences about how people may perceive, interpret, and mentally manipulate information they encounter in the environment. Information processing theorists also speculate about what internal mechanisms underlie human cognition (e.g., *working memory* and *long-term memory*) and about how people mentally process information (e.g., through *elaboration* and *visual imagery*). Initially, some information processing theorists believed that human thinking is similar to how a computer works (hence, they borrowed terms such as *encoding*, *storage*, and *retrieval* from computer lingo), but in recent years most theorists have largely abandoned the computer analogy.
Constructivism	Like information processing theorists, constructivists concern themselves with internal aspects of learning. And like Piaget, they propose that people create (rather than absorb) knowledge from their observations and experiences. Constructivists suggest that people combine much of what they learn into integrated bodies of knowledge and beliefs (e.g., these might take the form of *schemas* and *theories*) that may or may not be accurate and useful understandings of the world. Some constructivists focus on how individual learners create knowledge through their interactions with the environment; this approach is known as *individual constructivism*. Others emphasize that by working together, two or more people can often gain better understandings than anyone could gain alone; this approach is called *social constructivism*.

EXPERIENCING FIRSTHAND

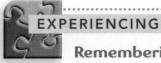

Remembering 12 Words

Read through the 12 words below *one time only*. Then cover up the page, and write down the words in the order they come to mind.

shirt	table	hat
carrot	bed	squash
pants	potatoes	stool
chair	shoe	bean

Did you write down the words in the order in which you read them? Probably not. If you are like most people, you recalled the words by category—perhaps clothing first, then vegetables, then furniture. From the order in which you wrote the words (i.e., from your *behavior*), we can draw an inference about an internal cognitive process that occurred as you learned the words: You mentally *organized* them into categories.

• *People are selective about what they mentally process and learn.* People are constantly bombarded with information. Consider the many stimuli you are encountering at this very moment. How many separate stimuli appear on these two open pages of your book? How many objects do you see in addition to the book? How many sounds are reaching your ears? How many objects—perhaps on your fingers, on your toes, at your back, or around your waist—do you feel? I suspect that you have been ignoring most of these stimuli until just now, when I specifically asked you to think about them.

It's useful to distinguish between *sensation*—one's ability to detect stimuli in the environment—and *perception*—one's interpretation of stimuli. For reasons you'll discover a bit later, it's virtually impossible to perceive (interpret) everything the body senses. Because learners can handle only so much information at a given time, they must choose a few things to focus on and ignore the rest.

As an analogy, consider the hundreds of items a typical adult receives in the mail each year, including all the packages, letters, bills, brochures, catalogs, flyers, advertisements, requests for donations, and sweepstakes announcements. Do you open, examine, and respond to every piece of mail? Probably not. If you're like me, you process only a few key items (e.g., packages, letters, bills, and some miscellaneous things that catch your eye). You may inspect other items long enough to know that you don't need them. You may even discard some items without opening them.

In much the same way, students encounter a great deal of new information every day—information delivered by way of teacher instruction, textbooks, bulletin boards, classmates' behaviors, and so on. They must inevitably make choices about which pieces of information are most important. They select a few stimuli to examine and respond to in depth, give other stimuli only a cursory glance, and ignore other stimuli altogether.

construction Mental process in which a learner takes many separate pieces of information and uses them to build an overall understanding or interpretation.

constructivism Theoretical perspective proposing that learners construct, rather than absorb, knowledge from their experiences.

• *Meanings and understandings are not derived directly from the environment; instead, they are constructed by the learner.* The process of **construction** lies at the core of many cognitive theories of learning: Learners take numerous, separate pieces of information and use them to create a general understanding or interpretation of the world around them (e.g., Brainerd & Reyna, 2005; Bransford & Franks, 1971; Neisser, 1967). Learning theories that focus primarily on the ways that learners construct knowledge are collectively known as **constructivism**.

To experience the process of construction firsthand, try the following exercise.

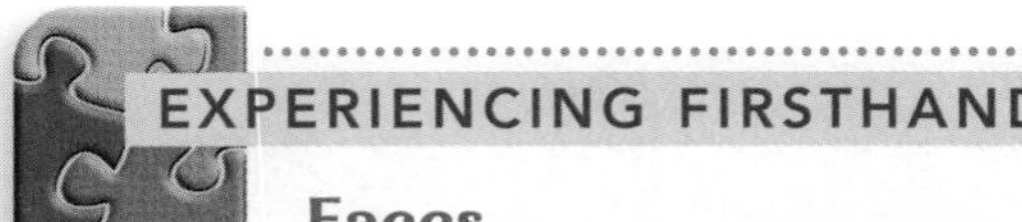

EXPERIENCING FIRSTHAND

Faces

Look at the three black-and-white figures shown here. What do you see in each one? Most people perceive the figure on the left as that of a woman, even though many of her features are missing. Enough features are visible—an eye, parts of the nose, mouth, chin, and hair—that you can construct a meaningful perception from them.

Is enough information available in the other two figures for you to construct two more faces? Construction of a face from the figure on the right may take a while, but it can be done.

Source: Figures from "Age in the Development of Closure Ability in Children" by C. M. Mooney, 1957, *Canadian Journal of Psychology,* 11, p. 220. Copyright 1957. Canadian Psychological Association. Reprinted with permission.

Objectively speaking, the three configurations of black splotches, and especially the two rightmost ones, leave a lot to the imagination. The woman in the middle is missing half of her face, and the man on the right is missing the top of his head. Yet knowing how human faces typically appear may have been enough to enable you to mentally add the missing features and perceive complete pictures. Curiously, once you have constructed faces from the figures, they then seem obvious. If you were to close this book now and not pick it up again for a week or more, you would probably see the faces almost immediately, even if you had had considerable difficulty perceiving them originally.

As teachers, we must remember that students won't necessarily learn information exactly as we present it to them. In fact, they will each interpret classroom subject matter in their own, idiosyncratic ways. And occasionally, they may construct *mis*information, as Kanesha does when she relates the *sternum* to the stern of a boat.

- *Maturational changes in the brain enable increasingly sophisticated cognitive processes with age.* In Chapter 2, we discovered several ways in which children's brains change over time. Such changes are almost certainly a key reason why children become capable of increasingly effective cognitive processes—longer attention spans, enhanced ability to organize and integrate information, and so on (Kuhn, 2006; Luna, Garver, Urban, Lazar, & Sweeney, 2004; C. A. Nelson et al., 2006). But rather than propose distinct stages of cognitive development (as Piaget did), most cognitive psychologists believe that children's cognitive development can best be characterized as gradual *trends.* As we proceed through the chapter, we'll identify a number of developmental trends in children's cognitive processes.

Table 6.2 summarizes the five assumptions just described and can help you apply them to your own teaching practice.

A Model of Human Memory

Central to cognitive psychologists' view of how people learn is the concept of **memory**. In some instances, we will use this term to refer to learners' ability to mentally save previously learned knowledge or skills over a period of time. In other instances, we will use it when talking about a particular location where learners put what they learn—perhaps *working memory* or *long-term memory.*

The process of putting what is being learned into memory is called **storage**. For example, each time you go to class, you undoubtedly *store* some of the ideas presented in a lecture or class discussion. You may store other information from class as well—perhaps the name of the person sitting next to you (George), the shape and size

memory Ability to mentally save something that has been previously learned; also, the mental "location" where such information is saved.

storage Process of putting new information into memory.

Principles/ Assumptions

TABLE 6.2
Basic Assumptions of Cognitive Psychology and Their Educational Implications

Assumption	Educational Implication	Example
Influence of cognitive processes	Encourage students to think about classroom subject matter in ways that will help them remember it.	When introducing the concept *mammal*, ask students to identify numerous examples.
Behavior as a reflection of cognitive processes	Ask students to explain their reasoning, and look closely at what they do and say to make educated guesses about how they are thinking about classroom topics.	When a student says that 16 + 19 = 25 and that 27 + 27 = 44, suspect that the student is forgetting to carry when solving two-digit addition problems.
Selectivity about what is learned	Help students to identify the most important things for them to learn and to understand why these things are important.	Give students questions they should try to answer as they read their textbooks. Include questions that ask them to apply what they read to their own lives.
Construction of meanings and understandings	Provide experiences that will help students make sense of the topics they are studying, and regularly monitor students' understandings.	When studying Nathaniel Hawthorne's *The Scarlet Letter*, have students convene in small groups to discuss possible reasons that the Reverend Dimmesdale refuses to acknowledge that he is the father of Hester Prynne's baby.
Increasing capacity for sophisticated cognitive processes with age	Take into account strengths and limitations in students' cognitive processing capabilities at different age levels.	When teaching kindergartners basic counting skills, accommodate their short attention span by keeping verbal explanations short and conducting a variety of active, hands-on counting activities.

of the classroom (rectangular, about 15 by 30 meters), or the pattern of the instructor's shirt (a ghastly combination of orange and purple horizontal stripes). Yet learners rarely store information exactly as they receive it. Instead, they engage in **encoding**, modifying the information in some way. For instance, when listening to a story, you might imagine what certain characters look like—thus encoding some verbal input as visual images. And when you see your instructor's orange and purple shirt, you might think, "My instructor really needs a wardrobe makeover"—thus assigning a specific *meaning* and *interpretation* to what you have seen.

At some point after you have stored information in your memory, you may discover that you need to use it. The process of remembering previously stored information—that is, finding it in memory—is called **retrieval**. The following exercise illustrates this process.

EXPERIENCING FIRSTHAND

Retrieval Practice

See how quickly you can answer each of the following questions:

1. What is your name?
2. What is the capital of France?
3. In what year did Christopher Columbus first sail across the Atlantic Ocean to reach the New World?
4. When talking about appetizers at a party, we sometimes use a French term instead of the word *appetizer*. What is that French term, and how is it spelled?

encoding Changing the format of new information as it is being stored in memory.

retrieval Process of finding information previously stored in memory.

FIGURE 6.1 A model of the human memory system

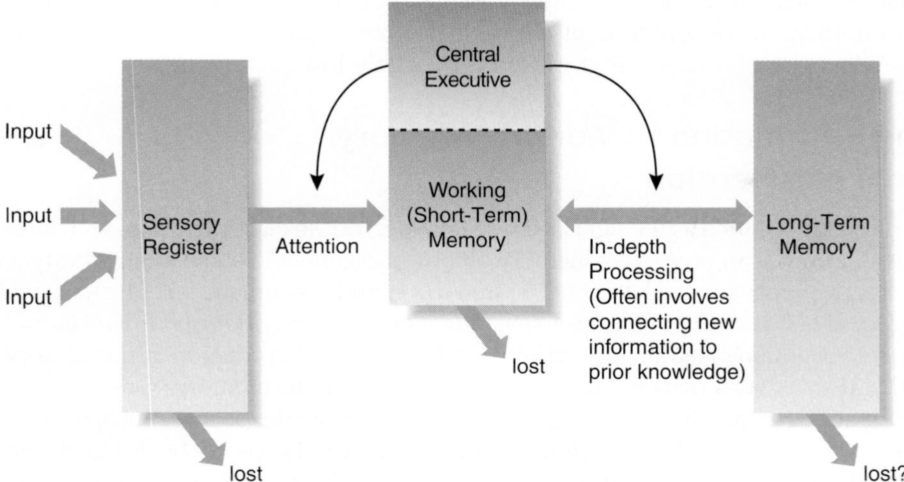

As you probably noticed when you tried to answer these questions, retrieving some kinds of information from memory—your name, for instance—is quick and easy. Other things—perhaps the capital of France (Paris) and the year of Columbus's first voyage (1492)—can be retrieved only after some thought and effort. Still other pieces of information, even though you may have stored them in memory at one time, may be almost impossible to retrieve. Perhaps the correct spelling of *hors d'oeuvre* falls into this category.

Although cognitive psychologists are fairly consistent in their use of such terms as *storage*, *encoding*, and *retrieval*, they don't all agree about the exact nature of human memory. However, many believe that memory may have three key components: a sensory register, a working (short-term) memory, and a long-term memory. A three-component model of human memory, based loosely on one proposed by Atkinson and Shiffrin in 1968 but modified to reflect more recent research findings, is presented in Figure 6.1. The model oversimplifies the nature of memory to some degree (more about this point later), but it provides a good way to organize much of what we know about how memory works.

Please note that in referring to three components of memory, I am *not* necessarily referring to three separate parts of the brain. The model of memory I describe here has been derived largely from studies of human behavior, rather than from studies of the brain.

The Nature of the Sensory Register

If you have ever played with a lighted sparkler at night, then you have seen the tail of light that follows a sparkler as you wave it about. If you have ever daydreamed in class, you may have noticed that when you tune back in to a lecture, you can still hear the three or four words that were spoken just *before* you started paying attention to your instructor again. The sparkler's tail and the words that linger are not out there in the environment. Instead, they are recorded in your sensory register.

The **sensory register** is the component of memory that holds the information you receive—the *input*—in more or less its original, *un*encoded form. Thus, visual input is stored in a visual form, auditory input in an auditory form, and so on (e.g., Coltheart, Lea, & Thompson, 1974; Cowan, 1995). The sensory register has a *large capacity:* It can hold a great deal of information at any one time.

sensory register Component of memory that holds incoming information in an unanalyzed form for a very brief period of time (two or three seconds at most, depending on the modality).

That's the good news. The bad news is that information stored in the sensory register doesn't last very long (Cowan, 1995; Wingfield & Byrnes, 1981). Visual information (i.e., what you see) probably lasts for less than a second. For example, as a child,

I never could spell out my entire first name (Jeanne) with a sparkler: The *J* had always faded before I got to the first *n*, no matter how quickly I wrote. Auditory information (i.e., what you hear) probably lasts slightly longer, perhaps for two or three seconds. To keep information for any time at all, then, learners need to move it to *working memory*. Whatever information isn't moved is probably lost, or forgotten.

Moving Information to Working Memory: The Role of Attention

Sensory information, such as the light cast by a sparkler, doesn't last very long, no matter what we do. But we can preserve a memory of it by encoding it in some minimal way—for instance, by perceiving the letters *Jea* written in a sparkler's curlicue tail. The first step in this process is **attention**: *Whatever someone mentally pays attention to moves into working memory*. Many cognitive psychologists believe that information in the sensory register that doesn't get a person's attention disappears from the memory system.

myeducationlab

Observe 10-year-old David's realization that attention affects memory in the video "Memory and Cognition: Early and Middle Childhood." When David says "My brain was turned off right now," he really means that his *attention* was turned off, or at least directed to something other than what the interviewer was saying. (To find this video, go to Chapter 6 of the Book-Specific Resources in MyEducationLab, select *Video Examples*, and then click on the title.)

Paying attention involves directing not only the appropriate sensory receptors (in the eyes, ears, etc.) but also the *mind* toward whatever needs to be learned and remembered. Imagine reading a textbook for one of your classes. Your eyes are moving down each page, but you are thinking about something altogether different—a recent argument with a friend, a high-paying job advertised in the newspaper, or your growling stomach. What will you remember from the textbook? Absolutely nothing. Even though your eyes were focused on the words in the book, you weren't *mentally* attending to the words.

Young children's attention often moves quickly from one thing to another and is easily drawn to objects and events unrelated to the task at hand. As children grow older, they become better able to focus their attention on a particular task and keep it there, and they are less distracted by irrelevant thoughts and events (S. M. Carlson & Moses, 2001; Dempster & Corkill, 1999; Higgins & Turnure, 1984). Nevertheless, they can rarely keep their minds on a single task *all* the time.

Even when learners are paying attention, they can attend to only a very small amount of information at any one time. In other words, attention has a *limited capacity* (Cherry, 1953; Cowan, 2007). For example, if you are sitting in front of the television with your textbook open in your lap, you can attend to the *Friends* rerun playing on TV *or* to your book but not to both simultaneously. And if you are preoccupied in class with your instructor's desperate need for a fashion makeover, you are unlikely to be paying attention to the content of the lecture.

myeducationlab

Hear 12-year-old Claudia describe things her teachers do that capture or lose her attention in the video "Motivation." (To find this video, go to Chapter 6 of the Book-Specific Resources in MyEducationLab, select *Video Examples*, and then click on the title.)

Exactly *how* limited is the limited capacity of human attention? People can often perform two or three well-learned, automatic tasks at once. For example, you can walk and chew gum simultaneously, and you can probably drive a car and drink a cup of coffee at the same time. But when a stimulus or event is detailed and complex (as both textbooks and *Friends* reruns are) or when a task requires considerable thought (as understanding a lecture and driving a car on an icy mountain road would), then people can usually attend to only *one* thing at a time (J. R. Anderson, 2005; Reisberg, 1997).

To some extent, we teachers can tell which students are paying attention to an ongoing activity by their overt behaviors (Grabe, 1986; Piontkowski & Calfee, 1979). But appearances can be deceiving. You can probably think of times when, as a student, you looked directly at a teacher without really hearing anything the teacher was saying. You can probably also think of times when you looked at a textbook without a single word on the page sinking in. Remember, attention is not just a behavior; it is also a mental process. It isn't enough that students' eyes and ears are directed toward their classroom material. Their minds must be directed toward it as well. The Into the Classroom feature "Getting and Keeping Students' Attention" presents several effective strategies for keeping students' minds on classroom topics.

attention Focusing of mental processing on particular stimuli.

working memory Component of memory that holds and actively thinks about and processes a limited amount of information for a short time.

The Nature of Working (Short-Term) Memory

Working memory is the component of memory where we hold attended-to information for a short time while we try to make sense of it. Working memory is also where

INTO THE Classroom

Getting and Keeping Students' Attention

- **Incorporate intriguing topics and tasks into your lessons.**

  In a unit on nutrition, a high school biology teacher has students determine the nutritional value of various menu items at a popular local fast-food restaurant.

- **Get students physically involved with the subject matter.**

  A middle school history teacher plans a day late in the school year when all of his classes "go back in time" to the American Civil War. In preparation for the event, the students spend several weeks learning about the Battle of Gettysburg, researching typical dress and meals of the era, gathering appropriate clothing and equipment, and preparing snacks and lunches. On the day of the "battle," students assume various roles: Union and Confederate soldiers, government officials, journalists, merchants, homemakers, doctors and nurses, and so on.

- **Incorporate a variety of instructional methods into lessons.**

  After explaining how to calculate the areas of squares and rectangles, a fourth-grade teacher has her students practice calculating areas in a series of increasingly challenging word problems. She then breaks the class into cooperative learning groups of three or four members. Each group is given a tape measure and calculator and asked to determine the area of the classroom floor, excluding those parts covered by several built-in cabinets that extend into the room. To complete the task, the students must divide the room into several smaller rectangles, compute the area of each rectangle separately, and add the subareas together.

- **Provide frequent breaks from sedentary activities, especially when working with students in the elementary grades.**

  To provide practice with the alphabet, a kindergarten teacher occasionally has students make letters with their bodies: one child standing with arms extended up and out to make a Y, two children bending over and joining hands to form an M, and so on.

- **In the middle school and high school grades, encourage students to take notes.**

  In a middle school science class, different cooperative learning groups have been specializing in and researching various endangered species. As each group gives an oral report about its species to the rest of the class, the teacher asks students in the audience to jot down questions about things they would like to know about the animal. Upon the completion of their prepared report, members of the presenting group address their classmates' questions.

- **Minimize distractions, especially when students must work quietly and independently.**

  The windows of several classrooms look out onto an area where a new parking lot is being created. Teachers in those classrooms have noticed that many of their students are being distracted by the construction activity outside. The teachers ask the principal to request that the construction company work elsewhere on the day that an important statewide assessment is scheduled to be administered.

Sources: Some strategies based on Di Vesta & Gray, 1972; Kiewra, 1989; Ku, Chan, Wu, & Chen, 2008; Pellegrini & Bjorklund, 1997; Posner & Rothbart, 2007.

much of our active cognitive processing actually occurs. For instance, it's where we think about the content of a lecture, analyze a textbook passage, or solve a problem. Basically, this is the component that does most of the mental work of the memory system—hence its name, *working* memory.

Rather than being a single entity, working memory probably has several components for holding and working with different kinds of information—for example, visual information, auditory information, and the underlying meanings of events—as well as a component that integrates multiple kinds of information. Working memory may also include a **central executive** that focuses attention, oversees the flow of information throughout the memory system, selects and controls complex voluntary behaviors, and inhibits counterproductive thoughts and actions (Aron, 2008; Baddeley, 2001; G. R. Lyon & Krasnegor, 1996; E. E. Smith, 2000).[1]

Information stored in working memory doesn't last very long—perhaps 5 to 20 seconds at most—unless the learner consciously does something with it (Baddeley, 2001; L. R. Peterson & Peterson, 1959). Accordingly, this component is sometimes

central executive Component of the human memory system that oversees the flow of information throughout the system.

[1]As you may have guessed, the functions of working memory are located largely in the front part of the cortex, which I've previously described as being the center for much of our conscious thinking (see Chapter 2). Certain other parts of the brain (e.g., the hippocampus) are involved as well (Aron, 2008; Byrnes, 2001; Dehaene, 2007).

called *short-term memory*. For example, imagine that you need to call a friend, so you look up the friend's number in the telephone book. Because you've paid attention to the number, it is presumably in your working memory. But you discover that someone else is using the phone, and you have no paper and pencil handy. To keep the number in your memory until you can dial it, you might simply repeat it to yourself over and over again. This process, known as **maintenance rehearsal**, keeps information in working memory for as long as you're willing to continue talking to yourself. But once you stop, the number will disappear fairly quickly.

For reasons that aren't entirely clear, the amount of information children can hold in working memory increases somewhat as they get older (Ben-Yehudah & Fiez, 2007; Kail, 2007). Yet even adults have only so much room to simultaneously hold and think about information. To see what I mean, put your working memory to work for a moment in the following exercise.

EXPERIENCING FIRSTHAND
Division Problem

Try computing the answer to this division problem in your head:

$59\overline{)49{,}383}$

Did you find yourself having trouble remembering some parts of the problem while you were dealing with other parts? Did you ever arrive at the correct answer of 837? Most people can't solve a division problem with this many digits unless they write it down on paper. The fact is, working memory just doesn't have enough space both to hold all that information and to perform mathematical calculations with it. Like attention, working memory has a *limited capacity*—perhaps just enough for a telephone number or very short grocery list (G. A. Miller, 1956; Posner & Rothbart, 2007; Simon, 1974). Thus, it lets you hold and think about only a very small amount of material at once.

As teachers, we must keep the limited capacity of working memory in mind as we plan and conduct lessons and activities. A mistake many new teachers make is to present a great deal of information very quickly, and their students' working memories simply can't handle it all. Instead, we should pace the presentation of important information slowly enough that students have time to process what they're seeing and hearing. In addition, we might repeat the same idea several times (perhaps rewording it each time), stop to write important points on the chalkboard, and provide numerous examples and illustrations.

Let students know which ideas are most important to remember, and pace instruction to give them sufficient time to think about each one.

Even when the pace of instruction is appropriate, however, students can probably never learn *everything* presented to them in a lecture, activity, or textbook (Calfee, 1981; E. D. Gagné, 1985). Although students must continually make choices about what to learn and what *not* to learn, they aren't always the best judges of what is important (Garner, Alexander, Gillingham, Kulikowich, & Brown, 1991; Mayer, 1984; R. E. Reynolds & Shirey, 1988). We can help them make the right choices by giving them guidelines about how and what to study and omitting unnecessary details from lessons.

I sometimes hear students talking about putting class material in "short-term memory" so that they can do well on an upcoming exam. Such a statement reflects the common misconception that this component of memory lasts for several days, weeks, or even months. Now you know otherwise. Working memory is obviously *not* the place to leave information that you need for an exam later in the week or even information you need for a class later in the day. For such information, storage in long-term memory—the final component of the memory system—is in order.

maintenance rehearsal Rapid repetition of a small amount of information to keep it fresh in working memory.

Moving Information to Long-Term Memory: Connecting New Information with Prior Knowledge

In the memory model depicted in Figure 6.1, the arrow between working memory and long-term memory points in both directions. The process of storing new information in long-term memory usually involves drawing on "old" information previously stored there—hence, temporarily revisiting the old information in working memory (Kirschner, Sweller, & Clark, 2006). To see this process in your own learning, try the following exercise.

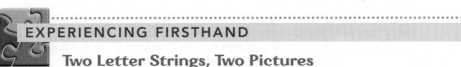

EXPERIENCING FIRSTHAND

Two Letter Strings, Two Pictures

1. Study the two strings of letters below until you can remember each of them perfectly:

   AIIRODFMLAWRS FAMILIARWORDS

2. Study the two pictures to the right until you can reproduce each one accurately from memory.

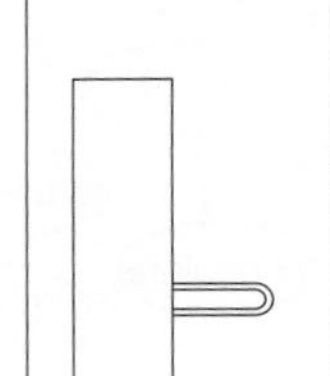

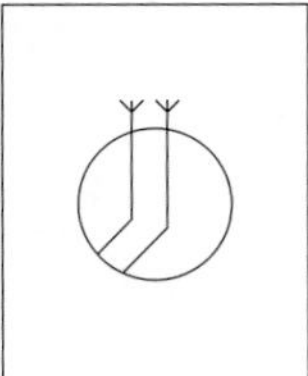

Source: Figures are from "Comprehension and Memory for Pictures" by G. H. Bower, M. B. Karlin, and A. Dueck, 1975, *Memory and Cognition, 3,* p. 217. Reprinted by permission of Psychonomic Society, Inc.

No doubt the second letter string was easier to learn because you could relate it to something you already knew: the words *familiar words.* How easily were you able to learn the two pictures? Do you think you could draw them from memory a week from now? Do you think you could remember them more easily if they had titles such as "A Very Short Man Playing a Trombone in a Telephone Booth" and "An Early Bird Who Caught a Very Strong Worm"? The answer to the last question is almost certainly yes, because the titles would help you relate the pictures to familiar shapes, such as those of trombones, telephone booths, and birds' feet (Bower, Karlin, & Dueck, 1975).

The Nature of Long-Term Memory

Long-term memory is where learners store their general knowledge and beliefs about the world, the things they have learned in school (e.g., the capital of France, the correct spelling of *hors d'oeuvre*), and their recollections of events in their personal lives. Long-term memory is also where learners store their knowledge about how to perform various actions, such as how to ride a bicycle, swing a baseball bat, and do long division.

Much of the information stored in long-term memory is interconnected. To see what I mean, try the following exercise.

EXPERIENCING FIRSTHAND

Starting with a Horse

What's the first word that comes to mind when you see the word *horse*? And what other word does that word remind you of? Beginning with the word *horse,* follow your train of thought, letting each word remind you of another one, for a sequence of at least eight words or phrases. Write down the words in order as they come to mind.

You probably found yourself easily following a train of thought from the word *horse,* perhaps something like the route I followed:

horse → cowboy → lasso → rope → knot → Girl Scouts → cookies → chocolate

long-term memory Component of memory that holds knowledge and skills for a relatively long time.

FIGURE 6.2 A possible train of thought from *horse* to *chocolate*

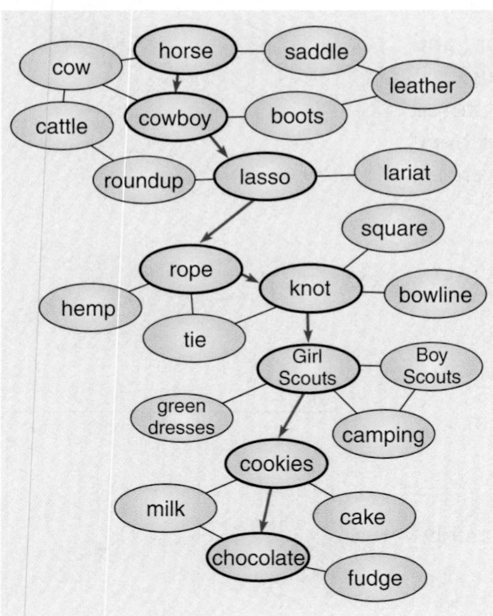

The last word in your sequence might be one with little or no obvious relationship to horses. Yet you can probably see a logical connection between each pair of items in the sequence. Related pieces of information in long-term memory are often interconnected, perhaps in a network similar to the one depicted in Figure 6.2.

Obviously, information stored in long-term memory lasts much longer than that in working memory. But exactly *how* long is long-term memory? As you well know, people often forget things they have known for a day, a week, or even longer. Historically, many psychologists believed that once information is stored in long-term memory, it remains there permanently in some form (Loftus & Loftus, 1980). More recently, however, some psychologists have come to the conclusion that information can slowly weaken and eventually disappear from long-term memory, especially if it isn't used regularly (e.g., Altmann & Gray, 2002; Brainerd & Reyna, 2005; Schacter, 1999).

In addition to its indefinitely long duration, long-term memory seems to be capable of holding as much information as a learner needs to store there. There is probably no such thing as running out of room. In fact, for reasons you'll discover shortly, the more information already stored in long-term memory, the easier it is to learn new things.

Critiquing the Three-Component Model

As mentioned earlier, the three-component model just described oversimplifies—and perhaps overcompartmentalizes—the nature of human memory (e.g., J. P. Spencer, Simmering, Schutte, & Schöner, 2007). For example, working memory (in particular, its central executive aspect) influences what we pay attention to. Thus, the flow of information from sensory register to working memory isn't as simple as the one-way arrow in Figure 6.1 suggests (Demetriou et al., 2002; Sergeant, 1996). In fact, attention may be a *part* of working memory, rather than the separate entity depicted in Figure 6.1 (Cowan, 2007; R. W. Engle, 2002; Wagner, 1996).

Furthermore, research yields mixed results about whether working memory and long-term memory are distinctly different entities (Baddeley, 2001; Cowan, 1995; Nee, Berman, Moore, & Jonides, 2008). Some psychologists have proposed that working and long-term memory simply reflect different **activation** states of a single memory (e.g., J. R. Anderson, 2005; Cowan, 1995; Sadoski & Paivio, 2001). According to this view, all information stored in memory is in either an active or inactive state. *Active* information, which may include both incoming information and information previously stored in memory, is what people are currently paying attention to and thinking about—information I have previously described as being in working memory. As attention shifts, other pieces of information in memory become activated, and the previously activated information gradually becomes inactive. The bulk of information stored in memory is in an *inactive* state, such that we aren't consciously aware of it; this is information I have previously described as being in long-term memory.

Despite its imperfections, the three-component model can help us remember aspects of learning and memory we should take into account as we teach. For example, the model highlights the importance of *attention* in learning, the *limited capacity* of attention and working memory, the *interconnectedness* of the knowledge learners acquire, and the importance of *relating* new information to things learned on previous occasions.

Long-Term Memory Storage

Regardless of whether there are three truly distinct components of memory, some aspects of memory are definitely long term. Certainly, human beings remember many things for a considerable length of time, and in this sense, at least, these things are in long-term memory.

activation Degree to which something in memory is being actively attended to and mentally processed.

It appears that information stored in long-term memory can be encoded in a variety of forms (e.g., Barsalou, Simmons, Barbey, & Wilson, 2003; Brainerd & Reyna, 2005; Sadoski & Paivio, 2001). Some information may be encoded in a *verbal* form, perhaps as actual words. Things you remember word for word—for instance, your name, your address, the nursery rhyme "Jack and Jill"—are all verbally encoded. Other information may be encoded as *imagery*, as it appears perceptually. For instance, if, in your mind, you can see the face of a relative, hear that person's voice, or conjure up a mental whiff of the person's favorite perfume or aftershave lotion, then you are retrieving images. Finally, a great deal of information in long-term memory is probably encoded *semantically*, as a set of underlying meanings.

All of the preceding examples are instances of **declarative knowledge**: knowledge that relates to the nature of how things are, were, or will be. Declarative knowledge encompasses both general world knowledge (collectively known as *semantic memory*) and recollections of specific life experiences (collectively known as *episodic memory*). Not everything in long-term is declarative in nature, however. People also acquire **procedural knowledge**; that is, they learn how to do things (e.g., J. R. Anderson, 1983; Phye, 1997; Tulving, 1983). You probably know how to ride a bicycle, wrap a birthday present, and multiply a three-digit number by a two-digit number. To perform such actions successfully, you must adapt your behavior to changing conditions. For example, when you ride a bicycle, you must be able to turn left or right when an object blocks your path, and you must be able to come to a complete stop when you reach your destination. Accordingly, procedural knowledge must often include information about how to respond under different circumstances—it involves knowing when to do certain things (either physically or mentally). In such instances, it's also known as **conditional knowledge**.

Most declarative knowledge is **explicit knowledge**: Once we recall it, we are quite conscious of what it is we know. But a good deal of procedural knowledge is **implicit knowledge**: We cannot consciously recall or explain it, but it affects our thinking or behavior nonetheless (J. R. Anderson, 2005; C. A. Nelson et al., 2006; Posner & Rothbart, 2007). Another difference is that declarative knowledge can sometimes be learned very quickly, perhaps after a single presentation, whereas procedural knowledge is often acquired slowly and only with considerable practice.

How Declarative Knowledge Is Learned

When talking about declarative knowledge, learning theorists distinguish between two general kinds of long-term memory storage processes—*rote learning* and *meaningful learning*—and among more specific storage processes that differ considerably in their effectiveness (see Table 6.3).

Rote Learning Learners engage in **rote learning** when they try to learn and remember something without attaching much meaning to it. For example, you would be engaging in rote learning if you tried to remember the letter string FAMILIARWORDS *without* trying to find some kind of sense in the sequence—patterns in the letters, perhaps, or similarities to words you know. You would also be engaging in rote learning if you tried to remember the shapes in the earlier "telephone booth" and "early bird" figures simply by trying to memorize where each line and curve is on the page.

One common form of rote learning is **rehearsal**, repeating something over and over within a short time frame (typically, a few minutes or less), either by saying it aloud or by continuously thinking about it in a more or less unaltered, verbatim fashion. Earlier, I described how maintenance rehearsal—verbally repeating something over and over—helps us keep information in working memory indefinitely. Contrary to what many students think, however, rehearsal is *not* a very effective way of storing information in long-term memory. If a learner repeats something often enough, it might eventually sink in, but the process is slow, laborious, and not much fun. Furthermore, for reasons I'll identify later, people who use rehearsal and other forms of rote learning often have trouble remembering what they have learned (J. R. Anderson, 2005; Craik & Watkins, 1973; Nickerson & Adams, 1979).

declarative knowledge Knowledge concerning the nature of how things are, were, or will be.

procedural knowledge Knowledge concerning how to do something (e.g., a skill).

conditional knowledge Knowledge concerning appropriate ways to respond (physically or mentally) under different circumstances.

explicit knowledge Knowledge that a person is consciously aware of and can verbally describe.

implicit knowledge Knowledge that a person cannot consciously recall or explain but that nevertheless affects the person's thinking or behavior.

rote learning Learning information in a relatively uninterpreted form, without making sense of it or attaching much meaning to it.

rehearsal Cognitive process in which information is repeated over and over within a short timeframe (typically a few minutes or less) as a possible way of learning and remembering it.

Compare/ Contrast

TABLE 6.3
Long-Term Memory Storage Processes

Rote learning: Learning primarily through repetition and practice, with little or no attempt to make sense of what's being learned			
Process	***Definition***	***Example***	***Effectiveness***
Rehearsal	Repeating information verbatim, either mentally or aloud	Word-for-word repetition of a formula or definition	Relatively ineffective: Storage is slow, and later retrieval is difficult
Meaningful learning: Making connections between new information and prior knowledge			
Process	***Definition***	***Example***	***Effectiveness***
Elaboration	Adding additional ideas to new information based on what one already knows	Thinking about possible reasons that historical figures made the decisions they did	Effective if the associations and additions made are appropriate and productive
Organization	Making connections among various pieces of new information	Studying how one's lines in a play relate to the play's overall story line	Effective if the organizational structure is legitimate and consists of more than just a list of discrete facts
Visual imagery	Forming a mental picture of something, either by actually seeing it or by envisioning how it might look	Imagining how various characters and events in a novel might have looked	Individual differences in effectiveness; especially beneficial when used in combination with elaboration or organization

Verbally rehearsing information is probably better than not actively processing it at all, and rehearsal may be one of the few strategies students can use when they have little prior knowledge to draw on to help them understand new material (E. Wood, Willoughby, Bolger, & Younger, 1993). For example, in the opening case study, Kanesha resorts to rehearsal in her efforts to remember such seemingly nonsensical bones as the coccyx, clavicle, and patella. Ideally, however, we should encourage students to use meaningful learning whenever possible.

Meaningful Learning In contrast to rote learning, **meaningful learning** involves recognizing a relationship between new information and something already stored in long-term memory.[2] When we use such words as *comprehension* and *understanding*, we are talking about meaningful learning. For example, in a video clip in MyEducationLab, 16-year-old Hilary describes some of the connections she makes in her Spanish and government classes:

> When I'm trying to study for a test, I try to associate the things that I'm trying to learn with familiar things. Like, if I have a Spanish vocabulary test, I'll try to . . . with the Spanish words, I'll try to think of the English word that it sounds like, because sometimes it does sound like the English word. And then our government teacher is teaching us the amendments and we're trying to memorize them. He taught us one trick for memorizing Amendment 2, which is the right to bear arms. He said, "Bears have two arms, so that's Amendment 2."

In the vast majority of cases, meaningful learning is more effective than rote learning for storing information in long-term memory (e.g., Ghetti & Angelini, 2008; Mar-

myeducationlab

Observe 16-year-old Hilary engaging in meaningful learning in the video "Memory and Cognition: Early and Late Adolescence." (To find this video, go to Chapter 6 of the Book-Specific Resources in MyEducationLab, select *Video Examples*, and then click on the title.)

meaningful learning Cognitive process in which learners relate new information to things they already know.

[2]The process of meaningful learning is similar to Piaget's concept of assimilation, discussed in Chapter 2.

ley, Szabo, Levin, & Glenberg, 2008; Mayer, 1996). It's especially effective when learners relate new ideas not only to what they already know about the world but also to what they know or believe about themselves—for instance, to self-descriptions or personal life experiences (Heatherton, Macrae, & Kelley, 2004; Rogers, Kuiper, & Kirker, 1977).

Three forms of meaningful learning prevalent in the research literature are elaboration, organization, and visual imagery. All three are *constructive* in nature: They involve combining several pieces of information into a meaningful whole.

Elaboration In **elaboration**, learners use their prior knowledge to embellish on a new idea, thereby storing more information than was actually presented. For example, when I took a course in Mandarin Chinese in high school, I learned that the Chinese word *wǒmen* means "we." "Aha," I thought to myself, "the sign on the restroom that *we* girls use says *wǒmen*" (albeit without the tone mark over the *o*). Similarly, a student who reads that allosaurs (a species of dinosaurs) had powerful jaws and sharp, pointed teeth might correctly deduce that allosaurs were meat eaters. And when a student who learns that the crew on Columbus's first trip across the Atlantic threatened to revolt, the student might speculate, "I'll bet the men were really frightened when they continued to travel west day after day without ever seeing signs of land."

On average, the more students elaborate on new material—that is, the more they use what they already know to help them understand and interpret the new material—the more effectively they will store and remember it. Thus, students who regularly elaborate on what they learn in school usually show higher achievement than those who simply take information at face value (J. R. Anderson, 2005; McDaniel & Einstein, 1989; Paxton, 1999; Waters, 1982).

One effective way to encourage elaboration in the classroom is to have students write about a topic—for instance, to summarize what they've learned, relate new concepts to their personal experiences, or express and defend certain positions on controversial topics (T. Shanahan, 2004). Another good strategy is to ask questions that require students to expand on something they've just learned (McCrudden & Schraw, 2007). For example, we might ask questions such as these:

- Explain why . . .
- How would you use . . . to . . . ?
- What is a new example of . . . ?
- What do you think would happen if . . . ?
- What is the difference between . . . and . . . ? (A. King, 1992, p. 309)

Still another approach is to have students work in pairs or small groups to formulate and answer their *own* elaborative questions. Different researchers call such group questioning either *elaborative interrogation* or *guided peer questioning* (Kahl & Woloshyn, 1994; A. King, 1994, 1999; Rosenshine, Meister, & Chapman, 1996; E. Wood et al., 1999). In the following dialogue, fifth graders Katie and Janelle are working together to study class material about tide pools. Katie's job is to ask Janelle questions that encourage elaboration:

> Encourage students to go beyond the specific information they have learned—to draw inferences, speculate about possible implications, defend a position about a controversial issue, and so on. For example, have them work in pairs or small groups to formulate and ask one another elaborative questions.

Katie: How are the upper tide zone and the lower tide zone different?

Janelle: They have different animals in them. Animals in the upper tide zone and splash zone can handle being exposed—have to be able to use the rain and sand and wind and sun—and they don't need that much water and the lower tide animals do.

Katie: And they can be softer 'cause they don't have to get hit on the rocks.

Janelle: Also predators. In the spray zone it's because there's predators like us people and all different kinds of stuff that can kill the animals and they won't survive, but the lower tide zone has not as many predators.

elaboration Cognitive process in which learners embellish on new information based on what they already know.

Katie: But wait! Why do the animals in the splash zone have to survive? (A. King, 1999, p. 97)

Notice that the two girls are continually relating the animals' characteristics to survival in different tide zones, and eventually Katie asks why animals in the splash zone even *need* to survive. Such analyses are quite sophisticated for fifth graders. Imagine what high school students, with their increasing capacity for abstract thought, might be able to do!

Organization On average, we learn and remember a body of new information more easily when we pull it together into a logical structure (e.g., Nesbit & Adesope, 2006; Novak, 1998; D. H. Robinson & Kiewra, 1995). Such **organization** involves making connections among various pieces of new information and forming an overall cohesive structure. For example, a learner might group information into categories, just as you probably categorized the 12 words (shirt, carrot, table, etc.) in the "Remembering 12 Words" exercise near the beginning of the chapter.

FIGURE 6.3 We can remember information more easily when it's organized in some way.

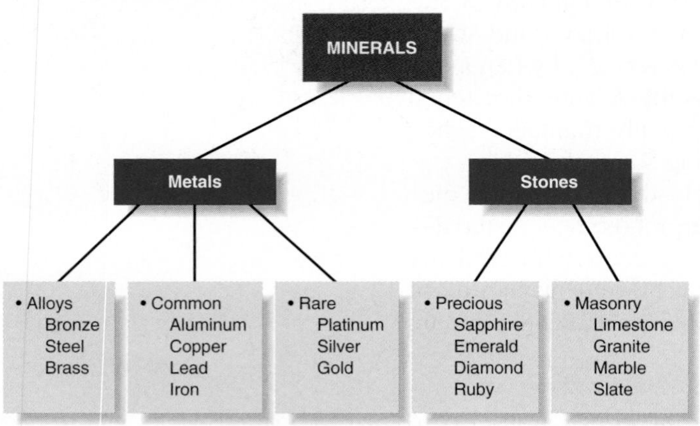

Source: Figure from "Hierarchical Retrieval Schemes in Recall of Categorized Word Lists" by G. H. Bower, M. C. Clark, A. M. Lesgold, and D. Winzenz, 1969, *Journal of Verbal Learning and Verbal Behavior, 8*, pp. 323–345, copyright 1969. Elsevier Science (USA), reproduced by permission of the publisher.

Another way of organizing information is to identify interrelationships among its various parts. For instance, when learning about *velocity*, *acceleration*, *force*, and *mass* in a physics class, a student might better understand these concepts by seeing how they are interconnected—perhaps by learning that velocity is the product of acceleration and time ($v = a \times t$) and that an object's force is determined by both its mass and its acceleration ($f = m \times a$). The trick is not simply to memorize the formulas (that would be rote learning) but rather to make sense of and understand the relationships that the formulas represent.

A classic experiment with college students illustrates how effective organization can sometimes be (Bower, Clark, Lesgold, & Winzenz, 1969). Students were given four study trials in which to learn 112 words falling into four categories (e.g., minerals, plants). For some students, the words were arranged in an organized fashion (Figure 6.3 shows an example). For other students, the words were arranged randomly. Look at the average number of words that each group remembered after one study period (about four minutes) and then after three additional study periods:

Number of Study Periods	*Organized Words*	*Unorganized Words*
1	73 (65%)	21 (19%)
4	112 (100%)	70 (63%)

Notice that after studying the words one time, students who were given the organized words remembered more than three times as many words as students who received them in mixed-up fashion. After four study periods, the students with the organized words remembered the entire list of 112!

Be explicit in showing how various ideas are interrelated.

As teachers, we can help students organize new material in a variety of ways. For instance, in physics, we might point out important interrelations (e.g., cause–effect) among various concepts and phenomena. And in biology, we might show how certain categories of living things are hierarchically nested within other, more general categories (e.g., ants and mosquitoes are both insects; crabs and crayfish are both crustaceans; insects and crustaceans are both arthropods). We can also present related pieces of information close together in time, because students are more likely to associate related ideas when they encounter the ideas together (Glanzer & Nolan, 1986; Hayes-Roth & Thorndyke, 1979).

organization Cognitive process in which learners make connections among various pieces of information they need to learn (e.g., by forming categories, identifying hierarchies, determining cause–effect relationships).

It's often helpful to give students specific structures they can use to organize information. For example, the weblike note-taking form shown in Figure 6.4 can help elementary students organize what they learn about tarantulas. Another effective structure is a two-dimensional matrix or table that enables students to compare several items with respect to various characteristics—for instance, how various geographical regions differ in topography, climate, economic activities, and cultural practices (R. K. Atkinson et al., 1999; Kiewra, DuBois, Christian, & McShane, 1988; D. H. Robinson & Kiewra, 1995). A third approach is to teach students how to create **concept maps**, diagrams that depicts the concepts of a unit and their interrelationships (Mintzes, Wandersee, & Novak, 1997; Nesbit & Adesope, 2006; Novak, 1998). Figure 6.5 shows concept maps constructed by two fifth graders after they watched a slide lecture on Australia. The concepts themselves are circled, and their interrelationships are indicated by lines with words or short phrases. Several concept-mapping software programs (e.g., Kidspiration, MindMapper Jr. for Kids) are available for creating and modifying concept maps quickly and easily.

FIGURE 6.4 Using a form his second-grade teacher has provided, 7-year-old Tony organizes what he has learned about tarantulas.

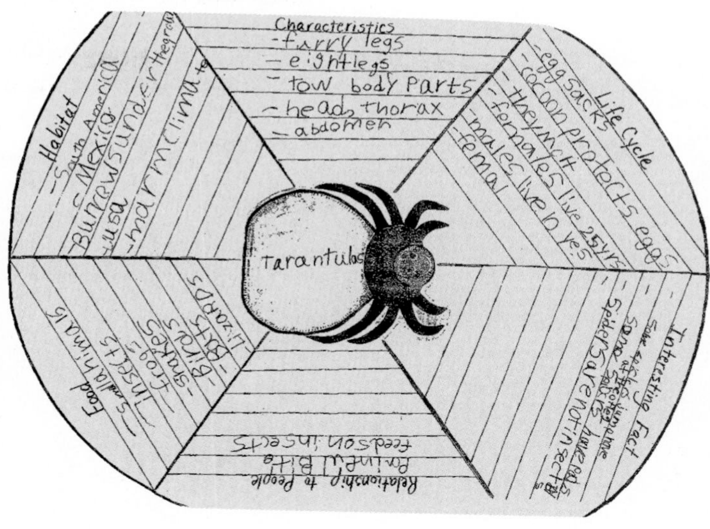

Students' use of such self-constructed organizational structures can both help students learn more effectively and also help teachers *assess* students' learning. For example, the two concept maps in Figure 6.5 reveal significant differences in depth and organization of knowledge about Australia. Furthermore, the map on the left has errors (e.g., Adelaide isn't part of Melbourne; it's a different city altogether). If geographic knowledge about Australia is an important instructional goal for the class, then this student clearly needs further instruction to correct such misunderstandings.

Give students specific tools to help them organize what they're learning.

Visual Imagery Earlier, I mentioned imagery as one possible way in which information might be encoded in long-term memory. Numerous research studies indicate that **visual imagery**—mental pictures that are formed of objects or ideas—can be a highly effective method of storing information (Dewhurst & Conway, 1994; Sadoski & Paivio, 2001; D. L. Schwartz & Heiser, 2006). To show you how effective visual imagery can be, on the next page I'll teach you a few of the Mandarin Chinese words I learned in high school.

FIGURE 6.5 Concept maps constructed by two fifth-grade students after watching a slide lecture on Australia

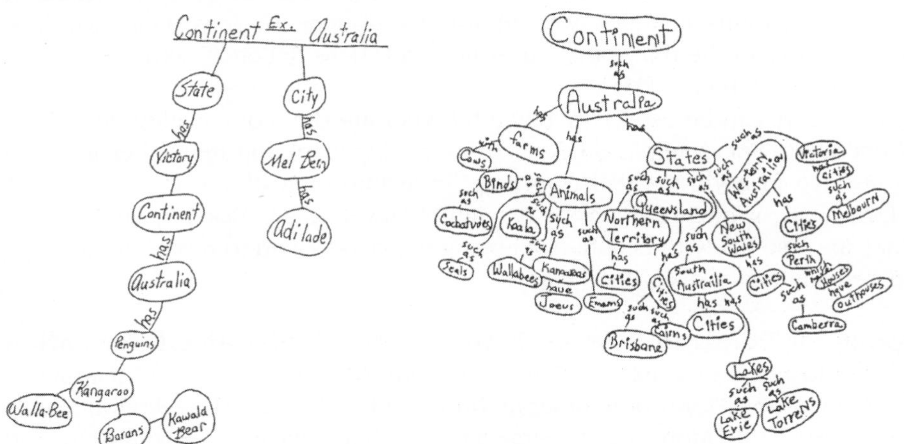

Source: From *Learning How to Learn* (pp. 100–101) by J. D. Novak and D. B. Gowin, 1984, Cambridge, England: Cambridge University Press. Copyright 1984 by Cambridge University Press. Reprinted with the permission of Cambridge University Press.

concept map Diagram of concepts and their interrelationships; used to enhance learning and memory of a topic.

visual imagery Process of forming mental pictures of objects or ideas.

EXPERIENCING FIRSTHAND

Five Chinese Words

Try learning these five Chinese words by forming the visual images I describe (don't worry about learning the marks over the words):

Chinese Word	***Meaning***	***English Image***
fáng	house	Picture a *house* with *fangs* growing on its roof and walls.
mén	door	Picture a restroom *door* with the word *MEN* painted on it.
ké	guest	Picture someone giving someone else (the *guest*) a *key* to the house.
fàn	food	Picture a plate of *food* being cooled by a *fan*.
shū	book	Picture a *shoe* with a *book* sticking out of it.

Now find something else to do for a couple of minutes. Stand up and stretch, get a glass of water, or use the restroom. But be sure to come back to your reading in just a minute or two.

Now that you're back, cover the list of Chinese words, English meanings, and visual images. Then try to remember what each word means:

ké fàn mén fáng shū

Did the Chinese words remind you of the visual images you stored? Did the images, in turn, help you remember the English meanings? You may have remembered all five words easily, or you may have remembered only one or two. People differ in their ability to use visual imagery: Some form images quickly and easily, whereas others form them only slowly and with difficulty (Behrmann, 2000; J. M. Clark & Paivio, 1991; Kosslyn, 1985).

In the classroom, we can promote the use of visual imagery in several ways. We can ask students to imagine how certain events in literature or history might have looked (Johnson-Glenberg, 2000; Sadoski & Paivio, 2001). We can provide visual materials (pictures, charts, graphs, etc.) that illustrate important but possibly abstract ideas (R. K. Atkinson et al., 1999; R. Carlson, Chandler, & Sweller, 2003; Verdi, Kulhavy, Stock, Rittschof, & Johnson, 1996). We can also ask students to draw their own illustrations or diagrams of the things they are studying (Edens & Potter, 2001; Van Meter, 2001; Van Meter & Garner, 2005).

Illustrate verbal instruction with visual materials (e.g., pictures, maps, diagrams).

myeducationlab

Learn one strategy for teaching students how to use visual imagery by completing the Understanding Research exercise "Teaching Reading Comprehension Strategies" in MyEducationLab. (To find this activity, go to the topic Cognition and Memory in MyEducationLab, click on *Assignments and Activities,* and then select *Understanding Research.*)

Visual imagery can be especially powerful when used in combination with other forms of encoding. For example, students more readily learn and remember information they receive in both a verbal form (e.g., a lecture or textbook passage) and a graphic form (e.g., a picture, map, or diagram) (Mayer, 2003; Moreno, 2006; Winn, 1991). They are also likely to benefit from being explicitly asked to represent information both verbally and visually (see Figure 6.6).

Developmental Trends in Storage Processes for Declarative Information

The tendency to relate new information to prior knowledge—meaningful learning—probably occurs in one form or another at virtually all age levels (Flavell et al., 2002; Siegler & Alibali, 2005). More specific strategies—such as rehearsal, organization, and visual imagery—are rare in the early elementary years but increase in both frequency

FIGURE 6.6 In a sixth-grade social studies unit, students created postcards that an imaginary friend might send them from ancient cultures. Here, 11-year-old Shea depicts ancient Ur both visually and verbally.

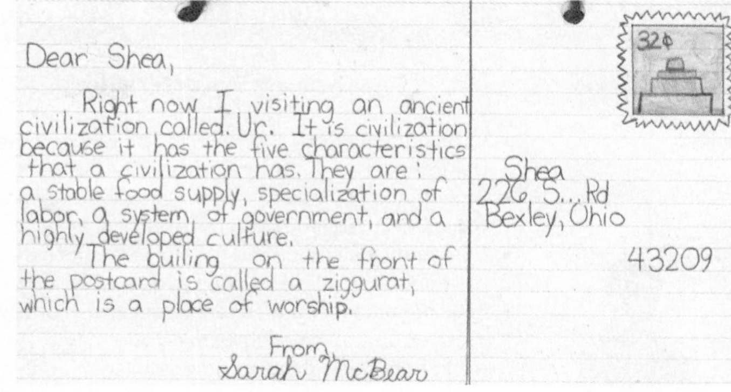

and effectiveness over the course of childhood and adolescence. The frequency of elaboration (especially as a process that learners *intentionally* use to help them remember something) picks up a bit later, often not until adolescence, and is more common in high-achieving students. Table 6.4 provides more detailed information on the nature of long-term memory storage processes at different grade levels.

myeducationlab

Observe developmental differences in students' ability to organize and remember a list of 12 words in the two "Memory and Cognition" videos. (To find these videos, go to Chapter 6 of the Book-Specific Resources in MyEducationLab, select *Video Examples*, and then click on the titles.)

How Procedural Knowledge Is Learned

Some of the procedures people learn—for example, baking a cake, serving a volleyball, driving a car with a stick shift—consist primarily of overt behaviors. Many others—for instance, writing a persuasive essay, solving for x in an algebraic equation, surfing the Internet—have a significant mental component as well. Most procedures probably involve a combination of physical behaviors and mental activities.

Procedural knowledge ranges from relatively simple actions (e.g., holding a pencil correctly or using scissors) to far more complex ones. Complex procedures are usually not learned in one fell swoop. Instead, they are acquired slowly over a period of time, often only with a great deal of practice (Charness, Tuffiash, & Jastrzembski, 2004; Ericsson, 2003; Proctor & Dutta, 1995).

Researchers are just beginning to identify the ways in which procedural knowledge is stored in memory. To some degree, of course, learners store physical procedures as actual behaviors (Keele, 1981; D. B. Willingham, 1999; D. B. Willingham & Goedert-Eschmann, 1999). Yet some procedures, especially complex ones, may first be learned as declarative knowledge—in other words, as *information* about how to execute a procedure rather than as the actual *ability* to execute it (J. R. Anderson, 1983, 2005; Beilock & Carr, 2003). When learners use declarative knowledge to guide them as they carry out a new procedure, their performance tends to be slow and laborious, the activity consumes a great deal of mental effort, and learners are apt to talk themselves through their actions. As they continue to perform the activity, however, their declarative knowledge gradually evolves into procedural knowledge. This knowledge becomes fine-tuned over time and eventually allows learners to perform an activity quickly, efficiently, and effortlessly (we'll talk more about such *automaticity* a bit later). People who show exceptional talent in a particular skill—say, in figure skating or playing the piano—typically practice a great deal, often a minimum of three to four hours a day over a period of 10 years or more (Ericsson, 1996; Horn, 2008).

Some of the storage processes we've already discussed play a role in acquiring procedural knowledge as well as declarative knowledge. For instance, verbally rehearsing a sequence of steps in a motor skill enhances people's ability to perform

TABLE 6.4
Typical Long-Term Memory Storage Processes at Different Grade Levels

Grade Level	Age-Typical Characteristics	Suggested Strategies
K–2	• Organization of physical objects as a way to remember them • Emergence of rehearsal to remember verbal material; used infrequently and relatively ineffectively • Emerging ability to use visual imagery to enhance memory, especially if an adult suggests this strategy • Few intentional efforts to learn, remember, or elaborate on verbal material; learning and memory result from other things children do (creating things, talking about events, listening to stories, etc.)	• Get students actively involved in topics, perhaps through hands-on activities, engaging reading materials, or fantasy play. • Relate new topics to students' prior experiences. • Model rehearsal as a strategy for remembering things over the short run. • Provide pictures that illustrate verbal material.
3–5	• Spontaneous, intentional, and increasingly effective use of rehearsal to remember things for a short time period • Increasing use of organization as an intentional learning strategy for verbal information • Increasing effectiveness in the use of visual imagery as a learning strategy	• Emphasize the importance of making sense of, rather than memorizing, information. • Encourage students to organize what they are studying; suggest possible organizational structures for topics. • Provide a variety of visual aids to facilitate visual imagery, and suggest that students create their own drawings or visual images of things they need to remember.
6–8	• Predominance of rehearsal as a learning strategy • Greater abstractness and flexibility in categories used to organize information • Emergence of elaboration as an intentional learning strategy	• Suggest questions that students might ask themselves as they study; emphasize questions that promote elaboration (e.g., "Why would ____ do that?" "How is ____ different from ____?"). • Assess true understanding, not rote memorization, in assignments and quizzes.
9–12	• Continuing reliance on rehearsal as an intentional learning strategy, especially by low-achieving students • Increasing use of elaboration and organization to learn, especially by high-achieving students	• Ask thought-provoking questions that engage students' interest and help students see the relevance of topics to their own lives. • Have students work in mixed-ability cooperative learning groups, in which high-achieving students can model effective learning strategies for low-achieving students.

Sources: J. E. Barnett, 2001; Bjorklund & Coyle, 1995; Bjorklund & Jacobs, 1985; Bjorklund, Schneider, Cassel, & Ashley, 1994; Cowan, Saults, & Morey, 2006; DeLoache & Todd, 1988; Fivush, Haden, & Adam, 1995; Flavell et al., 2002; Gathercole & Hitch, 1993; I. W. Gaskins & Pressley, 2007; Kail, 1990; Kosslyn, Margolis, Barrett, Goldknopf, & Daly, 1990; Kunzinger, 1985; Lehmann & Hasselhorn, 2007; Lucariello, Kyratzis, & Nelson, 1992; Marley et al., 2008; L. S. Newman, 1990; Plumert, 1994; Pressley, 1977, 1982; Pressley & Hilden, 2006; Schneider & Pressley, 1989; E. Wood et al., 1999.

the skill (Weiss & Klint, 1987). Seeing an illustration or live demonstration of a procedure, which presumably fosters visual imagery, is also beneficial (R. M. Gagné, 1985; Kitsantas, Zimmerman, & Cleary, 2000; Zimmerman & Kitsantas, 1999). In fact, imagining *oneself* performing a new skill (e.g., executing a gymnastics move or a basketball shot) can enhance acquisition of the skill, although this strategy is obviously not as effective as actual practice (Feltz, Landers, & Becker, 1988; Kosslyn, 1985).

Perhaps the most effective way to teach new procedures is to demonstrate them, including both the overt behaviors and the internal thought processes involved (e.g., Rittle-Johnson, 2006; Schunk, 1998) (more about such *modeling* in Chapter 10). The Into the Classroom feature "Helping Students Acquire New Procedures" illustrates several additional strategies for facilitating procedural learning.

Roles of Prior Knowledge and Working Memory in Long-Term Memory Storage

knowledge base One's existing knowledge about specific topics and the world in general.

Students are more likely to engage in meaningful learning when they have a relevant **knowledge base**—that is, when they have existing knowledge to which they can connect whatever new information and skills they are trying to master. Occasionally students' prior knowledge interferes with something they need to learn; this is the case

INTO THE Classroom

Helping Students Acquire New Procedures

Help students understand the logic behind the procedures they are learning.

As a teacher demonstrates the correct way to swing a tennis racket, she asks her students these questions: "Why is it important to have your feet apart rather than together? Why is it important to hold your arm straight as you swing?"

When skills are especially complex, break them into simpler tasks that students can practice one at a time.

Knowing that the task of driving a car can initially be overwhelming, a driver education teacher begins behind-the-wheel instruction by having students practice steering and braking in an empty school parking lot. Only later, after students have mastered these skills, does he have them drive in traffic on city streets.

Provide mnemonics that can help students remember a sequence of steps.

A math teacher shows students how to multiply in the expression $((3x + 4)(2x + 5))$ by working out the steps on the chalkboard. As she goes along, she explains what she's doing: "The word *FOIL* can help you remember what you need to do. You begin by multiplying the two *first* terms inside the parentheses—that would be $3x \times 2x$, or $6x^2$. Then, you multiply the two *outer* terms—$3x \times 5$—which gives you 15x. Next, you multiply the two *inner* terms—$4x \times 2x$—which gives you 8x. Finally, you multiply the two *last* terms—4×5, which equals 20. Add them all together, and you get $6x^2 + 23x + 20$."

Give students many opportunities to practice new skills, and provide the feedback they need to help them improve.

A science teacher asks his students to write lab reports after each week's lab activity. Because many of his students have had little or no previous experience in scientific writing, he writes numerous comments when he grades the reports. Some comments describe the strengths that he sees, and others provide suggestions for making the reports more objective, precise, and clear.

Sources: P. A. Alexander & Judy, 1988; J. R. Anderson, Reder, & Simon, 1996; Beilock & Carr, 2003; R. L. Cohen, 1989; Hattie & Timperley, 2007; Hecht, Close, & Santisi, 2003; Proctor & Dutta, 1995; Shute, 2008.

in the opening case study when Kanesha tries to remember where the sternum is located. In general, however, having a relevant knowledge base helps students encode and store classroom subject matter more effectively (P. A. Alexander, Kulikowich, & Schulze, 1994; Schneider, 1993; Shapiro, 2004). For example, students will better understand scientific principles if they have already seen those principles in action, either in their personal lives or in the classroom. And they will better understand how large some dinosaurs were if they have previously seen life-sized dinosaur skeletons at a museum of natural history. The more knowledge students have already stored in long-term memory, the easier it is for them to learn new information, because they have more things with which to associate the new information.

Provide concrete experiences (lab experiments, museum visits, etc.) to which students can relate academic topics.

Students' prior knowledge contributes to their learning in several ways:

- It helps them determine what is most important to learn and so helps them direct their *attention* appropriately.
- It helps them *elaborate* on information—for example, by filling in missing details, clarifying ambiguities, or drawing inferences.
- It provides a framework for *organizing* new information (Bjorklund, Muir-Broaddus, & Schneider, 1990; Haskell, 2001; Rumelhart & Ortony, 1977; P. T. Wilson & Anderson, 1986).

Children's knowledge about the world grows by leaps and bounds every year. This increasing knowledge base is one reason that adults and older children usually learn new things more easily than younger children: Older learners have more knowledge to help them understand and elaborate on new ideas and events (Flavell et al., 2002; Halford, 1989; Kail, 1990). As an example, consider the case of an Inuit (Eskimo) man named Tor in the following exercise.

EXPERIENCING FIRSTHAND

Tor of the Targa

Consider this scenario:

> Tor, a young man of the Targa tribe, was out hunting in the ancient hunting territory of his people. He had been away from his village for many days. The weather was bad and he had not yet managed to locate his prey. Because of the extreme temperature he knew he must soon return but it was a matter of honor among his people to track and kill the prey single-handed. Only when this was achieved could a boy be considered a man. Those who failed were made to eat and keep company with the old men and the women until they could accomplish this task.
>
> Suddenly, in the distance, Tor could make out the outline of a possible prey. It was alone and not too much bigger than Tor, who could take him single-handed. But as he drew nearer, a hunter from a neighboring tribe came into view, also stalking the prey. The intruder was older than Tor and had around his neck evidence of his past success at the hunt. "Yes," thought Tor, "he is truly a man." Tor was undecided. Should he challenge the intruder or return home empty handed? To return would mean bitter defeat. The other young men of the tribe would laugh at his failure. He decided to creep up on the intruder and wait his chance. (A. L. Brown, Smiley, Day, Townsend, & Lawton, 1977, p. 1460)

- On what kind of terrain was Tor hunting?
- What was the weather like?
- What kind of prey might Tor have been stalking?

You may have used your knowledge about Inuits to speculate that Tor was hunting polar bears or seals on snow and ice, possibly in freezing temperatures or a bad blizzard. But notice that the story itself didn't tell you any of these things; you had to *infer* them.

Like you, young adolescents may know a fair amount about how Inuit people live and can use that information to help them elaborate on and remember Tor's story better than younger children can (A. L. Brown et al., 1977). When young children have more knowledge than their elders, however, they often have the upper hand (Chi, 1978; Rabinowitz & Glaser, 1985). For example, when my son Alex and I used to read books about lizards together, Alex always remembered more than I did, because he was a self-proclaimed lizard expert and I knew very little about reptiles of any sort.

Calvin and Hobbes **by Bill Watterson**

Calvin is trying to learn new information meaningfully, but his efforts are in vain because the word *feudal* is not in his knowledge base.

Yet it isn't enough that students have the knowledge they need to make sense of new material. They must also be *aware* that some of their existing knowledge is relevant. They must retrieve that knowledge from long-term memory while thinking about the new material, so that they have both the old and the new in working memory simultaneously and can make the appropriate connections (Bellezza, 1986; Glanzer & Nolan, 1986).

prior knowledge activation Process of reminding learners of things they already know relative to a new topic.

As teachers, we should keep students' existing knowledge in mind and use it as a starting point whenever we introduce a new topic. Furthermore, we should explicitly remind students of things they know that bear directly on a topic of classroom study—an instructional strategy known as **prior knowledge activation** (Machiels-Bongaerts, Schmidt, & Boshuizen, 1993; Resnick, 1989; Spires & Donley, 1998). For instance, we might begin a first-grade unit about plants by asking students to describe what their parents do to keep flowers or vegetable gardens growing. In a secondary English literature class, we might introduce Sir Walter Scott's *Ivanhoe* (in which Robin Hood is a major character) by asking students to tell the tale of Robin Hood as they know it. We should also remember that students from diverse cultural backgrounds may have somewhat different knowledge bases and modify our starting point accordingly (Nelson-Barber & Estrin, 1995).

Begin instruction with what students already know, and help them make connections between the "new" and the "old."

Furthermore, we should encourage students to retrieve relevant knowledge *on their own* as they study. One approach is to model this strategy for students. For example, we might read aloud a portion of a textbook, stopping occasionally to tie an idea in the text to something previously studied in class or to something in our own personal experience. We can then encourage students to do likewise, giving suggestions and guiding their efforts as they proceed (Spires & Donley, 1998). Especially when working with students in the elementary grades, we might also want to provide specific questions that remind students to reflect on their existing knowledge and beliefs as they read and study:

Encourage students to think about what they already know about a topic.

- What do you already know about your topic?
- What do you hope to learn about your topic?
- Do you think what you learn by reading your books will change what you already know about your topic? (H. Thompson & Carr, 1995, p. 9)

With time and practice, students should eventually get in the habit of retrieving relevant prior knowledge with little or no assistance from us (Spires & Donley, 1998).

Encouraging a Meaningful Learning Set

We cannot always blame students when they take a relatively meaning*less*-learning approach to their studies. Inadvertently, some teachers tend to encourage students to learn school subjects by rote. Think back to your own experiences in school. How many times were you allowed to define a word by repeating its dictionary definition, rather than being expected to explain it in your own words? In fact, how many times were you *required* to learn something word for word? And how many times did an exam assess your knowledge of facts or principles without ever assessing your ability to relate those facts and principles to everyday life or to things learned in previous courses? Perhaps you had assignments and quizzes similar to the fill-in-the-blank questions shown in Figure 6.7. When

FIGURE 6.7 Seventh-grade science students are asked to complete these and other fill-in-the-blank questions as they watch a video about dinosaurs. The questions probably help students pay attention to the video. However, many of the questions encourage rote, rather than meaningful, learning.

1) One of the coolest things about dinosaurs is that of all the millions there were, we only know about a few thousand of them.
2) The word "fossil" comes from the Latin word meaning dug up.
3) What four things can fossils tell us about dinosaurs?
1 ate 3 what they did w/ young
2 look like 4 size/weight
4) Two steps in the process of fossilization are:
-need to die -then are covered in layers of sedimen
5) One of the processes which forms a fossil is pre-mineralized This means that minerals replace the bones of the dinosaur.
6) The evidence that dinosaurs once lived is found in discovering fossils.
7) Scientists can learn about dinosaurs by observing where their fossils are buried, how deep the fossils are, and what is buried nearby the dinosaur fossils.
8) Dinosaurs lived on earth for about 160 million years.
9) Dinosaurs died out about 65 million years ago.
10) One reason dinosaurs may have become extinct is a meteorite.

meaningful learning set Attitude that one can make sense of the information one is studying.

mnemonic Memory aid or trick designed to help learn and remember one or more specific pieces of information.

verbal mediator Word or phrase that forms a logical connection, or bridge, between two pieces of information.

keyword method Mnemonic technique in which an association is made between two ideas by forming a visual image of one or more concrete objects (*keywords*) that either sound similar to or symbolically represent those ideas.

superimposed meaningful structure Familiar shape, word, sentence, poem, or story imposed on information to facilitate recall.

students discover that assignments and assessments focus on recall of unrelated facts—rather than on understanding and applying an integrated body of knowledge—many rely on rote learning, believing that this approach will yield a higher score and that meaningful learning would be counterproductive (Crooks, 1988).

As teachers, we should not only encourage meaningful learning through the strategies already described—asking students to logically organize related ideas, think of new examples, speculate about implications, and so on—but we should also communicate that school topics are to be *understood* rather than memorized. In other words, we should encourage students to adopt a **meaningful learning set** (Ausubel, Novak, & Hanesian, 1978; M. A. Church, Elliot, & Gable, 2001). For instance, we might frequently ask students to explain their reasoning, and our assignments and assessment tasks should require true understanding, rather than rote memorization (Lundeberg & Fox, 1991; Middleton & Midgley, 2002; L. A. Shepard, Hammerness, Darling-Hammond, & Rust, 2005).

Using Mnemonics in the Absence of Relevant Prior Knowledge

Some things are hard to make sense of—that is, hard to learn meaningfully. For instance, why do bones in the human body have such names as *fibula, coccyx,* and *ulna*? Why is *Au* the chemical symbol for gold? Why is Augusta the capital of Maine? From most students' perspectives, there is no rhyme or reason to such facts.

Suggest helpful mnemonics when new information is difficult to learn meaningfully, and teach students how to create their own mnemonics.

When students have trouble finding relationships between new material and their prior knowledge or when a body of information seemingly has no logical organizational structure (as is true for many lists), special memory tricks known as **mnemonics** can help students remember classroom material more effectively. Three commonly used mnemonics—verbal mediation, the keyword method, and superimposed meaningful structures—are described in Figure 6.8.

Research consistently supports the effectiveness of using mnemonics in learning (e.g., R. K. Atkinson et al., 1999; M. S. Jones, Levin, Levin, & Beitzel, 2000; Pressley, Levin, & Delaney, 1982). Their effectiveness lies in their conformity with a basic principle of long-term memory storage: Learners find some sort of meaning—even if that meaning is sometimes a bit contrived—in what might otherwise be nonsensical information.

Often, students can create their own effective mnemonics. For example, in a sixth-grade science class, a girl named Ginny created a song about bones to the tune of Lou Bega's "Mambo no. 5." The first verse went like this:

> A little bit of cranium on my head
> A little bit of mandible on my jaw
> A little bit of scapula on my back
> A little bit of humerus on this bone
> A little bit of radius on the back
> A little bit of ulna on the front
> A little bit of carpals just like that
> A little bit of metacarpals on my hand
> A little bit of phalanges in the end
> A little bit of tibia on the front
> A little bit of fibula on the back
> A little bit of torso just like that
> A little bit of metatarsals on my foot
> A little bit of phalanges on the end
> Just wave your phalanges, yeah yeah yeah
> Just wave your phalanges, yeah. (Barton, Tan, & Rivet, 2008, pp. 82–83).

myeducationlab

You can hear Ginny sing this song on the Internet. To find the link, go to Chapter 6 of the Book-Specific Resources in MyEducationLab and then select *Video Examples*.

myeducationlab

Hear 10-year-old David describe a mnemonic for the Hebrew letter *pay* (פ) in "Memory and Cognition: Early and Middle Childhood." Also, watch middle school students work in small groups to develop mnemonics for the life cycle of a sheep liver fluke in "Group Work." (To find these videos, go to Chapter 6 of the Book-Specific Resources in MyEducationLab, select *Video Examples*, and then click on the titles.)

In addition to helping students store information and procedures in long-term memory, mnemonics also appear to help students retrieve these things when needed at a later time.

FIGURE 6.8 Common mnemonic techniques

Verbal Mediation

A **verbal mediator** is a word or phrase that creates a logical connection, or bridge, between two pieces of information. Verbal mediators can be used for paired pieces of information such as foreign language words and their English meanings, countries and their capitals, chemical elements and their symbols, and words and their spellings. Following are examples:

Information to Be Learned	Verbal Mediator
Handschuh is German for "glove."	A glove is a *shoe* for the *hand.*
Quito is the capital of Ecuador.	*Mosquitoes* are at the *equator.*
Au is the symbol for gold.	*Ay, you* stole my *gold* watch!
The word *principal* (a school administrator) ends with the letters *pal* (not *ple*).	The *principal* is my *pal.*
The *humerus* bone is the large arm bone above the elbow.	The *humorous* bone is just above the *funny* bone.
The Second Amendment to the U.S. Constitution is the right to *bear arms.*	A *bear* has *two arms.*

Keyword Method

Like verbal mediation, the **keyword method** aids memory by making a connection between two things. This technique is especially helpful when there is no logical verbal mediator to fill the gap—for example, when there is no obvious sentence or phrase to relate a foreign language word to its English meaning. The keyword method involves two steps, which we can illustrate using the Spanish word *amor* and its English meaning, "love":

1. Identify a concrete object to represent each piece of information. The object can be either a commonly used symbol (e.g., a heart to symbolize *love*) or a sound-alike word (e.g., a suit of armor to represent *amor*). Such objects are *keywords.*
2. Form a mental picture—that is, a visual image—of the two objects together. For example, to remember that *amor* means "love," we might picture a knight in a suit of armor with a huge red heart painted on his chest.

You used the keyword method when you completed the "Five Chinese Words" exercise earlier in the chapter. Here are additional examples:

Information to Be Learned	Visual Image
Das Pferd is German for horse.	Picture a *horse* driving a *Ford.*
Augusta is the capital of Maine.	Picture *a gust of* wind blowing through a horse's *mane.*
Tchaikovsky composed the ballet *Swan Lake.*	Picture a *swan* swimming on a *lake,* wearing a *tie* and *cough*ing.

Superimposed Meaningful Structure

A larger body of information, such as a list of items, can often be learned by superimposing a meaningful visual or verbal organizational structure on it—for instance, a familiar shape, word, sentence, rhythm, poem, or story. The following are examples of such **superimposed meaningful structures:**

Information to Be Learned	Superimposed Meaningful Structure
The shape of Italy	A boot
The Great Lakes (Huron, Ontario, Michigan, Erie, Superior)	HOMES
Lines on the treble clef (E G B D F)	Elvis's Guitar Broke Down Friday, *or* Every Good Boy Does Fine.
The distinction between stalagmites and stalactites	When the "mites" go up, the "tites" come down.
The number of days in each month	Thirty days has September, . . .

Superimposed meaningful structures can be used to remember procedures as well as declarative information. Here are three examples:

Procedure to Be Learned	Superimposed Meaningful Structure
Shooting a free throw in basketball	BEEF: Balance the ball, Elbows in, Elevate the arms, Follow through.
Simplifying a complex algebraic expression	Please Excuse My Dear Aunt Sally: First, simplify terms within **p**arentheses, then terms with an **e**xponent, then terms to be **m**ultiplied or **d**ivided, and finally terms to be **a**dded or **s**ubtracted.
Turning a screw (clockwise to tighten, counter-clockwise to loosen).	Righty, tighty. Lefty, loosey.

Long-Term Memory Retrieval

As you have already discovered, some of the information stored in long-term memory is easily retrieved later on. Other pieces of information are more difficult to find, and still others may never be found at all. Retrieving information from long-term memory appears to involve following a pathway of associations; it's a process of mentally going down Memory Lane. One idea reminds us of another idea—that is, one idea *activates* another—the second idea reminds us of a third idea, and so on. The process is similar to what happened when you followed your train of thought from the word *horse* earlier in the chapter. If the pathway of associations eventually leads us to what we're trying to remember, we do indeed remember it. If the path takes us in other directions, we're out of luck.

People are more likely to remember something later on if, in the process of storing it, they connect it with something else in long-term memory. And ideally, the new and the old will have a logical relationship. To illustrate this idea, let's return once again to all that mail that arrives in your mailbox. Imagine that, on average, you receive five important items—things you really want to save—every day. With six postal deliveries a week and 52 weeks a year (minus a dozen or so holidays), you would save about 1,500 pieces of mail each year. Over the course of 15 years, you would have more than 22,000 important things stashed somewhere in your home.

Imagine that one day, you hear that stock in a clothing company (Mod Bod Jeans, Inc.) has tripled in value. You remember that your wealthy Aunt Agnes sent you some Mod Bod stock certificates for your birthday several years ago, and you presumably decided they were important enough to save. But where in the world did you put them? How long will it take you to find them among all those important letters, bills, brochures, catalogs, flyers, and so on?

How easily you find the certificates—in fact, whether you find them at all—depends on how you've been storing your mail as you've accumulated it. If you've been storing it in a logical, organized fashion—for instance, all paid bills on a closet shelf, all mail order catalogs in a couple of cardboard boxes, and all items from relatives in a file cabinet (in alphabetical order by last name)—then you should quickly retrieve Aunt Agnes's gift. But if you simply tossed each day's mail randomly around the house, you will be searching for a long, long time, possibly without ever finding a trace of that Mod Bod stock.

Like a home with 15 years' worth of mail, long-term memory contains a great deal of information. And like your search for the Mod Bod certificates, the ease with which information is retrieved from long-term memory depends somewhat on whether the information has been stored in a logical place—that is, whether it's connected to related ideas. By making connections to existing knowledge—that is, by engaging in meaningful learning—we will know where to look for information when we need it. In contrast, learning something by rote is like throwing Aunt Agnes's gift randomly among thousands of pieces of unorganized mail: We may never retrieve it again.

Factors Affecting Retrieval

Even when people connect new information to their existing knowledge base, they can't always find it when they need it. Researchers have identified at least six factors affecting retrieval, described in the following sections.

Multiple Connections with Existing Knowledge and a Variety of Contexts Sometimes learners acquire and practice certain behaviors and ways of thinking in a very limited set of environments—say, in their math classes or science labs. When this happens, the learners may associate those behaviors and ways of thinking *only* with those particular environments and therefore fail to retrieve what they've learned in other contexts. This tendency for some responses and cognitive processes to be associated with and retrieved in a very limited range of circumstances is known as **situated learning** or **situated cognition** (J. S. Brown et al., 1989; Greeno, Collins, & Resnick, 1996; Lave & Wenger, 1991). For example, if students associate principles of geometry only with math classes, they may not retrieve those principles at times when geometry would come in handy—say, when trying to determine whether a 10-inch pizza that costs eight dollars is a better value than an 8-inch pizza that costs six dollars.

In general, learners are more likely to retrieve information when they have many possible pathways to it—in other words, when they have associated the information with many other things in their existing knowledge base and with many different contexts in which they might use it. Making multiple connections is like using cross-references in your mail storage system. You may have filed the Mod Bod certificates in the items-from-relatives file cabinet, but you may also have written their location on notes left in other places—perhaps with your birth certificate (after all, you received the stock on your birthday), with your income tax receipts, and in your safe-deposit box. By looking in any one of these logical places, you'll discover where to find the stock certificates.

As teachers, we can help students more effectively remember classroom subject matter over the long run if we show how it relates to numerous other things they already know. For example, we can show them how new material relates to one or more of the following:

- Concepts and ideas within the same subject area (e.g., showing how multiplication is related to addition)
- Concepts and ideas in other subject areas (e.g., talking about how scientific discoveries have affected historical events)
- Students' general knowledge of the world (e.g., drawing parallels between the Black Death of the fourteenth century and the modern-day AIDS epidemic)
- Students' personal experiences (e.g., finding similarities between the family feud in *Romeo and Juliet* and students' own interpersonal conflicts)
- Students' current activities and needs outside the classroom (e.g., showing how persuasive writing skills might be used to craft an essay for a college application)

Help students connect important ideas to a variety of disciplines and real-world situations.

Distinctiveness Learners are more likely to remember things that are unique in some way—for instance, things that are new, unusual, or perhaps a bit bizarre (D. Davidson, 2006; R. R. Hunt & Worthen, 2006). For example, second graders are more likely to remember a visit to the local firehouse than, say, their teacher's explanation of what a *noun* is. And when U.S. high school students recall what they've learned about events leading up to the American Revolution, they are more likely to remember the Boston Tea Party—a unique and colorful illustration of colonists' dissatisfaction with British taxation policies—than, say, the Quartering Act or the publication of Thomas Paine's *Common Sense.* Certainly, learners are more likely to pay attention to distinctive information, increasing the odds that they store it in long-term memory in the first place. But even when attention and initial learning have been the same, distinctive information is easier to retrieve than dull, ordinary information (Craik, 2006).

Make important ideas distinctive in some way, perhaps by illustrating them with vivid examples or engaging hands-on experiences.

Emotional Overtones As learners pay attention to and think about new information, their thoughts and memories sometimes become emotionally charged—a phenomenon known as **hot cognition**. For example, learners might get excited when they read about advances in science that could lead to effective treatments for spinal cord injuries, cancer, AIDS, or mental illness. Or they might feel sad when they read about living conditions in certain parts of the world. And they will, we hope, get angry when they learn about atrocities committed against African American slaves in the pre–Civil War days of the United States or about large-scale genocides carried out in more recent times in Europe, Africa, and Asia.

situated learning and cognition Knowledge, behaviors, and thinking skills acquired and used primarily within certain contexts, with limited or no retrieval and use in other contexts.

hot cognition Learning or cognitive processing that is emotionally charged.

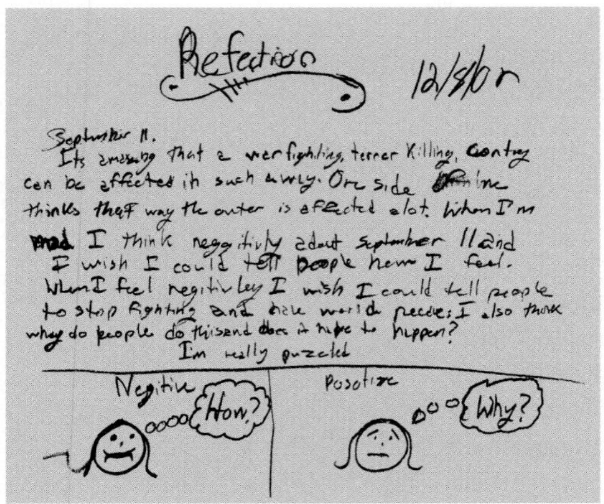

In this reflection, written more than a year after the 9/11 terrorist attacks on the World Trade Center and the Pentagon, 12-year-old Amaryth still has strong feelings about the attacks.

When information is emotionally charged in such ways, learners are more likely to pay attention to it, continue to think about it for an extended period, and repeatedly elaborate on it (Bower, 1994; Heuer & Reisberg, 1992; Zeelenberg, Wagenmakers, & Rotteveel, 2006). And over the long run, learners can usually retrieve material with high emotional content more easily than they can recall relatively nonemotional information (LaBar & Phelps, 1998; Phelps & Sharot, 2008; Reisberg & Heuer, 1992).[3] It appears that students' emotional reactions to classroom subject matter become integral parts of their network of associations in long-term memory (Bower & Forgas, 2001; Siegel, 1999).

Academic subject matter certainly doesn't need to be dry and emotionless. In addition to presenting subject matter that evokes emotional reactions, we can promote hot cognition by revealing our own feelings about a topic. For instance, we might bring in newspaper articles and other outside materials about which we are excited, or we might share the particular questions and issues about which we are personally concerned (Brophy, 2004; R. P. Perry, 1985).

Regular Practice As noted earlier, rehearsal—mindlessly repeating information over and over within the course of a few seconds or minutes—is a relatively ineffective way of getting information into long-term memory. But by "regular practice," I mean repetition over a lengthy time span: reviewing and using information and skills at periodic intervals over the course of a few weeks, months, or years. When practice is spread out in this manner—ideally in a variety of contexts—people of all ages learn something better and remember it longer (Dempster, 1991; Proctor & Dutta, 1995; Rohrer & Pashler, 2007).

When learners continue to practice things they have already mastered, they eventually achieve **automaticity**: They can retrieve what they've learned quickly and effortlessly and can use it almost without thinking (J. R. Anderson, 2005; Pashler, Rohrer, Cepeda, & Carpenter, 2007; Proctor & Dutta, 1995). As an example, think of driving a car, a complicated skill that you can probably perform easily. Your first attempts at driving many years ago may have required a great deal of mental effort. But perhaps now you can drive without having to pay much attention to what you are doing. Even if your car has a standard transmission, driving is, for you, an automatic activity.

FIGURE 6.9 Occasional rote practice of numerals and letters can be helpful in promoting automaticity, but too much conveys the message that learning basic skills is boring and tedious. Here, 5-year-old Gunnar has practiced writing numerals 1 through 9. Notice, however, that he got practice in writing 9 *backward*!

Learning something to the point of automaticity has a second advantage as well. Remember that working memory has a limited capacity: The active, thinking part of the human memory system can handle only so much at a time. Thus, when much of its capacity must be used for recalling single facts or carrying out simple procedures, little room is left for addressing more complex situations or tasks. One key reason for learning some facts and procedures to automaticity, then, is to free up working memory capacity for complex tasks and problems that require those simpler facts and procedures (D. Jones & Christensen, 1999; Proctor & Dutta, 1995; Stanovich, 2000). For example, second graders who are reading a story can better focus their efforts on understanding it if they don't have to sound out words like *before* and *after*. High school chemistry students can more easily interpret the expression Na_2CO_3 (sodium carbonate) if they don't have to stop to think about what the symbols *Na, C,* and *O* represent.

Unfortunately, automaticity is achieved in only one way: practice, practice, and more practice. Practice doesn't necessarily make perfect, but it does make knowledge more durable and more easily retrievable. When learners use information and skills

[3]Occasionally, people may have trouble retrieving highly anxiety-arousing memories. This phenomenon, known as *repression*, is most likely to occur with very traumatic personal events (Erdelyi, 1985; Pezdek & Banks, 1996). It's unlikely to be a factor in the retrieval of classroom subject matter.

frequently, they essentially pave their retrieval pathways—in some cases creating superhighways. This is *not* to say that we should continually assign drill-and-practice exercises involving isolated facts and procedures (e.g., see Figure 6.9). Such activities promote rote (rather than meaningful) learning, are often boring, and are unlikely to convince students of the value of the subject matter (Mac Iver et al., 1995). A more effective approach is to routinely incorporate basic knowledge and skills into a variety of meaningful and enjoyable activities—problem-solving tasks, group projects, games, brainteasers, and so on.

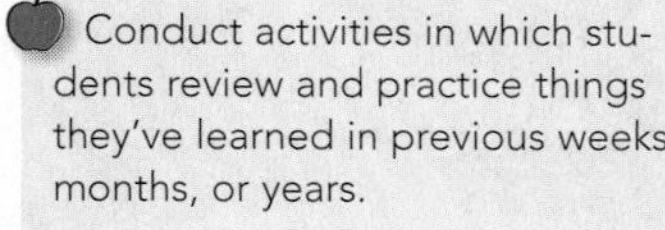
Conduct activities in which students review and practice things they've learned in previous weeks, months, or years.

Relevant Retrieval Cues If you were educated in North America, then at one time or another, you probably learned the names of the five Great Lakes. Yet right now you may initially have trouble retrieving all five, even though they are all still stored somewhere in your long-term memory. Perhaps Lake Michigan doesn't come to mind when you retrieve the other four. The *HOMES* mnemonic presented in Figure 6.8 provides a **retrieval cue**, or hint about where to "look" in long-term memory. The mnemonic tells you that one lake begins with the letter *M*, prompting you to search among the *M* words in your long-term memory until (we hope) you find *Michigan*. Learners are more likely to retrieve information when relevant retrieval cues are present to start their search of long-term memory in the right direction (e.g., Morris, Bransford, & Franks, 1977; Tulving & Thomson, 1973).

For another example of how retrieval cues can aid retrieval, try the following exercise.

EXPERIENCING FIRSTHAND

Recall versus Recognition

Earlier in the chapter, I described a process that can keep information in working memory indefinitely. Can you retrieve the name of that process from your long-term memory? See whether you can before you read any further.

If you can't remember the term, then try answering the same question posed in a multiple-choice format:

What do we call the process that keeps information in working memory for as long as you need it?

a. Facilitative construction
b. Internal organization
c. Short-term memorization
d. Maintenance rehearsal

Did you experience an aha-now-I-remember feeling? The correct answer is *d*. Perhaps the multiple-choice format provided a retrieval cue for you, directing you to the correct answer you had stored in long-term memory. Generally, it's easier to remember something in a **recognition task** in which you simply need to recognize correct information among incorrect statements or irrelevant information, rather than in a **recall task** in which the correct information must be retrieved in its entirety from long-term memory (Semb, Ellis, & Araujo, 1993).

As teachers, we won't always want to help students retrieve information by putting that information right in front of them. Nevertheless, there will be occasions when providing hints is certainly appropriate. For example, if a student asks what the symbol *Au* stands for, we might respond by saying "In class, we talked about *Au* coming from the Latin word *aurum*. Can you remember what *aurum* means?" Another example comes from one of my former teacher interns, Jess Jensen. A student in her eighth-grade history class had been writing about the Battle of New Orleans, which was a decisive victory for the United States in the War of 1812. The following exchange took place:

automaticity Ability to respond quickly and efficiently while mentally processing or physically performing a task.

retrieval cue Stimulus that provides guidance about where to look for a piece of information in long-term memory.

recognition task Memory task in which one must identify correct information among incorrect statements or irrelevant information.

recall task Memory task in which one must retrieve information from long-term memory with only minimal retrieval cues.

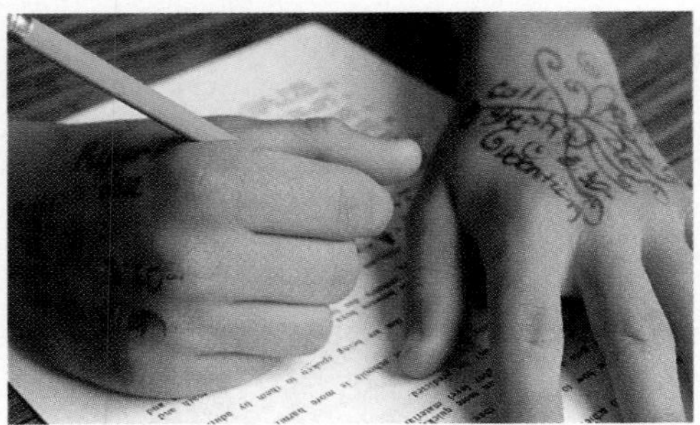

Ultimately, students must learn to develop their own retrieval cues. Here Max, a seventh grader, has written notes to himself on his hands.

Student: Why was the Battle of New Orleans important?

Jess: Look at the map. Where is New Orleans?

[The student locates New Orleans.]

Jess: Why is it important?

Student: Oh! It's near the mouth of the Mississippi. It was important for controlling transportation up and down the river.

In the early grades, teachers typically provide many retrieval cues for their students; for instance, they remind students about the tasks they need to do at certain times ("I hear the fire alarm. Remember, we all walk quietly during a fire drill," or "It's time to go home. Do you all have the field trip permission slip to take to your parents?"). But as students grow older, they must develop greater independence, relying more on themselves and less on their teachers for the things they need to remember. At all grade levels, we can teach students ways of providing retrieval cues for themselves. For example, if we expect first graders to get a permission slip signed, we might ask them to write a reminder on a piece of masking tape that they put on their jacket or lunch box. If we give junior high school students a major assignment due in several weeks, we might suggest that they tape a note with the due date to their bedside table or add an appropriate reminder to their cell phone calendar. One tenth grader developed several effective retrieval cues, each appropriate for certain situations:

Provide retrieval cues when appropriate. Also, teach students to develop their own retrieval cues for things they must remember to do.

> Homework is written down in my agenda book. If it is something to do when I get home, I will write it on my hand. If I have something to do in the next few days, I write it on a note card in my wallet, and whenever I go to get money, I will think to do it.

Wait Time By **wait time**, I mean the amount of time a teacher allows to pass after the teacher or a student says something before the teacher says something else. In many classrooms, wait time is insufficient for most students to retrieve information that might be relevant to a teacher's or classmate's question or comment. For instance, when teachers ask students a question, they typically wait for only a very short time—often a second or less—and if students don't respond in that short time, teachers tend to speak again, perhaps by asking different students the same question, rephrasing the question, or even answering the question themselves (Jegede & Olajide, 1995; M. B. Rowe, 1974, 1987). Teachers are equally reluctant to let much time elapse after students answer questions or make comments in class; on average, teachers allow one second or less of silence before responding to a statement or asking another question (Jegede & Olajide, 1995; M. B. Rowe, 1987).

Give students time to think about and formulate responses to challenging questions.

When teachers instead allow at least *three seconds* to elapse after their own questions and after students' comments, dramatic changes can occur in students' behaviors. More students—especially more females and minority-group members—participate in class, and students begin to respond to one another's comments and questions. In addition, students are more likely to support their reasoning with evidence or logic and more likely to speculate when they don't know an answer. Furthermore, they are more motivated to learn classroom subject matter, thereby increasing actual learning and decreasing behavior problems.

Such changes are due, in part, to the fact that with increased wait time, *teachers'* behaviors change as well. Teachers ask fewer simple questions (e.g., those requiring recall of facts) and more thought-provoking ones (e.g., those requiring elaboration). They also modify the direction of discussion to accommodate students' comments and questions, and they allow their classes to pursue a topic in greater depth than they had originally anticipated. Moreover, their expectations for many students, especially low-achieving ones, begin to improve (Giaconia, 1988; Mohatt & Erickson, 1981; M. B. Rowe, 1974, 1987; Tharp, 1989; Tobin, 1987).

wait time Length of time a teacher pauses, either after asking a question or hearing a student's comment, before saying something further.

When our objective is simple recall—that is, when students need to retrieve classroom material very quickly, to "know it cold"—then wait time should be short. Students may sometimes benefit from rapid-fire drill and practice to learn information and skills to automaticity. But when our instructional goals include more complex processing of ideas and issues, a longer wait time may give both our students and us the time needed to think things through.

Why Learners Sometimes Forget

Fortunately, people don't need to remember everything. For instance, you may have no reason to remember the Internet address of a website you looked at yesterday, the plot of last week's episode of a certain television show, or the due date of an assignment you turned in last semester. Much of the information learners encounter is, like junk mail, not worth keeping, and forgetting it enables learners to get rid of needless clutter (Schacter, 1999). But sometimes, learners have trouble recalling what they *do* need to remember. Let's look at five possible explanations for why students may sometimes forget important information.

Rapid-fire question–answer sessions can be helpful in promoting automaticity, but they don't always give students adequate time to generate complex, creative responses.

Failure to Store or Consolidate Information in Long-Term Memory As we've seen, a great deal of the information students encounter never reaches long-term memory. Perhaps students didn't pay attention to a piece of information, so it never went beyond the sensory register. Or perhaps after attending to it, they didn't continue to process it, so it went no further than working memory.

Even when information does reach long-term memory, it appears to need some time to "firm up" in the brain—a process called **consolidation**. An event that interferes with this consolidation—such as a serious brain injury—may cause a student to forget things that happened several seconds, minutes, hours, or even longer prior to the event (Bauer, DeBoer, & Lukowski, 2007; Wixted, 2005).

Decay Earlier in the chapter, we noted that information stored in long-term memory doesn't necessarily last forever. Much of it may weaken over time and possibly disappear altogether, especially if it isn't retrieved and used very often. Theorists often use the word **decay** to describe this gradual fading process.

Inadequate Search of Long-Term Memory A man at the supermarket looks familiar, but you can't remember who he is or where you met him. He smiles at you and says "Nice to see you again." Gulp! You desperately search your long-term memory for his name, but you have clearly forgotten who he is. A few days later, you have a bowl of chili for dinner. The chili reminds you of the Chili for Charity supper at which you worked a few months back. Of course! You and the man at the supermarket had stood side by side serving chili to hundreds of people that night. Oh yes, you now recall, his name is Melville Herman.

Like you, students often have retrieval difficulties: They simply can't find something that is actually in their long-term memory (e.g., Schacter, 1999). Sometimes they may stumble on the information later, while looking for something else. But at other times they never do retrieve it, perhaps because they've learned it by rote or don't have sufficient retrieval cues to guide their search of long-term memory.

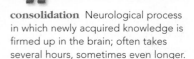

consolidation Neurological process in which newly acquired knowledge is firmed up in the brain; often takes several hours, sometimes even longer.

decay Gradual weakening of information stored in long-term memory, especially if the information is used infrequently.

Interference Sometimes people can easily retrieve things they've learned but don't know what goes with what. To experience this phenomenon yourself, try the following exercise.

EXPERIENCING FIRSTHAND

Six Chinese Words

Here are six more Mandarin Chinese words and their English meanings (for simplicity, I've omitted the pronunciation marks over the words). Read the words two or three times, and try to store them in your long-term memory. But don't do anything special to learn the words—for instance, don't intentionally develop mnemonics to help you remember them.

Chinese	***English***
jung	middle
ting	listen
sung	deliver
peng	friend
ching	please
deng	wait

Now cover up the list of words and test yourself. What is the Chinese word for *friend*? *please*? *listen*? *wait*?

Did you find yourself getting confused, perhaps forgetting which English meaning went with each Chinese word? If you did, then you were the victim of **interference**. The various pieces of information you stored in memory were interfering with one another—essentially, they were getting mixed up in your head. Interference is especially likely to occur when items are similar to one another and when they are learned by rote, rather than in a meaningful or mnemonic-based fashion (Dempster, 1985; Lustig & Hasher, 2001; Lustig, Konkel, & Jacoby, 2004). Interference was probably at work when Kanesha struggled to remember *tibia* and *fibula*—two similar-sounding bones in the lower leg—in the opening case study.

When important details are difficult to fill in logically or might easily be confused with one another, make sure students learn them well.

Reconstruction Error Retrieval isn't necessarily an all-or-nothing phenomenon. Sometimes students retrieve part of the information they're seeking from long-term memory but can't recall the rest. In such situations they may fill in the gaps using their general knowledge and assumptions about the world (Kolodner, 1985; Roediger & McDermott, 2000; P. T. Wilson & Anderson, 1986). But even though the gaps are filled in logically, they aren't always filled in correctly—a form of forgetting called **reconstruction error**. We'll look at the reconstructive nature of retrieval in greater detail in Chapter 7.

All of these explanations of forgetting underscore the importance of instructional strategies we previously identified: We must make sure students are paying attention, help them relate new material to things they already know, and give them opportunities to review, practice, and apply the material frequently.

interference Phenomenon whereby something stored in long-term memory inhibits one's ability to remember something else correctly.

reconstruction error Construction of a logical but incorrect memory by combining information retrieved from long-term memory with one's general knowledge and beliefs about the world.

Diversity in Cognitive Processes

Children and adolescents differ considerably in the various factors that influence their ability to learn and remember in the classroom—attention, working memory capacity, long-term memory storage processes, prior knowledge, and so on. For example, on average, girls have a slight edge over boys in keeping their attention focused on classroom activities and in performing certain kinds of memory tasks, such as remembering lists and specific life events (Das, Naglieri, & Kirby, 1994; Halpern, 2006; Halpern & LaMay, 2000). On average, too, children from middle- and high-income families tend to have stronger literacy and mathematical skills when they begin school than their lower-income peers, but children from low-income families are apt to bring a wealth of prior knowledge about other topics on which we can build (see Chapter 4).

Another important source of diversity is culture. Children's varying cultural backgrounds may have prepared them to handle different kinds of learning environments and tasks. For instance, African American and Hispanic students are more likely than European American students to be comfortable in environments in which several activities are going on at once and can more easily shift their attention from one activity to another (Correa-Chávez, Rogoff, & Mejía Arauz, 2005; Tyler et al., 2008). Students from North American, Middle Eastern, and East Asian cultures are apt to have had experience rote-memorizing specific facts and written materials (perhaps in the form of poems or religious teachings), whereas students from certain cultures in Africa, Australia, and Central America may have been encouraged to remember oral histories or particular locations and landmarks in the local terrain (Purdie & Hattie, 1996; Rogoff, 2001, 2003; Rogoff et al., 2007; Q. Wang & Ross, 2007).

The importance of wait time depends partly on students' cultural backgrounds as well. For example, some Native American students may wait several seconds before responding to a question as a way of showing respect for an adult (see Chapter 4). And English language learners—students who have grown up in a non-English-speaking environment and are still developing their proficiency in English—are apt to require more mental translation time than their native-English-speaking peers.

However, group differences don't account for all of the diversity we will see in students. Significant individual differences also exist *within* any group. For instance, some students are able to think about, encode, and respond to new events and ideas much more quickly than others can (Danthiir, Roberts, Schulze, & Wilhelm, 2005; Demetriou et al., 2002; Kail, 2000). And even students from very similar backgrounds will have unique knowledge bases on which to draw, leading them to elaborate differently on the ideas they encounter at school (e.g., Cothern, Konopak, & Willis, 1990; C. A. Grant & Gomez, 2001; R. E. Reynolds et al., 1982).

To maximize each student's learning and achievement in the classroom, we must take such individual and group differences into account. For example, we should be especially careful to engage the interest of—and also minimize distractions for—those students whose attention easily wanders. In addition, in our attempts to promote meaningful learning and other effective storage processes, we should relate classroom subject matter to the diverse background experiences that students have had. And we must allow sufficient wait time after questions and comments so that students can actively think about and elaborate on topics of discussion.

myeducationlab

Gain practice in facilitating effective long-term memory storage processes by completing the Building Teaching Skills and Dispositions exercise "Facilitating Effective Long-Term Memory Storage Processes" in MyEducationLab. (To find this exercise, go to the topic Cognition and Memory in MyEducationLab and click on *Building Teaching Skills and Dispositions.*)

Facilitating Cognitive Processing in Students with Special Needs

Chapter 5 introduced five general categories of students with special needs:

1. Students with specific cognitive or academic difficulties, such as learning disabilities and attention-deficit hyperactivity disorder (ADHD)
2. Students with social or behavioral problems, such as emotional and behavioral disorders and autism spectrum disorders
3. Students with general delays in cognitive and social functioning (i.e., intellectual disabilities, also known as mental retardation)
4. Students with physical or sensory challenges, such as chronic health conditions, visual impairments, and hearing loss
5. Students with advanced cognitive development (i.e., giftedness)

This chapter and the ones that follow include tables called *Students in Inclusive Settings* that apply chapter content to students in each of these five general categories. The first

Students in Inclusive Settings

TABLE 6.5
Facilitating Cognitive Processing in Students with Special Educational Needs

Category	Characteristics You Might Observe	Suggested Strategies
Students with specific cognitive or academic difficulties	• Deficiencies in one or more specific cognitive processes (e.g., perception, organization of related ideas into an integrated whole) • Distractibility, inability to sustain attention for some students • Difficulty screening out irrelevant stimuli • Less working memory capacity or less efficient use of working memory • Impulsivity in responding to classroom tasks • Exceptionally detailed memory for personally experienced events (for some students with ADHD)	• Analyze students' errors as a way of identifying possible processing difficulties. • Identify weaknesses in specific cognitive processes, and provide instruction that enables students to compensate for these weaknesses. • Keep distracting stimuli to a minimum, and make sure you have students' attention before giving instructions or presenting information. • Intersperse activities requiring sustained attention with opportunities for physical exercise. • Encourage greater reflection before responding—for instance, by reinforcing accuracy rather than speed, or by teaching self-instructions (see Chapter 10). • Present information in an organized fashion and make frequent connections to students' prior knowledge as ways of promoting more effective long-term memory storage. • Teach mnemonics to aid long-term memory storage and retrieval. • Acknowledge and capitalize on students' strengths (e.g., the detailed event memories that some students with ADHD have).
Students with social or behavioral problems	• Limited ability to focus attention because of off-task thoughts and behaviors (for some students with emotional and behavioral disorders) • Difficulty shifting attention quickly (for students with autism) • Exceptional ability to attend to small details; may be reflected in unusually detailed memory and drawings (for some students with autism) • Impulsivity; less ability to inhibit inappropriate social behaviors (sometimes due to neurological deficits) • Possible difficulties in other cognitive processes (e.g., undiagnosed learning disabilities)	• Capture students' attention by relating instruction to their personal interests. • Nurture and capitalize on the visual memory and artistic strengths that some students with autism have. • Refer students to a school psychologist for evaluation and diagnosis of possible learning disabilities. • As appropriate, use strategies listed above for students with specific cognitive or academic difficulties.
Students with general delays in cognitive and social functioning	• Slower cognitive processing • Difficulty with attention to task-relevant information • Reduced working memory capacity or less efficient use of working memory • Less intentional control of cognitive processes • Smaller knowledge base on which to build new learning • Greater difficulty retaining information for long periods	• Keep instructional materials simple, emphasizing relevant stimuli and minimizing irrelevant stimuli. • Provide clear instructions that focus students' attention on desired behaviors (e.g., "Listen," "Write," "Stop"). • Pace instruction to allow students enough time to think about and process information adequately (e.g., provide ample wait time after questions). • Assume little prior knowledge about new topics (i.e., begin at the beginning).
Students with physical or sensory challenges	• Normal cognitive processing ability in most students • Less-developed knowledge base to which new information can be related, due to limited experiences in the outside world • Better than average ability to recall details of abstract shapes (for older students who are deaf but proficient with sign language)	• Assume equal ability for acquiring new information and skills, but consider how students' physical or sensory challenges may interfere with some learning processes. • Provide basic life experiences that students may have missed because of their disabilities.
Students with advanced cognitive development	• Greater ability to attend to tasks for extended periods • More rapid cognitive processing • Greater intentional control of cognitive processes • Larger knowledge base, with specific contents dependent on students' cultural backgrounds • More interconnections among ideas in long-term memory • More rapid retrieval of information from long-term memory	• Proceed through topics more quickly or in greater depth. • Create interdisciplinary lessons to foster integration of material in long-term memory.

Sources: Barkley, 2006; Beirne-Smith et al., 2006; Bulgren, Schumaker, & Deshler, 1994; Butterfield & Ferretti, 1987; Cattani, Clibbens, & Perfect, 2007; B. Clark, 1997; Courchesne et al., 1994; Fletcher, Lyon, Fuchs, & Barnes, 2007; Geary, Hoard, Byrd-Craven, Nugent, & Numtee, 2007; Grandin & Johnson, 2005; Heward, 2009; J. Johnson, Im-Bolter, & Pascual-Leone, 2003; Landau & McAninch, 1993; E. P. Lorch et al., 1999; G. R. Lyon & Krasnegor, 1996; Meltzer, 2007; Mercer & Pullen, 2005; Moran & Gardner, 2006; Morgan & Jenson, 1988; Piirto, 1999; Posner & Rothbart, 2007; Pressley, 1995; Rabinowitz & Glaser, 1985; Skowronek, Leichtman, & Pillemer, 2008; H. L. Swanson et al., 1998; H. L. Swanson & Jerman, 2006; Turnbull et al., 2007.

of these tables, Table 6.5, identifies cognitive processing differences we are likely to see in students with special educational needs.

As you can see from the table, some students with disabilities have particular trouble attending to and effectively processing classroom subject matter. This is certainly true for students with learning disabilities (who, by definition, have deficits in certain cognitive processes), and it is often true for students with ADHD and general intellectual disabilities as well. In contrast, many children with autism spectrum disorders can be *very* attentive, sometimes to the point that they have trouble shifting to new tasks. And on average, gifted students have a longer attention span and can process new ideas more rapidly and elaboratively than many of their classmates.

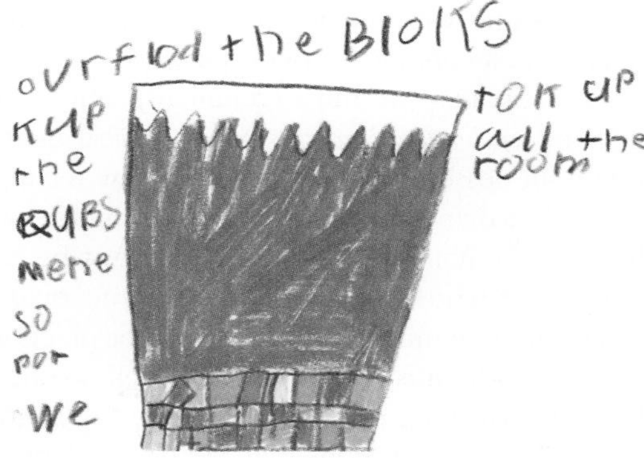

FIGURE 6.10 In a science activity in his third-grade class, 9-year-old Nicholas copied the scientific principle "No two pieces of matter can occupy the same space at the same time" onto a sheet of paper. He and a lab partner then filled a cup with water and dropped, one at a time, more than a dozen small metal cubes into the cup. Here, Nick recorded his observations with both words and a drawing.

As teachers, we must keep in mind that students with disabilities almost invariably have strengths as well as weaknesses. For example, some students with ADHD have a keen memory for events they have personally experienced and may generate more detailed narratives than their nondisabled classmates (Skowronek, Leichtman, & Pillemer, 2008). And some students with autism notice and remember many subtle nuances in the things they see and may produce highly detailed and skillful drawings that are unusual for their age-group (I. L. Cohen, 2007; S. Moran & Gardner, 2006).

The far-right column of Table 6.5 presents many useful strategies for working with students who have special educational needs. The first of these—analyzing students' errors for clues about possible processing difficulties—is illustrated in 9-year-old Nicholas's lab report in Figure 6.10. Nick's description of what he observed can be translated as "We poured so many cubes [that] the cup overflowed. The blocks took up all the room." We can only speculate why Nick wrote up the left side of the glass, across the top, and then down the other side. One possible explanation is that, with his limited language skills, Nick had not yet mastered the conventional direction of written English. This hypothesis seems unlikely, however, as other samples of Nick's writing (not shown here) correctly begin at the top of the page and proceed downward. Another possibility is that Nick was thinking about the direction of the water flow (up and out) as he wrote and either intentionally or unintentionally followed the water's direction in his writing. His limited working memory capacity may have been a factor here: Perhaps he had insufficient room in his working memory to think simultaneously about his observations plus the spellings of words and conventions of written English.

Virtually all students, including those without any identified special needs, occasionally have difficulty learning or remembering class material. Accordingly, many of the instructional strategies in Table 6.5—getting students' attention, analyzing their errors, teaching them mnemonics, and so on—need not be limited to use with students with special needs. *All* students can benefit from help in processing information more effectively.

The Big Picture

Cognitive psychology has much to offer teachers and students alike. Following are several key principles that can guide all members of any classroom community:

- ***Learners are actively involved in their own learning.*** As should be clear by now, learning involves creating self-constructed understandings, rather than thoughtlessly absorbing information from the environment. Hence, strictly one-way forms of instruction—for instance, talking *at* rather than *with* students—won't necessarily lead students to think about classroom topics in the same way that their teachers do.

- ***To learn and remember something effectively, learners must give it their undivided attention.*** That is, they must mentally focus on it and temporarily make it the center of their cognitive world. However, attention and working memory have a limited capacity (i.e., learners can attend to and think about only a small amount of information at one time), thus creating a major bottleneck in the human memory system. No matter how fascinating a topic may be, students can learn only so much so fast.

• ***In most circumstances, meaningful learning is more effective than rote learning.*** Effective learners try to make new information meaningful, logical, organized, and vivid—for instance, by identifying ways in which it's similar to things they already know, drawing inferences from it, finding connections among its various pieces, and forming visual images that capture some of its key qualities. When certain kinds of information have little underlying logic—as is the case, for example, with many capitals of states and countries and with many words in foreign languages—using mnemonic techniques provides a viable alternative.

As teachers, we must continually emphasize the importance of *understanding* classroom subject matter—seeing how it all ties together, recognizing new examples, and so on—rather than simply memorizing it in a relatively thought-free manner. This emphasis must be reflected not only in our words but also in our instructional activities, classroom assignments, and assessment practices. For instance, in high school science classes, we might embed thought-provoking questions into our explanations and lectures—perhaps questions that require students to evaluate, synthesize, or apply new ideas. In elementary math instruction, rather than ask students simply to memorize procedures for adding two two-digit numbers, we might ask them to identify at least three *different* ways they might solve a problem such as "15 + 45 = ?" or "29 + 68 = ?" and to justify their reasoning. And in middle school history, rather than assess students' knowledge with questions about names, places, and dates, we might ask students to explain why certain events happened and how those events altered the course of subsequent history. Such approaches will not only make students' learning more meaningful and effective but will also enhance their belief that classroom topics are interesting, enjoyable, and relevant to their own lives.

• ***Repetition over the long run has greater benefits than repetition in the short run.*** As you've learned, rehearsal—repeating something over and over within the course of a few seconds or minutes—is a useful way of keeping information in working memory but is relatively ineffective for storing it in long-term memory. Once information *is* in long-term memory, however, occasional repetition over the course of several weeks, months, or years can help to keep it there indefinitely. Furthermore, students are likely to achieve automaticity for important facts and skills—enabling them to retrieve those facts and skills quickly and efficiently—only if they practice using them at regular intervals and in different contexts.

• ***Long-term memory appears to have as much capacity as learners could ever need.*** Thanks to the process of meaningful learning, the more information that learners currently have in long-term memory, the more easily they can understand and remember new ideas. When it comes to acquiring new knowledge, then, the rich get richer and the poor (in knowledge) stay relatively poor. There appear to be no limits to the amount of information and the number of skills that human beings can learn.

Practice for Your Licensure Exam

How Time Flies

Ms. Llewellyn has recently completed her degree in U.S. history and has just begun her first year teaching at an American high school. In September, she begins her American history classes with a study of early Native American groups and European explorers of the Western Hemisphere. By early October, students are reading about the colonial settlements of the 1600s. By December, they have covered the French and Indian War, the Revolutionary War, and the Declaration of Independence. The winter months are spent studying the nineteenth century (e.g., the Industrial Revolution, the Civil War), and the spring is spent studying the twentieth century (e.g., both world wars, the Korean War, the Vietnam War, and recent U.S. conflicts in the Middle East).

In her daily class lectures, Ms. Llewellyn describes historical events in considerable detail, hoping to give her students a sense of their complexity. In addition to having students read the usual high school textbook, she assigns articles in the historical journals that she reads at home.

Occasionally, Ms. Llewellyn stops her lecture a few minutes before the bell rings to ask questions that check her students' recall of the day's topics. Although her students can usually remember the gist of the day's lecture, they have difficulty with the details, either mixing them up or forgetting them altogether. A few students remember so little that she can hardly believe they were in class that day. Her students perform even more poorly on monthly essay exams: It's obvious from their written responses that they remember little of what Ms. Llewellyn has taught them. "I explained things so clearly to them," she tells herself. "Perhaps these kids just don't want to learn."

1. **Multiple-choice question:**

   Three of the following are possible explanations of why Ms. Llewellyn's students have not performed as well as she had hoped. Which alternative is *not* consistent with what researchers have learned about memory and cognition?

   a. The students may have had trouble keeping their attention on the daily lectures.
   b. Ms. Llewellyn has not given students the drill and practice they need to memorize the material.
   c. The students may have insufficient background knowledge to make sense of the assigned journal articles.
   d. Ms. Llewellyn has presented the material too quickly for students to store it effectively in long-term memory.

2. **Constructed-response question:**

   Drawing on concepts and principles from contemporary cognitive psychology, what might you do differently than Ms. Llewellyn has done? Describe at least three strategies, being specific and concrete about what you would do.

Go to Chapter 6 of the Book-Specific Resources in **MyEducationLab** and click on "Practice for Your Licensure Exam" to answer these questions. Compare your responses with the feedback provided.

PRAXIS

Turn to Appendix C, "Matching Book and MyEducationLab Content to the Praxis Principles of Learning and Teaching Tests," to discover sections of this chapter that may be especially applicable to the Praxis tests.

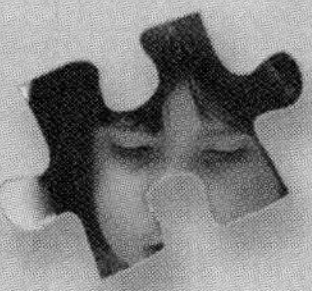

PEARSON myeducationlab

Now go to MyEducationLab (**www.myeducationlab.com**), where you can:

- Find learning outcomes for Cognition and Memory, along with the national standards that connect to these outcomes.
- Complete Assignments and Activities that can help you more deeply understand the chapter content.
- Engage in Building Teaching Skills and Dispositions exercises in which you can apply and practice core teaching skills identified in the chapter.
- Access Book-Specific Resources:
  - Check your comprehension of chapter content by going to the Study Plan, where you can find (a) Chapter Objectives; (b) Focus Questions that can guide your reading; (c) a Self-Check Quiz that can help you monitor your progress in mastering chapter content; (d) Review, Practice, and Enrichment exercises with detailed feedback that will deepen your understanding of various concepts and principles; (e) Flashcards that can give you practice in understanding and defining key terms; and (f) Common Beliefs and Misconceptions about Educational Psychology that will alert you to typical misunderstandings in educational psychology classes.
  - Video Examples of various concepts and principles presented in the chapter.
  - Supplementary Readings that enable you to pursue certain topics in greater depth.
  - A Practice for Your Licensure Exam exercise that resembles the kinds of questions appearing on many teacher licensure tests.

CHAPTER OUTLINE

CHAPTER OBJECTIVES

- **Objective 7.1:** Explain how constructive processes can occur during both storage and retrieval, as well as how they occur both in individual learners and in social and cultural groups.
- **Objective 7.2:** Describe the general nature of learners' concepts, schemas, scripts, theories, and worldviews; apply your knowledge about each of these forms of organized knowledge to instructional practice.
- **Objective 7.3:** Describe and illustrate seven general strategies you might use to facilitate students' construction of knowledge about classroom topics.
- **Objective 7.4:** Explain how and why students' existing misconceptions can interfere with effective learning, and identify several ways of helping students revamp their misconceptions into productive understandings.
- **Objective 7.5:** Apply your knowledge of constructive processes to identify effective instructional strategies for diverse cultural groups and for students with special educational needs.

Chapter 7

Knowledge Construction

CASE STUDY: The New World

Rita's fourth-grade class in Michigan recently had a unit on Michigan's history. Rita still knows little about U.S. history; she will study that subject as a fifth grader next year. But despite her limited background in history, Rita willingly responds to an interviewer's questions about the New World:

Interviewer: Our country is in the part of the world called America. At one time, America was called the New World. Do you know why it was called the New World?

Rita: Yeah. We learned this in social studies.

Interviewer: What did you learn?

Rita: Because they used to live in England, the British, and they didn't know about. . . . They wanted to get to China 'cause China had some things they wanted. They had some cups or whatever—no, they had furs. They had fur and stuff like that and they wanted to have a shorter way to get to China so they took it and they landed in Michigan, but it wasn't called Michigan. I think it was the British that landed in Michigan and they were there first and so they tried to claim that land, but it didn't work out for some reason so they took some furs and brought them back to Britain and they sold them, but they mostly wanted it for the furs. So then the English landed there and they claimed the land and they wanted to make it a state, and so they got it signed by the government or whoever, the big boss, then they were just starting to make it a state so the British just went up to the Upper Peninsula [a part of Michigan separated from the rest of the state by the Straits of Mackinac, which connect Lake Michigan and Lake Huron] and they thought they could stay there for a little while. Then they had to fight a war, then the farmers, they were just volunteers, so the farmers went right back and tried to get their family put together back again.

Interviewer: Did you learn all this in state history this year?

Rita: Um hum. (VanSledright & Brophy, 1992, p. 849; reprinted by permission)

- **Which parts of Rita's response accurately describe the history of the New World? Which parts are clearly inaccurate?**
- **At the time British colonists were first settling in Michigan, merchants in England were seeking a new trade route to the Far East so that they could more easily secure the tea, spices, and silk available there. Why might Rita initially suggest that the British wanted to get cups from China? Why might she then say that they wanted to get furs?**

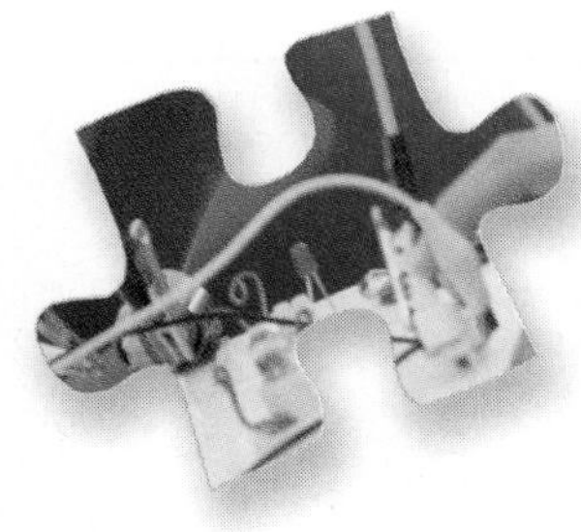

RITA HAS CERTAINLY LEARNED SOME FACTS about her state and its history. For example, she's aware that part of Michigan is called the Upper Peninsula, and she knows that many of the state's early European settlers were British. But she has used what she knows to weave a tale that could give a historian heart failure. To some extent, Rita's lack of information about certain other things is limiting her ability to make sense of what she has learned about Michigan's history. Specifically, Rita doesn't know that the British and the English were the *same people*. Thinking of them as two different groups, she assumes that the arrival of the latter group drove the former group to the Upper Peninsula. Occasionally, what Rita *does* know is also a source of difficulty. For instance, she apparently associates China with dinnerware (including cups), and she has learned that some early European explorers sought exotic animal furs to send back to their homeland. She uses such information to draw logical but incorrect inferences about why the British were so eager to find a new route to China.

Like Rita, we often create our own unique understandings of the world—understandings that may or may not be accurate. For example, think back to a time when you tried to carry on a conversation with someone in a noisy room—maybe at a party, in a bar where a band was playing, or in a workshop with loud machinery operating nearby. You probably couldn't hear everything the other person was saying, but perhaps you were able to get the gist of the message by combining what you *did* hear with things you could see (e.g., gestures and facial expressions) and with things you already knew about the topic under discussion. Even in quieter circumstances, learning and memory involve a process of **construction** that may rely heavily on prior knowledge—that is, on information previously stored in long-term memory.

Constructive Processes in Learning and Memory

Rita may have constructed her unique view of history at the time she learned it—that is, during storage. Alternatively, she may have constructed it while the adult was interviewing her—in other words, while she was retrieving what she'd previously learned. Knowledge construction often occurs during both storage and retrieval.

Construction in Storage

As an example of how construction might occur during long-term memory storage, try the following exercise.

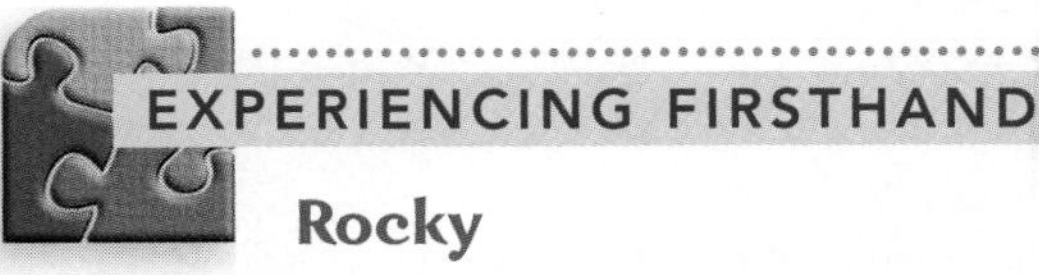

Rocky

Read the following passage *one time only:*

> Rocky slowly got up from the mat, planning his escape. He hesitated a moment and thought. Things were not going well. What bothered him most was being held, especially since the charge against him had been weak. He considered his present situation. The lock that held him was strong but he thought he could break it. He knew, however, that his timing would have to be perfect. Rocky was aware that it was because of his early roughness that he had been penalized so severely—much too severely from his point of view. The situation was becoming frustrating; the pressure had been grinding on him for too long. He was being ridden unmercifully. Rocky was getting angry now. He felt he was ready to make his move. He knew that his success or failure would depend on what he did in the next few seconds. (R. C. Anderson, Reynolds, Schallert, & Goetz, 1977, p. 372)

Now summarize what you've just read in two or three sentences.

construction Mental process in which a learner takes many separate pieces of information and uses them to build an overall understanding or interpretation.

What did you think the passage was about? A prison escape? A wrestling match? Or perhaps something else altogether? The passage about Rocky includes numerous facts but leaves a lot unsaid. For instance, it tells us nothing about where Rocky was, what kind of lock was holding him, or why timing was of the utmost importance. Yet you were probably able to use the information the passage *does* include to construct a reasonable understanding of Rocky's situation (R. C. Anderson et al., 1977).

Different people often construct different meanings from the same stimuli or events, in part because they each bring unique prior experiences and knowledge to the situation. For example, when the "Rocky" passage was used in an experiment with college students, physical education majors frequently interpreted it as a wrestling match, but music education majors (most of whom had little or no knowledge of wrestling) were more likely to think it was about a prison break (R. C. Anderson et al., 1977).

Furthermore, people often interpret what they see and hear based on what they expect to see and hear and what they pay attention to. As an illustration, consider this well-known nursery rhyme:

Little Bo Peep

Little Bo Peep has lost her sheep
And doesn't know where to find them.
Leave tham alone, and they'll come home,
Waggng their tails behind them.

Did you notice the two typographical errors in the rhyme: *tham* and *waggng*? If you didn't notice one or both of these errors (and many people don't), then your perception of the rhyme was influenced by the words you expected to see. Many people overlook typos when they read (even when intentionally proofreading for spelling errors), in part because they already have some idea of what they are likely to read and therefore don't look closely at all of the words. In virtually any situation, people can pay attention to only so many things, and the things that they closely attend to contribute more heavily to their unique constructions of what they have observed or experienced.

Prior knowledge and expectations are especially likely to influence learning when new information is ambiguous (e.g., Eysenck & Keane, 1990). To see what I mean, try another exercise.

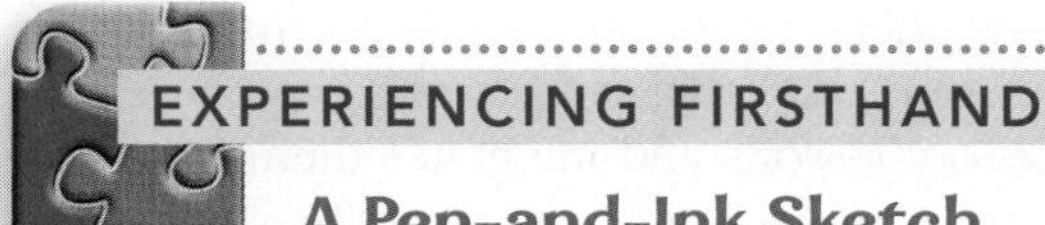

EXPERIENCING FIRSTHAND

A Pen-and-Ink Sketch

Take a close look at the figure shown here. Look at the details carefully. Notice the shape of the head, the facial features, and the relative proportion of one part to another. But what exactly *do* you see?

Source: Figure from "The Role of Frequency in Developing Perceptual Sets" by B. R. Bugelski and D. A. Alampay, 1961, *Canadian Journal of Psychology, 15*, p. 206. Copyright 1961. Canadian Psychological Association. Reprinted with permission.

Did you see a picture of a rat or mouse, or did you see a bald-headed man? In fact, the drawing isn't a very good picture of *anything;* too many details have been left out. Despite the missing pieces, however, people can usually make sense of the figure. Whether they see a man or a rodent depends, in large part, on whether they expect to see a human being or a nonhuman creature (Bugelski & Alampay, 1961). Interpretations of

FIGURE 7.1 As her journal entries show, 8-year-old Darcy initially interpreted her teacher's casual remark to the school nurse in a way very different from the teacher's intended meaning. Fortunately, the teacher could correct the misunderstanding a few days later.

October 22nd, 2001
I went to a new school today. My teacher's name is Mrs. Whaley. I accidentally cracked an egg on my head. Mrs. Whaley told the nurse that I was a showoff and a nuisance. I got really sad and wanted to run away from school, but I didn't leave.

. . .

October 27th, 2001
We presented our book reports today. I was the last one to present my book report. Whenever I did my book report, they laughed at me, but the teacher said they were laughing with me. I asked the teacher why she had called me a nuisance the first day. And she said, "Darcy, I didn't call you a nuisance. I was saying to Mrs. Larson that it was a nuisance to try to wash egg out of your hair." I was so happy. I decided to like Mrs. Whaley again.

ambiguous information are particularly susceptible to biases and expectations because so much of the information necessary for an accurate perception (if accuracy is possible) simply isn't available.

In the classroom, students construct their own idiosyncratic meanings and interpretations in virtually every area of the curriculum. For example, the process of reading is typically quite constructive: Students combine their prior knowledge with the ideas they acquire on the printed page and then draw what are—to them, at least—logical conclusions about what a text is saying (J. A. Dole, Duffy, Roehler, & Pearson, 1991; Otero & Kintsch, 1992). So, too, do students make their own personal sense of science, math, and social studies (R. Driver, Asoko, Leach, Mortimer, & Scott, 1994; L. B. Resnick, 1989; VanSledright & Brophy, 1992).

Students may also interpret nonacademic interactions in ways we don't anticipate. For example, the first day that 8-year-old Darcy attended third grade at a new school, she accidentally got egg in her hair. Her teacher, Mrs. Whaley, took her to the nurse's office to have the egg washed out. As revealed in the journal entries in Figure 7.1, Darcy initially misinterpreted Mrs. Whaley's comment about the situation. Not until five days later did she gain a more accurate understanding of what Mrs. Whaley had said. In communicating about either academic or nonacademic matters, we must take care to express our messages completely and unambiguously, leaving little room for misunderstanding.

To minimize misinterpretations, aim for completeness and clarity in your messages to students.

Construction in Retrieval

Have you ever remembered an event very differently from how a friend did, even though the two of you were equally active participants in the event? Were you and your friend both certain of the accuracy of your own memories and convinced that the other person remembered the situation incorrectly? Constructive processes in retrieval might explain this difference of opinion. Retrieval isn't necessarily an all-or-nothing phenomenon. Sometimes, we retrieve only certain parts of something we've previously learned. In such situations, we may construct our memory of an event by combining the tidbits we can recall with our general knowledge and assumptions about the world (Roediger & McDermott, 2000; Schacter, 1999).

When people fill gaps in the information they have retrieved based on what seems logical, they often make mistakes—a phenomenon known as **reconstruction error**. In the opening case study, Rita's version of Michigan history is a prime example: She retrieves certain facts from her history lessons and integrates them into what is, for her, a reasonable scenario. So, too, will our own students sometimes fall victim to reconstruction error, pulling together what they can recall in ways we may hardly recognize (Leichtman & Ceci, 1995; Roediger & McDermott, 2000). If important details are difficult to fill in logically, we must make sure students learn them well enough to retrieve them easily from long-term memory.

When important details are difficult to fill in logically, make sure students learn them well.

Up to this point, we have been talking about construction as a process that occurs within a single learner. Theories that focus on how individual people construct meaning from events are collectively known as **individual constructivism**.

reconstruction error Construction of a logical but incorrect memory by combining information retrieved from one's long-term memory with one's general knowledge and beliefs about the world.

individual constructivism Theoretical perspective that focuses on how individuals construct meaning from their experiences.

Knowledge Construction as a Social Process

Sometimes people work together, rather than separately, to construct meaning and knowledge. For instance, think about times when you've been confused about material in one of your high school or college classes. In such situations, did you ever work

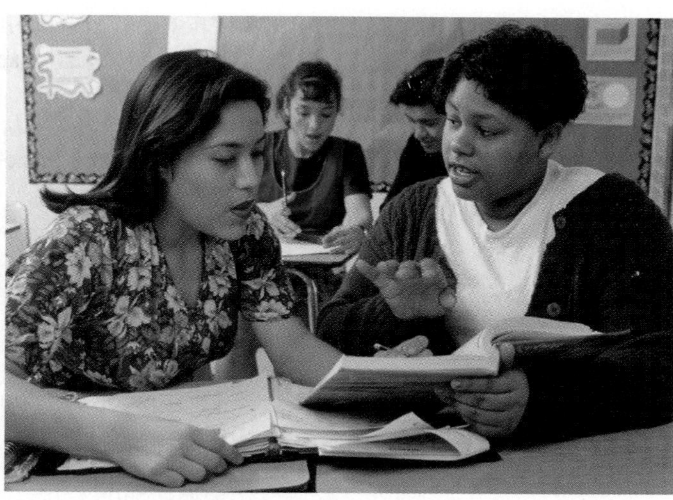
When students must explain their thinking to their peers, they often organize and elaborate on what they've learned. Such processes help them develop a more integrated and thorough understanding of classroom topics.

cooperatively with classmates (who perhaps were just as confused as you were) to make sense of the material *together?* Quite possibly, by sharing your various interpretations, you jointly constructed a better understanding of the subject matter than any of you could have constructed on your own. Unlike individually constructed knowledge, which may differ considerably from one individual to another, socially constructed knowledge is shared by two or more people simultaneously. A perspective known as **social constructivism** focuses on such collective efforts to impose meaning on the world.

On some occasions, meaning is jointly constructed by two or more people at a single time, as would be the case if you and a few classmates made sense of puzzling course material by working together in a study group. In other instances, social construction of meaning may take weeks, years, or even centuries, as is seen in the evolution of such academic disciplines as mathematics, science, history, economics, and psychology. Through these disciplines, people have developed concepts (e.g., *pi* [π], *molecule*, and *revolution*) and principles (e.g., *Pythagorean theorem*, *supply-and-demand*, and the *limited capacity of working memory*) to simplify, organize, and explain certain aspects of the world or its inhabitants. Literature, music, and the fine arts help us to impose meaning on the world as well—for example, by trying to portray the thoughts and feelings that characterize human experience. Here, we see the very critical role that *culture* plays in knowledge construction: To the extent that different groups of people use different concepts and principles to explain their physical experiences and to the extent that they have unique bodies of literature, music, and art to capture their psychological experiences, they will inevitably see the world in diverse ways (Y. Hong et al., 2000; O. Lee, 1999; Tomasello, 2000).

Two early developmental theorists, Jean Piaget and Lev Vygotsky, suggested that children can learn a great deal about the world by discussing various topics with other people (see Chapter 2). In many situations, social construction of knowledge involves students and a teacher working actively together to make better sense of information and events (e.g., see the discussion of *mediated learning experiences* in Chapter 2). In other cases, although the teacher may initiate and monitor a learning activity, students work primarily with one another to construct meaning about classroom subject matter—for instance, to explore, explain, discuss, and debate certain topics either in small groups or as an entire class. By working together in such a manner, students are, in essence, engaging in **distributed cognition**: They spread a learning task across many minds and can draw on multiple knowledge bases and ideas (Kuhn, 2001b; Palincsar & Herrenkohl, 1999; Salomon, 1993). Learners are apt to benefit in a variety of ways from sharing their ideas and perspectives with one another:

- They must clarify and organize their ideas well enough to explain and justify the ideas to others.
- They tend to elaborate on what they have learned—for example, by drawing inferences, generating hypotheses, and formulating questions to be answered.
- They are exposed to the views of others, who may have more accurate understandings.
- They can model effective ways of thinking about and studying academic subject matter for one another.
- They may discover flaws and inconsistencies in their own thinking, thereby identifying gaps in their understanding (e.g., see the discussion of *sociocognitive conflict* in Chapter 2).

social constructivism Theoretical perspective that focuses on people's collective efforts to impose meaning on the world.

distributed cognition Process whereby learners think about an issue or problem together, sharing ideas and working collaboratively to draw conclusions or develop solutions.

- They may discover how people from different cultural and ethnic backgrounds interpret the topic in different yet perhaps equally valid ways.
- With the support of their peers, they can gain practice in more sophisticated learning and reasoning skills, which they can eventually begin to use on their own (see the discussion of *internalization* in Chapter 2).
- They can also gain practice in the argumentation skills that experts in various disciplines use to advance the frontiers of knowledge—for instance, presenting evidence in support of conclusions and examining the strengths and weaknesses of various explanations.
- They may acquire a more sophisticated view of the nature of knowledge and learning. For example, they may begin to realize that acquiring knowledge involves acquiring an integrated set of ideas about a topic and that such knowledge is likely to evolve gradually over time (views of the nature of knowledge are known as *epistemic beliefs*; see Chapter 8). (Andriessen, 2006; Banks, 1991; P. Bell & Linn, 2002; Bendixen & Rule, 2004; M. Carr & Biddlecomb, 1998; Chinn, 2006; Hatano & Inagaki, 2003; K. Hogan, Nastasi, & Pressley, 2000; A. King, 1999; Kuhn & Udell, 2003; P. K. Murphy & Mason, 2006; Nussbaum, 2008; B. B. Schwarz, Neuman, & Biezuner, 2000; Sinatra & Pintrich, 2003; C. L. Smith, 2007; Vygotsky, 1978; N. M. Webb & Palincsar, 1996)

Group discussions about academic subject matter have social and motivational benefits as well as cognitive ones. Discussing a topic with classmates can help students acquire more effective interpersonal skills (see Chapter 3). It can also have an energizing effect on students and instill a genuine desire to understand a topic better (Hacker & Bol, 2004; P. K. Murphy & Mason, 2006). Controversial topics can be especially motivating, because students may be eager to resolve conflicting viewpoints, provided that they can effectively do so without alienating their peers (Chinn, 2006). Clearly, then, students have a great deal to gain from conversing with one another regularly about classroom subject matter.

Organizing Knowledge

In the process of constructing knowledge, whether derived individually or socially, learners make many connections among the specific things they experience and learn. In the first years of life, children's knowledge about a topic often involves isolated bits and pieces of information, but as children get older, their knowledge base becomes increasingly organized and integrated (Bjorklund, 1987; Flavell et al., 2002). Here, we'll look at several ways in which learners appear to organize the things they learn: concepts, schemas, scripts, theories, and worldviews.

Concepts

A **concept** is a way of mentally grouping objects or events that are similar in some way. Many concepts (e.g., *dog, run, hot*) are shared by people around the world. Many others (e.g., *quesadilla, burqa, spreadsheet*) are specific to certain cultures. And as noted in our earlier discussion of social constructivism, people in various academic disciplines have developed numerous discipline-specific concepts (e.g., *pi, molecule*) to help them make better sense of the phenomena they study.

Concepts are at the very core of our thinking; some theorists consider them to be our "smallest units of thought" (Ferrari & Elik, 2003, p. 25). If you have already read the discussion of Vygotsky's theory in Chapter 2, you should recall that concepts are important cognitive tools that help people think and act more effectively and efficiently. By combining numerous objects or events into single entities, concepts take

concept Mental grouping of objects or events that have something in common.

some of th ain off the limited capacity of working memory (Oakes & Rakison, 2003; Ormrod 08). For instance, the concept *molecule* takes very little "space" in working mem despite the many things we know about molecules: their very tiny size, their es ial role in the nature of matter, and so on.

Children and adolescents learn thousands of concepts during the school years. They acquire some concepts quickly and easily. They acquire others more gradually and continue to modify them over time. In some cases, children initially **undergeneralize** a concept, having too narrow a view about which objects or events the concept includes. For example, some children might think of an *animal* as something with four legs and fur and are therefore quite surprised when their teacher says that fish, birds, and insects are also animals (S. Carey, 1985). On other occasions, children may **overgeneralize** a concept, inappropriately including objects and events that aren't true members of the category. For instance, when students learn that a *noun* is "a person, place, or thing," some might reasonably conclude that *you* and *me* are nouns, rather than pronouns. Students don't fully understand a concept until they can identify both examples and nonexamples of it with complete accuracy.

undergeneralization Overly narrow view of the objects or events that a concept includes.

overgeneralization Overly broad view of the objects or events that a concept includes.

As Piaget and other developmental researchers have found, children become increasingly able to think about abstract ideas as they get older (see Chapter 2). This developmental trend is reflected in children's concept development, especially as children become more knowledgeable about a topic (J. M. Alexander, Johnson, Scott, & Meyer, 2008; R. M. Gagné, 1985; Liu, Golinkoff, & Sak, 2001). For instance, children may initially think of various family members (e.g., cousins, uncles, etc.) in terms of things they can actually observe (e.g., an *uncle* is any man who is nice and brings presents), rather than in terms of the nature of the relationship (Keil, 1989). Similarly, children may first develop a concrete understanding of a *circle* (i.e., a roundish thing); later, perhaps in a high school geometry class, they may develop an abstract concept of a circle (i.e., all points on a plane equidistant from another single point). Or they may first think of *summer* as a time when it's hot and there's no school; only later do they discover that, to scientists, the seasons are determined by the earth's tilt relative to the sun. As is true for the concepts *circle* and *summer*, formal instruction is one key means through which children acquire abstract understandings of concepts.

An important part of mastering concepts is learning how they are interrelated. For example, in the elementary grades, students learn that a *complete sentence* includes, at a minimum, both a *subject* (including a *noun* or *pronoun*) and a *predicate* (including a *verb* and perhaps also a *direct object*). In a middle school music class, students might learn that a *waltz* is a melody in *three-quarter time*. In some instances, concepts are nested within one another in a hierarchy. For instance, as a child, you learned that *dogs* and *cats* are both *mammals*, that *mammals* and *birds* are both *vertebrates*, and that *vertebrates* and *invertebrates* are both *animals*. The more general, all-encompassing concepts (those near the top of the hierarchy) tend to be relatively abstract, whereas the more specific ones (those near the bottom of the hierarchy) tend to be fairly concrete (Flavell et al., 2002; Rosch, Mervis, Gray, Johnson, & Boyes-Braem, 1976). As children grow older, they become more knowledgeable about such hierarchical relationships (e.g., recall the discussion of *class inclusion* in Chapter 2) (Flavell et al., 2002).

The Into the Classroom feature "Teaching Concepts" offers suggestions for fostering concept learning in a variety of academic disciplines. Given that students may initially acquire an almost-but-not-quite understanding of a concept (e.g., they may undergeneralize or overgeneralize), it's important that we not only describe and illustrate each new concept but also assess students' evolving comprehension of it—for instance, by asking students to identify examples and nonexamples and to generate their own examples. For instance, in Figure 7.2, 8-year-old Noah correctly classifies a butterfly as an insect; notice that he points out its six legs (which all insects must have) but doesn't mention its wings (which some insects *don't* have).

FIGURE 7.2 In his classification of a butterfly as an *insect*, 8-year-old Noah identifies one characteristic that all insects have—six legs—but correctly doesn't mention the wings, which are optional.

INTO THE Classroom

Teaching Concepts

- **Give a definition.**

  A high school geometry teacher defines a *sphere* as "the set of points in three-dimensional space that are equidistant from a single point."

- **Highlight the characteristics that all or most examples of a concept possess.**

  A teacher illustrates the concept *insect* with a line drawing that emphasizes its three body parts, three pairs of legs, and two antennae in bold black lines. The drawing downplays other, irrelevant characteristics that might be visible, such as the insect's color and the presence of wings.

- **Present a best example—a prototype that captures the key elements of the concept.**

  To illustrate the concept *democracy*, a social studies teacher describes a hypothetical, ideal government.

- **Present a wide range of examples.**

  On both a piano and a guitar, a music teacher plays a *primary chord* in several keys.

- **Present nonexamples, especially near misses, to show what the concept is *not*.**

  When a teacher describes what a *mammal* is, he explains why frogs and lizards don't fall into this category.

- **Ask students to identify examples and nonexamples from among numerous possibilities.**

  A language arts teacher gives students a list of sentences and asks them to identify the sentences containing a *dangling participle*.

- **Ask students to generate their own examples of the concept.**

  A teacher asks students to think of examples of *adjectives* they frequently use in their own speech.

- **Show students how various concepts are related to one another—their similarities and differences, their hierarchical relationships, and so on.**

  A science teacher explains that the concepts *velocity* and *acceleration* have somewhat different meanings, even though they both involve speed.

Sources: Best, Dockrell, & Braisby, 2006; Carmichael & Hayes, 2001; R. G. Cook & Smith, 2006; R. M. Gagné, 1985; Ormrod, 2008; Rosch, 1977; B. H. Ross & Spalding, 1994; Tennyson & Cocchiarella, 1986.

Schemas and Scripts

A **schema** is a tightly organized set of facts related to a particular concept or phenomenon; these facts tell us what is likely to be true about the concept or phenomenon (e.g., Rumelhart & Ortony, 1977; Schraw, 2006; D. T. Willingham, 2004).[1] For example, take a moment to consider what you know about horses. You know what horses look like, of course, and you can recognize one when you see one; hence, you have a concept for *horse*. But now think about the many other things you know about horses: What do they eat? How do they spend their time? Where are you most likely to see them? You can probably answer all of these questions quite easily, perhaps identifying horses' fondness for oats and carrots, their love of grazing and running, and their frequent appearance in pastures and at racetracks. The various things you know about horses are closely interconnected in your long-term memory in the form of a horse schema.

People have schemas not only about objects but also about events. When a schema involves a predictable sequence of events related to a particular activity, it is sometimes called a **script**. For example, read the following passage about John.

schema Tightly organized set of facts about a specific topic.

script Schema that involves a predictable sequence of events related to a common activity.

[1]Different theorists have somewhat different conceptions of the term *schema* (and many can be frustratingly vague in their use of the term). Some theorists use the term as a rough equivalent to the term *concept*. Others use the meaning I use here: a set of closely related facts *about* a concept or phenomenon.

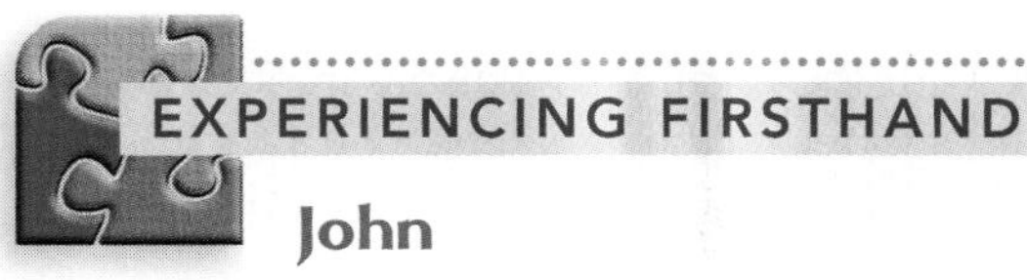

EXPERIENCING FIRSTHAND

John

Read this paragraph *one time only*:

> John was feeling bad today so he decided to go see the family doctor. He checked in with the doctor's receptionist, and then looked through several medical magazines that were on the table by his chair. Finally the nurse came and asked him to take off his clothes. The doctor was very nice to him. He eventually prescribed some pills for John. Then John left the doctor's office and headed home. (Bower, Black, & Turner, 1979, p. 190)

You probably had no trouble understanding the passage because you have been to a doctor's office and have a schema for how those visits usually go. You can therefore fill in a number of details that the passage doesn't tell you. For instance, you probably inferred that John actually *went* to the doctor's office, although the story omits this essential step. Likewise, you probably concluded that John took off his clothes in the examination room, not in the waiting room, even though the story never mentions where John did his striptease. When critical information is missing, as is true in the story about John, schemas and scripts often enable learners to fill in the gaps in a reasonable way.

Many schemas and scripts are unique to particular cultures. The next exercise illustrates this point.

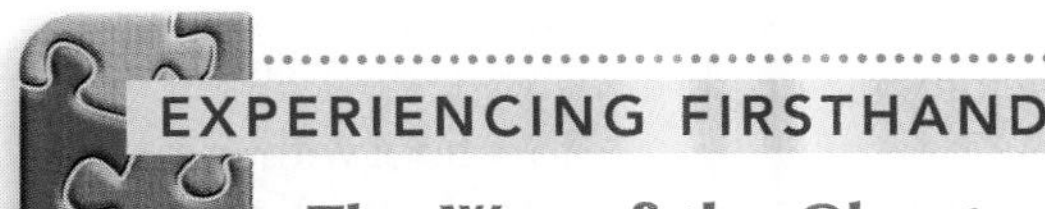

EXPERIENCING FIRSTHAND

The War of the Ghosts

Read the following story *one time only*:

> One night two young men from Egulac went down to the river to hunt seals, and while they were there it became foggy and calm. Then they heard war-cries, and they thought, "Maybe this is a war-party." They escaped to the shore, and hid behind a log. Now canoes came up, and they heard the noise of paddles, and saw one canoe coming up to them. There were five men in the canoe, and they said:
>
> "What do you think? We wish to take you along. We are going up the river to make war on the people."
>
> One of the young men said: "I have no arrows."
>
> "Arrows are in the canoe," they said.
>
> "I will not go along. I might be killed. My relatives do not know where I have gone. But you," he said, turning to the other, "may go with them."
>
> So one of the young men went, but the other returned home.
>
> And the warriors went on up the river to a town on the other side of Kalama. The people came down to the water, and they began to fight, and many were killed. But presently the young man heard one of the warriors say, "Quick, let us go home: that Indian has been hit." Now he thought: "Oh, they are ghosts." He did not feel sick, but they said he had been shot.
>
> So the canoes went back to Egulac, and the young man went ashore to his house, and made a fire. And he told everybody and said, "Behold I accompanied the ghosts, and we went to fight. Many of our fellows were killed, and many of those who attacked us were killed. They said I was hit, and I did not feel sick."
>
> He told it all, and then he became quiet. When the sun rose he fell down. Something black came out of his mouth. His face became contorted. The people jumped up and cried.
>
> He was dead. (Bartlett, F.C. *Remembering: A Study in Experimental and Social Psychology*. 1932, p 65. Cambridge, England: Cambridge University Press. Reprinted with the permission of Cambridge University Press.

Now cover the story, and write down as much of it as you can remember.

theory Integrated set of concepts and principles developed to explain a particular phenomenon.

Compare your own rendition of the story with the original. What differences do you notice? Your version is almost certainly the shorter of the two, and you probably left out many details. But did you also find yourself distorting certain parts of the story so that it made more sense to you?

As a Native American ghost story, "The War of the Ghosts" may be inconsistent with some of the schemas and scripts you've acquired, especially if you were raised in a non-Native American culture. In an early study of long-term memory (F. C. Bartlett, 1932), students at England's Cambridge University were asked to read the story twice and then to recall it at various times later on. Students' recollections of the story often included additions and distortions that made the story more consistent with English culture. For example, people in England rarely go "to the river to hunt seals" because seals are saltwater animals and most rivers have fresh water. Students might therefore say that the men went to the river to *fish*. Similarly, the ghostly element of the story did not fit comfortably with the religious beliefs of most Cambridge students and so was often modified. When one student was asked to recall the story six months after he had read it, he provided the following account:

> Four men came down to the water. They were told to get into a boat and to take arms with them. They inquired, "What arms?" and were answered "Arms for battle." When they came to the battle-field they heard a great noise and shouting, and a voice said: "The black man is dead." And he was brought to the place where they were, and laid on the ground. And he foamed at the mouth. (F. C. Bartlett, 1932, pp. 71–72)

Notice how the student's version of the story leaves out many of its more puzzling aspects—puzzling, at least, from his own cultural perspective.

Students from diverse cultural backgrounds typically come to school with somewhat different schemas and scripts (e.g., Lipson, 1983; R. E. Reynolds et al., 1982; Steffensen, Joag-Dev, & Anderson, 1979). As a result, they may interpret the same classroom materials or activities differently and, in some cases, may have trouble making sense of a particular lesson or reading assignment. As teachers, we need to find out whether students have the appropriate schemas and scripts to understand the subject matter we are teaching. When our students don't have such knowledge, we may sometimes need to back up and help them develop it before we forge ahead with new material.

Determine whether students have appropriate schemas and scripts to understand the topic at hand.

Theories

On a much larger scale, human beings—young children included—construct general understandings and belief systems, or **theories**, about various aspects of the world. People's theories include many concepts and the relationships among them (e.g., correlation, cause-and-effect). To see what some of your own theories are like, try the next exercise.

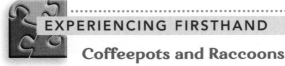

EXPERIENCING FIRSTHAND

Coffeepots and Raccoons

Consider each of the following situations:

A

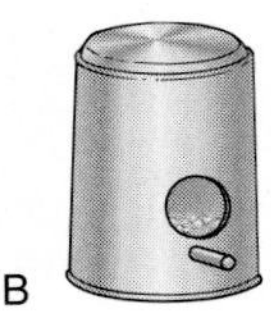

B

1. People took a coffeepot that looked like Drawing A. They removed the handle, sealed the top, took off the top knob, sealed the opening to the spout, and removed the spout. They also sliced off the base and attached a flat piece of metal. They attached a little stick, cut a window in the side, and filled the metal container with birdseed. When they were done, it looked like Drawing B. After these changes, was this a coffeepot or a bird feeder?
2. Doctors took the raccoon in Drawing C and shaved away some of its fur. They dyed what was left black. Then they bleached a single stripe all white down the

center of the animal's back. Then, with surgery, they put in its body a sac of super smelly odor, such as a skunk has. After they were all done, the animal looked like Drawing D. After the operation, was this a skunk or a raccoon?

Source: Both scenarios based on Keil, 1989, p. 184.

Chances are, you concluded that the coffeepot was transformed into a bird feeder but that the raccoon was still a raccoon despite its cosmetic makeover and major surgery. Even fourth graders come to these conclusions (Keil, 1986, 1989). How is it possible that the coffeepot could be made into something entirely different, whereas the raccoon could not?

Long before children reach school age, they begin to construct their own theories about various aspects of their physical, biological, psychological, and social worlds (Delval, 1994; S. A. Gelman, 2003; Inagaki & Hatano, 2006). Usually inherent in their theories is a basic distinction between human-made objects (e.g., coffeepots, bird feeders) and biological entities (e.g., raccoons, skunks). By age 8 or 9, children seem to conceptualize the two categories in fundamentally different ways: Human-made objects are defined largely by the functions they serve (e.g., brewing coffee, feeding birds), whereas biological entities are defined primarily by their origins (e.g., the parents who brought them into being, their DNA). Thus, when a coffeepot begins to hold birdseed rather than coffee, it becomes a bird feeder because its function has changed. But when a raccoon is cosmetically and surgically altered to look and smell like a skunk, it still has raccoon parents and raccoon DNA and so cannot possibly *be* a skunk (Keil, 1987, 1989). Thinking along similar lines, even preschoolers will tell you that you can't change a yellow finch into a bluebird by giving it a coat of blue paint or dressing it in a bluebird costume (Keil, 1989).

Students' theories about the world help them organize and make sense of personal experiences, classroom subject matter, and other new information (Reiner, Slotta, Chi, & Resnick, 2000; Wellman & Gelman, 1998). Their theories also seem to guide them in their efforts to master new concepts (S. A. Gelman & Kalish, 2006; Keil, 1987). For example, if you were trying to learn what a *horse* is, knowing that it's an animal would lead you to conclude that its location (stable, pasture, shopping mall, or whatever) is irrelevant. In contrast, if you were trying to learn what the *equator* is, knowing that it's something on a world map should lead you to suspect that location is of the utmost importance.

By and large, children's early, home-grown theories seem to emerge with little or no guidance from more knowledgeable individuals—hence, they are sometimes called *naive theories.* On many occasions these theories provide a good foundation on which formal instruction in science and other disciplines can build. But sometimes they include erroneous beliefs that can seriously impede new learning (more about this point later in the chapter).

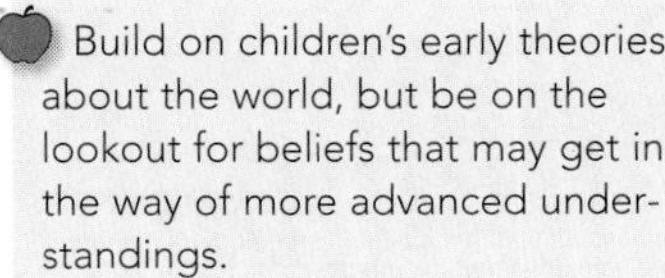
Build on children's early theories about the world, but be on the lookout for beliefs that may get in the way of more advanced understandings.

Learners' theories tend to be specific to particular domains; for instance, they may be related to the origins of living beings or the nature of human thinking (recall the discussion of *theory of mind* in Chapter 3). In contrast, learners' *worldviews* influence their meaning-making in a great many domains.

Worldviews

A **worldview** is a general set of beliefs and assumptions about reality—how things are and should be—that influences a learner's understanding of a wide variety of phenomena (Koltko-Rivera, 2004). The following are examples of assumptions that a worldview might encompass:

worldview General, culturally based set of assumptions about reality that influence understandings of a wide variety of phenomena.

- Life and the universe came into being through random acts of nature *or* as part of a divine plan and purpose.

- Human beings are at the mercy of the forces of nature *or* should strive to master the forces of nature *or* must learn to live in harmony with nature.
- People's successes and failures in life are the result of their own actions *or* divine intervention *or* fate *or* random occurrences.
- People are most likely to enhance their well-being by relying on scientific principles and logical reasoning processes *or* by seeking guidance from authority figures. (Kelemen, 2004; Koltko-Rivera, 2004; Losh, 2003; Medin, 2005)

To a considerable degree, such beliefs and assumptions are culturally transmitted, with different cultures communicating somewhat different beliefs and assumptions through adults' day-to-day interactions with children (see Chapter 4).

Worldviews are often such an integral part of everyday thinking that learners take them for granted and usually aren't consciously aware of them. In many cases, then, worldviews encompass *implicit*, rather than explicit, knowledge. Nevertheless, they influence learners' interpretations of current events and classroom subject matter. For instance, students might interpret a hurricane not as the unfortunate result of natural meteorological forces but instead as divine punishment for their own or other people's wrongdoings (O. Lee, 1999; see Chapter 4). And students might struggle with a science curriculum that explores how human beings can manipulate and gain control over natural events because their culture consistently emphasizes the importance of accepting and living in harmony with nature as it is (Atran et al., 2005; Medin, 2005; again see Chapter 4).

Promoting Effective Knowledge Construction

Knowing that learning involves constructive processes does not, in and of itself, inform us about how we can most effectively *promote* such processes (e.g., K. R. Harris & Alexander, 1998; Mayer, 2004; Nuthall, 1996). In the following sections, we'll explore several approaches that contemporary psychologists and educators have identified for helping students construct richer and more sophisticated knowledge bases.

Providing Opportunities for Firsthand Observation and Experimentation

Provide opportunities for students to observe and experiment firsthand with certain physical and biological phenomena.

By observing, interacting, and experimenting with the things around them, students can discover many characteristics and principles of the world on their own (Fosnot, 1996; Minogue & Jones, 2006; Moreno, 2006). For example, in one study, kindergarten students had one of two different experiences raising animals (Hatano & Inagaki, 1993). Some students had pet rabbits in their classrooms; they took turns feeding and caring for the rabbits using procedures their teacher had carefully prescribed for them. Other students cared for goldfish at home; these students had to make their own decisions and, in doing so, could experiment with feeding schedules, water purity, and other variables that might affect the fish's welfare. The children with the goldfish at home appeared to develop a better understanding of animals in general and were able to apply to other species what they learned with their own pets. When asked whether one could keep a baby frog the same size forever, one goldfish owner said, "No, we can't, because the frog will grow bigger as the goldfish grew bigger. My goldfish were small before, but now they are big" (Hatano & Inagaki, 1993, p. 121).

Presenting Experts' Perspectives

Although it may sometimes be beneficial to have students discover basic principles for themselves (as the goldfish owners did), we should also present experts' views—the concepts, principles, theories, and so on that society has developed to explain the physical and psychological aspects of human experience (R. Driver, 1995; Sweller,

Kirschner, & Clark, 2007; Vygotsky, 1934/1986). Students are most likely to construct a productive view of the world when they have the benefit of experiencing the world firsthand *and* the benefit of learning how experts have come to interpret human experience. For example, children can learn a great deal about various biological species and fragile ecosystems—and are likely to acquire positive attitudes toward science—when firsthand observations in class or on field trips are accompanied by scientific explanations of the phenomena at hand (e.g., Patrick, Mantzicopoulos, & Samarapungavan, 2009; Zaragoza & Fraser, 2008).

Expose students to the ways in which experts interpret various phenomena and events.

We need not present others' ideas in a didactic, this-is-how-it-is manner, however. Through asking appropriate questions and providing hints and suggestions, we can sometimes lead students to derive appropriate interpretations of objects and events by themselves. Teacher Katherine Maria took this approach in a series of discussions with 6½-year-old Jennifer about the nature of gravity. Katherine had been trying to help Jennifer understand that people and objects in the Southern Hemisphere don't fall off the earth just because, from the standpoint of someone looking at a globe, they are located on the earth's "bottom" side. Katherine reported the following interaction between Jennifer (J) and herself (K) to show the progress Jennifer was making in her understanding of gravity:

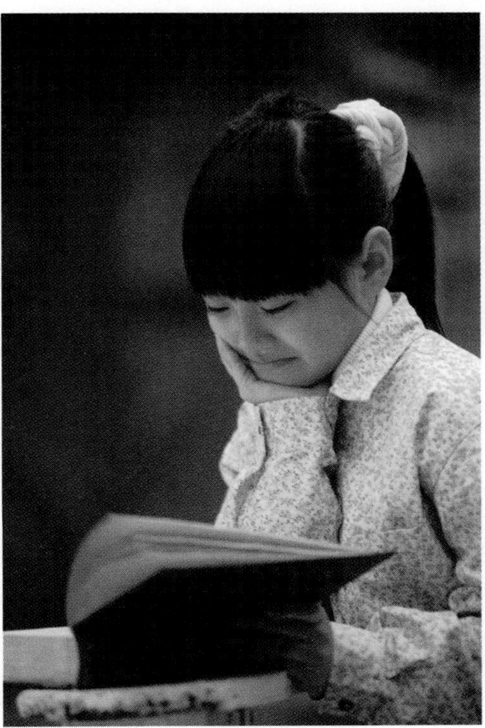

Students can more effectively construct meaningful interpretations of events when they consider how others have interpreted similar events. For example, children's literature offers a variety of perspectives on human perceptions, personalities, motives, and behaviors.

> I used [an] inflatable globe and a figure stuck to the lower part of South America to explain to Jennifer that I had visited this place and had not fallen off the earth. We then had [this] discussion: . . .
>
> *K:* What would happen if there was a hole in the earth and this person (the figure stuck to South America) dropped a ball through it?
> *J:* People might think that if you dropped a rock into the hole it might go back out.
> *K:* Why would they think that?
> *J:* Because it's at the bottom of the earth. . . . They think that maybe the gravity did that.
> *K:* But what does gravity pull you toward?
> *J:* Down.
> *K:* (sticking the figure on the top of the inflatable globe): If you're standing here, where is down?
>
> Jennifer points her finger in a downward direction. I move the figure to the South Pole.
>
> *K:* But suppose this was you. If you were here, where is down?
>
> Jennifer points to a spot in the middle of the globe.
>
> *K:* Yeah, so it's pulling toward the?
> *J:* Middle.
> *K:* Right. So where would the rock end up then?
> *J:* In the middle. (Maria, 1998, p. 13)

Emphasizing Conceptual Understanding

Let's look again at the opening case study. Rita has acquired a few tidbits about American history but has apparently learned them as separate, isolated facts and doesn't pull them together until an adult asks her to explain what she has learned. Unfortunately, such learning of isolated facts, without any sense of how they fit together, is all too common at both the elementary and secondary grade levels (e.g., Hollon, Roth, & Anderson, 1991; Lesgold, 2001; Paxton, 1999).

Ideally, students should instead gain a **conceptual understanding** of classroom topics; that is, they should form many logical connections among related concepts and principles. For example, rather than simply memorize basic mathematical computation procedures, students should learn how those procedures reflect underlying principles

conceptual understanding Meaningfully learned and well-integrated knowledge about a topic, including many logical connections among specific concepts and ideas.

Help students learn classroom subject matter as well-integrated bodies of knowledge that include many cause-and-effect relationships.

of mathematics. And rather than learn historical facts as a list of unrelated people, places, and dates, students should place those facts within the context of major social and religious trends, migration patterns, economic considerations, human personality characteristics, and so on. The more interrelationships students form within the subject matter they are learning—in other words, the better they *organize* it—the more easily they will be able to remember and apply it later on (L. M. Anderson, 1993; Bédard & Chi, 1992; J. J. White & Rumsey, 1994).

Constructing an integrated understanding of any complex topic inevitably takes time. Accordingly, many educators advocate the principle *Less is more:* Less material studied thoroughly (rather than superficially) is learned more completely and with greater understanding (e.g., Sizer, 1992, 2004). Following are several more specific strategies for promoting conceptual understanding of classroom subject matter:

- Organize units around a few core ideas or issues, always relating specific content back to this core.
- Explore each topic in depth—for example, by considering many examples, examining cause-and-effect relationships, and discovering how specific details relate to more general principles.
- Explain how new ideas relate to students' personal experiences and to things students have previously learned at school.
- Show students—through the statements made, the questions asked, the assignments given, and the criteria used to evaluate achievement—that conceptual understanding of classroom subject matter is far more important than knowledge of isolated facts.
- Ask students to teach what they have learned to others. Teaching others encourages them to focus on and pull together main ideas in a way that makes sense. (L. M. Anderson, 1993; Brophy, 2004; Brophy & Alleman, 1992; Hatano & Inagaki, 1993; Middleton & Midgley, 2002; Perkins & Ritchhart, 2004; Prawat, 1993; Roscoe & Chi, 2007; VanSledright & Brophy, 1992; J. J. White & Rumsey, 1994)

Encouraging Classroom Dialogue

Regularly engage students in small-group or whole-class discussions that encourage them to exchange views and build on one another's ideas.

We have already identified numerous advantages to having students talk with one another about classroom topics. In general, students remember new ideas and experiences more effectively and accurately when they talk about these things with others (Hacker, 1998; Schank & Abelson, 1995; Tessler & Nelson, 1994; Wasik, Karweit, Burns, & Brodsky, 1998). Accordingly, many contemporary theorists recommend that student discussions be a regular feature of classroom instruction. For example, in the "*The Scarlet Letter*" video clip in MyEducationLab, you can see how a high school English teacher encourages students to construct a more thorough understanding of the character Arthur Dimmesdale in Nathaniel Hawthorne's *The Scarlet Letter*. After reading a paragraph describing Dimmesdale, she tells her students:

> In your logs, jot down some of the important characteristics of that description. What's the diction that strikes you as being essential to understanding Dimmesdale's character? How do you see him? If you were going to draw a portrait of him, what would you make sure he had? Just write some things, or draw a picture if you'd like.

She then solicits diverse opinions ("well-dressed," "unsure of himself," "sweating really bad," "a nerd-type guy") that can help students jointly and individually construct a complex, multifaceted conception of Dimmesdale.

myeducationlab

Observe a teacher encourage knowledge construction in the video "Discussion of *The Scarlet Letter*." (To find this video, go to Chapter 7 of the Book-Specific Resources in MyEducationLab, select *Video Examples*, and then click on the title.)

Assigning Authentic Activities

Some contemporary cognitive theorists suggest that students can construct a more integrated and useful knowledge base if they learn classroom subject matter within the context of **authentic activities**, which are similar to those they might encounter in the outside world. For example, students' writing skills may show greater improvement in both quality and quantity when, instead of completing traditional workbook writing exercises, they write stories, essays, and letters to real people (E. H. Hiebert & Fisher, 1992). Students gain a more complete understanding of how to use and interpret maps when, instead of answering workbook questions about maps, they construct their *own* maps (Gregg & Leinhardt, 1994). And students are more likely to check their solutions to mathematics problems—in particular, to make sure their solutions make logical sense—when they use math for real-life tasks (Cognition and Technology Group at Vanderbilt, 1993; Rogoff, 2003).

Authentic activities can also be highly motivating for students (M. Barnett, 2005; Marks, 2000). As an example, consider one high school student's recollection of a ninth-grade moon-tracking activity:

> It was the first time I can remember in school doing something that wasn't in the textbook . . . like we were real scientists or something. We had to keep data sheets, measure the time and angle of the moonrise every day for a month. It drove my mom nuts because sometimes we'd be eating dinner, and I'd look at my watch and race out the door! We had to measure the river near us to see how it was affected by the moon. . . . I went down to the river more than I have in my whole life, I think. Then we had to do the calculations, that was another step, and we had to chart our findings. The test was to analyze your findings and tell what they meant about the relationship of the tides and the moon. . . . I felt that I did something real, and I could see the benefit of it. (Wasley, Hampel, & Clark, 1997, pp. 117–118)

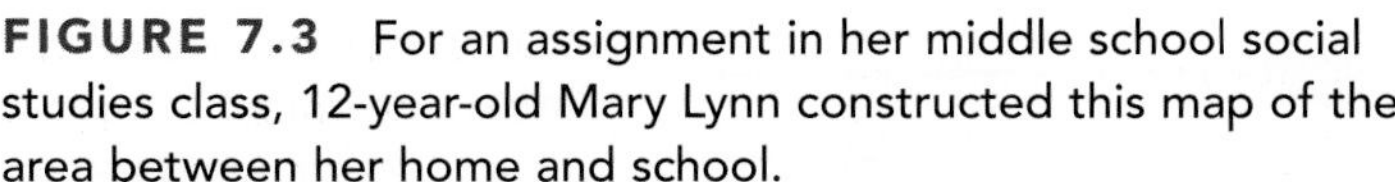

FIGURE 7.3 For an assignment in her middle school social studies class, 12-year-old Mary Lynn constructed this map of the area between her home and school.

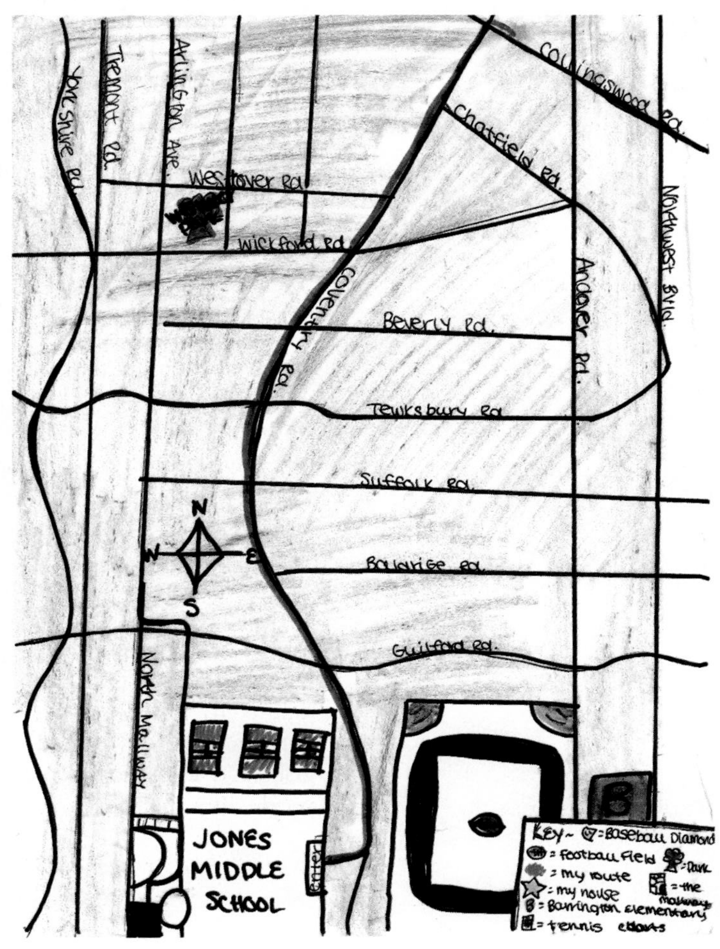

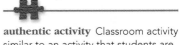

Incorporate classroom subject matter into real-world tasks.

Authentic activities can be developed for virtually any area of the curriculum. For example, we might ask students to do the following:

- Write an editorial
- Participate in a debate
- Design an electrical circuit
- Conduct an experiment
- Construct a map (e.g., see Figure 7.3)
- Perform in a concert
- Plan a family budget
- Converse in a foreign language
- Make a videotape
- Develop an Internet home page

In some instances, authentic activities take the form of **problem-based learning** or **project-based learning**, in which students acquire new knowledge and skills as they work on complex problems or projects similar to those they might find in the outside world (Hmelo-Silver, 2004, 2006; Krajcik & Blumenfeld, 2006; Polman, 2004). On occa-

authentic activity Classroom activity similar to an activity that students are apt to encounter in the outside world.

problem-based learning Classroom activity in which students acquire new knowledge and skills while working on a complex problem similar to one that might exist in the outside world.

project-based learning Classroom activity in which students acquire new knowledge and skills while working on a complex, multifaceted project that yields a concrete end product.

service learning Activity that promotes learning and development through contributing to the betterment of others and the outside community.

sion, authentic activities may also involve **service learning**—that is, projects that directly or indirectly enhance the quality of life in the outside community. To be effective in enhancing students' learning—and to be sources of pleasure and success rather than sources of frustration and failure—most complex authentic activities require considerable teacher guidance and support (Hmelo-Silver, Duncan, & Chinn, 2007; Mergendoller, Markham, Ravitz, & Larmer, 2006).

By placing classroom activities in real-world contexts, we help students discover the reasons that they are learning academic subject matter; accordingly, authentic activities may be especially valuable in working with students who are at risk for academic failure (see Chapter 4). Authentic activities also increase the likelihood that, later on, students will actually use the information and skills we have taught them (S. M. Barnett & Ceci, 2002; A. Collins et al., 1989; De Corte et al., 1996). An authentic activity is possibly most beneficial when it promotes complex thinking skills—for instance, synthesizing information, forming and testing hypotheses, or solving problems—and when its final outcome is multifaceted and somewhat unpredictable (Newmann & Wehlage, 1993; Paris & Turner, 1994). The Into the Classroom feature "Conducting Authentic Activities" offers several strategies that researchers and experienced educators have found to be effective.

Scaffolding Theory Construction

As we've seen, children begin forming theories about various aspects of their world long before they start school. Over time, as they gain knowledge and experience both in and out of school, they continue to expand on and revise these theories (e.g., D. B. Clark, 2006; Dixon & Kelley, 2007). One important goal of any academic curriculum is to guide students' theory development to be consistent with theories that experts have developed over decades or centuries of systematic research. Psychologists and educators have offered several suggestions for helping students construct productive theories:

Encourage and answer students' why and how questions. Young children ask many why and how questions: Why is the sky blue? How does a telephone call know which house to go to? Such questions often pop up in conversations with teachers and other adults. Although we might occasionally find these questions bothersome, they typically reflect children's genuine desire to make sense of their world and enhance their theories about what causes what and why things are the way they are (Elkind, 1987; Kemler Nelson, Egan, & Holt, 2004).

Ask students to make predictions about what will happen in classroom experiments. Especially in the science curriculum, experiments and demonstrations with concrete objects are often useful in illustrating important concepts and principles. Asking students to make predictions beforehand can activate their existing beliefs and misbeliefs relative to the topic at hand (A. L. Brown & Campione, 1994; diSessa & Minstrell, 1998). For example, in a physics lesson, we might give students a clay ball attached to a long metal spring and ask them to make a prediction:

> You hold the other end of the spring and put half of the clay ball into water. Will the spring (a) become shorter, (b) become longer, or (c) retain its length? (Hatano & Inagaki, 1991, p. 337)

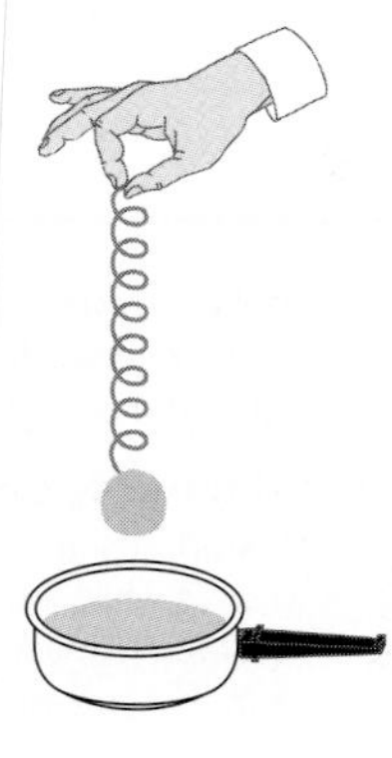

When the clay ball is partially immersed in water, will the spring change in length? If so, will it become shorter or longer?

Before immersing the clay halfway in water, students are apt to think about the problem in a variety of ways, as illustrated in the following examples:

- The water has the power to make things float. Therefore, I think the water will make the clay ball float to some extent.
- [The spring will be longer] because the water will be absorbed into the tiny particles which the clay ball consists of.
- The water has the power to make completely immersed things float, but not if they are only half immersed. (Hatano & Inagaki, 1991, pp. 337–338)

INTO THE Classroom

Conducting Authentic Activities

Simplify the task sufficiently for the age-group.

At a school in Seattle, Washington, students in kindergarten and the first and second grades work cooperatively with researchers to monitor dog "poop" along a nature trail in an important watershed area. Once every two months, the students and several adult volunteers count and map the various dog deposits they find on the trail and within seven feet to either side. Midway through the school year, the students place plastic-bag dispensers at various locations near the trail and continue their bimonthly monitoring in order to determine whether the dispensers and bags have any effect. Not only do the students gain an awareness of the harmful effects of pollution on natural resources, but they also gain confidence in their ability to have a positive impact on the health of their local environment.

Choose a task that requires students to integrate and apply what they've learned in two or more subject areas.

A third-grade class creates a "publishing company" that provides various printed materials (announcements, programs, banners, etc.) for activities and performances throughout their school. Students engage in many typical business activities; for instance, they interview for various jobs in the company, make sales calls to solicit business from other classes, design customer order forms, edit and proofread their work, and conduct customer satisfaction surveys.

Communicate that there is no single best or right approach or solution for a task.

A teacher of a high school life skills class gives students a list of prices of many items (meats, fruits, vegetables, milk, etc.) available at the local grocery store. Using the list, the food pyramid, and a budget of 30 dollars, students must plan a healthful breakfast, lunch, and dinner for a family of four.

Encourage students to experiment with new ideas and strategies.

A fifth-grade class has been studying a number of common plants and animals indigenous to their area. The students work in groups of two or three to create informational displays about several species for the city museum. Their teacher helps each group brainstorm ideas about how it might effectively portray a particular plant or animal for the general public.

Communicate high expectations for students' performance, but provide enough scaffolding to ensure students' success.

All 92 eighth graders at a middle school are required to contribute in a meaningful way to the annual eighth-grade musical. Some students are members of the cast, whereas others are involved in scenery construction, costume design, or lighting. Faculty members supervise each aspect of the project and provide guidance and assistance as needed, but the students are largely responsible for the quality of the production. As students from different social groups work with one another, social barriers and ill feelings between popular and unpopular students begin to break down. By opening night, the class has acquired a sense of cohesiveness and overall class spirit, and collectively, the students take much pride in their successful production.

Sources: Edelson & Reiser, 2006; Hmelo-Silver, Duncan, & Chinn, 2007; Kornhaber, Fierros, & Veenema, 2004 (publishing business example); Mergendoller, Markham, Ravitz, & Larmer, 2006; Newmann & Wehlage, 1993; Paris & Turner, 1994; Pickens, 2006 (dog poop example); M. Thompson & Grace, 2001 (class play example).

Clay is denser than water and so would completely sink if it were not held up by the spring. Yet the first response has some truth in it, because the water should offer more resistance than air would (thus, it would push the ball up more), making the spring shorter. The second and third responses reveal misunderstandings—that the clay would soak up some of the water and that half-immersion has no effect—which would warrant discussion and reconsideration.

Use analogies that help students relate new concepts and ideas to their prior knowledge. Especially when students cannot actually see particular concepts in action, analogies with familiar phenomena can help them in their theory construction (Clement, 1991; Mayer, 1999). For example, we might draw an analogy between *peristalsis*—the muscular contractions that gradually push food through the digestive tract—and the process of squeezing ketchup from a packet:

> You squeeze the packet near one corner and run your fingers along the length of the packet toward an opening at the other corner. When you do this, you push the ketchup through the packet, in one direction, ahead of your fingers, until it comes out of the opening. (Newby, Ertmer, & Stepich, 1994, p. 4)

FIGURE 7.4 In this picture 9-year-old Trisha integrates what she has learned about the water cycle.

Present physical or symbolic models that encapsulate key features of an entity or phenomenon. Providing a **model**—a concrete representation of a phenomenon that depicts its key components and their interrelationships—can often help students conceptualize a phenomenon as experts do (Glynn, Yeany, & Britton, 1991; C. V. Schwarz & White, 2005). For example, in your own schooling, you have undoubtedly seen models of the solar system that consist of a sun and eight or nine planets at various distances from it. The models are never to scale, as the distances between the various bodies are, relatively speaking, much smaller than they are in reality. Regardless, seeing a model can help you conceptualize how the sun and planets are organized and move in space. *Physical models* such as these involve tangible objects—a sun and planets, components of a molecule, parts of an eye, and so on. In contrast, *symbolic models*, such as diagrams and flowcharts, are graphic representations on paper or a computer. You can find examples in this book in Figure 2.2 (a model of neurons and their interconnections) and Figure 6.1 (a model of the human memory system).

Choose explanations that are compatible with students' level of cognitive development. Many widely accepted theories are quite abstract—probably too abstract for children, young adolescents, and many older adolescents to fully understand. In such instances, relatively concrete explanations, even if they aren't completely in line with contemporary scientific views, can sometimes help students make accurate predictions in practical situations (D. B. Clark, 2006; M. C. Linn & Muilenburg, 1996; M. C. Linn, Songer, & Eylon, 1996). For example, let's consider how heat is transmitted from one thing to another. A physicist would tell us that heat and its transference from one object to another are a function of how quickly atoms move and how much they collide with one another. A more concrete explanation is simply that heat "flows" from one thing to another. Although this explanation wouldn't pass muster in a college physics class, it can certainly help middle school students understand why it's important to use potholders when grabbing a pot of boiling water (M. C. Linn & Muilenburg, 1996).

Ask students to reflect on and interrelate the things they have learned. On average, students more effectively remember and apply newly acquired theories when they represent the relevant concepts and interrelationships on paper—for instance, by drawing pictures or diagrams or by explaining in lab reports or journal entries what they've observed (Edens & Potter, 2001; P. D. Klein, 2000). In Figure 7.4, 9-year-old Trisha pulls together what she has learned in a lesson about the water cycle.

Creating a Community of Learners

With the benefits of dialogue and other forms of student interaction in mind and with a goal of promoting the social construction of meaning, some psychologists and educators suggest that we create a **community of learners**, a class in which teachers and students collaborate to build a body of knowledge about a topic and help one another learn about it (A. L. Brown & Campione, 1994, 1996; A. Collins, 2006; R. A. Engle & Conant, 2002). A class that operates as a community of learners is likely to have characteristics such as these:

model A physical or symbolic representation of a phenomenon that depicts its key components and important interrelationships.

community of learners Class in which teachers and students actively and collaboratively work to create a body of knowledge and help one another learn.

- All students are active participants in classroom activities.
- The primary goal is to acquire a body of knowledge on a specific topic, with students contributing to and building on one another's efforts.
- Students draw on many resources—textbooks, magazines, the Internet, and one another—in their efforts to learn about the topic.
- Discussion and collaboration among two or more students occur regularly and play a key role in learning.
- Diversity in students' interests and rates of progress is expected and respected.
- Students and teacher coordinate their efforts in helping one another learn; no one has exclusive responsibility for teaching others.
- Everyone is a potential resource for others; different individuals are likely to serve as resources on different occasions, depending on the topics and tasks at hand. In some cases, students "major" in a particular topic and become local "experts" on it. Occasionally, people outside the classroom share their expertise as well.
- The teacher provides some guidance and direction for classroom activities, but students also contribute guidance and direction.
- Mechanisms are in place through which students can share what they've learned with others; students regularly critique one another's work.
- The process of learning is emphasized as much as, and sometimes more than, the finished product. (Bielaczyc & Collins, 1999; A. L. Brown & Campione, 1994, 1996; Campione, Shapiro, & Brown, 1995; Rogoff, 1994, 2003; Rogoff, Matusov, & White, 1996; Scardamalia & Bereiter, 2006)

Create a community atmosphere in which peer collaboration and mutual support are integral parts of classroom learning and achievement.

In one example of how a community of learners can be structured (A. L. Brown & Campione, 1994), students are divided into small groups to study different subtopics falling under a general theme; for instance, subtopics for the theme *changing populations* might be *extinct, endangered, artificial, assisted,* and *urbanized.* Each group conducts research and prepares teaching materials related to its subtopic. The class then reassembles into new groups that include at least one representative from each of the previous groups. Within these new groups, the students teach one another the things they have learned.

Another approach is to use a computer network to promote a community of learners (Bereiter & Scardamalia, 2006; Hewitt & Scardamalia, 1998; G. Stahl, Koschmann, & Suthers, 2006). In this electronic environment, students post their work (notes, short stories, reports, problem solutions, diagrams and flowcharts depicting scientific phenomena, etc.) as computer files that their classmates can read, react to, and possibly modify or build on. Students also interact in an ongoing computer-based chat room, in which they present questions or issues to which their classmates respond. In the following online discussion, consider how three students respond to another student's question: "How does heat affect solids?" Note that they use the headings "My theory" and "I need to understand" to structure their discussion:

JA: **My theory:** I think that heat makes solids burn or melt. I think that my prediction is right because I've seen solids melt and burn.

AR: **My theory:** I think that if a solid comes in contact with heat, it becomes hot. I also think it might change colour. Generally if any solid comes in contact with heat then it becomes hot. I think that the solid would become hot faster if it could conduct energy well. If an object didn't conduct energy well then it would heat up, but take a longer time than an object that conducts energy well. It might change colour because we think that if something is very hot it is white or red and sort of hot it is orange or yellow. There might be some truth to this.

AD: **My theory:** I think that it depends on how much heat there is. I also think that it depends on what sort of solid it is. For instance, the heat that might melt rubber might not melt metal. (This last sentence might be wrong, I'm just using it as an example.)

I need to understand: What makes wood burn instead of melt?

My theory: I think that it might have something to do with wood being organic, because I can't think of anything that is organic, and would melt. (Hewitt & Scardamalia, 1998, p. 85)

Such online discussions may be especially valuable for students who are shy or otherwise feel uncomfortable communicating with their classmates in a more public fashion (Hewitt & Scardamalia, 1998).

Working in communities of learners can give students a sense of the approach scientists and other scholars take to advance the frontiers of knowledge: They conduct individual and collaborative research, share ideas, build on one another's findings, and so on. And in fact, participating in such communities appears to promote fairly complex thinking and knowledge-building processes, often for extended periods (A. L. Brown & Campione, 1994, 1996; R. A. Engle, 2006; R. A. Engle & Conant, 2002; Scardamalia & Bereiter, 2006). Participating in a community of learners is also highly motivating for students, who often insist on going to school even when they are ill and are disappointed when summer vacation begins (Rogoff, 1994; Turkanis, 2001).

In addition to the cognitive and motivational benefits, working in a community of learners can foster effective peer relationships and social skills. It can also help create a sense of community in the classroom—a sense that teachers and students have shared goals, are mutually respectful and supportive of one another's efforts, and believe that everyone makes an important contribution to classroom learning.

However, we should note two potential weaknesses of communities of learners, as well as of group discussions more generally (A. L. Brown & Campione, 1994; Hynd, 1998b). For one thing, what students learn will inevitably be limited to the knowledge that they acquire and share with one another. In addition, students may occasionally pass on their own misconceptions to their classmates. Obviously, then, when we conduct classroom discussions or structure our classrooms as communities of learners, we must carefully monitor student interactions to make sure that students ultimately acquire thorough and accurate understandings of the subject matter they are studying.

When Knowledge Construction Goes Awry: Addressing Learners' Misconceptions

When learners construct their own understandings, there is, of course, no guarantee that they will construct accurate ones. Recall how, in the opening case study, Rita thinks that the British wanted to go to China to get furs and that they moved to the Upper Peninsula after the English arrived. Also, consider how 7-year-old Rob thinks mountains are formed:

Interviewer: How were the mountains made?

Rob: Some dirt was taken from outside and it was put on the mountain and then mountains were made with it.

Interviewer: Who did that?

Rob: It takes a lot of men to make mountains, there must have been at least four. They gave them the dirt and then they made themselves all alone.

Interviewer: But if they wanted to make another mountain?

Rob: They pull one mountain down and then they could make a prettier one. (Piaget, 1929, p. 348)

A **misconception** is a belief that is inconsistent with commonly accepted and well-validated explanations of phenomena or events. In science, for example, students' misconceptions might be at odds with data collected over the course of decades or centuries of scientific research. In history, students' understandings of certain events might be inconsistent with existing historical records and artifacts from the time period in question.

Research tells us that children and adolescents have a variety of misconceptions about the world around them. Table 7.1 presents common misconceptions that researchers have observed at various grade levels. Even well-educated adults are apt to have misconceptions about certain topics, as you probably learned firsthand when you took the OOPS test in Chapter 1.

Students' misconceptions probably have a variety of origins. In many instances, they arise out of students' own well-intended efforts to make sense of what they see (Vosniadou, 2003). Consider one teacher's anecdote about a young boy's interpretation of evaporating water in his class's fish tank:

> Wesley . . . recounted to me that they had to put water in the tank almost every week, and I had asked him where he thought that water went. Wesley had answered, "Into the rocks." (Hawkins, 1997, p. 337)

Like Wesley, students sometimes draw erroneous conclusions from how things *appear* to be (D. B. Clark, 2006; Duit, 1991; Reiner et al., 2000). For example, they may occasionally infer incorrect cause-and-effect relationships between two objects or events simply because the two things occur at the same time—thus confusing correlation with causation (Keil, 1991; Kuhn, 2001b).

Society and culture can foster misconceptions as well. Sometimes common expressions in language misrepresent the true nature of physical events (Duit, 1991; Mintzes, Trowbridge, Arnaudin, & Wandersee, 1991). For instance, when we talk about the sun rising and setting—that is, *moving* in some way—children may easily conclude that the sun revolves around the earth, rather than vice versa. In addition, fairy tales and television cartoon programs may misrepresent laws of physics (Glynn et al., 1991). Think of cartoon bad guys who run off cliffs and remain suspended in the air until they realize there's nothing holding them up, at which point they fall straight down; in the real world, of course, the combination of gravity and inertia would lead them to begin falling immediately but also to continue traveling forward until reaching the ground. Unfortunately, students can also acquire erroneous ideas from other people, including some teachers and textbook authors (Begg, Anas, & Farinacci, 1992; Duit, 1991).

Regardless of how students' misconceptions originate, they can wreak havoc on new learning (e.g., Kuhn, 2001b; Porat, 2004; Reiner et al., 2000). As a result of elaborating on new information—a process that usually facilitates learning—students may interpret or distort the information to be consistent with what they already "know" and thus continue to believe what they have always believed. For example, one eleventh-grade physics class was studying the idea that an object's mass and weight do *not*, by themselves, affect the speed at which the object falls. Students were asked to build egg containers that would keep eggs from breaking when dropped from a third-floor window. They were told that on the day of the egg drop, they would record the time it took for the eggs to reach the ground. Convinced that heavier objects fall faster, a student named Barry added several nails to his egg's container. Yet when he dropped it, classmates timed its fall at 1.49 seconds—a time very similar to that for other students' lighter containers. Rather than acknowledge that light and heavy objects fall at the same rate, Barry explained the result by rationalizing that "the people weren't timing real good" (Hynd, 1998a, p. 34).

When students have misunderstandings such as Barry's, we must work hard to promote **conceptual change**, a process of revising or overhauling an existing theory or belief system in such a way that new, discrepant information can be better understood and explained. Don't let the term *conceptual* mislead you here: For the most

myeducationlab

Discover the kinds of understandings and misunderstandings that fifth and sixth graders are likely to construct by completing the Understanding Research exercise "Knowledge Construction in History" in MyEducationLab. (To find this activity, go to the topic Knowledge Construction in MyEducationLab, click on *Assignments and Activities*, and then select *Understanding Research*.)

misconception Belief that is inconsistent with commonly accepted and well-validated explanations of phenomena or events.

conceptual change Significant revision of an existing theory or belief system, enabling new and discrepant information to be better understood and explained.

TABLE 7.1
Common Misunderstandings at Different Grade Levels

Grade Level	Examples of Age-Typical Beliefs	Suggested Strategies[a]
K–2	• Undergeneralization of the concept *animal* (e.g., using the term only for mammals) • Belief that natural features (e.g., lakes, mountains) are human made and that natural objects exist for particular purposes (e.g., rocks have rough edges that enable animals to scratch themselves) • Belief that the world is flat or that it's both round and flat (i.e., pancake shaped) • Belief that features on maps depict physical entities (e.g., lines separating states and countries are painted on the earth)	• Use the word *animal* in diverse contexts (e.g., in reference to fish or insects). • Describe physical causes of natural phenomena in a simple, concrete manner (e.g., "Lakes form when water from rivers collects in low parts of the ground"). • Use a globe to find various countries; talk about the earth as being a ball rather than a pancake. • Provide practice in using maps of the local neighborhood and community, showing how some features of maps are different from physical reality.
3–5	• Belief that space has an absolute up and down, so that people standing at the South Pole will fall off the earth • Belief that plants "eat" soil and fertilizer in much the same way that people eat meat and vegetables • Belief that in vision, something travels from the eye (rather than light traveling *to* the eye) • Belief that the problem of poverty can be easily solved by giving poor people a small amount of money	• Explain that gravity draws people to the center of the earth; show videos of people who live in the Southern Hemisphere. • Introduce the process of photosynthesis, contrasting the idea of plants making their own food with that of plants simply absorbing food as people do. • Ask students to draw a line depicting the direction that light travels when a person sees an object; have them explain why they drew the line in the direction they did. • Have students explore multiple reasons that some people are poor; brainstorm potentially enduring solutions to chronic poverty.
6–8	• Belief that an astronaut who opens the hatch of a spaceship will be sucked into space (in reality, the astronaut would be blown into space by the air within the spaceship) • Belief that tiny, light particles of matter have no weight • Belief that the presence of more digits always indicates a larger number (e.g., 2.34 > 2.8) • Assumption that in algebraic equations $(x + y)^2 = x^2 + y^2$, $\sqrt{a + b} = \sqrt{a} + \sqrt{b}$, and the like	• Begin to explore such physics concepts as *force* and *vacuum*, relating them to students' prior experiences (e.g., with wind and vacuum cleaners). • Demonstrate that even seemingly weightless pieces of Styrofoam tip a balance scale, and conduct class discussions about whether it would be possible for the Styrofoam to lose all of its weight as it becomes increasingly smaller. • Provide practice with more–less relationships among decimals and fractions; embed some practice within the context of hands-on problems involving real objects. • Study the appropriate order of calculations in an algebraic expression; contrast the correct results with the results obtained from using an inappropriate sequence.
9–12	• Belief that any moving object has a special force acting on or within it (in reality, force is needed only to *change* the direction or speed of movement) • Belief that the process of division always leads to a smaller number—for instance, that 5 ÷ 0.65 yields an answer less than 5 (actual solution is about 7.69) • Beliefs that Christopher Columbus was Spanish, was the first person to assert that the world was round, and landed on the mainland of North America	• Introduce the concept of *inertia*; show how it explains movement of planets and spaceships in outer space; explore explanations for apparent violations of this concept (e.g., friction slows an object's speed as it travels along a surface). • Provide practice with mathematical problems that yield counterintuitive solutions; ask students to explain why the solutions are correct. • When describing historical events, explicitly contrast students' beliefs with more accurate information (e.g., Columbus was Italian and landed on islands in the Caribbean; Aristotle suggested that the world was round more than 1,500 years before Columbus's birth).

[a] These strategies are merely possible starting points. Some misconceptions are such an integral part of students' belief systems that they require multiple strategies over a lengthy period.

Sources: Behr & Harel, 1988; S. Carey, 1985; Delval, 1994; diSessa, 1996; J. F. Eaton, Anderson, & Smith, 1984; Gardner, Torff, & Hatch, 1996; Geary, 2005; Haskell, 2001; Hynd, 2003; Kelemen, 1999; Liben & Myers, 2007; Piaget, 1929; K. J. Roth & Anderson, 1988; C. Shanahan, 2004; C. L. Smith, 2007; Sneider & Pulos, 1983; Tirosh & Graeber, 1990; Vosniadou, 1994.

part, we are talking not about changing specific, isolated concepts but rather about changing understandings of how various concepts and ideas are interrelated.

Obstacles to Conceptual Change

Teachers often present new information in class with the expectation that it will replace any erroneous beliefs students have about a topic. Yet students of all ages can hold quite stubbornly to their existing misconceptions about the world, even after considerable instruction that explicitly contradicts these misconceptions. Theorists have offered several possible explanations about why students' misconceptions can be so resistant to change:

- *Most children and adolescents have a confirmation bias.* Learners of all ages (even college students!) tend to look for information that confirms their existing beliefs and to ignore or discredit contradictory evidence—a phenomenon known as **confirmation bias** (e.g., De Lisi & Golbeck, 1999; Hynd, 1998b; P. K. Murphy & Mason, 2006). For example, when students in a high school science lab observe results that contradict what they expected to happen, they might complain that their equipment "isn't working right" or (as Barry did during the egg-dropping project) that classmates "weren't timing real good" (Hynd, 1998a, p. 34; Minstrell & Stimpson, 1996, p. 192).

myeducationlab

Observe an example of confirmation bias in the video "Designing Experiments." (To find this video, go to Chapter 7 of the Book-Specific Resources in MyEducationLab, select *Video Examples*, and then click on the title.)

- *Students' misconceptions may be consistent with their everyday experiences.* Well-established scientific theories are often fairly abstract and sometimes seem to contradict everyday reality (P. A. Alexander, 1997; D. B. Clark, 2006; M. C. Linn et al., 1996). For example, although the law of inertia tells us that force is needed to start an object in motion but not to *keep* it in motion, we know from experience that if we want to move a heavy object across the floor, we must continue to push it until we get it where we want it (R. Driver et al., 1994).

- *Some beliefs are integrated into cohesive theories, with many interrelationships existing among various ideas.* In such circumstances, changing misconceptions involves changing an entire organized body of knowledge—an entire theory or worldview—rather than a single belief (Derry, 1996; Koltko-Rivera, 2004; Sinatra & Pintrich, 2003; C. L. Smith, Maclin, Grosslight, & Davis, 1997). For example, the belief that the sun revolves around the earth may be part of a more general earth-centered view of things, perhaps one that includes the moon, stars, and other heavenly bodies revolving around the earth as well. In reality, of course, the moon revolves around the earth, the earth revolves around the sun, and other stars aren't directly involved with the earth in one way or another. Yet the earth-centered view is a much easier one to understand and accept (on the surface, at least), and everything fits so nicely together.

- *Students may fail to notice an inconsistency between new information and their existing beliefs.* Sometimes this happens because students learn the new information in a rote manner, without relating it to things they already know and believe. In other cases it occurs because existing misconceptions take the form of *implicit knowledge*—knowledge that students are not consciously aware of. In either situation, students don't realize that the new things they have learned contradict what they already believe, and they may continue to apply their misconceptions when interpreting new situations (Chambliss, 1994; Hynd, 2003; Keil & Silberstein, 1996; P. K. Murphy, 2007; Strike & Posner, 1992).

- *Students have a personal or emotional investment in their existing beliefs.* For one reason or another, students may be especially committed to certain beliefs, perhaps insisting "This theory is what I believe in! Nobody can make me change it!" (Mason, 2003, p. 228). In some instances, their beliefs may be an integral part of their religion or culture (Mosborg, 2002; Porat, 2004; Southerland & Sinatra, 2003). In other cases, students may interpret information that contradicts their existing understandings

confirmation bias Tendency to seek information that confirms, rather than discredits, current beliefs.

as a threat to their self-esteem (Linnenbrink & Pintrich, 2003; Minstrell & Stimpson, 1996; Sherman & Cohen, 2002).

Promoting Conceptual Change

For all of the reasons just identified, promoting conceptual change can be quite a challenge. Not only must we help students learn new things, but we must also help them *un*learn, or at least *inhibit*, their existing beliefs (Hynd, 2003).

The rightmost column of Table 7.1 offers specific suggestions for addressing a number of common misconceptions. The following are more general strategies that seem to have an impact; we may often need to use a combination of them, especially when students' counterproductive beliefs are integral parts of more general theories or worldviews:

Identify existing misconceptions before instruction begins. As teachers, we can more easily address students' misconceptions when we know what they *are* (P. K. Murphy & Alexander, 2004, 2008; Putnam, 1992). Thus, we should probably begin any new topic by assessing students' current beliefs about the topic—perhaps simply by asking a few informal questions and probing further if students' initial explanations are vague. The following conversation illustrates the kinds of beliefs that persistent questioning might reveal:

> ***Adult:*** What is rain?
>
> ***Child:*** It's water that falls out of a cloud when the clouds evaporate.
>
> ***Adult:*** What do you mean, "clouds evaporate"?
>
> ***Child:*** That means water goes up in the air and then it makes clouds and then, when it gets too heavy up there, then the water comes and they call it rain.
>
> ***Adult:*** Does the water stay in the sky?
>
> ***Child:*** Yes, and then it comes down when it rains. It gets too heavy.
>
> ***Adult:*** Why does it get too heavy?
>
> ***Child:*** 'Cause there's too much water up there.
>
> ***Adult:*** Why does it rain?
>
> ***Child:*** 'Cause the water gets too heavy and then it comes down.
>
> ***Adult:*** Why doesn't the whole thing come down?
>
> ***Child:*** Well, 'cause it comes down at little times like a salt shaker when you turn it upside down. It doesn't all come down at once 'cause there's little holes and it just comes out.
>
> ***Adult:*** What are the little holes in the sky?
>
> ***Child:*** Umm, holes in the clouds, letting the water out. (Stepans, 1991, p. 94)

This conception of a cloud as a salt shaker is hardly consistent with scientific views of rain and should definitely be addressed during instruction.

Informal preassessment will be especially important in your first few years of teaching. As you gain experience teaching a particular topic year after year, you may eventually find that you can anticipate what students' prior beliefs and misbeliefs about the topic are likely to be.

Look for—and then build on—elements of truth in students' existing understandings. Often students' current understandings have a partly-right-and-partly-wrong quality (diSessa, 1996, 2006). For example, in the preceding question-and-answer session about rain, the child correctly understands that (a) clouds have water, (b) evaporation is somehow involved in the water cycle, and (c) rain is the result of water being too heavy to remain suspended in air. Such knowledge provides a good starting point for further instruction. For instance, it would be important to explain where in the water cycle evaporation occurs (i.e., in cloud formation) and how a cloud actually *is* water, rather than being a shakerlike water container.

Convince students that their existing beliefs need revision. We can more effectively promote conceptual change when we show students how new information contradicts what they currently believe and when we demonstrate why their existing conceptions are inadequate. In Piaget's terminology, we need to create *disequilibrium*, perhaps with strategies such as these:

- Ask questions that lead students to find weaknesses in their current beliefs.
- Present phenomena that students cannot adequately explain with their existing understandings.
- Have students conduct experiments to test various hypotheses and predictions.
- Ask students to provide several explanations for puzzling phenomena and to discuss the pros and cons of each one.
- Show how one explanation of an event or phenomenon is more plausible (i.e., makes more sense) than others.
- Have students apply the new ideas to real-life situations and problems.
- Ask students to reflect on and describe how their beliefs about a topic have changed as a result of instruction. (Chinn & Malhotra, 2002; D. B. Clark, 2006; Howe, Tolmie, Greer, & Mackenzie, 1995; P. K. Murphy & Alexander, 2008; P. K. Murphy & Mason, 2006; Pine & Messer, 2000; Posner, Strike, Hewson, & Gertzog, 1982; K. J. Roth, 2002; C. Shanahan, 2004; C. L. Smith, 2007; Sinatra & Pintrich, 2003; Slusher & Anderson, 1996)

myeducationlab

Observe a teacher use several strategies—probing children's existing beliefs, asking them to make predictions, and presenting a phenomenon that some of them have difficulty explaining—to encourage conceptual change in the video "Properties of Air." (To find this video, go to Chapter 7 of the Book-Specific Resources in MyEducationLab, select *Video Examples*, and then click on the title.)

Such strategies might encompass a wide variety of instructional methods, including demonstrations, hands-on experiments, teacher explanations, small-group or whole-class discussions, and writing activities. But all of these strategies have one thing in common: a focus on meaningful learning rather than rote memorization.

Motivate students to learn correct explanations. Students will be most likely to engage in meaningful learning and undergo conceptual change when they are motivated to do so (Pintrich, Marx, & Boyle, 1993; Sinatra & Pintrich, 2003). At a minimum, they must be interested in the subject matter, see it as useful in helping them achieve their personal goals, set their sights on mastering it, and have sufficient self-confidence to believe they *can* master it (Andre & Windschitl, 2003; Hynd, 2003; Pintrich et al., 1993). (As we consider motivation in Chapter 11, we'll identify strategies for accomplishing these things.)

When pointing out errors or weaknesses in students' reasoning or beliefs, preserve their self-esteem. Ideally, a classroom should be socially and emotionally supportive of conceptual change (Bransford & Schwartz, 1999; Hatano & Inagaki, 2003; Sherman & Cohen, 2002). For instance, students must feel confident that their teacher and classmates will not ridicule them for expressing logical but incorrect ideas and that the ultimate goal of a lesson is understanding the subject matter, not simply performing well on a quiz or assignment. (We'll explore the latter point—aiming for true understanding—in greater depth in the discussion of *mastery versus performance goals* in Chapter 11.)

Students are more likely to undergo conceptual change about a topic when they genuinely *want* to make sense of it.

Monitor what students say and write for persistent misconceptions .Some misconceptions and partly-but-not-totally-correct understandings may persist despite our best efforts. Throughout a lesson, then, we should often check students' beliefs about the topic at hand, looking for subtle signs that their understanding isn't completely on target and giving corrective feedback when necessary. For example, in a lesson about vision, transparency, and opaque objects, fifth-grade teacher Ms. Ramsey uses an overhead projector to show students a picture of a girl standing by her house, with an eight-foot wall between her and the family car. The following discussion ensues:

Ms. Ramsey: Why can't the girl see around the wall?

Annie: The girl can't see around the wall because the wall is opaque.

Ms. Ramsey: What do you mean when you say the wall is opaque?

Annie: *You can't see through it. It is solid.*

Brian: (calling out) The rays are what can't go through the wall.

Ms. Ramsey: I like that answer better. Why is it better?

Brian: The rays of light bounce off the car and go to the wall. They can't go through the wall.

Ms. Ramsey: Where are the light rays coming from originally?

Students: The sun.

Annie: *The girl can't see the car because she is not far enough out.*

Ms. Ramsey: So you think her position is what is keeping her from seeing it. (She flips down the overlay with the answer.) Who was better?

Students: Brian.

Ms. Ramsey: (to Annie) Would she be able to see if she moved out beyond the wall?

Annie: Yes.

Ms. Ramsey: Why?

Annie: *The wall is blocking her view.*

Ms. Ramsey: Is it blocking her view? What is it blocking?

Student: Light rays.

Ms. Ramsey: Light rays that are doing what?

Annie: If the girl moves out beyond the wall, then the light rays that bounce off the car are not being blocked. (K. J. Roth & Anderson, 1988, pp. 129–130)

Notice that Ms. Ramsey is not satisfied with Annie's original answer that the wall is opaque. With further questioning, it becomes clear that Annie's understanding of opaqueness is off target: She talks about the girl's inability to "see through" the wall, rather than about the light's inability to pass through the wall. With Ms. Ramsey's continuing insistence on precision, Annie eventually incorporates *light rays* into her explanation (K. J. Roth & Anderson, 1988).

Assessment of students' comprehension is important *after* a lesson as well. We are more likely to detect and correct misconceptions when we ask students to *explain* and *apply* what they have learned (as Ms. Ramsey does in the preceding class discussion), rather than just spit back memorized facts, definitions, and formulas (D. B. Clark, 2006; Pine & Messer, 2000; K. J. Roth, 1990). For example, if we want students in a social studies class to understand that there are often valid and compelling perspectives on both sides of a controversial issue—rather than to believe that controversy is always a matter of the good guys versus the bad guys, we might ask them to engage in a debate in which they must convincingly present a perspective contrary to their own beliefs. Or if students in a creative writing class have previously learned that complete sentences are always essential in good writing and we want to convince them otherwise, we might ask them to find examples of how incomplete sentences are sometimes used quite effectively in short stories and novels.

As you can see, a variety of strategies can help nudge students toward conceptual change. But ultimately, students themselves are in control of the cognitive processes that enable them to make sense of new ideas and acquire more accurate understandings. Their understanding of what it actually *means* to learn something and their proficiency in directing their own learning efforts are key elements in their ability to revise their thinking about classroom subject matter. We will look more at these issues in our discussions of metacognition in Chapter 8 and self-regulated learning in Chapter 10.

myeducationlab

Gain practice in strategies for promoting effective knowledge construction by completing the Building Teaching Skills and Dispositions exercise "Promoting Knowledge Construction and Conceptual Change" in MyEducationLab. (To find this exercise, go to the topic Knowledge Construction in MyEducationLab and click on *Building Teaching Skills and Dispositions.*)

Diversity in Constructive Processes

We have explored a number of reasons that students inevitably interpret classroom subject matter in unique, idiosyncratic ways. To some degree, different students have different knowledge bases—including different concepts, schemas, scripts, theories, and worldviews—that they use to make sense of new situations (Medin, Unsworth, & Hirschfeld, 2007). You probably discovered this principle firsthand when you did "The War of the Ghosts" exercise. Consider also how, in the opening case study, Rita focuses on what European settlers were doing as she explains events in the New World. In contrast, a Native American student might look at this time period from the perspective of those whose land was being occupied and ultimately taken away by self-serving foreigners. Such a student's description of events in Michigan might reflect a theme of *invasion* rather than *settlement* (Banks, 1991).

In some cases, academic subject matter may conflict with students' most core beliefs, and ultimately with the very essence of who they are as individuals (O. Lee, 1999; Porat, 2004; Southerland & Sinatra, 2003). For example, students whose cultures attribute natural events (e.g., hurricanes) to supernatural causes may have trouble buying into more scientific, earthly explanations. In addition, students who strongly believe in the divine creation of humankind may readily dismiss any suggestion that the human race has evolved from more primitive species. And students whose cultures view certain historical battles as involving good guys triumphing over bad guys may disregard more balanced perspectives in which each side has legitimate needs and concerns. Under such circumstances, a more achievable goal may be to help students *understand* (rather than *accept*) academic scholars' explanations and lines of reasoning (Sinatra, Southerland, McConaughy, & Demastes, 2003; Southerland & Sinatra, 2003).

As we help students construct a meaningful understanding of the world around them, we can increase their multicultural awareness by promoting *multiple constructions* of the same situation. For instance, we might present the western migration across North America during the 1700s and 1800s from two different perspectives: that of European settlers and that of Native Americans already living on the land. One simple way to do this is to point out that migrating peoples are referred to as *pioneers* or *settlers* in most U.S. history books but might instead have been called *foreigners* or *invaders* by Native Americans (Banks, 1991). Ultimately, we must help students to understand the very complex nature of human knowledge and to appreciate the fact that there may be several possible interpretations of any single event.

Expose students to multiple, equally valid perspectives of historical and current events.

A community of learners may be especially useful when we have a diverse student population (Bielaczyc & Collins, 2006; Ladson-Billings, 1995b; Rothstein-Fisch & Trumbull, 2008). Such a community values the contributions of all students, using everyone's individual backgrounds, cultural perspectives, and unique abilities to enhance the overall learning and achievement of the class. It also provides a context in which students can form friendships across the lines of ethnicity, gender, socioeconomic status, and disability. As noted in Chapters 3 and 4, such friendships are critical for students' social development and multicultural understanding.

Accommodating Students with Special Needs

We often see evidence of diversity in constructive processes in students with special educational needs. For example, some of these students may construct counterproductive interpretations of social situations, perhaps seeing an innocent gesture as an act of aggression or hearing an insult when none was intended (recall the discussion of *hostile attributional bias* in Chapter 3). Table 7.2 identifies patterns in the constructive processes of students with special needs, along with suggestions for facilitating productive constructions in academic and social situations.

Students in Inclusive Settings

TABLE 7.2
Knowledge Construction in Students with Special Educational Needs

Category	Characteristics You Might Observe	Suggested Strategies
Students with specific cognitive or academic difficulties	• Possible gaps in knowledge that may limit meaningful understanding of some classroom topics • Occasional unusual or inappropriate interpretations of prose • Occasional misinterpretations of social situations	• Determine students' prior knowledge about a new topic; remind them of what they already know about it. • Monitor students' comprehension of prose; correct misinterpretations. • Encourage productive interpretations of others' social behaviors.
Students with social or behavioral problems	• Frequent misinterpretations of social situations (sometimes reflecting a hostile attributional bias) • Overly literal interpretations of things heard and read (for students with autism spectrum disorders)	• Encourage alternative interpretations of others' behaviors, and help students identify suitable courses of action based on the most reasonable interpretation of a given situation. • Monitor students' understandings of implied meanings, figurative language, and the like.
Students with general delays in cognitive and social functioning	• Smaller knowledge base on which to build • Difficulty constructing accurate interpretations when information is ambiguous or incomplete	• Assume little, if any, prior knowledge about topics unless you have evidence to the contrary; remind students of what they *do* know about a topic. • Present information clearly and unambiguously.
Students with physical or sensory challenges	• Limited knowledge base to which students can relate new information, due to fewer opportunities to interact with the outside world	• Provide the background experiences (e.g., field trips) that students need to make sense of classroom subject matter.
Students with advanced cognitive development	• Larger knowledge base on which to build • Rapid concept learning • Greater conceptual understanding of classroom material (e.g., greater understanding of cause-and-effect relationships) • Greater ability to make inferences	• Assign challenging tasks that enable students to develop and use their advanced understanding of topics. • Ask thought-provoking questions that encourage students to draw inferences from what they have learned.

Sources: Butterfield & Ferretti, 1987; Graham & Hudley, 1994; J. N. Hughes, 1988; Klin, Volkmar, & Sparrow, 2000; Lochman & Dodge, 1994; Myles & Simpson, 2001; Patton et al., 1996; Pelphrey & Carter, 2007; Piirto, 1999; Pressley, 1995; Schumaker & Hazel, 1984; Turnbull et al., 2007; J. P. Williams, 1991.

The Big Picture

As we've seen, human learning is a process of constructing, rather than "soaking up," information from the environment. As you work to help children and adolescents acquire new information and skills, keep the following points in mind:

- ***Learners construct knowledge both on their own and in collaboration with others.*** To some degree, learners create their own views of physical and social phenomena. Yet their knowledge and beliefs are shaped considerably by their social and cultural environments. For example, children draw on explanations that previous generations have developed—perhaps the concepts and theories of various academic disciplines or the folk wisdom of their local communities—to help them understand current situations and events. They also work in partnership with parents and teachers to make sense of puzzling phenomena, and they frequently collaborate with age-mates in their efforts to comprehend both classroom subject matter and nonschool topics. But regardless of the extent to which learners acquire their understandings either on their own or with the help of others, they all construct somewhat unique interpretations of the ideas and events they encounter both inside and outside the classroom.

- ***Learners integrate much of what they learn to make generalizations about their world.*** Such generalizations take a variety of forms—concepts, schemas, scripts, theories, worldviews—that help learners make sense of new situations and experiences. Some of these generalizations (e.g., concepts such as *dog* and *hot*) are found worldwide, but others (e.g., views about the causes of weather phenomena and interpretations of various historical events) are apt to vary from person to person and from culture to culture.

- ***Learners' constructions are sometimes productive and sometimes counterproductive.*** In some instances, children's diverse understandings may be equally valid and appropriate. But on other occasions, certain beliefs may interfere with children's long-term academic and social success—for example, beliefs that the earth is flat, that rote learning is more effective than meaningful learning, or that a classmate is trying to pick a fight. As teachers, we must help our students interpret the world around them in ways that will be productive over the long run.

Practice for Your Licensure Exam

Vision Unit

Ms. Kontos is teaching a unit on human vision to her fifth-grade class. She shows her students a diagram of the various parts of the human eye: lens, cornea, retina, and so on. She then explains that people can see objects because light from the sun or another light source bounces off those objects and into their eyes. To illustrate this idea, she shows them Picture A.

A

"Do you all understand how our eyes work?" she asks. Her students nod that they do.

The next day, Ms. Kontos gives her students Picture B.

B

She asks students to draw one or more arrows on the picture to show how light enables the child to see the tree. More than half of the students draw lines something like the one shown in Picture C.

C

Source: Case based on a study by J. F. Eaton et al., 1984.

1. **Constructed-response question:**

   Obviously, most of Ms. Kontos's students have not learned what she thought she had taught them about human vision.

   A. Explain why many students believe the opposite of what Ms. Kontos has taught them. Base your response on contemporary principles and theories of learning and cognition.

   B. Describe two different ways in which you might improve on this lesson to help students gain a more accurate understanding of human vision. Base your strategies on contemporary principles and theories of learning and cognition.

2. **Multiple-choice question:**

   Many elementary school children think of human vision in the way that Ms. Kontos's fifth graders do—that is, as a process that originates in the eye and goes outward toward objects that are seen. When students revise their thinking to be more consistent with commonly accepted scientific explanations, they are said to be

   a. acquiring a new script
   b. revising their worldview
   c. undergoing conceptual change
   d. acquiring procedural knowledge

Go to Chapter 7 of the Book-Specific Resources in **MyEducationLab,** and click on "Practice for Your Licensure Exam" to answer these questions. Compare your responses with the feedback provided.

PRAXIS

Turn to Appendix C, "Matching Book and MyEducationLab Content to the Praxis Principles of Learning and Teaching Tests," to discover sections of this chapter that may be especially applicable to the Praxis tests.

PEARSON myeducationlab

Now go to MyEducationLab (**www.myeducationlab.com**) where you can:

- Find learning outcomes for Knowledge Construction, along with the national standards that connect to these outcomes.
- Complete Assignments and Activities that can help you more deeply understand the chapter content.
- Engage in Building Teaching Skills and Dispositions exercises, in which you can apply and practice core teaching skills identified in the chapter.
- Access Book-Specific Resources:
  - Check your comprehension of chapter content by going to the Study Plan, where you can find (a) Chapter Objectives; (b) Focus Questions that can guide your reading; (c) a Self-Check Quiz that can help you monitor your progress in mastering chapter content; (d) Review, Practice, and Enrichment exercises with detailed feedback that will deepen your understanding of various concepts and principles; (e) Flashcards that can give you practice in understanding and defining key terms; and (f) Common Beliefs and Misconceptions about Educational Psychology that will alert you to typical misunderstandings in educational psychology classes.
- Video Examples of various concepts and principles presented in the chapter.
- A Practice for Your Licensure Exam exercise that resembles the kinds of questions appearing on many teacher licensure tests.

CHAPTER OUTLINE

- CASE STUDY: TAKING OVER
- METACOGNITION AND LEARNING STRATEGIES
  Effective Learning Strategies • Factors Affecting Strategy Use • Diversity, Disabilities, and Exceptional Abilities in Metacognition
- TRANSFER
  Factors Affecting Transfer
- PROBLEM SOLVING •
  Problem-Solving Strategies: Algorithms and Heuristics • Cognitive Factors Affecting Problem Solving • Using Computer Technology to Teach Problem-Solving Skills
- CREATIVITY
  Fostering Creativity
- CRITICAL THINKING
  Fostering Critical Thinking
- DIVERSITY IN CREATIVITY, CRITICAL THINKING, AND OTHER COMPLEX THINKING PROCESSES
  Accommodating Students with Special Needs
- THE BIG PICTURE
- PRACTICE FOR YOUR LICENSURE EXAM: INTERVIEW WITH EMILY

CHAPTER OBJECTIVES

- **Objective 8.1:** Describe the roles that metacognitive knowledge and skills play in children's and adolescents' learning and academic achievement, and explain how you can promote metacognitive development in your own students.
- **Objective 8.2:** Describe various forms that transfer might take and the conditions in which transfer is most likely to occur, and apply research findings about transfer to your classroom practices.
- **Objective 8.3:** Give examples of problems for which various problem-solving algorithms and heuristics might be effective, and describe several teaching strategies you can use to facilitate students' problem-solving success.
- **Objective 8.4:** Identify several strategies you can use to help your students use academic subject matter creatively as they encounter new tasks and problems.
- **Objective 8.5:** Describe at least four different forms that critical thinking can take, and explain how you can help your students critically evaluate what they see, hear, and read both inside and outside the classroom.
- **Objective 8.6:** Give examples of diversity you might see in creativity, critical thinking, and other complex thinking processes as a result of students' cultural backgrounds, disabilities, or advanced cognitive development.

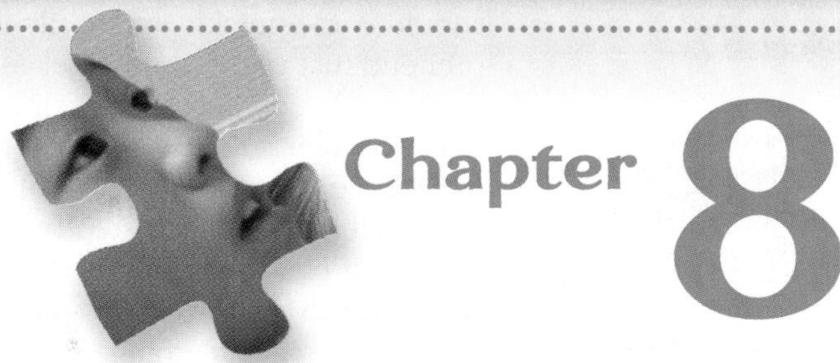

Chapter 8

Complex Cognitive Processes

CASE STUDY: Taking Over

When a ninth-grade math teacher goes on maternity leave in March, substitute teacher Ms. Gaunt takes over her classes. In accordance with Massachusetts state standards, the students are expected to master a variety of mathematical concepts and procedures, including working with exponents and irrational numbers, graphing linear equations, and applying the Pythagorean theorem. But many of the students have not yet mastered more basic concepts and operations, such as percentages, negative numbers, and long division. A few haven't even learned such number facts as $6 \times 3 = 18$ and $7 \times 8 = 56$.

Ms. Gaunt quickly discovers that not only do her students lack a solid foundation in basic math, but many also have beliefs and attitudes that impede their progress. Some think that their teacher's job is to ensure that students "get" math immediately and remember it forever. Thus, they neither work hard to understand the material nor take notes during classroom explanations. In fact, a few insist on individual tutoring during class time. On one occasion, when Ms. Gaunt is at Jason's desk demonstrating a procedure, she asks Mark, who is sitting beside Jason, to watch what she is doing and listen to what she is saying. "I don't need to," Mark responds. "After you're done explaining it to Jason, you can come and explain it to *me*."

Another problem is that most of the students are concerned only with getting the right answer as quickly as possible. They depend on calculators to do their mathematical thinking for them and complain when Ms. Gaunt insists that they solve a problem with pencil and paper instead. Students rarely check to see if their solutions make logical sense. For instance, in a problem such as this one,

> Louis can type 35 words a minute. He needs to type a final copy of his English composition, which is 4,200 words long. How long will it take Louis to type his paper?

a student might submit an answer of 147,000 minutes—an answer that translates into more than 100 days of around-the-clock typing—and not give the outlandishness of the solution a second thought. (It would actually take two hours to type the paper.)

In mid-April, Ms. Gaunt begins moving through lessons more rapidly so that she can cover the mandated ninth-grade math curriculum before the upcoming statewide math competency exam. "Students can't do well on the exam if they haven't even been exposed to some of the required concepts and procedures," she reasons. "Mastery probably isn't possible at this point, but I should at least *present* what students need to know. Maybe this will help a few of them with some of the test items."

- **Why are the students having difficulty mastering what the state of Massachusetts considers to be a ninth-grade mathematics curriculum?**
- **Can you identify at least three different factors that appear to be interfering with students' learning?**

Source: Case used courtesy of a friend who wishes to be anonymous; "Ms. Gaunt" is a pseudonym.

ONE FACTOR INTERFERING WITH THE STUDENTS' LEARNING is, of course, their lack of prerequisite knowledge and skills. Much of mathematics is hierarchical in nature—complex concepts and procedures build on simpler, more basic ones—and some of the students have little knowledge on which to build. Students' beliefs about learning and problem solving are also playing a role. The students think that learning

myeducationlab

Learn more about promoting learning and complex cognitive processes in a supplementary reading "Learning in the Content Areas." (To find this reading, go to Chapter 8 of the Book-Specific Resources in MyEducationLab, and then select *Supplementary Readings*.)

should come quickly and easily if the teacher does her job. They don't seem to comprehend that understanding classroom subject matter is a constructive process, involving considerable effort on their part, and that certain strategies (e.g., taking notes) can enhance their learning. And they view mathematical problem solving as a quick, mindless enterprise that involves plugging numbers into a calculator and writing down the result, rather than a step-by-step process that requires logical reasoning and frequent self-checking. Mastering basic facts and skills—which involves primarily **lower-level cognitive processes**—is important, to be sure. But students gain little if they cannot also *do* something with what they're learning. Our focus in this chapter will be on **higher-level cognitive processes**, those in which people do something fairly complex with what they are learning—perhaps actively studying it, applying it to a new situation or problem, using it to create a new product, or critically evaluating it. As we examine such processes, I hope that you'll think not only about how you might apply chapter content to help your future students learn and achieve at higher levels but also about how you—as a student yourself—might learn and achieve more successfully.

Metacognition and Learning Strategies

The term **metacognition** literally means "thinking about thinking." Metacognition encompasses knowledge and beliefs about the nature of human cognitive processes, reflection on one's own cognitive processes, and conscious attempts to engage in behaviors and thought processes that increase learning and memory.

To illustrate, you have undoubtedly learned by now that you can acquire only so much information so fast—for instance, you can't possibly absorb the contents of an entire textbook in an hour. You have also discovered that you can learn information more quickly and recall it more easily if you put it into some sort of organizational framework. And perhaps you have taken to heart one of the recommendations in Chapter 1: Periodically check yourself to make sure you remember and understand what you have read. In general, you are metacognitively aware of some things you can do (mentally) to learn new information effectively.[1]

The more learners know about thinking and learning—that is, the greater their *metacognitive awareness*—the better their learning and achievement will be (Hofer & Pintrich, 2002; Perkins, 1995; Schneider & Lockl, 2002). Furthermore, students who have a more sophisticated understanding of learning and thinking—for instance, students who realize that one's knowledge of a topic continues to evolve over time—are more likely to undergo conceptual change when it's warranted (Mason, Gava, & Boldrin, 2008; Sinatra & Pintrich, 2003).

In the early elementary grades, children have only a vague awareness of their own thinking and are apt to be overly optimistic about how much they can remember. With age, children become more introspective. In the following reflection, 9-year-old Eamon is unusually insightful about how he learns new ideas in science:

> I try to look for a fit. Like if it doesn't fit with any . . . of the ideas that I have in my head I just leave it and wait for other ideas to come in so that I can try to fit them together with my ideas. Maybe they will go with my ideas and then another idea will come in and I can fit it together with that idea and my understanding just keeps on enlarging. An idea usually does fit. (M. G. Hennessey, 2003, p. 123)

As children gain experience with a wide variety of learning tasks, they discover that some things are more difficult to learn than others and that, in general, they can't pos-

lower-level cognitive process Cognitive process that involves learning or remembering specific information or skills in more or less the same form in which they were initially presented.

higher-level cognitive process Cognitive process that involves going well beyond something specifically learned (e.g., by analyzing, applying, or evaluating it).

metacognition Knowledge and beliefs about the nature of human cognitive processes (including one's own), as well as conscious attempts to engage in behaviors and thought processes that increase learning and memory.

[1]One key ingredient in metacognition is *theory of mind*, a concept we examined in Chapter 3.

sibly remember everything they see or hear (Bjorklund & Green, 1992; Flavell et al., 2002; Schneider & Lockl, 2002).

Let's consider a classic early experiment with elementary school children as an example (Flavell, Friedrichs, & Hoyt, 1970). Children in four age-groups (ranging from preschool to fourth grade) were shown strips of paper that had pictures of one to ten objects on them. The children were asked to predict how many of the objects they could remember in the correct order for a short time period. Following are the average predictions of each age-group and the average number of objects the different groups actually did remember:

Age-Group	*Predicted Number*	*Actual Number*
Preschool	7.2	3.5
Kindergarten	8.0	3.6
Grade 2	6.0	4.4
Grade 4	6.1	5.5

Notice that all four age-groups predicted that they would remember more objects than they actually could. But the older children were more realistic about the limitations of their memories than the younger ones. The kindergartners predicted they would remember eight objects in correct order but actually remembered fewer than four!

Table 8.1 summarizes the typical nature of metacognition at various grade levels. You can also get a general sense of how metacognition changes with age by listening to 6-year-old Brent, 10-year-old David, 12-year-old Colin, and 16-year-old Hilary as they talk about learning, memory, and studying in the two "Memory and Cognition" video clips in MyEducationLab. For instance, when Brent is asked to explain what kinds of things he did to remember a list of 12 words, he says only "Think" and "Hold it in my brain." In contrast, Hilary is quite introspective about why she's done well on the task: "Just 'cause they're things that I have in the house and that we use every day . . . and just thinking it over, I guess. It helps when I picture things, too."

myeducationlab

Observe developmental trends in metacognitive awareness and estimations of memory ability in the two "Memory and Cognition" videos. (To find this video, go to Chapter 8 of the Book-Specific Resources in MyEducationLab, select *Video Examples*, and then click on the title.)

Effective Learning Strategies

An important component of metacognition is *controlling* one's own thinking and learning to some degree. Thanks, in part, to maturational changes in the brain, children and adolescents gradually become more capable of controlling and directing their cognitive processes in their efforts to learn something new (Eigsti et al., 2006; Kuhn & Franklin, 2006). When learners intentionally use a certain approach to learning and remembering something, they are using a **learning strategy**.

In Chapter 6, we identified several long-term memory storage processes, including rehearsal, elaboration, organization, and visual imagery. As children grow older, they increasingly discover the benefits of these processes and use them more frequently (see Table 6.4 in Chapter 6). Children gradually acquire additional strategies as well. For example, consider the simple idea that when you don't learn something the first time you study it, you need to study it again. This is a strategy that 8-year-olds use but 6-year-olds do not (Masur, McIntyre, & Flavell, 1973). With age and experience, children also become more aware of which strategies are effective in different situations (Lovett & Flavell, 1990; Schneider & Lockl, 2002; Short, Schatschneider, & Friebert, 1993). Even so, many students of all ages (college students included!) seem relatively uninformed about effective learning strategies (J. E. Barnett, 2001; Pintrich & De Groot, 1990; Schommer, 1994a).

Some learning strategies are **overt strategies**; in other words, they are behaviors we can actually see. Others, such as elaborating and forming visual images, are **covert strategies**; they are internal mental processes we often can*not* see (Kardash & Amlund, 1991).

learning strategy One or more cognitive processes used intentionally for a particular learning task.

overt strategy Learning strategy that is readily apparent in a learner's behavior (e.g., taking notes).

covert strategy Learning strategy that involves only mental activity and thus isn't reflected in a learner's observable behavior (e.g., forming a visual image of a new concept).

TABLE 8.1
Metacognition at Different Grade Levels

Grade Level	Age-Typical Characteristics	Suggested Strategies
K–2	• Awareness of thought in oneself and others, albeit in a simplistic form; limited ability to reflect on the specific nature of one's own thought processes • Considerable overestimation of what has been learned and how much can be remembered in the future • Belief that learning is a relatively passive activity • Belief that the absolute truth about any topic is "out there" somewhere, waiting to be discovered	• Talk often about thinking processes (e.g., "I *wonder* if . . ." "Do you *remember* when . . . ?"). • Provide opportunities for students to experiment with their memories (e.g., playing "I'm going on a trip and am going to pack ______," in which each student repeats items previously mentioned and then adds another item to the list). • Introduce simple learning strategies (e.g., rehearsal of spelling words, repeated practice of motor skills).
3–5	• Increasing ability to reflect on the nature of one's own thought processes • Some overestimation of memory capabilities • Emerging realization that learning is an active, constructive process and that people may misinterpret what they observe • Continuing belief in an absolute truth "out there"	• Provide simple techniques (e.g., self-test questions) that enable students to monitor their learning progress. • Examine scientific phenomena through hands-on activities and experimentation; ask students to make predictions about what will happen and to debate competing explanations for what they observe.
6–8	• Few and relatively ineffective study strategies (e.g., poor note-taking skills, little or no comprehension monitoring) • Belief that knowledge about a topic consists largely of a collection of discrete facts • Increasing realization that knowledge can be subjective and that conflicting perspectives may all have some validity (e.g., "people have a right to have their own opinions") • Increasing differentiation among the natures of different content domains (e.g., thinking that math involves right versus wrong answers, whereas social studies allows for diverse opinions)	• Teach and model effective strategies within the context of various subject areas. • Scaffold students' studying efforts (e.g., provide a structure for note taking, give students questions to answer as they study). • Introduce multiple perspectives about topics (e.g., asking whether Christopher Columbus was a brave explorer in search of new knowledge or an entrepreneur in search of personal wealth). • Explicitly ask students to reflect on their beliefs about the nature of various academic disciplines (e.g., "Can a math problem sometimes have two different right answers?").
9–12	• Growing (but incomplete) knowledge of which study strategies are effective in different situations; persistent use of rehearsal by some students • Increasing recognition that knowledge involves understanding interrelationships among ideas • Increasing recognition that mastering a topic or skill takes time and practice (rather than happening quickly as a result of innate ability) • Emerging understanding that conflicting perspectives should be evaluated on the basis of evidence and logic (seen in a small minority of high school students)	• Continue to teach and model effective learning strategies; ask students to describe their strategies to one another. • Design classroom assessments that emphasize understanding, integration, and application, rather than recall of discrete facts. • Present various subject areas as dynamic entities that continue to evolve with new discoveries and theories. • Have students apply objective criteria (e.g., hard evidence, logical reasoning processes) to weigh pros and cons of various explanations.

Sources: Andre & Windschitl, 2003; Astington & Pelletier, 1996; J. E. Barnett, 2001; Buehl & Alexander, 2006; Chandler, Hallett, & Sokol, 2002; Elder, 2002; Flavell et al., 1970, 2002; Hatano & Inagaki, 2003; P. M. King & Kitchener, 2002; Kuhn, Garcia-Mila, Zohar, & Andersen, 1995; Kuhn & Park, 2005; Kuhn & Weinstock, 2002; Lovett & Flavell, 1990; Markman, 1977; Meltzer, Pollica, & Barzillai, 2007; Muis, Bendixen, & Haerle, 2006; Perkins & Ritchhart, 2004; Schommer, 1994a, 1997; Short, Schatschneider, & Friebert, 1993; J. W. Thomas, 1993a; vanSledright & Limón, 2006; Wellman, 1985, 1990.

Overt Strategies To some degree, successful learning and classroom achievement are the result of certain behaviors, such as asking questions in times of confusion, keeping a calendar for assignments and due dates, devoting part of every evening to schoolwork, and so on. One especially effective overt strategy is *writing* about classroom subject matter (Bangert-Drowns, Hurley, & Wilkinson, 2004; Benton, 1997; P. D. Klein, 1999). Here, we look at research on two writing-based learning strategies: taking notes and creating summaries.

Taking Notes By the time students reach the upper elementary or middle school grades, note-taking skills begin to play a role in their classroom achievement. In general, students who take more notes learn and remember classroom subject matter better (Kiewra, 1989). However, the *quality* of the notes is equally important. Useful notes typically reflect the main ideas of a lesson or reading assignment (A. L. Brown, Campione, & Day, 1981; Kiewra, 1985; Peverly, Brobst, Graham, & Shaw, 2003).

Despite the advantages of note taking, many young adolescents take few or no class notes unless specifically instructed to take them (recall the infrequent note taking in Ms. Gaunt's ninth-grade math class), and the notes they do take differ considerably in quality. For example, in a unit on Greek mythology, seventh-grade language arts teacher Barbara Dee gave her students note-taking forms to use when taking notes about various myths. Figure 8.1 shows the notes that two students took about the King Midas myth. The notes on the left provide a good overall synopsis of the King Midas story and might reasonably help the student remember the story fairly accurately. In contrast, the notes on the right are too brief and disjointed to be useful.

Especially when students are first learning how to take notes in class, we should scaffold their efforts by giving them an idea about which things are most important to include (Meltzer, Pollica, & Barzillai, 2007; Pressley, Yokoi, van Meter, Van Etten, & Freebern, 1997). One approach is to provide a specific structure to use, much as Barbara Dee did in her unit on Greek mythology. Another strategy, especially if students are novice note takers, is to occasionally check their notebooks for accuracy and appropriate emphasis and give constructive feedback.

Scaffold students' early note-taking efforts.

Creating Summaries Research consistently indicates that writing a summary of the material being studied can enhance learning and memory (A. King, 1992; T. Shanahan, 2004; Wade-Stein & Kintsch, 2004). Creating a good summary is a fairly complex process, however. At a minimum, it includes distinguishing between important and unimportant information, synthesizing details into more general ideas, and identifying important relationships among the ideas. It's not surprising, then, that even many high school students have difficulty developing a good summary (Hidi & Anderson, 1986).

FIGURE 8.1 Two students' class notes on King Midas, taken in a seventh-grade language arts unit on Greek mythology.

Story Note taking Form

Title: King Midas and the golden touch

Author:

I. Characters (write a few notes after each character's name to describe them, make a abbreviation after the character's name for further notes)

a. King Midas– King of Phyrygia
b. Silenus - a demigod
c. Dionysus - god of whine
d. Daughter of King Midas
e.
f.
g.
h.
i.

II. Setting (write a few notes after the place to describe it, try to discover the time period)

a.
b.
c.

III. Events

a. ~~Someone~~ Silenus was tearing up km's rosebushs
b. Silenus tutored dionysus, dionysus watches over silenus
c. silenus got a feast from km, silenus stayed for awhile
d. Dionysus wants to pay km for being nice to silenus. Dionysus gives him a wish.
e. km picks gold now everything he touches turns to gold
f. km Turns daughter to gold. km waster everything in the Pactolus loses gold tuch.

IV. Conflict (what is the problem, who is involved)

a.
b.

V. Solution (how did the problem work itself out, was there a lesson to learn)

a.
b.

Story Note taking Form

Title: King midas and the golden touch

Author:

I. Characters (write a few notes after each character's name to describe them, make a abbreviation after the character's name for further notes)

a. King Midas
b. first guard
c. Second guard
d. Silenous
e. Dionysus
f. Dughter of the king
g.
h.
i.

II. Setting (write a few notes after the place to describe it, try to discover the time period)

a. Castle
b.
c.

III. Events

a. sylinus destroys roses
b. King gets him
c.
d.
e.
f.

IV. Conflict (what is the problem, who is involved)

a. every thing he touches turns to gold
b.

V. Solution (how did the problem work itself out, was there a lesson to learn)

a.
b.

Ask students to summarize what they're learning, and scaffold their early efforts.

Probably the best way of helping students acquire this strategy is to ask them on a regular basis to summarize what they hear and read (e.g., see Figure 8.2). For example, we might occasionally give homework assignments asking students to write a summary of a textbook chapter. Or we might ask them to work in cooperative learning groups to develop a brief oral presentation that condenses information they have learned about a topic. At first, we should restrict summary-writing assignments to short, simple, and well-organized passages involving material with which students are familiar; we can assign more challenging material as students become more proficient summarizers (Hidi & Anderson, 1986). Computer software is also available to scaffold the summarizing process (e.g., Wade-Stein & Kintsch, 2004).

FIGURE 8.2 Eight-year-old Neville summarizes a lesson about glaciers.

The weight of a glacier makes it move down the mountains toward the sea. Glaciers move so slowly that you cannot see them move. Sometimes they move ten feet in one day. They might move less then an inch in one day.

Covert Strategies Students' overt strategies—note taking, summarizing, and so on—are probably valuable only to the extent that effective cognitive processes, or *covert strategies,* underlie them (Kardash & Amlund, 1991). For example, high-achieving students tend to benefit more from note taking than low-achieving students, perhaps because the high-achieving students are more likely to elaborate on and organize what they're learning as they take notes (Kiewra, Benton, & Lewis, 1987; Ku, Chan, Wu, & Chen, 2008). In addition to engaging in meaningful learning processes (e.g., elaboration, organization), two covert strategies that may be especially critical for effective classroom learning and achievement are (a) accurately identifying important information and (b) regularly monitoring one's learning.

Identifying Important Information Because the human memory system isn't set up to remember *everything* presented in class or a textbook, students must be selective when studying classroom material. The things they choose to study—whether main ideas and critical pieces of information or, instead, isolated facts and trivial details—inevitably affect their learning and school achievement (Dee-Lucas & Larkin, 1991; J. A. Dole et al., 1991; R. E. Reynolds & Shirey, 1988).

Students often have trouble identifying the most important information in a lesson or reading assignment, especially when they don't know very much about the topic. Many are apt to zero in on superficial characteristics, such as what a teacher writes on the chalkboard or what a textbook author puts in *italics* or **boldface**. In the following excerpts from interviews conducted by students in my own educational psychology classes, Annie (a fifth grader) and Damon (an eighth grader) reveal their naiveté about how best to identify important ideas:

> *Adult:* When you read, how do you know what the important things are?
>
> *Annie:* Most of my books have words that are written darker than all of the other words. Most of the time the "vocab" words are important. In my science books, there are questions on the side of the page. You can tell that stuff is important because it is written twice. (Interview used courtesy of a student who wishes to be anonymous)

> *Adult:* What do you think are the important things to remember when your teacher is talking?
>
> *Damon:* The beginning sentences of their speech or if there's a formula or definition. (Interview used courtesy of Jenny Bressler)

Tell students what is most important to learn and remember.

As teachers, we can help students learn more effectively by letting them know what we think are the most important ideas to be gained from lectures and reading materials. We can, of course, simply tell them exactly what to study. But we can also get the same message across through more subtle means:

- Provide a list of objectives for a lesson.
- Write key concepts and relationships on the chalkboard.
- Ask questions that focus students' attention on key ideas.

Students, especially low-achieving ones, are more likely to learn the essential points of a lesson when such prompts are provided for them (Kiewra, 1989; McCrudden &

Schraw, 2007; R. E. Reynolds & Shirey, 1988; Schraw, Wade, & Kardash, 1993). As students become better able to distinguish between important and unimportant information on their own, we can gradually phase out our guidance.

Regularly Monitoring Learning One very powerful learning strategy is **comprehension monitoring**, a process of periodically checking oneself for recall and understanding. How well do *you* monitor your comprehension? The following exercise can help you find out.

High achievers typically know a good deal about how they learn, and they use this knowledge to guide their studying.

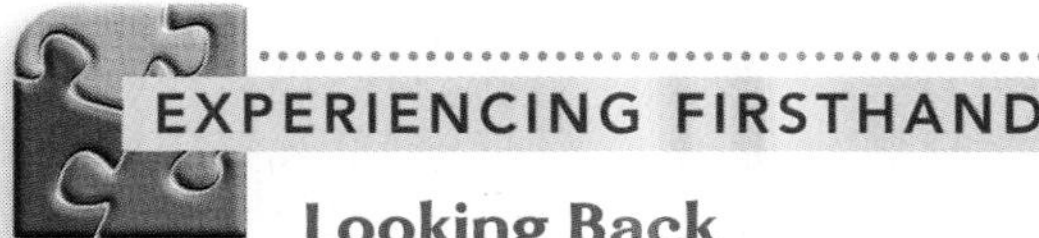

EXPERIENCING FIRSTHAND

Looking Back

Stop for a minute and ask yourself this question:

What have I learned from the last five pages of this textbook?

Jot down what you can recall on a sheet of scrap paper.

Now go back and look at the five pages just before this one. Do the notes you've just written include all of the major points covered in these pages? Is there something you thought you understood but realize now that you don't? Is there something you never learned at all—perhaps something you were supposedly "reading" when your mind was someplace altogether different?

Successful learners continually monitor their comprehension both *while* they study something and at some point *after* they've studied it (Dunlosky, Rawson, & McDonald, 2002; Hacker, Bol, Horgan, & Rakow, 2000; Weaver & Kelemen, 1997). Furthermore, when they realize they don't understand, they take steps to correct the situation, perhaps by rereading a section of a textbook or asking a question in class. In contrast, low achievers rarely check themselves or take appropriate action when they don't comprehend something. For instance, they seldom reread paragraphs they haven't completely understood the first time (L. Baker & Brown, 1984; Haller, Child, & Walberg, 1988; Stone, 2000).

Many children and adolescents engage in little, if any, comprehension monitoring (J. A. Dole et al., 1991; Nokes & Dole, 2004; J. W. Thomas, 1993a). When they don't monitor their learning and comprehension, they don't know what they know and what they don't know; consequently, they may think they have mastered something when they really haven't. Although this **illusion of knowing** is especially common in young children, it is seen in learners at all levels, even college students (L. Baker, 1989; Hacker, 1998; Schneider & Lockl, 2002). As paper-and-pencil exams become increasingly prevalent at upper grade levels, an illusion of knowing can lead students to overestimate how well they will perform on these assessments, especially if students don't know the subject matter very well (Hacker et al., 2000; Stone, 2000). My own students occasionally come to me expressing frustration with low test scores. "I knew the material so well!" they tell me. But when we sit down and begin to talk about the exam material, it usually becomes clear that, in fact, they have only a very vague understanding of some ideas and an incorrect understanding of others.

myeducationlab

Learn more about how high-achieving and low-achieving high school students study differently by completing the Understanding Research exercise "High School Students' Study Strategies" in MyEducationLab. (To find this exercise, go to the topic Complex Cognitive Processes in MyEducationLab, click on *Assignments and Activities*, and then select *Understanding Research*.)

Comprehension monitoring doesn't have to be a solitary activity, of course. If students work in small study groups, they can easily test one another on classroom material and may detect gaps or misconceptions in one another's understandings (Dunning et al., 2004; Hacker, 1998). Ideally, the questions they ask one another should encourage them to elaborate on, rather than simply recall, what they are studying. For example, we might teach them to ask questions beginning with such phrases as *Explain why, What do you think would happen if,* and *What is the difference between* (A. King, 1992, p. 309).

Yet to be truly effective learners, students must ultimately learn how to test *themselves* as well. One effective strategy is **self-explanation**, in which students frequently

comprehension monitoring Process of checking oneself to verify understanding and memory of newly acquired information.

illusion of knowing Thinking that one knows something that one actually does *not* know.

self-explanation Process of occasionally stopping to verbalize to oneself (and hence to better understand) material being read or studied.

stop to explain to themselves what they have learned (deLeeuw & Chi, 2003). Another, similar approach is **self-questioning**, in which students periodically stop to ask themselves questions—essentially internalizing the mutual question-asking process they have learned from small-group study sessions (Dunning et al., 2004; Martínez, Bannan-Ritland, Kitsantas, & Baek, 2008; Wong, 1985). Their self-questions should, of course, include not only simple, fact-based questions but also elaborative ones.

Teach students strategies for monitoring their own and others' learning progress.

Factors Affecting Strategy Use

As we've seen, students become increasingly capable of using effective learning strategies as they grow older, in part because they can better control and direct their cognitive processes. With age, too, comes an ever-expanding knowledge base that better enables students to engage in elaboration, identify important information in reading assignments, and effectively monitor their comprehension. Several other factors also influence students' choice and use of various strategies, as reflected in the following principles:

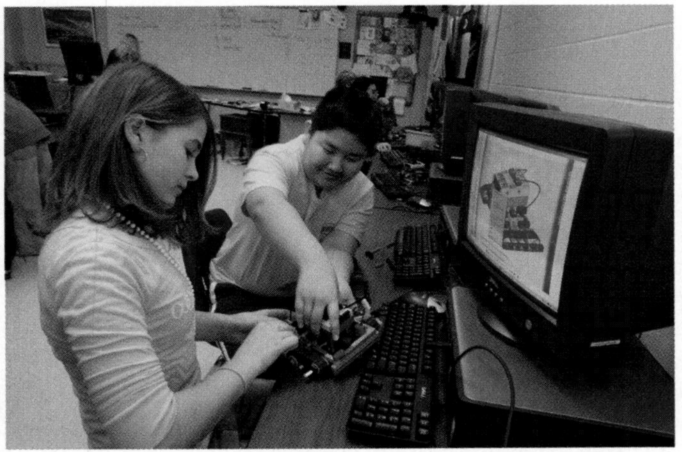

The strategies students use to learn school subject matter depend, in part, on what they're asked to do with the material while they're studying.

- *Learning strategies depend partly on the learning task at hand.* In some situations, teachers may assign tasks for which truly effective learning strategies are either counterproductive or impossible. For instance, if we insist that facts and definitions be learned verbatim, students will understandably be reluctant to engage in elaboration and other meaningful learning processes (Turner, 1995; Van Meter, Yokoi, & Pressley, 1994). And if we expect students to master a great deal of material for a single exam, they may have to devote their limited study time to getting a superficial impression of everything or to studying the easy material they're confident they can master, rather than to developing an in-depth understanding and integration of the subject matter as a whole (Son & Schwartz, 2002; J. W. Thomas, 1993b).
- *Students are likely to acquire and use new, more effective strategies only if they realize that their prior strategies have been ineffective.* Students will come to such a conclusion only if they have been regularly monitoring their comprehension in past learning tasks and have been aware of their learning difficulties. Comprehension monitoring, then, does not just affect students' understanding of classroom subject matter. It also plays a pivotal role in the development of *other* metacognitive strategies (Kuhn, Garcia-Mila, Zohar, & Andersen, 1995; Lodico, Ghatala, Levin, Pressley, & Bell, 1983; Loranger, 1994). In some cases, feedback that students are *not* mastering a learning task will spur them to adopt more effective strategies, at least for the short run (Starr & Lovett, 2000).
- *Students' beliefs about the nature of knowledge and learning influence their strategy choices.* I once had a conversation with my son Jeff, then an eleventh grader, about the Canadian Studies program that a local university had just added to its curriculum. Jeff's comments revealed a very simplistic view of what history is:

> *Jeff:* The Canadians don't have as much history as we [Americans] do.
>
> *Me:* Of course they do.
>
> *Jeff:* No, they don't. They haven't had as many wars.
>
> *Me:* History's more than wars.
>
> *Jeff:* Yeah, but the rest of that stuff is really boring.

Once Jeff reached college, he discovered that history is a lot more than wars and other "really boring" stuff. In fact, he majored in history and now, as a secondary school

self-questioning Process of asking oneself questions as a way of checking understanding of a topic.

teacher, actually *teaches* history. But it's unfortunate that he had to wait until college to discover the true nature of history as an academic discipline.

Students have misconceptions about other subject areas as well. For instance, in the opening case study, Ms. Gaunt's students think that mathematics consists of nothing more than a collection of procedures that yield right answers. In addition, students often have misconceptions about the nature of learning. For instance, Ms. Gaunt's students think they should be able to learn mathematical concepts and procedures quickly and easily, with little or no effort on their part, as long as their teacher does her job.

Students' beliefs about the nature of knowledge and learning are collectively known as **epistemic beliefs**. Such beliefs often influence studying and learning (Hofer & Pintrich, 1997; Muis, 2007; Schommer, Calvert, Gariglietti, & Bajaj, 1997). For example, when learners believe that learning happens quickly in an all-or-none fashion (as Ms. Gaunt's students apparently do), they are apt to think they have mastered something before they really have. Furthermore, they tend to give up quickly in the face of failure and express discouragement or distaste regarding the topic they are studying. In contrast, when learners believe that learning is a gradual process that often takes time and effort, they are likely to use a wide variety of learning strategies as they study and to persist until they have made sense of the material (D. L. Butler & Winne, 1995; Kardash & Howell, 2000; Muis, 2007; Schommer, 1990, 1994b).

As another example of variability in learners' epistemic beliefs, some students believe that when they read a textbook, they are passively absorbing information—often in the form of isolated facts—directly from the page to their minds. In contrast, other students recognize that learning from reading requires them to construct their own meanings by actively interpreting, organizing, and applying the information. Learners who realize that reading is a constructive, integrative process are more likely to engage in meaningful learning as they read and to undergo conceptual change when they encounter ideas that contradict their existing understandings (Mason et al., 2008; Muis, 2007; Schommer-Aikins, 2001; Sinatra & Pintrich, 2003).

Epistemic beliefs tend to evolve over the course of childhood and adolescence (Hofer, 2004; Kuhn & Park, 2005; Schommer et al., 1997). Children in the elementary grades typically believe in the certainty of knowledge: They think that for any topic, there is an absolute truth "out there" somewhere. As they reach the high school grades, some (but by no means all) of them begin to realize that knowledge is a subjective entity and that different perspectives on a topic are sometimes equally valid. Additional changes may occur at the high school level. For example, twelfth graders are more likely than ninth graders to believe that knowledge consists of complex interrelationships, rather than discrete facts, and that learning happens slowly, rather than quickly. Such developmental trends are reflected in some of the entries in Table 8.1.

As teachers, we must communicate to students what we ourselves have already learned about knowledge and learning (Hofer & Pintrich, 1997; P. M. King & Kitchener, 2002; Muis, Bendixen, & Haerle, 2006; Schommer, 1994b):

- Knowledge does not always mean having clear-cut answers to difficult, complex issues.

- Knowledge involves not only knowing facts, concepts, and ideas but also understanding interrelationships among these things.

- Learning involves active construction of knowledge, rather than just a passive absorption of it.

- Mastering a body of information or a complex skill sometimes requires persistence and hard work.

Communicate that true knowledge is complex, rather than simple, and that learning involves considerable thought and effort.

In communicating such messages—not only in what we say but also in what we do (e.g., what activities we assign, how we assess students' learning)—we increase

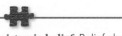

epistemic belief Belief about the nature of knowledge or knowledge acquisition.

the likelihood that students will apply effective learning strategies, critically evaluate classroom subject matter, and undergo conceptual change when appropriate (P. M. King & Kitchener, 2002; P. K. Murphy & Mason, 2006; Purdie, Hattie, & Douglas, 1996; Sinatra & Pintrich, 2003).

• *Different motives and goals call for different strategies.* Motivational factors clearly influence the extent to which students use effective strategies to learn and study (P. A. Alexander, Graham, & Harris, 1998; Nolen, 1996; Palmer & Goetz, 1988). Some students may be more interested in getting by with a passing grade than truly mastering classroom material. Others may think that meaningful learning and other effective strategies involve too much time and effort to be worthwhile. Still others may have so little faith in their learning ability that they expect to do poorly, regardless of the strategies they use. In our discussion of motivation in Chapter 11, we'll identify many things we can do to overcome such impediments to successful learning and achievement.

• *Ongoing instruction and guidance about effective strategies enhances learning and achievement.* With every transition to a higher educational level, teachers expect students to learn more material and to think about it in more sophisticated ways. Thus, the simple learning strategies that children acquire in grade school (e.g., rehearsal) become less and less effective with each passing year. All too often, however, teachers teach academic content areas—history, biology, math, and so on—without also teaching students how to *learn* in those content areas (Hamman, Berthelot, Saia, & Crowley, 2000; Nokes & Dole, 2004; Pressley et al., 1990). When left to their own devices, most students develop effective strategies very slowly (if at all) and thus, over the years, encounter increasing difficulty in their attempts to master classroom subject matter. And when they *don't* master it, they may not know why they have failed or how to improve their chances of succeeding the next time (Hacker et al., 2000; Loranger, 1994; O'Sullivan & Joy, 1994).

myeducationlab

Gain practice in helping students acquire effective learning and study strategies by completing the Building Teaching Skills and Dispositions exercise "Teaching Reading Comprehension Strategies" in MyEducationLab. (To find this exercise, go to the topic Complex Cognitive Processes in MyEducationLab and click on *Building Teaching Skills and Dispositions.*)

Using effective learning strategies makes such a difference in students' classroom achievement that we must not leave the development of these strategies to chance. How can we help students *learn how to learn*? The Into the Classroom feature "Promoting Effective Learning and Study Strategies" presents several research-based strategies. The most important of the strategies presented there is the first one: *When teaching academic content, simultaneously teach students how to effectively study and remember that content.* Students are more likely to use effective learning and study strategies when those strategies are taught not in separate how-to-study classes but rather as integral parts of everyday instruction about specific academic topics (Hattie, Biggs, & Purdie, 1996; Paris & Paris, 2001; Pressley, El-Dinary, Marks, Brown, & Stein, 1992; Pressley, Harris, & Marks, 1992).

Diversity, Disabilities, and Exceptional Abilities in Metacognition

Researchers have observed cultural differences in students' epistemic beliefs—in particular, their beliefs about what it means to *learn* something. From the perspective of mainstream Western culture, learning is largely a mental enterprise: People learn in order to understand the world and acquire new skills and abilities. But for many people in China, learning also has moral and social dimensions: It enables an individual to become increasingly virtuous and honorable and to contribute in significant ways to the betterment of society. From a traditional East Asian perspective, true learning is not a quick-and-easy process; rather, it comes only with a great deal of diligence, concentration, and perseverance (Dahlin & Watkins, 2000; H. Grant & Dweck, 2001; J. Li, 2005; J. Li & Fischer, 2004).

Learning strategies, too, may differ somewhat from culture to culture. Consistent with a belief that learning requires diligence and perseverance, many East Asian parents and teachers encourage frequent use of rehearsal and rote memorization as learn-

INTO THE Classroom

Promoting Effective Learning and Study Strategies

- **When teaching academic content, simultaneously teach students how to effectively study and remember that content.**

When a second-grade teacher presents the new spelling words for the week, he asks students to practice writing each word once by itself and once in a sentence. He also asks students to think about how some of the words are spelled similarly to words they already know (e.g., "The word *clown* ends in the letters o-w-n. What other words have you learned that end in those letters?"). And he teaches his students the mnemonic "*I* before *E* except after *C* . . ." to help them remember the spellings of such words as *believe* and *receive*.

- **Suggest a wide variety of strategies—taking notes, thinking of new examples, forming mnemonics, summarizing, administering self-check quizzes, and so on—each of which is apt to be useful in different situations and for different purposes.**

A high school social studies teacher acknowledges that some aspects of geography, such as the names of European capital cities, can be hard to remember. She suggests the keyword mnemonic and illustrates this process with the capital of Belgium, which is Brussels: "Think of a large *bell* with eyes and a mouth, and picture it eating some *Brussels* sprouts." But in addition, the teacher points out that many aspects of geography make sense and should be understood rather than memorized. For example, when presenting a map of Europe one day, she says, "Notice how most European capitals—for instance, Paris, Rome, Brussels, Prague—are on major rivers. Why do you suppose that is?"

- **Scaffold students' attempts to use new strategies—for instance, by modeling the strategies, giving clues about when to use them, and providing feedback on appropriate and inappropriate strategy use.**

A seventh-grade language arts teacher gives her students note-taking forms they can use to take notes in a unit on Greek mythology (see Figure 8.1).

- **Explain the usefulness of various strategies in an age-appropriate way.**

A ninth-grade history teacher asks his class, "Who can tell me why the American colonists were so upset about the Quartering Act of 1765? We talked about that last week. Does anyone remember?" When no one responds, the teacher continues, "A lot of kids don't realize this, but we human beings can't always remember everything we're taught. It's time we started getting serious about taking notes in this class." The teacher gives some initial pointers on how and when to take notes and continues to scaffold the students' note taking over the course of the school year, sometimes simply by saying "This is an important point that you should be sure to include in your notes."

- **Occasionally ask students to study instructional material in pairs or small cooperative learning groups.**

In a unit on the human muscular system, seventh graders are given "starters" (e.g., "Describe _____ in your own words"; "Compare _____ with respect to _____") to help them formulate elaboration-promoting questions to ask a study partner. The students then break into pairs to study together. Many of them generate and are able to answer such elaborative questions as "Why are muscles important?" and "How are the skeletal muscles and the cardiac muscles the same?"

- **Ask students to share their strategies with one another.**

At a school that serves a large number of minority-group students who are at risk for academic failure, faculty and students create a Minority Achievement Committee (MAC) program designed to make academic achievement a high priority. Participation in the program is selective (i.e., students must show a commitment to academic improvement) and prestigious. In regular meetings, high-achieving eleventh and twelfth graders describe, model, and encourage many effective strategies, and they help younger students who are struggling with their schoolwork.

Sources: P. A. Alexander et al., 1998; J. E. Barnett, Di Vesta, & Rogozinski, 1981; Borkowski, Carr, Rellinger, & Pressley, 1990; D. L. Butler & Winne, 1995; Hacker, 1998; Hattie, Biggs, & Purdie, 1996; Kahl & Woloshyn, 1994; A. King, 1992, 1994; A. King, Staffieri, & Adelgais, 1998 (muscular system example, pp. 139, 141); Kucan & Beck, 1997; Kuhn et al., 1995; McCrudden & Schraw, 2007; McGovern, Davis, & Ogbu, 2008 (Minority Achievement Club example); Meltzer, Pollica, & Barzillai, 2007; Nokes & Dole, 2004; Paris & Winograd, 1990; Pressley, Borkowski, & Schneider, 1987; Pressley, El-Dinary, et al., 1992; Pressley, Harris, & Marks, 1992; Pressley & Hilden, 2006; Rosenshine et al., 1996; Slater, 2004; Starr & Lovett, 2000; J. W. Thomas, 1993a; Vygotsky, 1978; C. E. Weinstein, Goetz, & Alexander, 1988; C. E. Weinstein & Hume, 1998; Winne, 1995; E. Wood et al., 1999.

ing strategies (Dahlin & Watkins, 2000; Ho, 1994; Purdie & Hattie, 1996). Rehearsal and memorization are also common in cultures that value verbatim learning of oral histories and passages of sacred text (e.g., the Koran, the Bible) (MacDonald, Uesiliana, & Hayne, 2000; Rogoff et al., 2007; Q. Wang & Ross, 2007). In contrast, many schools in mainstream Western culture are increasingly conducting activities and encouraging strategies that foster meaningful learning and conceptual understanding. Even so, Western schools typically insist that students learn certain things—such as multiplication tables and word spellings—by heart (Q. Wang & Ross, 2007).

Remember that students' learning strategies and beliefs about learning may be partly the result of their cultural backgrounds.

Accommodating Students with Special Needs We are especially likely to see diversity in metacognition in students who have special educational needs. Table 8.2

Students in Inclusive Settings

TABLE 8.2
Promoting Metacognitive Development in Students with Special Educational Needs

Category	Characteristics You Might Observe	Suggested Strategies
Students with specific cognitive or academic difficulties	• Less metacognitive awareness or control of learning • Use of few and relatively inefficient learning strategies • Increased strategy use after explicit instruction in strategies	• Teach effective learning strategies (e.g., taking notes, using mnemonics, finding general themes in reading material) within the context of lessons about particular topics. • Model effective strategies and scaffold students' efforts to use them (e.g., provide outlines to guide note taking, ask questions that encourage retrieval of prior knowledge).
Students with social or behavioral problems	• Limited metacognitive awareness of one's processing difficulties (for some students) • Few effective learning strategies (for some students)	• Provide guidance in using effective learning and study strategies (e.g., verbally model strategies, give outlines that guide note taking).
Students with general delays in cognitive and social functioning	• Lack of metacognitive awareness or control of learning • Lack of learning strategies, especially in the absence of strategies training	• Teach relatively simple learning strategies (e.g., rehearsal, specific mnemonics), and give students ample practice in using them.
Students with physical or sensory challenges	• No consistently observed deficits in metacognitive knowledge or strategies; specific deficits sometimes due to sensory impairments	• Address any deficits in metacognition with strategies you would use with nondisabled students, making appropriate accommodations for physical and sensory limitations.
Students with advanced cognitive development	• Use of relatively sophisticated learning strategies in comparison with peers	• Don't assume that students have adultlike learning strategies; assess their existing strategies and, as appropriate, encourage use of more effective strategies (e.g., elaboration, comprehension monitoring). • Provide opportunities for self-directed learning if students clearly have effective learning strategies they can use with little teacher guidance.

Sources: Beirne-Smith et al., 2006; Campione, Brown, & Bryant, 1985; Candler-Lotven et al., 1994; B. Clark, 1997; E. S. Ellis & Friend, 1991; Frasier, 1989; Graham & Harris, 1996; Grodzinsky & Diamond, 1992; Heward, 2009; Mastropieri & Scruggs, 2007; McGlynn, 1998; Meltzer, 2007; Mercer & Pullen, 2005; Piirto, 1999; Porath, 1988; Pressley, 1995; Scruggs & Mastropieri, 1992; H. L. Swanson, 1993; Turnbull et al., 2007; Wilder & Williams, 2001; Wong, 1991a.

presents characteristics you might see in these students. Notice that many students with cognitive disabilities—and some with emotional and behavioral disorders, as well—may exhibit little knowledge and use of effective learning strategies. In contrast, students who are gifted typically have more sophisticated learning strategies than their peers do.

For many students with disabilities, we may have to teach metacognitive skills explicitly and with considerable scaffolding—that is, with close guidance and assistance in the use of specific learning strategies (Meltzer, 2007). For example, we might provide partially filled-in outlines to guide students' note taking (see Figure 8.3). We might also tell students when particular strategies (e.g., elaboration, comprehension monitoring) are appropriate and model the use of such strategies with specific classroom subject matter. Finally, we must give students opportunities to practice their newly acquired strategies, along with feedback about how effectively they are using each one.

As teachers, we must remember that our students are likely to learn differently—and often less efficiently and successfully—than we do. Almost all of them can benefit from acquiring more sophisticated understandings of what knowledge and learning involve and from regularly practicing effective strategies for mastering school subject matter.

Keep in mind that your students are apt to be less effective learners than you are.

FIGURE 8.3 Example of a partially filled-in outline that can guide students' note taking.

MUSCLES

A. *Number of Muscles*
   1. There are approximately ____________ muscles in the human body.

B. *How Muscles Work*
   1. Muscles work in two ways:
      a. They ____________, or shorten.
      b. They ____________, or lengthen.

C. *Kinds of Muscles*
   1. ____________ muscles are attached to the bones by ____________.
      a. These muscles are ____________ (voluntary/involuntary).
      b. The purpose of these muscles is to ________________________
      ________________________.
   2. ____________ muscles line some of the body's ____________.
      a. These muscles are ________________ (voluntary/involuntary).
      b. The purpose of these muscles is to ________________________
      ________________________.
   3. The ____________ muscle is the only one of its kind.
      a. This muscle is ____________ (voluntary/involuntary).
      b. The purpose of this muscle is to ________________________
      ________________________.

Transfer

How students think about and study school subject matter has implications not only for how well they can understand and remember it but also for how effectively they can use and apply it on later occasions. Here, we are talking about **transfer**: the extent to which knowledge and skills acquired in one situation affect people's learning or performance in a subsequent situation. Following are examples:

- Elena is bilingual: She speaks both English and Spanish fluently. She begins a French course in high school and immediately recognizes many similarities between French and Spanish. "Aha," she thinks, "what I know about Spanish will help me learn French."
- In her middle school history class, Stella discovers that she does better on quizzes when she takes more notes. She decides to take more notes in her geography class as well, and once again the strategy pays off.
- Ted's fifth-grade class has been working with decimals for several weeks. His teacher asks, "Which number is larger, 4.4 or 4.14?" Ted recalls something he knows about whole numbers: Numbers with three digits are larger than numbers with only two digits. "The larger number is 4.14," he mistakenly concludes.

In most cases, prior learning *helps* learning or performance in another situation. Such **positive transfer** takes place when Elena's Spanish helps her learn French and when Stella's practice with note taking in history class improves her performance in geography class. In some instances, however, existing knowledge or skills actually *hinder* later learning. Such **negative transfer** is the case for Ted, who transfers a principle related to whole numbers to a situation in which it doesn't apply: comparing decimals.

transfer Phenomenon in which something a person has learned at one time affects how the person learns or performs in a later situation.

positive transfer Phenomenon in which something learned at one time facilitates learning or performance at a later time.

negative transfer Phenomenon in which something learned at one time interferes with learning or performance at a later time.

THE FAR SIDE® By GARY LARSON

Brain aerobics

Although general transfer certainly occurs, the general-mental-exercise view of transfer (formal discipline) has largely been discredited.

Sometimes we see **specific transfer**, in which the original learning task and the transfer task overlap in content. For example, Elena should have an easy time learning to count in French because the numbers (*un, deux, trois, quatre, cinq*) are very similar to the ones she already knows in Spanish (*uno, dos, tres, cuatro, cinco*). At other times, we may see **general transfer**, in which learning in one situation affects learning and performance in a somewhat dissimilar situation. Consider, for example, Stella's strategy of taking more notes in geography because of her success with note taking in history class. History and geography don't necessarily overlap in content, but a strategy acquired in one class can help with learning in another.

Historically, research studies have indicated that when application of academic subject matter is involved, specific transfer occurs far more often than general transfer (S. M. Barnett & Ceci, 2002; W. D. Gray & Orasanu, 1987). In fact, the question of whether general transfer occurs at all has been the subject of considerable debate over the years. Many early educators believed that certain subjects (e.g., Latin, Greek, mathematics, formal logic) have great potential for general transfer: Because these subjects require considerable attention to precision and detail, they might strengthen students' minds and thereby enable students to tackle other, unrelated tasks more easily. This **formal discipline** perspective of transfer persisted throughout the first several decades of the twentieth century. For instance, when I was in high school in the mid-1960s, most college-bound students at my school were encouraged to take both French and Latin—the only two languages my school offered. Taking French made a great deal of sense: Living in Massachusetts, we were within a day's drive of French-speaking Quebec. "But why should I take Latin?" I asked my guidance counselor. "I can use it only if I attend Catholic mass or run across phrases like 'caveat emptor' or 'e pluribus unum.' Hardly anyone speaks the language anymore." The counselor pursed her thin, red lips and gave me a look suggesting that she knew best. "Latin will discipline your mind," she told me. "It will help you learn better."

Most research has discredited this mind-as-muscle notion of transfer (Haskell, 2001; Perkins & Salomon, 1989; E. L. Thorndike, 1924). For example, practice in memorizing poems doesn't necessarily make one a faster poem memorizer (James, 1890). And studying computer programming, though often a worthwhile activity in its own right, doesn't necessarily help a person with dissimilar kinds of logical tasks (Mayer & Wittrock, 1996; Perkins & Salomon, 1989).

We're more likely to see general transfer when we broaden our notion of transfer to include application of general academic skills (e.g., reading, writing) and general learning strategies (e.g., note taking) that can be applied to a wide variety of topics and contexts (J. R. Anderson, Greeno, Reder, & Simon, 2000; S. M. Barnett & Ceci, 2002; Perkins, 1995; Posner & Rothbart, 2007). Furthermore, general beliefs, attitudes, and dispositions related to learning and thinking—for instance, recognition that learning often requires hard work, as well as open-mindedness to diverse viewpoints—can have a profound impact on later learning and achievement across multiple domains and so clearly illustrate general transfer at work (Bransford & Schwartz, 1999; De Corte, 2003; Pugh & Bergin, 2006; Pugh, Linnenbrink, Kelly, Manzey, & Stewart, 2006; also see the discussion of *dispositions* in Chapter 5). And some students develop a general desire to apply what they learn in the classroom—that is, they have a *spirit of transfer*—that consistently resurfaces in later instructional contexts (Haskell, 2001; Volet, 1999).

specific transfer Instance of transfer in which the original learning task and the transfer task overlap in content.

general transfer Instance of transfer in which the original learning task and the transfer task are different in content.

formal discipline View of transfer suggesting that the study of rigorous subject matter enhances one's ability to learn other, unrelated things.

Factors Affecting Transfer

Ideally, positive transfer to real-world contexts should be a major objective in classrooms at all grade levels. When learners can't use their basic math skills to compute correct change or balance a checkbook, when they can't use their knowledge of English grammar in a job application or business report, and when they can't apply their knowledge of science to an understanding of personal health or environmental problems, then we have to wonder whether the time spent learning the math, grammar, and science might have been better spent doing something else.

Although both specific and general transfer do occur, students often *don't* apply the academic content they learn in particular classes to other classes or to out-of-school situations (Mayer & Wittrock, 1996; Perkins, 1992; Renkl, Mandl, & Gruber, 1996). Learners are, of course, more likely to transfer what they learn at school when they approach each classroom topic with a conscious intention to apply it. But several other factors also influence the probability of transfer, often because they influence learners' ability to *retrieve* what they've learned when they need it:

- *The more meaningfully and thoroughly something is learned, the more likely it is to be transferred to a new situation.* Instructional time is clearly an important variable affecting transfer: The more time students spend studying a particular topic, the more likely they are to apply what they've learned on future occasions (P. A. Alexander & Judy, 1988; Haskell, 2001; Schmidt & Bjork, 1992; Voss, 1987). Ideally, students should have a *conceptual understanding* of the topic—that is, they should have the many things they've learned appropriately organized and interrelated. Here we see another instance of the *Less is more* principle introduced in Chapter 7: Students are more likely to transfer their school learning to new situations, including those beyond the classroom, when they study a few things in depth and learn them well, instead of studying many topics superficially (Bereiter, 1995; Brooks & Dansereau, 1987; Mayer & Wittrock, 1996).

Teach important topics in depth, with a focus on true understanding, not rote memorization.

The *Less is more* principle is clearly being violated in the opening case study. Ms. Gaunt decides that she must move fairly quickly if she is to cover all of the ninth-grade math curriculum, even if it means that few students will master any particular topic or procedure. Given the upcoming statewide mathematics exam, she may have little choice about the matter, but her students are unlikely to *use* what they're learning on future occasions.

- *Both positive and negative transfer are more common when a new situation is similar—or at least appears to be similar—to a previous one.* Perceived similarity increases the chances that a new situation will provide retrieval cues that point learners in the right direction as they search long-term memory for potentially relevant knowledge and skills (Bassok, 2003; Di Vesta & Peverly, 1984; Haskell, 2001). For instance, when Elena first encounters number words in her French class (*un, deux, trois, quatre, cinq*), they should quickly trigger recall of similar-sounding Spanish words (*uno, dos, tres, cuatro, cinco*).

However, we should note that the similarity of two situations, although usually promoting positive transfer, can sometimes lead to negative transfer instead (e.g., Sun-Alperin & Wang, 2008). To see what I mean, try the following exercise.

EXPERIENCING FIRSTHAND

A Division Problem

Quickly estimate an answer to this division problem:

$$60 \div 0.38$$

Is your answer larger or smaller than 60? If you applied your knowledge of division by whole numbers here, you undoubtedly concluded that the answer is smaller than 60. In fact, the answer is approximately 158, a number much *larger* than 60.

Does this exercise remind you of Ted's erroneous conclusion—that 4.14 is larger than 4.4—based on his knowledge of how whole numbers can be compared? Many students at all levels, even in college, show negative transfer of whole-number principles to situations involving decimals (Behr & Harel, 1988; Ni & Zhou, 2005; Tirosh & Graeber, 1990). Working with decimals appears, on the surface, to be similar to working with whole numbers. The only difference—but a very important one, as it turns out—is a tiny decimal point.

To minimize negative transfer, we teachers must be sure to point out differences between two superficially similar topics. For example, Ted's teacher could have identified some of the specific ways in which decimals are different from whole numbers. As another example, I find that students in my educational psychology classes often have trouble correctly understanding certain concepts (e.g., *maturation, socialization, short-term memory, reinforcement*), because the meanings of these words in psychology are quite different from their meanings in everyday conversation. So when I first introduce one of these concepts, I take great pains to contrast the different meanings. Even so, the everyday meanings continue to intrude into some students' thinking about course content, especially if the students don't continually monitor their own thinking and understanding (see also Dai, Gonyea, Malkani, Zhang, & Smith, 2005).

When concepts might be easily confused, explicitly point out their differences.

• *Principles and theories are more easily transferred than discrete facts.* Specific facts certainly do have an important place in the classroom. For instance, students should know what 2 + 3 equals, what the Berlin Wall signified, and where to find Africa on a globe. Yet by themselves, facts have limited utility in new situations. On average, general principles, rules, and theoretical explanations are more widely applicable than specific facts and information (Bransford & Schwartz, 1999; Haskell, 2001; Perkins & Salomon, 1987; M. Perry, 1991). The more we can emphasize general principles—for example, that adding two positive whole numbers always yields a larger number, that a country's citizens sometimes revolt when their government officials act unjustly, and that the cultures of various nations are influenced by their locations and climates—the more we facilitate students' ability to transfer what they learn.

Emphasize general principles more than discrete facts.

Especially as they get older, some students acquire an ability to apply general principles to topics quite different from those they've previously studied. For example, in one research study, fifth graders and college students were asked to develop a plan for increasing the population of bald eagles, an endangered species in their state (Bransford & Schwartz, 1999). None of the students in either age-group had previously studied strategies for eagle preservation, and the plans that both groups developed were largely inadequate. Yet in the process of developing their plans, the college students addressed more sophisticated questions than the fifth graders did. In particular, the fifth graders focused on the eagles themselves (e.g., How big are they? What do they eat?), whereas the college students looked at the larger picture (e.g., What type of ecosystem supports eagles? What about predators of eagles and eagle babies?) (Bransford & Schwartz, 1999, p. 67). Thus, the college students were drawing on an important principle they had acquired in their many years of science study: *Living creatures are more likely to survive and thrive when their habitat supports, rather than threatens, them.*

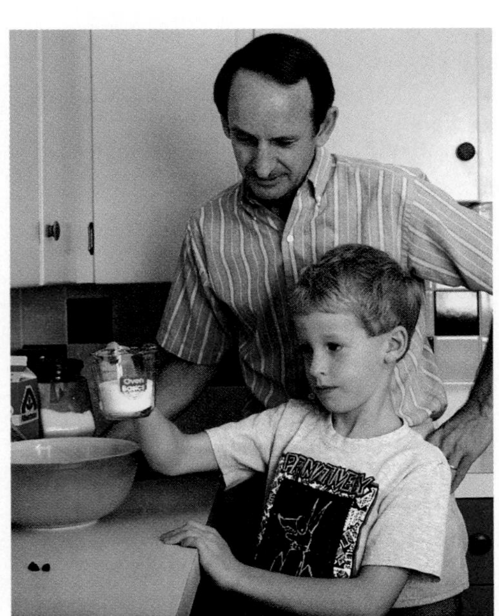
Children are more apt to transfer their knowledge of fractions and ratios to future situations if they perceive it to be context free and if they practice using it in a variety of real-world contexts.

• *Transfer is more common when information and skills are perceived as being relevant to diverse disciplines and real-world situations.* Unfortunately, many students tend to think of academic subject areas as being *context bound,* or as distinct disciplines that are completely separate from one another and from real-world concerns (P. A. Alexander & Judy, 1988; S. M. Barnett & Ceci, 2002; Perkins & Simmons, 1988; Renkl et al., 1996). For example, when baking cookies, an 11-year-old might ask a parent, "Do two one-quarters make two fourths? I know it does in math but what about in cooking?" (Pugh & Bergin, 2005, p. 16).

The context-bound nature of some school learning may prevent students from retrieving what they've learned in situations where it might be useful (recall the discussion of *situated learning and cognition* in Chapter

6). A study with high school students (Saljo & Wyndhamn, 1992) provides an illustration. Students were asked to figure out how much postage they should put on an envelope that weighed a particular amount, and they were given a table of postage rates that would enable them to determine the correct amount. When students were given the task in a social studies class, most of them used the postage table to find the answer. But when students were given the task in a math class, most of them ignored the postage table and tried to calculate the postage in some way, figuring it to several decimal places in some cases. Thus, the students in the social studies class were more likely to solve the problem correctly—as a former social studies teacher myself, I suspect that, in that context, they were well accustomed to looking for information in tables and charts. In contrast, many of the students in the math class drew on strategies they associated with math, using formulas and performing calculations, and thus overlooked the more efficient and accurate approach.

Fortunately, not all school learning remains "stuck" in school or in a particular classroom. People regularly use some of the skills they've learned at school in their daily lives—reading, arithmetic, map interpretation, and so on. But we can increase the transferability of school subject matter by regularly relating it to other disciplines and to the outside world (R. E. Clark & Blake, 1997; Perkins, 1992). For instance, we might show students how human digestion provides a justification for categorizing food into several basic food groups or how principles of economics have indirect impacts on global climate change. We should also give students many opportunities to practice using what they've learned in a variety of real-world situations (Z. Chen, 1999; Cox, 1997; Haskell, 2001; Reimann & Schult, 1996). By doing such things, students discover that much of what they learn at school truly has wide applicability outside the classroom—in other words, it becomes *context free* (A. Collins et al., 1989; Cox, 1997; Perkins & Salomon, 1989).

Regularly relate topics in one academic discipline to other academic disciplines and to the nonacademic world. Provide numerous opportunities to apply classroom content to authentic, real-world tasks.

• *Transfer increases when the cultural environment encourages and expects transfer.* All too often, it seems, students are encouraged to acquire school subject matter for mysterious purposes (e.g., "You'll need to know this in college" or "It will come in handy later in life"), with few insights into when and how they might find it useful. Teachers who regularly point out similarities among seemingly diverse tasks and situations and who communicate the importance of transfer increase the chances that learners will apply what they learn to new situations. Ideally, we should create a *culture* of transfer—a learning environment in which applying newly acquired information, skills, and cognitive strategies to diverse situations and real-world problems is both the expectation and the norm (R. A. Engle, 2006; Haskell, 2001; Pea, 1987). For instance, we might regularly encourage students to ask themselves, How might I use this information? as they listen, read, and study (Perkins, 1992; B. S. Stein, 1989; Sternberg & Frensch, 1993).

Create a classroom culture in which transfer is the expectation and the norm.

Problem Solving

By **problem solving**, I mean using (i.e., *transferring*) existing knowledge and skills to address an unanswered question or troubling situation. The world presents innumerable problems that differ widely in content and scope, as illustrated in the next exercise.

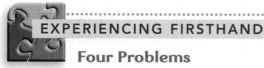

EXPERIENCING FIRSTHAND

Four Problems

How many of these problems can you solve?

1. You buy two apples for 25 cents each and one pear for 40 cents. How much change will you get back from a dollar bill?

problem solving Using existing knowledge and skills to address an unanswered question or troubling situation.

FIGURE 8.4 How long do the roof planks of this treehouse need to be?

2. You are building a treehouse with the shape and dimensions illustrated in Figure 8.4. You need to buy planks for a slanted roof. How long must the roof planks be to reach from one side of the treehouse to the other?
3. As a teacher, you want to illustrate the idea that metal battleships float even though metal is denser (and thus heavier) than water. You don't have a toy boat made of metal. What can you use instead to show students that a metal object with a hollow interior can float on water?
4. Tropical rainforests provide homes for many species of animals and plants (including some plants useful in modern medicine), and they help to reduce the rapid increase in carbon dioxide in the earth's atmosphere. Yet each day, tens of thousands of acres of tropical rainforest disappear, largely as a result of farmers' efforts to create new farmland by slashing and burning existing vegetation. What steps might be taken to curtail this alarming rate of deforestation?

Sometimes, problems are straightforward and easy to solve. Problem 1 requires only simple addition and subtraction procedures, which easily yield a correct solution: 10 cents. Problem 2 (Figure 8.4) is more difficult, partly because you probably don't encounter such problems very often. But if you have studied geometry, then you almost certainly learned the Pythagorean theorem: In any right triangle, the square of the hypotenuse equals the sum of the squares of the other two sides. Looking at the top part of the treehouse (from the dotted line upward) as a triangle, we can find the length for the roof planks (x) this way:

$$(\text{Slanted side})^2 = (\text{Horizontal side})^2 + (\text{Vertical side})^2$$
$$x^2 = 4^2 + (5 - 2)^2$$
$$x^2 = 16 + 9$$
$$x^2 = 25$$
$$x = 5$$

Problems don't always have a single correct solution, of course. A variety of objects (e.g., a metal baking dish, bucket, or thimble) might be used to solve Problem 3. And you might identify several possible ways of addressing Problem 4, but you probably wouldn't know which ones could successfully curtail rainforest destruction until you actually implemented them.

Problems differ considerably in the extent to which they are clearly specified and structured. At one end of this clarity-and-structure continuum is the **well-defined problem**, in which the goal is clearly stated, all information needed to solve the problem is present, and only one correct answer exists. Calculating correct change after a purchase (Problem 1) and determining the length of planks needed for a treehouse roof (Problem 2) are examples of well-defined problems. At the other end of the continuum is the **ill-defined problem**, in which the desired goal is unclear, information needed to solve the problem is missing, or several possible solutions exist. Finding a suitable substitute for a metal ship (Problem 3) is somewhat ill defined: Many objects might serve as a ship substitute, and some might work better than others. The rainforest destruction problem (Problem 4) is even less defined: The goal (curtailing deforestation) is ambiguous, we're missing a lot of information that would help us solve the problem (e.g., what alternatives might replace farmers' slash-and-burn practices?), and there is no single correct solution. On average, ill-defined problems are usually more difficult to solve than well-defined ones.

well-defined problem Problem in which the goal is clearly stated, all the information needed to solve the problem is present, and only one correct answer exists.

ill-defined problem Problem in which the desired goal is unclear, some information needed to solve the problem is missing, and/or several possible solutions to the problem exist.

Most problems presented in school are well defined. As an example, let's return to the typing problem in the opening case study:

> Louis can type 35 words a minute. He needs to type a final copy of his English composition, which is 4,200 words long. How long will it take Louis to type his paper?

Notice that all of the information that students need to solve the problem is given to them, and there's no irrelevant information to lead them astray. And there's only one correct answer, with no room for debate.

Yet the real world presents ill-defined problems far more often than well-defined ones, and students need practice in dealing with them (J. E. Davidson & Sternberg, 2003; L. B. Resnick, 1988). Although we can't expect students to totally solve a deforestation problem that has been plaguing ecologists for decades, we can certainly teach them strategies for tackling complex problems with no easy solutions. For instance, we can teach them how to break large, complex problems into smaller, better-defined ones (e.g., What viable alternatives might there be to slash-and-burn farming? How else might rainforest inhabitants earn a living?). And we can teach them techniques for finding information they may need to address a problem (e.g., using the library or Internet to locate the world's large rainforest regions and examine cultural practices in those regions).

Give students guidance and practice in dealing with ill-defined problems.

Problem-Solving Strategies: Algorithms and Heuristics

Some problems can be successfully solved with an **algorithm**, a specific sequence of steps that guarantees a correct solution. For example, by dividing 4,200 by 35, we can easily determine that Louis will need 120 minutes (2 hours) to type his English composition. And by using the Pythagorean theorem and simple algebra, we can correctly calculate the length of a treehouse's slanted roof.

However, the world presents many problems for which no algorithms exist. There are no rules or instructions we can follow to identify a substitute metal ship or to help us address worldwide rainforest destruction. In fact, few algorithms exist for solving problems outside the domains of mathematics and science. In the absence of an algorithm, learners must use one or more **heuristics**, general problem-solving strategies that may or may not yield a successful outcome. For example, one heuristic we might use in solving the deforestation problem is this: Identify a new behavior that adequately replaces the problem behavior (i.e., identify another way that rainforest farmers can meet their survival needs).

Both types of problem-solving strategies—algorithms and heuristics alike—are often specific to particular content domains. But here are several general problem-solving heuristics that are likely to be helpful in a variety of contexts:

Calvin and Hobbes **by Bill Watterson**

Some problems can be solved by an *algorithm*—a set of step-by-step instructions that guarantees a correct solution.

algorithm Prescribed sequence of steps that guarantees a correct problem solution.

heuristic General strategy that facilitates problem solving but doesn't always yield a solution.

FIGURE 8.5 In a third-grade activity, cooperative learning groups try to design an object that "flinks"—that is, one that neither floats to the top nor sinks to the bottom of a jar of water. Here, 8-year-old Tony describes his group's trial-and-error approach to the problem.

We all desided our jobs. Mrs. Pemperkin filled up our gar with a half of a gallen of water. We sent up our supllies person and he got stireafomb, clay, rubben bands, tacks, coubs and serandrap. First we tried a blook with clay on it it sunk. Then we trayed serandrap. combs and a tack it floted. We then tride clay and stairrafomb, it floted. Then gust thumb tacks sunk. Clay, stirafom and rubber bands, It flooted. Petter said every time he made something "This will bring us to victory!" Then we tried to make one with clay, stirerafomb, tacks, and rubber bands. Then we tried tacks and stirerafomb, it floted. Petter tried serannrap with clay, it flooted. Then we tride clay, tacks and wood, it floted. Then we tried paper towals, it floted. It was time to cleen up. we did not have a good time

- *Identify subgoals.* Break a large, complex task into two or more specific subtasks that can be more easily addressed.
- *Round complex numbers up or down.* Estimate mathematical solutions by converting hard-to-work-with numbers to simpler ones.
- *Use paper and pencil.* Draw a diagram, list a problem's components, or jot down potential solutions or approaches.
- *Draw an analogy.* Identify a situation analogous to the problem situation, and derive potential solutions from the analogy.
- *Brainstorm.* Generate a wide variety of possible approaches or solutions—perhaps including some that might seem outlandish or absurd—without initially evaluating any of them. After a lengthy list has been created, evaluate each item for its potential relevance and usefulness.
- *"Incubate" the situation.* Let a problem remain unresolved for a few hours or days, allowing time for a broad search of long-term memory for potentially productive approaches. (J. R. Anderson, 2005; J. E. Davidson & Sternberg, 1998, 2003; Halpern, 1997; Minsky, 2006)

Teaching Problem-Solving Strategies Occasionally students develop problem-solving strategies on their own. For instance, many children invent simple addition and subtraction strategies long before they encounter arithmetic at school (Bermejo, 1996; Ginsburg, Cannon, Eisenband, & Pappas, 2006; Siegler & Jenkins, 1989). But without some formal instruction in effective strategies, even the most inventive of students may occasionally resort to unproductive trial and error to solve problems (e.g., see Figure 8.5). Following are research-based recommendations for teaching problem-solving strategies:

For Teaching Algorithms

- Describe and demonstrate specific procedures and the situations in which each can be used.
- Provide worked-out examples of algorithms being applied, and ask students to explain what is happening in each step.
- Help students understand why particular algorithms are relevant and effective in certain situations.
- When a student's application of an algorithm yields an incorrect answer, look closely at what the student has done, and locate the trouble spot (e.g., see Figure 8.6).

FIGURE 8.6 Thirteen-year-old Malika incorrectly simplifies the expression $6(2x + y) + 2(x + 4y)$ as $14x + 10y$. The correct answer is $14x + 14y$. Where did Malika go wrong?

$6(2x+y)+2(x+4y)$
$12x+6y+2x+4y$
$14x+10y$

For Teaching Both Algorithms and Heuristics

- Teach problem-solving strategies within the context of specific subject areas (*not* as a topic separate from academic content) and sometimes within the context of authentic activities.
- Engage in joint problem-solving activities with students, modeling effective strategies and guiding students' initial efforts.

- Provide scaffolding for difficult problems (e.g., break them into smaller and simpler problems, give hints about possible strategies, or provide partial solutions).
- Ask students to explain what they're doing as they work through a problem.
- Have students solve problems in small groups, sharing ideas about problem-solving strategies, modeling various approaches for one another, and discussing the merits of each approach. (R. K. Atkinson, Derry, Renkl, & Wortham, 2000; Barron, 2000; Chinn, 2006; Crowley & Siegler, 1999; Gauvain, 2001; Kirschner et al., 2006; Mayer, 1985; Reimann & Schult, 1996; Renkl & Atkinson, 2003; Rittle-Johnson, 2006; Rogoff, 2003)

myeducationlab

Observe group problem solving in the video "Group Work: Secondary—Part 2." (To find this video, go to Chapter 8 of the Book-Specific Resources in MyEducationLab, select *Video Examples*, and then click on the title.)

Cognitive Factors Affecting Problem Solving

As we've discovered, well-defined problems are usually more easily solved than ill-defined ones, and problems that can be solved with algorithms are generally easier than those requiring heuristics. Factors we previously identified as affecting transfer—thorough understanding of a topic, perception of relevance to diverse academic disciplines and to real-world situations, and so on—affect problem solving as well (e.g., P. A. Alexander & Judy, 1988; Schoenfeld & Hermann, 1982). The following principles reveal additional factors at work in problem solving:

- *Working memory places an upper limit on how much students can think about at one time as they work on a problem.* You may recall from an exercise in Chapter 6 just how difficult it can be to solve a long division problem in your head. Remember, working memory has a limited capacity: At any one time, it can hold only a few pieces of information and accommodate only so much cognitive processing. If a problem requires a student to deal with too much information at once or to manipulate that information in a very complex way, working memory capacity may be insufficient for effective problem processing. When working memory capacity is exceeded, the problem cannot be solved (Johnstone & El-Banna, 1986; Perkins, 1995; H. L. Swanson, Jerman, & Zheng, 2008).

Students can overcome the limits of working memory in at least two ways. One obvious way is to create an external record of needed information—for example, by writing it on a piece of paper (as we often do with long division problems). Another approach is to learn some skills to automaticity—in other words, to learn them so well that they can be retrieved quickly and easily (N. Frederiksen, 1984a; Mayer & Wittrock, 1996). But in the case of automaticity, it's possible to have too much of a good thing, as we'll see in a moment.

Encourage students to write parts of a problem on paper.

Make sure students learn basic problem-solving skills to a level of automaticity.

- *How students encode a problem influences their approach in trying to solve it.* Any particular problem or situation might be represented in working memory—that is, *encoded*—in a variety of ways. As an example, see whether you can solve the problem in the following exercise.

EXPERIENCING FIRSTHAND
Pigs and Chickens

Consider this problem:

> Old MacDonald has a barnyard full of pigs and chickens. Altogether, there are 21 heads and 60 legs in the barnyard (not counting MacDonald's own head and legs). How many pigs and how many chickens are running around the barnyard?

Can you figure out the answer? If you are having trouble, think about the problem in the following way:

Some ways of encoding a problem promote more successful problem solving than others do.

Imagine that the pigs are standing upright on only their two hind legs, with their front two legs raised over their heads. Therefore, both the pigs and the chickens are standing on two legs. Figure out how many legs are on the ground and how many must be in the air. From this information, can you determine the number of pigs and chickens in the barnyard?

Because there are 21 heads, the total number of animals must be 21. Thus, there must be 42 legs on the ground (21 × 2), which leaves 18 pigs' legs in the air (60 − 42). There must therefore be 9 pigs (18 ÷ 2) and 12 chickens (21 − 9).

There are, of course, a variety of ways you might approach the pigs-and-chickens problem. But if you initially had trouble solving it, you may have been struggling to encode it in a way that led you to an easy solution. Students often have difficulty solving mathematical word problems because they don't know how to translate the problems into procedures or operations with which they are familiar (Mayer, 1992; L. B. Resnick, 1989; Reusser, 1990). For instance, you may initially have had trouble with the pigs-and-chickens problem because your algebra skills are a bit rusty.

At other times, students may encode a problem in a seemingly logical way that nevertheless fails to yield a workable result. As an example, take a stab at the problem in the following exercise.

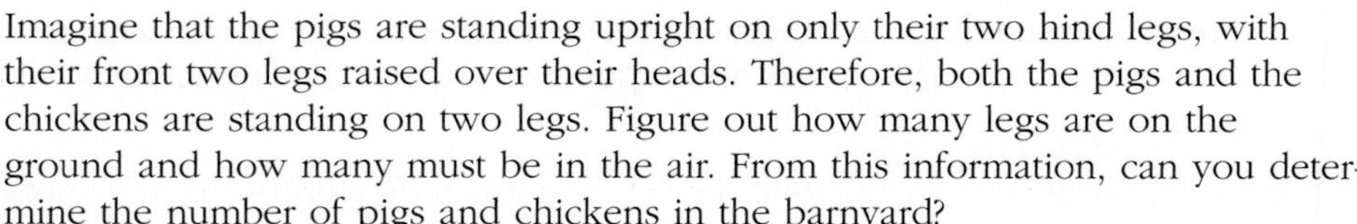

EXPERIENCING FIRSTHAND

Candle Problem

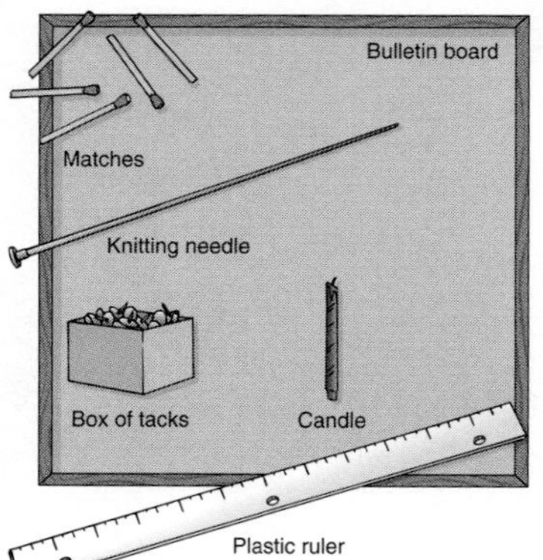

How might you stand a candle upright in front of a bulletin board attached to the wall? You don't want the candle to touch the bulletin board, because the flame might singe the board. Instead, you need to place the candle about a centimeter away from the board. How can you accomplish the task using some or all of the following materials: a small candle (birthday cake size), a metal knitting needle, matches, a box of thumbtacks, and a 12-inch ruler?

Source: Based on Duncker, 1945.

As it turns out, the ruler and knitting needle are useless in solving the problem. Piercing the candle with the knitting needle will probably break the candle, and you're unlikely to have much luck balancing the ruler on a few tacks. (I speak from experience here, as my own students have unsuccessfully tried both strategies.) The easiest solution is to turn the thumbtack box upside down or sideways, attach it to the bulletin board with tacks, and then attach the candle to the top of the box with either a tack or melted wax. Many people don't consider this possibility, however, because they encode the box only as a *container of tacks* and so overlook its potential use as a candle stand. When learners encode a problem in a way that excludes potential solutions, they are the victims of a **mental set**.

mental set Inclination to encode a problem in a way that excludes potential solutions.

Mental sets sometimes emerge when learners practice solving a particular kind of problem (e.g., doing subtraction problems in math or applying the formula $E = mc^2$ in physics) without also practicing other kinds of problems at the same time. Such repetitive practice can lead students to encode problems in a particular way without really thinking about them—in other words, it can lead to automaticity in encoding. Although automaticity in the basic information and skills needed for problem solving is often an advantage because it frees up working memory capacity, automaticity in *encoding* problems can lead students to solve them incorrectly (E. J. Langer, 2000; Luchins, 1942).

Several strategies can help students encode problems more effectively but not fall victim to counterproductive mental sets:

- Present problems in a concrete manner; for example, provide real objects that students can manipulate, or present an illustration of a problem's components.
- Encourage students to make problems concrete *for themselves;* for example, encourage them to draw a picture or diagram.
- Point out any aspects of problems that students can competently solve, and when those elements appear again in a different problem, indicate that the same information can be applied or the same approach to problem solution can be used.
- Give problems that look different on the surface yet require the same or similar problem-solving procedures.
- Mix the kinds of problems that students tackle in any single practice session.
- Have students work in cooperative groups to identify several ways of representing a single problem—perhaps as a formula, a table, and a graph.

(Anzai, 1991; Brenner et al., 1997; Z. Chen, 1999; L. S. Fuchs et al., 2003; E. J. Langer, 2000; Luchins & Luchins, 1950; Mayer, 1992; Mayfield & Chase, 2002; Prawat, 1989; Turner, Meyer, et al., 1998)

• *Complex problem solving requires considerable metacognitive involvement.* Metacognitive processes play an important role not only in studying but also in problem solving (M. Carr & Biddlecomb, 1998; J. E. Davidson & Sternberg, 1998, 2003; Dominowski, 1998). When problems are fairly complex and challenging, effective problem solvers tend to do many of the following:

- Identify one or more goals that must be accomplished to solve the problem.
- Break the problem into two or more subproblems.
- Plan a systematic, sequential approach to solving the problem and its subproblems.
- Continually monitor and evaluate progress toward the goal(s).
- Identify obstacles that may be impeding progress.
- Change to a new strategy if the current one isn't working.

Such actions enable learners to use problem-solving strategies flexibly and to determine when particular strategies aren't appropriate. In contrast, *in*effective problem solvers tend to apply problem-solving procedures mindlessly, without any real understanding of what they are doing or why they are doing it. In the opening case study, Ms. Gaunt's students rarely critique their problem solutions for logical sense; thus, they may not recognize that typing a 4,200-word paper is unlikely to take 100 days.

To some extent, students' metacognitive problem-solving processes depend on their conceptual understanding of the subject matter (M. Carr & Biddlecomb, 1998; J. E. Davidson & Sternberg, 1998). Yet students also benefit from instruction and guidance in metacognitive strategies. For example, we can do the following:

- Ask students to explain what they are doing and why they are doing it as they work on a problem.
- Give students questions they can ask themselves as they work on a problem (e.g., "Are we getting closer to our goal?" "Why is this strategy most appropriate?").
- Help students to identify common errors in their problem solving and to check regularly for these errors.

- Ask students to reflect on their problem solutions to determine whether the solutions make sense within the context of the original problems. (Dominowski, 1998; Johanning, D'Agostino, Steele, & Shumow, 1999; A. King, 1999, p. 101; Kramarski & Mevarech, 2003, p. 286; Roditi & Steinberg, 2007)

Such approaches can be especially effective when students work in pairs or small groups on challenging problems and must explain and defend their reasoning to one another.

Using Computer Technology to Teach Problem-Solving Skills

The strategies we've considered thus far have been largely "low tech." But we can also capitalize on computer technology to foster problem-solving skills. Following are several possibilities:

- Use computer-based tutoring programs to promote mathematical and scientific reasoning and problem solving.
- Show students how to use spreadsheets to analyze complex sets of data.
- Use computer simulations that allow students to formulate hypotheses, design experiments to test the hypotheses, and interpret the virtual results.
- Present complex real-world problems (i.e., authentic activities) that students must solve. (Cognition and Technology Group at Vanderbilt, 1990, 1996; Vye et al., 1998)

Numerous software packages and Internet resources can help us with the last of these strategies: presenting complex real-world problems. Here are three examples:

- *Gary Gadget: Building Cars.* Students assemble a car and drive to various destinations using a map; they occasionally encounter obstacles (e.g., a muddy road, a steep hill) that require making adjustments to the car.
- *Crazy Machines: The Wacky Contraptions Game.* Students use a collection of three-dimensional parts (e.g., pumps, pipes, generators, balls) to construct machines for various purposes (e.g., driving nails, moving heavy objects, shooting cannons).
- *Animal Hospital: Pet Vet 3D.* Students play the role of a veterinarian who must diagnose and treat a variety of sick pets and also handle the business side of a veterinary office (e.g., purchasing supplies, maintaining a reasonable workload).

Many Internet websites also provide problem-solving activities appropriate for children and adolescents. For example, the following websites offer problem-solving activities related to a wide range of topics:

- National Science Foundation (www.nsf.gov)
- Smithsonian Institution (www.smithsonianeducation.org)
- Educator's Reference Desk (www.eduref.org)
- Discovery Education (school.discoveryeducation.com)

Some of the activities on these websites are fairly traditional academic ones; others are more authentic in nature. Some of the activities also involve some degree of creativity—our next topic.

Creativity

Creativity, like problem solving, is a form of transfer, because it involves applying previously learned knowledge or skills to a new situation. Psychologists have offered varying opinions about the nature of creativity, but in general, it has two components:

- *New and original behavior.* Behavior not specifically learned from someone else
- *A productive result.* A product appropriate for and in some way valuable to one's culture (Plucker, Beghetto, & Dow, 2004; Ripple, 1989; Runco & Chand, 1995; R. K. Sawyer, 2003)

To illustrate these two components, let's say I am giving a lecture on creativity and want a creative way of keeping my students' attention. One possible approach would be to come to class stark naked. This approach certainly meets the first criterion for creativity (it's new and original) but not the second criterion (it isn't appropriate in our culture). An alternative strategy might be to give my students several challenging problems that require creative thinking. This approach is more likely to meet both criteria: Not only is it a relatively original way of teaching, but it is also appropriate and productive for students to learn about creativity by exploring the process firsthand.

Many complex tasks involve both problem solving and creativity. But the two processes differ somewhat in the extent to which they involve convergent versus divergent thinking (see Figure 8.7). To successfully tackle a problem, we typically pull together two or more pieces of information into an integrated whole that resolves the problem. This combining of information into a single idea or product is known as **convergent thinking**. In contrast, when we engage in creativity, we often begin with a single idea and take it in a variety of directions, at least one of which leads to something that is new, original, and culturally appropriate. This process of generating many different ideas from a single starting point is known as **divergent thinking**. To see the difference firsthand, try the next exercise.

FIGURE 8.7 Convergent versus divergent thinking

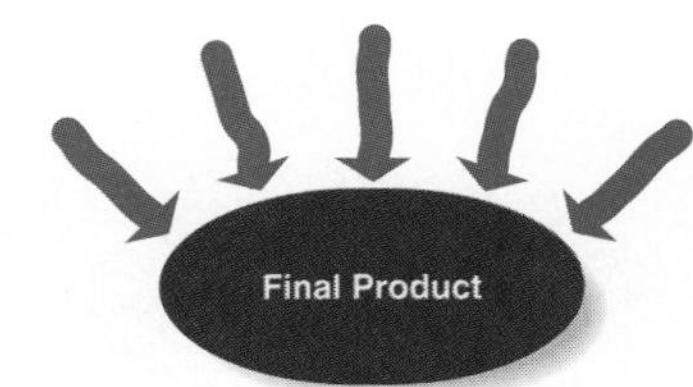

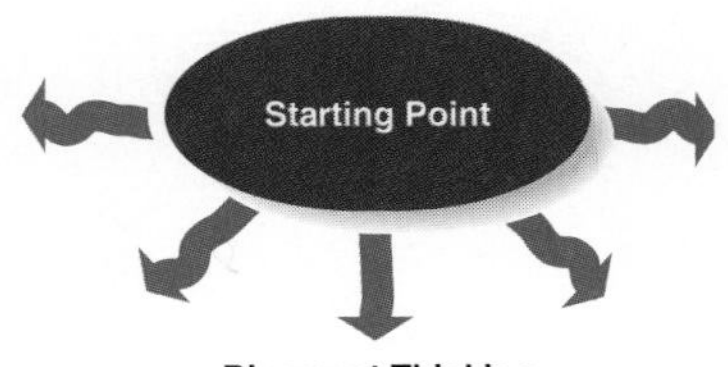

EXPERIENCING FIRSTHAND
Convergent and Divergent Thinking

On a sheet of paper, write your responses to each of the following:

1. Why are houses more often built with bricks than with stones?
2. What are some possible uses of a brick? Try to think of as many different and unusual uses as you can.
3. Add improvements to the wagon drawing so that the object will be more fun to play with.

Source: Items 2 and 3 modeled after Torrance, 1970.

To answer the first question, you must use convergent thinking to pull together the things you know about bricks, stones, and houses. But the other two items require divergent thinking about a single object: You must consider how a brick might be used in different contexts and how different parts of the wagon might be embellished—with some of your responses being novel and unique.

Contrary to popular belief, creativity is *not* a single entity that people either have or don't have. Rather, it's probably a combination of many specific thinking processes, motives, and behaviors. Among other things, creative individuals tend to have the following characteristics:

creativity New and original behavior that yields a productive and culturally appropriate result.

convergent thinking Process of pulling together several pieces of information to draw a conclusion or solve a problem.

divergent thinking Process of moving mentally in a variety of directions from a single idea.

- Considerable knowledge relevant to the task at hand
- An ability to interpret problems and situations in a flexible manner and to combine existing information and ideas in new ways
- High standards for evaluating their accomplishments
- A passion for—and therefore a willingness to invest much time and effort in—what they are doing (Csikszentmihalyi, 1996; Glover, Ronning, & Reynolds, 1989; Leung, Maddux, Galinsky, & Chiu, 2008; Runco & Chand, 1995; Russ, 1993; Simonton, 2000, 2004; Weisberg, 1993)

Furthermore, creativity is usually somewhat specific to particular situations and content areas (Glover et al., 1989; Ripple, 1989; Runco, 2004). Students may show creativity in art, writing, or science, for example, but may not be creative in all of these areas.

Fostering Creativity

Certain aspects of creative thinking may have their roots in hereditary factors, but environmental factors play an equally important role in the development of creativity (Esquivel, 1995; Ripple, 1989; Simonton, 2000). In fact, because creativity requires considerable expertise and fairly sophisticated thought processes, learners are apt to become increasingly creative as they grow older, gain diverse experiences and perspectives—ideally including *multicultural* experiences and perspectives—and have numerous opportunities to experiment with objects and ideas (Hatano & Oura, 2003; Leung et al., 2008; Simonton, 2004).

Research studies suggest several strategies for promoting creativity in the classroom:

Show students that creative thoughts and behaviors are valued. One way to do this is to encourage and reward unusual ideas and responses. For example, we can express excitement when students complete a project in a unique and unusual manner. And as we evaluate students' performance on classroom assessments, we should acknowledge responses that, although not what we were expecting, are legitimately correct. Engaging in creative activities ourselves also shows that we value creativity (B. A. Hennessey & Amabile, 1987; Lubart & Mouchiroud, 2003; Runco, 2004; Sternberg, 2003).

Focus students' attention on internal, rather than external, rewards. Students are more creative when they engage in activities they enjoy and can take pride in their accomplishments (B. A. Hennessey, 1995; Lubart & Mouchiroud, 2003). To foster creativity, then, we should occasionally give students opportunities to explore their own interests—those they will gladly pursue without having to be prodded. We can also foster creativity by downplaying the importance of grades, focusing students' attention instead on the internal satisfaction that their creative efforts bring (B. A. Hennessey, 1995; Perkins, 1990). For instance, we might say this to students in an art class:

> Please don't worry too much about grades. As long as you use the materials appropriately and give each assignment your best effort, you will do well in this class. The important thing is to find an art form that you enjoy and through which you can express yourself.

By making such a statement, we are essentially encouraging *intrinsic motivation*, a concept we'll look at more closely in Chapter 11.

Promote mastery of a subject area. Creativity in a particular subject area is more likely to occur when students have considerable mastery and conceptual understanding of a topic (Amabile & Hennessey, 1992; Haskell, 2001; Simonton, 2000). For example, if we want students to apply scientific principles in a creative manner—

perhaps as they complete a science fair experiment or develop a solution to an environmental problem—we should make sure that they first have those principles down pat.

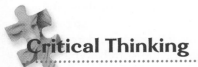

Ask thought-provoking questions. Students are more likely to think creatively when we ask **higher-level questions**: questions that require them to use previously learned information in new ways. Questions that require divergent thinking may be especially helpful (Feldhusen & Treffinger, 1980; Perkins, 1990; Torrance & Myers, 1970). For example, during a unit on the Pony Express, we might ask questions such as these:

- What are all the ways mail might have been transported across the United States at that time?
- Can you think of some very unusual way that no one else has thought of to transport mail today? (Feldhusen & Treffinger, 1980, p. 36)

Give students the freedom and security they need to take risks. To be creative, students must be willing to take risks—something they are unlikely to do if they are afraid of failing (Houtz, 1990; Sternberg, 2003). To encourage risk taking, we can allow students to engage in certain activities without evaluating their performance. We can also urge them to think of their mistakes and failures as an inevitable—but usually temporary—aspect of the creative process (B. A. Hennessey & Amabile, 1987; Pruitt, 1989). For example, when students are writing a short story, we might give them several opportunities to get our feedback, and perhaps the feedback of their peers as well, before they turn in a final product.

Provide the time that creativity requires. Students need time to experiment with new materials and ideas, to think in divergent directions, and to occasionally make mistakes. A critical aspect of promoting creativity, then, is to give them that time (Feldhusen & Treffinger, 1980; Pruitt, 1989; Sternberg, 2003). For example, when teaching a foreign language, we might ask small groups of students to write and videotape a television commercial spoken entirely in that language. This is hardly a project that students can do in a day. Rather, they may need several weeks to brainstorm ideas about characters and plot lines, write and revise a script, find or develop the props they need, and rehearse their lines. Creative ideas and products seldom emerge overnight.

Critical Thinking

The process of **critical thinking** involves evaluating the accuracy, credibility, and worth of information and lines of reasoning (Beyer, 1985; Heyman, 2008). It can take a variety of forms, depending on the context. The following exercise presents four possibilities.

EXPERIENCING FIRSTHAND
Colds, Cars, Chance, and Cheer

Read and respond to each of the following situations:

1. It's autumn, and the days are becoming increasingly chilly. You see the following advertisement in the newspaper:

   > Aren't you tired of sniffles and runny noses all winter? Tired of always feeling less than your best? Get through a whole winter without colds. Take Eradicold Pills as directed. (R. J. Harris, 1977, p. 605)

   Should you go out and buy a box of Eradicold Pills?
2. You have a beat-up old car and have invested several thousand dollars to get it

higher-level question Question that requires students to use previously learned information in a new way—that is, to engage in higher-level cognitive processes.

critical thinking Process of evaluating the accuracy, credibility, and worth of information and lines of reasoning.

in working order. You can sell the car in its present condition for $1,500, or you can invest a couple thousand dollars more on repairs and then sell it for $3,000. What should you do? (modeled after Halpern, 1998)

3. You have been rolling a typical six-sided die (i.e., one member of a pair of dice). You know for a fact that the die isn't "loaded" (i.e., it's not heavier on one side than another), yet in the past 30 rolls you have not rolled a number 4 even once. What are the odds that you will get a 4 on the next roll?

4. This research finding was presented by Dr. Edmund Emmer at the annual conference of the American Educational Research Association in 1994:

   Teachers who feel happy when they teach are more likely to have well-behaved students (Emmer, 1994).

   If you are a teacher, do such results suggest that you should try to feel happy when you enter the classroom each morning?

In each of these situations, you had to evaluate information and make some sort of judgment. In Item 1, I hope you weren't tempted to purchase Eradicold Pills, because the advertisement provided no proof that they reduce cold symptoms. The ad simply included the suggestion to "Take Eradicold Pills as directed" within the context of a discussion of undesirable symptoms—a common ploy in persuasive advertising.

As for Item 2, it makes more sense to sell the car now. If you sell the car for $3,000 after making $2,000 worth of repairs, you will make $500 less than you would otherwise. Many people mistakenly believe that their past investments justify making additional ones, when, in fact, past investments are irrelevant to the present state of affairs (Halpern, 1998).

In Item 3, the chance of rolling a 4 on an evenly balanced die is one in six. The outcomes of previous rolls are irrelevant, because each roll is independent of the others. But when a 4 hasn't shown up even once in 30 rolls, many people believe that a 4 is long overdue and so greatly overestimate its probability—a misconception known as the *gambler's fallacy*.

Now what about making sure you're happy each time you enter the classroom (Item 4)? One common mistake people make in interpreting research results is to think that an association (*correlation*) between two things means that one of those things must *cause* the other. As we noted in Chapter 1, however, correlation doesn't necessarily show causation. Perhaps teacher happiness directly influences students' classroom behavior, but there are other possible explanations for the correlation as well. For instance, perhaps good student behavior makes teachers feel happy (rather than vice versa), or perhaps teachers who feel upbeat use more effective teaching techniques and can better keep students on task as a result (Emmer, 1994).

The four situations presented in the preceding exercise illustrate several forms that critical thinking can take (Halpern, 1997, 1998, 2008; Nussbaum, 2008):

- *Verbal reasoning*. Understanding and evaluating persuasive techniques found in oral and written language. You engaged in verbal reasoning when deciding whether to purchase Eradicold Pills.
- *Argument analysis*. Discriminating between reasons that do and do not support a conclusion. You engaged in argument analysis when you considered possible pros and cons of investing an additional $2,000 in car repairs.
- *Probabilistic reasoning*. Determining the likelihood and uncertainties associated with various events. You engaged in probabilistic reasoning when you determined the probability of rolling a 4 on the die.
- *Hypothesis testing*. Judging the value of data and research results in terms of the methods used to obtain them and their potential relevance to certain conclusions. When hypothesis testing includes critical thinking, it involves considering questions such as the following:

- Was an appropriate method used to measure a particular outcome?
- Have other possible explanations or conclusions been eliminated?
- Can the results obtained in one situation be reasonably generalized to other situations?

You engaged in hypothesis testing when you evaluated Dr. Emmer's findings about teacher happiness.

Critical thinking takes different forms in different content domains.

The nature of critical thinking is different in various content domains. In writing, critical thinking may involve reading the first draft of a persuasive essay to look for errors in logical reasoning or for situations in which opinions have not been sufficiently justified. In science, it may involve revising existing theories or beliefs to account for new evidence; that is, it may involve conceptual change. In history, it may involve drawing inferences from historical documents, attempting to determine whether things *definitely* happened a particular way or only *maybe* happened that way.

As you might guess, critical thinking skills emerge gradually over the course of childhood and adolescence (Amsterlaw, 2006; Kuhn & Franklin, 2006; Metz, 2004; Pillow, 2002). Yet all too often, students at all grade levels (even college students) take the information they see in textbooks, advertisements, media reports, and elsewhere at face value. In other words, they engage in little or no critical analysis of the information. Students are more likely to look analytically and critically at new information if they believe that even experts' understanding of a topic continues to evolve as new evidence accumulates. They are *less* likely to engage in critical thinking if they believe that knowledge is an absolute, unchanging entity (Kardash & Scholes, 1996; Kuhn, 2001a; Schommer-Aikins, 2001). Thus, students' *epistemic beliefs* enter into the critical thinking process.

Fostering Critical Thinking

Critical thinking is a disposition as well as a set of higher-level thinking skills. In other words, some learners are more inclined than others to approach new ideas in a thoughtful, analytical, evaluative manner (Halpern, 2008; Perkins, Tishman, Ritchhart, Donis, & Andrade, 2000). Yet researchers have had some success in *nurturing* critical thinking in children and adolescents (Abrami et al., 2008; Kuhn & Franklin, 2006). Perhaps because critical thinking encompasses such a variety of cognitive skills, strategies for encouraging it are many and varied. Following are recommendations that researchers have offered:

- Teach fewer topics, but in greater depth—the *Less is more* principle once again.
- Encourage some intellectual skepticism—for instance, by urging students to question and challenge the ideas they read and hear—and communicate the message that our knowledge and understanding of any single topic will continue to change over time.
- Model critical thinking—for instance, by thinking aloud while analyzing a persuasive argument or scientific report.
- Give students numerous opportunities to practice critical thinking—for instance, by identifying flaws in the arguments of a persuasive essay, evaluating the quality and usefulness of a scientific finding, and using evidence and logic to support a particular viewpoint.
- Ask questions such as these to encourage critical thinking:
  - Who produced this document? What biases or predispositions did the author or authors have?
  - What persuasive technique is the author using? Is it valid, or is it designed to mislead the reader?

- What information contradicts information in other documents?
- What reasons support the conclusion? What reasons do *not* support the conclusion?
- What actions might I take to improve the design of this study? (Questions based on Halpern, 1998, p. 454; S. A. Stahl & Shanahan, 2004, pp. 110–111)

- Have students debate controversial issues from several perspectives, and occasionally ask them to defend a perspective quite different from their own.
- Help students understand that critical thinking involves considerable mental effort but that its benefits make the effort worthwhile.
- Embed critical thinking skills within the context of authentic activities as a way of helping students retrieve those skills later on, both in the workplace and in other aspects of adult life. (Chinn, Anderson, & Waggoner, 2001; Derry, Levin, Osana, & Jones, 1998; Halpern, 1998; Heyman, 2008; Kardash & Scholes, 1996; Kuhn, 2001a; Kuhn & Weinstock, 2002; Monte-Sano, 2008; Nussbaum, 2008; Onosko, 1989; Onosko & Newmann, 1994; Reiter, 1994)

The Into the Classroom feature "Fostering Critical Thinking" presents examples of what teachers might do in language arts, social studies, and science.

Using an Internet search engine such as Yahoo! or Google, you can find numerous computer software programs allegedly designed to promote critical thinking skills. Some of them may be effective, whereas others may not be. When considering them for possible use in your classroom, keep in mind that, like all complex cognitive processes, critical thinking skills are probably most effectively learned—and most likely to be transferred to new situations—when they're practiced within the context of specific academic topics (e.g., Kuhn & Franklin, 2006; S. A. Stahl & Shanahan, 2004).

It's important that students think critically not only about what they read and hear in the classroom but also about what they see online (e.g., see Figure 8.8). People with a wide variety of motives and ideologies post their ideas on websites, and students must learn to scrutinize every posting with a skeptical eye. One good resource for

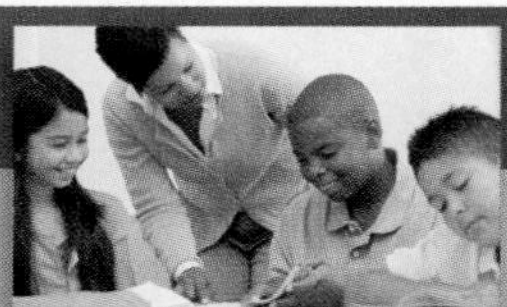

INTO THE Classroom

Fostering Critical Thinking

Teach elements of critical thinking.

In a unit on persuasion and argumentation, a junior high school language arts teacher explains that a sound argument meets three criteria: (a) The evidence presented to justify the argument is accurate and consistent; (b) the evidence is relevant to and provides sufficient support for the conclusion; and (c) little or no information has been omitted that, if present, would lead to a contradictory conclusion. The teacher then has students practice applying these criteria to a variety of persuasive and argumentative essays.

Foster epistemic beliefs that encourage critical thinking.

Rather than teach history as a collection of facts to be memorized, a high school history teacher portrays the discipline as an attempt by informed but inevitably biased scholars to interpret and make sense of historical events. On several occasions, he asks his students to read two or three different historians' accounts of the same incident and to look for evidence of personal bias in each one.

Embed critical thinking skills within the context of authentic activities.

In a unit on statistical and scientific reasoning, an eighth-grade science class studies concepts related to probability, correlation, and experimental control. Then, as part of a simulated legislative hearing, the students work in small groups to develop arguments for or against a legislative bill concerning the marketing and use of vitamins and other dietary supplements. To find evidence to support their arguments, the students apply what they've learned about statistics and experimentation as they read and analyze journal articles and government reports about the possible benefits and drawbacks of nutritional supplements.

Sources: Derry et al., 1998 (statistics example based on this study); Halpern, 1997 (criteria for a sound argument); Paxton, 1999 (history example).

FIGURE 8.8 As a ninth-grade social studies teacher at an English-language school in Thailand, my son Jeff asked his students to critically evaluate what they saw on certain Internet websites. Students submitted their responses electronically, allowing them to paste excerpts from the websites directly into their homework. Here are examples of the tasks and questions Jeff assigned. Used with courtesy of Jeff Ormrod.

Mad Media Investigation

Bad News?

- Begin by going to www.bangkokpost.com or the website of another major world news organization (New York Times, CNN, BBC, etc.).
- Look over all of the major headlines. How many of them are bad/negative news stories (violence, war, economic turndown, political figures doing bad things, etc.)?
- How many of the major headings are good/positive news stories (people giving to good causes, charities, human interest stories, etc.)?
- What types of pictures appear on the front page? Copy one here, and discuss what it shows and why the news organization might have chosen to use it.
- What do you think the main motivations of the news media might be?

Cash Clothes:

- Find an advertisement for a particular brand of clothing, and copy the image/example to this document.
- Where did you find this advertisement?
- What types of people would be using this website/magazine?
- Describe how the company is using the text, art, pictures, and graphics to sell its product.
- Does this advertisement make you want to do anything? to buy the product?

teachers is a website maintained by the Center for Media Literacy (www.medialit.org), where you can find free software that teaches students to ask themselves questions such as these:

- Who created this message?
- What values, lifestyles, and points of view are represented in, or omitted from, this message?
- Why is this message being sent? (Center for Media Literacy, n.d.)

In this age of widespread access to the Internet, critical thinking skills are now more *critical* than ever.

Diversity in Creativity, Critical Thinking, and Other Complex Thinking Processes

We might reasonably speculate that Western schools' focus on meaningful learning and conceptual understanding enhances students' ability to be creative. One recent study with college students found students from a European American background to be especially proficient in solving math problems requiring creative thinking (Schommer-Aikins & Easter, 2008). Perhaps more significant, however, was the finding that experiences in *two or more cultures* enhanced creative thinking and behaviors. Quite possibly, having such a multicultural background exposes learners to a broader range of concepts, ideas, and perspectives from which to draw when trying to think "outside the box" (Leung et al., 2008).

Critical thinking is another complex cognitive process that seems to depend somewhat on students' cultural backgrounds. Some cultures place high value on respecting one's elders or certain religious leaders, and in doing so, they may foster the belief that "truth" is a cut-and-dried entity that's best gained from authority figures (Losh, 2003; Qian & Pan, 2002; Tyler et al., 2008). Furthermore, a cultural emphasis on maintaining group harmony may discourage children from hashing out differences in perspectives, which critical thinking often entails (Kağitçibaşi, 2007; Kuhn & Park, 2005). Perhaps as a result of such factors, critical thinking may be less common in some groups (e.g., in some

Teach students tactful and respectful ways of critiquing other people's arguments and viewpoints. For example, suggest that they pose questions in a nonthreatening way, perhaps like this: "What if someone were to criticize your idea by saying _____? How might you answer that person?"

traditional Asian communities and in certain fundamentalist religious groups in the United States) than in others (Kuhn, Daniels, & Krishnan, 2003; Kuhn & Park, 2005). In some situations, then, we must walk a fine line between teaching students to critically evaluate persuasive arguments and scientific evidence, on the one hand, and to show appropriate respect and strive for group harmony in their community and culture, on the other.

Accommodating Students with Special Needs

In addition to differences that may be a function of cultural background, researchers have observed differences in complex thinking skills for students with various disabilities and for those who have advanced cognitive abilities. Table 8.3 presents some of the characteristics you are likely to see in students with special needs, along with recommendations for working with these students.

Students in Inclusive Settings

TABLE 8.3
Promoting Advanced Thinking Skills in Students with Special Educational Needs

Category	Characteristics You Might Observe	Suggested Strategies
Students with specific cognitive or academic difficulties	• Difficulty in transferring learned information to new situations • Difficulties in problem solving, perhaps because of limited working memory capacity, inability to identify important aspects of a problem, inability to retrieve appropriate problem-solving strategies, or limited metacognitive problem-solving skills	• Encourage and scaffold transfer of school topics. • Model effective problem-solving strategies, and scaffold students' efforts to use them (e.g., teach questions that students should ask themselves as they work their way through problems). • Present simple problems at first; then gradually move to more difficult problems as students gain proficiency and self-confidence. • Teach techniques for minimizing the load on working memory during problem solving (e.g., writing parts of a problem on paper, drawing a diagram of the problem).
Students with social or behavioral problems	• Deficiencies in social problem-solving skills	• Teach social problem-solving skills (see Chapter 10 for ideas).
Students with general delays in cognitive and social functioning	• Difficulty in transferring information and skills to new situations • Few effective problem-solving strategies • Little, if any, ability to think creatively or critically about classroom topics	• Teach new information and skills in the specific contexts and situations in which students should be able to use them. • Present simple problems, and guide students through each step in determining the solutions.
Students with physical or sensory challenges	• No consistent deficits in complex cognitive processes; deficits are sometimes due to students' limited experiences with tasks that require higher-level thinking	• Address any deficits in higher-level thinking skills with strategies you would use with nondisabled students, making appropriate accommodations for physical and sensory limitations.
Students with advanced cognitive development	• Greater transfer of learning to new situations • Greater effectiveness in problem solving, more sophisticated problem-solving strategies, greater flexibility in strategy use, and less susceptibility to mental sets • Divergent thinking (e.g., asking unusual questions, giving novel responses) • Greater potential for critical thinking	• Place greater emphasis on higher-level processes (e.g., transfer, problem solving) within the curriculum. • Teach higher-level thinking skills within the context of specific classroom topics, rather than in isolation from academic content. • Accept and encourage divergent thinking, including unanticipated yet appropriate responses. • Encourage critical analysis of ideas, opinions, and evidence.

Sources: Beirne-Smith et al., 2006; Brownell, Mellard, & Deshler, 1993; B. Clark, 1997; DuPaul & Eckert, 1994; E. S. Ellis & Friend, 1991; N. R. Ellis, 1979; Frasier, 1989; S. Goldstein & Rider, 2006; K. R. Harris, 1982; Heward, 2009; M. C. Linn et al., 1989; Maker, 1993; Mastropieri & Scruggs, 2007; Meichenbaum, 1977; Mercer & Pullen, 2005; Piirto, 1999; Pulos & Linn, 1981; Slife, Weiss, & Bell, 1985; Stanley, 1980; Torrance, 1989; Turnbull et al., 2007.

The Big Picture

If we focus classroom activities on learning isolated facts and if we also use assessment techniques that emphasize students' knowledge of those facts, then students will naturally begin to believe that school learning is a process of absorbing information in a rote fashion and regurgitating it later on. But if we instead focus class time and activities on *doing things with* information—for instance, applying, analyzing, and critically evaluating it—then students should acquire the cognitive processes and skills that will serve them well in the world beyond the classroom.

Throughout the chapter, we've identified numerous strategies for fostering effective learning strategies, transfer, problem solving, creativity, and critical thinking. Several basic principles summarize many of these strategies:

- ***Meaningful learning and conceptual understanding are more conducive to higher-level thinking skills than rote memorization.*** Students can better apply and critique classroom subject matter if they acquire a thorough and cohesive understanding of it. Thus, we have repeatedly encountered the *Less is more* principle: Teaching a few topics in depth is almost invariably more effective than skimming over the surface of a great many topics.

- ***Higher-level thinking skills are best learned within the context of specific academic topics.*** As teachers, we will occasionally run across packaged curricular programs designed to teach complex cognitive processes such as study strategies, problem solving, and critical thinking. But as a general rule, we are better advised to teach higher-level thinking skills within the context of academic subject matter—for example, teaching critical thinking and problem-solving skills as students study science and teaching creative thinking as students write short stories.

- ***Sophisticated beliefs about the nature of knowledge and learning increase the prevalence of higher-level thinking skills.*** Students' epistemic beliefs about a particular academic discipline—as well as about knowledge and learning more generally—have a significant impact on how they study, what they learn, how readily they apply classroom subject matter, and how often they critically evaluate it. For example, students are more likely to critically evaluate what they read and hear if they understand that knowledge about many topics continues to evolve over time as new evidence and perspectives appear on the scene. Some classroom topics are cut and dried, to be sure; 2 + 2 will always equal 4 (at least in a base-10 number system), mammals definitely have backbones (i.e., they are vertebrates), and Columbus's first trip across the Atlantic is well documented as having taken place in 1492. But our society's knowledge of other topics—for instance, the human brain, global climate change, and distant galaxies—grows by leaps and bounds every year.

- ***Group discussions and projects provide a supportive context in which to acquire and practice higher-level thinking skills.*** When students talk with one another, they must verbalize—and therefore become more metacognitively aware of—what and how they are thinking. They also hear other (possibly better) ideas, interpretations, problem-solving strategies, and critical analyses. Invariably, too, they scaffold one another's attempts at higher-level tasks that might be too difficult for any one of them to accomplish individually.

- ***Authentic activities can help promote transfer of thinking skills to real-life settings.*** We don't necessarily want to fill the school day with one authentic activity after another, as students may need the time and opportunities to practice certain things without much distraction—basic math facts, grammatical rules, symbols for various elements in chemistry, and so on (J. R. Anderson et al., 1996). However, unless authentic activities are a regular part of the school curriculum, students may find that thinking about school subject matter in sophisticated ways has little relevance to their lives in the outside world.

- ***Higher-level thinking skills must be a priority in assessment activities as well as in classroom instruction.*** It's fairly easy to construct assignments and tests that assess knowledge of basic facts and procedures. But it's ultimately more important that we assess what students can *do* with that knowledge.

Practice for Your Licensure Exam

Interview with Emily

In the ninth and tenth grades, Emily earns mostly Cs and Ds in her classes. When she reaches eleventh grade, however, she begins to work more diligently on her schoolwork, and by the first semester of twelfth grade, she is earning As and Bs. Ms. Tillman, a preservice teacher, interviews Emily about her study strategies:

Ms. T.: Now that you're receiving good grades, how do you study for a test?

Emily: Well, it's different for every subject. Now when I study for a math test, I do many practice problems. When I'm studying for a history or science test, I first review my notes. My favorite thing to do is make flashcards with the important facts. I then go through the flashcards many times and try to learn the facts on them.

Ms. T.: What do you mean, "learn" the facts on them?

Emily: I guess I try to memorize the facts. I'll go through the flashcards many times and say them over and over in my head until I remember them.

Ms. T.: How do you know when a fact is memorized?

Emily: I'll repeat a fact over and over in my head until I think I've memorized it. Then I'll leave and do something else, like get a snack. I know I've memorized something if I still remember it after taking my break.

Ms. T.: Do you consider yourself a good textbook reader?

Emily: Not really. Textbooks are pretty boring. I'll try to read everything in the textbook, but at times I find myself looking for boldface print. Phrases in bold print are important.

Ms. T.: What are some good methods for studying for a test?

Emily: I really like the flashcard method because it helps me to memorize facts. I also like to reread the text and my notes. Another good method is outlining the text, but this method takes too long so I rarely use it. (Interview used courtesy of Melissa Tillman)

1. **Constructed-response question:**

   In the interview, Emily reveals several strategies she uses to learn and remember school subject matter.

   A. Identify three specific strategies that Emily uses when she studies.

   B. For each strategy you've identified, describe the extent to which it's likely to help Emily remember and apply school subject matter over the long run. Base your explanation on contemporary principles and theories of learning, memory, and metacognition.

2. **Multiple-choice question:**

   Emily says, "My favorite thing to do is make flashcards with the important facts. I then go through the flashcards many times and try to learn the facts on them." This statement suggests that Emily views academic subject matter as being primarily a collection of discrete facts. Such a perspective is an example of which one of the following?

   a. Critical thinking
   b. Divergent thinking
   c. An illusion of knowing
   d. An epistemic belief

Go to Chapter 8 of the Book-Specific Resources in **MyEducationLab,** and click on "Practice for Your Licensure Exam" to answer these questions. Compare your responses with the feedback provided. 

PRAXIS

Turn to Appendix C, "Matching Book and MyEducationLab Content to the Praxis Principles of Learning and Teaching Tests," to discover sections of this chapter that may be especially applicable to the Praxis tests.

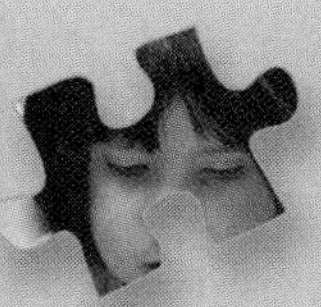

PEARSON myeducationlab

Now go to MyEducationLab (**www.myeducationlab.com**) where you can:

- Find learning outcomes for Complex Cognitive Processes, along with the national standards that connect to these outcomes.
- Complete Assignments and Activities that can help you more deeply understand the chapter content.
- Engage in Building Teaching Skills and Dispositions exercises in which you can apply and practice core teaching skills identified in the chapter.
- Access Book-Specific Resources:
  - Check your comprehension of chapter content by going to the Study Plan, where you can find (a) Chapter Objectives; (b) Focus Questions that can guide your reading; (c) a Self-Check Quiz that can help you monitor your progress in mastering chapter content; (d) Review, Practice, and Enrichment exercises with detailed feedback that will deepen your understanding of various concepts and principles; (e) Flashcards that can give you practice in understanding and defining key terms; and (f) Common Beliefs and Misconceptions about Educational Psychology that will alert you to typical misunderstandings in educational psychology classes.
- Video Examples of various concepts and principles presented in the chapter.
- Supplementary Readings that enable you to pursue certain topics in greater depth.
- A Practice for Your Licensure Exam exercise that resembles the kinds of questions appearing on many teacher licensure tests.

CHAPTER OUTLINE

CHAPTER OBJECTIVES

- **Objective 9.1:** Describe five basic assumptions underlying behaviorist views of learning, and apply these assumptions to classroom practice.
- **Objective 9.2:** Explain how learners can acquire involuntary responses through classical conditioning and how you might help them overcome those responses that interfere with classroom performance.
- **Objective 9.3:** Describe the effects that various kinds of consequences can have on behavior.
- **Objective 9.4:** Apply behaviorist principles to encourage productive student behaviors and discourage undesirable student behaviors both inside and outside the classroom.
- **Objective 9.5:** Use a behaviorist perspective to describe the diversity you are likely to see among students.
- **Objective 9.6:** Describe three kinds of situations in which behaviorist techniques are unlikely to be helpful.

Chapter 9

Behaviorist Views of Learning

CASE STUDY: The Attention Getter

James is the sixth child in a family of nine children. He likes many things; for instance, he likes rock music, comic books, basketball, and strawberry ice cream. But more than anything else, James likes attention.

James is a skillful attention getter. He gets his teacher's attention by making outrageous comments in class, throwing paper clips and erasers in the teacher's direction, and refusing to turn in classroom assignments. He gets the attention of classmates by teasing them, poking them, and writing obscenities on the restroom walls. By the middle of the school year, James is getting an extra bonus as well: His antics have increased to the point that he also gets the assistant principal's attention at least once a week.

- **Why do you think James chooses inappropriate behaviors, rather than more productive ones, as a way of getting other people's attention?**

AS YOU CONSIDER JAMES'S SITUATION, think back to your own experiences as a student in elementary and secondary school. Which students received the most attention: those who behaved well or those who behaved poorly? Chances are, it was the *mis*behaving students to whom your teachers and classmates paid the most attention (Landrum & Kauffman, 2006; J. C. Taylor & Romanczyk, 1994). James has undoubtedly learned that if he wants to be noticed—if he wants to stand out in a crowd—he must behave in ways that are difficult to ignore.

Throughout our lives, we acquire many, many new behaviors—how to use scissors, catch a softball, get other people's attention, and so on. In most cases, we develop such behaviors because our environment encourages us to do so. In this chapter, we'll examine a theoretical perspective known as **behaviorism**, which focuses on how environmental stimuli bring about changes in people's behaviors. We'll also use behaviorist ideas to understand how, as teachers, we can help students acquire behaviors that are perhaps more complex, productive, or prosocial than the ones they exhibit when they first enter our classrooms.

behaviorism Theoretical perspective in which learning and behavior are described and explained in terms of stimulus–response relationships.

Basic Assumptions of Behaviorism

When psychologists first began studying human learning and behavior systematically in the late 1880s, much of their work involved asking people to "look" inside their heads and describe what they were doing mentally (e.g., Ebbinghaus, 1885/1913; Galton, 1880; James, 1890). But beginning in the early 1900s, some psychologists criticized this approach as being subjective and scientifically unsound. In their minds, the human mind was a "black box" that simply could not be opened for inspection. Instead, these psychologists began to focus on two things that could be observed and objectively measured: environmental events, or **stimuli** (sometimes abbreviated as **S**), and people's behaviors, or **responses** (sometimes abbreviated as **R**). This focus gave rise to the behaviorist movement, which dominated much of psychology in the middle decades of the twentieth century, especially in North America.

In later decades, psychologists became increasingly inventive in their effects to study thinking processes with scientific rigor, and many left the behaviorist approach behind for more cognitively oriented approaches. Nevertheless, behaviorism is still very much alive and well, in large part because behaviorist concepts and principles can be quite useful in helping people of all ages acquire productive behaviors in classrooms and other settings.

Underlying the behaviorist perspective are several key assumptions:

- *People's behaviors are largely the result of their experiences with environmental stimuli.* Historically, many behaviorists have suggested that, with the exception of a few simple reflexes, a person is born as a "blank slate" (or in Latin, *tabula rasa*), with no inherited tendency to behave one way or another. Over the years, the environment "writes" on this slate, slowly molding, or **conditioning**, the person into someone who has unique characteristics and ways of behaving.

As teachers, we must keep in mind the very significant effect that students' past and present environments are likely to have on their behaviors. We can often use this basic principle to our advantage: By changing the classroom environment, we may also be able to change how students behave.

- *Learning involves a behavior change.* In Chapter 6, we defined *learning* as "a long-term change in mental representations or associations as a result of experience." Some behaviorists would quibble with this definition because we can't *see* mental changes. Instead, they suggest, we might define learning as a change in *behavior* due to experience. Such a view of learning can be especially useful in the classroom. Consider this scenario:

> Your students look at you attentively as you explain a difficult concept. When you finish, you ask "Any questions?" You look around the room, and not a single hand is raised. "Good," you think, "they all understand."

But *do* your students understand? On the basis of what you've just observed, you really have no idea whether they do or don't. Only observable behavior changes—perhaps an improvement in achievement test scores, a greater frequency of independent reading, or a reduction in off-task behaviors—can ultimately tell us that learning has occurred.

- *Learning involves forming associations among stimuli and responses.* By and large, behaviorist principles focus on relationships among observable events. For example, the opening case study illustrates one important behaviorist principle: People are more likely to learn and exhibit behaviors that bring about certain kinds of consequences. In particular, James increases his disruptive behaviors (*responses*) because those behaviors lead other people to behave in certain ways (i.e., their behaviors are *stimuli* for James).

If we were to take a strict "black box" perspective here, we wouldn't concern ourselves with what's going on inside James's head at all. But in recent decades,

stimulus (S) Specific object or event that influences an individual's learning or behavior.

response (R) Specific behavior that an individual exhibits.

conditioning Term commonly used by behaviorists for *learning*; typically involves specific environmental events leading to the acquisition of specific responses.

it has become increasingly evident, even to behaviorists, just how difficult it is to omit thinking from explanations of learning and behavior. Accordingly, some behaviorists have begun to incorporate cognitive processes and other internal phenomena into their theoretical explanations (e.g., DeGrandpre, 2000; Rescorla, 1988). As you read this chapter, you will find that I occasionally allude to internal phenomena in my discussion of behaviorist principles. In doing so, I am revealing my own biases as a cognitive psychologist, and pure behaviorists might object.

"Stimulus, response! Stimulus, response! Don't you ever *think?*"

• *Learning is most likely to take place when stimuli and responses occur close together in time.* When two events occur at more or less the same time—perhaps two stimuli or perhaps a stimulus and a response—we say that there is **contiguity** between them. The following examples illustrate contiguity:

> One of your instructors (Professor X) scowls at you as she hands back an exam she has just corrected. You discover that you have gotten a D− on the exam, and your entire body tenses up. The next time Professor X scowls at you, that same bodily tension returns.
>
> Another instructor (Professor Y) calls on you every time you raise your hand. Although you are fairly quiet in your other classes, you find yourself raising your hand and speaking up more frequently in this one.

In the first situation, Professor X's scowl and the D− on your exam are presented more or less simultaneously. Here, we see contiguity between two stimuli. In the second situation, your hand-raising response is followed immediately by Professor Y's request for your input. In this case, we see contiguity between a response and a subsequent stimulus (although calling on you is a response that Professor Y makes, it is a *stimulus* for *you*). In both situations, a behavior has changed: You've learned to tighten your muscles every time one instructor scowls, and you've learned to raise your hand and speak up more frequently in another instructor's class.

• *Many species of animals, including human beings, learn in similar ways.* Many behaviorist principles have been derived from research with nonhuman animals. For instance, as you'll see in a moment, our knowledge about classical conditioning first emerged from Ivan Pavlov's early work with dogs. And another well-known behaviorist, B. F. Skinner, worked almost exclusively with rats and pigeons. Students in my own educational psychology classes sometimes resent having human learning compared to that of laboratory rats. But the fact is that behaviorist principles developed from the study of nonhuman animals are often quite helpful in explaining human behavior.

Table 9.1 summarizes the five assumptions just described and draws general implications for classroom practice.

Building on Existing Stimulus–Response Associations: Classical Conditioning

Consider this situation:

> Alan has always loved baseball. But in a game last year, he was badly hurt by a wild pitch while he was up at bat. Now, although he still plays baseball, he gets

contiguity Occurrence of two or more events (e.g., two stimuli, or a stimulus and a response) at approximately the same time.

Principles/ Assumptions

TABLE 9.1
Basic Assumptions of Behaviorism and Their Educational Implications

Assumption	Educational Implication	Example
Influence of the environment	Create a classroom environment that fosters desirable student behaviors.	When a student consistently has trouble working independently, praise her inconspicuously every time she completes an assignment without having to be prompted.
Learning as a behavior change	Conclude that learning has occurred only when students exhibit a change in classroom performance.	Regularly assess students' learning, and look for ongoing progress in what they know and can do.
Focus on observable events (stimuli and responses)	Identify specific stimuli (including your own actions as a teacher) that may be influencing students' behaviors.	If a student frequently engages in disruptive classroom behavior, consider whether you might be encouraging such behavior by giving him attention every time he misbehaves.
Contiguity of events	If you want students to associate two events (stimuli, responses, or stimulus and response), make sure those events occur close together in time.	Include enjoyable yet educational activities in each day's schedule as a way of helping students associate school subject matter with pleasurable feelings.
Similarity of learning principles across species	Remember that research with nonhuman species often has relevance for classroom practice.	Reinforce a hyperactive student for sitting quietly for successively longer time periods—a *shaping* process based on early research studies with rats and pigeons.

anxious whenever it is his turn at bat, to the point that his heart rate increases and he often backs away from the ball instead of swinging at it.

One possible explanation of Alan's behavior is **classical conditioning**, a theory that explains how we sometimes learn new responses as a result of two stimuli being present at approximately the same time. Alan experienced two stimuli—an oncoming baseball and its painful impact—almost simultaneously. Alan's current responses to a pitched ball—his physiological reactions and his backing away—are ones he didn't exhibit before his painful experience with the baseball. Thus, learning has occurred.

Classical conditioning was first described by Ivan Pavlov (e.g., 1927), a Russian physiologist who was conducting research about salivation. Pavlov often used dogs in his research projects and presented meat to get them to salivate. He noticed that the dogs often began to salivate as soon as they heard the lab assistant coming down the hall, even though they could not yet smell the meat the assistant was carrying. Curious about this phenomenon, Pavlov conducted an experiment to examine more systematically how a dog learns to salivate in response to a new stimulus. His experiment went something like this:

1. Pavlov flashes a light. The dog does not salivate to the light stimulus. Using S for stimulus and R for response, we can symbolize Pavlov's first observation like this:

   S (light) → R (none)

2. Pavlov flashes the light again and presents meat immediately afterward. He repeats this procedure several times, and the dog salivates each time. The dog is demonstrating something it already knows how to do—salivate to meat—and has not yet learned anything new. We can symbolize Pavlov's second observation like so:

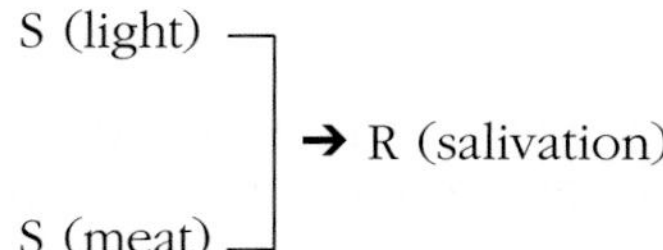

classical conditioning Form of learning in which a new, involuntary response is acquired as a result of two stimuli being presented at the same time.

3. Pavlov flashes the light once more but this time without any meat. The dog salivates; in other words, it has learned a new response to the light stimulus. We can symbolize Pavlov's third observation this way:

   S (light) ➔ R (salivation)

In more general terms, classical conditioning proceeds as follows:

1. It begins with a stimulus–response association that already exists—in other words, an *unconditioned* stimulus–response association. Pavlov's dog salivates automatically whenever it smells meat, and Alan becomes upset and backs away whenever he encounters a painful stimulus. No learning is involved in either case. When a stimulus leads to a particular response without prior learning, we say that an **unconditioned stimulus (UCS)** elicits an **unconditioned response (UCR)**.[1] The unconditioned response is typically an automatic, involuntary one, over which the learner has little or no control.
2. Conditioning occurs when a **neutral stimulus**—one that doesn't elicit any particular response—is presented immediately before the unconditioned stimulus. In the case of Pavlov's dog, a light is presented immediately before the meat. In the case of Alan, a baseball is pitched immediately before the painful impact. Conditioning is especially likely to occur when both stimuli are presented together on several occasions and when the neutral stimulus occurs *only* when the unconditioned stimulus is about to follow (R. R. Miller & Barnet, 1993; Rachlin, 1991; Rescorla, 1967). Sometimes one pairing is enough, especially if the unconditioned stimulus is a very painful or frightening one.
3. Before long, the new stimulus also elicits a response, usually one very similar to the unconditioned response. The neutral stimulus has become a **conditioned stimulus (CS)**, and the response to it has become a **conditioned response (CR)**. For example, Pavlov's dog acquires a conditioned response of salivation to a new, conditioned stimulus—the light. Likewise, Alan acquires conditioned responses of anxiety and backing away from a pitched baseball. Like the unconditioned response, the conditioned response is an involuntary one: It occurs automatically every time the conditioned stimulus is presented.

Classical Conditioning of Involuntary Emotional Responses

Classical conditioning can help us understand how people learn a variety of involuntary responses, especially responses associated with physiological functioning or emotion (Mineka & Zinbarg, 2006; Watson & Rayner, 1920). Following are three examples of how unpleasant emotional responses might be learned through classical conditioning. Notice that in each case, two stimuli are presented together: One stimulus already elicits a response, and the second stimulus begins to elicit a similar response as a result of the pairing.

- Bernard falls into a swimming pool and almost drowns. A year later, when his mother takes him to the local recreation center for a swimming lesson, he cries hysterically as she tries to drag him to the side of the pool.

  UCS: inability to breathe ➔ UCR: fear of asphyxiation
  CS: swimming pool ➔ CR: fear of the pool

unconditioned stimulus (UCS) Stimulus that elicits a particular response without prior learning.

unconditioned response (UCR) Response that is elicited by a particular (unconditioned) stimulus without prior learning.

neutral stimulus Stimulus that does not elicit any particular response.

conditioned stimulus (CS) Stimulus that begins to elicit a particular response through classical conditioning.

conditioned response (CR) Response that begins to be elicited by a particular (conditioned) stimulus through classical conditioning.

[1] As I do here, behaviorists often use the word *elicit,* meaning "draw forth or bring out," in describing classical conditioning. The word conveys the idea that learners have little or no control over their classically conditioned responses.

The best part of third grade was
divison
algerbra
mlltiplecation
math
realing

In a personal yearbook, Ashton identifies math and reading as being the best part of his third-grade year. He clearly associates these subjects with pleasure rather than discomfort.

- Bobby misses a month of school because of illness. When he returns to school, he doesn't know how to do the long division problems his teacher is now assigning. After a number of frustrating experiences with the assignments, he begins to feel anxious whenever he encounters a division task.

UCS: failure/frustration	➔	UCR: anxiety about failure
CS: long division	➔	CR: anxiety about long division

- Beth's teacher catches her writing a note to a friend during class. The teacher reads the note to the entire class, revealing some very personal and private information that embarrasses Beth. Beth now feels extremely uncomfortable whenever she goes into that teacher's classroom.

UCS: humiliation	➔	UCR: embarrassment in response to humiliation
CS: teacher/classroom	➔	CR: emotional discomfort in response to teacher/classroom

Create a classroom atmosphere in which students feel physically and psychologically safe and secure.

As teachers, we should create a classroom environment in which stimuli (including our own behaviors) are likely to elicit such responses as enjoyment or relaxation, *not* fear or anxiety. When students associate school with pleasant circumstances—positive feedback, enjoyable activities, and so on—they soon learn that school is a place they want to be. But when they encounter unpleasant stimuli in school—such as public humiliation or constant frustration and failure—they may eventually learn to fear or dislike a particular activity, subject area, teacher, or even school in general.

Common Phenomena in Classical Conditioning

Two common phenomena in classical conditioning are generalization and extinction. As you'll discover later in the chapter, variations of these phenomena occur in instrumental conditioning as well.

Remember that the feelings students develop in response to you, your classroom, and specific subject matter may generalize to other situations.

Generalization When people learn a conditioned response to a new stimulus, they may respond in the same way to similar stimuli—a phenomenon known as **generalization**. For example, a boy who learns to feel anxious about long division problems may generalize the anxiety response to other kinds of math problems. And a girl who experiences humiliation in one classroom may generalize her feelings of embarrassment to other classrooms as well. Thus, we see a second reason that students should associate pleasant feelings with classroom subject matter: Students' reactions to a particular topic, activity, or context may generalize—that is, they may *transfer*—to similar topics, activities, or contexts.

Extinction Pavlov discovered that conditioned responses don't necessarily last forever. By pairing a light with meat, he conditioned a dog to salivate to the light alone. But later, when he repeatedly flashed the light without following it with meat, the dog salivated less and less. Eventually, the dog no longer salivated to the flash of light. When a conditioned stimulus occurs repeatedly in the absence of the unconditioned stimulus—for example, when mathematics is never again associated with failure or when a teacher is never again associated with humiliation—the conditioned response may decrease and eventually disappear. In other words, **extinction** occurs.

Many conditioned responses do fade over time. Unfortunately, many others do not. A child's fear of water or anxiety about mathematics may persist for years. One reason that fears and anxieties persist is that learners tend to avoid situations that elicit negative emotional reactions. But if they stay away from a stimulus that makes them fearful, they never have a chance to experience the stimulus in the absence of the unconditioned stimulus with which it was originally paired. As a result, they have no opportunity to learn to be *un*afraid—no opportunity for the response to undergo extinction.

generalization Phenomenon in which a person learns a response to a particular stimulus and then makes the same response to a similar stimulus; in classical conditioning, involves making a conditioned response to a stimulus similar to a conditioned stimulus.

extinction Gradual disappearance of an acquired response; in classical conditioning, results from repeated presentation of a conditioned stimulus in the absence of the unconditioned stimulus.

Addressing Counterproductive Emotional Responses

As teachers, how can we reduce conditioned responses that interfere with students' learning and performance? One effective way to extinguish a negative emotional reaction to a particular conditioned stimulus is to introduce the stimulus slowly and gradually while a student is happy, relaxed, or in some other way feeling good rather than poorly (M. C. Jones, 1924; Ricciardi, Luiselli, & Camare, 2006; Wolpe & Plaud, 1997). For example, if Bernard is afraid of water, we might begin his swimming lessons someplace where he feels at ease—perhaps on dry land or in the wading pool—and move to a deeper pool only as he begins to feel more comfortable. And if Bobby gets overly anxious every time he encounters a math problem, we might revert to very easy problems—those he can readily solve—and gradually increase the difficulty of his assignments only as he demonstrates greater competence and self-confidence.

When a particular subject matter or task arouses anxiety, present it slowly and gradually while a student is happy and relaxed.

There's nothing like success to help students feel good about being in the classroom. One thing we can do to promote student success is structure the classroom environment so that appropriate behaviors lead to desirable consequences and inappropriate behaviors do not. Such *reinforcement* plays a central role in instrumental conditioning.

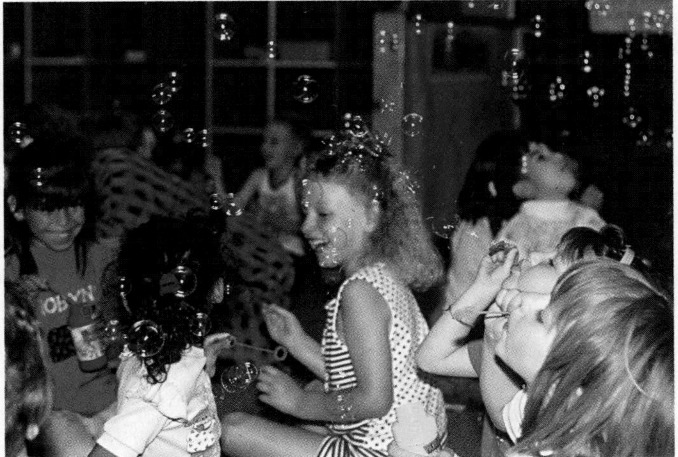

When students associate school with pleasant stimuli, they learn that school is a place they want to be.

Learning from Consequences: Instrumental Conditioning

Mark is a student in Ms. Ferguson's geography class. Let's look at what happens to him during the first week in October:

- *Monday.* Ms. Ferguson asks the class to locate Colombia on the globe. Mark knows where Colombia is, and he sits smiling, with his hands in his lap, hoping that Ms. Ferguson will call on him. Instead, Ms. Ferguson calls on another student.
- *Tuesday.* Ms. Ferguson asks the class where Colombia got its name. Mark knows that Colombia was named after Christopher Columbus, so he raises his hand a few inches. Ms. Ferguson calls on another student.
- *Wednesday.* Ms. Ferguson asks the class why Colombia's official language is Spanish, rather than, say, English or French. Mark knows that Colombians speak Spanish because many of the country's early European settlers came from Spain. He raises his hand high in the air. Ms. Ferguson calls on another student.
- *Thursday.* Ms. Ferguson asks the class why Colombia grows coffee but Canada does not. Mark knows that coffee can be grown only in certain climates. He raises his hand high and waves it wildly back and forth. Ms. Ferguson calls on him.
- *Friday.* Whenever Ms. Ferguson asks a question that Mark can answer, he raises his hand high and waves it wildly about.

Notice that several of Mark's behaviors bring no results. But waving his hand wildly brings the outcome he wants—a chance to speak in class—and so it increases in frequency.

When learners' behaviors either increase or decrease as a result of the consequences of those behaviors, **instrumental conditioning** is at work. Consequences

instrumental conditioning Form of learning in which a response either increases or decreases as a result of being followed by either reinforcement or punishment, respectively.

that *increase* the behaviors they follow are **reinforcers**, and the act of following a particular response with a reinforcer is known as **reinforcement**. Conversely, consequences that *decrease* the behaviors they follow constitute **punishment**. Both reinforcers and punishments are environmental *stimuli* that influence behavior.[2]

Notice that I have just defined both *reinforcer* and *punishment* in terms of their effects on behavior, rather than in terms of their relative pleasantness and desirability. Some learners increase certain behaviors for consequences that most of us would think of as unpleasant—consequences that we certainly wouldn't think of as "rewards." As an example, let's return to the opening case study. When James throws objects, makes outrageous comments, and so on, we can assume that his teacher is probably frowning, scolding, or even yelling at him, which we don't usually think of as desirable outcomes. Yet those consequences are leading to an increase in James's misbehaviors; thus, they are apparently reinforcing for him. Other people's attention, regardless of the form it might take, can be highly reinforcing for some students and often serves to maintain counterproductive classroom behaviors (Austin & Soeda, 2008; Flood, Wilder, Flood, & Masuda, 2002; McComas, Thompson, & Johnson, 2003).

Punishment, too, seems to be in the eye of the beholder. For example, some seemingly very desirable forms of attention, such as teacher praise, can be a must-to-avoid—and hence punishing—for adolescents who don't want their peers to think of them as a "goodie-two-shoes" or the teacher's pet (Burnett, 2001; Pfiffner, Rosen, & O'Leary, 1985).

Countless research studies have demonstrated that reinforcement can have powerful effects on students' learning and behavior in the classroom. The use of punishment in the classroom is more controversial; some forms do more harm than good. But under certain conditions, punishment can be both effective and appropriate, especially when students appear to have little motivation to change their behavior for the better.

Contrasting Classical Conditioning and Instrumental Conditioning

Classical conditioning and instrumental conditioning both involve stimuli and responses. But instrumental conditioning is different from classical conditioning in two important ways:

- *The response is voluntary rather than involuntary.* In classical conditioning, the response is involuntary: When a particular (conditioned) stimulus is present, the response usually follows automatically, with little choice on the learner's part. In instrumental conditioning, however, the response is typically voluntary: The learner can control whether or not to make it. For example, in the opening case study, James can choose whether to make inappropriate comments, throw erasers, or tease classmates; nothing in the classroom environment is forcing him to do these things.

  The voluntary nature of responses in instrumental conditioning is an important one for teachers to keep in mind. In order for such conditioning to occur, *learners must first make a response.* Many educational applications of behaviorist principles, then, involve getting students physically and actively engaged in working with academic subject matter.
- *Learning occurs as a result of a stimulus that comes after, rather than before, the response.* Classical conditioning results from the pairing of two stimuli: one (the

Get students physically and actively engaged in working with classroom topics.

reinforcer Consequence (stimulus) of a response that increases the frequency of the response it follows; the act of following a response with a reinforcer is known as **reinforcement**.

punishment Consequence (stimulus) that decreases the frequency of the response it follows.

[2] You may often see the term *operant conditioning* used in reference to the effects of reinforcers on behavior. In contrast, *instrumental conditioning* encompasses both the response-increasing effects of reinforcers and the response-decreasing effects of punishments.

UCS) that initially elicits a response and another (the CS) that begins to elicit the same or a similar response. Thus, these two stimuli *lead to* certain responses. In instrumental conditioning, however, the learner makes the first move, and an environmental stimulus (either a reinforcer or punishment) follows. Typically, there is a **contingency** between the response and the consequence: The consequence almost always follows the response and seldom occurs when the response hasn't been made. For example, a teacher who praises students only when they behave appropriately is making reinforcement contingent on desired behavior. In contrast, a teacher who laughs at the antics of a chronically misbehaving student is providing reinforcement even when an acceptable response hasn't occurred; consequently, the student's behavior is unlikely to improve.

Don't confuse *contingency* with the term *contiguity* introduced near the beginning of the chapter. Contingency involves an if-this-happens-then-that-happens relationship. In contrast, contiguity simply involves two things happening at about the same time. Effective instrumental conditioning usually involves contiguity as well as contingency; that is, the consequence occurs almost immediately after the response (J. A. Kulik & Kulik, 1988; Rachlin, 1991). The immediacy of reinforcement or punishment after a response is especially important when working with young children. It's less critical for older children and adolescents, who are better able to make a mental connection between what they do *now* with what happens to them *later* (more on this point shortly).

The Various Forms That Reinforcement Can Take

Reinforcers come in all shapes and sizes, and different ones are effective for different learners. We explore a few possibilities in the following exercise.

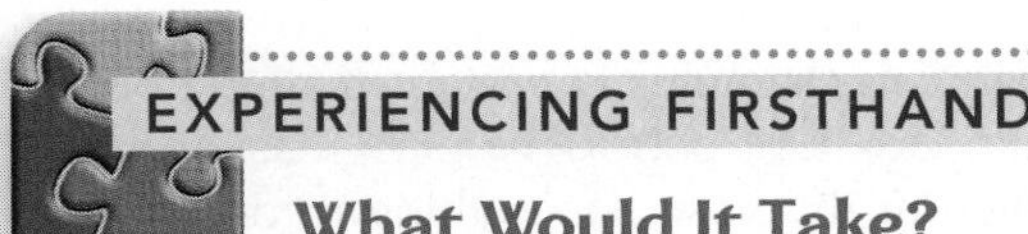

EXPERIENCING FIRSTHAND

What Would It Take?

1. Imagine that you are currently enrolled in my educational psychology class. As your instructor, I ask you if you would be willing to spend an hour after class tutoring two classmates who are having difficulty understanding course material. You have no other commitments for that hour, but you'd really like to spend the time at a nearby coffee shop, where several friends are having lunch. What would it take for you to spend the hour tutoring your classmates instead of joining your friends? Would you do it to gain my approval? Would you do it for a candy bar? How about if I gave you five dollars? Would you do it simply because it made you feel good to be helping someone else? Write down a reward—perhaps one I have listed or a different one altogether—that would persuade you to help your classmates instead of meeting your friends.
2. A few weeks later, I ask you to spend the weekend (eight hours a day on both Saturday and Sunday) tutoring the same two struggling classmates. What would it take this time to convince you to do the job? Would my approval do the trick? a candy bar? five dollars? five *hundred* dollars? Or would your internal sense of satisfaction be enough? Once again, write down what it would take for you to agree to help your classmates.

There are no right or wrong answers to this exercise. Different people would agree to tutor classmates for different reasons. But you were probably able to identify at least one consequence in each situation that would entice you to give up your free time to help others.

contingency Situation in which one event happens only after another event has already occurred; one event is *contingent* on the other's occurrence.

Primary versus Secondary Reinforcers Some reinforcers, such as a candy bar, are **primary reinforcers**, because they address a basic biological need. Food, water, sources of warmth, and oxygen are all primary reinforcers. To some extent, physical affection and cuddling seem to address built-in biological needs as well, and for an adolescent addicted to an illegal substance, the next "fix" is also a primary reinforcer (Harlow & Zimmerman, 1959; Lejuez, Schaal, & O'Donnell, 1998; Vollmer & Hackenberg, 2001).

Other reinforcers, known as **secondary reinforcers**, don't satisfy any physiological need. Praise, money, good grades, and trophies are examples. Such stimuli may become reinforcing over time through their association with other reinforcers. For example, if praise is occasionally associated with a special candy treat from Mother and if money often comes with a hug from Father, the praise and money eventually become reinforcing in and of themselves. In this way, seemingly unpleasant stimuli can become reinforcers. For instance, if James regularly associates a teacher's scolding with something he wants—more attention—then scolding may indeed become a reinforcer in its own right.

Secondary reinforcers are far more common in classrooms than primary reinforcers. In fact, making primary reinforcers (e.g., lunch, restroom breaks) contingent on certain levels of performance is generally *not* good teaching practice. When we use secondary reinforcers, however, we must remember that they are *learned* reinforcers, and not everyone has come to appreciate them. Although most students respond positively to such consequences as praise and good grades, a few students may not.

Keep in mind that not all students have learned to appreciate such secondary reinforcers as praise and good grades.

Positive versus Negative Reinforcement Up to this point, we have been speaking of reinforcement as the *presentation* of a particular reinforcing stimulus. But in some cases, we can also reinforce a behavior through the *removal* of a stimulus. Behaviorists use the terms *positive reinforcement* and *negative reinforcement*, respectively, for these two situations.

Positive Reinforcement Whenever a particular stimulus is *presented* after a behavior and the behavior increases as a result, **positive reinforcement** has occurred. Don't be misled by the word *positive*, which in this case has nothing to do with the pleasantness or desirability of the stimulus being presented. Positive reinforcement can occur even when the presented stimulus is one that others might think is *un*pleasant or *un*desirable. The word *positive* here simply means *adding* something to the situation. For instance, some students may make a response to get a teacher's praise, but others (like James in the opening case study) may behave in a way that gets them a scolding. Most students will work for As, but a few may actually prefer Cs or even Fs. (As a school psychologist, I once worked with a high school student who used Fs as a way to get revenge on his overly controlling parents.) Depending on the individual, any one of these stimuli—praise, a scolding, an A, or an F—can be a positive reinforcer. Following are examples of the forms that positive reinforcement can take:

Be aware that certain consequences that seem "negative" (e.g., scoldings, bad grades) may nevertheless be *positively* reinforcing for some students.

primary reinforcer Consequence that satisfies a biologically built-in need.

secondary reinforcer Consequence that becomes reinforcing over time through its association with another reinforcer.

positive reinforcement Consequence that brings about the increase of a behavior through the presentation (rather than the removal) of a stimulus.

Premack principle Phenomenon in which learners do less-preferred activities in order to engage in more-preferred activities.

- A *concrete reinforcer* is an actual object—something that can be touched (e.g., a snack, sticker, or toy).
- A *social reinforcer* is a gesture or sign (e.g., a smile, attention, praise, or "thank-you") that one person gives another, often to communicate positive regard.
- An *activity reinforcer* is an opportunity to engage in a favorite activity. Learners often do one thing, even something they don't like to do, if it enables them to do something they enjoy. This phenomenon is sometimes called the **Premack principle** (Premack, 1959, 1963). For example, children with attention-deficit hyperactivity disorder (ADHD) are more likely to sit quietly during a lesson if they know that doing so will enable them to engage in a physically more lively activity afterward (Azrin, Vinas, & Ehle, 2007).

- Sometimes the simple message that an answer is correct or that a task has been done well—*positive feedback*—is reinforcement enough. In fact, sometimes even *negative* feedback can be reinforcing if the overall message is a positive one. The Creating a Productive Classroom Environment feature "Using Feedback to Improve Learning and Behavior" offers suggestions based on research by behaviorists, cognitive psychologists, and motivation theorists.

The reinforcers just listed are **extrinsic reinforcers**, those provided by the external environment (often by other people). Yet some positive reinforcers are **intrinsic reinforcers**, those supplied by learners themselves or inherent in tasks being performed. When students perform certain behaviors in the absence of any observable reinforcers—when they read an entire book without putting it down, do extra classwork without being asked, or practice with a neighborhood rock group into the wee hours of the morning—they are probably working for the intrinsic reinforcement that such behaviors yield. Intrinsic reinforcers are *not* observable events and thus do not fit

extrinsic reinforcer Reinforcer that comes from the outside environment, rather than from within the learner.

intrinsic reinforcer Reinforcer that is provided by the learner or inherent in the task being performed.

Creating A PRODUCTIVE CLASSROOM ENVIRONMENT

Using Feedback to Improve Learning and Behavior

- **Be explicit about what students are doing well—ideally, at the time they are doing it.**

  When praising her students for appropriate classroom behavior, a second-grade teacher makes it quite clear which actions she is commending them for. For example, she says, "I like the way you're working quietly" and "You should see Ricky being so polite. Thank-you, Ricky, for not disturbing the rest of the class." (This example is depicted in the "Reading Group" Video Example in Chapter 9 of the Book-Specific Resources in MyEducationLab.)

- **Give concrete guidance about how students can improve their performance.**

  A high school physical education teacher tells a student, "Your time in the 100-meter dash wasn't as fast as it could have been. It's early in the season, though, and if you work on your endurance, I know you'll improve. Also, I think you might get a faster start if you stay low when you first come out of the starting blocks."

- **Communicate optimism that students *can* improve.**

  When a student in a middle school geography class gives her oral report on Mexico, she goes on at length about her family's recent trip to Puerto Vallarta, showing many photos, postcards, and souvenirs to illustrate her remarks. The other students soon become bored and communicate their displeasure through body language and occasional whispers across the aisle. At the end of class, the student is devastated that her report has been so poorly received. Her teacher takes her aside and gently says, "You included many interesting facts in your report, Julie, and all your pictures and artifacts really helped us understand Mexican culture. But you know how young teenagers are—they can have a pretty short attention span at times. I'll be assigning oral reports again next semester. Before you give yours, let's sit down and plan it so that your classmates will think, 'Wow, this is really interesting!' "

- **Don't overwhelm students with too much feedback; tell them only what they can reasonably attend to and remember at the time.**

  As a kindergarten teacher watches one of his students practice writing several alphabet letters, he helps the student hold her pencil in a way that gives her better control. He doesn't mention that she is writing her *B*s and *D*s backward; he will save this information for a later time, after she has mastered her pencil grip.

- **Minimize feedback when students already know exactly what they've done well or poorly.**

  A high school math teacher has a student who has been getting poor grades in large part because of insufficient effort. When he begins to buckle down and do his homework regularly, his quiz scores improve tremendously. As his teacher hands him his first quiz after his newfound diligence—a quiz on which he's earned a score of 96%—she says nothing but smiles and gives him a thumbs-up.

- **Teach students strategies for appropriately asking for teacher feedback.**

  A fourth-grade teacher has three students with intellectual disabilities in her class. She knows that these students may need more frequent feedback than their classmates. She teaches them three steps to take when they need her assistance: (a) They should raise their hands or walk quietly to her desk; (b) they should wait patiently until she has time to speak with them; and (c) they should make their needs known (e.g., "How am I doing?" "What do I do next?").

Sources: Bangert-Drowns, Kulik, Kulik, & Morgan, 1991; D. L. Butler & Winne, 1995; Craft, Alberg, & Heward, 1998, p. 402 (fourth-grade example); Feltz, Chase, Moritz, & Sullivan, 1999; Hattie & Timperley, 2007; K. A. Meyer, 1999; Pintrich & Schunk, 2002; Schunk & Pajares, 2005; Shute, 2008; Tunstall & Gipps, 1996.

With three math tests scheduled for later that day, dozens of students suddenly came down with mysterious illnesses.

Complaining about imaginary ailments is negatively reinforced if it enables students to avoid difficult classroom tasks. If such behavior occurs frequently, we should address the roots of the behavior—perhaps by helping students experience success far more often than failure and frustration.

comfortably within traditional behaviorist theory. Yet students clearly do engage in some behaviors solely for the intrinsic satisfaction those behaviors bring. For instance, in the preceding "What Would It Take?" exercise, if you agreed to help your classmates simply because doing so would make you feel good, you would be working for an intrinsic reinforcer.

From our perspective as teachers, positive feedback (an extrinsic reinforcer) and the feelings of pleasure and satisfaction that such feedback can bring (intrinsic reinforcers) are probably the most desirable forms of classroom reinforcement. But we must remember that the classroom successes that yield such forms of reinforcement can occur only when instruction has been carefully tailored to individual skill levels and abilities and only when students have learned to value academic achievement. When students are not motivated to achieve academic success for whatever reasons, then social reinforcers, activity reinforcers, and occasionally even concrete reinforcers can be used to increase desired classroom behaviors.

Negative Reinforcement Whereas positive reinforcement involves the presentation of a stimulus, **negative reinforcement** brings about the increase of a behavior through the *removal* of a stimulus (typically an unpleasant one, at least from the perspective of the learner). The word *negative* here is not a value judgment. It simply refers to the act of *taking away*, rather than adding, a stimulus.[3] When people make a response in order to get rid of something and the frequency of the response increases as a result, they are being negatively reinforced.

Imagine, for example, that you have a difficult assignment to complete for one of your classes. Because you don't like it hanging over your head, you complete it and give it to your instructor well before its due date. After you turn it in, you feel much better; you've gotten rid of that annoying "worry" feeling. If you find yourself completing future assignments early as well, then you've been negatively reinforced for your complete-something-before-due-date behavior.

We can see another possible example of negative reinforcement in the opening case study. When James misbehaves, his teacher sometimes sends him to the assistant principal's office. By doing so, the teacher may be negatively reinforcing his troublesome behavior. In particular, James *gets out of class*, thereby removing a stimulus—some aspect of the class environment—that may be aversive for him. (If James likes spending time with the assistant principal, he is receiving positive reinforcement as well.) Whereas some students misbehave in class primarily to get attention (a positive reinforcer), others often misbehave to escape something they don't want to do, such as a difficult assignment, and their escape behavior is negatively reinforced (McComas et al., 2003; K. A. Meyer, 1999; Mueller, Edwards, & Trahant, 2003). Students may learn other escape behaviors as well, as one student with a learning disability revealed:

> When it comes time for reading I do everything under the sun I can to get out of it because it's my worst nightmare to read. I'll say I have to go to the bathroom or that I'm sick and I have to go to the nurse right now. My teacher doesn't know that I'll

negative reinforcement Consequence that brings about the increase of a behavior through the removal (rather than the presentation) of a stimulus.

[3]You might draw an analogy between positive and negative reinforcement and positive and negative numbers. Positive numbers and positive reinforcement both *add* something to a situation. Negative numbers and negative reinforcement both *subtract* something from a situation.

be walking around campus. She thinks I am going to the bathroom or whatever my lame excuse is. All I really want to do is get out of having to read. (Zambo & Brem, 2004, p. 5)

As teachers, we should use negative reinforcement rarely, if at all. Ideally, we want to create a classroom environment in which there are few stimuli that students want to be rid of. Nevertheless, we should recognize that negative reinforcement *does* have an effect on behavior. Some students may finish an assignment more to get it out of the way than for any intrinsic satisfaction the assignment brings. Others may engage in a variety of responses—perhaps misbehaving or identifying imaginary reasons for leaving the classroom—as a way of avoiding the assignment altogether. When certain responses enable students to eliminate or escape unpleasant stimuli, those responses will increase in frequency.

When students consistently behave in ways that enable them to avoid or escape certain activities, identify and address the reasons that students find the activities aversive.

Looking at Reinforcement from a Developmental Perspective Children's preferences for various kinds of reinforcers tend to change with age. For example, concrete reinforcers (e.g., scratch-and-sniff stickers, small trinkets) can be effective with young children, but teenagers are more likely to appreciate opportunities to interact with friends. Table 9.2 presents forms of reinforcement that may be especially effective at various grade levels.

An important developmental trend is evident in Table 9.2 as well: As children get older, they become better able to handle **delay of gratification**. That is, they can forego small, immediate reinforcers for the larger reinforcers that their long-term efforts may bring down the road (Atance, 2008; L. Green et al., 1994; Rotenberg & Mayer, 1990). Whereas a preschooler or kindergartner is apt to choose a small reinforcer available now, rather than a larger and more attractive reinforcer she cannot get until tomorrow, an 8-year-old may be willing to wait a day or two for the more appealing item. Many adolescents can delay gratification for several weeks or even longer. For instance, as a 16-year-old, my son Jeff worked long hours stocking shelves at the local grocery store (hardly an intrinsically reinforcing activity!) to earn enough money to pay half the cost of a $400-a-night limousine for his high school prom.

Some children and adolescents are better able to delay gratification than others. Those who are willing and able to postpone reinforcement are less likely to yield to temptation, more carefully plan their future actions, and achieve at higher levels at school (Atance, 2008; Bembenutty & Karabenick, 2004; Shoda, Mischel, & Peake, 1990). However, even 4- and 5-year-olds can learn to delay gratification for a few hours if their teachers tell them that rewards for desired behaviors (such as sharing toys with other children) will be coming later in the day (Fowler & Baer, 1981). Teaching children effective waiting strategies—for instance, focusing attention on something else during the delay and using such self-talk as "If I wait a little longer, I will get something better"—enhances their ability to postpone gratification as well (Binder, Dixon, & Ghezzi, 2000).

When working with young children, try to reinforce desired behaviors immediately, even if only by pointing out that a desired consequence will be coming later.

The Various Forms That Punishment Can Take

All punishing consequences fall into one of two categories. **Presentation punishment** involves presenting a new stimulus, presumably something a learner finds unpleasant and doesn't want. Scoldings and teacher scowls are instances of presentation punishment *if* they lead to a reduction in the behavior they follow. **Removal punishment** involves removing an existing stimulus or state of affairs, presumably one a learner finds desirable and doesn't want to lose. Loss of a privilege, a fine or penalty (involving the loss of money or previously earned points), and grounding (i.e., restriction from certain pleasurable outside activities) are all examples of removal punishment.

Over the years, I have often seen or heard people use the term *negative reinforcement* when they are really talking about punishment. Remember, negative reinforce-

delay of gratification Ability to forego small, immediate reinforcers in order to obtain larger ones later on.

presentation punishment Punishment involving presentation of a new stimulus, presumably one a learner finds unpleasant.

removal punishment Punishment involving removal of an existing stimulus, presumably one a learner doesn't want to lose.

TABLE 9.2
Effective Reinforcers at Different Grade Levels

Grade Level	Age-Typical Characteristics	Suggested Strategies

K–2	• Preference for small, immediate reinforcers over larger, delayed ones
	• Examples of effective reinforcers:
	  • Concrete reinforcers (e.g., stickers, crayons, small trinkets)
	  • Teacher approval (e.g., smiles, praise)
	  • Privileges (e.g., going to lunch first)
	  • "Grown-up" responsibilities (e.g., taking absentee forms to the main office)
		• Give immediate praise for appropriate behavior.
		• Describe enjoyable consequences that may come later as a result of students' current behaviors.
		• Use colorful stickers to indicate a job well done; choose stickers that match students' interests (e.g., favorite cartoon characters).
		• Have students line up for recess, lunch, or dismissal based on desired behaviors (e.g., "Table 2 is the quietest and can line up first").
		• Rotate opportunities to perform classroom duties (e.g., feeding the goldfish, watering plants); make such duties contingent on appropriate behavior.

3–5	• Increasing ability to delay gratification (i.e., to put off small reinforcers in order to gain larger ones later on)
	• Examples of effective reinforcers:
	  • Concrete reinforcers (e.g., sweets, pencils, small toys)
	  • Teacher approval and positive feedback
	  • "Good citizen" certificates
	  • Free time (e.g., for drawing or playing games)
		• Use concrete reinforcers only occasionally, perhaps to add novelty to a classroom activity.
		• Award a certificate to a Citizen of the Week, explicitly identifying things the recipient has done especially well; be sure that every student gets at least one certificate during the school year.
		• Plan a trip to a local amusement park for students with good attendance records. (This is especially useful for students at risk for academic failure.)

6–8	• Increasing desire to have social time with peers
	• Examples of effective reinforcers:
	  • Free time with friends
	  • Acceptance and approval from peers
	  • Teacher approval and emotional support (especially critical after the transition to middle school or junior high)
	  • Specific positive feedback about academic performance (preferably given in private)
		• Make short periods of free time with peers (e.g., five minutes) contingent on accomplishing assigned tasks.
		• Spend one-on-one time with students, especially those who appear to be socially isolated.
		• Provide explicit feedback about what things students have done well (e.g., their use of colorful language in an essay or their prosocial behaviors with classmates).

9–12	• Considerable ability to postpone immediate pleasures in order to gain desired long-term outcomes
	• Concern about getting good grades (especially for students who are applying to selective colleges)
	• Examples of effective reinforcers:
	  • Opportunities to interact with friends
	  • Specific positive feedback about academic performance
	  • Public recognition for group performance (e.g., newspaper articles about a club's public service work)
	  • Positions of responsibility (e.g., being student representative to the Faculty Senate)
		• Acknowledge students' concerns about earning good grades, but focus their attention on the value of learning school subject matter for its own sake. (See the discussion of achievement goals in Chapter 11.)
		• Be sure that good grades are contingent on students' own work; take precautions to ensure that cheating and plagiarism are *not* reinforced.
		• Publicize accomplishments of extracurricular groups and athletic teams in local news media.
		• Provide opportunities for independent decision making and responsibility, especially when students show an ability to make wise decisions.

Sources: L. H. Anderman, Patrick, Hruda, & Linnenbrink, 2002; Atance, 2008; Cizek, 2003; Fowler & Baer, 1981; L. Green, Fry, & Myerson, 1994; Hine & Fraser, 2002; Krumboltz & Krumboltz, 1972; Rimm & Masters, 1974; Rotenberg & Mayer, 1990; M. G. Sanders, 1996.

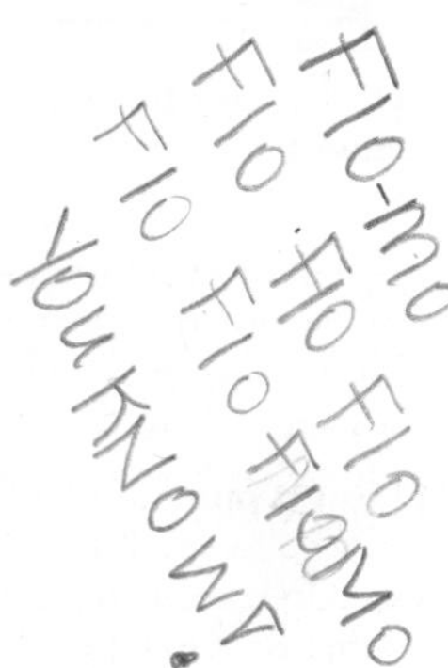

ment is *reinforcement*, which increases a response, whereas punishment has the opposite effect. Table 9.3 can help you understand that negative reinforcement, presentation punishment, and removal punishment are all very different concepts.

Consequences That Serve as Effective Punishments As a general rule, we should use relatively mild forms of punishment in the classroom (Landrum & Kauffman, 2006). Researchers and educators have identified several mild consequences that can be effective in reducing classroom misbehaviors.

Verbal Reprimands (Scolding) Although some students seem to thrive on teacher scolding because of the attention it brings, most students, especially if they are scolded

Compare/Contrast

TABLE 9.3
Distinguishing Among Positive Reinforcement, Negative Reinforcement, and Punishment

Consequence	Effect	Examples
Positive reinforcement	Response *increases* when a new stimulus (presumably one the learner finds desirable) is *presented.*	• A student *is praised* for writing an assignment in cursive. She begins to write other assignments in cursive as well. • A student *gets lunch money* by bullying a girl into surrendering hers. He begins bullying his classmates more frequently.
Negative reinforcement	Response *increases* when a previously existing stimulus (presumably one the learner finds undesirable) is *removed.*	• A student *no longer has to worry* about a research paper he has completed several days before the due date. He begins to do his assignments ahead of time whenever possible. • A student *escapes the principal's wrath* by lying about her role in recent school vandalism. After this incident, she begins lying to school faculty whenever she finds herself in an uncomfortable situation.
Presentation punishment	Response *decreases* when a new stimulus (presumably one the learner finds undesirable) is *presented.*	• A student *is scolded* for taunting other students. She taunts others less frequently after that. • A student *is ridiculed by classmates* for asking what they perceive to be a stupid question during a lecture. He stops asking questions in class.
Removal punishment	Response *decreases* when a previously existing stimulus (presumably one the learner finds desirable) is *removed.*	• A student *is removed from the softball team for a week* for showing poor sportsmanship. She rarely shows poor sportsmanship in future games. • A student *loses points on a test* for answering a question in a creative but unusual way. He takes fewer risks on future tests.

only infrequently, find verbal reprimands to be unpleasant and punishing (Landrum & Kauffman, 2006; Pfiffner & O'Leary, 1993; Van Houten, Nau, MacKenzie-Keating, Sameoto, & Colavecchia, 1982). In general, reprimands are most effective when they are immediate, brief, and unemotional. They also work best when they are given quietly in close proximity to the student, perhaps because they are less likely to draw the attention of classmates. Reprimands should be given in private whenever possible. When scolded in front of classmates, some students may relish the peer attention, and others (e.g., many Native American and Hispanic students) may feel totally humiliated (Fuller, 2001).

Response Cost The loss either of a previously earned reinforcer or of an opportunity to obtain reinforcement is known as **response cost**. A form of *removal punishment,* response cost is especially effective when used in combination with reinforcement of appropriate behavior and when learners who make a few missteps within an overall pattern of desirable behavior lose only a *little* of what they've earned (Conyers et al., 2004; Landrum & Kauffman, 2006; E. L. Phillips, Phillips, Fixsen, & Wolf, 1971).

Logical Consequences A **logical consequence** is something that follows naturally or logically from a student's misbehavior; in other words, it's punishment that fits the crime. For example, if a student destroys a classmate's possession, a reasonable consequence is for the student to replace it or pay for a new one. If two close friends talk so much that they aren't completing assignments, a reasonable consequence is for them to be separated. The use of logical consequences makes logical sense, and research vouches for its effectiveness (Dreikurs, 1998; Landrum & Kauffman, 2006; Nucci, 2001).

response cost Loss either of a previously earned reinforcer or of an opportunity to obtain reinforcement.

logical consequence Consequence that follows naturally or logically from a student's misbehavior.

Positive-Practice Overcorrection One desired result of administering punishment, of course, is that students learn more appropriate behavior in the process. **Positive-practice overcorrection** involves having a student repeat an action but this time doing it correctly, perhaps in an exaggerated fashion. For example, a student who runs dangerously down the school corridor might be asked to back up and then *walk* (perhaps at a normal pace or perhaps very slowly) down the hall. Similarly, a student in a drivers' education class who neglects to stop at a stop sign might be asked to drive around the block, return to the same intersection, and come to a complete stop (perhaps counting aloud to five) before proceeding. In general, positive-practice overcorrection is most likely to be effective when its duration is relatively short and when teachers portray it as a means for helping students acquire appropriate behavior, rather than as punishment per se (Alberto & Troutman, 2003; R. G. Carey & Bucher, 1983; M. D. Powers & Crowel, 1985).

Time-Out A misbehaving student given a **time-out** is placed in a dull, boring (but not scary) situation—perhaps a separate room designed especially for time-outs, a little-used office, or a remote corner of the classroom. A student in time-out has no opportunity to interact with classmates and no opportunity to obtain reinforcement. The length of the time-out is typically quite short (perhaps 2 to 10 minutes, depending on the student's age), but the student isn't released until any inappropriate behavior (e.g., screaming, kicking) has stopped.

Time-outs have been used successfully to reduce a variety of noncompliant, disruptive, and aggressive behaviors (e.g., Pfiffner, Barkley, & DuPaul, 2006; Rortvedt & Miltenberger, 1994; A. G. White & Bailey, 1990). Keep in mind, however, that a time-out is apt to be effective only if ongoing classroom activities are a source of pleasure and reinforcement for a student. If a time-out allows a student to escape difficult tasks or an overwhelming amount of noise and stimulation, it might actually be a form of negative reinforcement and thus *increase* undesirable behavior (Alberto & Troutman, 2003; McClowry, 1998; Pfiffner et al., 2006).

In-School Suspension Like time-out, **in-school suspension** involves placing a student in a quiet, boring room within the school building. However, it often lasts one or more school days and involves close adult supervision. Students receiving in-school suspension spend the day working on the same assignments that their nonsuspended peers do, enabling them to keep up with their schoolwork. But they have no opportunity for interaction with peers—an aspect of school that is reinforcing for most students.

Although in-school suspension programs have not been systematically investigated through controlled research studies, educators report that these programs are often effective in reducing chronic behavior problems. They are typically most effective when suspension sessions include instruction in appropriate behaviors and missing academic skills and when the supervising teacher acts as a supportive resource, rather than a punisher (Gootman, 1998; Huff, 1988; Pfiffner et al., 2006; J. S. Sullivan, 1989).

positive-practice overcorrection Consequence of a poorly performed response in which a learner must repeat the response correctly and appropriately, perhaps in an exaggerated manner.

time-out Consequence for misbehavior in which a student is placed in a dull, boring situation with no opportunity for reinforcement or social interaction.

in-school suspension Consequence for misbehavior in which a student is placed in a quiet, boring room within the school building, typically to do schoolwork under close adult supervision.

Consequences That May Undermine Desired Behavior Changes Several forms of punishment are typically *not* recommended because they have adverse side effects, convey a counterproductive message, or actually serve as reinforcers for some students.

Physical Punishment Most experts advise against physical punishment for school-age children (e.g., W. Doyle, 1990; Hyman et al., 2006; Landrum & Kauffman, 2006). Furthermore, its use in the classroom is *illegal* in many places. Even mild physical punishment, such as a spank or slap with a ruler, can lead to such undesirable outcomes as resentment of the teacher, avoidance of school tasks, lying, aggression, vandalism, and truancy. When carried to extremes, physical punishment constitutes child abuse and can cause long-term physical damage, psychological problems, or both.

Psychological Punishment Any consequence that seriously threatens a student's sense of self-worth is **psychological punishment** and is not recommended (Brendgen, Wanner, Vitaro, Bukowski, & Tremblay, 2007; G. A. Davis & Thomas, 1989; Hyman et al., 2006). Fear tactics, embarrassing remarks, and public humiliation can lead to some of the same side effects as physical punishment can (e.g., resentment of the teacher, inattention to school tasks, truancy) and can inflict long-term psychological harm. By deflating students' sense of self, psychological punishment can also lower their expectations for future performance and their motivation to learn and achieve.

Extra Classwork Asking a student to complete makeup work for time missed in school is a reasonable and justifiable request. But assigning extra classwork or homework beyond that required for other students is inappropriate if it is assigned simply to punish a student for wrongdoing (H. Cooper, 1989; Corno, 1996). Such punishment has a very different side effect: It communicates the message that schoolwork is unpleasant.

Do *not* use physical punishment, public humiliation, or extra classwork to discourage undesirable behaviors.

Out-of-School Suspension Teachers and administrators are negatively reinforced when they suspend a problem student. After all, they get rid of something they don't want—a problem! But out-of-school suspension is usually *not* an effective means of changing a student's behavior (Fenning & Bohanon, 2006; Moles, 1990; J. D. Nichols, Ludwin, & Iadicola, 1999). First of all, being suspended from school may be exactly what the student wants, in which case inappropriate behaviors are being reinforced, rather than punished. Second, because many students with chronic behavior problems also tend to do poorly in their schoolwork, suspension involves a loss of valuable instructional time and interferes with any psychological attachment to school. Thus, it decreases students' chances for academic and social success even further and increases the probability that students will drop out before graduation (Christenson & Thurlow, 2004; J. D. Nichols et al., 1999; Skiba & Rausch, 2006).

Advocate for in-school alternatives to out-of-school suspension for wrongdoing.

Consequences with Mixed Reviews Two additional forms of punishment get mixed reviews regarding effectiveness. In some situations, *missing recess* is a logical consequence for students who fail to complete their schoolwork during regular class time because of off-task behavior. Yet research indicates that, especially at the elementary level, students can more effectively concentrate on school tasks if they have frequent breaks and opportunities to release pent-up energy (Maxmell, Jarrett, & Dickerson, 1998; Pellegrini & Bohn, 2005; Pellegrini, Huberty, & Jones, 1995). And although imposing *after-school detention* for serious misbehavior is common practice at many schools, some students simply cannot stay after school hours, perhaps because they have transportation issues, must take care of younger siblings until parents get home from work, or are justifiably afraid to walk through certain neighborhoods after dark (J. D. Nichols et al., 1999). Unless we can address such concerns, imposing after-school detention is potentially unreasonable and inequitable.

Keep in mind the downsides of having students miss recess and imposing after-school detention.

Strategies for Encouraging Productive Behaviors

One early behaviorist, B. F. Skinner, argued that punishment was a relatively ineffective means of changing behavior—it might temporarily suppress a response but could never eliminate it—and urged teachers to focus their efforts on reinforcing desirable behaviors, rather than punishing undesirable ones (e.g., Skinner, 1954, 1968; Skinner & Epstein, 1982). Following Skinner's lead, most contemporary behaviorists suggest that we emphasize the positive, looking for and reinforcing what's *right* with student behavior.

As teachers, we must be sure that productive student behaviors—for instance, contributing to class discussions, keeping work areas tidy and organized, and working

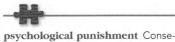

psychological punishment Consequence that seriously threatens self-esteem and general psychological well-being.

GARFIELD / Jim Davis

As teachers, we must be careful that we don't inadvertently reinforce undesirable behaviors—for instance, by paying attention to students only when they misbehave.

Be careful that you don't inadvertently reinforce undesirable behaviors.

cooperatively with classmates—are reinforced in some way. At the same time, we should be careful *not* to reinforce inappropriate and counterproductive behaviors. If we repeatedly allow Carol to turn in assignments late because she says she forgot her homework and if we often let Colin get his way by bullying his classmates on the playground, then we are reinforcing (and hence increasing) Carol's irresponsibility and Colin's aggressiveness.

Using Reinforcement Effectively

The following strategies are consistent with behaviorist principles and research findings:

Specify desired behaviors at the beginning. Behaviorists recommend that we describe, up front, the behaviors we want students to learn and demonstrate. They further urge us to describe these end results—the **terminal behaviors**—in specific, concrete, observable terms. Rather than talk about the need for students to "Learn world history," we might instead talk about them being able to "Describe the antecedents and consequences of World War II." Rather than say that students should "Learn responsibility," we might instead talk about their need to "Follow instructions, bring the necessary books and supplies to class every day, and turn in assignments by the due dates." By specifying terminal behaviors at the beginning of instruction, we give both ourselves and our students targets to shoot for, and we can better determine whether we are making progress toward those targets.

In recent years, educators have increasingly recognized the importance of spelling out ahead of time the most important things that students should learn in the classroom. You are apt to see a variety of terms for this idea—perhaps *instructional goals, objectives, competencies, benchmarks,* and *standards.*

Make sure that all students regularly receive reinforcement for desired behaviors. In the opening case study, James engages in a variety of inappropriate behaviors to gain the attention of his teacher, his classmates, and sometimes the assistant principal. Students are far more likely to misbehave if they have little social contact with others *unless* they misbehave (McGill, 1999). We might reasonably guess that James would prefer more appropriate interactions with adults and peers, yet for whatever reasons, he seldom has such interactions—perhaps because his academic performance rarely gains his teacher's praise or perhaps because he lacks the social skills to make and maintain friendships. In working with James, then, his teacher should identify the academic and social skills he might be missing, help him acquire those skills, and then, of course, reinforce him for using the skills.

In our attempts to improve the behaviors of some students, however, we must be careful that we don't unintentionally slight other, equally deserving students. Furthermore, we must keep in mind that some students may be unable to exhibit particular

terminal behavior Form and frequency of a desired response that a teacher hopes to foster through reinforcement.

behaviors through little or no fault of their own. Consider the case of a young immigrant girl who had to adjust very quickly from a 10:00–5:00 school day in Vietnam to a 7:45–3:45 school day in the United States:

> Every week on Friday after school, the teacher would give little presents to kids that were good during the week. And if you were tardy, you wouldn't get a present. . . . I would never get one because I would always come to school late, and that hurt at first. I had a terrible time. I didn't look forward to going to school. (Igoa, 1995, p. 95)

Ultimately, school should be a place where *all* students can, in one way or another, earn reinforcement for appropriate behaviors and academic progress.

Use extrinsic reinforcers only when desired behaviors will not otherwise occur. It's neither possible nor necessary to reinforce every good deed. Furthermore, many extrinsic reinforcements lose their effectiveness when used repeatedly (Michael, 2000; Murphy, McSweeney, Smith, & McComas, 2003). The best reinforcers are intrinsic ones, such as the pleasure one gets from reading, the pride one feels after accomplishing a challenging task, and the internal satisfaction one feels while helping others. Students will willingly engage in activities that are enjoyable or that satisfy their curiosity, and they will readily behave in ways that lead to success and to feelings of mastery and accomplishment.

Success isn't always achieved easily and effortlessly, however. Many of the tasks students tackle in school—reading and writing, solving mathematical word problems, playing a musical instrument, and so on—can be difficult and frustrating, especially at first. When students struggle with a task and encounter frequent failure, we should probably provide some extrinsic reinforcement (praise, colorful stickers, free time, etc.) for the small improvements they make. And when we find that we must break down a complex task into smaller pieces that are easier to accomplish but are less fulfilling in their own right (e.g., if we assign drill-and-practice activities to foster automaticity in basic reading or math skills), we will probably need to reinforce students' many seemingly meaningless successes. However, once students have mastered tasks and skills to a level that brings them frequent success and feelings of genuine accomplishment, extrinsic reinforcers may no longer be necessary (J. Cameron, 2001; Covington, 1992; Deci, Koestner, & Ryan, 2001; Hidi & Harackiewicz, 2000).

Determine whether particular "reinforcers" are truly reinforcing for students. We will look at motivation in more detail in Chapter 11, but for now, we should note that motivation plays a significant role in determining the consequences that students find reinforcing (McGill, 1999; Michael, 2000). Some students work at academic tasks simply for the feelings of success and accomplishment that such activities bring, but others work diligently at the same tasks only if doing so leads to social benefits—perhaps the respect of classmates or the opportunity to spend time with friends.

The use of reinforcement is far more effective when reinforcers are tailored to individual students than when the same consequences are used for everyone (e.g., Pfiffner et al., 1985). In some cases, we can let students choose their *own* reinforcers and perhaps even choose different reinforcers on different occasions. One useful strategy for a class with many chronic misbehavers is a **token economy**, in which students who exhibit desired behaviors receive *tokens* (i.e., poker chips, specially marked pieces of colored paper, etc.) that they can later use to "purchase" a variety of *backup reinforcers*—perhaps small treats, free time in the reading center, or a prime position in the lunch line. Children do seem to prefer having some choice in the reinforcers for which they work (Geckeler, Libby, Graff, & Ahearn, 2000; Tiger, Hanley, & Hernandez, 2006). Furthermore, the tokens often become effective reinforcers in and of themselves (Hundert, 1976). Perhaps they become secondary reinforcers through repeated association with other reinforcing objects and events, or perhaps they are effective simply because they provide feedback that students are doing something right.

token economy Technique in which desired behaviors are reinforced by tokens that learners can use to "purchase" a variety of other reinforcers.

Use concrete reinforcers, such as toys and candy, only if less tangible reinforcers are ineffective.

By and large, however, we should stay away from concrete reinforcers (e.g., toys and candy) as much as possible. Such reinforcers can be expensive and distract students' attention away from their schoolwork. Fortunately, many less tangible reinforcers—such as positive feedback, special privileges, and favorite activities—and reinforcement at home for school behaviors can be quite effective with school-age children and adolescents (e.g., Feltz et al., 1999; Homme, deBaca, Devine, Steinhorst, & Rickert, 1963; Kelley & Carper, 1988). The Creating a Productive Classroom Environment feature "Identifying Effective Reinforcers for Different Students" offers several suggestions that are likely to be useful at one time or another.

Make response-consequence contingencies explicit. Reinforcement is typically more effective when students know exactly which behaviors will lead to which consequences. For example, kindergarten students are more likely to respond appropriately when they are told, "The quietest group will be first to get in line for recess." And high school students are more likely to complete their Spanish assignments if they know that regularly doing so will enable them to take a field trip to a local Cinco de Mayo festival.

One concrete way of communicating expectations for behavior and response-reinforcement contingencies is a **contingency contract**. To develop such a contract, the teacher meets with a student to discuss a problem behavior (e.g., talking to friends during independent seatwork or making rude comments to classmates). The teacher and the student then identify and agree on desired behaviors that the student will demonstrate (e.g., completing seatwork assignments within a certain time frame or speaking with classmates in a friendly, respectful manner). The two also agree on one or more reinforcers for those behaviors (e.g., a certain amount of free time or points earned toward a particular privilege or prize). Together, the teacher and the student write and sign a contract that describes the behaviors the student will perform and the reinforcers that will result. Contingency contracts can be highly effective in improving a wide variety of academic and social behaviors (Brooke & Ruthren, 1984; D. L. Miller & Kelley, 1994; Rueger & Liberman, 1984; Welch, 1985).

Playing a team sport is an example of a behavior reinforced by a group contingency: The team wins together or loses together.

When you want to encourage the same behavior in a group of students, consider using a group contingency. Up to this point, we've been talking about reinforcing students for their own individual behaviors. But positive reinforcement can also take the form of a **group contingency**: Students are reinforced only when *everyone* in a particular group (perhaps a cooperative learning group, perhaps an entire class) achieves at a certain level or behaves appropriately. The following are two examples of whole-class contingencies:

- A class of 32 fourth graders was doing poorly on weekly spelling tests, with an average of only 12 students (38%) earning perfect spelling test scores in any given week. Hoping for improvement, their teacher announced that any student with a perfect test score would get free time later in the week. The new reinforcement program had a noticeable effect: The average number of perfect spelling tests rose to 25 a week (78%). But then the teacher added a group contingency: Whenever the entire class achieved perfect spelling tests by Friday, the class could listen to the radio for 15 minutes. The group contingency produced an average of 30 perfect spelling tests (94%) a week (Lovitt, Guppy, & Blattner, 1969).
- Another fourth-grade teacher was dealing with an unusually unruly class: In any given minute, chances were good that one or more students would be talking out of turn or getting out of their seats. In a desperate move, the teacher divided the class into two teams that competed in a "good behavior game." Each time a student was observed talking out of turn or getting out of his or

contingency contract Formal agreement between a teacher and a student that identifies behaviors the student will exhibit and the reinforcers that will follow.

group contingency Situation in which everyone in a group must make a particular response before reinforcement occurs.

Creating A PRODUCTIVE CLASSROOM ENVIRONMENT

Identifying Effective Reinforcers for Different Students

- **Give students choices among two or more alternatives.**

  A high school teacher is working with a boy who has a significant intellectual disability and chronic behavior problems. On different occasions, she gives him different choices about which of two things he'd prefer to do. For example, she might give him a choice between (a) talking with her versus playing alone with favorite items, (b) working with her on an assigned task versus sitting by himself with nothing to do, or (c) working with her on an assigned task versus playing alone with favorite items. From the student's pattern of choices, the teacher concludes that her attention is an effective reinforcer for the student.

- **Ask students (or perhaps their parents) about consequences they would find especially appealing.**

  A first-grade teacher always includes his students in parent–teacher conferences. At one such conference, the teacher expresses his delight about the progress a student has made in the last few weeks but adds, "I've seen a lot of inconsistency in Janie's performance. Sometimes she works very hard, but at other times she doesn't put much effort into her schoolwork, and occasionally she doesn't complete assignments at all." Together, the teacher, Janie, and her parents agree that successfully completed assignments will earn her points toward the bicycle she has been asking her parents for.

- **Make use of the Premack principle: Students will often engage in behaviors they don't especially enjoy so that they can do something else they *do* enjoy.**

  After class one day, a ninth-grade teacher commends a student for his desire to make other people laugh. Then she points out the downside of his sense of humor: "Unfortunately, your jokes can distract your classmates from what they're supposed to be doing, and sometimes I have a hard time getting class discussions back on topic." She promises the student that if he can keep his attention and remarks focused on classroom subject matter throughout a class period, she will give him the last two or three minutes of the period to tell the class a joke or two.

- **Provide a small amount of free time contingent on desired behaviors.**

  A fifth-grade teacher allows students to engage in favorite activities during the free time they earn each day. Some students work on the classroom computer, others work on art projects, and still others converse with friends.

- **Observe students' behaviors and written work, keeping a lookout for activities and consequences that students seem to appreciate.**

  At home one night, 11-year-old Amie writes the entry below in the class journal that she and her teacher regularly use to communicate. The entry reveals that Amie clearly enjoys playing soccer; in other words, soccer is intrinsically reinforcing for her. It appears, too, that Amie appreciates attention from her coach, probably because (a) he might have her play more and (b) she would like feedback about what she's doing well and how she might improve her skills.

  Today I had a soccer game to see who would go to the state finals. Unfortenly we lost. I was very disapontated, not because we lost, but because my coach only put me in for 10 mins. I feel that the coach was ignoring me and was just focused on winning. I wish the coach would take notice of me on the side lines and not just focuse on winning.

Source: W. K. Berg et al., 2007 (student with intellectual disability example).

her seat, the student's team received a mark on the chalkboard. The team receiving fewer marks during a lesson won special privileges—for example, being first in the lunch line or having free time at the end of the day. If both teams had five marks or fewer, everyone won privileges. Misbehaviors dropped almost immediately to less than 20% of their initial frequency (Barrish, Saunders, & Wolf, 1969; also see Taub & Pearrow, 2006).

myeducationlab

Observe a group contingency for a cooperative learning group in the video "Cooperative Learning." (To find this video, go to Chapter 9 of the Book-Specific Resources in MyEducationLab, select *Video Examples*, and then click on the title.)

Group contingencies are clearly effective in improving academic achievement and classroom behavior *if* everyone in the group is capable of making the desired response (Heck, Collins, & Peterson, 2001; Kellam, Rebok, Ialongo, & Mayer, 1994; S. L. Robinson & Griesemer, 2006). Peer pressure and social reinforcers seem to play a role here. Misbehaving students are encouraged by other students to change their behaviors and are frequently praised when the changes occur (D. W. Johnson & Johnson, 1987; O'Leary & O'Leary, 1972; Slavin, 1983). Furthermore, when students' own success is riding on the success of their classmates, students who have mastered a topic begin to tutor those who are struggling with it (e.g., Pigott, Fantuzzo, & Clement, 1986).

When imposing a group contingency, make sure that everyone in the group is capable of making the desired response.

Whenever we use group contingencies, however, we must closely monitor students' behaviors to make sure that any peer pressure is socially appropriate—for instance, that students aren't ridiculing or bullying their low-performing classmates.

Administer reinforcement consistently until a desired behavior occurs at a desired rate. As you might guess, desired responses increase more quickly when they are reinforced every time they occur—that is, when the responses lead to **continuous reinforcement**. Continuous reinforcement is most important when students are first learning a new behavior, particularly one that doesn't come easily to them. If a new skill is especially difficult, we may need to begin by reinforcing *effort* (e.g., time on task) and switch to reinforcing *accuracy* only after students have gained some proficiency (Lannie & Martens, 2004).

Once a behavior is well established, wean students from extrinsic reinforcement, but do so very gradually. Just as reinforced behaviors increase in frequency, nonreinforced behaviors often *de*crease in frequency and may eventually disappear altogether. Like the decrease of a conditioned response in classical conditioning, the decrease and eventual disappearance of a nonreinforced response in instrumental conditioning is known as **extinction**.

Intrinsic reinforcement can, of course, maintain many productive behaviors over the long run, both in the classroom and in the outside world. But as we've already noted, students don't necessarily find *all* desired behaviors enjoyable in and of themselves. When certain behaviors have no intrinsic appeal, **intermittent reinforcement**—reinforcing a behavior on some occasions but not others—provides a viable alternative.

As an illustration, let's consider Molly and Maria, two students who almost never participate in class discussions. Their teacher, Mr. Oliver, decides to reinforce the girls for raising their hands. Each time Molly raises her hand, Mr. Oliver calls on her and praises her response, thus giving her continuous reinforcement. But when Maria raises her hand, Mr. Oliver doesn't always notice her. He calls on Maria whenever he sees her hand in the air, but he doesn't often look in her direction—so Maria is receiving intermittent reinforcement. Molly's hand raising should increase more rapidly than Maria's.

Now let's move ahead a few weeks. Thanks to Mr. Oliver's attentiveness to Molly and Maria, both girls are at this point volunteering frequently in class. Consequently, Mr. Oliver turns his attention to several other students who have been failing to participate. Foolishly, he no longer reinforces Molly and Maria for raising their hands. As you might expect, the girls begin to participate less; in other words, we see signs of extinction. But which girl's class participation will extinguish more quickly?

Once students exhibit a desired behavior frequently, continue to reinforce it intermittently to encourage persistence and prevent extinction.

If you predicted that Molly's volunteering will decrease more rapidly than Maria's, you are correct. Responses that have previously been continuously reinforced tend to extinguish relatively quickly once reinforcement stops. But because Maria has been receiving intermittent reinforcement, she's accustomed to being occasionally ignored and may not realize that reinforcement has stopped altogether. Behaviors that have previously been reinforced intermittently decrease slowly, if at all, once reinforcement stops. In other words, these behaviors are more *resistant to extinction* (e.g., Freeland & Noell, 1999).

Once students have mastered a desired behavior and are using it regularly, we should continue to reinforce it intermittently, especially if it doesn't otherwise lead to intrinsic reinforcement. Mr. Oliver doesn't need to call on Molly and Maria every time they raise their hands, but he should certainly call on them once in a while. In a similar manner, we might occasionally reinforce diligent study habits, completed homework assignments, prosocial behaviors, and so on—even for the best of students—as a way of encouraging these responses to continue.

Monitor students' progress. When we use reinforcement in the classroom, behaviorists urge us to determine, as objectively as possible, whether our efforts are bringing about the desired results. More specifically, they urge us to assess the fre-

continuous reinforcement Reinforcement of a response every time it occurs.

extinction (in instrumental conditioning) Gradual disappearance of an acquired response as a result of repeated lack of reinforcement.

intermittent reinforcement Reinforcement of a response only occasionally, with some occurrences of the response *not* being reinforced.

quency of the desired terminal behavior both before and during our attempts to increase it. The frequency of a behavior *before* we intentionally begin reinforcement is known as its **baseline** level. Some behaviors occur frequently even when they are not being explicitly reinforced, whereas other behaviors occur rarely or not at all.

By comparing the baseline frequency of a response with its frequency after we begin reinforcing it, we can determine whether our strategy is actually bringing about a behavior change. As an example, let's look once again at James in the opening case study. He rarely turns in classroom assignments; this is a behavior with a low baseline. An obvious reinforcer to use with James is attention—a consequence that, until now, has effectively reinforced such counterproductive behaviors as blurting out answers in class and throwing objects across the room. When we make our attention contingent on James's turning in assignments, rather than on his refusing to do so, we might see an almost immediate increase in the number of assignments we receive from James. If we see no significant change in James's behavior, we might need to consider alternative reinforcers. We should also consider and address possible reasons (e.g., poor reading skills) that may make it difficult for him to do his assignments.

Shaping New Behaviors

What if a desired behavior has a baseline level of *zero*? How can we encourage a behavior that a student never exhibits at all? Behaviorists suggest one possible solution: gradually **shaping** the behavior. Shaping involves reinforcing a series of responses—known as *successive approximations*—that increasingly resemble the terminal behavior. To shape a new response, we take these steps:

1. Reinforce any response that in some way resembles the terminal behavior.
2. Reinforce a response that more closely approximates the terminal behavior (while no longer reinforcing the previously reinforced response).
3. Reinforce a response that resembles the terminal behavior even more closely.
4. Continue reinforcing closer and closer approximations to the terminal behavior.
5. Reinforce only the terminal behavior.

Shape a low-frequency behavior by reinforcing closer and closer approximations over time.

Each response in the sequence is reinforced every time it occurs until we see it regularly. Only at that point do we begin reinforcing a behavior that more closely approaches the desired end result.

As an example, imagine that we have a second grader who can't seem to sit still long enough to get much of anything done. We would ultimately like her to sit still for 20-minute periods, but we may first have to reinforce her for staying in her seat for just 2 minutes, gradually increasing the sitting time required for reinforcement as she makes progress.

We can use shaping to help students acquire academic skills as well as appropriate classroom behaviors. When complex skills are involved, the shaping process may occur very slowly over several months or years. For example, kindergartners and first graders are taught to print their letters on wide-lined paper, and they are praised for well-formed letters whose bottoms rest on one line and whose tops touch a higher line. As children progress through the grade levels, the space between the lines becomes smaller, and teachers become fussier about how well letters are formed. Most children begin to write consistently sized and carefully shaped letters using only a lower line, and eventually, they need no line at all. In Figure 9.1 we see how my son Jeff's handwriting was gradually shaped from first to fourth grade.

In much the same way, we can (and teachers often do) use shaping to teach students to work independently on classroom assignments. We begin by giving first graders structured tasks that may take only 5 to 10 minutes to complete. As students move through the elementary school years, we expect them to work independently

baseline Frequency of a response before it is systematically reinforced.

shaping Process of reinforcing successively closer and closer approximations to a desired terminal behavior.

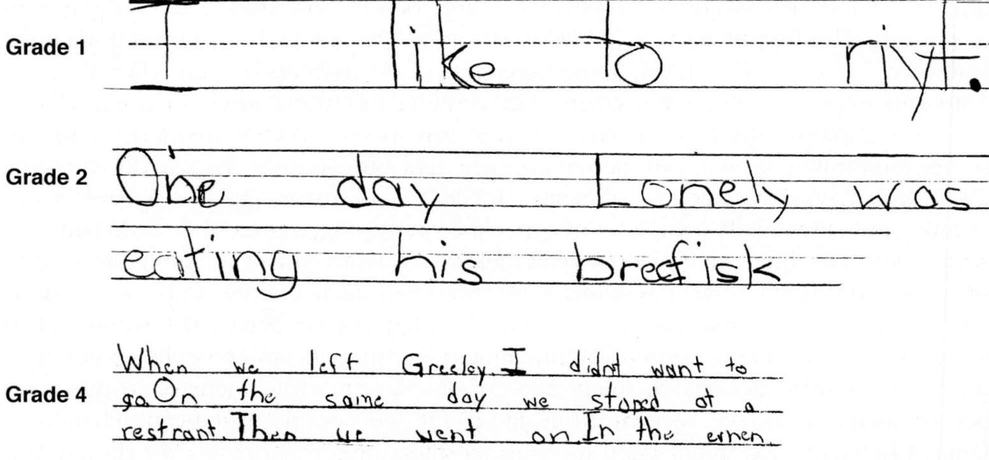

FIGURE 9.1 As Jeff moved through the elementary grades, his teachers gradually shaped his handwriting, both by reducing the spacing between lines and later by omitting some of the lines.

myeducationlab

Observe several examples of cueing in the video "Reading Group." (To find this video, go to Chapter 9 of the Book-Specific Resources in MyEducationLab, select *Video Examples*, and then click on the title.)

for longer periods and begin to give them short assignments to do at home. By the time students reach high school, they have extended study halls and complete lengthy assignments on their own after school hours. In the college years, student assignments require a great deal of independence and self-direction.

Bringing Antecedent Stimuli and Responses into the Picture

In our discussion of instrumental conditioning so far, we've focused on the consequences of behaviors. But stimuli and responses that *precede* a desired behavior (i.e., **antecedent stimuli** and **antecedent responses**) can also have an effect. Here we will look at several phenomena—cueing, setting events, generalization, and discrimination—that involve antecedent stimuli, as well as one phenomenon—behavioral momentum—that involves antecedent responses.

Quickly and unobtrusively cue students about appropriate behaviors, perhaps through a flick of the light switch or short verbal reminder.

Cueing Students are more likely to behave appropriately when they are given reminders (often called *cues* or *prompts*) that certain behaviors are expected (Emmer, Evertson, & Worsham, 2000; Northup et al., 1995; Shabani et al., 2002). Such **cueing** sometimes involves a nonverbal signal, such as flicking overhead lights off and on to remind students to use their "indoor voices." At other times, cueing involves a verbal reminder about what students should be doing. Subtle hints are often effective for older students (e.g., "I see some art supplies that still need to be put away"), whereas more explicit hints may be necessary for younger children (e.g., "Table 3 needs to clean up its art supplies before it can go to lunch").

antecedent stimulus Stimulus that increases the likelihood that a particular response will follow.

antecedent response Response that increases the likelihood that a certain other response will follow.

cueing Use of a verbal or nonverbal signal to indicate that a certain behavior is desired or that a certain behavior should stop.

setting event Complex environmental condition in which a particular behavior is most likely to occur.

Setting Events In cueing, we use specific stimuli to prompt students to behave in particular ways. An alternative approach is to create an overall environment—a **setting event**—that is apt to induce desired behaviors. For example, young children are more likely to interact with peers during free-play time if they have a relatively small area in which to play and if the toys available to them (e.g., balls, puppets, toy housekeeping materials) encourage cooperation and group activity (W. H. Brown, Fox, & Brady, 1987; Frost et al., 1998; S. S. Martin, Brady, & Williams, 1991). Similarly, the nature of the games children are asked to play influences the behaviors they exhibit:

Cooperative games promote cooperative behavior, whereas competitive games promote aggressive behavior (Bay-Hinitz, Peterson, & Quilitch, 1994).

Create an environment in which desired behaviors are more likely to occur of their own accord.

Generalization Once children have learned that a response is likely to be reinforced in one set of circumstances (which serve as antecedent stimuli), they are apt to make the same response in a similar situation. In other words, they show **generalization**. For example, after an especially fidgety student has learned to sit quietly and attentively for 20-minute periods in her second-grade classroom, she may generalize that behavior to her third-grade classroom the following year. And once a student has learned cursive writing at school, he is apt to use cursive in his out-of-school writing tasks. Generalization of newly acquired behaviors is most likely to occur when students have opportunities to practice those behaviors in a variety of settings (Haring & Liberty, 1990; B. M. Johnson et al., 2006; Stokes & Baer, 1977).

Provide opportunities for students to practice desired behaviors in a variety of settings.

This process of generalization should remind you of the generalization that occurs in classical conditioning: In both cases, an individual learns a response to one stimulus and then responds in the same way to a similar stimulus. The major difference is one of learner control: Generalization involves an automatic, involuntary response in classical conditioning but a voluntary response in instrumental conditioning.

Discrimination Sometimes people learn that responses are reinforced only when certain environmental conditions (i.e., certain antecedent stimuli) are present. This ability to distinguish between conditions in which a particular behavior will and will not be reinforced is known as **discrimination**. For example, first graders might learn that they can go to the restroom only after their teacher has given them permission. And teenage boys should certainly learn that slapping a peer on the fanny may be quite acceptable when celebrating an athletic victory with teammates but is usually *not* acceptable when greeting a female classmate in the hall.

Occasionally students overgeneralize, exhibiting newly learned behaviors in situations where such behaviors are inappropriate. In such cases, we must teach them to discriminate between suitable and unsuitable stimulus conditions. We should describe in very concrete terms the circumstances in which certain behaviors are and are not acceptable. And we must then be sure to reinforce students for engaging in those behaviors *only* when the conditions are right.

Describe conditions under which certain behaviors are appropriate, and reinforce the behaviors only when they *are* appropriate.

Sometimes we can use cueing to help students determine when certain behaviors are allowed. For example, in one recent study, children in three elementary classrooms were having trouble determining when they could and could not request a teacher's assistance. Their teachers began to wear green and red leis at different times and told them, "While I am wearing the green lei, I will be able to answer your questions. While I am wearing the red lei, I will not be able to answer your questions." This simple procedure minimized student requests at inopportune moments (Cammilleri, Tiger, & Hanley, 2008, p. 301).

Take advantage of behavioral momentum by assigning easy tasks as a lead-in to similar but more challenging ones.

Behavioral Momentum In many cases, students are more likely to make desired responses if they are already making similar responses—a phenomenon known as **behavioral momentum** (Ardoin, Martens, & Wolfe, 1999; Belfiore, Lee, Vargas, & Skinner, 1997; Mace et al., 1988). For example, imagine that we have low-achieving high school students with a history of refusing to do math assignments. Such students are more likely to attempt difficult three-digit multiplication problems after they have first worked on a few simple one-digit problems (Belfiore et al., 1997). Similarly, we might ask students to tidy up a messy classroom after they have already cleaned their own desktops or to try a backward roll after they have already executed a forward roll successfully. In general, we can promote behavioral momentum by assigning relatively easy or enjoyable tasks that lead naturally into more complex and potentially frustrating ones.

generalization (in instrumental conditioning) Phenomenon in which a person makes a voluntary response to a stimulus that is similar to one previously associated with a response-reinforcement contingency.

discrimination Phenomenon in which a student learns that a response is reinforced in the presence of one stimulus but not in the presence of another similar stimulus.

behavioral momentum Increased tendency for a learner to make a particular response immediately after making similar responses.

Strategies for Discouraging Undesirable Behaviors

Our focus so far has been primarily on promoting desirable behaviors. But we will also need to address *un*desirable behaviors—those that interfere with students' own learning and achievement and possibly also with the learning and achievement of classmates. Behaviorists offer several possible approaches, including extinction, cueing, reinforcement of incompatible behaviors, and punishment.

Creating Conditions for Extinction

Identify and try to remove reinforcers that may be maintaining an undesirable behavior.

One way to reduce the frequency of an inappropriate response is simply to make sure it is never reinforced. For instance, a class clown whose antics are ignored may stop distracting his classmates, and an aggressive child who never gets what she wants by hitting or shoving others may become less aggressive.

There are three points to keep in mind about extinction, however. First, once reinforcement stops, a previously reinforced response may initially *increase* for a short time (Lerman & Iwata, 1995; McGill, 1999). To illustrate how this might occur, imagine that you have a cantankerous television set that gives you a clear picture only when you bang it on the side once or twice. Eventually, something changes in the inner workings of your set, such that banging is no longer an effective remedy. As you desperately try to get a clear picture, you may bang your TV quite a bit before abandoning that response. In much the same way, the class clown who is now being ignored may engage in more disruptive behavior at first, and the aggressive child who no longer obtains desired results may initially act out more frequently. Fortunately, such increases are usually temporary, but they can certainly try our patience and perhaps tempt us into inadvertently reinforcing counterproductive behaviors.

Second, if teacher attention has been the primary consequence reinforcing a behavior, we must make sure that in our efforts to extinguish the behavior we don't ignore the student altogether. The trick is to give misbehaving students attention when they are doing something well or, instead, at seemingly random intervals throughout the school day (Austin & Soeda, 2008).

Third, we may sometimes have situations in which removing a reinforcer has no noticeable effect on a student's inappropriate behavior. In such situations—when extinction doesn't occur—chances are good that we haven't been able to remove *all* reinforcers. Perhaps the behavior is leading to a naturally reinforcing consequence; for instance, a class clown's peers may continue to snicker even if the teacher ignores his jokes. Or perhaps the response is intrinsically reinforcing; for instance, a student's physically aggressive behavior may release pent-up energy (and thus may feel good), even if it doesn't otherwise get her what she wants.

Subtle actions can often be effective cues. While this teacher is temporarily preoccupied, her hand on a student's shoulder provides a gentle reminder about what he should and should not be doing.

Cueing Inappropriate Behaviors

Just as we can use cueing to remind students about what they should be doing, we can also cue them about what they should *not* be doing (Emmer, 1987; Northup et al., 1995; Woolfolk & Brooks, 1985). For example, we might use *body language*—perhaps making eye contact or raising an eyebrow—or *physical proximity*—moving closer to the student and standing there until the problem behavior stops. When subtlety doesn't work, a brief *verbal cue* may be in order—stating a student's name or (if necessary) pointing out an inappropriate behavior (e.g., "Lucy, put the magazine away").

Use physical and verbal cues to discourage inappropriate behavior.

Reinforcing Incompatible Behaviors

Often we can reduce the frequency of an unproductive behavior simply by reinforcing an *alternative* behavior. Ideally, the two behaviors are **incompatible behaviors**, which cannot be performed simultaneously. To discover examples of incompatible behaviors in your own life, try the following exercise.

EXPERIENCING FIRSTHAND

Asleep on Your Feet

Have you ever tried to sleep while standing up? Horses can do it, but most of us humans really cannot. In fact, there are many pairs of responses that are impossible to perform simultaneously. Take a minute to identify something you can't possibly do when you perform each of these activities:

When you . . .	*You cannot simultaneously . . .*
Sit down	____________________
Eat crackers	____________________
Take a walk	____________________

Obviously, there are no single right answers in this exercise. As one possibility, you might have said that sitting is incompatible with standing. Eating crackers is incompatible with singing—or at least with singing *well*. Taking a walk is incompatible with taking a nap. In each case, it is physically impossible to perform both activities at exactly the same time.

When our attempts at extinction or cueing are unsuccessful, reinforcement of one or more behaviors that are incompatible with a problem behavior is often quite effective (K. Lane, Falk, & Wehby, 2006; Lerman, Kelley, Vorndran, Kuhn, & LaRue, 2002). This is the approach we're taking when we reinforce a hyperactive student for sitting quietly: Sitting is incompatible with getting-out-of-seat and roaming-around-the-room behaviors. It's also an approach we might use to deal with forgetfulness (we reinforce students when they remember to do what they are supposed to do), being off-task (we reinforce on-task behavior), and verbal abusiveness (we reinforce prosocial statements). And consider how we might deal with a chronic litterbug:

Encourage and reinforce responses that are incompatible with undesirable behaviors.

> Walt is a junior high school student who consistently leaves garbage (banana peels, sunflower seed shells, etc.) on the lunchroom floor, in school corridors, and on the playground. When the school faculty establishes an Antilitter Committee, it puts Walt on the committee, and the committee eventually elects him as its chairman. Under Walt's leadership, the committee institutes a massive antilitter campaign, complete with posters and lunchroom monitors, and Walt receives considerable recognition for the campaign's success. Curiously (or perhaps not), school personnel no longer find Walt's garbage littering the school grounds (Krumboltz & Krumboltz, 1972).

Using Punishment When Necessary

Some misbehaviors require an immediate remedy—for instance, they might interfere significantly with classroom learning or reflect total disregard for other people's rights and welfare. Consider this example:

incompatible behaviors Two or more behaviors that cannot be performed simultaneously.

> Bonnie doesn't handle frustration very well. Whenever she encounters an obstacle she can't immediately overcome, she responds by hitting, punching, kicking, or breaking something. One day, during a class Valentine's Day party, she accidentally drops her cupcake upside-down on the floor. When she discovers that the cupcake is no longer edible, she throws her carton of milk across the room, hitting another child on the head.

Use punishment when alternative approaches have been ineffective.

Bonnie's troublesome behaviors are difficult to extinguish because they aren't being reinforced to begin with—at least not extrinsically. They are also behaviors with no obvious incompatible responses that can be reinforced. And we can reasonably assume that Bonnie's teacher has frequently cued her about her inappropriate behavior. When other strategies are inapplicable or ineffective, punishment is a potentially viable alternative.

A frequent criticism of using punishment is that it is inhumane, or somehow cruel and barbaric. Indeed, certain forms of punishment, such as physical abuse and public humiliation, do constitute inhumane treatment. We must be *extremely careful* in our use of punishment in the classroom. If administered judiciously, however, some forms of mild punishment can lead to a rapid reduction in misbehavior without causing physical or psychological harm. And when we can decrease counterproductive classroom behaviors quickly and effectively—especially when those behaviors are harmful to self or others—punishment may, in fact, be one of the most humane approaches we can take (Lerman & Vorndran, 2002). Following are several guidelines for using punishment effectively and humanely:

Choose a consequence that is truly punishing without being overly severe. Any unpleasant consequence must be strong enough to discourage students from engaging in the punished behavior in the future (Landrum & Kauffman, 2006; Lerman & Vorndran, 2002). But unnecessarily harsh punishments—those that far surpass the severity of the crime—are apt to lead to such undesirable side effects as resentment, hostility, aggression, and escape behavior. Furthermore, although severe punishment can quickly suppress a response, that response may reappear at its original level once the punisher has left the scene (Appel & Peterson, 1965; Azrin, 1960; Landrum & Kauffman, 2006). The ultimate purpose of administering punishment is to communicate that the limits of acceptable behavior have been exceeded, *not* to exact revenge and retaliation.

Inform students ahead of time that certain behaviors will be punished, and explain how those behaviors will be punished. When students are informed of response-punishment contingencies ahead of time, they are less apt to engage in forbidden behaviors; they are also less apt to be surprised or resentful if punishment must be administered (G. D. Gottfredson & Gottfredson, 1985; Moles, 1990). Ultimately, students should learn that their behaviors influence the consequences they experience—that they have some control over what happens to them (more on this point in our discussion of *attributions* in Chapter 11).

Follow through with specified consequences. A mistake some teachers make is to continually threaten punishment without ever following through. One warning is desirable, but repeated warnings are not. Consider the teacher who says "If you bring that rubber snake to class one more time, Tommy, I'll take it away from you" but never does take the snake away. This teacher is giving the message that no response-punishment contingency really exists.

Administer punishment privately, especially when other students aren't aware of the transgression. By administering punishment in private, we protect students from public embarrassment and humiliation. We also eliminate the possibility that the punishment will draw the attention of classmates—a potential reinforcer for the very behavior we are trying to eliminate.

Some mild forms of punishment, such as a brief time-out in a quiet corner of the classroom, can reduce counterproductive behaviors, but we must monitor their effectiveness for different students.

- ***Emphasize that it's the behavior—not the student—that is unacceptable, and explain why it's unacceptable.*** We must explain exactly why a certain behavior cannot be tolerated in the classroom—perhaps because it interferes with learning, threatens other students' safety or self-esteem, or damages school property. In other words, punishment should be accompanied by *induction* (see Chapter 3). Punishment is far more effective when accompanied by one or more reasons that the punished behavior is unacceptable (Cheyne & Walters, 1970; Parke, 1974; D. G. Perry & Perry, 1983).

- ***Administer punishment within the context of a generally warm, supportive environment.*** Punishment is more effective when the person administering it has previously established a good working relationship with the student (Landrum & Kauffman, 2006; Nucci, 2001). The message should ultimately be this: "I care for you and want you to succeed, and your current behavior is interfering with your success."

- ***Simultaneously teach and reinforce desirable alternative behaviors.*** Punishment of misbehavior is almost always more effective when appropriate behaviors are being reinforced at the same time (Landrum & Kauffman, 2006; Lerman & Vorndran, 2002). Furthermore, by reinforcing desirable responses as well as punishing undesirable ones, we give students the positive, optimistic message that, yes, behavior can and will improve. Ultimately, the overall classroom atmosphere we create must be a positive one that highlights the good things students do and deemphasizes the bad (e.g., R. E. Smith & Smoll, 1997).

- ***Monitor the punishment's effectiveness.*** Remember that punishment is defined by its effect on behavior. True punishment decreases the response it follows and typically does so quite rapidly (R. V. Hall et al., 1971; Landrum & Kauffman, 2006). If a given consequence doesn't decrease the response it is meant to punish, the consequence may not be aversive to the individual being "punished." In fact, it may even be reinforcing.

Addressing Especially Difficult Classroom Behaviors

Behaviorist principles can be extremely helpful in tackling difficult and chronic behavior problems. In this section, we consider three related approaches for addressing especially challenging behaviors. Often they are planned and carried out by one or more teachers in consultation with a school psychologist or other specialist.

Applied Behavior Analysis

Applied behavior analysis (ABA) is a group of procedures that systematically apply behaviorist principles in changing behavior. (You may also see such terms as *behavior modification, behavior therapy,* and *contingency management.*) ABA is based on the assumptions that (a) behavior problems result from past and present environmental circumstances and that (b) modifying a learner's present environment will promote more productive responses. When teachers and therapists use ABA to help a student acquire more appropriate classroom behavior, they typically use strategies such as these:

applied behavior analysis (ABA) Systematic application of behaviorist principles in educational and therapeutic settings.

- Describe both the present behaviors and the desired terminal behaviors in observable, measurable terms.
- Identify one or more effective reinforcers.

- Develop a specific intervention or treatment plan, which may involve reinforcement of desired behaviors, shaping, extinction, reinforcement of incompatible behaviors, punishment, or some combination of these.
- Give explicit instruction related to desired behaviors.
- Measure the frequency of desired and undesired behaviors both before treatment (i.e., at baseline level) and during treatment in order to monitor the treatment's effectiveness; modify the program, if necessary.
- Take steps to promote generalization of newly acquired behaviors (e.g., by having the student practice the behaviors in a variety of realistic situations).
- Gradually phase out the treatment (e.g., through intermittent reinforcement) after desired behaviors are occurring regularly.

The systematic use of behaviorist strategies such as these can lead to significant improvements in academic performance and classroom behavior. For example, when we reinforce students for academic accomplishments, we are apt to see noticeable progress in such areas as reading, spelling, creative writing, and math (Piersel, 1987). And when we reinforce appropriate classroom behaviors—paying attention, interacting cooperatively and prosocially with classmates, and so on—misbehaviors decrease (S. N. Elliott & Busse, 1991; E. McNamara, 1987; Ormrod, 2008). In many situations, ABA is effective when other approaches have not been (Evertson & Weinstein, 2006; O'Leary & O'Leary, 1972; Piersel, 1987).

One likely reason that ABA often works so well is that students know exactly what is expected of them. Consistent use of reinforcement for appropriate responses gives a clear message about which behaviors are acceptable and which are not. Another likely reason is that through the gradual process of *shaping*, students begin to practice new behaviors only when they are truly ready to acquire them; thus, their probability of achieving success and reinforcement is quite high.

Functional Analysis and Positive Behavioral Support

When a problem behavior persists, try to identify functions that the behavior serves for the student.

myeducationlab

Gain practice in identifying antecedents and consequences by completing the Building Teaching Skills and Dispositions exercise "Applying Behaviorist Principles" in MyEducationLab. (To find this exercise, go to the topic Behaviorist Perspectives in MyEducationLab, and click on *Building Teaching Skills and Dispositions*.)

functional analysis Examination of inappropriate behavior and its antecedents and consequences to determine functions that the behavior might serve for the learner.

Traditional ABA focuses largely on changing response-reinforcement contingencies to bring about more appropriate behavior. In recent years, some theorists have suggested that we also consider the purposes, or *functions*, that students' inappropriate behaviors may serve (e.g., Potoczak, Carr, & Michael, 2007; Van Camp et al., 2000). Such an approach is known as **functional analysis** (you may also see the terms *functional assessment* and *functional behavioral assessment*). Functional analysis involves collecting data regarding the specific conditions (i.e., antecedent stimuli) in which students tend to misbehave and also the consequences (i.e., reinforcers, punishments, or both) that typically follow the misbehaviors. Thus, we would collect data related to the three parts of a stimulus–response–stimulus sequence:

Antecedent ➔ Behavior ➔ Consequence

As an example, we have speculated that in the opening case study, James misbehaves to get the attention he apparently cannot get in any other way and possibly also to escape certain classroom tasks. Functional analyses have shown that students with chronic classroom behavior problems often misbehave when they are asked to do difficult or unpleasant tasks (this is the *antecedent*) and that their misbehavior either (a) allows them to avoid having to do these tasks or (b) gains the attention of their teacher or peers (these are possible *consequences*) (K. M. Jones, Drew, & Weber, 2000; McComas et al., 2003; K. A. Meyer, 1999; Van Camp et al., 2000).

Positive behavioral support (PBS) takes the process a step further: After identifying the purposes that inappropriate behaviors may serve, a teacher—or more often, a team of teachers and other professionals—develops and carries out a plan to encourage appropriate behaviors. In particular, positive behavioral support involves strategies such as these:

- Teach behaviors that can serve the same purpose as (and can therefore replace) inappropriate behaviors.
- Modify the classroom environment to minimize conditions that might trigger inappropriate behaviors.
- Establish a predictable daily routine as a way of minimizing anxiety and making the student feel more comfortable and secure.
- Give the student opportunities to make choices; in this way, the student can often gain desired outcomes without having to resort to inappropriate behavior.
- Make adaptations in the curriculum, instruction, or both to maximize the likelihood of academic success (e.g., build on the student's interests, present material at a slower pace, or intersperse challenging tasks among easier and more enjoyable ones).
- Monitor the frequency of various behaviors to determine whether the intervention is working or, instead, requires modification. (Crone & Horner, 2003; Koegel et al., 1996; Ruef, Higgins, Glaeser, & Patnode, 1998)

myeducationlab

Examine an illustration of functional analysis by completing the Understanding Research exercise "Conducting a Functional Analysis" in MyEducationLab. (To find this activity, go to the topic Behaviorist Perspectives in MyEducationLab, click on *Assignments and Activities*, and then select *Understanding Research*.)

As an illustration of how functional analysis and positive behavioral support might be used in combination, let's consider 9-year-old Samantha:

> Samantha had been identified as having a mild form of autism and moderate speech disabilities. She frequently ran out of her third-grade classroom, damaging school property and classmates' belongings in her flight. When a teacher or other adult tried to intervene, she would fight back by biting, hitting, kicking, or pulling hair. On such occasions, school personnel often called her parents and asked that they come to take her home.
>
> By systematically collecting data on Samantha's classroom performance, a team of teachers and specialists discovered that her destructive and aggressive behaviors typically occurred when she was given a difficult assignment or was expecting such an assignment. Departures from the regular schedule or the absence of favorite teachers further increased the probability of inappropriate responses.
>
> The team hypothesized that Samantha's undesirable behaviors served two purposes: They (a) helped her avoid unpleasant academic tasks and (b) enabled her to gain the attention of valued adults. The team suspected, too, that Samantha felt as if she had little or no control over classroom activities and that she yearned for more social interaction with her teachers and classmates (DeVault, Krug, & Fake, 1996).

Armed with this information, the team took several steps to address the roots of Samantha's inappropriate behaviors and help her acquire more productive ones:

- Samantha was given a consistent and predictable daily schedule that included frequent breaks from potentially challenging academic tasks and numerous opportunities to interact with others.
- Samantha was given goal sheets from which she could choose the academic tasks she would work on, the length of time she would work on them, and the reinforcer she would receive for achieving each goal.
- Samantha was taught how to ask for assistance when she needed it—a strategy she could use instead of fleeing from the classroom when she encountered a challenging task.

positive behavioral support (PBS) Variation of traditional applied behavior analysis that involves identifying the purposes of undesirable behaviors and encouraging alternative behaviors that more appropriately accomplish those purposes.

- When Samantha felt she needed a break from academic tasks, she could ask to spend some time in the "relaxation room," a quiet and private space where she could sit in a beanbag chair and listen to soothing audiotapes.
- If Samantha tried to leave the classroom, an adult would place her immediately in the relaxation room, where she could calm down without a great deal of adult attention.
- Samantha was given explicit instruction in how to interact appropriately with classmates. Initially, she earned points for appropriate social behaviors and could trade them for special treats (e.g., a family trip to Dairy Queen or a video store). Eventually, her new social skills led to natural consequences—friendly interactions with peers—that made extrinsic reinforcers unnecessary (DeVault et al., 1996).

Samantha's problem behaviors didn't disappear overnight, but they showed a dramatic decline over the next few months. By the time Samantha was 12 years old and in sixth grade, her grades consistently earned her a place on the honor roll, and she had a group of friends with whom she participated in several extracurricular activities. Her teachers described her as being sociable, inquisitive, and creative. Her principal called her a "model student" (DeVault et al., 1996).

Positive behavioral support clearly has elements of behaviorist theory, including its focus on structuring an environment that reinforces desired behaviors and extinguishes undesirable ones. At the same time, it also incorporates contemporary theories of motivation, as reflected in its attempts to minimize anxiety, provide opportunities for choice making, and promote mastery of classroom tasks.[4] The importance of doing all of these things will become clearer when we discuss motivation in Chapter 11.

Diversity in Student Behaviors and Reactions to Consequences

When we take a behaviorist perspective, we realize that each of our students brings a unique set of previous environments and experiences to the classroom, and such diversity is undoubtedly a key reason for the different behavior patterns we see. For one thing, students have been reinforced and punished—by parents, previous teachers, peers, and so on—for different kinds of behaviors. Some students may have been reinforced for completing tasks in a careful and thorough manner, whereas others may have been reinforced for completing tasks quickly but sloppily. Some students may have been reinforced for initiating interactions with age-mates; others may have been punished (perhaps in the form of peer rejection) for similar outgoing behavior. In some instances, diversity in students' classroom behaviors is the result of the different behaviors that various cultures encourage (i.e., reinforce) and discourage (i.e., punish) in children.

We see differences, too, in the consequences that students find reinforcing and punishing. In some cultures, reprimands are often used to communicate concern and affection. For example, on one occasion, a teacher in Haiti was reprimanding her students for proceeding across a parking lot without her. The following conversation ensued:

> *Teacher:* Did I tell you to go?
>
> *Children:* No.

---

[4]For more information and additional examples of PBS in action, go to the website of the Association for Positive Support at www.apbs.org.

Teacher: Can you cross this parking lot by yourselves?

Children: No.

Teacher: That's right. There are cars here. They're dangerous. I don't want you to go alone. Why do I want you to wait for me, do you know?

Claudette: Yes . . . because you like us. (Ballenger, 1992, p. 205)

Students from certain other cultures may be unaccustomed to direct praise for good performance, perhaps because adults in their culture express their approval in other ways—for instance, by telling other people how skillful a child is (Greenfield et al., 2006; Kitayama, Duffy, & Uchida, 2007; Rogoff, 2003). And many Native American students may feel uncomfortable when praised for their work as individuals yet feel quite proud when they receive praise for group success (Fuller, 2001). Such preference for group praise is consistent with the cooperative spirit in which these students have grown up (see Chapter 4).

Keep in mind that students from some cultures are unaccustomed to praise for their individual accomplishments.

Accommodating Students with Special Needs

A behaviorist approach allows us to consider characteristics of students with special needs from a somewhat different perspective than we have taken in previous chapters. Table 9.4 illustrates how responses, reactions to reinforcement, generalization, and discrimination might sometimes be different in students with special needs.

Strengths and Potential Limitations of Behavioral Approaches

Behaviorist techniques are especially helpful when we need to address chronic and challenging classroom behavior problems. Although such approaches as applied behavior analysis, functional analysis, and positive behavioral support can sometimes be fairly time consuming and labor intensive, they are often effective when other approaches have failed.

Psychologists have had mixed feelings about the value of behaviorist techniques in addressing *academic* problems, however. Reinforcement and other behaviorist strategies often do lead to improved academic performance, but we should keep the following drawbacks in mind:

- *Attempts to change behaviors ignore cognitive factors that are potentially interfering with learning.* When cognitive deficiencies (e.g., limited background knowledge, poor reading skills, ineffective study strategies) hinder students' ability to acquire certain skills, reinforcement alone may be insufficient to bring about significant improvement. As an example, let's return one final time to the opening case study. Perhaps James has poor reading skills that, because of shame or embarrassment, he wants to hide from his teacher and classmates. If so, he may sometimes misbehave to escape tasks that, to him, seem impossible. For those students who have significant weaknesses in their knowledge or cognitive abilities, instructional strategies based on cognitive theories (described in Chapters 6 through 8) may be more effective.

- *Reinforcement for accomplishing academic tasks may encourage students to do things quickly rather than well.* In general, reinforcement solely for accomplishing a particular task, perhaps at a minimally acceptable level, focuses students' attention and effort more on completing the activity than on *learning* from it. Especially if we want students to engage in complex, higher-level thinking—for instance, to elaborate on and think creatively about the subject matter—then extrinsic reinforcement simply for task accomplishment may be counterproductive (Deci & Ryan, 1985; B. A. Hennessey & Amabile, 1987; McCaslin & Good, 1996).

Students in Inclusive Settings

TABLE 9.4
Encouraging Appropriate Behaviors in Students with Special Educational Needs

Category	Characteristics You Might Observe	Suggested Strategies
Students with specific cognitive or academic difficulties	• Inappropriate classroom behaviors (for some students) • Less ability to delay gratification (for students with ADHD) • Avoidance behaviors common when confronting challenging tasks • Difficulty discriminating among similar stimuli, especially when perceptual deficits exist	• Be explicit about and consistently reinforce desired classroom behaviors. • Emphasize differences among similar stimuli (e.g., the letters *b*, *d*, *p*, and *q*), and provide opportunities to practice making subtle discriminations. • Promote generalization of new responses (e.g., by pointing out similarities among different situations and by teaching skills in real-world contexts).
Students with social or behavioral problems	• Inappropriate responses, especially in social situations; difficulty determining when and where particular responses are appropriate • A history of inappropriate behaviors being reinforced (e.g., intrinsically or by teacher attention) • Responsiveness to teacher praise if given in private (for students with emotional and behavioral disorders) • Little or no appreciation of others' praise and approval (for some students with autism spectrum disorders) • Difficulty generalizing appropriate responses to new situations	• Explicitly and concretely describe desired behaviors. • Give precise feedback regarding students' behaviors. • Reinforce desired behaviors using teacher attention, private praise, activity reinforcers, and group contingencies (for students with emotional and behavioral disorders). • Reinforce accomplishments immediately, using concrete reinforcers or activity reinforcers; combine them with praise so that praise eventually becomes reinforcing in and of itself (for students with more severe forms of autism). • Shape desired behaviors over time; expect gradual improvement, rather than immediate perfection. • Punish inappropriate behaviors (e.g., using time-out or response cost); consider applied behavior analysis or positive behavioral support for persistently challenging behaviors. • Promote generalization of new responses to appropriate situations (e.g., by teaching skills in real-world contexts and providing opportunities to role-play new responses).
Students with general delays in cognitive and social functioning	• Appreciation of and responsiveness to extrinsic reinforcers • Difficulty delaying gratification; behavior more likely to improve when reinforcement is immediate rather than delayed • Inappropriate responses in social situations • Difficulty discriminating between important and unimportant stimuli • Difficulty generalizing responses from one situation to another	• Explicitly teach and cue appropriate behaviors. • Reinforce accomplishments immediately (e.g., using concrete reinforcers, activity reinforcers, praise). • Use continuous reinforcement during the acquisition of new responses. • Shape complex behaviors slowly over time; expect gradual improvement rather than immediate perfection. • Reprimand minor misbehaviors; use time-out or response cost for more serious and chronic misbehaviors. • Emphasize the stimuli to which you want students to attend. • Promote generalization of new responses (e.g., by teaching skills in real-world contexts and by reinforcing generalization).
Students with physical or sensory challenges	• Loss of some previously learned behaviors if students have had traumatic brain injury	• Shape desired behaviors slowly over time; expect gradual improvement rather than immediate perfection.
Students with advanced cognitive development	• Unusual and sometimes creative responses to classroom tasks	• Keep an open mind about acceptable responses to classroom assignments. • Encourage and reinforce creative responses.

Sources: Barbetta, 1990; Barbetta, Heward, Bradley, & Miller, 1994; Beirne-Smith et al., 2006; Buchoff, 1990; Cuskelly, Zhang, & Hayes, 2003; E. S. Ellis & Friend, 1991; Gearheart et al., 1992; S. Goldstein & Rider, 2006; Heward, 2009; Hobson, 2004; Hoerger & Mace, 2006; Landau & McAninch, 1993; Mercer & Pullen, 2005; Morgan & Jenson, 1988; Neef et al., 2005; Patton et al., 1996; Pfiffner et al., 2006; Piirto, 1999; Pressley, 1995; Turnbull et al., 2007.

• *Extrinsic reinforcement of an activity that students already find intrinsically reinforcing may undermine their enjoyment of the activity.* Students often engage in behaviors because of the intrinsic reinforcers (e.g., feelings of success or pleasure) that those behaviors bring. Some research studies indicate that enjoyable activities can be increased through extrinsic reinforcement but will then *decrease* to a below-baseline frequency once the reinforcers are removed. Extrinsic reinforcers are most likely to have this adverse effect when students perceive them as being controlling or manipulative, rather than as promoting improvement and progress (see Chapter 11).

Communicate genuine appreciation for what students have done. Try not to come across as controlling or manipulative.

Before using extrinsic reinforcers, then, we should be sure that such reinforcers are truly necessary—that students have little or no intrinsic desire to acquire the academic skills and classroom behaviors essential for their school success. For example, perhaps students initially find a new activity boring, difficult, or frustrating and need external encouragement to continue. Extrinsic reinforcement can also be quite useful when students otherwise have no desire to behave in ways that help to keep the classroom orderly and productive. With continuing practice, however, their competence and skills should improve, and they may begin to find certain activities and behaviors worth engaging in for their own sake.

The Big Picture

Three general ideas sum up much of our discussion of behaviorism in this chapter:

• ***Many human behaviors reflect a sequence of stimulus-response associations.*** Conditions already present in a learner's environment—antecedent stimuli—tend to evoke certain kinds of responses either involuntarily (in classical conditioning) or voluntarily (in instrumental conditioning). Those responses may, in turn, lead to changes in the learner's environment—for instance, they may lead to reinforcement or punishment. If we think of reinforcing and punishing consequences as *stimuli* (because indeed, they are), then we see a continuing interaction between a learner and his or her environment:

$$S \rightarrow R \rightarrow S \rightarrow R \rightarrow S \rightarrow R \rightarrow \ldots$$

• ***An intervention in any part of this sequence can help learners acquire more productive behaviors.*** Sometimes an intervention involves altering the classroom environment (the stimulus conditions). For instance, we might present a stimulus that evokes unpleasant feelings (e.g., as math does for some students) in conjunction with one or more stimuli that elicit feelings of enjoyment or relaxation. In other cases, an intervention involves teaching students more effective ways of responding to the environment. For example, we can increase students' on-task behavior and simultaneously decrease their off-task behavior by giving them reinforcement (e.g., attention) only when they are on task. And we can help them gain reinforcement from their peers (e.g., enjoyable group activities) by teaching and shaping increasingly effective social skills.

• ***Helpful as stimulus—response principles may be, by themselves, they give us an incomplete picture of human learning.*** For example, although reinforcement may increase the amount of time that students study, it doesn't necessarily increase the effectiveness of that study time. Cognitive psychology provides more guidance as to how we can help students learn information more effectively, remember it longer, and apply it to new situations more readily. Furthermore, one very big factor within that "black box" we cannot open—learners' *interpretations* of various stimuli in their environment—play a critical role in determining how they respond to those stimuli at any given time. The perspective we look at in the next chapter—social cognitive theory—will help us bring cognition into the picture as we continue our exploration of stimulus–response relationships.

Practice for Your Licensure Exam

Hostile Helen

Mr. Washington has a close-knit group of friends in one of his high school vocational education classes. He is concerned about one particular student in this group, a girl named Helen. Helen uses obscene language in class. She's also rude and disrespectful to Mr. Washington, and she taunts and insults classmates outside her own circle of friends. In addition, Helen is physically aggressive toward school property; she defaces furniture, kicks equipment, punches walls, and so on.

At first, Mr. Washington tries to ignore Helen's hostile and aggressive behaviors, but this strategy doesn't lead to any improvement in her behavior. He then tries praising Helen on those rare occasions when she does behave appropriately, but this strategy doesn't seem to work either.

1. Multiple-choice question:

Mr. Washington initially tries to ignore Helen's inappropriate behavior. This approach best reflects which one of the following concepts from behaviorism?

a. Extinction
b. Response cost
c. Functional analysis
d. Negative reinforcement

2. Multiple-choice question:

Later, Mr. Washington tries praising Helen for appropriate behaviors. This approach best reflects which one of the following behaviorist concepts?

a. Setting event
b. Discrimination
c. Positive behavioral support
d. Reinforcement of incompatible behaviors

3. Constructed-response question:

Many research studies indicate that behaviorist principles *can* be effective in bringing about significant improvements in students' classroom behavior, yet neither of Mr. Washington's strategies has an effect on Helen's classroom behavior.

A. Suggest at least three different reasons that Mr. Washington's strategies might not be having much effect.

B. Describe how you might use behaviorist learning principles to bring about a behavior change in Helen. Be specific about what you would do.

Go to Chapter 9 of the Book-Specific Resources in **MyEducationLab**, and click on "Practice for Your Licensure Exam" to answer these questions. Compare your responses with the feedback provided.

PRAXIS

Turn to Appendix C, "Matching Book and MyEducationLab Content to the Praxis Principles of Learning and Teaching Tests," to discover sections of this chapter that may be especially applicable to the Praxis tests.

PEARSON myeducationlab

Now go to MyEducationLab (**www.myeducationlab.com**) where you can:

- Find learning outcomes for Behaviorist Perspectives, along with the national standards that connect to these outcomes.
- Complete Assignments and Activities that can help you more deeply understand the chapter content.
- Engage in Building Teaching Skills and Dispositions exercises in which you can apply and practice core teaching skills identified in the chapter.
- Access Book-Specific Resources:
    - Check your comprehension of chapter content by going to the Study Plan, where you can find (a) Chapter Objectives; (b) Focus Questions that can guide your reading; (c) a Self-Check Quiz that can help you monitor your progress in mastering chapter content; (d) Review, Practice, and Enrichment exercises with detailed feedback that will deepen your understanding of various concepts and principles; (e) Flashcards that can give you practice in understanding and defining key terms; and (f) Common Beliefs and Misconceptions about Educational Psychology that will alert you to typical misunderstandings in educational psychology classes.
- Video Examples of various concepts and principles presented in the chapter.
- A Practice for Your Licensure Exam exercise that resembles the kinds of questions appearing on many teacher licensure tests.

CHAPTER OUTLINE

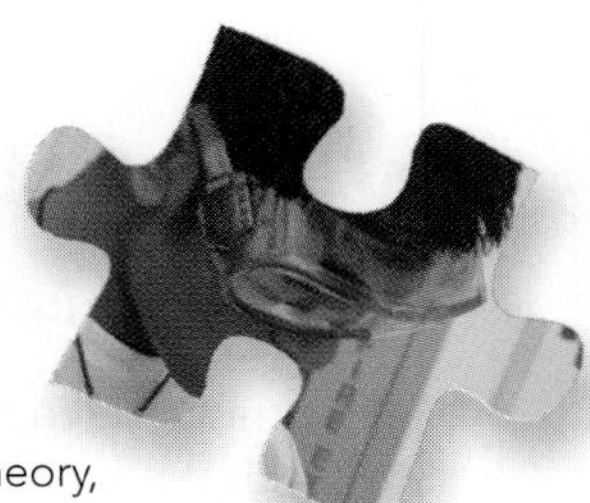

CHAPTER OBJECTIVES

- **Objective 10.1:** Describe five basic assumptions underlying social cognitive theory, and apply these assumptions to classroom practice.
- **Objective 10.2:** Explain how cognitive processes and vicarious experiences influence the effects that reinforcement and punishment have on learners' behavior.
- **Objective 10.3:** Describe the potential effects of modeling on students' behaviors, and explain how you can use modeling effectively in your classroom.
- **Objective 10.4:** Describe the nature and origins of self-efficacy, and explain how you might promote high self-efficacy both in your students as learners and in yourself as a teacher.
- **Objective 10.5:** Identify important components of self-regulated behavior and self-regulated learning, and apply your knowledge of self-regulation to help diverse learners effectively control their behavior, master academic subject matter, and address interpersonal problems.
- **Objective 10.6:** Explain and illustrate how environment, behavior, and personal variables mutually influence one another through reciprocal causation.
- **Objective 10.7:** Compare and contrast perspectives of learning associated with cognitive psychology, behaviorism, and social cognitive theory.

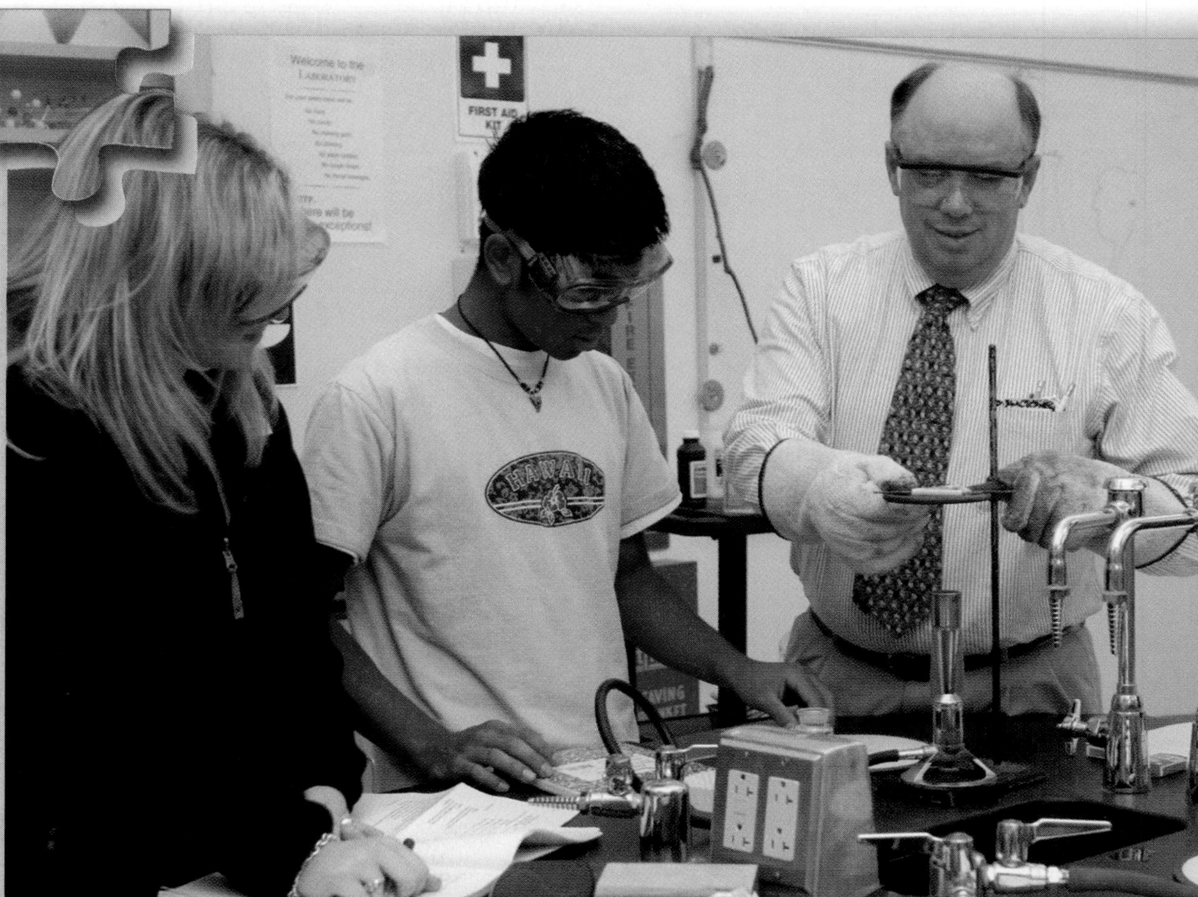

Chapter 10

Social Cognitive Views of Learning

CASE STUDY: Parlez-Vous Français?

Nathan has enrolled in French I only because his mother insists that he take it. On the first day of French class, Nathan notices that most of his classmates are girls; the few boys are students he doesn't know very well. He sits sullenly in the back row, recalling that three male friends who took French last year got mostly Ds and Fs on quizzes and homework and that two of them dropped the class after one semester. "I do great in math and science," he thinks to himself, "but I'm just no good at learning languages. Besides, learning French is a *girl* thing."

Although Nathan comes to class every day, his mind often wanders as his teacher demonstrates correct pronunciations and explains simple syntactical structures. He makes feeble attempts at homework assignments but quickly puts them aside whenever he encounters something he doesn't immediately understand.

Sure enough, Nathan is right: He can't do French. He gets a D− on the first exam.

- **What has Nathan learned about French by observing other people?**

NATHAN HAS APPARENTLY NOT BENEFITED very much from his teacher's demonstrations and explanations. But he has learned something from observing his *peers:* Knowing what happened to three male friends and seeing mostly girls in his class, he concludes that he is doomed to failure, in part because French is a "girl thing."

We human beings learn a wide variety of behaviors by observing the people in our lives and in the media. We also learn which behaviors are likely to get us ahead—and which are not—by seeing their consequences for others. In part by watching what others do, we develop a sense of what our own capabilities are likely to be, and we begin to direct our behavior toward goals we think we can achieve.

In this chapter, we will explore **social cognitive theory**, a perspective that can help us understand what and how people learn by observing others and how, in the process, they begin to take control of their own behavior. Originally called *social learning theory*, social cognitive theory has its early roots in behaviorism and thus addresses the effects of reinforcement and punishment to some extent. Over the past few decades, however, it has increasingly incorporated cognitive processes into its explanations of learning—hence its current name, social *cognitive* theory—and it now includes a blend of ideas from behaviorism and cognitive psychology.

social cognitive theory Theoretical perspective that focuses on how people learn by observing others and how they eventually assume control over their own behavior.

model Person who demonstrates a behavior for someone else.

self-efficacy Belief that one is capable of executing certain behaviors or achieving certain goals.

Social cognitive theory has developed in large part through the research efforts of Albert Bandura at Stanford University. You will find references to Bandura and others who have built on his ideas (e.g., Dale Schunk, Barry Zimmerman) throughout the chapter.

Basic Assumptions of Social Cognitive Theory

In the opening case study, we see evidence of the first of several assumptions underlying social cognitive theory:

- *People can learn by observing others.* From the perspective of instrumental conditioning (Chapter 9), learning is often a process of trial and error: People try many different responses, increasing those that bring desirable consequences and leaving unproductive ones behind. Social cognitive theorists argue that learners don't necessarily have to experiment in such a trial-and-error manner. Instead, they can acquire many new responses simply by observing the behaviors of other individuals, or **models**. For example, a student might learn how to solve a long division problem, spell the word *synonym* correctly, or mouth off at a teacher simply by watching someone else do these things first.

- *Learning is an internal process that may or may not lead to a behavior change.* Some of the things that people learn appear in their behavior immediately, other things affect their behavior at a later time, and still others never influence their behavior at all. For example, you might attempt to swing a tennis racket as soon as you learn the correct form. But you probably won't demonstrate that you've learned how to apologize tactfully until a later time when an apology is necessary. And you might *never* walk through campus nude, no matter how many times you see someone else do it. Rather than define learning as a change in behavior (as many behaviorists do), social cognitive theorists (like cognitive psychologists) view learning as an internal mental process that may or may not be reflected in the learner's behavior.

- *Cognitive processes influence motivation as well as learning.* Like cognitive psychologists, social cognitive theorists recognize the importance of particular cognitive processes—attention, encoding, and so on—for learning and remembering new information. But social cognitive theorists point out that cognition is an important ingredient in *motivation* as well. From the perspective of social cognitive theory, people set mental *goals* toward which they direct their behavior, and their goals are based to some degree on their *expectations* about what they might reasonably be able to accomplish. People's expectations about their ability to execute certain behaviors or reach certain goals—that is, their **self-efficacy**—play a key role in how hard they try, how long they persist at challenging tasks, and ultimately how much they learn and achieve.

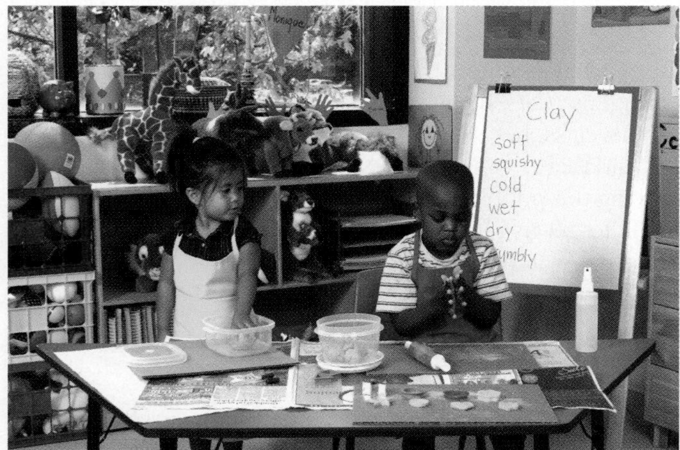

Children learn many new behaviors simply by watching adults or peers perform them successfully.

- *People and their environments mutually influence each other.* Some learning theorists, especially behaviorists, focus primarily on how the environment can affect learners. But the reverse is true as well: Learners affect their environments, often quite consciously and intentionally. To some degree, learners influence their environments through their *behaviors.* For instance, the responses students make (e.g., the academic classes they choose, the extracurricular activities they pursue, the company they keep) determine the learning opportunities they will have and the consequences they will experience. Internal cognitive processes, personality characteristics, and other things that in some way reside inside learners come into play as well (social cognitive theorists refer to these things as *person* variables). For instance, students are apt to focus their attention on (and thus learn from) only certain aspects of their environment, and their idiosyncratic interpretations of why they have been reinforced or punished will influence the specific effects that such consequences have.

Ultimately, all three of these variables—environment, behavior, and person—influence one another in the manner shown in Figure 10.1. Social cognitive theorists use the term **reciprocal causation** when referring to this constant interplay among environment, behavior, and person variables (Bandura, 1989, 2006; Schunk & Pajares, 2004; Zimmerman & Schunk, 2003).

- *Behavior becomes increasingly self-regulated.* In the first few years of life, children's actions are controlled and guided to a considerable degree by others: parents, older siblings, child care providers, teachers, and so on. But as children grow older, most of them increasingly take charge of their lives, not only making decisions about the goals toward which they will strive but also directing and monitoring their behaviors and thought processes to accomplish their goals. In other words, most children increasingly engage in **self-regulation**.

Table 10.1 summarizes the assumptions just listed and offers examples of their implications for classroom practice.

reciprocal causation Interdependence of environmental, behavioral, and personal variables in influencing learning and development.

self-regulation Process of setting goals for oneself and engaging in behaviors and cognitive processes that lead to goal attainment.

FIGURE 10.1 In social cognitive theory, environmental, behavioral, and personal variables mutually influence one another.

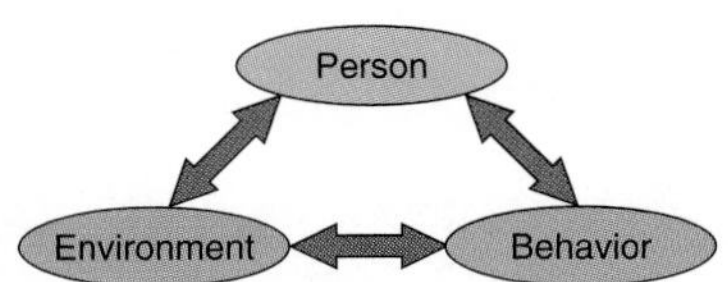

Principles/Assumptions

TABLE 10.1
Basic Assumptions of Social Cognitive Theory and Their Educational Implications

Assumption	Educational Implication	Example
Learning by observation	Help students acquire new behaviors more quickly by demonstrating those behaviors yourself.	Demonstrate appropriate ways to deal with and resolve interpersonal conflicts. Then ask students to role-play conflict resolution in small groups, and compliment those who use prosocial strategies.
Learning as an internal process that may or may not be reflected in behavior	Remember that new learning doesn't always reveal itself immediately but may instead be reflected in students' behaviors at a later time.	When one student engages in disruptive classroom behavior, take appropriate steps to discourage it. Otherwise, classmates who have witnessed the misbehavior may be similarly disruptive in the future.
Cognitive processes in motivation	Encourage students to set productive goals for themselves, especially goals that are challenging yet achievable.	When teaching American Sign Language to help students communicate with a classmate who is deaf, ask them to predict how many new words and phrases they can learn each week.
Reciprocal influences among environmental, behavioral, and personal variables	Encourage students to make choices that will lead to beneficial learning experiences.	Describe the benefits of taking an advanced writing course, not only as a means of enhancing writing skills but also as a way of discovering whether one might enjoy a career in writing.
Increasing self-regulation with age	Teach students strategies through which they can better control their own behavior and direct their own learning.	Give students concrete suggestions about how they can remind themselves to bring needed supplies to school each day.

The Social Cognitive View of Reinforcement and Punishment

As we discovered in Chapter 9, behaviorists propose that the consequences of people's voluntary behaviors—in particular, whether those behaviors are followed by reinforcement or punishment—are directly responsible for behavior change and learning. Reinforcement and punishment are less critical in social cognitive theory, but they do have several indirect effects on learning and behavior (e.g., Bandura, 1977, 1986; T. L. Rosenthal & Zimmerman, 1978). Cognitive factors come into play in these indirect effects, as reflected in the following ideas:

Be explicit about which behaviors have led to which consequences.

• *Consequences have an effect on behavior only if learners are aware of the contingency.* From a social cognitive perspective, reinforcement increases the frequency of a behavior only if learners think or know that the behavior is being reinforced (Bandura, 1986). Likewise, punishment decreases a behavior only if learners realize that it is the direct result of something *they* have done. As teachers, then, we should be very clear about what we are reinforcing and punishing, so that students know the real response-reinforcement contingencies operating in the classroom. For instance, if Sam gets an A on an essay but we don't let him know *why* he's earned that grade, he won't necessarily know how to get an A the next time. To improve Sam's performance, we might tell him that the essay earned an A because he supported his opinion with a logical train of thought. Similarly, if we say "Good game!" to Sandra after a basketball game even though she scored only one basket, she may understandably be a bit confused. We might tell her instead that we were pleased with her high energy level and cooperation with other team members throughout the game.

Be explicit about future response-reinforcement and response-punishment contingencies as well.

• *Learners form expectations about the likely consequences of future actions and behave accordingly.* Learners often base their expectations on existing patterns of reinforcement, nonreinforcement, and punishment. For example, perhaps you have taken a course in which all the exam questions came from material presented in the textbook, without a single question coming from class lectures. After the first exam, did you find yourself reading the textbook carefully but skipping class frequently? Or perhaps you have taken a course in which the exams were based almost entirely on class lectures and activities. In that situation, did you go to class regularly but rarely open your textbook? When a particular response is reinforced every time it is made, learners typically expect to be reinforced for behaving the same way in the future. In a similar manner, when a response frequently leads to punishment—as insulting an instructor or skipping class on a test day might—learners will probably expect that response to be punished on later occasions as well.

Sometimes, however, learners form their expectations about what things will be reinforced and punished on the basis of very little hard data. For example, a high school student might believe, perhaps erroneously, that bragging about his high test scores will gain him the admiration of his classmates (i.e., a reinforcer). Another student might believe that her classmates will ridicule and reject (i.e., punish) her for being smart, even though they wouldn't actually do so.

Regardless of whether expectations about future contingencies are accurate, they influence learners' choices about how to behave and *not* behave. To see what I mean, try the next exercise.

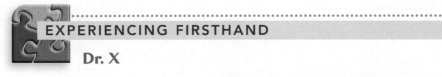

EXPERIENCING FIRSTHAND

Dr. X

How many of the following questions can you answer about your educational psychology instructor? I'm going to call your instructor "Dr. X."

1. Is Dr. X right handed or left handed?
2. Is Dr. X a flashy dresser or a more conservative dresser?
3. What kind of shoes does Dr. X wear to class?
4. Does Dr. X wear a wedding ring?
5. Does Dr. X bring a briefcase to class each day?

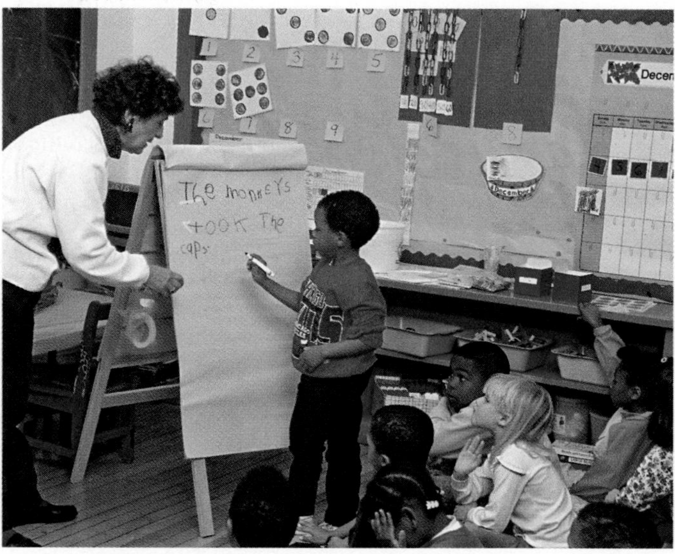

Students make decisions about how to behave based, in part, on the responses for which their peers are reinforced or punished.

If you've been attending class regularly, you probably know the answers to at least two of these questions; perhaps you can answer all five. But I'm guessing that you've never mentioned what you've learned to anyone else because you've had no reason to believe that demonstrating your knowledge about these matters would be reinforced.

When learners *do* expect reinforcement for such knowledge, it suddenly surfaces. For example, every time I teach educational psychology, I take a minute sometime during the semester to hide my feet behind the podium and ask my students to tell me what my shoes look like. Students first look at me as if I have two heads, but after a few seconds of awkward silence, at least a half dozen of them (usually those who regularly sit in the first two rows) begin to describe my shoes, right down to the rippled soles, scuffed leather, and beige stitching.

Students learn many things in the classroom. They learn facts and figures, they learn ways of getting their teacher's attention, and they may even learn which classmate stores Twinkies in his desk or what kind of shoes the teacher wears to school. Of all the things they learn, students are most likely to demonstrate the things they think will bring them reinforcement.

When learners choose to behave in a way that might bring future reinforcement, they are working for an **incentive**, which is never guaranteed. For instance, students never know that they are going to get an A on a test when they study for it or that they will win a position on the Student Council simply because they run for office. An incentive is an expected or hoped-for consequence, one that may or may not actually occur.

- *Learners' expectations are influenced by what happens to other people as well as to themselves.* When I was in the third grade, I entered a Halloween costume contest dressed as Happy Tooth, a character in several toothpaste commercials at the time. I didn't win the contest; a "witch" won first prize. So the following year I entered the same contest dressed as a witch, figuring I was a shoo-in for first place. In this situation, I experienced reinforcement not directly but rather *vicariously*—that is, through watching what happened to someone else.

Learners who observe someone else being reinforced for a particular behavior are likely to exhibit that behavior more frequently themselves—a phenomenon known as **vicarious reinforcement**. For instance, by watching the consequences their classmates experience, students might learn that studying hard leads to good grades, that being elected to class office brings status and popularity, or that neatness counts.

Conversely, when learners see someone else get punished for a certain behavior, they are less likely to behave that way themselves—a phenomenon known as **vicarious punishment**. For example, when a coach benches a football player for unsportsmanlike conduct, other players are unlikely to mimic such behavior. Unfortunately, vicarious punishment can suppress desirable behaviors as well as undesirable

incentive Hoped-for but not guaranteed future consequence of behavior.

vicarious reinforcement Phenomenon in which a response increases in frequency when another person is observed being reinforced for that response.

vicarious punishment Phenomenon in which a response decreases in frequency when another person is observed being punished for that response.

ones. For example, when a teacher belittles a student's question by calling it "silly," other students may be reluctant to ask questions of their own.[1]

As teachers, we must be extremely careful that we don't vicariously reinforce undesirable behaviors or vicariously punish desirable ones. If we give too much attention to a misbehaving student, others who want our attention may misbehave as well. Or if we ridicule a student who volunteers an incorrect answer or erroneous belief, classmates will hardly be eager to voice their own ideas.

• *Expectations about future consequences affect how thoroughly and in what ways learners cognitively process new information.* To get a sense of how this might happen, try the following exercise.

EXPERIENCING FIRSTHAND

Planning Ahead

Quickly skim the contents of the upcoming section on modeling to get a general idea of the topics it includes. Once you have done so, imagine yourself in each of these situations:

1. Your instructor announces, "The section on modeling won't be on your test, but please read it anyway." How thoroughly and carefully will you read that section? Jot down a brief answer to this question.
2. The next day your instructor announces, "I misled you yesterday. In reality, half of next week's test will be on modeling." *Now* how thoroughly and carefully will you read that section of the chapter? Once again, jot down a brief answer.

If you don't expect to be reinforced for knowing about modeling, you may very well *not* read the chapter's discussion of it. (Perhaps you'll read it later, you tell yourself, but you have many other things to do right now.) If, instead, you discover that getting an A in your educational psychology class depends on knowing the material about modeling really well, you are apt to read the material slowly and attentively, possibly trying to learn and remember every detail.

When learners believe they will be reinforced for learning something, they are more likely to pay attention to it and mentally process it in an effective manner. When they don't expect to be reinforced for learning something, they are far less likely to think about or process it in any significant way. As an example of the latter situation, let's return to the opening case study. Nathan is convinced that he can't learn French, thanks, in part, to his friends' low French grades (which served as vicarious punishment for him). As a result, Nathan pays little attention to what his teacher says in class, and he makes only a halfhearted effort to complete his homework assignments. His low expectations almost guarantee his poor performance—a self-fulfilling prophecy.

• *The nonoccurrence of an expected consequence—whether for oneself or for someone else—can have a reinforcing or punishing effect in and of itself.* What happens when learners' expectations aren't met—for instance, when an expected reinforcement never comes? When, as a fourth grader, I entered the Halloween costume contest as a "witch," I lost once again—this time to a girl wearing a metal colander on her head and claiming to be *Sputnik*, the first satellite launched into space

[1]The effects of vicarious reinforcement and vicarious punishment are sometimes referred to as the *response facilitation effect* and *response inhibition effect*, respectively.

by what was then the Soviet Union. That was the last time I entered a Halloween contest. I had expected reinforcement and felt cheated because I didn't get it. Social cognitive theorists propose that the nonoccurrence of expected reinforcement is a form of punishment (e.g., Bandura, 1986). When people think that a certain response is going to be reinforced but it *isn't* reinforced, they are less likely to exhibit the response in the future.

Just as the nonoccurrence of expected reinforcement is a form of punishment, the nonoccurrence of expected punishment is a form of reinforcement (Bandura, 1986). Perhaps you can think of a time when you broke a rule, expecting to be punished, but you got away with your crime. Or perhaps you can remember seeing someone else break a rule without being caught. When nothing bad happens after a forbidden behavior, people may actually feel as if the behavior has been reinforced.

Thus, when students work hard to achieve a desired result—perhaps a compliment, a high grade, or a special privilege—and the anticipated result doesn't materialize, they will be unlikely to work as hard the next time around. And when students break school rules but aren't punished for doing so, they are likely to break the rules again—and so are the other students who are aware that the behavior has gone unpunished.[2] It's important that we, as teachers, follow through with promised reinforcements for desirable student behaviors. It's equally important that we impose any reasonable consequences students have come to expect for inappropriate behaviors. (See Chapter 9 for guidelines and cautions on the use of punishment.)

Follow through with the consequences students have been led to expect for certain behaviors.

Modeling

As human beings, we have some ability to imitate others almost from the moment of birth (T. F. Field, Woodson, Greenberg, & Cohen, 1982; Kugiumutzakis, 1988; Meltzoff, 2005). In fact, the brain seems to be specially equipped for imitation. In recent years, researchers have found that certain neurons in the brain become active either (a) when learners observe others engaging in a particular behavior or (b) when learners engage in that same behavior. Such neurons, appropriately known as *mirror neurons*, suggest that the brain is prewired for making connections between observing and doing (Arbib, 2005; Iacoboni & Woods, 1999; Murata et al., 1997).

Many of the models from whom we learn are **live models**: real people whom we observe doing something. But we are also influenced by **symbolic models**: real or fictional characters portrayed in books, in films, on television, and through various other media. For instance, students can learn valuable lessons from studying the behaviors of important figures in history or reading stories about people who have accomplished great things in the face of adversity. Social cognitive theorists sometimes use the term **modeling** to describe what a model does (i.e., demonstrate a behavior) and at other times to describe what the observer does (i.e., imitate the behavior). To minimize confusion, I will often use the verb *imitate*, rather than *model*, when referring to what the observer does.

Behaviors and Skills That Can Be Learned Through Modeling

People do, of course, learn a wide variety of psychomotor behaviors—from relatively simple actions (e.g., brushing teeth) to far more complex ones (e.g., performing dance

live model Currently living individual whose behavior is observed in person.

symbolic model Real or fictional character portrayed in the media that influences an observer's behavior.

modeling Demonstrating a behavior for another person *or* observing and imitating another person's behavior.

[2] The tendency for learners to engage in forbidden behavior when they see others incur no adverse consequences for it is known as the *response disinhibition effect*. In this situation, the learners have presumably already mastered the behavior, but the expectation of punishment has previously inhibited it. With this expectation removed, the behavior is disinhibited and may increase in frequency.

In the Bleachers
by Steve Moore

Not all the people in children's lives model desirable behaviors. A child is most apt to imitate undesirable behaviors that appear to have no adverse consequences and that seem to lead to reinforcement.

Source: IN THE BLEACHERS © 2001 Steve Moore. Reprinted with permission of UNIVERSAL PRESS SYNDICATE. All rights reserved.

routines or gymnastics skills)—by observing what others do (Magill, 1993; Poche, McCubbrey, & Munn, 1982; Vintere, Hemmes, Brown, & Poulson, 2004). But observations of others also enable people to acquire many behaviors with cognitive or emotional components. For example, learners are apt to do the following:

- Become better readers when their parents read frequently at home (Hess & McDevitt, 1989)
- Learn to fear particular stimuli or situations if others show fear in those circumstances (Mineka & Zinbarg, 2006)
- Better resist the enticements of a stranger when a peer has modeled effective resistance strategies (Poche, Yoder, & Miltenberger, 1988)
- Be less likely to tolerate racist statements if people around them refuse to tolerate such statements (Blanchard, Lilly, & Vaughn, 1991)

Considerable research has been conducted concerning the impact of models in three areas: academic skills, aggression, and interpersonal behaviors.

Academic Skills Students learn many academic skills, at least in part, by observing what others do. For instance, they may learn how to solve long division problems or write a cohesive composition partly by observing how their teachers and peers do these things (Braaksma, Rijlaarsdam, & van den Bergh, 2002; R. J. Sawyer, Graham, & Harris, 1992; Schunk & Hanson, 1985). Modeling of academic skills can be especially effective when the model demonstrates not only how to *do* a task but also how to *think about* the task—in other words, when the model engages in **cognitive modeling** (R. J. Sawyer et al., 1992; Schunk, 1981, 1998; Schunk & Swartz, 1993). As an example, consider how a teacher might model the thinking processes involved in the long division problem in the margin:

$4\overline{)276}$

> First I have to decide what number to divide 4 into. I take 276, start on the left and move toward the right until I have a number the same as or larger than 4. Is 2 larger than 4? No. Is 27 larger than 4? Yes. So my first division will be 4 into 27. Now I need to multiply 4 by a number that will give an answer the same as or slightly smaller than 27. How about 5? 5 × 4 = 20. No, too small. Let's try 6. 6 × 4 = 24. Maybe. Let's try 7. 7 × 4 = 28. No, too large. So 6 is correct. (Schunk, 1998, p. 146)

Aggression Numerous research studies have indicated that children become more aggressive when they observe aggressive or violent models (Bandura, 1965; N. E. Goldstein, Arnold, Rosenberg, Stowe, & Ortiz, 2001; Guerra, Huesmann, & Spindler, 2003). Children learn aggression not only from live models but also from the symbolic models they see in films, on television, and in video games (C. A. Anderson et al., 2003; Carnagey, Anderson, & Bartholow, 2007). In fact, children's aggressive behaviors tend to take the same *forms* as the aggression they see (Bandura, Ross, & Ross, 1963; Mischel & Grusec, 1966). Boys in particular are apt to copy other people's aggressive actions (Bandura et al., 1963; Bushman & Anderson, 2001; Lowry, Sleet, Duncan, Powell, & Kolbe,1995).

A classic study by Bandura, Ross, and Ross (1961) dramatically illustrates the power of modeling for both encouraging and discouraging aggressive behavior. Preschoolers were taken, one at a time, to a playroom that contained a wide variety of toys. They were seated at a table where they could draw pictures. Some of the children then observed an adult (an aggressive model) enter the room and engage in numerous aggressive behaviors toward an inflatable punching doll—for instance, kicking the doll

cognitive modeling Demonstrating how to think about as well as how to do a task.

in the air, straddling it and hitting it on the head with a wooden mallet, and making statements like "Pow!" "Kick him," and "Punch him in the nose." Other children instead observed an adult (a nonaggressive model) come in and play in a constructive way with building blocks. Still other children saw no model while in the playroom. The children were then led to another room where they were mildly frustrated: Just as they began to play with some very attractive and entertaining toys, the toys were taken away. Finally, the children were taken to a third room that contained both nonaggressive and aggressive toys (including the inflatable punching doll and wooden mallet). Those children who had seen the aggressive model were the most aggressive of the three groups; in fact, they mimicked many of the same behaviors they had seen the aggressive model display. Those children who had seen a nonaggressive model were even less aggressive than the no-model group. With regard to aggression, then, models can have an impact either way: Aggressive models lead to increased aggression in children, and nonaggressive models lead to decreased aggression.

Interpersonal Behaviors By observing and imitating others, learners acquire many interpersonal skills. For example, in small groups with classmates, children may adopt one another's strategies for conducting discussions about literature, perhaps learning how to solicit one another's opinions ("What do you think, Jalisha?"), express agreement or disagreement ("I agree with Kordell because . . ."), and justify a point of view ("I think it shouldn't be allowed, because . . .") (R. C. Anderson et al., 2001, pp. 14, 16, 25). And children with mild or moderate forms of autism are apt to play more effectively with age-mates after watching a videotape of a nondisabled peer using good social skills in play activities (Nikopoulos & Keenan, 2004).

As noted in Chapter 3, children can also learn prosocial behaviors—showing compassion, sharing possessions with others, and, in general, putting others' needs and well-being before their own—when they see models who exhibit prosocial behavior. In one study (Rushton, 1980), children observed an adult playing a bowling game and reinforcing himself with tokens for high performance. Some children then saw the adult donate half of his earned tokens to a poor boy named Bobby, pictured on a poster in the room; other children observed the adult keeping all of his winnings for himself despite knowing about Bobby. After that, the children had the opportunity to play the game and reward themselves with tokens. The more tokens they earned, the better the prize they could purchase. They could make a donation to Bobby, but doing so meant that they would be able to purchase a lesser prize for themselves. Children who had watched generous models were more likely to donate some of their own tokens to Bobby than were children who had watched selfish models. This difference was true not only in the initial experimental session but also in a follow-up session two months later.

Characteristics of Effective Models

Of course learners don't always imitate the behaviors of people they see around them and in the media. Influential models typically have several characteristics (Bandura, 1986; T. L. Rosenthal & Bandura, 1978; Schunk, 1987). First, they are *competent* at the behavior or skill in question. Learners usually want to behave like people who do something well rather than poorly. For instance, children may try to imitate the basketball skills of a professional basketball player, and adolescents may make note of especially effective techniques they observe in art or literature (see Figure 10.2). Even preschoolers have some ability to discriminate between competent and incompetent models (Want & Harris, 2001).

Second, influential models typically have *prestige and power*. Some effective models—a world leader, a renowned athlete, a popular rock star—are famous at a national or international level. The prestige and power of other models—a head cheerleader, the captain of the high school hockey team, a gang leader—may be more localized. As an example of such local influence, children are more likely to interact with

FIGURE 10.2 Students in Barbara Dee's seventh-grade language arts class chose these examples of effective figurative writing from books they were reading. Such examples can serve as models for students' own writing efforts.

"The blackness of the night came in, like snakes around the ankles."
—Caroline Cooney, *Wanted*, p. 176

"Flirtatious waves made passes at the primly pebbled beach."
—Lilian Jackson Braun, *The Cat Who Saw Stars*, p. 120

"Water boiled up white and frothy, like a milkshake."
—Lurlene McDaniel, *For Better, for Worse, Forever*, p. 60

"Solid rocket boosters suddenly belched forty-four million horsepower."
—Ben Mikaelsen, *Countdown*, p. 148

"I try to swallow the snowball in my throat."
—Laurie Halse Anderson, *Speak*, p. 72

students who have disabilities when they see popular classmates initiating such interactions (Sasso & Rude, 1987).

Third, and perhaps most importantly, influential models exhibit *behaviors relevant to learners' own circumstances*. Learners are most likely to adopt behaviors they believe will be useful for themselves as well as for the model. For example, a middle school student is more likely to mimic the attire of popular classmates if she thinks she can become popular by wearing such attire. She has less reason to dress this way if she thinks her thick glasses and adolescent acne will prevent her from being popular regardless of what she wears. And remember Nathan's belief that French is a "girl thing"? Learners must believe that a particular behavior is appropriate for their gender, with different individuals having varying views about which activities are "gender appropriate" (Grace, David, & Ryan, 2008; Leaper & Friedman, 2007).

IN THE BLEACHERS
by Steve Moore

"Don't cry, Megan. Remember, it's not whether Daddy wins the brawl in the stands that's important. It's how you played the game."

When we work with children, our actions often speak louder than our words.

As classroom teachers, we are likely to be perceived by most students as competent, prestigious, and powerful; that is, we are likely to be influential models for them. Thus, we teach not only by what we say but also by what we do. It is critical, then, that we model appropriate behaviors and *don't* model inappropriate ones. Do we model fairness to all students or favoritism to a few? Do we model enthusiasm and excitement about the subject matter or merely tolerance for a dreary topic the class must muddle through as best it can? Do we expound on the virtues of innovation and creativity yet use the same curriculum materials year after year? Our actions often speak louder than our words (e.g., J. H. Bryan, 1975).

Yet our students won't always perceive our behaviors as being relevant to their own circumstances. For instance, students from cultures and socioeconomic groups very different from our own may think that certain topics or skills have little value in their own lives and communities. Students of both genders may view certain content domains and careers as being only for males or "girl things." And students with disabilities may believe that they are incapable of accomplishing the things a nondisabled teacher demonstrates. Ideally, students need to see models who are similar to them in obvious ways—for instance, in race, cultural background, socioeconomic status, gender, and (if applicable) disability—being successful in a variety of activities and domains (C. L. Martin & Ruble, 2004; Pang, 1995; L. E. Powers, Sowers, & Stevens, 1995).

Expose students to successful male and female models from diverse cultural and socioeconomic backgrounds. Also expose them to models who have achieved success despite disabilities.

Essential Conditions for Successful Modeling

Even when models are competent and prestigious and even when they exhibit behaviors that students see as appropriate for themselves, successful learning from models doesn't always occur. According to social cognitive theorists (e.g., Bandura, 1986), four conditions are necessary before a student can successfully learn from observing modeled behavior: attention, retention, motor reproduction, and motivation.

FIGURE 10.3 Often students can more easily remember a complex behavior, such as the arm movements for the elementary backstroke, when those behaviors have verbal labels.

Attention In the opening case study, Nathan paid little attention to his French teacher. To learn effectively, *the learner must pay attention to the model* and, in particular, to critical aspects of the modeled behavior. For instance, students must observe carefully as we show proper procedures in the science lab or demonstrate the elementary backstroke, and they must listen attentively as we pronounce *Comment allez-vous?*

Retention After paying attention, *the learner must remember what the model does.* If you have already read the discussion of cognitive processes in Chapter 6, you know that students are more likely to recall information they have encoded in memory in more than one way—perhaps as both a visual image and a verbal representation. As teachers, then, we may often want to describe what we're doing as we demonstrate behaviors. We may also want to give descriptive labels to complex behaviors that might otherwise be difficult to remember (Vintere et al., 2004; Ziegler, 1987). To illustrate, in teaching swimming, an easy way to help students remember the sequence of arm positions in the elementary backstroke is to teach them the labels *chicken, airplane,* and *soldier* (see Figure 10.3).

Motor Reproduction In addition to attending and remembering, *the learner must be physically capable of reproducing the modeled behavior.* When a student lacks the ability to reproduce an observed behavior, motor reproduction obviously cannot occur. For instance, first graders who watch a high school student throw a softball don't have the muscular coordination to mimic the throw. And high school students who haven't yet learned to roll their *r*'s will have trouble repeating the Spanish teacher's tongue twister: "*Erre con erre cigarro, erre con erre barril. Rápido corren los carros del ferrocarril.*"

It's often useful to have students imitate a desired behavior immediately after they see it modeled and to give them guidance and feedback that can help them improve their performance. This approach—sometimes known as *coaching*—is often more effective than modeling alone (S. N. Elliott & Busse, 1991; Kitsantas et al., 2000; Schunk & Swartz, 1993). When considering this approach, however, we must keep in mind a point made in Chapter 4: Students from some ethnic groups (e.g., many Native Americans) may prefer to practice new behaviors in private at first and show us what they have learned only after they have achieved sufficient mastery.

Motivation Finally, *the learner must be motivated to demonstrate the modeled behavior.* Some students may be eager to show what they have observed and remembered; for example, they may have seen the model reinforced for a certain behavior and thus have already been vicariously reinforced. But other students may not have any motivation to demonstrate something they have seen a model do, perhaps because they don't see the model's actions as being appropriate for them.

When all four factors—attention, retention, motor reproduction, and motivation—are present, modeling can be an extremely effective teaching technique. The Into the Classroom feature "Promoting Learning Through Modeling" offers several strategies that can maximize its effectiveness.

Not only does modeling teach learners new behaviors and skills, but it can also boost their self-confidence that they can accomplish challenging tasks. When a student from a low-income neighborhood meets someone from the same neighborhood who has become a successful physician and when a student with a physical disability meets an individual with cerebral palsy who is a top executive at the local bank, these students may begin to believe that they, too, are capable of such achievements. Students who believe in their own ability to succeed have high *self-efficacy*.

INTO THE Classroom

Promoting Learning Through Modeling

- **Make sure you have students' attention when modeling a desired behavior.**

  A middle school science teacher wants to show his class how to prepare a slide of swamp water for inspection under a microscope. He meets with students in groups of three or four so that everyone can closely observe what he does.

- **Describe what you are doing as you model a desired behavior.**

  As a fourth-grade teacher shows students how to use word processing software to edit their compositions, she explains every step she takes to insert new text, cut unwanted text, use the thesaurus and spell-check functions, and so on. She also distributes a handout that describes, step by step, how to perform each of these procedures, and she shows where to find important commands and functions on the computer screen.

- **When teaching a complex behavior or sequence of behaviors, provide descriptive labels that students can repeat to themselves to help them remember what they need to do.**

  To help students remember the new dance steps she demonstrates, a dance teacher instructs them to say such things as "One, two, gallop, gallop" and "One leg, other leg, turn, and turn" while performing the steps.

- **Have students perform a desired behavior immediately after you model it; give them guidance and feedback to help them improve their performance.**

  After an elementary art teacher shows students how to work effectively with watercolor paints, she walks around the classroom, giving pointers on how to blend colors for desired shades and how to keep differently colored areas from bleeding into one another.

- **Show students how the skills you model can help them in their own lives.**

  After demonstrating how to use rounding to estimate sums, a middle school math teacher presents examples of how students might quickly estimate the total cost of several purchases at a local discount store.

- **Invite respected professionals to the classroom to demonstrate skills in their areas of expertise.**

  A high school journalism teacher invites a local newspaper reporter to show students how he determines the order in which he presents information in a newspaper article.

- **Have students read about or observe positive role models in such media as books and films.**

  In a unit on civic responsibility and community service, a high school social studies teacher has students read excerpts from Barack Obama's *Dreams from My Father*.

- **Introduce students to models who have successfully crossed traditional gender boundaries in certain professions.**

  When exploring various professions over the course of the school year, a second-grade teacher invites several adults in the community—including a female police officer and a male nurse—to come to class and describe what they do in their jobs.

- **Include competent children in the role models you present.**

  Once a week, a kindergarten teacher invites a third- or fourth-grade student to come and read storybooks to his class. The older children delight in their ability to show off their reading skills and work especially hard to make the stories lively and entertaining.

Sources: R. L. Cohen, 1989; S. N. Elliott & Busse, 1991; Féry & Morizot, 2000; Gerst, 1971; Kitsantas et al., 2000; Mace, Belfiore, & Shea, 1989; Obama, 2004; T. L. Rosenthal, Alford, & Rasp, 1972; Schunk, 1989c; Schunk & Hanson, 1985; Schunk & Swartz, 1993; Shute, 2008; Vintere et al., 2004, p. 309 (dance example); Ziegler, 1987.

Self-Efficacy

In general, *self-efficacy* is a person's self-constructed judgment about his or her ability to execute certain behaviors or reach certain goals. To get a sense of your own self-efficacy for various activities, try the following exercise.

EXPERIENCING FIRSTHAND

Self-Appraisal

Take a moment to answer the following questions:

1. Do you believe you'll be able to understand and apply educational psychology by reading this textbook and thinking carefully about its content? Or do you believe you're going to have trouble with the material regardless of how much you study?
2. Do you think you could learn to execute a reasonable swan dive from a high diving board if you were shown how to do it and given time to practice? Or do you think you're such a klutz that no amount of training and practice would help?
3. Do you think you could walk barefoot over hot coals unscathed? Or do you think the soles of your feet would be burned to a crisp?

People are more likely to engage in certain behaviors when they believe they will be able to execute the behaviors successfully—that is, when they have high self-efficacy (e.g., Bandura, 1997). For example, I hope you have high self-efficacy for learning educational psychology, believing that, with careful thought about what you read, you will be able to understand and apply the ideas in this textbook. You may or may not believe that with instruction and practice, you would eventually be able to perform a passable swan dive. You are probably quite skeptical that you could ever walk barefoot over hot coals, so my guess is that you have low self-efficacy regarding this activity.

As noted in Chapter 3, self-efficacy is a component of one's overall sense of self. It may seem similar to such concepts as *self-concept* and *self-esteem*, but it's different from these other two concepts in important ways (Bong & Skaalvik, 2003; Pietsch, Walker, & Chapman, 2003; Schunk & Pajares, 2005). When psychologists talk about self-concept and self-esteem, they are typically describing a fairly general self-view that pervades a broad range of activities (e.g., "Am I a good student?") and may encompass feelings as well as beliefs (e.g., "How proud am I of my classroom performance?"). In contrast, self-efficacy is more task or situation specific and involves judgments (rather than feelings) almost exclusively (e.g., "Can I master long division?").

How Self-Efficacy Affects Behavior and Cognition

Students' sense of self-efficacy affects their choice of activities, their goals, and their effort and persistence in classroom activities. Ultimately, then, it also affects their learning and achievement (Bandura, 1982, 2000; Schunk & Pajares, 2005).

Choice of Activities Imagine yourself on registration day, perusing the hundreds of courses in the semester schedule. You fill most of your schedule with required courses, but you have room for an elective. Only two courses are offered at the time slot you want to fill. Do you sign up for Advanced Psychoceramics, a challenging seminar taught by the world-renowned Dr. Josiah S. Carberry? Or do you sign up for an

A student must have high self-efficacy about her ability to make friends before she will actually try to make them (e.g., Patrick et al., 2002).

English literature course known across campus as being an "easy A"? Perhaps you find the term *psychoceramics* a bit intimidating, and you think you can't possibly pass such a course, especially if Dr. Carberry is as grouchy and demanding as everyone claims. So you settle for the literature course, knowing it's one in which you can succeed.

People tend to choose tasks and activities at which they believe they can succeed and to avoid those at which they think they will fail. Eventually, students also place greater *value* on activities in which they think they will do well (e.g., Bandura, 1986; more on this point in Chapter 11).

Goals People set higher goals for themselves when they have high self-efficacy in a particular domain. For instance, adolescents' choices of careers and occupational levels reflect subject areas in which they have high, rather than low, self-efficacy (Bandura et al., 2001). Their choices are often consistent with traditional gender stereotypes: Boys are more likely to have high self-efficacy for—and so aspire to careers in—science and technology, whereas girls are more likely to have high self-efficacy for—and so choose careers in—education, health, and social services (Bandura et al., 2001).

Interpret reluctance and lack of persistence as possible indicators of low self-efficacy.

Effort and Persistence People with a high sense of self-efficacy are more likely to exert effort when attempting a new task. They are also more likely to persist—to "Try, try again"—when they confront obstacles to their success. In contrast, students with low self-efficacy about a task will put in little effort and give up quickly in the face of difficulty. For example, in the opening case study, Nathan is convinced he can't learn French. With such low self-efficacy, he quickly abandons French homework assignments when he encounters something he doesn't immediately understand.

PEARSON myeducationlab

Observe 12-year-old Claudia's high self-efficacy for math in the video "Motivation." (To find this video, go to Chapter 10 of the Book-Specific Resources in MyEducationLab, select *Video Examples*, and then click on the title.)

Learning and Achievement People with high self-efficacy tend to learn and achieve more than those with low self-efficacy. This is true even when the two groups initially have similar ability levels (Bandura, 1986; Eccles, Wigfield, et al., 1989; Klassen, 2002). In other words, when several individuals have equal ability, those who believe they can do a task are more likely to accomplish it successfully than those who don't believe they are capable of success. Students with high self-efficacy may achieve at superior levels partly because they engage in cognitive processes that promote learning—paying attention, organizing, elaborating, and so on (Bong & Skaalvik, 2003; Liem, Lau, & Nie, 2008; Schunk & Pajares, 2005).

Some Overconfidence—but Not Too Much—Can Be Beneficial Most 4- to 6-year-olds are quite confident about their ability to perform various tasks (R. Butler, 1990, 2005; Eccles et al., 1998). As they move through the elementary grades, however, they can better recall their past successes and failures, and they become increasingly aware of and concerned about how their performance compares with that of their peers. Presumably as a result of these changes, students gradually become less confident, although usually more realistic, about what they can and cannot do (R. Butler, 2005; Dijkstra, Kuyper, van der Werf, Buunk, & van der Zee, 2008; Wigfield & Wagner, 2005).

Ideally, learners should have a reasonably accurate sense of what they can and cannot accomplish, putting them in a good position to capitalize on their strengths and address their weaknesses (Försterling & Morgenstern, 2002; J. Wang & Lin, 2005). However, a tad of overconfidence can often be beneficial, because it may entice learners to take on challenging activities that will help them develop new skills and abilities (Assor & Connell, 1992; Bandura, 1997; Pajares, 2005). Within this context, it's useful to distinguish between *self-efficacy for learning* ("I can learn this if I put my mind to it") and *self-efficacy for performance* ("I already know how to do this") (Lodewyk & Winne, 2005; Schunk & Pajares, 2004). Self-efficacy for learning (for what one can eventually do with effort) should be on the optimistic side, while self-efficacy for performance should be more in line with current ability levels.

myeducationlab

Learn how self-efficacy for learning and self-efficacy for performance might be different by completing the Understanding Research exercise "Self-Efficacy and Achievement" in MyEducationLab. (To find this activity, go to the topic Social Cognitive Perspectives in MyEducationLab, click on *Assignments and Activities*, and then select *Understanding Research*.)

Sometimes students—girls especially—underestimate their chances of success, perhaps because they have had a few bad experiences or are especially attuned to how their own performance falls short relative to that of peers (D. A. Cole, Martin, Peeke, Seroczynski, & Fier, 1999; Dijkstra et al., 2008; Schunk & Pajares, 2005). For example, a girl who gets a C in science from a teacher with exceptionally strict grading criteria may erroneously believe that she is no good in science. Or a new boy at school whose attempts at being friendly are rejected by two or three thoughtless classmates may erroneously believe that no one likes him. In such circumstances, students set unnecessarily low goals for themselves and give up easily in the face of small obstacles.

But it's also possible to have too much of a good thing. When learners are *too* overconfident, they may set themselves up for failure by forming unrealistically high expectations or exerting insufficient effort to succeed (Bandura, 1997; Paris & Cunningham, 1996; Sweeny, Carroll, & Shepperd, 2006). Moreover, students will hardly be inclined to address weaknesses they don't realize they have (McKeachie, 1987; Pintrich, 2003).

FIGURE 10.4 Nine-year-old Sophie has been charting her monthly progress in remembering multiplication facts. Although she has had minor setbacks, her general progress is upward. (She was absent for February's assessment.)

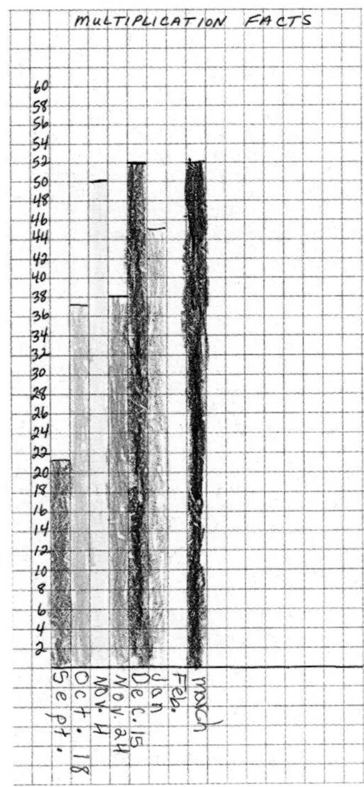

Factors in the Development of Self-Efficacy

Several factors appear to affect the development of self-efficacy, including one's previous successes and failures, other people's messages, others' successes and failures, and successes and failures that one experiences as a member of a particular group.

A Learner's Previous Successes and Failures Without a doubt, the most important factor affecting learners' self-efficacy for an activity is the extent to which they have succeeded at that activity or at similar activities in the past (Bandura, 1986; J. Chen & Morris, 2008; Usher & Pajares, 2008). For example, Edward is more likely to believe he can learn to divide fractions if he has already mastered multiplication of fractions. Elena will be more confident about her ability to play field hockey if she has already developed skills in soccer. However, students show developmental differences in *how far back* they look when they consider their prior successes and failures. Perhaps because of more limited cognitive abilities, children in the early elementary grades typically recall only their most recent experiences when judging their competence to perform a particular activity. In contrast, older children and adolescents are apt to consider a long-term pattern of successes and failures (Eccles et al., 1998).

As you can see, then, one important strategy for enhancing students' self-efficacy is to help them be successful at a variety of tasks in different content domains. Ideally, we should tailor task difficulty to students' current self-efficacy levels: Students with little or no confidence in their ability to perform in a particular domain may initially respond more favorably when we give them tasks at which they will almost certainly do well (Stipek, 1996). But ultimately, students develop higher self-efficacy when they can successfully accomplish *challenging*, rather than easy, tasks. We can best enhance their self-efficacy under challenging circumstances if we provide some degree of structure—that is, *scaffolding*—to help pave the way for successful performance (Falco, 2008; Lodewyk & Winne, 2005).

Adjust the initial difficulty of tasks to students' existing self-efficacy levels. Then gradually increase the challenge, providing structure to guide students' efforts.

Nonetheless, mastery of important knowledge and skills, even fairly basic ones, often comes only slowly over time. Consequently, it's sometimes important to define success in terms of *improvement*, rather than mastery (R. Butler, 1998a). In such instances, we may need to provide concrete mechanisms that highlight day-to-day progress—for instance, giving students progress charts they can fill in themselves (e.g., see Figure 10.4) and providing frequent verbal or written feedback about the little things students are doing well.

Once students have developed a high sense of self-efficacy, an occasional failure is unlikely to dampen their optimism very much. In fact, when these students encounter small setbacks on the way to achieving success, they learn that they *can* succeed if they try, and they also develop a realistic attitude about failure—that at worst, it's a temporary setback, and at best, it can give them useful information about how to improve their performance. In other words, students develop **resilient self-efficacy** (Bandura, 1989; Dweck, 2000). When students *consistently* fail at an activity, however, they are apt to have little confidence about their ability to succeed at the activity in the future.

myeducationlab

Observe an example of efficacy-enhancing feedback in the video "Author's Chair." (To find this video, go to Chapter 10 of the Book-Specific Resources in MyEducationLab, select *Video Examples*, and then click on the title.)

Messages from Others When students' successes aren't obvious, we can enhance their self-efficacy by explicitly pointing out ways in which they've previously done well or are now excelling. Occasionally, we may also be able to boost students' self-efficacy by giving them reasons to believe they can be successful in the future (Usher & Pajares, 2008). Statements such as "You can do this problem if you work at it" and "I bet Judy will play with you if you just ask her" might give students a slight boost in self-confidence. The effects of optimistic predictions will be modest and short lived, however, unless students' efforts at a task ultimately do meet with success (Schunk, 1989a; Valentine, DuBois, & Cooper, 2004).

Sometimes the messages we give students are implied, rather than directly stated, yet such messages can have just as much impact on self-efficacy. Even negative feedback can promote high self-efficacy *if* it gives guidance about how to improve and communicates confidence that improvement is likely—in other words, if it boosts *self-efficacy for learning* (Deci & Ryan, 1985; Parsons, Kaczala, & Meece, 1982; Pintrich & Schunk, 2002). Consider the following example:

Communicate your confidence in students' abilities even in your feedback about students' weaknesses.

> In the first draft of your research paper, many of your paragraphs don't lead logically to the ones that follow. A few headings and transitional sentences would make a world of difference. Let's find a time to discuss how you might use these techniques to improve the flow of your paper.

This statement indirectly communicates the message "With a little effort and new strategies, I know you can do better."

In some cases, we communicate our beliefs about students' competence through our actions rather than our words. For example, if we offer after-school assistance to students who are struggling to master a particular mathematical procedure or musical technique, we are communicating that with a little persistence, improvement is possible. We must be careful not to go overboard, however. If we give struggling students considerably more assistance than they really need, we may inadvertently communicate the message "I don't think you can do this on your own" (Schunk, 1989b).

Try not to give students more help than they actually need to succeed.

Successes and Failures of Other Individuals We often form opinions about our own abilities by observing the successes and failures of other people, especially those with ability levels similar to our own (Dijkstra et al., 2008; Usher & Pajares, 2008; Zeldin & Pajares, 2000). For instance, you are more likely to enroll in Dr. Carberry's Advanced Psychoceramics class if most of your friends have done well in the course, but if, instead, numerous friends have dropped the course in frustration, you may suspect that your own chances of succeeding are pretty slim. Children and adolescents, too, consider the successes and failures of their classmates, especially those of similar ability, when appraising their own chances of success. For example, recall Nathan's pessimism about learning French in the opening case study—pessimism based largely on the experiences of three low-achieving friends.

Another way of enhancing students' self-efficacy, then, is to point out that others like them have mastered the knowledge and skills at hand (Schunk, 1983, 1989c). For example, a class of chemistry students who are horrified at the number of chemical symbols they must learn can perhaps be reassured with a statement such as this:

resilient self-efficacy Belief that one can perform a task successfully even after experiencing setbacks.

> I know it seems like a lot to learn in such a short time. My students last year thought so, too, but they found that they could learn the symbols within three weeks if they studied a few new symbols each day.

Students often have higher self-efficacy about challenging tasks when they can work with peers, rather than alone.

But even more than *telling* students about others' successes, *seeing* is believing. Students who observe similar-ability peers successfully reach a goal are especially likely to believe that they, too, can achieve that goal. Hence, students sometimes develop greater self-efficacy when they see a fellow student model a behavior than when they see their teacher model it. In one study (Schunk & Hanson, 1985), elementary school children who were having trouble with subtraction were given 25 subtraction problems to complete. Children who had seen another student successfully complete the problems got an average of 19 correct, whereas those who saw a teacher complete the problems got only 13 correct, and those who saw no model at all solved only 8! It may be even more beneficial for students to see one or more peers struggling with a task or problem at first (as they themselves might do) and then eventually mastering it (Braaksma et al., 2002; Kitsantas et al., 2000; Schunk, Hanson, & Cox, 1987; Schunk & Pajares, 2005).

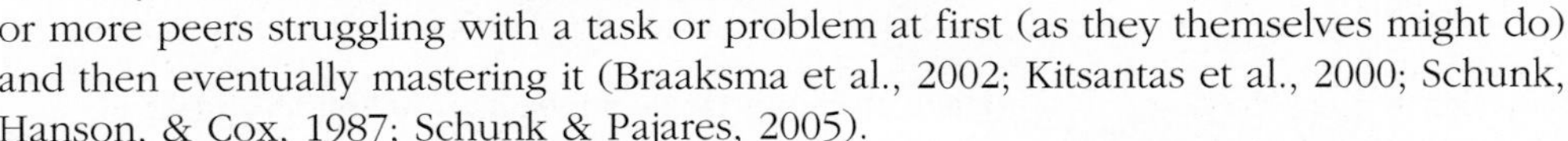

What we *don't* want to do, however, is to define success in terms of how students' performance compares with that of their peers—perhaps identifying the "best" writer, science student, or basketball player. Such comparison sets up a competitive situation in which the majority of students must inevitably lose. Most students have higher self-efficacy and achieve at higher levels if they *don't* evaluate their own performance in terms of how they stack up against others (Covington, 1992; Graham & Golen, 1991; Shih & Alexander, 2000; Stipek, 1996).

Minimize students' awareness of classmates' performance levels.

Successes and Failures as Part of a Group In earlier chapters, we discovered that learners can often think more intelligently and acquire a more complex understanding of a topic when they collaborate with peers to master and apply classroom subject matter. (See the discussions of distributed intelligence in Chapter 5 and knowledge construction as a social process in Chapter 7.) Collaboration with peers has a possible additional benefit: Learners may have greater self-efficacy when they work in a group rather than alone. Such **collective self-efficacy** depends not only on students' perceptions of their own and others' capabilities but also on their perceptions of how effectively they can work together and coordinate their roles and responsibilities (Bandura, 1997, 2000; George & Feltz, 1995).

Whether we ask students to tackle challenging tasks as individuals or in small groups, we must keep in mind that the school day shouldn't necessarily pose one challenge after another. Such a state of affairs would be absolutely exhausting, and probably quite discouraging as well. Instead, we should strike a balance between easy tasks, which will boost students' self-confidence over the short run, and the challenging tasks so critical for developing a long-term sense of high self-efficacy (Spaulding, 1992; Stipek, 1993, 1996). The Into the Classroom feature "Enhancing Students' Self-Efficacy" presents several strategies that researchers have consistently found to be effective.

collective self-efficacy People's beliefs about their ability to be successful when they work together on a task.

Teacher Self-Efficacy

Not only should our students have high self-efficacy about their ability to succeed in the classroom, but so, too, should we, as teachers, have high self-efficacy about our

INTO THE Classroom

Enhancing Students' Self-Efficacy

- **Teach basic knowledge and skills to mastery.**

  A biology teacher makes sure all students clearly understand the basic structure of DNA before moving to mitosis and meiosis, two topics that require a knowledge of DNA structure.

- **Assure students that they can be successful at challenging tasks, and point out that others like them have been successful in the past.**

  Early in the school year, students in beginning band express frustration in learning to play their instruments. Their teacher reminds them that, like themselves, students in last year's beginning band started out with little knowledge but eventually mastered their instruments. A few weeks later, the beginning band class attends a concert at which the school's advanced band (last year's beginning band class) plays a medley from the Broadway musical *Wicked.*

- **Have students see peers with similar ability accomplish challenging tasks.**

  To convince students from low-income, minority-group families that they can do almost anything if they put their minds to it, a high school math teacher shows his class the film *Stand and Deliver.* The film depicts the true story of 18 Mexican American high school students from a low-income neighborhood in East Los Angeles who, through hard work and perseverance, earned college credit by passing the national Advanced Placement (AP) calculus exam.

- **Help students track their progress on challenging tasks.**

  As first graders are learning how to weave on small, circular looms, one student approaches her teacher in tears, frustrated that her first few rows are full of mistakes. The teacher responds, "Look, Dorothy, this is the history, your own history, of learning to weave. You can look at this and say, 'Why, I can see how I began, here I didn't know how very well, I went over two instead of one; but I learned, and then—it is perfect all the way to the end!' " The student returns to her seat, very much comforted, and finishes her piece. She follows it with another, flawless one and proudly shows it to her teacher.

- **After students have mastered basic skills, present some tasks at which they can succeed only with effort and perseverance.**

  A physical education teacher tells his students, "Today we've determined how far each of you can go in the broad jump. We will continue to practice good form a little bit each week. Some of your future efforts will be more successful than others, but let's see if every one of you can jump at least two inches farther when I test you again at the end of the month."

- **Have students tackle especially challenging tasks in small cooperative groups.**

  A fifth-grade teacher has students work in groups of three or four to write research papers about early colonial life in North America. The teacher makes sure that the students in each group collectively have the skills in library research, writing, word processing, and art necessary to complete the task. She also makes sure that every student has some unique skills to contribute to the group effort.

Sources: Bandura, 1986, 1989, 1997, 2000; R. Butler, 1998a; Eccles et al., 1998; Hawkins, 1997, p. 332 (weaving example); Lodewyk & Winne, 2005; Mathews, 1988; Menéndez, 1988 (*Stand and Deliver* example); Schunk, 1983, 1989a, 1989c; Usher & Pajares, 2008; Zeldin & Pajares, 2000.

ability to *help* them succeed. As noted in Chapter 1, students are more likely to achieve at high levels when their teachers have confidence that they can help students master classroom topics. Some of this teacher confidence may take the form of collective self-efficacy: When teachers at a school believe that, as a group, they can make a significant difference in the lives of their students, students, too, have higher self-efficacy and are more likely to achieve at high levels (Goddard, 2001; Goddard, Hoy, & Woolfolk Hoy, 2000; Tschannen-Moran et al., 1998).

Collaborate with colleagues to identify effective ways of fostering *all* students' academic and social success at school.

When teachers have high self-efficacy about their effectiveness in the classroom—both individually and collectively—they influence students' achievement in several ways:

- These teachers are more willing to experiment with new teaching strategies that can better help students learn.
- These teachers have higher expectations for—and thus set higher goals for—students' performance.
- These teachers put more effort into their teaching and are more persistent in helping students learn. (Bandura, 1997; Roeser, Marachi, & Gehlbach, 2002; Tschannen-Moran et al., 1998)

Such effects should look familiar: Just as self-efficacy affects students' choice of activities, goals, effort, and persistence, so, too, does it affect *teachers'* choices, goals, effort, and persistence.

As is true for our students, however, it's possible to have too much of a good thing. Occasionally teachers have so much confidence in their existing knowledge and skills that they find little benefit in professional development activities that would enhance their effectiveness (Guskey, 1988; Middleton & Abrams, 2004; Tschannen-Moran et al., 1998). We teachers are *learners* as well, and we will always have room for improvement in our classroom strategies (e.g., Hammerness, Darling-Hammond, & Bransford, 2005).

Self-Regulation

Although high self-efficacy can certainly enhance students' classroom performance, it is by no means the only thing that affects their performance. Students must also master the knowledge and skills that make high performance levels possible. Some knowledge and skills are specific to particular topics and academic domains, but one set of skills—self-regulation skills—can have a pervasive influence on students' achievement across the board. To get a sense of your own self-regulation skills, try the following exercise.

EXPERIENCING FIRSTHAND

Self-Reflection About Self-Regulation

In each of the following situations, choose the alternative that most accurately describes your attitudes, thoughts, and behaviors as a college student. No one will see your answers except you, so be honest!

1. With regard to my final course grades, I am trying very hard to
   a. Earn all As.
   b. Earn all As and Bs.
   c. Keep my overall grade point average at or above the minimally acceptable level at my college.
2. As I am reading or studying a textbook,
   a. I often notice when my attention is wandering, and I immediately get my mind back on my work.
   b. I sometimes notice when my attention is wandering, but not always.
   c. I often get so lost in daydreams that I waste a lot of time.
3. Whenever I finish a study session,
   a. I write down how much time I have spent on my schoolwork.
   b. I make a mental note of how much time I have spent on my schoolwork.
   c. I don't really think much about how much time I have spent on my schoolwork.
4. When I turn in an assignment,
   a. I usually have a good idea of the grade I will get on it.
   b. I am often surprised by the grade I get.
   c. I don't think much about the quality of what I have done.
5. When I do exceptionally well on an assignment,
   a. I feel good about my performance and might reward myself in some way.
   b. I feel good about my performance but don't do anything special for myself afterward.
   c. I don't feel much different than I did before I received my grade.

Regardless of how you answered Item 1, you could probably identify a particular goal toward which you are striving. Your response to Item 2 should give you an idea of how much you monitor and try to control your thoughts when you are studying. Your responses to Items 3 and 4 tell you something about how frequently and accurately you evaluate your performance. And your response to Item 5 indicates whether you are likely to reinforce yourself for desired behaviors.

The standards and goals we set for ourselves, the ways in which we monitor and evaluate our own cognitive processes and behaviors, and the consequences we impose on ourselves for our successes and failures—all of these are aspects of self-regulation. If our thoughts and actions are under *our* control, rather than that of the people and circumstances around us, we are self-regulating individuals (Zimmerman, 1998).

Thanks, in part, to brain maturation over the course of childhood and adolescence, most learners become increasingly self-regulating as they grow older (Rothbart, Sheese, & Posner, 2007; L. Steinberg, 2007). Table 10.2 presents typical advancements in the elementary and secondary school years. Some of the entries in the table, such as self-instructions and self-evaluation of actions, reflect self-regulation in *behavior.* Others, such as ability to control attention and self-motivation, reflect self-regulation in *learning.* We'll look here at both self-regulated behavior and self-regulated learning, as well as at self-regulated problem solving.

Self-Regulated Behavior

FIGURE 10.5 Components of self-regulated behavior

Before the Response:
- Self-Determined Standards and Goals

During the Response:
- Emotion Regulation
- Self-Instructions
- Self-Monitoring

After the Response:
- Self-Evaluation
- Self-Imposed Contingencies

When we behave in particular ways and observe how our environment reacts—reinforcing some behaviors and punishing or otherwise discouraging others—we begin to distinguish between desirable and undesirable responses. As we develop an understanding about which responses are appropriate and which are not (for us, at least), most of us increasingly control and monitor our own behavior (Bandura, 1986). In other words, we engage in **self-regulated behavior**. Six key aspects of self-regulated behavior are presented in Figure 10.5. Let's look at the nature and potential implications of each one.

Self-Determined Standards and Goals As self-regulating human beings, we tend to have general standards for our behavior—standards that serve as criteria for evaluating our performance in specific situations. We also establish certain goals that we value and toward which we direct many of our behaviors. Meeting our standards and reaching our goals give us considerable self-satisfaction, enhancing our self-efficacy and spurring us on to greater heights (Bandura, 1986, 1989).

Different individuals inevitably adopt different standards and goals for themselves; for instance, one may strive for straight As, whereas another may be content with a record of Cs. Learners' standards and goals are often modeled after those they see other people adopt (Bandura, 1986; E. A. Locke & Latham, 1990; R. B. Miller & Brickman, 2004). For instance, at the high school I attended, many students wanted to go to the best college or university they possibly could. In such an environment, others began to share the same academic aspirations. But at a different high school, getting a job after graduation (or perhaps *instead* of graduation) might have been the aspiration more commonly modeled by classmates.

Students are typically more motivated to work toward goals—and thus more likely to accomplish those goals—when they have set the goals for themselves, instead of having goals imposed on them (M. E. Ford, 1992; Spaulding, 1992; also see the discussion of *self-determination* in Chapter 11.) One way to help students develop self-regulation, then, is to provide situations in which they set their own goals. For example, we might ask them to decide how many addition facts they are going to learn by Friday, what topic they wish to study for a research project, or which gymnastic skills they would like to master.

self-regulated behavior Self-chosen and self-directed behavior that leads to the fulfillment of personally constructed standards and goals.

TABLE 10.2
Self-Regulation at Different Grade Levels

Grade Level	Age-Typical Characteristics	Suggested Strategies
K–2	• Some internalization of adults' standards for behavior; some ability to inhibit behaviors known to be inappropriate • Emerging ability to set self-chosen goals for learning and achievement • Some use of self-instructions (self-talk) to guide behavior • Some self-evaluation of effectiveness and appropriateness of actions; feelings of guilt about wrongdoings • Individual differences in self-control of impulses, emotions, and attention; peer relationships and classroom performance affected by amount of self-control in these areas	• Discuss rationales for classroom rules. • Show students how some behaviors can help them reach their goals and how other behaviors interfere with goal attainment. • Organize the classroom so that students can carry out some activities on their own (e.g., have reading centers where children can listen to storybooks on tape). • Give students some leeway to solve minor interpersonal problems on their own; intervene if the problems escalate. • When students show impulsiveness or poor emotional control, provide consistent guidelines and consequences for behavior.
3–5	• Improving ability to assess one's own performance and progress • Guilt and shame about unsatisfactory performance and moral transgressions • Emerging self-regulated learning strategies (e.g., conscious attempts to focus attention, ability to do short assignments independently at home) • Persistent difficulties with self-control for some students	• Encourage students to assess their own performance; provide criteria they can use to evaluate their work. • Ask students to engage in simple, self-regulated learning tasks (e.g., small-group cooperative learning activities, homework assignments); provide some structure to guide students' efforts. • Encourage students to use their peers as resources when they need help with a task. • If students have ongoing difficulty with self-control, teach self-instructions that can help them control their behavior.
6–8	• Increasing ability to plan future actions, due in part to increased capacity for abstract thought • Increasing mastery of some self-regulating learning strategies, especially those that involve overt behaviors (e.g., keeping a calendar of assignments and due dates) • Self-motivational strategies (e.g., minimizing distractions, devising ways to make a boring task more interesting and enjoyable, reminding oneself about the importance of doing well) • Considerable variability in self-regulating abilities (e.g., in completing homework)	• Assign homework and other tasks that require independent learning. • Provide concrete strategies for keeping track of learning tasks and assignments (e.g., provide monthly calendars on which students can write due dates). • Provide explicit guidance about how to learn and study effectively (e.g., give students questions they should answer as they complete reading assignments at home). • Give students frequent opportunities to assess their own learning; have them compare your evaluations with their own.
9–12	• More long-range goal setting • Continuing development of strategies for emotion regulation, especially in contexts that evoke strong emotions (e.g., sports, dramatic productions) • Increasing mastery of covert (internal) learning strategies (e.g., self-initiated elaboration on new ideas, comprehension monitoring) • Continuing variability in ability to self-regulate learning, especially in independent learning activities; few self-regulating learning strategies among many low-achieving high school students • For a minority of older adolescents, persistent difficulties in self-regulation of behavior that may adversely affect classroom behavior and peer relationships	• Relate classroom learning tasks to students' long-range personal and professional goals. • Encourage students to experiment with various emotions and emotional control strategies through role playing and drama. • Describe and model effective cognitive strategies for reading, learning, and studying. • Assign complex independent learning tasks, providing the necessary structure and guidance for students who are not yet self-regulating learners.

Sources: Blair, 2002; Bronson, 2000; Corno & Mandinach, 2004; Damon, 1988; Eccles et al., 1998; Fries, Dietz, & Schmid, 2008; Hampson, 2008; Kochanska et al., 2002; Meichenbaum & Goodman, 1971; S. D. Miller, Heafner, Massey, & Strahan, 2003; Larson & Brown, 2007; Paris & Paris, 2001; Posner & Rothbart, 2007; Valiente, Lemery-Calfant, Swanon, & Reiser, 2008; Wolters & Rosenthal, 2000.

Have students set some of their own goals in the classroom. Encourage them to set challenging yet realistic goals; caution them against always striving for perfection.

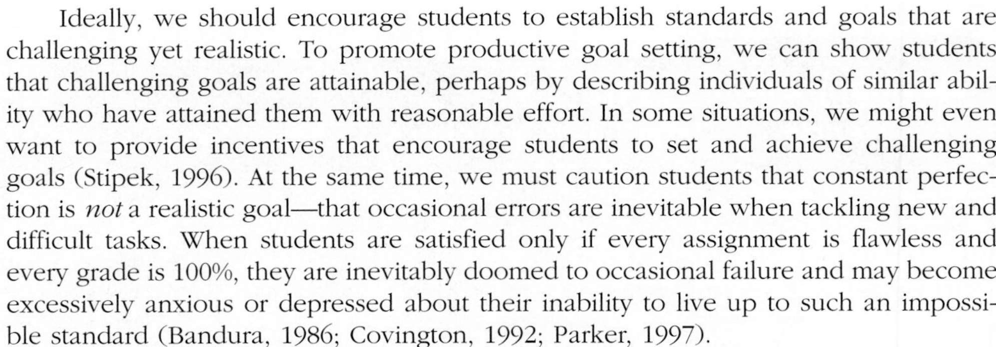

Ideally, we should encourage students to establish standards and goals that are challenging yet realistic. To promote productive goal setting, we can show students that challenging goals are attainable, perhaps by describing individuals of similar ability who have attained them with reasonable effort. In some situations, we might even want to provide incentives that encourage students to set and achieve challenging goals (Stipek, 1996). At the same time, we must caution students that constant perfection is *not* a realistic goal—that occasional errors are inevitable when tackling new and difficult tasks. When students are satisfied only if every assignment is flawless and every grade is 100%, they are inevitably doomed to occasional failure and may become excessively anxious or depressed about their inability to live up to such an impossible standard (Bandura, 1986; Covington, 1992; Parker, 1997).

myeducationlab

Listen to 10-year-old Daniel, 13-year-old Crystal, and 15-year-old Greg describe their strategies for emotion regulation in the video "Emotions." (To find this video, go to Chapter 10 of the Book-Specific Resources in MyEducationLab, select *Video Examples*, and then click on the title.)

Emotion Regulation A second important aspect of self-regulated behavior is **emotion regulation**: keeping in check or modifying any feelings that might lead to counterproductive responses—perhaps anger, resentment, or excessive excitement. Effective emotion regulation often involves a two-pronged approach (Pekrun, 2006; J. M. Richards, 2004; Silk, Steinberg, & Morris, 2003). First, learners control the extent to which they *express their feelings*. In addition, self-regulating individuals often *reinterpret events* in order to put a positive spin on what might otherwise be anger- or sadness-provoking circumstances. For instance, a student who gets an unexpectedly low quiz score might treat it as a wake-up call to study more diligently in the future. And a student who doesn't make the varsity soccer team might think, "Maybe this is a blessing in disguise, because it gives me more time to help out at the Boys' Club after school."

To some extent, students' ability to control their emotions depends on neurological maturation (M. D. Lewis & Stieben, 2004; Wisner Fries & Pollak, 2007). However, as teachers, we can also encourage strategies that help students control any feelings that might lead them to behave in ways they will later regret. For instance, we might suggest that students count to 10 in order to calm down before responding to a provocation on the playground. And we can help them brainstorm possible "silver linings" in disappointing circumstances.

Teach strategies for keeping counterproductive emotions in check.

Self-Instructions Consider the formerly forgetful student who, before leaving the house each morning, now asks herself, "Do I have everything I need for my classes? I have my math homework for Period 1, my history book for Period 2, my change of clothes for gym during Period 3 . . ." And consider the once impulsive student who now pauses before beginning a new assignment and says to himself, "OK, what am I supposed to do? Let's see. . . . I need to read the directions first. What do the directions tell me to do?"

Sometimes students simply need reminders of what to do in particular situations. By teaching students how to talk themselves through these situations using **self-instructions**, we provide them with a means through which *they remind themselves* about appropriate actions. Such a strategy is often effective for students who otherwise seem to behave without thinking (Carter & Doyle, 2006; W. M. Casey & Burton, 1982; Meichenbaum, 1985).

One effective way of teaching students to give themselves instructions involves five steps (Meichenbaum, 1977):

1. *Cognitive modeling.* The teacher models self-instruction by repeating instructions aloud while simultaneously performing the activity.
2. *Overt, external guidance.* The teacher repeats the instructions aloud while the student performs the activity.
3. *Overt self-guidance.* The student repeats the instructions aloud while performing the activity.
4. *Faded, overt self-guidance.* The student whispers the instructions while performing the activity.
5. *Covert self-instruction.* The student silently thinks about the instructions while performing the activity.

emotion regulation Process of keeping in check or intentionally altering feelings that might lead to counterproductive behavior.

self-instructions Instructions that one gives oneself while performing a complex behavior.

As you can see in these steps, the teacher initially serves as a model both for the behavior and the self-instructions. Gradually, the responsibility for performing and, later, self-guiding the activity is turned over to the student. Steps 3 through 5 in the process may remind you of Vygotsky's concepts of *self-talk* and *inner speech* (see Chapter 2).

By following these five steps, impulsive elementary school children can effectively learn to slow themselves down and think through what they are doing (Meichenbaum & Goodman, 1971). For example, notice how one formerly impulsive student was able to talk his way through a matching task in which he needed to find two identical pictures among several very similar ones:

self-monitoring Process of observing and recording one's own behavior.

self-evaluation Process of judging one's own performance or behavior.

Teach students instructions they can use to guide themselves through difficult tasks.

> I have to remember to go slowly to get it right. Look carefully at this one, now look at these carefully. Is this one different? Yes, it has an extra leaf. Good, I can eliminate this one. Now, let's look at this one. I think it's this one, but let me first check the others. Good, I'm going slow and carefully. Okay, I think it's this one. (Meichenbaum & Goodman, 1971, p. 121)

Self-Monitoring Another important part of self-regulation is to observe oneself in action—a process known as **self-monitoring** (or *self-observation*). To make progress toward important goals, we must be aware of how well we are currently doing. And when we see ourselves making progress toward our goals, we are more likely to continue with our efforts (Schunk & Zimmerman, 1997).

Students aren't always astute monitors of their own behavior, however. For instance, they aren't always aware of how frequently they do something incorrectly or ineffectively or of how infrequently they do something well. Specific, concrete mechanisms can often help students attend to the things they do and don't do. For example, if Raymond is speaking out of turn too often, we can ask him to make a checkmark on a sheet of paper every time he catches himself speaking out of turn. And if Olivia has trouble staying on task during assigned activities, we can ask her to stop and reflect on her behavior every few minutes (perhaps with the aid of an egg timer or electronic beeper) to determine whether she was staying on task during each interval. Figure 10.6 provides an example of the type of form we might give Olivia to record her observations.

Have students observe and record information about their own behavior.

Research clearly indicates that such self-focused observation and recording can bring about changes (sometimes dramatic ones) in students' behavior. For example, self-monitoring can be used to increase students' attention to their work (i.e., their *time on task*) and the number of assignments they complete. Self-monitoring is also effective in reducing aggression and disruptive behaviors such as talking out of turn and getting out of one's seat (Belfiore & Hornyak, 1998; Mace & Kratochwill, 1988; Reid, Trout, & Schartz, 2005; Webber, Scheuermann, McCall, & Coleman, 1993).

FIGURE 10.6 Example of a self-monitoring sheet for staying on task

Self-Observation Record for Olivia

Every ten minutes, put a mark to show how well you have been staying on task.

+ means you were almost always on task
1/2 means you were on task about half the time
– means you were hardly ever on task

9:00-9:10	9:10-9:20	9:20-9:30	9:30-9:40	9:40-9:50	9:50-10:00
+	+	–	+	1/2	–
10:00-10:10	10:10-10:20	10:20-10:30	10:30-10:40	10:40-10:50	10:50-11:00
1/2	–	recess		+	1/2
11:00-11:10	11:10-11:20	11:20-11:30	11:30-11:40	11:40-11:50	11:50-12:00

Self-Evaluation Both at home and in school, students' behaviors are frequently judged by others—by parents, teachers, classmates, and so on. To become self-regulating, however, students must begin to engage in **self-evaluation**, judging their *own* behavior. Students' ability to evaluate themselves with some degree of objectivity and accuracy is critical for their long-term success in the adult world (e.g., Vye et al., 1998).

Once students have developed appropriate standards and goals and once they have developed

self-imposed contingency Self-reinforcement or self-punishment that follows a behavior.

objective techniques for observing and monitoring their own behavior, we can help them evaluate their own performance in a variety of ways. Following are three possible strategies:

- Have students write in daily or weekly journals in which they address the strengths and weaknesses of their performance.
- Arrange small-group peer conferences in which several students discuss their reactions to one another's work.
- Have students assemble portfolios of what they consider their best work, with a self-evaluation of each entry (see Chapter 15 for details). (Paris & Ayres, 1994; Paris & Paris, 2001)

Once students have set appropriate standards and objective methods of self-observation, ask them to evaluate their own performance.

In addition, we can provide self-assessment instruments that show students what to look for as they evaluate their work, and we can occasionally have them compare their self-assessments with others' independent judgments of their performance (DuPaul & Hoff, 1998; Mitchem & Young, 2001; Reid et al., 2005; D. J. Smith, Young, West, Morgan, & Rhode, 1988). Figure 10.7 presents a form one teacher has used to help her students learn to evaluate their performance in a cooperative group activity.

Self-Imposed Contingencies **Self-imposed contingencies** involve giving oneself reinforcement or punishment for one's behavior. For example, how do you feel when you accomplish a difficult task—perhaps earning an A in a challenging course, getting elected president of an organization, or making a three-point shot in a basketball game? And how do you feel when you fail in your endeavors—perhaps getting a D on an exam because you forgot to study, thoughtlessly hurting a friend's feelings, or missing an easy goal in a soccer game? When you accomplish something you've set out to do, especially if the task is complex and challenging, you probably feel quite proud of yourself and give yourself a mental pat on the back. In contrast, when you fail to accomplish a task, you're probably unhappy with your performance; you may also feel guilty, regretful, or ashamed (Harter, 1999; Krebs, 2008).

FIGURE 10.7 After a cooperative group activity with three classmates, Rochelle and her teacher use the same criteria to rate Rochelle's performance and that of her group. With the two sets of ratings side by side, Rochelle can evaluate the accuracy of her self-assessments.

Project description Travel Guide

Evaluate with a 1 for weak, a 2 for fair, a 3 for good, a 4 for very good, and a 5 for excellent.

Student	Teacher	
4	4	1. The task was a major amount of work in keeping with a whole month of effort.
5	4	2. We used class time quite well.
4	5	3. The workload was quite evenly divided. I did a fair proportion.
4	5	4. I showed commitment to the group and to a quality project.
5	4	5. My report went into depth; it didn't just give the obvious, commonly known information.
5	5	6. The project made a point: a reader (or viewer) could figure out how all of the details fitted together to help form a conclusion.
5	5	7. The project was neat, attractive, well assembled. I was proud of the outcome.
4	5	8. We kept our work organized; we made copies; we didn't lose things or end up having to redo work that was lost.
5	4	9. The work had a lot of original thinking or other creative work.
4	4	10. The project demonstrated mastery of basic language skills—composition, planning, oral communication, writing.
45	45	Total

As children and adolescents become increasingly self-regulating, they, too, begin to reinforce themselves (perhaps by feeling proud or telling themselves they did a good job) when they accomplish their goals. And they may punish themselves (perhaps by feeling sorry, guilty, or ashamed) when they do something that doesn't meet their own performance standards. But self-imposed contingencies aren't necessarily confined to emotional reactions. Many self-regulating individuals reinforce themselves in far more concrete ways when they do something well (Bandura, 1977). I once had a colleague who went shopping every time she completed a research article or report (she had one of the best wardrobes in town). I am more frugal. When I finish writing each major section of a chapter, I either help myself to a piece of chocolate or take a half hour to watch one of my favorite quiz shows (as a result, I am chubbier than my colleague, but I have a wealth of knowledge of game-show trivia and would almost certainly beat her in a game of Trivial Pursuit).

Thus, an additional way to help students become more self-regulating is to teach them self-reinforcement. When students begin to reinforce themselves for appropriate responses—perhaps giving themselves some free time, allowing themselves to engage in a favorite activity, or simply praising themselves—their study habits and classroom behavior sometimes improve significantly (K. R. Harris, 1986; Hayes et al., 1985; Reid et al., 2005). In one research study, students who were performing poorly in arithmetic were taught to give themselves points when they did well on their assignments; they could later use the points to "buy" a variety of items and privileges. Within a few weeks, these students were doing as well as their classmates on both in-class assignments and homework (H. C. Stevenson & Fantuzzo, 1986).

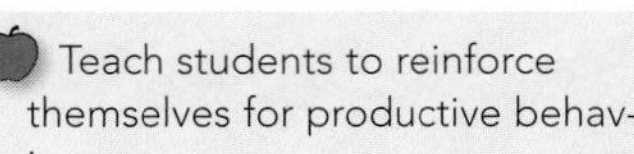
Teach students to reinforce themselves for productive behavior.

The most diligent workers and highest achievers in the classroom, on the athletic field, and elsewhere are likely to be individuals who can effectively self-regulate their behavior (Duckworth & Seligman, 2005; Trautwein, Lüdtke, Kastens, & Köller, 2006; Zimmerman & Kitsantas, 2005). But we certainly don't have to leave the development of self-regulated behavior to chance. As we teach students strategies for taking charge of their own actions, we should keep several points in mind:

- Students must be cognitively capable of achieving the goals they have set.
- Students must be motivated to change their behavior.
- Students' expectations for change must be realistic and practical; dramatic overnight improvements are rare.
- Students must have high self-efficacy for making the necessary changes.

Acquiring effective self-regulation skills is often a slow, gradual process, but with reasonable guidance and scaffolding, virtually all students can master them.

Self-Regulated Learning

Social cognitive theorists and cognitive psychologists alike are beginning to realize that to be truly effective learners, students must engage in some of the self-regulating behaviors just described. In fact, not only must students regulate their own behaviors, but they must also regulate their *cognitive processes*. In particular, **self-regulated learning** includes the following processes, many of which are metacognitive in nature:

- *Goal setting*. Self-regulating learners know what they want to accomplish when they read or study—perhaps to learn specific facts, gain a broad conceptual understanding of a topic, or simply acquire enough knowledge to do well on a classroom exam. Typically they tie their goals for a particular learning activity to longer-term goals and aspirations (Nolen, 1996; Winne & Hadwin, 1998; Wolters, 1998; Zimmerman, 2004).

self-regulated learning Regulation of one's own cognitive processes and studying behaviors in order to learn successfully.

- *Planning.* Self-regulating learners determine ahead of time how best to use the time and resources they have available for learning tasks (Zimmerman, 2004; Zimmerman & Risemberg, 1997).
- *Self-motivation.* Self-regulating learners typically have high self-efficacy regarding their ability to accomplish a learning task successfully. They use a variety of strategies to keep themselves on task—perhaps embellishing the task to make it more fun, reminding themselves of the importance of doing well, or promising themselves a reward when they are finished (Corno, 1993; Wolters, 2003; Zimmerman, 2004).
- *Attention control.* Self-regulating learners try to focus their attention on the subject matter at hand and to clear their minds of potentially distracting thoughts and emotions (Harnishfeger, 1995; J. Kuhl, 1985; Winne, 1995).
- *Flexible use of learning strategies.* Self-regulating learners choose different learning strategies depending on the specific goals they hope to accomplish. For example, how they read a magazine article depends on whether they are reading it for entertainment or studying for an exam (Meltzer et al., 2007; van den Broek, Lorch, Linderholm, & Gustafson, 2001; Winne, 1995).
- *Self-monitoring.* Self-regulating learners continually monitor their progress toward their goals for studying—for instance, engaging in the *comprehension monitoring* of which I spoke in Chapter 8—and change their learning strategies or modify their goals as necessary (D. L. Butler & Winne, 1995; Carver & Scheier, 1990; Zimmerman, 2004).
- *Appropriate help-seeking.* Truly self-regulating learners don't necessarily try to do everything on their own. On the contrary, they recognize when they need other people's help and seek such assistance. They are especially likely to ask for the kind of help that will enable them to work more independently in the future (R. Butler, 1998b; R. S. Newman, 2008; A. M. Ryan, Pintrich, & Midgley, 2001).
- *Self-evaluation.* Self-regulating learners determine whether what they have learned addresses their original goals. Ideally, they also use their self-evaluations to adjust their use of various learning strategies on future occasions (Schraw & Moshman, 1995; Winne & Hadwin, 1998; Zimmerman & Schunk, 2004).

As you can see in Table 10.2, a few elements of self-regulated learning (e.g., conscious attempts to focus attention and ability to complete short learning tasks at home) emerge in the upper elementary grades, and additional ones (e.g., planning, self-motivation) appear in the middle school and high school years. To some extent, self-regulated learning probably develops from opportunities to engage in age-appropriate independent learning activities and to observe other people modeling effective self-regulation strategies (Paris & Paris, 2001; Vye et al., 1998; Zimmerman, 2004).

But if we take Vygotsky's perspective for a moment, we might suspect that self-regulated learning also has roots in socially regulated learning (Stright, Neitzel, Sears, & Hoke-Sinex, 2001; Vygotsky, 1934/1986; Zimmerman, 1998). At first, other people (e.g., teachers and parents) might help children learn by setting goals for a learning activity, keeping children's attention focused on the learning task, suggesting effective learning strategies, monitoring learning progress, and so on. Over time, children assume increasing responsibility for these processes. That is, they begin to set their own goals, stay on task with little prodding from others, identify potentially effective strategies, and evaluate their own learning.

Developmentally speaking, a reasonable bridge between other-regulated learning and self-regulated learning is **co-regulated learning**, in which an adult and one or more children share responsibility for directing the various aspects of the learning process (McCaslin & Good, 1996; Zimmerman, 2004). For instance, a teacher and students might agree on the specific goals of a learning endeavor, or the teacher might describe the criteria that indicate successful learning and then have students evaluate their own performance in light of those criteria. Initially the teacher might provide considerable structure, or scaffolding, for the students' learning efforts. Then,

co-regulated learning Process through which an adult and child share responsibility for directing various aspects of the child's learning.

in true Vygotskian fashion, such scaffolding is gradually removed as students become more proficient self-regulators.

When children and adolescents are self-regulating learners, they set more ambitious academic goals for themselves, learn more effectively, and achieve at higher levels in the classroom (D. L. Butler & Winne, 1995; Corno et al., 2002; Zimmerman & Risemberg, 1997). Self-regulation becomes increasingly important in adolescence and adulthood, when many learning activities—reading, doing homework, surfing the Internet, and so on—occur in isolation from other people and thus require considerable self-direction (Trautwein et al., 2006; Winne, 1995; Zimmerman & Kitsantas, 2005). Even at the upper grade levels, however, few students develop a high level of self-regulated learning, perhaps, in part, because traditional instructional practices do little to encourage it (Paris & Ayres, 1994; Zimmerman & Risemberg, 1997).

Self-regulated learning often emerges from *co-regulated learning,* in which a teacher and learner share responsibility for directing various aspects of the learning process—setting goals, identifying effective strategies, evaluating progress, and so on.

Promoting Self-Regulated Learning To promote self-regulated learning, we must, of course, teach students the kinds of cognitive processes that facilitate learning and memory (see the discussion of *metacognition* in Chapter 8). In addition, researchers have suggested the following strategies:

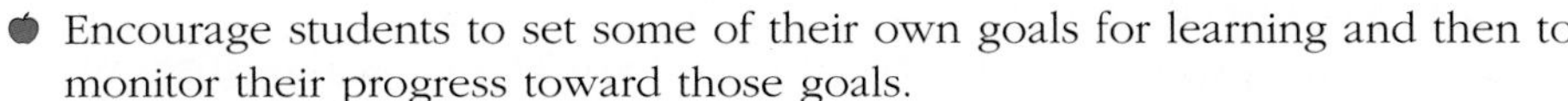

- Encourage students to set some of their own goals for learning and then to monitor their progress toward those goals.
- Give students opportunities to work without teacher direction or assistance; include both independent learning activities, in which students study by themselves (e.g., seatwork assignments, homework), and group activities, in which students help one another learn (e.g., peer tutoring, cooperative learning).
- Occasionally assign activities in which students have considerable leeway regarding goals and use of time (e.g., research papers, creative projects).
- Teach time management strategies (e.g., setting aside specific times to study at home, prioritizing assignments based on difficulty and due dates).
- Provide the scaffolding students need to acquire self-regulation skills (e.g., give them checklists they can use to identify what they need to do each day and to determine when they have completed all assigned work).
- Model self-regulating cognitive processes by thinking aloud while using such processes, and then give students constructive feedback as they engage in similar processes.
- Encourage students to seek short-term, focused help to overcome temporary difficulties in understanding.
- Consistently ask students to evaluate their own performance, and have them compare their self-assessments to any teacher assessments. (Belfiore & Hornyak, 1998; Bronson, 2000; Falco, 2008; A. King, 1997; McCaslin & Good, 1996; Meltzer et al., 2007; R. S. Newman, 2008; Paris & Paris, 2001; N. E. Perry, 1998; N. E. Perry, VandeKamp, Mercer, & Nordby, 2002; Schunk & Zimmerman, 1997; J. W. Thomas, 1993b; Winne & Hadwin, 1998; Wong, Hoskyn, Jai, Ellis, & Watson, 2008; Zimmerman & Risemberg, 1997)

PEARSON myeducationlab

Gain practice in identifying and fostering students' self-regulation skills by completing the Building Teaching Skills and Dispositions exercise "Encouraging Self-Regulation" in MyEducationLab. (To find this exercise, go to the topic Social Cognitive Perspectives in MyEducationLab, and click on *Building Teaching Skills and Dispositions.*)

Self-Regulated Problem Solving

Effectively directing one's own efforts in tackling complex problems—that is, **self-regulated problem solving**—involves many of the same components as self-regulated learning: goal setting, self-motivation, attention control, self-monitoring, self-

self-regulated problem solving Use of self-directed strategies to address complex problems.

evaluation, and so on (Zimmerman & Campillo, 2003). And just as teacher scaffolding facilitates the development of self-regulated learning skills, so, too, does it facilitate the acquisition of self-regulated problem-solving strategies. For example, to encourage brainstorming and perhaps elicit greater creativity in solving problems, we might suggest that students give themselves instructions such as these:

> I want to think of something no one else will think of, something unique. Be free-wheeling, no hang-ups. I don't care what anyone thinks; just suspend judgment. I'm not sure what I'll come up with; it will be a surprise. The ideas can just flow through me. (Meichenbaum, 1977, p. 62)

We might also provide a general structure for students to follow as they approach complex problems—for example, by encouraging them to ask themselves such questions as "Why am I using this strategy?" and "Am I sure this answer makes sense?" (Berardi-Coletta, Buyer, Dominowski, & Rellinger, 1995; Desoete, Roeyers, & De Clercq, 2003).

Teach students the mental steps they can follow to solve complex problems more effectively.

Self-regulated problem solving is important not only for solving academic problems but for solving social problems as well. For instance, to help students deal more effectively with interpersonal conflicts, we might teach them to take these steps:

1. Define the problem.
2. Identify several possible solutions.
3. Predict the likely consequences of each solution.
4. Choose the best solution.
5. Identify the steps required to carry out the solution.
6. Carry out the steps.
7. Evaluate the results. (S. N. Elliott & Busse, 1991; Meichenbaum, 1977; Weissberg, 1985; Yell, Robinson, & Drasgow, 2001)

Following such steps often helps students who have interpersonal problems—for instance, students who are either socially withdrawn or overly aggressive—to develop more effective social skills (K. R. Harris, 1982; Meichenbaum, 1977; Yell et al., 2001).

Another approach is to provide training in **peer mediation**, in which students *help one another* solve interpersonal problems. More specifically, this approach teaches students how to mediate conflicts among classmates by asking opposing sides to express their differing points of view and then work together to devise a reasonable resolution (M. Deutsch, 1993; D. W. Johnson & Johnson, 1996, 2006; Stevahn, Johnson, Johnson, Oberle, & Wahl, 2000). In one study involving several second-through fifth-grade classrooms (D. W. Johnson, Johnson, Dudley, Ward, & Magnuson, 1995), students were trained to help peers resolve interpersonal conflicts by asking the opposing sides to do the following:

1. Define the conflict (the problem).
2. Explain their own perspectives and needs.
3. Explain the other person's perspectives and needs.
4. Identify at least three possible solutions to the conflict.
5. Reach an agreement that addresses the needs of both parties.

Teach students strategies for effectively mediating classmates' interpersonal conflicts.

peer mediation Approach to conflict resolution in which a student (serving as a *mediator*) asks peers in conflict to express their differing viewpoints and then work together to devise a reasonable resolution.

Students took turns serving as mediator for their classmates, such that everyone had experience resolving the conflicts of others. As a result, the students more frequently resolved their own interpersonal conflicts in ways that addressed the needs of both parties, and they were less likely than students in an untrained control group to ask for adult intervention.

In peer mediation, then, we see another example of Vygotsky's notion that many effective cognitive processes have their roots in social interactions. In a peer mediation session, students model effective conflict resolution skills for one another, and they may eventually internalize the skills they use in solving others' problems to solve their *own* problems.

Peer mediation is most effective when students of diverse ethnic backgrounds, socioeconomic groups, and achievement levels all serve as mediators (Casella, 2001a; K. M. Williams, 2001b). Furthermore, this approach is typically most useful for relatively small, short-term interpersonal problems (e.g., hurt feelings, conflicts over use of limited academic resources, etc.). Even the most proficient of peer mediators may be ill prepared to handle conflicts that involve deep-seated and emotionally charged attitudes and behaviors, such as homophobia and sexual harassment (Casella, 2001a). In such cases, the guidance and intervention of teachers and other school personnel may be necessary.

Diversity in Self-Regulation

Children differ considerably in their ability to regulate their behavior and cognitive processes. To some extent, an aspect of temperament known as **effortful control** seems to play a role. In particular, some children are better able than others to inhibit dominant responses when other, less dominant responses might be more productive (Bates & Pettit, 2007; Rothbart et al., 2007). Children who show high levels of effortful control can better plan ahead, focus their attention where they need to, and keep inappropriate emotional reactions in check. Such children also tend to be better behaved in class and to achieve at higher levels than their classmates with less self-control (Blair & Razza, 2007; Liew, McTigue, Barrois, & Hughes, 2008; Valiente, Lemery-Calfant, Swanon, & Reiser, 2008).

But culture, too, seems to make a difference. Some cultural groups—for instance, many East Asian cultures—place particular importance on emotional restraint and self-discipline. Children growing up in these cultures are apt to be hard workers who can focus their attention and work independently on assigned tasks for long periods (P. M. Cole, Tamang, & Shrestha, 2006; Morelli & Rothbaum, 2007; Tyler et al., 2008).

Promoting Self-Regulation in Students at Risk Some students have few outside role models for effective study habits—that is, few people in their out-of-school lives who can show them the self-regulated learning skills they will need to succeed in high school and postsecondary education (J. Chen & Morris, 2008). As a result, these students may have little knowledge about how to accomplish goals such as graduating, attending college, and eventually becoming successful professionals (Belfiore & Hornyak, 1998; B. L. Wilson & Corbett, 2001). In one study (B. L. Wilson & Corbett, 2001), researchers interviewed middle school students in a low-income neighborhood in inner-city Philadelphia. Many of these students aspired to a professional career (e.g., doctor, lawyer, or teacher) but were certainly not on track toward their career goals: They misbehaved in class, completed homework inconsistently, and often skipped school. They had an overly simplistic notion of what it would take to turn their lives around, as this interview with one of the students reveals:

> ***Adult:*** Are you on track to meet your goals?
>
> ***Student:*** No. I need to study more.
>
> ***Adult:*** How do you know that?
>
> ***Student:*** I just know by some of my grades. [mostly Cs]
>
> ***Adult:*** Why do you think you will be more inclined to do it in high school?
>
> ***Student:*** I don't want to get let back. I want to go to college.
>
> ***Adult:*** What will you need to do to get better grades?
>
> ***Student:*** Just do more and more work. I can rest when the school year is over. (B. L. Wilson & Corbett, 2001, p. 23)

effortful control Ability to inhibit dominant responses in favor of other, less-dominant ones that might be more productive; thought to be an aspect of temperament that is influenced by biology and brain maturation.

FIGURE 10.8 On this daily log sheet, 13-year-old Lea has kept track of her math assignments, their due dates, and her performance on them.

First Quarter

	Math Grade Log	Name Lea Demers		Total
				(as needed)
	Assignment	Due Date	Points/Points Possible	
1	Anagram Name	8-27	5/5	5/5
2	1-1 #2-42 even	8/26	5/5	10/10
3	Your Life in Math	8/27	5/5	15/15
4	1-2 #2-52 evens	8/30	5/5	20/20
5	1-3 #2-46 even	8/31	5/5	25/25
6	1-5 #1-36	9/1	5/5	30/30
7	Quiz 1-1 to 1-3	9/2	20/25	50/55
8	4-4's Problem	9/1	6/5	56/60
9	TI Programming A	9/3	5/5	61/65
10	Quiz 1-5 to 1-8	9/10	23/25	84/90
11	1-7 #1-48	9/7	5/5	89/95

This student wanted to get a college education, but in his view, all that he needed to do was "study more" and "do more and more work." Motivation and effort are important, to be sure, but so are planning, time management, regular self-monitoring and self-evaluation, and appropriate help-seeking—things that this student seemed to have little awareness of (B. L. Wilson & Corbett, 2001).

Fortunately, explicit instruction in self-regulating strategies can help students at risk begin to acquire more effective study habits (Cosden et al., 2001; Eilam, 2001; Graham & Harris, 1996; S. D. Miller et al., 2003). Sometimes instruction can take place in structured after-school homework programs, in which students have considerable scaffolding in acquiring such basic skills as keeping track of homework assignments and due dates, identifying the specific tasks involved in each assignment, developing a plan to complete all assignments in a timely manner, and locating helpful resources. But we can also provide scaffolding for self-regulated activities during regular school hours—for instance, distributing forms that students can use to keep track of what they have done and still need to do. A daily log sheet, such as that presented in Figure 10.8, can be used to help middle school students keep track of their math assignments and monitor their performance. The form has its limits, because it focuses students' attention entirely on the number of problems they are getting correct. It provides no place for students to record the types of problems they get wrong, the kinds of errors they make, or any other information that might help them improve. For students with few self-regulation strategies, however, using such a form can start them on the road to effective self-monitoring.

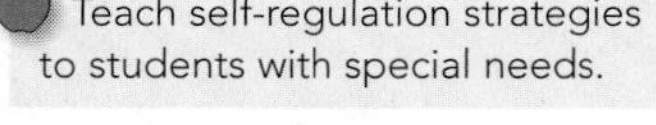

Teach self-regulation strategies to students with special needs.

Supporting Students with Special Needs Students with disabilities often grow up in tightly controlled and structured environments, and some of them have brain abnormalities that make self-regulation difficult. Thus, many of these students may especially benefit from explicit instruction in self-regulation strategies and scaffolded opportunities to self-regulate some of their own activities (Coch et al., 2007; Wehmeyer et al., 2007). For instance, we might encourage students with disabilities to set and strive for their own goals, especially goals that are concrete, specific, and accomplishable within a short time period. These students are also well served when we teach them self-monitoring, self-reinforcement techniques, and self-regulated problem-solving skills (C. E. Cunningham & Cunningham, 2006; Mithaug & Mithaug, 2003; Reid et al., 2005; J. R. Sullivan & Conoley, 2004).

Table 10.3 presents a social cognitive perspective of characteristics commonly seen in students with special needs. It also presents numerous strategies for promoting the academic and social success of these students.

Revisiting Reciprocal Causation

In our discussion of social cognitive theory, we've discovered how environmental factors—reinforcement, teacher scaffolding, and so on—might influence learners' behaviors. We've also identified personal factors (e.g., self-efficacy, self-determined standards and goals) that learners bring with them to new tasks. From a social cognitive perspective, all three of these factors—environment, behavior, and person—mutually influence one another in a phenomenon known as *reciprocal causation.* Several examples of these reciprocal influences are presented in the "General Examples" column in Table 10.4.

Students in Inclusive Settings

TABLE 10.3
Applying Social Cognitive Theory with Students Who Have Special Educational Needs

Category	Characteristics You Might Observe	Suggested Strategies
Students with specific cognitive or academic difficulties	• Difficulty predicting the consequences of specific behaviors • Low self-efficacy for academic tasks in areas where there has been a history of failure • Less self-regulation of learning and behavior	• Help students form more realistic expectations about the consequences of their behaviors. • Scaffold students' efforts on academic tasks to increase the probability of success. • Identify students' areas of strength, and give them opportunities to tutor peers in those areas. • Teach self-regulation strategies (e.g., goal setting and planning, self-monitoring, self-instructions, self-reinforcement).
Students with social or behavioral problems	• Unusual difficulty in learning from models and other aspects of the social environment (for many students with autism spectrum disorders) • Difficulties in planning a productive course of action and in predicting the likely consequences of specific behaviors • Friendships with peers who are poor models of effective social skills and prosocial behavior (for some students with emotional and behavioral disorders) • Less self-regulation of emotions and behaviors • Deficits in social problem solving	• Model appropriate classroom behaviors; combine modeling with explicit verbal instruction, and use visual aids to communicate desired behaviors. • Discuss possible consequences of various courses of action when social conflicts arise. • Provide opportunities for students to interact with peers who model effective social and prosocial behaviors. • Videotape students as they exhibit appropriate behaviors, and then have them observe themselves as models for such behaviors. • Teach self-regulation strategies (e.g., self-monitoring, self-instructions, self-regulated problem solving). • Help students recognize and interpret other people's body language and other social cues.
Students with general delays in cognitive and social functioning	• Low self-efficacy for academic tasks • Tendency to watch others for guidance about how to behave • Low goals for achievement (possibly as a way of avoiding failure) • Little or no self-regulation of learning and behavior	• Scaffold students' efforts on academic tasks to increase the probability of success. • Model desired behaviors; identify peers who can also serve as appropriate models. • Encourage students to set high yet realistic goals for achievement. • Promote self-regulation (e.g., by teaching self-monitoring, self-instructions, self-reinforcement).
Students with physical or sensory challenges	• Few opportunities to develop self-regulation skills because of health limitations and/or a tightly controlled environment	• Teach skills that promote self-sufficiency and independence. • Teach students to make positive self-statements (e.g., "I can do it!") to enhance their self-efficacy for acting independently.
Students with advanced cognitive development	• High self-efficacy for academic tasks • High goals for performance • More effective self-regulated learning • A history of easy successes and, hence, little experience dealing productively with failure (for some students)	• Provide the academic support that students need to reach high goals. • Provide opportunities for independent study. • Provide challenging tasks, including some at which students may initially fail; teach constructive strategies for dealing with failure (e.g., persistence, using errors to guide future practice efforts).

Sources: Bandura, 1989; Beirne-Smith et al., 2006; Biemiller, Shany, Inglis, & Meichenbaum, 1998; Coch, Dawson, & Fischer, 2007; C. E. Cunningham & Cunningham, 2006; Dapretto et al., 2006; E. S. Ellis & Friend, 1991; Fletcher et al., 2007; Kehle, Clark, Jenson, & Wampold, 1986; Meltzer, 2007; Mercer & Pullen, 2005; Mithaug & Mithaug, 2003; Morgan & Jenson, 1988; J. R. Nelson, Smith, Young, & Dodd, 1991; Nikopoulos & Keenan, 2004; Piirto, 1999; Reid et al., 2005; Sands & Wehmeyer, 1996; Schumaker & Hazel, 1984; Schunk et al., 1987; Silk et al., 2003; J. R. Sullivan & Conoley, 2004; Turnbull et al., 2007; Usher & Pajares, 2008; Webber & Plotts, 2008; Yell et al., 2001; Zimmerman, 2004.

Compare/Contrast

TABLE 10.4
Mutual Influences (Reciprocal Causation) Among Environment, Behavior, and Person

		General Examples	Examples in Lori's Case: Scene 1	Examples in Lori's Case: Scene 2
Effect of environment	On behavior	Reinforcement and punishment affect future behavior.	Teacher's ignoring Lori leads to future classroom failure.	New instructional methods lead to improved academic performance.
	On person	Feedback from others affects sense of self-efficacy.	Teacher's ignoring Lori perpetuates low self-efficacy.	New instructional methods capture Lori's interest and attention.
Effect of behavior	On environment	Specific behaviors affect the amount of reinforcement and punishment received.	Poor classroom performance leads the teacher to meet privately with Lori and then eventually to ignore her.	Increasing self-regulation and better academic performance lead to more reinforcement from the teacher.
	On person	Success and failure affect expectations for future performance.	Poor classroom performance leads to low self-efficacy.	Increasing self-regulation and better academic performance lead to higher self-efficacy.
Effect of person	On environment	Self-efficacy affects choices of activities and therefore also affects the specific environment encountered.	Attention to classmates rather than classroom activities affects the specific environmental stimuli and events perceived and experienced.	Attention to classroom activities leads to greater benefits derived from teacher's instruction.
	On behavior	Attention, retention, and motivation affect the degree to which a learner imitates behaviors modeled by others.	Attention to classmates, rather than classroom activities, leads to academic failure.	Greater self-efficacy and increased motivation lead to more persistent study habits.

As a concrete illustration of how environment, behavior, and personal factors are continually intertwined, let's consider Scene 1 in the case of a student named Lori:

Scene 1

Lori often comes late to Mr. Broderick's seventh-grade social studies class, and she is usually ill prepared for the day's activities. In class, she spends more time interacting with friends (e.g., whispering, passing notes) than engaging in assigned tasks. Lori's performance on most exams and assignments is unsatisfactory (when she turns in her work at all).

One day in mid-October, Mr. Broderick takes Lori aside to express his concern about her lack of classroom effort. He suggests that Lori could do better if she paid more attention in class. He also offers to work with her twice a week after school to help her understand class material. Lori is less optimistic, describing herself as "not smart enough to learn this stuff."

For a week or so after meeting with Mr. Broderick, Lori seems to buckle down and exert more effort, but she never does stay after school for extra help. And before long, she is back to her old habits. Mr. Broderick eventually concludes that Lori is a lost cause and decides to devote his time and effort to helping more motivated students.

Lori's low self-efficacy (a *person* factor) is probably one reason she spends so much class time engaged in task-irrelevant activities (*behaviors*). The fact that she devotes her attention (another *person* factor) to her classmates, rather than to her teacher, affects the particular stimuli she experiences (her *environment*). Lori's non-self-regulated behaviors and resulting poor performance on assignments and exams (*behaviors*) affect both her self-efficacy (*person*) and Mr. Broderick's treatment of her (*environment*). By eventually concluding that Lori is a lost cause, Mr. Broderick begins to ignore Lori (*environment*), contributing further to her failure (*behavior*) and even lower self-efficacy (*person*). (See the "Scene 1" column in Table 10.4 for examples of such interactive effects.) Clearly, Lori is showing signs of being at risk for long-term academic failure.

Now imagine that after reading several research articles about how to work with students at risk, Mr. Broderick develops greater optimism that he can break the vicious cycle of reciprocal causation for students such as Lori. Midway through the school year, he makes the following changes in his classroom:

- He communicates clearly and consistently that he expects all students in his classroom to succeed.
- He incorporates students' personal experiences and interests into the study of social studies.
- He identifies specific, concrete tasks that students will accomplish each week.
- He provides guidance and structure for how each task should be accomplished.
- To teach simple self-regulation strategies, he asks students to set goals for each learning task, suggests that they reinforce themselves with 15 minutes of a favorite activity after finishing a homework assignment, and shows them how to track their academic progress on graph paper.
- After consulting with the school's reading specialist and school psychologist, he helps students develop more effective reading and learning strategies.
- He gives a quiz every Friday so that students can self-assess some of the things they've learned each week.
- When students perform well on weekly quizzes, he reminds them that they are responsible for their performance.

Let's see what happens next, as we consider Scene 2:

Scene 2

By incorporating students' personal experiences and interests into daily lesson plans, Mr. Broderick starts to capture Lori's interest and attention. She begins to realize that social studies has implications for her own life, and she becomes more involved in classroom activities. With the more structured assignments, better guidance about how to study class material, and frequent quizzes, Lori finds herself succeeding in a subject in which she previously experienced only failure. Mr. Broderick is equally pleased with her performance, something he tells her frequently through his facial expressions, verbal feedback, and willingness to provide help whenever she needs it.

By the end of the school year, Lori is studying course material more effectively and completing her assignments regularly. She is actually looking forward to next year's social studies class, confident that she will continue to do well.

Once again, we see the interplay among environment, behavior, and person. Mr. Broderick's new instructional methods (*environment*) engage Lori's attention (*person*), foster self-regulation, and enhance academic performance (*behaviors*). Lori's improved classroom performance, in turn, influences Mr. Broderick's treatment of her (*environment*) and her own self-efficacy (*person*). Her improved self-efficacy, her greater attention to classroom activities, and her increased motivation to succeed (all *person* variables) affect her ability to benefit from Mr. Broderick's instruction (*environment*) and her classroom success (*behavior*). (See the "Scene 2" column in Table 10.4 for examples of such interactive effects.)

Comparing the Three General Perspectives of Learning

If you have read Chapters 6 through 10 in sequence, then you have now examined three general theoretical perspectives of learning: cognitive psychology (encompassing both information processing theory and constructivism), behaviorism, and social cognitive theory. Table 10.5 identifies some of the major ways in which the three perspectives are similar and different.

It's important to reiterate a point made in Chapter 6: *Diverse perspectives of learning often complement, rather than contradict, one another, and together, they give us a richer, more multifaceted picture of human learning than any single perspective can give us by itself.* All three perspectives provide valuable lessons about how to help students achieve in the classroom. For instance, principles from cognitive psychology give us ideas about how we can help students remember information and apply it to new situations and problems. Principles from behaviorism yield strategies for helping students develop and maintain more productive classroom behaviors. Principles from social cognitive theory show us how we can effectively model the skills we want students to acquire and how we can promote greater self-regulation. And principles from all three perspectives are useful for motivating students to succeed in the classroom, as you will discover in Chapter 11.

Compare/Contrast

TABLE 10.5
Comparing the Three Perspectives of Learning

Issue	Cognitive Psychology	Behaviorism	Social Cognitive Theory
Learning is defined as . . .	An internal mental phenomenon that may or may not be reflected in behavior	A behavior change	An internal mental phenomenon that may or may not be reflected in behavior
The focus of investigation is on . . .	Cognitive processes	Stimuli and responses that can be readily observed	Both behavior and cognitive processes
Principles of learning describe how . . .	People mentally process new information and construct knowledge from their experiences	People's behaviors are affected by environmental stimuli	People's observations of those around them affect their behavior and cognitive processes
Consequences of behavior . . .	Are not a major focus of consideration	Must be experienced directly if they are to affect learning	Can be experienced either directly or vicariously
Learning and behavior are controlled . . .	Primarily by cognitive processes within the individual	Primarily by environmental circumstances	Partly by the environment and partly by cognitive processes (people become increasingly self-regulating—and therefore less controlled by the environment—over time)
Educational implications focus on how we can help students . . .	Process information in effective ways and construct accurate and complete knowledge about classroom topics	Acquire more productive classroom behaviors	Learn by observing others and acquire effective self-regulation skills

The Big Picture

As you look back at the sections on basic assumptions, reinforcement and punishment, modeling, self-efficacy, and self-regulation, you should find three general ideas permeating much of social cognitive theory:

- ***People learn a great deal from their observations of others.*** The process of learning new behaviors from models is the most obvious example, but observation has other effects as well. For instance, people learn what behaviors are most likely to lead to reinforcement and punishment in part by watching what happens to others (i.e., through vicarious experiences). In addition, people develop beliefs about which tasks they are and are not capable of doing (i.e., they develop high or low self-efficacy) in part by watching their peers succeed or fail at those tasks. And as people become increasingly self-regulating, the standards they set for their own behavior are often modeled after those they have seen others adopt.

- ***People have considerable control over their learning and behavior.*** Much of social cognitive theory focuses on how people can be masters of their environments. For instance, people can often choose the activities in which they participate, thereby controlling the particular experiences they have. Furthermore, when people observe models demonstrating certain behaviors, they control what and if they learn by paying attention (or not) and by encoding what they see (or not) in particular ways. Moreover, when people self-regulate, they take charge of their own behavior and learning—for instance, by setting their own goals, monitoring their own progress, and evaluating their own performance. Their self-efficacy for various tasks encompasses their beliefs about *how well* they can master and control their environment.

- ***Motivation has a significant impact on learning and performance.*** As we examined the assumptions that underlie social cognitive theory, we noted that people's behavior is often goal directed. Furthermore, people form expectations about the probable future consequences of various behaviors by observing the typical outcomes of the behaviors, and they are likely to exhibit the behaviors that others model only if they think that doing so will benefit them. To be truly motivated—that is, to consciously choose certain activities, work hard at them, and persist in the face of failure—people must have high self-efficacy and believe they will eventually achieve success. Ultimately, many people take charge of their own motivation—for instance, by imposing their own response-reinforcement contingencies and by using a variety of strategies for keeping themselves on task during independent learning activities.

Practice for Your Licensure Exam

Teacher's Lament

"Sometimes a teacher just can't win," complains Mr. Adams, a sixth-grade teacher. "At the beginning of the year, I told my students that homework assignments would count for 20% of their grades. Yet some students hardly ever turned in any homework, even though I continually reminded them about their assignments. After reconsidering the situation, I decided that I probably shouldn't use homework as a criterion for grading. After all, in this poor, inner-city neighborhood, many kids don't have a quiet place to study at home.

"So in November, I told my class that I wouldn't be counting homework assignments when I calculated grades for the first report card. Naturally, some students—the ones who hadn't been doing their homework—seemed relieved. But the students who *had* been doing it were absolutely furious! And now hardly anyone turns in homework anymore."

1. **Multiple-choice question:**

   Which one of the following statements best uses principles from social cognitive theory to explain why the students who had regularly been doing their homework were so upset?

   a. Switching grading policies midstream, as Mr. Adams did, was a form of negative reinforcement.
   b. The nonoccurrence of expected reinforcement for completing homework was a form of punishment.
   c. By not giving credit for homework assignments, Mr. Adams significantly reduced students' self-efficacy regarding academic subject matter.
   d. Reciprocal causation was at work: The students were essentially retaliating against their teacher for his unexpected change in grading policy.

2. **Constructed-response question:**

   What might Mr. Adams do to encourage and help all students to complete homework assignments? Basing your discussion on principles of self-regulation, describe at least three different strategies in specific, concrete terms.

Go to Chapter 10 of the Book-Specific Resources in **MyEducationLab**, and click on "Practice for Your Licensure Exam" to answer the questions presented in the exercise. Compare your responses with the feedback provided.

PRAXIS

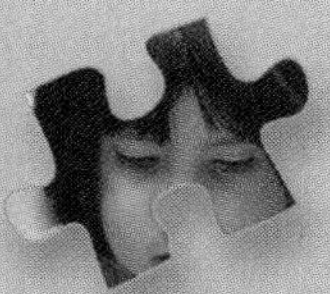

Turn to Appendix C, "Matching Book and MyEducationLab Content to the Praxis Principles of Learning and Teaching Tests," to discover sections of this chapter that may be especially applicable to the Praxis tests.

The Big Picture

As you look back at the sections on basic assumptions, reinforcement and punishment, modeling, self-efficacy, and self-regulation, you should find three general ideas permeating much of social cognitive theory:

- ***People learn a great deal from their observations of others.*** The process of learning new behaviors from models is the most obvious example, but observation has other effects as well. For instance, people learn what behaviors are most likely to lead to reinforcement and punishment in part by watching what happens to others (i.e., through vicarious experiences). In addition, people develop beliefs about which tasks they are and are not capable of doing (i.e., they develop high or low self-efficacy) in part by watching their peers succeed or fail at those tasks. And as people become increasingly self-regulating, the standards they set for their own behavior are often modeled after those they have seen others adopt.

- ***People have considerable control over their learning and behavior.*** Much of social cognitive theory focuses on how people can be masters of their environments. For instance, people can often choose the activities in which they participate, thereby controlling the particular experiences they have. Furthermore, when people observe models demonstrating certain behaviors, they control what and if they learn by paying attention (or not) and by encoding what they see (or not) in particular ways. Moreover, when people self-regulate, they take charge of their own behavior and learning—for instance, by setting their own goals, monitoring their own progress, and evaluating their own performance. Their self-efficacy for various tasks encompasses their beliefs about *how well* they can master and control their environment.

- ***Motivation has a significant impact on learning and performance.*** As we examined the assumptions that underlie social cognitive theory, we noted that people's behavior is often goal directed. Furthermore, people form expectations about the probable future consequences of various behaviors by observing the typical outcomes of the behaviors, and they are likely to exhibit the behaviors that others model only if they think that doing so will benefit them. To be truly motivated—that is, to consciously choose certain activities, work hard at them, and persist in the face of failure—people must have high self-efficacy and believe they will eventually achieve success. Ultimately, many people take charge of their own motivation—for instance, by imposing their own response-reinforcement contingencies and by using a variety of strategies for keeping themselves on task during independent learning activities.

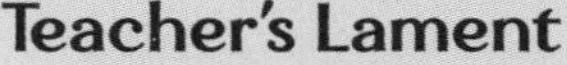

Practice for Your Licensure Exam

Teacher's Lament

"Sometimes a teacher just can't win," complains Mr. Adams, a sixth-grade teacher. "At the beginning of the year, I told my students that homework assignments would count for 20% of their grades. Yet some students hardly ever turned in any homework, even though I continually reminded them about their assignments. After reconsidering the situation, I decided that I probably shouldn't use homework as a criterion for grading. After all, in this poor, inner-city neighborhood, many kids don't have a quiet place to study at home.

"So in November, I told my class that I wouldn't be counting homework assignments when I calculated grades for the first report card. Naturally, some students—the ones who hadn't been doing their homework—seemed relieved. But the students who *had* been doing it were absolutely furious! And now hardly anyone turns in homework anymore."

1. **Multiple-choice question:**

   Which one of the following statements best uses principles from social cognitive theory to explain why the students who had regularly been doing their homework were so upset?

   a. Switching grading policies midstream, as Mr. Adams did, was a form of negative reinforcement.
   b. The nonoccurrence of expected reinforcement for completing homework was a form of punishment.
   c. By not giving credit for homework assignments, Mr. Adams significantly reduced students' self-efficacy regarding academic subject matter.
   d. Reciprocal causation was at work: The students were essentially retaliating against their teacher for his unexpected change in grading policy.

2. **Constructed-response question:**

   What might Mr. Adams do to encourage and help all students to complete homework assignments? Basing your discussion on principles of self-regulation, describe at least three different strategies in specific, concrete terms.

Go to Chapter 10 of the Book-Specific Resources in **MyEducationLab**, and click on "Practice for Your Licensure Exam" to answer the questions presented in the exercise. Compare your responses with the feedback provided.

PRAXIS

Turn to Appendix C, "Matching Book and MyEducationLab Content to the Praxis Principles of Learning and Teaching Tests," to discover sections of this chapter that may be especially applicable to the Praxis tests.

Now go to MyEducationLab (**www.myeducationlab.com**) where you can:

- Find learning outcomes for Social Cognitive Perspectives, along with the national standards that connect to these outcomes.
- Complete Assignments and Activities that can help you more deeply understand the chapter content.
- Engage in Building Teaching Skills and Dispositions exercises in which you can apply and practice core teaching skills identified in the chapter.
- Access Book-Specific Resources:
    - Check your comprehension of chapter content by going to the Study Plan, where you can find (a) Chapter Objectives; (b) Focus Questions that can guide your reading; (c) a Self-Check Quiz that can help you monitor your progress in mastering chapter content; (d) Review, Practice, and Enrichment exercises with detailed feedback that will deepen your understanding of various concepts and principles; (e) Flashcards that can give you practice in understanding and defining key terms; and (f) Common Beliefs and Misconceptions about Educational Psychology that will alert you to typical misunderstandings in educational psychology classes.
    - Video Examples of various concepts and principles presented in the chapter.
    - A Practice for Your Licensure Exam exercise that resembles the kinds of questions appearing on many teacher licensure tests.

CHAPTER OUTLINE

- CASE STUDY: PASSING ALGEBRA
- THE NATURE OF MOTIVATION
  Extrinsic versus Intrinsic Motivation
- BASIC HUMAN NEEDS
  Arousal • Competence and Self-Worth • Self-Determination • Relatedness • Universality and Diversity in Basic Needs • A Possible Hierarchy of Needs: Maslow's Theory
- COGNITIVE FACTORS IN MOTIVATION
  Interests • Expectancies and Values • Goals • Attributions • Teacher Expectations and Attributions • Diversity in Cognitive Factors Affecting Motivation
- AFFECT AND ITS EFFECTS
  How Affect and Motivation Are Interrelated • How Affect Is Related to Learning and Cognition • Anxiety in the Classroom • Diversity in Affect
- THE BIG PICTURE
- PRACTICE FOR YOUR LICENSURE EXAM: WHEN PERFECT ISN'T GOOD ENOUGH

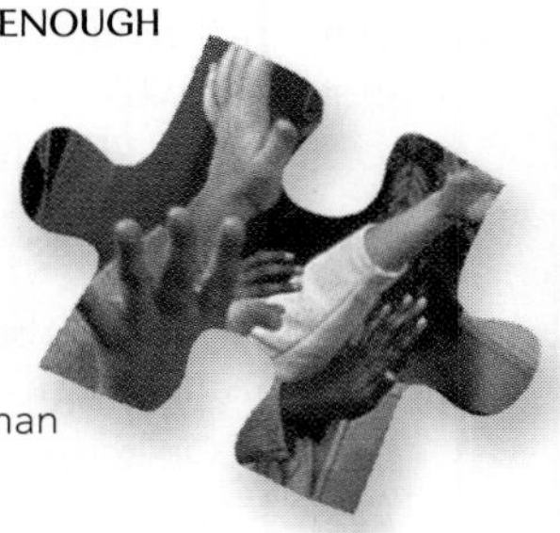

CHAPTER OBJECTIVES

- **Objective 11.1:** Draw on diverse theoretical perspectives to describe the general nature and effects of motivation.
- **Objective 11.2:** Describe several basic needs that seem to drive much of human behavior, and identify numerous strategies for helping students address these needs at school.
- **Objective 11.3:** Explain the roles that interests, expectancies, values, goals, and attributions play in students' motivation, and apply your knowledge of these factors to your own classroom practices.
- **Objective 11.4:** Describe how various forms of affect are intertwined with motivation, learning, and cognition, and explain how you can promote productive affective states in your students.

Chapter 11

Motivation and Affect

CASE STUDY: Passing Algebra

Fourteen-year-old Michael has been getting failing grades in his eighth-grade algebra class, prompting his family to ask graduate student Valerie Tucker to tutor him. In his initial tutoring session, Michael tells Ms. Tucker that he has no hope of passing algebra because he has little aptitude for math and his teacher doesn't teach the subject matter very well. In his mind, he is powerless to change either his own ability or his teacher's instructional strategies, making continuing failure inevitable.

As Ms. Tucker works with Michael over the next several weeks, she encourages him to think more about what *he* can do to master algebra and less about what his teacher may or may not be doing to help him. She points out that he did well in math in earlier years and so certainly has the ability to learn algebra if he puts his mind to it. She also teaches him a number of strategies for understanding and applying algebraic principles. Michael takes a giant step forward when he finally realizes that his own efforts play a role in his classroom success:

> Maybe I can try a little harder. . . . The teacher is still bad, but maybe some of this other stuff can work. (Tucker & Anderman, 1999, p. 5)

When Michael sees gradual improvement on his algebra assignments and quizzes, he becomes increasingly aware that the specific strategies he uses are just as important as his effort:

> I learned that I need to understand information before I can hold it in my mind. . . . Now I do things in math step by step and listen to each step. I realize now that even if I don't like the teacher or don't think he is a good teacher, it is my responsibility to listen. I listen better now and ask questions more. (Tucker & Anderman, 1999, p. 5)

As Michael's performance in algebra continues to improve in later weeks, he gains greater confidence that he *can* master algebra after all, and he comes to realize that his classroom success is ultimately up to him:

> The teacher does most of his part, but it's no use to me unless I do my part. . . . Now I try and comprehend, ask questions and figure out how he got the answer. . . . I used to just listen and not even take notes. I always told myself I would remember but I always seemed to forget. Now I take notes and I study at home every day except Friday, even if I don't have homework. Now I study so that I know that I have it. I don't just hope I'll remember. (Tucker & Anderman, 1999, p. 6)

- **On what factors does Michael initially blame his failure? What effects do his early beliefs appear to have on his classroom behavior and study habits?**
- **To what factors does Michael later attribute his success? How have his changing beliefs affected his learning strategies?**

MICHAEL INITIALLY BELIEVES he is failing algebra because of two things he can't control: his own low ability and his teacher's poor instruction. As a result, he doesn't listen very attentively or take notes in class. With Ms. Tucker's guidance, however, he gains a better understanding of algebra and learns how to use it to solve mathematical problems. He also discovers that increased effort and better strategies (e.g., taking notes, asking questions when he doesn't understand, studying regularly, etc.) *do* affect his classroom performance. Suddenly Michael himself—not his teacher and not some genetically predetermined inability that lurks within him—is in control of the situation. As a result, his confidence skyrockets, and he works hard to master algebra.

In our discussions of development and learning in previous chapters, we've focused primarily on the question, What can children and adolescents do and learn? As we turn to motivation in this chapter, we'll focus on a very different question: How likely are children and adolescents to do what they're capable of doing and to learn what they're capable of learning? Later in the chapter, we'll also look at the nature of emotions—which psychologists often refer to as *affect*—and consider how they come into play in both learning and motivation.

The Nature of Motivation

Motivation is something that energizes, directs, and sustains behavior; it gets students moving, points them in a particular direction, and keeps them going. In particular, motivation has several effects on learners' behavior:

- It directs behavior toward particular goals.
- It leads to increased effort and energy in pursuit of those goals.
- It increases initiation of and persistence in certain activities, even in the face of occasional interruptions and frustrations.
- It affects cognitive processes, such as what learners pay attention to and how much they think about and elaborate on it.
- It determines which consequences are reinforcing and punishing. (Csikszentmihalyi & Nakamura, 1989; Larson, 2000; Maehr, 1984; Maehr & Meyer, 1997; Pintrich et al., 1993; Pintrich & Schunk, 2002; Pugh & Bergin, 2006)

We often see students' motivation reflected in personal investment and in cognitive, emotional, and behavioral engagement in certain activities (Fredricks, Blumenfeld, & Paris, 2004; Maehr & McInerney, 2004). In general, then, motivation increases students' **time on task**, an important factor affecting their learning and achievement in a particular domain (Larson, 2000; E. Skinner, Furrer, Marchand, & Kindermann, 2008; Wigfield, 1994).

Virtually all students are motivated in one way or another. One student may be keenly interested in classroom subject matter and seek out challenging course work, participate actively in class discussions, and earn high marks on assigned projects. Another student may be more concerned with the social side of school, interacting with classmates frequently, attending extracurricular activities almost every day, and perhaps running for a student government office. Still another student may be focused on athletics, excelling in physical education classes, playing or watching sports most afternoons and weekends, and faithfully following a physical fitness regimen. Yet another student—perhaps because of an undetected learning disability, a shy temperament, or a seemingly uncoordinated body—may be motivated to avoid academics, social situations, or athletic activities.

Yet motivation isn't necessarily something that learners bring *to* school; it can also arise from environmental conditions *at* school. When we talk about how the environment can enhance a learner's motivation to learn particular things or behave in partic-

motivation Inner state that energizes, directs, and sustains behavior.

time on task Amount of time that students are actively engaged in a learning activity.

ular ways, we are talking about **situated motivation** (Paris & Turner, 1994; Rueda & Moll, 1994; Turner & Patrick, 2008). As you'll see throughout the chapter, we teachers can do many things to motivate students to learn and behave in ways that promote their long-term success and productivity.

situated motivation Phenomenon in which aspects of the immediate environment enhance motivation to learn particular things or behave in particular ways.

Researchers have approached the study of motivation from several angles, which are summarized in Table 11.1. Within the last two or three decades, the cognitive and social cognitive perspectives have dominated theory and research in motivation (A. M. Ryan, 2000; Winne & Marx, 1989); consequently, they will also dominate our discussion in this chapter. But we must keep in mind that no single theory gives us a complete picture of human motivation. Each of the perspectives summarized in Table 11.1 provides pieces of the motivation "puzzle," offering useful ideas about how we can motivate students in classroom settings.

Compare/Contrast

TABLE 11.1
General Theoretical Approaches to the Study of Motivation

Theoretical Perspective	General Description
Trait theories	Relatively enduring characteristics and personality traits play a significant role in motivation. For example, learners have different *temperaments* that predispose them to seek or avoid novel experiences and social situations. Furthermore, significant *individual differences* exist in learners' motives—for instance, in their desires to achieve at high levels, to interact frequently with other people, and to obtain other people's approval for their achievements and behaviors.
Behaviorist theories	Motivation is often the result of *drives*: internal states caused by a lack of something necessary for optimal functioning. Consequences of behavior (reinforcement, punishment) are effective to the extent that they either decrease or increase these drive states. In recent years, some behaviorists have added a *purposeful* element to the behaviorist perspective: They suggest that learners intentionally behave in order to achieve certain end results (e.g., see the discussion of functional analysis in Chapter 10).
Humanism	Learners have within themselves a tremendous *potential for psychological growth* and continually strive to fulfill this potential. When given a caring and supportive environment, learners strive to understand themselves, to enhance their abilities, and to behave in ways that benefit both themselves and others. Initially, humanism arose largely in reaction to behaviorists' environment-driven portrait of human motivation and was grounded largely in philosophy, rather than in research findings. In recent years, however, a more research-based perspective known as *positive psychology* has begun to emerge.
Social cognitive theories	In the first few years of life, learners are motivated largely by the consequences that follow either their own behaviors or the behaviors of other people. With age and experience, they acquire *self-efficacy beliefs*—that is, beliefs about their ability to achieve desired results in different domains. As many learners become increasingly self-regulating over time, they begin to set *goals* for themselves, and much of their motivation comes from within, rather than from external consequences.
Cognitive theories	A variety of cognitive factors—sometimes in combination with emotional factors—affect learners' perceptions of themselves, of various topics, and of the world at large. Such perceptions, in turn, influence learners' inclinations to engage or not engage in particular tasks and activities. For example, learners tend to be more intrinsically motivated when they believe they have some control and choice in their activities—in other words, when they have a sense of *self-determination.* Also, learners identify what are, in their minds, the likely causes of their successes and failures, and these *attributions* influence their subsequent behaviors.
Sociocultural theories	Many aspects of motivation are the result of social and cultural factors, such as the norms for behavior that parents, peers, and others communicate and encourage. For example, children may initially engage in certain behaviors in order to get parental approval, but many gradually *internalize* the importance of these behaviors and engage in them even in the absence of external pressure and reinforcement. Furthermore, motivation is often *situated* in particular sociocultural contexts. For example, students are more likely to think actively and elaboratively about academic topics when the overall classroom community encourages and supports such thinking.

Extrinsic versus Intrinsic Motivation

Not all forms of motivation have exactly the same effects on human learning and performance. Consider these two students in an advanced high school writing class:

> Sheryl doesn't enjoy writing and is taking the class for only one reason: Earning an A or B in the class will help her earn a scholarship at State University, which she desperately wants to attend.
>
> Shannon has always liked to write. Doing well in the class will certainly help her get a scholarship at State University. More importantly, however, Shannon wants to become a better writer and knows that the skills she can gain in the class will be useful in her future profession as a journalist. Besides, she's learning many new techniques for making what she writes more vivid and engaging.

Sheryl exhibits **extrinsic motivation**: She is motivated by factors external to herself and unrelated to the task she is performing. Learners who are extrinsically motivated may want the good grades, money, or recognition that particular activities and accomplishments bring. Essentially, they are motivated to perform a task as a means to an end, not as an end in itself.

In contrast, Shannon exhibits **intrinsic motivation**: She is motivated by factors within herself and inherent in the task she is performing. Learners who are intrinsically motivated may engage in an activity because it gives them pleasure, helps them develop a skill they think is important, or seems to be the ethically and morally right thing to do. Some learners with high levels of intrinsic motivation become so focused on and absorbed in an activity that they lose track of time and completely ignore other tasks—a phenomenon known as **flow** (Csikszentmihalyi, 1990, 1996; Csikszentmihalyi, Abuhamdeh, & Nakamura, 2005).

myeducationlab

Observe high levels of intrinsic motivation in a second-grade class in the video "Author's Chair." (To find this video, go to Chapter 11 of the Book-Specific Resources in MyEducationLab, select *Video Examples*, and then click on the title.)

Learners are most likely to show the beneficial effects of motivation when they are *intrinsically* motivated to engage in classroom activities. Intrinsically motivated learners tackle assigned tasks willingly and are eager to learn classroom material, are more likely to process information in effective ways (e.g., by engaging in meaningful learning), and are more likely to achieve at high levels. In contrast, extrinsically motivated learners may have to be enticed or prodded, may process information only superficially, and may be interested in performing only easy tasks and meeting minimal classroom requirements (A. E. Gottfried, Fleming, & Gottfried, 2001; Reeve, 2006; Schiefele, 1991; Tobias, 1994).

In the early elementary grades, students are often eager and excited to learn new things at school. But sometime between grades 3 and 9, their intrinsic motivation to learn and master school subject matter declines (Covington & Müeller, 2001; Lepper, Corpus, & Iyengar, 2005; Otis, Grouzet, & Pelletier, 2005). This decline is probably the result of several factors. As students get older, they are increasingly reminded of the importance of good grades (extrinsic motivators) for promotion, graduation, and college admission, causing them to focus their efforts on earning high grade point averages. Furthermore, they become more cognitively able to set and strive for long-term goals, and they begin to evaluate school subjects in terms of their relevance to such goals, rather than in terms of any intrinsic appeal. In addition, students may grow increasingly impatient with the overly structured, repetitive, and boring activities they often encounter at school (Battistich, Solomon, Kim, Watson, & Schaps, 1995; Larson, 2000).

extrinsic motivation Motivation resulting from factors external to the individual and unrelated to the task being performed.

intrinsic motivation Motivation resulting from internal personal characteristics or inherent in the task being performed.

flow Intense form of intrinsic motivation involving complete absorption in and concentration on a challenging activity.

Extrinsic motivation isn't necessarily a bad thing, however. Often, learners are simultaneously motivated by *both* intrinsic and extrinsic factors (J. Cameron & Pierce, 1994; Covington, 2000; Lepper et al., 2005). For example, although Shannon enjoys her writing course, she also knows that getting a good grade will help her get a scholarship at State U. Furthermore, good grades and other external rewards for high achievement may confirm for Shannon that she is mastering school subject matter (Hynd, 2003).

In some instances, extrinsic motivation—perhaps in the form of extrinsic reinforcers for academic achievement or desired behavior—may be the *only* thing that can get students on the road to successful classroom learning and productive behavior. Yet intrinsic motivation is ultimately what will sustain students over the long run. It will encourage them to make sense of and apply what they are studying and will increase the odds that they will continue to read and learn about writing, science, history, and other academic subject matter long after they have left their formal education behind.

Basic Human Needs

Over the years, motivation theorists have speculated that people have certain basic needs. Some needs (e.g., food, water, and shelter) are obviously necessary for physical survival. But theorists have speculated that fulfilling certain other needs may be important for psychological well-being and that these needs may be key ingredients in intrinsic motivation. Here we'll look at four such psychological needs: the needs for arousal, competence, self-determination, and relatedness.

Arousal

Several classic studies conducted in the 1950s and 1960s suggest that human beings have a basic need for stimulation—in other words, a **need for arousal** (E. M. Anderman, Noar, Zimmerman, & Donohew, 2004; Berlyne, 1960; Heron, 1957; Labouvie-Vief & González, 2004). As an example, try the following exercise.

Take Five

For the next five minutes, you are going to be a student who has nothing to do. *Remain exactly where you are*, put your book aside, and *do nothing*. Spend at least five minutes on this "task."

What kinds of responses did you make during your five-minute break? Did you fidget a bit, perhaps wiggling tired body parts or scratching newly detected itches? Did you interact in some way with something or someone else, perhaps tapping on a table or talking to another person in the room? Did you get out of your seat altogether—something I specifically asked you *not* to do? The exercise has, I hope, shown you that you tend to feel better when *something*, rather than nothing at all, is happening to you.

Some theorists have suggested that not only do people have a basic need for arousal, but they also strive for a certain *optimal level* of arousal at which they feel best (e.g., E. M. Anderman et al., 2004; Berlyne, 1960). Too little stimulation is unpleasant, but so is too much. You might enjoy watching a television game show or listening to music, but you would probably rather not have three television sets, five CD players, and a live rock band all blasting in your living room at once. Different people have different optimal levels: Some individuals are *sensation seekers*, who thrive on physically thrilling and possibly dangerous experiences (Cleveland, Gibbons, Gerrard, Pomery, & Brody, 2005; V. F. Reyna & Farley, 2006). Others prefer a quieter existence. I, for one, like physical stimulation a bit on the dull side: You'll never catch me hang-gliding or bungee-jumping. At the same time, I like a lot of *cognitive* stimulation in the form of regular exposure to new ideas, occasional debates with colleagues about controversial issues, and so on (e.g., see Cacioppo et al., 1996).

need for arousal Ongoing need for either physical or cognitive stimulation.

The need for arousal explains some of the things students do in the classroom. For instance, it explains why many students happily pull out a favorite book and read if they finish an in-class assignment before their classmates. But it also explains why students sometimes engage in off-task behaviors during boring lessons—for instance, passing notes and playing practical jokes. Obviously, students are most likely to stay on task when classroom activities keep them sufficiently aroused that they have little need to look elsewhere for stimulation.

Plan classroom activities that keep students continually active, either physically or cognitively.

Competence and Self-Worth

Human beings also appear to have a basic **need for competence**—a need to believe that they can deal effectively with their environment (Boggiano & Pittman, 1992; Elliot & Dweck, 2005; Reeve, Deci, & Ryan, 2004; R. White, 1959). To achieve this sense of competence, children spend a great deal of time engaged in exploring and attempting to gain mastery over various aspects of their world.

One motivation theorist has proposed that one of people's highest priorities is *protecting* their general belief that they are good, capable individuals—something he calls **self-worth** (Covington, 1992). Occasionally, people seem more concerned about maintaining *consistent* self-perceptions, even if those self-perceptions are negative (Cassidy, Ziv, Mehta, & Feeney, 2003; Hay, Ashman, van Kraayenoord, & Stewart, 1999). By and large, however, viewing oneself favorably and demonstrating competence for others do appear to be high priorities (Rhodewalt & Vohs, 2005; Sedikides & Gregg, 2008; T. D. Wilson & Gilbert, 2008).

Other people's judgments and approval play a key role in children's development of a sense of competence and self-worth, especially in the early years (Harter, 1999; Rudolph, Caldwell, & Conley, 2005). Regularly achieving success in new and challenging activities—as Michael eventually does in mathematics in the opening case study—is another important way of maintaining, perhaps even enhancing, a sense of competence and self-worth (Deci & Moller, 2005; N. E. Perry, Turner, & Meyer, 2006; Reeve et al., 2004).

But consistent success isn't always possible, especially when learners must undertake especially difficult tasks. In the face of such tasks, an alternative way to maintain self-worth is to *avoid failure*, because failure gives the impression of low ability (Covington & Müeller, 2001; Urdan & Midgley, 2001). Failure avoidance manifests itself in a variety of ways: Learners might refuse to engage in a task, minimize the task's importance, or set exceedingly low expectations for performance (Covington, 1992; Harter, 1990; Rhodewalt & Vohs, 2005).

When learners cannot avoid tasks at which they expect to do poorly, they have several strategies at their disposal. They may make excuses that seemingly justify their poor performance (Covington, 1992; Urdan & Midgley, 2001). They may also do things that actually *undermine* their chances of success—a phenomenon known as **self-handicapping**. Self-handicapping takes a variety of forms, including the following:

- *Reducing effort.* Putting forth an obviously insufficient amount of effort to succeed
- *Setting unattainably high goals.* Working toward goals that even the most capable individuals couldn't achieve
- *Taking on too much.* Assuming so many responsibilities that no one could possibly accomplish them all
- *Procrastinating.* Putting off a task until success is virtually impossible
- *Cheating.* Presenting others' work as one's own
- *Using alcohol or drugs.* Taking substances that will inevitably reduce performance (E. M. Anderman, Griesinger, & Westerfield, 1998; Covington, 1992; E. E. Jones & Berglas, 1978; A. J. Martin, Marsh, Williamson, & Debus, 2003; Riggs, 1992; Urdan, Ryan, Anderman, & Gheen, 2002)

need for competence Basic need to believe that one can deal effectively with one's overall environment.

self-worth General belief about the extent to which one is a good, capable individual.

self-handicapping Behavior that undermines one's own success as a way of protecting self-worth during potentially difficult tasks.

It might seem paradoxical that learners who want to be successful would actually try to undermine their own success. But if they believe they are unlikely to succeed no matter what they do—and especially if failure will reflect poorly on their intelligence and ability—such behaviors increase their chances of *justifying* the failure and thereby protecting their self-worth (Covington, 1992; Sedikides & Gregg, 2008; Urdan et al., 2002). Self-handicapping is seen as early as elementary school and becomes increasingly common in the high school and college years (Urdan, 2004; Urdan & Midgley, 2001; Wolters, 2003).

A Book That canged me

The Book that canged me was At The Plat With Ken Jriffey Jr. This Book canged me becouse it was my first book that had over onehondred pagis after that I read On The Cort With Mikeol Jorden. I asow liked it becouse it was by Matt Crister the frst spotswiter for Kids.

Mastering new challenges is one important means of gaining a sense of competence and self-worth. In writing about "A Book That C[h]anged Me," 8-year-old Anthony expresses pride in reading his first book of more than 100 pages. Notice Anthony's emerging interest in sports: One book, *At the Plat[e]*, is about baseball, and the other, *On the Co[u]rt*, is about basketball.

Revisiting Self-Efficacy On the surface, the concepts of competence and self-worth are similar to the concept of *self-efficacy* described in Chapters 3 and 10. In theory, however, there is a key difference between the need for competence and self-worth, on the one hand, and the need for self-efficacy, on the other. Having a sense of competence and self-worth may be a basic human need. In contrast, social cognitive theorists have suggested that self-efficacy is certainly a good thing, but they don't go so far as to speculate that it's an essential driving force of human nature. However, one point on which virtually all motivation theorists agree is that students' confidence about their ability to handle day-to-day tasks is an important variable influencing motivation—especially *intrinsic* motivation—in the classroom (Boggiano & Pittman, 1992; Elliot & Dweck, 2005; Harter, Whitesell, & Kowalski, 1992; Mac Iver, Stipek, & Daniels, 1991; Reeve et al., 2004).

Enhancing Students' Sense of Competence and Self-Worth In Chapters 3 and 10, we identified a variety of strategies for enhancing students' sense of self and self-efficacy, and those strategies should enhance students' sense of competence and self-worth as well. For instance, we should do the following:

- Help students achieve success, especially on challenging tasks.
- Give students concrete mechanisms through which they can track their progress over time.
- Minimize competitions and other situations in which students might judge themselves unfavorably in comparison with peers.

myeducationlab

Observe Elena's and Greg's desires for challenge in the video "Motivation." (To find this video, go to Chapter 11 of the Book-Specific Resources in MyEducationLab, select *Video Examples*, and then click on the title.)

Ideally, learners' sense of competence and self-worth should be based on a reasonably accurate appraisal of what they can and cannot accomplish. Learners who underestimate their abilities set unnecessarily low goals for themselves and give up easily after only minor setbacks. Those who overestimate their abilities—perhaps because they have been lavished with praise by parents or teachers or perhaps because school assignments have been consistently easy and unchallenging—may set themselves up for failure by forming unrealistically high expectations, exerting insufficient effort, or not addressing their weaknesses (Försterling & Morgenstern, 2002; Lockhart et al., 2002; Paris & Cunningham, 1996; H. W. Stevenson et al., 1990).

As teachers, we are more likely to encourage students to tackle realistically challenging tasks—and thus enhance students' sense of competence and intrinsic motivation—when we create an environment in which students feel comfortable taking risks and making mistakes (Clifford, 1990; Fredricks et al., 2004). We can also provide greater rewards for succeeding at challenging tasks than for achieving easy successes; for example, we might give students a choice between doing an easy task or a more difficult one but give them more points for accomplishing the difficult one (Clifford,

Create an environment that encourages students to take risks—for instance, through the kinds of feedback you give and the criteria you use to assign grades.

1990; Lan, Repman, Bradley, & Weller, 1994). Once students are intrinsically motivated, they seem to *prefer* challenges rather than easy tasks (Csikszentmihalyi et al., 2005; Reeve, 2006). In general, challenges and intrinsic motivation mutually enhance one another, leading to a "vicious cycle" of the most desirable sort.

To date, most research on competence, self-worth, and self-handicapping has focused on academic tasks and accomplishments. We must keep in mind, however, that academic achievement isn't always the most important thing affecting students' sense of competence and self-worth. For many students, such factors as physical appearance, peer approval, and social success are more influential (Eccles et al., 1998; Rudolph et al., 2005). To the extent that we can, then, we should support students' successes in the nonacademic as well as the academic aspects of their lives.

Help students achieve a sense of competence in social as well as academic activities.

Self-Determination

Some theorists suggest that human beings not only want to feel competent but also want to have a sense of autonomy and self-direction regarding the things they do and the courses their lives take. In other words, human beings may have a basic **need for self-determination** (d'Ailly, 2003; deCharms, 1972; Reeve et al., 2004; R. M. Ryan & Deci, 2000). For instance, when we think "I *want* to do this" or "I would *find it valuable* to do that," we have a high sense of self-determination. In contrast, when we think "I *have to*" or "I *should*," we are telling ourselves that someone or something else is making decisions for us. To experience the latter situation, try the following exercise.

EXPERIENCING FIRSTHAND
Painting Between the Lines

Imagine that I give you a set of watercolor paints, a paintbrush, two sheets of paper (a fairly small one glued on top of a larger one), and some paper towels. I ask you to paint a picture of your house, apartment building, or dormitory and then give you the following instructions:

> Before you begin, I want to tell you some things you will have to do. There are rules that I have about painting. You have to keep the paints clean. You can paint only on this small sheet of paper, so don't spill any paint on the big sheet. And you must wash out your brush and wipe it with a paper towel before you switch to a new color of paint, so that you don't get the colors all mixed up. In general, I want you to be a good art student and not make a mess with the paints (based on Koestner, Ryan, Bernieri, & Holt, 1984, p. 239).

How much fun do you think your task would be? After reading my rules, how eager are you to begin painting?

My rules about painting are somewhat restrictive, aren't they? In fact, they are quite *controlling:* They make it clear that I am in charge of the situation and that you, as the artist, have little choice about how to go about your task. By diminishing your sense of self-determination, my rules would undermine any intrinsic motivation you might have to paint the picture I asked of you, and you would probably be less creative in your painting than you might be otherwise (Amabile & Hennessey, 1992; Koestner et al., 1984; Reeve, 2006).

In general, students with a sense of self-determination are more intrinsically motivated to engage in school activities, tend to achieve at higher levels, and are more likely to complete their high school education (Hardré & Reeve, 2003; Reeve, Bolt, & Cai, 1999; Shernoff, Knauth, & Makris, 2000; Vansteenkiste, Lens, & Deci, 2006). Even kindergartners seem to prefer classroom activities of their own choosing; their perceptions of autonomy versus control are often seen in their notions of *play* and *work* (E. J. Langer, 1997;

need for self-determination Basic need to believe that one has some autonomy and control regarding the course of one's life.

Paley, 1984). The following conversation with several girls in Ms. Paley's kindergarten class illustrates this point:

Students are more likely to be intrinsically motivated when they have a sense of self-determination about what they are doing.

Mary Ann: The boys don't like to work.

Ms. Paley: They're making a huge train setup right now.

Mary Ann: That's not work. It's just playing.

Ms. Paley: When do girls play?

Charlotte: In the doll corner.

Ms. Paley: How about at the painting table?

Mary Ann: That's work. You could call it play sometimes, but it's really schoolwork.

Ms. Paley: When is it work and when is it play?

Clarice: If you paint a real picture, it's work, but if you splatter or pour into an egg carton, then it's play.

Charlotte: It's mostly work, because that's where the teacher tells you how to do stuff. (Paley, 1984, pp. 30–31)

Enhancing Students' Sense of Self-Determination Naturally, we can't always give students total freedom about what they will and will not do in the classroom. Nor can we always convince them that classroom activities are really play rather than work. Nevertheless, we can do a number of things to enhance students' sense of self-determination about school-related tasks and assignments:

Provide opportunities for independent work and decision making. Opportunities to work and make decisions independently not only foster self-regulation skills (see Chapter 10) but also enhance students' sense of self-determination. For instance, we might have students tackle challenging tasks through small-group work or practice new skills through computer-based instruction, and we can give students considerable autonomy in the extracurricular activities we supervise (Larson, 2000; Stefanou, Perencevich, DiCintio, & Turner, 2004; Swan, Mitrani, Guerrero, Cheung, & Schoener, 1990).

Giving students autonomy in some activities doesn't mean removing *all* structure, however (H. A. Davis, 2003; Larson, 2000; Reeve, 2006). Some scaffolding—tailored to students' developmental levels, of course—is essential not only for helping students master important topics and skills but also for enhancing their sense of self-determination. For example, we can establish general routines and procedures that students should follow as they work, thereby minimizing the need to give explicit instructions for each and every assignment (Spaulding, 1992). And if we clearly communicate expectations for performance (e.g., by providing evaluation criteria in advance), students will know exactly what they need to do to be successful (Reeve, 2006).

Present rules and instructions in an informational rather than controlling manner. Virtually every classroom needs a few rules and procedures to ensure that students act appropriately and activities run smoothly. The challenge is to present these rules and procedures without communicating a message of *control.* Instead, we can present them as *information*—for instance, as conditions that can help students accomplish classroom objectives (Deci, 1992; Koestner et al., 1984; Reeve et al., 2004). Here are two examples:

- "We can make sure everyone has an equal chance to speak and be heard if we listen without interrupting and if we raise our hands when we want to contribute to the discussion."
- "I'm giving you a particular format to follow when you do your math homework. If you use this format, it will be easier for me to find your answers and to figure out how I can help you improve."

myeducationlab

Watch the video "Classroom Rules." Would you characterize the teacher's style as *informational* or *controlling*? (To find this video, go to Chapter 11 of the Book-Specific Resources in MyEducationLab, select *Video Examples*, and then click on the title.)

FIGURE 11.1 In this assignment, a sixth-grade language arts teacher enhances students' sense of self-determination by offering several options for demonstrating understanding of a science fiction book.

Choose One!

SCIENCE FICTION BOOK PROJECTS

____ Write a "Dear Abby" letter from one of the main characters, in which he or she asks for advice on solving his or her main problem. Then answer the letter.

____ Draw a time line of the main events of the book.

____ Create a comic book or a comic strip page that features a major scene from the book in each box.

____ Make a collage of objects and printed words from newspapers and magazines that give the viewer a feeling for the mood of the book.

____ Your book probably takes place in an unusual or exotic setting, so illustrate and write a travel brochure describing that location.

____ Imagine yourself as a scientist who has been asked to explain the unusual events in the book. Write up a report in scientific style.

____ With other students who have read the same book, plan a bulletin board display. Write a plot summary; character and setting descriptions; discussions of special passages. Each group member must contribute one artistic piece—for example, new book cover, bookmark, poster, banner, some of the ideas listed above. Arrange the writing and artwork under a colorful heading announcing the book.

Give students opportunities to make choices. Sometimes there is only one way to accomplish a particular instructional objective. But at other times, a variety of routes will lead to the same destination. For instance, we might allow students, either individually or as a group, to make choices—within reasonable limits—about some or all of the following:

- Rules and procedures to make the class run more smoothly
- Specific topics for research or writing projects
- Specific works of literature to be read
- Due dates for some assignments
- The order in which specific tasks are done during the school day
- Ways of achieving mastery of a particular skill or of demonstrating that it has been mastered (e.g., see Figure 11.1)
- Criteria by which some assignments will be evaluated (Kohn, 1993; Meece, 1994; Patall, Cooper, & Wynn, 2008; Reed, Schallert, Beth, & Woodruff, 2004; Stipek, 1993)

When students can make choices about such matters, they gain a sense of ownership about classroom activities (Schraw, Flowerday, & Lehman, 2001; Stefanou et al., 2004). And they are more likely to be interested in what they are doing, work diligently, complete assignments quickly and efficiently, and take pride in their work (Deci & Ryan, 1992; Lepper & Hodell, 1989; Patall et al., 2008; Turner, 1995). Furthermore, students who are given choices—even students with serious behavior problems—are less likely to misbehave in class (Dunlap et al., 1994; S. Powell & Nelson, 1997; B. J. Vaughn & Horner, 1997).

> **myeducationlab**
>
> Observe examples of noncontrolling evaluation in the video "Author's Chair." (To find this video, go to Chapter 11 of the Book-Specific Resources in MyEducationLab, select *Video Examples*, and then click on the title.)

Evaluate students' performance in a noncontrolling way. As teachers, we will inevitably need to evaluate students' accomplishments. But external evaluations can undermine students' intrinsic motivation, especially if they are communicated in a controlling manner (Deci & Moller, 2005; Harter et al., 1992). Ideally, we should present evaluations of students' work not as judgments to remind students of how they *should* perform but as information that can help them improve their knowledge and skills (Stipek, 1996). Furthermore, we can give students criteria by which they can evaluate *themselves* (see Chapters 10 and 14).

need for relatedness Basic need to feel socially connected to others and to secure others' love and respect.

Be selective about when and how you use extrinsic reinforcers. Our discussion of behaviorism in Chapter 9 emphasized the importance of relying on *intrinsic* reinforcers—such as students' own feelings of pride and satisfaction about their accomplishments—as often as possible. One problem with *extrinsic* reinforcers (praise, favorite activities, etc.) is that they may undermine self-determination and intrinsic motivation, especially if students perceive them as controlling behavior and limiting choices (Deci & Moller, 2005; Lepper & Hodell, 1989; Reeve, 2006). Extrinsic reinforcers may also communicate the message that classroom tasks are unpleasant chores (why else would a reinforcer be necessary?) rather than activities to be carried out and enjoyed for their own sake (B. A. Hennessey, 1995; Stipek, 1993).

Extrinsic reinforcers appear to have no adverse effects when they're unexpected—for instance, when students get special recognition for a community service project—or when the reinforcers are not contingent on specific behaviors—for instance, when they're used simply to make an activity more enjoyable (J. Cameron, 2001; Deci et al., 2001; Reeve, 2006). They can even be beneficial if used to encourage students not only to do something but also to do it *well* (J. Cameron, 2001). And if they communicate that students *have* done something well (as a high grade might indicate) or have made considerable improvement, they can enhance students' sense of competence and focus students' attention on mastering the subject matter (J. Cameron, 2001; Deci & Moller, 2005; Hynd, 2003).

Sometimes students may initially find a new topic or skill boring or frustrating and may therefore need external encouragement to continue (J. Cameron, 2001; Deci et al., 2001; Hidi & Harackiewicz, 2000). On such occasions, one effective strategy is to praise students in a manner that communicates information but doesn't show an intent to control behavior (Deci, 1992; R. M. Ryan, Mims, & Koestner, 1983). Following are two examples:

- "Your description of the main character in your short story is so detailed and vivid! It really makes her come alive."
- "Your poster clearly describes every step you took in your science experiment. Your use of a bar graph makes the differences between your treatment and control groups easy to see and interpret."

Another strategy is to teach students to reinforce themselves for their accomplishments, a practice that clearly keeps control in students' hands (see the discussion of *self-imposed contingencies* in Chapter 10.).

Relatedness

To some degree, we are all social creatures: We live, work, and play with our fellow human beings. Some psychologists have proposed that people of all ages have a fundamental **need for relatedness**—a need to feel socially connected and to secure the love and respect of others (Connell & Wellborn, 1991; Fiske & Fiske, 2007; Reeve et al., 2004; R. M. Ryan & Deci, 2000). The need for relatedness seems to be especially strong in early adolescence (B. B. Brown et al., 1986; Juvonen, 2000; A. M. Ryan & Patrick, 2001). Many young adolescents prefer to hang out in tight-knit groups and often worry about what others think of them; some are quite susceptible to peer influence (see Chapter 3).

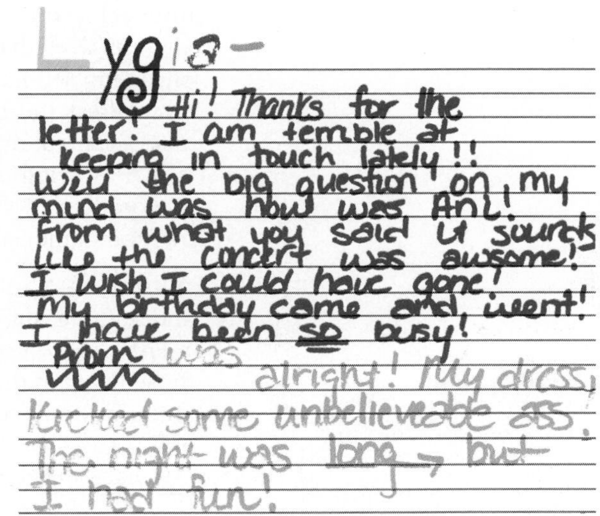

Lygia-
Hi! Thanks for the letter! I am terrible at keeping in touch lately!! Well the big question on my mind was how was Ani! From what you said it sounds like the concert was awsome! I wish I could have gone! My birthday came and went! I have been so busy! Prom was alright! My dress kicked some unbelievable ass. The night was long, but I had fun!

Passing notes in class is one way that some students regularly address their need for relatedness.

At school, the need for relatedness manifests itself in a wide variety of behaviors. Many children and adolescents place high priority on interacting with friends, often at the expense of getting schoolwork done (Dowson & McInerney, 2001; W. Doyle, 1986a;

Wigfield, Eccles, Mac Iver, Reuman, & Midgley, 1991). They may also be concerned about projecting a favorable public image—that is, looking smart, popular, athletic, or cool. By looking good in the eyes of others, students not only satisfy their need for relatedness but also enhance their sense of self-worth (Harter, 1999; Juvonen, 2000). Yet another way in which they might address the need for relatedness is to work for the betterment of others—for instance, by helping peers who are struggling with classroom assignments (Dowson & McInerney, 2001; Lawlor & Schonert-Reichl, 2008).

Enhancing Students' Sense of Relatedness As teachers, we must remember that maintaining good relationships with other people is apt to be among most students' highest priorities. Thus, students are more likely to be academically motivated and successful—and more likely to stay in school rather than drop out—when they believe that their peers and teachers like and respect them (Furrer & Skinner, 2003; Goodenow, 1993; Hymel et al., 1996; A. M. Ryan & Patrick, 2001).

Give students frequent opportunities to interact as they study classroom topics.

Ideally, we should find ways to help students simultaneously learn academic subject matter *and* address their eagerness to interact with peers (Wentzel & Wigfield, 1998). Group-based activities—such as discussions, debates, role playing, cooperative learning tasks, and competitions among two or more teams of equal ability[1] —all provide the means through which students can satisfy their need for relatedness while also acquiring new knowledge and skills (Blumenfeld, Kempler, & Krajcik, 2006; Brophy, 1987; Urdan & Maehr, 1995).

Continually communicate the message that you like and respect your students.

Students' relationships with their teachers are equally important. Thus, we should show students that we like them, enjoy being with them, and are concerned about their well-being (D. K. Meyer & Turner, 2006; Patrick et al., 2002). We can communicate our fondness for students in numerous ways—for instance, by expressing an interest in their outside activities and accomplishments, providing extra help or support when they need it, or lending a sympathetic ear in times of trouble. Such caring messages may be especially important for students from minority-group backgrounds: Such students are more likely to succeed at school if we show interest in their lives and concern for their individual needs (Phelan, Davidson, & Cao, 1991).

myeducationlab

Gain practice in addressing students' needs for arousal, competence, self-determination, and relatedness by completing the Building Teaching Skills and Dispositions exercise "Addressing Students' Basic Needs" in MyEducationLab. (To find this exercise, go to the topic Motivation and Affect in MyEducationLab, and click on *Building Teaching Skills and Dispositions*.)

Universality and Diversity in Basic Needs

The four basic needs we've just examined are probably universal among people throughout the world (e.g., Bao & Lam, 2008; Berlyne, 1960; Deci & Moller, 2005; Fiske & Fiske, 2007). However, researchers have identified distinct cultural differences in how people strive to address three of these needs—in particular, the needs for competence, self-determination, and relatedness.

Achieving a Sense of Competence and Self-Worth In mainstream Western culture, achieving a sense of self-worth often involves being good at certain things and also *thinking* that one is good at these things. In such a context, learners are likely to engage in self-handicapping as a means of justifying poor performance. But not all cultures stress the importance of positive self-evaluation. For instance, many people in East Asian cultures place greater importance on how well other people view an individual as living up to society's high standards for behavior. In such cultures, the focus is more likely to be on correcting existing weaknesses—that is, on *self-improvement*—than on demonstrating current strengths (Chiu & Hong, 2005; Heine, 2007; J. Li, 2005).

Achieving a Sense of Self-Determination The amounts and forms of autonomy and self-determination may differ considerably from group to group (d'Ailly, 2003; Fiske & Fiske, 2007; Rogoff, 2003). For example, adults in some Native American groups (e.g., those living in the Navajo Nation in the southwestern United States) give children more autonomy and control over decision making and do so at an earlier age than do many

[1]Competitions among students of differing ability levels typically motivate only the high-ability students in the group. However, when a competitive event involves teams of equal overall ability, students may have a reasonably high sense of *collective self-efficacy* (see Chapter 10) and be motivated accordingly.

adults in mainstream Western culture (Deyhle & LeCompte, 1999; see the opening case study in Chapter 4). In contrast, many African American adults who live in low-income neighborhoods give children less autonomy than other American adults, apparently as a way of ensuring children's safety in a potentially hostile environment (Hale-Benson, 1986; McLoyd, 1998).

Cultural differences have also been observed in one important aspect of self-determination: opportunities to make choices. In particular, although young people around the world find choice-making opportunities highly motivating, those from Asian cultures often prefer that people they trust (e.g., parents, teachers, respected peers) make the choices for them (Hufton, Elliott, & Illushin, 2002; Iyengar & Lepper, 1999; Vansteenkiste, Zhou, Lens, & Soenens, 2005). Perhaps Asian children see trusted others as people who can make *wise* choices, which will ultimately lead to higher levels of learning and competence.

Ethnic background can be an important factor influencing students' motivation, yet all students have certain basic motives, such as the need for competence, self-determination, and relatedness.

Achieving a Sense of Relatedness Researchers have found several cultural differences in how children and adolescents address their need for relatedness. In comparison to other groups, Asian children tend to spend less time with peers; they place greater importance on excelling in schoolwork and gaining others' approval and respect for high achievement (Dien, 1998; J. Li, 2005; L. Steinberg, 1996). In contrast, some students from certain other minority groups (boys especially) may experience peer pressure *not* to achieve at high levels, perhaps because high achievement reflects conformity to mainstream Western culture (B. B. Brown, 1993; Graham, 1997; Ogbu, 2008b).

An additional factor is family ties: Students from many cultural and ethnic groups (e.g., many Native American, Hispanic, and Asian communities, as well as some rural European American communities) have especially strong loyalties to family and may have been brought up to achieve for their respective communities, rather than just for themselves as individuals. Statements such as "Think how proud your family will be!" and "If you go to college and get a good education, you can really help your community!" are likely to be especially effective for such students (Dien, 1998; Kağitçibaşi, 2007; Suina & Smolkin, 1994; Timm & Borman, 1997).

Point out the value of students' school achievement for their families and communities.

The need for relatedness can sometimes be at odds with the need for self-determination. In particular, achieving relatedness can involve doing what *others* want one to do, whereas achieving self-determination involves doing what one *personally* wants to do. Many East Asians resolve this apparent conflict by willingly agreeing to adjust personal behaviors and goals to meet social demands and maintain overall group harmony (Iyengar & Lepper, 1999; Kağitçibaşi, 2007; J. Li & Fischer, 2004).

A Possible Hierarchy of Needs: Maslow's Theory

What happens when people have difficulty reconciling their various needs? One early humanist, Abraham Maslow, suggested that people tend to prioritize their needs in a fairly consistent manner. His theory predates much of the research on the four basic needs we've examined in this chapter, but two (possibly three) of them are reflected in the five basic needs he identified:

1. *Physiological.* Needs related to physical survival (food, water, oxygen, warmth, etc.)
2. *Safety.* The need to feel safe and secure in one's environment
3. *Love and belonging.* The need to have affectionate relationships with others and to be accepted as part of a group
4. *Esteem.* The need to feel good about oneself (*self-esteem*) and also to believe that others also perceive oneself favorably (*esteem from others*)
5. *Self-actualization.* The need to reach one's full potential—to become all that one is capable of becoming

FIGURE 11.2 Maslow's hierarchy of needs

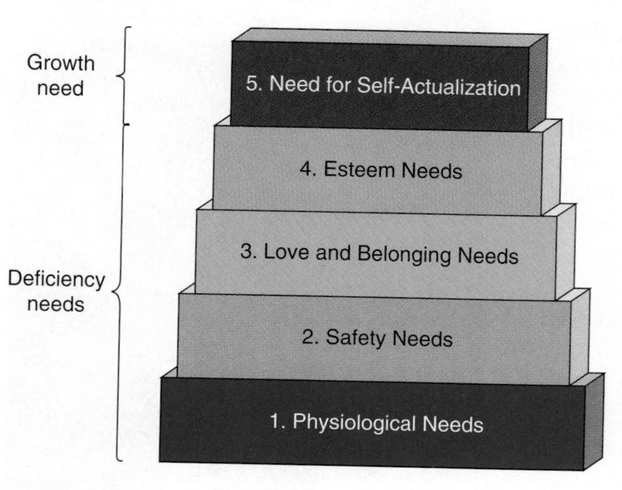

We can reasonably speculate that the need for relatedness underlies Maslow's love-and-belonging and esteem-from-others needs and that the need for competence underlies his self-esteem and self-actualization needs. Furthermore, the need for arousal may sometimes have a physiological basis—perhaps simply in the form of a need to release pent-up energy.

Maslow proposed that the five needs form a hierarchy, as illustrated in Figure 11.2. Specifically, people try to satisfy their physiological needs first, then their need for safety, and still later their needs for love, belonging, and esteem. Only when such needs have been met do they strive for self-actualization, exploring areas of interest, learning simply for the sheer pleasure of it, and so on. For example, a boy with a need for releasing pent-up energy (a physiological need) may become excessively restless in class even though he is scolded by his teacher for his hyperactivity (and thereby does *not* get his need for esteem from others met). A girl with an unfulfilled need for love and belonging may decide not to enroll in intermediate algebra—a class that would satisfy her desire to learn more math—if the peers whose friendships she most values tell her the class is only for nerds. I once knew a boy living in a Philadelphia ghetto who was eager to go to school but often stayed home to avoid the violent gangs that hung out on the local street corner. This boy's need for safety took precedence over any need for self-actualization he might have had.

The first four needs in the hierarchy—physiological, safety, love and belonging, and esteem—relate to things that a learner may lack; hence, Maslow called them *deficiency needs.* Deficiency needs can be met only by external sources—by people and events in one's environment. And once these needs are fulfilled, there's no reason to satisfy them further. In contrast, the last need, self-actualization, is a *growth need:* Rather than address a deficiency in a learner's life, it enhances the learner's growth and development. The need for self-actualization is never completely satisfied; learners seeking to self-actualize continue to strive for further fulfillment. And self-actualizing activities are intrinsically motivating: Learners engage in them because doing so gives them pleasure and satisfies their desire to know and grow. In Maslow's view, total self-actualization is rarely, if ever, achieved, and then typically only by mature adults.

Remember that students are unlikely to work hard on classroom assignments if more basic needs, such as physiological and safety needs, have not already been met.

Unfortunately, Maslow's hierarchy of needs was based on very little hard evidence; thus, many theorists continue to regard his theory as being more conjecture than fact. Nevertheless, it provides a helpful reminder for us as teachers: Students are unlikely to pursue classroom tasks with much interest or energy until more basic needs—needs such as an adequate diet, a safe classroom environment, and the positive regard of their teacher and classmates—have been addressed.

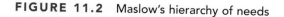

Cognitive Factors in Motivation

Let's return to the opening case study, in which Michael changes from a student who is failing math to one who pays close attention in class, regularly does his homework, and seeks help with things he doesn't understand. Michael's dramatic turnaround illustrates a point made at the beginning of the chapter: *Motivation affects cognitive processes.* But the case illustrates the reverse as well: *Cognitive processes affect motivation.* Michael's initial beliefs about his math ability (i.e., his self-efficacy) and his explanations for his poor performance (low ability and poor instruction) contribute to a lackadaisical attitude: He simply *hopes* he'll remember—but usually forgets—his teacher's explanations. Later, when Michael's appraisal of the situation changes—when his self-efficacy increases and he attributes success to effort and better strategies—he is a much more engaged and proactive learner. As we explore various cognitive elements of motivation in the upcoming sections, we will often see that cognition and motivation interact in their effects on learning and behavior.

Interests

When we say that learners have **interest** in a particular topic or activity, we mean that they find the topic or activity intriguing and engaging. Interest, then, is a form of intrinsic motivation. Interest is typically accompanied by cognitive arousal and such feelings as pleasure and excitement (Ainley, 2006; Hidi, Renninger, & Krapp, 2004; Silvia, 2008).

interest Perception that an activity is intriguing and enticing; typically accompanied by both cognitive engagement and positive affect.

situational interest Interest evoked temporarily by something in the environment.

personal interest Long-term, relatively stable interest in a particular topic or activity.

Learners who are interested in a particular topic devote more attention to it and become more cognitively engaged in it (Hidi & Renninger, 2006; M. A. McDaniel, Waddill, Finstad, & Bourg, 2000). They are also likely to learn it more meaningfully—for instance, by relating it to prior knowledge, interrelating ideas, drawing inferences, and identifying potential applications (Pintrich & Schrauben, 1992; Renninger, Hidi, & Krapp, 1992; Schraw & Lehman, 2001; Tobias, 1994). And unless they are emotionally attached to their current beliefs, learners who are interested in what they are studying are more likely to undergo conceptual change when it's warranted (Andre & Windschitl, 2003; Linnenbrink & Pintrich, 2003; Mason, Gava, & Boldrin, 2008). As you might guess, then, students who are interested in what they study show higher academic achievement and are more likely to remember the subject matter over the long run (Garner, Brown, Sanders, & Menke, 1992; Hidi & Harackiewicz, 2000; Renninger et al., 1992).

Psychologists distinguish between two general types of interest. **Situational interest** is evoked by something in the immediate environment. Things that are new, different, unexpected, or especially vivid often generate situational interest, as do things that involve a high activity level or intense emotions (Hidi, 1990; M. Mitchell, 1993; Renninger et al., 1992). Learners also tend to be intrigued by topics related to people and culture (e.g., disease, violence, holidays), nature (e.g., dinosaurs, weather, the sea), and current events (e.g., television shows, popular music, substance abuse, gangs) (Zahorik, 1994). Works of fiction (e.g., novels, short stories, movies) are more interesting and engaging when they include themes and characters with which students can personally identify (Hidi & Harackiewicz, 2000; Schank, 1979; Wade, 1992). Textbooks and other works of nonfiction are more interesting when they are easy to understand and relationships among ideas are clear (Schraw & Lehman, 2001; Wade, 1992). And challenging tasks are often more interesting and engaging than easy ones (Danner & Lonky, 1981; Harter, 1978; S. D. Miller & Meece, 1997).

myeducationlab

Observe examples of situational interest in the video "Motivation"; in particular, notice 6-year-old Joey's interest in physical activities, 9-year-old Elena's curiosity about new words, and 12-year-old Claudia's eagerness for hands-on activities. (To find this video, go to Chapter 11 of the Book-Specific Resources in MyEducationLab, select *Video Examples*, and then click on the title.)

Other interests lie within: Learners tend to have personal preferences about the topics they pursue and the activities in which they engage. Such **personal interests** are relatively stable over time and lead to consistent patterns in the choices students make (J. M. Alexander, Johnson, Leibham, & Kelley, 2008; Nolen, 2007; Y.-M. Tsai, Kunter, Lüdtke, Trautwein, & Ryan, 2008). Even in the early elementary grades, many children have specific interests—perhaps reptiles, ballet, or outer space—that persist over time. By and large, learners form interests in activities that they can do well and that are stereotypically "appropriate" for their gender and socioeconomic group (Hidi et al., 2004; Wigfield, 1994). Often, personal interest and knowledge perpetuate each other: Interest in a topic fuels a quest to learn more about it, and the increased knowledge and skills gained, in turn, promote greater interest (Blumenfeld et al., 2006; Nolen, 2007; Tobias, 1994).

Ultimately, personal interest is more beneficial than situational interest, because it sustains engagement, effective cognitive processing, and improvement over the long run (P. A. Alexander et al., 1994; Durik & Harackiewicz, 2007; Hidi et al., 2004). Yet situational interest is important as well, because it captures learners' attention and often provides a seed from which personal interest can grow (Hidi & Renninger, 2006; M. Mitchell, 1993).

Promoting Interest in Classroom Subject Matter Almost all students learn more when a topic is interesting; students with little background knowledge in the topic are especially likely to benefit (P. A. Alexander, 1997; Garner, Alexander, Gillingham, Kulikowich, & Brown, 1991). Unfortunately, students often report that they find little of interest in classroom subject matter, especially after they reach the middle school and high school grades (Gentry, Gable, & Rizza, 2002; Larson, 2000).

Ask students to apply newly acquired skills to areas of personal interest.

As teachers, we can certainly capitalize on students' personal interests by allowing some flexibility in the topics about which they read, learn, write, and study (e.g.,

FIGURE 11.3 We can often capitalize on students' personal interests by allowing flexibility in the topics students explore as they work on basic skills. Twelve-year-old Connor gained practice in basic research and graphing skills by surveying fellow students about a favorite topic: cars. His findings are shown here.

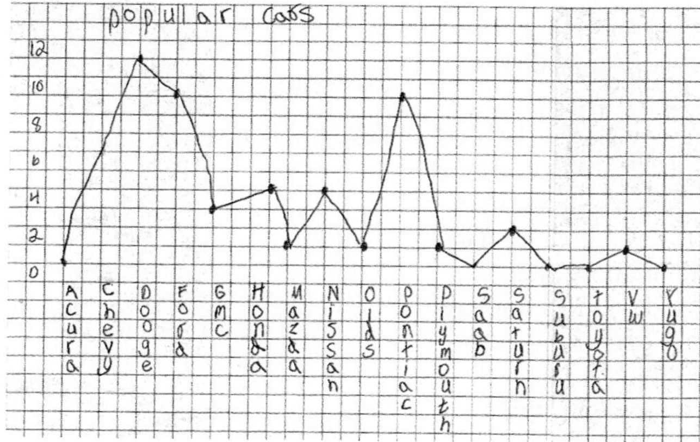

see Figure 11.3). On other occasions, we can temporarily pique students' interest—and perhaps also stimulate the beginnings of more enduring personal interests—through the activities we develop and the ways we present information. Following are several strategies that often evoke interest in classroom topics:

- Model excitement and enthusiasm about classroom topics.
- Occasionally incorporate novelty, variety, fantasy, or mystery into lessons and procedures.
- Encourage students to identify with historical figures or fictional characters and to imagine what these people might have been thinking or feeling.
- Provide opportunities for students to respond actively to the subject matter—perhaps by manipulating and experimenting with physical objects, creating new inventions, debating controversial issues, representing ideas in art or drama, or teaching something they've learned to peers. (Ainley, 2006; Andre & Windschitl, 2003; Brophy, 2004; Certo, Cauley, & Chafin, 2002; Chinn, 2006; Hidi & Renninger, 2006; Hidi, Weiss, Berndorff, & Nolan, 1998; Lepper & Hodell, 1989; Levstik, 1994; Pool, Dittrich, & Pool, 2008; Zahorik, 1994)

myeducationlab

Gain practice in engaging students' interest by completing the Building Teaching Skills and Dispositions exercise "Promoting Interest in Classroom Subject Matter" in MyEducationLab. (To find this exercise, go to the topic Motivation and Affect in MyEducationLab, and click on *Building Teaching Skills and Dispositions.*)

Figure 11.4 presents examples of how we might promote intrinsic motivation in a variety of content domains.

Expectancies and Values

Some theorists (e.g., Feather, 1982; Jacobs et al., 2005; Wigfield & Eccles, 2000) have proposed that motivation for performing a particular task depends on two variables, both of which are fairly subjective. First, learners must have a high expectation, or **expectancy**, that they will be successful. Certainly their prior history of success and failure at a particular task—and thus their self-efficacy—has a strong influence. But other factors also affect expectancy level, including the perceived difficulty of a task, the availability of resources and support, the quality of instruction (remember Michael's concerns about his algebra teacher), and the amount of effort that will be necessary (Dweck & Elliott, 1983; Wigfield & Eccles, 1992; Zimmerman, Bandura, & Martinez-Pons, 1992). From such factors, learners come to conclusions—perhaps correct, perhaps not—about their chances of success.

Equally important, and equally subjective, is **value**: Learners must believe there are direct or indirect benefits in performing a task. Theorists have suggested four possible reasons that value might be high or low: importance, utility, interest, and cost (Eccles, 2005; Wigfield & Eccles, 1992, 2000). Some activities are valued because they are associated with desirable personal qualities; that is, they are viewed as *important*. For example, a boy who wants to be smart and thinks that smart people do well in school will place a premium on academic success. Other activities have high value because they are seen as a means to a desired goal; that is, they have *utility*. For instance, although my daughter Tina found mathematics confusing and frustrating, she struggled through four years of high school math because many colleges require that much math. Still other activities are valued simply because they bring pleasure and enjoyment; in other words, they are *interesting*.

However, we can also envision circumstances in which learners will probably not value an activity very much. Some activities may require a lot more effort than they are worth; this is the *cost* factor. For example, although you could eventually become

expectancy Belief about the likelihood of success in an activity given present ability levels and external circumstances that may either help or hinder performance.

value Belief regarding the extent to which an activity has direct or indirect benefits.

FIGURE 11.4 Examples of strategies for generating interest in various content domains

- *Art.* Have students make mosaics from items they've found on a scavenger hunt around the school building.
- *Biology.* Hold a class debate about the ethical implications of conducting medical research on animals.
- *Geography.* Present household objects not found locally, and ask students to guess where they might be from.
- *Health education.* In a lesson about alcoholic beverages, have students role-play being at a party and being tempted to have a beer or wine cooler.
- *History.* Have students read children's perspectives of historical events (e.g., Anne Frank's diary during World War II, Zlata Filipovic's diary during the Bosnian War).
- *Language arts.* Examine lyrics in popular hip-hop music, looking for grammatical patterns and literary themes.
- *Mathematics.* Have students play computer games to improve their automaticity for number facts.
- *Music.* In a unit on musical instruments, let students experiment with a variety of simple instruments.
- *Physical education.* Incorporate steps from hip-hop, swing, or country line dancing into an aerobics workout.
- *Physical science.* Have each student make several paper airplanes using different designs and then fly them to see which design travels the farthest.
- *Reading.* Turn a short story into a play, with each student taking a part.
- *Spelling.* Depart from standard word lists on occasion, instead asking students to learn how to spell the names of favorite television shows or classmates' surnames.

Sources: Some ideas derived from Alim, 2007; Brophy, 1986; Lepper & Hodell, 1989; Spaulding, 1992; Stipek, 1993; Wlodkowski, 1978.

an expert on some little-known topic (e.g., the nature of rats' dreams, animal-eating plants of Borneo), gaining expertise might require far more time and energy than you're willing to expend. Other activities might seem costly as a result of their association with bad feelings. For example, if learners become frustrated often enough in their efforts to understand mathematics, they may eventually begin to steer clear of the subject whenever possible. And of course, anything likely to threaten a learner's sense of self-worth is a "must" to avoid.

Students are likely to engage in a particular behavior only if they have some expectancy of success *and* find some value in the behavior. Aside from this *both-are-necessary* condition, expectancies and values are related to different aspects of students' behavior and performance (Durik, Vida, & Eccles, 2006; Mac Iver et al., 1991; Wigfield, Tonks, & Eccles, 2004). Values affect the choices students make (e.g., which courses they select, whether they participate in extracurricular activities). In contrast, expectancies are related to students' effort and achievement (e.g., their grade point average).

In the early elementary years, students often pursue activities they find interesting and enjoyable, regardless of their expectancies for success (Wigfield, 1994). As they get older, however, their values and expectancies become somewhat interdependent. In particular, they increasingly attach value to activities for which they have high expectancy for success and which they think will help them meet long-term goals. At the same time, they begin to *devalue* the things they do poorly (Jacobs, Lanza, Osgood, Eccles, & Wigfield, 2002; Wigfield, 1994). Sadly, the value students find in many school subjects (e.g., math, English, music, and sports) declines markedly over the school years (Eccles et al., 1998; Jacobs et al., 2002; Wigfield et al., 1991, 2004). As one 16-year-old put it, "School's fun because you can hang out with your friends, but I know I won't use much of this stuff when I leave here" (Valente, 2001).

Internalizing Cultural Values over the Course of Development Learners' social and cultural environments also influence their values. As children grow older, they tend to adopt many of the priorities and values of the people around them. Such **internalized motivation** typically develops gradually over the course of childhood and adolescence, perhaps in the sequence depicted in Figure 11.5 (Deci & Moller, 2005; Deci & Ryan, 1995; R. M. Ryan & Deci, 2000). Initially, children may engage in certain activities primarily because of the external consequences that result. For instance, they may do schoolwork to earn praise or avoid being punished for poor grades. With time, other people's approval becomes increasingly important for

internalized motivation Adoption of other people's priorities and values as one's own.

Find a reasonable balance between giving students autonomy in their actions and imposing reasonable limits on their behavior.

children's sense of self. Eventually, children begin to internalize the pressure to perform certain activities and to see these activities as important in their own right. Such internalization of values is most likely to occur if adults who espouse those values (parents, teachers, etc.) do the following:

- Engage in and thereby model valued activities themselves
- Provide a warm, responsive, and supportive environment (addressing children's need for relatedness)
- Offer some autonomy in decision making (addressing children's need for self-determination)
- Set reasonable limits for behavior and provide information about why certain behaviors are important (Deci & Moller, 2005; Eccles, 2007; Jacobs et al., 2005; R. M. Ryan, Connell, & Grolnick, 1992; R. M. Ryan & Deci, 2000)

FIGURE 11.5 Sequence in which internalized motivation may develop

1. External regulation: Learners are initially motivated to behave in certain ways, based primarily on the external consequences that will follow the behaviors; that is, the learners are extrinsically motivated.

2. Introjection: Learners begin to behave in ways that gain the approval of others, partly as a way of protecting and enhancing their sense of self. They feel guilty when they violate certain standards for behavior but do not fully understand the rationale behind these standards.

3. Identification: Learners now see some behaviors and activities as being personally important or valuable for them.

4. Integration: Learners integrate certain behaviors and activities into their overall system of motives and values. In essence, these behaviors become a central part of their sense of self.

Source: Based on Deci & Moller, 2005; Deci & Ryan, 1995.

Fostering the development of internalized motivation, then, involves striking a delicate balance between giving students opportunities to experience self-determination yet also providing guidance about desired behaviors.

Internalized motivation is similar, in one respect, to intrinsic motivation: Both forms of motivation come from inside the learner, rather than from outside factors in the immediate, here-and-now environment. But there's an important difference: Because intrinsic motivation seems to arise spontaneously within the learner, it can increase or decrease somewhat unpredictably. In contrast, because internalized motivation is a product of ongoing social and cultural factors and eventually becomes an integral part of learners' sense of self, it has considerable stability and is therefore fairly dependable over time (Otis et al., 2005; Reeve et al., 2004).

The more students have internalized the value of learning and academic success, the more cognitively engaged they become in school subject matter and the better their overall classroom achievement is likely to be (Otis et al., 2005; Ratelle, Guay, Vallerand, Larose, & Senécal, 2007; R. M. Ryan & Deci, 2000; Walls & Little, 2005). Internalized motivation is also an important aspect of self-regulated learning: It underlies a general work ethic in which learners spontaneously engage in activities that, although not always fun or immediately gratifying, are essential for reaching long-term goals (Harter, 1992; McCombs, 1996; R. M. Ryan et al., 1992).

Fostering Expectancies and Values in the Classroom As teachers, we must certainly give students reasons to expect success with classroom tasks—for instance, providing the necessary resources, support, and strategies (recall how, in the opening case study, Ms. Tucker taught Michael strategies for mastering algebra). But we must also help students find value in school activities. Motivation theorists and experienced teachers have offered several suggestions for fostering genuine appreciation for academic subject matter:

- Convey how certain concepts and principles can help students make better sense of the world around them.
- Relate information and skills to students' present concerns and long-term goals.
- Clearly identify the particular knowledge and skills that students will gain from lessons.
- Embed the use of new skills within the context of meaningful, real-world (i.e., authentic) tasks.
- Model how you yourself value academic activities—for example, by describing how you apply the things you've learned in school.

Enhance students' expectancies for success by providing the necessary resources, support, and strategies.

- Above all, refrain from asking students to engage in activities with little long-term benefit—for instance, memorizing trivial facts for no good reason, reading material that is clearly beyond students' comprehension levels, and so on. (C. Ames, 1992; Brophy, 2004, 2008; Brophy & Alleman, 1991; Ferrari & Elik, 2003; Finke & Bettle, 1996; Newmann & Wehlage, 1993; Stefanou et al., 2004)

Goals

Much of human behavior is directed toward particular goals. Some goals (e.g., "I want to finish reading my dinosaur book") are short-term and transitory; others (e.g., "I want to be a paleontologist") are long-term and relatively enduring. Children and adolescents typically have a wide variety of goals: Being happy and healthy, doing well in school, gaining popularity with peers, winning athletic competitions, and finding a long-term mate are just a few of the many possibilities (M. E. Ford & Smith, 2007; Schutz, 1994). Here we'll look at research related to several common types of goals: achievement goals, work-avoidance goals, social goals, and career goals.

Achievement Goals Early motivation theorists proposed that *achievement motivation* is a general trait that learners exhibit consistently in a variety of areas. In contrast, most contemporary theorists believe that achievement motivation may instead be somewhat specific to particular tasks and occasions. It can also take different forms, depending on people's specific goals. For example, let's consider what three different boys might be thinking during the first day of a basketball unit in Mr. Wesolowski's physical education class:

> *Tim:* This is my chance to show all the guys what a great basketball player I am. If I stay near the basket, Travis and Tony will keep passing to me, and I'll score a lot of points. I can really impress Wesolowski and my friends.
>
> *Travis:* I hope I don't screw this up. If I shoot at the basket and miss, I'll look like a real loser. Maybe I should just stay outside the three-point line and keep passing to Tim and Tony.
>
> *Tony:* I really want to become a better basketball player. I can't figure out why I don't get more of my shots into the basket. I'll ask Wesolowski to give me feedback about how I can improve my game. Maybe some of my friends will have suggestions as well.

All three boys want to play basketball well; that is, they all have *achievement goals.* But they have different reasons for wanting to play well. Tim is concerned mostly about looking good in front of his teacher and classmates and therefore wants to maximize opportunities to demonstrate his skill on the court. Travis, too, is concerned about the impression he'll make, but he just wants to make sure he doesn't look *bad.* In contrast, Tony isn't thinking about how his performance will appear to others. Instead, he's interested mainly in developing his basketball skills and doesn't expect immediate success. For Tony, making mistakes is an inevitable part of learning a new skill, not a source of embarrassment or humiliation.

Tony's approach to basketball illustrates a **mastery goal**: a desire to acquire additional knowledge or master new skills. Tim and Travis each have a **performance goal**: a desire to present themselves as competent in the eyes of others. More specifically, Tim has a **performance-approach goal**: He wants to look good and receive favorable judgments from others. In contrast, Travis has a **performance-avoidance goal**: He wants to avoid looking bad and receiving unfavorable judgments. Sometimes achievement goals—especially performance goals—have an element of social comparison, with learners being concerned about how their accomplishments compare to those of their peers (Elliot, 2005; Midgley et al., 1998; Régner, Escribe, & Dupeyrat, 2007).

Mastery goals, performance-approach goals, and performance-avoidance goals are not necessarily mutually exclusive. Learners may simultaneously have two kinds or even all three (Covington & Müeller, 2001; Hidi & Harackiewicz, 2000; Meece &

mastery goal Desire to acquire new knowledge or master new skills.

performance goal Desire to demonstrate high ability and make a good impression.

performance-approach goal Desire to look good and receive favorable judgments from others.

performance-avoidance goal Desire not to look bad or receive unfavorable judgments from others.

myeducationlab

Observe examples of mastery goals in the videos "Portfolio" and "Author's Chair." (To find these videos, go to Chapter 11 of the Book-Specific Resources in MyEducationLab, select *Video Examples*, and then click on the title.)

myeducationlab

Learn more about the possible benefits of combining mastery goals and performance-approach goals by completing the Understanding Research exercise "Combining Achievement Goals" in MyEducationLab. (To find this activity, go to the topic Motivation and Affect in MyEducationLab, click on *Assignments and Activities*, and then select *Understanding Research*.)

Holt, 1993). Returning to our basketball example, we could imagine a fourth boy, Trey, who wants to improve his basketball skills *and* look good in front of his classmates *and* not come across as a klutz.

Effects of Mastery and Performance Goals In most instances, having mastery goals is the optimal situation. As Table 11.2 illustrates, learners with mastery goals tend to engage in the very activities that will help them learn: They pay attention in class, process information in ways that promote effective long-term memory storage, and learn from their mistakes. Furthermore, learners with mastery goals have a healthy perspective about learning, effort, and failure: They realize that learning is a process of trying hard and continuing to persevere even in the face of temporary setbacks. Consequently, these learners are the ones who are most likely to stay on task and who benefit the most from their classroom experiences (Kumar et al., 2002; Sins, van Joolingen, Savelsbergh, & van Hout-Wolters, 2008; Wentzel & Wigfield, 1998).

In contrast, learners with performance goals—especially those with performance-*avoidance* goals—tend to steer clear of the challenges so important for learning, give up easily in the face of failure, and are apt to engage in self-handicapping when they expect to do poorly. Performance-*approach* goals are a mixed bag: They sometimes have very positive effects, especially in combination with mastery goals, spurring learners on to achieve at high levels (Linnenbrink, 2005; Rawsthorne & Elliot, 1999; Wolters, 2004). Yet by themselves, performance-approach goals may be less beneficial than mastery goals: Learners may exert only the minimum effort necessary, use relatively superficial learning strategies (e.g., rote memorization), and occasionally cheat on assessments (E. M. Anderman, Griesinger, & Westerfield, 1998; Midgley, Kaplan, & Middleton, 2001). Performance-approach goals appear to be most detrimental when learners are younger (e.g., in the elementary grades) and have low self-efficacy for classroom tasks (Hidi & Harackiewicz, 2000; Kaplan & Midgley, 1997; Midgley et al., 2001).

Developmental Trends in Achievement Goals Before children reach school age, they seem to focus largely on mastery goals (Dweck & Elliott, 1983). However, performance goals become increasingly prevalent as children progress through the elementary and secondary school grades (Blumenfeld, 1992; W. Doyle, 1986b; Elliot & McGregor, 2000; Harter, 1992). By the time students reach high school, they may find pleasure in learning new things, but many are concerned primarily about getting good grades and prefer short, easy tasks to lengthier, more challenging ones. Performance goals are also common in team sports, where the focus often is more on winning and gaining public recognition than on developing new skills (G. C. Roberts, Treasure, & Kavussanu, 1997).

When children begin school at age 5 or 6, two things happen that orient them more toward performance goals (Dweck & Elliott, 1983). For one thing, they suddenly have many peers with whom they can compare their own behavior; as a result, they may begin to define success more in terms of doing better than classmates than in terms of task mastery. In addition, children may have trouble evaluating their progress on the complex cognitive skills they are learning (reading, writing, mathematical computations, etc.) and therefore must rely on others (e.g., teachers) to make judgments about their competence and progress. As children reach adolescence, two additional factors kick in: They become increasingly concerned about what other people think of them (recall our discussion of the *imaginary audience* in Chapter 3), and they recognize that performing at high levels—in particular, getting good grades—is critical for their future educational and professional opportunities (Covington & Müeller, 2001; Juvonen, 2000; Midgley, 1993).

Many teaching and coaching practices also contribute to the development of performance goals (Midgley, 2002). For instance, consider these common practices:

- Reinforcing students only for correct answers
- Posting only the "best" work on a bulletin board

Compare/ Contrast

TABLE 11.2
Typical Differences Between Learners with Mastery Versus Performance Goals

Learners with Mastery Goals	Learners with Performance Goals (Especially Those with Performance-Avoidance Goals)
Are more likely to be interested in and intrinsically motivated to learn course material	Are more likely to be extrinsically motivated and may be tempted to cheat to obtain good grades
Believe that competence develops over time through practice and effort; persist in the face of difficulty	Believe that competence is a stable characteristic (i.e., people either have talent or they don't); think that competent people shouldn't have to try very hard; give up quickly when facing difficulty
Choose tasks that maximize opportunities for learning; seek out challenges	Choose tasks that maximize opportunities for showing competence; avoid tasks and actions that might reveal incompetence (e.g., asking for help)
Exhibit more self-regulated learning and behavior	Exhibit less self-regulation
Use learning strategies that promote true understanding (e.g., elaboration, comprehension monitoring) and effective problem solving	Use learning strategies that promote only rote learning (e.g., word-for-word memorization); may procrastinate on assignments
Are more likely to undergo conceptual change when confronted with convincing evidence that contradicts current beliefs	Are less likely to undergo conceptual change, in part because they are less likely to notice the discrepancy between new information and existing beliefs
React to easy tasks with feelings of boredom or disappointment	React to success on easy tasks with feelings of pride or relief
Seek feedback that accurately describes their ability and helps them improve	Seek feedback that flatters them
Willingly collaborate with peers when doing so is likely to enhance learning	Collaborate with peers primarily when doing so can help them look competent or enhance their social status
Evaluate their own performance in terms of the progress they make	Evaluate their own performance in terms of how they compare with others
View errors as a normal and useful part of the learning process; use errors to improve performance	View errors as a sign of failure and incompetence; engage in self-handicapping to provide apparent justification for errors and failures
Are satisfied with their performance if they try hard and make progress	Are satisfied with their performance only if they succeed
View a teacher as a resource and guide to help them learn	View a teacher as a judge and as a rewarder or punisher
Remain relatively calm during tests and other classroom assessments	Are often quite anxious about tests and other assessments
Are more likely to be enthusiastic about and become actively involved in school activities	Are more likely to distance themselves from the school environment

Sources: Ablard & Lipschultz, 1998; E. M. Anderman et al., 1998; E. M. Anderman & Maehr, 1994; Corpus, McClintic-Gilberg, & Hayenga, 2006; Dweck, 1986; Dweck & Elliott, 1983; Dweck, Mangels, & Good, 2004; L. S. Fuchs et al., 1997; Gabriele, 2007; Gabriele & Boody, 2001; Graham & Weiner, 1996; Hardré, Crowson, DeBacker, & White, 2007; Jagacinski & Nicholls, 1984, 1987; Kaplan & Midgley, 1999; Lau & Nie, 2008; Levy-Tossman & Kaplan, 2004; Liem, Lau, & Nie, 2008; Linnenbrink & Pintrich, 2002, 2003; E. A. Locke & Latham, 2006; McGregor & Elliot, 2002; Meece, 1994; Middleton & Midgley, 1997; P. K. Murphy & Alexander, 2000; Newman & Schwager, 1995; Nolen, 1996; Rawsthorne & Elliot, 1999; A. M. Ryan et al., 2001; Schiefele, 1991; Shernoff & Hoogstra, 2001; Shim, Ryan, & Anderson, 2008; Sideridis, 2005; Skaalvik, 1997; Southerland & Sinatra, 2003; Turner, Thorpe, & Meyer, 1998; Urdan, 2004; Urdan & Midgley, 2001; Urdan, Midgley, & Anderman, 1998; Wolters, 2004.

Students with mastery goals recognize that competence comes only from effort and practice.

- Grading tests on a curve
- Reminding students of the importance of good grades for college admissions
- Giving special recognition to sports teams that consistently defeat their rivals

All of these strategies are undoubtedly well intentioned, but they encourage students to focus their attention more on performance than on learning.

Fostering Productive Achievement Goals To some degree, performance goals are probably inevitable in today's schools and in society at large. Children and adolescents often use their peers' performance as a criterion for evaluating their own performance, many colleges look at grade point averages and test scores when screening applicants, and many adult tasks (e.g., finding employment, working in private industry, playing professional sports, etc.) are inherently competitive in nature. Ultimately, however, mastery goals are the ones most likely to lead to effective learning and performance over the long run.

Sometimes mastery goals come from within, especially when students both value and have high self-efficacy for learning a topic (Bandura, 1997; Liem, Lau, & Nie, 2008; P. K. Murphy & Alexander, 2000). But classroom practices such as the following can also encourage mastery goals:

- Show how mastery of certain topics is relevant to students' long-term personal and professional goals.
- Insist that students *understand*, rather than simply memorize, classroom material.
- Communicate the belief that effective learning requires exerting effort and making mistakes.
- Give students short-term, concrete goals—known as **proximal goals**—toward which to work; identify mastery goals that are challenging yet accomplishable with reasonable effort.
- Ask students to set some of their *own* proximal goals for learning.
- Provide regular feedback that enables students to assess their progress toward goals.
- Offer specific suggestions about how students can improve.
- Give praise that focuses on mastery of content rather than on comparison with classmates.
- Encourage students to use their peers not as a reference point for their own progress but rather as a source of ideas and assistance. (E. M. Anderman & Maehr, 1994; Brophy, 2004; Corpus, Tomlinson, & Stanton, 2004; E. A. Locke & Latham, 2006; Middleton & Midgley, 2002; R. B. Miller & Brickman, 2004; Page-Voth & Graham, 1999; N. E. Perry & Winne, 2004; Schunk & Pajares, 2005; Turner, Meyer, et al., 1998; Urdan et al., 2002)

Focusing on mastery goals, especially when these goals relate to students' own lives and needs, may especially benefit students from diverse ethnic backgrounds and students at risk for academic failure (E. S. Alexander, 2008; García, 1992; Wlodkowski & Ginsberg, 1995).

proximal goal Concrete goal that can be accomplished within a short time period; may be a stepping stone toward a long-term goal.

Work-Avoidance Goals As we have seen, learners sometimes want to avoid looking bad as they perform classroom tasks. But on other occasions, they may want to avoid doing classroom tasks *at all*, or they may try to put as little effort as possible into those tasks. In other words, learners may have a **work-avoidance goal** (Coddington & Guthrie, 2008; Dowson & McInerney, 2001; Jagacinski, Kumar, Lam, & Lustenberger, 2008). Students with work-avoidance goals use a variety of strategies to minimize their workload; for instance, they engage in off-task behavior, ask for help on easy tasks, complain loudly about challenging assignments, and select the least taxing alternatives whenever choices are given (Dowson & McInerney, 2001; Hemmings, 2004). These students rarely use effective learning strategies or pull their weight in small-group activities (Dowson & McInerney, 2001; Gallini, 2000).

A couple of conditions seem to foster work-avoidance goals. First, students are apt to have low self-efficacy for assigned tasks (Urdan et al., 2002). Second, they may see no payoffs for mastering the subject matter (Garner, 1998). In other words, students are most likely to have work-avoidance goals when they have neither intrinsic nor extrinsic motivation to achieve instructional goals. Thus, students with work-avoidance goals may be our biggest challenges, and we will need to use a variety of motivational strategies—probably extrinsic reinforcement as well as strategies that promote interest and mastery goals—to get them truly engaged in and eventually committed to mastering academic subject matter (Brophy, 2004).

Keep in mind that you may initially have to use extrinsic reinforcers to motivate students who have work-avoidance goals.

Social Goals Earlier, we noted that virtually all people have a need for relatedness—a need to feel socially connected with their fellow human beings. Consistent with this fundamental need, children and adolescents are apt to have a variety of social goals as they interact with others. Such goals typically include some or all of the following:

- Forming and maintaining friendly or intimate social relationships
- Gaining other people's approval
- Achieving status, popularity, and prestige among peers
- Becoming part of a cohesive, mutually supportive group; gaining a sense of belonging in the classroom
- Adhering to the rules and conventions of the group (e.g., being a good citizen)
- Meeting social obligations and keeping interpersonal commitments
- Assisting and supporting others and ensuring their welfare (Dowson & McInerney, 2001; M. E. Ford & Smith, 2007; Hicks, 1997; Hinkley, McInerney, & Marsh, 2001; Patrick et al., 2002; Schutz, 1994; Wentzel, Filisetti, & Looney, 2007)

myeducationlab

In some cases, students' sense of self-worth depends heavily on the approval they get from others. Learn more about this relationship by completing the Understanding Research exercise "Need for Approval and Emotional Well-Being" in MyEducationLab. (To find this activity, go to the topic Motivation and Affect in MyEducationLab, click on *Assignments and Activities*, and then select *Understanding Research*.)

The specific nature of students' social goals affects their classroom behavior and academic performance—sometimes for the better but sometimes for the worse. If students are seeking friendly relationships with classmates or are concerned about others' welfare, they may eagerly engage in such activities as cooperative learning and peer tutoring (Dowson & McInerney, 2001; Wentzel et al., 2007). But if they are more concerned about gaining the *approval* of their peers, they may go out of their way to behave in ways they think will please others, possibly compromising their own standards for behavior in the process and possibly also alienating peers because they are trying too hard to be liked (M. Bartlett, Rudolph, Flynn, Abaied, & Koerber, 2007; Boyatzis, 1973; Rudolph et al., 2005).

Meanwhile, of course, many students are also eager to form productive social relationships with their teachers. Ideally, we would hope that they would see us teachers primarily as sources of support and guidance who can help them master academic subject matter and adjust comfortably to the school environment. But some may be more concerned with gaining our approval, in which case they are likely to shoot for performance goals and may self-handicap in activities at which they expect to do poorly (H. A. Davis, 2003; Hinkley et al., 2001; S. C. Rose & Thornburg, 1984).

work-avoidance goal Desire either to avoid classroom tasks or to complete them with minimal effort.

Career Goals Many students include career goals among their long-term goals. Young children set such goals with little thought and change them frequently; for instance, a 6-year-old may want to be a firefighter one week and a professional baseball player the next. But by late adolescence, some of them have reached tentative and relatively stable decisions about the career path they want to pursue (Lapan, Tucker, Kim, & Kosciulek, 2003; Marcia, 1980). Even in low-income, inner-city neighborhoods, many adolescents aspire to professional careers—perhaps in medicine, law, teaching, or computer science (B. L. Wilson & Corbett, 2001).[2]

Many students, especially those brought up in fairly traditional cultures, tend to limit themselves to gender-stereotypical careers (Lippa, 2002; Olneck, 1995; S. M. Taylor, 1994). Even though traditional notions about what professions are and are not "appropriate" for men and for women are slowly melting away, the majority of college students enrolled in engineering programs continue to be males, and the majority of education majors continue to be females. Certainly gender stereotypes are not the only things affecting students' career goals; students' expectations for success, values, and social goals are also involved (e.g., Eccles, 2009). However, as teachers, we best serve our students when we open their eyes to the many rewarding careers they might consider, expose them to adults of both genders and numerous ethnic groups who are successfully pursuing those careers, and help them achieve the academic successes necessary to convince them that they, too, have what it takes to do well in a variety of professions.

Encourage students to consider a variety of possible careers, including those that have traditionally been associated with the opposite gender.

Coordinating Multiple Goals Most students have numerous goals at any one time and use a variety of strategies to juggle them (Covington, 2000; Dodge, Asher, & Parkhurst, 1989; Urdan & Maehr, 1995). Sometimes students find activities that allow them to address two or more goals simultaneously; for instance, they can address both achievement goals and social goals by forming a study group to prepare for a test. Sometimes students pursue one goal while temporarily putting others on the back burner; for example, they might complete a required reading assignment while bypassing more interesting but unassigned material. And occasionally students may modify their idea of what it means to achieve a particular goal; for instance, an ambitious high school student who initially hopes to earn all As in three advanced classes may eventually concede that earning Bs in two of them may be more realistic.

In other situations, students may entirely abandon one goal to satisfy another (McCaslin & Good, 1996; Phelan et al., 1994). For instance, students who want to do well in school may choose *not* to perform at their best in order to maintain relationships with peers who don't value academic achievement (B. B. Brown, 1993; Ogbu, 2008b). And students with mastery goals in particular content domains may find that the multiple demands of school coerce them into focusing on performance goals (e.g., getting good grades) rather than studying the subject matter as thoroughly as they'd like. Brian, a junior high school student, expresses his concern about leaving his mastery goals behind as he strives for performance goals:

> I sit here and I say, "Hey, I did this assignment in five minutes and I still got an A+ on it." I still have a feeling that I could do better, and it was kind of cheap that I didn't do my best and I still got this A. . . . I think probably it might lower my standards eventually, which I'm not looking forward to at all. . . . I'll always know, though, that I have it in me. It's just that I won't express it that much. (S. Thomas & Oldfather, 1997, p. 119)

Surgeon
I want to be a surgeon
because I can help people
if the get sick and can
treat them so they will feel bett
And can save their lives. I will
study hard for lots of years.

Many children begin thinking about careers in the preschool and early elementary years. Here, 7-year-old Ashton explains why he wants to be a surgeon. His explanation reflects social goals as well as a career goal.

[2]Unfortunately, many students from low-income backgrounds don't have the self-regulation skills to achieve their lofty aspirations (R. B. Miller & Brickman, 2004; B. L. Wilson & Corbett, 2001). For example, see the section "Diversity in Self-Regulation" in Chapter 10.

Naturally, our students will be most successful when their multiple goals all lead them in the same direction (M. E. Ford, 1992; Wentzel, 1999). For example, students might work toward mastery goals by learning and practicing new skills within the context of group projects (thus meeting their social goals) and with evaluation criteria that allow for taking risks and making mistakes (thus also meeting their performance goals). Students are *un*likely to strive for mastery goals when assignments ask little of them (recall Brian's concern about the minimal requirements for an A), when we insist that they compete with one another for resources or high test scores (thereby interfering with their social goals), or when any single failure has a significant impact on their final grades (thereby thwarting their progress toward performance goals).

Attributions

Another cognitive factor affecting motivation is the extent to which learners make mental connections between the things they do and the things that happen to them. Learners' beliefs about what behaviors and other factors influence various events in their lives—including their perceptions about the causes of their successes and failures—are known as **attributions**. To gain insight into the kinds of attributions you yourself might form, try the following exercise.

EXPERIENCING FIRSTHAND

Carberry and Seville #1

1. Professor Josiah S. Carberry has just returned the first set of exams, scored and graded, in your Advanced Psychoceramics class. You discover that you've received one of the few high test scores in the class: an A−. Why did you do so well when most of your classmates did poorly? On a sheet of paper, jot down several possible explanations for why you might have received a high grade in Carberry's class.
2. An hour later, you get the results of the first test in Professor Barbara F. Seville's Sociocosmetology class, and you learn that you *failed* it! Why did you do so poorly? Jot down several possible reasons for your F on Seville's test.
3. You will be taking second exams in both psychoceramics and sociocosmetology in about three weeks. How much will you study for each exam?

Here are some possible explanations for your A− in Carberry's class:

- You studied hard.
- You're smart.
- You have a natural talent for psychoceramics.
- You were lucky. Carberry asked the right questions; if he'd asked different questions, you might not have done so well.
- All those hours you spent brown-nosing Carberry in his office, asking questions about psychoceramics and requesting copies of the articles he's written (which you never actually read), really paid off.

In contrast, here are some possible reasons you failed the exam in Seville's class:

- You didn't study enough.
- You studied the wrong things.
- You've never had a knack for sociocosmetology.

attribution Personally constructed causal explanation for a particular event, such as a success or failure.

- The student next to you was constantly distracting you with his wheezing and coughing.
- You were unlucky. Seville asked the wrong questions; if she'd asked different questions, you would have done better.
- It was a bad test: The questions were ambiguous and tested knowledge of trivial facts.

The amount of time you spend studying for your upcoming exams will depend to some degree on how you've interpreted your earlier test grades. Let's first consider your A− on Professor Carberry's exam. If you think you did well because you studied hard, you will probably spend a lot of time studying for the second test as well. If you think you did well because you're smart or because you're a whiz at psychoceramics, you may not study quite as much. If you believe your success was a matter of luck, you may not study much at all, but you might wear your lucky sweater when you take the next exam. And if you think the A− reflects how much Carberry likes you, you may decide that time spent flattering him is more important than time spent studying.

Now let's consider your failing grade on Professor Seville's exam. Once again, the reasons you identify for your test grade will influence the ways in which you prepare for her second exam—if, in fact, you prepare at all. If you believe you didn't study enough or didn't study the right things, you may spend more time studying the next time. If you think your poor grade was due to a temporary situation—you were ill, the student sitting next to you was distracting you, or Seville asked the wrong questions—then you may study in much the same way that you did before, hoping you'll do better the second time around. If you believe that your failure was due to your low aptitude for sociocosmetology or to the fact that Seville writes lousy tests, you may study even less than you did before. After all, what good will it do to study when your poor test performance is beyond your control?

Learners form attributions for many events in their daily lives—not only about why they do well or poorly on tests and assignments but also about why they are popular or unpopular with peers, why they are skilled athletes or total klutzes, and so on. Their attributions vary in three primary ways (Weiner, 1986, 2000, 2004, 2005):

1. *Locus: Internal versus external.*[3] Learners sometimes attribute the causes of events to *internal* things—to factors within themselves. Thinking that a good grade is due to your own hard work and believing that a poor grade is due to your lack of ability are examples of internal attributions. At other times, learners attribute events to *external* things—to factors outside themselves. Concluding that you won a spelling bee only because you were asked to spell easy words and interpreting a classmate's scowl as a sign of her bad mood (rather than a response to something you might have done to her) are examples of external attributions.
2. *Stability: Stable versus unstable.* Sometimes learners believe that events are due to *stable* factors—to things that probably won't change much in the near future. For example, if you believe that you do well in science because of your innate intelligence or that you have trouble making friends because you're overweight, then you are attributing events to stable, relatively long-term causes. But sometimes learners believe that events result from *unstable* factors—things that can change from one time to the next. Thinking you won a tennis game because of a lucky break and believing you got a bad test grade because you were tired when you took the test are examples of attributions involving unstable factors.
3. *Controllability: Controllable versus uncontrollable.* On some occasions, learners attribute events to *controllable* factors—things that they (or perhaps someone

[3]This dimension is sometimes referred to as *locus of control*; however, as you can see in the discussion here, *locus* and *control* are two distinct dimensions (Weiner, 1986, 2000).

else) can influence and change. For example, if you think a classmate invited you to his birthday party because you always smile and say nice things to him and if you think that you probably failed a test simply because you didn't study the right things, then you are attributing these events to controllable factors. On other occasions, learners attribute events to *uncontrollable* factors—to things over which they have no influence. If you think that you were chosen for the lead in the school play only because you look right for the part or that you played a lousy game of basketball because you were sick, then you are attributing these events to uncontrollable factors.

IN THE BLEACHERS
by Steve Moore

"And remember, kids: If you play to the best of your ability and still lose the game, just blame it all on the umpire."

By blaming the umpire for a loss, children can more easily maintain a sense of self-worth. However, such external attributions are counterproductive when the true causes of success and failure are actually internal and within children's control.

Attributions are an excellent example of knowledge construction in action: Learners interpret new events in light of existing knowledge and beliefs about themselves and the world and then develop what seems to be a reasonable explanation of what has happened. Because attributions are self-constructed, they may or may not reflect the true state of affairs. For instance, a student may blame a low test grade on a tricky test or an unfair teacher when the cause was really the student's own lack of effort or ineffective learning strategies.

In general, learners tend to attribute their successes to internal causes (e.g., high ability, hard work) and their failures to external causes (e.g., luck, other people's actions) (Marsh, 1990; Rhodewalt & Vohs, 2005; Whitley & Frieze, 1985). By patting themselves on the back for the things they do well and putting the blame elsewhere for poor performance, they are able to maintain their sense of self-worth. But when learners *consistently* fail at tasks—especially when they see their peers succeeding at those same tasks—they are apt to put the blame on a stable and uncontrollable internal factor: their own low ability (Hong, Chiu, & Dweck, 1995; Schunk, 1990; Weiner, 1984).

In the opening case study, Michael initially attributes his failure in algebra to two stable factors over which he has no control: low aptitude (an internal attribution) and poor instruction (an external attribution). But as his tutor helps him understand algebraic principles and procedures, enabling him to experience success in class, he begins to attribute his performance to two unstable, internal factors that he *can* control: effort and better strategies:

> I realize now that even if I don't like the teacher or don't think he is a good teacher, it is my responsibility to listen. . . . The teacher does most of his part, but it's no use to me unless I do my part. . . . Now I try and comprehend, ask questions and figure out how he got the answer. (Tucker & Anderman, 1999, pp. 5–6)

How Attributions Influence Affect, Cognition, and Behavior Attributions influence a number of factors that either directly or indirectly affect learners' future performance. First, attributions influence learners' *emotional reactions to success and failure*. For instance, learners are apt to feel proud about their successes and guilty and ashamed about their failures only if they attribute these outcomes to internal causes—for instance, to things they themselves have done. Unpleasant as guilt and shame might feel, such emotions often spur learners to address their shortcomings. If, instead, learners think someone else was to blame for an undesirable outcome, they are apt to be angry—an emotion that's unlikely to lead to productive follow-up behaviors (Hareli & Weiner, 2002; Pekrun, 2006).

Second, attributions have an impact on *expectations for future success and failure*. When learners attribute their successes and failures to stable factors—perhaps to innate ability or inability—they expect their future performance to be similar to their current performance. In contrast, when they attribute successes and failures to

Students are usually happy when they succeed at classroom tasks, but they also feel proud and satisfied if they attribute their successes to internal causes.

*un*stable factors—for instance, to effort or luck—their current success rate has little influence on their future expectations (Dweck, 2000; Schunk, 1990; Weiner, 1986). The most optimistic learners—those with the highest expectations for future success—are the ones who attribute their successes to stable, dependable (and usually internal) factors, such as innate ability and an enduring work ethic, and attribute their failures to unstable factors, such as lack of effort or inappropriate strategies (Fennema, 1987; Pomerantz & Saxon, 2001; Weiner, 1984).

Third, attributions affect *effort and persistence.* Learners who believe their failures result from their own lack of effort (a controllable cause) are apt to try harder and persist in the face of difficulty. Learners who, instead, attribute failure to a lack of innate ability (an uncontrollable cause) give up easily and sometimes can't even perform tasks they have previously done successfully (Dweck, 2000; Eccles [Parsons], 1983; Feather, 1982; Weiner, 1984).

Finally, attributions influence *learning strategies and classroom performance.* Learners who expect to succeed in the classroom and believe that academic success is a result of their own doing are more likely to apply effective learning and self-regulation strategies, especially when they're taught these strategies. In contrast, learners who expect failure and believe that their academic performance is largely out of their hands often reject effective learning strategies in favor of rote-learning approaches (Mangels, 2004; D. J. Palmer & Goetz, 1988; Zimmerman, 1998). Given all of these effects, it should not surprise you to learn that students with internal, controllable attributions for classroom success—rather than external ones they can't control—are more likely to achieve at high levels and graduate from high school (L. E. Davis, Ajzen, Saunders, & Williams, 2002; Dweck, Mangels, & Good, 2004; Pintrich, 2003).

Let's consider how some of the factors just discussed play out in the opening case study. Michael initially attributes his failure in algebra to both his own low ability and his teacher's poor instruction—attributions that probably evoke both shame and anger. Furthermore, because the perceived causes of his failure are both stable and out of his control, he expects future failure no matter what he does and therefore has little reason to exert much effort (e.g., he doesn't take notes). As Michael acquires new study skills and gains a better understanding of algebraic concepts and procedures, he achieves greater success and realizes that his success is the direct result of his own hard work. His new internal and controllable attributions lead him to use effective strategies and be a more self-regulating learner:

> Now I do things in math step by step and listen to each step. . . . I used to just listen and not even take notes. I always told myself I would remember but I always seemed to forget. Now I take notes and I study at home every day except Friday, even if I don't have homework. Now I study so that I know that I have it. I don't just hope I'll remember. (Tucker & Anderman, 1999, pp. 5–6)

Developmental Trends in Attributions Young children become increasingly able to distinguish among the various possible causes of their successes and failures: effort, ability, luck, task difficulty, and so on (Dweck & Elliott, 1983; Eccles et al., 1998; Nicholls, 1990). One distinction they increasingly get a handle on is that between effort and ability. In the early elementary school grades, children think of effort and ability as positively correlated: People who try harder are more competent. Thus, they tend to attribute their successes to hard work and are usually optimistic about their chances for future success as long as they try hard. Sometime around age 9, they begin to understand that effort and ability often compensate for each other and that people with less ability may need to exert greater effort. Many begin to attribute their successes and failures to an inherited ability—for instance, intelligence—which they perceive to be fairly stable and beyond their control. If they are usually successful at school tasks, they have high self-efficacy for such tasks. If, instead, they often fail, their self-efficacy is likely to plummet (Dweck, 1986; Eccles [Parsons], 1983; Schunk, 1990). Table 11.3 summarizes developmental trends in attributions and other aspects of motivation.

The degree to which intelligence is the result of environment (and thus able to improve with instruction and practice) or heredity (and thus stable and uncontrollable) is a matter of some controversy among psychologists (see Chapter 5). Even children and adolescents have differing opinions on the matter (Dweck, 2000; Dweck & Molden, 2005). Those with an **incremental view** believe that intelligence can and does improve with effort and practice. In contrast, those with an **entity view** believe that intelligence is a distinct ability that is built in and relatively permanent. A student named Sarah clearly reveals an entity view in her explanation of why she has trouble in mathematics:

> My dad is very good at math, and my brother, I, and my mom aren't good at math at all, we inherited the "not good at math gene" from my mom and I am good in English but I am not good in math. (K. E. Ryan, Ryan, Arbuthnot, & Samuels, 2007, p. 5)

Students with an incremental view of intelligence and specific academic abilities are likely to adopt mastery goals in the classroom, to work hard at their studies, and to earn increasingly high grades. In contrast, students with an entity view adopt performance goals, quickly lose interest in a topic that doesn't come easily to them, self-handicap in the face of failure, and earn lower grades over time (Blackwell, Trzesniewski, & Dweck, 2007; Dweck & Leggett, 1988; Dweck & Molden, 2005).

Portray intelligence and more specific abilities as characteristics that can change with effort and persistence.

Why does one student see a failure as a temporary setback due to her own insufficient effort, whereas another thinks it reveals a lack of ability and thus signals more failures to come, and still another blames the failure on the teacher's capricious and unpredictable actions? To some extent, learners' attributions are the result of their previous history of successes and failures (Covington, 1987; Hong et al., 1995; Klein, 1990). Learners who have frequently succeeded when they've tried hard are likely to credit success to internal factors such as effort or high ability. Those who have usually failed despite their best efforts are apt to attribute success to something beyond their control—perhaps to an ability they don't possess or to such external factors as luck or a teacher's arbitrary judgment.

Yet factors in learners' current environment also play a role. When a classroom task appears to be complex and exceptionally challenging—and especially if classmates are struggling with it as well—failure can easily be attributed to task difficulty rather than to internal causes. But if peers are performing a task with ease, learners are likely to attribute their own failures to low ability (Schunk, 1990; Weiner, 1984). Another source of information is the attributions adults communicate for learners' successes and failures, as we'll discover shortly.

Mastery Orientation versus Learned Helplessness As children grow older, they gradually develop predictable patterns of attributions and expectations for their future performance. Consider these two students, keeping in mind that *their actual academic ability is the same*:

> Jared is an enthusiastic, energetic learner. He works hard at school activities and takes obvious pleasure in doing well. He likes challenges, especially the brain-teaser problems his teacher assigns as extra-credit work each day. He can't always solve the problems, but he takes failure in stride and is eager for more problems the following day.

incremental view of intelligence Belief that intelligence can improve with effort and practice.

entity view of intelligence Belief that intelligence is a distinct ability that is relatively permanent and unchangeable.

TABLE 11.3
Motivation at Different Grade Levels

Grade Level	Age-Typical Characteristics	Suggested Strategies
K–2	• Focus more on acquiring competence than on self-evaluating it • Rapidly changing interests; often provoked by familiar experiences, fantasy, or entertaining activities • Pursuit of interesting and enjoyable activities regardless of expectancy for success • Emerging tendency to distinguish between effort and ability as causes of success and failure; belief that high effort is a sign of high ability • Tendency to attribute success to hard work and practice, leading to optimism about what can be accomplished	• Engage students' interest in important topics through hands-on, playlike activities. • Entice students into reading, writing, and other basic skills through high-interest books and subject matter (e.g., animals, superheroes, princes and princesses). • Show students how they have improved over time; point out how their effort and practice have contributed to their improvement.
3–5	• Increasing concern about self-evaluating competence as well as acquiring it • Emergence of fairly stable interests • Increasing focus on performance goals • Recognition that effort and ability compensate for each other—that people with lower ability must work harder to succeed • Increasing belief in innate ability as a significant and uncontrollable factor affecting learning and achievement • Increasing awareness of the kinds of attributions that will elicit positive reactions from others (e.g., "I didn't feel well during the test")	• Allow students to pursue personal interests in independent reading and writing tasks. • Demonstrate your own fascination and enthusiasm about classroom topics; communicate that many topics are worth learning about for their own sake. • Identify strengths in every student; provide sufficient support to enable students to gain proficiency in areas of weakness.
6–8	• Decline in general sense of competence (relative to peers) in many academic domains • Increasing tendency to self-handicap as a way of maintaining self-worth during difficult tasks • Increasingly gender-stereotypical interests • Increasing tendency to value activities associated with long-term goals and high expectancies for success • For many students, decline in perceived value of many content domains, such as English, math, and music • Increasing focus on social goals (e.g., interacting with peers, making a good impression) • Emerging realization that high effort cannot totally make up for low ability—that some tasks may be impossible regardless of effort	• Promote interest in classroom topics by presenting puzzling phenomena and building on students' personal interests. • Relate classroom subject matter to students' long-term goals (e.g., through authentic activities). • Provide opportunities for social interaction as students study and learn (e.g., through role-playing activities, classroom debates, cooperative learning projects). • Focus students' attention on their improvement; minimize opportunities for them to compare their performance to that of classmates.
9–12	• Increasing integration of certain interests and values into overall sense of self • For most students, prevalence of performance goals (e.g., getting good grades) rather than mastery goals • Increase in cheating as a means of accomplishing performance goals • Increasing focus on postgraduation goals (e.g., college, careers); for some students, insufficient self-regulation strategies to achieve these goals	• Provide opportunities to address interests and values through out-of-class projects and extracurricular activities (e.g., community service work). • Make it possible for students to attain good grades through reasonable effort and effective strategies; minimize competitive grading practices (e.g., grading on a curve). • Discourage cheating (see Chapter 14 for specific strategies). • Teach self-regulation strategies that can help students reach their long-term goals (see Chapter 10 for specific strategies).

Sources: Brophy, 2004; Cizek, 2003; Dweck & Elliott, 1983; Elliot & Dweck, 2005; Eccles et al., 1998; Hidi et al., 2004; Jacobs et al., 2002; Juvonen, 2000; Nicholls, 1990; Nicholls, Cobb, Yackel, Wood, & Wheatley, 1990; Patrick et al., 2002; Urdan, 2004; Wigfield, 1994; Wigfield et al., 1991; B. L. Wilson & Corbett, 2001; Wolters, 2003; Youniss & Yates, 1999.

> Jerry is an anxious, fidgety student who doesn't have much confidence in his ability to accomplish school tasks successfully. In fact, he is always underestimating what he can do: Even when he has succeeded, he doubts that he can do it again. He prefers filling out drill-and-practice worksheets that help him practice skills he's already mastered, rather than attempting new tasks and problems. As for those daily brainteasers Jared likes so much, Jerry sometimes takes a stab at them but gives up quickly if the answer isn't obvious.

Over time, some learners, like Jared, develop an "I can do it" attitude known as a **mastery orientation**—a general sense of optimism that they can master new tasks and succeed in a variety of endeavors. Other learners, like Jerry, develop an "I *can't* do it" attitude known as **learned helplessness**—a general sense of futility about their chances for future success. You might think of this distinction, which really reflects a continuum rather than an either–or dichotomy, as a difference between *optimists* and *pessimists* (C. Peterson, 1990, 2006; Seligman, 1991).

Even when learners with a mastery orientation and those with learned helplessness have equal ability initially, those with a mastery orientation behave in ways that lead to higher achievement over the long run. In particular, they set ambitious goals, seek challenging situations, and persist in the face of failure. Learners with learned helplessness behave very differently. Because they underestimate their ability, they set goals they can easily accomplish, avoid the challenges likely to maximize their learning and cognitive growth, and respond to failure in counterproductive ways (e.g., giving up quickly) that almost guarantee future failure (Dweck, 2000; Graham, 1989; C. Peterson, 2006; Seligman, 1991).

By age 5 or 6, some children begin to show a consistent tendency either to persist at a task and express confidence that they can master it, on the one hand, or to abandon a task quickly and say they don't have the ability to do it, on the other (Burhans & Dweck, 1995; Ziegert, Kistner, Castro, & Robertson, 2001). However, children younger than 8 rarely exhibit extreme forms of learned helplessness, perhaps because they still believe that success is due largely to their own efforts (Eccles et al., 1998; Lockhart et al., 2002; Paris & Cunningham, 1996). By early adolescence, a general sense of helplessness becomes more common. Some middle schoolers believe they cannot control the things that happen to them (e.g., they are apt to have an entity view of intelligence) and are at a loss for strategies about how to avert future failures (Dweck, 2000; Paris & Cunningham, 1996; C. Peterson, Maier, & Seligman, 1993). In the opening case study, Michael's initial pessimism about his chances of future success in his algebra class suggests some degree of learned helplessness, at least about mathematics.

Many of the strategies we've previously identified for enhancing self-efficacy and a sense of competence (e.g., promoting mastery on challenging tasks) should promote a mastery orientation as well. In addition, students should know that they have a variety of resources—their teacher, their peers, self-instructional computer programs, volunteer tutors, and so on—to which they can turn in times of difficulty. In general, students must have sufficient academic support to believe "I can do this if I really want to."

When working with students who have learned helplessness, be consistent and persistent in your efforts to help them succeed.

Teacher Expectations and Attributions

Teachers typically draw conclusions about their students relatively early in the school year, forming opinions about each one's strengths, weaknesses, and potential for academic success. In many instances, teachers size up their students fairly accurately: They know which ones need help with reading skills, which ones have short attention spans, and so on, and they can adapt their instruction and assistance accordingly (Goldenberg, 1992; T. L. Good & Brophy, 1994; T. L. Good & Nichols, 2001). Yet even the best teachers sometimes make errors in their judgments. For example, teachers often underestimate the abilities of students who come from certain ethnic minority groups or low-income families (Banks & Banks, 1995; McLoyd, 1998; Tenenbaum & Ruck, 2007; Woolfolk Hoy, Davis, & Pape, 2006).

mastery orientation General, fairly pervasive belief that one is capable of accomplishing challenging tasks.

learned helplessness General, fairly pervasive belief that one is incapable of accomplishing tasks and has little or no control of the environment.

Furthermore, many teachers have an entity view of intelligence: They believe that students' performance is often due to abilities that are relatively fixed and enduring (Dweck & Molden, 2005; Oakes & Guiton, 1995; C. Reyna, 2000). This entity attribution leads them to form fairly stable expectations for students' performance, which, in turn, lead them to treat different students differently. For example, when teachers have high expectations for students, they present more challenging topics, interact with students more frequently, and give more positive and specific feedback. In contrast, when teachers have low expectations for certain students, they present easy tasks, offer few opportunities for speaking in class, and give little feedback about students' responses (Babad, 1993; T. L. Good & Brophy, 1994; Graham, 1990; R. Rosenthal, 1994).

Continually ask yourself whether you are giving inequitable treatment to students for whom you have low expectations. Also reflect on your beliefs about students' intelligence: Are you taking an incremental view that gives you optimism about future progress?

Teachers' beliefs about the reasons for students' performance often reveal themselves in the things they say to students (Dweck & Molden, 2005; Weiner, 2000). Consider the following interpretations of a student's success:

- "You did it! You're so smart!"
- "Your hard work has really paid off, hasn't it?"
- "You've done very well. It's clear that you really know how to study."
- "Terrific! This is certainly your lucky day!"

And now consider these interpretations of a student's failure:

- "Maybe this just isn't something you're good at. Perhaps we should try a different activity."
- "Why don't you practice a little more and then try again?"
- "Let's see if we can come up with some study strategies that might work better for you."
- "Maybe you're just having a bad day."

myeducationlab

Observe a teacher communicate controllable attributions in the video "Author's Chair."

(To find this video, go to Chapter 11 of the Book-Specific Resources in MyEducationLab, select *Video Examples*, and then click on the title.)

All of these comments are presumably intended to make a student feel good. But notice the different attributions they imply—in some cases, stable and uncontrollable abilities (being naturally smart or incapable); in other cases, controllable and therefore changeable behaviors (hard work, lack of practice, effective or ineffective study strategies); and in still other cases, external, uncontrollable causes (a lucky break, a bad day).

Teachers communicate their attributions for students' successes and failures in more subtle ways as well—for instance, through the emotions they convey (C. Reyna & Weiner, 2001; Weiner, 2005). Teachers and other adults are often sympathetic and forgiving when children fail because of something beyond their control (illness, lack of ability, etc.) but frequently get angry when children fail simply because they didn't try very hard. As an example, let's return once more to the opening case study, in which Michael is initially doing poorly in his eighth-grade algebra class. Imagine that you are Michael's teacher. Imagine, too, that you believe Michael has low ability: He just doesn't have a "gift" for math. When you see him consistently getting Ds and Fs on assignments and quizzes, you might reasonably conclude that his poor performance is beyond his control, leading you to communicate pity and sympathy in your interactions with him. But now imagine, instead, that you believe Michael has *high* math ability: He definitely has what it takes to do well in your class. When you see his poor marks on assignments and quizzes, you naturally assume he isn't trying very hard. In your eyes, Michael has complete control over the amount of effort he exerts; thus, you might express anger or annoyance when he doesn't do well. Under such circumstances, some teachers might even punish him for his poor performance (C. Reyna & Weiner, 2001).

How Teacher Expectations and Attributions Affect Students' Achievement Most children and adolescents readily pick up on their teachers' subtle messages about their own and others' abilities (R. Butler, 1994; T. L. Good & Nichols, 2001; R. S. Weinstein, 1993). When teachers repeatedly give them low-ability messages, they may begin to see themselves as their teachers do and to behave accordingly (Marachi, Friedel, & Midgley, 2001; Murdock, 1999). In such cases, teachers' expectations and attributions may lead to a **self-fulfilling prophecy**: What teachers expect students to achieve becomes what students actually do achieve.

Teachers who hold high expectations for their students are more likely to give specific feedback about the strengths and weaknesses of students' responses.

A classic early study by Rosenthal and Jacobson (1968) provides an example. In May 1964, researchers administered something they called the "Harvard Test of Inflected Acquisition" to elementary school students in a low-income neighborhood. Just before school resumed the following fall, the researchers gave teachers the names of students who, according to the test results, would probably show dramatic achievement gains during the school year. In fact, the researchers had chosen these academic "spurters" entirely at random—essentially pulling their names out of a hat. Despite the researchers' bogus predictions, the chosen children made greater achievement gains during the school year than their nonchosen classmates, and teachers rated these children in more favorable terms (e.g., as being more intellectually curious). The results were especially dramatic for children in grades 1 and 2.

Certainly, teacher expectations don't always lead to self-fulfilling prophecies. In some cases, teachers follow up on their initially low assessments of students' abilities by offering the instruction and assistance that students need to improve, and students *do* improve (Dweck & Molden, 2005; Goldenberg, 1992). In other cases, students may develop an "I'll show *you*" attitude that spurs them on to greater effort and achievement than a teacher anticipated (T. L. Good & Nichols, 2001). In still other cases, assertive parents step in and offer evidence that their children are more capable than a teacher initially thought (T. L. Good & Nichols, 2001).

So how prevalent and dramatic are self-fulfilling prophecies? Research on this topic yields mixed results (Eccles et al., 1998; Goldenberg, 1992; R. Rosenthal, 1994, 2002). Some research indicates that girls, students from low-income families, and students from ethnic minority groups are more susceptible to teacher expectations than are boys from European American backgrounds (Graham, 1990; Jussim, Eccles, & Madon, 1996). Teacher expectations also appear to have a greater influence in the early elementary school years (grades 1 and 2), the first year of secondary school, and, more generally, the first few weeks of school—in other words, at times when students are entering new and unfamiliar school environments (Jussim et al., 1996; Kuklinski & Weinstein, 2001; Raudenbush, 1984).

Be especially careful not to form unwarranted expectations for students at transition points in their academic careers.

As teachers, we are most likely to motivate students to achieve at high levels when we have optimistic expectations for their performance (within realistic limits, of course) and when we attribute their successes and failures to things over which either they or we have control (*their* effort, *our* instructional methods, etc.). The Into the Classroom feature "Forming Productive Expectations and Attributions for Student Performance" presents several strategies for helping teachers and students alike keep an optimistic outlook on students' abilities and chances of future success. Communicating attributions to controllable factors may be especially important. We must be careful when we attribute either success or failure to *effort,* however. There are at least two occasions when effort attributions can backfire. To see what I mean, try the next exercise.

self-fulfilling prophecy Situation in which expectations for an outcome either directly or indirectly lead to the expected result.

INTO THE Classroom

Forming Productive Expectations and Attributions for Student Performance

- **Remember that teachers can definitely make a difference.**

The teachers at a historically low-achieving middle school in a poor, inner-city neighborhood meet once a month to learn about teaching strategies that are especially effective with children from low-income families. They are encouraged by the many research studies indicating that children at all socioeconomic levels can achieve at high levels when instruction takes their existing skills into account and when teachers provide reasonable guidance and support. They experiment with various strategies in their own classrooms and share especially effective strategies at their group meetings.

- **Look for strengths in every student.**

A 9-year-old girl who lives in a homeless shelter seems to have learned little about rules for punctuation and capitalization, and her spelling is more typical of a first grader than a fourth grader. Nonetheless, the stories she writes often have unusual plot twists and creative endings. Her teacher suspects that her frequent moves from one school to another have left big gaps in her knowledge of written language and so finds a parent volunteer who can work with her on her writing several times a week.

- **Consider multiple possible explanations for students' low achievement and classroom misbehavior.**

Several seventh-grade teachers are sharing their experiences with a student who, at age 8, suffered a traumatic brain injury when he fell off a kitchen counter and landed on his head. His art and music teachers describe him as "very disruptive" in class and believe that he intentionally misbehaves in order to draw attention to himself. In contrast, his math and science teachers have found that he can easily stay on task—and can also achieve at average to above-average levels—as long as they provide reasonable structure for assignments and classroom behavior. They also realize that some children with brain injuries have trouble inhibiting inappropriate behaviors through no fault of their own.

- **Communicate optimism about what students can accomplish.**

In September, a high school teacher tells his class, "Next spring, I will ask you to write a 15-page research paper. Fifteen pages may seem like a lot now, but in the next few months, we'll work on the various skills you'll need to research and write your paper. By April, 15 pages won't seem like a big deal at all!"

- **Objectively assess students' progress, and be open to evidence that contradicts your initial assessments of students' abilities.**

A kindergarten teacher initially has low expectations for the daughter of migrant workers, a girl named Lupita who has previously had little access to books, toys, and other educational resources. When a videocamera captures Lupita's strong leadership ability and skill in assembling puzzles, the teacher realizes that she has considerable potential and so works hard to help her acquire the math and literacy skills she will need to be successful in first grade. (See the opening case study, "Hidden Treasure," in Chapter 3.)

- **Attribute students' successes to a combination of high ability and controllable factors such as effort and learning strategies.**

In a unit on basketball, a middle school physical education teacher tells students, "From what I've seen so far, you all have the capability to play a good game of basketball. And it appears that many of you have been practicing regularly after school."

- **Attribute students' successes to effort only when they have actually exerted considerable effort.**

A teacher observes that his students have completed a particular assignment more quickly and easily than he expected. He briefly acknowledges their success and then moves on to a more challenging task.

- **Attribute students' failures to factors that are controllable and easily remedied.**

A high school student seeks his teacher's advice about how he might improve his performance in her class. "I know you can do better, Frank," she replies. "I wonder if part of the problem might be that, with your part-time job and all of your extracurricular activities, you just don't have enough time to study. Let's sit down before school tomorrow and look at what and how much you're doing to prepare for class."

- **When students fail despite making obvious effort, attribute their failures to a lack of effective strategies and help them acquire such strategies.**

A student in an advanced science class is having difficulty with the teacher's challenging weekly quizzes. The student works diligently on her science every night and attends the after-school help sessions her teacher offers, but to no avail. The teacher observes that the student is trying to learn the material by rote—an ineffective strategy for answering the higher-level questions typically presented on the quizzes—and teaches her strategies that promote more meaningful learning.

Sources: Brophy, 2006; Carrasco, 1981 (Lupita example); H. M. Cooper & Good, 1983; Curtis & Graham, 1991; Dweck, 2000; Goldenberg, 1992; Graham, 1991; Hawley, 2005 (brain injury example); J. A. Langer, 2000; Pressley et al., 1987; Roeser et al., 2002; C. E. Weinstein, Hagen, & Meyer, 1991; R. S. Weinstein, Madison, & Kuklinski, 1995.

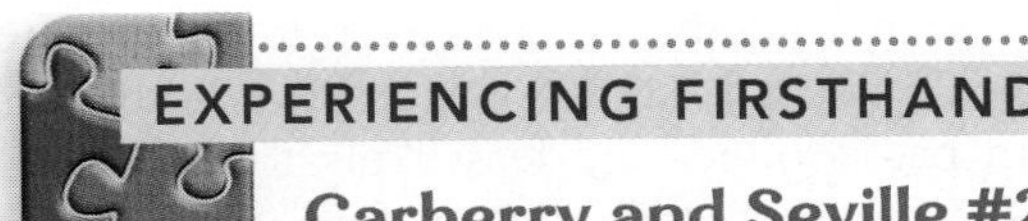

Carberry and Seville #2

1. Imagine that Professor Carberry wants you to learn to spell the word *psychoceramics* correctly. He gives you 10 minutes of intensive training in the spelling of the word. He then praises you profusely when you are able to spell it correctly. In which of the following ways would you be most likely to respond?
   a. You are delighted that he approves of your performance.
   b. You proudly show him that you've also learned how to spell *sociocosmetology*.
   c. You wonder, "Hey, is this all he thinks I can do?"
2. Now imagine that you drop by Professor Seville's office to find out why you did so poorly on her sociocosmetology exam. Professor Seville is warm and supportive, suggesting that you simply try harder next time. But the fact is, you tried as hard as you could the *first* time. Which one of the following conclusions would you be most likely to draw?
   a. You need to try even harder next time.
   b. You need to exert the same amount of effort the next time and just keep your fingers crossed that you'll make some lucky guesses.
   c. Perhaps you just weren't meant to be a sociocosmetologist.

Chances are good that you answered *c* to both questions. Let's first consider the situation in which Carberry spent 10 minutes teaching you how to spell *psychoceramics*. When students succeed at a very easy task and are then praised for their effort, they may get the unintended message that their teacher doesn't have much confidence in their ability (Graham, 1991; Schunk & Pajares, 2004). Attributing students' successes to effort is apt to be beneficial only when students have, in fact, exerted a great deal of effort.

Now consider the second scenario, in which Seville encouraged you to try harder even though you had previously studied very hard indeed. When students fail at a task on which they have expended a great deal of effort and are then told that they didn't try hard enough, they are likely to conclude that they simply don't have the ability to perform the task successfully (Curtis & Graham, 1991; Robertson, 2000; Stipek, 1996). In such circumstances, it's usually better to attribute their failure to ineffective strategies. Students can and do acquire more effective learning and study strategies over time, especially when they are specifically trained to use these strategies (see Chapter 8). By teaching effective strategies, not only do we promote students' academic success, but we also promote their beliefs that they can *control* their success (C. E. Weinstein, Madison, & Kuklinski, 1991).

Diversity in Cognitive Factors Affecting Motivation

We've already seen examples of diversity in cognitive factors affecting motivation—for instance, in personal interests, values, achievement goals, and general attributional style. Here our focus will be on diversity in students of various cultural and ethnic backgrounds, genders, and income levels, as well as in students with special educational needs.

Cultural and Ethnic Differences Most cultural and ethnic groups place a high value on getting a good education (P. J. Cook & Ludwig, 2008; Fuligni & Hardway, 2004; Phalet, Andriessen, & Lens, 2004; Spera, 2005). But to some degree, different cultural groups seem to encourage different kinds of values related to school learning. For example, many Asian cultures (e.g., in China, Japan, and Russia) emphasize learning for learning's sake: With knowledge comes personal growth, better understanding of the world, and greater potential to contribute to society. Important for these cultures, too, are hard work and persistence in academic studies, even if such studies are not intrinsically enjoyable (Hufton et al., 2002; J. Li, 2006; Morelli & Rothbaum, 2007). Students from European American backgrounds are less likely to be diligent when classroom topics have little intrinsic appeal, but they often find value in academic subject matter that piques their curiosity and in assignments that require creativity, independent thinking, or critical analysis (Hess & Azuma, 1991; Kuhn & Park, 2005).

Learners from diverse cultural backgrounds may also define academic success differently and, as a result, may set different achievement goals. For instance, on average, Asian American students aim for higher grades than do students from other ethnic groups, in part because they believe their parents would be angry about grades lower than A− (L. Steinberg, 1996). Even so, Asian American students—and African American students as well—tend to focus more on mastery goals (i.e., truly understanding what they are studying) than European American students do (Freeman, Gutman, & Midgley, 2002; Qian & Pan, 2002; Shim & Ryan, 2006). And students brought up in cultures that value group achievement over individual achievement (e.g., many Asian, Native American, Mexican American, and Pacific Islander cultures) tend to focus their mastery goals not on how much they alone can improve but instead on how much they *and their peers* can improve—or in some instances on how much their actions can contribute to the betterment of the larger social group or society (Chiu & Hong, 2005; Kağitçibaşi, 2007; J. Li, 2005, 2006).

Learners' cultural and ethnic backgrounds influence their attributions as well. For instance, students from families with traditional Asian cultural beliefs are more likely than students from mainstream Western culture to attribute classroom success and failure to unstable factors—effort in the case of academic achievement, and temporary situational factors in the case of appropriate or inappropriate behaviors (J. Li & Fischer, 2004; Lillard, 1997; Weiner, 2004). Also, some studies have found a greater tendency for African American students to develop a sense of learned helplessness about their ability to achieve academic success (Graham, 1989; Holliday, 1985). To some extent, racial prejudice may contribute to their learned helplessness: Students may begin to believe that because of the color of their skin, they have little chance of success no matter what they do (S. Sue & Chin, 1983; van Laar, 2000).

Gender Differences In general, girls are more concerned than boys are about doing well in school: They work harder on assignments, earn higher grades, and more often graduate from high school (see Chapter 4). But some students perceive certain domains (e.g., writing, instrumental music) to be "for girls" and other domains (e.g., math, science) to be "for boys," dampening their interest and efforts in seemingly opposite-gender content areas (Bandura et al., 2001; Eccles, 2005; Jacobs et al., 2002; Pajares & Valiante, 1999).

Another commonly observed gender difference is the tendency for girls (especially high-achieving girls) to be more discouraged by failure experiences than boys are (Dweck, 1986, 2000). We can explain this difference, at least in part, by looking at gender differences in attributions. Some research results indicate that boys tend to attribute their successes to a fairly stable ability and their failures to a lack of effort, thus revealing an "I know I can do this" attitude. Girls show the reverse pattern: They attribute their successes to effort and their failures to lack of ability, believing "I don't know whether I can keep on doing it, because I'm not very good at this type of thing." Such differences are most often observed in stereotypically male domains, (e.g., mathematics and sports) and can appear even when boys' and girls' previous levels of achievement in the domains have been equivalent (Eccles & Jacobs, 1986; Leaper & Friedman, 2007; Stipek, 1984; Vermeer, Boekaerts, & Seegers, 2000).

As we work to encourage high levels of motivation in all of our students, we may want to focus our efforts in somewhat different directions for males and females. For boys, who have less concern about doing well in school, we may need to stress the importance of academic achievement for their own long-term goals and make a particular effort to pique their interest in classroom activities. For girls, we may have to go the extra mile to convince them that their classroom successes are the result not only of their efforts but also of their natural abilities—a stable and dependable internal attribution.

Help boys discover the relevance of their classroom learning and performance to their long-term goals. Encourage girls to consider a wide range of career options, and help them discover that they have "what it takes" to be successful in traditionally male domains.

Socioeconomic Differences Many students from low socioeconomic backgrounds want to do well in school (Payne, 2005; Shernoff, Schneider, & Csikszentmihalyi, 2001; B. L. Wilson & Corbett, 2001). However, teachers' attitudes, instructional practices, and relationships with students have a significant influence on whether these students choose to pursue academic success; this is especially true for students at high risk for academic failure (L. W. Anderson & Pellicer, 1998; Kumar et al., 2002; Maehr & Anderman, 1993; Murdock, 1999). Students from low-income families flourish in schools in which teachers have high expectations, engage students in high-interest activities and subject matter, emphasize mastery goals over performance goals, and make students feel that they are valued members of the classroom community (more on this *sense of community* in Chapter 13).

In addition, we can increase the perceived value of school activities by making them relevant to students' own lives, experiences, and needs (P. A. Alexander et al., 1994; Knapp, Turnbull, & Shields, 1990; Wlodkowski & Ginsberg, 1995). All too often, students at schools in low-income neighborhoods encounter instruction that focuses on rote learning and lower-level skills (e.g., memorization of facts)—instruction that is unlikely to entice even the most motivated students (Becker & Luthar, 2002; Portes, 1996). The following interview with middle school students in an inner-city Philadelphia school illustrates the problem:

Remember that meaningful, personally relevant classroom tasks are especially important for motivating students from lower-income families.

> ***Adult:*** How often do you write in English class?
>
> ***Student:*** Every day.
>
> ***Adult:*** What kinds of things are you writing?
>
> ***Student:*** We copy notes from the board and we do dictionary work. We also answer questions from our workbook.
>
> ***Adult:*** Do you ever write your own stories?
>
> ***Student:*** No. (B. L. Wilson & Corbett, 2001, p. 52)

Not only is such instruction unengaging, but it's also unlikely to prepare students for the demands of a challenging high school or college curriculum (Ogbu, 2003; Suskind, 1998). It's essential that we help students acquire the skills and strategies they will need to achieve their long-term goals for higher education and careers—higher-level thinking skills, self-regulation strategies, and so on. In addition, if students have had little direct contact with college life or high-income professions, we must promote a realistic understanding of what college achievement and professional success involve. When speaking with a group of middle school boys who hoped to go to college, one researcher encountered considerable naiveté about college life:

> They got a dazed look in their eyes when I talked about the reality of actually getting into college: filling out an application, the importance of getting good grades, and so on. So, I asked them what they thought college was like. The response was nearly unanimous—it was all about partying—drinking, smoking weed, and hanging out. Never did it come up that they would attend classes or do homework. College meant partying, and that was why they wanted to go. They thought, also, that college would help them get a job at which they could make a lot of money. This explained to me why students who say they hate school still wish to attend college. (K. M. Williams, 2001a, p. 106)

Such misconceptions are perhaps not surprising if we consider how college life is often portrayed in television and films. For adolescent viewers, college parties certainly yield more interesting plot lines than going to class and studying at the library.

Communicate that academic success requires hard work not only in the secondary grades but in college as well.

Students in Inclusive Settings

TABLE 11.4
Enhancing Motivation in Students with Special Educational Needs

Category	Characteristics You Might Observe	Suggested Strategies
Students with specific cognitive or academic difficulties	• Less intrinsic motivation to succeed at academic tasks, due in part to a low sense of self-efficacy and competence • Reluctance to ask questions or seek assistance, especially in the secondary grades • Little or no persistence when confronting difficult tasks • Tendency to attribute poor achievement to low ability, rather than to more controllable factors; learned helplessness regarding some classroom tasks	• Use extrinsic reinforcers to encourage effort and achievement, gradually phase out reinforcers as students show signs of intrinsic motivation. • Establish short-term goals for achievement that students perceive as challenging yet accomplishable. • Offer assistance when you think students may really need it, but refrain from offering help when you know students are capable of succeeding on their own. • Teach effective learning strategies and encourage students to attribute their successes to such strategies.
Students with social or behavioral problems	• Desire to succeed in the classroom, despite behaviors that may seemingly indicate a lack of motivation • Tendency to interpret praise as an attempt at control (for students who exhibit defiance or oppositional behavior) • Stronger desire for power over classmates than for establishing friendships (for some students with emotional and behavioral disorders) • Little or no apparent interest in social interaction (for some students with autism spectrum disorders) • Perception of classroom tasks as having little relevance to personal needs and goals • Tendency to attribute negative consequences to uncontrollable factors (things "just happen")	• Provide the guidance and support students need to succeed at classroom tasks. • When students are concerned about control issues, use subtle reinforcers (e.g., leave notes commending productive behaviors) rather than more obvious and seemingly controlling ones. • Provide choices about academic activities as a way of increasing a sense of self-determination. • Help students discover the benefits of equitable and prosocial interactions with peers. • Relate the curriculum to students' specific needs and interests. • Teach behaviors that lead to desired consequences; stress cause-and-effect relationships between actions and outcomes.
Students with general delays in cognitive and social functioning	• On average, less intrinsic motivation than nondisabled age-mates; occasional curiosity about certain topics • Responsiveness to extrinsic motivators • Tendency to give up easily in the face of difficulty • Limited or no ability to conceptualize long-term goals • Tendency to attribute poor achievement to low ability or to external sources rather than to more controllable factors; in some situations, a sense of learned helplessness	• Use extrinsic reinforcers to encourage productive behaviors; gradually phase out reinforcers as students show signs of intrinsic motivation. • Reinforce persistence as well as success. • Set specific, short-term (proximal) goals for performance. • Help students see the relationship between their own actions and resulting consequences.
Students with physical or sensory challenges	• Low sense of self-determination about the course of their lives • Fewer opportunities to satisfy the need for relatedness, especially with peers	• Teach self-regulating behaviors and independence skills. • Identify classmates who can serve as "study buddies" to help students with assigned tasks or provide companionship at lunch and recess. • Collaborate with parents to promote interaction with classmates outside school.
Students with advanced cognitive development	• High self-efficacy and sense of competence • Eagerness for challenges; boredom when classroom tasks don't challenge their abilities • Persistence in the face of failure (although some may give up easily if they aren't accustomed to failure) • Possible self-handicapping if there is a strong desire to affiliate with low-achieving peers • Social isolation (for some students who are exceptionally gifted) • Variety of interests, sometimes pursued with a passion • Higher than average goal-directedness • Internal, optimistic attributions for classroom achievement • Tendency to adopt an entity view of intelligence; can lead to learned helplessness if failure is encountered after an early string of successes (especially for girls)	• Provide opportunities for students to pursue complex tasks and activities over an extended period. • Give assignments that students find stimulating and challenging. • Keep students' exceptional achievements confidential if their friends don't value high achievement. • Provide opportunities to pursue individual interests, perhaps with other students who have similar interests or perhaps in an apprenticeship with an outside mentor. • Encourage students to set high goals without expecting perfection.

Sources: Beirne-Smith et al., 2006; Brophy, 2004; M. Carr & Borkowski, 1989; B. Clark, 1997; Covington, 1992; G. Dawson & Bernier, 2007; Duchardt, Deshler, & Schumaker, 1995; Dunlap et al., 1994; Dweck, 2000; Foster-Johnson, Ferro, & Dunlap, 1994; Friedel, 1993; S. Goldstein & Rider, 2006; T. L. Good & Brophy, 1994; A. E. Gottfried, Fleming, & Gottfried, 1994; D. A. Greenspan, Solomon, & Gardner, 2004; Heward, 2009; Hoge & Renzulli, 1993; Jacobsen et al., 1986; Knowlton, 1995; Mercer & Pullen, 2005; Patrick, 1997; Patton et al., 1996; Piirto, 1999; S. Powell & Nelson, 1997; Sanborn, 1979; G. F. Schultz & Switzky, 1990; Shavinina & Ferrari, 2004; Turnbull et al., 2007; Wehmeyer et al., 2007; Winner, 1997, 2000a, 2000b; Wong, 1991a.

Accommodating Students with Special Needs Students with special educational needs are typically among those who show the greatest diversity in motivation. For example, students with learning disabilities or general intellectual disabilities may be easily discouraged by challenging tasks; some may even show signs of learned helplessness if their efforts consistently meet with failure (Jacobsen, Lowery, & DuCette, 1986; Mercer & Pullen, 2005; Seligman, 1975). In contrast, students who are gifted may become easily bored or annoyed if classroom activities do *not* challenge their abilities (Bleske-Rechek, Lubinski, & Benbow, 2004; Winner, 2000b). Table 11.4 presents these and other motivational characteristics in students with special needs.

Affect and Its Effects

A close partner of motivation is **affect**: the emotions and general moods that a learner brings to bear on a task. Virtually any form of affect has both psychological elements (subjective feelings) and physiological elements (changes in heart rate, perspiration, muscular tension, etc.). Some forms of affect—such as happiness, excitement, and pride—feel both psychologically and physiologically pleasant. Other forms—such as fear, anger, and shame—feel both psychologically and physiologically aversive.

All forms of affect, of course, have their basis in the brain, and each form has a specific function (Izard, 2007; Minsky, 2006; Pekrun, 2006). For example, when we face a dangerous situation, our fearful reaction includes an increased heart rate and muscular tension that spur us to take action, typically a *fight-or-flight response*. In contrast, when we find ourselves enjoying the company of others, we are apt to smile, laugh, and in other ways nurture interpersonal relationships.

How Affect and Motivation Are Interrelated

Without doubt, people's automatic emotional reactions to certain events—for instance, a quick, fearful retreat from someone who is wielding a gun or knife—are designed to keep them alive (Damasio, 1994; Öhman & Mineka, 2003). But affect also plays a significant role in the more planful, goal-directed aspects of human motivation. As a general rule, people act in ways they think will help them feel happy and comfortable, rather than sad, confused, or angry (Mellers & McGraw, 2001; J. L. Tsai, 2007).

Some emotions, known as **self-conscious emotions**, are closely tied to people's self-evaluations and thus affect their sense of self-worth (M. Lewis & Sullivan, 2005; Pekrun, 2006). When people evaluate their behaviors and accomplishments as being consistent with their culture's standards for appropriate and desirable behavior, they are apt to feel pride. When, in contrast, they see themselves as failing to live up to those standards—for instance, when they thoughtlessly cause harm to someone else—they are apt to feel guilt and shame.

Affect and motivation are interrelated in other ways as well. Learners are more likely to be intrinsically (rather than extrinsically) motivated when they experience pleasure in what they're doing. They tackle challenging tasks more willingly and effectively when they enjoy what they're doing, and their successful efforts often bring on feelings of excitement and pride (Linnenbrink & Pintrich, 2004; Pekrun, Goetz, Titz, & Perry, 2002; R. E. Snow, Corno, & Jackson, 1996). Learners are especially likely to feel excited about their successes if they didn't expect to be successful, but they will also experience more intense negative emotions about their failures—and often about the activity in question—if they didn't expect to fail (Bower & Forgas, 2001; Shepperd & McNulty, 2002). Their specific reactions will depend on how they *interpret* the outcomes of events—in particular, whether they hold themselves, other people, environmental circumstances, or something else responsible for what has happened (recall our earlier discussion of *attributions*).

In general, how learners feel depends on whether their needs are being met and their goals are being accomplished. In the "Emotions" video clip in MyEducationLab, you can find numerous examples of this relationship between affect and motivation.

affect Feelings, emotions, and moods that a learner brings to bear on a task.

self-conscious emotion Affective state based on self-evaluations regarding the extent to which one's actions meet society's standards for appropriate and desirable behavior; examples are pride, guilt, and shame.

myeducationlab

See how affect and motivation are often closely connected in the video "Emotions." (To find this video, go to Chapter 11 of the Book-Specific Resources in MyEducationLab, select *Video Examples*, and then click on the title.)

For example, 10-year-old Daniel explains that one common source of anger is "not getting what you want." For 13-year-old Crystal, people are happy if they "have a boyfriend or girlfriend or if they get one." For 15-year-old Greg, friends and good grades are a source of happiness, and disrupted peer relationships can be a source of anger or sadness.

How Affect Is Related to Learning and Cognition

The parts of the brain that underlie and support various emotions have many interconnections with those parts that underlie and support cognition (Benes, 2007; Phelps & Sharot, 2008). As a result, affective reactions are often closely intertwined with human thinking and learning (Damasio, 1994; D. K. Meyer & Turner, 2002; Ochsner & Lieberman, 2001). For example, while learning how to perform a task, learners simultaneously learn whether or not they like doing it (Zajonc, 1980). Learners who feel frustrated and anxious when they struggle to master new material (as Michael initially does in the opening case study) are apt to develop a dislike for the subject matter (Carver & Scheier, 1990; Goetz, Frenzel, Hall, & Pekrun, 2008; Stodolsky, Salk, & Glaessner, 1991). An exchange between Brian, one of my educational psychology students, and his 16-year-old sister, Megan, illustrates the effects of mastery and nonmastery on students' feelings about what they are studying:

> ***Brian:*** How do you know when you have learned something?
>
> ***Megan:*** I know that I have learned something when I get really excited about that topic while I am talking to a person about it. When I haven't learned something I tend to say that I hate it, because I don't understand it. When I am excited and can have a discussion about something is when I know that I fully understand and have studied enough on that topic. (Interview used courtesy of Brian Zottoli)

Get students emotionally involved with classroom subject matter.

As we discovered in Chapter 6, learners can also associate specific topics and pieces of information with certain emotions—a phenomenon known as **hot cognition**. On average, learners are more likely to pay attention to, think actively about, and remember emotionally charged information (Bower, 1994; Heuer & Reisberg, 1992; Zeelenberg, Wagenmakers, & Rotteveel, 2006). Sometimes the nature of a topic itself evokes hot cognition, perhaps because it invokes feelings of sympathy for people in dire straits or a sense of outrage about blatant violations of ethical standards. Information that conflicts with what learners currently know or believe can also evoke hot cognition. In particular, such information can cause learners considerable mental discomfort, something that Piaget called *disequilibrium* but many contemporary theorists call **cognitive dissonance**. This dissonance typically leads learners to try to resolve the inconsistency in some way, perhaps undergoing conceptual change or perhaps ignoring or discrediting the new information (Buehl & Alexander, 2001; Harmon-Jones, 2001; Zohar & Aharon-Kraversky, 2005).

myeducationlab

Observe a teacher creating cognitive dissonance in the video "Properties of Air." (To find this video, go to Chapter 11 of the Book-Specific Resources in MyEducationLab, select *Video Examples*, and then click on the title.)

How effectively learners think about and make sense of new information depends, in part, on their general affect while they are studying (Bower, 1994; Pekrun, 2006; R. E. Snow et al., 1996). They are most likely to engage in meaningful learning and think creatively about a topic if they are in an emotionally positive frame of mind. If they feel generally sad or frustrated—or perhaps if they are bored with the subject matter—they are apt to process new information in more superficial, inflexible ways (e.g., by using rehearsal). One critical way to promote positive affect in the classroom, of course, is to address students' basic needs (e.g., for competence, relatedness, etc.). Motivation researchers have suggested several additional ways in which we might increase positive affect:

hot cognition Learning or cognitive processing that is emotionally charged.

cognitive dissonance Feeling of mental discomfort caused by new information that conflicts with current knowledge or beliefs.

- Occasionally incorporate gamelike features into classroom tasks and activities (e.g., crossword puzzles for practicing new spelling words, a television game-show format for a history class review).

- Adjust task difficulty to a level that students think they can handle.
- Have students ask themselves questions that help them focus on the positive aspects of classroom activities and school in general (e.g., "What excites me about _____?" "What did I enjoy about _____?"). (Brophy, 2004; Pekrun, 2006; Townsend, 2008)

One form of affect—anxiety—can have either positive or negative effects on learning and cognition, depending on the circumstances. Because so many students experience anxiety at school and because instructional practices and the classroom environment can contribute significantly to students' anxiety levels, we will look at this particular form of affect more closely.

Anxiety in the Classroom

Imagine that you are enrolled in Professor Josiah S. Carberry's course in Advanced Psychoceramics. Today is your day to give a half-hour presentation on the topic of psychoceramic califractions. You have read several books and numerous articles on your topic and undoubtedly know more about psychoceramic califractions than any of your classmates. Furthermore, you have meticulously prepared a set of note cards to which you can refer during your presentation. As you sit in class waiting for your turn to speak, you should be feeling calm and confident. But instead you're a nervous wreck: Your heart is pounding wildly, your palms are sweaty, and your stomach is in a knot. When Professor Carberry calls you to the front of the room and you begin to speak, you have trouble remembering what you planned to say, and you can't read your note cards because your hands are shaking so much.

It's not as if you want to be nervous about speaking in front of your psychoceramics class. Moreover, you can't think of a single reason that you should be nervous. After all, you're an expert on your topic, you're not having a bad-hair day, and your classmates are unlikely to snicker or throw rotten tomatoes if you make a mistake. So what's the big deal? What happened to the self-assured student who was practicing in front of the mirror last night?

You are a victim of **anxiety**: You have a feeling of uneasiness and apprehension about an event because you're not sure what its outcome will be. This feeling can be accompanied by a variety of physiological symptoms, including a rapid heartbeat, increased perspiration, and muscular tension. Anxiety is similar to fear, in the sense that both involve fairly high levels of arousal. But the two emotions are different in one important respect: Although we are usually afraid of something in particular (e.g., a roaring lion or intense electrical storm), we usually don't know exactly why we're anxious (Lazarus, 1991). It's difficult to deal with anxiety when we can't pinpoint its cause.

Almost everyone is anxious at one time or another. Many students become anxious just before a test they know will be difficult, and most get nervous when they have to give a prepared speech to other people. Such temporary feelings of anxiety are instances of **state anxiety**. However, some students are anxious a good part of the time, even when the situation isn't especially dangerous or threatening. For example, some students get excessively nervous even before very easy exams, and others may be so anxious about mathematics that they can't concentrate on even the simplest math assignment. A learner who shows a pattern of responding with anxiety even in nonthreatening situations has **trait anxiety**, a chronic condition that often interferes with maximal performance.

anxiety Feeling of uneasiness and apprehension concerning a situation with an uncertain outcome.

state anxiety Temporary feeling of anxiety elicited by a threatening situation.

trait anxiety Pattern of responding with anxiety even in nonthreatening situations.

How Anxiety Affects Learning and Performance Imagine, for a moment, that you aren't anxious at all—not even the slightest bit—about your grade in Professor Carberry's psychoceramics class. Will you study for Carberry's tests? Will you turn in the assigned research papers? If you have no anxiety whatsoever, you might not even buy the textbook or go to class. And you probably won't get a very good grade in your psychoceramics class.

A small amount of anxiety often improves performance: It is known as **facilitating anxiety**. A little anxiety spurs students into action. For instance, it can make them go to class, read the textbook, do assignments, and study for exams (see Figure 11.6). It also leads students to approach their classwork carefully and to think carefully before making a response (Shipman & Shipman, 1985). In contrast, a great deal of anxiety usually interferes with effective performance: It is known as **debilitating anxiety**. Excessive anxiety distracts learners and interferes with their attention to the task at hand.

At what point does anxiety stop facilitating and begin to debilitate performance? Very easy tasks—things that learners can do almost without thinking (e.g., running)—are typically facilitated by a high level of anxiety. But more difficult tasks—those that require considerable thought and mental effort—are best performed with only a small or moderate level of anxiety (Kirkland, 1971; Landers, 2007; Yerkes & Dodson, 1908). A high level of anxiety in a difficult situation can interfere with several aspects of cognition that are critical for successful learning and performance:

- Paying attention to what needs to be learned
- Processing information effectively (e.g., organizing or elaborating on it)
- Retrieving information and demonstrating skills that have previously been learned (Cassady, 2004; Covington, 1992; Eysenck, 1992; Hagtvet & Johnsen, 1992; Sarason, 1980)

When asking students to perform difficult tasks, encourage them to do their best, but don't make them unnecessarily anxious about their performance.

Anxiety is especially likely to interfere with such cognitive processes when a task places heavy demands on either working memory or long-term memory—for instance, when a task involves problem solving or creativity. In such situations, learners may be so preoccupied with the possibility of doing poorly that they can't get their minds on what they need to accomplish (Ashcraft, 2002; Beilock, 2008; Eysenck, 1992; Turner, Thorpe, & Meyer, 1998; Zeidner & Matthews, 2005).

Sources of Anxiety Learners sometimes develop feelings of anxiety about particular situations through the process of classical conditioning (see Chapter 9). They are also more likely to experience anxiety, especially debilitating anxiety, when they face a **threat**: a situation in which they believe they have little or no chance of succeeding. Facilitating anxiety is more common when learners face a **challenge**: a situation in which they believe they can probably achieve success with a significant yet reasonable amount of effort (Combs, Richards, & Richards, 1976; Csikszentmihalyi & Nakamura, 1989; Deci & Ryan, 1992).

Children and adolescents are apt to have some degree of anxiety—possibly facilitating, possibly debilitating—in many of the following circumstances:

- *A situation in which physical safety is at risk*—for example, being regularly exposed to violence at school or in the neighborhood
- *A situation in which self-worth is threatened*—for example, hearing unflattering remarks about one's race or gender
- *Concern about physical appearance*—for example, feeling too fat or too thin or reaching puberty either earlier or later than peers
- *A new situation*—for example, moving from one school to another midway through the school year
- *Judgment or evaluation by others*—for example, receiving a low grade from a teacher or being disliked or excluded by peers
- *Frustrating subject matter*—for example, having a history of difficulty with mathematics word problems
- *Excessive classroom demands*—for example, being expected to learn a great deal of material in a very short time

facilitating anxiety Level of anxiety (usually relatively low) that enhances performance.

debilitating anxiety Anxiety of sufficient intensity that it interferes with performance.

threat Situation in which a learner believes there is little or no chance of success.

challenge Situation in which a learner believes that success is possible with sufficient effort.

- *Classroom tests*—for example, facing a test that affects one's chances for promotion or graduation (more about such high-stakes tests in Chapter 15)
- *Concern about the future*—for example, not knowing how to make a living after graduation from high school (Ashcraft, 2002; Cassady, 2004; Chabrán, 2003; Covington, 1992; DuBois et al., 2002; Harter, 1992; Hembree, 1988; N. J. King & Ollendick, 1989; Matthews et al., 2006; Phelan et al., 1994; Sarason, 1980; Stipek, 1993; Stodolsky et al., 1991; Wigfield & Meece, 1988; K. M. Williams, 2001a; Zeidner & Matthews, 2005)

Learners' particular concerns change somewhat as they grow older. Table 11.5 describes developmental trends in anxiety, as well as in affect more generally, across childhood and adolescence. Developmentally speaking, the most anxiety-arousing period is probably the transition from elementary school to a secondary school format—usually at the beginning of middle school or junior high, but sometimes at the beginning of high school. We look at this issue next.

FIGURE 11.6 This writing sample by 14-year-old Loretta illustrates how anxiety can sometimes improve learning and achievement.

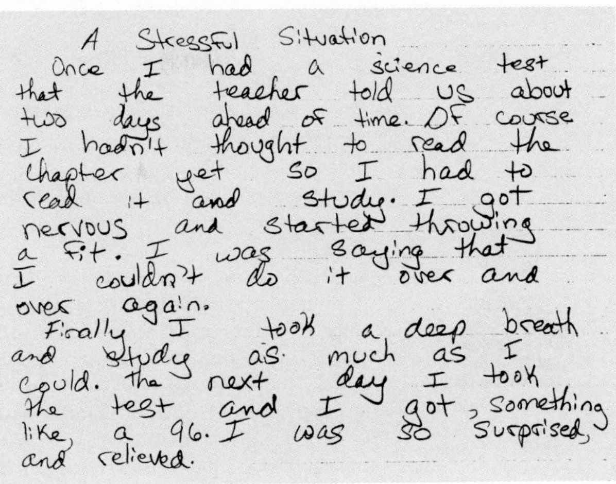

A Stressful Situation

Once I had a science test that the teacher told us about two days ahead of time. Of course I hadn't thought to read the chapter yet so I had to read it and study. I got nervous and started throwing a fit. I was saying that I couldn't do it over and over again.

Finally I took a deep breath and study as much as I could. the next day I took the test and I got, something like, a 96. I was so surprised, and relieved.

Making the Transition to a Secondary School Format Elementary school classrooms are often warm, nurturing places in which teachers get to know 20 or 30 students very well. Students in elementary classrooms also get to know one another quite well: They often work together on academic tasks and may even see themselves as members of a classroom "family." But somewhere around fifth to seventh grade, many students move from elementary school to a middle school or junior high school. As they do so, they simultaneously encounter numerous changes in the nature of their schooling:

- The school is larger and has more students.
- Students have several teachers, and each teacher has many students. Thus, teacher–student relationships are more superficial and less personal than in elementary school, and teachers are less aware of how well individual students are mastering classroom subject matter.
- There is more whole-class instruction, with less individualized instruction that takes into account each student's academic needs.
- Classes are less socially cohesive. Students may not know their classmates very well and may be reluctant to ask peers for assistance.
- Students have fewer opportunities to make choices about the topics they pursue and the tasks they complete. At the same time, they have more independence and responsibility regarding their learning. For example, they may be expected to complete a relatively unstructured assignment over a two- or three-week period, and they must take the initiative to seek help when they are struggling.
- Teachers place greater emphasis on students' demonstrating rather than acquiring competence, reflecting a shift from mastery goals to performance goals. Thus, making mistakes is more costly for students.
- Standards for assigning grades are more rigorous, so students may earn lower grades than they did in elementary school. Grades are often assigned on a comparative and competitive basis, with only the highest-achieving students getting As and Bs.
- High-stakes tests—tests that affect promotion to the next grade level—become increasingly common. (H. A. Davis, 2003; Eccles & Midgley, 1989; Harter, 1996; Hine & Fraser, 2002; Midgley, Middleton, Gheen, & Kumar, 2002; Wentzel & Wigfield, 1998; Wigfield et al., 1996)

TABLE 11.5
Affect at Different Grade Levels

Grade Level	Age-Typical Characteristics	Suggested Strategies
K–2	• Possible culture shock and intense anxiety upon beginning school, especially if students have had little or no preschool experience • Possible separation anxiety when parents first leave the classroom (especially in the first few days of kindergarten) • Reduced anxiety when teachers and other adults are warm and supportive • Only limited control of overt emotional behaviors (e.g., may cry easily if distressed or act impulsively if frustrated)	• Ask parents about routines and procedures followed at home; when appropriate, incorporate them into classroom procedures. • If possible, provide an opportunity for students to meet you a few days or weeks before school begins. • Be warm, caring, and supportive with all students (but check school policies about giving hugs and other forms of physical affection). • Address inappropriate behaviors gently but firmly (see suggestions in Chapters 9 and 13).
3–5	• Increasing control of overt emotional behaviors • Emergence of math anxiety for some students, especially if they are given little support or assistance with math tasks • Tendency for close friends (especially girls) to talk about and ruminate on negative emotional events; continues into adolescence • Possible stress as a result of others' racist and sexist behaviors (e.g., racial slurs, unkind remarks about emerging sexual characteristics); continues into adolescence	• Ensure that students master basic concepts and procedures before proceeding to more complex material that depends on those concepts and procedures. (This is especially important in teaching math, a subject area in which advanced knowledge and skills build on more basic ones.) • Monitor students' behaviors for subtle signs of serious anxiety or depression; talk with students privately if they are anxious or upset, and consult with the school counselor if necessary. • Insist that students show respect for all class members' characteristics, feelings, and backgrounds; do not tolerate racist or sexist remarks or actions.
6–8	• General decline in positive emotions; extreme mood swings, partly as a result of hormonal changes accompanying puberty • Increased anxiety and potential depression accompanying the transition to middle school or junior high school • Decrease in enjoyment of school (especially for boys) • Increasing concern and anxiety about how one appears to others (*imaginary audience*; see Chapter 3)	• Expect mood swings, but monitor students' behavior for signs of long-term depression. • Make a personal connection with every student; express confidence that students can succeed with effort, and offer support to facilitate success. • Occasionally incorporate gamelike features into classroom activities. • Provide opportunities for students to form supportive friendships with classmates (e.g., assign cooperative learning projects).
9–12	• Continuing emotional volatility (especially in grades 9 and 10) • Considerable anxiety if the transition to a secondary school format has been delayed until high school • Susceptibility to serious depression in the face of significant stress • Increasing prevalence of debilitating anxiety regarding tests, especially high-stakes tests • Feelings of uncertainty about life after graduation	• Be especially supportive if students have just made the transition from elementary school (e.g., show personal interest in students' well-being, teach effective study skills). • Be on the lookout for signs that a student may be considering suicide (see the warning signs in Chapter 5). • Give frequent classroom assessments so that no single test score is a "fatal" one; help students prepare for high-stakes tests. • Present multiple realistic options for postgraduation career paths.

Sources: Arnett, 1999; Ashcraft, 2002; Brophy, 2004; Chabrán, 2003; DuBois et al., 2002; Eccles & Midgley, 1989; Elkind, 1981; Gentry et al., 2002; K. T. Hill & Sarason, 1966; Hine & Fraser, 2002; Kuhl & Kraska, 1989; Lapsley, 1993; Larson, Moneta, Richards, & Wilson, 2002; Midgley, Middleton, Gheen, & Kumar, 2002; Roderick & Camburn, 1999; A. J. Rose, 2002; Rudolph, Lambert, Clark, & Kurlakowsky, 2001; R. E. Snow et al., 1996; Spear, 2000; R. M. Thomas, 2005; Tomback, Williams, & Wentzel, 2005.

Furthermore, previously formed friendships can be disrupted as students move to new (and perhaps different) schools (Pellegrini & Long, 2004; Wentzel, 1999). And of course, students are also dealing with the physiological changes that accompany puberty and adolescence.

This multiple whammy of changes often leads to decreased confidence, a lower sense of self-worth, less intrinsic motivation, and considerable anxiety. Focus on peer relationships increases, and academic achievement drops. Some students become emotionally disengaged from the school environment and may eventually drop out of school altogether (Eccles & Midgley, 1989; Gentry et al., 2002; Urdan & Maehr, 1995; Wigfield et al., 1996).

If students remain in a close-knit elementary school environment in early adolescence, their attitudes and motivation are more likely to remain positive, and they are less likely to experience anxiety or depression (Midgley et al., 2002; Rudolph, Lambert, Clark, & Kurlakowsky, 2001). By the time they reach ninth grade, however, they almost inevitably make the transition to a secondary school format, where they experience many of the changes that their peers in other school districts experienced a few grades earlier—more demanding expectations, increased emphasis on demonstrating competence, less supportive teacher–student relationships, lack of class cohesiveness, and so on (Midgley et al., 2002; Roderick & Camburn, 1999; Tomback, Williams, & Wentzel, 2005). Students in lower-income, inner-city school districts (especially males and minorities) are particularly at risk for making a rough transition from an elementary to a secondary school format, elevating their risk for dropping out before graduation.

Students entering the middle school grades face new challenges—more stringent evaluation criteria, less individualized instruction, greater competition in classes and sports, and so on—while also undergoing the unsettling physiological changes of puberty.

In theory, middle schools were developed to ease the transition to a secondary school format. Ideally, they are designed to accommodate the unique needs of preadolescents and early adolescents, including their anxieties about more demanding academic expectations, the changing nature of peer relationships, and their own rapidly maturing bodies. Effective middle schools give attention to students' personal, emotional, and social development as well as to academic achievement, and they are attuned to students' individual differences and unique academic needs. They teach learning and study skills that help students move toward increasing independence as learners. At many middle schools, teams of four or five teachers work with a subset of the student population (perhaps 75 to 125 students per team), coordinating activities and exchanging information about how particular students are progressing. Such strategies can ease students' transition to a secondary school setting (Hine & Fraser, 2002; Midgley et al., 2002).

Students who make a smooth transition to a secondary school format are more likely to be successful there and, as a result, are more likely to graduate from high school (Roderick & Camburn, 1999; Wigfield et al., 1996). The Into the Classroom feature "Easing the Transition to Middle and Secondary School" suggests several strategies for teachers at the middle school and high school levels.

Keeping Students' Anxiety at a Facilitative Level Even when students aren't making a significant transition from one educational setting to another, they may have many reasons to be anxious at school. We can address their concerns about social matters—for instance, their worries about peer acceptance and respect—by teaching social skills and planning activities that foster frequent and productive student interactions (see Chapter 3). And we can address their concerns about an uncertain future by teaching skills that will be marketable in the adult world and providing assistance with college applications.

But perhaps most importantly, we must take steps to ensure that students don't become overly anxious about classroom tasks and subject matter. Because anxiety, like all emotions, is largely beyond students' immediate control, simply telling them to calm down is unlikely to be effective. The key is to prevent, rather than "cure," debilitating anxiety. Following are several strategies that should keep students' anxiety at a facilitative level:

- Communicate clear, concrete, and realistic expectations for performance.
- Match instruction to students' cognitive levels and capabilities (e.g., use concrete materials to teach mathematics to students not yet capable of abstract thought).

INTO THE Classroom

Easing the Transition to Middle and Secondary School

- **Provide a means through which every student can feel part of a small, close-knit group.**

  During the first week of school, a ninth-grade math teacher establishes *base groups* of three or four students who provide support and assistance for one another throughout the school year. At the beginning or end of every class period, the teacher gives group members five minutes to help one another with questions and concerns about daily lessons and homework assignments.

- **Find time to meet one-on-one with every student.**

  Early in the school year, while students are working on a variety of cooperative learning activities, a middle school social studies teacher schedules individual appointments with each of his students. In these meetings, he searches for interests that he and his students share and encourages the students to seek him out whenever they need help with academic or personal problems. Throughout the semester, he continues to touch base with individual students (often during lunch or before or after school) to see how they're doing.

- **Teach students the skills they need to be successful independent learners.**

  After discovering that few of her students know how to take effective class notes, a high school science teacher distributes a daily notes "skeleton" that guides them through the note-taking process that day. The skeleton includes headings such as "Topic of the Lesson," "Definitions," "Important Ideas," and "Examples." As students' class notes improve over the course of the school year, the teacher gradually reduces the amount of structure she provides.

- **Assign grades on the basis of mastery, not on comparisons with peers, and provide reasonable opportunities for improvement.**

  A junior high school language arts teacher requires students to submit two drafts of every essay and short story he assigns; he gives students the option of submitting additional drafts as well. He judges each composition on several criteria, including quality of ideas, organization and cohesiveness, word usage, grammar, and spelling. He explains and illustrates each of these criteria and gives ample feedback on every draft that students turn in.

- When students have a high level of trait anxiety, provide considerable structure to guide their activities.
- Provide supplementary sources of support for learning challenging topics and skills until mastery is attained (e.g., provide additional practice, individual tutoring, or a structure for taking notes).
- Teach strategies that can enhance students' learning and performance (e.g., effective study skills).
- Assess students' performance independently of how well their classmates are doing, and encourage students to assess their own performance in a similar manner.
- Provide feedback about specific behaviors, rather than global evaluations of classroom performance.
- Allow students to correct errors so that no single mistake is ever a "fatal" one. (Brophy, 1986; Hembree, 1988; K. T. Hill & Wigfield, 1984; McCoy, 1990; Sarason, 1980; Stipek, 1993; Tryon, 1980; Zeidner, 1998)

In Chapter 14, we'll identify additional strategies for keeping students' anxiety at reasonable levels during tests and other classroom assessments.

Diversity in Affect

Some people seem to be consistently more emotionally upbeat than others—an individual difference variable that is probably rooted in biology to some degree (Costa &

McCrae, 1992; C. Peterson, 2006). In addition, researchers have observed some consistent differences in affect in students of different cultural and ethnic backgrounds, genders, and socioeconomic levels.

stereotype threat Awareness of a negative stereotype about one's own group and accompanying uneasiness that low performance will confirm the stereotype; leads (often unintentionally) to a reduction in performance.

Cultural and Ethnic Differences On average, cultural groups differ in the degree to which they show their feelings in their behaviors and facial expressions. For example, whereas Americans and Mexicans are often quite expressive, people from East Asian cultures tend to be more reserved and controlled (Camras, Chen, Bakeman, Norris, & Cain, 2006; P. M. Cole & Tan, 2007; Morelli & Rothbaum, 2007). Cultures probably differ most in the extent to which they tolerate overt expressions of anger. Mainstream Western culture encourages children to act and speak up if someone infringes on their rights and needs, and expressing anger in a nonviolent way is considered quite acceptable. In many Southeast Asian cultures, however, any expression of anger is viewed as potentially undermining adults' authority or disrupting social harmony (Mesquita & Leu, 2007; J. L. Tsai, 2007; Zahn-Waxler, Friedman, Cole, Mizuta, & Hiruma, 1996). Children brought up in some Buddhist communities are encouraged to not even *feel* anger (P. M. Cole, Bruschi, & Tamang, 2002; P. M. Cole et al., 2006; Solomon, 1984). For instance, if unfairly embarrassed or accused, a child who has grown up in the Tamang culture of Nepal might respond, "Tilda bomo khaba?" ("Why be angry?"), because the event has already occurred and being angry about it serves no purpose (P. M. Cole et al., 2002, p. 992).

Even seemingly "positive" emotions are not always viewed favorably. Some cultures that place a high priority on social harmony discourage children from feeling pride about personal accomplishments, because such an emotion focuses attention on an individual rather than on the overall group (Eid & Diener, 2001). And for some cultural groups, joy and happiness can sometimes be too much of a good thing. For instance, many Chinese and Japanese advocate striving for contentment and serenity—relatively calm emotions—rather than joy (Mesquita & Leu, 2007; J. L. Tsai, 2007).

Finally, learners from various cultural backgrounds may have somewhat different sources of anxiety. For instance, some children and adolescents from Asian American families may feel so much family pressure to perform well in school that they experience debilitating test anxiety (Pang, 1995). And children who are recent immigrants are often anxious about a variety of things in their new country: how to behave, how to interpret others' behaviors, how to make friends, and, more generally, how to make sense of the strange new culture in which they now find themselves (P. M. Cole & Tan, 2007; Dien, 1998; Igoa, 1995).

Keep in mind that students from Asian American families may be especially prone to debilitating test anxiety.

Anxiety may be at the root of a phenomenon known as **stereotype threat**, in which students from stereotypically low-achieving groups perform more poorly on classroom assessments than they otherwise would simply because they are aware that their group traditionally *does* do poorly (J. Aronson & Steele, 2005; K. E. Ryan & Ryan, 2005; J. L. Smith, 2004). When students are aware of the unflattering stereotype—and especially when they know that the task they are performing reflects their ability in an important domain—their heart rate and other physiological correlates of anxiety go up and their performance goes down (J. Aronson et al., 1999; McKown & Weinstein, 2003; Osborne & Simmons, 2002). We are more likely to see the negative effects of stereotype threat when students interpret their performance on a task as an evaluation of their competence or overall self-worth (Davies & Spencer, 2005; Huguet & Régner, 2007; McKown & Weinstein, 2003). Furthermore, stereotype threat is more apt to occur when students have an entity view of ability—that is, a belief that ability is relatively fixed and permanent—rather than an incremental view (Ben-Zeev et al., 2005; Dweck et al., 2004; C. Good, Aronson, & Inzlicht, 2003).

Gender Differences In general, girls express their emotions more openly than boys do. However, girls sometimes hide angry feelings in order to preserve social harmony with others, whereas boys are often quite willing to show their anger (Eisenberg et al., 1996; Lippa, 2002; Sadker & Sadker, 1994). Girls are also more anxious about their classroom performance (which may partly explain their greater diligence in

Seek professional help in anger management training if a student frequently lashes out in anger.

Be especially supportive and reassuring when a student experiences extreme stress at school or elsewhere.

schoolwork) and have greater difficulty coping with stress (Frydenberg & Lewis, 2000; Marsh, Martin, & Cheng, 2008; Pomerantz, Altermatt, & Saxon, 2002). For instance, girls are more prone to test anxiety than boys are; some become victims of stereotype threat, earning lower scores than they should on tests in stereotypically "male" domains such as math (Hong, O'Neil, & Feldon, 2005; Huguet & Régner, 2007). Clearly, then, girls and boys alike need our social and emotional support but for somewhat different reasons.

Socioeconomic Differences As a result of their impoverished and unpredictable life circumstances—uncertainty about future food and housing, frequent incidents of neighborhood violence, and so on—students from low-income families are, on average, more prone to anxiety and depression than their higher-income classmates (see Chapter 4). Such chronically stressful conditions can have adverse effects on students' physiological functioning (e.g., elevated heart rate, high levels of stress-related hormones) (Ashiabi & O'Neal, 2008; G. W. Evans & Kim, 2007). Accordingly, these students are apt to have a greater than average need for our emotional and social support, and they are the ones who are most likely to benefit from a consistently warm and nurturing classroom environment (Becker & Luthar, 2002; Masten, 2001; Milner, 2006).

Be especially attentive to the emotional needs of children from low-income families.

The Big Picture

Motivation enhances learning and achievement in a variety of ways. Effectively motivated learners pay attention, process information meaningfully, persist in the face of failure, use their errors to help them improve their skills, and seek ever more challenging tasks. Yet the reverse is true as well: Successful learning and achievement foster the development of productive motivational patterns. When students discover that they can usually accomplish academic tasks successfully, they bring to class a sense of competence and a desire to master new information and skills. Thus, motivation and learning go hand in hand, with each playing a critical role in the development of the other.

Affect frequently comes into the mix as well. Affect is closely intertwined with motivation; for instance, fear can evoke a fight-or-flight response, and a little bit of anxiety or guilt can spur learners to address their shortcomings and wrongdoings. Furthermore, affect is often an integral part of what students learn; for instance, learners may begin to associate certain topics and content domains with various feelings (enjoyment, dislike, outrage, etc.).

Three key principles sum up much of our discussion in this chapter:

- ***All children and adolescents are motivated in one way or another.*** Occasionally I hear educators, policy makers, or the public at large talking about "unmotivated" students. In reality, all young people have needs and desires they are motivated to satisfy. For instance, virtually all students want to feel physically safe in their environment, to believe they are competent human beings, and to socially and emotionally connect with other people. Some students may perceive school to be a place in which they can satisfy such needs, but others may find that one or more of their needs—perhaps for physical well-being, self-worth, or relatedness—is actually thwarted in the classroom.

- ***Motivation to do well in school is grounded in a variety of cognitive factors that build up slowly over time.*** A common misconception about motivation in the classroom is that students can turn it on or off at will, much as one would flip a light switch. In fact, motivation, especially intrinsic motivation, is the result of many cognitive factors—including interests, expectancies, values, goals, and attributions—that often change only slowly over time. In the opening case, two things change for Michael over the course of his tutoring sessions: His expectancy for mastering algebra increases, and his attributions for his performance begin to reflect controllable rather than uncontrollable factors. These two elements don't change overnight but gradually become more optimistic and productive as Ms. Tucker helps Michael discover that, by applying effort and good strategies, he *can* be successful in his math class.

- ***Conditions in the classroom play a major role in students' motivation to learn and achieve.*** The concept of *situated motivation* highlights the fact that well-chosen instructional practices can nurture students' eagerness to tackle academic topics and master the knowledge and skills that will serve them well over the long run. Many strategies for enhancing students' motivation in the classroom can be summed up in six words: *task, autonomy, recognition, grouping, evaluation,* and *time* (J. L. Epstein, 1989; Maehr & Anderman, 1993). This multifaceted TARGET approach to motivation is presented in Table 11.6. If you look closely at the entries in the table, you'll find that they reflect many of the concepts we've addressed in this chapter, including competence and self-worth, self-determination, relatedness, hot cognition, interests, expectancies, values, goals, and attributions.

Principles/ Assumptions

TABLE 11.6
Six TARGET Principles of Motivation

Principle	Educational Implications	Example
Classroom **tasks** affect motivation.	• Present new topics through tasks that students find interesting, engaging, and perhaps emotionally charged. • Encourage meaningful rather than rote learning. • Relate activities to students' lives and goals. • Provide sufficient support that students can be successful.	• Ask students to conduct a scientific investigation about an issue that concerns them.
The amount of **autonomy** students have affects motivation, especially intrinsic motivation.	• Give students some choice about what and how they learn. • Teach self-regulation strategies. • Solicit students' opinions about classroom practices and policies. • Have students take leadership roles in some activities.	• Let students choose from among several ways of accomplishing an instructional objective, being sure that each choice offers sufficient scaffolding to make success likely.
The amount and nature of the **recognition** students receive affect motivation.	• Acknowledge not only academic successes but also personal and social successes. • Commend students for improvement as well as for mastery. • Provide concrete reinforcers for achievement only when students have little or no intrinsic motivation to learn. • Show students how their own efforts and strategies are directly responsible for their successes.	• Commend students for completing a successful community service project.
The **grouping** procedures in the classroom affect motivation.	• Provide frequent opportunities for students to interact (e.g., cooperative learning activities, peer tutoring). • Plan activities to which all students can make valuable contributions. • Teach the social skills that students need to interact effectively with peers. • Create an atmosphere of mutual caring, respect, and support.	• Have students work in small groups to tackle a challenging issue or problem for which there is no single right answer.
The forms of **evaluation** in the classroom affect motivation.	• Make evaluation criteria clear; specify them in advance. • Minimize or eliminate competition for grades (e.g., don't grade on a curve). • Give specific feedback about what students are doing well. • Give concrete suggestions about how students can improve. • Teach students how to evaluate their own work.	• Give students concrete criteria with which they can evaluate the quality of their writing.
How teachers schedule **time** affects motivation.	• Give students enough time to master important topics and skills. • Let students' interests dictate some activities in the weekly schedule. • Include variety in the school day (e.g., intersperse high-energy activities among more sedentary ones). • Include opportunities for independent learning in the school day.	• After explaining a new concept, present a hands-on activity that lets students see the concept in action.

Sources: J. L. Epstein, 1989; Maehr & Anderman, 1993.

Practice for Your Licensure Exam

When Perfect Isn't Good Enough

Mrs. Gaskill's second graders are just beginning to learn how to write the letters of the alphabet in cursive. Every day Mrs. Gaskill introduces a new cursive letter and shows her students how to write it correctly. She also shows them some common errors in writing the letter—for instance, claiming that she's going to make the "perfect f" but then making it much too short and crossing the lines in the wrong place—and the children delight in finding her mistakes. After the class explores the shape of a letter, Mrs. Gaskill asks her students to practice the letter, first by writing it in the air using large arm movements and then by writing it numerous times on a sheet of lined paper.

Meanwhile, Mrs. Gaskill has decided to compare the effects of two kinds of praise on the children's performance. She has placed a small colored sticker on each child's desk to indicate membership in one of two groups. When children in Group 1 write a letter with good form, she gives them a happy-face token, says "Great!" or "Perfect!" and either smiles at them or gives them a pat on the back. When children in Group 2 write a letter with good form at least once, she gives them a happy-face token and says something like "You sure are working hard," "You can write beautifully in cursive," or "You are a natural at this." When children in either group fail to meet her standards for cursive writing, she gives them whatever corrective feedback they need.

Thus, the only way in which Mrs. Gaskill treats the two groups differently is in what she says to them when they do well, either giving them fairly cryptic feedback (for Group 1) or telling them that they are trying hard or have high ability (for Group 2). Despite such a minor difference, Mrs. Gaskill finds that the children in Group 2 say they enjoy cursive writing more, and they use it more frequently in their spelling tests and other writing tasks. Curiously, too, the children in Group 1 often seem disappointed when they receive their seemingly positive feedback. For instance, on one occasion a girl who writes beautifully but has the misfortune of being in Group 1 asks, "Am *I* a natural at this?" Although the girl consistently gets a grade of "+" for her cursive writing, she never writes in cursive voluntarily throughout the three-week period in which Mrs. Gaskill conducts her experiment.

1. **Multiple-choice question:**

   Which one of the following observations best supports the conclusion that the children in Group 2 have greater *intrinsic* motivation than the children in Group 1?

   a. The children in Group 2 get more detailed feedback.
   b. The children in Group 2 seem happier when Mrs. Gaskill reinforces them.
   c. The children in Group 1 seem disappointed about the feedback they get.
   d. The children in Group 2 use cursive writing more frequently in other assignments.

2. **Constructed-response question:**

   Explain why the praise given to Group 2 might be more motivating than the praise given to Group 1. Base your explanation on contemporary principles and theories of motivation.

3. **Constructed-response question:**

   Might the feedback given to Group 1 ("e.g., Great!" "Perfect!") be more effective if Mrs. Gaskill used it for all, rather than just some, of her students? Explain your reasoning. (The section "Factors Influencing Sense of Self" in Chapter 3 might help you answer this question.)

Go to Chapter 11 of the Book-Specific Resources in **MyEducationLab**, and click on "Practice for Your Licensure Exam" to answer these questions. Compare your responses with the feedback provided.

Source: Study described by Gaskill, 2001.

PRAXIS

Turn to Appendix C, "Matching Book and MyEducationLab Content to the Praxis Principles of Learning and Teaching Tests," to discover sections of this chapter that may be especially applicable to the Praxis tests.

PEARSON myeducationlab

Now go to MyEducationLab (**www.myeducationlab.com**) where you can:

- Find learning outcomes for Motivation and Affect, along with the national standards that connect to these outcomes.
- Complete Assignments and Activities that can help you more deeply understand the chapter content.
- Engage in Building Teaching Skills and Dispositions exercises in which you can apply and practice core teaching skills identified in the chapter.
- Access Book-Specific Resources:
  - Check your comprehension of chapter content by going to the Study Plan, where you can find (a) Chapter Objectives; (b) Focus Questions that can guide your reading; (c) a Self-Check Quiz that can help you monitor your progress in mastering chapter content; (d) Review, Practice, and Enrichment exercises with detailed feedback that will deepen your understanding of various concepts and principles; (e) Flashcards that can give you practice in understanding and defining key terms; and (f) Common Beliefs and Misconceptions about Educational Psychology that will alert you to typical misunderstandings in educational psychology classes.
- Video Examples of various concepts and principles presented in the chapter.
- A Practice for Your Licensure Exam exercise that resembles the kinds of questions appearing on many teacher licensure tests.

CHAPTER OUTLINE

CHAPTER OBJECTIVES

- **Objective 12.1:** Describe several processes involved in instructional planning, and explain how planning and instruction are closely intertwined.
- **Objective 12.2:** Explain how you can effectively promote students' learning through expository approaches to instruction.
- **Objective 12.3:** Explain how you can get students actively involved in working with classroom subject matter through hands-on, "head-on," and practice activities.
- **Objective 12.4:** Describe various strategies you might use to help students learn through the questions you ask and through student–student interactions and collaborative endeavors.
- **Objective 12.5:** Choose appropriate instructional strategies for different kinds of students and for different instructional goals and objectives.

Chapter 12

Instructional Strategies

CASE STUDY: Oregon Trail

Michele Minichiello's fifth-grade class is learning about the westward migration of American settlers during the middle 1800s. Today's lesson is about one well-traveled route, the Oregon Trail.[1]

"The covered wagons were about 4 feet by 10 feet," Ms. Minichiello tells her class. She has two students use masking tape to mark a 4-by-10-foot rectangle on the classroom carpet. "How much room would that give you for your family and supplies?" The students agree that people would have to be quite choosy about what they brought with them on the trip west.

"Let's brainstorm some of the things the settlers might have packed," Ms. Minichiello says. The students volunteer many possibilities—food, water, blankets, rifles, medicine, spare wagon parts—and Ms. Minichiello writes them on the chalkboard. She asks the class to be more specific about the items on the board (e.g., what kinds of food? how much of each kind?) and then passes out reading materials that list the supplies a typical family would actually pack for the journey. As the students read and discuss the materials in small cooperative learning groups, Ms. Minichiello circulates among them to show old photographs of how the inside of a covered wagon looked when occupied by a family and its possessions.

Once the students have finished their reading, Ms. Minichiello directs their attention to their own supply list on the chalkboard and asks them to compare it to the list of typical supplies presented in the reading materials. The students notice many discrepancies:

Lacy: We need much more flour.
Janie: [Referring to an item listed in the reading materials] I don't think they should bring 100 pounds of coffee.
Curt: [Also referring to the reading materials] I don't think they need 50 pounds of lard.
Ms. M: What were some of the things the pioneers had to be prepared for?

After the class discusses possible reasons for the various items the settlers brought with them, Ms. Minichiello asks students to put themselves in the settlers' shoes:

Ms. M: If *you* were taking such a trip now—if you were moving far away from where you live now—what things would you bring with you?
Misha: Computer.
Lou: Cell phone.
Dana: Refrigerator.
Cerise: My dog.
Ms. M: Imagine that your family isn't doing well, and so you decide to travel to a distant planet. It's very expensive to travel there. You can take only *one* item, so pick the one item you would take. Assume there will be food and a place to sleep. Take five minutes to pick one item, and explain why you would take it.

Ms. Minichiello distributes index cards on which the students can write their responses. After a few minutes she asks, "Who found that it was hard to pick just one item?" Almost all of the students raise their hands. "What I wanted you to realize is that if you had been a child back then, it would have been really hard to leave most of your things behind."

- **What specific instructional strategies does Ms. Minichiello use to engage and motivate her students?**

[1] I observed Michele's lesson when I was supervising her teaching internship, and she gave me permission to describe it here. The students' names are pseudonyms.

MS. MINICHIELLO USES SEVERAL STRATEGIES to engage and motivate her students:

- She makes the lesson a very social, interactive one.
- She arouses interest by engaging students in a physical activity (marking the dimensions of a wagon on the floor) and asking them to imagine what the settlers might have been thinking and feeling.
- She creates cognitive dissonance by presenting a supply list quite different from the one the class has generated.
- She poses a challenging task ("Pick one item.").

Furthermore, Ms. Minichiello encourages effective long-term memory storage processes, such as visual imagery, organization, and elaboration:

- She uses a masking tape "wagon" and photographs to make the subject matter concrete and vivid.
- She has the class consider cause-and-effect relationships that justify the supply list ("What were some of the things the pioneers had to be prepared for?").
- She asks the students to relate the settlers' situation to one they themselves might face.

Much of Ms. Minichiello's lesson reflects **teacher-directed instruction**, in which the teacher calls most of the shots, choosing which topics will be addressed, directing students' activities, and so on. Even when she asks fairly open-ended questions (e.g., "If *you* were taking such a trip now, . . . what things would you bring with you?"), she is nudging students toward the kinds of conclusions she wants them to draw about life on the Oregon Trail. But one of her strategies—her use of small cooperative learning groups for studying reading materials about the westward journey—reflects **learner-directed instruction**, in which students have considerable control regarding the specific issues they address and the ways they address those issues.[2]

Ultimately, our decisions about whether to use teacher-directed or learner-directed strategies—or to combine the two approaches, as Ms. Minichiello does—should be based on our goals for instruction and on the knowledge and skills our students bring to the situation. As you read this chapter, then, don't think about choosing a single "best" instructional strategy. Instead, think about how different strategies may be more or less suitable in different contexts and how you might often combine them effectively in a single lesson.

To organize our discussion in this chapter, I've grouped instructional strategies under four general headings. The first step any teacher must take, of course, is *planning*—deciding in advance both what needs to be accomplished and how best to accomplish it. We'll then look at three general categories of instructional methods: *expository strategies* (directly presenting the information to be learned); *hands-on, "head-on," and practice activities* (having students actively work with and apply the subject matter); and *interactive and collaborative strategies* (having students discuss certain topics and in other ways help one another learn). These three general approaches to instruction are not intended to be mutually exclusive. For instance, expository strategies sometimes have a hands-on element and student–student interactions. And some hands-on activities are very collaborative in nature, with students working on challenging tasks in small cooperative groups.

teacher-directed instruction Approach to instruction in which the teacher is largely in control of the content and course of the lesson.

learner-directed instruction Approach to instruction in which students have considerable control regarding the issues they address and the ways they address them.

[2]Some educational psychologists instead use the terms *teacher-centered* and *learner-centered instruction*. The American Psychological Association's 14 *Learner-Centered Psychological Principles* encompass many of the concepts and principles identified in earlier chapters. You can find these principles at the APA's website at www.apa.org; type "learner-centered principles" in the search box.

Keep in mind that planning and instruction are invariably intertwined. For instance, planning takes place not only before instruction but also *during* instruction; as teachers, we must continue to revise our plans (mentally, at least) as a lesson or instructional unit proceeds. Furthermore, planning and instruction each interact with two other critical aspects of classroom practice: creating a productive classroom environment (the topic of Chapter 13) and assessing students' performance (the topic of Chapters 14 and 15). As you'll discover in this and the following chapters, planning, instruction, the classroom environment, and assessment practices not only influence one another but also influence and are influenced by student characteristics and behaviors (see Figure 12.1). As we make our day-to-day decisions in the classroom, we must always take into account what we know about each of our students.

FIGURE 12.1 Planning, instruction, the classroom environment, assessment, and student characteristics are all interdependent and mutually influence one another.

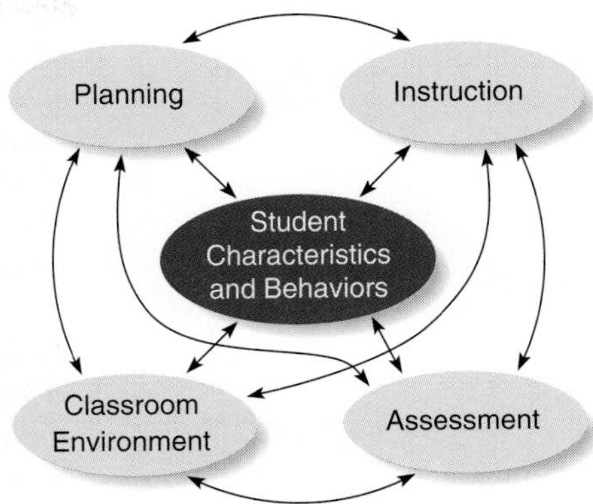

Planning for Instruction

Good teachers engage in considerable advance planning: They identify the knowledge and skills they want students to acquire, determine an appropriate sequence in which to teach such knowledge and skills, and develop classroom lessons and activities that will maximize learning and keep students motivated and on task. Ideally, they also coordinate their plans with other teachers—for example, identifying common goals toward which they will all strive or developing interdisciplinary units that involve two or more classes and subject areas. And they regularly share their plans and upcoming activities with their students.

Identifying the Goals of Instruction

An essential part of planning instruction is identifying the specific things students should accomplish during a lesson or unit, as well as the things they should accomplish over the course of a semester or school year. Educators use a variety of terms for such results, including *goals, objectives, competencies, proficiencies, targets, benchmarks,* and *outcomes.* In this book, I'll typically use the term **instructional goals** when referring to general, long-term outcomes of instruction. I'll use the term **instructional objectives** when referring to more specific outcomes of a particular lesson or unit.

Regardless of the terminology used, experts agree that the desired results of instruction should influence what we teach, how we teach it, and how we assess students' learning and achievement (e.g., Darling-Hammond & Bransford, 2005; Kuhn, 2007). In fact, as a general rule, we should *begin* the planning process by determining what we ultimately want students to know and be able to do. One popular approach is a **backward design**, in which teachers proceed through this sequence (Wiggins & McTighe, 2005):

1. Identify the desired results in terms of knowledge and skills that students should ultimately attain.
2. Determine acceptable evidence—in the form of performance on various classroom assessment tasks—to verify that students have achieved those results.
3. Plan learning experiences and instructional activities that enable students to demonstrate—through their performance on the assessment tasks—attainment of the desired results.

With such an approach, we essentially *begin at the end* and then choose assessment tasks and instructional strategies that are specifically related to that end. For example, if the objective for a unit on addition is *knowledge* of number facts, we may want to use drill and practice (perhaps flashcards or gamelike computer software) to enhance

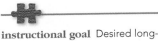

instructional goal Desired long-term outcome of instruction.

instructional objective Desired outcome of a lesson or unit.

backward design Approach to instructional planning in which a teacher first determines the desired end result (i.e., what knowledge and skills students should acquire) and then identifies appropriate assessments and instructional strategies.

Consider your instructional goals and objectives when choosing your instructional methods.

students' automaticity for these facts, and we may want to use a timed test to measure students' ability to recall the facts quickly and easily. But if our objective is *application* of number facts, we may instead want to focus instruction and assessment methods on word problems or on activities involving real objects and hands-on measurements.

Students, too, benefit from knowing the objectives of a lesson or unit. When they know what we hope they will accomplish, they can make more informed decisions about how to focus their efforts and allocate their study time, and they can more effectively monitor their comprehension as they read and study (Gronlund & Brookhart, 2009; McAshan, 1979). For example, if we tell students that we expect them to apply mathematics concepts and procedures to everyday situations, they will probably think about and study mathematics very differently than if we tell them to memorize definitions and formulas.

Aligning Instructional Goals with National, International, and State Standards People have varying opinions about the kinds of things students should learn in elementary and secondary school classrooms. For example, you may have heard some parents, taxpayers, and policy makers advocating for increasing students' factual knowledge—a perspective sometimes referred to as *back to the basics* or *cultural literacy* (e.g., Hirsch, 1996). Certainly some factual knowledge is essential for students' long-term academic and professional success. But equally important are the higher-level thinking skills (e.g., problem solving, critical thinking) and general *habits of mind* (e.g., scientific reasoning, drawing inferences from historical documents) that are central to various academic disciplines (P. A. Alexander, 1997; Brophy, 2008; R. K. Sawyer, 2006).

myeducationlab

Find web links to content area standards developed by the 50 U.S. states and various discipline-specific professional organizations in MyEducationLab. (To find these links, go to MyEducationLab, click on the *Resources* tab at the top of the screen, and select "Licensure and Standards.")

One source of guidance comes from content area **standards** identified by national and international discipline-specific professional groups (e.g., National Council of Teachers of English, National Council for Geographic Education). Such standards are typically in the form of general statements regarding the knowledge and skills that students should acquire at various grade levels, as well as the characteristics their accomplishments should reflect. Also, in the United States, state departments of education—as well as some local school districts—have established comprehensive lists of standards in reading, writing, math, science, and social studies and sometimes also in such domains as art, music, foreign languages, and physical education. As an illustration, Table 12.1 presents examples of North Carolina's standards—which state educators call *competency goals*—for English Language Arts in grades 1, 4, 7, and 11 (see columns 1 and 2 of the table).

Existing standards for particular content domains are certainly useful in helping us focus instruction on important educational goals in various content domains. However, such standards have several limitations to keep in mind. First, many are based on topics and skills that are *typically taught* at various grade levels, rather than on developmental research concerning what students can reasonably accomplish at different ages (e.g., vanSledright & Limón, 2006). Second, some sets of standards are so lengthy that they might lead us to provide only fragmented, superficial coverage of topics, rather than follow the *Less-is-more* principle advocated in previous chapters (e.g., Schmidt, 2008). But perhaps most importantly, these standards largely overlook goals that lie *outside* particular content areas—effective learning strategies, self-regulation techniques, good social skills, and so on.

Writing Useful Goals and Objectives Given the limitations of existing content-area standards, we cannot rely on them exclusively: We must also develop some of our own goals and objectives. Ideally, we should identify goals and objectives that can give us concrete guidance as we plan instructional activities and assessment procedures. The Into the Classroom feature "Identifying Appropriate Goals and Objectives" offers suggestions for writing useful ones. The third column in Table 12.1 applies some of these suggestions in translating the examples of North Carolina's competency goals into more specific classroom goals and objectives, and the rightmost column in the table identifies relevant instructional strategies. (We'll identify assessment strategies for the same standards and goals in a separate table in Chapter 14.)

standards General statements regarding the knowledge and skills that students should gain and the characteristics that their accomplishments should reflect.

TABLE 12.1
Examples of How You Might Align Classroom Goals, Objectives, and Instructional Strategies with State Standards at Different Grade Levels

Grade Level	Examples of North Carolina's Grade-Specific Competency Goals for English Language Arts	Examples of More Specific Goals and Objectives You Might Write Related to the State Goals	Examples of Instructional Strategies That Address These Goals and Objectives
Grade 1	Read and comprehend both fiction and nonfiction text appropriate for grade one using: • Prior knowledge • Summary • Questions • Graphic organizers (Competency Goal 2.03)	Use prior knowledge to draw correct inferences from a work of literature in which the author has omitted important information.	• Read high-interest stories, stopping frequently to ask questions that require students to go beyond the text itself (e.g., to speculate about what a character might be feeling).
	Respond and elaborate in answering what, when, where, and how questions. (Competency Goal 2.07)	Identify main characters, setting, and general plot line in a short story.	• Have students create props for and act out a story they have recently read.
Grade 4	Interact with the text before, during, and after reading, listening, and viewing by: • Setting a purpose using prior knowledge and text information • Making predictions • Formulating questions • Locating relevant information • Making connections with previous experiences, information, and ideas (Competency Goal 2.02)	Make predictions about how the plot line might unfold in a novel.	• As a reading group discusses Carl Hiaasen's *Hoot*, ask students to speculate about how the plot might progress and to identify clues in the text that support their predictions.
	Make inferences, draw conclusions, make generalizations, and support by referencing the text. (Competency Goal 2.05)	Identify cause-and-effect relationships in assigned readings in a history textbook.	• When students are reading their history textbook, ask *why* questions that encourage cause-and-effect connections (e.g., "Why did Columbus's crew want to turn back after several weeks on the open sea?").
Grade 7	Respond to informational materials that are read, heard, and/or viewed by: • Monitoring comprehension for understanding of what is read, heard, and/or viewed • Analyzing the characteristics of informational works • Summarizing information • Determining the importance of information • Making connections to related topics/information • Drawing inferences and/or conclusions • Generating questions (Competency Goal 2.01)	Use the organizational structure of a science textbook to facilitate learning and studying its content.	• Before students read a chapter in their science textbook, have them use its headings and subheadings to (a) create a general outline of the chapter and (b) generate questions they hope to answer as they read the chapter. Then, for homework, ask them to read and take notes on the chapter, using the outline and self-questions as guides for note taking.
	Analyze the purpose of the author or creator by: • Monitoring comprehension for understanding of what is read, heard, and/or viewed • Examining any bias, apparent or hidden messages, emotional factors, and/or propaganda techniques • Exploring and evaluating the underlying assumptions of the author/creator • Understanding the effects of the author's craft on the reader/viewer/listener (Competency Goal 4.01)	Identify persuasive techniques used in advertisements for commercial products in magazines and online websites.	• Give students an advertisement for a self-improvement product (e.g., a diet pill or exercise equipment); have them work in small cooperative learning groups to (a) identify the advertiser's motives and (b) evaluate the quality of evidence for the product's effectiveness.

Continues

TABLE 12.1 CONTINUED

Grade Level	Examples of North Carolina's Grade-Specific Competency Goals for English Language Arts	Examples of More Specific Goals and Objectives You Might Write Related to the State Goals	Examples of Instructional Strategies That Address These Goals and Objectives
Grade 11	Demonstrate the ability to read, listen to, and view a variety of increasingly complex print and non-print informational texts appropriate to grade level and course literary focus, by: • Selecting, monitoring, and modifying as necessary reading strategies appropriate to readers' purpose • Identifying and analyzing text components . . . and evaluating their impact on the text • Providing textual evidence to support understanding of and reader's response to text • Demonstrating comprehension of main ideas and supporting details • Summarizing key events and/or points from text • Making inferences, predicting, and drawing conclusions based on text • Identifying and analyzing personal, social, historical or cultural influences, contexts, or biases . . . (portions of Competency Goal 2.03 for English III)	Identify authors' political and cultural biases in their descriptions of current events.	• Ask students to identify the unstated assumptions underlying two news magazines' depictions of the same event (e.g., an assumption that one group is good or right and another is bad or wrong).
	Assess the power, validity, and truthfulness in the logic of arguments given in public and political documents by: • Identifying the intent and message of the author or artist • Recognizing how the author addresses opposing viewpoints • Articulating a personal response to the message and method of the author or artist • Evaluating the historical significance of the work (Competency Goal 4.03 for English III)	Identify and evaluate methods of persuasion used in editorials in the news media.	• Describe common techniques in persuasive writing, and have students find them in newspaper editorials.

Source: Competency Goals (second column) are from a website maintained by North Carolina's Department of Public Instruction and are provided with permission from the Public Schools of North Carolina. Standards are curent as of June 30, 2009, from www.dpi.state.nc.us/curriculum/languagearts/scos/. Please note that North Carolina is currently revising its Standard Course of Study; thus, the Competency Goals may change within the next few years.

An especially important suggestion in the Into the Classroom feature is to *include goals and objectives with varying levels of complexity and sophistication.* One tool that can help us keep a broad view of what students should learn and be able to do is a recent revision of **Bloom's taxonomy**, a list of six general cognitive processes that vary from simple to complex:

Bloom's taxonomy Taxonomy of six cognitive processes, varying in complexity, that lessons might be designed to foster.

1. *Remember:* Recognizing or recalling information learned at an earlier time and stored in long-term memory
2. *Understand:* Constructing meaning from instructional materials and messages (e.g., drawing inferences, identifying new examples, summarizing)
3. *Apply:* Using knowledge in a familiar or new situation

INTO THE Classroom

Identifying Appropriate Goals and Objectives

Consult local, state, national, and international standards, but don't rely on them exclusively.

In identifying instructional goals for the year, a middle school science teacher considers both the state science standards and the standards developed by the National Academy of Sciences. In addition, he identifies specific goals related to two issues directly affecting students in his inner-city school district: air pollution and poor nutrition.

Identify both short-term objectives and long-term goals.

An elementary school teacher wants students to learn how to spell 10 new words each week. She also wants them to write a coherent and grammatically correct short story by the end of the school year.

In addition to goals related to specific topics and content areas, identify goals related to students' general long-term academic success.

A middle school social studies teacher realizes that early adolescence is an important time for developing the learning and study strategies that students will need in high school and college. Throughout the school year, he continually introduces new strategies for learning and remembering classroom subject matter—effective ways students might organize their notes, mnemonic techniques they might use to help them remember specific facts, questions they might try to answer as they read a textbook chapter, and so on.

Include goals and objectives with varying levels of complexity and sophistication.

A high school physics teacher wants students not only to understand basic kinds of machines (e.g., levers, wedges) but also to recognize examples of these machines in their own lives and to use them to solve real-world problems.

Consider physical, social, motivational, and affective outcomes as well as cognitive outcomes.

A physical education teacher wants his students to know the basic rules of basketball and to dribble and pass the ball appropriately. He also wants them to acquire a love of basketball, effective ways of working cooperatively with teammates, and a general desire to stay physically fit.

Describe goals and objectives not in terms of what the teacher will do during a lesson but in terms of what *students* should be able to do at the *end* of instruction.

A Spanish teacher knows that students often confuse the verbs *estar* and *ser* because both are translated into English as "to be." She identifies this objective for her students: "Students will correctly conjugate *estar* and *ser* in the present tense and use each one in appropriate contexts."

When writing short-term objectives, identify specific behaviors that will reflect accomplishment of the objectives.

In a unit on the food pyramid, an elementary school teacher identifies this objective for students: "Students will create menus for a breakfast, a lunch, and a dinner that, in combination, include all elements of the pyramid in appropriate proportions."

When writing long-term goals that involve complex topics or skills, list a few abstract outcomes and give examples of specific behaviors that reflect each one.

Faculty members at a middle school identify this instructional goal for all students at their school: "Students will demonstrate effective classroom listening skills—for example, by taking thorough and accurate notes, answering teacher questions correctly, and seeking clarification when they don't understand."

Provide opportunities for students to identify some goals and objectives of their own.

A high school art teacher asks each student to choose a particular medium to focus on during the semester (e.g., pastels, oils, clay) and to identify at least three skills to improve while working with the chosen medium. She helps students develop concrete goals toward which they will work and specific criteria they can use to evaluate their progress.

Sources: Brophy, 2008; Brophy & Alleman, 1991; N. S. Cole, 1990; Gronlund & Brookhart, 2009; Popham, 1995; Wiggins & McTighe, 2005.

4. *Analyze:* Breaking information into its constituent parts and perhaps also identifying interrelationships among the parts
5. *Evaluate:* Making judgments about information using certain criteria or standards
6. *Create:* Putting together knowledge, procedures, or both to form a coherent, structured, and possibly original whole (L. W. Anderson et al., 2001)

This taxonomy is hardly an exhaustive list of what students should be able to do while learning classroom subject matter; for instance, it doesn't include psychomotor skills or productive attitudes related to a topic. Even so, it can certainly remind us that there is much more to school learning and academic achievement than remembering discrete facts.

myeducationlab

Find additional taxonomies in the supplementary reading "Using Taxonomies to Formulate Instructional Goals and Objectives." (To find this reading, go to Chapter 12 of the Book-Specific Resources in MyEducationLab, and then select *Supplementary Readings.*)

task analysis Process of identifying the specific behaviors, knowledge, or cognitive processes necessary to master a particular subject area or skill.

Conducting a Task Analysis

In addition to identifying goals and objectives for instruction, we need to determine how best to break down complex topics and skills into manageable chunks. Consider these four teachers:

- Ms. Begay plans to teach her third graders how to solve arithmetic word problems. She also wants to help them learn more effectively from the things they read.
- Mr. Marzano, a middle school physical education teacher, is beginning a unit on basketball. He wants his students to develop enough proficiency in the sport to feel comfortable playing both on organized school basketball teams and in less formal games with friends and neighbors.
- Mr. Wu, a junior high school music teacher, needs to teach his new trumpet students how to play a recognizable version of "Seventy-Six Trombones" in time for the New Year's Day parade.
- Ms. Flores, a high school social studies teacher, is going to introduce the intricacies of the federal judicial system to her classes.

These teachers have something in common: They want to teach complex topics or skills. All four should probably conduct a **task analysis**, identifying the specific knowledge and behaviors necessary to master the subject matter in question. The task analysis can then guide them as they select the most appropriate methods and sequence in which to teach that subject matter.

Figure 12.2 illustrates three general approaches to task analysis (Jonassen, Hannum, & Tessmer, 1989):

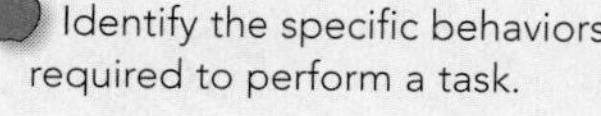

1. *Behavioral analysis.* One way of analyzing a complex task is to identify the specific behaviors required to perform it (much as a behaviorist might do). For example, Mr. Marzano can identify the specific physical movements involved in dribbling, passing, and shooting a basketball. Similarly, Mr. Wu can identify the behaviors that students must master to play a trumpet successfully: holding the instrument with the fingers placed appropriately on the valves, blowing correctly into the mouthpiece, and so on.

2. *Subject matter analysis.* Another approach is to break down the subject matter into the specific topics, concepts, and principles that it includes. For example, Ms. Flores can identify various aspects of the judicial system (concepts such as *innocent until proven guilty* and *reasonable doubt*, the roles that judges and juries play, etc.) and their interrelationships. And Mr. Wu, who needs to teach his new trumpet students

FIGURE 12.2 Three ways of analyzing a task

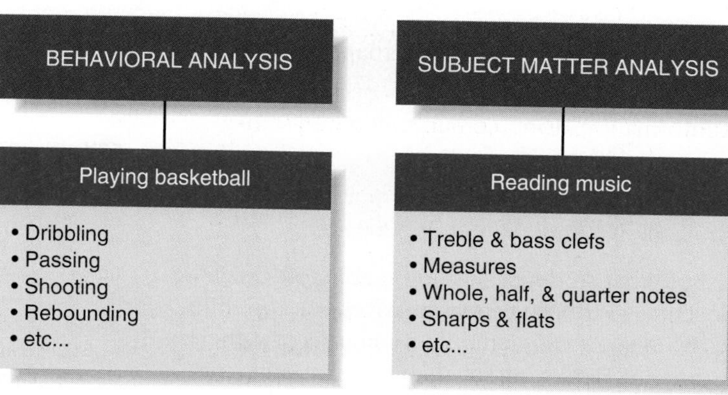

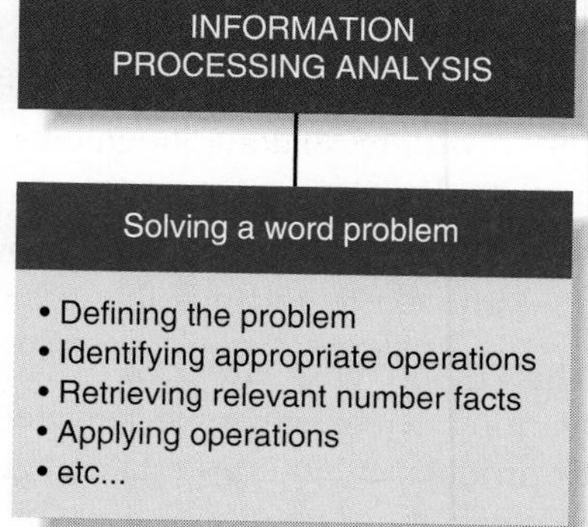

how to read music as well as how to play the instrument, can identify the basic elements of written music that students must be able to interpret, such as the treble and bass clefs and whole, half, and quarter notes. Subject matter analysis is especially important when the subject matter being taught includes many interrelated ideas and concepts that students should learn meaningfully and with conceptual understanding.

Break down the subject matter in terms of specific topics, ideas, concepts, and so on.

3. *Information processing analysis.* A third approach is to specify the cognitive processes involved in a task. To illustrate, Ms. Begay can identify the mental processes involved in successfully solving an arithmetic word problem—for instance, correct encoding of the problem (e.g., determining whether it requires addition, subtraction, etc.) and rapid retrieval of basic number facts. She can also identify specific cognitive strategies useful in reading comprehension, such as finding main ideas, elaborating, and summarizing.

Break down a task in terms of the specific cognitive processes it requires.

To get an idea of what a task analysis involves, try the following exercise.

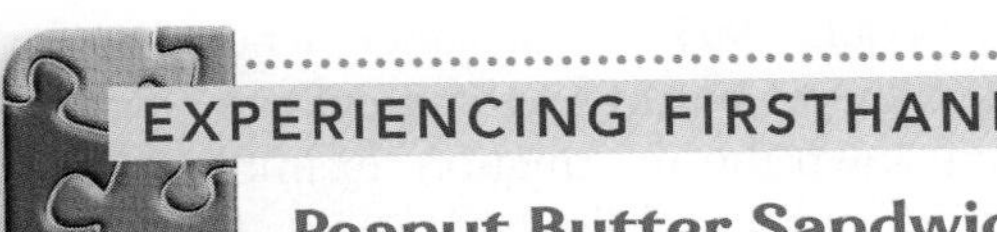

EXPERIENCING FIRSTHAND

Peanut Butter Sandwich

Conduct a task analysis for the process of making a peanut butter sandwich:

1. Decide whether your approach should be a behavioral analysis, a subject matter analysis, or an information processing analysis.
2. Using the approach you've selected, break the sandwich-making task into a number of small, teachable steps.
3. (Optional) If you're hungry and have the necessary materials close at hand, make an actual sandwich following the steps you've identified. Did your initial analysis omit any important steps?

Chances are good that you chose a behavioral analysis, because making a peanut butter sandwich is largely a behavioral, rather than a mental, task. For instance, you must know how to unscrew the peanut butter jar lid, get an appropriate amount of peanut butter on your knife, spread the peanut butter gently enough that you don't tear the bread, and so on.

Conducting task analyses for complex skills and topics has at least two advantages (Desberg & Taylor, 1986; Jonassen et al., 1989). First, when we identify a task's specific components—whether behaviors, concepts and ideas, or cognitive processes—we gain a better sense of what things students need to learn and the order in which they can most effectively learn them. Second, a task analysis helps us choose appropriate instructional strategies. For example, if one necessary component of solving arithmetic word problems is the rapid retrieval of math facts from memory, repeated practice of these facts may be critical for developing automaticity. If another aspect of such problem solving is identifying the relevant procedure to apply (e.g., addition, subtraction, etc.), then we must promote a true understanding of mathematical concepts and principles, perhaps by using concrete manipulatives or authentic activities.

Sometimes a task analysis will lead us to conclude that we can most effectively teach a complex task by teaching some or all of its components separately. For instance, Mr. Wu may initially ask his beginning trumpet students to practice blowing into the mouthpiece correctly without worrying about the specific notes they produce. On other occasions, however, it may be more appropriate to teach the desired knowledge and behaviors entirely within the context of the overall task; by doing so, we make the subject matter more meaningful for students. For example, Ms. Begay should almost certainly teach her students the processes involved in learning effectively from reading materials—elaborating, summarizing, and so on—primarily within the context of authentic reading tasks.

Developing a Lesson Plan

After identifying goals for instruction and perhaps conducting a task analysis as well, effective teachers develop a **lesson plan** to guide them during instruction. A lesson plan typically includes the following:

- The goal(s) or objective(s) of the lesson
- Instructional materials (e.g., textbooks, handouts) and equipment required
- Instructional strategies to be used and the sequence in which they will be used
- Assessment method(s) planned

myeducationlab

Get a sense of what a lesson plan looks like in the supplementary reading "Example of a Lesson Plan." (To find this reading, go to Chapter 12 of the Book-Specific Resources in MyEducationLab, and then select *Supplementary Readings*.) Also, use the online Lesson Plan Builder to guide you as you create lesson plans appropriate for your age-group and subject matter. (To find this helpful tool, go to MyEducationLab and click on the *Resources* tab at the top of the screen.)

In your first few months of teaching, create fairly detailed lesson plans to guide you, but be flexible when circumstances call for adjustments.

Any lesson plan should, of course, take into account the students who will be learning—their developmental levels, prior knowledge, cultural backgrounds, and so on.

As a beginning teacher, you will probably want to develop fairly detailed lesson plans that describe how you are going to help your students learn the subject matter in question (Calderhead, 1996; Sternberg & Horvath, 1995). For instance, when I began teaching middle school geography—and also when I began teaching college psychology—I spent many hours each week writing down the information, examples, questions, and student activities I wanted to use during the following week. But as you gain experience teaching certain topics, you will learn which strategies work effectively and which do not, and you may use some of the effective ones frequently enough that you can retrieve them quickly and easily from long-term memory. Consequently, as time goes on, you will find that planning lessons becomes far less time consuming and that you can do a lot of your planning in your head rather than on paper (Calderhead, 1996).

We should usually think of a lesson plan more as a guide than as a recipe—in other words, as something that can and should be adjusted as events unfold (Calderhead, 1996; Corno, 2008). For example, during the course of a lesson, we may find that students have less prior knowledge than we expected; thus, we may need to back up and teach material we thought they had already mastered. Or if students express curiosity or have intriguing insights into a particular topic, we may want to spend more time exploring it than we had originally intended.

As we proceed through the school year, our long-range plans will also change somewhat. For instance, we may find that our initial task analyses of desired knowledge and skills were overly simplistic, or we may discover that our initial expectations for students' achievement are either unrealistically high or unnecessarily low. We must continually revise our plans as instruction proceeds and as classroom assessments reveal how well students are learning and achieving.

Setting Up a Class Website

For reasons we've previously identified, students learn and perform more effectively when they know in advance what their teachers expect them to learn and be able to do. Students should also have advance notice about upcoming activities and assessments. A long-standing practice at the secondary and college levels is to give students a printed syllabus that lists topics, homework assignments, due dates, and scheduled quizzes. But in this age of widespread access to computer technology, many teachers can now share such information—and much more—on class-specific Internet websites within their school's overall website.

Figure 12.3 shows the opening screen for a website my son Jeff created for his sixth-grade information technology (IT) class at Prem Tinsulanonda International School in Thailand. Notice that the course resources include two documents—a course outline and assessment criteria—that students can download. Scrolling farther down in the website, students can get information on various units and assignments for the course. A sidebar presents a calendar with due dates and a place to upload or view students' completed assignments. Jeff created the site using free-of-charge software

lesson plan Teacher-constructed guide for a lesson that identifies instructional goals, necessary materials, instructional strategies, and one or more assessment methods.

FIGURE 12.3 Opening screen of a website for a ninth-grade information technology class

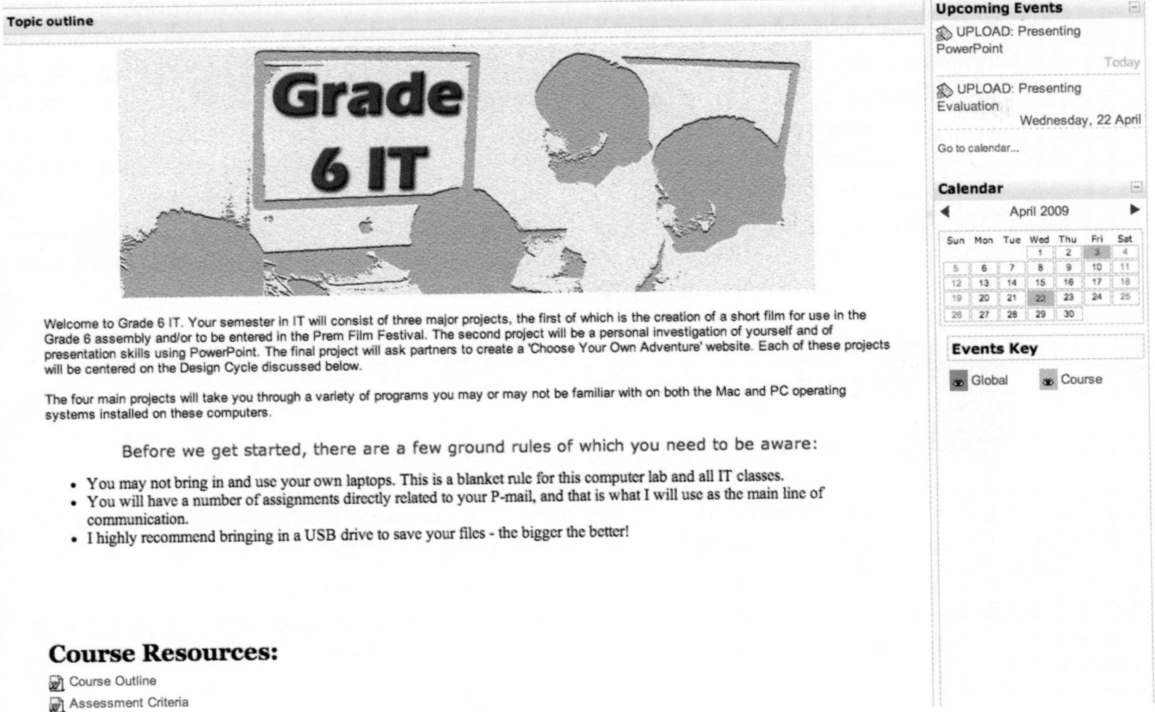

Source: Used courtesy of Jeff Ormrod.

called Moodle (www.moodle.org); similar software is available through Sakai (sakaiproject.org).

Expository Strategies

Traditionally, the most common approach to teaching has been **expository instruction**, in which information is presented (i.e., *exposed*) in essentially the same form in which students are expected to learn it. Ms. Minichiello's lesson about the Oregon Trail has several elements of expository instruction: She presents the dimensions of a typical covered wagon, distributes reading materials about how the settlers packed for the long trip west, and shows photographs of pioneer families and their temporary covered-wagon homes. As we'll see in the upcoming sections, some forms of expository instruction (e.g., textbooks) are exclusively one way in nature, with information going only from an expert to learners. But most forms incorporate some exchange of information between a teacher (or perhaps a virtual teacher, such as a computer) and learners.

Lectures and Textbooks

Some theorists have criticized lectures and textbooks for putting students in a physically passive role (e.g., Skinner, 1968). But cognitive psychologists argue that students are often *mentally* active during such seemingly passive activities as listening and reading (Ausubel et al., 1978; Mayer, 2004; Weinert & Helmke, 1995). The degree to which students learn from expository instruction depends on the particular cognitive processes they engage in—the extent to which they pay attention, focus on meaningful (rather than rote) learning, monitor their comprehension, and so on.

expository instruction Approach to instruction in which information is presented in more or less the same form in which students are expected to learn it.

Unfortunately, lectures and textbooks don't always present information in ways that promote learning. For instance, you can probably think of high school or college instructors whose lectures were dry, disorganized, confusing, or in some other way nonmotivating and noninformative. And analyses of school textbooks in such diverse disciplines as history, geography, and science have found the focus of many texts to be on teaching specific facts, with little attention to helping students learn the facts in a meaningful way (Alleman & Brophy, 1992; I. L. Beck & McKeown, 1994, 2001; Chambliss & Calfee, 1989).

What strategies can we use to help students learn from classroom lectures and reading assignments? The following exercise might give you a few ideas about techniques that work for *you* as a learner.

EXPERIENCING FIRSTHAND

Finding Pedagogy in the Book

1. Look back at two or three of the preceding chapters. Find places where specific things I've done have helped you learn and remember the material more effectively. What strategies did I use to facilitate your cognitive processing?
2. In those same chapters, can you find places where you had difficulty processing the material presented? If so, what might I have done differently in those instances?

I'm hoping that the Experiencing Firsthand exercises have helped you relate new topics to your own knowledge and experiences. I'm hoping, too, that the case studies and student work samples have made abstract ideas more concrete and easy to understand. Perhaps some of the tables and graphics have helped you organize concepts and principles. But if you've found certain parts of the book confusing or difficult to understand, I encourage you to let me know.[3]

The Into the Classroom feature "Using Expository Instruction Effectively" suggests several research-based strategies for promoting effective cognitive processing and learning through explanations, lectures, and other expository approaches. Expository instruction has a distinct advantage: It enables us to present information quickly and efficiently. However, a major disadvantage is that, by itself, it doesn't allow us to assess students' progress in learning the subject matter. When we need to make sure that students master information and skills that are prerequisites for later lessons, the three strategies we consider next—mastery learning, direct instruction, and computer-based instruction—are possible alternatives.

Mastery Learning

Imagine that a class of 27 students, listed in Figure 12.4, is beginning a unit on fractions. The class progresses through several lessons as follows:

- *Lesson 1.* The class studies the basic idea that a fraction represents a part of a whole: The denominator indicates the number of pieces into which the whole has been divided, and the numerator indicates how many of those pieces are present. By the end of the lesson, 23 children understand what a fraction is. But Sarah, LaShaun, Jason K., and Jason M. are either partly or totally confused.

[3] I'm always eager to hear my readers' suggestions for improving the book. You can reach me at *jormrod@alumni.brown.edu*.

INTO THE Classroom

Using Expository Instruction Effectively

Use an *advance organizer*—a verbal or graphic introduction that lays out the general organizational framework of upcoming material—to help students make meaningful connections among the things they learn.

A high school biology teacher introduces a unit on vertebrates by saying, "Vertebrates all have backbones. We'll be talking about five phyla of vertebrates—mammals, birds, reptiles, amphibians, and fish—that differ from one another in several ways, including whether their members are warm blooded or cold blooded; whether they have hair, scales, or feathers; and whether they lay eggs or bear live young."

Make ongoing connections between new information and things students already know.

A middle school geography teacher draws an analogy between how a glacier grows and how pancake batter behaves as it's poured into a frying pan: "As more and more substance is added to the middle, the edges spread farther and farther out."

Informally assess students' existing understandings of the topic to determine whether they have misconceptions that require conceptual change.

When beginning a unit on the solar system, a fourth-grade teacher asks her students, "What do we mean when we say that the sun *sets*? Does the sun really go down at the end of the day?" Several students respond that the sun does indeed go down and then travels to the other side of the world. The teacher isn't surprised (as this is a common misconception) but works hard to show students that the earth's rotation gives the appearance of the sun moving around it, when actually the opposite is true: The earth revolves around the sun.

Present new ideas in a logical, organized manner that enables students to make appropriate interconnections among them.

While describing the contributions of different vitamins and minerals to people's health and well-being, a ninth-grade health teacher writes each nutrient and its benefits in a two-column table on the chalkboard.

Give students numerous signals about the things that are most important for them to learn and remember.

A high school government teacher begins a unit about the U.S. government system by writing the phrase "Checks and Balances" on the chalkboard and underlining it with big, bold strokes. "This is a key principle that guided delegates to the Constitutional Convention as they wrote the Constitution. We're going to look at how each of the three branches of government—executive, legislative, and judicial—places limits on the power of the other two branches. Be sure to include at least four examples of checks and balances in your class notes for today." Later in the class session, the teacher assigns a textbook chapter for homework and distributes a list of questions that students should be able to answer after they've finished reading the chapter.

Use visual aids to help students encode material visually as well as verbally.

In a lesson on the Oregon Trail, a fifth-grade teacher shows photographs of wagon trains and typical covered wagons to help students get a sense of how arduous the westward migration was for many pioneer families.

Pace your presentation slowly enough to give students adequate time to think about and meaningfully process the information.

To demonstrate how to make a pinch pot from a ball of clay, an elementary school art teacher proceeds through the steps slowly and deliberately, explaining what he's doing every step of the way: "First I roll the clay into a nice round ball—as round as I can make it, with no cracks or rough edges. . . . Okay, see how I've done that? Now I hold the ball in both hands and gently push my thumbs into the middle, slowly pushing them farther and farther in, but being sure that I don't push them out the other side of the ball. . . . And then I gradually push the sides of the ball outward, continually turning the ball so that I make the sides of my pot an even thickness all the way around."

At the end of a lecture or reading assignment, summarize the key points of the lesson as a way of helping students organize the material and identify its main ideas.

A high school English teacher sums up a lesson on the poems of Emily Dickinson by describing the characteristics that make Dickinson's poetry so unique and powerful.

Sources: Bulgren, Deshler, Schumaker, & Lenz, 2000; Carney & Levin, 2002; Corkill, 1992; Dansereau, 1995; Donnelly & McDaniel, 1993; E. L. Ferguson & Hegarty, 1995; Hansen & Pearson, 1983; J. Hartley & Trueman, 1982; Krajcik, 1991; Ku, Chan, Wu, & Chen, 2008; J. R. Levin & Mayer, 1993; M. C. Linn et al., 1996; R. F. Lorch, Lorch, & Inman, 1993; Mayer, 1989; Mayer & Gallini, 1990; M. A. McDaniel & Einstein, 1989; Newby, Ertmer, & Stepich, 1994; Pittman & Beth-Halachmy, 1997; R. E. Reynolds & Shirey, 1988; Sadoski & Paivio, 2001; Scevak, Moore, & Kirby, 1993; M. Y. Small, Lovett, & Scher, 1993; Tennyson & Cocchiarella, 1986; Verdi & Kulhavy, 2002; Wade, 1992; P. T. Wilson & Anderson, 1986; Winn, 1991; Wittwer & Renkl, 2008; Zook, 1991; Zook & Di Vesta, 1991.

• *Lesson 2.* The class studies the process of reducing fractions to lowest terms (e.g., 2/4 can be reduced to 1/2, 12/20 can be reduced to 3/5). By the end of the lesson, 20 children understand this process. But Alison, Reggie, and Jason S. haven't mastered the idea that they need to divide both the numerator and denominator by the same number. Sarah, LaShaun, and the other two Jasons still don't understand what fractions *are* and therefore have trouble with this lesson as well.

advance organizer Introduction to a lesson that provides an overall organizational scheme for the lesson.

FIGURE 12.4 How the sequential and hierarchical nature of knowledge about fractions can affect students' learning

Students	**Lesson 1:** Concept of Fraction	**Lesson 2:** Reducing to Lowest Terms (Builds on Lesson 1)	**Lesson 3:** Adding Fractions with Same Denominators (Builds on Lesson 1)	**Lesson 4:** Adding Fractions & Reducing to Lowest Terms (Builds on Lessons 2 & 3)
Sarah	- - -➤	- - -➤	- - -➤	- - -➤
LaShaun	- - -➤	- - -➤	- - -➤	- - -➤
Jason K.	- - -➤	- - -➤	- - -➤	- - -➤
Jason M.	- - -➤	- - -➤	- - -➤	- - -➤
Alison	⟶	- - -➤	⟶	- - -➤
Reggie	⟶	- - -➤	⟶	- - -➤
Jason S.	⟶	- - -➤	⟶	- - -➤
Matt	⟶	⟶	- - -➤	- - -➤
Charlie	⟶	⟶	- - -➤	- - -➤
Maria F.	⟶	⟶	- - -➤	- - -➤
Maria W.	⟶	⟶	- - -➤	- - -➤
Muhammed	⟶	⟶	⟶	- - -➤
Aretha	⟶	⟶	⟶	- - -➤
Karen	⟶	⟶	⟶	- - -➤
Kevin	⟶	⟶	⟶	⟶
Nori	⟶	⟶	⟶	⟶
Marcy	⟶	⟶	⟶	⟶
Janelle	⟶	⟶	⟶	⟶
Joyce	⟶	⟶	⟶	⟶
Ming Tang	⟶	⟶	⟶	⟶
Georgette	⟶	⟶	⟶	⟶
LaVeda	⟶	⟶	⟶	⟶
Mark	⟶	⟶	⟶	⟶
Seth	⟶	⟶	⟶	⟶
Joanne	⟶	⟶	⟶	⟶
Rita	⟶	⟶	⟶	⟶
Shauna	⟶	⟶	⟶	⟶

- *Lesson 3.* The class studies the process of adding two fractions, for now looking only at fractions with equal denominators (e.g., $\frac{2}{5} + \frac{2}{5} = \frac{4}{5}$, $\frac{1}{20} + \frac{11}{20} = \frac{12}{20}$). By the end of the lesson, 19 children can add fractions with the same denominator. But Matt, Charlie, Maria F., and Maria W. keep adding the denominators together as well as the numerators (e.g., figuring that $\frac{2}{5} + \frac{2}{5} = \frac{4}{10}$). And Sarah, LaShaun, Jason K., and Jason M. still don't know what fractions actually are.

- *Lesson 4.* The class combines the processes of adding fractions and reducing fractions to lowest terms. They must first add two fractions together and then, if necessary, reduce the sum to its lowest terms (e.g., after adding $\frac{1}{20} + \frac{11}{20}$, they must reduce the sum of $\frac{12}{20}$ to $\frac{3}{5}$). Here we lose Muhammed, Aretha, and Karen, because they keep forgetting to reduce the sum to its lowest terms. And of course, we've already lost Sarah, LaShaun, Alison, Reggie, Matt, Charlie, the two Marias, and the three Jasons on prerequisite skills. *We now have 13 of our original 27 students understanding what they are doing—less than half the class* (see the rightmost column of Figure 12.4).

Mastery learning, in which students must demonstrate competence in one topic before proceeding to the next, minimizes the likelihood of leaving some students behind as we proceed to increasingly challenging material (e.g., Bloom, 1981; Guskey, 1985; Zimmerman & Didenedetto, 2008). This approach is based on three underlying assumptions:

- Almost every student can learn a particular topic to master.
- Some students need more time to master a topic than others.
- Some students need more assistance than others.

As you can see, mastery learning represents a very optimistic approach to instruction: It assumes that most children *can* learn school subject matter if given sufficient time and instruction to do so.[4]

Mastery learning usually includes the following components:

1. *Small, discrete units.* The subject matter is broken up into numerous lessons, with each lesson covering a small amount of material and aimed at accomplishing a small number of instructional objectives (perhaps one to three).
2. *A logical sequence.* Units are sequenced so that basic, foundational concepts and procedures are studied before more complex ones.
3. *Demonstration of mastery at the end of each unit.* Students move to a new unit only after they show mastery of the preceding one (e.g., by taking a test). Mastery is defined in specific, concrete terms (e.g., answering at least 90% of test items correctly).
4. *Additional activities for students needing extra help or practice to attain mastery.* Support and resources are tailored to individual needs and might include alternative approaches to instruction, different materials, specially tailored assignments, study groups, or individual tutoring.

Students engaged in mastery learning often proceed through units at their own speed; hence, different students may be studying different units at any given time. But it's also

To promote mastery, break the subject matter into small, logically sequenced units, assess students' mastery of each one, and provide additional instruction and practice as needed.

mastery learning Approach to instruction in which students learn one topic thoroughly before moving to a subsequent one.

[4]Don't confuse mastery *learning* with mastery *goals.* Here, we're talking about an instructional strategy. In contrast, mastery goals reflect students' focus on gaining competence in the subject matter, rather than on, say, simply getting a good grade (see Chapter 11).

possible for an entire class to proceed through a sequence at the same rate: Students who master a unit more quickly than their classmates can pursue various enrichment activities, or they can serve as tutors for those still working on the unit (Block, 1980; Guskey, 1985).

Research indicates that mastery learning has several advantages over nonmastery approaches. In particular, students tend to have a better attitude toward the subject matter, learn more, and perform at a higher level on classroom assessments. The benefits are especially striking for low-ability students (C. C. Kulik, Kulik, & Bangert-Drowns, 1990; Shuell, 1996).

Furthermore, elements of mastery learning are consistent with several theoretical perspectives. Operant conditioning theorists tell us that complex behaviors are often acquired more easily through *shaping*, whereby a simple response is reinforced until it occurs frequently (i.e., until it is mastered), then a slightly more difficult response is reinforced, and so on. Cognitive psychologists point out that information and skills that need to be retrieved rapidly or used in complex problem-solving situations must be practiced and learned thoroughly so that *automaticity* is attained. And as social cognitive theorists have noted, the ability to perform a particular task successfully and easily is likely to enhance students' sense of *self-efficacy* for performing similar tasks.

Mastery learning is most appropriate when the subject matter is hierarchical in nature—that is, when certain concepts and skills provide the foundation for future learning. If instructional goals deal with such basics as word recognition, rules of grammar, arithmetic, or key scientific concepts, instruction designed to promote mastery learning may be in order. However, the very notion of mastery may be inappropriate for some long-term instructional goals. Skills such as critical thinking, scientific reasoning, and creative writing may continue to improve throughout childhood and adolescence without ever being completely mastered.

direct instruction Approach to instruction that uses a variety of techniques (e.g., explanations, questions, guided and independent practice) in a fairly structured manner to promote learning of basic skills.

Direct Instruction

An approach incorporating elements of both expository instruction and mastery learning is **direct instruction**, which uses a variety of techniques to keep students continually and actively engaged in learning and applying classroom subject matter (e.g., Englemann & Carnine, 1982; R. M. Gagné, 1985; Tarver, 1992; Weinert & Helmke, 1995). To some extent, direct instruction is based on behaviorist ideas: It requires learners to make frequent responses and provides immediate reinforcement of correct responses through teacher feedback. But direct instruction also considers principles from cognitive psychology, including the importance of attention and long-term memory storage processes in learning, the limited capacity of working memory, and the value of learning basic skills to automaticity (Rosenshine & Stevens, 1986).

Different theorists describe and implement direct instruction somewhat differently. But in general, this approach involves small and carefully sequenced steps, fast pacing, and a great deal of teacher–student interaction. Each lesson typically involves most or all of the following components (Rosenshine & Stevens, 1986):

1. *Review of previously learned material.* The teacher reviews relevant content from previous lessons, checks homework assignments involving that content, and reteaches any information or skills that students have not yet mastered.
2. *Statement of the objectives of the lesson.* The teacher describes one or more concepts or skills that students should master in the new lesson.
3. *Presentation of new material in small, logically sequenced steps.* The teacher presents a small amount of information or a specific skill, perhaps through a verbal explanation, modeling, and one or more examples. The teacher may also provide an advance

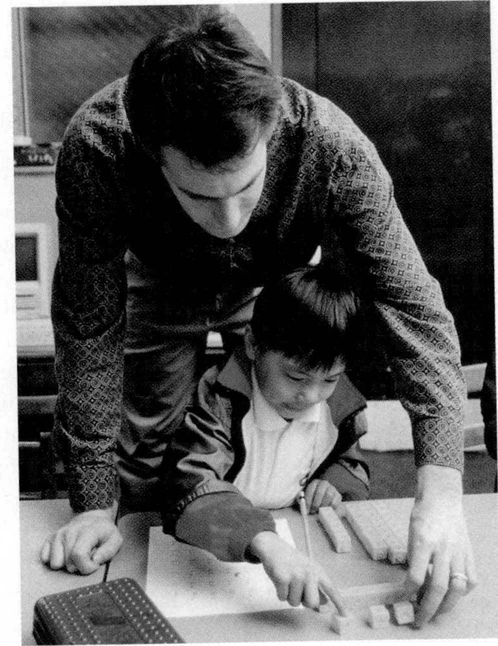

Direct instruction typically involves many opportunities to practice new skills, often with considerable teacher guidance in the early stages.

organizer, ask questions, or in other ways scaffold students' efforts to process and remember the material.

4. *Guided student practice and assessment after each step.* Students have numerous opportunities to practice what they are learning, perhaps by answering questions, solving problems, or performing modeled procedures. The teacher gives hints during students' early responses, provides immediate feedback about their performance, makes suggestions about how to improve, and provides remedial instruction as needed. After students have completed guided practice, the teacher checks to be sure they have mastered the information or skill in question, perhaps by having them summarize what they've learned or answer a series of follow-up questions.
5. *Independent practice.* Once students have acquired some mastery (e.g., by correctly answering 80% of questions), they engage in further practice either independently or in small cooperative learning groups. By doing so, they work toward achieving automaticity for the material in question.
6. *Frequent follow-up reviews.* Over the course of the school year, the teacher provides opportunities for students to review previously learned material, perhaps through homework assignments, writing tasks, or paper-and-pencil quizzes.

Explicitly teach basic skills, giving lots of guidance, scaffolding, and practice. Once students have achieved mastery, provide additional opportunities for them to practice the skills in less structured settings.

The teacher moves back and forth among these steps as necessary to ensure that all students are truly mastering the subject matter.

Like mastery learning, direct instruction is most suitable for teaching information and skills that are well defined and best taught in a step-by-step sequence (Rosenshine & Stevens, 1986). Because of the high degree of teacher–student interaction, direct instruction is often implemented more easily with small groups rather than with an entire class. Especially when conducted with small groups, it can lead to substantial gains in achievement of both basic skills and higher-level thinking processes, high student interest and self-efficacy for the subject matter in question, and a low rate of student misbehavior (Rittle-Johnson, 2006; Rosenshine & Stevens, 1986; Tarver, 1992; Weinert & Helmke, 1995). Using direct instruction *exclusively* may be too much of a good thing, however, particularly if we don't vary instructional methods to maintain students' interest and engagement—for instance, if we just present one worksheet after another (Mac Iver et al., 1995; Wasley et al., 1997).

Computer-Based Instruction

Computer-based instruction (CBI)—instruction presented through carefully designed computer programs—typically includes many elements of mastery learning and direct instruction. For instance, learners encounter new information in a step-by-step fashion, have considerable scaffolding and practice in new skills, and get regular feedback on their progress.

In its earliest forms in the 1970s and 1980s, CBI was based largely on behaviorist principles of active responding, shaping, and reinforcement: Students progressed through a series of lockstep computer frames that presented small amounts of new information, asked for responses to questions, and then provided feedback. More contemporary CBI software typically reflects cognitivist principles as well as those of behaviorism. For example, effective programs capture and hold students' attention, encourage meaningful learning, and present diverse examples and practice exercises that promote transfer to new situations (P. F. Merrill et al., 1996; Moreno, 2006; Moreno, Mayer, Spires, & Lester, 2001).

Some computer-based instructional programs provide drill and practice of basic knowledge and skills (e.g., math facts, typing, fundamentals of music), helping students develop automaticity in these areas. Others act as *intelligent tutors* that skillfully guide students through complex subject matter and can anticipate and address a wide variety of misconceptions and learning difficulties (Koedinger & Corbett, 2006; Lajoie & Derry, 1993; Mathan & Koedinger, 2005). Still others teach and scaffold complex study strategies, metacognitive skills, and self-regulation (Azevedo, 2005a; Graesser,

myeducationlab

Early instructional software based largely on behaviorist principles was more commonly called *computer-assisted instruction*, or *CAI*. Learn more about CAI and its paper-and-pencil predecessor, *programmed instruction*, in the supplementary reading "Programmed Instruction and Computer-Assisted Instruction." (To find this reading, go to Chapter 12 of the Book-Specific Resources in MyEducationLab, and then select *Supplementary Readings*.)

computer-based instruction (CBI) Academic instruction provided by means of specially designed computer software.

McNamara, & VanLehn, 2005; Quintana, Zhang, & Krajcik, 2005; Wade-Stein & Kintsch, 2004).

CBI can be used either instead of or in addition to more traditional instructional methods. Well-designed CBI programs are often quite effective in helping students learn academic subject matter (e.g., H. S. Kim & Kamil, 2004; Slavin & Lake, 2008; Wise & Olson, 1998). CBI can also be highly motivating, piquing situational interest and giving students the independence and frequent successes that can enhance their feelings of self-determination and competence (Blumenfeld et al., 2006; Snir, Smith, & Raz, 2003; Swan et al., 1990).

A downside of CBI is that it gives students few opportunities for social interaction and thus does little to address students' need for relatedness (Winn, 2002). Yet it offers several advantages that we often don't have with other approaches. For one thing, computer-based instructional programs can include animations, video clips, and spoken messages—components that are not possible with traditional printed materials. Second, a computer can record and maintain ongoing data for students, including such information as how far each of them has progressed in a program, how quickly they respond to questions, and how often they are right and wrong. With such data, we can monitor each student's progress and identify students who appear to be struggling with the material. Finally, a computer can be used to provide instruction when flesh-and-blood teachers are not available. For example, CBI is often used in **distance learning**, a situation in which learners receive much or all of their technology-based instruction at a location physically separate from that of their instructor.

distance learning Technology-based instruction in which students are at a location physically separate from that of their instructor.

Instructional Websites

Students' access to new information through computer technology isn't necessarily limited to computer programs in their own schools and classrooms. Many expository materials appropriate for elementary and secondary students are also available on the Internet. A good example is Human Anatomy Online (www.innerbody.com), which presents information about the various human anatomical systems. When first entering the website, the student chooses a particular system (e.g., skeletal, digestive, muscular, cardiovascular) and is linked to focused descriptions of that system and its various components. For example, a student might first choose the digestive system and then, on subsequent screens, learn more about such things as teeth, the esophagus, the spleen, and the small intestine. The site also includes animated depictions of certain body parts (e.g., heart, lungs, ear) in action. Figure 12.5 illustrates this site with a screen from the ear animation.

Internet search engines such as Google (www.google.com) and Yahoo! (www.yahoo.com) enable students and teachers to find websites on virtually any topic. Another good general resource is Wikipedia (www.wikipedia.org), an ever-expanding online encyclopedia to which virtually anyone can contribute about a limitless number of topics. Keepin mind, however, that students don't always have the knowledge and self-regulation skills they need to learn effectively as they explore the many resources the Internet has to offer (Azevedo, 2005b; K. Hartley & Bendixen, 2001; Kuiper, Volman, & Terwel, 2005). Furthermore, the Internet has no good quality-control mechanism to ensure that information is accurate, especially when posted by individuals, rather than by government agencies or professional organizations. (For instance, entries in Wikipedia, although generally accurate, occasionally include inaccuracies added by nonexperts.) An additional concern is that some students may venture into unproductive domains, perhaps finding research papers they can pass off as their own (thereby plagiarizing), stumbling upon sites that preach racist attitudes or offer pornographic images, or sharing personal information with people who might jeopardize their well-being (Nixon, 2005; Schofield, 2006).

FIGURE 12.5 The Internet offers many good instructional sites. For example, at Human Anatomy Online, students can see animated depictions of such body parts as the heart, lungs, mouth and throat, and ear.

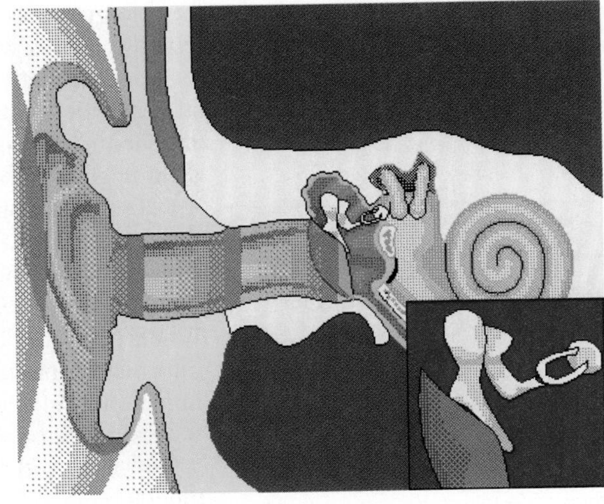

Source: Image ear5.gif from Human Anatomy Online (www.innerbody.com) provided by Pickering Brothers, LLC.

FIGURE 12.6 Students may need some scaffolding to develop their information literacy skills—for instance, specific questions to answer as they look at a website about maple sugaring.

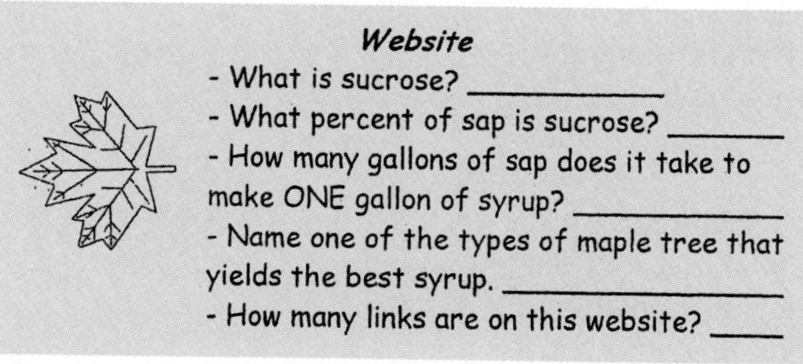
Website
- What is sucrose? ___________
- What percent of sap is sucrose? _______
- How many gallons of sap does it take to make ONE gallon of syrup? ___________
- Name one of the types of maple tree that yields the best syrup. ___________
- How many links are on this website? _____

Source: Used courtesy of Carol Lincoln.

Clearly, then, students often need considerable scaffolding as they conduct online research about a topic, and their journeys into cyberspace should be closely monitored. For example, elementary school librarian Carol Lincoln gives students precise, step-by-step directions on how to use the "Searchasaurus" search engine of EBSCO Information Services, telling students what icons to click on, what words to type in a search box, and so on. When students reach the website she has in mind, she provides specific questions that guide their learning (e.g., see Figure 12.6). In such an activity, she enhances not only students' knowledge about a particular topic but also their **information literacy**—their knowledge and skills related to finding, using, evaluating, organizing, and presenting information acquired from diverse sources. As students become more proficient in information literacy skills, they can proceed with greater independence, perhaps working in small cooperative learning groups to research certain topics in depth.

Scaffold students' early research on the Internet, and monitor their explorations to ensure that they don't venture into inappropriate websites and subject matter.

Hands-On, "Head-On," and Practice Activities

In the opening case study, Ms. Minichiello doesn't just describe the dimensions of a covered wagon; she also has students measure the dimensions for themselves in order to get a firsthand view of a migrating family's typical living space. In general, when we talk about hands-on, head-on, and practice activities, we are talking about having students actively *do* something with what they are learning. The term *head-on activity* is my own creation; I simply mean an activity that engages students' minds more than their hands. Hands-on, head-on, and practice activities can take a variety of forms, as we will see in upcoming sections.

Discovery and Inquiry Learning

Unlike expository instruction, in which information is presented in its final form, **discovery learning** is a process through which students interact with their environment and derive information for themselves—perhaps by randomly exploring and manipulating objects or perhaps by performing systematic laboratory experiments. For example, in the student artifact shown in Figure 12.7, 10-year-old Berlinda describes her group's dissection of a pig's lung. Notice that she has responded to the activity emotionally as well as cognitively (e.g., "grose" [gross], "cool"), and this *hot cognition* will undoubtedly help her remember what she has observed. Discovery learning activities can be incorporated into other forms of instruction; for instance, the Experiencing Firsthand exercises in this very expository book have, I hope, helped you discover a number of important principles on your own.

Learners sometimes remember and transfer information more effectively when they construct it for themselves rather than simply reading or hearing about it (de Jong & van Joolingen, 1998; M. A. McDaniel & Schlager, 1990; D. S. McNamara & Healy, 1995). We can easily explain this finding using principles of cognitive psychology. When learners discover something on their own, they may give more thought to the information or skill than they would otherwise, and so they are more likely to engage in meaningful learning. Furthermore, when learners *see* something happen in addition to reading or hearing about it, they can encode it in long-term memory visually as well as verbally. And from a developmental perspective, many students, especially those in the elementary grades, understand concrete experiences more easily than abstract ideas (see Chapter 2).

myeducationlab

Learn more about information literacy in the supplementary reading "Promoting Information Literacy Skills." (To find this reading, go to Chapter 12 of the Book-Specific Resources in MyEducationLab, and then select *Supplementary Readings*.)

information literacy Knowledge and skills that help a learner find, use, evaluate, organize, and present information about a particular topic.

discovery learning Approach to instruction in which students derive their own knowledge about a topic through firsthand interaction with the environment.

How effective is discovery learning in the classroom? Unfortunately, research doesn't give us a clear answer. Ideally, to determine whether discovery learning works better than other approaches, we would need to compare two groups of students who differ on only *one* variable: the extent to which discovery learning is a part of their instructional experience. But few research studies have made this crucial comparison, and the studies that have been conducted have yielded inconsistent results. Nevertheless, some general conclusions about discovery learning can be gleaned from research findings:

- When we consider *overall academic achievement*, discovery learning isn't necessarily better or worse than more expository approaches to instruction; research yields mixed findings on this issue.
- When we consider *higher-level thinking skills*, discovery learning is sometimes preferable for fostering transfer, problem solving, creativity, and self-regulated learning.
- When we consider *motivational and affective benefits*, discovery learning often promotes a more positive attitude toward teachers and schoolwork than does traditional instruction; in other words, students like school better. (E. L. Ferguson & Hegarty, 1995; Giaconia & Hedges, 1982; Klahr & Nigam, 2004; Marshall, 1981; Mayer, 1974; Patrick et al., 2009; P. L. Peterson, 1979; Rittle-Johnson, 2006; Roughead & Scandura, 1968; Shymansky, Hedges, & Woodworth, 1990; B. Y. White & Frederiksen, 1998; Zaragoza & Fraser, 2008)

FIGURE 12.7 Ten-year-old Berlinda's report about her group's dissection of a pig lung

Pig Lungs Dissection

It was 10:40 a.m. on Friday November 1, 1996. We were going to dissect a set of lungs which had belonged to a pig. I could read just about everyones minds. Ew. Grose. It's bloody. This thing stinks!

Our table was given an esophogus with felt wet and smooth. The main blood vessel which felt hard, almost as though someone had stuck a toothpick inside of it. The tracea which felt felt wet and slitely textured. The heart which, well you couldn't tell. Two lungs which felt a little pit like silly pudy. As 11:30 rolled around most of us had changed our thoughts. It was now cool, neat, and still bloody.

A variation of discovery learning, **inquiry learning**, typically has the goal of helping students acquire more effective *reasoning processes* either instead of or in addition to acquiring new information. For example, to help students learn to separate and control variables in scientific investigations, we might have them design and conduct experiments related to, say, factors affecting how fast a pendulum swings or how far a ball travels after rolling down an incline. And we might foster critical thinking skills in history by having students read historical documents with the mind-set that they are reading *interpretations* rather than facts and therefore must look for evidence that either supports or disconfirms those interpretations. Such activities can often promote more advanced reasoning skills, especially when combined with appropriate instruction and scaffolding (Kuhn, 2007; Kuhn & Pease, 2008; Lorch et al., 2008; Monte-Sano, 2008).

Discovery and inquiry activities need not be limited to materials we have in the classroom, of course. With access to the Internet, our options are virtually unlimited. For example, my middle school geography students and I once used the U.S. Geological Survey website (www.usgs.gov) to track the path of a hurricane as it made its way through the Caribbean and up the Atlantic Coast. Similarly, data available from the U.S. Census Bureau (www.census.gov) can enable students to explore issues related to population growth and poverty. And data from the Centers for Disease Control and Prevention (www.cdc.gov) can enable students to delve into issues related to AIDS, cancer, and other health-threatening conditions.

At the same time, we must note three potential problems with discovery-learning and inquiry-learning activities (Karpov, 2003; Schauble, 1990; B. Y. White & Frederiksen, 2005). First, students don't always have sufficient metacognitive skills to effectively direct their explorations and monitor their findings. Second, students sometimes construct incorrect understandings from their discovery and inquiry activities; for instance, they may misinterpret or distort the evidence they gather in an experiment, possibly finding support for existing misconceptions (see the discussion of *confirmation bias* in Chapter 7). Finally, such activities often take considerably more

inquiry learning Approach to instruction in which students seek new information through the intentional application of higher-level thinking processes (e.g., scientific reasoning, critical thinking).

time than expository instruction, and teachers may feel torn between providing hands-on experiences, on the one hand, and covering all the topics in the school-mandated curriculum, on the other. In my own experience, students typically remember what they learn in hands-on activities so much more effectively than what they learn through expository instruction that the extra time devoted to these activities is time well spent (another instance of the *Less-is-more* principle).

The Into the Classroom feature "Using Discovery and Inquiry Learning Activities Effectively" offers several suggestions for maximizing the advantages and minimizing potential shortcomings of these approaches.

In-Class Assignments

Students are typically asked to accomplish a wide variety of in-class tasks and assignments over the course of the school year—completing worksheets, solving problems, writing lab reports, acting out short stories, and so on. Our number-one criterion in giving such assignments must be to help students accomplish important instructional goals. Some of these goals may be at the *remember* or *understand* level in Bloom's taxonomy. For instance, we may want students to conjugate the

INTO THE Classroom

Using Discovery and Inquiry Learning Activities Effectively

- **Identify a concept or principle about which students can learn something significant through interaction with their physical or social environment.**

  A fifth-grade teacher realizes that rather than tell students how to calculate the area of a triangle, he can help them discover the procedure for themselves by applying what they've previously learned about the area of a rectangle.

- **Make sure students have the necessary prior knowledge to discover new ideas and principles.**

  A high school physics class studies basic principles of velocity, acceleration, and force. In a follow-up lab activity, students place metal balls of various weights and sizes at the top of an inclined plane and observe each ball's progress as it rolls down the slope. A computer attached to the plane enables the students to measure the rate of acceleration for each ball, thereby also enabling them to determine whether either weight or size influences acceleration. From the data, the students can draw conclusions about the effects of gravity.

- **Show puzzling results to arouse curiosity.**

  A science teacher shows her class two glasses of water. In one glass, an egg floats at the water's surface; in the other glass, an egg rests on the bottom. The students give a simple and logical explanation for the difference: One egg has more air inside and so must be lighter. But then the teacher switches the eggs into opposite glasses. The egg that the students believe to be heavier now floats, and the supposedly lighter egg sinks to the bottom. The students are quite surprised and demand to know what is going on. (Ordinarily, because water is less dense than an egg, an egg placed in it will quickly sink. But in this situation, one glass contains salt water, a mixture denser than an egg and thus capable of keeping it afloat.)

- **Structure the experience sufficiently that students can proceed logically toward discoveries you want them to make.**

  To demonstrate the effects of prejudice, a middle school social studies teacher creates a situation in which some students, because of an arbitrarily chosen physical characteristic they possess, experience the prejudice of classmates. After 15 minutes—long enough for students to feel the sting of prejudice but not so long as to damage peer relationships—he stops the activity and asks students to share their reactions to the experience.

- **Have students record their findings.**

  Students in a biology class collect data from a local stream and use hand-held wireless computer-networking devices to send their findings to a central class computer. Once back in the classroom, the students consolidate and graph the data and look for general patterns and trends.

- **Help students relate their findings to concepts and principles in the academic discipline they are studying.**

  After students in a social studies class have collected data on average incomes and voting patterns in different counties within their state, their teacher asks, "How can we interpret these data, given what we've learned about the relative wealth of members of the two major political parties?"

Sources: Bruner, 1966; de Jong & van Joolingen, 1998; N. Frederiksen, 1984a; Hardy, Jonen, Möller, & Stern, 2006; Kirschner et al., 2006; Minstrell & Stimpson, 1996; Moreno, 2006; E. L. Palmer, 1965 (egg example); Pea & Maldonado, 2006 (stream example); Schwartz & Martin, 2004; B. Y. White & Frederiksen, 1998, 2005.

French verb *être* ("to be"), know members of different biological classes and orders, or be familiar with current events around the globe. Other goals will be higher-level ones. For instance, we may want students to write a well-organized persuasive essay, use scientific principles to interpret everyday phenomena, or apply arithmetic operations to real-world problems.

Prioritize in-class assignments based on their relevance to important instructional goals.

Especially when higher-level goals are involved, we should assign tasks that help students learn classroom material in a meaningful, integrated manner. Often, we will want to assign the **authentic activities** described in Chapter 7. Such activities encourage *transfer* of school subject matter to real-world contexts (see Chapter 8) and can increase the *value* that students attach to academic subject matter (see Chapter 11). Complex, multifaceted authentic activities are probably best completed in small groups, in which students can share ideas, ask one another questions, and offer explanations of their thinking (Hickey, 1997; Newmann & Wehlage, 1993; Paris & Turner, 1994). Furthermore, because authentic activities are typically less structured and more complex than traditional classroom tasks, they are apt to require a good deal of teacher scaffolding (Hmelo-Silver, 2006; Mergendoller et al., 2006; van Merriënboer, Kirschner, & Kester, 2003).

It usually isn't desirable to fill the entire school day with authentic tasks, however. For one thing, students can often master basic skills more effectively when they practice them in relative isolation from more complex activities (J. R. Anderson et al., 1996). When learning to play the violin, for example, students need to master their fingering before they join an orchestra, and when learning to play softball, students need to practice hitting, throwing, and catching the ball before they can have an enjoyable game. In addition, some authentic tasks are too expensive and time consuming to warrant regular use in the classroom (Bereiter & Scardamalia, 2006; M. M. Griffin & Griffin, 1994). It is probably most important that in-class activities encourage effective cognitive processing (e.g., organization, elaboration) and that students understand the relevance of what they are learning for larger tasks they will face down the road (J. R. Anderson et al., 1996; Bransford et al., 2006).

Regardless of whether in-class activities are authentic or more traditional, we are most likely to facilitate students' learning and achievement when we do the following:

- Clearly define each task and its purpose.
- Capture students' attention and interest.
- Begin at an appropriate difficulty level—ideally, assigning tasks that challenge students to "stretch" existing knowledge and skills (i.e., tasks within each student's *zone of proximal development*; see Chapter 2).
- Accommodate diversity in students' abilities and needs.
- Provide sufficient scaffolding to ensure success.
- Increase difficulty and complexity as students gain proficiency.
- Provide opportunities for frequent teacher monitoring and feedback.
- Assess students' work in ways that reward high quality but also allow for some experimentation and risk taking.
- Encourage students to reflect on and evaluate their work. (Brophy & Alleman, 1991, 1992; Brophy & Good, 1986; W. Doyle, 1983; Dymond, Renzaglia, & Chun, 2007; Edelson & Reiser, 2006)

Computer Simulations and Applications

Earlier we talked about computer-based instruction as a means of introducing new information and skills. We can also use computer technology to give students valuable hands-on experiences with a variety of academic topics and skills—for instance, by using simulations and such computer tools as word processing programs, databases, and spreadsheets. Often the tasks involved are sufficiently complex and challenging that students must work on them in small groups rather than as individuals, and many

authentic activity Classroom activity similar to an activity that students are apt to encounter in the outside world.

FIGURE 12.8 In the instructional software program Science Court, students explore a variety of science topics in a simulated courtroom environment. The screen shown here is a scene from "Living Things."

Source: From "Living Things," *Science Court,* www.tomsnyder.com/products/products.asp?subject=science<http://www.tomsnyder.com/products/products.asp?subject=science>. Reprinted with permission from Tom Snyder Productions.

students find such computer-based small-group work especially motivating (Lou, Abrami, & d'Apollonia, 2001).

Simulations Some computer programs promote higher-level thinking skills (e.g., problem solving, scientific inquiry skills) within gamelike or seemingly authentic contexts. Following are examples:

- *Sim City.* Learners plan and build cities (including transportation networks, commercial and residential districts, energy plants, etc.) and generate income to support continuing development (e.g., through taxes and legalized gambling); they observe and must decide how to respond to budget shortfalls, opinion polls, changes in traffic patterns, and the like (simcity.ea.com).
- *StockTrak.* Learners "invest" in various stocks in the stock market and track profits and losses in their virtual "portfolios" over time (www.stocktrak.com).
- *Science Court.* In a courtlike setting, learners confront common misconceptions about science, examine evidence, and make predictions(www.tomsnyder.com/products/products.asp?Subject=Science). Figure 12.8 shows a scene from a courtroom "trial" on the nature of living things.

Use well-designed computer simulations when actual hands-on activities are impractical or impossible.

Computer-based simulations are often both motivating and challenging (thereby keeping students on task for extended periods) and can significantly enhance students' problem-solving and reasoning skills (de Jong & van Joolingen, 1998; Kuhn & Pease, 2008; Vye et al., 1998; Zohar & Aharon-Kraversky, 2005).

Some computer simulations involve many students—and sometimes many schools—working together on common problems. For example, in an Internet-based simulation called GlobalEd (www.globaled.uconn.edu), middle school social studies classes become representatives for particular countries (e.g., one class might be France, another might be Nigeria), with different members of a class tackling different global issues (e.g., international conflicts, human rights, environmental issues). Students study their countries and issues and then electronically communicate with representatives from other "countries" (i.e., students in other schools) to share perspectives and negotiate treaties. Not only does the simulation enhance students' understanding of global issues, but it also enhances their perspective-taking ability and interest in social studies as a discipline (Gehlbach et al., 2008).

FIGURE 12.9 Daniel, a fifth grader who struggles with reading and writing, wrote this cohesive paragraph with the help of a word processing program. A spell checker enabled him to spell most but not all of the words correctly. (He meant to use *very* and *sight*, not *vary* and *site*.)

When I was young it was almost impossible to read. One of my teachers told me I could learn to read if I worked hard. Learning to read was like climbing Mount Rushmore. It took a very long time but I finally got it. My Mom said she was vary proud. Reading was hard for me. It took five years for me to learn to read. Every day I would go to the learning center to learn my 400 site words. It was hard for me to learn these words but I did it. Reading is one of the most important things I have learned so far in my life.

Computer Tool Applications Basic computer skills are essential in today's society. For instance, many professions require expertise with such *computer tools* as word processing, desktop publishing, databases, and spreadsheets. Consequently, our instructional objectives may often include computer skills as well as skills in traditional academic subject areas. However, we can often address instructional goals in both computer literacy and traditional content domains simultaneously. Consider these examples:

- Concept mapping and brainstorming software can help students generate and organize ideas as they study for a test or write a research paper.
- Word processing programs can enhance the quality of students' essays and short stories (e.g., see Figure 12.9).
- Database programs can help students organize information about trees or planets.

- Spreadsheets can enable students to predict changes in weather patterns or declines in endangered species populations.
- Music editors let students create musical compositions and experiment with different notes, keys, instrumental sounds, and time signatures.
- With geographic mapping software (known as *geographic information systems software*, or *GIS*), students can map data on pollutants or environmental wetlands. (Egbert, 2009; Guinee, 2003; P. F. Merrill et al., 1996; Sitko, 1998)

Have students use computer tools to complete tasks in various content domains.

We must keep in mind, however, that such strategies are most likely to be effective when students have already acquired some automaticity in keyboarding and other basic computer skills.

Homework

Assign homework to enhance automaticity of basic knowledge and skills, encourage review, introduce students to new but relatively simple material, or help students make connections between class material and the outside world.

Students can accomplish only so much during class time, and homework provides a means through which we can, in essence, extend the school day. On some occasions we may want to use homework to give students extra practice with familiar information and procedures (perhaps as a way of promoting review and automaticity) or to introduce them to new but simple material (H. Cooper, 1989). In other situations we might give homework assignments that ask students to apply classroom material to their outside lives. For example, in a unit on lifestyle patterns, we might ask second graders to compare their own homes with homes of earlier time periods (e.g., caves, log cabins) and to identify modern conveniences that make their lives easier and more comfortable (Alleman & Brophy, 1998). On still other occasions we might encourage students to bring items and ideas from home (e.g., a jar with tadpoles from a local pond, events that occurred over the weekend) and use them as the basis for in-class activities (Corno, 1996; C. Hill, 1994). When we ask students to make connections between classroom material and the outside world through homework assignments, we are potentially promoting transfer.

Unfortunately, researchers have conducted few carefully controlled studies on the impact of completing homework on learning and achievement (H. Cooper, Robinson, & Patall, 2006; Trautwein & Köller, 2003). Existing data indicate that doing homework probably has a small effect on achievement in the middle school and high school grades but little or no effect at the elementary level (H. Cooper, Lindsay, Nye, & Greathouse, 1998; H. Cooper et al., 2006; H. Cooper & Valentine, 2001). Although homework in the elementary grades may not enhance achievement very much, it can help students develop some of the study strategies and self-regulation skills they will need in later years (H. Cooper & Valentine, 2001; Zimmerman, 1998). Undoubtedly, the *quality* of assignments—for instance, whether they encourage rote memorization or meaningful learning and elaboration—makes an appreciable difference both in what and how much students learn and in what kinds of learning and self-regulating strategies they develop (Trautwein et al., 2006).

For many students, doing homework isn't an intrinsically enjoyable activity. These students are more likely to do homework because they want to please their teacher or stay out of trouble than because they want to master a topic (Trautwein & Lüdtke, 2007; J. M. T. Walker, 2001; Xu, 2008). Yet even when intrinsically motivated to complete homework, not all students have the self-regulation skills they need to stay on task at home (Bembenutty & Karabenick, 2004; Eilam, 2001; Fries, Dietz, & Schmid, 2008). Furthermore, some students may have few resources (e.g., reference books, computers, etc.) and little or no family support to enable them to complete certain kinds of assignments (H. Cooper, 1989; Garbe & Guy, 2006; Hoover-Dempsey et al., 2001).

Remember that some students have few resources at home to help them complete homework assignments.

We can maximize the benefits of homework by following a few simple guidelines:

- Use assignments primarily for instructional and diagnostic purposes; minimize the degree to which homework is used to assess learning and determine final class grades.

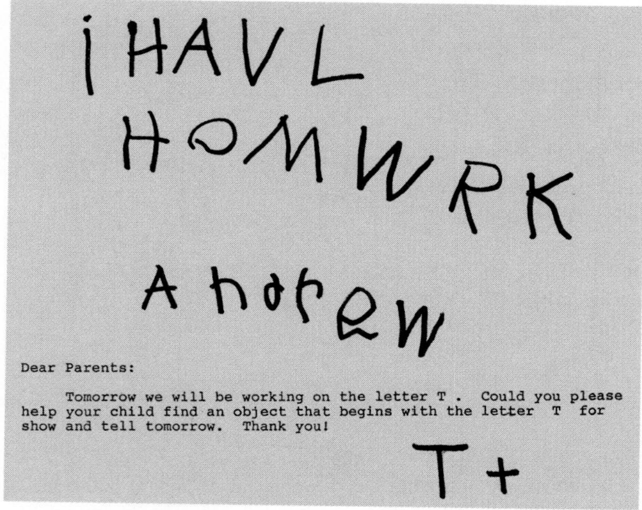

i HAVL
HOMWRK
Dear Parents:
Tomorrow we will be working on the letter T . Could you please help your child find an object that begins with the letter T for show and tell tomorrow. Thank you!
T+

Young children don't always have the self-regulation skills they need to complete homework on their own. Six-year-old Andrew and his teacher jointly constructed the homework reminder shown here.

- Provide the information and structure students need to complete assignments with little or no assistance from others.
- Give a mixture of required and voluntary assignments. (Voluntary assignments should help to give students a sense of self-determination and control, enhancing their intrinsic motivation.)
- Discuss homework assignments in class the following day or as soon after that as possible.
- When students have poor self-regulation skills or limited resources at home, establish supervised after-school homework programs. (Belfiore & Hornyak, 1998; H. Cooper, 1989; Cosden et al., 2001; Garbe & Guy, 2006; Patall, Cooper, & Wynn, 2008; Trautwein et al., 2006)

We should remember, too, that homework is appropriate only to help students achieve important educational goals—*never* to punish students for misbehavior (see Chapter 9).

Interactive and Collaborative Approaches

Social interactions in the classroom—not only teacher–student interactions but also student–student interactions—have numerous benefits for learning. For instance, when students talk about and exchange ideas, they must organize and elaborate on their thoughts, may discover gaps and inconsistencies in their understandings, and may encounter explanations that are more accurate and useful than their own (see Chapter 7). Of the six interactive instructional strategies we'll consider in upcoming sections, five are predominantly learner directed. The first—teacher questions—is teacher directed but often paves the way for learner-directed discussions.

Teacher Questions

Some teacher questions are **lower-level questions** that ask students to retrieve information they've already acquired. Such questions have several benefits:

Ask lower-level questions to check for basic understanding and recall.

- They give us a good idea of what prior knowledge and misconceptions students have about a topic.
- They help keep students' attention on the lesson in progress.
- They help us assess whether students are learning class material successfully or are confused about particular points. (Even very experienced teachers sometimes overestimate what students are actually learning during expository instruction.)
- They give students the opportunity to monitor their *own* comprehension—to determine whether they understand the information being presented or, instead, should ask for help or clarification.
- When students are asked questions about material they've studied earlier, they must review that material, which should promote greater recall later on.

(Airasian, 1994; Brophy, 2006; F. W. Connolly & Eisenberg, 1990; P. W. Fox & LeCount, 1991; Wixson, 1984)

lower-level question Question that requires students to retrieve and recite what they have learned in essentially the same way they learned it.

Following is an example of how one eighth-grade teacher promoted review of a lesson on ancient Egypt by asking questions:

> *Teacher:* The Egyptians believed the body had to be preserved. What did they do to preserve the body in the earliest times?
>
> *Student:* They dried them and stuffed them.
>
> *Teacher:* I am talking about from the earliest times. What did they do? Carey.
>
> *Carey:* They buried them in the hot sands.
>
> *Teacher:* Right. They buried them in the hot sands. The sand was very dry, and the body was naturally preserved for many years. It would deteriorate more slowly, at least compared with here. What did they do later on after this time?
>
> *Student:* They started taking out the vital organs.
>
> *Teacher:* Right. What did they call the vital organs then?
>
> *Norm:* Everything but the heart and brain.
>
> *Teacher:* Right, the organs in the visceral cavity. The intestines, liver, and so on which were the easiest parts to get at.
>
> *Teacher:* Question?
>
> *Student:* How far away from the Nile River was the burial of most kings? (Aulls, 1998, p. 62)

myeducationlab

Observe the wide variety of purposes that teacher questions can serve in the videos "Properties of Air," "Classroom Rules," "Civil War Discussion," "Group Work," "*Scarlet Letter*," and "Charles's Law." (To find these videos, go to Chapter 12 of the Book-Specific Resources in MyEducationLab, select *Video Examples*, and then click on the titles.)

At the end of the dialogue, a *student* asks a question—one that requests information not previously presented. The student is apparently trying to elaborate on the material, perhaps speculating that only land a fair distance from the Nile would be dry enough to preserve bodies for a lengthy period. We can encourage such elaboration, and therefore also encourage new knowledge construction, by asking **higher-level questions**—those that require students to go beyond the information they have learned (Brophy, 2006; Minstrell & Stimpson, 1996; Pogrow & Londer, 1994). For instance, a higher-level question might ask students to think of their own examples of a concept, use a new principle to solve a problem, or speculate about possible explanations for a cause-and-effect relationship. As an illustration, consider these questions from a lesson on the telegraph:

> Was the need for a rapid communications system [in North America] greater during the first part of the nineteenth century than it had been during the latter part of the eighteenth century? Why do you think so? (Torrance & Myers, 1970, p. 214)

To answer these questions, students must recall what they know about the eighteenth and nineteenth centuries (including the increasing movement of settlers to distant western territories) and pull that knowledge together in a way they have perhaps never done before.

Ask higher-level questions to encourage elaboration, transfer, problem solving, and critical thinking.

Asking questions during a group lesson or as follow-up to an independent reading assignment often enhances students' learning (Allington & Weber, 1993; Liu, 1990; Redfield & Rousseau, 1981). This is especially true when we ask higher-level questions that call for inferences, applications, justifications, or solutions to problems. However, we must give students adequate time to respond to our questions. Just as students need time to process new information, they also need time to consider questions and retrieve information relevant to possible answers (see the discussion of *wait time* in Chapter 6). Furthermore, even when students can retrieve an answer almost immediately, those from some cultural and ethnic backgrounds may intentionally allow several seconds to elapse before responding as a way of being courteous and showing respect for the speaker (see Chapter 4).

higher-level question Question that requires students to use previously learned information in a new way—that is, to engage in higher-level cognitive processes.

Class Discussions

myeducationlab

Observe examples of whole-class and small-group discussions in the videos "Properties of Air," "Civil War Discussion," "Group Work," and "*The Scarlet Letter*." (To find these videos, go to Chapter 12 of the Book-Specific Resources in MyEducationLab, select *Video Examples*, and then click on the titles.)

Teacher questions, especially higher-level questions, often get the ball rolling in class discussions, which can be fruitful in virtually any academic discipline. For example, in language arts, students might discuss various interpretations of classic works of literature, addressing questions with no easy answers and, in the process, finding parallels to their own lives (Applebee, Langer, Nystrand, & Gamoran, 2003; Eeds & Wells, 1989; L. M. McGee, 1992). In science classes, discussions of various and conflicting explanations of observed phenomena can enhance scientific reasoning skills, promote conceptual change, and help students understand that science is a dynamic and continually evolving set of concepts and principles rather than just a collection of discrete facts (P. Bell & Linn, 2002; K. Hogan et al., 2000; Schwarz et al., 2000). (The preceding point should remind you of the discussion of *epistemic beliefs* in Chapter 8.) And in mathematics, discussions that focus on alternative approaches to solving the same problem can promote more complete understanding, more creative problem solutions, and better transfer to new situations and problems (M. M. Chiu, 2008; Cobb et al., 1991; Webb et al., 2008).

Although students typically do most of the talking in class discussions, teachers nevertheless play a critical role. Researchers have offered several guidelines for promoting effective discussions:

Focus on topics that lend themselves to multiple perspectives, explanations, or approaches. Such topics appear to have several benefits: Students are more likely to express their views, seek out new information that resolves seemingly contradictory data, reevaluate their own positions on issues, and develop a meaningful and well-integrated understanding of the subject matter (Applebee et al., 2003; E. G. Cohen, 1994; K. Smith, Johnson, & Johnson, 1981).

Make sure students have enough prior knowledge about a topic to discuss it intelligently. This knowledge might come either from previous class sessions or from students' personal experiences (Bruning, Schraw, & Ronning, 1995). In many cases, it comes from studying a particular topic in depth (Onosko, 1996).

Create a classroom atmosphere conducive to open debate and the constructive evaluation of ideas. Students are more likely to share their ideas and opinions if their teacher is supportive of multiple viewpoints and if disagreeing with classmates is socially acceptable (A.-M. Clark et al., 2003; Hadjioannou, 2007; Walshaw & Anthony, 2008). To promote such an atmosphere, we might do the following:

- Communicate that understanding a topic at the end of a discussion is more important than having a correct answer at the beginning of the discussion.
- Communicate that asking questions reflects curiosity, that differing perspectives on a controversial topic are both inevitable and healthy, and that changing one's opinion on a topic is a sign of thoughtful reflection.
- Encourage students to explain and justify their reasoning and to try to understand one another's explanations.
- Suggest that students build on one another's ideas whenever possible.
- Encourage students to be open in their agreement or disagreement with classmates—that is, to agree to disagree.
- Stress that, although it is acceptable to critique ideas, it is *not* acceptable to criticize people.
- When students' perspectives reflect misconceptions or errors in reasoning, gently guide them toward more productive understandings.
- Depersonalize challenges to a student's line of reasoning by framing questions in a third-person voice—for example, "What if someone were to respond to your claim by saying . . . ?"

- Occasionally ask students to defend a position that is the opposite of what they actually believe.
- Require students to develop compromise solutions that take into account opposing perspectives. (Cobb & Yackel, 1996; Hatano & Inagaki, 1993, 2003; Hadjioannou, 2007; Herrenkohl & Guerra, 1998; K. Hogan et al., 2000; Lampert et al., 1996; Nussbaum, 2008; Onosko, 1996; Reiter, 1994; Staples, 2007; Walshaw & Anthony, 2008; Webb et al., 2008)

Many students feel more comfortable discussing issues in a small group rather than in front of the entire class.

When students become comfortable with disagreeing in a congenial way, they often find the interactions highly motivating (Certo, Miller, Reffitt, Moxley, & Sportsman, 2008; A.-M. Clark et al., 2003; Hadjioannou, 2007). One fourth grader, whose class regularly had small-group discussions about literature, put it this way:

> I like it when we get to argue, because I have a big mouth sometimes, and I like to talk out in class, and I get really tired of holding my hand up in the air. Besides, we only get to talk to each other when we go outside at recess, and this gives us a chance to argue in a nice way. (A.-M. Clark et al., 2003, p. 194)

Use small-group discussions as a way of encouraging all students to participate. Students gain more from a class discussion when they actively participate in it (Lotan, 2006; A. M. O'Donnell, 1999). And they are more likely to speak openly when their audience is a handful of classmates rather than the class as a whole—a difference especially noticeable for girls and for students with disabilities (A.-M. Clark et al., 2003; Théberge, 1994). On some occasions, then, we may want to have students discuss an issue in small groups first—thereby allowing them to test and possibly gain support for their ideas in a relatively private context—before bringing them together for a whole-class discussion (Minstrell & Stimpson, 1996; Onosko, 1996).

Provide a structure to guide the discussion. Discussions are more productive when they have some sort of structure. For example, we might do the following:

- Set a particular goal toward which students should work.
- Assign different roles to different class members (e.g., some might evaluate the quality of evidence presented, others might evaluate the validity of conclusions, etc.).
- Before conducting an experiment, ask students to make and defend predictions about what will happen; later, ask them to explain what *did* happen and why. (Calfee, Dunlap, & Wat, 1994; Hatano & Inagaki, 1991; Herrenkohl & Guerra, 1998; Palincsar & Herrenkohl, 1999; B. Y. White & Frederiksen, 1998)

At the same time, we must recognize that the most effective group discussions are often those in which students have some control over the direction of discourse—perhaps asking their own questions, initiating new issues related to the topic, or taking a creative but risky approach or viewpoint (Aulls, 1998; M. M. Chiu, 2008; K. Hogan et al., 2000). Learner-directed discussions are also more likely to encourage effective group interaction skills (R. C. Anderson et al., 2001). For instance, when elementary school students meet in small, self-directed groups to discuss children's literature, they may develop and model such skills as expressing agreement ("I agree with Kordell because . . ."), disagreeing tactfully ("Yeah, but they could see the fox sneak in"), justifying an opinion ("I think it shouldn't be allowed, because if he got to be king, who knows what he would do to the kingdom"), and seeking everyone's participation ("Ssshhh! Be quiet! Let Zeke talk!") (R. C. Anderson et al., 2001, pp. 16, 25; Certo et al., 2008; A.-M. Clark et al., 2003).

Ultimately, the amount of structure we impose must depend on how much scaffolding students need to have a productive discussion. For instance, we may want to be more directive with a small discussion group that seems to be unfocused and floundering than with one in which students are effectively articulating, critiquing, and building on one another's ideas (K. Hogan et al., 2000).

Provide closure at the end of the discussion. Even when the topic of discussion has no single right answer, a class discussion should have some form of closure that helps students tie various ideas together. For instance, when I conduct discussions about controversial topics in my own classes, I spend a few minutes at the end of class identifying and summarizing the key issues that students have raised. Another strategy is to have students explain how a particular discussion has helped them understand a topic more fully (Onosko, 1996).

Reciprocal Teaching

Student discussions not only encourage students to think about and process classroom subject matter more thoroughly, but they can also promote more effective metacognitive strategies during reading and listening activities (A. L. Brown & Reeve, 1987; Nussbaum, 2008; Paris & Winograd, 1990). One form of discussion, **reciprocal teaching**, is especially effective in this regard. It focuses on promoting four metacognitive strategies:

1. *Summarizing:* Identifying the gist and main ideas of a reading passage
2. *Questioning:* Asking oneself questions to make sure one understands a reading passage; in other words, engaging in comprehension monitoring
3. *Clarifying:* Taking active steps to make sense of confusing or ambiguous parts of a passage, perhaps by rereading or making logical inferences
4. *Predicting:* Anticipating what is likely to come next based on cues in the text (e.g., headings) and ideas that have already been presented (A. L. Brown & Palincsar, 1987; Palincsar & Brown, 1984, 1989; Palincsar & Herrenkohl, 1999)

When reading a story or textbook with students, ask questions that promote summarizing, questioning, clarifying, and predicting. Gradually turn the role of teacher over to students.

In a typical reciprocal teaching session, a teacher and several students meet in a group to read a piece of text, occasionally stopping to discuss and process the text aloud. Initially the teacher leads the discussion, asking questions about the text to promote summarizing, questioning, clarifying, and predicting. But gradually the role of "teacher" is turned over to different students, who then take charge of the discussion and ask one another the kinds of questions their teacher has modeled. Eventually students can read and discuss a text almost independently of their teacher: They work together to construct meaning and check one another for comprehension and possible misunderstandings, and they become increasingly flexible in how they apply their newly acquired strategies (A. L. Brown & Palincsar, 1987; Palincsar & Herrenkohl, 1999).

In most instances of reciprocal teaching, students take turns reading sections of the text being discussed. Sometimes, however, the teacher reads the text, especially when working with novice readers. As an illustration, let's look at a reciprocal teaching session in which six first graders and their teacher are discussing a text about snowshoe rabbits. The teacher has just read a description of a mother rabbit giving birth to and caring for several babies. In the discussion that follows, a student named Kam takes the role of "teacher." As you read the dialogue, look for examples of summarizing, questioning, clarifying, and predicting—there is at least one instance of each.

reciprocal teaching Approach to teaching reading and listening comprehension in which students take turns asking teacherlike questions of classmates.

Kam: When was the babies born?

Teacher: That's a good question to ask. Call on someone to answer that question.

Kam: Robby? Milly?

Milly: Summer.

Teacher: What would happen if the babies were born in the winter? Let's think.

Several children make a number of responses, including "The baby would be very cold," "They would need food," "They don't have no fur when they are just born."

Kam: I have another question. How does she get the babies safe?

Kris: She hides them.

Kam: That's right, but something else. . . .

Teacher: There is something very unusual about how she hides them that surprised me. I didn't know this.

Travis: They are all in a different place.

Teacher: Why do you think she does this?

Milly: Probably because I heard another story, and when they're babies they usually eat each other or fight with each other.

Teacher: That could be! And what about when that lynx comes?

Several children comment that that would be the end of all the babies.

Travis: If I was the mother, I would hide mine, I would keep them all together.

Kris: If the babies are hidden and the mom wants to go and look at them, how can she remember where they are?

Teacher: Good question. Because she does have to find them again. Why? What does she bring them?

Milly: She needs to bring food. She probably leaves a twig or something.

Teacher: Do you think she puts out a twig like we mark a trail?

Several children disagree and suggest that she uses her sense of smell. One child, recalling that the snowshoe rabbit is not all white in the winter, suggests that the mother might be able to tell her babies apart by their coloring.

Teacher: So we agree that the mother rabbit uses her senses to find her babies after she hides them. Kam, can you summarize for us now?

Kam: The babies are born in the summer. . . .

Teacher: The mother . . .

Kam: The mother hides the babies in different places.

Teacher: And she visits them . . .

Kam: To bring them food.

Travis: She keeps them safe.

Teacher: Any predictions?

Milly: What she teaches her babies . . . like how to hop.

Kris: They know how to hop already.

Teacher: Well, let's read and see. (Used courtesy of A. Palincsar)

Reciprocal teaching provides a mechanism through which both the teacher and the students can model effective reading and learning strategies; hence, this approach has an element of social cognitive theory. But when we consider that we are encouraging effective cognitive processes by first having students practice them aloud in group sessions, we realize that Vygotsky's theory of cognitive development is also at work here: Students should eventually *internalize* the processes that they first use in their discussions with others. Furthermore, the structured nature of a reciprocal teaching session scaffolds students' efforts to make sense of what they read and hear. For example, in the preceding dialogue the teacher models elaborative questions and connections to prior knowledge (e.g., "What would happen if the babies were born in the winter?") and provides general guidance and occasional hints about how students should process the text ("Kam, can you summarize for us now?"). Also notice in the dialogue how students support one another in their efforts to make sense of what they are learning (e.g., Kam says, "That's right, but something else").

Reciprocal teaching promotes more effective reading and listening comprehension skills in students at all grade levels, and in English language learners as well as native English speakers (Alfassi, 2004; Johnson-Glenberg, 2000; K. D. McGee, Knight, & Boudah, 2001; Palincsar & Brown, 1989; Rosenshine & Meister, 1994; Slater, 2004). In an early study of reciprocal teaching (Palincsar & Brown, 1984), six seventh graders with a history of poor reading comprehension participated in 20 reciprocal teaching sessions, each lasting about 30 minutes. Despite this relatively short intervention, students showed remarkable improvement in their reading comprehension skills. Furthermore, they generalized their new reading strategies to other classes, sometimes even surpassing the achievement of their classmates (A. L. Brown & Palincsar, 1987; Palincsar & Brown, 1984).

We shouldn't think of reciprocal teaching as something that only reading teachers use. It's also been successfully used in science classes (where teachers have adapted it for whole-class discussions of passages in science textbooks) and math classes (where teachers have adapted it to help students make sense of complex word problems) (A. L. Brown & Palincsar, 1987; van Garderen, 2004). Furthermore, reciprocal teaching sessions can be conducted online as well as in the classroom (Reinking & Leu, 2008). Using reciprocal teaching effectively may take some practice, however. It may also require a concerted effort to make sure that students do, in fact, generate and model higher-level questions as well as lower-level ones (e.g., Hacker & Tenent, 2002).

Cooperative Learning

In your many years as a student, you've undoubtedly had a variety of incentives to do well in your classes. In the following exercise, you'll experience three possibilities.

EXPERIENCING FIRSTHAND
Purple Satin

Imagine yourself as a student in each of the three classrooms described here. How would you behave in each situation?

1. On Monday, Mr. Alexander tells your class, "Let's find out which students can learn the most in this week's unit on the human digestive system. The three students getting the highest scores on Friday's test will get free tickets to the Purple Satin concert this weekend." Purple Satin is a popular musical group. You would give your eyeteeth to hear them perform, but the concert has been sold out for months.
2. Ms. Bernstein introduces her lesson this way: "I'm hoping that all of you will master the basics of human digestion this week. If you get a score of at least 90% on Friday's test, I'll give you a free ticket to the Purple Satin concert."
3. Mr. Camacho begins the same lesson like this: "Beginning today, you'll be working in groups of three to study the human digestive system. On Friday, I'll give you a test to see how much you've learned. If all three members of your group score at least 90% on the test, your group will get free tickets to the Purple Satin concert."

In which class(es) are you likely to work hard to get free tickets to Purple Satin? How might you work differently in the three situations?

The first class (Mr. Alexander's) is obviously a very competitive one: Only the three best students are getting tickets to the concert. Will you try to earn one of those tickets? It all depends on what you think your chances are of being a top scorer on

Friday's test. If you've been doing well on tests all year, you'll undoubtedly study harder than ever during this week's unit. If, instead, you've been doing poorly in class despite your best efforts, you probably won't work for something you're unlikely to get. But in either case, will you help your fellow students learn about the digestive system? Not if you want to go to the concert yourself!

In Ms. Bernstein's class, there's no competition for concert tickets. As long as you get a score of 90% or higher on the test, you'll get a ticket. But will you help your classmates understand what the pancreas does or learn the difference between the large and small intestines? Maybe—*if* you have the time and are feeling charitable.

Now consider Mr. Camacho's class. Whether or not you get a concert ticket depends on how well you *and two other students* score on Friday's test. Are you going to help those two students learn about salivation and digestive enzymes? And can you expect them, in turn, to help you understand where the liver fits into the whole system? Absolutely!

In **cooperative learning**,[5] students work in small groups to achieve a common goal. Unlike an individualistic classroom, such as Ms. Bernstein's (in which one student's success is unrelated to the achievement of others), or a competitive classroom, such as Mr. Alexander's (in which one student's success depends partly on the *failure* of others), students in a cooperative learning environment such as Mr. Camacho's work together to achieve joint successes.

On some occasions cooperative groups are formed on a short-term basis to accomplish specific tasks—perhaps to study new material, solve a problem, or complete an assigned project. In other instances, groups are formed to work toward long-term classroom goals. For example, **base groups** are cooperative groups that work together for an entire semester or school year, clarifying assignments for one another, helping one another with class notes, and giving one another a general sense of support and belonging in the classroom (D. W. Johnson & Johnson, 1991).

Create cooperative base groups in which students can get support from two or three classmates throughout the school year.

When students engage in cooperative learning, they reap the many benefits of student dialogue, including greater comprehension and integration of the subject matter, exposure to new strategies, and increased perspective taking. Furthermore, when students help one another learn, they provide scaffolding for one another's efforts and thus tend to have higher self-efficacy for accomplishing challenging tasks (Good, McCaslin, & Reys, 1992; A. M. O'Donnell & O'Kelly, 1994; Webb & Palincsar, 1996; Wiley & Bailey, 2006).

Research indicates that cooperative learning activities—when designed and structured appropriately—are effective in many ways. Students of all ability levels show higher academic achievement; females, members of ethnic minority groups, and students at risk for academic failure are especially likely to benefit (Ginsburg-Block, Rohrbeck, & Fantuzzo, 2006; Lou et al., 1996; Qin, Johnson, & Johnson, 1995; Rohrbeck, Ginsburg-Block, Fantuzzo, & Miller, 2003; Slavin & Lake, 2008). Cooperative learning activities may also promote higher-level cognitive processes: Students essentially think aloud, modeling various learning and problem-solving strategies for one another and developing greater metacognitive knowledge as a result (Good et al., 1992; A. King, 1999; Paris & Winograd, 1990). Furthermore, students are more likely to believe that their classmates like them, and friendships across racial and ethnic groups and between students with and without disabilities are apt to form (Marsh & Craven, 1997; J. D. Nichols, 1996; Pfeifer, Brown, & Juvonen, 2007; R. J. Stevens & Slavin, 1995; Webb & Palincsar, 1996).

Cooperative learning activities have several potential pitfalls, however. Some students may be more interested in meeting social and performance goals (e.g., creating a good impression, getting the right answer quickly) than they are in mastering the material; consequently, their willingness to assist others or ask for help may be compromised (Levy, Kaplan, & Patrick, 2000; M. C. Linn et al., 1996; Moje & Shepardson,

cooperative learning Approach to instruction in which students work with a small group of peers to achieve a common goal and help one another learn.

base group Cooperative learning group in which students work together for an entire semester or school year to provide mutual support for one another's learning.

[5]Some theorists distinguish between *cooperative* learning and *collaborative* learning, with different theorists drawing the dividing line somewhat differently. I'm using *cooperative learning* broadly to include collaborative approaches to learning.

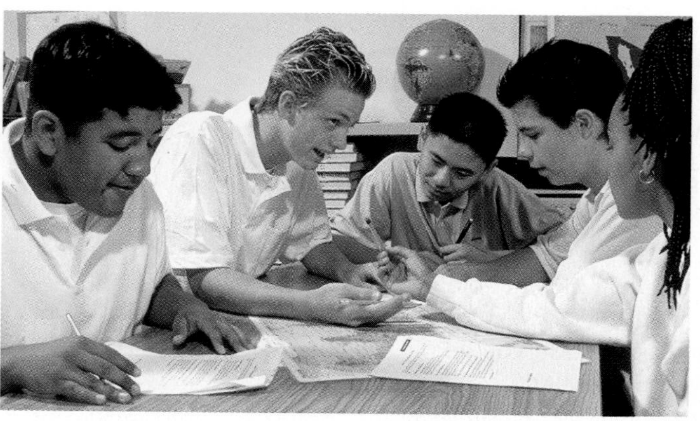

Cooperative learning has personal and social benefits as well as academic ones. For instance, it often promotes self-efficacy, intrinsic motivation, social skills, and cross-cultural friendships.

1998). Furthermore, students who do most of the work and most of the talking are likely to learn more than other group members (Blumenfeld, 1992; Gayford, 1992; Webb, 1989). In addition, students may occasionally agree to use an incorrect strategy or method that a particular group member has suggested, or they may share misconceptions about the topic they are studying (Good et al., 1992; Stacey, 1992). And in some cases students simply don't have the skills to help one another learn (D. M. Hogan & Tudge, 1999; Webb & Mastergeorge, 2003). Clearly, then, we must keep a close eye on group discussions, providing additional structure and guidance when necessary to promote maximal learning and achievement.

Following are several strategies that tend to enhance the effectiveness of cooperative learning groups:

Form groups based on which students are likely to work effectively with one another. Cooperative groups are typically comprised of two to six members; groups of three to four students are especially effective (Hatano & Inagaki, 1991; Lou et al., 1996). In most cases *we* should form the groups, identifying combinations of students that will be productive (D. W. Johnson & Johnson, 1991; Lotan, 2006). Some advocates of cooperative learning suggest that groups be heterogeneous, with each group including high achievers and low achievers, boys and girls, and children of various ethnic backgrounds. Others disagree, arguing that too much heterogeneity makes ability differences among students too obvious and discourages low-ability students from actively participating (Lotan, 2006; Moje & Shepardson, 1998; A. M. O'Donnell & O'Kelly, 1994; S. E. Peterson, 1993; Webb, Nemer, & Zuniga, 2002).

myeducationlab

Examine one study's findings on the effects of group composition by completing the Understanding Research exercise "Effects of Ability Level on Students' Collaborative Work" in MyEducationLab. (To find this activity, go to the topic Planning and Instruction in MyEducationLab, click on *Assignments and Activities*, and then select *Understanding Research*.)

Research regarding the effects of heterogeneous cooperative groups has yielded mixed results. Some studies indicate that heterogeneous groups benefit both high-achieving students (who can sharpen their knowledge by explaining it to peers) and low-achieving students (who benefit from hearing such explanations) (Lou et al., 1996; R. J. Stevens & Slavin, 1995; Webb, Nemer, Chizhik, & Sugrue, 1998; Webb & Palincsar, 1996). However, other studies indicate that high-achieving students don't always gain from working with their low-achieving classmates and may occasionally even lose ground (D. M. Hogan & Tudge, 1999; Lou et al., 1996; Webb et al., 2002). Given such mixed messages from research, our best strategy is probably to experiment with varying degrees of heterogeneity in cooperative groups and determine which approach works best in our own circumstances.

Give group members one or more common goals toward which to work. At the beginning of a cooperative learning activity, we should specify clearly and concretely what each group should accomplish (Crook, 1995; D. W. Johnson & Johnson, 1991). For instance, when my daughter Tina was enrolled in high school Spanish, the goal of one cooperative activity was to write and videotape an episode of a television soap opera spoken entirely in Spanish. The students knew that these *telenovelas* would eventually be shown at an "Academy Awards" banquet for the students and parents, and "Oscars" would be presented for best picture, best screenplay, and so on. (Tina won for best actress, no surprise to me given her frequent displays of emotional drama at home.) Another example, this one used in an eighth-grade social studies class, is presented in Figure 12.10.

Provide clear guidelines about how to behave. Students have more productive interactions when we describe appropriate behaviors for their discussions (Blumenfeld, Marx, Soloway, & Krajcik, 1996; A.-M. Clark et al., 2003; Windschitl, 2002). We might provide guidelines such as these for cooperative learning activities:

- Make sure that everyone has an equal chance to participate.
- Give reasons for your ideas and suggestions.

FIGURE 12.10 To be effective, cooperative learning groups should work toward common goals. Here, eighth-grade history teacher Mark Nichols identifies several things students need to accomplish as they prepare their group presentations about colonial America.

Colonial Economies

Textbook Chapters:

Planting Colonies–Chapter 4

- -Spain Builds a Large Empire (Mr. Nichols)
- -French and Dutch Colonies (Group 1)
- -English Settlers in Virginia (Group 2)
- -The Pilgrims at Plymouth (Group 3)

English Colonies Take Root–Chapter 5

- -New England Colonies (Group 4)
- -Middle Colonies (Group 5)
- -Southern Colonies (Group 6)
- -Governing the Colonies (Group 7)

Group Responsibilities:

Groups will be established with 3-4 students.

Each group will be responsible for reading and thoroughly understanding their assigned sub-chapter.

Each group will prepare an outline of the chapter which will be typed in final draft format. Copies will be made for each student in class.

Each group will create an artistic example of their material and a board game to be played at the end of the presentations.

The day before your group presentation you are to instruct the class to read your sub-chapter and prepare a homework assignment for the class.

A presentation of the material will be made to the class, which will include going over the homework assignment, the outline, and explanation of your creative display of the sub-chapter information. Class members are required to question the presenting group on their material.

An open note test will be given at the end of this unit in order to ensure understanding of the material.

- Listen to others politely and attentively.
- Ask clear, precise questions when you don't understand.
- Encourage others and offer assistance as needed.
- Address differences of opinion in respectful and constructive ways.
- Whenever possible, identify compromises that integrate diverse perspectives.
- Change your mind if the arguments and evidence presented indicate that you should do so.
- Make sure that everyone eventually understands the material. (E. G. Cohen, 1994; M. Deutsch, 1993; Gillies & Ashman, 1998; Lotan, 2006; Lou et al., 1996; A. M. O'Donnell & O'Kelly, 1994; Webb & Farivar, 1999)

myeducationlab

Observe a math class discussion of appropriate group behavior in the video "Cooperative Learning." (To find this video, go to Chapter 12 of the Book-Specific Resources in MyEducationLab, select *Video Examples*, and then click on the title.)

Structure tasks so that group members must depend on one another for success. Students must believe it is to their advantage that they cooperate with one another and that all group members do well (Ginsburg-Block et al., 2006; Lou et al., 1996; van Drie, van Boxtel, & van der Linden, 2006). Tasks that involve creative problem solving and have more than one right answer are especially likely to encourage students to work cooperatively (Blumenfeld et al., 1996). In some situations, each student might have a unique and essential function within the group, perhaps serving as group leader, recorder, critic, peacekeeper, and so on (A. L. Brown & Palincsar, 1989; D. W. Johnson & Johnson, 1991; Lotan, 2006). In other situations, the **jigsaw technique** is useful: New information is divided equally among all group members, and each student must teach his or her portion to the others (E. Aronson & Patnoe, 1997). Still another approach is to assign projects that require such a wide range of talents and skills that every group member is likely to have something truly unique and useful to contribute to the group's overall success (E. G. Cohen, 1994; Schofield, 1995).

jigsaw technique Instructional technique in which materials are divided among members of a cooperative group, with different students being responsible for learning different content and teaching it to other group members.

When students are novices at cooperative learning, it is often helpful to give them a set of steps—a script to follow, if you will—that guides their interaction (Gillies, 2003; A. M. O'Donnell, 1999, 2006; Webb & Palincsar, 1996). In an approach known as **scripted cooperation**, students work together in pairs to read and study expository text. One member of the pair might act as *recaller*, summarizing the contents of a textbook passage, while the other student acts as *listener*, correcting any errors and recalling additional important information. The two students switch roles for the subsequent passage. Such an approach can help students improve learning strategies such as elaboration, summarizing, and comprehension monitoring (Dansereau, 1988; A. M. O'Donnell, 1999).

Serve primarily as a monitor and resource. During any cooperative learning activity, we must monitor both the content and the behaviors of group interactions (D. W. Johnson & Johnson, 1991; Meloth & Deering, 1999). For example, we might consider issues such as these:

- Are students working toward a common goal?
- Are they all actively participating?
- Are their ideas and strategies productive ones?
- Are they asking one another questions when they don't understand?
- Are they behaving in respectful ways toward one another?

We must also take corrective actions when necessary. For instance, if students seem to be buying into their peers' misconceptions about the subject matter, a gentle intervention may steer a discussion in a more fruitful direction—for instance, "Lydia thinks such-and-such; do the rest of you agree with that?" And if students make hurtful remarks to peers, a reminder about the rules for behavior—and in some cases a request for an apology—may be in order.

In addition, we may occasionally need to offer assistance if group members are unable to provide information or insights that are critical for accomplishing the group's goal. Too much intervention can be counterproductive, however: Students tend to talk less with one another when their teacher joins the group (E. G. Cohen, 1994).

Make students individually accountable for their achievement, but also reinforce them for group success. Students are more likely to learn assigned subject matter during cooperative learning activities when they know they will have to demonstrate individual mastery or accomplishment of the group's goal—for example, answering questions in class, taking a quiz, or making a unique and easily identifiable contribution to an overall group product. Such an approach minimizes the likelihood that some students will do most or all of the work while others contribute little or nothing (Finn, Pannozzo, & Achilles, 2003; Ginsburg-Block et al., 2006; Karau & Williams, 1995).

In addition to holding students accountable for their own learning and achievement, we might also reinforce group members for the success of the group as a whole—a *group contingency* in action (see Chapter 9) (Lou et al., 1996; Slavin, 1990; Stipek, 1996). Such group rewards often promote higher achievement overall, perhaps because students have a vested interest in one another's performance and thus make a concerted effort to help fellow group members understand the subject matter (R. J. Stevens & Slavin, 1995). One commonly used approach is to give students a quiz over material they have studied in cooperative learning groups and award bonus points if all group members perform at or above a certain level.

myeducationlab

Observe a combination of individual accountability and group rewards in the video "Cooperative Learning." (To find this video, go to Chapter 12 of the Book-Specific Resources in MyEducationLab, select *Video Examples*, and then click on the title.)

At the end of an activity, have groups evaluate their effectiveness. Once cooperative learning groups have accomplished their goals, we should have them look analytically and critically (perhaps with our assistance) at the ways in which they have functioned effectively and the ways in which they need to improve (E. G. Cohen, 1994; M. Deutsch, 1993; D. W. Johnson & Johnson, 1991). We might ask groups to consider some of the same issues we kept in mind as we monitored the activity—for instance, whether everyone participated equally, whether group members asked one another questions when they didn't understand, and whether they behaved respectfully toward one another. In Figure 12.11, 12-year-old Amaryth reflects on her group's effectiveness in a collaborative task. Notice her concerns: "not really focused," "not lisening [listening] to each other," "yelling a lot." As you can see, members of her group still have much to learn about how to work well together.

scripted cooperation Technique in which cooperative learning groups follow a set of steps, or script, that guides members' verbal interactions.

Peer Tutoring

One of the reasons cooperative learning enhances classroom achievement is that students tutor one another in the subject matter they are studying. Such **peer tutoring** is often an effective learner-directed approach to teaching fundamental knowledge and skills. On some occasions we might have students within a single class tutor one another. At other times we might have older students teach younger ones—perhaps fourth or fifth graders teaching students in kindergarten or first grade.

FIGURE 12.11 In an entry in her class journal, 12-year-old Amaryth reflects on the effectiveness of a cooperative learning group. (She misspells *group* as "gobe.")

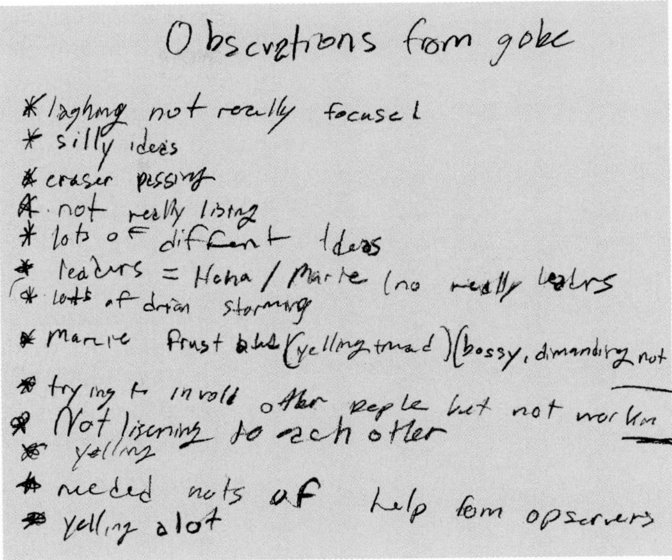

Peer tutoring can lead to considerable gains in academic achievement (Ginsburg-Block et al., 2006; D. R. Robinson, Schofield, & Steers-Wentzell, 2005; Roscoe & Chi, 2007). One possible reason for its effectiveness is that it give students many opportunities to make the active responses that, from a behaviorist perspective, are so essential to learning. Furthermore, it provides a context in which struggling students may be more comfortable asking questions when they don't understand something. In one study (Graesser & Person, 1994), students asked 240 times as many questions during peer tutoring as they did during whole-class instruction!

Peer tutoring typically benefits tutors as well as those being tutored (D. Fuchs, Fuchs, Mathes, & Simmons, 1997; Inglis & Biemiller, 1997; D. R. Robinson et al., 2005). Students are more intrinsically motivated to learn something if they know they'll have to teach it to someone else, and they are apt to engage in considerable elaboration as they study and explain it (Benware & Deci, 1984; A. M. O'Donnell, 2006; Roscoe & Chi, 2007). Furthermore, in the process of directing and guiding other students' learning and problem solving, tutors may, in a Vygotskian fashion, internalize these processes and so become better able to direct and guide their *own* learning and problem solving. In other words, peer tutoring can foster greater self-regulation in the tutors (Biemiller et al., 1998).

When one student tutors another, the tutor often learns as much from the experience as the student being tutored.

Peer tutoring has nonacademic benefits as well. Cooperation and other social skills improve, behavior problems diminish, and friendships form among students of different ethnic groups and between students with and without disabilities (Cushing & Kennedy, 1997; DuPaul, Ervin, Hook, & McGoey, 1998; Greenwood, Carta, & Hall, 1988; D. R. Robinson et al., 2005).

Like other interactive approaches to instruction, peer tutoring is most effective when teachers follow certain guidelines in using it. Following are several recommendations based on research findings:

Make sure that tutors have mastered the material they are teaching and that they use sound instructional techniques. Good tutors have a conceptual understanding of the subject matter they are teaching and can provide explanations that focus on such understanding; poor tutors are more likely to describe procedures without explaining why the procedures are useful (L. S. Fuchs et al., 1996; Roscoe & Chi, 2007). Good tutors also use teaching strategies that are likely to promote learning: They ask questions, give hints, provide feedback, and so on (Lepper, Aspinwall, Mumme, & Chabay, 1990).

Students don't always have the knowledge and skills that will enable them to become effective tutors, especially in the elementary grades (Greenwood et al., 1988; Kermani & Moallem, 1997; D. Wood, Wood, Ainsworth, & O'Malley, 1995). Consequently, most tutoring sessions should be limited to subject matter that the tutors know well (we'll see an exception in a moment). Training in effective tutoring skills is also helpful—for instance, showing tutors how to establish rapport with the children they are tutoring, how to break a task into simple steps, how and when to give feedback, and so on (Fueyo & Bushell, 1998; Inglis & Biemiller, 1997; Kermani & Moallem, 1997; D. R. Robinson et al., 2005).

peer tutoring Approach to instruction in which one student provides instruction to help another student master a classroom topic.

Provide a structure for students' interactions. Providing a structure for tutoring sessions can often help students facilitate their classmates' learning (Fantuzzo, King, & Heller, 1992; L. S. Fuchs et al., 1996; Mathes, Torgesen, & Allor, 2001). As an example, in one study (D. Fuchs et al., 1997), 20 second- through sixth-grade classes participated in a project called Peer-Assisted Learning Strategies (PALS), designed to foster more effective reading comprehension skills. In each class, students were ranked by reading ability, and the ranked list was divided into two parts. The first-ranked student in the top half of the list was paired with the first-ranked student in the bottom half of the list, the second student in the top half was paired with the second student in the bottom half, and so on. Through this procedure, students who were paired together had moderate but not extreme differences in reading level. Each pair read text at the level of the weaker reader and engaged in the following activities:

- *Partner reading with retell.* The stronger reader read aloud for five minutes, and then the weaker reader read the same passage of text. Reading something that had previously been read presumably enabled the weaker reader to read the material easily. After the double reading, the weaker reader described the material just read.
- *Paragraph summary.* The students both read a passage one paragraph at a time. Then, with help from the stronger reader, the weaker reader tried to identify the subject and main idea of the paragraph.
- *Prediction relay.* Both students read a page of text, and then, with help from the stronger reader, the weaker reader summarized the text and also made a prediction about what the next page would say. The pair then read the following page, and the weaker reader confirmed or disconfirmed the prediction, summarized the new page, made a new prediction, and so on.

This procedure enabled students in the PALS program to make significantly more progress in reading than students who had traditional reading instruction, even though the amount of class time devoted to reading was similar for both groups. The researchers speculated that the PALS students performed better because they had more frequent opportunities to make verbal responses to what they were reading, received more frequent feedback about their performance, and, in general, were more frequently encouraged to use effective reading strategies.

At the middle and secondary school levels, we can incorporate a tutoring component into paired study sessions by teaching students the kinds of questions they might ask one another as they jointly study science, social studies, and other academic disciplines. In one approach (A. King, 1997, 1999), students are given question "starters" to help them formulate higher-level questions (e.g., "What is the difference between _____ and _____?" "What do you think would happen to _____ if _____ happened?") (A. King, 1997, p. 230). In the following dialogue, two seventh graders use question starters as they work together to learn more about muscles, a topic that neither of them previously knew much about:

Jon: How does the muscular system work, Kyle?

Kyle: Well . . . it retracts and contracts when you move.

Jon: Can you tell me more?

Kyle: Um . . . well . . .

Jon: Um, why are muscles important, Kyle?

Kyle: They are important because if we didn't have them we couldn't move around.

Jon: But . . . how do muscles work? Explain it more.

Kyle: Um, muscles have tendons. Some muscles are called skeletal muscles. They are in the muscles that—like—in your arms—that have tendons that hold your muscles to your bones—to make them move and go back and forth. So you can walk and stuff.

Jon: Good. All right! How are the skeletal muscles and the cardiac muscles the same? . . .

Kyle: Well, they're both a muscle. And they're both pretty strong. And they hold things. I don't really think they have much in common.

Jon: Okay. Why don't you think they have much in common?

Kyle: Because the smooth muscle is—I mean the skeletal muscle is voluntary and the cardiac muscle is involuntary. Okay, I'll ask now. What do you think would happen if we didn't have smooth muscles?

Jon: We would have to be chewing harder. And so it would take a long time to digest food. We would have to think about digesting because the smooth muscles—like the intestines and stomach—are *in*voluntary. . . .

Kyle: Yeah, well—um—but, do you think it would *hurt* you if you didn't have smooth muscles?

Jon: Well, yeah—because you wouldn't have muscles to push the food along—in the stomach and intestines—you'd get plugged up! Maybe you'd hafta drink liquid—just liquid stuff. Yuk. (A. King, Staffieri, & Adelgais, 1998, p. 141)

Notice how the boys ask each other questions that encourage elaboration and metacognitive self-reflection (e.g., "Why don't you think they have much in common?" "Do you think it would *hurt* you if you didn't have smooth muscles?"). Through such structured interactions, students at the same grade and ability levels can provide valuable scaffolding for one another's learning (A. King, 1998).

Be careful that your use of higher-achieving students to tutor lower-achieving students is not excessive or exploitative. As we have seen, tutors often gain just as much from tutoring sessions as the students they are tutoring. Nevertheless, we must not assume that high-achieving students will always learn from a tutoring session; we should regularly monitor the effects of a peer tutoring program to make sure that all students are reaping its benefits.

Make sure that all students have opportunities to tutor other individuals. This is often easier said than done, as a few students may show consistently lower achievement than most of their peers. One effective approach is to ask low-achieving students to tutor classmates with disabilities (Cushing & Kennedy, 1997; DuPaul et al., 1998; D. Fuchs et al., 1997). Another possibility is to teach low-achieving students specific tasks or procedures that they can share with their higher-achieving but in this case uninformed classmates (E. G. Cohen, Lockheed, & Lohman, 1976; Webb & Palincsar, 1996). Still another is to have students teach basic skills to younger children (Inglis & Biemiller, 1997). In fact, students with significant social or behavioral problems (e.g., emotional and behavioral disorders, autism spectrum disorders) can make significant gains in both academic and social skills when they have opportunities to tutor children several years younger than they are (J. R. Sullivan & Conoley, 2004).

Technology-Based Collaborative Learning

Effective student interactions don't necessarily have to be face to face. Through such mechanisms as electronic mail (e-mail), web-based chat rooms, electronic bulletin boards, and web logs (blogs), computer technology enables students to communicate with peers in their own classroom or elsewhere, exchange perspectives, and brainstorm and build on one another's ideas (e.g., Fabos & Young, 1999; Noss & Hoyles, 2006; Stahl, Koschmann, & Suthers, 2006). Technology also allows subject matter experts to be occasionally pulled into the conversation (A. L. Brown & Campione, 1996; Winn, 2002).

Use computer networks to expand students' communication with peers and outside experts.

Software created at the University of Toronto provides an example of how technology can enhance student interaction and knowledge construction. This software, called Knowledge Forum (www.knowledgeforum.com), enables students to commu-

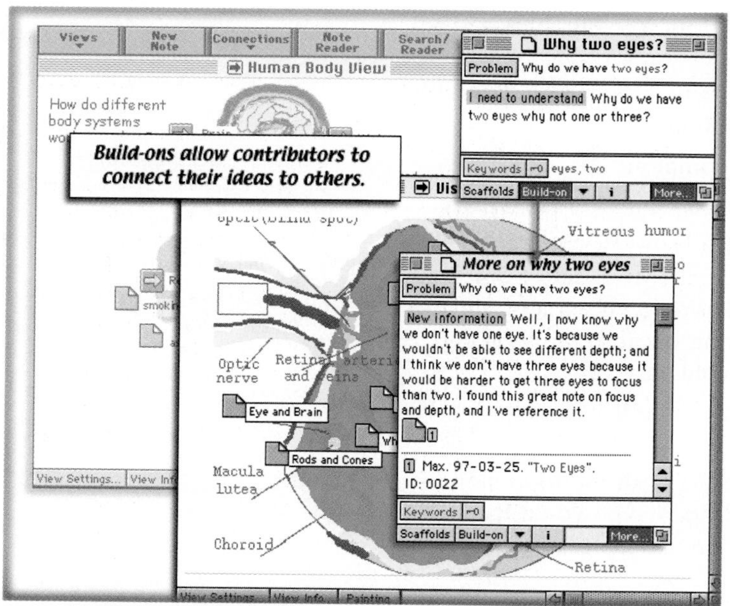

This Knowledge Forum software allows students to exchange and interconnect ideas not only with their classmates but also with peers and adults at other institutions.

Source: Knowledge Forum® <www.KnowledgeForum.com> was designed by Marlene Scardamalia, Carl Bereiter, and the CSILE/Knowledge-Building Team at the Ontario Institute of Studies in Education at the University of Toronto (OISE-UT) and is published by Learning in Motion, Inc.

nicate regularly using a classwide or cross-institution database; it essentially creates a computer-based *community of learners* (Hewitt & Scardamalia, 1996, 1998; Lamon, Chan, Scardamalia, Burtis, & Brett, 1993; Scardamalia & Bereiter, 2006). Using the database, students share their questions, ideas, notes, writing products, and graphic constructions. Their classmates (and sometimes a subject matter expert as well) respond regularly, perhaps giving feedback, building on ideas, offering alternative perspectives, or synthesizing what has been learned.

Research regarding the use of Knowledge Forum has generally been quite favorable. Students are concerned about truly understanding classroom subject matter (rather than simply "getting things done"), they actively try to relate new material to what they already know (i.e., they adopt mastery goals, rather than performance goals), and they show greater ability to remember, synthesize, and apply classroom subject matter (Bereiter & Scardamalia, 2006; Lamon et al., 1993; Scardamalia & Bereiter, 2006). In addition, the ongoing student interactions can often foster more sophisticated epistemic beliefs about the subject matter in question (Scardamalia & Bereiter, 2006). For example, in an anthropology unit "Prehistory of the New World" conducted in a fifth- and sixth-grade classroom, students worked in groups of three or four to study particular topics and then shared their findings through their computer database (Hewitt, Brett, Scardamalia, Frecker, & Webb, 1995). One group, which studied various theories about how human beings first migrated from Asia to the Americas, reported the following:

> **What We Have Learned**
>
> We know that we have learned lots on this project, but the more that we learn the more we get confused about which is fact and which is fiction. The problem within this problem is that there isn't any real proof to say when they came or how. The theory that is most believed is the Bering Strait theory in which people from Asia walked over a land bridge. Another theory is they kayaked the distance between the two continents. We have also unfortunately found racist theories done by people who hate people unlike their own saying that the people of the New World are these people because of human sacrifices and only this race of people would do that.
>
> We have made are [our] own theories using information we found and trying to make sense of it. We have heard some people say they come from outer space but this theory is pretty much out of the question. I don't think the Native peoples or the Inuit would like to hear that theory either. How they came isn't easily answered for some of the theories but it does make since [sense] with the Bering Strait theory. (Hewitt et al., 1995, p. 7)

Notice the sophisticated epistemic beliefs that the group's summary reveals: The students recognize that, as a discipline, anthropology isn't just a set of facts but also encompasses varying perspectives that may or may not be correct. Furthermore, the students acknowledge that different theories may have greater or lesser usefulness in explaining the evidence that anthropologists have gathered.

Another option for technology-based collaborative learning is the GLOBE Program (www.globe.gov), through which student groups around the world collaborate on inquiry-based projects related to environmental and earth sciences. Students in participating schools and classrooms collect and analyze data about various environmental topics (e.g., climate change, watershed dynamics), write reports, and share their findings with students and professional scientists elsewhere.

As the Internet becomes increasingly accessible to learners worldwide, then, not only do we have limitless sources of information on which to draw, but we also have limitless mechanisms for communicating and collaborating with other people in faraway settings about issues of common interest. Multinational student–student collaborations are an excellent way to get young learners thinking and acting as *global* citizens as well as citizens of a particular community and country.

myeducationlab

Gain practice in identifying effective strategies in both teacher-directed and learner-directed instruction by completing the Building Teaching Skills and Dispositions exercise "Identifying Effective Instructional Strategies" in MyEducationLab. (To find this exercise, go to the topic Planning and Instruction in MyEducationLab, and click on *Building Teaching Skills and Dispositions.*)

Taking Student Diversity into Account

To some degree, the instructional strategies we choose should correspond to students' ages and developmental levels. For instance, strategies that involve a lot of active responding and frequent feedback (e.g., mastery learning, direct instruction) may be especially appropriate for younger students (Rosenshine & Stevens, 1986). Lectures (which are often somewhat abstract) and homework assignments tend to be more effective with older students (Ausubel et al., 1978; H. Cooper et al., 2006).

The knowledge and skills that students bring to a topic should also be a consideration (Gustafsson & Undheim, 1996; Rosenshine & Stevens, 1986). Structured, teacher-directed approaches are probably most appropriate when students know little or nothing about the subject matter. But when students have mastered basic knowledge and skills, especially when they are self-regulating learners, they should begin directing some of their own learning, perhaps in group discussions, authentic activities, or instructional Internet websites.

When choosing instructional strategies, take into account students' developmental levels, background knowledge, and degree of self-regulated learning.

In general, however, *all* students should have experience with a wide variety of instructional methods. For instance, although some students may need to spend considerable time on basic skills, too much time in structured, teacher-directed activities can minimize opportunities to choose what and how to study and learn and, as a result, can prevent students from developing a sense of self-determination (Battistich et al., 1995). In addition, authentic activities, although often more unstructured and complex than more traditional classroom tasks, can give students of all levels a greater appreciation for the relevance and meaningfulness of classroom subject matter.

Considering Group Differences

Students' cultural and ethnic backgrounds may occasionally have implications for our choice of instructional strategies. For instance, students from cultures that place a high premium on interpersonal cooperation (e.g., many Hispanic and Native American communities) are apt to achieve at higher levels in classrooms with many interactive and collaborative activities (Castagno & Brayboy, 2008; García, 1994, 1995; Webb & Palincsar, 1996). In contrast, recent immigrants from some Asian countries may be more accustomed to teacher-directed instruction than to learner-directed classroom activities, and students who have only limited proficiency in English may be reluctant to speak up in class discussions (Igoa, 1995; Walshaw & Anthony, 2008). When working with English language learners, technology can often come to our assistance, perhaps in the form of bilingual software for teaching basic skills, English-language tutorials, and word processing programs with spell checkers and grammar checkers (Egbert, 2009; P. F. Merrill et al., 1996).

Identify teaching strategies that are compatible with students' cultural backgrounds.

We must take gender differences into account as well. Many boys thrive on competition, but girls tend to do better when instructional activities are interactive and cooperative. However, girls can be intimidated by whole-class discussions; they are more likely to participate when discussions and activities take place in small groups (Théberge, 1994). Because boys sometimes take charge of small-group activities, we may occasionally want to form all-female groups. By doing so, we are likely to

Use cooperative approaches to enhance the achievement of females and students from ethnic minority groups.

increase girls' participation in group activities and to encourage them to take leadership roles (Fennema, 1987; MacLean et al., 1995).

Our choice of instructional strategies may be especially critical when we work in schools in low-income, inner-city neighborhoods. Students in such schools often experience more than their share of drill-and-practice work in basic skills—work that's hardly conducive to fostering excitement about academic subject matter (Duke, 2000; R. Ferguson, 1998; Portes, 1996). Mastering basic knowledge and skills is essential, to be sure, but we can frequently incorporate such activities into engaging lessons that ask students to apply what they're learning to personal interests, real-world contexts, and local community concerns (Eccles, 2007; Lee-Pearce, Plowman, & Touchstone, 1998; M. McDevitt & Chaffee, 1998). For example, in a curriculum called Kids Voting USA, students in kindergarten through grade 12 have age-appropriate lessons about voting, political parties, and political issues, and they relate what they learn to local election campaigns (M. McDevitt & Chaffee, 1998). Depending on the grade level, they might conduct their own mock elections, analyze candidates' attacks on opponents, or give speeches about particular propositions on the ballot. Students who participate in the program are more likely to attend regularly to media reports about an election, initiate discussions about the election with friends and family members, and be knowledgeable about candidates and election results. In fact, their knowledge and excitement about politics is contagious, because even their *parents* begin to pay more attention to the news, talk more frequently about politics, and acquire more knowledge about candidates and political issues.

Interactive and collaborative strategies are particularly valuable when our instructional goals include promoting social development as well as academic achievement. As we have seen, such interactive approaches as cooperative learning and peer tutoring encourage friendly relationships across ethnic groups. Furthermore, cooperative learning groups—especially when they work on tasks involving a number of different skills and abilities—can foster an appreciation for the various strengths that students with diverse backgrounds are likely to contribute (E. G. Cohen, 1994; E. G. Cohen & Lotan, 1995). And virtually any collaborative approach to instruction—cooperative learning, reciprocal teaching, peer tutoring—can help students begin to look beyond the obvious diversity among them and recognize that they are ultimately more similar than different (Schofield, 1995).

Accommodating Students with Special Needs

Include your instructional strategies in the individualized education programs (IEPs) you develop for students with special needs.

We must often modify our instructional goals and strategies for students who have exceptional cognitive abilities or disabilities, a practice known as **differentiated instruction**. For example, to ensure that all students are working on tasks appropriate for their current skill levels (i.e., tasks within their zones of proximal development), we may need to identify more basic goals for some students (e.g., those with intellectual disabilities) and more challenging goals for others (e.g., those who are gifted). In addition, different instructional strategies may be more or less useful for students with different kinds of special needs. For instance, strictly expository instruction (e.g., a lecture or textbook chapter) can provide a quick and efficient means of presenting new ideas to students who process information quickly and abstractly but might be incomprehensible and overwhelming to students with low cognitive ability. Similarly, inquiry-learning and discussion-based approaches are often effective in enhancing the academic achievement of students with high ability but may be detrimental to the achievement of lower-ability students who have not yet mastered basic concepts and skills (Corno & Snow, 1986; Lorch et al., 2008). In contrast, mastery learning and direct instruction have been shown to be effective with students who have learning difficulties but might prevent rapid learners from progressing at a rate commensurate with their potential (Arlin, 1984; Rosenshine & Stevens, 1986; J. A. Stein & Krishnan, 2007).

differentiated instruction Practice of individualizing instructional methods—and possibly also individualizing specific content and instructional goals—to align with each student's existing knowledge, skills, and needs.

Table 12.2 reviews some of the characteristics of students with special needs identified in previous chapters. It also presents some instructional strategies we can use to accommodate these characteristics.

Students in Inclusive Settings

TABLE 12.2
Identifying Appropriate Instructional Goals and Strategies for Students with Special Educational Needs

Category	Characteristics You Might Observe	Suggested Strategies
Students with specific cognitive or academic difficulties	• Uneven patterns of achievement • Difficulty with complex cognitive tasks in some content domains • Difficulty processing or remembering information presented in particular modalities • Poor listening skills, reading skills, or both • Greater than average difficulty in completing homework	• Tailor goals to individual students' strengths and weaknesses. • Identify the specific cognitive skills involved in a complex task; consider teaching each skill separately. • Use mastery learning, direct instruction, CBI, cooperative learning, and peer tutoring to help students master basic knowledge and skills. • Provide information through multiple modalities (e.g., videotapes, audiotapes, graphic materials); also provide advance organizers and study guides. • Have students use computer tools (e.g., grammar and spell checkers) to compensate for areas of weakness. • Assign homework that provides additional practice in basic skills; provide extra scaffolding (e.g., solicit parents' help, explicitly teach effective study habits). • Use reciprocal teaching to promote listening and reading comprehension.
Students with social or behavioral problems	• Frequent off-task behaviors • Inability to work independently for extended periods • Poor social skills	• Use small-group direct instruction and peer tutoring as ways of providing one-on-one attention. • Keep unsupervised seatwork assignments to a minimum. • Use cooperative learning to foster social skills and friendships. • Give explicit guidelines about how to behave during interactive learning activities; closely monitor students' behavior in small groups. • As appropriate, use strategies listed above for students with specific cognitive or academic difficulties.
Students with general delays in cognitive and social functioning	• Difficulty with complex tasks • Difficulty thinking abstractly • Need for a great deal of repetition and practice of basic information and skills • Difficulty transferring information and skills to new situations	• Identify realistic goals related to both academic and social development. • Break complex behaviors into simpler responses that students can easily learn. • Present information as concretely as possible (e.g., by engaging students in hands-on experiences). • Use direct instruction and CBI to provide extended practice in basic skills. • Embed basic skills within simple authentic tasks to promote transfer to the outside world. • Use peer tutoring to promote friendships with nondisabled classmates; also identify skills these students have mastered and can teach to classmates or younger students.
Students with physical or sensory challenges	• Average intelligence in most instances • Tendency to tire easily (for some) • Limited motor skills (for some) • Difficulty with speech (for some)	• Aim for instructional goals similar to those for nondisabled students unless there's a compelling reason to do otherwise. • Allow frequent breaks from strenuous or intensive activities. • Use CBI (with any needed mechanical adaptations) to enable students to progress through material at their own pace and make active responses during instruction. • When students have difficulty speaking, use other means (perhaps technology) to enable them to participate actively in class discussions and cooperative learning groups.
Students with advanced cognitive development	• Rapid learning • Greater frequency of responses at higher levels of Bloom's taxonomy (e.g., analysis, evaluation) • Greater ability to think abstractly; earlier appearance of abstract thinking • Greater conceptual understanding of classroom material • Ability to learn independently	• Identify goals and objectives that challenge students and encourage them to develop to their full potential. • Use expository instruction (e.g., lectures) as a way of transmitting abstract information about particular topics quickly and efficiently. • Provide opportunities to pursue topics in greater depth (e.g., through assigned readings, CBI, or homogeneous cooperative groups). • Teach strategies that enable students to learn on their own (e.g., teach the scientific method, library skills, effective use of Internet websites). • Ask predominantly higher-level questions. • Introduce students to safe Internet outlets where they can communicate with others who have similar interests and abilities. • Use advanced students as peer tutors only if both the tutors and learners will benefit.

Sources: Strategies based on suggestions from T. Bryan, Burstein, & Bryan, 2001; Carnine, 1989; Connor, 2006; DuNann & Weber, 1976; Egbert, 2009; Fiedler et al., 1993; Fletcher et al., 2007; Greenwood et al., 1988; Heward, 2009; C. C. Kulik et al., 1990; Mercer & Pullen, 2005; P. F. Merrill et al., 1996; Morgan & Jenson, 1988; Piirto, 1999; A. Robinson, 1991; Ruef et al., 1998; Schiffman, Tobin, & Buchanan, 1984; Spicker, 1992; R. J. Stevens & Slavin, 1995; J. R. Sullivan & Conoley, 2004; Tarver, 1992; Turnbull et al., 2007; J. W. Wood & Rosbe, 1985.

The Big Picture

Historically, many theorists and practitioners have looked for—and, in some cases, believe they have found—the single best way to teach children and adolescents. The result has been a series of movements in which educators have advocated a particular instructional approach and then, a few years later, have advocated a very different approach.

I've often wondered why the field of education is characterized by such pendulum swings, and I've developed several hypotheses. Perhaps some people are looking for an *algorithm* for teaching—a specific procedure they can follow to guarantee high achievement. Or perhaps they confuse theory with fact, thinking that the latest theoretical fad must certainly be the correct explanation of how children learn or develop and thus concluding that the teaching strategies associated with that theory must be far more powerful than all other approaches. Or perhaps they just have an overly simplistic view of what the goals of our educational system should be.

As should be clear by now, *there is no single best approach to classroom instruction.* Each of the instructional strategies we've examined has its merits, and each is useful in different situations. I urge you to keep three points in mind as you choose instructional strategies in your own classroom:

- ***The choice of instructional strategies must depend to some degree on the goals of instruction.*** Some instructional methods are most appropriate for teaching basic skills, others are better for promoting higher-level cognitive processes, and so on. Table 12.3 lists several general instructional goals teachers are likely to have and suggests instructional strategies that might be appropriate for each one. Notice that many of the strategies we've examined in this chapter appear in two or more rows in the table, reflecting the multiple purposes for which they might flexibly be used.

- ***The choice of instructional strategies must also depend on students' characteristics and needs.*** Our choice of instructional strategies must certainly be tailored to students' current age and ability levels and to their existing knowledge about a topic. We must take temperamental and motivational characteristics into consideration as well. For example, some children and adolescents have trouble sitting still and concentrating during lengthy lectures, and many students of all ages find hands-on activities more motivating and engaging than abstract textbook readings.

- ***Effective teachers regularly use a variety of instructional strategies.*** A successful classroom—one in which students are acquiring and using school subject matter in truly meaningful ways—is undoubtedly a classroom in which a variety of approaches to instruction can be found. As you gain experience as a classroom teacher, you will become increasingly adept at using many (perhaps all) of the strategies we've explored in this chapter. I hope you will experiment with different approaches to determine which ones work most effectively for your own instructional goals, academic discipline(s), and students. Such experimentation will ultimately be beneficial not only for your students' academic growth but also for your own professional growth.

Compare/Contrast

TABLE 12.3
Choosing an Instructional Strategy

When Your Goal Is to Help Students . . .	Consider Using . . .
Master and review basic skills	• Mastery learning • Direct instruction • Computer-based instruction (some programs) • Lower-level teacher questions • Cooperative learning • Peer tutoring • Homework assignments (those in which students practice skills they've previously learned at school)
Gain firsthand, concrete experience with a particular topic	• Discovery learning • Computer simulations
Gain an organized, relatively abstract body of knowledge about a topic	• Lectures • Textbooks and other assigned readings • Computer-based instruction (some programs) • Instructional websites on the Internet
Connect school subject matter to real-world contexts and problems	• Authentic activities • Inquiry learning • Technology-based collaborative learning • Homework assignments (those in which students are asked to relate what they're learning at school to specific issues at home or in the community)
Acquire advanced understandings about a topic and/or develop higher-level cognitive processes (e.g., problem solving, critical thinking, scientific reasoning)	• Inquiry learning • Authentic activities • Computer simulations (some programs) • Higher-level teacher questions • Class discussions • Cooperative learning • Technology-based collaborative learning • Peer tutoring (which requires tutors to organize and elaborate on previously learned information and skills)
Acquire increased metacognitive awareness and more effective reading and self-regulation strategies	• Computer-based instruction (some programs) • Reciprocal teaching • Cooperative learning • Peer tutoring (which can enhance self-regulation for tutors) • Homework assignments (those appropriately scaffolded to foster planning, self-monitoring, etc.)
Acquire computer literacy skills	• Computer-based instruction • Instructional websites on the Internet • Computer simulations • Computer tool applications • Technology-based collaborative learning
Acquire effective strategies for interacting and working with others	• Class discussions • Cooperative learning • Peer tutoring • Technology-based collaborative learning • Computer simulations (those in which students from many classrooms interact in a joint pursuit of knowledge)

Practice for Your Licensure Exam

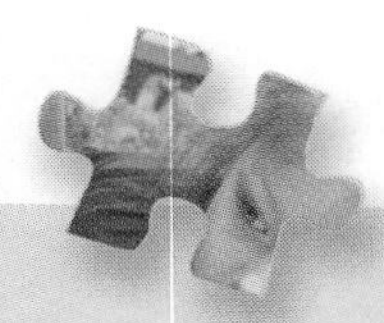

Cooperative Learning Project

One Monday morning, Ms. Mihara begins the unit "Customs in Other Lands" in her fourth-grade class. She asks students to choose two or three students with whom they would like to work to study a particular country. After the students have assembled into six small groups, she assigns each group a country: Australia, Colombia, Ireland, Greece, Japan, or South Africa. She tells the students, "Today we will go to the school library, where your group can find information on the customs of your country and check out materials you think will be useful. Every day over the next two weeks, you will have time to work with your group. A week from Friday, each group will give an oral report to the class."

During the next few class sessions, Ms. Mihara runs into many more problems than she anticipated. She realizes that the high achievers have gotten together to form two of the groups, and many socially oriented, "popular" students have flocked to two others. The remaining two groups are comprised of whichever students were left over. Some groups get to work immediately on their task, others spend their group time joking and sharing gossip, and still others are neither academically nor socially productive.

As the unit progresses, Ms. Mihara hears more and more complaints from students about their task: "Janet and I are doing all the work; Karen and Mary Kay aren't helping at all," "Eugene thinks he can boss the rest of us around because we're studying Ireland and he's Irish," "We're spending all this time but just can't seem to get anywhere!" And the group reports at the end of the unit differ markedly in quality: Some are carefully planned and informative, whereas others are disorganized and have little substance.

"So much for this cooperative learning stuff," Ms. Mihara mumbles to herself. "If I want students to learn something, I'll just have to teach it to them myself."

1. **Constructed-response question:**

   Describe two things you might do to improve Ms. Mihara's cooperative learning activity. Base your improvements on research findings related to cooperative learning or on contemporary principles and theories of learning, development, or motivation.

2. **Multiple-choice question:**

   Ms. Mihara never identifies an instructional objective for her unit "Customs in Other Lands." Which one of the following objectives reflects commonly accepted guidelines about how instructional objectives should be formulated?

   a. The teacher should expose students to many differences in behaviors and beliefs that exist in diverse cultures (e.g., eating habits, ceremonial practices, religious beliefs, moral values).
   b. The teacher should use a variety of instructional practices, including (but not limited to) lectures, direct instruction, textbook readings, and cooperative learning activities.
   c. Students should study a variety of cultural behaviors and beliefs, including those of countries in diverse parts of the world.
   d. Students should demonstrate knowledge of diverse cultural practices—for example, by describing three distinct ways in which another culture is different from their own.

Go to Chapter 12 of the Book-Specific Resources in **MyEducationLab** and click on "Practice for Your Licensure Exam" to answer these questions. Compare your responses with the feedback provided.

PRAXIS

Turn to Appendix C, "Matching Book and MyEducationLab Content to the Praxis Principles of Learning and Teaching Tests," to discover sections of this chapter that may be especially applicable to the Praxis tests.

PEARSON myeducationlab

Now go to MyEducationLab (www.myeducationlab.com) where you can:

- Find learning outcomes for Planning and Instruction, along with the national standards that connect to these outcomes.
- Complete Assignments and Activities that can help you more deeply understand the chapter content.
- Engage in Building Teaching Skills and Dispositions exercises in which you can apply and practice core teaching skills identified in the chapter.
- Access Book-Specific Resources:
    - Check your comprehension of chapter content by going to the Study Plan, where you can find (a) Chapter Objectives; (b) Focus Questions that can guide your reading; (c) a Self-Check Quiz that can help you monitor your progress in mastering chapter content; (d) Review, Practice, and Enrichment exercises with detailed feedback that will deepen your understanding of various concepts and principles; (e) Flashcards that can give you practice in understanding and defining key terms; and (f) Common Beliefs and Misconceptions about Educational Psychology that will alert you to typical misunderstandings in educational psychology classes.
- Video Examples of various concepts and principles presented in the chapter.
- Supplementary Readings that enable you to pursue certain topics in greater depth.
- A Practice for Your Licensure Exam exercise that resembles the kinds of questions appearing on many teacher licensure tests.

CHAPTER OUTLINE

- **CASE STUDY: A CONTAGIOUS SITUATION**
- **CREATING A SETTING CONDUCIVE TO LEARNING**
  Arranging the Classroom • Establishing and Maintaining Productive Teacher–Student Relationships • Creating an Effective Psychological Climate • Setting Limits • Planning Activities That Keep Students on Task • Monitoring What Students Are Doing • Modifying Instructional Strategies • Taking Developmental Differences into Account • Taking Individual and Group Differences into Account
- **COORDINATING EFFORTS WITH OTHERS**
  Working with Other Faculty Members • Working with the Community at Large • Working with Parents
- **DEALING WITH MISBEHAVIORS**
  Ignoring Behavior • Cueing Students • Discussing Problems Privately with Students • Teaching Self-Regulation Strategies • Conferring with Parents • Conducting Planned, Systematic Interventions • Taking Students' Cultural Backgrounds into Account
- **ADDRESSING AGGRESSION AND VIOLENCE AT SCHOOL**
  A Three-Level Approach • Addressing Gang-Related Problems
- **THE BIG PICTURE**
- **PRACTICE FOR YOUR LICENSURE EXAM: THE GOOD BUDDY**

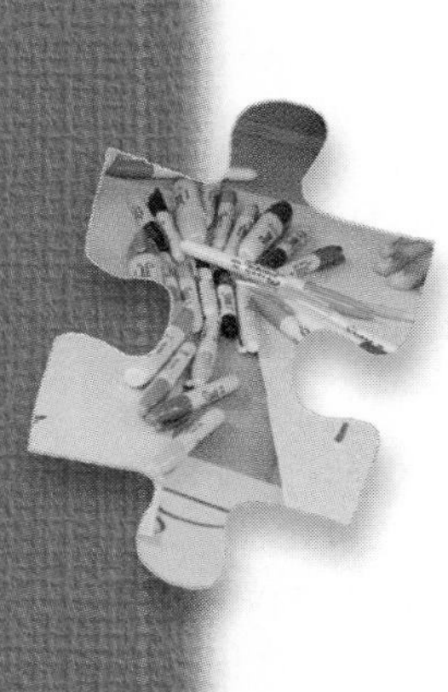

CHAPTER OBJECTIVES

- **Objective 13.1:** Identify numerous strategies for creating a classroom environment conducive to students' academic achievement and social and emotional well-being.
- **Objective 13.2:** Explain how you can coordinate your efforts with colleagues, community agencies, and parents to maximize students' academic and personal development.
- **Objective 13.3:** Identify six general approaches to dealing with student misbehaviors and the circumstances and cultural contexts in which each approach might be appropriate.
- **Objective 13.4:** Describe a three-level plan that can effectively reduce aggression and violence in the overall school community, as well as additional strategies you might use to address gang-related hostilities.

Chapter 13

Creating a Productive Learning Environment

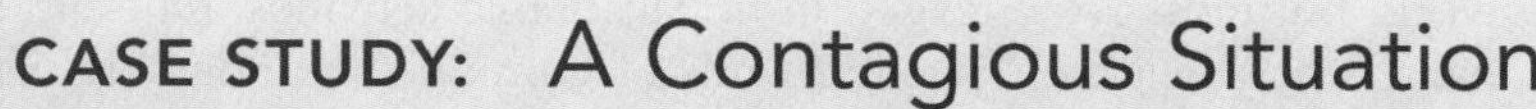

CASE STUDY: A Contagious Situation

After receiving a teaching certificate in May, Ms. Cornell accepted a position as a fifth-grade teacher at Twin Pines Elementary School. She has spent the summer planning her classroom curriculum, identifying her instructional goals for the year, and developing numerous activities to help students achieve those goals. Today, on the first day of school, she has jumped headlong into the curriculum she has planned. But three problems quickly present themselves—in the forms of Eli, Jake, and Vanessa.

These three students seem determined to disrupt the class at every possible opportunity. They move about the room without permission, intentionally annoying others as they walk to the pencil sharpener or wastebasket. They talk out of turn, sometimes being rude and disrespectful to their teacher and classmates and at other times belittling the activities Ms. Cornell has so carefully planned. They rarely complete in-class assignments, preferring instead to engage in horseplay or practical jokes. They seem especially prone to misbehavior during downtimes in the daily schedule—for example, at the beginning and the end of the school day, before and after recess and lunch, and whenever Ms. Cornell is preoccupied with other students.

Ms. Cornell continues to follow her daily lesson plans, ignoring her problem students and hoping they will begin to shape up. Yet the disruptive behavior continues, with the three of them delighting in one another's antics. Furthermore, the misbehavior begins to spread to other students. By the middle of October, Ms. Cornell's classroom is out of control, and instructional objectives are rarely accomplished. The few students who still seem intent on learning something are having a difficult time doing so.

- **In what ways has Ms. Cornell planned in advance for her classroom? In what ways has she *not* planned?**

AS A FIRST-YEAR TEACHER, Ms. Cornell is well prepared in some respects but not at all prepared in others. She has carefully identified her instructional goals and planned relevant lessons. But she has neglected to think about how she might keep students on task or how she might adjust her lessons based on how students are progressing. And she has not considered how she might nip behavior problems in the bud, before they begin to interfere with instruction and learning. In the absence of such planning, no curriculum can be very effective—not even one grounded firmly in contemporary theories of learning, development, and motivation.

Skillful teachers not only choose instructional strategies that promote effective learning and cognitive processes, but they also create an environment that keeps students busily engaged in productive learning activities. They certainly deal with the inappropriate behaviors that occur, but their emphasis is on *preventing* such behaviors. As we explore classroom management strategies in this chapter, our focus, too, will be on prevention. We will frequently return to the opening case study and consider how Ms. Cornell might have gotten the school year off to a better start.

Creating a Setting Conducive to Learning

In general, **classroom management** involves creating and maintaining a classroom environment conducive to students' learning and achievement. Students clearly learn more in some classrooms than in others. Consider these four classes as examples:

- Mr. Aragon's class is calm and orderly. The students are working independently at their seats, and all of them appear to be concentrating on individually tailored tasks. Occasionally students approach Mr. Aragon to seek clarification of an assignment or to get feedback about a task they've completed, and he confers quietly with them.
- Mr. Boitano's class is chaotic and noisy. A few students are doing their schoolwork, but most are engaged in nonacademic activities. One girl is painting her nails, a boy nearby is picking wads of gum off the underside of his desk, three students are exchanging gossip, and several others are reenacting the Battle of Waterloo with rubber bands and paper clips.
- Mr. Cavalini's class is as noisy as Mr. Boitano's. But rather than exchanging gossip or waging war, students are debating (often loudly and passionately) the pros and cons of nuclear energy. After 20 minutes of heated discussion, Mr. Cavalini stops the conversation, lists students' various arguments on the board, and then explains in simple philosophical terms why there is no easy or single "correct" resolution of the issue.
- Mr. Durocher believes that students learn most effectively when rules for their behavior are clearly spelled out, so he has 53 rules that cover almost every conceivable occasion: "Always use a ballpoint pen with blue or black ink," "Don't submit assignments on torn-out pages from spiral notebooks," "Don't ask questions irrelevant to the day's topic," and so on. He punishes each infraction severely enough that students follow the rules to the letter. As a result, his students are a quiet and obedient (if somewhat anxious) bunch, but they never seem to learn as much as Mr. Durocher knows they are capable of learning.

Two of these classrooms are quiet and orderly; the other two are active and noisy. But as you can see, the activity and noise levels are not good indicators of how much students are learning. Students are learning in Mr. Aragon's quiet class and in Mr. Cavalini's noisier one. At the same time, neither the students in Mr. Boitano's loud, chaotic battlefield nor those in Mr. Durocher's peaceful dictatorship seem to be learning much at all. A well-managed classroom is one in which students are consistently engaged in productive learning activities and in which students' behaviors rarely interfere with the achievement of instructional goals (Brophy, 2006; W. Doyle, 1990; Emmer & Evertson, 1981). It is *not* one in which students' every move is closely controlled.

Creating and maintaining an environment in which students are continually engaged in productive activities can be a challenging task indeed. After all, we must tend to the unique needs of many different students, must sometimes coordinate several activities at the same time, and must often make quick decisions about how to respond to unanticipated events (W. Doyle, 1986a). Furthermore, we must vary our classroom management techniques considerably depending on the particular instructional strategies in progress; for instance, hands-on approaches to instruction require

classroom management Establishment and maintenance of a classroom environment that's conducive to learning and achievement.

very different management techniques than expository approaches do (Emmer & Stough, 2001). It isn't surprising, then, that many beginning teachers mention classroom management as their number-one concern (Evertson & Weinstein, 2006; V. Jones, 1996; Veenman, 1984).

A good general model of effective classroom management is *authoritative parenting*, which I described in Chapter 3. Authoritative parents tend to do the following:

A well-managed classroom isn't necessarily one in which everyone is quiet but rather one in which everyone is consistently engaged in learning.

- Provide a loving and supportive home environment
- Hold high expectations and standards for children's behavior
- Explain why some behaviors are acceptable and others are not
- Consistently enforce household rules
- Include children in decision making
- Provide age-appropriate opportunities for independence

As we explore classroom management strategies, we'll often see one or more of these characteristics at work.

I've organized the discussion in this chapter around eight general management strategies:

- Create a physical arrangement that helps to focus students' attention on classroom lessons and academic subject matter.
- Establish and maintain good working relationships with students.
- Create a psychological climate in which students feel they belong and are intrinsically motivated to learn.
- Set reasonable limits for behavior.
- Plan activities that encourage on-task behavior.
- Regularly monitor what students are doing.
- Modify instructional strategies when necessary.
- Take developmental differences and student diversity into account in making classroom management decisions.

In the following sections, we'll identify specific ways to implement each of these strategies.

Arranging the Classroom

Good management begins well before the first day of class. As we arrange tables and chairs, decide where to put instructional materials and equipment, and think about where each student will sit, we should consider the effects that various arrangements are likely to have on students' behavior. Four strategies are especially helpful:

Arrange furniture in ways that encourage student interaction when appropriate and discourage it when counterproductive. When I was a child, student desks and chairs were bolted to the floor in tidy rows—an arrangement that was compatible only with a traditional lecture format. Fortunately, the great majority of classrooms now have movable furniture, giving us considerable flexibility in how we might arrange and occasionally rearrange things. Several clusters of desks and chairs facing one another are useful for small-group work, whereas traditional rows are often more effective in keeping students on task during individual assignments (Carter & Doyle, 2006). However, we should be sensitive to cultural differences here: Students who are accustomed to cooperating regularly with peers (e.g., students from many Native American communities) might find an everyone-faces-the-teacher arrangement strange and unnerving (Lipka, 1994).

Minimize possible distractions. Marla is more likely to poke classmates with her pencil if she has to brush past them to get to the pencil sharpener, and David is more likely to gossip with a friend if the friend is sitting right beside him. As teachers, we should arrange our classrooms in ways that minimize the likelihood of such behaviors—for instance, by establishing traffic patterns that allow students to move around the room without disturbing one another and by seating overly chatty friends on opposite sides of the room. We should also keep intriguing materials out of sight and reach until we need them (Emmer, Evertson, & Worsham, 2000; Sabers, Cushing, & Berliner, 1991).

Place chronically misbehaving or uninvolved students close at hand.

Arrange the classroom so that it is easy to interact with students. Our arrangement of desks, tables, and chairs should make it easy for us to converse with virtually any student as necessary (G. A. Davis & Thomas, 1989). It's often beneficial to place chronically misbehaving or uninvolved students close at hand: Students seated near us are more likely to pay attention, interact with us, and become actively involved in classroom activities (W. Doyle, 1986a; Woolfolk & Brooks, 1985).

Identify locations that allow easy monitoring of students' behavior. As we proceed through various lessons and activities—even when working with a single individual or small group—we should ideally be able to see *all* of our students (Emmer et al., 2000; Gettinger & Kohler, 2006). By occasionally surveying the classroom for possible signs of confusion, frustration, or boredom, we can more easily detect minor student difficulties and misbehaviors before they develop into serious problems.

Establishing and Maintaining Productive Teacher–Student Relationships

Research consistently indicates that the quality of teacher–student relationships is one of the most important factors—perhaps *the* most important factor—affecting students' emotional well-being, motivation, and learning during the school day. When students have positive, supportive relationships with teachers, they have higher self-efficacy and more intrinsic motivation to learn. They also engage in more self-regulated learning, behave more appropriately in class, and achieve at higher levels (J. N. Hughes, Luo, Kwok, & Loyd, 2008; Marzano, 2003; Patrick, Ryan, & Kaplan, 2007; Pianta, Belsky, Vandergrift, Houts, & Morrison, 2008; Roeser, Eccles, & Sameroff, 2000).

Without a doubt, high-quality teacher–student relationships help students satisfy their *need for relatedness*—their need to feel socially connected with one another (see Chapter 11). Although some students may misbehave as a way of gaining our attention (this might be the case with Eli, Jake, and Vanessa), in my own experiences as a parent, teacher, and school psychologist, I've never met a child or adolescent who, deep down, didn't want to have positive, productive relationships with school faculty members.

The following strategies must be central in our efforts to have productive working relationships with students:

Regularly communicate caring and respect for students as people. To some extent, we can communicate our affection and respect through the many little things we do each day (Allday & Pakurar, 2007; Certo et al., 2002). For example, we can give students a smile and warm greeting at the beginning of the day. We can compliment them when they get a flattering haircut, excel in an extracurricular activity, or receive recognition in the local newspaper. We can be good listeners when they come to school angry or upset. One high school student described caring teachers this way:

> You might see them in the hallway and they ask how you're doing, how was your last report card, is there anything you need. Or, maybe one day you're looking a little upset. They'll pull you to the side and ask you what's wrong, is there anything I can do. (Certo et al., 2002, p. 15)

Such caring gestures can be especially important for students who have few dependably supportive relationships at home (Diamond, 1991; Juvonen, 2006; O'Connor & McCartney, 2007).

Remember that caring and respect involve much more than simply showing affection. Some beginning teachers erroneously think that good teaching involves little more than showing that they really like their students—in other words, being "warm and fuzzy" (L. H. Anderman, Patrick, Hruda, & Linnenbrink, 2002, p. 274; Goldstein & Lake, 2000; Patrick & Pintrich, 2001). In fact, to show students that we *truly* care about and respect them, we must take steps such as the following:

- Be well prepared for class and in other ways demonstrate a love of teaching and an eagerness to take teaching responsibilities seriously.
- Communicate high yet realistic expectations for student performance, and provide the support students need to meet those expectations.
- Include students in decision making and evaluation of their work.
- Acknowledge that students can occasionally have an "off" day, and don't hold it against them. (Certo et al., 2002; H. A. Davis, 2003; H. A. Davis, Schutz, & Chambless, 2001; J. M. T. Walker & Hoover-Dempsey, 2006)

Another important strategy is to establish means through which we and our students can frequently communicate one on one. One option, especially for older students, is electronic mail (e-mail), perhaps through a mechanism such as Gaggle (www.gaggle.net), which prevents students from wandering into potentially inappropriate websites in cyberspace. Another option is the use of two-way *dialogue journals*, in which individual students and their teacher both write one or more times each week. Figure 13.1 shows several entries in 6-year-old Matt's journal; each entry is followed by a response (indented) from his first-grade teacher. Notice that Matt feels comfortable enough with his teacher to engage in some playful one-upmanship ("I can go fast[e]r then you"). Although his writing skills are far from perfect—for instance, he writes *especially downhill skiing* as "spshal don hilscein"—they are certainly adequate to communicate his thoughts. Notice, too, that his teacher doesn't correct his misspellings. Her primary purposes are to encourage him to write and to open the lines of communication; giving negative feedback about spelling might interfere with both of these goals. Instead, the teacher simply models correct spelling in her own entries.

Establish mechanisms through which you can communicate regularly and privately with every student.

Work hard to improve relationships that have gotten off to a bad start. Occasionally students may come to us with an apparent chip on the shoulder, distrusting us from day one because of previous hurtful relationships with parents, teachers, or other adults (H. A. Davis, 2003; Hyman et al., 2006; Pianta, 1999). At other times, we may get relationships off to a bad start through our own actions—perhaps because we've incorrectly attributed low achievement to a lack of effort rather than a lack of skill or perhaps because we've accused a temperamentally high-energy child of being intentionally disobedient (Darch & Kame'enui, 2004; B. K. Keogh, 2003; Silverberg, 2003). Unfortunately, students who have the poorest relationships with their teachers are often the ones most in need of good ones (Juvonen, 2006; Stipek & Miles, 2008).

Regardless of how nonproductive relationships start, we must work hard to turn them into productive ones. The first step, of course, is to *identify* nonproductive relationships, recognizing signs such as these:

- We have hostile feelings (e.g., dislike, anger) toward a student.
- We rarely interact with a student.
- Our messages to a student usually involve criticism or fault finding.

FIGURE 13.1 Two-way dialogue journals provide one effective means of maintaining one-on-one communication with all students. In these excerpts from 6-year-old Matt's journal, Matt and his first-grade teacher discover common outside interests.

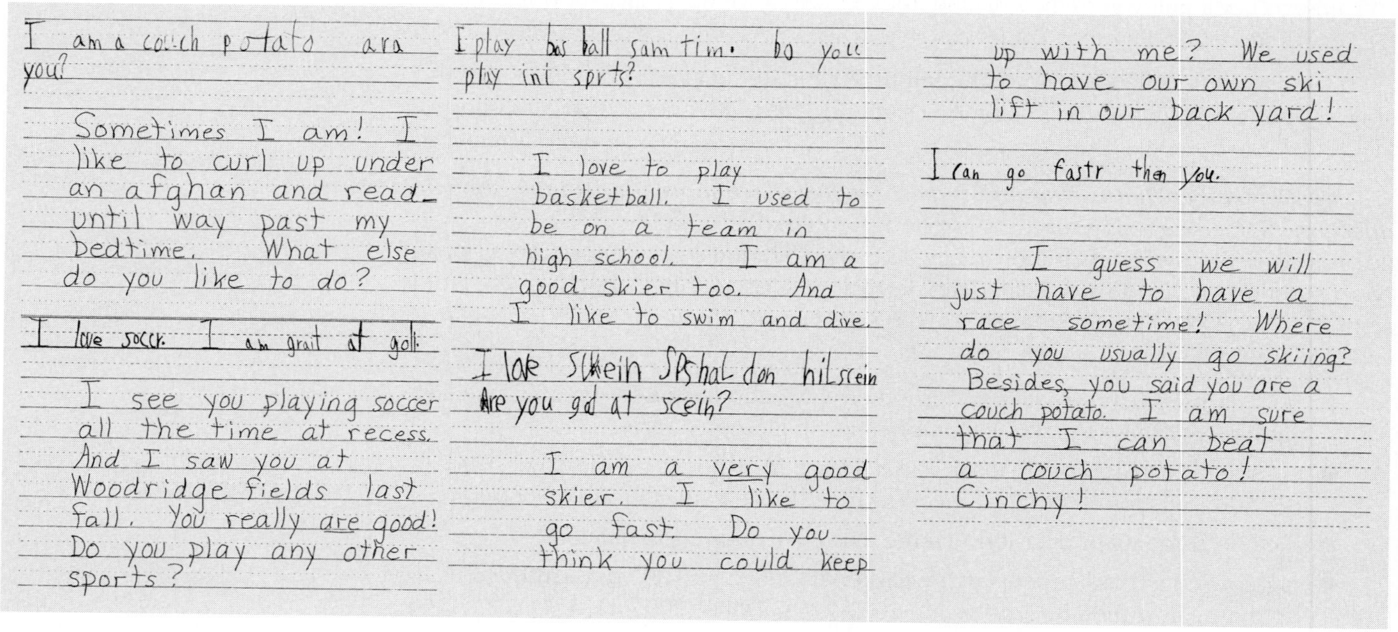

I am a couch potato ara you?

Sometimes I am! I like to curl up under an afghan and read until way past my bedtime. What else do you like to do?

I love soccr. I am grait at goli.

I see you playing soccer all the time at recess. And I saw you at Woodridge fields last fall. You really are good! Do you play any other sports?

I play bas ball sam tim. Do you play ini sprts?

I love to play basketball. I used to be on a team in high school. I am a good skier too. And I like to swim and dive.

I lak SIkein SRshal don hilscein Are you gd at scein?

I am a very good skier. I like to go fast. Do you think you could keep up with me? We used to have our own ski lift in our back yard!

I can go fastr then you.

I guess we will just have to have a race sometime! Where do you usually go skiing? Besides, you said you are a couch potato. I am sure that I can beat a couch potato! Cinchy!

- We have a sense of learned helplessness about our ability to work effectively with a student. (Pianta, 1999; Sutherland & Morgan, 2003)

Once we have identified troublesome relationships, several strategies can help us repair them:

- Meet one on one with a student to talk openly about the problem and possible ways to fix it (more on this point later in the chapter).
- Think actively—perhaps in a brainstorming session with one or more colleagues—about alternative hypotheses that might explain a student's behavior and about potential solutions that these hypotheses suggest.
- Spend time with a student in a relaxed, noninstructional context—perhaps a mutually enjoyable recreational activity—that can allow more positive feelings to emerge (Pianta, 1999, 2006; Silverberg, 2003; Sutton & Wheatley, 2003).

Creating an Effective Psychological Climate

Caring and supportive teacher–student relationships are important contributors to the overall **classroom climate**—the general psychological environment that permeates classroom interactions. Ultimately, we want a classroom in which students feel safe and secure, make learning a high priority, and are willing to take the risks and make the mistakes so critical for maximal cognitive growth (Brand, Felner, Shim, Seitsinger, & Duman, 2003; Hamre & Pianta, 2005). Such an environment minimizes discipline problems and seems to be especially important for students at risk for academic failure and dropping out of school (Freiberg & Lapointe, 2006; V. E. Lee & Burkam, 2003; Pianta, 1999). Following are several critical strategies:

Establish a goal-oriented, businesslike, yet nonthreatening atmosphere. Although caring relationships with students are essential, we and our students must all recognize that we are in school to get certain things accomplished (G. A. Davis & Thomas, 1989). Classroom activities need not be boring and tedious, however. On the contrary, they should be interesting and engaging—sometimes even exciting. But

classroom climate Overall psychological atmosphere of the classroom.

entertainment and excitement should not be goals in and of themselves. Rather, they are means to a more important goal: mastering academic subject matter.

Despite our emphasis on business, the classroom atmosphere should never be uncomfortable or threatening. Students who are excessively anxious are unlikely to give us their best (see Chapter 11). Strategies such as the following enable us to be businesslike without being threatening:

- Hold students accountable for achieving instructional objectives but without placing them under continual surveillance.
- Point out students' mistakes without making them feel like failures.
- Admonish students for misbehavior without holding grudges against them from one day to the next. (C. R. Rogers, 1983; Spaulding, 1992)

Communicate and demonstrate that school tasks and academic subject matter have value. As teachers, we give students messages about the value of school subject matter by both what we say and what we do (Brophy, 2008; W. Doyle, 1983). For instance, if we ask students to spend hours each day engaged in what seems like meaningless busy work and if we assess learning primarily through tests that encourage rote memorization, we are indirectly telling students that classroom tasks are merely things that need to be "gotten over with" (E. H. Hiebert & Raphael, 1996; Stodolsky et al., 1991). Furthermore, if we continually focus students' attention on performance goals—what their test grades are, how their work compares to that of their classmates, and so on—we increase their anxiety about academic achievement and indirectly increase the frequency of disruptive behavior (Kumar et al., 2002; Marachi et al., 2001; A. M. Ryan & Patrick, 2001). If, instead, we continually communicate that learning classroom subject matter can help students make better sense of the outside world, if we assess learning in ways that require meaningful learning, and if we focus on how well each student is improving over time, we show students that knowing the subject matter can potentially enhance the quality of their lives.

Give students some control over classroom activities. To make sure students accomplish important instructional goals, we must direct the course of classroom activities to some degree. Nevertheless, we can give students control over some aspects of classroom life—for example, through strategies such as these:

- Give advance notice of upcoming activities and assignments, enabling students to plan ahead.
- Create a regular routine for completing assignments, enabling students to do them with only minimal guidance.
- Allow students to set their own deadlines for some assignments, enabling them to establish a manageable time frame.
- Provide occasional opportunities for students to make choices about how to complete assignments or spend class time, enabling them to set some of their own priorities. (Spaulding, 1992)

Through such strategies, we promote the sense of self-determination so important for intrinsic motivation (see Chapter 11) along with the development of self-regulated learning skills so essential for students' long-term academic success (see Chapter 10).

Promote a general sense of community and belongingness. An increasingly popular instructional strategy is to create a *community of learners*, a classroom in which the teacher and students collaborate to build a body of knowledge about a topic and help one another learn about that topic (see Chapter 7). Ultimately, we also want to create a general **sense of community** in the classroom—a sense that we and our students have shared goals, are mutually respectful and supportive of one another's efforts, and believe that everyone makes an important contribution to classroom learning (Hom & Battistich, 1995; D. Kim, Solomon, & Roberts, 1995; Osterman, 2000). Creating a sense of community engenders feelings of **belongingness**: Students see themselves as important and valued members of the classroom (E. M. Anderman, 2002).

sense of community Shared belief that teacher and students have common goals, are mutually respectful and supportive, and all make important contributions to classroom learning.

belongingness General sense that one is an important and valued member of the classroom.

Create a sense of shared goals, interpersonal respect, and mutual support.

Students achieve at higher levels in the classroom when they have a sense of community—that is, when they have shared goals and are respectful and supportive of one another's efforts.

When students share a sense of community, they are more likely to exhibit prosocial behavior, stay on task, be enthusiastic about classroom activities, and achieve at high levels. Furthermore, a sense of classroom community is associated with lower rates of emotional distress, disruptive classroom behavior, truancy, and dropping out (Hom & Battistich, 1995; Juvonen, 2006; Osterman, 2000; Patrick, Ryan, & Kaplan, 2007). And consistent experiences with caring and equitable classroom communities help students internalize attitudes essential for a successful democratic society, including a commitment to fairness and justice for everyone (C. A. Flanagan, Cumsille, Gill, & Gallay, 2007).

Perhaps the most important characteristic of a sense of classroom community is that students always treat one another with kindness and respect. When classmates are *not* kind and respectful—for example, when they ridicule or bully certain other class members—their victims are apt to withdraw either physically or mentally from classroom activities (see Chapter 3). In the following interview, a middle school student named Barnie describes how painful the ridicule of classmates can be:

Adult: Are there times when you feel you are really different from your classmates?

Barnie: Yeah, all the time. . . . Because they all answer the questions, when I raise my hand I always get it wrong. Last week I was in a group, a smart group and I am not that smart. And I mostly get all the wrong answers and they yell at me.

Adult: What do they say?

Barnie: "You're dumb! You're stupid!"

Adult: What do you tell them?

Barnie: That's the way I am.

Adult: Can you tell me about any other times when you felt different?

Barnie: When I am in the gym, I cannot run as fast as everybody and they all laugh at me. . . . It feels like I am the worst student ever. (Kumar et al., 2002, p. 161)

Do not tolerate statements or behaviors that show lack of concern or respect for other class members.

As teachers, we must make it very clear that remarks or behaviors that deride or denigrate other class members are totally unacceptable both inside and outside the classroom. The Creating a Productive Classroom Environment feature "Creating and Enhancing a Sense of Classroom Community" offers several strategies that can enhance students' sense that they are important and valued members of the classroom.

Setting Limits

In the opening case study, Ms. Cornell failed to provide guidelines for how students should behave, something she should have done the first week of school. Students must know that certain behaviors simply won't be tolerated—especially those that cause physical or psychological harm, damage school property, or interfere with others' learning and performance. And over the long run, setting reasonable limits on classroom behavior helps students become productive members of adult society. In other words, imposing limits on students' behavior is one important way in which schools help *socialize* children to work effectively in their cultural groups (see Chapter 3).

Creating A PRODUCTIVE CLASSROOM ENVIRONMENT

Creating and Enhancing a Sense of Classroom Community

- **Consistently communicate the message that all students deserve the respect of their classmates and are important members of the classroom community.**

  A middle school language arts class includes several students with reading disabilities—disabilities that are obvious in much of the students' oral and written work in class. The teacher doesn't publicly identify the students with disabilities, because doing so would violate their right to confidentiality about their diagnoses. However, she frequently communicates the message that students in any single age-group vary widely in their literacy skills, usually through no fault of their own. She also continually stresses that it's the class's responsibility to help *everyone* improve their reading and writing skills over the course of the school year.

- **Create mechanisms through which students can all help to make the classroom run smoothly and efficiently.**

  A kindergarten teacher creates several "helper" roles (e.g., distributing art supplies, feeding the class goldfish, taking messages to the main office) that he assigns to different students on a rotating basis.

- **Emphasize such prosocial values as sharing and cooperation, and provide opportunities for students to help one another.**

  As students work on in-class assignments each day, a seventh-grade math teacher often asks, "Who has a problem that someone else might be able to help you solve?"

- **Make frequent use of interactive and collaborative teaching strategies (e.g., class discussions, cooperative learning activities, etc.).**

  In assigning students to cooperative learning groups, a high school social studies teacher usually puts any student with poor social skills (e.g., a student with Asperger syndrome) in a group with two or three more socially proficient students. Before the groups begin their work, the teacher reminds the class that everyone should focus both on completing the assigned task and on helping other group members master the topic at hand. She also reminds students of the class's rules for cooperative group work: "Listen to others politely and attentively," "Address differences of opinion in respectful and constructive ways," and so on.

- **Solicit students' ideas and opinions, and incorporate them into class discussions and activities.**

  A first-grade teacher regularly has students vote on the storybooks they would like her to read during "settling-down" time after lunch each day. She first reads the book that gets the most votes, but she assures students who voted differently that she will read their choices later in the week. "It's important that everyone in this class has a say in what we read," she often tells them.

- **Use competition only to create an occasional sense of playfulness in the class and only when all students have an equal chance of winning.**

  A high school Spanish teacher assigns a long-term cooperative group project in which students write and videotape Spanish soap operas (*telenovelas*). A few weeks later, the teacher holds an "Academy Awards Banquet"—a potluck dinner for the students and their families. At the banquet, the teacher shows all of the videos and awards a variety of "Oscars." She gives every student an Oscar for some aspect of his or her performance, but she also gives one group an Oscar for best telenovela.

- **Encourage students to be on the lookout for classmates on the periphery of ongoing activities (perhaps students with disabilities) and to ask these children to join in.**

  Teachers at an elementary school all adhere to and enforce the same no-exclusion policy on the playground: Any student who wants to be involved in a play activity *can* be involved.

- **Work on social skills with students whose interpersonal behaviors may victimize or alienate others.**

  A third grader often behaves rudely, sometimes aggressively, toward classmates who have something she wants. For example, when waiting for her turn to use the classroom computer, the girl may yell "*I* need to use it now!" or, instead, may shove its current user out of his or her chair. In a private conference after school, her teacher points out that patience and turn taking are sometimes necessary to enable all students to have equal opportunities to use classroom equipment and supplies. The teacher suggests several strategies the girl might use to make her needs known in more socially appropriate ways—for instance, by politely asking "When do you think you might be finished with the computer? Can I use it after you're through?" The teacher also has the student practice the strategies in various role-playing scenarios.

- **Watch for incidents of bullying and other forms of peer harassment, and administer appropriate consequences to the perpetrators.**

  A middle school science teacher has a student who is consistently disruptive and often demeans his classmates. She knows that the boy comes from a dysfunctional family and has, for most of his life, been shuffled from the home of one relative to that of another. She communicates her concern for the student ("I know you're going through a lot; how can I help you be successful in my class?"), but she also calls him to task for his inappropriate behaviors. For instance, when he refers to a classmate as a "faggot," she responds emphatically, "You know that such language is unacceptable. Please see me at the end of the period." After class, she reminds the student that everyone in her class deserves respect and then insists that he give the offended classmate both oral and written apologies. But she also reassures him that she will not hold this incident against him, especially if, in the future, he works hard to be more respectful and compassionate.

Sources: C. Ames, 1984; Emmer et al., 2000; Espelage & Swearer, 2004; Hamovitch, 2007; D. Kim, Solomon, & Roberts, 1995; Lickona, 1991; Osterman, 2000; A. M. Ryan & Patrick, 2001; Sapon-Shevin, Dobbelaere, Corrigan, Goodman, & Mastin, 1998 (playground example); Stipek, 1996; Turnbull et al., 2000.

As we set limits, however, we must remember that students are more likely to be intrinsically motivated to master classroom subject matter if we preserve their sense of autonomy and self-determination. With this caution in mind, I offer the following recommendations:

Establish a few rules and procedures at the beginning of the year. Effective classroom managers establish and communicate certain rules and procedures right from the start (Borko & Putnam, 1996; W. Doyle, 1990; Gettinger & Kohler, 2006). For instance, they identify acceptable and unacceptable behaviors and describe the consequences of noncompliance (e.g., see Figure 13.2). They also develop consistent procedures and routines for such things as completing seatwork, asking for help, and turning in assignments. And they have procedures in place for nonroutine events such as school assemblies, field trips, and fire drills. Taking time to clarify rules and procedures seems to be especially important in the early elementary grades, when students may not be very familiar with how things are typically done at school (Carter & Doyle, 2006; Evertson & Emmer, 1982; Gettinger & Kohler, 2006).

myeducationlab

Observe how a second-grade teacher solicits students' ideas about useful classroom rules in the video "Classroom Rules." (To find this video, go to Chapter 13 of the Book-Specific Resources in MyEducationLab, select *Video Examples*, and then click on the title.)

Ideally, students should understand that rules and procedures are not based on our personal whims but are, instead, designed to help the classroom run smoothly and efficiently. One way of promoting such understanding is to include students in decision making about the rules and procedures by which the class will operate (Fuller, 2001; Lickona, 1991). For example, we might solicit students' suggestions for making sure that unnecessary distractions are kept to a minimum and that everyone has a chance to speak during class discussions. By incorporating students' ideas and listening to their concerns about the limits we set, we help them understand the reasons for—and also enhance their sense of ownership of—those limits (Evertson, Emmer, & Worsham, 2000; M. Watson, 2008).

Keep in mind that rules and procedures are easier to remember—and therefore easier to follow—if they are relatively simple and few in number (G. A. Davis & Thomas, 1989; Emmer & Gerwels, 2006). Effective classroom managers tend to stress only the most important rules and procedures at the beginning of the school year. They introduce other rules and procedures later on as needed (W. Doyle, 1986a). You should also keep in mind that, although some order and predictability are essential for student productivity, too much order can make a classroom a routine, boring place—one without any element of fun and spontaneity. We don't necessarily need rules and procedures for everything!

Present rules and procedures in an informational rather than a controlling manner. We are more likely to maintain students' sense of self-determination if we present rules and procedures as items of information rather than as forms of control

FIGURE 13.2 Effective teachers typically begin the school year with a few rules to help classroom activities run smoothly. Such rules often include variations on those listed here.

1. *Bring all needed materials to class.* Students should have books, homework assignments, permission slips, and any needed supplies for planned activities.
2. *Be in your seat and ready to work when the bell rings.* Students should be at their desks, have paper out and pencils sharpened, and be physically and mentally ready to work.
3. *Respect and be polite to all people.* Students should listen attentively when someone else is speaking, behave appropriately for a substitute teacher, and refrain from insults, fighting, and other disrespectful or hostile behaviors.
4. *Respect other people's property.* Students should keep the classroom clean and neat, refrain from defacing school property, ask for permission to borrow another's possessions, and return those possessions in a timely fashion.
5. *Obey all school rules.* Students must obey the rules of the school building as well as the rules of the classroom.

Sources: Emmer et al., 2000, pp. 22–23; Evertson, Emmer, & Worsham, 2000, p. 23.

(see Chapter 11). Figure 13.3 presents several examples of rules and procedures presented in an informational manner. Each of these statements includes the reasons for imposing certain guidelines—a strategy that is likely to increase students' compliance with the rules (recall the discussion of *induction* in Chapter 3). The following scenario provides a simple illustration of how giving a reason can make all the difference in the world:

> Gerard has little tolerance for frustration. Whenever he asks Ms. Donnelly for assistance, he wants it *now*. If she is unable to help him immediately, he screams, "You're no good!" or "You don't care!" and shoves other students' desks as he walks angrily back to his seat.
>
> At one point during the school year, the class has a unit on interpersonal skills. One lesson in the unit addresses *timing*—the most appropriate and effective time to ask for another person's assistance with a problem.
>
> A week later, Gerard approaches Ms. Donnelly for help with a math problem. She is working with another student but turns briefly to Gerard and says, "Timing." She waits expectantly for Gerard's usual screaming. Instead, he responds, "Hey, Ms. D., I get it! I can ask you at another time!" He returns to his seat with a smile on his face. (Based on Sullivan-DeCarlo, DeFalco, & Roberts, 1998, p. 81)

Periodically review the usefulness of existing rules and procedures. As the school year progresses, we will almost inevitably discover that some rules and procedures need revision. For instance, we may find that rules about when students can and cannot move around the room are overly restrictive or that procedures for turning in homework don't accommodate students who must leave class early for doctors' appointments, school athletic events, and the like.

Regularly scheduled class meetings provide one mechanism through which we and our students can periodically review classroom rules and procedures (D. E. Campbell, 1996; Glasser, 1969; Striepling-Goldstein, 2004). Consider this scenario as an example:

> Every Friday afternoon at 2:00, Ms. Ayotte's students move their chairs into a large circle for their weekly class meeting. First on the agenda is a review of the past week's successes, including both academic achievements and socially productive

FIGURE 13.3 We are more likely to motivate students to follow classroom rules and procedures when we communicate those rules and procedures as information *without* conveying a desire to impose a lot of control.

We might say this (as information) . . .	Rather than this (as control)
"You'll get your independent assignments done more quickly if you get right to work."	"Please be quiet and do your own work."
"As we practice for our fire drill, it's important to line up quickly and be quiet so that we can hear the instructions we are given and will know what to do."	"When the fire alarm sounds, line up quickly and quietly, and then wait for further instructions."
"This assignment is designed to help you develop the writing skills you will need after you graduate. Because it's unfair to other authors to copy their work word for word, we will practice putting ideas into our own words and giving credit to authors whose ideas we borrow. Passing off another's writing or ideas as your own can lead to suspension in college or a lawsuit in the business world."	"Cheating and plagiarism are not acceptable in this classroom."

> events. Next, the group identifies problems that have emerged during the week and brainstorms possible ways to avert such problems in the future. Finally, the students consider whether existing classroom rules and procedures are serving their purpose and, if not, either modify existing rules and procedures or establish new ones. During the first few meetings, Ms. Ayotte leads the discussions, but once students have become familiar and comfortable with the process, she relinquishes control of the meetings to one or another of her students on a rotating basis.

When it is necessary to change classroom rules and procedures, include students in the decision making.

By providing frequent opportunities for students to review classroom policies, we find another way of giving them a sense of ownership about the policies. Furthermore, more advanced moral reasoning may gradually emerge, perhaps as a result of occasional moral dilemmas with which students must wrestle (Nucci, 2006, 2009; Power et al., 1989; also see the discussion of moral development in Chapter 3).

Acknowledge students' feelings about classroom requirements. There will undoubtedly be times when we must ask students to do things they would prefer not to do. Rather than pretend that students are eager to do what we ask of them, we are better advised to acknowledge their displeasure and lack of motivation (Deci & Ryan, 1985; Reeve, 2006). For example, we might tell students that we know how difficult it can be to sit quietly during a lengthy school assembly or to spend an entire evening on a particular assignment. At the same time, we can explain that the behaviors we request of students, although not always intrinsically enjoyable, can help them achieve their own long-term goals. By acknowledging students' feelings about tasks they would rather not do but also pointing out the benefits of those tasks, we increase the likelihood that students will willingly comply (Deci & Ryan, 1985; Reeve, 2006).

Enforce rules consistently and equitably. Classroom rules are apt to be effective only when they're consistently enforced. For example, in the opening case study, Ms. Cornell imposes no consequences when her three troublesome students misbehave. Not only do their antics continue, but other students, realizing that "anything goes" in Ms. Cornell's classroom, follow suit. As we discovered in our discussion of social cognitive theory in Chapter 10, imposing no adverse consequence for inappropriate behavior—especially when that consequence has been spelled out in advance—can actually be a form of *reinforcement* for the misbehavior.

Consistency in enforcing classroom rules should apply not only across occasions but also across *students*. As teachers, we will almost inevitably like some students more than others (e.g., we're apt to prefer high achievers), but we must keep our preferences to ourselves. Students can be quite resentful of teachers who grant special favors to and perhaps overlook rule infractions of a few favorite students (Babad, 1995; Babad, Avni-Babad, & Rosenthal, 2003; J. Baker, 1999). And students who are unfairly accused or punished are, of course, even more resentful, as one high school student explains:

> Because like if you had a past record or whatever like in middle school if you got in trouble like at all, they would think that you're a slight trouble maker and if you got in trouble again, they would always . . . if you were anywhere that something bad happened or something against the rules or whatever, they pick you first because they think that you have a past. So they wouldn't like pick the kids that had never done anything. (Certo et al., 2002, p. 25)

Thus, consistency and equitable treatment for all students—or the lack thereof—is apt to have a significant effect on teacher–student relationships and overall classroom climate (Babad et al., 2003; J. Baker, 1999; Certo et al., 2002).

Planning Activities That Keep Students on Task

As effective teachers plan their lessons, they think not only about how to facilitate students' learning and cognitive processing but also how to *motivate* students to learn. In Chapter 11, we identified many strategies for fostering motivation to master academic subject matter. But in addition, expert teachers offer the following suggestions for keeping students on task:

Students who are actively engaged in classroom activities rarely exhibit problem behaviors.

Make sure that students are always productively engaged in worthwhile activities. In the "Take Five" Experiencing Firsthand exercise in Chapter 11, I asked you to do nothing—absolutely nothing—for a five-minute period. Chances are good that you found yourself filling in the time somehow, perhaps looking around the room, tapping on the table, fiddling with nearby objects, and so on. Virtually all human beings have a basic *need for arousal*—a need for some degree of stimulation. At school, children and adolescents should find their stimulation in ongoing tasks and activities. If, instead, they have a lot of free time on their hands, they will generate stimulation of their own, sometimes in the form of misbehaviors.

Effective classroom managers make sure there is little unscheduled time in which nothing is going on. Following are several strategies for keeping students productively engaged:

- Have something specific for students to do each day, even on the first day of class.
- Have materials organized and equipment set up before class.
- Select activities that ensure *all* students' involvement and participation.
- Maintain a brisk pace throughout each lesson (but not one so fast that students can't keep up).
- Ensure that students' comments are relevant and helpful but not excessively long winded. (For instance, take chronic time-monopolizers aside for a private discussion about giving classmates a chance to speak.)
- Spend only short periods of class time assisting individual students unless other students are capable of working independently and productively in the meantime.
- Ensure that students who finish an assigned task quickly have something else to do (e.g., writing in a class journal or reading a book). (G. A. Davis & Thomas, 1989; W. Doyle, 1986a; Emmer et al., 2000; Emmer & Gerwels, 2006; Evertson & Harris, 1992; Gettinger, 1988; Munn, Johnstone, & Chalmers, 1990)

Choose tasks at an appropriate difficulty level for students' knowledge and skills. Students are more likely to work diligently at their classwork when they have activities and assignments appropriate for their current knowledge and skills (Mac Iver et al., 1995; Moore & Edwards, 2003; S. L. Robinson & Griesemer, 2006). They are apt to misbehave when they are asked to do things that they perceive—either accurately or not—as being too difficult for them. Thus, classroom misbehaviors are more often observed with students who have a history of struggling in their schoolwork (W. Doyle, 1986a; Miles & Stipek, 2006). In the opening case study, Eli, Jake, and Vanessa may very well have such a history.

Avoiding overly difficult tasks does *not* mean that we should plan activities so easy that students aren't challenged and learn nothing new in doing them. One workable strategy is to *begin* the school year with relatively easy tasks that students can readily complete. Such tasks enable students to practice normal classroom routines and procedures and gain a sense that they can enjoy and succeed in classroom activities. Once a supportive classroom climate has been established and students are comfortable with classroom procedures, we can gradually introduce more difficult and challenging assignments (W. Doyle, 1990; Emmer et al., 2000; Evertson & Emmer, 1982).

Begin the school year with easy and familiar tasks, introducing more difficult tasks after a supportive classroom climate has been firmly established.

Provide some structure for activities and assignments. Even when lessons are largely learner-directed, students typically need some structure and guidance. As an example of how important structure can be, try the following exercise.

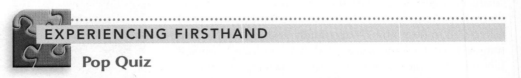

EXPERIENCING FIRSTHAND

Pop Quiz

Get a blank sheet of paper and a pen or pencil, and complete these two tasks:

- *Task A:* Using single words or short phrases, list six characteristics of an effective teacher.
- *Task B:* Explain the general effects of school attendance on children's lives.

Don't continue reading until you have either (a) completed each task or (b) spent at least five minutes on it.

After you have completed both tasks, answer each of the following questions with either "Task A" or "Task B":

1. For which task did you have a better understanding of what you were being asked to do?
2. During which task did your mind more frequently wander to irrelevant topics?
3. During which task did you engage in more off-task behaviors (e.g., looking around the room, doodling, getting out of your seat)?

I'm guessing that you found the first task relatively straightforward, whereas the second wasn't at all clear-cut. Did the ambiguity of Task B lead to more irrelevant thoughts and off-task behaviors? Off-task behavior occurs more frequently when activities are so loosely structured that students don't have a clear sense of what they are supposed to do.

Effective teachers tend to give assignments with some degree of structure. For example, they give clear directions about how to proceed and provide a great deal of feedback about appropriate responses, especially during the first few weeks of the school year (W. Doyle, 1990; Evertson & Emmer, 1982; Gettinger & Kohler, 2006). However, we need to strike a happy medium here: We don't want to structure classroom tasks to the point that students never make their own decisions about how to proceed or to the point that only lower-level thinking skills are required. In addition to keeping students on task, we also want them to have a sense of self-determination, engage in some self-regulation, and develop and use higher-level cognitive processes—for example, to think analytically, critically, and creatively (W. Doyle, 1986a; Nichols, 2004; Weinert & Helmke, 1995).

The concept of *scaffolding* is useful here: We can provide a great deal of structure for tasks early in the school year, gradually removing it as students become better able to structure tasks for themselves. For example, when introducing students to cooperative learning, we might break down each group task into several subtasks, giving clear directions about how each subtask should be carried out and assigning every group member a particular role to serve in the group. As the school year progresses and students become more adept at working cooperatively with their classmates, we can gradually become less directive about how group tasks are accomplished.

Plan for transition times in the school day. In the opening case study, Eli, Jake, and Vanessa often misbehave at the beginning and the end of the school day, as well as before and after recess and lunch. Misbehaviors occur most frequently during transition times—as students end one activity and begin a second or as they move from one classroom to another. Effective classroom managers take steps to ensure that transitions proceed quickly and without a loss of momentum (W. Doyle, 1984; Gettinger & Kohler, 2006). For example, they establish procedures for moving from one activity to the next, and they ensure that there is little slack time in which students have nothing to do. And especially in the secondary grades, when students change classes every hour or so, effective classroom managers typically have a task for students to complete as soon as they enter the classroom.

How can we plan for the various transitions that occur throughout the school day? Here are some examples:

- An elementary school teacher has students follow the same procedure each day as lunchtime approaches: (a) place completed assignments in a basket on the teacher's desk, (b) put away supplies, (c) get lunches from the coatroom, and (d) line up quietly by the door.
- A middle school math teacher has students copy the next homework assignment as soon as they come into class.
- A high school English composition teacher writes a topic or question on the chalkboard at the beginning of each class period. When students come to class, they know that they should immediately begin to write on the topic or question of the day.
- A high school physical education teacher has students begin each class session with five minutes of stretching exercises.

Although very different in nature, all of these strategies have the same goal: keeping students focused on productive behaviors.

Some students may have particular difficulty moving from one activity to another, especially if they are deeply engaged in what they are doing. Accordingly, it's often helpful to give students advance warning that a transition is coming, describe for them what the subsequent activity will be, and remind them of the usual procedures for switching from one task to another (Carter & Doyle, 2006; Emmer & Gerwels, 2006).

myeducationlab

Gain practice in helping students stay focused on productive academic tasks by completing the Building Teaching Skills and Dispositions exercise "Maintaining On-Task Behavior" in MyEducationLab. (To find this exercise, go to the topic Classroom Management in MyEducationLab, and click on *Building Teaching Skills and Dispositions.*)

Monitoring What Students Are Doing

Effective teachers communicate something called **withitness**: They know—and their students *know* that they know—what students are doing at all times. These teachers regularly scan the classroom and make frequent eye contact with individual students. They know what misbehaviors are occurring *when* those misbehaviors occur, and they know who the perpetrators are (Gettinger & Kohler, 2006; T. Hogan et al., 2003; Kounin, 1970). Consider the following classroom example:

> In one second-grade classroom, an hour and a half of each morning is devoted to reading. Students spend part of this time with their teacher in small reading groups and the remainder of the time working on independent assignments tailored to their individual reading skills. As the teacher works with each reading group at the front of the classroom, she situates herself with her back to the wall so that she can simultaneously keep an eye on students working independently at their seats. She sends a quick and subtle signal—perhaps a stern expression, a finger to the lips, or a callout of a student's name—to any student who gets off task.

When we demonstrate such withitness, especially at the beginning of the school year, students are more likely to stay on task and display appropriate classroom behavior. Not surprisingly, they are also more likely to achieve at high levels (W. Doyle, 1986a; Gettinger & Kohler, 2006; Woolfolk & Brooks, 1985).

Continually monitor what students are doing, and let students know that *you* know what's going on in your classroom.

myeducationlab

Observe this classroom in action in the video "Reading Group." (To find this video, go to Chapter 13 of the Book-Specific Resources in MyEducationLab, select *Video Examples*, and then click on the title.)

withitness Classroom management strategy in which a teacher gives the impression of knowing what all students are doing at all times.

Modifying Instructional Strategies

As we have repeatedly seen, principles of effective classroom management go hand in hand with principles of learning and motivation. When students are learning and achieving successfully and when they clearly want to pursue the class's instructional goals, they are apt to be busily engaged in productive activities for most of the school day (W. Doyle, 1990). In contrast, when students have difficulty understanding classroom subject matter or little interest in learning it, they are likely to exhibit the nonproductive or counterproductive classroom behaviors that result from frustration or boredom.

Consider whether instructional strategies or classroom assignments might be partly to blame for off-task behaviors.

When students misbehave, beginning teachers often think about what the students are doing wrong. In contrast, experienced teachers are more apt to think about what *they themselves* could do differently to keep students on task, and they modify their plans accordingly (Emmer & Stough, 2001; Sabers et al., 1991; H. L. Swanson, O'Connor, & Cooney, 1990). Thus, when behavior problems arise, we should think as the experts do, considering questions such as these:

- How can I change my instructional strategies to stimulate students' interest in a topic?
- Are instructional materials so difficult or unstructured that students are becoming frustrated? Alternatively, are they so easy or lock-step that students are bored?
- What are students really concerned about? For example, are they more concerned about interacting with their classmates than in gaining new knowledge and skills? How can I address students' motives and goals (e.g., their desire to interact with peers) while simultaneously helping them achieve classroom objectives?

Answering such questions enables us to focus our efforts on our ultimate goal: *helping students learn.*

Occasionally current events on the international, national, or local scene (e.g., a terrorist attack, a presidential election, or a tragic car accident involving classmates) may take priority. When students' minds are justifiably preoccupied with something other than the topic of instruction, they will have difficulty paying attention to that topic and are likely to learn little about it. In such circumstances, we may want to abandon our lesson plans altogether, at least for a short while.

Taking Developmental Differences into Account

Take developmental differences into account in planning your classroom management strategies.

To some degree, the age levels of our students must influence our classroom management decisions. Many children in the early elementary grades haven't had enough experience with formal education to know all the unspoken rules that govern classroom interactions: Students should remain silent when a teacher or other adult is talking, only the student who is called on should answer a question, and so on (Mehan, 1979; R. K. Payne, 2005). In addition, children just beginning kindergarten or first grade may find their new school environment to be unsettling and anxiety arousing, as do many adolescents making the transition to middle school or high school (see Chapter 11). And of course, as children grow older, they gain increasing social skills, which affect their ability to interact effectively with their teacher and classmates (see Chapter 3). Table 13.1 presents these and other developmental differences, along with examples of how we might accommodate them in our classroom practices.

Taking Individual and Group Differences into Account

Earlier I mentioned the importance of consistency and equity in enforcing classroom rules. But when it comes to *preventing* off-task behavior, optimal strategies may differ considerably from one student to the next. For instance, during independent seatwork assignments, some students may work quite well with classmates close by, whereas others may be easily distracted unless they can work in a quiet spot, perhaps near their

TABLE 13.1
Effective Classroom Management at Different Grade Levels

Grade Level	Age-Typical Characteristics	Suggested Strategies
K–2	• Anxiety about being in school, especially in the first few weeks and especially for students without preschool experience • Lack of familiarity with unspoken rules about appropriate classroom behavior • Short attention span and high level of distractibility • Little self-regulation • Strong desire for teacher affection and approval • Noticeable individual differences in social skills	• Invite students and their parents to visit the classroom before the school year begins. • Especially during the first week of school, place high priority on establishing a warm, supportive relationship with every student. • Be explicit about acceptable classroom behavior; correct inappropriate behavior gently but consistently. • Keep assigned tasks relatively short and focused. • Give students frequent opportunities to release pent-up energy. • Create a gathering place (e.g., a carpet) where students can sit close at hand for whole-class discussions. • Create areas where students can work independently on tasks of their choosing (e.g., a reading center where students can listen to storybooks on tape).
3–5	• Continuing desire for teacher approval but with increasing concern about peer approval as well • Greater attentiveness to teachers who are emotionally expressive (e.g., teachers who often smile and show obvious concern in times of distress) • Increasing self-regulation skills • Increasing ability to reflect on one's own and others' thoughts and motives (i.e., increasing social cognition) • Increasing disengagement from school if students have consistently encountered academic and social failure	• Use two-way journals to communicate regularly with students about academic, social, and emotional issues. • In both words and actions, regularly show students that you're concerned about their academic progress and emotional well-being. • Provide increasing opportunities for independent work but with enough structure to guide students' efforts. • In times of disagreement or conflict, ask students to reflect on one another's thoughts and feelings. • Make an extra effort to establish close, supportive relationships with students who appear to be apathetic and socially disengaged.
6–8	• Considerable anxiety about the transition to middle school, due in part to less close and less supportive relationships with teachers • Decrease in intrinsic motivation to learn academic subject matter • Tendency to challenge school norms regarding dress, hairstyle, and the like (for some students) • Increase in cheating behavior; less common if students think teachers respect them and are committed to helping them learn • Heightened concern about ability to fit in and be accepted by peers • Increase in bullying behaviors	• Find occasions to see students outside class (e.g., chaperone dances, attend sporting events). • Plan lessons that are engaging and relevant to students' lives and needs. • Prohibit modes of dress that may threaten students' safety and well-being (e.g., gang insignia, racist T-shirts, sexually revealing attire), but otherwise give students some freedom of expression in what they wear. • Provide sufficient academic support that students have no reason to cheat; nevertheless, be on the lookout for possible cheating (see Chapter 14). • Don't tolerate bullying and other forms of aggression; address their underlying causes (see the discussion of aggression in Chapter 3). • Reach out to students who seem socially unconnected (e.g., invite them to join you for lunch in your classroom).
9–12	• Anxiety about the transition to high school, especially if the seventh and eighth grades were part of elementary school • Increasing understanding that abiding by school rules and shared social conventions is important for helping the school function effectively • Social and romantic relationships that often become sources of distraction • Considerable self-regulation ability (in some but not all students) • High incidence of cheating, in part because peers think it's acceptable • Disdain for classmates who work too hard for teacher approval (i.e., brown-nosers) • Tendency for some adolescents to think that misbehaving in class will gain peers' admiration • Increase in violent behaviors, especially at schools in low-income neighborhoods	• Remember that, even in high school, students achieve at a higher level when they have close, supportive relationships with teachers. • Regularly plan activities that involve social interaction; if possible, move desks and chairs to allow students to interact more easily. • When students have few self-regulation skills, provide guidance and support to keep them on task. • Describe what cheating is and why it's unacceptable (see Chapter 14). • Communicate approval privately, rather than publicly. • Proactively address violence (see the section "Addressing Aggression and Violence at School" in this chapter).

Sources: Many characteristics and suggestions are derived from discussions in earlier chapters. Others are based on Blugental, Lyon, Lin, McGrath, & Bimbela, 1999; Carter & Doyle, 2006; Cizek, 2003; Emmer & Gerwels, 2006; Fingerhut & Christoffel, 2002; Hamre & Pianta, 2005; Mehan, 1979; Murdock, Hale, & Weber, 2001; Nucci, 2009; Pellegrini, 2002.

teacher's desk. And during small-group work, some groups may function effectively on their own, whereas others may need considerable guidance and supervision.

One important individual difference factor affecting classroom behavior is *temperament*: the extent to which a student is naturally inclined to be energetic, irritable, impulsive, and so on (see Chapter 3). To be truly effective classroom managers, we must realize that students' vastly different classroom behaviors may be due, in part, to biological predispositions that aren't entirely within their control (e.g., W. Johnson, McGue, & Iacono, 2005). Such a realization should influence our beliefs about why students are acting as they are—that is, it should influence our *attributions*—and these beliefs will, in turn, affect our willingness to adapt classroom strategies to foster productive classroom behavior (B. K. Keogh, 2003; A. Miller, 2006).

Remember that some students from diverse backgrounds may need explicit guidance about how they should behave at school.

Cultural and Ethnic Differences Students who have grown up in diverse cultural and ethnic groups aren't always familiar with the unspoken standards for behavior in Western schools (Igoa, 1995; Tyler et al., 2008). Furthermore, some students may be unfamiliar with questions and hints that only indirectly tell them how they should behave—for instance, "Sally, would you like to sit down?" Such students are apt to be better behaved (and also less confused) if we are more explicit in our requests—for instance, "Sally, please sit down and focus on your schoolwork" (Woolfolk Hoy & Weinstein, 2006, p. 186).

A warm, supportive classroom climate may be especially important for students from diverse ethnic backgrounds.

But perhaps most important for students from diverse backgrounds is a warm, supportive classroom atmosphere (Castagno & Brayboy, 2008; García, 1995; Meehan, Hughes, & Cavell, 2003). For example, African American students in one eighth-grade social studies class were asked why they liked their teacher so much. Their responses were quite revealing:

> "She lets us express our opinions!"
>
> "She looks us in the eye when she talks to us!"
>
> "She smiles at us!"
>
> "She speaks to us when she sees us in the hall or in the cafeteria!" (Ladson-Billings, 1994a, p. 68)

Simple gestures such as these go a long way toward establishing the kinds of teacher–student relationships that lead to a productive learning environment.

It's also essential that we create a sense of community in the classroom—a sense that we and our students share common goals and are mutually supportive of everyone's reaching those goals. This sense of community is consistent with the cooperative spirit evident in many Hispanic, Native American, and African American groups (Ladson-Billings, 1994a; Tyler et al., 2008).

Make a special effort to establish good relationships with emotionally distant and chronically misbehaving students, especially boys.

Gender Differences On average, girls form closer, more affectionate relationships with their teachers than boys do. Most nonproductive teacher–student relationships involve male, rather than female, students, probably for a variety of reasons (Pianta, 2006; Tutwiler, 2007). Boys are more prone to physical aggression than girls, and they are more likely than girls to be oppositional and defiant when asked to engage in tasks they would rather not do. And in general, boys are temperamentally more active, to the point that they often have trouble sitting still for lengthy periods (W. O. Eaton & Enns, 1986). Notice what happened to one fourth grader (now a successful college professor) when his teacher took his temperament into consideration:

> One day when I was especially restless . . . I could see Miss Rickenbrood circling to the back of the room. I wasn't aware of having done anything in particular, but I knew her eyes were on me. After a few minutes she leaned over and whispered in my ear, "Tom, would you like to go outside and run?"
>
> I was stunned. To go outside and run? On my own? When it wasn't recess? What could have possessed this woman to ignore all school rules and allow me to run? I

said yes and quietly went to put on my coat. As I recall, I didn't actually run in the playground (people would be watching from inside the building), but stood outside in the doorway, in the cold, marveling at my freedom. I returned to class after about ten minutes, settled for the rest of the day. (Newkirk, 2002, pp. 25–26)

Socioeconomic Differences Having teachers' affection, respect, and support is even more important for students who face exceptional hardships at home—poverty, violent inner-city neighborhoods, homelessness, and so on. Some of these students may be prone to anger and disrespectful behavior in the classroom, undoubtedly as a result of their difficult circumstances outside school (R. K. Payne, 2005). Yet when students from economically impoverished backgrounds have one or more caring, trustworthy adults in their lives—and when they regularly come to a classroom that is warm, predictable, and dependable—they often have a strong sense of self-worth and self-determination. Hence, they are better equipped to succeed both in the classroom and in the outside world. In other words, they are more likely to be *resilient*—to rise above their adverse circumstances (see Chapter 4) (Becker & Luthar, 2002; Felner, Seitsinger, Brand, Burns, & Bolton, 2007; Masten, 2001; Milner, 2006; Polakow, 2007; D. A. O'Donnell et al., 2002).

When students face exceptional challenges at home, make an extra effort to create an affectionate, supportive, predictable, and safe environment at school.

Accommodating Students with Special Needs In general, students with special needs can more easily adapt to a general education setting when the classroom is orderly and well structured. Even more so than their nondisabled peers, students with disabilities benefit from classrooms in which procedures for performing certain tasks are specified, expectations for student behavior are clear, and misbehaviors are treated consistently (Heward, 2009; Pfiffner, Barkley, & DuPaul, 2006; Scruggs & Mastropieri, 1994). Table 13.2 offers many suggestions for accommodating students with special needs.

Earlier in the chapter, I mentioned that consistency and equitable treatment for all students are critical for establishing effective teacher–student relationships and a positive classroom climate. How do we reconcile this point with the need to accommodate individual differences, especially the often-challenging behaviors of some students with disabilities? The key lies in knowing *when* and *how* to accommodate students' unique needs. To behave appropriately, students with disabilities sometimes need more guidance and support than their nondisabled classmates. But unless there are extenuating circumstances, students with disabilities must incur the same consequences as everyone else when their behaviors are out of line.

Coordinating Efforts with Others

As we work to promote students' learning and development, we will be far more effective if we coordinate our efforts with the other people in students' lives. In particular, we must work cooperatively with other faculty members, with the community at large, and, most importantly, with parents.

Working with Other Faculty Members

As teachers, we are apt to spend much of the school day working in our individual classrooms. Nevertheless, we can be far more effective when we do the following:

- Communicate and collaborate regularly with other classroom teachers and with specialists (e.g., librarians, counselors).
- Identify common goals regarding what students should learn and achieve.
- Work together to identify obstacles to students' learning and to develop strategies for overcoming those obstacles.
- Establish a shared set of strategies for encouraging productive student behaviors.

Students in Inclusive Settings

TABLE 13.2
Maintaining a Productive Classroom Environment for Students with Special Educational Needs

Category	Characteristics You Might Observe	Suggested Strategies
Students with specific cognitive or academic difficulties	• Difficulty staying on task • Misbehaviors such as hyperactivity, impulsiveness, disruptiveness, and inattentiveness (in some students) • Poor time management skills and/or a disorganized approach to accomplishing tasks (in some students)	• Closely monitor students during independent assignments. • Make sure students understand their assignments; if appropriate, give them extra time to complete the assignments. • Make expectations for behavior clear, and enforce classroom rules consistently. • Reinforce (e.g., praise) desired behaviors immediately; be specific about the behaviors you are reinforcing. • For hyperactive students, plan short activities that help them settle down after periods of physical activity (e.g., after recess, lunch, or physical education). • For impulsive students, teach self-instructions (see Chapter 10). • Teach strategies for organizing time and work (e.g., tape a schedule of daily activities to students' desks, provide folders students can use to carry assignments between school and home).
Students with social or behavioral problems	• Frequent overt misbehaviors, such as acting out, aggression, noncompliance, destructiveness, or stealing (in some students) • Difficulty inhibiting impulses • Misbehaviors triggered by changes in the environment or daily routine or by sensory overstimulation (for students with autism) • Difficulty interacting effectively with classmates • Difficulty staying on task • Tendency to engage in power struggles with teachers (for some students)	• Specify in precise terms what behaviors are acceptable and unacceptable in the classroom; establish and enforce rules for behavior. • Maintain a predictable schedule; warn students ahead of time about changes in the routine. • Use self-regulation techniques and behaviorist approaches to promote productive classroom behaviors. • Teach social skills (see Chapter 3). • Closely monitor students during independent assignments. • Give students a sense of self-determination about some aspects of classroom life; minimize the use of coercive techniques. • Make an extra effort to show students that you care about them as human beings.
Students with general delays in cognitive and social functioning	• Occasional disruptive classroom behavior (for some students) • Dependence on others for guidance about how to behave • More appropriate classroom behavior when expectations are clear	• Establish clear, concrete rules for classroom behavior. • As necessary, remind students about appropriate behavior; keep directions simple. • Use structured behaviorist approaches to promote desired behaviors. • Give explicit feedback about what students are and are not doing appropriately.
Students with physical or sensory challenges	• Social isolation from classmates (for some students) • Difficulty accomplishing tasks as quickly as other students • Difficulty understanding directions and other spoken messages about desired behaviors (for students with hearing loss)	• Establish a strong sense of community within the classroom. • When appropriate, give extra time to complete assignments. • Keep unnecessary classroom noise to a minimum if one or more students have hearing loss.
Students with advanced cognitive development	• Off-task behavior in some students, often due to boredom during easy assignments and activities	• Assign tasks appropriate to students' cognitive abilities.

Sources: Achenbach & Edelbrock, 1981; Barkley, 2006; Beirne-Smith et al., 2006; Buchoff, 1990; B. Clark, 1997; Dempster & Corkill, 1999; Diamond, 1991; Friedel, 1993; D. A. Granger, Whalen, Henker, & Cantwell, 1996; Heward, 2009; Koegel et al., 1996; Landau & McAninch, 1993; Mercer & Pullen, 2005; Morgan & Jenson, 1988; Ogden & Germinario, 1988; Patton et al., 1996; Pellegrini & Horvat, 1995; Piirto, 1999; M. C. Reynolds & Birch, 1988; Turnbull et al., 2007; Winner, 1997.

- Make a group commitment to promote equality and multicultural sensitivity throughout the school community. (Battistich, Solomon, Watson, & Schaps, 1997; D. C. Gottfredson, 2001; J. A. Langer, 2000; Levine & Lezotte, 1995; T. J. Lewis, Newcomer, Trussell, & Richter, 2006)

Ideally, we should create not only a sense of community within our individual classrooms but also an overall **sense of school community** (Battistich et al., 1995, Battistich, Solomon, Watson, & Schaps, 1997; M. Watson & Battistich, 2006). Students should get the same message from every member of the faculty: that we are working together to help them become informed, successful, and productive citizens and that they can and should *help one another* as well.

Collaborate with colleagues to create an overall sense of school community.

A sense of school community also involves close student–student relationships across various classrooms and grade levels. Cross-class peer tutoring, participation in extracurricular activities, student involvement in school decision making, frequent use of school mascots and other traditional school symbols—all of these help to create a sense that students are members of a mutually supportive school "family" (Juvonen, 2006; Nucci, 2009; D. R. Robinson et al., 2005).

When teachers and students share an overall sense of school community, students have more positive attitudes toward school, are more motivated to achieve at high levels, exhibit more prosocial behavior, and interact more often with peers from diverse backgrounds. Furthermore, teachers have higher expectations for students' achievement and a greater sense of self-efficacy about their teaching effectiveness (Battistich et al., 1995, 1997; J. A. Langer, 2000). In fact, when teachers work together, they may have higher *collective self-efficacy*: a belief that by working as a group, they can definitely have an impact on students' learning and achievement. Moreover, this collective self-confidence is related to students' performance (Bandura, 2000; Goddard et al., 2000; Hoy, Tarter, & Woolfolk Hoy, 2006). Such a team spirit has an additional advantage for beginning teachers: It provides the support structure (i.e., scaffolding) they may need, especially when working with students who are at risk for school failure. New teachers report greater confidence in their ability to help students learn and achieve when they collaborate regularly with their colleagues (Chester & Beaudin, 1996).

Working with the Community at Large

Students almost always have regular contact with other institutions besides school—possibly youth groups, community organizations, social services, churches, hospitals, mental health clinics, and local judicial systems. And some students live in cultural environments very different from our own. As teachers, we will be most effective if we understand the environments in which our students live and if we think of ourselves as part of a larger team that promotes children's and adolescents' long-term development. For example, we must educate ourselves about students' cultural backgrounds, perhaps by taking course work and getting involved in local community events (see Chapter 1). We must also keep in contact with other people and institutions that play major roles in students' lives, coordinating our efforts whenever possible (J. L. Epstein, 1996).

Work cooperatively with other agencies that play key roles in students' lives.

Working with Parents

Above all, we must work cooperatively with students' parents and other primary caregivers. We can best think of our relationships with these individuals as *partnerships* in which we collaborate to promote students' long-term development and learning (Hidalgo, Siu, Bright, Swap, & Epstein, 1995). Such relationships may be especially important when working with students from diverse cultural backgrounds (Hidalgo et al., 1995; Salend & Taylor, 1993). And they are *essential* when working with students who have special educational needs (see Chapter 5). Good parent–teacher

sense of school community
Shared belief that all faculty and students within a school are working together to help everyone learn and succeed.

relationships increase the probability of positive outcomes if students are struggling in their academic work or having difficulties with their classroom behavior (e.g., J. N. Hughes & Kwok, 2007).

Remember that some students' primary caregivers are people other than their parents.

We must keep in mind that families come in a variety of forms and that students' primary caregivers are not always their parents. For example, in some ethnic minority communities, grandmothers take primary responsibility for raising children (Stack & Burton, 1993; M. Wilson, 1989). For simplicity, I will use the term *parents* in our discussion, but I am, in fact, referring to all primary caregivers.

Remember that communication with parents should be a two-way street, with information traveling in both directions.

Communicating with Parents To work effectively with parents, we should open lines of communication with them as soon as classes begin—perhaps even before that—and stay in regular contact with them throughout the school year. We should inform them of their children's accomplishments and keep them apprised of any behaviors that are consistently interfering with learning and achievement. Regular communication also provides a means through which parents can give *us* information, which might prompt ideas about how we can best assist or motivate their children. At the least, such information can help us understand why these students sometimes behave as they do. In addition, regular communication enables us to coordinate our classroom strategies with those that parents use at home. Following are several common means of teacher–parent communication.

Consider including students in parent–teacher conferences.

Parent–Teacher Conferences In most school districts, formal parent–teacher conferences are scheduled one or more times a year. We may often want to include students in conferences—essentially making them parent–teacher–student conferences—and in some instances we might even ask students to *lead* the conferences (Popham, 1995; Stiggins, 2008). By holding student-led conferences, we increase the likelihood that parents will come to the conferences, we encourage students to reflect on their own academic progress, and we give students practice in communication and leadership skills. Furthermore, teachers, students, and parents alike are apt to leave such meetings with a shared understanding of the progress that has been made and of subsequent steps that need to be taken.

Accommodate cultural differences in parent–teacher conferences. For instance, invite extended family members to come, and include a trusted individual who can translate for non-native-English speakers.

When a student's parents speak a language other than English, we will want to include in the conversation someone who can converse fluently with the parents in their native tongue—ideally, someone whom the parents trust. And in cultures in which extended families play a key role in children's lives, we may want to include other family members as well—perhaps grandparents, aunts, or uncles. Additional suggestions for conducting effective conferences are presented in Figure 13.4.

Use informal notes and classroom newsletters in addition to more formal reports.

Written Communication Written communication can take a variety of forms. It can be a welcome-to-my-class letter sent to students and parents before the school year begins. It can be a weekly teacher-constructed checklist or grade sheet that documents a student's academic progress. It can be a quick, informal note acknowledging a significant accomplishment. Or it can be a general newsletter describing noteworthy classroom activities, expectations for homework, common behaviors and needs for various age groups, and so on. All of these mechanisms have two things in common: They let parents know what is happening at school and convey a genuine desire to stay in touch with families.

A parent letter written by second-grade teacher Ann Reilly provides an illustration (see Figure 13.5). The letter was written on September 14, 2001, three days after terrorist attacks on the World Trade Center and Pentagon and during a week when students were taking a districtwide standardized test. The letter communicates a great deal of information: what topics the class is studying, how parents will get results of the standardized test, and why the class is not talking much about the terrorist attacks. It communicates attitudes as well; for instance, Ms. Reilly is eager to keep the lines of communication with parents open, is approachable (she signs the letter "Ann"), and cares about how well her students are doing (e.g., "I don't like telling them that they are on their own" during classroom assessments). She also suggests several simple

FIGURE 13.4 Suggestions for conducting effective parent–teacher conferences

Suggestions for Any Parent–Teacher Conference

- Schedule the conference at a time that accommodates parents' jobs and other obligations.
- Prepare ahead of time; for example, organize your notes, review information you have about the student, create an agenda for the meeting, and have examples of the student's work on hand.
- Create a warm, nonjudgmental atmosphere. For instance, express your appreciation that the parents have come, actively encourage them to express their thoughts and perspectives, and give them enough time to do so. Remember that your objective is to work cooperatively and constructively with parents to create the best educational program possible for their child.
- Describe your goals and expectations for the student.
- Avoid educational jargon with which parents may be unfamiliar; describe the student's performance in ways a noneducator can understand.
- Actively seek information from parents—for instance, by asking them to describe their child's strong points and favorite activities.
- End on a positive note—perhaps with a review of the student's many strengths and the progress he or she has made.
- Follow through with anything you have said you will do.

Additional Suggestions for a Student-Led Conference

- Meet with the student ahead of time to agree on appropriate work samples to share.
- Model and role-play effective conferences in class, and give students time to practice with their classmates.
- Schedule a backup audience (e.g., a former teacher or trusted friend) who can sit in if the student's parents don't attend.
- Offer additional time in which you can meet without the student present if the parents so desire.
- Talk with the student afterward about what went well and how the two of you might improve the next conference.

Sources: C. Davis & Yang, 2005; M. D. Miller, Linn, & Gronlund, 2009; Polloway & Patton, 1993; Salend & Taylor, 1993; Stiggins, 2008.

ways in which parents might contribute to the class: volunteering to help with spelling assessment, donating tissues, and providing instructions for making baby wipes. Because she teaches in a school district in which most parents have Internet access either at home or at work, she has given parents her e-mail address. Suggesting the use of e-mail would be less appropriate in communities in which many families cannot afford computers or parents have limited knowledge of English.

Telephone Conversations In the elementary grades, telephone calls are a useful way of introducing oneself as a child's teacher for the coming school year and following up on a parent–teacher conference that parents have missed (C. Davis & Yang, 2005; Striepling-Goldstein, 2004). And at all grade levels, telephone calls are often appropriate when issues require immediate attention. We might call a parent to express concern when a student's behavior deteriorates unexpectedly without apparent provocation. But we might also call to express excitement about an important step forward. Parents, too, should feel free to call us. Because many parents are at work during the school day, it's often helpful to accept and encourage calls at home during the early evening hours.

Make a quick telephone call to inform parents of exciting new accomplishments or potential areas of concern.

Parent Discussion Groups In some instances, we may want to assemble a group of parents to discuss issues of mutual interest—perhaps specific topics that might be included in the classroom curriculum or effective strategies that parents can use to promote their children's academic, personal, and social development (J. L. Epstein, 1996;

Hold parent discussion groups for topics of general interest.

FIGURE 13.5 Example of a teacher's letter to parents

9/14/01

Dear Parents,

I have been lucky so far and have not had to go back for jury duty. I have two more weeks to go [in terms of possibly being summoned for duty] and hope I will continue to be in the classroom.

We have been trying to keep the routine pretty regular, despite one or two testing sessions per day. The children have been pretty focused, although it is difficult when they are unfamiliar with the format and look to us for help. I don't like telling them that they are on their own. We are done, thank goodness. I believe you will receive results in the mail.

Homework and spelling will resume next week. I could also use my regular volunteers to help get through the spelling assessments. The times you have been coming are still fine. Call or e-mail me if you need the available times for helping.

We finished our unit on germs and sanitation, although we did not get into any discussions about Anthrax. It seems that you are keeping the children protected at home from details of the scary news, as we are at school. We kept our discussions to common illnesses that they are aware of and how they can avoid them with proper sanitation.

A few classrooms are doing activities to raise money for many of the children involved in the tragedy. Sarah [the teacher intern] and I decided not to work with our children on a fundraiser because we don't want to get into anxiety-producing discussions. It is hard to help young children understand that they are safe where they are and that it is unlikely that they will be involved in such things.

Next week, we will be starting a Nutrition Unit and beginning to read some Halloween stories. We will continue working to become automatic with math facts, along with our regular routine of phonics lessons, DOL [daily oral language], reading, writing, spelling, etc.

We are running out of Kleenex and could use some donations. We would also like some boxes of baby wipes to use in cleaning hands and desks when there is not time for the entire class to wash. Someone mentioned to me that there is a homemade recipe for baby wipes out there somewhere. Is there a parent who knows and would be willing to share?

Have a great weekend.

Ann

Source: Used courtesy of Ann Reilly.

Fosnot, 1996; Rudman, 1993). Also, some teachers have successfully used *parent coffee nights*, during which they explain a new instructional strategy, or *author teas*, during which students read poetry and short stories they have written.

Getting Parents Involved in School Activities Ultimately, the best means of communicating and collaborating with parents is to get them—and perhaps other family members as well—actively involved in school life and in children's learning (G. A. Davis & Thomas, 1989; J. L. Epstein, 1996; Levine & Lezotte, 1995). Students whose parents are involved in school activities have better attendance records, higher achievement, and more positive attitudes toward school. Although the reasons for the correlation are not entirely clear, it appears to be due partly to the fact that parents who actively participate in school activities can more effectively coordinate their efforts at home with teachers' efforts in the classroom (N. E. Hill & Craft, 2003; N. E. Hill & Taylor, 2004; Mattingly, Prislin, McKenzie, Rodrigues, & Kayzar, 2002; Spera, 2005).

Parental involvement in school activities can take a variety of forms. For instance, we might do the following:

- Invite parents to an open house or musical performance in the evening.
- Request parents' help with a fund-raiser on a Saturday afternoon.
- Seek volunteers to help with field trips, special projects, or individual tutoring during the school day.
- Use parents and other community members as resources to provide a multicultural perspective of the local community. (C. Davis & Yang, 2005; McCarty & Watahomigie, 1998; Minami & Ovando, 1995; H. L. Smith, 1998)

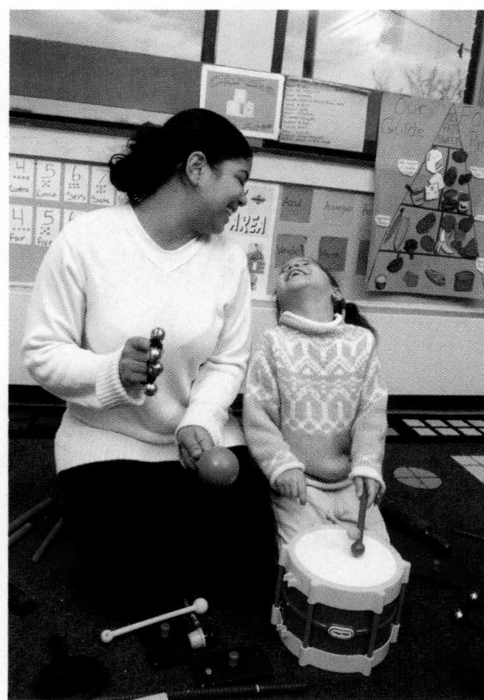

Students tend to be more successful at school when their parents are actively involved in school activities.

Most parents are apt to become involved in such activities only when they have a specific invitation to do so and when they know that school personnel genuinely want them to be involved (C. L. Green, Walker, Hoover-Dempsey, & Sandler, 2007; Serpell, Baker, & Sonnenschein, 2005). Some parents—especially those from certain minority groups or lower-income families—may not take a general, open-ended invitation seriously, as one African American mother reveals:

> If we are talking about slavery times . . . the slaves were all around, plantation owner came to the plantation [and said] "Oh, we're having a party over next door, come on over!" He would say, "Come on over," there was an invitation without any qualification as to who was to come. The African Americans, the slaves would not come because they knew the invitation was not for them. . . . They were not expected to participate. (A. A. Carr, 1997, p. 2)

A personal invitation can often make all the difference, as the same mother explains:

Extend personal invitations to school events.

> The thing of it is, had someone not walked up to me and asked me specifically, I would not hold out my hand and say, "I'll do it." . . . You get parents here all the time, black parents that are willing, but maybe a little on the shy side and wouldn't say I really want to serve on this subject. You may send me the form, I may never fill the form out. Or I'll think about it and not send it back. But you know if that principal, that teacher, my son's math teacher called and asked if I would. . . . (A. A. Carr, 1997, p. 2)

Keep in mind that parents' involvement in their children's schooling doesn't necessarily mean participating in activities at school. Parents can also be invaluable in helping children with homework. When they are well educated themselves, they can often provide assistance with specific assignments—identifying appropriate resources, providing practice with basic skills, checking written work, and so on. But even parents who have few academic skills can provide valuable support—for instance, by communicating the importance of doing well, providing a quiet place to study, and making television viewing contingent on homework completion. The more parents do such things, the higher their children's achievement is likely to be (N. E. Hill, Castellino, et al., 2004; S. Hong & Ho, 2005; J.-S. Lee & Bowen, 2006; Patall, Cooper, & Robinson, 2008). Furthermore, many parents are open to teacher suggestions about how they might best be of assistance (N. E. Hill & Taylor, 2004; J. M. T. Walker & Hoover-Dempsey, 2006).

Offer suggestions about the things parents might do to help their children with homework.

Encouraging Reluctant Parents Despite our best efforts, a few parents will remain uninvolved in their children's education; for instance, they may never attend scheduled parent–teacher conferences. But before we jump too quickly to the conclusion that these parents are also *uninterested* in their children's education, we must recognize several possible reasons that parents might be reluctant to make contact with us. Some may have an exhausting work schedule or lack adequate child care. Others may know little English, have difficulty finding their way through the school system, or believe it's inappropriate to bother teachers with their concerns. Still others may have had such bad experiences when they themselves were students that they feel uncomfortable in a school building. And a few parents may be victims of mental illness or substance abuse, limiting their ability to support their children financially, academically, or otherwise (Carbrera, Shannon, West, & Brooks-Gunn, 2006; Cazden, 2001; Hernandez, Denton, & Macartney, 2008; J.-S. Lee & Bowen, 2006; Ogbu, 2003; Petterson & Albers, 2001).

Identify alternative sources of academic support when a student's family is unable to provide it themselves.

Experienced educators have offered numerous suggestions for getting reluctant parents more involved in their children's schooling:

- Make an extra effort to gain parents' trust and confidence—for instance, by demonstrating that their contributions are valued and that faculty members would never try to make them look foolish.

"I can't talk right now! I'm helping Stevie with his science project, which is due at 8 a.m. tomorrow!"

Like this mother, some parents don't have a clear understanding of how they can best help their children with homework. In such circumstances, tactful suggestions about what to do and *not* to do are often useful.

Source: CLOSE TO HOME © John McPherson. Reprinted with permission of UNIVERSAL PRESS SYNDICATE. All rights reserved.

- Encourage parents to be assertive when they have questions or concerns.
- Invite other important family members (e.g., grandparents, aunts, uncles) to participate in school activities, especially if a student's cultural background is one that places high value on the extended family.
- Give parents suggestions about learning activities they can easily do with their children at home.
- Find out what parents do exceptionally well (e.g., carpentry, cooking), and ask them to share their talents with the students.
- Provide opportunities for parents to volunteer for jobs that don't require them to leave home (e.g., to be someone whom students can call when unsure of homework assignments).
- Identify specific individuals (e.g., bilingual parents) who can translate for those who speak little or no English.
- Make home visits *if* such visits are welcomed.
- Offer resources for parents at the school building (e.g., contacts with social and health services; classes in English, literacy, home repairs, arts and crafts). (Castagno & Brayboy, 2008; C. Davis & Yang, 2005; J. L. Epstein, 1996; Finders & Lewis, 1994; Hidalgo et al., 1995; Howe, 1994; G. R. López, 2001; Salend & Taylor, 1993; Sanders, 1996; J. M. T. Walker & Hoover-Dempsey, 2006)

Another potentially effective strategy is to reinforce *parents* as well as students when the students do well at school. One administrator at a school serving many immigrant students put it this way:

Give recognition to parents whose children do well at school.

> One of the things we do . . . is that we identify those students that had perfect attendance, those students that passed all areas of the [statewide achievement tests] and were successful. We don't honor the student, we honor the parents. We give parents a certificate. Because, we tell them, "Through your efforts, and through your hard work, your child was able to accomplish this." (G. R. López, 2001, p. 273)

Don't penalize students for things that their parents do or don't do.

A few parents will resist all of our efforts to get them involved, and a small subset of them may truly have little interest in helping their children do well (e.g., Lamborn, Mounts, Steinberg, & Dornbusch, 1991). Especially in such circumstances, we must never penalize students for their parents' actions or inactions. And we must realize that, as teachers, *we* are apt to be among the most important academic and emotional resources in these students' lives.

Considering Cultural Differences When Working with Parents As we work with students' parents, we must be aware that people from different cultural and ethnic groups sometimes have radically different ideas about how—and also how *much*—to control their children's behavior. For example, many parents from Asian cultures expect children to obey adult authority figures without question; such parents often think that Western teachers are much too lenient with students (Dien, 1998; Hidalgo et al., 1995; Tudge et al., 1999). In contrast, parents in some Native American cultures believe that children have a right to make their own decisions; from their perspective, good parenting involves providing gentle suggestions and guidance rather than insisting that children behave in certain ways (Deyhle & LeCompte, 1999; see the opening case study in Chapter 4). Yet a common disciplinary strategy in both Asian and Native American cultural groups is ostracism: If a child's misbehaviors are seen as bringing shame on the family or the community, the child is ignored for an extended period (Pang, 1995; Salend & Taylor, 1993).

Ultimately, we must recognize that the vast majority of parents want what's best for their children and recognize the value of a good education (Corbett, Wilson, & Williams, 2002; Gallimore & Goldenberg, 2001; Okagaki, 2001; Spera, 2005). It's essential, then, that we not leave parents out of the loop when we're concerned about how their children are performing in school. And as we talk with them, we must listen to their attitudes and opinions with an open mind and try to find common ground on which to develop strategies for helping their children thrive in the classroom (Good & Nichols, 2001; Salend & Taylor, 1993).

Communicate your confidence in each student's ability to succeed, as well as your commitment to working cooperatively with parents.

Dealing with Misbehaviors

Despite our best efforts to create a classroom environment conducive to learning—an environment in which all students feel psychologically safe and are actively engaged in productive activities—one or more students will occasionally behave in undesirable ways. For purposes of our discussion, we will define a **misbehavior** as any action that can potentially disrupt learning and planned classroom activities, puts one or more students' physical safety or psychological well-being in jeopardy, or violates basic moral and ethical standards. Some misbehaviors are relatively minor and have little long-term impact on students' achievement. Such behaviors as talking out of turn, writing brief notes to classmates during a lecture, and submitting homework assignments after their due date—especially if these behaviors occur infrequently—generally fall in this category. Other misbehaviors are far more serious, as they definitely interfere with the learning or well-being of one or more students. For example, when students scream at their teachers, hit their classmates, or habitually refuse to participate in ongoing activities, then classroom learning—certainly that of the guilty party, and sometimes that of other students as well—can be adversely affected, as can the overall classroom climate.

Typically, only a few students are responsible for the great majority of misbehaviors in any single classroom (W. Doyle, 2006). Such students are apt to be among our greatest challenges, and it can be all too tempting to write them off as lost causes. Yet we must work vigorously to turn them in more productive directions: Without active intervention by teachers and other caring adults, students who are consistently disruptive or in other ways off task in the early grades may continue to show behavior problems in later years as well (Emmer & Gerwels, 2006; Vitaro, Brendgen, Larose, & Tremblay, 2005).

As teachers, we need to plan ahead about how we will address students' misbehaviors. Although we must certainly be consistent in the consequences we impose for blatant rule infractions (recall our earlier discussion of consistency and equity), a variety of strategies can be useful in reducing counterproductive behaviors over the long run. We'll examine six such strategies, each of which is appropriate under different circumstances: ignoring a behavior, cueing a student, discussing a problem privately with a student, teaching self-regulation strategies, conferring with parents, and planning and conducting a systematic intervention.

misbehavior Action that disrupts learning and planned classroom activities, puts students' physical safety or psychological well-being in jeopardy, or violates basic moral standards.

Ignoring Behavior

On some occasions, our best course of action is *no* action, at least nothing of a disciplinary nature (G. A. Davis & Thomas, 1989; W. Doyle, 2006). For example, consider these situations:

- Dimitra rarely breaks classroom rules. But on one occasion, after you have just instructed students to work quietly and independently at their seats, you see her briefly whisper to the girl beside her. None of the other students seems to notice that Dimitra has disobeyed your instructions.
- Herb is careless in chemistry lab and accidentally knocks over a small container of liquid (a harmless one, fortunately). He quickly apologizes and cleans up the mess.

Will these behaviors interfere with Dimitra's or Herb's academic achievement? Probably not.

Whenever we stop an instructional activity to deal with a misbehavior, even for a few seconds, we may disrupt the momentum of the activity and draw students' attention to their misbehaving classmate(s). If we respond every time someone gets a little bit out of line, our own actions may be more distracting than the actions we are trying to curtail. Furthermore, by drawing peers' attention to a particular student's behavior, we may unintentionally be reinforcing it.

Ignoring misbehavior is often reasonable in circumstances such as these:

- When the behavior is a rare occurrence and probably won't be repeated
- When the behavior is unlikely to spread to other students
- When the behavior is the result of unusual and temporary conditions (e.g., the last day of school before a holiday, unsettling events in a student's personal life)
- When the behavior is typical for a particular age-group (e.g., kindergartners becoming restless after sitting for an extended time, sixth-grade boys and girls resisting holding one another's hands during dance instruction)
- When the behavior's natural consequence is unpleasant enough to deter a student from repeating it
- When the behavior isn't interfering with classroom learning (G. A. Davis & Thomas, 1989; W. Doyle, 1986a, 2006; Dreikurs & Cassel, 1972; Munn et al., 1990; Silberman & Wheelan, 1980; Wynne, 1990)

Ignore minor infractions that are unlikely to be repeated or to spread to other students.

Dimitra's behavior—briefly whispering to a classmate during independent seatwork—is unlikely to spread to her classmates because they didn't see her do it, and it probably isn't an instance of cheating because it occurred before she began working on the assignment. Herb's behavior—knocking over a container of liquid in chemistry lab—has, in and of itself, resulted in an unpleasant consequence: He must clean up the mess. In both situations, ignoring the misbehavior is probably the best thing to do.

Cueing Students

In some situations, off-task behaviors, although not serious in nature, *do* interfere with classroom learning and must be discouraged. Consider these situations as examples:

- As you're explaining a difficult concept, Marjorie is busily writing. At first, you think she's taking notes, but then you see her pass the paper across the aisle to Kang. A few minutes later, you see Kang pass the same sheet back to Marjorie. It appears that the two students are writing personal notes when they should be attending to the lesson.
- You have separated your class into small groups for a cooperative learning activity. One group is frequently off task and probably won't complete its task if its members don't get down to business soon.

Effective classroom managers handle such minor behavior problems as unobtrusively as possible: They don't stop the lesson, distract other students, or call unnecessary attention to the inappropriate behavior (W. Doyle, 1990, 2006; Emmer, 1987). In many cases, they use **cueing**: They give a brief signal—perhaps a stern look or a simple verbal directive—to communicate that the misbehavior has been noticed and should stop. Ideally, such cues focus students' attention on what *should* be done, rather than on what *isn't* being done (Emmer et al., 2000; Good & Brophy, 1994). For instance, instead of chastising students for being overly noisy during a cooperative group activity, a teacher might say, "As you exchange ideas, remember to use your *indoor voices* so that you don't distract other groups."

Gently cue students about desired behaviors.

Discussing Problems Privately with Students

Sometimes brief cues are insufficient to change a student's misbehavior. Consider these situations:

- Alonzo is almost always a few minutes late to your third-period algebra class. When he finally arrives, he takes several more minutes to pull his textbook and other class materials out of his backpack. You have often reminded him about the importance of coming to class on time, yet his tardiness continues.
- Trudy rarely completes classroom assignments; in fact, she often doesn't even begin them. On many previous occasions, you have gently tried to get her on task but usually without success. Today, when you look Trudy in the eye and ask her point blank to get to work, she defiantly responds, "I'm not going to do it. You can't make me!"

In such situations, talking privately with the student is the next logical step. The discussion should be *private* for several reasons. First, as noted earlier, calling peers' attention to a problem behavior may actually reinforce the behavior rather than discourage it. Or, instead, the attention of classmates may cause a student to feel excessively embarrassed or humiliated—feelings that may make the student overanxious about being in the classroom in the future. Finally, when we spend too much class time dealing with a single misbehaving student, other students are apt to get off task as well (W. Doyle, 2006; Emmer & Gerwels, 2006; Scott & Bushell, 1974).

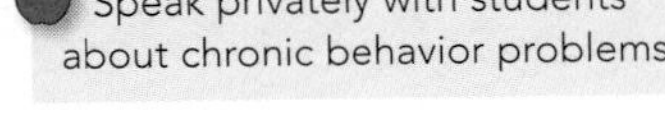

Speak privately with students about chronic behavior problems.

Private conversations with individual students give us, as teachers, a chance to explain why certain behaviors must stop. They also give students a chance to explain why they behave as they do. For instance, Alonzo might explain his chronic tardiness by revealing that he has diabetes and must check his blood sugar level between his second- and third-period classes. He can perform the procedure himself but would prefer to do it in the privacy of the school nurse's office. Meanwhile, Trudy might describe her long-standing frustration with subject matter and assignments she perceives as being impossible to make sense of. A boy with a reading disability once voiced such frustration in an interview with a researcher:

> They [teachers] used to hand us all our homework on Mondays. One day my teacher handed me a stack about an inch thick and as I was walking out of class there was a big trash can right there and I'd, in front of everybody including the teacher, just drop it in the trash can and walk out. I did this because I couldn't read what she gave me. It was kind of a point that I wanted to get the teacher to realize. That while I'm doing it, inside it kind of like hurt because I really wanted to do it but I couldn't and just so it didn't look like I was goin' soft or anything like that I'd walk over to the trash and throw it in. (Zambo & Brem, 2004, p. 6)

Students' explanations can often provide clues about how best to deal with their behavior over the long run. For example, given his diabetes, Alonzo's continued tardiness to class might be inevitable. Perhaps we could reassign him to a seat by the door, enabling him to join class unobtrusively when he arrives, and we might ask the student next to him to quietly fill him in on the lesson in progress. Trudy's frustration

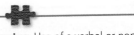

cueing Use of a verbal or nonverbal signal to indicate that a certain behavior is desired or that a certain behavior should stop.

If cueing a misbehaving student is ineffective, having a private conversation with the student might be the best next step. From a motivational standpoint, how might private discussions with students be helpful?

with her schoolwork suggests that she needs additional scaffolding to help her succeed. It also hints at a possible undiagnosed learning disability that might warrant a referral to the school psychologist or other diagnostician.

Students won't always provide explanations that lead to such logical solutions, however. For example, it may be that Alonzo is late to class simply because he wants to spend a few extra minutes hanging out with friends in the hall. Or perhaps Trudy says she doesn't want to do her assignments because she's "sick and tired" of other people always telling her what to do. In such circumstances, it's essential that we not get into a power struggle with the student—a situation in which one person wins by dominating the other in some way (Diamond, 1991; Emmer et al., 2000). Several strategies can minimize the likelihood of a power struggle:

- Speak in a calm, matter-of-fact manner, describing the problem as you see it. ("You haven't turned in a single assignment in the past three weeks. You and I would both like for you to do well in my class, but that can't happen unless we *both* work to make it happen.")
- Listen empathetically to what the student has to say, being openly accepting of his or her feelings and opinions. ("I get the impression that you don't enjoy classroom activities very much. I'd really like to hear your concerns.")
- Summarize what you think the student has told you, and seek clarification if necessary. ("It sounds as if you'd rather not let your classmates know how much trouble you're having with your schoolwork. Is that the problem, or is it something else?")
- Give **I-messages**; that is, describe the effects of the problem behavior, including your personal reactions to it, in a calm, relatively nonaccusatory manner. ("When you come to class late each day, I worry that you're getting further and further behind, and sometimes I even feel a little hurt that you don't seem to value your time in my classroom.")
- Give the student a choice from among two or more acceptable options. ("Would you rather try to work quietly at your group's table, or would it be easier if you sat somewhere by yourself to complete your work?")
- Especially when working with an adolescent, try to identify a solution that allows the student to maintain credibility in the eyes of peers. ("I suspect you might be worrying that your friends will think less of you if you comply with my request. What might we do to address this problem?") (Colvin, Ainge, & Nelson, 1997; Emmer et al., 2000; Keller & Tapasak, 2004; Lane et al., 2006)

Ultimately, we must communicate (a) our interest in the student's long-term school achievement, (b) our concern that the misbehavior is interfering with that achievement, and (c) our commitment to working cooperatively with the student to alleviate the problem.

I-message Statement that communicates the adverse effects of a student's misbehavior, including one's own reactions to it, in a calm, relatively nonaccusatory manner; its intent is to convey information, not to lay blame.

Teaching Self-Regulation Strategies

When students express their *own* concern about their problem behaviors, teaching self-regulation strategies can be helpful. Consider the following situations as examples:

- Brett's performance on assigned tasks is usually rather poor. You know he's capable of better work, because he occasionally submits work of exceptionally high quality. The root of Brett's problem seems to be that he is off task most of the time—perhaps sketching pictures of sports cars, mindlessly fiddling with objects he has found on the floor, or simply daydreaming. Brett would really like to improve his academic performance, but he doesn't seem to know how to do it.

- Georgia often talks without permission—for instance, blurting out answers to questions, interrupting classmates who are speaking, and initiating off-task conversations at inopportune times. On several occasions, you have spoken with Georgia, and she always vows to exercise more self-control in the future. Her behavior improves for a day or so, but after that, her mouth is off and running once again.

Brett's off-task behavior interferes with his own learning, and Georgia's excessive chattiness interferes with the learning of her classmates. Cueing and private discussions haven't led to any improvement. But both Brett and Georgia have something going for them: They *want* to change their behavior.

Self-regulation strategies are discussed in detail in Chapter 10, but a brief review of a few of them might be helpful here. *Self-monitoring* is especially useful when students need a reality check about the severity of the problem. Brett may think he's on task far more often than he really is; thus, we might give him a timer set to beep every five minutes and ask him to write down whether he has been on task each time he hears a beep. Georgia may not realize how frequently she prevents her classmates from speaking; thus, we might ask her to make a checkmark on a tally sheet every time she talks without permission.

If self-monitoring alone doesn't do the trick, *self-instructions* are often effective. For example, self-instructions such as the following might help Georgia acquire some self-restraint in classroom discussions:

1. *Button* my lips.
2. *Raise* my hand.
3. *Wait* until I'm called on.

Encourage self-regulation by teaching such strategies as self-monitoring, self-instructions, and self-imposed contingencies.

Finally, both students might use *self-imposed contingencies* to give themselves a motivational boost. For example, Brett might award himself a point for each 15-minute period he's been on task. Georgia might give herself 5 points at the beginning of each school day and then subtract a point each time she speaks out of turn. By accumulating a certain number of points, the students could earn opportunities to engage in favorite activities.

Self-regulation strategies have several advantages. They help us avoid power struggles with students about who's in charge. They increase students' sense of self-determination and consequently also increase their intrinsic motivation to learn and achieve in the classroom. Furthermore, self-regulation techniques benefit students over the long run, promoting productive behaviors that are apt to continue after students have moved on from a particular classroom or school. And when we teach students to monitor and modify their own behavior, rather than depend on us to do it for them, we become free to do other things—for example, to teach!

Conferring with Parents

We may sometimes need to consult with students' parents or other primary caregivers about a serious or chronic behavior problem. Consider these situations:

- You give your students short homework assignments almost every night. Carolyn has turned in only about one-third of them. You're pretty sure she's capable of doing the work, and you know from previous parent–teacher conferences that her parents give her the time and support she needs to get her assignments done. You've spoken with Carolyn several times about the problem, but she shrugs you off as if she doesn't really care whether or not she does well in your class.

- Students have frequently found things missing from their desks or personal storage bins shortly after Roger has been in the vicinity. A few students have told you that they've seen Roger take things that belong to others, and many of the missing objects have later turned up in Roger's possession. When you confront him about your suspicion that he's been stealing from classmates, he adamantly denies it. He says he has no idea how Cami's gloves or Marvin's baseball trading cards ended up in his desk.

Confer with parents about chronic problems that have serious implications for students' long-term success.

Conferring with parents is especially important when students' behavior problems show a pattern over time and have serious implications for students' long-term academic or social success. In some instances, a simple telephone call may be sufficient (Emmer et al., 2000). For example, Carolyn's parents may be unaware that she hasn't been doing her homework (she's been telling them she doesn't have any) and may be able to take the steps necessary to ensure that it gets done. In other cases, a school conference may be more productive. For example, you may want to discuss Roger's stealing habits with both Roger and his parent(s) together—something you can do more effectively when you all sit face to face in the same room.

Some ways of talking with parents are far more effective than others. Put yourself in a parent's shoes in the following exercise.

EXPERIENCING FIRSTHAND

Putting Yourself in a Parent's Shoes

Imagine that you're the parent of a seventh grader named Tommy. As you and Tommy are eating dinner one evening, the telephone rings. You get up and answer the phone:

You: Hello?

Ms. J: This is Ms. Johnson, Tommy's teacher. May I talk with you for a few minutes?

You: Of course. What can I do for you?

Ms. J: Well, I'm afraid I've been having some trouble with your son, and I thought you should know about it.

You: Really? What's the problem?

Ms. J: Tommy hardly ever gets to class on time. When he does arrive, he spends most of his time talking to his friends rather than paying attention to what I'm saying. It seems as if I have to speak to him three or four times every day about his behavior.

You: How long has all this been going on?

Ms. J: For several weeks now. And the problem is getting worse rather than better. I'd really appreciate it if you'd talk with Tommy about the situation.

You: Thank you for letting me know about this, Ms. Johnson.

Ms. J: You're most welcome. Good night.

You: Good night, Ms. Johnson.

Take a few minutes to jot down some of the things that, as a parent, you might be thinking after this telephone conversation.

You may have had a variety of thoughts in response to your conversation with Ms. Johnson. Here are some possibilities:

- Why isn't Tommy taking his schoolwork more seriously?
- Isn't Tommy doing anything *right*?

- Has Ms. Johnson tried anything besides reprimanding Tommy for his behavior? Or is she laying all of this on *my* shoulders?
- Tommy's a good kid. I should know, because I raised him. For some reason, Ms. Johnson doesn't like him and is therefore finding fault with anything he does.

Only the first of these four reactions is likely to lead to a productive response on your part.

Notice how Ms. Johnson focused strictly on the negative aspects of Tommy's classroom performance. As a result, you (as Tommy's parent) may possibly have felt anger toward your son or guilt about your ineffective parenting skills. Alternatively, if you maintained your confidence in your son's scholastic abilities and in your own ability as a parent, you may have begun to wonder about Ms. Johnson's ability to teach and motivate seventh graders. Sadly, too many teachers reach out to parents only to talk about students' weaknesses—never their strengths—as the following interview with Jamal illustrates:

> *Adult:* Has your grandpa [Jamal's primary caregiver] come to school?
>
> *Jamal:* Yup, when the teachers call him.
>
> *Adult:* What did they call him for?
>
> *Jamal:* The only time they call him is when I am being bad, the teacher will call him, he will come up here and have a meeting with the teacher.
>
> *Adult:* If you are being good do the teachers call?
>
> *Jamal:* No. (Kumar et al., 2002, p. 164)

Ideally, a teacher–parent discussion about problem behaviors is initiated within the context of an ongoing relationship that is characterized by mutual trust and respect and a shared concern for the student's learning and well-being. For instance, making a phone call to parents is most likely to yield productive results if we already have a good working relationship with them and are confident that they won't overreact with harsh, excessive punishment of their child. Furthermore, when communicating with parents, our overall messages about their child should be positive and optimistic. For instance, we might describe negative aspects of a student's classroom performance within the context of the many things the student does *well.* (Rather than start out by complaining about Tommy's behavior, Ms. Johnson might have begun by saying that Tommy is a bright and capable young man with many friends and a good sense of humor.) And we must be clear about our commitment to working *together* with parents to help a student succeed in the classroom. The Into the Classroom feature "Talking with Parents About a Student's Misbehaviors" presents several strategies for effectively approaching parents about a challenging behavior problem.

Conducting Planned, Systematic Interventions

On occasion, students may be either unwilling or unable to change their own behavior. And for one reason or another, consulting with parents may not yield effective solutions. Consider these situations:

- Tucker finds many reasons to roam about the room—he "has to" sharpen a pencil, "has to" get his homework out of his backpack, "has to" get a drink of water, and so on. Naturally, Tucker gets very little work done, and his classmates are continually distracted by his perpetual motion. You've tried everything, it seems—regularly reminding him about the importance of staying on task, pointing out how much his behavior interferes with classmates' learning, and asking him to keep track of his out-of-seat behaviors—but have seen no improvement. His mother agrees with you that something needs to be done but is at a loss for constructive ideas.

INTO THE Classroom

Talking with Parents About a Student's Misbehaviors

Consult with parents if a collaborative effort might bring about a behavior change.

At a parent–teacher–student conference, a high school math teacher expresses his concern that a student often falls asleep in class. Because the student has a computer and a telephone line in her room, her father speculates that perhaps she is surfing the Internet when she should be in bed. He looks at his daughter inquisitively, and her guilty facial expression reveals that his suspicion is justified. With the teacher's prompting, the father and the student identify an appropriate policy for home computer use—one that includes moving the computer to another room, where its use can be more closely monitored.

Begin with a description of the child's many strengths.

A teacher talks on the telephone with the father of one of her students. She describes several areas in which the student has made considerable progress and then asks for advice about strategies for helping him stay on task and be more conscientious about his work.

Describe the problem in terms of inappropriate behaviors, *not* in terms of undesirable personality characteristics.

When describing a student's poor record of turning in homework assignments, her teacher says, "Carolyn has turned in only one-third of the homework I've assigned this year. She's missed only two school days this year, so I know she's been healthy. And she's certainly capable of doing the work." At no point does the teacher suggest that Carolyn is lazy, unmotivated, or stubborn.

Don't place blame; instead, acknowledge that raising children is rarely easy.

When talking with the mother of a middle school student, a teacher mentions that the student seems to be more interested in talking with classmates than in getting her schoolwork done. The mother says she has encountered a similar problem at home: "Marnie's always been a much more social girl than I ever was. It's like pulling teeth just getting her off the telephone to do her homework, and then we end up having a shouting match that gets us nowhere!" The teacher sympathetically responds, "Students seem to become especially concerned about social matters once they reach adolescence. How about if you, Marnie, and I meet some day after school to talk about the problem? Perhaps by working together the three of us can find a way to solve it."

Ask for information, and express your desire to work together to address the problem.

When a teacher finds that a student has regularly been taking items from classmates' personal storage bins, she sets up an appointment to meet with the student and his grandmother (the student's primary caregiver). "I like Roger a lot," she says. "He has a great sense of humor, and his smile often lights up my day. I can't understand why he might want to 'borrow' items from other children without asking them first. His actions have cost him several friendships. Do either of you have any ideas about how we might tackle the problem? I'd like to do whatever I can to help Roger repair his reputation in the eyes of his classmates."

Agree on a strategy.

While reviewing a student's academic progress at a parent–teacher conference, an elementary teacher says, "Mark has a tendency to fiddle with things at his desk—for example, twisting paperclips, playing with rubber bands, or making paper airplanes—when he should be getting his work done. As a result, he often doesn't complete his assignments." The student's father replies, "I've noticed the same thing when he works on his homework, but I bring a lot of paperwork home from the office every night and don't have time to constantly hound him to stay on task." The teacher and father talk more about the problem and agree that reinforcement for completed assignments might be helpful. Mark will earn points for high scores that will help him "buy" the new bicycle he's been asking his father for.

Sources: Christenson & Sheridan, 2001; C. Davis & Yang, 2005; Emmer et al., 2000; Evertson et al., 2000; A. Miller, 2006; Woolfolk Hoy, Davis, & Pape, 2006.

- Janet's verbal abusiveness is getting out of hand. She regularly insults her peers with sexually explicit language and sometimes calls you X-rated names. You've tried praising her on occasions when she's been pleasant to others, and you've had several private conferences with her. She seems to appreciate your attention and concern, but her abusive remarks continue. Meanwhile, Janet's parents adamantly deny that their "little angel" could possibly be acting up at school.

Plan a systematic intervention when other, simpler interventions have been unsuccessful.

When a misbehavior is clearly interfering with one or more students' learning and achievement and simple intervention strategies haven't been productive, an intensive, systematic intervention is probably in order. Behaviorist approaches such as applied behavior analysis and positive behavioral support are frequently quite useful in such circumstances (see Chapter 9). These approaches can be especially effective when combined with other strategies—for instance, fostering perspective-taking ability and other aspects of social cognition, teaching effective social skills, and providing self-regulation strategies (e.g., D. C. Gottfredson, 2001; T. R. Robinson, Smith, Miller, &

Brownell, 1999). Combining behaviorist principles with other, more cognitively oriented techniques is sometimes called **cognitive behavioral therapy**.

How might we use behaviorist techniques to improve Tucker's classroom behavior? One approach would be to identify one or more effective reinforcers—given Tucker's constant fidgeting, opportunities for physical activity might be reinforcing—and then gradually shape more sedentary behavior. In addition, because some out-of-seat responses are quite appropriate (e.g., getting a reference book from the bookshelf, delivering a completed assignment to the teacher's "In" basket), we might give Tucker a reasonable allotment of "tickets" he can use to "purchase" out-of-seat behaviors during the day. An alternative strategy might be to conduct a functional analysis to determine the particular purpose that out-of-seat behavior serves for Tucker. Perhaps it allows him to avoid difficult tasks or to release the physical energy his body seems to overproduce. If we discover that Tucker acts out only when he expects challenging assignments, we should provide the instruction and support he needs to accomplish those assignments successfully—for instance, by teaching him some effective learning or problem-solving strategies. If, instead, we find that Tucker's hyperactivity emerges in a wide variety of situations, we might suspect a physiological cause and give him numerous opportunities to release pent-up energy during the school day.

myeducationlab

Discover how a functional analysis might help to determine existing reinforcers of problem behaviors by completing the Understanding Research exercise "Identifying Reinforcers Through Functional Analysis" in MyEducationLab. (To find this activity, go to the topic Classroom Management in MyEducationLab, click on *Assignments and Activities*, and then select *Understanding Research*.)

Cognitive behavioral therapy might be helpful for Janet as well. In this case, we might suspect that Janet lacks the social skills she needs to interact effectively with others; we might therefore begin by teaching her such skills through modeling, role playing, and so on. Once we know that Janet possesses effective interpersonal skills, we can begin to reinforce her for using those skills (perhaps with praise, as she has responded positively to such feedback in the past). Meanwhile, we should also punish (perhaps with a time-out) any relapses into old, abusive behavior patterns.

Table 13.3 summarizes the six strategies we've examined for addressing student misbehaviors, along with the circumstances in which each strategy is likely to be useful.

Taking Students' Cultural Backgrounds into Account

As we determine which behaviors are truly unacceptable in our classrooms, we must remember that some behaviors that our own culture deems inappropriate may be quite appropriate in another culture (e.g., Gay, 2006). In the following exercise, we look at some examples.

EXPERIENCING FIRSTHAND

Identifying Misbehaviors

As you read each scenario below, consider these questions:

- Would you classify the behavior as a *misbehavior?*
- What cultural group(s) might find the behavior appropriate? (Draw on the discussion of group differences in Chapter 4.)
- How might you deal with the behavior?

Scenarios

1. A student is frequently late for school, sometimes arriving more than an hour after the bell has rung.
2. Two students are sharing answers as they take a quiz.
3. Several students are exchanging insults that become increasingly derogatory.

cognitive behavioral therapy Planned, systematic combination of behaviorist techniques and cognition-based strategies (e.g., modeling, self-regulation techniques) as a means of bringing about desired behaviors.

Principles/ Assumptions

TABLE 13.3
Strategies for Addressing Inappropriate Classroom Behaviors

Strategy	Situations in Which It's Appropriate	Examples
Ignoring the behavior	• The misbehavior is unlikely to be repeated. • The misbehavior is unlikely to spread to other students. • Unusual circumstances have temporarily elicited the misbehavior. • The misbehavior doesn't seriously interfere with learning.	• One student discreetly passes a note to another student just before the end of class. • A student accidentally drops her books, startling other students and temporarily distracting them from their work. • An entire class is hyperactive on the last afternoon before spring break.
Cueing the student	• The misbehavior is a minor infraction but definitely interferes with students' learning. • Behavior is likely to improve with a subtle reminder.	• A student forgets to close his notebook at the beginning of a test. • Members of a cooperative learning group are talking so loudly that they distract students in other groups. • Several students are exchanging jokes during an independent seatwork assignment.
Discussing the problem privately with the student	• Cueing has been ineffective in changing the behavior. • If made clear, the reasons for the misbehavior might suggest possible strategies for addressing it.	• A student is frequently late to class. • A student refuses to do certain kinds of assignments. • A student shows a sudden drop in motivation for no apparent reason.
Promoting self-regulation	• The student has a strong desire to improve his or her behavior.	• A student doesn't realize how frequently she interrupts her classmates. • A student seeks help in learning to control his anger. • A student acknowledges that his inability to stay on task is adversely affecting the good grades he wants to get.
Conferring with parents	• A chronic behavior problem is likely to interfere with long-term academic and/or social success. • The source of the problem may possibly lie outside school walls. • Parents are likely to work collaboratively with school faculty members to bring about a behavior change.	• A student does well in class but rarely turns in required homework assignments. • A student falls asleep in class almost every day. • A student is caught stealing classmates' lunches.
Conducting a planned, systematic intervention	• The misbehavior has continued over a period of time and significantly interferes with student learning. • Other, less intensive approaches (e.g., cueing, private conferences) have been ineffective. • The student seems unwilling or unable to use self-regulation techniques.	• A student has unusual difficulty sitting still for age-appropriate time periods. • A student's obscene remarks continue even though her teacher has spoken with her about the behavior on several occasions. • A member of the soccer team displays bursts of anger and aggression that are potentially dangerous to other players.

Tardiness (Example 1) interferes with learning because the student loses valuable instructional time; thus, it might reasonably be construed as a misbehavior. However, a student who is chronically tardy may live in a community that doesn't observe strict schedules and timelines—a pattern common in some Hispanic and Native American communities. Furthermore, arrival time may not be entirely within the student's control; for instance, perhaps the student has household responsibilities or transportation issues that make punctuality difficult. A private conversation with the student, perhaps followed up by a conference with family members, might be the most effective way to determine the root of the problem and identify potential solutions.

Sharing answers during a quiz (Example 2) is a misbehavior *if* students have been specifically instructed to do their own work. Because a quiz helps a teacher determine what students have and have not learned, inaccurate quiz scores affect the teacher's instructional planning and thus indirectly affect future learning. (Inappropriately sharing answers also lowers the *validity* of quiz scores; see Chapter 15.) Although the behavior represents cheating to many people, it may reflect the cooperative spirit and emphasis on group achievement evident in the cultures of many Native American and Mexican American students. An adverse consequence is in order *if* we have previously explained what cheating is in a way that students understand and *if* we have clearly described the situations in which collaboration is and isn't appropriate—in other words, if the students know full well that their behavior violates classroom policy. But if we have *not* laid such groundwork, we must take the incident as a lesson for ourselves about what we must do to prevent such behavior from occurring again.

Exchanging insults (Example 3) might be psychologically harmful for the students involved and might adversely affect the overall classroom climate. Alternatively, however, it might simply be an instance of "playing the dozens," a playful verbal interaction involving creative one-upmanship common in some African American communities. How we handle the situation depends on the spirit in which the students seem to view the exchange. Their body language—whether they're smiling or scowling, whether they seem relaxed or tense—will tell us a great deal. If the insults truly signal escalating hostilities, immediate intervention is in order—perhaps separating the students, imposing an appropriate consequence, and following up with a private conference. If, instead, the insults reflect creative verbal play, we may simply need to establish reasonable boundaries (e.g., indoor voices should be used, racial or ethnic slurs are unacceptable).

Remember that some behaviors that are considered unacceptable in your culture may be quite acceptable in a student's culture. When such behaviors interfere with classroom achievement, be patient and understanding as you help the student acquire behaviors consistent with school expectations.

Addressing Aggression and Violence at School

In recent years, the news media have focused considerable attention on violent school crime (e.g., students murdering classmates), leading many to believe that aggression in our schools is on the rise. In reality, violent aggression involving serious injury or death is relatively rare on school grounds and, in the United States at least, has *declined* over the past 15 to 20 years (Bureau of Justice Statistics, 2005; DeVoe et al., 2003; DeVoe, Peter, Noonan, Snyder, & Baum, 2005). Most aggression at school involves psychological harm, minor physical injury, or destruction of property. For instance, it might involve sexual or racial harassment, bullying, or vandalization of student lockers (G. Bender, 2001; Casella, 2001b; Pellegrini, 2002).

If we consider *only* violent aggression that causes serious injury or death, then school is probably the safest place that young people can be (DeVoe et al., 2003, 2005; Garbarino, Bradshaw, & Vorrasi, 2002; U.S. Secret Service National Threat Assessment Center, 2000). But if we consider *all* forms of aggression (mild as well as severe), then aggression among children and adolescents occurs more frequently at school than at any other location—especially in areas where adult supervision is minimal (e.g., hallways, restrooms, parking lots) (Astor, Meyer, & Behre, 1999; Casella, 2001b; Finkelhor & Ormrod, 2000). The relative prevalence of aggression at school is almost certainly due to two factors. First, children and adolescents spend a great deal of time at school, more so than in any other place except home. Second, the sheer number of students attending even the smallest of schools makes some interpersonal conflict almost inevitable.

The roots of school aggression and violence are many and diverse. A variety of cognitive factors (e.g., lack of perspective taking, misinterpretation of social cues, poor social problem-solving skills, etc.) predispose some students to aggressive behavior (see Chapter 3). Furthermore, perhaps because of the home or neighborhood environment in which they live, some students believe that aggression is an appropriate and effective way of resolving conflicts. Developmental factors come into play as well; for instance, many young children and a few adolescents have poor impulse control, and in early adolescence, the unsettling transition to middle school may lead some students to bully weaker age-mates as a way of gaining social status with peers (Espelage et al., 2003; National Center for Education Statistics, 2007; Pellegrini, 2002). The school culture is also involved; for example, at some high schools, students believe it to be quite acceptable to threaten or fight with a peer who tries to steal one's boyfriend or girlfriend (K. M. Williams, 2001a, 2001b). Finally, aggression is a common reaction to frustration, and some students are repeatedly frustrated in their efforts to be academically and socially successful at school (G. Bender, 2001; Casella, 2001b; Miles & Stipek, 2006).

A Three-Level Approach

Don't tolerate *any* form of aggression at school. For instance, be on the lookout for bullying and other forms of psychological intimidation. (See Chapter 3 for recommendations on addressing the causes and emotional consequences of peer bullying.)

Regardless of the roots of the behavior, we must not tolerate *any* form of aggression or violence on school grounds. Students can learn and achieve at optimal levels only if they know they are both physically and psychologically safe at school. And if they *don't* feel safe, they're at increased risk for dropping out before high school graduation (Rumberger, 1995). To be truly effective in combating aggression and violence, we must attack it on three levels, depicted graphically in Figure 13.6 (Dwyer & Osher, 2000; Hyman et al., 2006; H. M. Walker et al., 1996).[1]

Level I: Creating a Nonviolent School Environment One-shot antiviolence campaigns have little lasting effect on school aggression and violence (Burstyn & Stevens, 2001). Instead, creating a peaceful, nonviolent school environment must be a long-term effort that includes the following strategies:

- Make a joint, schoolwide commitment to supporting all students' academic and social success.
- Provide a challenging and engaging curriculum.
- Form caring, trusting faculty–student relationships.
- Insist on genuine and equal respect—among students as well as faculty—for people of diverse backgrounds, races, and ethnicities.
- Establish schoolwide policies and practices that foster appropriate behavior (e.g., give clear guidelines for behavior, consistently apply consequences for infractions, provide instruction in effective social interaction and problem-solving skills).
- Involve students in school decision making.
- Provide mechanisms through which students can communicate their concerns openly and without fear of reprisal.
- Emphasize prosocial behaviors (e.g., sharing, helping, cooperating).
- Establish close working relationships with community agencies and families.
- Openly discuss safety issues. (Burstyn & Stevens, 2001; Dwyer & Osher, 2000; Dwyer, Osher, & Warger, 1998; Learning First Alliance, 2001; Meehan et al., 2003; G. M. Morrison, Furlong, D'Incau, & Morrison, 2004; Pellegrini, 2002; U.S. Secret Service National Threat Assessment Center, 2000; J. S. Warren et al., 2006)

FIGURE 13.6 A three-level approach to preventing aggression and violence in schools

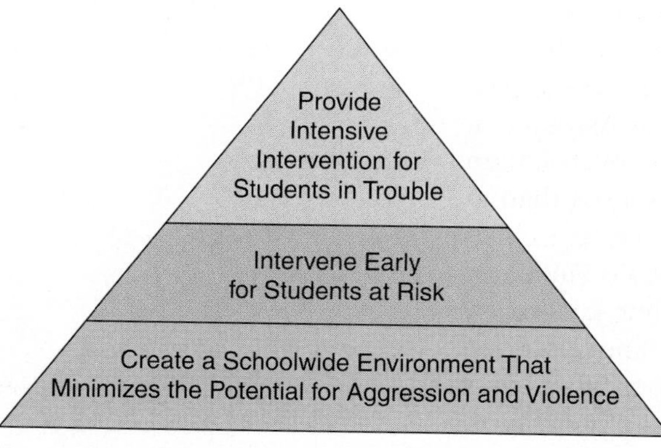

Source: Based on a figure in *Safeguarding Our Children: An Action Guide* (p. 3), by K. Dwyer and D. Osher, 2000, Washington, DC: U.S. Departments of Education and Justice, American Institutes for Research.

[1]For a more in-depth discussion of the three levels, I urge you to read *Safeguarding Our Children: An Action Guide*, by K. Dwyer and D. Osher (2000). You can download a copy from a variety of Internet websites, including www.ed.gov/admins/lead/safety/actguide/index.html.

Most of these strategies should look familiar, as they've been mentioned frequently throughout the book. The final strategy on the list—openly discussing safety issues—encompasses a variety of more specific strategies, such as these:

- Explain what bullying is (i.e., that it involves harassing and intimidating peers who cannot easily defend themselves) and why it's unacceptable.
- Solicit students' input about potentially unsafe areas that require more faculty supervision (e.g., an infrequently used restroom or back stairwell).
- Convey your willingness to hear students' complaints about troublesome classmates. (Such complaints can provide important clues about which students are most in need of assistance and intervention.)
- Most importantly, take active steps to address students' safety concerns.

Level II: Intervening Early for Students at Risk Usually, when educators use the term *students at risk*, they are referring to students who are at risk for academic failure (see Chapter 4). But students can be at risk for *social* failure as well. For instance, they may have few or no friends, be overtly bullied or rejected by many of their peers, or in other ways find themselves excluded from the social life of the school.

Perhaps 10% to 15% of students need some sort of intervention to help them interact effectively with peers, establish good working relationships with teachers, and become bona fide members of the school community (Dwyer & Osher, 2000; H. M. Walker et al., 1996). Such intervention cannot be a one-size-fits-all approach but must instead be tailored to students' particular strengths and needs. For some students, intervention might take the form of social skills training. For other students, it might mean getting them actively involved in school clubs or extracurricular activities. For still others, it may require a well-planned, systematic effort to encourage and reinforce productive behaviors, perhaps through applied behavior analysis or positive behavioral support. Regardless of type, interventions are most effective when they occur *early*—before students go too far down the path of antisocial behavior—and when they are developed by a multidisciplinary team of teachers and other professionals who bring various areas of expertise to the planning table (Dryfoos, 1997; Dwyer & Osher, 2000).

Provide individually tailored guidance and support when students experience consistent social failure at school.

Level III: Providing Intensive Intervention for Students in Trouble For a variety of reasons, minor interventions aren't always sufficient when students are predisposed to be aggressive and violent. For instance, some students have serious mental illnesses that interfere with their ability to think rationally, cope appropriately with everyday frustrations, and control impulses. Typically, schools must work closely and collaboratively with other community groups—perhaps mental health clinics, police and probation officers, and social services—to help students at high risk for aggression and violence (Dwyer & Osher, 2000; Greenberg et al., 2003; Hyman et al., 2006).

As teachers, our frequent interactions with students put us in an ideal position to identify those children and adolescents most in need of intensive intervention and get them back on track for academic and social success. As you gain teaching experience, you will begin to get a good sense of which characteristics are and are not normal for a particular age-group. You should especially be on the lookout for the early warning signs of violence presented in Figure 13.7.

Although we must be ever vigilant for signals that a student may be planning to cause harm to others, it is essential that we keep several points in mind. First, as mentioned earlier, extreme violence is *very rare* in schools; unreasonable paranoia about potential school violence will prevent us from working effectively with students. Second, the great majority of students who exhibit one or a few of the warning signs listed in Figure 13.7 will *not* become violent (U.S. Secret Service National Threat Assessment Center, 2000). And most importantly, we must *never* use the warning signs as a reason to unfairly accuse, isolate, or punish a student or to exclude a student from the education that all children and adolescents deserve (Dwyer et al., 1998).

Keep the common warning signs of violence in mind. Use them as possible indicators that a student needs significant assistance in developing emotional well-being and social success.

FIGURE 13.7 Early warning signs of possible violent behavior

Experts have identified numerous warning signs that a student may be contemplating violent actions against others. By themselves, most of the signs are unlikely to signal a violent attack, but several of them in combination should lead us to consult with school administrators and specially trained professionals.

- *Social withdrawal.* Over time, a student interacts less and less frequently with teachers and all or most peers.
- *Excessive feelings of isolation, rejection, or persecution.* A student directly or indirectly expresses the belief that he or she is friendless, disliked, or unfairly picked on; such feelings may be the result of long-term physical or psychological bullying by peers.
- *Rapid decline in academic performance.* A student shows a dramatic change in academic performance and seems unconcerned about doing well. Cognitive and physical factors (e.g., learning disabilities, ineffective study strategies, brain injury) have been ruled out as causes of the decline.
- *Poor coping skills.* A student has little ability to deal effectively with frustration, takes the smallest affront personally, and has trouble bouncing back after minor disappointments.
- *Lack of anger control.* A student frequently responds with uncontrolled anger to even the slightest injustice and may misdirect anger at innocent bystanders.
- *Sense of superiority, self-centeredness, and lack of empathy.* A student depicts himself or herself as smarter or in some other way better than peers, is preoccupied with his or her own needs, and has little regard for the needs of others.
- *Lengthy grudges.* A student is unforgiving of others' transgressions, even after considerable time has elapsed.
- *Violent themes in drawings and written work.* Violence predominates in student's artwork, stories, or journal entries, and perhaps certain individuals (e.g., a parent or particular classmate) are regularly targeted in these fantasies. (Keep in mind that occasional violence in writing and art isn't unusual, especially for boys.)
- *Intolerance of individual and group differences.* A student shows intense disdain for and prejudice against people of a certain race, ethnicity, gender, sexual orientation, religion, or disability.
- *History of violence, aggression, and other discipline problems.* A student has a long record of seriously inappropriate behavior extending over several years.
- *Association with violent peers.* A student associates regularly with a gang or other antisocial peer group.
- *Inappropriate role models.* A student speaks with admiration about Satan, Adolf Hitler, Osama bin Laden, or some other malevolent figure.
- *Frequent alcohol or drug use.* A student who abuses alcohol or drugs may have reduced self-control; in some cases, substance abuse signals significant mental illness.
- *Inappropriate access to firearms.* A student has easy access to guns and ammunition and may regularly practice using them.
- *Threats of violence.* A student has openly expressed an intent to harm someone else, perhaps in explicit terms or perhaps through ambiguous references to "something spectacular" happening at school on a particular day. ***This warning sign requires immediate action.***

Sources: Dwyer et al., 1998; O'Toole, 2000; U.S. Secret Service National Threat Assessment Center, 2000; M. W. Watson, Andreas, Fischer, & Smith, 2005.

Addressing Gang-Related Problems

A frequent source of aggression at some schools is gang-related hostility. Although gangs are more prevalent in low-income, inner-city schools, they are sometimes found in suburban and rural schools as well (Howell & Lynch, 2000).

The three-level approach to combating school aggression and violence just described can go a long way toward suppressing violent gang activities, but we will often need to take additional measures as well. Recommended strategies include the following:

- Develop, communicate, and enforce clear-cut policies regarding potential threats to other students' safety.
- Identify the specific nature and scope of gang activity in the student population.

- Forbid clothing, jewelry, and behaviors that signify membership in a particular gang (e.g., bandanas, shoelaces in gang colors, certain hand signs).[2]
- Actively mediate between-gang and within-gang disputes. (Kodluboy, 2004)

A case study at one middle school (Sanchez & Anderson, 1990) illustrates just how effective the last of these strategies—mediation—can be in addressing gang-related aggression. Many students belonged to one of several gangs that seemed to "rule the school." Fights among rival gangs were common, and nongang members were frequent victims of harassment. Dress codes, counseling, and suspensions of chronic trouble makers had little impact on students' behavior. In desperation, two school counselors suggested that the school implement a mediation program, beginning with three large gangs that were responsible for most of the trouble. Interpersonal problems involving two or more gangs would be brought to a mediation team, comprised of five school faculty members and three representatives from each of the three gangs. Team members had to abide by the following rules:

1. Really try to solve the problem.
2. No name-calling or put-downs.
3. No interrupting.
4. Be as honest as possible.
5. No weapons or acts of intimidation.
6. All sessions to be confidential until an agreement is reached or mediation is called off. (Sanchez & Anderson, 1990, p. 54)

To lay the groundwork for productive discussions, faculty members of the mediation team met separately with each of the three gangs to establish feelings of rapport and trust, explain how the mediation process would work, and gain students' cooperation with the plan.

In the first mediation session, common grievances were aired. Students agreed that they didn't like being insulted or intimidated, that they worried about their physical safety, and that they all wanted one another's respect. In several additional meetings during the next two weeks, the team reached agreement that a number of behaviors would be unacceptable at school: There would be no put-downs, name calling, hateful stares, threats, shoving, or gang graffiti. After the final meeting, each gang was called separately into the conference room. Its representatives on the mediation team explained the agreement, and other members of the gang were asked to sign it. Despite some skepticism, most members of all three gangs signed the agreement.

A month later, it was clear that the process had been successful. Members of rival gangs nodded pleasantly to one another or gave one another a high-five sign as they passed in the hall. Gang members no longer felt compelled to hang out in groups for safety's sake. Members of two of the gangs were seen playing soccer together one afternoon, and there had been no gang-related fights all month.

As should be apparent from our discussion in this chapter, helping growing children and adolescents develop into successful, productive adults can occasionally be quite a challenge. But in my own experience, discovering that you actually *can* make a difference in students' lives—including the lives of some who are at risk for academic or social failure—is one of the most rewarding aspects of being a teacher.

---

[2]A potential problem with this strategy is that it may violate students' civil liberties. For guidance on how to walk the line between ensuring students' safety and giving them reasonable freedom of expression, see Kodluboy (2004) and Rozalski and Yell (2004).

The Big Picture

Five general principles sum up much of our discussion of classroom management in this chapter:

- ***Effective teachers establish caring, supportive relationships with their students.*** Being caring and supportive doesn't just mean showing affection—although showing affection for every student certainly *is* important. Being caring and supportive also means being well prepared for class each day, holding high expectations for students' achievement, and providing whatever scaffolding each student needs to meet those expectations. All students truly want to succeed at school, and virtually all of them respond favorably to teachers who clearly have their best interests at heart.

- ***Effective teachers nurture productive student-student relationships as well.*** Students need to succeed socially as well as academically. Ideally, they should feel a genuine *sense of community*: a sense that all members of the class make meaningful contributions and deserve one another's respect and support. When some students have trouble fitting in—perhaps because they have poor social skills, are excessively shy, or have grown up in a culture very different from that of their classmates—we must think creatively about how we can help them establish and maintain good relationships with their peers.

- ***Effective teachers think proactively about how to minimize behavior problems.*** When it comes to classroom management, remember the old adage that "An ounce of prevention is worth a pound of cure." As teachers, we will be far more effective if we plan ahead about how to keep students on task throughout the school day. We can do this in a variety of ways—for example, by planning activities that motivate students to engage productively with classroom subject matter, setting reasonable limits for behavior, and taking into account the developmental characteristics of the specific age-group with whom we are working.

- ***Effective teachers are consistent and equitable in their enforcement of rules, but they accommodate individual differences when helping students adhere to the rules.*** To function effectively, any classroom needs certain rules for behavior, and we must not play favorites when enforcing rule infractions. Yet we can individualize our efforts to *prevent* behavior problems. For instance, we might seat chronically distractible students away from peers who might lure them into off-task activities, and we may occasionally need to institute preplanned, systematic interventions for students who have a long history of counterproductive behaviors.

- ***Effective teachers are team players.*** As teachers, we are just one part (albeit a very important part) of a team of faculty, parents, and other community members who are helping children and adolescents acquire behaviors that will serve them well in the adult world. It is especially important that we stay in regular contact with students' parents, sharing information in both directions about the progress students are making and coordinating efforts at school with those at home.

Practice for Your Licensure Exam

The Good Buddy

Mr. Schulak has wanted to be a teacher for as long as he can remember. In his many volunteer activities over the years—coaching a girls' basketball team, assisting with a Boy Scout troop, teaching Sunday school—he has discovered how much he enjoys working with children. Children obviously enjoy working with him as well: Many occasionally call or stop by his home to shoot baskets, talk over old times, or just say hello. Some of them even call him by his first name.

Now that Mr. Schulak has completed his college degree and obtained his teaching certificate, he has accepted a teaching position at his hometown's junior high school. He's delighted to find that he already knows many of his students, and he spends the first few days of class renewing his friendships with them. But by the end of the week, he realizes that his classes have accomplished little of an academic nature.

The following Monday, Mr. Schulak vows to get down to business. He begins each of his six class sessions by describing his instructional goals for the weeks to come and then introduces the first lesson. Unfortunately, many of his students are resistant to settling down and getting to work. They want to move from one seat to another, talk with friends, toss wadded-up paper "basketballs" across the room, and do anything *except* the academic tasks that Mr. Schulak has in mind. In his second week as a new teacher, Mr. Schulak has already lost control of his classroom.

1. **Constructed-response question:**

   Mr. Schulak is having considerable difficulty bringing his class to order.

   A. Identify two critical things that Mr. Schulak has *not* done to get the school year off to a good start.

   B. Describe two strategies that Mr. Schulak might now use to remedy the situation.

2. **Multiple-choice question:**

   Mr. Schulak is undoubtedly aware that good teachers show that they care about and respect their students. Which one of the following statements describes the kind of teacher–student relationship that is most likely to foster students' learning and achievement?

   a. The teacher communicates optimism about students' potential for success and offers the support necessary for that success.
   b. The teacher spends a lot of time engaging in recreational activities with students after school and on weekends.
   c. The teacher focuses almost exclusively on what students do well and ignores or downplays what students do poorly.
   d. The teacher listens patiently to students' concerns but reminds them that he or she alone will ultimately decide what transpires in the classroom.

Go to Chapter 13 of the Book-Specific Resources in **MyEducationLab,** and click on "Practice for Your Licensure Exam" to answer these questions. Compare your responses with the feedback provided.

PRAXIS

Turn to Appendix C, "Matching Book and MyEducationLab Content to the Praxis Principles of Learning and Teaching Tests," to discover sections of this chapter that may be especially applicable to the Praxis tests.

PEARSON myeducationlab

Now go to MyEducationLab **(www.myeducationlab.com)** where you can:

- Find learning outcomes for Classroom Management, along with the national standards that connect to these outcomes.
- Complete Assignments and Activities that can help you more deeply understand the chapter content.
- Engage in Building Teaching Skills and Dispositions exercises in which you can apply and practice core teaching skills identified in the chapter.
- Access Book-Specific Resources:
  - Check your comprehension of chapter content by going to the Study Plan, where you can find (a) Chapter Objectives; (b) Focus Questions that can guide your reading; (c) a Self-Check Quiz that can help you monitor your progress in mastering chapter content; (d) Review, Practice, and Enrichment exercises with detailed feedback that will deepen your understanding of various concepts and principles; (e) Flashcards that can give you practice in understanding and defining key terms; and (f) Common Beliefs and Misconceptions about Educational Psychology that will alert you to typical misunderstandings in educational psychology classes.
  - Video Examples of various concepts and principles presented in the chapter.
  - A Practice for Your Licensure Exam exercise that resembles the kinds of questions appearing on many teacher licensure tests.

CHAPTER OUTLINE

CHAPTER OBJECTIVES

- **Objective 14.1:** Describe the various forms that classroom assessment can take and the various purposes it can serve for teachers and students.
- **Objective 14.2:** Define and apply four RSVP characteristics of good assessment: reliability, standardization, validity, and practicality.
- **Objective 14.3:** Describe the nature, advantages, and limitations of informal assessments in the classroom.
- **Objective 14.4:** Explain how to design, use, and evaluate formal paper–pencil and performance assessments in ways that optimize RSVP characteristics and maximize students' learning and performance.
- **Objective 14.5:** Describe group differences and characteristics of students with special educational needs that have implications for classroom assessment practices.

Chapter 14

Classroom Assessment Strategies

CASE STUDY: The Math Test

Ms. Ford is teaching a middle school math class to students with low mathematical ability. She has just returned a set of graded test papers, and the following class discussion ensues:

Ms. Ford: When I corrected these papers, I was really, really shocked at some of the scores. And I think you will be too. I thought there were some that were so-so, and there were some that were devastating, in my opinion.

Student: [Noise increasing.] Can we take them over?

Ms. Ford: I am going to give them back to you. This is what I would like you to do: Every single math problem that you got wrong, for homework tonight and tomorrow, it is your responsibility to correct these problems and turn them in. In fact, I will say this, I want this sheet back to me by Wednesday at least. All our math problems that we got wrong I want returned to me with the correct answer.

Student: Did anybody get 100?

Ms. Ford: No.

Student: Nobody got 100? [Groans]

Ms. Ford: OK, boys and girls, shhh. I would say, on this test in particular, boys and girls, if you received a grade below 75 you definitely have to work on it. I do expect this quiz to be returned with Mom or Dad's signature on it. I want Mom and Dad to be aware of how we're doing.

Student: No!

Student: Do we have to show our parents? Is it a requirement to pass the class?

Ms. Ford: If you do not return it with a signature, I will call home. (J. C. Turner, Meyer, et al., 1998, pp. 740–741)

- **What information have the test results actually given Ms. Ford?**
- **What inferences does Ms. Ford make based on this information?**

THE ONE THING MS. FORD KNOWS FOR SURE is that her students have performed poorly on her recent math test. From this fact, she assumes that they have not mastered the knowledge and skills the test was designed to assess—an assumption that is appropriate *only* if the test is a good measure of what students have learned in her class. Ms. Ford appears to be angry rather than sympathetic about the poor test results. If we consider our discussion of teacher attributions in Chapter 11, we might reasonably conclude that she attributes students' poor performance to a lack of effort or some other factor that they can control.

Classroom assessment practices are intertwined with virtually every other aspect of classroom functioning (look once again at Figure 12.1 on p. 415). They affect our future planning and instruction (e.g., what we teach, how we teach it, and whether we back up to teach something a second time), the classroom climate (e.g., whether it feels psychologically safe or threatening), and students' motivation and affect (e.g., whether students develop mastery goals or performance goals, whether they feel confident or anxious). Only when we consider the integral role that assessment plays in the classroom can we truly harness its benefits to help students achieve important instructional goals. It's essential, then, that we give considerable thought to how we assess students' learning and achievement, both informally through daily observations of their behavior and more formally through preplanned assignments and tests.

The Many Forms of Assessment

What exactly does assessment involve? The following definition sums up its major features:

> **Assessment** is a process of observing a sample of a student's behavior and drawing inferences about the student's knowledge and abilities.

Several parts of this definition are important to note. First, assessment involves an observation of *behavior*. As behaviorists have pointed out, it's impossible to look inside students' heads and see what knowledge lurks there; we can see only how students perform in particular situations. Second, an assessment typically involves just a *sample* of behavior; we certainly can't observe and keep track of every single thing that every single student does during the school day. Finally, assessment involves drawing *inferences* from observed behaviors to make judgments about students' overall classroom achievement—a tricky business at best. It is critical, then, that we select behaviors that can provide reasonably accurate estimates of what students know and can do.

Notice that our definition of assessment doesn't include anything about decision making. By themselves, educational assessments are merely *tools* that can help people make decisions about students and sometimes about teachers, instructional programs, and schools as well. When people use these tools for the wrong purpose or when they interpret assessment results in ways the results were never meant to be interpreted, it is the *people*—not the assessment instruments—that are to blame.

Think of classroom assessments primarily as tools that can help you improve classroom instruction and students' learning. Let assessment results guide, rather than dictate, your decision making.

Classroom assessments can take a variety of forms, which are summarized in Figure 14.1. Let's look more closely at each one.

assessment Process of observing a sample of a student's behavior and drawing inferences about the student's knowledge and abilities.

informal assessment Assessment that results from a teacher's spontaneous, day-to-day observations of how students perform in class.

formal assessment Preplanned, systematic attempt to ascertain what students know and can do.

paper–pencil assessment Assessment in which students provide written responses to written items.

performance assessment Assessment in which students demonstrate their knowledge and skills in a nonwritten fashion.

Informal versus Formal Assessment

An **informal assessment** involves a spontaneous, unplanned observation of something a student says or does. For example, when Mitchell asks "How come people in Australia don't fall into space?" he reveals a misconception about gravity. And when Jaffa continually squints at the chalkboard, we might wonder if she needs an appointment with an eye doctor. In contrast, a **formal assessment** is planned in advance and used for a specific purpose—perhaps to determine what students have learned from a geography unit or whether they can apply the Pythagorean theorem to real-world geometry problems. Formal assessment is *formal* in several respects: a particular time is set aside for it, students can prepare for it ahead of time, and it is intended to yield information about particular instructional goals or content area standards.

Paper–Pencil versus Performance Assessment

As teachers, we may sometimes choose **paper–pencil assessment**, in which we present questions or problems that students must address on paper. But we may also find it helpful to use **performance assessment**, in which students demonstrate (i.e., perform) their abilities—for example, by giving an oral presentation in a language arts class, jumping hurdles in a physical education class, or identifying acids and bases in a chemistry lab.

FIGURE 14.1 The various forms that educational assessment can take

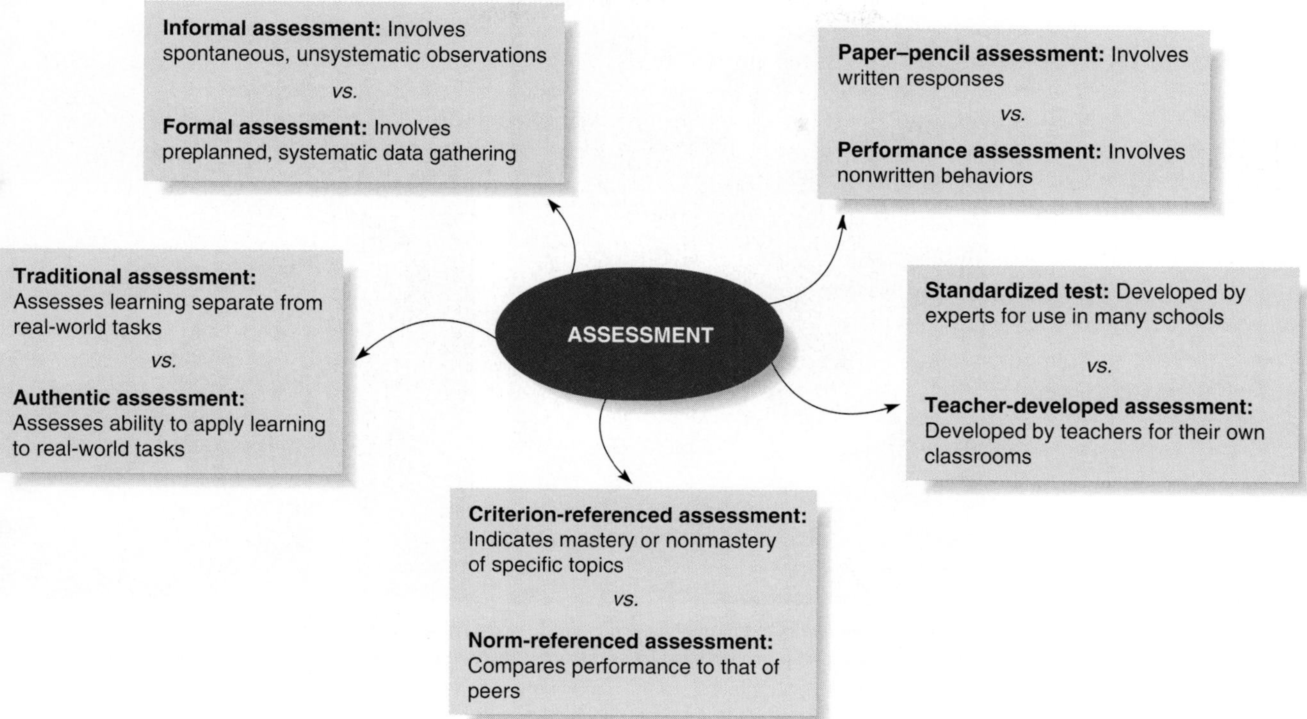

Traditional versus Authentic Assessment Historically, most educational assessments have focused on measuring knowledge and skills in relative isolation from tasks typically found in the outside world. Spelling quizzes, mathematics word problems, and physical fitness tests are examples of such **traditional assessment**. Yet ultimately, students must be able to transfer their knowledge and skills to complex tasks outside the classroom. The notion of **authentic assessment**—measuring students' knowledge and skills in a real-life (i.e., *authentic*) context—has gained considerable popularity in recent years. Keep in mind, however, that the distinction I've just made represents a *continuum* rather than an either–or situation: Assessment tasks can resemble real-world situations to varying degrees.

Some authentic assessment tasks involve paper and pencil. For example, we might ask students to write a letter to a friend or develop a school newspaper. But in many cases, authentic assessment is based on nonwritten performance and closely integrated with instruction. For instance, we might ask students to bake a cake, converse in a foreign language, or successfully maneuver a car into a parallel parking space. Often, teachers ask students to create *portfolios* that present a collection of authentic artifacts they've created—perhaps short stories, newspaper editorials, audiotapes of oral or musical performances, videotapes of dramatic performances, and so on (more on portfolios in Chapter 15).[1]

traditional assessment Assessment that focuses on measuring basic knowledge and skills in relative isolation from tasks typical of the outside world.

authentic assessment Assessment of students' knowledge and skills in a context similar to one in the outside world.

standardized test Test developed by test construction experts and published for use in many different schools and classrooms.

teacher-developed assessment instrument Assessment tool developed by an individual teacher for use in his or her own classroom.

Standardized Tests versus Teacher-Developed Assessments Sometimes classroom assessments involve tests developed by test construction experts and published for use in many different schools and classrooms. Such tests, commonly called

[1]Educators are not in complete agreement in their use of the terms *performance assessment* and *authentic assessment*; many treat them more or less as synonyms. However, I find it useful to consider separately whether an assessment involves *performance* (rather than paper and pencil) and whether it involves a complex, real-world (*authentic*) task. Thus, I do *not* use the two terms interchangeably.

Authentic assessments closely resemble real-world tasks. For example, in a semester-long unit on aerodynamics, a group of sixth graders constructs and then successfully launches a hot-air balloon.

standardized tests, can be quite helpful in assessing students' general achievement and ability levels (more on these tests in Chapter 15). But when we want to assess students' learning and achievement related to specific instructional objectives—for example, whether students have mastered long division or can apply what they've just learned in a social studies lesson—we will usually want to construct our own **teacher-developed assessment instruments**.

Criterion-Referenced versus Norm-Referenced Assessments Some assessment instruments, known as **criterion-referenced assessments**, are designed to tell us exactly what students have and have not accomplished relative to predetermined standards or criteria. A simple example is a test covering a fourth-grade class's 20 spelling words for the week: A score of 20 indicates a perfect paper, a score of 15 indicates 15 correct spellings, and so on. With such a test, we would know precisely which words each student does and does not know how to spell.

In contrast, **norm-referenced assessments** reveal how well each student's performance compares with the performance of peers—perhaps classmates or perhaps age-mates across the nation. For instance, ninth graders might take a nationwide mathematics test yielding percentile ranks that indicate how well each student has performed in comparison with other ninth graders around the country. Such scores don't tell us specifically what students have or have not learned in math; instead, they tell us how well each student stacks up against others at the same age or grade level.

Strictly speaking, any assessment has the potential to tell us *both* what students have learned and how they compare with peers. In reality, however, experienced educators tend to construct the two types of assessments somewhat differently. Ideally, questions and tasks on a criterion-referenced assessment are closely tied to the curriculum and to the particular knowledge and skills that we hope students have acquired. If all students have mastered the subject matter to the same degree, then it's entirely possible for them all to get the same score. If we want to know how students differ from one another (and we'll soon identify some circumstances in which we would want to know that), then we must have an instrument that will yield considerable variability in scores. In such an instrument, we are apt to have questions and tasks that vary widely in difficulty level, including some that only a few students can respond to correctly.

criterion-referenced assessment Assessment instrument designed to determine what students know and can do relative to predetermined standards or criteria.

norm-referenced assessment Assessment instrument that indicates how students perform relative to a peer group.

Using Assessment for Different Purposes

As noted in our earlier definition, assessment involves drawing inferences, and such inferences often have an evaluative component. Educators distinguish between two general forms of evaluation. On some occasions, we must engage in **formative evaluation**, assessing what students know and can do *before or during instruction*.[2] Ongoing formative evaluations can help us determine what students already know and believe about a topic (e.g., see Figure 14.2), whether they need further practice on a particular skill, and so on, and we can develop or revise our lesson plans accordingly. At other times, we must engage in **summative evaluation**, conducting an assessment *after instruction* to make final determinations about what students have achieved. Summative evaluations are used to determine whether students have mastered the content of a lesson or unit, what final grades we should assign, which students are eligible for more advanced classes, and the like.

FIGURE 14.2 Some assessments reflect *formative evaluation*, because they give us helpful information before or during instruction. Here 8-year-old Richard reveals his current knowledge and beliefs before his class begins a unit about the moon.

What I already know about the moon:
Solar ~~Lunar~~ eclipse: Sun, Earth and moon are all in a line.
It is big.
Gravitational pull effects tides.
It has craters. People have ben on it.
It looks like a face.
It can be blue and yellow.

With these two basic kinds of evaluation in mind, let's consider how we might use educational assessments for five possible purposes.

Guiding Instructional Decision Making

Both summative and formative evaluations can guide instructional decision making. Any upcoming summative evaluations—annual citywide or statewide tests of basic skills, for example—must inevitably guide us somewhat as we prioritize topics and skills on which to focus. Then, after we've identified our priorities, formative evaluations can help us determine a suitable point at which to begin instruction. Furthermore, conducting formative evaluations throughout a lesson or unit can give us ongoing information about the appropriateness of our instructional goals and the effectiveness of our instructional strategies. For instance, if we find that almost all students are completing assignments quickly and easily, we might set our goals a bit higher. If, instead, we discover that many students are struggling with material we have presented in class lectures, we might consider trying a different instructional approach—perhaps a more concrete, hands-on one.

Diagnosing Learning and Performance Problems

Why is Louis having trouble learning to read? Why does Gretel misbehave every time she is given a challenging assignment? We ask such questions when we suspect that certain students might learn differently from their classmates and may possibly require special educational services. A variety of standardized tests have been designed specifically to identify the unique academic and personal needs that some students have. Most of these tests require explicit training in their use and thus are often administered and interpreted by specialists (e.g., school psychologists, counselors, speech and language pathologists). As a general rule, the tests tend to be norm-referenced rather than criterion-referenced in order to identify students who are well above or well below their age-group with respect to certain abilities or characteristics.

Yet teacher-developed assessments can provide considerable diagnostic information as well, especially when they reveal consistent error patterns and areas of difficulty (e.g., see Figure 14.3). In other words, teacher-developed assessments can—and ideally *should*—give us information we can use to help students improve (Baek, 1994; Baxter, Elder, & Glaser, 1996; Covington, 1992).

formative evaluation Evaluation conducted before or during instruction to facilitate instructional planning and enhance students' learning.

summative evaluation Evaluation conducted after instruction to assess students' final achievement.

[2] You may sometimes see the term *curriculum-based assessment* used in reference to ongoing, formative assessments of students' learning during instruction.

FIGURE 14.3 In these and other work samples, 7-year-old Casey shows consistent difficulty in making connections between the sounds he hears and the sounds he represents in his writing—a difficulty that, in his case, reflects a learning disability known as *dyslexia*.

Determining What Students Have Learned from Instruction

We typically need to use formal assessments to determine whether students have achieved instructional goals or met certain content area standards. Such information is essential if we are using a mastery-learning approach to instruction; it's also important for assigning final grades. School counselors and administrators, too, may use assessment results to make placement decisions, such as which students are most likely to do well in advanced classes, which might need additional course work in basic skills, and so on.

Evaluating the Quality of Instruction

Use the results of classroom assessments not only to assess what students have learned but also to reflect on the effectiveness of your instructional strategies.

Final measures of student achievement are also useful in evaluating the quality of instruction. When most students perform poorly after an instructional unit (as Ms. Ford's students did in the opening case study), we must consider not only what our students might have done differently but also what we, as teachers, might have done differently. For instance, perhaps we moved too quickly through material or provided insufficient opportunities for students to practice critical skills. In any event, consistently low assessment results should tell us that some modification of instruction is in order.

Promoting Learning

Whenever we conduct formative evaluations to help us develop or modify our lesson plans, we are obviously using assessment to facilitate students' learning. But summative evaluation can influence learning as well, often in the following ways:

- *Assessments can motivate students to study and learn.* On average, students study class material more, review it more regularly, and learn it better when they are told they will be tested on it or in some other way held accountable for it, rather than when they are simply told to learn it (Dempster, 1991; N. Frederiksen, 1984b; Halpin & Halpin, 1982). Yet *how* students are assessed is as important as *whether* they're assessed. Assessments are especially effective as motivators when they are criterion-referenced, are closely aligned with instructional goals and objectives, and challenge students to do their best (Mac Iver et al., 1995; Maehr & Anderman, 1993; L. H. Meyer, Weir, McClure, & Walkey, 2008). Students' self-efficacy and attributions affect their perceptions of the challenge, of course: Students must believe that success on an assigned task is possible if they exert reasonable effort and use appropriate strategies.

Although regular classroom assessments can be highly motivating, they are, in and of themselves, usually *extrinsic* motivators. Thus, they may direct students' attention to performance goals and undermine any intrinsic motivation to learn. Assessments are especially likely to encourage performance goals when students perceive them to be primarily an evaluation of their performance rather than a mechanism for helping them master classroom subject matter (Danner, 2008; Grolnick & Ryan, 1987; Paris & Turner, 1994).

With the potentially motivating effects of classroom assessments in mind, let's return to the opening case study. From the classroom dialogue alone, it's impossible to know whether Ms. Ford's comments motivate the students to work harder on their math. Ms. Ford is almost certainly *not* promoting *intrinsic* motivation: By focusing on students' test scores and parents' approval or disapproval, she is fostering performance goals rather than mastery goals. Furthermore, notice how controlling, even threatening, some of her statements are: "It is your responsibility to correct these problems and turn them in. . . . All our math problems that we got wrong I want returned to me with the correct answer. . . . If you do not return [the quiz] with a [parent's] signature, I will call home." Such comments are likely to undermine students' sense of self-determination (see Chapter 11) and will hardly endear students to the discipline of mathematics. (How Ms. Ford attempts to communicate students' test scores to parents is yet another issue; we'll return to this point in Chapter 15.)

- *Assessments can influence students' cognitive processes as they study.* Different kinds of assessment tasks can lead students to study and learn quite differently (N. Frederiksen, 1984b; Lundeberg & Fox, 1991; L. Shepard, Hammerness, Darling-Hammond, & Rust, 2005). For instance, students typically spend more time studying the things they think they will be addressed on an assessment than the things they think the assessment won't cover. Furthermore, their expectations about the kinds of tasks they will need to perform and the questions they will need to answer will influence whether they memorize isolated facts, on the one hand, or construct a meaningful, integrated body of information, on the other.

As an example, look at the sixth-grade test about rocks shown in Figure 14.4. Part A (i.e., identifying rocks shown at the front of the room) might be assessing either basic knowledge or application (transfer) to new situations, depending on whether the students have seen those particular rock specimens before. The rest of the test clearly focuses on memorized facts—stages of the rock cycle, definitions of terms, and so on—and is likely to encourage students to engage in rote learning as they study for future tests. For instance, consider the last item: "Every rock has a ______." Students can answer this item correctly only if they have learned the material verbatim: The missing word here is "story."

Classroom assessments can also influence students' views about the nature of various academic disciplines; that is, they can influence the *epistemic beliefs* of which I spoke in Chapter 8. For example, if we give quizzes that assess knowledge of specific facts, students are apt to conclude that a discipline is just that: a collection of undisputed facts. If, instead, we ask students to take a position on a controversial issue and justify their position with evidence and logic, they get a very different message: that the discipline involves an integrated set of understandings that must be supported with reasoning and are subject to change over time.

Remember that, to some degree, assessment *is* instruction: It tells students what things are most important for them to learn. Accordingly, classroom assessment tasks should be closely aligned with instructional goals and content area standards.

In general, sound assessment practices are closely tied to instruction: They reflect instructional goals and content area standards, guide instructional strategies, and provide a means through which we can track students' progress through the curriculum. In a very real sense, assessment *is* instruction: It gives students clear messages about what things are most important for them to know and be able to do.

- *Assessments can serve as learning experiences in and of themselves.* In general, the very process of completing an assessment on class material helps students review

FIGURE 14.4 Much of this sixth-grade geology test focuses on knowledge of specific facts and may encourage students to memorize, rather than understand, information about rocks.

A. Write whether each of the rocks shown at the front of the room is a sedimentary, igneous, or metamorphic rock.
1. ____________________
2. ____________________
3. ____________________

B. The following are various stages of the rock cycle. Number them from 1 to 9 to indicate the order in which they occur.
___ Heat and pressure
___ Crystallization and cooling
___ Igneous rock forms
___ Magma
___ Weathering and erosion into sediments
___ Melting
___ Sedimentary rock forms
___ Pressure and cementing
___ Metamorphic rock forms

C. Write the letter for the correct definition of each rock group.

1. ___ Igneous	a. Formed when particles of eroded rock are deposited together and become cemented.
2. ___ Sedimentary	b. Produced by extreme pressures or high temperatures below the earth's surface.
3. ___ Metamorphic	c. Formed by the cooling of molten rock material from within the earth.

D. Fill in the blank in each sentence.
1. The process of breaking down rock by the action of water, ice, plants, animals, and chemical changes is called ____________________ .
2. All rocks are made of ____________________ .
3. The hardness of rocks can be determined by a ____________________ .
4. Continued weathering of rock will eventually produce ____________________ .
5. Every rock has a ____________________ .

[The test continues with several additional fill-in-the-blank and short-answer items.]

classroom material and learn it better. Assessment tasks are especially valuable if they ask students to elaborate on or apply the material in a new way (Fall, Webb, & Chudowsky, 2000; Foos & Fisher, 1988; Pashler et al., 2007).

• *Assessments can provide valuable feedback about learning progress.* Simply knowing one's final score on a test or assignment isn't terribly helpful. To facilitate students' learning—and ultimately to enhance their self-efficacy for mastering the subject matter—assessment feedback must include concrete information about where students have succeeded, where they have had difficulty, and how they might improve (Baron, 1987; Krampen, 1987; Pintrich & Schunk, 2002).

• *Assessments can encourage intrinsic motivation and self-regulation if students play an active role in the assessment process.* As noted earlier, classroom assessments are typically extrinsic motivators that provide only an externally imposed reason for learning school subject matter. Yet students learn more effectively when they are *intrinsically* motivated, and they are more likely to be intrinsically motivated if they have some sense of autonomy and self-determination about classroom activities. Furthermore, if students are to become self-regulating learners, they must acquire skills in self-monitoring and self-evaluation (see Chapter 10). For such reasons, students should be regular and active participants in the assessment of their own learning and performance. We'll pursue this point further in a later section of the chapter.

The Into the Classroom feature "Using Classroom Assessments to Promote Learning and Achievement" presents several examples of how we might use classroom assessments to foster effective cognitive processes and enhance student learning.

INTO THE Classroom

Using Classroom Assessments to Promote Learning and Achievement

- **Give a formal or informal pretest to determine where to begin instruction.**

  When beginning a new unit on cultural geography, a teacher gives a pretest designed to identify misconceptions that students may have about various cultural groups—misconceptions he can then address during instruction.

- **Choose or develop an assessment instrument that reflects the actual knowledge and skills you want students to achieve.**

  When planning how to assess students' achievement, a teacher initially decides to use questions from the test-item manual that accompanies the class textbook. When he looks more closely at these test items, however, he discovers that they measure only knowledge of isolated facts. Instead, he develops several authentic assessment tasks that better reflect his primary instructional goal: Students should be able to apply what they've learned to real-world problems.

- **Construct assessment instruments that reflect how you want students to think about and cognitively process information as they study.**

  A teacher tells her students, "As you study for next week's vocabulary test, remember that I will be asking you to put each definition in your own words and to give your own example to show what each word means."

- **Use an assessment task as a learning experience in and of itself.**

  A high school science teacher has students collect samples of the local drinking water and test them for bacterial content. She is assessing her students' ability to use procedures she has taught them, but she also hopes that they will discover the importance of protecting the community's natural resources.

- **Use an assessment to give students specific feedback about what they have and have not mastered.**

  As a teacher grades students' persuasive essays, he writes numerous notes in the margins to indicate places where students have analyzed a situation logically or illogically, identified a relevant or irrelevant example, proposed an appropriate or inappropriate solution, and so on.

- **Provide criteria that students can use to evaluate their own performance.**

  The teacher of a Foods and Nutrition class gives her students a checklist of qualities to look for in the pies they have baked.

Important Qualities of Good Assessment

As a student, have you ever been assessed in a way you thought was unfair? If so, *why* was it unfair?

1. Did the teacher evaluate students' responses inconsistently?
2. Were some students assessed under more favorable conditions than others?
3. Was the assessment a poor measure of what you had learned?
4. Was the assessment so time consuming that after a while you no longer cared how well you performed?

In light of your experiences, what characteristics seem to be essential for a good classroom assessment instrument? The four numbered questions just posed reflect, respectively, four *RSVP* characteristics of good classroom assessment: reliability, standardization, validity, and practicality.

Reliability

reliability Extent to which an assessment yields consistent information about the knowledge, skills, or characteristics being assessed.

The **reliability** of an assessment instrument or procedure is the extent to which it yields consistent information about the knowledge, skills, or characteristics being assessed. To get a sense of what reliability involves, try the following exercise.

EXPERIENCING FIRSTHAND

Fowl Play

Here is a sequence of events in the life of biology teacher Ms. Fowler:

- *Monday.* After completing a lesson on the bone structures of both birds and dinosaurs, Ms. Fowler asks her students to write an essay explaining why many scientists believe that birds are descended from dinosaurs. After school she tosses the pile of essays on the back seat of her cluttered '57 Chevy.
- *Tuesday.* Ms. Fowler looks high and low for the essays both at home and in her classroom, but she can't find them anywhere.
- *Wednesday.* Because Ms. Fowler wants to use the assignment to determine what her students have learned, she asks the class to write the same essay a second time.
- *Thursday.* Ms. Fowler discovers Monday's essays on the back seat of her Chevy.
- *Friday.* Ms. Fowler grades both sets of essays. She is surprised to find little consistency between them. The students who wrote the best essays on Monday didn't necessarily do well on Wednesday, and some of Monday's poorest performers did quite well on Wednesday.

Which results should Ms. Fowler use: Monday's or Wednesday's? Why?

When we assess students' learning and achievement, we must be confident that our assessment results will be essentially the same regardless of whether we give the assessment on Monday or Wednesday, whether the weather is sunny or rainy, or whether we evaluate students' responses while we're in a good mood or a foul frame of mind. Ms. Fowler's assessment instrument has poor reliability, because the results it yields are completely different from one day to another. So which day's results should she use? I've asked you a trick question: There is no way of knowing which set of results is more accurate.

Any single assessment instrument will rarely yield *exactly* the same results for the same student on two different occasions, even if the knowledge or ability being assessed remains the same. Many temporary conditions unrelated to the knowledge or ability being measured are apt to affect students' performance and almost inevitably lead to some fluctuation in assessment results. For instance, the inconsistencies in Ms. Fowler's two sets of student essays might have been due to temporary factors such as these:

- *Day-to-day changes in students*—for example, changes in health, motivation, mood, and energy level

  The week of the assessments, the 24-hour Netherlands flu was making the rounds in Ms. Fowler's classroom.

- *Variations in the physical environment*—for example, variations in room temperature, noise level, and outside distractions

  On Monday, the students who sat by the window in Ms. Fowler's classroom enjoyed peace and quiet. But on Wednesday, they had to contend with noisy construction machinery tearing up the pavement outside.

- *Variations in administration of the assessment*—for example, variations in instructions, timing, and the teacher's responses to students' questions

  On Monday, a few students wrote the essay after school because they had attended a dress rehearsal for the school play during class time. Ms. Fowler explained the task more clearly to them than she had to the other students, and she gave them as much time as they needed to finish. On Wednesday, a different group of students had to write the essay after school because of an across-town band concert during class time. Ms. Fowler explained the task very hurriedly to them and collected the essays before they had finished.

- *Characteristics of the assessment instrument*—for example, the length, clarity, and difficulty of tasks (assessments with many items tend to be more reliable because careless errors on one or two items have less impact on overall results; assessments with ambiguous and very difficult tasks tend to have low reliability because students are apt to make random guesses about answers)

  The essay topic—"Explain why many scientists believe that birds are descended from dinosaurs"—was sufficiently vague that students interpreted it differently from one day to the next.

- *Subjectivity in scoring*—for example, judgments made on the basis of vague, imprecise criteria

  Ms. Fowler graded both sets of essays while watching *Chainsaw Murders at Central High* on television Friday night. She gave higher scores during kissing scenes, lower scores during stalking scenes.

All of the factors just listed lead to a certain amount of *error* in students' test scores and other assessment results. Rarely is an assessment result a dead-on measure of what students have learned and can do.

Informal observations of student performance can often give us valuable information about how students are progressing. But ultimately we should draw firm conclusions about students' achievement only when we know our assessment methods are *reliable*, yielding consistent results about particular students time after time.

Psychologists distinguish among different kinds of reliability, which take different error factors into account. *Test–retest reliability* is the extent to which an assessment instrument yields similar results over a short time interval. *Scorer reliability* is the extent to which different people assessing students' performance agree in their judgments. *Internal consistency reliability* is the extent to which different parts of a single instrument all measure the same characteristic. Appendix B explains how we can determine each of these reliabilities; it also explains how we can estimate the amount of error that a particular assessment result might have.

Whenever we draw conclusions about students' learning and achievement, we must be confident that the information on which we're basing our conclusions isn't overly distorted by temporary, irrelevant factors. Several strategies can increase the likelihood that an assessment yields reliable results:

- Include a variety of tasks, and look for consistency in students' performance from one task to another.
- Define each task clearly enough that students know exactly what they are being asked to do.
- Identify specific, concrete criteria with which to evaluate students' performance.
- Try not to let preexisting expectations for students' performance influence judgments of *actual* performance.
- Avoid assessing students' achievement when they are unlikely to give their best performance—for instance, when they are ill.
- Administer the assessment in similar ways and under similar conditions for all students.

My last recommendation suggests that assessment procedures also be *standardized*—the second of the RSVP characteristics.

Standardization

Standardization refers to the extent to which an assessment involves similar content and format and is administered and scored in the same way for everyone. In most situations, students should all get the same instructions, perform identical or similar tasks, have the same time limit, and work under the same constraints. Furthermore, students' responses should be scored as consistently as possible. For example, unless there are extenuating circumstances, we shouldn't use tougher standards for one student than for another.

At the beginning of the chapter, I mentioned that many tests constructed and published by testing experts are called *standardized* tests. This label indicates that such tests have explicit procedures for administration and scoring that are consistently applied wherever the tests are used. Yet standardization is important in teacher-developed assessments as well: It reduces the error in our assessment results, especially error due to variation in test administration or subjectivity in scoring. The more an assessment is standardized for all students, then, the higher its reliability. Equity is an additional consideration: Under most circumstances, it's only fair to ask all students to be evaluated under similar conditions. We find an obvious exception to this guideline in the assessment of students with special educational needs; we'll consider appropriate accommodations for such students near the end of the chapter.

Validity

Earlier you learned about *reliability*. Let's see whether you can apply (i.e., transfer) your understanding of reliability in the following exercise.

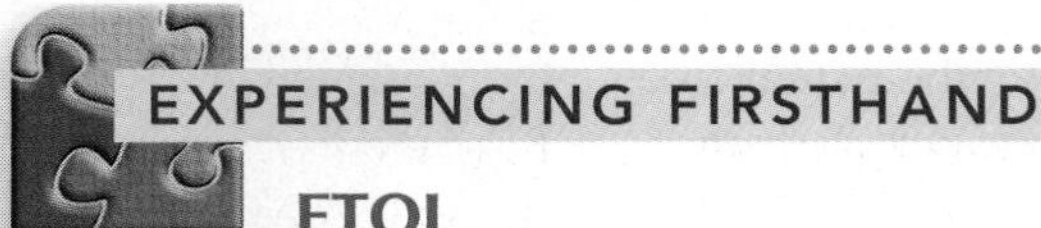

EXPERIENCING FIRSTHAND

FTOI

I have developed a new test called the FTOI: the Fathead Test of Intelligence. It consists of only a tape measure and a *table of norms* that shows how children and adults of various ages typically perform on the test.

Administration of the FTOI is quick and easy. You simply measure a person's head circumference just above the eyebrows (firmly but not too tightly) and compare your measure against the average head circumference for the person's age-group. Large heads (comparatively speaking) receive high IQ scores. Smaller heads receive low scores.

Does the FTOI have high reliability? Answer the question before you read further.

No matter how often you measure the circumference of a person's head, you are going to get a similar score: Fatheads will continue to be fatheads, and pinheads will always be pinheads. So the answer to my question is *yes*: The FTOI has high reliability because it yields consistent results. If you answered *no*, you were probably thinking that the FTOI isn't a very good measure of intelligence. But that's a problem with the instrument's *validity*, not its reliability.

The **validity** of an assessment instrument is the extent to which it measures what it's intended to measure and allows us to draw appropriate inferences about the characteristic or ability in question. Does the FTOI measure intelligence? Are scores on a standardized, multiple-choice achievement test good indicators of how much students have learned during the school year? Does students' performance at a school concert reflect what they have achieved in their instrumental music class? When our assess-

standardization Extent to which an assessment involves similar content and format and is administered and scored similarly for everyone.

validity Extent to which an assessment actually measures what it is intended to measure and allows appropriate inferences about the characteristic or ability in question.

ments don't do these things well—when they are poor measures of students' knowledge and abilities—we have a validity problem.

As noted earlier, numerous irrelevant factors are apt to influence how well students perform in assessment situations. Some of these—students' health, environmental distractions, inconsistencies in scoring, and so on—are temporary conditions that lead to fluctuation in assessment results from one time to the next and thereby lower reliability. But other irrelevant factors—perhaps reading ability or chronic test anxiety—are more stable, and thus their effects on assessment results will be relatively constant. For example, if Joe has poor reading skills, he may get consistently low scores on paper–pencil, multiple-choice achievement tests regardless of how much he has actually achieved in science, math, or social studies. And if Jane suffers debilitating anxiety every time she performs in front of an audience, her performance at a public concert may not be a good reflection of how well she can play the cello. When our assessment results continue to be affected by the same irrelevant variables, the validity of the results is in doubt.

Psychologists distinguish among different kinds of validity, each of which is important in different situations. Three kinds of particular interest to educators and other practitioners are content validity, predictive validity, and construct validity.

Content Validity As classroom teachers, we will usually be most concerned with **content validity**: the extent to which assessment questions and tasks are a representative sample of the overall body of knowledge and skills we are assessing. High content validity is *essential* whenever we are using an assessment instrument for summative evaluation purposes—that is, to determine what knowledge and skills students have ultimately acquired from instruction. Assessments with high content validity are (like effective instruction) closely aligned with instructional goals and any schoolwide and government-mandated standards (Haywood & Litz, 2007; NASSP, 2004; L. Shepard et al., 2005). In some situations—for instance, when the desired outcome is the simple recall of facts—we might ask students to respond to multiple-choice or short-answer questions on a paper–pencil test. In other situations—for instance, when the goal is to critique a literary work or to use principles of physics to explain everyday phenomena—essay questions that require students to follow a logical line of reasoning are appropriate. However, for some skills—for instance, cooking a hard-boiled egg, executing a front dismount from the parallel bars, identifying specific microorganisms through a microscope—only performance assessment can give us reasonable content validity. In the end, we may find that we can best assess students' achievement with a combination of paper–pencil and performance tasks (R. L. Linn, 1994; Messick, 1994a; D. B. Swanson, Norman, & Linn, 1995).

Align classroom assessment instruments and procedures both with mandated content area standards and with your own specific goals, objectives, and curriculum.

As an illustration of how we might align classroom assessments with standards, goals and objectives, and instruction, let's return to North Carolina's competency goals for English Language Arts. In Chapter 12, Table 12.1 showed how we might translate some of the state's competency goals for certain grade levels into specific instructional goals and objectives and how we might then tie instructional lessons and tasks to those goals and objectives. Table 14.1 repeats the entries in Table 12.1 but has an additional (rightmost) column suggesting possible ways of determining whether students have achieved the instructional goals and objectives. The entries in the new column are all intended to serve as *formal, summative assessments.* But notice that the entries to their immediate left (in the "Examples of Instructional Strategies" column) also require students to do, say, or write something—thus providing opportunities for *informal assessments* and *formative evaluation* of students' current knowledge and ongoing progress.

Regardless of the specific nature of our assessment tasks, taken together they must comprise a *representative* sample of the content domain we're assessing. The most widely recommended strategy is to construct a blueprint that identifies the specific things we want to assess and the proportion of questions or tasks that should address each one. This blueprint frequently takes the form of a **table of specifications**: a two-way grid that indicates both what topics should be covered and what students should be able to do with each topic. Each cell of the grid indicates the relative importance

content validity Extent to which an assessment includes a representative sample of tasks within the content domain being assessed.

table of specifications Two-way grid indicating the topics to be covered in an assessment and the things students should be able to do with those topics.

TABLE 14.1
Examples of How You Might Align Classroom Assessments with State Standards and Classroom Goals, Objectives, and Instruction at Different Grade Levels

Grade Level	Examples of North Carolina's Grade-Specific Competency Goals for English Language Arts	Examples of More Specific Goals and Objectives You Might Write Related to the State Goals	Examples of Instructional Strategies That Address These Goals and Objectives *and* Informally Assess Students' Progress	Examples of Formal Assessments That Align with the Goals, Objectives, and Classroom Instruction
Grade 1	Read and comprehend both fiction and nonfiction text appropriate for grade one using: • Prior knowledge • Summary • Questions • Graphic organizers (Competency Goal 2.03)	Use prior knowledge to draw correct inferences from a work of literature in which the author has omitted important information.	Read high-interest stories, stopping frequently to ask questions that require students to go beyond the text itself (e.g., to speculate about what a character might be feeling).	Ask students to read a simple story; alternatively, read them the story. Ask each student to draw inferences about certain missing details—for instance, "If [a character] was planting a garden, what time of year must it have been?" and "Why do you think [a character] was sad?"
	Respond and elaborate in answering what, when, where, and how questions. (Competency Goal 2.07)	Identify main characters, setting, and general plot line in a short story.	Have students create props for and act out a story they have recently read.	Meet with students in small groups and ask each group member to describe a story in his or her own words. Follow up with questions such as "What happened next?" and "Why did [a character] do that?" to determine the extent to which each student has understood important elements of the story.
Grade 4	Interact with the text before, during, and after reading, listening, and viewing by: • Setting a purpose using prior knowledge and text information • Making predictions • Formulating questions • Locating relevant information • Making connections with previous experiences, information, and ideas (Competency Goal 2.02)	Make predictions about how the plot line might unfold in a novel.	As a reading group discusses Carl Hiaasen's *Hoot*, ask students to speculate about how the plot might progress and to identify clues in the text that support their predictions.	After students have read the first few chapters of Natalie Babbitt's *Tuck Everlasting* (in which the Tuck family has drunk from a well that gives everlasting life), ask them to write an essay speculating on problems the Tucks' immortality might create for them. Later, after they learn that Mae Tuck has killed someone, ask them to speculate about the implications of her arrest and to back up their predictions with clues in the text.
	Make inferences, draw conclusions, make generalizations, and support by referencing the text. (Competency Goal 2.05)	Identify cause-and-effect relationships in assigned readings in a history textbook.	When students are reading their history textbook, ask *why* questions that encourage cause-and-effect connections (e.g., "Why did Columbus's crew want to turn back after several weeks on the open sea?").	Ask students to create concept maps that show interrelationships (including cause-and-effect) among various events during a particular period in history.

TABLE 14.1 (CONTINUED)

Grade Level	Examples of North Carolina's Grade-Specific Competency Goals for English Language Arts	Examples of More Specific Goals and Objectives You Might Write Related to the State Goals	Examples of Instructional Strategies That Address These Goals and Objectives *and* Informally Assess Students' Progress	Examples of Formal Assessments That Align with the Goals, Objectives, and Classroom Instruction
Grade 7	Respond to informational materials that are read, heard, and/or viewed by: • Monitoring comprehension for understanding of what is read, heard, and/or viewed • Analyzing the characteristics of informational works • Summarizing information • Determining the importance of information • Making connections to related topics/information • Drawing inferences and/or conclusions • Generating questions (Competency Goal 2.01)	Use the organizational structure of a science textbook to facilitate learning and studying its content.	Before students read a chapter in their science textbook, have them use its headings and subheadings to (a) create a general outline of the chapter and (b) generate questions they hope to answer as they read the chapter. Then, for homework, ask them to read and take notes on the chapter, using the outline and self-questions as guides for note taking.	Ask students to write a two-page summary of a chapter in their science book, using chapter headings and subheadings to organize their discussion.
	Analyze the purpose of the author or creator by: • Monitoring comprehension for understanding of what is read, heard, and/or viewed • Examining any bias, apparent or hidden messages, emotional factors, and/or propaganda techniques • Exploring and evaluating the underlying assumptions of the author/creator • Understanding the effects of the author's craft on the reader/viewer/listener (Competency Goal 4.01)	Identify persuasive techniques used in advertisements for commercial products in magazines and online websites.	Give students an advertisement for a self-improvement product (e.g., a diet pill or exercise equipment); have them work in small cooperative learning groups to (a) identify the advertiser's motives and (b) evaluate the quality of evidence for the product's effectiveness.	Have students examine an Internet website that promotes an allegedly health-promoting product. Ask them to identify, either orally or in writing, possible flaws in the evidence and logic the website uses to convince people to purchase the product.
Grade 11	Demonstrate the ability to read, listen to, and view a variety of increasingly complex print and non-print informational texts appropriate to grade level and course literary focus, by: • Selecting, monitoring, and modifying as necessary reading strategies appropriate to readers' purpose • Identifying and analyzing text components . . . and evaluating their impact on the text	Identify authors' political and cultural biases in their descriptions of current events.	Ask students to identify the unstated assumptions underlying two news magazines' depictions of the same event (e.g., an assumption that one group is good or right and another is bad or wrong).	Give students a magazine article describing a recent event in the national or international news. Ask them to underline five sentences that reveal the author's cultural and/or political biases and to describe those biases in a two-page essay.

Continues

TABLE 14.1 (CONTINUED)

Grade Level	Examples of North Carolina's Grade-Specific Competency Goals for English Language Arts	Examples of More Specific Goals and Objectives You Might Write Related to the State Goals	Examples of Instructional Strategies That Address These Goals and Objectives *and* Informally Assess Students' Progress	Examples of Formal Assessments That Align with the Goals, Objectives, and Classroom Instruction
Grade 11 (continued)	• Providing textual evidence to support understanding of and reader's response to text • Demonstrating comprehension of main ideas and supporting details • Summarizing key events and/or points from text • Making inferences, predicting, and drawing conclusions based on text • Identifying and analyzing personal, social, historical, or cultural influences, contexts, or biases . . . (portions of Competency Goal 2.03 for English III)			
	Assess the power, validity, and truthfulness in the logic of arguments given in public and political documents by: • Identifying the intent and message of the author or artist • Recognizing how the author addresses opposing viewpoints • Articulating a personal response to the message and method of the author or artist • Evaluating the historical significance of the work (Competency Goal 4.03 for English III)	Identify and evaluate methods of persuasion used in editorials in the news media.	• Describe common techniques in persuasive writing, and have students find them in newspaper editorials.	• Ask students to (a) identify five specific persuasive techniques used in the U.S. Declaration of Independence and (b) explain their particular purposes and probable effectiveness in the American colonies in 1776.

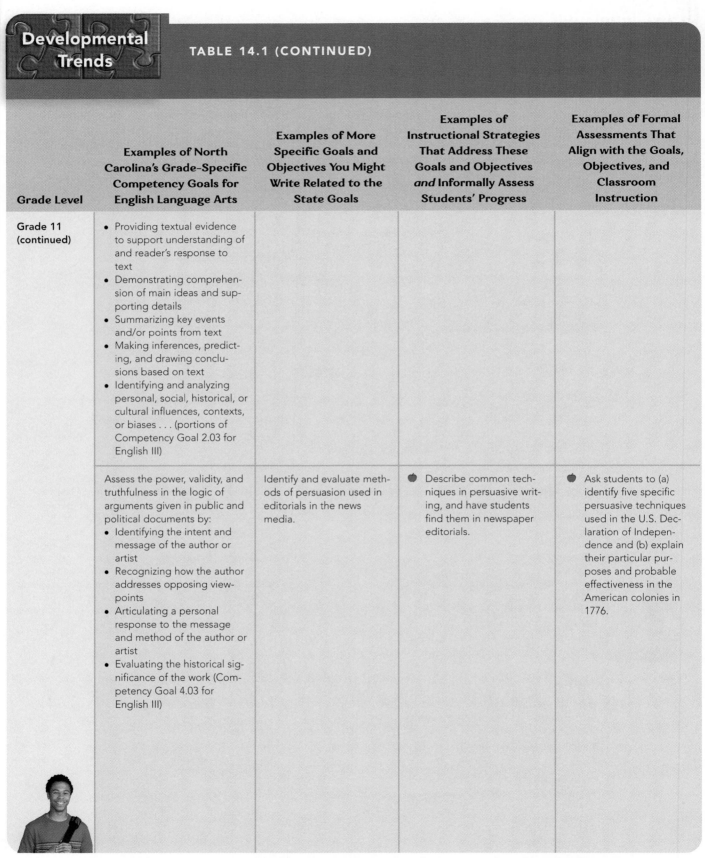

Source: Competency Goals (second column) are from a website maintained by North Carolina's Department of Public Instruction. Retrieved June 30, 2009, from www.dpi.state.nc.us/curriculum/languagearts/scos/. Please note that North Carolina is currently revising its Standard Course of Study; thus, the Competency Goals may change within the next few years.

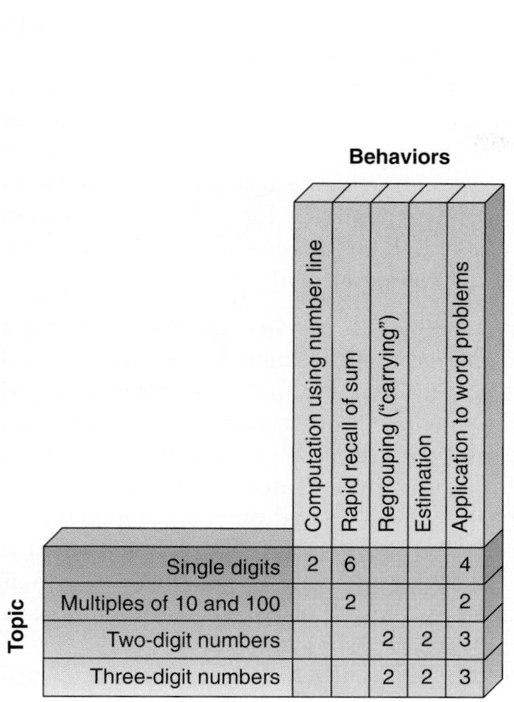

Topic	Computation using number line	Rapid recall of sum	Regrouping ("carrying")	Estimation	Application to word problems
Single digits	2	6			4
Multiples of 10 and 100		2			2
Two-digit numbers			2	2	3
Three-digit numbers			2	2	3

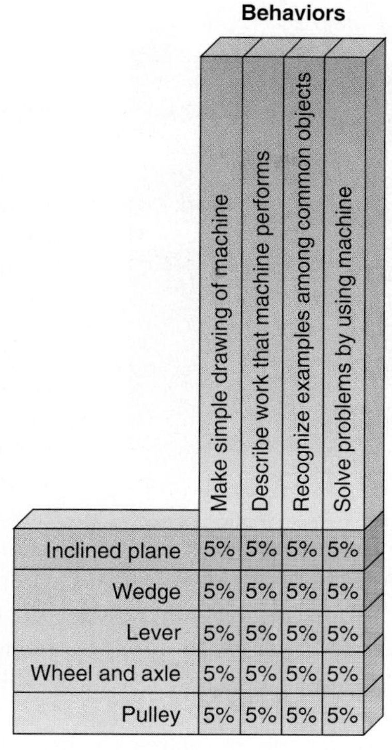

Topic	Make simple drawing of machine	Describe work that machine performs	Recognize examples among common objects	Solve problems by using machine
Inclined plane	5%	5%	5%	5%
Wedge	5%	5%	5%	5%
Lever	5%	5%	5%	5%
Wheel and axle	5%	5%	5%	5%
Pulley	5%	5%	5%	5%

FIGURE 14.5 Two examples of a table of specifications. *Left*: This table provides specifications for a 30-item paper–pencil test on addition. It assigns different weights (i.e., different numbers of items) to different topic–behavior combinations, with some combinations intentionally not being measured at all. *Right*: This table provides specifications for a combination paper–pencil and performance assessment on simple machines. It assigns equal importance (i.e., the same percentage of points) to each topic–behavior combination.

of each topic–behavior combination, perhaps as a particular number or percentage of tasks or test items to be included in the overall assessment. Figure 14.5 shows two examples: one for a paper–pencil test on addition and a second for a combined paper–pencil and performance assessment on simple machines. Once we have created a table of specifications, we can develop paper–pencil items or performance tasks that reflect both the topics and the behaviors we want to assess. And in doing so, we can have some confidence that our assessment instrument has content validity for the domain it's intended to represent.

To enhance the content validity of an assessment instrument, develop a table of specifications that can guide your selection of topics and tasks.

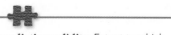

Content validity is important not only for teacher-developed assessments but also for any published achievement tests we use in our schools. Because these tests have already been constructed, we can follow the steps for ensuring content validity in reverse order. By looking at the items on the test, we can identify the topics covered and the behaviors required (e.g., recalling information, applying procedures, solving problems). Once again, we can construct a table of specifications, indicating the number of test items that fall in each cell.[3] We can then decide whether the table of specifications matches our curriculum closely enough that the test has content validity for our particular situation—that is, whether the test reflects what we actually have done in our classrooms.

Predictive Validity Shantel is thinking about a career in mathematics. But even though she's doing well in her eighth-grade math class, she worries that she will eventually have trouble with advanced courses in trigonometry and calculus. To get an idea of her chances for future math success, Shantel takes the Mathematics Aptitude Test (MAT) that her school counselor makes available to her. Shantel does quite well on the MAT, bolstering her confidence that she will succeed in a mathematics career. But does the MAT actually measure a student's potential for success as a mathematician? This is a question of **predictive validity**: the extent to which an assessment instrument accurately predicts future performance in some arena.

predictive validity Extent to which the results of an assessment predict future performance in a particular domain.

[3]Sometimes such a table appears in the test manual or can be obtained from the test publisher.

This teacher may be making inferences about her student's motivation to master basic writing skills. When we want to draw conclusions about underlying traits such as motivation, we must consider the *construct validity* of our assessment methods.

Publishers of standardized, norm-referenced ability tests often determine mathematically the accuracy with which test scores predict later success in certain domains (for details, see Appendix B). Keep in mind, however, that a test has no *single* predictive validity. Its validity in a given situation depends on the specific behavior being predicted, the age-group being tested (e.g., many tests have greater predictive validity for older students than for younger ones), and the amount of time between the test and the predicted performance.

Construct Validity In psychology, a *construct* is a hypothesized internal trait that cannot be directly observed but must instead be inferred from consistencies observed in people's behavior. *Motivation*, *self-efficacy*, and *intelligence* are all constructs; we can't actually *see* any of these things but must instead draw conclusions about them from what students do and don't do. For example, we might use our observations of students' on-task and off-task behavior to make inferences about their self-efficacy for various classroom topics and skills. Similarly, we might use tasks that ask students to reason abstractly to make inferences about their intelligence.

By **construct validity**, then, we mean the extent to which an assessment instrument actually measures an abstract, unobservable characteristic. Construct validity is of most concern when we're trying to draw general conclusions about students' traits and abilities so that we can better adapt instructional methods and materials to meet their individual needs. The problem with the Fathead Test of Intelligence (FTOI) I described earlier is one of poor construct validity: Despite its high reliability, the scores it yields have little—probably nothing—to do with intelligence.

How do we determine whether a test or other assessment instrument measures something we cannot see? Assessment experts have developed a variety of strategies for doing so. For instance, they might determine how well assessment results correlate with other measures of the same trait (e.g., do scores on one intelligence test correlate with scores on other IQ tests?). They might also find out whether older students perform better than younger students on instruments measuring traits that presumably increase with age (e.g., do 12-year-olds correctly answer more items on an intelligence test than 6-year-olds?). Or they might compare the performance of two groups that are known to be different with respect to the trait in question (e.g., do nondisabled 12-year-olds perform better on an intelligence test than 12-year-olds with intellectual disabilities?). When data from a variety of sources are consistent with what we would expect if the instrument was a measure of the characteristic in question, we conclude that it probably does have construct validity.

One principle that applies to all three forms of validity is this: *Virtually any assessment tool is more valid for some purposes than for others* (e.g., Kane, 2008). A mathematics achievement test may be a valid measure of how well students can solve paper–pencil arithmetic problems but a terrible measure of how well they can apply arithmetic to real-life situations. And a paper–pencil test on the rules of tennis may accurately assess students' knowledge of how many games are in a set, what *deuce* means, and so on, but it probably won't tell us much about how well students can actually play the game.

construct validity Extent to which an assessment accurately measures an unobservable educational or psychological characteristic.

practicality Extent to which an assessment instrument or procedure is inexpensive and easy to use and takes only a small amount of time to administer and score.

Practicality

The final RSVP characteristic is **practicality**, the extent to which assessment instruments and procedures are easy to use.[4] Practicality encompasses issues such as the following:

[4]Many psychologists use the term *usability*, but I think *practicality* better communicates this idea.

- How much time will it take to develop the questions and/or tasks to be administered?
- Can the assessment be administered to many students at once, or is one-on-one administration required?
- Are expensive materials involved?
- How much time will the assessment take away from instructional activities?
- How quickly and easily can students' performance be evaluated?

There is often a trade-off between practicality and characteristics such as validity and reliability. For example, a true–false test on tennis would be easier to construct and administer, but a performance assessment in which students actually demonstrated their tennis skills—even though it would take more time and energy—would undoubtedly be a more valid measure of how well students have mastered the game.

The four RSVP characteristics are summarized in Table 14.2. Of these, *validity is the most important:* We must use assessment techniques that validly assess students' achievement of instructional goals and objectives. Even so, it's important to note that *reliability is a necessary condition for validity.* Assessments can yield valid results only when they also yield consistent results—results that are only minimally affected by variations in administration, subjectivity in scoring, and so on. Reliability doesn't guarantee validity, however, as the earlier FTOI exercise illustrated. Standardization can enhance the reliability of assessment results and hence can indirectly enhance

Compare/ Contrast

TABLE 14.2
RSVP Characteristics of Good Assessment

Characteristic	Definition	Relevant Questions to Consider
Reliability	The extent to which an assessment instrument or procedure yields consistent results for each student	• How much are students' scores affected by temporary conditions unrelated to the characteristic being measured (*test–retest reliability*)? • Do different people score students' performance similarly (*scorer reliability*, also known as *interrater reliability*)? • Do different parts of a single assessment instrument lead to similar conclusions about a student's achievement (*internal consistency reliability*)? • Are all students assessed on identical or similar content?
Standardization	The extent to which assessment instruments and procedures are similar for all students	• Are all students asked to perform the same types of tasks? • Is everyone given the same instructions? • Do all students have the same time limit? • Is everyone's performance evaluated using the same criteria?
Validity	The extent to which an assessment instrument or procedure measures what it's intended to measure and enables appropriate inferences to be made	• Does the assessment tap a representative sample of the content domain being assessed (*content validity*)? • Do students' scores predict their later success in a domain (*predictive validity*)? • Does the instrument measure a particular psychological or educational characteristic (*construct validity*)?
Practicality	The extent to which an assessment instrument or procedure is easy and inexpensive to use	• How much class time does the assessment take to administer? • How quickly and easily can students' responses be scored? • Is special training required to administer or score the assessment? • Does the assessment require specialized materials that must be purchased?

validity. Practicality should be a consideration only when validity, reliability, and standardization aren't seriously jeopardized.

Informal Assessment

From our daily observations of students' classroom behaviors, we can discover a great deal about what students have and have not learned, enabling us to make reasonable decisions about how future instruction should proceed. For example, we can do the following:

- Ask questions during a lesson (see the Into the Classroom feature "Asking Questions to Assess Learning and Achievement Informally").
- Listen to what and how much students contribute to whole-class and small-group discussions; make note of the kinds of questions they ask.
- Have students write daily or weekly entries in personal journals.
- Observe how well students perform physical tasks.
- Identify the kinds of activities in which students engage voluntarily.
- Watch for body language that may reflect students' feelings about particular classroom tasks.
- Observe students' interactions with peers in class, at lunch, and on the playground.
- Look at the relative frequency of on-task and off-task behaviors; look for patterns in when students are off task.

Informal assessment has several advantages. First and foremost, it offers continuing feedback about the effectiveness of the day's instructional tasks and activities. Second, it's easily adjusted at a moment's notice; for example, when students reveal misconceptions about a particular topic, we can ask follow-up questions that probe

INTO THE Classroom

Asking Questions to Assess Learning and Achievement Informally

- **Direct questions to the entire class, not just to a few students who seem eager to respond.**

The girls in a high school science class rarely volunteer when their teacher asks questions. Although the teacher often calls on students who raise their hands, he occasionally calls on those who do not, and he makes sure that he calls on *every* student at least once a week.

- **When a question has only a few possible answers, have students vote on the particular answers they think are correct.**

When beginning a lesson on dividing one fraction by another, a middle school math teacher writes this problem on the chalkboard:

$3/4 \div 1/2 = ?$

She asks, "Before we talk about how we solve this problem, how many of you think the answer will be less than 1? How many think it will be greater than 1? How many think it will be exactly 1?" She tallies the number of hands that go up after each question and then says, "Hmmm, most of you think the answer will be less than 1. Let's look at how we solve a problem like this. Then each of you will know whether you were right or wrong."

- **Ask follow-up questions to probe students' reasoning.**

In a geography lesson on Canada, a fourth-grade teacher points to the St. Lawrence River on a map and asks, "Which way does the water flow: toward the ocean or away from it?" One student shouts out, "Away from it." "Why do you think so?" the teacher asks. The student's explanation reveals a common misconception: that rivers can flow only from north to south, never vice versa.

their beliefs and reasoning processes. Third, informal assessment provides information that may either support or call into question the data we obtain from more formal assessments such as paper–pencil tests; for instance, it might provide more optimistic assessments of English language learners. Finally, ongoing observations of students' behaviors provide clues about social, emotional, and motivational factors affecting students' classroom performance and may often be the only practical means through which we can assess such goals as "Shows courtesy" and "Enjoys reading." In the portfolio excerpt shown in Figure 14.6, a kindergarten teacher describes 6-year-old Meghan's progress in work habits and social skills—areas that the teacher can probably assess only through informal observation.

FIGURE 14.6 This page from 6-year-old Meghan's kindergarten portfolio shows her teacher's assessment of her work habits and social skills.

Group Participation and Work Habits

- **Demonstrates attentiveness as a listener through body language or facial expressions-** Meghan is still developing this skill. Sometimes it is difficult for her to listen when she is sitting near her friends.
- **Follows directions.**
- **Enters ongoing discussion on the subject.** -Sometimes needs to be encouraged to share her ideas.
- **Makes relevant contributions to ongoing activities.**
- **Completes assigned activities.** -Meghan is very responsible about her assignments.
- **Shows courtesy in conversations and discussions by waiting for turn to speak.**

Meghan enjoys lunch with her friends.

RSVP Characteristics of Informal Assessment

When we get information about students' characteristics and achievements through informal means, we must be aware of the strengths and limitations of this approach with respect to reliability, standardization, validity, and practicality.

Reliability Most informal assessments are quite short, and such snippets of students' behavior aren't always reliable indicators of their overall accomplishments and dispositions. Perhaps we happen to ask Manuel the *only* question to which he doesn't know the answer. Perhaps we happen to notice Naomi being off task during the *only* time she is off task. Perhaps we misinterpret something Jacquie says after school. When we use informal assessment to draw conclusions about what students know and can do, we should base our conclusions on many observations over a long period. And given the fact that our long-term memories can never be totally accurate, dependable records of our observations (see Chapter 6), we should keep ongoing, written records of what we see and hear (M. D. Miller, Linn & Gronlund, 2009; Stiggins, 2008).

> Don't take any single observation of a student's behavior too seriously; instead, look for patterns of behavior over time.

> Keep a written record of what students say and do, especially if final assessments will depend heavily on in-class observations.

Standardization Our informal assessments will rarely, if ever, be standardized; for example, we will ask different questions of different students, and we will probably observe each student's behavior in different contexts. Hence, such assessments will definitely *not* give us the same information for each student. In most cases, then, we cannot make legitimate comparisons among students merely on the basis of a few casual observations.

Validity Even when students' behavior is consistent over time, it won't always give us accurate data about what students know and can do. For instance, Tom may intentionally answer questions incorrectly so that he doesn't come across as a know-it-all, and Margot may be reluctant to say anything because of a chronic stuttering problem. In general, when we use in-class questions to assess students' learning, we must keep in mind that some students—especially females and students from certain ethnic minority groups—will be less eager to respond than others (B. Kerr, 1991; Rogoff, 2003; Sadker & Sadker, 1994; also see Chapter 4).

Our personal biases and expectations also come into play in informal assessments (Farwell & Weiner, 1996; Ritts, Patterson, & Tubbs, 1992; Stiggins, 2008). As we discovered in our discussion of knowledge construction in Chapter 7, we human beings typically impose meanings on what we see and hear based on the things we already know or believe to be true. For instance, we are likely to expect academic or social competence from students we like or admire and thus perceive their actions in an overly positive light—a phenomenon known as the **halo effect**. In much the same way, we might expect inappropriate behavior from students with a history of misbehavior, and our observations might be biased accordingly—a phenomenon aptly called the **horns effect**.

halo effect Phenomenon in which people are more likely to perceive positive behaviors in someone they like or admire.

horns effect Phenomenon in which people are more likely to perceive negative behaviors in someone for whom they have little affection or respect.

In addition, as noted in Chapter 11, teachers' expectations for students are sometimes influenced by students' ethnic backgrounds or socioeconomic status, and such expectations may unfairly bias judgments of students' performance. In one experimental study (Darley & Gross, 1983), college students were told that they were participating in a study on teacher evaluation methods and then shown a videotape of a fourth grader named Hannah. Two versions of the videotape gave differing impressions about Hannah's socioeconomic status: Her clothing, the kind of playground on which she played, and information about her parents' occupations indirectly conveyed to some students that she was from a high socioeconomic background and to others that she was from a low socioeconomic background. All students watched Hannah taking an oral achievement test (on which she performed at grade level) and were asked to rate her on several characteristics. Students who had been led to believe that Hannah came from a wealthy family rated her ability well above grade level, whereas students believing that she came from a poor family evaluated her as being below grade level. The two groups of students also rated Hannah's work habits, motivation, social skills, and general maturity differently.

Ask yourself whether your existing beliefs and expectations might be biasing your interpretations of students' performance.

Practicality The greatest strength of informal assessment is its practicality. It involves little or none of our time either before or after the fact (except when we keep written records of our observations). It is also quite flexible: We can adjust our assessment procedures on the spot as circumstances change.

Despite informal assessment's practicality, we have noted serious problems regarding its reliability, standardization, and validity. Hence, we should treat any conclusions we draw only as *hypotheses* that we must either confirm or disconfirm through other means. In the end, we must rely more heavily on formal assessment techniques to determine whether our students have achieved instructional goals and met content area standards.

Treat the conclusions you draw from informal assessment as hypotheses that need confirmation through more formal means.

Paper–Pencil Assessment

When we need to conduct a formal assessment, paper–pencil assessment is typically easier and faster—and thus has greater practicality—than performance assessment. Questions that require brief responses—such as short-answer, matching, true–false, and multiple-choice—are often suitable for assessing students' knowledge of single, isolated facts. Paper–pencil tasks that require extended responses—essays, for instance—lend themselves more easily to assessing such higher-level skills as problem solving, critical thinking, and synthesis of ideas. However, item type alone doesn't tell us whether we are assessing lower-level or higher-level skills. For example, we can construct multiple-choice items that assess higher-level skills, as the following item for a physics test illustrates:

> An inventor has just designed a new device for cutting paper. Without knowing anything else about his invention, you can reasonably guess that it is which type of machine?
>
> a. A lever

Think creatively about possible paper–pencil tasks that require higher-level thinking skills.

b. A movable pulley
c. An inclined plane
d. A wedge
(The correct answer is *d.*)

With a little ingenuity, we can even develop paper–pencil tasks that assess students' ability to apply classroom subject matter to real-world tasks, as illustrated in Figure 14.7.

One important consideration in designing paper–pencil assessments is whether to use recognition tasks, recall tasks, or a combination of the two. A **recognition task** (e.g., a multiple-choice, true–false, or matching question) asks students to identify a correct answer within the context of incorrect statements or irrelevant information. In contrast, a **recall task** (e.g., a short-answer question, essay, or word problem) requires students to generate the correct answer themselves.

recognition task Memory task in which one must identify correct information among incorrect statements or irrelevant information.

recall task Memory task in which one must retrieve information from long-term memory with only minimal retrieval cues.

Recognition items have two major advantages. First, we can include a relatively large number of questions in a single assessment, enabling us to tap into a large, representative sample of an instructional unit and hence potentially increasing content validity. In addition, we can score students' responses quickly and consistently, thus addressing our need for practicality and reliability. However, recognition tasks tend to overestimate achievement: Students can sometimes guess correctly when they don't know the material very well.

When our instructional goal involves retrieving knowledge and skills *without* the benefit of seeing the correct answer within the context of distracting information—and especially when we want to examine students' reasoning processes—recall tasks generally have greater validity than recognition tasks. Also, students tend to study classroom material more thoroughly when they're preparing for recall test questions, and they remember the material better (D'Ydewalle, Swerts, & De Corte, 1983; Roediger & Karpicke, 2006; G. Warren, 1979). But because students may require considerable time to respond to each recall item, we will be able to present fewer items in a single assessment session (adversely affecting reliability) and will tap a more limited sample of the content domain (potentially affecting content validity). In addition, we will typically take longer to score such items (a practicality issue) and will make more errors in scoring them (another reliability issue).

Use recognition tasks to assess students' ability to identify facts, especially when the content domain is large. Use recall tasks when it's important to assess students' ability to retrieve information on their own. Consider combining both kinds of tasks into a single assessment instrument.

FIGURE 14.7 Example of a paper–pencil assessment task that requires students to apply classroom subject matter to a real-world situation

You are to play the role of an advisor to President Nixon after his election to office in 1968. As his advisor, you are to make a recommendation about the United States' involvement in Vietnam.

Your paper is to be organized around three main parts: An introduction that shows an understanding of the Vietnam War up to this point by explaining who is involved in the war and what their objectives are; also in the Introduction, you are to state a recommendation in one or two sentences to make the advice clear.

The body of the paper should be written to convince the President to follow your advice by discussing: (a) the pros of the advice, including statistics, dates, examples, and general information; . . . (b) the cons of the advice, letting the President know that the advisor is aware of how others might disagree. Anticipate one or two recommendations that others might give, and explain why they are not the best advice.

The conclusion makes a final appeal for the recommendation and sells the President on the advice.

Source: From Newman, 1997, p. 368.

Constructing the Assessment Instrument

Experts have offered numerous suggestions for constructing paper–pencil assessment items.

True–False and Other Alternative-Response Items An *alternative-response item* is one for which there are only two or three possible answers (e.g., *true* versus *false*, *fact* versus *opinion*). Although such items are typically used to assess knowledge of discrete facts, they can also be used for assessing certain higher-level skills (M. D. Miller et al., 2009). The items that follow illustrate an alternative-response format for assessing students' ability to identify cause-and-effect relationships in science:

In each of the following statements, both parts of the statement are true. You are to decide whether the second part explains why the first part is true. If it does, circle Yes. If it does not, circle No.

Yes (No) 1. Leaves are essential *because* they shade the tree trunk.

Yes (No) 2. Whales are mammals *because* they are large.

(Yes) No 3. Some plants do not need sunlight *because* they get their food from other plants. (M. D. Miller et al., 2009, p. 181)

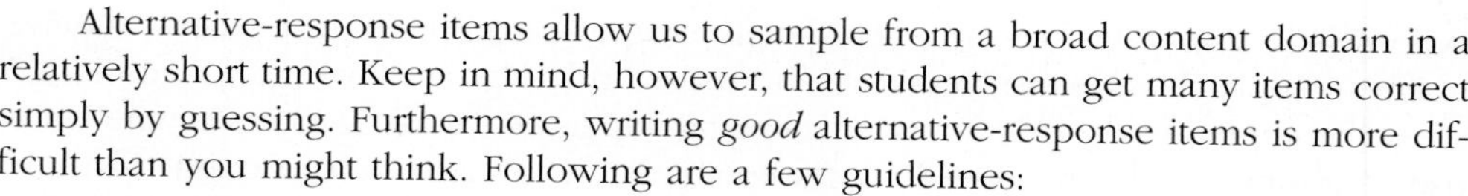

Alternative-response items allow us to sample from a broad content domain in a relatively short time. Keep in mind, however, that students can get many items correct simply by guessing. Furthermore, writing *good* alternative-response items is more difficult than you might think. Following are a few guidelines:

- ***Rephrase ideas; don't present them word for word from a textbook.*** Students are more likely to engage in meaningful learning as they study if they know that we will be assessing true understanding, rather than rote memorization.

- ***Write statements that clearly reflect one alternative or the other (e.g., statements that are clearly true or false).*** Knowledgeable students should be able to respond to each item with certainty; there should be nothing partly-right-and-partly-wrong about them. When items contain words with imprecise meanings (e.g., *sometimes, often*), even the best students may occasionally resort to random guessing, adversely affecting test reliability.

- ***Avoid excessive use of negatives, especially for false statements.*** Consider these true–false items:

  The south poles of two magnets don't repel each other.

  In the history of human civilization, the beginning of animal domestication was unrelated to human settlement patterns.

Did the negatives (i.e., the *don't* in the first item and the *un-* in the second one) confuse you? Negative words and prefixes in true–false items (e.g., *not, never, un-*) often lead to confusion, especially when the statements themselves are false. (Both of the items just presented are false.)

Matching Items A *matching item* presents two columns of information; students must match each item in the first column with an appropriate item in the second. Matching items lend themselves most readily to ideas that can be easily paired—words and their meanings, countries and their capitals, and so on. Following are two guidelines to keep in mind when constructing such items:

- ***Keep the items in each column homogeneous.*** Consider this matching task from a test about World War II:

Match each item on the right with its description on the left:

a. German battleship that sank numerous British ships	1. George Patton
b. Year in which the Japanese attacked Pearl Harbor	2. *Graf Spee*
c. Country invaded by Germany in 1939	3. Poland
d. General who led U.S. troops into Italy	4. 1941

Because each column contains only one person, one country, one year, and one name-of-something in italics, the correct responses are easy to deduce. A better item would be one in which the items in each column are members of the same category—perhaps all dates, generals, capital cities, or definitions.

- ***Have more items in one column than in the other, and include the option of using some items more than once.*** When a matching item involves the same number of items in both columns, with each item in column A matching one and only one item in column B, students can use a process of elimination to identify the matched pairs they don't otherwise know. The following test question prevents this elimination strategy:

> Match each function with the component of the digestive system where it occurs. Items on the right can be used more than once.
>
> | | |
> |---|---|
> | 1. Production of enzyme secreted to the mouth | a. Colon |
> | 2. Mixing of food with digestive enzymes | b. Gall bladder |
> | 3. Production of bile | c. Stomach |
> | 4. Production of insulin | d. Salivary glands |
> | 5. Storage place for food | e. Liver |
> | | f. Large intestine |
> | | g. Pancreas |

Alternative *c*, "Stomach" is the correct choice for both 2 and 5, and three items on the right aren't correct responses at all.

Multiple-Choice Items A *multiple-choice item* consists of a question or incomplete statement (the *stem*) followed by several alternatives. In most cases, only one alternative correctly answers the question or completes the statement; the other (incorrect) alternatives are *distractors*.

Of the various recognition items we might use, most assessment experts recommend multiple-choice items for two reasons. First, the number of items students can answer correctly simply by guessing is relatively low, especially in comparison with true–false and other alternative-response items. (When multiple-choice items have four possible answers, students can get only about 25% of them correct through guessing alone.) Second, of all the recognition-item types, the multiple-choice format lends itself most readily to measuring higher-level thinking skills.

Following are several guidelines to keep in mind when writing multiple-choice items:

> **myeducationlab**
>
> Find many examples of multiple-choice items that assess higher-level skills (e.g., transferring concepts to new situations) in the Self-Check Quizzes in MyEducationLab. (To find these quizzes, go to any chapter of the Book-Specific Resources, click on *Study Plan*, and select *Self-Check Quiz*.)

Present distractors that will be clearly wrong to students who know the material but plausible to students who haven't mastered it. For example, imagine that students have been told that a *manacle* is "a device used to restrain a person's hands or wrists." They later see the following item on a vocabulary test:

> Which one of the following words or phrases is closest in meaning to the word *manacle*?
>
> a. Handcuffs
>
> b. Out of control
>
> c. Eyeglass correcting the vision of a single eye
>
> d. Saltwater creature that clings to hard surfaces

Students who haven't learned the true meaning of *manacle* (Alternative *a*) might think the word is somehow related to *mania* (and hence choose Alternative *b*) or might mistake it for *monocle* (Alternative *c*) or *barnacle* (Alternative *d*).

Avoid using negatives in both the stem and the alternatives. Having negatives such as *not* and *don't* in two places at once amounts to a double negative, which students may have trouble interpreting. Consider the following question for an educational psychology course:

> Which one of the following is *not* a characteristic of most gifted children (in comparison with their classmates)?
>
> a. They are not as old.
>
> b. They are physically uncoordinated.

Developing paper–pencil items that reflect important instructional goals often takes considerable thought and creativity.

c. They do not feel uncomfortable in social situations.
d. They do not perform poorly on standardized achievement tests.

Confused? It's difficult to sort through all the *not* and *un-* language to determine which three statements are true and which one is false. The answer is *b:* Contrary to a popular stereotype, students who are gifted are, on average, just as coordinated as their nongifted peers.

Use "all of the above" or "none of the above" seldom, if at all. In writing multiple-choice items, novice teachers often list three correct answers and then add "all of the above" as the fourth choice. Students quickly figure this out: When in doubt, they think, choose "all of the above." Furthermore, when we tell students to choose the "best" or "most accurate" answer and then give them "all of the above" or "none of the above" as an alternative, they may understandably become confused about how to respond.

Avoid giving logical clues about the correct answer. To get a sense of how a student might use simple logic to answer a multiple-choice question, try the following exercise.

EXPERIENCING FIRSTHAND

Califractions

Imagine that you are enrolled in Professor Carberry's psychoceramics course. Early in the semester, before you've had a chance to read the assigned chapter, Professor Carberry gives you a surprise quiz on califractions. Below are the first three quiz items; there is only one correct answer for each:

1. Because they are furstier than other califractions, califors are most often used to
   a. Reassignment of matherugs
   b. Disbobble a fwing
   c. Mangelation
   d. In the burfews
2. Calendation is a process of
   a. Combining two califors
   b. Adding two califors together
   c. Joining two califors
   d. Taking two califors apart
3. The furstiest califraction is the
   a. Califor
   b. Calderost
   c. Calinga
   d. Calidater

You could possibly answer all three questions without knowing anything about califractions. Because Item 1 says "califors are most often used to," the answer must begin with a verb and so must be Alternative *b* (Alternatives *a* and *c* begin with nouns—*reassignment* and *mangelation*—and *d* begins with a preposition). Item 2 includes three similar-meaning alternatives (*a, b, c*); because the item can have only one right answer, the correct choice must be *d.* And the answer to Item 3 (the "furstiest califraction") must be *a,* because Item 1 has already told you that califors are furstier than other califractions.

Following are several ways to minimize clues about correct answers in multiple-choice items:

- Make all alternatives grammatically consistent with the stem, so that each one forms a complete sentence when combined with the stem.
- Make all alternatives distinctly different in meaning.
- Don't present information in one item that gives away the answer to another.
- Make all alternatives equally long and precise. (Novice test writers tend to make the correct alternative longer and more specific than the distractors.)

Short-Answer and Completion Items A *short-answer item* poses a question to be answered with a single word or number, a phrase, or a couple of sentences. A *completion item* presents a sentence with a blank for students to fill in. Both formats require recall rather than recognition but lend themselves most readily to assessing lower-level skills. In addition, scoring students' responses becomes more subjective, thereby decreasing reliability. Following are two guidelines to keep in mind when writing short-answer and completion items:

Specify the type of response required. Consider this item from a middle school science test:

> Explain why it is colder in winter than in summer.

A student could conceivably write several paragraphs on this topic. Fortunately, the teacher who wrote the item had given students some guidance about how to respond to it and the other short-answer items on her test:

> Provide a short answer (1–2 sentences) for each of the following questions. You must use complete and clearly stated sentences. Please use part of the question to introduce your response.

For completion items, include only one or two blanks per item. Several blanks in a single item can make the item difficult or impossible to interpret. To see what I mean, try filling in the blanks in this statement about material presented earlier in the chapter:

> Constructing an assessment instrument with high _____ can be accomplished by developing a _____ that describes both the _____ and the _____.

There are so many blanks that it's hard to know what information is being called for. (The answers I had in mind are "content validity," "table of specifications," "topic to be covered," and "student behaviors related to each topic," or words to that effect.)

Problems and Interpretive Exercises In a *problem*, students must manipulate or synthesize data and develop a solution to a new problem situation. In an *interpretive exercise*, students are given new material (e.g., a table, graph, map, or section of text) and asked to analyze and draw conclusions from it.[5] Problems and interpretive exercises often involve higher-level thinking skills (e.g., analysis, synthesis, critical thinking) and are especially suitable for assessing students' ability to transfer what they've learned to new situations (e.g., see Figure 14.8). The following two guidelines apply to both problems and interpretive exercises:

Use new examples and situations. When you present problems or interpretive material that students have already encountered, students may respond correctly simply because they've memorized the answers. We can truly assess transfer only when we ask students to apply what they've learned to a novel context.

---

[5]You can sometimes use true–false or multiple-choice questions in interpretive exercises, enabling greater reliability and practicality in scoring (M. D. Miller et al., 2009).

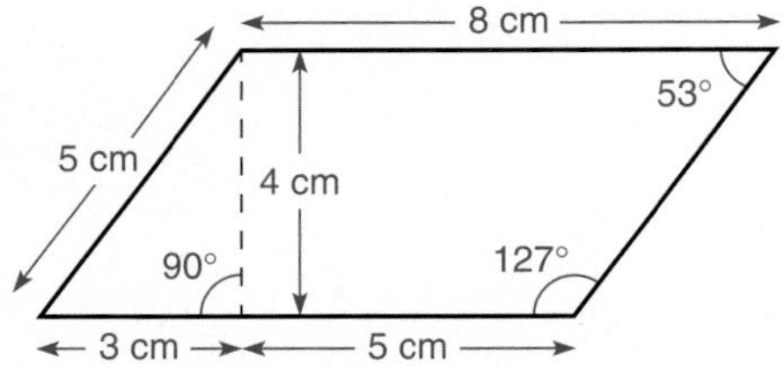

Include irrelevant information. At some point in your schooling, you almost certainly learned how to calculate the area of a parallelogram. If you did, calculate the area of the parallelogram shown in the margin. If you can recall the formula (Area = Base × Height), you should easily arrive at the answer (8 × 4, or 32 square cm). But if you've forgotten the procedure, you might be led astray by some of the information the figure provides.

Our purpose in adding extraneous information isn't to make a problem or exercise more difficult but rather to make it as similar as possible to a real-life situation. The outside world typically presents a lot of information that has little or nothing to do with the task at hand, and students must ultimately be able to determine what is relevant.

FIGURE 14.8 An interpretive exercise that asks students to apply what they've learned in geography to a new situation

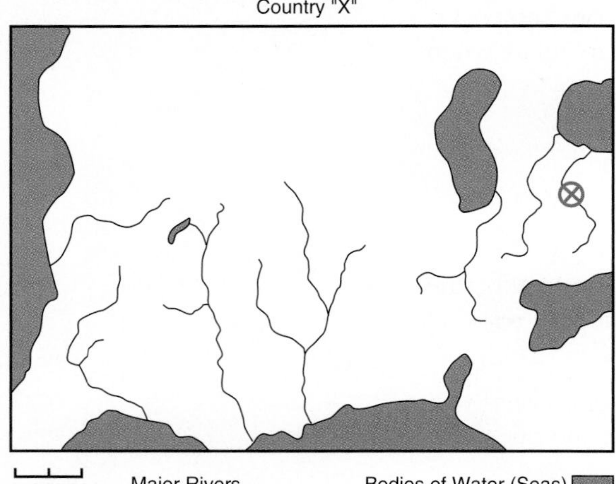

- If people living at the point marked "X" on the map began to migrate *or* expand, where would they go and what direction might they take?
- What would be the distribution of population in country "X"; that is, where would many people live, few, and so on?
- Where would large cities develop in country "X"?
- How would you judge the country's economic potential; that is, what areas might be best for development, which worst, and so on?

Source: Questions and figure are from *Teaching Creatively: Learning Through Discovery* by B. G. Massialas and J. Zevin, 1983, pp. 121, 127, Malabar, FL: Krieger. Reprinted by permission.

Essay Tasks An *essay task* requires a lengthy verbal response—at least a paragraph and perhaps as much as several pages. Essays are especially useful when we want students to show their writing ability or demonstrate higher-level thinking skills (e.g., to analyze a piece of literature or to compare and contrast two points of view) in a written format.

Essay items have two serious limitations, however. First, students can respond to only a small number of questions in a single assessment, limiting sampling of the content domain and hence limiting content validity. Second, scoring essays is time consuming and subjective (thus somewhat unreliable), especially when the questions require lengthy, relatively unstructured responses. Several guidelines can help to maximize the information obtained from students' essays while simultaneously ensuring reasonable validity and reliability:

Combine lengthy essay items with other items that require less time. Assessments consisting of only one or two lengthy essay questions rarely reflect a representative sample of a content domain, and errors in scoring can seriously impact students' overall scores. In most situations, then, we should probably use one of two approaches: (a) present several shorter essay questions or (b) combine one or two lengthy essays with other item types that can be answered quickly and easily.

Provide a structure for responding. Consider this essay question in an American history class:

> List three causes of the American Revolution.

One student might take the word *list* literally and simply write "Stamp Act, Boston Massacre, Quartering Act." But another student might write several pages describing Britain's increasing restriction of navigation, the colonists' resentment of taxation without representation, and King George III's apparent lack of concern about the colonists' welfare. Students' responses to unstructured tasks may go in so many different directions that scoring them consistently and reliably is virtually impossible. Especially in situations in which a great deal of material is potentially relevant, students need some guidance about the length and completeness of desired responses and about the things they should specifically address. For example, to assess what students have learned about the causes of the American Revolution, we might give them this task:

> Identify three policies or events during the 1760s and/or 1770s that contributed to the outbreak of the American Revolution. For each one, explain in three to five sentences how it increased tension between England and the American colonies.

Having students use reference materials during a formal assessment is quite appropriate if instructional goals focus on the ability to find and apply rather than simply recall information.

Ask questions with answers that can clearly be scored as correct or incorrect. Consider this essay question:

> How might you address the problem of the world's diminishing rainforests?

The question asks for students' opinions, which will be difficult to score as right or wrong. However, we don't necessarily have to limit our essay questions to those with only one correct answer. Consider this revision of the rainforest question:

> Develop and explain a possible solution to the problem of the world's diminishing rainforests. Show how your solution addresses at least two of the economic, social, or political factors contributing to rainforest devastation.

Students' responses can be judged on how well their proposed solutions address factors that contribute to deforestation—factors that were presumably discussed in class or presented in the textbook.

General Guidelines for Constructing Paper–Pencil Assessments Several general guidelines apply to constructing virtually any paper–pencil assessment instrument:

Define tasks clearly and unambiguously. Regardless of whether students know how to respond to assessment tasks, they should at least understand what we are asking them to do.

Consider giving students access to certain reference materials. In some cases, we may want students to have only one resource—their own long-term memories—as they carry out an assessment activity. But in others, it may be appropriate to let them use reference materials (perhaps a dictionary, atlas, or magazine article) as they work. An assessment task in which reference materials are allowed is especially appropriate when our objective is for students to locate, use, or analyze information rather than memorize it.

Identify scoring criteria in advance. We should identify correct responses—or at least the components of a good response—at the same time we develop our assessment tasks. In most cases we should also share our scoring criteria with students; doing so gives them guidance in how best to prepare and maximize their performance. Furthermore, we should develop policies to guide scoring when students give partially correct answers, respond correctly but include additional *in*correct information, or write responses with numerous grammatical and spelling errors.

Place shorter and easier items before more challenging ones. Some students approach paper–pencil tests strategically, answering quick and easy items first, regardless of the order in which the items are sequenced. But others address items in the order they appear, sometimes spending so much time on one item (e.g., a lengthy essay) that they leave little time to tackle other, shorter ones. By beginning an assessment with short, relatively easy items, we put students at ease and ensure that they show us something of what they know before they get bogged down in an especially challenging task (Gronlund & Waugh, 2009).

Set parameters for students' responses. Obviously, students can't read our minds about how we want them to respond to paper–pencil items. In addition to constructing the items themselves, then, we should provide information about the following:

- *Time limits*—for example, how long students should spend on each item and whether they have a fixed time in which to complete the overall assessment

myeducationlab

Subtracting points for wrong answers is controversial, as you can learn in the supplementary reading "Correcting for Guessing in Paper–Pencil Assessments." (To find this reading, go to Chapter 14 of the Book-Specific Resources in MyEducationLab, and then select *Supplementary Readings*.)

- *Nature of desired responses*—for example, whether students should choose a single best answer for each multiple-choice question or instead mark all correct alternatives
- *Method of recording responses*—for example, whether students should indicate their answers on the instrument itself or on a separate answer sheet
- *Acceptability of guessing*—for example, whether students should guess if they're not sure of an answer or will be penalized for wrong answers

Administering the Assessment

The validity of a classroom assessment instrument depends not only on how we have constructed the instrument but also on how we administer it. Following are three strategies that should increase the validity of our results when we administer a paper–pencil assessment:

Provide a quiet and comfortable environment. Students are more likely to perform at their best when they have adequate lighting, reasonable work space, and minimal distractions. Such comfort factors may be especially important for students who are easily distracted, unaccustomed to formal assessments, or uninterested in exerting much effort—for instance, students who are at risk for academic failure and dropping out of school (Popham, 1990).

Encourage students to ask questions when tasks aren't clear. Despite our best intentions, we may sometimes present assessment tasks that are ambiguous or misleading. Thus, we should encourage students to seek clarification whenever they are uncertain about what we're asking them to do. Such encouragement is especially important for students from ethnic minority groups, many of whom may be reluctant to ask questions during formal assessments (L. R. Cheng, 1987).

myeducationlab

Learn more about factors affecting high school students' decisions to cheat or not to cheat by completing the Understanding Research exercise "Cheating in High School Students" in MyEducationLab. (To find this activity, go to the topic Assessment in MyEducationLab, click on *Assignments and Activities*, and then select *Understanding Research*.)

Take reasonable steps to discourage cheating. The prevalence of cheating increases as students get older, and by high school the great majority of students are apt to cheat at one time or another (Cizek, 2003). Students cheat for a variety of reasons. Some may be more interested in doing well on an assessment than in actually learning the subject matter; for them, performance goals predominate over mastery goals. Others may believe that teachers' or parents' expectations for their performance are so high as to be unattainable and that success is out of their control unless they *do* cheat. In addition, students may perceive certain assessments (tests especially) to be poorly constructed, arbitrarily graded, or in some other way a poor reflection of what they have learned. Often, too, peers may communicate through words or actions that cheating is quite acceptable (Cizek, 2003; Danner, 2008; E. D. Evans & Craig, 1990; Murdock & Anderman, 2006).

When students cheat on assessments, their scores don't accurately reflect what they know and can do—hence, the scores have little or no validity. Furthermore, cheating can be habit forming if students discover that it enables them to get good grades with minimal effort (Cizek, 2003). The best approach is prevention—making sure students don't cheat in the first place—through strategies such as these:

In the weeks or days before the assessment

- Focus students' attention on mastery goals rather than performance goals.
- Make success without cheating a realistic possibility.
- Construct assessment instruments with obvious validity for important instructional goals.
- Create two or more instruments that are equivalent in form and content but have different answers (e.g., arrange the same set of multiple-choice questions in two different orders).
- Explain exactly what cheating is and why it is unacceptable.
- Describe the consequence you will impose for cheating.

During the assessment

- Have teacher-assigned seats during any assessments that require individual (rather than group) work.
- Seat students as far away from one another as possible.
- Remain attentive to what students are doing throughout the assessment session but without hovering over particular students.

If, despite reasonable precautions, cheating does occur, we must administer the consequence we have previously described. This consequence should be severe enough to discourage a student from cheating again yet not so severe that the student's motivation and chances for academic success are affected over the long run. (I typically require a student to redo the task, usually for less credit than he or she would have earned otherwise.) Students' final grades should ultimately reflect what they have and have not learned, however. For this reason, one expert (Stiggins, 2008) recommends that the consequence for cheating *not* be a failing grade for an entire course in which a student has, in other graded assignments, demonstrated mastery of the subject matter.

Identify an appropriate consequence for cheating—one severe enough to discourage cheating yet not so severe that it undermines motivation. Alert students to this consequence and administer it consistently when cheating occurs.

Scoring Students' Responses

As we evaluate students' performance on an assessment task, we must continue to be concerned about the four RSVP characteristics. Furthermore, we must keep in mind that our most important goal isn't to evaluate but rather to *help students learn.* Each of the following strategies is valuable in achieving one or both of these ends:

Specify scoring criteria in concrete terms. Whenever scoring involves making a subjective judgment of a complex performance—for instance, when it involves evaluating a lengthy essay or lab report—we should list the components that a correct response must include or the characteristics we will consider as we judge it. Such a list is sometimes called a **rubric**. Figure 14.9 shows a simple rubric that one fourth-grade teacher uses for scoring students' performance on mathematics word problems. Notice that she provides spaces for both herself and the student to evaluate the performance (more about students' self-assessments later). Notice, too, that the rubric includes qualitative, subjectively scorable criteria (e.g., neatness of work, explanation of the problem solution) as well as more objectively scorable criteria (e.g., the correct answer).

FIGURE 14.9 In this rubric for scoring solutions to mathematics word problems in a fourth-grade class, both teacher and student evaluate various aspects of the student's performance.

Elements	Possible Points	Points Earned: Self	Points Earned: Teacher
1. You highlighted the question(s) to solve.	2	___	___
2. You picked an appropriate strategy.	2	___	___
3. Work is neat and organized.	2	___	___
4. Calculations are accurate.	2	___	___
5. Question(s) answered.	2	___	___
6. You have explained in words how you solved the problem.	5	___	___
Total	___	___	___

Unless specifically assessing writing skills, score grammar and spelling separately from the content of students' responses to the extent possible. This recommendation is especially important when assessing students with limited writing skills, such as English language learners and students with disabilities (Hamp-Lyons, 1992; Scarcella, 1990).

Before beginning to score, skim a few students' responses, looking for unanticipated responses and revising the criteria if necessary. As a general rule, we should use the criteria we have told students we'll use. Occasionally, however, we may need to adjust one or more criteria—or perhaps add or subtract one or two criteria—to accommodate unexpected responses and enhance our ability to score all responses consistently, fairly, and reliably. Any adjustments should be made *before we begin scoring,* rather than midway through scoring a stack of papers.

rubric List of components that a student's performance on an assessment should ideally include; used to guide scoring.

Score item by item rather than paper by paper. When scoring involves some subjectivity, we can score students' responses more reliably if we score them item by item—scoring all responses to the first question, then all responses to the second question, and so on.

Try not to let prior expectations for students' performance influence judgments of their actual performance. The halo and horns effects described earlier can come into play in formal assessments as well as informal ones. The more variable and complex students' responses are on a paper–pencil assessment, the greater the difficulty we will have in scoring responses objectively and reliably. Strategies such as shuffling papers after grading one question and using small self-stick notes to cover students' names can help us prevent our expectations from inappropriately influencing our judgments.

myeducationlab

Gain practice in evaluating students' classroom assignments by completing the Building Teaching Skills and Dispositions exercise "Assessing Students' Written Work" in MyEducationLab. (To find this exercise, go to the topic Assessment in MyEducationLab, and click on *Building Teaching Skills and Dispositions.*)

Accompany any overall scores with detailed feedback. As we score students' responses, we should remember that our assessments should not only determine students' current achievement levels but also promote their *future* achievement. Accordingly, we should provide detailed comments that tell students what they've done well, where their weaknesses lie, and how they can improve (Hattie & Timperley, 2007; Krampen, 1987).

RSVP Characteristics of Paper–Pencil Assessment

How do paper–pencil assessments measure up in terms of the four RSVP characteristics? Let's consider each characteristic in turn.

Reliability When paper–pencil assessment tasks have definite right and wrong answers, we can usually evaluate students' responses with a high degree of consistency. In contrast, when we must make subjective judgments about the relative rightness or wrongness of students' responses, reliability inevitably goes down a bit.

Standardization As a general rule, paper–pencil instruments are easily standardized. We can give all students similar tasks and instructions, provide similar time limits and environmental conditions, and score everyone's responses in essentially the same way. But we probably don't want to go overboard in this respect. For example, we might sometimes allow students to choose a writing topic, perhaps as a way of increasing their sense of self-determination (see Chapter 11). We may also need to tailor assessment tasks to the particular abilities and disabilities of students with special needs.

Standardize paper–pencil assessments as much as possible, but make appropriate accommodations for students with disabilities.

Validity When we ask questions that require only short, simple responses, we can sample students' knowledge about many topics within a short period of time. In this sense, then, such questions can give us greater content validity. Yet such items won't always reflect our instructional goals. To assess students' ability to apply what they've learned to new situations and ill-defined, real-world problems, we may need to be satisfied with a few tasks requiring lengthy responses, even if those tasks provide a somewhat limited sample of the content domain.

Practicality Paper–pencil assessment is typically more practical than performance assessment; for instance, we can assess all students at the same time, and in many instances we can score students' responses fairly quickly. Thus, paper–pencil assessment should be our method of choice *if* it can yield a valid measure of what students know and can do. But in situations in which paper–pencil tasks are not a good reflection of what students have learned, we may need to sacrifice practicality to gain the greater validity that a performance assessment provides.

Choose paper–pencil assessment over performance assessment *if* a paper–pencil instrument can yield a valid measure of students' achievement.

Performance Assessment

Some skills, such as public speaking, can be assessed only with performance tasks.

A wide variety of performance tasks can be used to assess students' mastery of classroom subject matter. Here are just a few of the many possibilities:

- Creating a sculpture
- Executing a cartwheel
- Conducting an experiment
- Engaging in a debate
- Playing a musical instrument
- Giving a dramatic performance
- Role-playing a job interview
- Fixing a malfunctioning machine

Performance assessment lends itself especially well to the assessment of complex achievements, such as those that involve coordinating a number of skills simultaneously. It can also be quite helpful in assessing higher-level cognitive processes, such as problem solving, creativity, and critical thinking. Furthermore, performance tasks are often more meaningful, thought provoking, and authentic—and thus often more motivating—than paper–pencil tasks (Darling-Hammond, Ancess, & Falk, 1995; DiMartino & Castaneda, 2007; Khattri & Sweet, 1996; Paris & Paris, 2001).

Choosing Appropriate Performance Tasks

Our selection of appropriate performance assessment tasks must, of course, be closely aligned with our instructional goals and objectives. We must also consider whether a particular task will enable us to make reasonable generalizations about what our students know and can do in the content domain in question (Popham, 1995; Wiggins, 1992). We now look at four distinctions that can help us zero in on the most appropriate tasks for our purposes.

Products versus Processes Some performance assessments focus on tangible *products* that students create—perhaps a pen-and-ink drawing, scientific invention, or poster display. In situations with no tangible product, we must look instead at the specific *processes and behaviors* that students exhibit—perhaps giving an oral presentation, demonstrating a forward roll, or playing an instrumental solo.

Sometimes we might be interested in students' *thinking* processes. For example, if we want to determine whether students have acquired certain logical thinking abilities (e.g., conservation, separation and control of variables), we might present tasks similar to those Piaget used and, through a series of probing questions, ask students to explain their reasoning (recall the description of the *clinical method* in Chapter 2). And we can often learn a great deal about how students conceptualize and reason about scientific phenomena when we ask them to manipulate physical objects (e.g., chemicals in a chemistry lab, electrical circuit boards in a physics class), make predictions about what will happen under varying circumstances, and explain their results (Baxter et al., 1996; diSessa, 2007; Magnusson, Boyle, & Templin, 1994; Quellmalz & Hoskyn, 1997).

Individual versus Group Performance Many performance tasks require *individual* students to complete them with little or no assistance. Other tasks are sufficiently complex that they're best accomplished by a *group* of students. For instance, we might assess high school students' mastery of a unit on urban geography by using a field-based cooperative group project such as the following:

1. Select one of the neighborhoods marked on the city map.
2. Identify its current features by doing an inventory of its buildings, businesses, housing, and public facilities. Also, identify current transportation patterns and traffic flow. From the information made available, identify any special problems this neighborhood has, such as dilapidated housing, traffic congestion, or a high crime rate.
3. As a group, consider various plans for changing and improving your neighborhood. (Newmann, 1997, p. 369)

Such a task requires students to collect data systematically, use the data to draw conclusions and make predictions, and, in general, think as an urban planner would (Newmann, 1997).

One challenge in using group tasks for assessment purposes is determining how to evaluate each student's contribution. Often teachers consider individual students' behaviors and achievements (e.g., what and how much a student contributes to the group effort, how much the student has learned by the end of the project, etc.) in addition to or instead of the entire group's accomplishments (Lester, Lambdin, & Preston, 1997; Stiggins, 2008).

Restricted versus Extended Performance Some performance tasks are quite short; that is, they involve *restricted performance.* For instance, in a beginning instrumental music class, we might ask each student to play the C-major scale to make sure everyone has mastered the scale on his or her instrument. In a chemistry class, we might ask students to demonstrate mastery of basic safety procedures before beginning their lab experiments.

We assess *extended performance* when we want to determine what students are capable of doing over several days or weeks. Extended performance tasks might provide opportunities for students to collect data, engage in collaborative problem solving, and edit and revise their work. Many extended performance tasks embody authentic assessment: They closely resemble the situations and problems that students might eventually encounter in the outside world. Because extended performance tasks take a great deal of time, we should use them for assessing achievement related only to our most important and central instructional goals (Alleman & Brophy, 1997; De Corte et al., 1996; Lester et al., 1997).

Static versus Dynamic Assessment Whether paper–pencil or performance tasks, most assessments focus on identifying students' existing abilities and achievements. When used in isolation from other assessments, they don't specifically address how students learn and change over time; thus, you might think of them as *static assessments.* Static assessment is consistent with Vygotsky's concept of *actual developmental level,* reflecting the tasks a child can do easily on his or her own (see Chapter 2).

An alternative approach is **dynamic assessment**, in which a teacher assesses students' ability to learn something new, typically in a one-on-one situation that includes instruction, assistance, or some other form of scaffolding (e.g., Lidz & Gindis, 2003; L. A. Shepard, 2000; H. L. Swanson & Lussier, 2001). Such an approach reflects Vygotsky's *zone of proximal development* and can give us an idea of what students might be able to accomplish with appropriate structure and guidance. Hence, it's typically more appropriate for formative evaluation than for summative evaluation. When used as a tool for formative evaluation, dynamic assessment can provide a wealth of qualitative information about children's abilities, cognitive strategies, and approaches to learning. For instance, it can give us insights into the following:

dynamic assessment Systematic examination of how readily and in what ways a student can acquire new knowledge or skills, usually with adult assistance or some other form of scaffolding.

- Students' readiness for instruction in particular topics and skills
- Students' motivational and affective patterns (e.g., self-efficacy, achievement goals, attributions, anxiety)

- Students' work habits (e.g., impulsiveness, persistence, reactions to frustration and failure)
- Potential obstacles to students' learning (e.g., distractibility, poor reading comprehension skills, lack of effective self-monitoring and self-evaluation skills) (Bransford & Schwartz, 1999; L. S. Fuchs, Compton, et al., 2008; Hamers & Ruijssenaars, 1997; Haywood & Lidz, 2007; Tzuriel, 2000)

FIGURE 14.10 In this "Birthday Graph" exercise, first-grade teacher Susan O'Byrne gained information about students' writing and graphing skills.

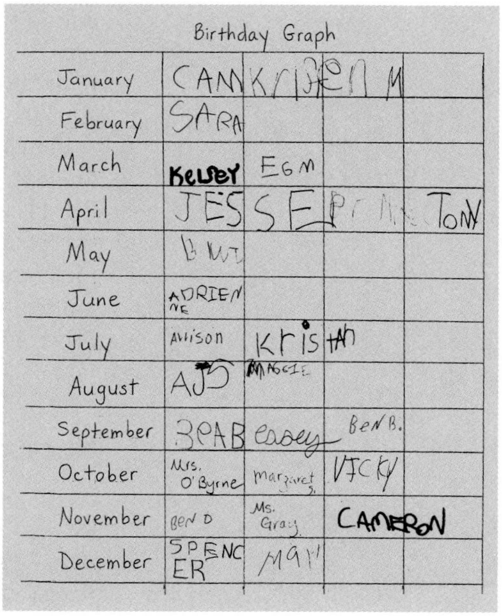

Planning and Administering the Assessment

Three guidelines presented earlier for paper–pencil assessment are equally relevant to performance assessment:

- Define tasks clearly and unambiguously.
- Identify scoring criteria in advance.
- Encourage students to ask questions when tasks aren't clear.

Three additional guidelines pertain specifically to performance assessment:

Consider incorporating the assessment into normal instructional activities. We can sometimes make more efficient use of class time if we combine instruction and assessment into a single activity (Baxter et al., 1996; Boschee & Baron, 1993). For example, in a unit on bar graphs, first-grade teacher Susan O'Byrne gave each of her students a two-dimensional grid, with the months of the year written in the leftmost column. She instructed students to write their own name in a box beside their birthday month and then to circulate around the room to get each classmate's signature in a box in the appropriate row. Ideally, this procedure would yield a horizontal bar graph depicting the number of children born in each month.

The completed "Birthday Graph," shown in Figure 14.10, reveals that some, but not all, students understood the nature of simple bar graphs. Many students (e.g., Cam, Allison, Spencer) wrote their names inside a single box on the grid. However, a few students (e.g., Kristen, Jesse, Kristah) used two boxes to write their names, perhaps because they (a) hadn't mastered the idea that one person equals one box or (b) couldn't write small enough to fit their name inside a box and didn't know how to solve this problem. Also, one student (Meg, with a March birthday) had not yet learned that she must always write words, including her name, in a left-to-right direction.

When we incorporate performance assessments into instructional activities, we must keep in mind that we won't be able to completely standardize conditions for all students and we won't necessarily see students' best work. Furthermore, although it's quite appropriate to give students assistance or feedback during instruction, it may be inappropriate to do so during a summative evaluation of what they have achieved (L. M. Carey, 1994). In some situations, then, we may want to conduct an assessment separately from instructional activities, announce it in advance, and give students guidance beforehand about how they can maximize their performance.

When using performance assessment for summative evaluation, keep the assessment separate from instruction.

Provide some structure to guide students' efforts, but not so much structure that it reduces the authenticity of the task. Especially if we're conducting a summative evaluation, we should probably structure performance assessments to some degree. For example, we can provide detailed directions about what students should accomplish, what materials and equipment they can use, and how much time they have to get the job done (Gronlund & Waugh, 2009; E. H. Hiebert, Valencia, & Afflerbach, 1994). Such structure helps to standardize the assessment and therefore enables us to evaluate students' performance more reliably. A *lot* of structure can decrease the validity of a performance task, however. Imposing a great deal of structure is particularly problematic when we intend performance tasks to be authentic ones that resemble real-world situations—which often *don't* have much structure.

Plan classroom management strategies for the assessment activity. As we conduct a performance assessment, we should put into practice two important principles of classroom management presented in Chapter 13: Effective teachers are continually aware of what their students are doing (the notion of *withitness*), and they make sure that students are always productively engaged. When we can assess only a few students (or perhaps only one) at a time, we must make sure that the other students are actively involved in a learning activity (L. M. Carey, 1994). For example, in an English class, when one student is giving an oral presentation, we might have the other students jot down notes about the topic being presented—facts they find interesting, ideas they disagree with, questions they wonder about. Or in a unit on soccer, when a few students are demonstrating their ability to dribble and pass the ball as they run down the field, we might have other students work in pairs to practice their footwork.

Scoring Students' Responses

Occasionally responses to performance assessment tasks are objectively scorable; for example, we can easily time students' performance in a 100-meter dash and count students' errors on a typing test. But more often we will find ourselves making subjective decisions as we assess students' performance. There are no clear-cut right or wrong responses when students give oral reports, create clay sculptures, or engage in heated debates on controversial issues. Consequently, if we aren't careful, our judgments may be unduly influenced by our expectations for each student (L. M. Carey, 1994; Gronlund & Waugh, 2009).

Especially for summative evaluations, we should carefully consider the criteria to use in judging students' responses and develop a rubric that identifies these criteria. A rubric can guide us during the evaluation process and later serve as a written record of what we have observed. The following strategies can help us design and use scoring rubrics effectively when we conduct performance assessments:

When using several criteria to evaluate students' performance, describe each criterion in concrete terms and develop a checklist or rating scale to guide scoring. Some tasks lend themselves well to **checklists**, on which we indicate whether specific behaviors or qualities are present or absent. Other tasks are more appropriately evaluated with **rating scales**, on which we rate aspects of the performance on one or more continua (see Figure 14.11). Both approaches enhance the reliability of scoring and have instructional benefits as well: They identify specific areas of difficulty and thereby give students feedback about how performance can be improved.

Some rubrics include rating scales that specify the meaning of each point of the scale. For example, in a unit on ancient civilizations, one ninth-grade social studies teacher had cooperative learning groups create tourist guidebooks depicting one of several locations (e.g., for ancient Egypt, China, or Central America). His rubric for grading the guidebooks is shown in Figure 14.12. Notice how the rubric provides guidance for assigning three possible labels ("Proficient," "Adequate," and "Poor") to three different aspects of the guidebooks ("Elements of Civilization," "Evidence," and "Visuals").

Decide whether analytic or holistic scoring better serves your purpose(s) in conducting the assessment. When we need detailed information about students' performance, we may want to use **analytic scoring**, in which we evaluate various aspects of the performance separately, perhaps with a checklist or several rating scales. In contrast, when we need to summarize students' performance in a single score, we

checklist Assessment tool with which a teacher evaluates student performance by indicating whether specific behaviors or qualities are present or absent.

rating scale Assessment tool with which a teacher evaluates student performance by rating aspects of the performance on one or more continua.

analytic scoring Scoring a student's performance on an assessment by evaluating various aspects of it separately.

FIGURE 14.11 Examples of checklists and rating scales

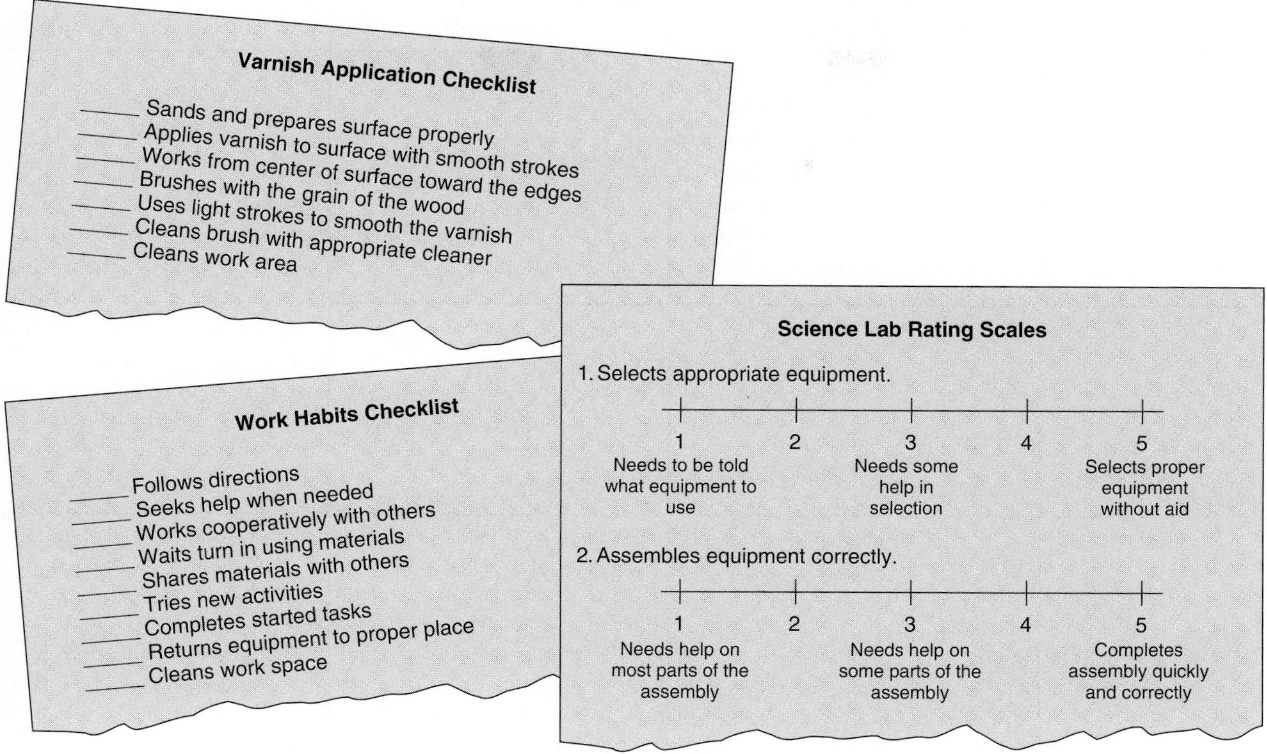

Source: "Varnish Application Checklist" from M. D. Miller et al., 2009, p. 283; "Work Habits Checklist" from R. L. Linn & Miller, 2005, p. 274; "Science Lab Rating Scales?" from Gronlund, 2004, p. 111.

should probably use **holistic scoring**, in which we consider all relevant criteria but make a single judgment; for instance, we might have a single rating scale of "1" to "5" or "Poor" to "Proficient" that describes typical overall performance at various points along the scale. Analytic scoring tends to be more useful in conducting formative evaluations and promoting students' learning, whereas holistic scoring is often used in summative evaluations.

Limit scoring criteria to the most important aspects of the desired response. Scoring criteria should focus on aspects of the performance that are critical indicators of proficiency and most relevant to instructional goals and objectives (M. D. Miller et al., 2009; Wiggins, 1992). The criteria should also be relatively few in number (perhaps five or six) so that we can keep track of them as we observe each student's performance (Airasian, 1994; Gronlund & Waugh, 2009; Popham, 1995). Remember the limited capacity of working memory: Human beings (including teachers!) can think about only so many things at a single time (see Chapter 6).

Make note of any significant aspects of a student's performance that the rubric doesn't address. Whenever we break down performance on a complex task into discrete behaviors, we can lose valuable information in the process (Delandshere & Petrosky, 1998). Thus, when we use rubrics to assist us in scoring performance, we may occasionally want to jot down other noteworthy characteristics of students' performance. This aspect of our scoring process will be neither standardized nor reliable, of course, but it can sometimes be useful in identifying students' unique strengths and needs and can therefore assist us in future instructional planning.

holistic scoring Summarizing a student's performance on an assessment with a single score.

FIGURE 14.12 Rubric for evaluating guidebooks in ninth-grade social studies unit on ancient civilizations

	Proficient	Adequate	Poor
Elements of Civilization	The guidebook shows a clear understanding of what a civilization is and how the group's particular civilization developed with respect to each factors characterizing a civilization.	The guidebook shows some understanding of what a civilization is. Each of the civilization factors is discussed at least briefly.	The guidebook shows little or no understanding of what a civilization is. Many factors are missing.
Evidence	The guidebook reflects class notes, class handouts, homework, and a variety of outside sources to achieve a comprehensive overview of the civilization.	The guidebook reflects class notes, class handouts, and homework to achieve a mostly complete overview of the civilization.	The guidebook does not reflect class notes, class handouts, homework, or any outside sources.
Visuals	Visuals have been well chosen and relate to the elements of civilization being discussed. There is a thorough analysis of each image and how it relates to the topic and culture.	Visuals relate to the elements of civilization being discussed.	Irrelevant or no visuals have been included in the guidebook.

Source: Used courtesy of Jeff Ormrod.

RSVP Characteristics of Performance Assessment

Compared with traditional paper–pencil assessment, performance assessment techniques are relative newcomers on the educational scene, and educators continue to wrestle with concerns related to reliability, standardization, validity, and practicality.

Reliability Researchers have reported varying degrees of reliability in performance assessments (e.g., Crehan, 2001; Hay, 2008; Haywood & Lidz, 2007; R. L. Linn, 1994). Assessment results are often inconsistent over time, and different teachers may rate the same performance differently.

There are probably several reasons for the low reliability of many performance assessments (L. M. Carey, 1994; Parkes, 2001; Wiley & Haertel, 1996). First, students don't always behave consistently; even in a task as simple as shooting a basketball, a student is likely to make a basket on some occasions but not on others. Second, we sometimes need to evaluate various aspects of complex behaviors rather quickly; things may happen so fast that we miss important parts of a student's performance. Finally, one form of reliability, *internal consistency* (see Table 14.2), is simply inappropriate for complex, multifaceted behaviors.

Given these limitations, a single performance assessment may very well *not* be a reliable indicator of what students have achieved. Accordingly, we should ask students to demonstrate behaviors related to important instructional goals on more than one occasion. And when an important summative evaluation is involved, we should ideally have more than one rater evaluate each student's performance (L. M. Carey, 1994; M. D. Miller et al., 2009; R. M. Thorndike, 1997).

Remember that a single performance assessment may not be a standardized or reliable indicator of what students have achieved.

Standardization Some performance assessments are easily standardized, but others are not. If we want to assess typing ability, we can easily make instructions, tasks, and time limits the same for everyone. In contrast, if we want to assess artistic creativity, we may want to let students choose the materials they use and the particular products they create. In such nonstandardized situations, it's especially important to use multiple assessments and look for consistency in students' performance across several occasions.

Validity As previously noted, performance assessment tasks can sometimes provide more valid indicators of what students have accomplished relative to instructional goals. Researchers have found, however, that students' responses to a *single* performance assessment task often are *not* a good indication of their overall achievement (Koretz, Stecher, Klein, & McCaffrey, 1994; R. L. Linn, 1994; Parkes, 2001; Shavelson, Baxter, & Pine, 1992). Content validity is the issue here: If we have time for students to perform only one or two complex tasks, we may not get a representative sample of what they have learned and can do. In addition, any biases that affect our judgment (e.g., beliefs about particular students' abilities) can distort our evaluations of students' performance—the halo and horns effects at work once again. To ensure that our conclusions are reasonably valid, then, we will typically want to administer several different performance tasks or perhaps the same task under different conditions (R. L. Linn, 1994; Messick, 1994a; Stiggins, 2008).

Remember that a single performance task may not provide a sufficiently representative sample of the content domain.

Practicality Unfortunately, performance assessments are often less practical than more traditional paper–pencil assessments (L. M. Carey, 1994; Hambleton, 1996; Popham, 1995). Administering an assessment can be quite time consuming, especially when we must observe students one at a time or when they must perform relatively complex (perhaps authentic) tasks. In addition, we may need considerable equipment to conduct the assessment—perhaps enough for every student to have a personal set. Clearly, then, we must carefully consider whether the benefits of a performance assessment outweigh its impracticality (Messick, 1994a; Tzuriel, 2000; Worthen & Leopold, 1992). Ultimately, the best strategy overall may be to use *both* paper–pencil and performance assessments when drawing conclusions about students' achievement.

Think about how you might use a combination of paper–pencil and performance tasks to assess what students know and can do.

Table 14.3 presents a summary of our RSVP analyses of informal assessment, formal paper–pencil assessment, and formal performance assessment.

Additional Considerations in Formal Assessment

In our discussion of formal assessment so far, our focus has been on the design, administration, and scoring of particular paper–pencil and performance tasks. We now step back and look at more general issues related to formal assessment.

Including Students in the Assessment Process

Students become increasingly skillful in self-assessment as they grow older (van Kraayenoord & Paris, 1997), but even students in the elementary grades have some ability to evaluate their own performance (e.g., see Figure 14.13). However, all students, especially those in the early elementary grades, can more effectively self-assess their work when teachers scaffold their efforts—for example, by suggesting specific things to look for in their work. To help students acquire self-regulated learning skills and gain a sense of self-determination about classroom activities, we should think of assessment as something we do *with* students rather than *to* them (Paris & Ayres, 1994; L. Shepard et al., 2005; Vye et al., 1998).

Following are strategies for including students in the assessment process and helping them develop important self-monitoring and self-evaluation skills:

- Make evaluation criteria explicit and easily observable.
- Solicit students' ideas about evaluation criteria and rubric design.
- Provide examples of good and not-so-good products, and ask students to compare them on the basis of several criteria.

myeducationlab

Observe 8-year-old Keenan assess her progress in writing in the video "Portfolio." Notice how her teacher scaffolds her efforts. (To find this video, go to Chapter 14 of the Book-Specific Resources in MyEducationLab, select *Video Examples*, and then click on the title.)

FIGURE 14.13 At the end of third grade, 9-year-old Philip reviewed the work he had completed over the course of the year and identified his strengths and weaknesses.

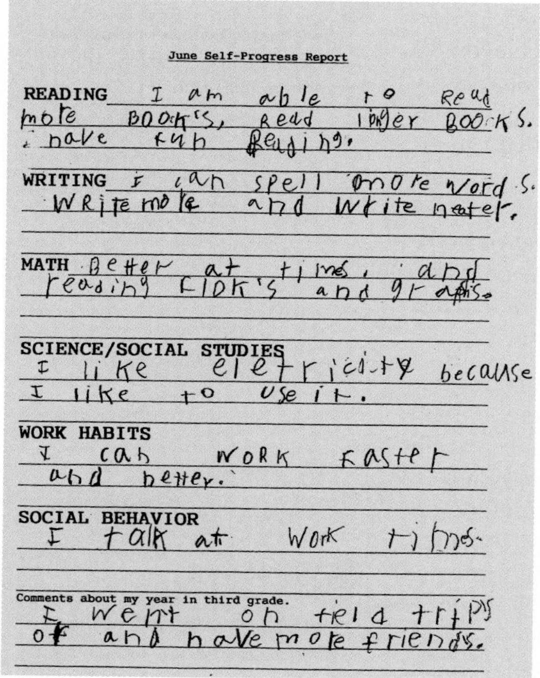

June Self-Progress Report

READING I am able to Read more BOOK'S, Read longer BOOKS. I have fun Reading.

WRITING I can spell more words. Write more and write neater.

MATH Better at times, and reading clok's and graphs.

SCIENCE/SOCIAL STUDIES I like eletricity because I like to use it.

WORK HABITS I can work faster and better.

SOCIAL BEHAVIOR I talk at work times.

Comments about my year in third grade. I went on feld trips of and have more friends.

- Have students compare self-ratings with teacher ratings (e.g., note the "Self" and "Teacher" columns in the rubric for word problems in Figure 14.9).
- Have students keep ongoing records of their performance and chart their progress over time.
- Have students reflect on their work in daily or weekly journal entries, where they can keep track of knowledge and skills they have and have not mastered, as well as learning strategies that have and have not been effective.
- Have students compile portfolios of their work (see Chapter 15).
- Ask students to write practice questions similar to those they expect to see on upcoming quizzes and tests.
- Ask students to lead parent conferences (see the discussion of *parent–teacher conferences* in Chapter 13). (A. L. Brown & Campione, 1996; DiMartino & Castaneda, 2007; Paris & Ayres, 1994; L. A. Shepard, 2000; Stiggins, 2008; Valencia, Hiebert, & Afflerbach, 1994)

Teaching Testwiseness

If you did well on the califractions quiz earlier in the chapter, you have some degree of **testwiseness**: You use test-taking strategies that enhance your test performance. Testwiseness includes strategies such as these:

- *Clarifying the task(s) to be performed*—for example, carefully reading the directions and every question
- *Using time efficiently*—for example, allocating enough time for each task and saving difficult items for last
- *Deductive reasoning*—for example, eliminating two alternatives that say the same thing and using information from one question to answer another
- *Avoiding sloppy errors*—for example, checking answers a second time and erasing any stray pencil marks on a computer-scored answer sheet
- *Guessing*—for example, eliminating obviously wrong alternatives and then guessing one of the others, or guessing randomly if time runs out and there's no penalty for guessing (Millman, Bishop, & Ebel, 1965; Petersen, Sudweeks, & Baird, 1990; L. Shepard et al., 2005)

Give students practice in responding to unfamiliar test-item formats (e.g., true–false, multiple-choice).

As a well-educated adult, you probably have considerable testwiseness, in part because you've had a lot of experience with a wide variety of tests and other assessments. But we must remember that many students—especially younger ones and those whose prior schooling has been in a different culture—may have had little experience with assessment formats such as true–false and multiple-choice questions. In some instances we may be able to make our classroom assessment tasks similar to those with which students have had previous experience. But when this isn't possible or appropriate, we should give students practice with the format of any test items or performance tasks we use (Popham, 1990).

To some degree we can also help students prepare for classroom assessments by teaching them useful test-taking strategies—temporarily skipping difficult items, double-checking to be sure answers are marked in the correct spots, and so on. We should keep in mind, however, that such testwiseness typically makes only a small difference in students' test performance (Geiger, 1997; Scruggs & Lifson, 1985). Furthermore, test-taking skills and student achievement are positively correlated: Students

testwiseness Test-taking know-how that enhances test performance.

test anxiety Excessive anxiety about a particular test or about assessment in general.

Compare/Contrast

TABLE 14.3
Evaluating RSVP Characteristics of Different Kinds of Assessment

Kind of Assessment	Reliability	Standardization	Validity	Practicality
Informal assessment	A single, brief assessment is not a reliable indicator of achievement. We must look for consistency in a student's performance across time and in different contexts.	Informal observations are rarely, if ever, standardized. Thus, we should not compare one student to another on the basis of informal assessment alone.	Students' public behaviors in the classroom are not always valid indicators of their achievement (e.g., some students may try to hide high achievement from their peers).	Informal assessment is definitely practical: It is flexible and can occur spontaneously during instruction.
Formal paper–pencil assessment	Objectively scorable items are highly reliable. We can enhance the reliability of subjectively scorable items by specifying scoring criteria in concrete terms.	In most instances, paper–pencil instruments are easily standardized for all students. Giving students choices (e.g., regarding topics to write about or questions to answer) may increase motivation but reduces standardization.	Numerous questions requiring short, simple responses can provide a more representative sample of the content domain. But tasks requiring lengthier responses may sometimes more closely match instructional goals.	Paper–pencil assessment is usually practical: All students can be assessed at once, and no special materials are required.
Formal performance assessment	Performance assessment tasks are often difficult to score reliably. We can enhance reliability by specifying scoring criteria in concrete terms.	Some performance assessment tasks are easily standardized, whereas others are not.	Performance tasks may sometimes be more consistent with instructional goals than paper–pencil tasks are. But a single performance task may not provide a representative sample of the content domain; several tasks may be necessary to ensure adequate content validity.	Performance assessment is typically less practical than other approaches: It may involve special materials, and it can take a fair amount of class time, especially if students must be assessed one by one.

with many test-taking strategies tend to be higher achievers than students with few strategies. In other words, very few students get low test scores *only* because they are poor test takers (Scruggs & Lifson, 1985). In most cases, then, we can best serve students by teaching them the knowledge and skills a given assessment is designed to measure, rather than spending an inordinate amount of time teaching them how to take tests (J. R. Frederiksen & Collins, 1989; L. Shepard et al., 2005).

Teach test-taking strategies, but not at the expense of adequate instruction in the knowledge and skills being assessed.

Keeping Test Anxiety in Check

A small amount of anxiety about tests and other important assessments can enhance performance (see Chapter 11). But some students become extremely anxious in assessment situations—they have **test anxiety**—to the point that their scores significantly underestimate what they've learned (Cassady & Johnson, 2002; Hembree, 1988). Such students appear to be concerned primarily about the *evaluative* aspect of assessments, worrying that someone will find them to be "stupid" or in some other way inadequate (Harter, Whitesell, & Kowalski, 1992; B. N. Phillips, Pitcher, Worsham, & Miller, 1980; Wine, 1980). Test anxiety interferes not only with retrieval and performance at the time of an assessment but also with encoding and storage when learners are preparing for the assessment (Cassady & Johnson, 2002; Hagtvet & Johnsen, 1992). Thus, highly test-anxious students don't just *test* poorly; they also *learn* poorly.

Minimize debilitating test anxiety by helping students master academic subject matter.

Speed Tests!
Speed Tests make every-
one a nervous reck before
I pasted Speed Test I I
would barle eat and had
troble sleeping. Now, this very
day I find out I pasted
Speed Test II and maybe
I pasted Speed Test III!
Oh God please, oh please
let me passe Speed Test
III. Effen if I never passi
Speed Test 15 teen I want
you to know I tried my
hardest.

In this reflection on "Speed Tests"—those in which many questions must be answered in a very short time—8-year-old Connie describes how overwhelming test anxiety can be.

Excessive, debilitating test anxiety is especially common in students from ethnic minority groups and students with disabilities (R. Carter, Williams, & Silverman, 2008; Putwain, 2007; Whitaker Sena, Lowe, & Lee, 2007). On average, students with the highest test anxiety are those who have performed poorly in school in the past. One important strategy for helping students overcome excessive test anxiety, then, is to help them acquire the skills they need to master course material in the first place (Kirkland, 1971; Naveh-Benjamin, 1991; Tryon, 1980). In addition, we must present classroom assessments in ways that motivate students to do their best without succumbing to debilitating anxiety. Table 14.4 distinguishes between classroom assessment practices that are likely to lead to facilitating anxiety and those that may elicit debilitating anxiety.

Encouraging Risk Taking

Ideally, students should feel comfortable enough about classroom assessments that they feel free to take risks and make mistakes. Only under these circumstances will students tackle the challenging tasks that can maximize their learning and cognitive development. We encourage risk taking—and lower anxiety levels as well—when our assessment strategies give students some leeway to be wrong without penalty (Clifford, 1990). And certainly no single assessment should ever be "sudden death" for a student who earns a low score. Following are three recommended strategies for encouraging risk taking during classroom assessments:

Assess students' achievement frequently rather than infrequently. Frequent assessment is important for several reasons. First, it provides ongoing information to both students and teachers about the progress students are making and about areas of weakness needing attention. Second, students are less likely to experience debilitating anxiety if they complete a number of assessments that each contribute only a small amount to their final grade. Third, frequent assessment motivates students, especially those with lower ability, to study regularly. Fourth, when students no longer feel pressure to perform well on every test and assignment, they are less likely to cheat to obtain good grades. Finally and most importantly, students who are assessed frequently learn and achieve at higher levels than students who are assessed infrequently (Crooks, 1988; E. D. Evans & Craig, 1990; Glover, 1989; Roediger & Karpicke, 2006; Sax, 1989).

Provide opportunities to correct errors. Especially when an assessment includes most or all of the content domain in question, students may learn as much—possibly even more—by correcting the errors they've made on an assessment task. For example, in an approach known as *mastery reform*, some math teachers have students correct their errors, as follows:

1. *Identification of the error.* Students describe in a short paragraph exactly what they don't yet know how to do.
2. *Statement of the process.* Using words rather than mathematical symbols, students explain the steps involved in the procedure they are trying to master.
3. *Practice.* Students demonstrate their mastery of the procedure with three new problems similar to the problem(s) they previously solved incorrectly.
4. *Statement of mastery.* Students state in a sentence or two that they have now mastered the procedure.

By completing these steps, students can replace a grade on a previous assessment with the new, higher one. One high school math teacher has told me that this approach has a more general, long-term benefit as well: Many of his students eventually incorporate the four steps into their regular, internalized learning strategies.

Compare/Contrast

TABLE 14.4
Keeping Students' Anxiety at a Facilitative Level during Classroom Assessments

What to Do	What *Not* to Do
Point out the value of the assessment as a feedback mechanism to improve learning.	Stress the fact that students' competence is being evaluated.
Administer a practice assessment or pretest that gives students an idea of what the final assessment instrument will be like.	Keep the nature of the assessment a secret until the day it's administered.
Encourage students to do their best but not necessarily to expect perfection; for instance, say, "We're here to learn, and you can't do that without making mistakes."	Remind students that failing will have dire consequences.
Provide or allow the use of memory aids (e.g., a list of formulas or a single note card containing key facts) when instructional goals don't require students to commit information to memory.	Insist that students commit even trivial facts to memory.
Eliminate time limits unless speed is an important part of the skill being measured.	Give more questions or tasks than students can possibly respond to in the time allotted.
Continually survey the room, and be available to answer students' questions.	Hover over students, watching them closely as they complete the assessment.
Use unannounced assessments (i.e., pop quizzes) only for formative evaluation (e.g., to determine an appropriate starting point for instruction).	Give occasional pop quizzes to motivate students to study regularly and to punish those who do not.
Use the results of several assessments to make decisions (e.g., to assign grades).	Evaluate students on the basis of a single assessment.

Sources: Brophy, 1986, 2004 ("We're here to learn" suggestion on p. 274); Cizek, 2003; Gaudry & Bradshaw, 1971; K. T. Hill, 1984; K. T. Hill & Wigfield, 1984; Popham, 1990; Sax, 1989; Sieber, Kameya, & Paulson, 1970; Spaulding, 1992; Stipek, 1993.

When appropriate, allow students to retake assessments. As noted in the discussion of mastery learning in Chapter 12, some students will invariably need more time than others to master a topic and may therefore need to be assessed on the same material more than once. In addition, students are less likely to have debilitating test anxiety when they know they will have a second try at an assessment task if they need one. Yet allowing retakes has disadvantages as well. When students know they can retake an assessment if they get a low score the first time, they may prepare less well than they would otherwise. Furthermore, students who are allowed to retake the *same* instrument may work on the specific things the assessment covers without studying equally important but nonassessed material. (Remember, most assessment tasks can be only a small sample of the content in question.)

If we truly want students to master course material but also to take risks in their learning and classroom performance, we may want to make retakes a regular practice. To encourage students to take the first assessment seriously and to discourage them from focusing only on the content of specific test items as they study for the retake, we might construct two assessment instruments for the same content domain, using one as the initial assessment and the other for retakes (this is what I currently do in my undergraduate classes). If this strategy is too time consuming to be practical, we can allow students to redo the same assessment a second time and average the two scores earned.

To encourage risk taking and reduce anxiety about classroom assessments, assess students frequently and give them opportunities to correct errors. Here a teacher uses a student's errors on a paper–pencil assessment to guide her future learning efforts.

Evaluating an Assessment after the Fact: Item Analysis

Not only must we assess our students' learning and achievement, but we must also *assess our assessments.* In the process of scoring students' performance on an assessment instrument, we may discover that some items or tasks simply don't provide the information we had hoped they would. For example, it may become obvious that one item isn't measuring the knowledge or skill we had in mind (a validity problem) and that another is hard to score consistently (a reliability problem that indirectly affects validity as well).

Conduct an item analysis as one source of evidence for the validity and reliability of an assessment instrument.

We can't always predict which items and tasks are going to be good ones and which are not. For this reason, assessment experts frequently recommend conducting an **item analysis** after an assessment has been administered and scored. Such an analysis typically involves an examination of both the difficulty level and the discriminative power of each item on the assessment instrument.

Item Difficulty We can determine the difficulty of each item simply by finding out how many students responded to it correctly. The **item difficulty (*p*)** of an item is the proportion of students who responded correctly relative to the total number of students who took the assessment:

$$p = \frac{\text{Number of students getting the item correct}}{\text{Number of students taking the assessment}}$$

This formula yields a number between 0.0 and 1.0. A high p value indicates that the item was relatively easy for students; for example, a p of 0.85 means that 85% of the students answered it correctly. A low p value indicates that the item was difficult; for example, a p of 0.10 means that only 10% gave a correct response.

On a norm-referenced assessment, p values tell us which items have a difficulty level that's best for comparing the performance of individual students. In this situation, ideal p values are somewhere between 0.30 and 0.70, indicating that the items are difficult enough that some, but not all, students get them wrong. When, instead, almost all students answer an item in the same way—either correctly (a very high p) or incorrectly (a very low p)—we get little or no information about how students differ from one another.

In contrast, there is no optimal item difficulty for a criterion-referenced assessment. In this case, p values help us determine how effectively we are accomplishing our instructional objectives. If most students have responded to an item correctly and we can rule out other factors (e.g., guessing, implausible distractors) that may have contributed to the high success rate, we can conclude that students have mastered the knowledge or skill the item represents. A low p value tells us either that students haven't learned what we are assessing or that the item doesn't accurately reflect what students *have* learned.

item analysis Follow-up analysis of patterns in students' responses to various items on an assessment instrument.

item difficulty (*p*) Index reflecting the proportion of students getting a particular assessment item correct.

item discrimination (*D*) Index reflecting the relative proportions of high-scoring versus low-scoring students getting a particular assessment item correct.

Item Discrimination Imagine that you are scoring a 30-item multiple-choice test you have just given your class. You notice that the best students—those who have done well on most of the test—have answered Question 12 incorrectly. You also notice that several students who got very low test scores got Question 12 correct. This doesn't make sense: You would expect the students who do well on any one item to be the same ones who perform well on the test overall. When the "wrong" students are getting an item correct—that is, when the item inaccurately identifies informed versus uninformed students—we have a problem with **item discrimination**.

To determine item discrimination (*D*), we use the approach just described. That is, we identify two groups of students—those who have gotten the highest overall scores and those who have gotten the lowest overall scores—putting about 20% to

30% of the total number of students in each group. We then compare the proportions of students in the two groups getting each item correct, using this formula:

$$D = \frac{\text{Number of high-scoring students getting item correct}}{\text{Total number of high-scoring students}} - \frac{\text{Number of low-scoring students getting item correct}}{\text{Total number of low-scoring students}}$$

The D formula yields a number ranging from -1.0 to $+1.0$. Positive D values tell us that more high-scoring students than low-scoring students have done well on an item; in other words, the item discriminates between knowledgeable and unknowledgeable students, which is exactly what we want. In contrast, negative D values reflect circumstances similar to the situation with Question 12 just described: Low-scoring students answered the item correctly but high-scoring students did not. A negative D is often a sign that something is wrong with the item; perhaps it misleads knowledgeable students to choose what was intended to be an incorrect response, or perhaps we have marked an incorrect answer on the answer key.

Follow up on negative *D* values; for example, disregard performance on items that high-achieving students have consistently responded to incorrectly, and recalculate overall scores accordingly.

Let's return to an assumption we made in the Question 12 situation: The students who do well on any single item should be the same ones who perform well overall. Here we are talking about *internal consistency reliability*, the extent to which different parts of an assessment instrument all measure more or less the same thing. However, when the items or tasks on an assessment instrument are all designed to measure very *different* things—as is often true for performance assessments—D values are less helpful in evaluating an item's effectiveness.

Many teachers save good assessment items for use on future occasions. For example, they might paste each item on an index card, with scoring criteria and item analysis data listed on the reverse side, or they might save the items electronically in a specially marked folder on their computer. As teachers accumulate items over the years, they eventually have a large enough collection that they don't have to use any one item very often.

Save good test questions and assessment tasks for use in future years; take precautions to prevent students from getting unauthorized access to them.

Taking Student Diversity into Account in Classroom Assessments

As we have seen, standardization of assessment instruments and procedures is important for fairness, reliability, and (indirectly) validity in our assessment results. Yet standardization has a downside: It limits our ability to accommodate students' diverse backgrounds and needs, capitalize on their individual strengths, and help them compensate for areas of weakness.

Standardization in classroom assessment practices is essential if, for some reason, we need to compare a student's performance to that of others. But in many other situations—for example, when we are trying to ascertain an appropriate starting point for instruction or specific weaknesses that each student needs to address—standardization is less critical. In some instances, in fact, we may find that the best way of assessing one student's learning is a relatively *ineffective* way of assessing another's.

Accommodating Group Differences

Let's remind ourselves of a few sources of diversity identified in previous chapters; let's also remember that these are *average* differences:

- Boys tend to talk more in class than girls do.
- Girls tend to work harder on classroom assignments than boys do; girls are also more test anxious than boys are.

- Students raised in mainstream Western culture recognize the value placed on individual achievement, but those from some other cultures are more accustomed to working as a group than to working alone.
- Many students brought up in mainstream Western culture are quite accustomed to showing others what they know and can do, but students from some cultural backgrounds are accustomed to practicing skills in private until they have achieved mastery.
- English language learners need considerable time—perhaps five to seven years—to master the levels of English vocabulary and syntax necessary to fully understand and learn from English-based instruction.
- Students from very low socioeconomic backgrounds may lack adequate nutrition and health care to perform their best in the classroom.
- Students at risk for academic failure may find that academic subject matter has little relevance to their own lives.

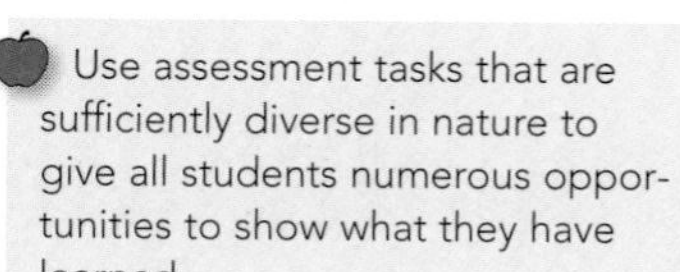
Use assessment tasks that are sufficiently diverse in nature to give all students numerous opportunities to show what they have learned.

All of these factors may, of course, affect students' ability to learn and achieve in the classroom. But they may also affect how students perform on our informal and formal assessments *independently* of their learning and achievement. This is just one of the many reasons that we should consider multiple assessments—as well as several different kinds of assessments—to assign grades and make other important assessment decisions (e.g., Haywood & Lidz, 2007; Spinelli, 2008; Sternberg, 2005). In addition, we should scrutinize our assessment tasks to be sure that they don't unfairly put some students at a disadvantage because of diversity in their life experiences. (Such inequity reflects *cultural bias*, a concept we'll look at in Chapter 15.) Ultimately, our assessment practices must be fair and equitable for students of all groups and backgrounds.

Accommodating Students with Special Needs

As noted in Chapter 5, in the United States the Individuals with Disabilities Education Act (IDEA) mandates that schools make appropriate accommodations for students with physical, mental, social, or emotional disabilities. This mandate applies not only to instruction but to assessment practices as well. Consequently, we may sometimes have to disregard our concern about standardization so that we can gain more *valid* assessments of what students with special needs know and can do. For example, we may often have to develop separate assessment instruments when students' individualized education programs (IEPs) specify instructional goals and objectives different from those for other students. Suggestions for additional accommodations for students with special needs are presented in Table 14.5.

The Big Picture

Ongoing assessment of students' progress is—and *must* be—a critical part of our role as teachers. As we assess students' learning and achievements, we should keep several points in mind:

- ***Assessments must be closely aligned with important instructional goals and objectives.*** Classroom assessments are worthless if they focus on students' accomplishments that are easy to measure but don't tell us what we really need to know—for instance, if they involve paper–pencil quizzes that ask students to recall trivial, isolated facts. Ultimately, we must not only teach but also *assess* the skills and abilities students will need to be successful in the outside world—for example, the ability to apply classroom subject matter to real-world situations.

- ***Classroom assessment practices have a significant influence on what and how students learn.*** Regardless of our primary purpose in assessing students' learning and achievement, the nature of our assessment instruments—what topics they address, whether they focus on lower-level or higher-level skills, and so on—will communicate messages about what's most important for students to learn and

Students in Inclusive Settings

TABLE 14.5
Using Classroom Assessments with Students Who Have Special Educational Needs

Category	Characteristics You Might Observe	Suggested Strategies
Students with specific cognitive or academic difficulties	• Poor listening, reading, and/or writing skills • Inconsistent performance due to off-task behaviors (for some students with learning disabilities or ADHD) • Difficulty processing specific kinds of information • Higher than average test anxiety	• Make paper–pencil instruments easy to read and respond to; for instance, type (rather than handwrite) tests, space items far apart, and have students respond directly on their test papers rather than on separate answer sheets. • If appropriate for the disability, provide extra time for students to complete assessment tasks and/or minimize reliance on literacy skills (e.g., read aloud paper–pencil test items and have students respond orally). • When students have a limited attention span, break lengthy assignments into several shorter tasks. • Let students take tests in a quiet place (e.g., the school's resource room) • Provide extra scaffolding to guide students' efforts; give explicit directions about what students are expected to do. • Be sure students are motivated to do their best but not overly anxious. • Score responses separately for content and quality of writing. • Look at students' errors for clues about specific cognitive processing difficulties. • Use informal assessments to confirm or disconfirm the results of formal assessments.
Students with social or behavioral problems	• Inconsistent performance on classroom assessments due to off-task behaviors or lack of motivation (for some students)	• Make modifications in assessment procedures as necessary (see the strategies just presented for students with specific cognitive or academic difficulties). • Use informal assessments to confirm or disconfirm the results of formal classroom assessments.
Students with general delays in cognitive and social functioning	• Slow learning and cognitive processing • Limited, if any, reading skills • Poor listening skills	• Be explicit about what you are asking students to do. • Make sure all reading materials are appropriate for students' reading levels. • Use performance assessments that require little reading or writing. • Allow considerable time for students to complete assigned tasks.
Students with physical or sensory challenges	• Mobility problems (for some students with physical challenges) • Tendency to tire easily (for some students with physical challenges) • Less developed language abilities (for some students with hearing loss)	• Use written rather than oral assessments (for students with hearing loss). • Minimize reliance on visual materials (for students with visual impairments). • Use appropriate technology to facilitate students' performance. • Provide extra time for students to complete assessments. • Limit assessments to short time periods, and give frequent breaks. • Use simple language if students have language difficulties.
Students with advanced cognitive development	• Greater ability to perform exceptionally complex tasks • Unusual, sometimes creative responses to classroom assessment instruments • Tendency to hide giftedness to avoid possible ridicule by peers (in some students)	• Use performance assessments to assess complex activities. • Establish scoring criteria that allow for unusual and creative responses. • Provide opportunities for students to demonstrate their achievements privately, especially if they are concerned that peers might disapprove of their high ability level.

Sources: Barkley, 2006; Beirne-Smith et al., 2006; D. Y. Ford & Harris, 1992; Mercer & Pullen, 2005; D. P. Morgan & Jenson, 1988; Piirto, 1999; Sireci, Scarpati, & Li, 2005; Stein & Krishnan, 2007; Turnbull et al., 2007; Whitaker Sena et al., 2007.

how students should study classroom subject matter. As we develop our classroom assessment tasks, then, we should continually ask ourselves questions such as these:

- Do assigned tasks reflect what is really most important for students to know and do?
- Do the tasks encourage students to engage in higher-level cognitive processes—for instance, problem solving, creativity, and critical thinking?
- Are scoring criteria stringent enough to ensure that students feel challenged yet not so stringent that students will perceive success to be impossible?
- Are students involved in assessing their own performance often enough that they are acquiring the skills they will ultimately need to be self-regulating learners?

Even when we are conducting summative evaluations of what students have learned, our ultimate goal should be to *help students learn better.*

• ***Classroom assessment practices also affect students' motivation and emotions.*** How we assess students' learning and achievement will, to some degree, determine whether they adopt mastery goals or performance goals and whether they have facilitating or debilitating levels of anxiety about classroom tasks. Ideally, our assessment practices should provide sufficient "wiggle room" that students feel comfortable taking on the challenges and making the mistakes so critical for their optimal learning and development.

• ***Classroom assessments are useful yet imperfect tools.*** No matter how well planned and executed, any single assessment almost invariably has limitations with respect to two or more of the RSVP characteristics: reliability, standardization, validity, and practicality. As a general rule, then, we should use a wide variety of assessments—both informal and formal, both paper–pencil and performance-based—to assess students' progress, improve classroom instruction, and maximize students' achievement over the long run.

Practice for Your Licensure Exam

Pick and Choose

Knowing that frequent paper–pencil quizzes will encourage students to study and review class material regularly, Mr. Bloskas tells his middle school science students that they will have a quiz every Friday. As a first-year teacher, he has had little experience developing test questions; thus, he decides to use the questions in the test-item manual that accompanies the class textbook. The night before the first quiz, Mr. Bloskas selects 30 multiple-choice and true–false items from the manual, making sure they cover the specific topics he has addressed in class.

Mr. Bloskas's students complain that the questions are "picky." As he looks carefully at his quiz, he realizes they are right: The quiz measures nothing more than memorization of trivial details. So when he prepares the second quiz, Mr. Bloskas casts the test-item manual aside and writes two essay questions that ask students to apply principles they have studied to new, real-life situations.

The following Friday, students complain even more loudly about the second quiz: "This is too hard!" "We never studied this stuff!" "I liked the first quiz better!" Later, as Mr. Bloskas scores the essays, he's appalled to discover how poorly his students have performed. "Back to the publisher's picky test items," he tells himself.

1. **Constructed-response question:**

   When identifying classroom assessment tasks, teachers must be sure that the tasks have validity, especially *content validity.*

   A. Compare the content validity of Mr. Bloskas's two quizzes.

   B. Describe an approach Mr. Bloskas might use to create quizzes that have reasonable content validity for his classes.

2. **Multiple-choice question:**

   The alternatives below present four possible explanations for the students' negative reactions to the second quiz. Drawing on contemporary theories of learning and motivation, choose the most likely explanation.

   a. Multiple-choice and true–false items are more likely than essay questions to enhance students' sense of self-determination.
   b. Learners are most likely to behave and study in ways that they expect will lead to reinforcement.
   c. Multiple-choice and true–false items are apt to foster learning goals, whereas essay questions are more likely to foster performance goals.
   d. Multiple-choice and true–false items assess information in short-term memory, whereas essay questions are more apt to assess information in long-term memory.

Go to Chapter 14 of the Book-Specific Resources in **MyEducationLab**, and click on "Practice for Your Licensure Exam" to answer these questions. Compare your responses with the feedback provided.

PRAXIS

Turn to Appendix C, "Matching Book and MyEducationLab Content to the Praxis Principles of Learning and Teaching Tests," to discover sections of this chapter that may be especially applicable to the Praxis tests.

PEARSON myeducationlab

Now go to MyEducationLab (**www.myeducationlab.com**) where you can:

- Find learning outcomes for Assessment, along with the national standards that connect to these outcomes.
- Complete Assignments and Activities that can help you more deeply understand the chapter content.
- Engage in Building Teaching Skills and Dispositions exercises in which you can apply and practice core teaching skills identified in the chapter.
- Access Book-Specific Resources:
  - Check your comprehension of chapter content by going to the Study Plan, where you can find (a) Chapter Objectives; (b) Focus Questions that can guide your reading; (c) a Self-Check Quiz that can help you monitor your progress in mastering chapter content; (d) Review, Practice, and Enrichment exercises with detailed feedback that will deepen your understanding of various concepts and principles; (e) Flashcards that can give you practice in understanding and defining key terms; and (f) Common Beliefs and Misconceptions about Educational Psychology that will alert you to typical misunderstandings in educational psychology classes.
  - Video Examples of various concepts and principles presented in the chapter.
  - Supplementary Readings that enable you to pursue certain topics in greater depth.
  - A Practice for Your Licensure Exam exercise that resembles the kinds of questions appearing on many teacher licensure tests.

CHAPTER OUTLINE

CHAPTER OBJECTIVES

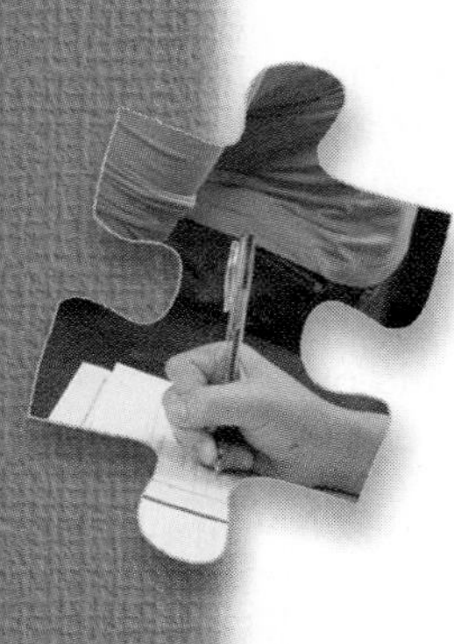

- **Objective 15.1:** Describe the nature, advantages, and disadvantages of three types of test scores: raw scores, criterion-referenced scores, and norm-referenced scores.
- **Objective 15.2:** Describe the guidelines you should follow in summarizing students' achievement with final grades and portfolios.
- **Objective 15.3:** Describe four different kinds of standardized tests, and explain how you might appropriately use and interpret such tests.
- **Objective 15.4:** Explain how high-stakes testing and accountability practices can affect instruction and classroom learning, and suggest several strategies for maximizing the benefits of these practices.
- **Objective 15.5:** Explain how you might accommodate cultural and linguistic diversity and special educational needs in your efforts to summarize students' achievement.
- **Objective 15.6:** Distinguish between the circumstances in which you should and should not reveal students' assessment results, and explain how you can effectively communicate these results to students and parents.

Chapter 15

Summarizing Students' Achievement and Abilities

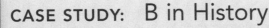

CASE STUDY: B in History

Twelve-year-old Ellie is the top student in Ms. Davidson's sixth-grade class. She is bright, motivated, and conscientious about completing her in-class work and homework assignments, and she has consistently earned straight As on report cards in previous years.

At the end of the school day on a Friday in November, Ms. Davidson tells her class, "As you all know, our first-quarter grading period ended last week. Today I have your report cards for you to take home to your parents. I'm especially proud of one student who always puts forth her best effort, and her grades are almost perfect." She smiles at Ellie with obvious affection and hands her a report card. "Here you are. Just one B, Ellie, in history. I'm sure you'll be able to bring it up to an A next quarter."

Despite the praise, Ellie is devastated. She is blindsided by the B; she had no idea it was coming. Embarrassed beyond words, she successfully fights back tears but looks down at her desk while Ms. Davidson distributes the other report cards. When the final school bell rings, Ellie quickly gathers her backpack and heads out the door, forgoing the usual after-school good-byes to her friends.

- **Ellie's parents are unlikely to be concerned about her single B; they are more worried about Ellie's younger brother, a second grader who still cannot read and probably has an undiagnosed learning disability. Why, then, might Ellie be so upset? Suggest at least two possible explanations.**
- **Was it appropriate for Ms. Davidson to announce Ellie's grades to the class? Why or why not?**

ALTHOUGH ELLIE UNDOUBTEDLY KNOWS that she's made occasional errors on history assessments, she's apparently been unaware of how those errors might add up to a B rather than an A. And with her past straight-A record, she's set an extremely high standard for herself. Only perfection is good enough—an unrealistic standard held by perhaps 25% of high-achieving sixth graders (Parker, 1997). In addition, Ms. Davidson has announced Ellie's imperfection to the entire class. As a young adolescent, Ellie isn't sure which is worse: that her peers know she's earned the highest grades in the class or that they know she's not perfect in history. Not only does Ms. Davidson's announcement make Ellie extremely uncomfortable, but it also violates her right to confidentiality. In fact, as we'll discover later in the chapter, making a student's grades public, as Ms. Davidson does, is illegal, at least in the United States.

As teachers, we must eventually determine what students have accomplished during the course of a school term or academic year. As we do so, we must keep the four RSVP characteristics in mind. In particular, an overall indicator of achievement should be *reliable*, reflecting a consistent pattern of achievement rather than a rare, chance occurrence. It should also be *standardized*: Except for extenuating circumstances (e.g., the special needs of students with disabilities), the same criteria should apply to everyone. In addition, any summary of achievement should be *valid*; that is, it should accurately reflect what students have learned and achieved. Finally, it must be *practical* in terms of the time and effort it requires.

Our first order of business in this chapter will be to consider how we might summarize students' performance on a single assessment instrument. After that, we'll consider ways to summarize students' achievement on a broader scale.

Summarizing the Results of a Single Assessment

One way to summarize students' performance on a single assessment is to write brief verbal descriptions of things they have done well and things they need to work on—descriptions that can ultimately help students improve their knowledge and skills. Yet writing a summary of every student's performance on every classroom assessment would be extremely time consuming (a practicality issue). More often, then, teachers use numbers or letter grades to summarize how students have performed on individual assessments. To simplify our discussion, we'll focus on numbers, which we'll call *scores*. The scores on individual assessments, whether teacher-developed instruments or standardized tests, typically take one of three forms: raw scores, criterion-referenced scores, and norm-referenced scores.

FIGURE 15.1 Example of a criterion-referenced checklist rubric in a beginning swimming class

Springside Parks and Recreation Department
Beginner Swimmer Class

Students must demonstrate proficiency in each of the following:

- ☐ Jump into chest-deep water
- ☐ Hold breath under water for 8 seconds
- ☐ Float in prone position for 10 seconds
- ☐ Glide in prone position with flutter kick
- ☐ Float on back for 10 seconds
- ☐ Glide on back with flutter kick
- ☐ Demonstrate crawl stroke and rhythmic breathing while standing in chest-deep water
- ☐ Show knowledge of basic water safety rules

Raw Scores

A **raw score** is a score based solely on the number or percentage of points earned or items answered correctly. For example, a student who correctly answers 15 items on a 20-item multiple-choice test might get a score of 75%. A student who gets 3 points, 8 points, and 5 points on three essay questions, respectively, might get an overall score of 16. Raw scores are easy to calculate, and they appear to be easy to understand. But in fact, we sometimes have trouble knowing what raw scores really mean. Are scores of 75% and 16 good scores or bad ones? Without knowing what kinds of tasks an assessment includes, we have no easy way of interpreting a raw score.

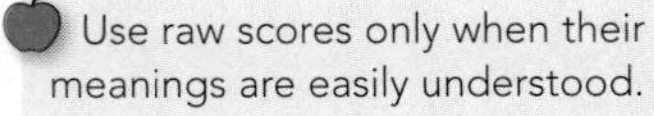
Use raw scores only when their meanings are easily understood.

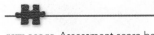

Criterion-Referenced Scores

As you might guess, criterion-referenced scores and norm-referenced scores are used, respectively, with criterion-referenced and norm-referenced assessment instruments. More specifically, a **criterion-referenced score** indicates what students have achieved in relation to specific instructional objectives or content area standards. Some criterion-referenced scores are *either–or* scores indicating that a student has mastered or not mastered a skill, met or not met an objective, or passed or failed a unit. Figure 15.1 illustrates this approach in a beginning swimming class. Other criterion-referenced scores indicate various levels of competence or achievement. For example, Figure 15.2 presents a rubric for grading students' written work. Using this rubric, a

raw score Assessment score based solely on the number or point value of correctly answered items.

criterion-referenced score Assessment score that specifically indicates what a student knows or can do.

FIGURE 15.2 Example of a criterion-referenced rating-scale rubric for summarizing the quality of high school students' writing samples

Score	Ideas and Content	Organization	Voice	Word Choice	Sentence Fluency	Conventions
5	• Clear, focused topic. • Relevant and accurate supporting details.	• Clear intro and body and satisfying conclusion. • Thoughtful transitions clearly show how ideas are connected. • Sequencing is logical and effective.	• Tone furthers purpose and appeals to audience. • Appropriately individual and expressive.	• Words are specific and accurate. • Language and phrasing is natural, effective, and appropriate.	• Sentence construction produces natural flow and rhythm.	• Grammar and usage are correct and contribute to clarity and style.
3	• Broad topic. • Support is generalized or insufficient.	• Recognizable beginning, middle, and end. • Transitions often work well; sometimes connections between ideas are fuzzy. • Sequencing is functional.	• Tone is appropriate for purpose and audience. • Not fully engaged or involved.	• Words are adequate and support the meaning. • Language is general but functional.	• Sentences are constructed correctly.	• Grammar and usage mistakes do not impede meaning.
1	• Unclear topic. • Lacking or irrelevant support.	• No apparent organization. • Lack of transitions. • Sequencing is illogical.	• Not concerned with audience or fails to match purpose. • Indifferent or inappropriate.	• Improper word choice/usage makes writing difficult to understand. • Language is vague or redundant.	• Sentences are choppy, incomplete, or unnatural.	• Grammar and usage mistakes distract the reader or impede meaning.

Source: From *Breaking Ranks II: Strategies for Leading High School Reform* by the National Association of Secondary School Principals (NASSP), p. 103. Copyright 2004, National Association of Secondary School Principals, Reston, VA. www.principals.org<htttp://www.principals.org> Reprinted with permission.

teacher would give every student's paper six criterion-referenced scores (for "Ideas and Content," "Organization," etc.), each of them on a scale of 1 to 5.

Norm-Referenced Scores

A **norm-referenced score** is derived by comparing a student's performance on an assessment with the performance of others—perhaps that of classmates or perhaps that of students in a nationwide *norm group*. The set of scores obtained from the comparison group comprises the **norms** for the assessment. A norm-referenced score tells us little about what a student specifically knows and can do; instead, it tells us whether a student's performance is typical or unusual for his or her age or grade level.

Most scores on published standardized tests are norm-referenced scores. In some cases the scores are derived by comparing a student's performance with that of students at a variety of grade or age levels; such comparisons give us grade- or age-equivalent scores. In other cases the scores are based on comparisons only with students of the *same* age or grade; these comparisons give us either percentile scores or standard scores.

norm-referenced score Assessment score that indicates how a student's performance compares with the performance of others.

norms In assessment, data regarding the typical performance of various groups of students on a standardized test or other norm-referenced measure of a particular characteristic or ability.

FIGURE 15.3 Hypothetical norm-group data for the Reading Achievement Test (RAT)

Norms for Grade Levels		Norms for Age Levels	
Grade	Average Raw Score	Age	Average Raw Score
5	19	10	18
6	25	11	24
7	30	12	28
8	34	13	33
9	39	14	37
10	43	15	41
11	46	16	44
12	50	17	48

Grade-Equivalent and Age-Equivalent Scores Imagine that Shawn takes a standardized test, the Reading Achievement Test (RAT). He gets 46 of the 60 test items correct; thus, 46 is his raw score. We turn to the norms reported in the test manual and find the average raw scores for students at different grade and age levels (see Figure 15.3). Shawn's raw score of 46 is the same as the average score of eleventh graders in the norm group, so he has a **grade-equivalent score** of 11. His score is also halfway between the average score of 16-year-old and 17-year-old students, so he has an **age-equivalent score** of about 16½. Shawn is 13 years old and in the eighth grade, so he has obviously done well on the RAT.

In general, grade- and age-equivalent scores are determined by matching a student's raw score to that of a particular grade or age level in the norm group. A student who performs on a reading test as well as the average second grader will get a grade-equivalent score of 2, regardless of the student's actual grade level. A student who gets the same raw score on a physical fitness test as the average 10-year-old will get an age-equivalent score of 10, regardless of whether that student is 5, 10, or 15 years old.

Grade- and age-equivalent scores are frequently used because they seem so simple and straightforward. But they have a serious drawback: They give us no idea of the typical *range* of performance for students at a particular grade or age level. For example, a raw score of 34 on the RAT gives us a grade-equivalent score of 8, but obviously not all eighth graders will get raw scores of exactly 34. It's possible (and, in fact quite likely) that many eighth graders will get raw scores several points above or below 34—yielding grade-equivalent scores of 9 or 7, perhaps even 10 or higher, or 6 or lower. Yet grade-equivalent scores are often used inappropriately as a standard for performance. Parents, some government officials, and the public at large may believe that *all* students should perform at grade level on an achievement test. Given the normal variability in virtually any classroom, this goal is impossible to meet.

Percentile Ranks A **percentile rank** (the shortened form is **percentile**) is the percentage of people at the same age or grade level getting a raw score less than or equal to the student's raw score. To illustrate, let's once again consider Shawn's performance on the RAT. Because Shawn is in the eighth grade, we turn to the eighth-grade norms in the RAT test manual. If we discover that a raw score of 46 is at the 98th percentile for eighth graders, we know that Shawn has done as well as or better than 98% of eighth graders in the norm group. Similarly, a student getting a percentile rank of 25 has performed better than 25% of the norm group, and a student getting a score at the 60th percentile has done better than 60%. It's important to note that a percentile rank refers to a percentage of *people*, not to the percentage of correct items—a common misconception among teacher education students (Lennon et al., 1990).

Percentile ranks are relatively easy to understand and therefore used frequently in reporting test results. But they have a major weakness: They distort actual differences among students. For example, consider the RAT percentile ranks of these four boys:

Student	***Percentile Rank***
Ernest	45
Frank	55
Giorgio	89
Wayne	99

In *actual achievement* (as measured by the RAT), Ernest and Frank are probably very similar to one another, even though their percentile ranks are 10 points apart. However, a 10-point difference at the upper end of the scale probably reflects a substan-

grade-equivalent score Test score matching a particular student's performance with the average performance of students at a certain grade level.

age-equivalent score Test score matching a particular student's performance with the average performance of students of a certain age.

percentile rank (percentile) Test score indicating the percentage of peers in the norm group getting a raw score less than or equal to a particular student's raw score.

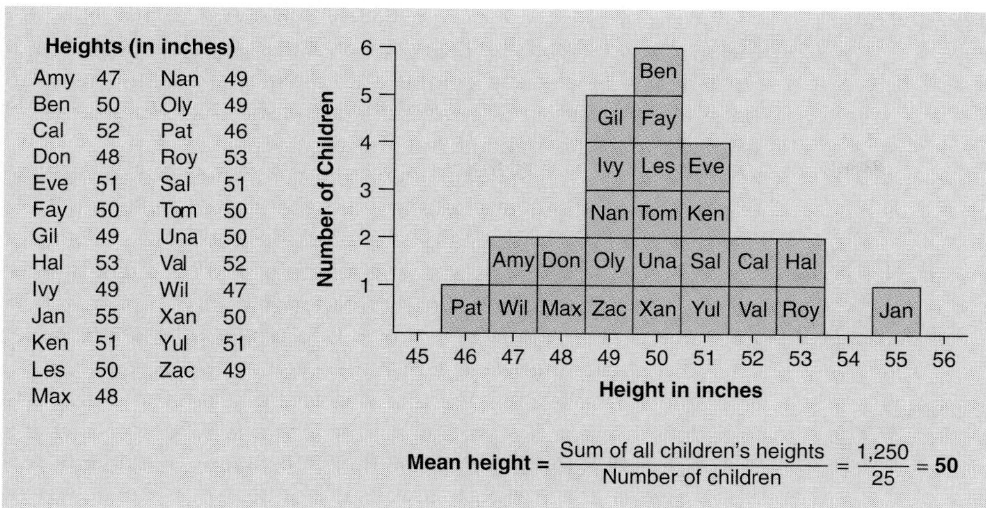

FIGURE 15.4 Heights of children in Ms. Oppenheimer's third-grade class

tial difference in achievement: Giorgio's percentile rank of 89 tells us that he knows quite a bit, but Wayne's percentile rank of 99 tells us that he knows an exceptional amount.

In general, percentiles tend to *over*estimate differences in the middle range of the characteristic being measured: Scores a few points apart reflect similar achievement or ability. Meanwhile, percentiles *under*estimate differences at the upper and lower extremes: Scores only a few points apart often reflect significant differences in achievement or ability. We can avoid these problems with percentiles by using standard scores.

Standard Scores The school nurse measures the heights of the 25 students in Ms. Oppenheimer's third-grade class; these heights are presented on the left side of Figure 15.4. The nurse then creates a graph of the children's heights, shown on the right side of Figure 15.4. Notice that the graph is high in the middle and low at both ends. This shape tells us that most of Ms. Oppenheimer's students are more or less average in height, with only a handful of very short students (e.g., Pat, Amy, Wil) and just a few very tall ones (e.g., Hal, Roy, Jan).

Many psychologists believe that educational and psychological characteristics (including academic achievement and abilities) typically follow the same pattern we see for height: Most people are close to average, with fewer and fewer people being counted as we move farther from this average. This theoretical pattern of educational and psychological characteristics, known as the **normal distribution** (or **normal curve**), is shown in the margin. Standard scores reflect this normal distribution: Many students have scores in the middle range, and only a few have very high or very low scores.

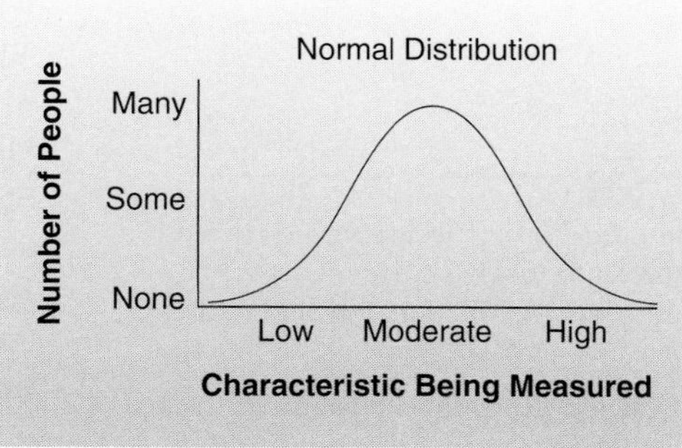

normal distribution (normal curve) Theoretical pattern of educational and psychological characteristics, in which most individuals score in the middle range and only a few score at either extreme.

mean (M) Mathematical average of a set of scores.

standard deviation (SD) Statistic indicating the amount of variability characterizing a set of scores.

Before we examine standard scores in more detail, we need to understand two numbers used to derive these scores: the mean and the standard deviation. The **mean (M)** is the *average* of a set of scores: We add all the scores together and divide by the total number of scores (or people). For example, if we add the heights of all 25 students in Ms. Oppenheimer's class and divide the sum by 25, we get a mean height of 50 inches (see the calculation at the bottom of Figure 15.4).

The **standard deviation (SD)** indicates the *variability* of a set of scores. A small number tells us that, generally speaking, the scores are close together, and a large number tells us that they are spread far apart. For example, third graders tend to be more similar in height than eighth graders; some eighth graders are less than five feet tall, whereas others may be almost six feet tall. The standard deviation for the heights

FIGURE 15.5 Normal distribution divided by the mean and the standard deviation

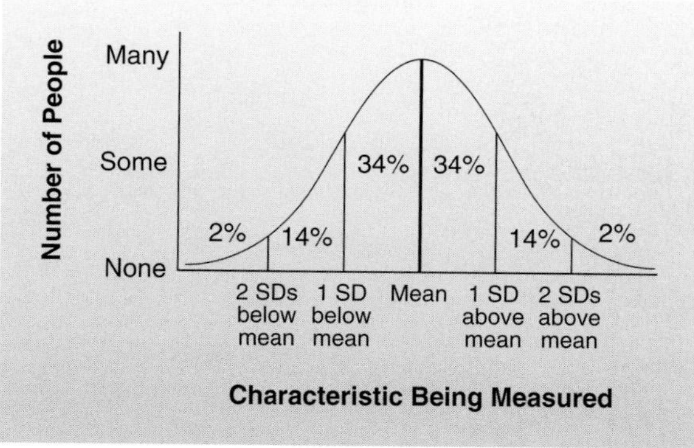

of third graders is therefore smaller than the standard deviation for the heights of eighth graders. The formula for calculating a standard deviation is fairly complex; fortunately, we don't need to know the formula in order to understand the role that a standard deviation plays in standard scores.

The mean and standard deviation can be used to divide the normal distribution into several parts, as shown in Figure 15.5. The vertical line in the middle of the curve shows the mean; for a normal distribution, it's both the midpoint and the highest point of the curve. The thinner lines to either side of the mean reflect the standard deviation: We count out 1 standard deviation higher and lower than the mean and mark each of those spots with a line, and then we count another standard deviation to either side and draw another line in each of those spots. When we divide a normal distribution in this way, the percentages of students getting scores in each part are always the same. Approximately two-thirds (68%) get scores within 1 standard deviation of the mean (34% in each direction). As we go farther away from the mean, we find fewer and fewer students, with 28% being between 1 and 2 standard deviations away (14% on each side) and only about 4% being more than 2 standard deviations away (2% at each end).

myeducationlab

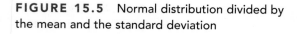

Learn how to calculate a standard deviation in the supplementary reading "Calculating Standard Deviations." (To find this reading, go to Chapter 15 of the Book-Specific Resources in MyEducationLab, and then select *Supplementary Readings.*)

Now that we better understand the normal distribution and two statistics that describe it, let's return to standard scores. A **standard score** reflects a student's position in the normal distribution: It tells us how far the student's performance is from the mean in terms of standard deviation units. Unfortunately, not all standard scores use the same scale: Scores used for various tests have different means and standard deviations. Four commonly used standard scores, depicted graphically in Figure 15.6, are the following:

IQ scores are frequently used to report students' performance on intelligence tests. They have a *mean of 100* and, for most tests, a *standard deviation of 15*. If you look back at Figure 5.1 in Chapter 5, you'll see that the curve is broken up by thirds of a standard deviation unit. The lines for 85 and 115 reflect 1 standard deviation from the mean score of 100. The lines for 70 and 130 reflect 2 SDs from the mean.

ETS scores are used on tests published by the Educational Testing Service, such as the SAT Reasoning Test and the Graduate Record Examination (GRE). They have a *mean of 500* and a *standard deviation of 100*. However, no scores fall below 200 or above 800.

Stanines (short for *standard nines*) are often used to report standardized achievement test results. They have a *mean of 5* and a *standard deviation of 2*. Because they are always reported as whole numbers, each score reflects a *range* of test performance, indicated by the shaded and nonshaded portions of the upper-right-hand curve in Figure 15.6.

***z*-scores** are the standard scores that statisticians most often use. They have a *mean of 0* and a *standard deviation of 1*.

standard score Test score indicating how far a student's performance is from the mean in terms of standard deviation units.

IQ score Score on an intelligence test, as determined by comparing a person's performance on the test with that of others in the same age-group; for most tests, it's a standard score with a mean of 100 and a standard deviation of 15.

ETS score Standard score with a mean of 500 and a standard deviation of 100.

stanine Standard score with a mean of 5 and a standard deviation of 2; always reported as a whole number.

***z*-score** Standard score with a mean of 0 and a standard deviation of 1.

Often the publishers of standardized achievement tests use two or more kinds of scores to report students' test results. For example, the left side of Figure 15.7 shows a computer printout with 12-year-old Ingrid's percentile and stanine scores on achievement tests in several content domains. These scores reveal average to below-average achievement in spelling and math computation, average to above-average achievement in math concepts, and well-above-average achievement in reading comprehension, science, and social studies. The "National Percentile Bands" (shown as rows of Xs within some of the green lines), which are more commonly called *confidence intervals*, reflect the amount of error (due to imperfect reliability) that's apt to be affecting Ingrid's percentile scores. (You can learn more about confidence intervals in Appendix B.)

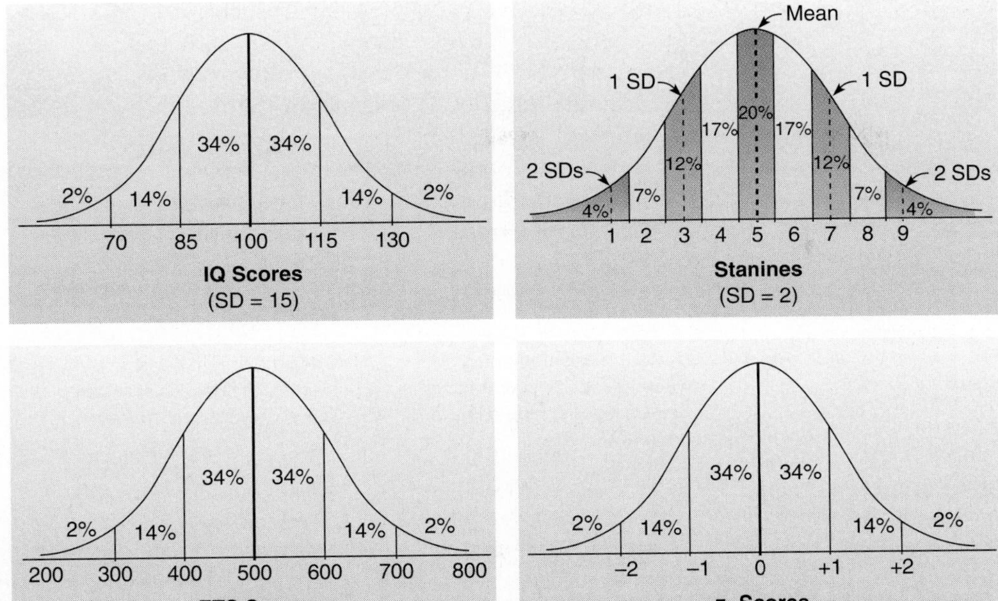

FIGURE 15.6 Distributions of four types of standard scores

Notice how the numbers at the bottom of the computer printout (1, 5, 10, 20, etc.) are unevenly spaced. Remember a point made earlier about percentile ranks: They overestimate differences near the mean and underestimate differences at the extremes. The uneven spacing is the test publisher's way of showing this fact: It squishes the middle percentile scores closer together and spreads high and low percentile scores farther apart. In this way, the publisher tries to give students and parents an idea about where students' test scores fall in a normal distribution.

Table 15.1 provides a summary of raw scores, criterion-referenced scores, and norm-referenced scores.

Using Criterion-Referenced versus Norm-Referenced Scores in the Classroom

Use criterion-referenced scores to indicate mastery of specific instructional goals and objectives.

In most instances, criterion-referenced scores communicate what teachers and students alike most need to know: whether instructional goals and content area standards have been achieved. Criterion-referenced scores focus attention on mastery goals and, by

FIGURE 15.7 Computer printout revealing 12-year-old Ingrid's scores on standardized achievement tests in several content domains

NATIONAL PERCENTILE BANDS

WELL BELOW AVERAGE : BELOW AVERAGE : AVERAGE : ABOVE AVERAGE : WELL ABOVE AVERAGE

	STANINE	PERCENTILE	1 5 10 20 30 40 50 60 70 80 90 95 99
READING COMPREHENSION	8	92	XXXXXXXXXXXXXX (≈85–99)
SPELLING	4	39	XXXXXXXXXXXX (≈30–50)
MATH COMPUTATION	4	37	XXXXXXXXXX (≈30–45)
MATH CONCEPTS	5	57	XXXXXXXXXXXX (≈48–68)
SCIENCE	8	90	XXXXXXXXXXXXXXX (≈80–97)
SOCIAL STUDIES	7	84	XXXXXXXX (≈76–90)
			1 5 10 20 30 40 50 60 70 80 90 95 99

Compare/ Contrast

TABLE 15.1
Scores Used to Summarize the Results of a Single Assessment

Type of Score	Method of Determining Score	Uses	Potential Drawbacks
Raw score	Counting the number (or calculating a percentage) of correct responses or points earned	Often used in teacher-developed assessment instruments	Scores may be difficult to interpret without knowledge of how performance relates either to a specific criterion or to a norm group.
Criterion-referenced score	Comparing performance to one or more criteria or standards for success	Useful when determining whether specific instructional objectives or standards have been achieved	Concrete criteria for assessing mastery of complex skills are sometimes difficult to identify.
Grade- or age-equivalent score (norm-referenced)	Equating a student's performance to the average performance of students at a particular grade or age level	Useful when explaining norm-referenced test performance to people who are unfamiliar with standard scores	Scores are frequently misinterpreted (especially by parents), may be inappropriately used as a standard that all students must meet, and are often inapplicable when achievement is being assessed in adolescence or adulthood.
Percentile rank (norm-referenced)	Determining the percentage of students at the same age or grade level who obtained the same score or lower scores	Useful when explaining norm-referenced test performance to people who are unfamiliar with standard scores	Scores overestimate differences near the mean and underestimate differences at the extremes.
Standard score (norm-referenced)	Determining how far the performance is from the mean (for the age or grade level) in terms of standard deviation units	Useful when describing a student's standing within the norm group	Scores are not easily understood by people who don't have some basic knowledge of statistics.

showing improvement over time, should enhance students' self-efficacy for learning academic subject matter. When criterion-referenced scores are difficult to determine—perhaps because an assessment addresses too many objectives simultaneously—raw scores are usually the second-best choice for teacher-developed assessments.

Norm-referenced scores—or, in everyday language, *grading on the curve*—may occasionally be appropriate if we truly need to indicate how students have performed relative to one another. For instance, we might find these scores helpful when designating first chairs in an instrumental music class (e.g., best violinist, best flutist, etc.) or when choosing the best entries for a regional science fair. We may also need to resort to a norm-referenced approach when assessing complex skills (e.g., writing poetry, demonstrating advanced athletic skills, or critically analyzing works of literature) that are difficult to describe as "mastered" or "not mastered."

We should probably *not* use norm-referenced scores for teacher-developed assessments on a regular basis, however. Such scores create a competitive situation, because students do well only if their performance surpasses that of their classmates. Thus, norm-referenced scores focus students' attention primarily on performance goals rather than on mastery goals and may possibly encourage students to cheat on assessment tasks (E. M. Anderman et al., 1998; Brophy, 2004; Mac Iver et al., 1995). Furthermore, the competitive atmosphere that norm-referenced scores create is inconsistent with the *sense of community* described in Chapter 13.

Use norm-referenced scores only when you truly need to compare the performances of various students.

Determining Final Class Grades

Most schools use letter and number grades to summarize students' overall achievement in particular content domains. Such grades have several limitations. First, different teachers use different criteria to assign grades; for instance, some are more lenient than others, and some stress rote memorization whereas others stress higher-level skills (L. Shepard et al., 2005). Second, in classes that include children of diverse backgrounds and needs, different students may be working to accomplish different instructional goals. Third, typical grading practices promote performance goals rather than mastery goals and may encourage students to go for the "easy A" instead of taking risks (Stipek, 1993; S. Thomas & Oldfather, 1997). Finally, students under pressure to achieve high grades may resort to undesirable behaviors (e.g., cheating, plagiarism) to attain those grades (Cizek, 2003).

Despite such problems, final grades continue to be the most common method of summarizing students' classroom achievement, in large part because school districts need an economical way of keeping track of students' overall performance to assist in decision making and communication with parents and colleges. The following recommendations can enhance the validity and usefulness of final class grades:

Take the job of grading seriously. Consider these scenarios:

- A high school math teacher who uses a formula to determine final grades makes numerous errors in his calculations. As a result, some students get lower grades than they've earned.
- A middle school Spanish teacher asks her teenage son to calculate her students' final grades. Some columns in her grade book are for scores students have earned when they've retaken a test on which they initially did poorly; students who did well on tests the first time have blanks in these columns. Not understanding the teacher's system, her son treats all blank spaces as zeros. The highest achievers—students who have many blank spots in the teacher's grade book—are quite surprised to discover that they've earned a D or F for the semester.

A math teacher who makes mathematical errors? A Spanish teacher who relies on a teenager to determine final grades? Preposterous? No, both scenarios are true stories. Students' final class grades are often the *only* data that appear in their school records. We must take the time and make the effort to ensure that those grades are accurate.

Many computer software programs are now available to assist with record keeping and grading. In addition to helping us keep track of a sizable body of assessment information, such software makes it easier to share our records with students on a regular basis (e.g., see Figure 15.8). We cannot use grading software mindlessly, however. For example, if we make errors when entering information or don't take into account the idiosyncrasies of our record-keeping system, we might as well have the Spanish teacher's son calculate our grades for us!

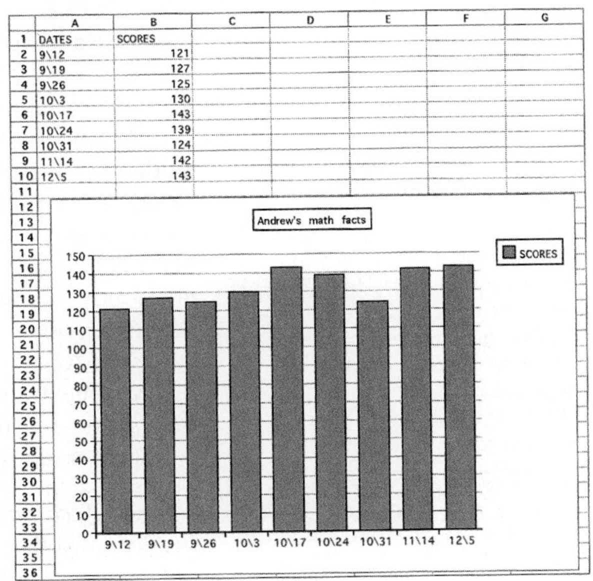

FIGURE 15.8 Computer software can often help us—and our students as well—keep track of students' performance on classroom assessments. Here we see 10-year-old Andrew's performance on regular quizzes of math facts. Each quiz is worth 150 points.

Base grades on achievement. Tempting as it might be to reward well-behaved, cooperative students with good grades and to punish chronic misbehavers with Ds or Fs, grades should ultimately reflect how much students have *learned.* Awarding good grades simply for good behavior may mislead students and their parents to believe that students are making better progress than they really are. And awarding low grades as punishment for disruptive behavior leads students to conclude, perhaps with good reason, that their teacher's grading system is arbitrary and meaningless (Brookhart, 2004; Cizek, 2003; L. Shepard et al., 2005).

Base grades on hard data. Subjective teacher judgments of students' achievement are imperfect assessments at best, and some teachers are better judges than others. Furthermore, although teachers can generally judge the achievement of high-ability students with some accuracy, they are less accurate when they subjectively assess the achievement of historically low-ability students (Gaines & Davis, 1990; Hoge & Coladarci, 1989). For these reasons and for the sake of our students—who learn more and achieve at higher levels when we tell them what we expect in concrete terms—we should base grades on objective information derived from formal assessments, *not* on subjective impressions of what students appear to know.

Use many assessments to determine grades, but don't count everything. Using multiple assessments to determine final grades can help us compensate for the imperfect reliability and validity of any single assessment instrument. At the same time, we probably don't want to consider *everything* students do. As noted in Chapter 14, we must create an atmosphere in which students feel free to take risks and make mistakes. Thus, we may not want to include students' early efforts at new tasks, which are likely to involve considerable trial and error. And many assessments may be more appropriately used for formative evaluation purposes—to help students learn—than for summative evaluation (Brookhart, 2004; Frisbie & Waltman, 1992; L. Shepard et al., 2005).

Identify a reasonable grading system, and stick to it. Consider this situation:

> At the beginning of the school year, Ms. Giroux tells her middle school students that final class grades will be based on the quiz scores they earn throughout the semester. But after a couple of months, she realizes that if she relies *only* on quiz scores, most students will get a D or F for the semester. To help students boost their grades, she asks them to turn in all of their homework assignments, which can contribute up to 20 percentage points toward final grades. The students protest loudly and angrily: Thinking there was no reason to keep completed homework assignments, many students have already discarded their previous work.

If most students are getting Ds and Fs, something is definitely wrong. Perhaps Ms. Giroux's instructional methods aren't as effective as other approaches might be. Perhaps she's moving so quickly through the curriculum that students never have time to master a topic. Perhaps her tests reflect unrealistic expectations about what students should be able to do.

As teachers, we can't always anticipate how best to teach a new topic or how well students will perform on particular assessments. Nevertheless, if we want to give students a sense that they have some control over their grades (recall our discussion of *internal attributions* in Chapter 11), we must tell them early in the semester or school year what our grading criteria will be. In addition, by providing concrete information about how we will be assigning grades, we avoid unpleasant surprises when students actually receive their grades (recall Ellie's sense of devastation in the opening case study). If we find that our initial criteria are overly stringent, we may need to lighten up in some way, perhaps by adjusting cutoffs or allowing retakes of critical assessments. But we must never change our criteria in midstream in a way that unfairly penalizes some students or imposes additional, unanticipated requirements.

myeducationlab

For ideas on possible grading systems you might use, see the supplementary reading "Combining Assessment Results to Determine Final Grades." (To find this reading, go to Chapter 15 of the Book-Specific Resources in MyEducationLab, and then select *Supplementary Readings*.)

Accompany grades with qualitative information about students' performance. Whether final grades take the form of letters or numbers, they are, at best, only general indicators of some *quantity* of what students have learned. Thus, it's often helpful to accompany grades with *qualitative* information—for instance, information about students' particular academic strengths, work habits, attitudes, social skills, unique contributions to the classroom community, and so on (e.g., see Figure 15.9). Students and parents alike often find such qualitative feedback just as informative as final class grades—sometimes even more informative. The feedback should be fairly explicit, however; comments such as "A pleasure to have in class" communicate little (Brookhart, 2004, p. 183).

FIGURE 15.9 Examples of qualitative feedback one second-grade teacher gave her students at the end of the school year

- To Amanda: You are a good friend to everyone in the class. You look out for people's feelings and work hard to make others feel good.
- To Andrea: You have a beautiful singing voice and are a very animated performer. You show self-confidence in all that you do.
- To Angus: You are always willing to lend a hand to teachers and peers alike. You have practical advice and reasonable solutions to many questions and situations that arise.
- To Charlotte: You are a very thoughtful worker. You always give 100% on everything you do. Your positive attitude and great work ethic are a wonderful addition to the class.
- To Colin: I love your sense of humor. You make me laugh with your great riddles and jokes. The humor in your stories is very creative and keeps your audience wanting to know more about the story.

Considering Improvement, Effort, and Extra Credit

Some educators suggest that students be graded at least partly on the basis of how much they improve, how hard they try, or how much extra work they do. Let's consider the implications of incorporating each of these factors into final class grades.

Considering Improvement As we discovered in our discussions of self-efficacy and intrinsic motivation in Chapters 10 and 11, motivation theorists stress the importance of focusing students' attention more on their own improvement than on how their performance compares with that of peers. But assessment experts have made two good arguments against basing final grades solely on students' improvement over the course of a semester or school year. First, students who have, in an earlier grade, mastered some of the topics in the year's curriculum will have less room for improvement than their classmates. Second, when we use improvement as a criterion, students trying to "beat the system" may quickly realize that they can achieve high grades simply by performing as poorly as possible at the beginning of the year (Airasian, 1994; Sax, 1989).

How do we balance what motivation theorists recommend, on the one hand, with what assessment experts recommend, on the other? Following are several possible strategies:

- Assign greater weight to assessments conducted at the end of the semester or school year, after *all* students have had a reasonable opportunity to achieve instructional goals.
- Give students a chance to correct their errors and, in doing so, to demonstrate mastery.
- Administer retakes of assessments, perhaps using items or tasks different from those presented the first time.
- Reinforce improvement in other ways—for instance, with free time or special privileges. (Lester et al., 1997; L. Shepard et al., 2005)

Considering Effort Most assessment experts urge us *not* to base final grades on the amount of effort students appear to exert in their studies. For one thing, students who begin the year already performing at a high level are penalized because they may not have to work as hard as their less knowledgeable classmates. Furthermore, student effort is something we can evaluate only subjectively and imprecisely at best (Brookhart, 2004; L. Shepard et al., 2005).

Evaluate students' effort separately from their achievement.

An alternative is to have students work for individualized instructional goals appropriate for their existing ability levels (Brookhart, 2004; Mac Iver et al., 1991).

myeducationlab

Observe a strategy for reinforcing improvement separately from achievement in the video "Cooperative Learning." (To find this video, go to Chapter 15 of the Book-Specific Resources in MyEducationLab, select *Video Examples*, and then click on the title.)

Such an approach is workable *if*, when we report students' final grades, we also report the instructional goals on which the grades are based. In fact, this approach is widely used for students with special educational needs, whose goals are described in their individualized education programs (IEPs).

Obviously, we enhance students' motivation when we acknowledge their effort in some significant way (Brookhart, 2004; Pintrich & Schunk, 2002). Some school systems have multidimensional grading systems that allow teachers to assign separate grades to the various aspects of students' classroom performance. Such mechanisms as letters to parents, parent–teacher conferences, and letters of recommendation provide additional means by which we can describe the multifaceted nature of students' classroom performance.

Giving Extra Credit Over the years, I have occasionally had students appear at my office door, asking—sometimes begging—for an opportunity to improve their grades at the last minute by completing extra-credit projects. My response is invariably *no* for a very good reason: My course grades are based on the extent to which students achieve instructional goals for the course, as determined by their performance on assessments that are the same or equivalent (therefore standardized and fair) for all students. Extra-credit projects assigned to only one or two students (typically those who are achieving at a low level) are insufficient to demonstrate mastery of the subject matter and are not standardized for the entire class.

Be sure that any extra-credit assignments relate to instructional goals and are available to all students.

Extra-credit work is occasionally appropriate *provided that* (a) the work relates to instructional goals and (b) all students have the same opportunity to complete it (Padilla-Walker, 2006; L. Shepard et al., 2005). It is *not* appropriate when its only purpose is to help a failing student earn a passing grade.

Choosing Criterion-Referenced or Norm-Referenced Grades

Many experts recommend that final grades reflect mastery of classroom subject matter and instructional goals—in other words, that final grades be criterion-referenced. Criterion-referenced grades are especially appropriate during the elementary years: Much of the elementary curriculum consists of basic skills that are either mastered or not mastered, and there is little need to use grades as a basis for comparing students to one another.

The issue becomes more complicated at the secondary level: Students' grades are sometimes used to choose college applicants, award scholarships, and so on. Historically, then, some secondary school teachers have used norm-referenced grades—for instance, giving As to the top 10% of each class, Bs to the next 20%, Cs to the middle 40%, and so on. My personal recommendation is that high school grades be criterion-referenced to the extent possible. The most critical decisions for which grades are used—decisions about promotion and graduation—should be based on students' mastery or nonmastery of the school curriculum, not on their standing relative to others. Furthermore, because different classes of students often differ in ability level, a strictly norm-referenced approach might grade a student's performance in one class (e.g., Honors Math) as a C, whereas the same performance in another class (e.g., General Math) might warrant an A. (Under such circumstances, a student striving for a high grade point average would be foolish to enroll in the Honors section.) Finally, only a very few students (i.e., the highest achievers) find a norm-referenced grading system motivating; most students quickly resign themselves to achieving at an average level at best (see the discussion of factors affecting self-efficacy in Chapter 10).[1]

Assign final grades that are criterion-referenced unless there is a compelling reason to do otherwise.

---

[1]Over the past several decades, teachers have gradually moved from norm-referenced grading (i.e., grading on the curve) to criterion-referenced grading. This focus on mastery of instructional goals and objectives, rather than on comparing students, accounts in part for the increasing grade point averages (i.e., "grade inflation") about which some public figures complain.

When setting up a criterion-referenced grading system, we should determine as concretely as possible what we want each grade to communicate. For example, if assigning traditional letter grades, we might use criteria such as the following:

Grade	***Criteria***
A	The student has a firm command of both basic and advanced knowledge and skills in the content domain. He or she is well prepared for future learning tasks.
B	The student has mastered all basic knowledge and skills. Mastery at a more advanced level is evident in some but not all areas. In most respects, he or she is ready for future learning tasks.
C	The student has mastered basic knowledge and skills but has difficulty with more advanced aspects of the subject matter. He or she lacks a few of the prerequisites critical for future learning tasks.
D	The student has mastered some but not all of the basics in the content domain. He or she lacks many prerequisites for future learning tasks.
F	The student shows little or no mastery of instructional objectives and cannot demonstrate the most elementary knowledge and skills. He or she lacks most of the prerequisites essential for success in future learning tasks. (Based on criteria described by Frisbie & Waltman, 1992)

Only when final grades reflect criteria such as these can they legitimately be used for instructional decision making.

Including Students in the Grading Process

Let's return to the opening case study, in which Ellie is completely blindsided by her B in history. Obviously, Ellie has been aware of her scores on history assignments and quizzes, but she apparently hasn't been aware of how those scores would be combined into an overall grade. Although Ellie's teacher has presumably been tracking her progress over time, Ellie herself has not been.

In previous chapters, we've repeatedly seen the benefits of self-assessment for self-regulation and motivation. But in the end, we teachers must be the ones to determine students' final grades, as most students are apt to give themselves grades based on what they would *like* rather than what they have objectively *earned* (e.g., see Figure 15.10). Yet final grades should not seemingly come out of the blue. Students must know, in advance and in concrete terms, our criteria for assigning grades, and we must frequently update students about their progress toward earning the grades they want (e.g., as the computer printout does in Figure 15.8). Under these conditions, students *do* have a say in the grades they earn—by working hard to master classroom subject matter.

FIGURE 15.10 In her rationale for getting an A for the term, 15-year-old Lexee focuses on effort, punctuality, and class participation rather than on achievement.

I think that I deserve an A+ for this term. I tried my best just some of the grammar things were hard for me so I got a few lower grades. oops! I'll list the other two reasons.
-I got everything in on time.
-I tried to participate as much as possible in class.

Using Portfolios

Whenever we boil down students' achievement into single indicators such as letter or number grades, we lose valuable information about students' specific strengths and weaknesses, inclinations and disinclinations, and so on. In contrast, portfolios enable us to capture the complex, multifaceted nature of students' accomplishments and interests. A **portfolio** is a collection of a student's work systematically collected over a lengthy time period. It might include writing samples, student-constructed

portfolio Collection of a student's work compiled systematically over a lengthy time period.

FIGURE 15.11 In a kindergarten portfolio, Meghan and her teacher included two digital photographs to illustrate Meghan's developing math skills.

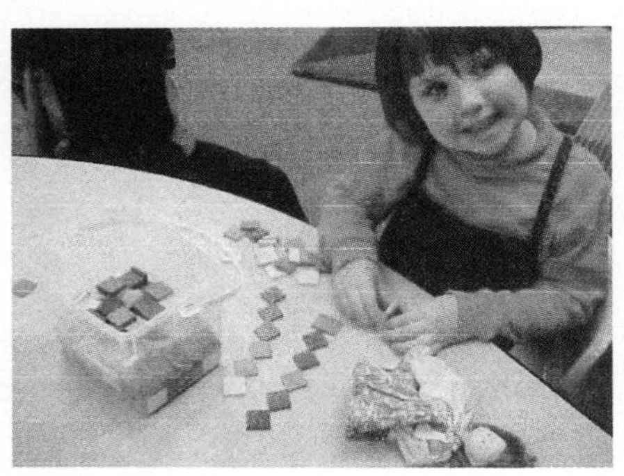

Meghan makes arrangements of six in math.

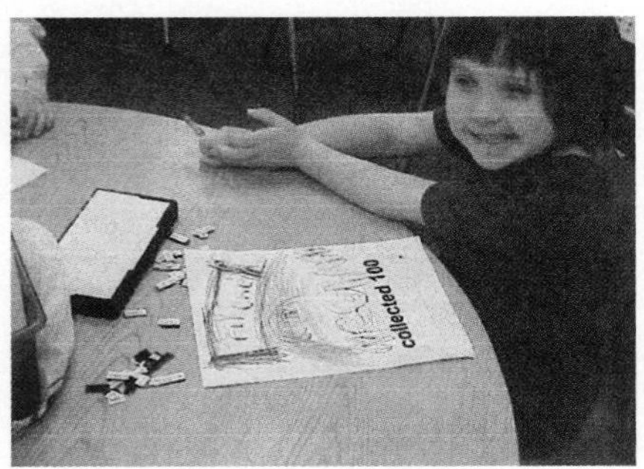

Meghan displays her collection of 100.

objects (e.g., sculptures, inventions), photographs, audio or video recordings, or any combination of these. For example, in the excerpt from a kindergarten portfolio shown in Figure 15.11, 6-year-old Meghan and her teacher used photographs to reveal Meghan's emerging math skills.

The samples of student work included in a portfolio are often called *artifacts*. In most cases students decide for themselves which artifacts to include in their portfolios (Paulson, Paulson, & Meyer, 1991; Popham, 1995; Spandel, 1997). The decision-making process can give students a sense of ownership of their portfolios and enhance their sense of self-determination and intrinsic motivation to learn.

In addition to specific artifacts, most school portfolios include student reflections that (a) identify the purpose(s) and goals of the portfolio, (b) describe each artifact and the reason(s) it was included, and (c) summarize what the collection of artifacts reveals about the student's achievement. For example, in Figure 15.12, 14-year-old Kurt describes and evaluates the writing samples he has included in a portfolio for his eighth-grade language arts class (his portfolio includes two or more drafts of each piece of writing). Student reflections encourage them to look at and judge their own work in ways that teachers typically do. Thus, they can promote the self-monitoring and self-evaluation skills so essential for self-regulated learning (Arter & Spandel, 1992; R. S. Johnson, Mims-Cox, & Doyle-Nichols, 2006; Vucko & Hadwin, 2004).

Types and Purposes of Portfolios

Portfolios take a variety of forms. Following are several types commonly used in school settings:

- *Working portfolio*—Shows competencies up to the present time; is dynamic in content, with new artifacts that show greater proficiency gradually replacing older, less skillful ones
- *Developmental portfolio*—Includes several artifacts related to a particular set of skills; shows how a student has improved over time
- *Course portfolio*—Includes assignments and reflections for a single course; typically also includes a summarizing reflection in which the student identifies his or her general accomplishments in the course
- *Best-work portfolio*—Includes artifacts intended to showcase the student's particular achievements and unique talents (R. S. Johnson et al., 2006; Spandel, 1997)

These categories aren't necessarily mutually exclusive. For instance, a course portfolio might have a developmental component, showing how a student has improved in, say, persuasive writing skills over the school year. And a best-work portfolio may be a work-in-progress for quite some time, thereby having the dynamic nature of a working portfolio.

myeducationlab

See 8-year-old Keenan using her developmental portfolio to track her progress in writing skills in the video "Portfolio." (To find this video, go to Chapter 15 of the Book-Specific Resources in MyEducationLab, select *Video Examples*, and then click on the title.)

Some portfolios are most appropriate for formative evaluation, whereas others are appropriate for summative evaluation (R. S. Johnson et al., 2006; Spandel, 1997). Developmental portfolios, which include products from the entire school year or perhaps an even longer period, can show whether students are making reasonable progress toward long-term instructional goals; as such, they are often best used for formative evaluation. Best-work portfolios are better suited for summative evaluation; for instance, they might be used to communicate students' final accomplishments to parents, school administrators, college admissions officers, or potential employers.

Traditionally, most portfolios have been actual physical entities that include paper artifacts (e.g., writing samples, artwork) and perhaps also audiovisual mate-

FIGURE 15.12 In this self-reflection, 14-year-old Kurt explains why he has chosen certain pieces to include in his eighth-grade language arts portfolio.

SELF-EVALUATION

The three pieces of writing in my portfolio that best represent who I am are: 1) "Author Ben Hoff," which is a story in the language of Ben Hoff; 2) "Quotes from The Tao of Pooh"; and 3) "Discrimination."

What "Author Ben Hoff" shows about me as a learner or a writer is that I am able to analyze and absorb the types and styles of an author and then transfer what I learn onto paper in a good final understandable piece of writing. This piece has good description, a good plot line, gets the point across, has a basic setting, and is understandable. I did not change too much of this piece from one draft to the next except punctuation, grammar and spelling. I did, however, add a quote from The Tao of Pooh.

"Quotes from The Tao of Pooh" shows that I am able to pull out good and significant quotes from a book, understand them, and put them into my own words. Then I can make them understandable to other people. This piece gets the point across well and is easy to understand. I really only corrected spelling and punctuation from one draft to the next.

"Discrimination" shows me that I am learning more about discrimination and how it might feel (even though I have never experienced really bad discrimination). I found I can get my ideas across through realistic writing. This piece has good description and was well written for the assignment. Besides correcting some punctuation and spelling, I changed some wording to make the story a little more clear.

For all three pieces, the mechanics of my writing tend to be fairly poor on my first draft, but that is because I am writing as thoughts come into my mind rather than focusing on details of grammar. Then my final drafts get better as I get comments and can turn my attention to details of writing.

The four most important things that I'm able to do as a writer are to: 1) get thoughts pulled into a story; 2) have that story understandable and the reader get something from it; 3) have the reader remember it was a good piece of writing; and 4) like the piece myself.

rials (e.g., audiotapes, videotapes) and three-dimensional creations (e.g., sculptures, inventions). But such a collection can occasionally become quite cumbersome and difficult to transport from one place to another. An alternative gaining increasing popularity is an *electronic portfolio* (sometimes simply called an *e-folio*), in which portfolio contents—writing samples, audiovisual materials, photographs of creations, and so on—are stored and presented via a portable electronic storage device (e.g., CD, DVD, or flash drive).

Benefits and Limitations of Portfolios

Portfolios have several benefits, some of which we've already identified:

- They capture the wide-ranging, complex nature of students' achievement, with a particular emphasis on higher-level skills.
- They can show growth over time—something that a single assessment at a single time cannot do.
- They can demonstrate students' performance on real-world, authentic assessment tasks (e.g., science experiments, service-learning projects).
- They provide practice in self-monitoring and self-evaluation, thereby enhancing students' self-regulation skills.
- They give students a sense of accomplishment and self-efficacy about areas that have been mastered, while also possibly alerting students to areas needing improvement.
- They provide a mechanism through which teachers can easily intertwine assessment with instruction: Students often include products that their teachers have assigned primarily for instructional purposes.
- Because the focus of portfolios is on complex skills, teachers are more likely to *teach* those skills. (Banta, 2003; Darling-Hammond et al., 1995; DiMartino & Castaneda, 2007; R. S. Johnson et al., 2006; Koretz et al., 1994; Paulson et al., 1991; Spandel, 1997)

RSVP characteristics are often a source of concern with portfolios, however, especially if they are used to evaluate (rather than simply communicate) students' learning and achievement (Arter & Spandel, 1992; R. S. Johnson et al., 2006; Koretz et al., 1994; Popham, 1995). When portfolios must be scored in a holistic manner, the scoring is often unreliable, with different teachers rating them differently. In addition, there is an obvious standardization problem: Because each portfolio includes a unique set of products, each student is evaluated on the basis of a unique body of information. Validity may or may not be a problem: Some portfolios may include enough work samples to adequately represent what students have accomplished relative to instructional goals, but others may be unrepresentative. And because portfolios are apt to take a great deal of teacher time, they are less practical than other methods of summarizing achievement.

Keep in mind the limitations of portfolios with respect to the RSVP characteristics.

All of this is not to say that we should shy away from using portfolios. But when we ask students to compile them, we should make sure the potential benefits outweigh the disadvantages. And we must interpret them cautiously if they are to serve as summative reflections of what students have accomplished.

Helping Students Construct Portfolios

Creating a portfolio is typically a lengthy process that stretches out over several weeks or months; some best-work portfolios may evolve over several years. So that students aren't overwhelmed by such a complex undertaking, it's often helpful to break the portfolio construction process into a series of steps, scaffolding students' efforts at each step:

Break the construction of portfolios into a sequence of manageable steps.

1. *Planning.* Decide on the purpose(s) the portfolio will serve—for instance, which instructional goals and/or content area standards it will address and whether it will be used primarily for formative or summative evaluation; identify a preliminary plan of attack for creating the portfolio.
2. *Collection.* Save artifacts that demonstrate progress toward or achievement of particular goals and standards.
3. *Selection.* Review the saved artifacts and choose those that best reflect achievement of the specified goals and standards.
4. *Reflection.* Write explanations and self-evaluations of each artifact; describe how the artifacts show current competencies and growth over time; relate achievements to previously identified goals and standards.
5. *Projection.* Identify new goals toward which to strive.
6. *Presentation.* Share the portfolio with an appropriate audience (e.g., classmates, parents, college admissions personnel). (Six steps based on R. S. Johnson et al., 2006)

The Into the Classroom feature "Summarizing Students' Achievements with Portfolios" offers and illustrates several suggestions for scaffolding students' efforts in creating portfolios.

Standardized Tests

Final grades and portfolios are derived directly from tasks that students complete in the classroom. A different approach to summarizing what students know and can do is the standardized test, developed by test construction experts and published for use in many different schools and classrooms.

Standardized tests are *standardized* in several ways: All students receive the same instructions, have the same time limits, respond to the same (or very similar) questions or tasks, and have their responses evaluated relative to the same criteria. Standardized tests come with test manuals that include the instructions to give students, the time

INTO THE Classroom

Summarizing Students' Achievements with Portfolios

- **Identify in advance the specific purpose(s) for which a portfolio will be used.**

  A third-grade teacher and her students agree to create portfolios that will show parents and other family members how much their writing skills improve over the school year. Throughout the year students save their fiction and nonfiction, and eventually they choose pieces that best demonstrate mastery of some writing skills and progress on others. The children proudly present their portfolios at parent–teacher–student conferences at the end of the year.

- **Align portfolio contents with important instructional goals and/or content area standards.**

  At a high school in Ohio, twelfth graders complete graduation portfolios with three components, each of which reflects one or more of the school's instructional goals for all graduates:

  - *A lifelong-learning skills section.* Includes artifacts showing one's best work in writing, math, science, and at least one other discipline or interest area, plus a personal reflection describing oneself as a learner.
  - *A democratic citizenship section.* Includes evidence of active citizenship (e.g., taking a stand on a public issue, engaging in public service) at school or in the community, plus a personal reflection on one's readiness for becoming a productive citizen in society.
  - *A career-readiness section.* Includes a résumé, a sample job or college application, recent letters of reference, and a personal reflection on one's readiness for postgraduation work or study.

- **Identify specific criteria that should guide students' selections; possibly include students in the criteria identification process.**

  A middle school geography teacher leads his class in a discussion of criteria that students might use to identify artifacts for a course portfolio. After reviewing the instructional goals for the course, the class agrees that each portfolio should include at least one artifact demonstrating each of the following:

  - Map interpretation skills
  - Map construction skills
  - Understanding of interrelationships between physical environments and socioeconomic practices
  - Knowledge of cultural differences within the nation
  - Recognition that all cultures have many positive qualities

- **Ask students to select the contents of their portfolios; provide the scaffolding they need to make wise choices.**

  A fifth-grade teacher meets one-on-one with each of his students to help them choose artifacts that best reflect their achievements for the year. To give students an idea of the kinds of things they might include, he shows them several portfolios that students have created in previous years. He shares only those portfolios that previous students and parents have given him permission to use in this way.

- **Have students include reflections on the products they include.**

  At the beginning of the school year, a ninth-grade journalism teacher tells students that they will be creating portfolios that show progress in journalistic writing during the semester. She asks them to save all of their drafts— "Even simple notes and sketchy outlines," she says. Later in the semester, as students begin to compile their portfolios, she asks them to look at their various drafts of each piece and to describe how the progression from one draft to the next shows their gradual mastery of journalistic skills. She occasionally assigns these reflections as homework so that students spread the portfolio construction task over a four-week period and therefore don't leave everything until the last minute.

- **Give students a general organizational scheme to follow.**

  When a high school requires students to complete portfolios as one of their graduation requirements, students get considerable guidance from their homeroom teachers. These teachers also provide a handout describing the elements each portfolio should include: title page, table of contents, introduction to the portfolio's contents, distinct sections for each content domain included, and final reflection summarizing the student's achievements.

- **Determine whether a physical format or electronic format is more suitable for the circumstances.**

  At a high school that places particular emphasis on visual and performing arts, students create electronic portfolios that showcase their talents in art, drama, dance, and/or instrumental music. They digitally photograph, videotape, or audiotape their projects and performances, and they create word processing documents that describe and evaluate each one. They then divide their electronic documents into several logical categories, each of which they put in a separate electronic folder on a flash drive, DVD, or CD.

- **When using portfolios for final evaluations, develop a rubric for scoring it.**

  At a high school in New York City, a key instructional goal is for students to acquire certain dispositions and thinking processes—which the school collectively calls *habits of mind*—in their academic work. One of these habits of mind is the use of credible, convincing evidence to support statements and positions. The school develops a four-point rating scale to evaluate students' work on this criterion. A score of 4 is given to work that reflects "Generalizations and ideas supported by specific relevant and accurate information, which is developed in appropriate depth." At the other end of the scale, a score of 1 is given to work that reflects "Mostly general statements; little specific evidence relating to the topic."

Sources: Darling-Hammond et al., 1995, p. 39 (New York City high school example); DiMartino & Castaneda, 2007, pp. 40–41 (Ohio high school example); R. S. Johnson et al., 2006; Paulson et al., 1991; Popham, 1995; Spandel, 1997.

limits to impose, and explicit scoring criteria to use. If the tests are norm-referenced (and most are), their manuals also provide norms for various age or grade levels. And the manuals often provide information about test reliability for various populations and age-groups, as well as information from which we can draw inferences about test validity for our own purpose and situation.

Types of Standardized Tests

School districts use four kinds of standardized tests fairly frequently: tests of achievement, general scholastic aptitude and intelligence, specific aptitudes and abilities, and school readiness.[2]

Achievement Tests Standardized achievement tests are designed to assess how much students have learned from what they have specifically been taught. The test items are intended to reflect the curriculum common to most schools; for example, a history test will focus on national or world history rather than the history of a particular state or province. The overall test scores usually reflect achievement in a very broad sense: They tell us how much a student has learned about mathematics or language mechanics (relative to a norm group) but not necessarily whether the student specifically knows how to multiply fractions or use commas appropriately.

Standardized achievement tests are useful in at least two ways (Ansley, 1997). First, they tell us how well our own students' achievement compares with that of students elsewhere—information that may indirectly tell us something about the effectiveness of our instructional programs. Second, they help us track students' general progress over time and alert us to potential trouble spots. For example, imagine that Lucas gets average test scores year after year but then suddenly performs well below average in the eighth grade, even though the test and norm group are the same as in previous years. At this point, we would want to ascertain whether the low performance is a temporary fluke (e.g., perhaps Lucas was sick on the test day) or, instead, due to more enduring factors that need our attention.

Use standardized achievement tests to track students' general progress in a content domain and to evaluate the effectiveness of your instructional program relative to other programs across the country.

Most standardized achievement tests are highly reliable; that is, they lead to fairly consistent results for individual students, especially for students in the upper elementary and secondary grades. However, our main concern whenever we assess achievement is *content validity*, which we need to determine for *our own situation*. We can determine the content validity of a standardized achievement test by comparing a table of specifications (provided in the test manual or constructed by us) to our own curriculum. A test has high content validity only if the topics and thinking skills emphasized in test items match our curriculum, instructional goals, and content area standards.

Determine the content validity of a standardized achievement test for your own curriculum, instructional goals, and content area standards.

General Scholastic Aptitude and Intelligence Tests Whereas achievement tests are designed to assess what students have specifically learned from what they've been taught, **scholastic aptitude tests** are designed to assess a general *capacity* to learn. Traditionally, many of these tests have been called *intelligence tests*. However, some experts are beginning to shy away from the latter term, in part because psychologists don't agree about what intelligence *is* and in part because many people mistakenly believe that IQ scores reflect inherited ability almost exclusively (M. D. Miller et al., 2009; also see Chapter 5). Other commonly used terms are *general aptitude test*, *school ability test*, and *cognitive ability test*.

Regardless of what we call them, tests that fall in this category are used mainly for prediction—that is, to estimate how well students are likely to learn and perform

scholastic aptitude test Test designed to assess a general capacity to learn and used to predict future academic achievement.

[2] You can find examples of commonly used standardized tests at the websites for CTB and McGraw-Hill (www.ctb.com) and Riverside Publishing (www.riverpub.com).

in future academic situations. Typically these tests are designed to assess how much students have learned and deduced from their general, everyday experiences. For example, they may assess understanding of vocabulary words that most students are likely to have encountered at one time or another. They may include analogies intended to assess how well students can recognize similarities among well-known relationships. They may ask students to analyze pictures or manipulate concrete objects. And most of them include measures of general knowledge and tasks that require deductive reasoning and problem solving.

specific aptitude test Test designed to predict future ability to succeed in a particular content domain.

school readiness test Test designed to assess cognitive skills important for success in a typical kindergarten or first-grade curriculum.

Like standardized achievement tests, scholastic aptitude tests tend to be quite reliable, especially for older students. Of greater concern, however, is their *predictive validity*—the accuracy with which they can help us estimate students' future achievement. Their predictive validity for future academic success varies considerably depending on the situation and population at hand, but in general you should think of these tests as providing only rough estimates of how students are likely to perform in school in the next two or three years. Keep in mind, too, that many factors not measured by these tests—for instance, motivation, self-regulation skills, and the quality of instruction—also influence students' learning and classroom performance.

Specific Aptitude and Ability Tests General scholastic aptitude tests are useful when we want to predict overall academic performance. But when we are interested in how well students are apt to perform in a particular area (e.g., math, music, or auto mechanics), measures of specific aptitudes and abilities—often called **specific aptitude tests**—are more appropriate. Some aptitude tests are designed to predict future performance in just one content domain. Others, called *multiple aptitude batteries*, yield subscores for a variety of domains simultaneously.

Some standardized tests are administered one on one. Such tests enable the examiner to observe a student's attention span, motivation, and other factors that may affect academic performance. For this reason, individually administered tests are typically used when identifying cognitive disabilities and other special educational needs.

Aptitude tests are sometimes used by school personnel to select students for specific instructional programs—for example, to identify those students most likely to succeed in a particular course. Such tests may also be used for counseling students about future educational plans and career choices. But two caveats are important to keep in mind when using these tests for such purposes. First, their predictive validity in academic contexts tends to be lower than that for general scholastic aptitude tests—that is, they yield only very rough estimates of students' future academic performance in the domain in question. Second, they are based on the assumption that the ability being measured is a fairly stable one—an assumption that may or may not be accurate. Rather than trying to identify students with high aptitudes for particular subject areas, then, some educators argue that we should focus more on *developing* abilities in *all* students (Boykin, 1994; P. D. Nichols & Mittelholtz, 1997; Sternberg, 2002). Accordingly, specific aptitude tests now appear less frequently in wide-scale school testing programs than they once did.

School Readiness Tests A **school readiness test** is designed to determine whether children have acquired the knowledge and skills essential for success in kindergarten or first grade—for instance, knowledge of colors, shapes, letters, and numbers. When used in combination with other information, school readiness tests can be quite helpful if we're looking for significant developmental delays that require immediate attention (Bracken & Walker, 1997; Lidz, 1991). On their own, however, they have limited predictive validity: The scores they yield typically correlate only moderately with children's academic performance even a year or so later (Duncan et al., 2007; La Paro & Pianta, 2000; C. E. Sanders, 1997; Stipek, 2002).

School readiness tests can often give us a rough idea of where to begin instruction with individual children. But as a general rule, we should *not* use them to identify children who should postpone formal schooling. By age 5, almost all children are probably ready for some form of structured educational program. Rather than focus on determining which children might have trouble in a particular educational curricu-

Use the results of school readiness tests more for instructional planning than for making decisions about which children are ready to begin school.

myeducationlab

Learn more about the pros and cons of readiness tests by completing the Understanding Research exercise "Usefulness of School Readiness Tests" in MyEducationLab. (To find this activity, go to the topic Assessment in MyEducationLab, click on *Assignments and Activities*, and then select *Understanding Research*.)

lum and environment, we better serve children when we determine how to adapt the curriculum and environment to fit each child's developmental progress and particular needs (Farran, 2001; Lidz, 1991; Stipek, 2002).

Table 15.2 summarizes the four categories of standardized tests just described.

Technology and Assessment

Increasingly we are seeing the use of computer technology to administer standardized tests. Computer technology and other technological advances provide several options that are either impractical or impossible with paper–pencil tests:

- They allow **adaptive testing**, which adjusts the difficulty level of items as students proceed through a test and can thereby zero in on students' specific strengths and weaknesses fairly quickly.
- They can present animations, simulations, videos, and audiotaped messages that greatly expand the kinds of knowledge and skills they can assess.
- They enable easy assessment of how students approach specific problems and how quickly they accomplish specific tasks.
- They allow the possibility of assessing students' abilities under varying levels of support (e.g., by providing one or more hints as needed to guide students' reasoning).
- They can provide on-the-spot objective scoring and analyses of students' performance.

Computer-based assessments tend to have reliability and validity levels similar to those of traditional paper–pencil tests (M. D. Miller et al., 2009). Their use should, of course, be limited to students who are familiar and comfortable with computers and have adequate keyboarding skills.

Guidelines for Choosing and Using Standardized Tests

As teachers, we will sometimes have input into the selection of standardized tests for our districts, and we will often be involved in administering them. Following are guidelines for choosing and using a standardized test appropriately:

Choose a test with high validity for your particular purpose and high reliability for students similar to your own. I described four categories of standardized tests as if they are distinctly different entities, but in fact the differences among them are not always clear cut. To some extent, all of these tests assess what a student has already learned, and all of them can be used to predict future performance. Our best bet is to choose the test that has the greatest validity for our particular purpose, regardless of what the test might be called. Of course, we also want a test that has been shown to be highly reliable with a population similar to ours.

Make sure the test's norm group is relevant to your own population. Scrutinize the test manual's description of the norm group used for the test, with questions like these in mind:

- Does the norm group include students of both genders and students of the same ages, educational levels, and cultural backgrounds as those of your own students?
- Is it a representative sample of the population at large or in some other way appropriate for any comparisons you plan to make?

adaptive testing Computer-based assessment in which students' performance on early items determines which items are presented subsequently.

Compare/Contrast

TABLE 15.2
Commonly Used Standardized Tests

Kind of Test	Purpose	Recommendations
Achievement tests	To assess how much students have learned from what they have been specifically taught	• Use these tests primarily for assessing broad areas of achievement rather than specific knowledge and skills.
Scholastic aptitude and intelligence tests	To assess students' general capability to learn; to predict their general academic success over the short run	• Use test scores as rough predictors of performance in the near future, *not* as predictors of learning potential over the long run. • Use tests designed for one-on-one administration if a student's verbal skills are limited or if exceptional giftedness or a significant disability is suspected.
Specific aptitude and ability tests	To predict how well students are likely to perform in a specific content domain	• Use test scores as rough predictors of performance in the near future, *not* as predictors of learning potential over the long run. • Because predictive validities for many of these tests are low, use test scores only in combination with other information about students.
School readiness tests	To determine whether young children have the prerequisite skills to be successful in a typical kindergarten or first-grade curriculum	• Use test results only in combination with other information about children. • Use test results primarily for instructional planning, *not* for deciding whether students are ready to begin formal schooling.

- Have the normative data been collected recently enough that they reflect how students typically perform in the current year?

When we determine norm-referenced test scores by comparing students with an inappropriate norm group, the scores are meaningless. For example, I recall a situation in which teacher education students at a major state university were required to take basic skills tests in language and mathematics. Because the tests had been normed on a high school population, the university students' performance was compared to that of high school seniors—a practice that made no sense whatsoever.

Take students' age and development into account. As we discovered in Chapter 14, a variety of irrelevant factors—motivation, mood, energy level, and so on—affect students' performance on tests and other assessments. When factors such as these are relatively stable characteristics, they affect test validity. When they are temporary and variable from day to day (perhaps even hour to hour), they affect test reliability and thus also indirectly affect validity. Such sources of error in students' test scores and other assessment results are especially common in young children, who may have limited language skills, short attention spans, little motivation to do their best, and low tolerance for frustration (Bracken & Walker, 1997; Messick, 1983). Furthermore, young children's erratic behaviors may make it difficult to maintain standardized testing conditions (Wodtke, Harper, & Schommer, 1989).

In adolescence, other variables can affect the validity of standardized test scores. For instance, especially in high school, some students become quite cynical about the validity and usefulness of standardized paper–pencil tests. Thus, they may read test items superficially, if at all, and a few may complete answer sheets simply by following a certain pattern (e.g., alternating between A and B) or filling in bubbles to make pictures or designs (Paris, Lawton, Turner, & Roth, 1991). Table 15.3 describes these and other developmental differences affecting students' performance on standardized tests.

Make sure students are adequately prepared to take the test. In most instances, we will want to prepare students ahead of time for a standardized test. For example, we can do the following:

- Explain the general nature of the test and the tasks it involves (e.g., if applicable, mention that students aren't expected to know all of the answers and that many students won't have enough time to respond to every item).
- Encourage students to do their best, but without describing the test as a life-or-death matter.
- Give students practice with the test's format and item types (e.g., demonstrate how to fill in computer-scored answer sheets).
- Give suggestions about effective test-taking strategies, but don't overdo it; remember that your time is best spent helping students master the content domain being assessed (see the discussion of *testwiseness* in Chapter 14).
- Encourage students to get a full night's sleep and eat a good breakfast before taking the test. (Kirkland, 1971; Popham, 1990; Sax, 1989; Scruggs & Lifson, 1985; L. Shepard et al., 2005)

When administering the test, follow the directions closely and report any unusual circumstances. Once a test session begins, we should follow the test administration procedures to the letter, distributing test booklets as directed, asking students to complete any practice items provided, keeping time faithfully, and responding to questions in the prescribed manner. If we don't replicate the conditions under which the norm group has taken a test, any norm-referenced scores derived from the test will be meaningless. When unanticipated events significantly alter the test environment (e.g., when electrical power unexpectedly goes out), they jeopardize the validity of the test results and must be reported. We should also make note of any students who are behaving in ways unlikely to lead to maximum performance—appearing exceptionally nervous, staring out the window for long periods, marking answers haphazardly, and so on (M. D. Miller et al., 2009).

Interpreting Standardized Test Scores

As noted near the beginning of the chapter, scores on most standardized tests are norm-referenced. Typically, the scores are grade- or age-equivalent scores, percentile ranks, standard scores, or some combination of these. But we must be careful that we don't place too much stock in the *exact* scores that tests yield. Following are several guidelines to keep in mind when interpreting and using standardized test scores:

Have a clear and justifiable rationale for establishing any cutoffs for acceptable performance. If we want to use test results to make *either–or* decisions—for instance, whether a student should move to a more advanced math class, be exempt from a basic writing course, and so on—we must have a clear rationale for the cutoff scores we use. The process can be relatively easy for criterion-referenced scores, provided that they truly reflect mastery and nonmastery of the subject matter. It's far more difficult for norm-referenced scores: At what point does a student's performance become acceptable? At the 20th percentile? At a stanine of 6? Without more information about the knowledge and skills such scores represent, there's no way of knowing what is an acceptable score.

Compare two standardized test scores only when those scores are derived from the same or equivalent norm group(s). Because different standardized tests almost always have different norm groups, we can't really compare students' perfor-

TABLE 15.3
Characteristics Affecting Standardized Test Performance at Different Grade Levels

Grade Level	Age-Typical Characteristics	Suggested Strategies
K–2	• Short attention span; significant individual differences in ability to stay focused on test items • Little intrinsic motivation to perform well on tests • Inconsistency in test performance from one occasion to another	• Don't use school readiness tests to determine which children are "ready" for elementary school; instead, plan early school experiences that can prepare students for future learning. • Leave assessment for diagnostic purposes (e.g., to identify students with special needs) in the hands of trained professionals who have experience in assessing young children. • Do not make long-term predictions about achievement on the basis of standardized test scores. • Use multiple measures when important decisions about students' education must be made.
3–5	• Unquestioning acceptance of standardized tests as valid measures of ability or achievement • Increasing ability to stay focused on a paper–pencil assessment instrument • Increasing facility with machine-scorable answer sheets • Considerable variability in testwiseness	• Stress the value of standardized tests for tracking students' progress and identifying areas in which students may need extra instruction and support. • Give students plenty of practice using machine-scorable answer sheets. • Explicitly teach basic test-taking strategies (e.g., skipping difficult test items and returning to them later if time allows).
6–8	• Increase in debilitating test anxiety (for some students) • Wide variability in test-taking strategies • Emerging skepticism about the value of standardized tests (for some students)	• Explain that standardized tests provide only a rough idea of what students know and can do; reassure students that test results won't be the only things affecting instructional decision making. • Encourage students to do their best on a test; assure them that test results will be used not to judge them but rather to help them learn more effectively. • Provide some practice in test-taking skills, but remember that students' performance depends more on their knowledge and abilities in content domains than on their general test-taking ability.
9–12	• Increasing cynicism about the validity and usefulness of standardized tests (especially common in low-achieving students) • Decreasing motivation to perform well on standardized tests; in some instances, may reflect self-handicapping as a way of justifying poor performance	• Acknowledge that standardized tests aren't perfect, but explain that they *can* help teachers and administrators assess school effectiveness and plan future instruction. • Be alert for signs that a student may intentionally subvert an assessment or has already done so; speak privately with the student about his or her concerns, and offer your support to enhance test performance.

Sources: Bracken & Walker, 1997; S. M. Carver, 2006; Dempster & Corkill, 1999; Lidz, 1991; Messick, 1983; Paris et al., 1991; Petersen et al., 1990; Sarason, 1980; Scruggs & Lifson, 1985; Stipek, 2002.

mance on one test with their performance on another. For example, if Susan takes the Basic Skills Test (BST), we can compare her score on the BST Reading subtest with her score on the BST Mathematics subtest because both scores are from the same test and have been derived from the same norms. But we cannot compare Susan's BST scores with her scores on a different standardized achievement test, such as the Reading Achievement Test (RAT) that Shawn took, because the two sets of scores are likely to be based on entirely different norm groups. (Appendix B offers additional insights on comparing test scores.)

Never use a single test score to make important decisions. No test—no matter how carefully constructed and widely used—has perfect reliability and validity. Every test is fallible, and students may do poorly on a test for a variety of reasons. Thus, we should never—and I do mean *never*—use a single assessment instrument or a single test score to make important decisions about individual students. Nor should

> **PEARSON myeducationlab**
> Gain practice in making sense of students' achievement test scores by completing the Building Teaching Skills and Dispositions exercise "Interpreting Standardized Achievement Test Results" in MyEducationLab. (To find this exercise, go to the topic Assessment in MyEducationLab, and click on *Building Teaching Skills and Dispositions.*)

we use single test scores to make important decisions about large groups of students or about the teachers who teach them.

High-Stakes Testing and Accountability

In recent years a great deal of emphasis—entirely *too* much emphasis, in my opinion—has been placed on students' performance on standardized achievement tests. Many politicians, business leaders, and other public figures have lamented students' low achievement test scores and called for a major overhaul of our educational system.[3]

Some students do seem to progress through several grade levels without acquiring basic skills in reading, writing, and math; a few even graduate from high school without these skills. To address such problems, many states and school districts now use students' performance on tests or other assessments as a basis for promoting them to the next grade level or for awarding them high school diplomas. Typically, educators begin by identifying certain content area standards (sometimes using the word *competencies*) that students' final achievement should reflect. They then assess students' performance levels (sometimes known as *outcomes*) at the end of instruction, and only those students whose performance meets the predetermined standards move forward.[4]

Whenever we use a single assessment instrument to make major decisions about students, we are using a **high-stakes test**. Because high-stakes tests are typically used to make judgments about mastery of school subject matter, they require criterion-referenced scores. For example, a high-stakes test might yield a score such as "In progress," "Proficient," or "Advanced" with respect to a student's knowledge and skills in a particular subject area.

Students' scores on high-stakes tests are sometimes used to make important decisions not only about the students themselves but also about their teachers and schools (e.g., decisions about salaries and school funding). In such circumstances—that is, when teachers, administrators, and other school personnel are mandated to accept responsibility for students' performance on high-stakes assessments—we are talking about **accountability**.

The U.S. No Child Left Behind Act

In the United States, the **No Child Left Behind Act** of 2001—sometimes known simply as **NCLB**—now mandates both high-stakes testing and accountability in all public elementary and secondary schools. It also mandates that all states establish

> challenging academic content standards in academic subjects that—
> (I) specify what children are expected to know and be able to do;
> (II) contain coherent and rigorous content; and
> (III) encourage the teaching of advanced skills (P.L. 107-110, Sec. 1111).

School districts must annually assess students in grades 3 through 8 and at least once during grades 10 through 12 to determine whether students are making *adequate yearly progress* in meeting state-determined standards in reading, math, and science. The nature of this progress is defined by the state (and thus differs from state to state), but assessment results must clearly show that all students—including those from diverse racial and socioeconomic groups—are making significant gains in knowledge

high-stakes testing Practice of using students' performance on a single assessment to make major decisions about students, school personnel, or overall school quality.

accountability An obligation of teachers and other school personnel to accept responsibility for students' performance on high-stakes assessments; often mandated by policy makers calling for school reform.

No Child Left Behind Act (NCLB) U.S. legislation passed in 2001 that mandates regular assessments of basic skills to determine whether students are making adequate yearly progress in relation to state-determined standards in reading, math, and science.

[3]In the United States, a report entitled *A Nation at Risk*, published by the National Commission on Excellence in Education in 1983, has been especially influential.

[4]You may see such terms as *minimum competency testing* and *outcomes-based education* used in reference to this approach.

and skills. (Students with significant cognitive disabilities may be given alternative assessments, but these students must show improvement commensurate with their ability levels.) Schools that demonstrate progress receive rewards, such as teacher bonuses and increased funding. Schools that don't demonstrate progress are subject to sanctions and corrective actions (e.g., bad publicity, administrative restructuring, dismissal of staff members), and their students have the option of attending a better public school at the school district's expense.[5]

Such efforts to monitor schools' instructional effectiveness and students' academic progress are certainly well intentioned. Ideally, they can help schools determine whether instructional methods need revision and whether teachers need retooling. They can also help teachers identify students who aren't acquiring the basic skills necessary for successful participation in the adult world. And the focus on improving the achievement of historically low-achieving groups is long overdue. However, the current emphasis on boosting students' test scores is fraught with difficulties in implementation, and solutions to these difficulties are only beginning to emerge.

Problems with High-Stakes Testing

Experts have identified several problems with the use of high-stakes tests to make decisions about students, teachers, and schools:

- *The tests don't always reflect important instructional goals.* High-stakes achievement tests don't always have good content validity for the contexts in which they're used (Hursh, 2007; O'Reilly & McNamara, 2007). Even if well constructed, they may reflect only a small portion of a school's curriculum and instructional goals. For instance, the emphasis in the No Child Left Behind Act and in some state-level and district-level assessments is primarily on achievement in certain content domains (e.g., NCLB focuses on reading, math, and science), with little regard for achievement in other disciplines or for content of particular relevance to cultural minority groups (Castagno & Brayboy, 2008; Siskin, 2003a; R. M. Thomas, 2005). Furthermore, the preponderance of multiple-choice and other objectively scorable items on many standardized tests limits the extent to which these tests assess higher-level thinking skills and performance on authentic, real-life tasks (Amrein & Berliner, 2002b; L. A. Shepard, 2000; R. M. Thomas, 2005).

- *Teachers spend a great deal of time teaching to the tests.* When teachers are held accountable for their students' performance on a particular test, many of them understandably devote many class hours to the topics and skills that the test assesses, and students may focus their studying accordingly (W. Au, 2007; Hursh, 2007; R. L. Linn, 2000). The result is often that students perform at higher levels on a high-stakes test *without* improving their achievement and abilities more generally (Amrein & Berliner, 2002b; R. M. Ryan & Brown, 2005; Jacob, 2003). If a test truly measures the things that are most important for students to learn—including such higher-level skills as transfer, problem solving, and critical thinking—then focusing on those things is quite appropriate. If the test primarily assesses rote knowledge and lower-level skills, however, then such emphasis can undermine the improvements we *really* want to see in students' achievement (Amrein & Berliner, 2002b; W. Au, 2007; L. Shepard et al., 2005).

Teach to the test *if* it reflects important instructional goals.

Let's briefly return to the opening case study in Chapter 8. Ninth-grade math teacher Ms. Gaunt knows that her students must take the statewide mathematics competency exam at the end of the school year. In order to cover all of the material on the exam, she eventually abandons her efforts to help students master basic concepts and procedures—essentially throwing out the *Less-is-more* principle. "Students can't do

[5]You can learn more about the No Child Left Behind Act at the U.S. Department of Education's website (www.ed.gov/nclb). You can also find a good summary of this legislation in R. M. Thomas (2005).

Although it's important to help low-achieving students achieve the competencies they need to pass high-stakes tests, we must not neglect high-ability students, who need challenging activities to maximize their intellectual growth.

well on the exam if they haven't even been exposed to some of the required concepts and procedures," Ms. Gaunt reasons. "Mastery probably isn't possible at this point, but I should at least *present* what students need to know. Maybe this will help a few of them with some of the test items." Such superficial coverage is common when the results of high-stakes tests must be at the top of teachers' priority lists (W. Au, 2007; R. M. Thomas, 2005; Valli & Buese, 2007).

• *Teachers and schools may focus much of their attention on helping some students while shortchanging others.* The focus of NCLB and many state- and district-level assessment policies is on maximizing the number of students who meet certain minimal criteria for acceptable performance. From this perspective, the key to doing well as a school is to push as many low-achieving students as possible over the minimal cutoff for success. In the process, students who fall way below that cutoff and students who are already well above it may be given short shrift; for instance, schools may devote little instructional time or resources to students who are most in need of them (Balfanz, Legters, West, & Weber, 2007; A. D. Ho, 2008; A. C. Porter & Polikoff, 2007).

• *School personnel have disincentives to follow standardized testing procedures and to assess the progress of chronically low achievers.* In a high-stakes situation, teachers and administrators sometimes conclude that *dis*honesty is the best policy. Imagine that you are a teacher or school administrator who wants to maximize the average test scores of students in a particular class or at a particular grade level. Might you give students more than the allotted time to finish the test? Might you provide hints about correct answers or possibly even *give* students correct answers? Might you find reasons to exempt certain students from taking the test—perhaps finding a place for them in a special education program or retaining them at a grade level where they won't be assessed? Such practices occur when teachers and administrators are under pressure to raise students' test scores (Hursh, 2007; Jacob, 2003; R. M. Ryan & Brown, 2005; R. M. Thomas, 2005).

A few years after NCLB was instituted, I spoke with a high school principal in a small rural school district in northern New England. Although he certainly saw benefits to regularly assessing students' progress in basic skills, he revealed that one group of minority students at his school had not shown the NCLB-mandated yearly progress during the preceding school year. "We have very few minority students at our school and only five students in that particular group," he told me. "As a result of difficult family circumstances, one of those five—a 16-year-old—lives on his own and comes to school only about 40% of the time. His performance on the annual assessment pulled the average scores for his group way down. If we truly wanted our test results to look good for the group, we should just have let him drop out—something he was inclined to do anyway. Instead, we did everything we could to keep him in school." The school's decision was certainly in the student's best interest, but it was a costly one in terms of the achievement results it reported for the school year.

• *Different criteria lead to different conclusions about which students and schools are performing at high levels.* When we base school funding, salary increases, and other incentives on students' test performance, exactly what criterion do we use? A predetermined, absolute level of achievement? Improvement over time? Superior performance relative to other school districts? There is no easy answer to this question. Yet depending on which criterion we use, we will reach different conclusions as to which students and schools are and are not performing well (R. L. Linn, 2000; R. M. Thomas, 2005). Compounding the problem is the fact that students in lower-income communities achieve at lower levels, on average, than those in higher-income communities even when both groups have excellent teachers and schools (Hursh, 2007; R. L. Linn, 2000).

- *Too much emphasis is placed on punishing low-performing schools; not enough is placed on helping those schools improve.* Many advocates of school reform think that a quick, easy fix to students' low achievement levels is simply to reward schools whose students do well and to punish schools whose students do not (J. Lee & Wong, 2004; L. A. Shepard, 2000). This strategy is unlikely to be effective, especially if some of the factors affecting students' academic performance (e.g., health, family support, peer group norms, etc.) are beyond teachers' and administrators' control. In fact, there is *no* convincing evidence that simply holding school personnel accountable for students' performance on high-stakes assessments—without also providing sufficient support to make change possible—has a significant and positive influence on teachers' instructional strategies or on students' learning and achievement (Amrein & Berliner, 2002b; Firestone & Mayrowetz, 2000; R. L. Linn, 2000; Stringfield & Yakimowski-Srebnick, 2005). Furthermore, the threat of harsh consequences for insufficient improvement in test scores can adversely affect teachers' morale and may lead some teachers, including some very good ones, to leave teaching altogether (Amrein & Berliner, 2002a; Finnigan & Gross, 2007; Stringfield & Yakimowski-Srebnick, 2005).

- *Students' motivation affects their performance on the tests, and consistently low test performance can, in turn, affect their motivation.* For a variety of reasons—perhaps because they have low self-efficacy, attribute poor performance to factors beyond their control, or intentionally self-handicap in order to rationalize their poor performance—some students have little motivation to do well on high-stakes tests, and others become so anxious that they *can't* do as well as they should (Chabrán, 2003; Siskin, 2003b). Furthermore, when students get consistently low test scores—and especially when their scores pose obstacles to promotion and graduation—they may find little value in staying in school. In the majority of U.S. states that require certain test scores for high school graduation, dropout rates have increased in recent years, especially for students from ethnic minority groups and students from low-income neighborhoods (Amrein & Berliner, 2002a, 2002b; Kumar et al., 2002, R. M. Ryan & Brown, 2005).

Potential Solutions

Public concern about students' achievement levels isn't going away any time soon, nor should it. Many students *are* achieving at low levels, especially those in low-income school districts, those with diverse cultural backgrounds, and those with special educational needs (see Chapters 4 and 5). Consequently, I offer several potential solutions—I say *potential* solutions that, in combination, may help to alleviate the problems just identified:

Identify and assess those things most important for students to know and do. If we're going to base important decisions about students, teachers, and schools on assessment results, we must make sure that we're assessing aspects of achievement most critical for students' long-term success both in school and in the adult world. For instance, students should not only acquire basic skills in literacy and math but also gain a solid understanding of how their government works, what social factors affect the welfare and behaviors of their fellow human beings, and how they can productively use their leisure time and contribute to the general betterment of society (R. M. Thomas, 2005). I don't pretend that assessing such things is easy, but it's essential if we're going to rely on assessment results to determine whether schools are truly meeting students' long-term needs.

Advocate for a focus on individual students' progress rather than age-group averages. Instead of maximizing the number of students who demonstrate minimally acceptable levels of achievement, we should assess the degree to which every student makes progress during the school year (e.g., A. D. Ho, 2008). This may not be the best approach to assigning final grades (recall my earlier concerns about basing grades on improvement), but it's a reasonable approach to evaluating teachers and schools. For example, in the state of New Hampshire's Follow the Child initiative, schools identify individual students' needs—their physical, personal, and social needs as well as their academic ones—and track students' individual progress in these areas over time. When particular students lag behind, the question is not how to punish teachers or schools but rather how to improve things on the students' behalf. Although the state doesn't yet have hard data on the initiative's effectiveness, Commissioner of Education Lyonel Tracy reports that school attendance and participation in extracurricular activities have increased, and inappropriate social behaviors (e.g., bullying) and school dropout rates have decreased.[6]

Advocate for support, not punishment, for "failing" schools. Students who perform poorly on high-stakes assessments are often those who attend schools with limited resources—small budgets, poorly trained teachers, outdated equipment, and so on (J. Lee & Wong, 2004; Tuerk, 2005). Punishing these schools by giving them reduced budgets, lower teacher salaries, and other sanctions is apt to make matters worse, not better.

As teachers, we must help educate the public about the limitations of standardized tests, especially those that are used in making important decisions about students and instructional programs.

Educate the public about what standardized tests can and cannot do for us. What I've seen and heard in the media leads me to think that many public figures and policy makers overestimate how much standardized achievement tests can tell us: They assume that such instruments are highly accurate, comprehensive measures of students' academic achievement. True, these tests are usually developed by experts in test construction, but no test is completely reliable, and its validity will vary considerably, depending on the context in which it's being used. It behooves all of us—teachers, school administrators, parents, and so on—to learn about the limitations of standardized tests and to educate our fellow citizens accordingly.

Look at alternatives to traditional objective tests. Especially when a test will be administered to many students at once, its format is apt to be objective and machine scorable, and multiple-choice items are often used. Well-constructed multiple-choice tests have the capacity to assess higher-level thinking skills (see Chapter 14), but they inevitably limit how effectively we can assess certain information and skills; for instance, they can tell us little about students' ability to write well (Traub, 1993). Thus, some experts argue that we should use authentic assessments either instead of or in addition to more traditional paper–pencil tests (e.g., DiMartino, 2007; Resnick & Resnick, 1992; L. Shepard et al., 2005). We should be aware, however, that states and school districts that have used authentic measures for large-scale assessments of student achievement have encountered difficulties with reliability and validity. Thus, we must tread cautiously as we move in this direction (e.g., S. Burger & Burger, 1994; Khattri & Sweet, 1996; Koretz et al., 1994; R. L. Linn, 1994; L. Shepard et al., 2005).

Advocate for the use of multiple measures in any high-stakes decisions. No matter what kind of assessment techniques we use, no single technique is likely to give us a comprehensive picture of what students have learned and achieved. Even if a single assessment could give us such a picture, perfect reliability is an elusive goal: Students' test results are inevitably subject to temporary swings in motivation, attention, mood, health, and other factors. To base life-altering decisions about students on a single test score is unconscionable.

---

[6]For more information on Follow the Child, go to www.ed.state.nh.us/education.

Taking Student Diversity into Account

bias (in assessment) Factor in an assessment instrument or procedure that consistently and differentially influences students' performance for reasons unrelated to the characteristic being measured; as a result, reduces the validity of the assessment.

cultural bias Extent to which assessment tasks either offend or unfairly penalize some students because of their ethnicity, gender, or socioeconomic status.

Whenever we administer standardized tests of achievement and ability, we must remember that students often differ from one another in ways that affect their performance in assessment situations. If two students have *learned equally* yet *perform differently* on an assessment, the information we obtain from the assessment has **bias** and questionable validity. One factor that can come into play is the *cultural bias* of an assessment, which can be detrimental not only for students from particular cultural backgrounds but also for students of a particular gender or socioeconomic group. We must also take into account cultural and linguistic differences that can adversely affect students' performance on a standardized test. And we may need to make special accommodations for students who have special educational needs.

Cultural Bias in Test Content

An assessment instrument has **cultural bias** if any of its items either offend or unfairly penalize some students on the basis of their ethnicity, gender, or socioeconomic status (e.g., Buck, Kostin, & Morgan, 2002; Popham, 1995). To get a sense of this phenomenon, try the following exercise.

EXPERIENCING FIRSTHAND

Predicting the Future

Imagine that you are taking a test designed to predict your success in future situations. Here are the first three questions on the test:

1. When you enter a hogan, in which direction should you move around the fire?
2. Why is turquoise often attached to a baby's cradleboard?
3. If you need black wool for weaving a rug, which one of the following alternatives would give you the blackest color?
   a. Dye the wool with a mixture of sumac, ochre, and piñon gum.
   b. Dye the wool with a mixture of indigo, lichen, and mesquite.
   c. Use the undyed wool of specially bred black sheep.

Try to answer these questions before you read further.

Did you have trouble answering some or all of the questions? All three questions were written from the perspective of a particular culture—that of the Navajos in the 1960s. Unless you have had considerable exposure to this culture, you would probably perform poorly on the test. By the way, the three answers are (1) clockwise, (2) to ward off evil, and (3) Alternative *a* ("Dye the wool with a mixture of sumac, ochre, and piñon gum") (Gilpin, 1968).

Is the test culturally biased? That depends. If the test is designed to assess your ability to succeed in a Navajo community, then the questions may be very appropriate. But if it's designed to assess your ability to accomplish instructional goals for which knowledge of Navajo culture is totally irrelevant, then such questions are culturally biased.

Two points about cultural bias are important to note. First, the term includes biases related to gender and socioeconomic status as well as to culture and ethnicity. For example, consider the following assessment items:

1. Mary is making a patchwork quilt from 36 squares of fabric, as shown in the margin. Each square has a perimeter of 20 inches. Mary sews the squares

together using a half-inch seam allowance. She then sews the assembled set of squares to a large piece of cotton that will serve as the flip side of the quilt, again using a half-inch seam allowance. How long is the perimeter of the finished quilt?

2. Would you rather swim in an ocean, a lake, or a swimming pool? Write a two-page essay defending your choice.

Question 1 assumes a fair amount of knowledge about sewing (e.g., knowing what a seam allowance is); this is knowledge that some students, especially girls, are more likely to have than others. Question 2 would obviously be difficult for students who haven't swum in all three environments and would be even more difficult for those who have never swum at all; students from low-income, inner-city families might easily fall into one of these two categories.

A second important point is that an assessment instrument is culturally biased if it *offends* a particular group. For example, imagine a test question that implies that boys are more competent than girls or a question that has a picture in which members of a particular ethnic group are engaging in criminal behavior. Such questions have cultural bias because some groups of students may be offended by the items and may thus be distracted from doing their best on the test. These students might also take the stereotypes to heart, which would adversely affect their sense of self.

An assessment instrument isn't necessarily biased simply because one group gets higher scores on it than another group. It's biased only if the groups' scores are different when the characteristic we're trying to measure *isn't* different for the groups or if the instrument has higher predictive validity for one group than for another. Yes, we may sometimes see group differences in students' scores on assessment instruments, but these differences often reflect inequities in students' previous experiences that will affect their future educational performance. For example, if high school girls earn lower scores on standardized math tests than high school boys do (on average), the difference may be partly due to the fact that (again, on average) parents more actively encourage boys than girls to learn math (Bleeker & Jacobs, 2004; Halpern et al., 2007; Tiedemann, 2000). Similarly, if students from low-income families have had few opportunities to venture beyond their immediate neighborhood (e.g., fewer trips to science museums, less educational travel to other states or countries, etc.), their more limited exposure to diverse environments is likely to impact both their test performance *and* their classroom achievement.

Most publishers of large-scale standardized tests employ individuals who represent numerous minority groups and who actively screen test items for possible sources of cultural bias (M. D. Miller et al., 2009). Furthermore, most scholastic aptitude tests show similar predictive validity for various ethnic and cultural groups, provided that the members of those groups are native English speakers (R. T. Brown, Reynolds, & Whitaker, 1999; Sattler, 2001; Zwick & Sklar, 2005). Nevertheless, before using any standardized test, school personnel should scrutinize it carefully for any items that might be offensive to either gender or to any cultural group, as well as for items that might be more difficult for one group than another for reasons unrelated to the characteristic being measured. And, of course, we should continually be on the lookout for any unintentional cultural bias in the classroom assessment instruments that we construct.

Scrutinize assessment instruments carefully for tasks that some students might find offensive or might have difficulty answering solely because of their ethnic background, gender, or socioeconomic status.

Cultural and Ethnic Differences

Even when test content isn't culturally biased, traditional group-administered standardized tests—the paper–pencil variety that involve time limits and computer-scorable answer sheets—put students from some cultural and ethnic backgrounds at a disadvantage. For example, timed tests that require answering many questions very quickly can be troublesome for Native American students whose communities have socialized them to carefully think and reflect before responding to questions (Tyler et al., 2008; also see Chapter 4). And children from some African American communities (especially those in parts of the southeastern United States) may have little prior experience with questions to which the adult already knows the answer (Heath, 1980, 1989; again see Chapter 4). In addition, debilitating test anxiety is more common among students from cultural and ethnic minority groups (e.g., R. Carter et al., 2008; Putwain, 2007). One possible contributor to this anxiety is a phenomenon known as **stereotype threat**, in which students from stereotypically low-achieving groups perform more poorly on classroom assessments than they otherwise would simply because they are aware that their group traditionally *does* do poorly (J. Aronson & Steele, 2005; J. L. Smith, 2004; see Chapter 11 for more details).

For such reasons, less traditional assessment methods—perhaps dynamic assessment (described in Chapter 14) or portfolios—can often provide a more optimistic picture of minority-group students' achievements and abilities (Haywood & Lidz, 2007; R. S. Johnson et al., 2006). When circumstances *require* traditional paper–pencil tests (e.g., as is usually the case for NCLB-related assessments), students should have plenty of advance practice in taking such tests. And to ease students' anxiety, we should encourage them to think of the tests as only rough measures of abilities that will almost certainly improve with future schooling and effort (e.g., C. Good et al., 2003).

When students' cultural backgrounds put them at a disadvantage in taking traditional group-administered standardized tests, assess their achievements and abilities in other ways. If a standardized paper–pencil test is mandated, give students practice in taking that kind of test, and encourage them to think of the ability being measured as something that will improve with time and practice.

Language Differences and English Language Learners

In the earlier discussion of cultural bias, I stated that most scholastic aptitude tests show similar predictive validity for various groups *provided that the members of those groups are native English speakers.* Without question, students' experience and facility with English affects their performance on English-based assessments of achievement and ability, including high-stakes tests (Carhill et al., 2008; Solórzano, 2008). Poor reading and writing skills are likely to interfere with success on paper–pencil tests, and poor speaking skills may adversely influence students' ability to perform well on oral exams. For example, Spanish-speaking students perform better on math tests when the tests are written in Spanish rather than English (García, 2005). For immigrant students in particular, "any test in English is a test *of* English" (García, 2005).

When students have little proficiency in English, minimize the use of written or spoken English to assess knowledge and skills that are not linguistic in nature.

A particular concern is the use of high-stakes tests with English language learners. When children come to school having been brought up speaking a language other than English, it typically takes them considerable time—perhaps five to seven years—to gain sufficient proficiency in English to perform at their best in English-speaking classrooms (see Chapter 2). Yet many school districts require these students to take high-stakes tests in English long before they achieve this proficiency (Solórzano, 2008; W. E. Wright, 2006). Clearly, such a policy leads to significant underestimations of English language learners' academic achievement. Ideally, we should modify the nature of high-stakes tests in ways that yield greater content validity. Following are examples of practices for which we should advocate for English language learners in high-stakes situations:

- Translate a test into students' native languages.
- Administer a test one-on-one, perhaps eliminating time limits, presenting questions orally, and allowing students to respond in their native languages.
- Use alternative assessment methods (e.g., dynamic assessment, portfolios) to document achievement.
- Exclude students' test scores when computing averages that reflect the overall achievement of a school or a particular subgroup within the school. (Haywood & Lidz, 2007; R. S. Johnson et al., 2006; Solórzano, 2008; W. E. Wright, 2006)

stereotype threat Awareness of a negative stereotype about one's own group and accompanying uneasiness that low performance will confirm the stereotype leads (often unintentionally) to a reduction in performance.

Accommodating Students with Special Needs

We must keep students' unique needs and disabilities in mind whenever we want to assess their abilities and summarize their achievements. For instance, if the instructional goals for a particular student are different from those for the rest of the class, our grading criteria should be altered accordingly, perhaps to be in line with the student's IEP. However, letter grades alone communicate very little definitive information about what students have learned and achieved; if we change the criteria for a particular student, the grades may communicate even less information. Portfolios—perhaps including teacher checklists, photographs, audiotapes, and videotapes, as well as students' written work—can be particularly helpful for conveying the progress and achievements of students with a variety of disabilities and special needs (Mastropieri & Scruggs, 2007; Venn, 2000).

We may also have to modify standardized testing procedures to accommodate students with special educational needs. In the United States, the Individuals with Disabilities Education Act (IDEA) mandates appropriate accommodations for students' disabilities. Such accommodations might involve one or more of the following:

- For a student with limited proficiency in English, administer assessments in his or her native language.
- Modify the presentation format of the assessment (e.g., using Braille or American Sign Language to present test items and other assessment tasks).
- Modify the response format (e.g., dictating answers, allowing use of a word processor).
- Modify the timing (e.g., giving extra time or frequent breaks).
- Modify the assessment setting (e.g., having a student take a standardized paper–pencil test alone in a quiet room).
- Administer part but not all of an instrument.
- Use instruments different from those given to nondisabled classmates, to be more compatible with students' ability levels and needs. (American Educational Research Association, American Psychological Association, & National Council on Measurement in Education, 1999)

We can often use students' IEPs for guidance about appropriate accommodations for each student. Table 15.4 offers additional suggestions for using standardized tests with students who have special needs.

When we modify educational assessment instruments for students with special needs, we must recognize that there is a trade-off between two of our RSVP characteristics. On the one hand, we are violating the idea that an assessment instrument should be standardized with respect to content, administration, and scoring criteria. On the other hand, if we fail to accommodate the disabilities that some students have, we will inevitably get results that have little validity. There's no magic formula for determining the right balance between standardization and validity for students with special needs; as teachers, we must use our best professional judgment (and perhaps also seek the advice of specialists) in each situation.

Keep in mind that published peer-group norms for a standardized test may no longer be applicable when the test is modified in a significant way.

We must keep in mind, too, that modifying assessment instruments or procedures for a standardized test may render the test's norms irrelevant; hence, any norm-referenced scores we derive may be uninterpretable. When our purpose is to *identify* students' learning and performance difficulties, standardized testing procedures and norm-referenced scores are often quite appropriate. But when we are later concerned about how to modify instructional methods and materials to *address* those difficulties, criterion-referenced scores and a close inspection of students' responses to particular tasks and items may be more helpful.

Confidentiality and Communication about Assessment Results

As a student yourself, how public would you like various assessments of your achievement, abilities, and other characteristics to be? Perhaps the following exercise can give you insights into your own thoughts and feelings about this issue.

Students in Inclusive Settings

TABLE 15.4
Using Standardized Tests with Students Who Have Special Educational Needs

Category	Characteristics You Might Observe	Suggested Strategies
Students with specific cognitive or academic difficulties	• Poor listening, reading, and/or writing skills (for some students) • Tendency for test scores to underestimate overall achievement levels (if students have poor reading skills) • Inconsistent performance due to off-task behaviors (e.g., hyperactivity, inattentiveness), affecting reliability and validity of scores (for some students with learning disabilities or ADHD) • Higher than average test anxiety	• Modify test administration procedures to accommodate disabilities identified in students' IEPs (e.g., when administering a districtwide essay test, allow students with writing disabilities to use a word processor and spell checker). • Have students take tests in a room with minimal distractions. • Make sure students understand what they are being asked to do. • Be sure students are motivated to do their best but not overly anxious. • Use classroom assessments (both formal and informal) to confirm or disconfirm results of standardized test results. • Record and report all modifications of standardized procedures.
Students with social or behavioral problems	• Inconsistent performance due to off-task behaviors or lack of motivation, affecting reliability and validity of scores (for some students)	• Modify test administration procedures to accommodate disabilities identified in students' IEPs (e.g., when students are easily distracted, administer tests individually in a quiet room). • Be sure students are motivated to do their best but are not overly anxious. • Use classroom assessments (both formal and informal) to confirm or disconfirm results of standardized test results. • Record and report all modifications of standardized procedures.
Students with general delays in cognitive and social functioning	• Slow learning and cognitive processing • Limited or no reading skills • Poor listening skills	• Choose instruments appropriate for students' cognitive abilities and reading and writing skills. • Minimize the use of instruments that are administered to an entire class at once; rely more on instruments that are administered one on one. • Make sure students understand what they are being asked to do.
Students with physical or sensory challenges	• Mobility problems (for some students with physical challenges) • Tendency to tire easily (for some students with physical challenges) • Less developed language skills, affecting reading and writing ability (for some students with hearing loss)	• Obtain modified test materials for students with visual impairments (e.g., large-print or Braille test booklets). • Modify test administration procedures to accommodate students' unique needs (e.g., have a sign language interpreter give directions to students with hearing loss, or have students with limited muscle control dictate their answers). • If reading and writing skills are impaired, read test items to students. • Break lengthy assessments into segments that can be administered on separate occasions. • Schedule tests at times when students feel rested and alert. • Record and report all modifications of standardized procedures. • Don't compare a student's performance to that of the norm group if significant modifications have been made.
Students with advanced cognitive development	• Greater interest and engagement in challenging tests • Tendency in some students to hide giftedness to avoid possible ridicule by peers (e.g., some minority students may want to avoid "acting white") • In some instances, ability levels beyond the scope of typical tests for the grade level	• Keep assessment results confidential. • When students consistently earn perfect or near-perfect scores (e.g., percentile ranks of 99), request individualized testing that can more accurately assess their very high ability levels. • Use dynamic assessments as an alternative to traditional ability tests to identify giftedness in students from diverse cultural or linguistic backgrounds.

Sources: Barkley, 2006; Beirne-Smith et al., 2006; D. Y. Ford & Harris, 1992; A. W. Gottfried et al., 1994; Haywood & Lidz, 2007; Mastropieri & Scruggs, 2007; Mercer & Pullen, 2005; M. S. Meyer, 2000; B. N. Phillips et al., 1980; Piirto, 1999; Pitoniak & Royer, 2001; Stein & Krishnan, 2007; Turnbull et al., 2007; Venn, 2000; Whitaker Sena et al., 2007.

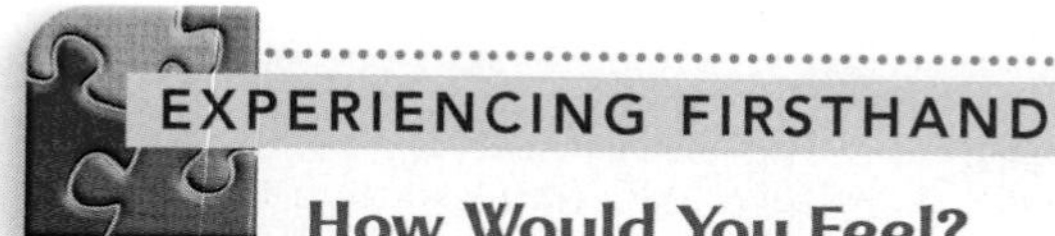

EXPERIENCING FIRSTHAND

How Would You Feel?

How would you feel if one of your instructors did the following?

- Returned test papers in the order of students' test scores, so that those with highest scores were handed out first and you received yours *last*
- Told your other instructors how poorly you had done on the test, so that they could be on the lookout for other stupid things you might do
- Looked through your school records and discovered that you scored 92 on an IQ test you took last year and, furthermore, that a personality test revealed some unusual sexual fantasies

You would probably be outraged if your instructor did any of these things. Test results and class grades should be confidential. But exactly *how* confidential? When should people know the results of students' assessments, and who should know them?

In the United States, we get legal guidance on these questions from the **Family Educational Rights and Privacy Act (FERPA)**, passed by the U.S. Congress in 1974. This legislation limits normal school testing practices primarily to the assessment of achievement and scholastic aptitude—two things that are clearly within the school's domain. Furthermore, it restricts access to students' assessment results to the few individuals who really need to know them: the students who earn them, their parents, and school personnel directly involved with students' education and well-being. Assessment results can be shared with other individuals (e.g., a family doctor or a psychologist in private practice) *only* if the student (if at least 18 years old) or a parent gives written permission.

This legislative mandate for confidentiality has several implications for school assessment practices. For example, we *cannot* do the following:

- Ask students to reveal their political affiliations, sexual behavior or attitudes, illegal behaviors, potentially embarrassing psychological problems, or family incomes. (One exception is questions about income to determine eligibility for financial assistance.)
- Post test scores in ways that allow students to learn one another's scores. (For example, we cannot post scores in alphabetical order or according to birthdays or social security numbers.)
- Distribute papers in any way that allows students to observe one another's scores. (For example, we cannot let students search through a stack of scored papers to find their own.)[7]

Keep students' assessment results confidential; for example, don't post assessment results in ways that allow students to discover how their classmates have performed.

Keeping students' assessment results confidential makes educational as well as legal sense. Students getting low test scores may feel embarrassed or ashamed if classmates know their scores, and they may become more anxious about their future class performance than they would otherwise have been. Students with high scores may also suffer from having the results made public: At many schools, it isn't cool to be

Family Educational Rights and Privacy Act (FERPA) U.S. legislation passed in 1974 that gives students and parents access to school records and limits other people's access to those records.

[7]Many educators initially interpreted FERPA as forbidding teachers to have students grade one another's test papers. In 2002, however, the U.S. Supreme Court ruled that this practice does not violate FERPA because the test scores obtained are not yet a part of students' permanent school records (*Owasso Independent School District* v. *Falvo*, 534 U.S. 426). Nevertheless, having students grade one another's classroom assessments—thereby revealing some students' exceptionally high or low performance—can have adverse effects on students' sense of psychological well-being in the classroom. For this reason, I strongly urge you *not* to have students swap and grade one another's papers.

smart, and high achievers may perform at lower levels to avoid risking peer rejection. And, of course, publicizing students' assessment results focuses students' attention on performance goals—how they appear to others—rather than on mastering the subject matter.

In the opening case study, the teacher announces Ellie's grades to the entire class. Although well intended, the teacher's remarks are illegal; they violate FERPA, which applies to final grades as well as to individual assessments. Furthermore, making Ellie's grades public isn't in Ellie's best interest. Rather than motivate her to work harder (after all, she's already highly motivated), it distresses her to the point that she no longer feels comfortable in the classroom.

An additional provision of FERPA is that parents and students (if at least 18 years old) have the right to review test scores and other school records. And school personnel must present and interpret this information in a way that parents and students can understand.

Communicating Assessment Results to Students and Parents

In the opening case study in Chapter 14, math teacher Ms. Ford distributes disappointing test results. Notice the approach she takes to communicate students' performance to parents:

> *Ms. Ford:* If you received a grade below 75 you definitely have to work on it. I do expect this quiz to be returned with Mom or Dad's signature on it. I want Mom and Dad to be aware of how we're doing.
>
> *Student:* No!
>
> *Student:* Do we have to show our parents? Is it a requirement to pass the class?
>
> *Ms. Ford:* If you do not return it with a signature, I will call home. (J. C. Turner, Meyer, et al., 1998, p. 741)

Ms. Ford obviously wants parents to know that their children aren't doing well in her class. However, there are three drawbacks to her approach. First, many students may find it easier to forge an adultlike signature than to deliver bad news to their parents. Second, parents who do see their children's test papers won't have much information to help them interpret the results (are the low scores due to little effort? poor study strategies? poor instruction?). And third, Ms. Ford focuses entirely on the problem—low achievement—without offering any suggestions for *solving* it.

Ultimately, we must think of ourselves as working in cooperation with students and parents for something that all of us want: students' academic success (see Chapter 13). Our primary goal in communicating classroom assessment results is to share information that will help us achieve that end—something Ms. Ford neglects to do. Furthermore, because virtually all of her students have done poorly on the test, Ms. Ford should consider whether something *she* has done—or not done—might account for the low scores. For instance, perhaps she allocated insufficient class time to certain concepts and skills, used ineffective strategies in teaching them, or constructed an exceptionally difficult test.

When we need to report standardized test results, we face a different challenge. How do we explain the results to students and parents who in all likelihood have never read a chapter on assessment in an educational psychology textbook? Following are several guidelines that experts offered many years ago (Durost, 1961; Ricks, 1959) but that still have relevance today:

Make sure you understand the results yourself. When conveying information about standardized test results, we need to know something about a test's reliability and validity for the situation in which we have used it. We also need to know the general nature of the test scores—for instance, whether they are criterion-referenced or norm-referenced and, if norm-referenced, how to interpret them.

Remember that in many cases it's sufficient to describe the test and students' performance in broad, general terms. To illustrate, we might describe an achievement test as a general measure of how much a student has learned in science compared to what other students around the country have learned, or we might describe a scholastic aptitude test as something that provides a rough idea of how well a student is likely to do in a particular instructional program. It's sometimes possible to describe a student's performance without mentioning test scores at all. For example, we might say, "Your daughter scores like students who do well in college math courses" or "Your son had more than average difficulty on the spelling subtest; this is an area in which he may need extra help in the next few years." However, if parents want to know their child's specific test scores, in the United States FERPA requires that we reveal those scores and help parents understand what they mean.

When reporting specific test scores, use percentile ranks and stanines, rather than grade equivalents or IQs. Many parents mistakenly believe that a child's grade-equivalent score reflects the grade level that the child should actually be in; consequently, they may argue for advanced placement of high-achieving children or feel distressed that low-achieving children are in over their heads. And many parents interpret IQ scores as reflecting a permanent, unchangeable ability rather than a rough estimate of a child's present cognitive functioning. By reporting test scores as percentile ranks or stanines, we are less likely to have parents jumping to such erroneous conclusions. Many parents are familiar with percentile ranks, and many others can easily grasp the notion of a percentile if it's explained to them. But because percentile ranks misrepresent actual differences among students (i.e., by overestimating differences in the middle range and underestimating differences at the extremes), we may also want to provide stanine scores. Although most parents are unfamiliar with standard scores in general, we can often present stanines in a graphic and concrete fashion, as illustrated in Figure 15.13.

FIGURE 15.13 Graphic technique for explaining stanines to parents

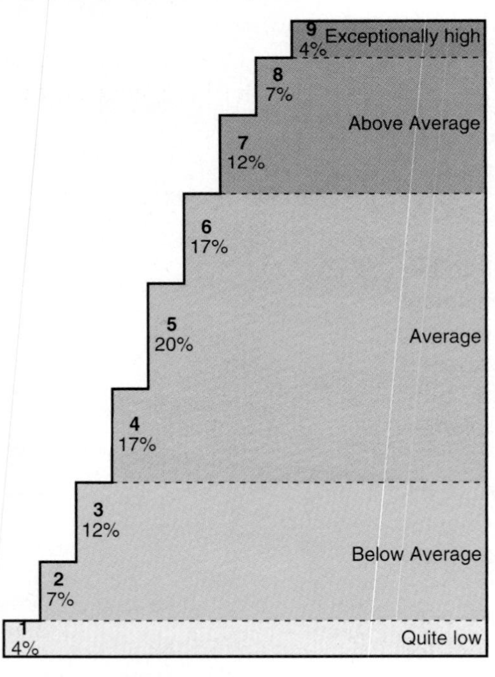

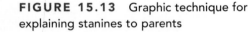

Source: Based on Durost, 1961.

When test results include confidence intervals, such as those depicted in the computer printout in Figure 15.7 (p. 559), it's helpful to explain them to parents. By reporting confidence intervals along with specific test scores, we communicate an important point about classroom assessment: Any test score has some error associated with it.

Whenever we assess students' achievement and abilities, we must remember that our primary purpose is to *help students learn and achieve more effectively* (Stiggins, 2008). When students perform well on classroom assessments and standardized tests, we have cause for celebration, because we know that our instructional strategies are working as they should. But when students perform poorly, our primary concern—and that of students and parents as well—should be how to improve the situation.

The Big Picture

As you wrestle with the issue of how best to summarize students' achievement in your own classroom, I urge you to keep three key principles in mind:

- ***Considerable information is lost any time that students' performance is summarized as a single grade or test score.*** For practical reasons, it's often necessary to summarize students' achievement with single number or letter grades. Furthermore, school administrators and government officials must sometimes administer standardized achievement tests to get a rough idea of how students in a particular school district, state, or province are doing relative to their peers elsewhere. Yet final grades and standardized test scores hardly tell the whole story of what students have accomplished. Through portfolios, parent–teacher conferences, and other means, then, we should supplement grades and scores with information both about students' specific strengths and talents and about areas needing further instruction and practice. And as we plan future lessons and determine how best to tailor instruction to meet students' unique needs, the nitty-gritty details of students' performance on assessment tasks—the specific things students do and do not know, the mistakes they make, the misconceptions they reveal—are probably most helpful of all.

- ***All summative evaluations of students' achievement must have high content validity.*** High content validity means, ultimately, that any overall indicator of academic achievement—whether a final grade, portfolio, or standardized test score—encapsulates what a student has accomplished with respect to important instructional goals. This principle is perhaps most important for high-stakes tests—tests that potentially have long-term implications for students' success both inside and outside the classroom. When we see this principle being violated in ways that can adversely affect students' learning and well-being, we must be vocal advocates for policy change.

- ***Most assessment instruments focus on cognitive factors affecting learning and achievement, giving short shrift to other factors that may be equally influential.*** Most standardized tests and teacher-developed assessments are designed to assess students' competence in particular content domains. They may also require language skills (e.g., reading and writing ability), logical thinking skills, testwiseness, and other cognitive abilities. Occasionally, noncognitive factors (e.g., test anxiety) enter into the equation, but generally classroom assessment instruments do *not* reflect motivational and affective variables—goals, dispositions, interests, attitudes, and so on—that are important factors in students' learning and long-term success. No matter how valid and reliable our assessments may be, they are unlikely to give us a complete picture of how well our students are doing and why.

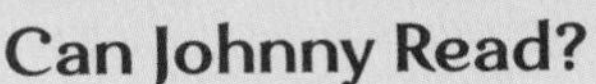

Practice for Your Licensure Exam

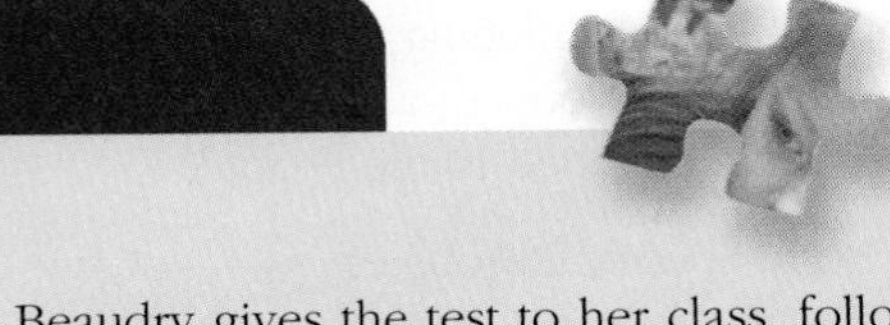

Can Johnny Read?

Ms. Beaudry is serving on a committee to study reading curricula in her school district. As part of her work with the committee, she plans to administer a standardized reading achievement test to determine whether her sixth graders have mastered the reading skills she has been trying to teach them this year. She's been given the opportunity to select the test from three instruments approved for purchase in her district. She scrutinizes the test manuals carefully and eliminates one test when she sees that it has poor test–retest reliability. She looks closely at tables of specifications for the other two tests and eventually selects the Colorado Reading Test (CRT) as the most reliable and valid measure for her own class.

Ms. Beaudry gives the test to her class, following the prescribed administration procedures closely. Because the test consists entirely of multiple-choice items, she is able to score the results quickly and easily that night. She computes each student's raw score and then turns to the norms in the test manual to obtain stanine scores. Her students' stanines range from 3 to 8. "Hmmm, what now?" she asks herself. "After all of this, I still don't know if my students have learned what I've been trying to teach them."

1. **Constructed-response question:**

   Ms. Beaudry chooses the wrong test for her purpose. What specifically does she do wrong?

2. **Multiple-choice question:**

   Ms. Beaudry uses tables of specifications to determine the validity of two of the tests for her own situation. Which one of the following statements best describes a typical table of specifications?

   a. It describes the ideal curriculum for a particular content domain and grade level.
   b. It provides specific, item-by-item scoring criteria that enable objective, reliable scoring.
   c. It indicates the topics covered by an assessment and the things that students should be able to do related to each topic.
   d. It presents the average performance of students at various grade and age levels, thereby enabling conversion of a raw score to one or more norm-referenced scores.

Go to Chapter 15 of the Book-Specific Resources in **MyEducationLab**, and click on "Practice for Your Licensure Exam" to answer these questions. Compare your responses with the feedback provided.

PRAXIS

Turn to Appendix C, "Matching Book and MyEducationLab Content to the Praxis Principles of Learning and Teaching Tests," to discover sections of this chapter that may be especially applicable to the Praxis tests.

PEARSON **myeducationlab**

Now go to MyEducationLab (**www.myeducationlab.com**) where you can:

- Find learning outcomes for Assessment, along with the national standards that connect to these outcomes.
- Complete Assignments and Activities that can help you more deeply understand the chapter content.
- Engage in Building Teaching Skills and Dispositions exercises in which you can apply and practice core teaching skills identified in the chapter.
- Access Book-Specific Resources:
  - Check your comprehension of chapter content by going to the Study Plan, where you can find (a) Chapter Objectives; (b) Focus Questions that can guide your reading; (c) a Self-Check Quiz that can help you monitor your progress in mastering chapter content; (d) Review, Practice, and Enrichment exercises with detailed feedback that will deepen your understanding of various concepts and principles; (e) Flashcards that can give you practice in understanding and defining key terms; and (f) Common Beliefs and Misconceptions about Educational Psychology that will alert you to typical misunderstandings in educational psychology classes.
  - Video Examples of various concepts and principles presented in the chapter.
  - Supplementary Readings that enable you to pursue certain topics in greater depth.
  - A Practice for Your Licensure Exam exercise that resembles the kinds of questions appearing on many teacher licensure tests.

APPENDIX A

Describing Associations with Correlation Coefficients

- Do students with high self-esteem perform better in school than students with low self-esteem?
- Which students are more likely to answer questions correctly: those who answer questions quickly or those who are slow to respond?
- When students take two different intelligence tests in the same week, how similar are their scores on the two tests likely to be?
- Are intellectually gifted students more emotionally well adjusted than their classmates of average intelligence?

Each of these questions asks about an association between two variables—whether it be an association between self-esteem and school achievement, between speed and accuracy in answering questions, between two sets of intelligence test scores, or between giftedness and emotional adjustment. The nature of such associations is sometimes summarized by a statistic known as a **correlation coefficient**.

A correlation coefficient is a number between −1 and +1; most correlation coefficients are decimals (either positive or negative) somewhere between these two extremes. A correlation coefficient for two variables tells us about both the direction and the strength of the association between those variables:

1. *Direction*. The direction of the association is indicated by the *sign* of the correlation coefficient—in other words, by whether the number is positive or negative. A positive number indicates a *positive correlation:* As one variable increases, the other variable also increases. For example, there is a positive correlation between self-esteem and school achievement: Students with higher self-esteem achieve at higher levels (e.g., Marsh, Gerlach, Trautwein, Lüdtke, & Brettschneider, 2007). In contrast, a negative number indicates a *negative correlation:* As one variable increases, the other variable decreases instead. For example, there is a negative correlation between speed and accuracy in answering questions: Students who take longer to answer questions tend to make fewer errors in answering them (e.g., Shipman & Shipman, 1985). Figure A.1 graphically depicts each of these relationships.

2. *Strength*. The strength of the association is indicated by the *size* of the correlation coefficient. A number close to either +1 or −1 (e.g., +.89 or −.76) indicates a *strong* correlation: The two variables are closely related, so that knowing the level of one variable allows us to predict the level of the other variable with some accuracy. For example, we often find a strong relationship between two intelligence tests taken within a short time. Students tend to get similar scores on both tests, especially if the tests cover similar kinds of content (e.g., McGrew, Flanagan, Zeith, & Vanderwood, 1997). In contrast, a number close to 0 (e.g., +.15 or −.22) indicates a *weak* correlation: Knowing the level of one variable allows us to predict the level of the other variable but not with much accuracy. For example, there is a weak association

correlation coefficient Statistic that indicates the strength and direction of an association between two variables.

FIGURE A.1 Each "face" in these two graphs represents 1 student in a group of 50 students. The location of the face tells the extent to which a student is high or low on the two characteristics indicated. There is a *positive correlation* between self-esteem and school achievement: Students with higher self-esteem tend to achieve at higher levels. There is a *negative correlation* between the length of time it takes for students to respond to questions and the number of errors in their answers: Students who take longer to answer questions tend to have fewer errors in their responses.

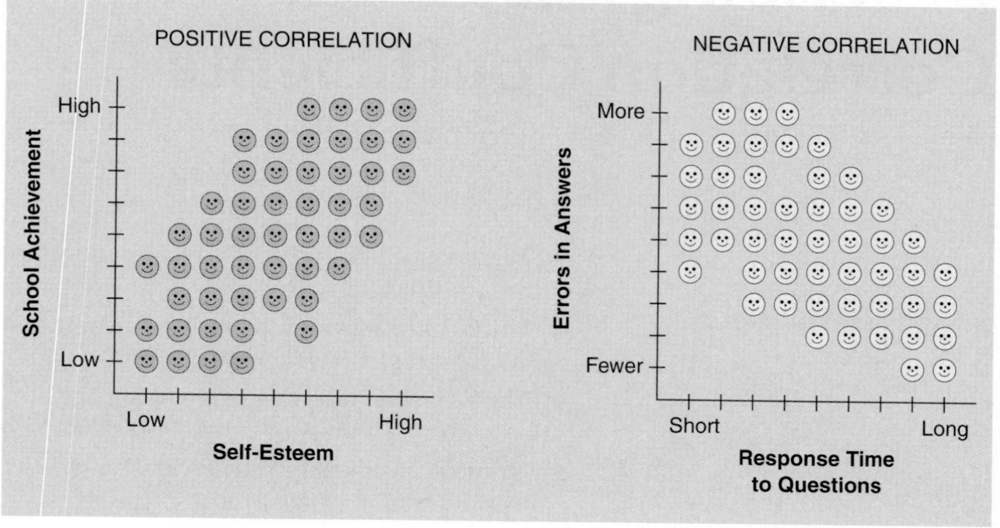

between intellectual giftedness and emotional adjustment: In general, students with higher IQ scores show greater emotional maturity than students with lower scores (e.g., Janos & Robinson, 1985), but many students are exceptions to this rule. Correlations in the middle range (e.g., those in the .40s and .50s—either positive or negative) indicate a *moderate* correlation.

As teachers, we will often encounter correlation coefficients in research articles in our professional books and journals. For instance, we might read that students' visual–spatial thinking ability is positively correlated with their success in a mathematics class or that there's a negative correlation between class size and students' achievement test scores. Whenever we see such evidence of correlation, we must remember one very important point: *Correlation does not necessarily indicate causation.* For example, we cannot say that visual–spatial thinking ability specifically *leads to* greater mathematical ability, nor can we say that large class size specifically *interferes with* classroom achievement. Each of these italicized phrases implies a causal relationship between two variables that doesn't necessarily exist. As indicated in Chapter 1, only carefully designed experimental studies enable us to draw conclusions about the extent to which one thing causes or influences another.

Many calculators are now programmed to compute correlation coefficients. Computing a correlation coefficient by hand is somewhat complicated but certainly not impossible. If you are interested in learning more, you can find the formula in most introductory statistics textbooks. You can also find it on many Internet websites by using a search engine such as Google or Yahoo!

APPENDIX B

Determining Reliability and Predictive Validity

If you have read Appendix A, you have already learned something about **correlation coefficients**: statistics that indicate the strength and direction of an association between two variables. A correlation coefficient is always a number between −1 and +1. A coefficient close to either +1 or −1 (e.g., +.89 or −.76) indicates a strong correlation, whereas a number close to 0 (e.g., +.15 or −.22) indicates a weak correlation. A *positive* coefficient (i.e., one preceded by either a plus sign or no sign at all) indicates a positive association: As one variable increases, the other variable also increases. A negative coefficient (i.e., one preceded by a minus sign) indicates a negative association: As one variable increases, the other variable *decreases.*

Psychologists sometimes use correlation coefficients to determine the reliability and predictive validity of an assessment instrument.

Determining Reliability

The **reliability** of a test or other assessment instrument is the extent to which it yields consistent information about the knowledge, skills, or characteristics we are trying to assess. To mathematically calculate the reliability of an assessment instrument, we begin by getting two scores on the same instrument for the same group of students. We can get these two sets of scores in at least three different ways, with each approach giving us a somewhat different angle on the instrument's reliability.

If we use the same instrument to assess students on two different occasions (as Ms. Fowler does in the "Fowl Play" exercise in Chapter 14), we get information about **test–retest reliability**, the extent to which the instrument yields similar results over a short time interval. If we ask two or more people to judge students' performance (i.e., to grade the same set of essays, rate the same gymnastic performance, etc.), we get information about **scorer reliability**, the extent to which different people agree in their judgments of students' performance. If we compute two or more subscores for different items on the same instrument and look at how similar those subscores are, we get information about **internal consistency reliability**, the extent to which different parts of the instrument all measure the same characteristic.

Once we have two sets of scores for a single group of students, we can determine how similar the two sets are by computing a correlation coefficient; in this case, it's more frequently called a *reliability coefficient.* A reliability coefficient typically ranges from 0 to +1.[1] A number close to +1 indicates high reliability: The two sets of test scores are very similar. Although a perfect reliability coefficient of 1.00 is rare, many standardized achievement and ability tests have reliabilities of .90 or above,

correlation coefficient Statistic that indicates the strength and direction of an association between two variables.

reliability Extent to which an assessment yields consistent information about the knowledge, skills, or characteristics being assessed.

test–retest reliability Extent to which a particular assessment instrument yields similar results over a short time interval.

scorer reliability Extent to which different people agree in their judgments of students' performance on an assessment; sometimes called *interrater reliability.*

internal consistency reliability Extent to which different parts of an assessment instrument all measure the same characteristic.

[1]A negative coefficient is possible but would be obtained only when an *inverse* relationship between the two sets of scores exists—that is, when students who get the highest scores one time get the lowest scores the other time and vice versa. Such an outcome is highly unlikely.

reflecting a high degree of consistency in the scores they yield. As reliability coefficients decrease, they indicate more error in the assessment results—error due to temporary and, in most cases, irrelevant factors. Publishers of standardized achievement and ability tests typically calculate and report reliability coefficients for the various scores and subscores that the tests yield.

Estimating Error in Assessment Results A reliability coefficient tells us, in general, the degree to which temporary errors contribute to fluctuations in students' assessment results. But how much error is apt to be present in a *single* score? In other words, how close is a particular student's score to what it really should be?

A number known as the **standard error of measurement (SEM)** allows us to estimate how close or far off the score might be. The standard error of measurement is calculated from the reliability coefficient; you can find details by searching "calculating standard error of measurement" through a search engine such as Google or Yahoo! (Be careful *not* to click on sites that address standard error of the *mean*, which is a statistic used for an entirely different purpose.)

Let's look at a concrete example. Imagine that Susan takes an academic achievement test known as the Basic Skills Test (BST). Imagine, too, that with her current level of reading ability, Susan should ideally get a score of 40 on the BST Reading subtest. Susan's ideal score of 40 is her **true score**: This is what she would theoretically get if we could measure her reading achievement with complete accuracy. But Susan misinterprets a few test items, answering them incorrectly when, in fact, she knows the correct answers, so she actually gets a score of only 37. Because we cannot see inside Susan's head, we have no way of determining what her true score is; we know only that she's earned a 37 on the test. To estimate the amount of error in her score, we consult the BST test manual to find the standard error of measurement for the Reading subtest: 5 points. We can then guess that Susan's true score probably lies somewhere within a range that is one SEM to either side of her test score: 37 ± 5, or between 32 and 42.

Because almost any assessment score includes a certain amount of error, assessment results are sometimes reported not as specific scores but as a range, or **confidence interval**, extending 1 SEM to either side of the actual test score. By reporting confidence intervals along with specific test scores, we communicate an important point about the tests we give: Any test score has some error associated with it. Figure B.1 shows how we might report Susan's scores on the Reading and other subtests of the BST. Notice that the confidence intervals for the different subtests are different lengths, because each subtest has a different standard error of measurement.

When we use a single SEM to determine the confidence interval, there is a 68% chance that the student's true score lies within that interval. If we instead use 2 SEMs to determine the interval (e.g., for Susan's reading score, such an interval would be 27 to 47), we can be 95% confident that the true score lies within it.[2]

If two or more test scores come from the same test battery (and therefore involve the same norm group), we can use the 68% confidence intervals for the scores to make meaningful comparisons. Overlapping confidence intervals for any two subtests indicate that the student has performed equally well in the two areas. But if the intervals show no overlap, we can reasonably conclude that the student has done appreciably better in one area than the other. Using this approach with Susan's BST scores, we can conclude that Susan has performed best on the math and science subtests, less well on the social studies subtest, and least well on the reading and spelling subtests. We would *not* say that she has done better in science than in math or that she has done better in reading than in spelling, because the confidence intervals overlap for those two pairs of scores.

standard error of measurement (SEM) Statistic estimating the amount of error in a test score or other assessment result.

true score Hypothetical score a student would obtain if an assessment measured a characteristic or ability with complete accuracy.

confidence interval Range around an assessment score reflecting the amount of error that is likely to be affecting the score's accuracy.

---

[2]If you have some knowledge of descriptive statistics, it may help you to know that the SEM is the standard deviation for the hypothetical distribution of all possible scores that a student with a particular true score might get.

FIGURE B.1 Graphic representation of Susan's scores on the Basic Skills Test (BST)

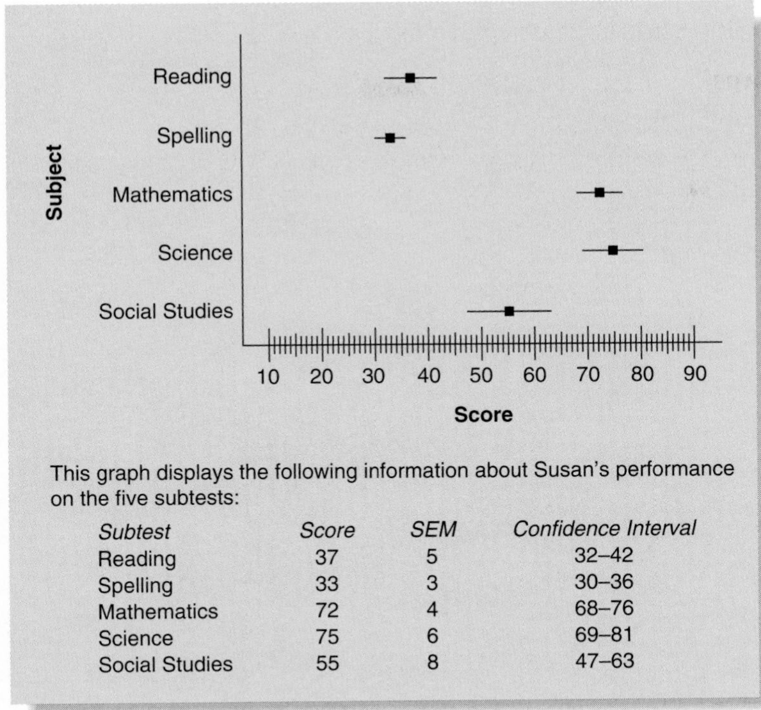

This graph displays the following information about Susan's performance on the five subtests:

Subtest	*Score*	*SEM*	*Confidence Interval*
Reading	37	5	32–42
Spelling	33	3	30–36
Mathematics	72	4	68–76
Science	75	6	69–81
Social Studies	55	8	47–63

Determining Predictive Validity

The **predictive validity** of an assessment instrument (you may also see the term *criterion validity*) is the extent to which the instrument accurately predicts future performance in some domain. Publishers of standardized, norm-referenced ability tests often determine the accuracy with which test scores predict later success in certain content areas. To do so, they first give a test to a group of people; a few months or years later, they measure the same group's success or competence in the behavior being predicted (i.e., the criterion behavior). They then calculate the correlation coefficient between the test scores and the criterion behavior. As is true for a reliability coefficient, this *validity coefficient* is typically a number between 0 and +1, with higher numbers indicating greater predictive validity. Tests with relatively high predictive validity for a particular behavior (e.g., validity coefficients in the .60s and .70s are usually considered high) predict that behavior fairly well. Those with lower predictive validity (e.g., coefficients in the .30s and .40s) are less accurate and will lead to less accurate predictions.

Any test's predictive validity can vary considerably depending on the specific criterion being predicted; for example, many scholastic aptitude tests more accurately predict academic performance in the near future (e.g., within the next two or three years) than in the distant future. Predictive validity also depends somewhat on the age-group in question; for instance, validity coefficients tend to be higher for students in the upper elementary and secondary grades than they are for young children. Typical validity coefficients for general scholastic aptitude tests (including intelligence tests) range between .40 and .70. Those for specific aptitude tests often fall below .50.

predictive validity Extent to which the results of an assessment predict future performance in a particular domain; sometimes called *criterion validity*.

APPENDIX C

Matching Book and MyEducationLab Content to the Praxis® *Principles of Learning and Teaching* Tests

In the United States, state teacher licensing requirements in many states include passing Praxis tests published by Educational Testing Service (ETS). Among the Praxis tests are four Principles of Learning and Teaching (PLT) tests, one each for teachers seeking licensure for early childhood and for grades K–6, 5–9, and 7–12. This text, *Educational Psychology: Developing Learners*, addresses most of the topics covered in the PLT tests. The left column of Table C.1 presents the topics covered on the tests, as identified in *The Praxis Series: Official Guide* (Educational Testing Service, 2008, pp. 348–364). The middle column of the table indicates the chapters and sections in *Educational Psychology: Developing Learners* that are relevant to these topics. The right column suggests relevant exercises and readings in MyEducationLab.

The Praxis Series™ Assessments* involve reading and analyzing case studies. For this reason, the case studies and "Practice for Your Licensure Exam" exercises presented in *Educational Psychology: Developing Learners* may be especially helpful as you prepare for these tests. The opening case study in each chapter is addressed in several places throughout the chapter. The "Practice for Your Licensure Exam" exercise presents a second case study and poses questions that encourage you to apply the chapter content. You will find additional case study material in some of the resources in MyEducationLab.

You may also want to obtain your own copy of *The Praxis Series: Official Guide.* It provides practice case studies and offers suggestions for analyzing them and responding to test questions. You can purchase a copy through various online vendors, including the following:

- Educational Testing Service
  www.ets.org/store.html
- McGraw Hill
  www.mhprofessional.com
- Amazon
  www.amazon.com
- Barnes and Noble
  www.barnesandnoble.com

At some of these websites, you may need to type "Praxis Official Guide" in the "Search" box.

**The Praxis Series, Profesional Assessments for Beginning Teachers* is a registered trademark of Educational Testing Service (ETS). Praxis is a trademark of ETS. Praxis materials are reprinted by permission of ETS. Permission to reprint does not constitute review or endorsement by Educational Testing Service of this publication.

Table C.1.

Matching Book and MyEducationLab Content to the PRAXIS™ *Principles of Learning and Teaching* Tests

Topics in the Praxis Principles of Learning and Teaching (PLT) Tests	Location of Topics in Ormrod's *Educational Psychology* (7th ed.)	Location of Topics and Practice Opportunities in MyEducationLab
I. Students as Learners		
A. Student Development and the Learning Process		
▶ Theoretical foundations about how learning occurs: how students construct knowledge, acquire skills, and develop habits of mind	**Chapter 2:** "Piaget's Basic Assumptions" (pp. 27–29); "Vygotsky's Basic Assumptions" (pp. 39–42) **Chapters 6–10:** Entire chapters (pp. 179–215, 217–247, 249–283, 285–321, 323–359)	**Supplementary Reading** "Learning in the Content Areas" (go to Book-Specific Resources for Chapter 8)
▶ Examples of important theorists: • Albert Bandura	**Chapter 10:** Entire chapter (pp. 323–359); see especially "Basic Assumptions of Social Cognitive Theory" (pp. 324–325)	
• Jerome Bruner	See "Bruner" citations in the Name Index.	
• John Dewey		
• Jean Piaget	**Chapter 2:** "Piaget's Theory of Cognitive Development" (pp. 26–27); **Practice for Your Licensure Exam: "Stones Lesson"** (pp. 58)	**Understanding Research** exercise "Class Inclusion" (go to the topic "Cognitive and Linguistic Development" and click on *Assignments and Activities*)
• Lev Vygotsky	**Chapter 2:** "Vygotsky's Theory of Cognitive Development" (pp. 38–39); **Practice for Your Licensure Exam: "Stones Lesson"** (p. 58)	**Building Teaching Skills and Dispositions** exercise "Using Cognitive Tools and Strategies to Scaffold Learning" (go to the topic "Cognitive and Linguistic Development" and click on *Building Teaching Skills and Dispositions*)
• Howard Gardner	**Chapter 5:** "Gardner's Multiple Intelligences" (pp. 139–141); Table 5.1 (p. 140)	
• Abraham Maslow	**Chapter 11:** "A Possible Hierarchy of Needs: Maslow's Theory" (pp. 373–374)	
• B. F. Skinner	**Chapter 9: Case Study: "The Attention Getter"** (p. 285); "Learning from Consequences: Instrumental Conditioning" (pp. 291–301); "Shaping New Behaviors" (pp. 307–308)	**Supplementary Reading** "Programmed Instruction and Computer-Assisted Instruction" (go to Book-Specific Resources for Chapter 12)
▶ Important terms that relate to learning theory: • Constructivism	**Chapter 2:** "Piaget's Basic Assumptions" (pp. 27–29); "Social Construction of Meaning" (pp. 44–45) **Chapter 6:** "Basic Assumptions of Cognitive Psychology" (pp. 180–183); "How Declarative Knowledge Is Learned" (pp. 191–197); "Reconstruction Error" (p. 210) **Chapter 7: Case Study: "The New World"** (p. 217); "Constructive Processes in Learning and Memory" (pp. 218–222); "Promoting Effective Knowledge Construction" (pp. 228–236); "When Knowledge Construction Goes Awry: Addressing Learners' Misconceptions" (pp. 236–243); "Diversity in Constructive Processes" (pp. 243–244); **Practice for Your Licensure Exam: "Vision Unit"** (p. 246)	**Building Teaching Skills and Dispositions** exercise "Promoting Knowledge Construction and Conceptual Change" (go to the topic "Knowledge Construction" and click on *Building Teaching Skills and Dispositions*) **Understanding Research** exercise "Knowledge Construction in History" (go to the topic "Knowledge Construction" and click on *Assignments and Activities*) **Supplementary Reading** "Learning in the Content Areas" (go to Book-Specific Resources for Chapter 8)
• Metacognition	**Chapter 8: Case Study: "Taking Over"** (p. 249); "Metacognition and Learning Strategies" (pp. 250–261); "Cognitive Factors Affecting Problem Solving" (pp. 269–272); **Practice for Your Licensure Exam: "Interview with Emily"** (p. 282)	**Building Teaching Skills and Dispositions** exercise "Encouraging Self-Regulation" (go to the topic "Social Cognitive Perspectives" and click on *Building Teaching Skills and Dispositions*)

Table C.1. continued

Matching Book and MyEducationLab Content to the PRAXIS™ *Principles of Learning and Teaching* Tests

Topics in the Praxis Principles of Learning and Teaching (PLT) Tests	Location of Topics in Ormrod's *Educational Psychology* (7th ed.)	Location of Topics and Practice Opportunities in MyEducationLab
I. Students as Learners–continued		
A. Student Development and the Learning Process–continued		
	Chapter 12: "Reciprocal Teaching" (pp. 440–442)	**Understanding Research** exercise "Self-Discipline and Academic Achievement" (go to the topic "Student Diversity" and click on *Assignments and Activities*) **Understanding Research** exercise "Teaching Reading Comprehension Strategies" (go to the topic "Cognition and Memory" and click on *Assignments and Activities*) **Understanding Research** exercise "High School Students' Study Strategies" (go to the topic "Complex Cognitive Processes" and click on *Assignments and Activities*) **Supplementary Reading** "Learning in the Content Areas" (go to Book-Specific Resources for Chapter 8)
• Readiness	**Chapter 2:** "Role of the Brain in Learning and Development" (pp. 23–26) **Chapter 15:** "School Readiness Tests" (pp. 571–572)	**Understanding Research** exercise "Usefulness of School Readiness Tests" (go to the topic "Assessment" and click on *Assignments and Activities*)
• Schemata	**Chapter 2:** "Piaget's Basic Assumptions" (pp. 27–29) **Chapter 7:** "Schemas and Scripts" (pp. 224–226)	
• Transfer	**Chapter 8:** "Transfer" (pp. 261–265)	
• Scaffolding	**Chapter 2:** "Scaffolding" (pp. 45–47) **Chapter 7:** "Scaffolding Theory Construction" (pp. 232–234) **Chapter 13:** "Planning Activities That Keep Students on Task" (pp. 470–473)	**Supplementary Reading** "Learning in the Content Areas" (go to Book-Specific Resources for Chapter 8)
• Bloom's taxonomy	**Chapter 12:** "Identifying the Goals of Instruction" (pp. 415–419)	**Supplementary Reading** "Using Taxonomies to Formulate Instructional Goals and Objectives" (go to Book-Specific Resources for Chapter 12)
• Zone of proximal development	**Chapter 2:** "Vygotsky's Basic Assumptions" (pp. 39–42)	**Building Teaching Skills and Dispositions** exercise "Using Cognitive Tools and Strategies to Scaffold Learning" (go to the topic "Cognitive and Linguistic Development" and click on Building Teaching Skills and Dispositions)
• Intrinsic and extrinsic motivation	**Chapter 9:** "Positive Reinforcement" (pp. 294–296); "Strengths and Potential Limitations of Behavioral Approaches" (pp. 317–319) **Chapter 11: Case Study: "Passing Algebra"** (p. 361); "Extrinsic versus Intrinsic Motivation" (pp. 364–365); "Basic Human Needs" (pp. 365–374); "Interests" (pp. 375–376); "Expectancies and Values" (pp. 375–376); "Achievement Goals" (pp. 390–380); **Practice for Your Licensure Exam: "When Perfect Isn't Good Enough"** (p. 410)	**Building Teaching Skills and Dispositions** exercise "Promoting Interest in Classroom Subject Matter" (go to the topic "Motivation and Affect" and click on *Building Teaching Skills and Dispositions*) **Understanding Research** exercise "Self-Discipline and Academic Achievement" (go to the topic "Student Diversity" and click on *Assignments and Activities*)

(continued)

Table C.1. continued

Matching Book and MyEducationLab Content to the PRAXIS™ *Principles of Learning and Teaching* Tests

Topics in the Praxis Principles of Learning and Teaching (PLT) Tests	Location of Topics in Ormrod's *Educational Psychology* (7th ed.)	Location of Topics and Practice Opportunities in MyEducationLab
I. Students as Learners–continued		
A. Student Development and the Learning Process–continued		
▶ Human development in the physical, social, emotional, moral, and cognitive domains:	**Chapters 2–3:** Entire chapters (pp. 19–59, 61–98) **Chapters 4–15:** Developmental Trends tables (pp. 122, 198, 238, 252, 298, 343, 390, 404, 417–418, 475, 516–518, 575) **Chapter 4:** "Origins of Gender Differences" (pp. 121–124) **Chapter 5:** "Nature and Nurture in the Development of Intelligence" (pp. 144–145) **Chapter 6:** "Developmental Trends in Storage Processes for Declarative Information" (pp. 196–197) **Chapter 10:** "Factors in the Development of Self-Efficacy" (pp. 337–339) **Chapter 11:** "Developmental Trends in Achievement Goals" (pp. 380–382); "Developmental Trends in Attributions" (pp. 385–389) **Chapter 13:** "Taking Developmental Differences into Account" (p. 474) **Chapter 15:** "Guidelines for Choosing and Using Standardized Tests" (pp. 572–574)	**Understanding Research** exercise "Class Inclusion" (go to the topic "Cognitive and Linguistic Development" and click on *Assignments and Activities*) **Supplementary Reading** "Physical Development Across Childhood and Adolescence" (go to Book-Specific Resources for Chapter 2) **Supplementary Reading** "Learning in the Content Areas" (go to Book-Specific Resources for Chapter 8; see especially **Case Study: "The Birth of a Nation"** and the various "Developmental Changes" sections)
• The theoretical contributions of important theorists such as Erik Erikson, Lawrence Kohlberg, Carol Gilligan, Jean Piaget, Abraham Maslow, Albert Bandura, and Lev Vygotsky	**Chapter 2:** "Piaget's Theory of Cognitive Development" (pp. 26–27); "Vygotsky's Theory of Cognitive Development" (pp. 38–39) **Chapter 3:** Figure 3.2 (pp. 72–73); "Developmental Trends in Morality and Prosocial Behavior" (pp. 90–95); "Diversity in Moral and Prosocial Development" (pp. 95–97) **Chapter 10:** Entire chapter (pp. 323–359) **Chapter 11:** "A Possible Hierarchy of Needs: Maslow's Theory" (pp. 373–374)	**Building Teaching Skills and Dispositions** exercise "Using Cognitive Tools and Strategies to Scaffold Learning" (go to the topic "Cognitive and Linguistic Development" and click on *Building Teaching Skills and Dispositions*) **Understanding Research** exercise "Self-Efficacy and Achievement" (go to the topic "Social Cognitive Perspectives" and click on *Assignments and Activities*) **Supplementary Reading** "Ecological Systems Perspectives of Child Development" (go to Book-Specific Resources for Chapter 2)
• The major progressions in each developmental domain and the ranges of individual variation within each domain	**Chapter 2:** "Piaget's Stages of Cognitive Development" (pp. 29–34); "Contemporary Extensions and Applications of Piaget's Theory" (pp. 36–38); "Trends in Language Development" (pp. 50–53) **Chapter 3:** "Developmental Changes in Sense of Self" (pp. 70–74); "Development of Peer Relationships and Interpersonal Understanding" (pp. 75–76); "Developmental Trends in Morality and Prosocial Behavior" (pp. 90–95) **Chapters 2–15:** Developmental Trends tables (pp. 51, 75, 83, 91, 122, 198, 238, 252, 298, 343, 390, 404, 417–418, 475, 516–518, 575)	**Building Teaching Skills and Dispositions** exercise "Encouraging Self-Regulation" (go to the topic "Social Cognitive Perspectives" and click on *Building Teaching Skills and Dispositions*) **Understanding Research** exercise "Class Inclusion" (go to the topic "Cognitive and Linguistic Development" and click on *Assignments and Activities*) **Supplementary Reading** "Physical Development Across Childhood and Adolescence" (go to Book-Specific Resources for Chapter 2)
• The impact of students' physical, social, emotional, moral, and cognitive development on their learning and how to address these factors when making instructional decisions	**Chapters 2–3:** See "apple" icons throughout **Chapter 2: Case Study: "Apple Tarts"** (p. 19); **Practice for Your Licensure Exam: "Stones Lesson"** (p. 58) **Chapter 3: Case Study: "Hidden Treasure"** (p. 61); **Practice for Your Licensure Exam: *"The Scarlet Letter"*** (p. 100)	**Building Teaching Skills and Dispositions** exercise "Using Cognitive Tools and Strategies to Scaffold Learning" (go to the topic "Cognitive and Linguistic Development" and click on *Building Teaching Skills and Dispositions*) **Understanding Research** exercise "Supporting

Table C.1. continued

Matching Book and MyEducationLab Content to the PRAXIS™ *Principles of Learning and Teaching* Tests

Topics in the Praxis Principles of Learning and Teaching (PLT) Tests	Location of Topics in Ormrod's *Educational Psychology* (7th ed.)	Location of Topics and Practice Opportunities in MyEducationLab
I. Students as Learners		
A. Student Development and the Learning Process–continued		
	Chapter 5: "Emotional and Behavioral Disorders" (pp. 162–164); "Intellectual Disabilities" (pp. 166–168)	Children at Risk" (go to the topic "Student Diversity" and click on *Assignments and Activities*) **Understanding Research** exercise "Need for Approval and Emotional Well-Being" (go to the topic "Motivation and Affect" and click on *Assignments and Activities*) **Understanding Research** exercise "Usefulness of School Readiness Tests" (go to the topic "Assessment" and click on *Assignments and Activities*) **Supplementary Reading** "Learning in the Content Areas" (go to Book-Specific Resources for Chapter 8)
• How development in one domain, such as physical, may affect performance in another domain, such as social	**Chapter 2:** "Role of the Brain in Learning and Development" (pp. 23–26) **Chapter 3:** "Temperament" (pp. 62–63); "Developmental Changes in Sense of Self" (pp. 70–74); "Social Cognition" (pp. 81–83); "Factors Influencing Moral and Prosocial Development" (p. 95) **Chapter 4:** "Characteristics of Students at Risk" (pp. 130–131)	**Building Teaching Skills and Dispositions** exercise "Fostering Perspective Taking and Social Skills" (go to the topic "Personal, Social, and Moral Development" and click on *Building Teaching Skills and Dispositions*) **Supplementary Reading** "Physical Development Across Childhood and Adolescence" (go to Book-Specific Resources for Chapter 2)
B. Students as Diverse Learners		
▶ Differences in the ways students learn and perform:	**Chapter 2:** "Diversity" sections (pp. 35–36, 43–44, 53); "Second-Language Learning and English Language Learners" (pp. 53–56) **Chapter 3:** "Personality Development" (pp. 62–66); "Diversity" sections (pp. 74–75, 87, 95–97) **Chapters 4–5:** Entire chapters (pp. 102–135, 136–177) **Chapter 6:** "Diversity in Cognitive Processes" (pp. 210–213) **Chapter 7:** "Diversity in Constructive Processes" (pp. 243–244) **Chapter 8:** "Diversity in Creativity, Critical Thinking, and Other Complex Thinking Processes" (pp. 279–280) **Chapter 9:** "Diversity in Student Behaviors and Reactions to Consequences" (pp. 316–317) **Chapter 10:** "Diversity in Self-Regulation" (pp. 351–352) **Chapter 11:** "Universality and Diversity in Basic Needs" (pp. 372–373); "Diversity in Cognitive Factors Affecting Motivation" (pp. 395–399); "Diversity in Affect" (pp. 406–408) **Chapter 12:** "Taking Student Diversity into Account" (pp. 451–453) **Chapter 13:** "Taking Individual and Group Differences into Account" (pp. 474–477); "Taking Students' Cultural Backgrounds into Account" (pp. 493–495)	**Understanding Research** exercise "High School Students' Study Strategies" (go to the topic "Complex Cognitive Processes" and click on *Assignments and Activities*) **Supplementary Reading** "Learning in the Content Areas" (go to Book-Specific Resources for Chapter 8)

(continued)

Table C.1. continued

Matching Book and MyEducationLab Content to the PRAXIS™ *Principles of Learning and Teaching Tests*

Topics in the Praxis Principles of Learning and Teaching (PLT) Tests	Location of Topics in Ormrod's *Educational Psychology* (7th ed.)	Location of Topics and Practice Opportunities in MyEducationLab
I. Students as Learners–continued		
B. Students as Diverse Learners–continued		
	Chapter 14: "Taking Student Diversity into Account in Classroom Assessments" (pp. 547–548) **Chapter 15:** "Taking Student Diversity into Account" (pp. 581–584)	
• Learning styles	**Chapter 5:** "Cognitive Styles and Dispositions" (pp. 147–149) **Chapter 6:** "Diversity in Cognitive Processes" (pp. 210–213)	**Understanding Research** exercise "Self-Discipline and Academic Achievement" (go to the topic "Student Diversity" and click on *Assignments and Activities*)
• Multiple intelligences	**Chapter 5:** "Gardner's Multiple Intelligences" (pp. 139–141)	
• Performance modes: • Concrete operational thinkers • Visual and aural learners	**Chapter 2:** Table 2.1 (p. 30); "Concrete Operations Stage" (pp. 31–32) **Chapter 5:** "Cognitive Styles and Dispositions" (pp. 147–149); "Learning Disabilities" (pp. 154–158) **Chapter 6:** "Visual Imagery" (pp. 195–196) **Chapter 8: Practice for Your Licensure Exam: "Interview with Emily"** (p. 282)	**Understanding Research** exercise "Teaching Reading Comprehension Strategies" (go to the topic "Cognition and Memory" and click on *Assignments and Activities*)
• Gender differences	**Chapter 3:** "Gender Differences" sections (pp. 74, 87, 96) **Chapter 4:** "Gender Differences" (pp. 121–125); **Practice for Your Licensure Exam: "The Active and the Passive"** (pp. 134–135) **Chapter 10: Case Study: "Parlez-Vous Français?"** (p. 323) **Chapter 11:** "Gender Differences" sections (pp. 396–397, 407–408) **Chapter 12:** "Considering Group Differences" (pp. 451–452) **Chapter 13:** "Gender Differences" (pp. 476–477) **Chapter 15:** "Cultural Bias in Test Content" (pp. 581–582)	
• Cultural expectations and styles	**Chapter 2:** "Considering Diversity from the Perspective of Vygotsky's Theory" (pp. 43–44) **Chapter 3: Case Study: "Hidden Treasure"** (p. 61); "Parents' Behaviors" (pp. 63–64); "Cultural Expectations and Socialization" (p. 65); "Cultural and Ethnic Differences" sections (pp. 65, 74–75, 87, 96–97) **Chapter 4: Case Study: "Why Jack Wasn't in School"** (p. 103); "Cultural and Ethnic Differences" (pp. 104–118); **Practice for Your Licensure Exam: "The Active and the Passive"** (pp. 134–135) **Chapter 5:** "Cultural and Ethnic Diversity in Intelligence" (p. 145) **Chapter 6:** "Diversity in Cognitive Processes" (pp. 210–213)	**Building Teaching Skills and Dispositions** exercise "Accommodating Cultural Differences" (go to the topic "Student Diversity" and click on *Building Teaching Skills and Dispositions*) **Understanding Research** exercise "Navigating Adolescence" (go to the topic "Personal, Social, and Moral Development" and click on *Assignments and Activities*)

Table C.1. continued

Matching Book and MyEducationLab Content to the PRAXIS™ *Principles of Learning and Teaching Tests*

Topics in the Praxis Principles of Learning and Teaching (PLT) Tests	Location of Topics in Ormrod's *Educational Psychology* (7th ed.)	Location of Topics and Practice Opportunities in MyEducationLab
I. Students as Learners–continued		
B. Students as Diverse Learners–continued		
	Chapter 7: "Worldviews" (pp. 227–228); "Diversity in Constructive Processes" (pp. 243–244) **Chapter 8: "**Diversity in Creativity, Critical Thinking, and Other Complex Thinking Processes" (pp. 279–280) **Chapter 9: "**Diversity in Student Behaviors and Reactions to Consequences" (pp. 316–317) **Chapter 10:** "Diversity in Self-Regulation" (pp. 351–352) **Chapter 11:** "Universality and Diversity in Basic Needs" (pp. 372–373); "Diversity in Cognitive Factors Affecting Motivation" (pp. 395–399); "Diversity in Affect" (pp. 406–408) **Chapter 12:** "Taking Student Diversity into Account" (pp. 451–453) **Chapter 13:** "Taking Students' Cultural Backgrounds into Account" (pp. 493–495) **Chapter 14:** "Teaching Testwiseness" (pp. 542–543); "Accommodating Group Differences" (pp. 547–548) **Chapter 15:** "Cultural Bias in Test Content" (pp. 581–582); "Cultural and Ethnic Differences" (pp. 582–583)	
▶ Areas of exceptionality in student learning:	**Chapter 5:** Entire chapter (pp. 136–177); see especially **Case Study: "Tim"** (p. 137) and **Practice for Your Licensure Exam: "Quiet Amy"** (pp. 176–177) **Chapters 6–15:** Students in Inclusive Settings tables (pp. 212, 244, 260, 280, 318, 353, 398, 453, 478, 585) **Chapters 6–15:** "Special Needs" sections (pp. 211–213, 317–318, 352, 399, 452, 477, 548, 583–584)	**Understanding Research** exercise "Conducting a Functional Analysis" (go to the topic "Behavioral Perspectives" and click on *Assignments and Activities*) **Understanding Research** exercise "Identifying Reinforcers Through Functional Analysis" (go to the topic "Classroom Management" and click on *Assignments and Activities*)
• Visual and perceptual differences	**Chapter 5:** Figure 5.3 (p. 154); "Autism Spectrum Disorders" (pp. 164–165)	
• Special physical or sensory challenges	**Chapter 5:** "Students with Physical and Sensory Challenges" (pp. 168–172)	
• Learning disabilities	**Chapter 5:** "Learning Disabilities" (pp. 154–158)	**Supplementary Reading** "Learning in the Content Areas" (go to Book-Specific Resources for Chapter 8)
• Attention-deficit disorder (ADD); Attention-deficit hyperactivity disorder (ADHD)	**Chapter 5: Case Study: "Tim"** (p. 137); "Attention-Deficit Hyperactivity Disorder (ADHD)" (pp. 158–159)	**Supplementary Reading** "Learning in the Content Areas" (go to Book-Specific Resources for Chapter 8)
• Functional mental retardation	**Chapter 5:** "Intellectual Disabilities" (pp. 166–168)	**Supplementary Reading** "Adaptive Behaviors and Mental Retardation" (go to Book-Specific Resources for Chapter 5)

(continued)

Table C.1. continued

Matching Book and MyEducationLab Content to the PRAXIS™ *Principles of Learning and Teaching Tests*

Topics in the Praxis Principles of Learning and Teaching (PLT) Tests	Location of Topics in Ormrod's *Educational Psychology* (7th ed.)	Location of Topics and Practice Opportunities in MyEducationLab
I. Students as Learners–continued		
B. Students as Diverse Learners–continued		
• Behavioral disorders	**Chapter 5:** "Emotional and Behavioral Disorders" (pp. 162–164)	**Understanding Research** exercise "Identifying Reinforcers Through Functional Analysis" (go to the topic "Classroom Management" and click on *Assignments and Activities*)
• Developmental delays	**Chapter 5:** "Students with General Delays in Cognitive and Social Functioning" (pp. 166–168)	
▶ Legislation and institutional responsibilities relating to exceptional students: • Americans with Disabilities Act (ADA)		
• Individuals with Disabilities Education Act (IDEA)	**Chapter 5: "**Public Law 94-142: The Individuals with Disabilities Education Act (IDEA)" (pp. 150–152)	
• Inclusion, mainstreaming, and "least restrictive environment"	**Chapter 5:** "Educating Students with Special Needs in General Education Classrooms" (pp. 149–154) **Chapters 6–15:** Students in Inclusive Settings tables (pp. 212, 244, 260, 280, 318, 353, 398, 453, 478, 585)	
• IEP (individual education plan), including what, by law, must be included in each IEP	**Chapter 5:** Figure 5.2 (p. 151) **Chapter 12:** "Accommodating Students with Special Needs" (p. 452) **Chapter 14:** "Accommodating Students with Special Needs" (p. 548) **Chapter 15:** "Considering Effort" (pp. 563–564); "Accommodating Students with Special Needs" (pp. 583–584)	
• Section 504 of the Rehabilitation Act		
• Due process	**Chapter 5:** "Public Law 94-142: Individuals with Disabilities Education Act (IDEA)" (pp. 150–154)	
• Family involvement	**Chapter 5:** "Public Law 94-142: Individuals with Disabilities Education Act (IDEA)" (pp. 150–154); "General Recommendations for Working with Students Who Have Special Needs" (p. 175) **Chapter 13:** "Working with Parents" (pp. 479–485)	
▶ Approaches for accommodating various learning styles, intelligences, exceptionalities, including:	**Chapter 5:** Entire chapter (pp. 136–177) **Chapter 6:** "Diversity in Cognitive Processes" (pp. 210–213) **Chapters 6–15:** Students in Inclusive Settings tables (pp. 212, 244, 260, 280, 318, 353, 398, 453, 478, 585)	
• Differentiated instruction	**Chapter 12:** "Accommodating Students with Special Needs" (p. 452)	

Table C.1. continued

Matching Book and MyEducationLab Content to the PRAXIS™ *Principles of Learning and Teaching Tests*

Topics in the Praxis Principles of Learning and Teaching (PLT) Tests	Location of Topics in Ormrod's *Educational Psychology* (7th ed.)	Location of Topics and Practice Opportunities in MyEducationLab
I. Students as Learners–continued		
B. Students as Diverse Learners–continued		
• Alternative assessments	**Chapter 14:** "The Many Forms of Assessment" (pp. 504–506); "Performance Assessment" (pp. 535–541) **Chapter 15:** "Using Portfolios" (pp. 565–568)	
• Testing modifications	**Chapter 14:** Table 14.5 (p. 549) **Chapter 15:** "Accommodating Students with Special Needs" (pp. 583–584); Table 15.4 (p. 585)	
▶ The process of second-language acquisition and strategies to support the learning of students for whom English is not a first language	**Chapter 2:** "Second-Language Learning and English Language Learners" (pp. 53–57) **Chapter 12:** "Considering Group Differences" (pp. 451–452) **Chapter 14:** "Informal Assessment" (pp. 522–534) **Chapter 15:** "Language Differences and English Language Learners" (p. 583)	
▶ How students' learning is influenced by individual experiences, talents, and prior learning, as well as language, culture, family, and community values, including:	**Chapter 3: Case Study: "Hidden Treasure"** (p. 61); "Parents' Behaviors" (pp. 63–64); "Cultural Expectations and Socialization" (p. 65) **Chapter 4: Case Study: "Why Jack Wasn't in School"** (p. 103); "Cultural and Ethnic Differences" (pp. 104–118) **Chapter 5:** "Cultural and Ethnic Diversity in Intelligence" (p. 145); "Cognitive Styles and Dispositions" (pp. 147–149) **Chapter 6:** "Roles of Prior Knowledge and Working Memory in Long-Term Memory Storage" (pp. 198–201); "Diversity in Cognitive Processes" (pp. 210–213) **Chapter 7:** "Knowledge Construction as a Social Process" (pp. 220–222) **Chapter 8: Case Study: "Taking Over"** (p. 249); **Chapter 12:** "Considering Group Differences" (pp. 451–452)	**Understanding Research** exercise "Knowledge Construction in History" (go to the topic "Knowledge Construction" and click on *Assignments and Activities*) **Supplementary Reading** "Ecological Systems Perspectives of Child Development" (go to Book-Specific Resources for Chapter 2)
• Multicultural backgrounds	**Chapter 3:** "Cultural Expectations and Socialization" (p. 65); Creating a Productive Classroom Environment box "Encouraging Positive Interactions Among Diverse Individuals and Groups" (p. 89) **Chapter 4: Case Study: "Why Jack Wasn't in School"** (p. 103); "Cultural and Ethnic Differences" (pp. 104–118)	**Building Teaching Skills and Dispositions** exercise "Accommodating Cultural Differences" (go to the topic "Student Diversity" and click on *Building Teaching Skills and Dispositions*) **Understanding Research** exercise "Navigating Adolescence" (go to the topic "Personal, Social, and Moral Development" and click on *Assignments and Activities*)
• Age-appropriate knowledge and behavior	**Chapter 2:** "Piaget's Stages of Cognitive Development" (pp. 29–34); "Trends in Language Development" (pp. 50–53) **Chapter 3:** "Developmental Changes in Sense of Self" (pp. 70–74); "Perspective Taking" (p. 82); "Developmental Trends in Morality and Prosocial Behavior" (pp. 90–95) **Chapters 4–15:** Developmental Trends tables (pp. 122, 198, 238, 252, 298, 343, 390, 404, 417–418, 475, 516–518, 578)	

(continued)

Table C.1. continued

Matching Book and MyEducationLab Content to the PRAXIS™ *Principles of Learning and Teaching Tests*

Topics in the Praxis Principles of Learning and Teaching (PLT) Tests	Location of Topics in Ormrod's *Educational Psychology* (7th ed.)	Location of Topics and Practice Opportunities in MyEducationLab
I. Students as Learners–continued		
B. Students as Diverse Learners–continued		
• The student culture at the school	**Chapter 3:** "Roles of Peers in Children's Development" (p. 76); "Characteristics of Peer Relationships" (pp. 77–81) **Chapter 4:** "Navigating Different Cultures at Home and at School" (pp. 105–107)	**Understanding Research** exercise "Navigating Adolescence" (go to the topic "Personal, Social, and Moral Development" and click on *Assignments and Activities*) **Understanding Research** exercise "Cheating in High School Students" (go to the topic "Assessment" and click on *Assignments and Activities*)
• Family backgrounds	**Chapter 3:** "Parents' Behaviors" (p. 63) **Chapter 4:** "Socioeconomic Differences" (pp. 125–130)	**Understanding Research** exercise "Supporting Children at Risk" (go to the topic "Student Diversity" and click on *Assignments and Activities*)
• Linguistic patterns and differences	**Chapter 2:** "Language Development" (pp. 49–57) **Chapter 5:** "Speech and Communication Disorders" (pp. 159–161)	
• Cognitive patterns and differences	**Chapter 5:** "Cognitive Styles and Dispositions" (pp. 147–149) **Chapter 6:** "Diversity in Cognitive Processes" (pp. 210–213) **Chapter 7:** "Diversity in Constructive Processes" (pp. 243–244) **Chapter 8: Practice for Your Licensure Exam: "Interview with Emily"** (p. 282)	**Understanding Research** exercise "Self-Discipline and Academic Achievement" (go to the topic "Student Diversity" and click on *Assignments and Activities*) **Understanding Research** exercise "High School Students' Study Strategies" (go to the topic "Complex Cognitive Processes" and click on *Assignments and Activities*)
• Social and emotional issues	**Chapter 3:** "Personality Development" (pp. 62–63); "Development of a Sense of Self" (pp. 66–75); "Social Cognition" (pp. 81–84); "Aggression" (pp. 84–86); "Factors Influencing Moral and Prosocial Development" (p. 95) **Chapter 5:** "Emotional and Behavioral Disorders" (pp. 162–164); "Autism Spectrum Disorders" (pp. 164–165) **Chapter 10:** "Emotion Regulation" (p. 344) **Chapter 11:** "Affect and Its Effects" (pp. 399–408) **Chapter 14:** "Keeping Test Anxiety in Check" (pp. 543–544)	**Understanding Research** exercise "Navigating Adolescence" (go to the topic "Personal, Social, and Moral Development" and click on *Assignments and Activities*) **Understanding Research** exercise "Need for Approval and Emotional Well-Being" (go to the topic "Motivation and Affect" and click on *Assignments and Activities*)
C. Student Motivation and the Learning Environment		
▶ Theoretical foundations about human motivation and behavior:	**Chapter 11:** Entire chapter (pp. 361–411)	
• Abraham Maslow	**Chapter 11:** "A Possible Hierarchy of Needs: Maslow's Theory" (pp. 373–374)	
• Albert Bandura	**Chapter 10:** Entire chapter (pp. 323–359)	
• B. F. Skinner	**Chapter 9: Case Study: "The Attention Getter"** (p. 285); "Learning from Consequences: Instrumental Conditioning" (pp. 291–301); "Shaping New Behaviors" (pp. 307–308)	**Supplementary Reading** "Programmed Instruction and Computer-Assisted Instruction" (go to Book-Specific Resources for Chapter 12)

Table C.1. continued

Matching Book and MyEducationLab Content to the PRAXIS™ *Principles of Learning and Teaching Tests*

Topics in the Praxis Principles of Learning and Teaching (PLT) Tests	Location of Topics in Ormrod's *Educational Psychology* (7th ed.)	Location of Topics and Practice Opportunities in MyEducationLab
I. Students as Learners–continued		
C. Student Motivation and the Learning Environment–continued		
▶ Important terms that relate to motivation and behavior:		
• Hierarchy of needs	**Chapter 11:** "A Possible Hierarchy of Needs: Maslow's Theory" (pp. 373–374)	
• Correlational and causal relationships	**Chapter 11: Case Study: "Passing Algebra"** (p. 361); "Attributions" (pp. 385–391)	
• Intrinsic motivation	**Chapter 9:** "Strengths and Potential Limitations of Behavioral Approaches" (pp. 317–319) **Chapter 11:** "Extrinsic versus Intrinsic Motivation" (pp. 364–365); "Basic Human Needs" (pp. 365–374); "Interests" (pp. 375–376); "Expectancies and Values" (pp. 376–379); "Achievement Goals" (pp. 379–380)	**Building Teaching Skills and Dispositions** exercises "Addressing Students' Basic Needs" and "Promoting Interest in Classroom Subject Matter" (go to the topic "Motivation and Affect" and click on *Building Teaching Skills and Dispositions*) **Understanding Research** exercise "Self-Discipline and Academic Achievement" (go to the topic "Student Diversity" and click on *Assignments and Activities*)
• Extrinsic motivation	**Chapter 9:** "Learning from Consequences: Instrumental Conditioning" (pp. 291–301) **Chapter 11:** "Extrinsic versus Intrinsic Motivation" (pp. 364–365); "Achievement Goals" (pp. 379–380) **Chapter 14:** "Promoting Learning" (pp. 508–510)	
• Learned helplessness	**Chapter 11:** "Mastery Orientation versus Learned Helplessness" (pp. 389–391)	
• Self-efficacy	**Chapter 3:** "Development of a Sense of Self" (pp. 66–75) **Chapter 10: Case Study: "Parlez-Vous Français?"** (p. 323); "Self-Efficacy" (pp. 335–341)	**Understanding Research** exercise "Self-Efficacy and Achievement" (go to the topic "Social Cognitive Perspectives" and click on *Assignments and Activities*)
• Operant conditioning	**Chapter 9:** "Learning from Consequences: Instrumental Conditioning" (pp. 291–301)	
• Reinforcement	**Chapter 9: Case Study: "The Attention Getter"** (p. 285); "The Various Forms That Reinforcement Can Take" (pp. 293–297); "Using Reinforcement Effectively" (pp. 302–307); "Reinforcing Incompatible Behaviors" (p. 311) **Chapter 10:** "The Social Cognitive View of Reinforcement and Punishment" (pp. 326–329); **Practice for Your Licensure Exam: "Teacher's Lament"** (pp. 357–358) **Chapter 13:** "Conducting Planned, Systematic Interventions" (pp. 491–493)	**Understanding Research** exercise "Conducting a Functional Analysis" (go to the topic "Behavioral Perspectives" and click on *Assignments and Activities*)
• Positive reinforcement	**Chapter 9:** "Positive Reinforcement" (pp. 294–296)	**Understanding Research** exercise "Identifying Reinforcers Through Functional Analysis" (go to the topic "Classroom Management" and click on *Assignments and Activities*)

(continued)

Table C.1. continued

Matching Book and MyEducationLab Content to the PRAXIS™ *Principles of Learning and Teaching Tests*

Topics in the Praxis Principles of Learning and Teaching (PLT) Tests	Location of Topics in Ormrod's *Educational Psychology* (7th ed.)	Location of Topics and Practice Opportunities in MyEducationLab
I. Students as Learners–continued		
C. Student Motivation and the Learning Environment–continued		
• Negative reinforcement	**Chapter 9:** "Negative Reinforcement" (pp. 296–297)	**Understanding Research** exercise "Identifying Reinforcers Through Functional Analysis" (go to the topic "Classroom Management" and click on *Assignments and Activities*)
• Shaping successive approximations	**Chapter 9:** "Shaping New Behaviors" (pp. 307–308)	**Supplementary Reading** "Programmed Instruction and Computer-Assisted Instruction" (go to Book-Specific Resources for Chapter 12)
• Prevention	**Chapter 9:** "Functional Analysis and Positive Behavioral Support" (pp. 314–316) **Chapter 13:** "Creating a Setting Conducive to Learning" (pp. 460–477); "Addressing Aggression and Violence at School" (pp. 495–499)	
• Extinction	**Chapter 9:** "Creating Conditions for Extinction" (p. 310); **Practice for Your Licensure Exam: "Hostile Helen"** (p. 320) **Chapter 13:** "Ignoring Behavior" (pp. 485–486)	
• Punishment	**Chapter 9:** "The Various Forms That Punishment Can Take" (pp. 293–297); "Using Punishment When Necessary" (pp. 311–313) **Chapter 10:** "The Social Cognitive View of Reinforcement and Punishment" (pp. 326–329); **Practice for Your Licensure Exam: "Teacher's Lament"** (pp. 357–358)	
• Continuous reinforcement	**Chapter 9:** "Using Reinforcement Effectively" (pp. 302–307)	
• Intermittent reinforcement	**Chapter 9:** "Using Reinforcement Effectively" (pp. 302–307)	
▶ How knowledge of human motivation and behavior should influence strategies for organizing and supporting individual and group work in the classroom	**Chapter 11:** Entire chapter (pp. 361–411)	**Building Teaching Skills and Dispositions** exercise "Applying Behaviorist Principles" (go to the topic "Behavioral Perspectives" and click on *Building Teaching Skills and Dispositions*) **Building Teaching Skills and Dispositions** exercise "Addressing Students' Basic Needs" (go to the topic "Motivation and Affect" and click on *Building Teaching Skills and Dispositions*) **Understanding Research** exercise "Combining Achievement Goals" (go to the topic "Motivation and Affect" and click on *Assignments and Activities*)
▶ Factors and situations that are likely to promote or diminish students' motivation to learn; how to help students become self-motivated	**Chapter 9:** "Strengths and Potential Limitations of Behavioral Approaches" (pp. 317–319) **Chapter 10:** "Self-Regulated Learning" (pp. 347–349); "Diversity in Self-Regulation" (pp. 351–352) **Chapter 11:** Entire chapter (pp. 361–411)	**Building Teaching Skills and Dispositions** exercise "Promoting Interest in Classroom Subject Matter" (go to the topic "Motivation and Affect" and click on *Building Teaching Skills and Dispositions*)

Table C.1. continued

Matching Book and MyEducationLab Content to the PRAXIS™ *Principles of Learning and Teaching Tests*

Topics in the Praxis Principles of Learning and Teaching (PLT) Tests	Location of Topics in Ormrod's *Educational Psychology* (7th ed.)	Location of Topics and Practice Opportunities in MyEducationLab
I. Students as Learners–continued		
C. Student Motivation and the Learning Environment–continued		
	Chapter 13: "Teaching Self-Regulation Strategies" (pp. 488–489)	**Understanding Research** exercise "Navigating Adolescence" (go to the topic "Personal, Social, and Moral Development" and click on *Assignments and Activities*) **Understanding Research** exercises "Need for Approval and Emotional Well-Being" **and** "Combining Achievement Goals" (go to the topic "Motivation and Affect" and click on *Assignments and Activities*) **Understanding Research** exercise "Cheating in High School Students" (go to the topic "Assessment" and click on *Assignments and Activities*)
▶ Principles of effective classroom management and strategies to promote positive relationships, cooperation, and purposeful learning, including:	**Chapters 3, 5, 9, 13:** Creating a Productive Classroom Environment boxes (pp. 67 89, 166, 295, 305, 467) **Chapter 3:** "Social Cognition" (pp. 81–83); "Aggression" (pp. 84–86); "Promoting Healthy Peer Relationships" (pp. 87–90) "Encouraging Moral and Prosocial and Development in the Classroom" (pp. 97–99) **Chapter 7:** "Creating a Community of Learners" (pp. 234–236) **Chapter 11:** "Relatedness" (pp. 371–372) **Chapter 13:** "Establishing and Maintaining Productive Teacher–Student Relationships" (pp. 462–464); "Creating an Effective Psychological Climate" (pp. 464–466); "Addressing Aggression and Violence at School" (pp. 495–499)	**Building Teaching Skills and Dispositions** exercise "Applying Behaviorist Principles" (go to the topic "Behavioral Perspectives" and click on *Building Teaching Skills and Dispositions*) **Building Teaching Skills and Dispositions** exercise "Maintaining On-Task Behavior" (go to the topic "Classroom Management" and click on *Building Teaching Skills and Dispositions*) **Understanding Research** exercise "Supporting Children at Risk" (go to the topic "Student Diversity" and click on *Assignments and Activities*)
• Establishing daily procedures and routines	**Chapter 13:** "Setting Limits" (pp. 466–470); **Practice for Your Licensure Exam: "The Good Buddy"** (pp. 500–501)	
• Establishing classroom rules	**Chapter 10:** "The Social Cognitive View of Reinforcement and Punishment" (pp. 326–329) **Chapter 13:** "Setting Limits" (pp. 466–470)	
• Using natural and logical consequences	**Chapter 9:** "Logical Consequences" (p. 299)	
• Providing positive guidance	**Chapter 3:** "Promoting Healthy Peer Relationships" (pp. 87–90) **Chapter 9:** "Shaping New Behaviors" (pp. 307–308); "Cueing Inappropriate Behaviors" (pp. 310–311); "Reinforcing Incompatible Behaviors" (p. 311); "Functional Analysis and Positive Behavioral Support" (pp. 314–316)	
• Modeling conflict resolution, problem solving, and anger management	**Chapter 10:** "Self-Regulated Problem Solving" (pp. 349–351) **Chapter 13:** "Addressing Aggression and Violence at School" (pp. 495–499)	

(continued)

Table C.1. continued

Matching Book and MyEducationLab Content to the PRAXIS™ *Principles of Learning and Teaching Tests*

Topics in the Praxis Principles of Learning and Teaching (PLT) Tests	Location of Topics in Ormrod's *Educational Psychology* (7th ed.)	Location of Topics and Practice Opportunities in MyEducationLab
I. Students as Learners–continued		
C. Student Motivation and the Learning Environment–continued		
• Giving timely feedback	**Chapter 9:** Creating a Productive Classroom Environment box "Using Feedback to Improve Learning and Behavior" (p. 295); "Cueing Inappropriate Behaviors" (pp. 310–311) **Chapter 11:** "Fostering Productive Achievement Goals" (p. 382); **Practice for Your Licensure Exam: "When Perfect Isn't Good Enough"** (p. 416) **Chapter 13:** "Cueing Students" (pp. 486–487); "Discussing Problems Privately with Students" (pp. 487–488) **Chapter 14:** "Scoring Students' Responses" sections (pp. 533–534, 538–539)	
• Maintaining accurate records	**Chapter 14:** "RSVP Characteristics of Informal Assessment" (pp. 523–524)	
• Communicating with parents and caregivers	**Chapter 13:** "Working with Parents" (pp. 479–485); "Conferring with Parents" (pp. 489–491)	
• Using objective behavior descriptions	**Chapter 9:** "Using Reinforcement Effectively" (pp. 302–307); "Addressing Especially Difficult Classroom Behaviors" (pp. 313–316)	
• Responding to student misbehavior	**Chapter 9:** "Strategies for Discouraging Undesirable Behaviors" (pp. 310–313); "Addressing Especially Difficult Classroom Behaviors" (pp. 313–316) **Chapter 13:** "Dealing with Misbehaviors" (pp. 485–495); "Taking Students' Cultural Backgrounds into Account" (pp. 493–495); "Addressing Aggression and Violence at School" (pp. 495–499)	
• Arranging of classroom space	**Chapter 13:** "Arranging the Classroom" (pp. 461–462)	
• Pacing and structuring the lesson	**Chapter 5:** "Intellectual Disabilities" (pp. 166–168) **Chapter 6:** "Wait Time" (pp. 208–209); **Practice for Your Licensure Exam: "How Time Flies"** (pp. 214–215) **Chapter 12:** "Conducting a Task Analysis" (pp. 420–421); Into the Classroom box "Using Expository Instruction Effectively" (p. 425) **Chapter 13:** "Planning Activities That Keep Students on Task" (pp. 470–473)	
II Instruction and Assessment		
A. Instructional Strategies		
▶ The major cognitive processes associated with student learning, including:	**Chapters 6–8:** Entire chapters (pp. 179–215, 217–247, 249–283)	**Building Teaching Skills and Dispositions** exercise "Facilitating Effective Long-Term Memory Storage Processes" (go to the topic "Cognition and Memory" and click on *Building Teaching Skills and Dispositions*)

Table C.1. continued

Matching Book and MyEducationLab Content to the PRAXIS™ *Principles of Learning and Teaching Tests*

Topics in the Praxis Principles of Learning and Teaching (PLT) Tests	Location of Topics in Ormrod's *Educational Psychology* (7th ed.)	Location of Topics and Practice Opportunities in MyEducationLab
II. Instruction and Assessment–continued		
A. Instructional Strategies–continued		
		Building Teaching Skills and Dispositions exercise "Promoting Knowledge Construction and Conceptual Change" (go to the topic "Knowledge Construction" and click on *Building Teaching Skills and Dispositions*) **Supplementary Reading** "Learning in the Content Areas" (go to Book-Specific Resources for Chapter 8)
• Critical thinking	**Chapter 5:** "Cognitive Styles and Dispositions" (pp. 147–149) **Chapter 8:** "Critical Thinking" (pp. 275–279)	**Understanding Research** exercise "Self-Efficacy and Achievement" (go to the topic "Social Cognitive Perspectives" and click on *Assignments and Activities*)
• Creative thinking	**Chapter 8:** "Creativity" (pp. 273–275)	
• Higher-order thinking	**Chapter 8:** Entire chapter (pp. 249–283) **Chapter 12:** "Identifying the Goals of Instruction" (pp. 415–419)	
• Inductive and deductive thinking	**Chapter 2:** "Piaget's Stages of Cognitive Development" (pp. 29–34) **Chapter 8:** "Critical Thinking" (pp. 275–278)	**Supplementary Reading** "Learning in the Content Areas" (go to Book-Specific Resources for Chapter 8)
• Problem-structuring and problem-solving	**Chapter 8: Case Study: "Taking Over"** (p. 249); "Problem Solving" (pp. 265–272)	**Building Teaching Skills and Dispositions** exercise "Teaching Problem-Solving Skills" (go to the topic "Complex Cognitive Processes" and click on *Building Teaching Skills and Dispositions*) **Supplementary Reading** "Learning in the Content Areas" (go to Book-Specific Resources for Chapter 8)
• Invention	**Chapter 8:** "Creativity" (pp. 273–275)	
• Memorization and recall	**Chapter 6:** Entire chapter (pp. 179–215) **Chapter 8: Practice for Your Licensure Exam: "Interview with Emily"** (p. 282)	
• Social reasoning	**Chapter 3:** "Social Cognition" (pp. 81–84); "Aggression" (pp. 84–86); "Developmental Trends in Morality and Prosocial Behavior" (pp. 90–95); "Gender Differences" (p. 74); **Practice for Your Licensure Exam: *"The Scarlet Letter"*** (pp. 100–101)	**Building Teaching Skills and Dispositions** exercise "Fostering Perspective Taking and Social Skills" (go to the topic "Personal, Social, and Moral Development" and click on *Building Teaching Skills and Dispositions*)
• Representation of ideas	**Chapter 6:** "The Nature of Long-Term Memory" (pp. 189–190); "How Declarative Knowledge Is Learned" (pp. 191–197) **Chapter 7:** "Organizing Knowledge" (pp. 222–227)	**Understanding Research** exercise "Knowledge Construction in History" (go to the topic "Knowledge Construction" and click on *Assignments and Activities*)
▶ Major categories of instructional strategies, including:	**Chapter 12:** Entire chapter (pp. 413–457)	

(continued)

Table C.1. continued

Matching Book and MyEducationLab Content to the PRAXIS™ *Principles of Learning and Teaching Tests*

Topics in the Praxis Principles of Learning and Teaching (PLT) Tests	Location of Topics in Ormrod's *Educational Psychology* (7th ed.)	Location of Topics and Practice Opportunities in MyEducationLab
II. Instruction and Assessment–continued		
A. Instructional Strategies–continued		
• Cooperative learning	**Chapter 12:** "Cooperative Learning" (pp. 442–446); **Practice for Your Licensure Exam: "Cooperative Learning Project"** (p. 456)	
• Direct instruction	**Chapter 12:** "Direct Instruction" (pp. 427–428)	
• Discovery learning	**Chapter 12:** "Discovery and Inquiry Learning" (pp. 430–432)	
• Whole-group discussion	**Chapter 7:** "Knowledge Construction as a Social Process" (pp. 220–222); "Encouraging Classroom Dialogue" (p. 230) **Chapter 12:** "Class Discussions" (pp. 438–440)	**Supplementary Reading** "Learning in the Content Areas" (go to Book-Specific Resources for Chapter 8)
• Independent study	**Chapter 5:** "Giftedness" (see especially subsection "Adapting Instruction," pp. 172–174) **Chapter 12:** "Computer-Based Instruction" (pp. 428–429); "Instructional Websites" (pp. 429–430); "Homework" (pp. 435–436)	**Supplementary Readings** "Programmed Instruction and Computer-Assisted Instruction" and "Promoting Information Literacy Skills" (go to Book-Specific Resources for Chapter 12)
• Interdisciplinary instruction	**Chapter 6:** "Multiple Connections with Existing Knowledge and a Variety of Contexts" (pp. 204–205) **Chapter 8:** "Factors Affecting Transfer" (pp. 263–265)	
• Concept mapping	**Chapter 6:** "Organization" (pp. 194–195)	
• Inquiry method	**Chapter 7:** "Providing Opportunities for Firsthand Observation and Experimentation" (p. 228); "Scaffolding Theory Construction" (pp. 232–234) **Chapter 12:** "Discovery and Inquiry Learning" (pp. 430–432)	**Supplementary Reading** "Learning in the Content Areas" (go to Book-Specific Resources for Chapter 8)
• Questioning	**Chapter 4:** "Responding to Questions" (p. 110) **Chapter 8:** "Fostering Creativity" (pp. 274–275) **Chapter 12:** "Teacher Questions" (pp. 436–437)	
• Play	**Chapter 2:** "Vygotsky's Basic Assumptions" (pp. 39–42)	
• Learning centers		
• Small-group work	**Chapter 2: Case Study: "Apple Tarts"** (p. 19) **Chapter 7:** "Creating a Community of Learners" (pp. 234–236) **Chapter 12:** "Cooperative Learning" (pp. 442–446); "Peer Tutoring" (pp. 447–449)	**Understanding Research** exercise "Teaching Reading Comprehension Strategies" (go to the topic "Cognition and Memory" and click on *Assignments and Activities*)
• Revisiting	**Chapter 6:** "Regular Practice" (pp. 206–207)	
• Reflection	**Chapter 10:** "Self-Evaluation" (pp. 345–346) **Chapter 14:** "Including Students in the Assessment Process" (pp. 541–542)	

Table C.1. continued

Matching Book and MyEducationLab Content to the PRAXIS™ *Principles of Learning and Teaching* Tests

Topics in the Praxis Principles of Learning and Teaching (PLT) Tests	Location of Topics in Ormrod's *Educational Psychology* (7th ed.)	Location of Topics and Practice Opportunities in MyEducationLab
II. Instruction and Assessment–continued		
A. Instructional Strategies–continued		
• Project approach	**Chapter 7:** "Assigning Authentic Activities" (pp. 231–232) **Chapter 12:** "In-Class Assignments" (pp. 432–433); "Cooperative Learning" (pp. 442–446); **Practice for Your Licensure Exam: "Cooperative Learning Project"** (p. 456)	
▶ Principles, techniques, and methods associated with various instructional strategies, including:	**Chapter 12:** Entire chapter (pp. 413–457)	**Building Teaching Skills and Dispositions** exercise "Facilitating Effective Long-Term Memory Storage Processes" (go to the topic "Cognition and Memory" and click on *Building Teaching Skills and Dispositions*) **Building Teaching Skills and Dispositions** exercise "Promoting Knowledge Construction and Conceptual Change" (go to the topic "Knowledge Construction" and click on *Building Teaching Skills and Dispositions*) **Building Teaching Skills and Dispositions** exercise "Identifying Effective Instructional Strategies" (go to the topic "Planning and Instruction" and click on *Building Teaching Skills and Dispositions*)
• Direct instruction:	**Chapter 12:** "Direct Instruction" (pp. 427–428)	
• Madeline Hunter's "Effective Teaching Model"		
• David Ausubel's "Advance Organizers"	**Chapter 12:** Into the Classroom box "Using Expository Instruction Effectively" (p. 425)	
• Mastery learning	**Chapter 12:** "Mastery Learning" (pp. 424–427)	
• Demonstrations	**Chapter 10:** Into the Classroom box "Promoting Learning Through Modeling" (p. 334)	
• Mnemonics	**Chapter 6:** "Using Mnemonics in the Absence of Relevant Prior Knowledge" (pp. 202–203)	
• Note taking	**Chapter 8:** "Overt Strategies" (pp. 252–253)	
• Outlining	**Chapter 8:** "Accommodating Students with Special Needs" (p. 280)	
• Use of visual aids	**Chapter 5:** "Visual Impairments" (pp. 169–170); "Hearing Loss" (pp. 170–171) **Chapter 6:** "Visual Imagery" (pp. 195–196) **Chapter 12:** Into the Classroom box "Using Expository Instruction Effectively" (p. 425)	

(continued)

Table C.1. continued

Matching Book and MyEducationLab Content to the PRAXIS™ *Principles of Learning and Teaching* Tests

Topics in the Praxis Principles of Learning and Teaching (PLT) Tests	Location of Topics in Ormrod's *Educational Psychology* (7th ed.)	Location of Topics and Practice Opportunities in MyEducationLab
II. Instruction and Assessment–continued		
A. Instructional Strategies–continued		
• Student-centered models:	**Chapter 12:** Discussion of *learner-directed instruction* at beginning of chapter (pp. 414–415)	
• Inquiry model	**Chapter 7:** "Providing Opportunities for Firsthand Observation and Experimentation" (p. 228); "Scaffolding Theory Construction" (pp. 232–234) **Chapter 12:** "Discovery and Inquiry Learning" (pp. 430–432)	
• Discovery learning	**Chapter 12:** "Discovery and Inquiry Learning" (pp. 430–432)	
• Cooperative learning (pair–share, jigsaw, STAD teams, games, tournaments)	**Chapter 12:** "Cooperative Learning" (pp. 442–446)	
• Collaborative learning	**Chapter 7:** "Creating a Community of Learners" (pp. 234–236) **Chapter 12:** "Peer Tutoring" (pp. 447–449); "Technology-Based Collaborative Learning" (pp. 449–451)	**Understanding Research** exercise "Effects of Ability Level on Students' Collaborative Work" (go to the topic "Planning and Instruction" and click on *Assignments and Activities*)
• Concept models (concept development, concept attainment, concept mapping)	**Chapter 6:** "Organization" (pp. 194–195) **Chapter 7:** "Concepts" (pp. 222–223)	
• Discussion models	**Chapter 2: Case Study: "Apple Tarts"** (p. 19) **Chapter 12:** "Class Discussions" (pp. 438–440)	**Understanding Research** exercise "Teaching Reading Comprehension Strategies" (go to the topic "Cognition and Memory" and click on *Assignments and Activities*)
• Laboratories	**Chapter 7:** "Providing Opportunities for Firsthand Observation and Experimentation" (p. 238); "Scaffolding Theory Construction" (pp. 232–234) **Chapter 12:** "Discovery and Inquiry Learning" (pp. 430–436)	**Supplementary Reading** "Learning in the Content Areas" (go to Book-Specific Resources for Chapter 8; see especially **Case Study: "All Charged Up"**)
• Project-based learning	**Chapter 7:** "Assigning Authentic Activities" (pp. 231–232) **Chapter 12:** "Cooperative Learning" (pp. 442–446); **Practice for Your Licensure Exam: "Cooperative Learning Project"** (p. 456)	
• Simulations	**Chapter 12:** "Computer Simulations and Applications" (pp. 433–435)	

Table C.1. continued

Matching Book and MyEducationLab Content to the PRAXIS™ *Principles of Learning and Teaching Tests*

Topics in the Praxis Principles of Learning and Teaching (PLT) Tests	Location of Topics in Ormrod's *Educational Psychology* (7th ed.)	Location of Topics and Practice Opportunities in MyEducationLab
II. Instruction and Assessment–continued		
A. Instructional Strategies–continued		
▶ Methods for enhancing student learning through the use of a variety of resources and materials:		
• Computers, Internet resources, Web pages, e-mail	**Chapter 5:** "Students with Physical and Sensory Challenges" (see especially subsection "General Recommendations," pp. 168–172) **Chapter 7:** "Creating a Community of Learners" (pp. 234–236) **Chapter 8:** "Using Computer Technology to Teach Problem-Solving Skills" (p. 272) **Chapter 12:** "Computer-Based Instruction" (pp. 428–429); "Instructional Websites" (pp. 429–430); "Computer Simulations and Applications" (pp. 433–435); "Technology-Based Collaborative Learning" (pp. 449–451)	**Supplementary Reading** "Programmed Instruction and Computer-Assisted Instruction" (go to Book-Specific Resources for Chapter 12)
• Audiovisual technologies such as videotapes and compact discs	**Chapter 12:** "Computer-Based Instruction" (pp. 428–429); "Computer Simulations and Applications" (pp. 433–435)	
• Local experts	**Chapter 5:** "Giftedness" (see especially subsection "Adapting Instruction," pp. 172–174)	
• Primary documents and artifacts	**Chapter 8:** Into the Classroom box "Fostering Critical Thinking" (p. 278)	**Supplementary Reading** "Learning in the Content Areas" (go to Book-Specific Resources for Chapter 8)
• Field trips	**Chapter 4:** "Fostering Resilience" (pp. 128–129) **Chapter 5:** "Students with Physical and Sensory Challenges" (see especially subsection "General Recommendations," pp. 168–172)	
• Libraries		**Supplementary Reading** "Promoting Information Literacy Skills" (go to Book-Specific Resources for Chapter 12)
• Service learning	**Chapter 3:** "Encouraging Moral and Prosocial Development in the Classroom" (pp. 97–99) **Chapter 7:** "Assigning Authentic Activities" (pp. 231–232)	
B. Planning Instruction		
▶ Techniques for planning instruction to meet curriculum goals, including the incorporation of learning theory, subject matter, curriculum development, and student development:	**Chapter 12:** "Planning for Instruction" (pp. 415–423) **Chapter 13: Case Study: "A Contagious Situation"** (p. 459)	

(continued)

Table C.1. continued

Matching Book and MyEducationLab Content to the PRAXIS™ *Principles of Learning and Teaching* Tests

Topics in the Praxis Principles of Learning and Teaching (PLT) Tests	Location of Topics in Ormrod's *Educational Psychology* (7th ed.)	Location of Topics and Practice Opportunities in MyEducationLab
II. Instruction and Assessment–continued		
B. Planning Instruction–continued		
• National and state learning standards	**Chapter 8: Case Study: "Taking Over"** (p. 249) **Chapter 12:** "Aligning Instructional Goals with National, International, and State Standards" (p. 416) **Chapter 14:** Table 14.1 (pp. 516–518) **Chapter 15:** "High-Stakes Testing and Accountability" (pp. 576–580)	
• State and local curriculum frameworks	**Chapter 12:** "Aligning Instructional Goals with National, International, and State Standards" (p. 416) **Chapter 15:** "High-Stakes Testing and Accountability" (pp. 576–580)	
• State and local curriculum guides		
• Scope and sequence in specific disciplines	**Chapter 12:** "Conducting a Task Analysis" (pp. 420–421)	**Supplementary Reading** "Using Taxonomies to Formulate Instructional Goals and Objectives" (go to Book-Specific Resources for Chapter 12)
• Units and lessons—rationale for selecting content topics	**Chapter 12:** "Developing a Lesson Plan" (p. 422)	**Supplementary Reading** "Example of a Lesson Plan" (go to Book-Specific Resources for Chapter 12) **Lesson Plan Builder** (go to the Resources tab at the top of the screen)
• Behavioral objectives: affective, cognitive, psychomotor	**Chapter 12:** Into the Classroom box "Identifying Appropriate Goals and Objectives" (p. 419)	**Supplementary Reading** "Using Taxonomies to Formulate Instructional Goals and Objectives" (go to Book-Specific Resources for Chapter 12)
• Learner objectives and outcomes	**Chapter 11:** "Achievement Goals" (pp. 379–383) **Chapter 12:** Into the Classroom box "Identifying Appropriate Goals and Objectives" (p. 419)	
• Emergent curriculum		
• Antibias curriculum	**Chapter 4:** "Creating a Culturally Inclusive Classroom Environment" (pp. 113–118)	
• Themes/projects	**Chapter 7:** "Emphasizing Conceptual Understanding" (pp. 229–230)	
• Curriculum webbing		
▶ Techniques for creating effective bridges between curriculum goals and students' experiences:	**Chapter 12:** "Planning for Instruction" (pp. 415–423)	
• Modeling	**Chapter 10:** "Essential Conditions for Successful Modeling" (pp. 333–334)	

Table C.1. continued

Matching Book and MyEducationLab Content to the PRAXIS™ *Principles of Learning and Teaching* Tests

Topics in the Praxis Principles of Learning and Teaching (PLT) Tests	Location of Topics in Ormrod's *Educational Psychology* (7th ed.)	Location of Topics and Practice Opportunities in MyEducationLab
II. Instruction and Assessment–continued		
B. Planning Instruction–continued		
• Guided practice	**Chapter 2:** "Scaffolding" (pp. 45–47); "Guided Participation in Adult Activities" (pp. 47–48); "Apprenticeships" (pp. 48–49)	
• Independent practice, including homework	**Chapter 10:** "Self-Regulated Learning" (pp. 347–349) **Chapter 12:** "Homework" (pp. 435–436)	
• Transitions	**Chapter 13:** "Planning Activities That Keep Students on Task" (pp. 470–473)	
• Activating students' prior knowledge	**Chapter 6:** "Moving Information to Long-Term Memory: Connecting New Information with Prior Knowledge" (p. 189); "Roles of Prior Knowledge and Working Memory in Long-Term Memory Storage" (pp. 198–201) **Chapter 12:** Into the Classroom box "Using Expository Instruction Effectively" (p. 425)	**Understanding Research** exercise "Knowledge Construction in History" (go to the topic "Knowledge Construction" and click on *Assignments and Activities*)
• Anticipating preconceptions	**Chapter 7:** "When Knowledge Construction Goes Awry: Addressing Learners' Misconceptions" (pp. 236–243); **Practice for Your Licensure Exam: "Vision Unit"** (p. 246)	**Building Teaching Skills and Dispositions** exercise "Promoting Knowledge Construction and Conceptual Change" (go to the topic "Knowledge Construction" and click on *Building Teaching Skills and Dispositions*) **Understanding Research** exercise "Knowledge Construction in History" (go to the topic "Knowledge Construction" and click on *Assignments and Activities*)
• Encouraging exploration and problem-solving	**Chapter 2:** "Piaget's Basic Assumptions" (pp. 27–29) **Chapter 7:** "Providing Opportunities for Firsthand Observation and Experimentation" (p. 228) **Chapter 8:** "Problem Solving" (pp. 265–272) **Chapter 12:** "Discovery and Inquiry Learning" (pp. 430–432)	**Building Teaching Skills and Dispositions** exercise "Teaching Problem-Solving Skills" (go to the topic "Complex Cognitive Processes" and click on *Building Teaching Skills and Dispositions*)
• Building new skills on those previously acquired	**Chapter 6:** "How Procedural Knowledge Is Learned" (pp. 197–198) **Chapter 9:** "Shaping New Behaviors" (pp. 307–308) **Chapter 12:** "Mastery Learning" (pp. 424–427)	
• Predicting	**Chapter 7:** "Scaffolding Theory Construction" (pp. 232–234)	**Supplementary Reading** "Learning in the Content Areas" (go to Book-Specific Resources for Chapter 8)
C. Assessment Strategies		
▶ Measurement theory and assessment-related issues:	**Chapters 14–15:** Entire chapters (pp. 503–551, 553–590)	
• Types of assessments	**Chapter 14:** "The Many Forms of Assessment" (pp. 504–506)	**Building Teaching Skills and Dispositions** exercise "Assessing Students' Written Work" (go to the topic "Assessment" and click on *Building Teaching Skills and Dispositions*)

(continued)

Table C.1. continued

Matching Book and MyEducationLab Content to the PRAXIS™ *Principles of Learning and Teaching* Tests

Topics in the Praxis Principles of Learning and Teaching (PLT) Tests	Location of Topics in Ormrod's *Educational Psychology* (7th ed.)	Location of Topics and Practice Opportunities in MyEducationLab
II. Instruction and Assessment–continued		
C. Assessment Strategies–continued		
• Standardized tests: norm referenced or criterion referenced	**Chapter 14:** "The Many Forms of Assessment" (pp. 504–506) **Chapter 15:** "Standardized Tests" (pp. 568–576); "High-Stakes Testing and Accountability" (pp. 576–580)	**Understanding Research** exercise "Usefulness of School Readiness Tests" (go to the topic "Assessment" and click on *Assignments and Activities*)
• Achievement tests	**Chapter 15:** "Achievement Tests" (p. 570); **Practice for Your Licensure Exam: "Can Johnny Read?"** (pp. 589–590)	
• Aptitude tests	**Chapter 15:** "General Scholastic Aptitude and Intelligence Tests" (pp. 570–571); "Specific Aptitude and Ability Tests" (p. 571)	
• Structured observations	**Chapter 14:** "Performance Assessment" (see especially subsection "Planning and Administering the Assessment," pp. 535–541)	
• Anecdotal notes	**Chapter 14:** "Informal Assessment" (pp. 522–524)	
• Assessments of prior knowledge	**Chapter 12:** Into the Classroom box "Using Expository Instruction Effectively" (p. 425)	
• Student responses during a lesson	**Chapter 14:** "Informal Assessment" (pp. 522–524)	
• Portfolios	**Chapter 15:** "Using Portfolios" (pp. 565–568)	**Building Teaching Skills and Dispositions** exercise "Encouraging Self-Regulation" (go to the topic "Social Cognitive Perspectives" and click on *Building Teaching Skills and Dispositions*)
• Essays written to prompts	**Chapter 14:** "Essay Tasks" (pp. 530–531)	
• Journals	**Chapter 13:** "Establishing and Maintaining Productive Teacher–Student Relationships" (pp. 462–464) **Chapter 14:** "Including Students in the Assessment Process" (pp. 541–542)	
• Self-evaluations	**Chapter 10:** "Self-Evaluation" (pp. 345–346) **Chapter 14:** "Including Students in the Assessment Process" (pp. 541–542) **Chapter 15:** "Including Students in the Grading Process" (p. 565); "Using Portfolios" (pp. 565–568)	**Building Teaching Skills and Dispositions** exercise "Encouraging Self-Regulation" (go to the topic "Social Cognitive Perspectives" and click on *Building Teaching Skills and Dispositions*)
• Performance assessments	**Chapter 14:** "Performance Assessment" (pp. 535–541)	
• Characteristics of assessments:	**Chapter 14: Practice for Your Licensure Exam: "Pick and Choose"** (p. 550) **Chapter 15: Practice for Your Licensure Exam: "Can Johnny Read?"** (pp. 589–590)	**Building Teaching Skills and Dispositions** exercise "Assessing Students' Written Work" (go to the topic "Assessment" and click on *Building Teaching Skills and Dispositions*)

Table C.1. continued

Matching Book and MyEducationLab Content to the PRAXIS™ *Principles of Learning and Teaching* Tests

Topics in the Praxis Principles of Learning and Teaching (PLT) Tests	Location of Topics in Ormrod's *Educational Psychology* (7th ed.)	Location of Topics and Practice Opportunities in MyEducationLab
II. Instruction and Assessment–continued		
C. Assessment Strategies–continued		
• Validity	**Chapter 14:** "Validity" (pp. 514–520); "RSVP Characteristics of Informal Assessment" (pp. 523–524); "RSVP Characteristics of Paper–Pencil Assessment" (p. 534); "RSVP Characteristics of Performance Assessment" (pp. 540–541) **Chapter 15:** "Using Portfolios" (pp. 565–568)	**Understanding Research** exercise "Usefulness of School Readiness Tests" (go to the topic "Assessment" and click on *Assignments and Activities*)
• Reliability	**Chapter 14:** "Reliability" (pp. 511–514); "RSVP Characteristics of Informal Assessment" (pp. 523–524); "RSVP Characteristics of Paper–Pencil Assessment" (p. 534); "RSVP Characteristics of Performance Assessment" (pp. 540–541) **Chapter 15:** "Using Portfolios" (pp. 565–568)	
• Norm-referenced	**Chapter 14:** "Criterion-Referenced versus Norm-Referenced Assessments" (p. 506) **Chapter 15:** "Norm-Referenced Scores" (pp. 555–559); "Using Criterion-Referenced versus Norm-Referenced Scores in the Classroom" (pp. 559–560); "Choosing Criterion-Referenced or Norm-Referenced Grades" (pp. 564–565)	
• Criterion-referenced	**Chapter 14:** "Criterion-Referenced versus Norm-Referenced Assessments" (p. 506) **Chapter 15:** "Criterion-Referenced Scores" (pp. 554–555); "Using Criterion-Referenced versus Norm-Referenced Scores in the Classroom" (pp. 559–560); "Choosing Criterion-Referenced or Norm-Referenced Grades" (pp. 564–565)	
• Mean, median, mode	**Chapter 15:** "Standard Scores" (pp. 557–559)	
• Sampling strategy	**Chapter 14:** "Content Validity" (pp. 515–519)	
• Scoring assessments:	**Chapter 14:** "Reliability" (pp. 511–514); "Scoring Students' Responses" sections (pp. 533–534, 538–540)	
• Analytical scoring	**Chapter 14:** "Performance Assessment" (see especially subsection "Scoring Students' Responses," pp. 535–541)	
• Holistic scoring	**Chapter 14:** "Performance Assessment" (see especially subsection "Scoring Students' Responses," pp. 535–541)	
• Rubrics	**Chapter 14:** "Scoring Students' Responses" sections (pp. 533–534, 538–540)	
• Reporting assessment results	**Chapter 15:** "Summarizing the Results of a Single Assessment" (pp. 554–560); "Communicating Assessment Results to Students and Parents" (pp. 587–588)	**Supplementary Reading** "Correcting for Guessing in Paper–Pencil Assessments" (go to Book-Specific Resources for Chapter 14)

(continued)

Table C.1. continued

Matching Book and MyEducationLab Content to the PRAXIS™ *Principles of Learning and Teaching* Tests

Topics in the Praxis Principles of Learning and Teaching (PLT) Tests	Location of Topics in Ormrod's *Educational Psychology* (7th ed.)	Location of Topics and Practice Opportunities in MyEducationLab
II. Instruction and Assessment–continued		
C. Assessment Strategies–continued		
	Appendix B: "Estimating Error in Assessment Results" (pp. B-1–B-3)	**Supplementary Reading** "Calculating Standard Deviations" (go to Book-Specific Resources for Chapter 15)
• Percentile ranks	**Chapter 15:** "Percentile Ranks" (pp. 556–557)	
• Stanines	**Chapter 15:** "Standard Scores" (pp. 557–559)	
• Mastery levels	**Chapter 15:** "Criterion-Referenced Scores" (pp. 554–555)	
• Raw score	**Chapter 15:** "Raw Scores" (p. 554)	
• Scaled score		
• Grade equivalent score	**Chapter 15:** "Grade-Equivalent and Age-Equivalent Scores" (p. 556)	
• Standard deviation	**Chapter 15:** "Standard Scores" (pp. 557–559)	
• Standard error of measurement	**Appendix B:** "Estimating Error in Assessment Results" (pp. B-1–B-3)	
• Use of assessments:	**Chapter 14:** "Using Assessment for Different Purposes" (pp. 507–511)	
• Formative evaluation	**Chapter 14:** "Using Assessment for Different Purposes" (pp. 507–511)	**Building Teaching Skills and Dispositions** exercise "Assessing Students' Written Work" (go to the topic "Assessment" and click on *Building Teaching Skills and Dispositions*)
• Summative evaluation	**Chapter 14:** "Using Assessment for Different Purposes" (pp. 507–511)	**Supplementary Reading** "Combining Assessment Results to Determine Final Grades" (go to Book-Specific Resources for Chapter 15)
• Diagnostic evaluation	**Chapter 14:** "Diagnosing Learning and Performance Problems" (p. 507)	
• Understanding measurement theory and assessment-related issues	**Chapter 14:** "Important Qualities of Good Assessment" (pp. 511–522); "Additional Considerations in Formal Assessment" (pp. 541–547) **Chapter 15:** "Considering Improvement, Effort, and Extra Credit" (pp. 563–564); "High-Stakes Testing and Accountability" (pp. 576–580); "Cultural Bias in Test Content" (pp. 581–582)	**Understanding Research** exercise "Cheating in High School Students" (go to the topic "Assessment" and click on *Assignments and Activities*)
• Interpreting and communicating results of assessments	**Chapter 15:** "Confidentiality and Communication About Assessment Results" (pp. 584–588)	

Table C.1. continued

Matching Book and MyEducationLab Content to the PRAXIS™ *Principles of Learning and Teaching* Tests

Topics in the Praxis Principles of Learning and Teaching (PLT) Tests	Location of Topics in Ormrod's *Educational Psychology* (7th ed.)	Location of Topics and Practice Opportunities in MyEducationLab
III. Communication Techniques		
▶ Basic effective verbal and nonverbal communication techniques	**Chapter 11:** "Enhancing Students' Sense of Self-Determination" (pp. 369–371); "Teacher Expectations and Attributions" (pp. 391–395); **Practice for Your Licensure Exam: "When Perfect Isn't Good Enough"** (p. 410) **Chapter 13:** "Establishing and Maintaining Productive Teacher–Student Relationships" (pp. 462–464); "Creating an Effective Psychological Climate" (pp. 464–466); "Setting Limits" (pp. 466–470); "Working with Parents" (pp. 479–485); "Discussing Problems Privately with Students" (pp. 487–488) **Chapter 14: Case Study: "The Math Test"** (p. 503) **Chapter 15:** "Communicating Assessment Results to Students and Parents" (pp. 587–588)	
▶ Effect of cultural and gender differences on communications in the classroom	**Chapter 4:** "Examples of Cultural and Ethnic Diversity" (pp. 107–113); "Research Findings Regarding Gender Differences" (see especially subsections "Interpersonal Behaviors and Relationships," pp. 118–121, and "Classroom Behaviors," pp. 120–121)	
▶ Types of questions that can stimulate discussion in different ways for particular purposes:	**Chapter 12:** "Teacher Questions" (pp. 436–437)	
• Probing for learner understanding	**Chapter 6:** "Elaboration" (pp. 193–195) **Chapter 7:** "Emphasizing Conceptual Understanding" (pp. 229–230)	
• Helping students articulate their ideas and thinking processes	**Chapter 6:** "Wait Time" (pp. 208–209) **Chapter 7:** "Promoting Conceptual Change" (pp. 240–243)	
• Promoting risk-taking and problem-solving	**Chapter 8:** "Problem Solving" (pp. 265–272) **Chapter 13:** "Creating an Effective Psychological Climate" (pp. 464–466)	
• Facilitating factual recall	**Chapter 6:** "Factors Affecting Retrieval" (pp. 204–209)	**Understanding Research** exercise "Knowledge Construction in History" (go to the topic "Knowledge Construction" and click on *Assignments and Activities*)
• Encouraging convergent and divergent thinking	**Chapter 8:** "Creativity" (pp. 273–275)	
• Stimulating curiosity	**Chapter 2:** "Piaget's Basic Assumptions" (pp. 27–29); **Practice for Your Licensure Exam: "Stones Lesson"** (p. 58) **Chapter 11:** "Promoting Interest in Classroom Subject Matter" (pp. 375–376) **Chapter 12:** "Discovery and Inquiry Learning" (pp. 430–432)	

(continued)

Table C.1. continued

Matching Book and MyEducationLab Content to the PRAXIS™ *Principles of Learning and Teaching* Tests

Topics in the Praxis Principles of Learning and Teaching (PLT) Tests	Location of Topics in Ormrod's *Educational Psychology* (7th ed.)	Location of Topics and Practice Opportunities in MyEducationLab
III. Communication Techniques–continued		
• Helping students to question	**Chapter 8:** "Regularly Monitoring Learning" (pp. 255–256); "Critical Thinking" (pp. 275–279)	
• Promoting a caring community	**Chapter 7:** "Creating a Community of Learners" (pp. 234–236) **Chapter 11:** "Relatedness" (pp. 371–372) **Chapter 13:** "Creating an Effective Psychological Climate" (pp. 464–466); "Working with Other Faculty Members" (pp. 477–479)	
IV. Profession and Community		
A. The Reflective Practitioner		
▶ Types of resources available for professional development and learning:		
• Professional literature	**Chapter 1:** "Developing as a Teacher" (pp. 12–13)	
• Colleagues	**Chapter 13:** "Working with Other Faculty Members" (pp. 477–479)	
• Professional associations	**Chapter 1:** "Developing as a Teacher" (pp. 12–13)	
• Professional development activities	**Chapter 1:** "Developing as a Teacher" (pp. 12–13)	
▶ Ability to read, understand, and apply articles and books about current research, views, ideas, and debates regarding best teaching practices	**Chapter 1:** "Understanding Research" (pp. 4–5); **Practice for Your Licensure Exam: "New Software"** (pp. 15–16)	All **Understanding Research** exercises (go to various topic areas listed on the left-hand side and click on *Assignments and Activities*)
▶ Why personal reflection on teaching practices is critical, and approaches that can be used to reflect and evaluate:	**Chapter 1:** "Developing as a Teacher" (pp. 12–13) **Chapter 3: Case Study: "Hidden Treasure"** (p. 61) **Chapter 4:** "Creating a Culturally Inclusive Classroom Environment" (pp. 113–118) **Chapter 11:** "Teacher Expectations and Attributions" (pp. 391–395)	
• Code of ethics		
• Advocacy for learners	**Chapter 4:** "Supporting Students at Risk" (p. 132)	
B. The Larger Community		
▶ The role of the school as a resource to the larger community:	**Chapter 13:** "Working with the Community at Large" (p. 479); "Getting Parents Involved in School Activities" (pp. 482–483)	
• Teacher as a resource	**Chapter 13:** "Communicating with Parents" (pp. 480–482)	

Table C.1. continued

Matching Book and MyEducationLab Content to the PRAXIS™ *Principles of Learning and Teaching* Tests

Topics in the Praxis Principles of Learning and Teaching (PLT) Tests	Location of Topics in Ormrod's *Educational Psychology* (7th ed.)	Location of Topics and Practice Opportunities in MyEducationLab
IV. Profession and Community–continued		
B. The Larger Community–continued		
▶ Factors in the students' environment outside of school (family circumstances, community environments, health and economic conditions) that may influence students' life and learning	**Chapter 3:** "Parents' Behaviors" (pp. 63–64) **Chapter 4: Case Study: "Why Jack Wasn't in School"** (p. 103); "Navigating Different Cultures at Home and at School" (pp. 105–107); "Family Relationships and Expectations" (p. 112); "Socioeconomic Differences" (pp. 125–130); "Students at Risk" (pp. 130–132) **Chapter 5:** "Nature and Nurture in the Development of Intelligence" (pp. 144–145)	**Supplementary Reading** "Ecological Systems Perspectives of Child Development" (go to Book-Specific Resources for Chapter 2)
▶ Basic strategies for developing and utilizing active partnerships among teachers, parents/guardians, and leaders in the community to support the educational process:	**Chapter 5:** "General Recommendations for Working with Students Who Have Special Needs" (p. 175) **Chapter 13:** "Coordinating Efforts with Others" (pp. 477–485); "Addressing Aggression and Violence at School" (pp. 495–499)	
• Shared ownership		
• Shared decision making	**Chapter 5:** "Public Law 94-142: Individuals with Disabilities Education Act (IDEA)" (pp. 150–152)	
• Respectful/reciprocal communication	**Chapter 13:** "Working with Parents" (pp. 479–485)	
▶ Major laws related to students' rights and teacher responsibilities:		
• Equal education		
• Appropriate education for students with special needs	**Chapter 5:** "Public Law 94-142: Individuals with Disabilities Education Act (IDEA)" (pp. 150–152)	
• Confidentiality and privacy	**Chapter 15: Case Study: "B in History"** (p. 553); "Confidentiality and Communication About Assessment Results" (pp. 584–588)	
• Appropriate treatment of students		
• Reporting in situations related to possible child abuse	**Chapter 3:** "Child Maltreatment" (pp. 64–65)	

Glossary

accommodation Process of dealing with a new event by either modifying an existing scheme or forming a new one.

accountability An obligation of teachers and other school personnel to accept responsibility for students' performance on high-stakes assessments; often mandated by policy makers calling for school reform.

acculturation Gradual process of adopting the values and customs of a new culture.

action research Research conducted by teachers and other school personnel to address issues and problems in their own schools or classrooms.

activation Degree to which something in memory is being actively attended to and mentally processed.

actual developmental level Upper limit of tasks that a learner can successfully perform independently.

adaptive behavior Behavior related to daily living skills and appropriate conduct in social situations; used as a criterion for identifying students with intellectual disabilities.

adaptive testing Computer-based assessment in which students' performance on early items determines which items are presented subsequently.

advance organizer Introduction to a lesson that provides an overall organizational scheme for the lesson.

affect Feelings, emotions, and moods that a learner brings to bear on a task.

African American English Dialect of some African American communities that includes some pronunciations, idioms, and grammatical constructions different from those of Standard English.

age-equivalent score Test score matching a particular student's performance with the average performance of students of a certain age.

aggressive behavior Action intentionally taken to hurt another either physically or psychologically.

algorithm Prescribed sequence of steps that guarantees a correct problem solution.

analytic scoring Scoring a student's performance on an assessment by evaluating various aspects of it separately.

antecedent response Response that increases the likelihood that a certain other response will follow.

antecedent stimulus Stimulus that increases the likelihood that a particular response will follow.

anxiety Feeling of uneasiness and apprehension concerning a situation with an uncertain outcome.

applied behavior analysis (ABA) Systematic application of behaviorist principles in educational and therapeutic settings.

apprenticeship Mentorship in which a novice works intensively with an expert to learn how to perform complex new skills.

arousal See *need for arousal.*

Asperger syndrome Mild form of autism in which students have normal intelligence and language skills but show significant deficits in social cognition and social skills.

assessment Process of observing a sample of a student's behavior and drawing inferences about the student's knowledge and abilities.

assimilation Process of dealing with a new event in a way that is consistent with an existing scheme.

attachment Strong, affectionate bond formed between a child and a caregiver.

attention Focusing of mental processing on particular stimuli.

attention-deficit hyperactivity disorder (ADHD) Disorder marked by inattention, hyperactivity, impulsive behavior, or some combination of these characteristics.

attribution Personally constructed causal explanation for a particular event, such as a success or failure.

authentic activity Classroom activity similar to an activity that students are apt to encounter in the outside world.

authentic assessment Assessment of students' knowledge and skills in a context similar to one in the outside world.

authoritarian parenting Parenting style characterized by rigid rules and expectations for behavior that children are asked to obey without question.

authoritative parenting Parenting style characterized by emotional warmth, high standards for behavior, explanation and consistent enforcement of rules, and inclusion of children in decision making.

autism spectrum disorders Disorders marked by impaired social cognition, social skills, and social interaction, as well as by repetitive behaviors; extreme forms are often associated with significant cognitive and linguistic delays and highly unusual behaviors.

automaticity Ability to respond quickly and efficiently while mentally processing or physically performing a task.

backward design Approach to instructional planning in which a teacher first determines the desired end result (i.e., what knowledge and skills students should acquire) and then identifies appropriate assessments and instructional strategies.

base group Cooperative learning group in which students work together for an entire semester or school year to provide mutual support for one another's learning.

baseline Frequency of a response before it is systematically reinforced.

basic interpersonal communication skills (BICS) Proficiency in English sufficient for day-to-day conversation with English speakers but *not* sufficient for academic success in an English-only curriculum.

behavioral momentum Increased tendency for a learner to make a particular response immediately after making similar responses.

behaviorism Theoretical perspective in which learning and behavior are described and explained in terms of stimulus–response relationships.

belongingness General sense that one is an important and valued member of the classroom.

bias (in assessment) Factor in an assessment instrument or procedure that consistently and differentially influences students' performance for reasons unrelated to the characteristic being measured; as a result, reduces the validity of the assessment.

bilingual education Second-language instruction in which students are instructed in academic subject areas in their native language while simultaneously being taught to speak and write in the second language.

Bloom's taxonomy Taxonomy of six cognitive processes, varying in complexity, that lessons might be designed to foster.

bully Child or adolescent who frequently threatens, harasses, or causes injury to particular peers.

central executive Component of the human memory system that oversees the flow of information throughout the system.

challenge Situation in which a learner believes that success is possible with sufficient effort.

checklist Assessment tool with which a teacher evaluates student performance by indicating whether specific behaviors or qualities are present or absent.

child maltreatment Consistent neglect or abuse of a child that jeopardizes the child's physical and psychological well-being.

classical conditioning Form of learning in which a new, involuntary response is acquired as a result of two stimuli being presented at the same time.

class inclusion Recognition that an object simultaneously belongs to a particular category and to one of its subcategories.

classroom climate Overall psychological atmosphere of the classroom.

classroom management Establishment and maintenance of a classroom environment conducive to learning and achievement.

clinical method Procedure in which an adult presents a task or problem and asks a child a series of questions about it, tailoring later questions to the child's responses to previous ones.

clique Moderately stable friendship group of perhaps three to ten members.

cognitive academic language proficiency (CALP) Mastery of English vocabulary and syntax sufficient for English language learners to achieve academic success in an English-only curriculum.

cognitive apprenticeship Mentorship in which a teacher and a student work together on a challenging task and the teacher provides guidance in how to think about the task.

cognitive behavioral therapy Planned, systematic combination of behaviorist techniques and cognition-based strategies (e.g., modeling, self-regulation techniques) as a means of bringing about desired behaviors.

cognitive development Development of increasingly sophisticated thinking, reasoning, and language with age.

cognitive dissonance Feeling of mental discomfort caused by new information that conflicts with current knowledge or beliefs.

cognitive modeling Demonstrating how to think about as well as how to do a task.

cognitive process Particular way of thinking about and mentally responding to a certain event or piece of information.

cognitive psychology General theoretical perspective that focuses on the mental processes underlying learning and behavior.

cognitive style Characteristic way in which a learner tends to think about a task and process new information; typically comes into play automatically rather than by choice.

cognitive tool Concept, symbol, strategy, procedure, or other culturally constructed mechanism that helps people think about and respond to situations more effectively.

collective self-efficacy People's beliefs about their ability to be successful when they work together on a task.

community of learners Class in which teachers and students actively and collaboratively work to create a body of knowledge and help one another learn.

comprehension monitoring Process of checking oneself to verify understanding and memory of newly acquired information.

computer-based instruction (CBI) Academic instruction provided by means of specially designed computer software.

concept Mental grouping of objects or events that have something in common.

concept map Diagram of concepts and their interrelationships; used to enhance the learning and memory of a topic.

conceptual change Significant revision of an existing theory or belief system, enabling new and discrepant information to be better understood and explained.

conceptual understanding Meaningfully learned and well-integrated knowledge about a topic, including many logical connections among specific concepts and ideas.

concrete operations stage Piaget's third stage of cognitive development, in which adultlike logic appears but is limited to concrete reality.

conditional knowledge Knowledge concerning appropriate ways to respond (physically or mentally) under different circumstances.

conditioned response (CR) Response that begins to be elicited by a particular (conditioned) stimulus through classical conditioning.

conditioned stimulus (CS) Stimulus that begins to elicit a particular response through classical conditioning.

conditioning Term commonly used by behaviorists for *learning;* typically involves specific environmental events leading to the acquisition of specific responses.

confidence interval Range around an assessment score reflecting the amount of error that is likely to be affecting the score's accuracy.

confirmation bias Tendency to seek information that confirms, rather than discredits, current beliefs.

conservation Recognition that if nothing is added or taken away, amount stays the same regardless of alterations in shape or arrangement.

consolidation Neurological process in which newly acquired knowledge is firmed up in the brain; often takes several hours, sometimes even longer.

construction Mental process in which a learner takes many separate pieces of information and uses them to build an overall understanding or interpretation.

constructivism Theoretical perspective proposing that learners construct, rather than absorb, a body of knowledge from their experiences.

construct validity Extent to which an assessment accurately measures an unobservable educational or psychological characteristic.

content validity Extent to which an assessment includes a representative sample of tasks within the content domain being assessed.

contiguity Occurrence of two or more events (e.g., two stimuli, or a stimulus and a response) at approximately the same time.

contingency Situation in which one event happens only after another event has already occurred; one event is *contingent* on the other's occurrence.

contingency contract Formal agreement between a teacher and a student that identifies behaviors the student will exhibit and the reinforcers that will follow.

continuous reinforcement Reinforcement of a response every time it occurs.

control group Group of people in a research study who are given either no intervention or one that is unlikely to have an effect on the dependent variable (i.e., a *placebo* treatment).

controversial student Student whom some peers strongly like and other peers strongly dislike.

conventional morality Uncritical acceptance of society's conventions regarding right and wrong.

conventional transgression Action that violates a culture's general expectations regarding socially appropriate behavior.

convergent thinking Process of pulling together several pieces of information to draw a conclusion or solve a problem.

cooperative learning Approach to instruction in which students work with a small group of peers to achieve a common goal and help one another learn.

co-regulated learning Process through which an adult and child share responsibility for directing various aspects of the child's learning.

correlation Extent to which two variables are associated, such that when one variable increases, the other either increases or decreases somewhat predictably.
correlational study Research study that explores associations among variables.
correlation coefficient Statistic that indicates the strength and direction of an association between two variables.
cortex Upper part of the brain; site of complex, conscious thinking processes.
covert strategy Learning strategy that involves only mental activity and thus is not reflected in a learner's observable behavior (e.g., forming a visual image of a new concept).
creativity New and original behavior that yields a productive and culturally appropriate result.
criterion-referenced assessment Assessment instrument designed to determine what students know and can do relative to predetermined standards or criteria.
criterion-referenced score Assessment score that specifically indicates what a student knows or can do.
criterion validity See *predictive validity.*
critical period See *sensitive period.*
critical thinking Process of evaluating the accuracy, credibility, and worth of information and lines of reasoning.
crowd Large, loose-knit social group that shares certain common interests and behaviors.
crystallized intelligence Knowledge and skills accumulated from prior experience, schooling, and culture.
cueing Use of a verbal or nonverbal signal to indicate that a certain behavior is desired or that a certain behavior should stop.
cultural bias Extent to which assessment tasks either offend or unfairly penalize some students because of their ethnicity, gender, or socioeconomic status.
cultural mismatch Situation in which a child's home culture and the school culture hold conflicting expectations for behavior.
culturally responsive teaching Intentional use of instructional strategies consistent with students' culturally preferred ways of learning and behaving.
culture Behaviors and belief systems of a long-standing social group.
culture shock Sense of confusion when a student encounters a new environment with behavioral expectations very different from those previously learned.
cyberbullying Engaging in relational aggression via wireless technologies or the Internet.
debilitating anxiety Anxiety of sufficient intensity that it interferes with performance.
decay Gradual weakening of information stored in long-term memory, especially if the information is used infrequently.
declarative knowledge Knowledge concerning the nature of how things are, were, or will be.
delay of gratification Ability to forego small, immediate reinforcers in order to obtain larger ones later on.
descriptive study Research study that enables researchers to draw conclusions about the current state of affairs but not about correlational or cause–and–effect relationships.
developmental milestone Appearance of a new, more advanced behavior that indicates significant progress in a child's development.
dialect Form of a language that has certain unique pronunciations and grammatical structures and is characteristic of a particular region or ethnic group.
differentiated instruction Practice of individualizing instructional methods—and possibly also individualizing specific content and instructional goals—to align with each student's existing knowledge, skills, and needs.
direct instruction Approach to instruction that uses a variety of techniques (e.g., explanations, questions, guided and independent practice) in a fairly structured manner to promote learning of basic skills.
discovery learning Approach to instruction in which students derive their own knowledge about a topic through firsthand interaction with the environment.
discrimination Phenomenon in which a student learns that a response is reinforced in the presence of one stimulus but not in the presence of another, similar stimulus.
disequilibrium State of being unable to address new events with existing schemes; typically accompanied by some mental discomfort.
disposition General inclination and desire to approach and think about learning and problem-solving tasks in a particular way; typically has a motivational component in addition to cognitive components.
distance learning Technology-based instruction in which students are at a location physically separate from that of their instructor.
distributed cognition Process whereby learners think about an issue or problem together, sharing ideas and working collaboratively to draw conclusions or develop solutions.
distributed intelligence Thinking facilitated by physical objects and technology, concepts and symbols of one's culture, and/or social collaboration and support.
divergent thinking Process of moving mentally in a variety of directions from a single idea.
dynamic assessment Systematic examination of how readily and in what ways a student can acquire new knowledge or skills, usually with adult assistance or some other form of scaffolding.
educational psychology Academic discipline that (a) systematically studies the nature of learning, child development, motivation, and related topics and (b) applies its research findings to the identification and development of effective instructional practices.
effortful control Ability to inhibit dominant responses in favor of other, less dominant ones that might be more productive; thought to be an aspect of temperament that is influenced by biology and brain maturation.
elaboration Cognitive process in which learners embellish on new information based on what they already know.
emotional and behavioral disorders Emotional states and behaviors that consistently and significantly disrupt academic learning and performance.
emotion regulation Process of keeping in check or intentionally altering feelings that might lead to counterproductive behavior.
empathy Experience of sharing the same feelings as someone in unfortunate circumstances.
encoding Changing the format of new information as it is being stored in memory.
English language learner (ELL) School-age child who is not fully fluent in English because of limited exposure to English prior to enrollment in an English-speaking school.
entity view of intelligence Belief that intelligence is a distinct ability that is relatively permanent and unchangeable.
epistemic belief Belief about the nature of knowledge or knowledge acquisition.
equilibration Movement from equilibrium to disequilibrium and back to equilibrium, a process that promotes development of more complex thought and understandings.
equilibrium State of being able to address new events with existing schemes.
ethnic group People who have common historical roots, values, beliefs, and behaviors and who share a sense of interdependence.
ethnic identity Awareness of one's membership in a particular ethnic or cultural group and willingness to adopt behaviors characteristic of the group.

ETS score Standard score with a mean of 500 and a standard deviation of 100.

evidence-based practice An instructional method or other classroom strategy that research has consistently shown to bring about significant gains in students' development and/or academic achievement.

expectancy Belief about the likelihood of success in an activity given present ability levels and external circumstances that may either help or hinder performance.

experimental study Research study that involves the manipulation of one variable to determine its possible effect on another variable, allowing conclusions to be drawn about cause–and–effect relationships.

explicit knowledge Knowledge that a person is consciously aware of and can verbally describe.

expository instruction Approach to instruction in which information is presented in more or less the same form in which students are expected to learn it.

externalizing behavior Symptom of an emotional or behavioral disorder that has a direct effect on other people (e.g., aggression, lack of self-control).

extinction Gradual disappearance of an acquired response. In classical conditioning, results from repeated presentation of a conditioned stimulus in the absence of the unconditioned stimulus; in instrumental conditioning, results from repeated lack of reinforcement.

extrinsic motivation Motivation resulting from factors external to the individual and unrelated to the task being performed.

extrinsic reinforcer Reinforcer that comes from the outside environment, rather than from within the learner.

facilitating anxiety Level of anxiety (usually relatively low) that enhances performance.

Family Educational Rights and Privacy Act (FERPA) U.S. legislation passed in 1974 that gives students and parents access to school records and limits other people's access to those records.

flow Intense form of intrinsic motivation involving complete absorption in and concentration on a challenging activity.

fluid intelligence Ability to acquire knowledge quickly and adapt effectively to new situations.

formal assessment Preplanned, systematic attempt to ascertain what students know and can do.

formal discipline View of transfer suggesting that the study of rigorous subject matter enhances one's ability to learn other, unrelated things.

formal operational egocentrism Inability of adolescents in Piaget's formal operations stage to separate their own abstract logic from the perspectives of others and from practical considerations.

formal operations stage Piaget's fourth and final stage of cognitive development, in which logical reasoning processes are applied to abstract ideas as well as to concrete objects.

formative evaluation Evaluation conducted before or during instruction to facilitate instructional planning and enhance students' learning.

functional analysis Examination of inappropriate behavior and its antecedents and consequences to determine functions that the behavior might serve for the learner.

g Theoretical general factor in intelligence that influences one's ability to learn and perform in a wide variety of contexts.

gang Cohesive social group characterized by initiation rites, distinctive colors and symbols, territorial orientation, and feuds with rival groups.

gender schema Self-constructed, organized body of beliefs about the traits and behaviors of males or females.

general transfer Instance of transfer in which the original learning task and the transfer task are different in content.

generalization Phenomenon in which a person learns a response to a particular stimulus and then makes the same response to a similar stimulus. In classical conditioning, involves making a conditioned response to a stimulus similar to a conditioned stimulus; in instrumental conditioning, involves making a voluntary response to a stimulus that is similar to one previously associated with a response–reinforcement contingency.

giftedness Unusually high ability or aptitude in one or more areas, to such a degree that students require special educational services to help them meet their full potential.

goodness of fit Situation in which classroom conditions and expectations are compatible with students' temperaments and personality characteristics.

grade-equivalent score Test score matching a particular student's performance with the average performance of students at a certain grade level.

group contingency Situation in which everyone in a group must make a particular response before reinforcement occurs.

group differences Consistently observed differences (on average) among diverse groups of students (e.g., students of different genders or ethnic backgrounds).

guided participation A child's performance, with guidance and support, of an activity in the adult world.

guilt Feeling of discomfort about having caused someone else pain or distress.

halo effect Phenomenon in which people are more likely to perceive positive behaviors in someone they like or admire.

hearing loss Malfunction of the ears or associated nerves that interferes with perception of sounds within the frequency range of normal human speech.

heuristic General strategy that facilitates problem solving but doesn't always yield a solution.

higher-level cognitive process Cognitive process that involves going well beyond something specifically learned (e.g., by analyzing, applying, or evaluating it).

higher-level question Question that requires students to use previously learned information in a new way—that is, to engage in higher-level cognitive processes.

high-stakes testing Practice of using students' performance on a single assessment to make major decisions about students, school personnel, or overall school quality.

holistic scoring Summarizing a student's performance on an assessment with a single score.

horns effect Phenomenon in which people are more likely to perceive negative behaviors in someone for whom they have little affection or respect.

hostile attributional bias Tendency to interpret others' behaviors as reflecting hostile or aggressive intentions.

hot cognition Learning or cognitive processing that is emotionally charged.

identity Self-constructed definition of who one is and what things are important to accomplish in life.

ill-defined problem Problem in which the desired goal is unclear, some information needed to solve the problem is missing, and/or several possible solutions to the problem exist.

illusion of knowing Thinking that one knows something that one actually does *not* know.

imaginary audience Belief that one is the center of attention in any social situation.

I-message Statement that communicates the adverse effects of a student's misbehavior, including one's own reactions to it, in a calm, relatively nonaccusatory manner; its intent is to convey information, not to lay blame.

immersion Second-language instruction in which students hear and speak that language almost exclusively in the classroom.

implicit knowledge Knowledge that a person cannot consciously recall or explain but that nevertheless affects the person's thinking or behavior.

incentive Hoped-for but not guaranteed future consequence of behavior.

inclusion Practice of educating all students, including those with severe and multiple disabilities, in neighborhood schools and general education classrooms.

incompatible behaviors Two or more behaviors that cannot be performed simultaneously.

incremental view of intelligence Belief that intelligence can improve with effort and practice.

individual constructivism Theoretical perspective that focuses on how people, as individuals, construct meaning from their experiences.

individual differences Diversity in abilities and characteristics (intelligence, personality, etc.) among students at a particular age and within any given group.

individualized education program (IEP) Written description of an appropriate instructional program for a student with special needs.

Individuals with Disabilities Education Act (IDEA) U.S. federal legislation granting educational rights from birth until age 21 for people with cognitive, emotional, or physical disabilities.

induction Explanation of why a certain behavior is unacceptable, often with a focus on the pain or distress that someone has caused another.

information literacy Knowledge and skills that help a learner find, use, evaluate, organize, and present information about a particular topic.

informal assessment Assessment that results from a teacher's spontaneous, day-to-day observations of how students perform in class.

information processing theory Theoretical perspective that focuses on the specific ways in which learners mentally think about, or process, new information and events.

inner speech Process of talking to and guiding oneself mentally rather than aloud.

inquiry learning Approach to instruction in which students seek new information through the intentional application of higher-level thinking processes (e.g., scientific reasoning, critical thinking).

in-school suspension Consequence for misbehavior in which a student is placed in a quiet, boring room within the school building, typically to do schoolwork under close adult supervision.

instructional goal Desired long-term outcome of instruction.

instructional objective Desired outcome of a lesson or unit.

instrumental conditioning Form of learning in which a response either increases or decreases as a result of being followed by either reinforcement or punishment, respectively; instrumental conditioning brought about by reinforcement is sometimes called *operant conditioning*.

intellectual disability Disability characterized by significantly below-average general intelligence and deficits in adaptive behavior, both of which first appear in infancy or childhood; also known as *mental retardation*.

intelligence Ability to apply prior knowledge and experiences flexibly to accomplish challenging new tasks.

intelligence test General measure of current level of cognitive functioning; often used to predict academic achievement in the short run.

interest Perception that an activity is intriguing and enticing; typically accompanied by both cognitive engagement and positive affect.

interference Phenomenon whereby something stored in long-term memory inhibits one's ability to remember something else correctly.

intermittent reinforcement Reinforcement of a response only occasionally, with some occurrences of the response *not* being reinforced.

internal consistency reliability Extent to which different parts of an assessment instrument all measure the same characteristic.

internalization Process through which a learner gradually incorporates socially based activities into his or her internal cognitive processes.

internalized motivation Adoption of other people's priorities and values as one's own.

internalizing behavior Symptom of an emotional or behavioral disorder that significantly affects the student with the disorder but has little or no direct effect on other people (e.g., depression, social withdrawal).

interrater reliability See *scorer reliability*.

intrinsic motivation Motivation resulting from internal personal characteristics or inherent in the task being performed.

intrinsic reinforcer Reinforcer that is provided by the learner or inherent in the task being performed.

IQ score Score on an intelligence test, as determined by comparing a person's performance with that of others in the same age-group; for most tests, it's a standard score with a mean of 100 and a standard deviation of 15.

IRE cycle Adult–child interaction marked by adult initiation (usually involving a question), child response, and adult evaluation.

item analysis Follow-up analysis of patterns in students' responses to various items on an assessment instrument.

item difficulty (*p*) Index reflecting the proportion of students getting a particular assessment item correct.

item discrimination (*D*) Index reflecting the relative proportions of high-scoring versus low-scoring students getting a particular assessment item correct.

jigsaw technique Instructional technique in which materials are divided among members of a cooperative group, with different students being responsible for learning different content and teaching it to other group members.

keyword method Mnemonic technique in which an association is made between two ideas by forming a visual image of one or more concrete objects (*keywords*) that either sound similar to or symbolically represent those ideas.

knowledge base One's existing knowledge about specific topics and the world in general.

learned helplessness General, fairly pervasive belief that one is incapable of accomplishing tasks and has little or no control of the environment.

learner-directed instruction Approach to instruction in which students have considerable control regarding the issues they address and the ways they address them.

learning Long-term change in mental representations or associations as a result of experience.

learning disabilities Deficiencies in one or more specific cognitive processes but not in overall cognitive functioning.

learning strategy One or more cognitive processes used intentionally for a particular learning task.

least restrictive environment Most typical and standard educational environment that can reasonably meet the needs of a student with a disability.

lesson plan Teacher-constructed guide for a lesson that identifies instructional goals, necessary materials, instructional strategies, and one or more assessment methods.

level of potential development Upper limit of tasks that a learner can successfully perform with the assistance of a more competent individual.

live model Currently living individual whose behavior is observed in person.

logical consequence Consequence that follows naturally or logically from a student's misbehavior.

long-term memory Component of memory that holds knowledge and skills for a relatively long time.

lower-level cognitive process Cognitive process that involves learning or remembering specific information or skills in more or less the same form in which they were initially presented.

lower-level question Question that requires students to retrieve and recite what they have learned in essentially the same way they learned it.

maintenance rehearsal Rapid repetition of a small amount of information to keep it fresh in working memory.

mastery goal Desire to acquire new knowledge or master new skills.

mastery learning Approach to instruction in which students learn one topic thoroughly before moving to a subsequent one.

mastery orientation General, fairly pervasive belief that one is capable of accomplishing challenging tasks.

maturation Occurrence of genetically controlled physical advancements as a child develops.

mean (M) Mathematical average of a set of scores.

meaningful learning Cognitive process in which learners relate new information to things they already know.

meaningful learning set Attitude that one can make sense of the information one is studying.

mediated learning experience Discussion between an adult and a child in which the adult helps the child make sense of an event they have mutually experienced.

memory Ability to mentally save something that has been previously learned; also, the mental "location" where such information is saved.

mental retardation See *intellectual disability.*

mental set Inclination to encode a problem in a way that excludes potential solutions.

metacognition Knowledge and beliefs about the nature of human cognitive processes (including one's own), as well as conscious attempts to engage in behaviors and thought processes that increase learning and memory.

metalinguistic awareness Ability to think consciously about the nature and functions of language.

misbehavior Action that disrupts learning and planned classroom activities, puts students' physical safety or psychological well-being in jeopardy, or violates basic moral standards.

misconception Belief that is inconsistent with commonly accepted and well-validated explanations of phenomena or events.

mnemonic Memory aid or trick designed to help students learn and remember one or more specific pieces of information.

model In science, physical or symbolic representation of a phenomenon that depicts its key components and important interrelationships. In social cognitive theory, an individual (live or symbolic) who demonstrates a behavior for someone else.

modeling Demonstrating a behavior for another person *or* observing and imitating another person's behavior.

moral dilemma Situation in which two or more people's rights or needs may be at odds and the morally correct action is not clear cut.

morality One's general standards about right and wrong behavior.

moral transgression Action that causes harm or infringes on the needs or rights of others.

motivation Inner state that energizes, directs, and sustains behavior.

multicultural education Instruction that integrates throughout the curriculum the perspectives and experiences of numerous cultural groups.

myelination Growth of a fatty sheath (myelin) around the axons of neurons, enabling faster transmission of messages.

need for arousal Ongoing need for either physical or cognitive stimulation.

need for competence Basic need to believe that one can deal effectively with one's overall environment.

need for relatedness Basic need to feel socially connected to others and to secure others' love and respect.

need for self-determination Basic need to believe that one has some autonomy and control regarding the course of one's life.

negative reinforcement Consequence that brings about the increase of a behavior through the removal (rather than the presentation) of a stimulus.

negative transfer Phenomenon in which something learned at one time interferes with learning or performance at a later time.

neglected student Student about whom most peers have no strong feelings, either positive or negative.

neo-Piagetian theory Theoretical perspective that combines elements of Piaget's theory with more contemporary research findings and theoretical concepts and that suggests that development in specific content domains is often stagelike in nature.

neuron Cell in the brain or another part of the nervous system that transmits information to other cells.

neurotransmitter Chemical substance through which one neuron sends a message to another.

neutral stimulus Stimulus that does not elicit any particular response.

No Child Left Behind Act (NCLB) U.S. legislation passed in 2001 that mandates regular assessments of basic skills to determine whether students are making adequate yearly progress in relation to state-determined standards in reading, math, and science.

normal distribution (normal curve) Theoretical pattern of educational and psychological characteristics in which most individuals score in the middle range and only a few score at either extreme.

norm-referenced assessment Assessment instrument that indicates how students perform relative to a peer group.

norm-referenced score Assessment score that indicates how a student's performance compares with the performance of others.

norms In assessment, data regarding the typical performance of various groups of students on a standardized test or other norm-referenced measure of a particular characteristic or ability.

operant conditioning See *instrumental conditioning.*

organization Cognitive process in which learners make connections among various pieces of information they need to learn (e.g., by forming categories, identifying hierarchies, determining cause–and–effect relationships).

overgeneralization Overly broad view of the objects or events that a concept includes.

overt strategy Learning strategy that is readily apparent in a learner's behavior (e.g., taking notes).

paper–pencil assessment Assessment in which students provide written responses to written items.

pedagogical content knowledge Knowledge about effective methods of teaching a specific topic or content area.

peer mediation Approach to conflict resolution in which a student (serving as *mediator*) asks peers in conflict to express their differing viewpoints and then work together to devise a reasonable resolution.

peer pressure Phenomenon whereby age-mates strongly encourage some behaviors and discourage others.

peer tutoring Approach to instruction in which one student provides instruction to help another student master a classroom topic.

people-first language Language usage in which a student's disability is identified *after* the student is named.

percentile rank (percentile) Test score indicating the percentage of peers in the norm group getting a raw score less than or equal to a particular student's raw score.

performance-approach goal Desire to look good and receive favorable judgments from others.

performance assessment Assessment in which students demonstrate their knowledge and skills in a nonwritten fashion.

performance-avoidance goal Desire not to look bad or receive unfavorable judgments from others.

performance goal Desire to demonstrate high ability and make a good impression.

personal development Development, with age, of distinctive behavioral styles and increasingly complex self-understandings.

personal fable Belief that one is completely unlike anyone else and so cannot be understood by others.

personal interest Long-term, relatively stable interest in a particular topic or activity.

personality Characteristic ways in which an individual behaves and thinks in a wide range of circumstances.

personal space Personally or culturally preferred distance between two people during social interaction.

perspective taking Ability to look at a situation from someone else's viewpoint.

phonological awareness Ability to hear the distinct sounds that comprise spoken words.

physical aggression Action that can potentially cause bodily injury.

physical and health impairments General physical or medical conditions that interfere so significantly with school performance that special accommodations are required.

popular student Student whom many peers like and perceive to be kind and trustworthy.

portfolio Collection of a student's work compiled systematically over a lengthy time period.

positive behavioral support Variation of traditional applied behavior analysis that involves identifying the purposes of undesirable behaviors and encouraging alternative behaviors that more appropriately accomplish those purposes.

positive reinforcement Consequence that brings about the increase of a behavior through the presentation (rather than the removal) of a stimulus.

positive transfer Phenomenon in which something learned at one time facilitates learning or performance at a later time.

positive-practice overcorrection Consequence of a poorly performed response in which a learner must repeat the response correctly and appropriately, perhaps in an exaggerated manner.

postconventional morality Thinking in accordance with self-developed, abstract principles regarding right and wrong.

practicality Extent to which an assessment instrument or procedure is inexpensive and easy to use and takes only a small amount of time to administer and score.

pragmatics Use of socially effective and culturally appropriate behaviors in verbal interactions with others.

predictive validity Extent to which the results of an assessment predict future performance in a particular domain; sometimes called *criterion validity.*

preconventional morality Lack of internalized standards about right and wrong; decision making based primarily on what seems best for oneself.

Premack principle Phenomenon in which learners do less-preferred activities in order to engage in more-preferred activities.

preoperational egocentrism Inability of children in Piaget's preoperational stage to view situations from another person's perspective.

preoperational stage Piaget's second stage of cognitive development, in which children can think about objects and events beyond their immediate view but do not yet reason in logical, adultlike ways.

presentation punishment Punishment involving presentation of a new stimulus, presumably one a learner finds unpleasant.

primary reinforcer Consequence that satisfies a biologically built-in need.

prior knowledge activation Process of reminding learners of things they already know relative to a new topic.

proactive aggression Deliberate aggression against another as a means of obtaining a desired goal.

problem-based learning Classroom activity in which students acquire new knowledge and skills while working on a complex problem similar to one that might exist in the outside world.

problem solving Using existing knowledge and skills to address an unanswered question or troubling situation.

procedural knowledge Knowledge concerning how to do something (e.g., a skill).

project-based learning Classroom activity in which students acquire new knowledge and skills while working on a complex, multifaceted project that yields a concrete end product.

prosocial behavior Behavior directed toward promoting the well-being of people other than oneself.

proximal goal Concrete goal that can be accomplished within a short time period; may be a stepping stone toward a long-term goal.

psychological punishment Consequence that seriously threatens self-esteem and general psychological well-being.

punishment Consequence (stimulus) that decreases the frequency of the response it follows.

qualitative research Research yielding information that cannot be easily reduced to numbers; typically involves an in-depth examination of a complex phenomenon.

quantitative research Research yielding information that is inherently numerical in nature or can easily be reduced to numbers.

rating scale Assessment tool with which a teacher evaluates student performance by rating aspects of the performance on one or more continua.

raw score Assessment score based solely on the number or point value of correctly answered items.

reactive aggression Aggressive response to frustration or provocation.

recall task Memory task in which one must retrieve information from long-term memory with only minimal retrieval cues.

reciprocal causation Interdependence of environmental, behavioral, and personal variables in influencing learning and development.

reciprocal teaching Approach to teaching reading and listening comprehension in which students take turns asking teacherlike questions of classmates.

recognition task Memory task in which one must identify correct information among incorrect statements or irrelevant information.

reconstruction error Construction of a logical but incorrect memory by combining information retrieved from one's long-term memory with one's general knowledge and beliefs about the world.

recursive thinking Thinking about what other people may be thinking about oneself, possibly through multiple iterations.

reflective teaching Regular, ongoing examination and critique of one's assumptions and instructional strategies, and revision of them as necessary to enhance students' learning and development.

rehearsal Cognitive process in which information is repeated over and over within a short timeframe (typically a few minutes or less) as a possible way of learning and remembering it.

reinforcer Consequence (stimulus) of a response that increases the frequency of the response it follows; the act of following a response with a reinforcer is known as *reinforcement.*

rejected student Student whom many peers identify as being an undesirable social partner.

relatedness See *need for relatedness.*

relational aggression Action that can adversely affect interpersonal relationships.

reliability Extent to which an assessment yields consistent information about the knowledge, skills, or characteristics being assessed.

removal punishment Punishment involving removal of an existing stimulus, presumably one a learner doesn't want to lose.
resilient self-efficacy Belief that one can perform a task successfully even after experiencing setbacks.
resilient student Student who succeeds in school and in life despite exceptional hardships at home.
response (R) Specific behavior that an individual exhibits.
response cost Loss either of a previously earned reinforcer or of an opportunity to obtain reinforcement.
response to intervention (RTI) Approach to diagnosing a learning disability in which students are identified for in-depth assessment after failing to master certain basic skills despite both whole-class and remedial small-group instruction that research has shown to be effective for most students.
retrieval Process of finding information previously stored in memory.
retrieval cue Stimulus that provides guidance about where to "look" for a piece of information in long-term memory.
rote learning Learning information in a relatively uninterpreted form, without making sense of it or attaching much meaning to it.
rubric List of components that a student's performance on an assessment should ideally include; used to guide scoring.
scaffolding Support mechanism that helps a learner successfully perform a challenging task (in Vygotsky's theory, a task within the learner's zone of proximal development).
schema Tightly organized set of facts about a specific topic.
scheme In Piaget's theory, organized group of similar actions or thoughts that are used repeatedly in response to the environment.
scholastic aptitude test Test designed to assess a general capacity to learn and used to predict future academic achievement.
school readiness test Test designed to assess cognitive skills important for success in a typical kindergarten or first-grade curriculum.
scorer reliability Extent to which different people agree in their judgments of students' performance on an assessment; sometimes called *interrater reliability.*
script Schema that involves a predictable sequence of events related to a common activity.
scripted cooperation Technique in which cooperative learning groups follow a set of steps, or script, that guides members' verbal interactions.
secondary reinforcer Consequence that becomes reinforcing over time through its association with another reinforcer.
self-concept See *sense of self.*
self-conscious emotion Affective state based on self-evaluations regarding the extent to which one's actions meet society's standards for appropriate and desirable behavior; examples are pride, guilt, and shame.
self-determination See *need for self-determination.*
self-efficacy Belief that one is capable of executing certain behaviors or achieving certain goals.
self-esteem See *sense of self.*
self-evaluation Process of judging one's own performance or behavior.
self-explanation Process of occasionally stopping to verbalize to oneself (and hence to better understand) material being read or studied.
self-fulfilling prophecy Situation in which expectations for an outcome either directly or indirectly lead to the expected result.
self-handicapping Behavior that undermines one's own success as a way of protecting self-worth during potentially difficult tasks.
self-imposed contingency Self-reinforcement or self-punishment that follows a behavior.
self-instructions Instructions that one gives oneself while performing a complex behavior.
self-monitoring Process of observing and recording one's own behavior.
self-questioning Process of asking oneself questions as a way of checking one's understanding of a topic.
self-regulated behavior Self-chosen and self-directed behavior that leads to the fulfillment of personally constructed standards and goals.
self-regulated learning Regulation of one's own cognitive processes and studying behaviors in order to learn successfully.
self-regulated problem solving Use of self-directed strategies to address complex problems.
self-regulation Process of setting goals for oneself and engaging in behaviors and cognitive processes that lead to goal attainment.
self-socialization Self-motivated tendency to conform to what one believes are other people's expectations for behavior.
self-talk Process of talking to oneself as a way of guiding oneself through a task.
self-worth General belief about the extent to which one is a good, capable individual.
sense of community Shared belief that teacher and students have common goals, are mutually respectful and supportive, and all make important contributions to classroom learning.
sense of school community Shared belief that all faculty and students within a school are working together to help everyone learn and succeed.
sense of self Perceptions, beliefs, judgments, and feelings about oneself as a person; includes *self-concept* and *self-esteem.*
sensitive period Age range during which a certain aspect of a child's development is especially susceptible to environmental conditions (you may sometimes see the term *critical period*).
sensorimotor stage Piaget's first stage of cognitive development, in which schemes are based largely on behaviors and perceptions.
sensory register Component of memory that holds incoming information in an unanalyzed form for a very brief period of time (two or three seconds at most, depending on the modality).
service learning Activity that promotes learning and development through contributing to the betterment of others and the outside community.
setting event Complex environmental condition in which a particular behavior is most likely to occur.
severe and multiple disabilities Combination of two or more disabilities that, taken together, require significant classroom adaptations and highly specialized educational services.
shame Feeling of embarrassment or humiliation after failing to meet certain standards for moral behavior.
shaping Process of reinforcing successively closer and closer approximations to a desired terminal behavior.
situated learning and cognition Knowledge, behaviors, and thinking skills acquired and used primarily within certain contexts, with limited or no retrieval and use in other contexts.
situated motivation Phenomenon in which aspects of the immediate environment enhance motivation to learn particular things or behave in particular ways.
situational interest Interest evoked temporarily by something in the environment.
social cognition Process of thinking about how other people are likely to think, act, and react.
social cognitive theory Theoretical perspective that focuses on how people learn by observing others and how they eventually assume control over their own behavior.
social constructivism Theoretical perspective that focuses on people's collective efforts to impose meaning on the world.
social development Development, with age, of increasingly sophisticated understandings of other people and of society as a whole, as well as increasingly effective interpersonal skills and more internalized standards for behavior.

social information processing Mental processes involved in making sense of and responding to social events.
socialization Process of molding a child's behavior and beliefs to be appropriate for his or her cultural group.
sociocognitive conflict Situation in which one encounters and has to wrestle with ideas and viewpoints inconsistent with one's own.
sociocultural theory Theoretical perspective emphasizing the importance of society and culture in promoting cognitive development.
socioeconomic status (SES) One's general social and economic standing in society; encompasses family income, occupation, and educational level.
specific aptitude test Test designed to predict future ability to succeed in a particular content domain.
specific language impairment Disability characterized by abnormalities in the production or comprehension of spoken language, to the point that special educational services are required.
specific transfer Instance of transfer in which the original learning task and the transfer task overlap in content.
speech and communication disorders Impairments in spoken language or language comprehension that significantly interfere with classroom performance.
standard deviation (SD) Statistic indicating the amount of variability characterizing a set of scores.
Standard English Form of English generally considered acceptable at school, as reflected in textbooks and grammar instruction.
standard error of measurement (SEM) Statistic estimating the amount of error in a test score or other assessment result.
standardization Extent to which an assessment involves similar content and format and is administered and scored similarly for everyone.
standardized test Test developed by test construction experts and published for use in many different schools and classrooms.
standards General statements regarding the knowledge and skills that students should gain and the characteristics that their accomplishments should reflect.
standard score Test score indicating how far a student's performance is from the mean in terms of standard deviation units.
stanine Standard score with a mean of 5 and a standard deviation of 2; always reported as a whole number.
state anxiety Temporary feeling of anxiety elicited by a threatening situation.
stereotype Rigid, simplistic, and erroneous view of a particular group of people.
stereotype threat Awareness of a negative stereotype about one's own group and accompanying uneasiness that low performance will confirm the stereotype; leads (often unintentionally) to a reduction in performance.
stimulus (S) Specific object or event that influences an individual's learning or behavior.
storage Process of putting new information into memory.
student at risk Student with a high probability of failing to acquire minimal academic skills necessary for success in the adult world.
students with special needs Students different enough from their peers that they require specially adapted instructional materials and practices to maximize their learning and achievement.
subculture Group that resists the ways of the dominant culture and adopts its own norms for behavior.
subtractive bilingualism Phenomenon in which immersion in a new-language environment leads to deficits in a child's native language.
summative evaluation Evaluation conducted after instruction to assess students' final achievement.
superimposed meaningful structure Familiar shape, word, sentence, poem, or story imposed on information to facilitate recall.
symbolic model Real or fictional character portrayed in the media that influences an observer's behavior.
sympathy Feeling of sorrow for another person's distress, accompanied by concern for the person's well-being.
synapse Junction between two neurons that allows transmission of messages from one to the other.
synaptic pruning Universal process in brain development in which many previously formed synapses wither away.
synaptogenesis Universal process in early brain development in which many new synapses form spontaneously.
syntax Set of rules that one uses, often unconsciously, to put words together into sentences.
table of specifications Two-way grid indicating the topics to be covered in an assessment and the things students should be able to do with those topics.
task analysis Process of identifying the specific behaviors, knowledge, or cognitive processes necessary to master a particular subject area or skill.
teacher-developed assessment instrument Assessment tool developed by an individual teacher for use in his or her own classroom.
teacher-directed instruction Approach to instruction in which the teacher is largely in control of the content and course of the lesson.
temperament Genetic predisposition to respond in particular ways to one's physical and social environments.
terminal behavior Form and frequency of a desired response that a teacher hopes to foster through reinforcement.
test anxiety Excessive anxiety about a particular test or about assessment in general.
test-retest reliability Extent to which a particular assessment instrument yields similar results over a short time interval.
testwiseness Test-taking know-how that enhances test performance.
theory Integrated set of concepts and principles developed to explain a particular phenomenon.
theory of mind General understanding of one's own and other people's mental and psychological states (thoughts, feelings, etc.).
threat Situation in which a learner believes there is little or no chance of success.
time on task Amount of time that students are actively engaged in a learning activity.
time-out Consequence for misbehavior in which a student is placed in a dull, boring situation with no opportunity for reinforcement or social interaction.
token economy Technique in which desired behaviors are reinforced by tokens that learners can use to "purchase" a variety of other reinforcers.
traditional assessment Assessment that focuses on measuring basic knowledge and skills in relative isolation from tasks typical of the outside world.
trait anxiety Pattern of responding with anxiety even in nonthreatening situations.
transfer Phenomenon in which something a person has learned at one time affects how the person learns or performs in a later situation.
treatment group Group of people in a research study who are given a particular experimental intervention (e.g., a particular method of instruction).
true score Hypothetical score a student would obtain if an assessment measured a characteristic or ability with complete accuracy.
unconditioned response (UCR) Response that is elicited by a particular (unconditioned) stimulus without prior learning.

unconditioned stimulus (UCS) Stimulus that elicits a particular response without prior learning.
undergeneralization Overly narrow view of the objects or events that a concept includes.
universals Similar patterns in how children change and progress over time regardless of their specific environment.
validity Extent to which an assessment actually measures what it is intended to measure and allows appropriate inferences about the characteristic or ability in question.
value Belief regarding the extent to which an activity has direct or indirect benefits.
verbal mediator Word or phrase that forms a logical connection, or bridge, between two pieces of information.
vicarious punishment Phenomenon in which a response decreases in frequency when another person is observed being punished for that response.
vicarious reinforcement Phenomenon in which a response increases in frequency when another person is observed being reinforced for that response.
visual imagery Process of forming mental pictures of objects or ideas.
visual impairments Malfunctions of the eyes or optic nerves that prevent normal vision even with corrective lenses.
visual-spatial ability Ability to imagine and mentally manipulate two- and three-dimensional figures.
wait time Length of time a teacher pauses, either after asking a question or hearing a student's comment, before saying something else.
well-defined problem Problem in which the goal is clearly stated, all the information needed to solve the problem is present, and only one correct answer exists.
withitness Classroom management strategy in which a teacher gives the impression of knowing what all students are doing at all times.
work-avoidance goal Desire either to avoid classroom tasks or to complete them with minimal effort.
working memory Component of memory that holds and actively thinks about and processes a limited amount of information for a short time period.
worldview General, culturally based set of assumptions about reality that influence understandings of a wide variety of phenomena.
zone of proximal development (ZPD) Range of tasks that a learner can perform with the help and guidance of others but cannot yet perform independently.
***z*-score** Standard score with a mean of 0 and a standard deviation of 1.

References

Ablard, K. E., & Lipschultz, R. E. (1998). Self-regulated learning in high-achieving students: Relations to advanced reasoning, achievement goals, and gender. *Journal of Educational Psychology, 90*, 94–101.

Abrami, P. C., Bernard, R. M., Borokhovski, E., Wade, A., Surkes, M. A., Tamim, R., et al. (2008). Instructional interventions affecting critical thinking skills and dispositions: A stage 1 meta-analysis. *Review of Educational Research, 78*, 1102–1134.

Achenbach, T. M., & Edelbrock, C. S. (1981). Behavioral problems and competencies reported by parents of normal and disturbed children aged four through sixteen. *Monographs of the Society for Research in Child Development, 46*(1, Serial No. 188).

Ackerman, P. L., & Lohman, D. F. (2006). Individual differences in cognitive functions. In P. A. Alexander & P. H. Winne (Eds.), *Handbook of educational psychology* (2nd ed., pp. 139–161). Mahwah, NJ: Erlbaum.

Adalbjarnardottir, S., & Selman, R. L. (1997). "I feel I have received a new vision": An analysis of teachers' professional development as they work with students on interpersonal issues. *Teaching and Teacher Education, 13*, 409–428.

Aikens, N. L., & Barbarin, O. (2008). Socioeconomic differences in reading trajectories: The contribution of family, neighborhood, and school contexts. *Journal of Educational Psychology, 100*, 235–251.

Ainley, M. (2006). Connecting with learning: Motivation, affect, and cognition in interest processes. *Educational Psychology Review, 18*, 391–405.

Ainsworth, M. D. S., Blehar, M. C., Waters, E., & Wall, S. (1978). *Patterns of attachment*. Hillsdale, NJ: Erlbaum.

Airasian, P. W. (1994). *Classroom assessment* (2nd ed.). New York: McGraw-Hill.

Alapack, R. (1991). The adolescent first kiss. *Humanistic Psychologist, 19*, 48–67.

Alberto, P. A., & Troutman, A. C. (2003). *Applied behavior analysis for teachers* (6th ed.). Upper Saddle River, NJ: Merrill/Prentice Hall.

Alderman, M. K. (1990). Motivation for at-risk students. *Educational Leadership, 48*(1), 27–30.

Alessandri, S. M., & Lewis, M. (1993). Parental evaluation and its relation to shame and pride in young children. *Sex Roles, 29*, 335–343.

Alexander, E. S. (2008). *How to hope: A model of the thoughts, feelings, and behaviors involved in transcending challenge and uncertainty*. Saarbrücken, Germany: VDM Verlag.

Alexander, J. M., Johnson, K. E., Leibham, M. E., & Kelley, K. (2008). The development of conceptual interests in young children. *Cognitive Development, 23*, 324–334.

Alexander, J. M., Johnson, K. E., Scott, B., & Meyer, R. D. (2008). Stegosaurus and spoonbills: Mechanisms for transfer across biological domains. In M. F. Shaughnessy, M. V. E. Vennemann, & C. K. Kennedy (Eds.), *Metacognition: A recent review of research, theory, and perspectives* (pp. 63–83). Happauge, NY: Nova.

Alexander, K. L., Entwisle, D. R., & Dauber, S. L. (1995). *On the success of failure*. New York: Cambridge University Press.

Alexander, P. A. (1997). Mapping the multidimensional nature of domain learning: The interplay of cognitive, motivational, and strategic forces. In P. R. Pintrich & M. L. Maehr (Eds.), *Advances in motivation and achievement* (Vol. 10). Greenwich, CT: JAI Press.

Alexander, P. A. (2003). The development of expertise: The journey from acclimation to proficiency. *Educational Researcher, 32*(8), 10–14.

Alexander, P. A., Graham, S., & Harris, K. R. (1998). A perspective on strategy research: Progress and prospects. *Educational Psychology Review, 10*, 129–154.

Alexander, P. A., & Judy, J. E. (1988). The interaction of domain-specific and strategic knowledge in academic performance. *Review of Educational Research, 58*, 375–404.

Alexander, P. A., Kulikowich, J. M., & Schulze, S. K. (1994). How subject-matter knowledge affects recall and interest. *American Educational Research Journal, 31*, 313–337.

Alfassi, M. (2004). Reading to learn: Effects of combined strategy instruction on high school students. *Journal of Educational Research, 97*, 171–184.

Algozzine, B., Browder, D., Karvonen, M., Test, D. W., & Wood, W. M. (2001). Effects of interventions to promote self-determination for individuals with disabilities. *Review of Educational Research, 71*, 219–277.

Alim, H. S. (2007). "The Whig party don't exist in my hood": Knowledge, reality, and education in the hip hop nation. In H. S. Alim & J. Baugh (Eds.), *Talkin Black talk: Language, education, and social change* (pp. 15–29). New York: Teachers College Press.

Alim, H. S., & Baugh, J. (Eds.). (2007). *Talkin black talk: Language, education, and social change*. New York: Teachers College Press.

Allday, R. A., & Pakurar, K. (2007). Effects of teacher greetings on student on-task behavior. *Journal of Applied Behavior Analysis, 40*, 317–320.

Alleman, J., & Brophy, J. (1992). Analysis of the activities in a social studies curriculum. In J. Brophy (Ed.), *Advances in research on teaching: Vol. 3. Planning and managing learning tasks and activities*. Greenwich, CT: JAI Press.

Alleman, J., & Brophy, J. (1997). Elementary social studies: Instruments, activities, and standards. In G. D. Phye (Ed.), *Handbook of classroom assessment: Learning, achievement, and adjustment*. San Diego, CA: Academic Press.

Alleman, J., & Brophy, J. (1998). Strategic learning opportunities during out-of-school hours. *Social Studies and the Young Learner, 10*(4), 10–13.

Allen, J. P., Porter, M., McFarland, C., McElhaney, K. B., & Marsh, P. (2007). The relation of attachment security to adolescents' paternal and peer relationships, depression, and externalizing behavior. *Child Development, 78*, 1222–1239.

Allen, L., & Aber, J. L. (2006). The development of ethnic identity during adolescence. *Developmental Psychology, 42*, 1–10.

Allington, R. L., & Weber, R. (1993). Questioning questions in teaching and learning from texts. In B. K. Britton, A. Woodward, & M. Binkley (Eds.), *Learning from textbooks: Theory and practice*. Mahwah, NJ: Erlbaum.

Allison, K. W. (1998). Stress and oppressed social category membership. In J. Swim & C. Stangor (Eds.), *Prejudice: The target's perspective* (pp. 149–170). San Diego, CA: Academic Press.

Altermatt, E. R., Jovanovic, J., & Perry, M. (1998). Bias or responsivity? Sex and achievement-level effects on teachers' classroom questioning practices. *Journal of Educational Psychology, 90*, 516–527.

Altermatt, E. R., & Pomerantz, E. M. (2003). The development of competence-related and motivational beliefs: An investigation of similarity and influence among friends. *Journal of Educational Psychology, 95*, 111–123.

Altmann, E. M., & Gray, W. D. (2002). Forgetting to remember: The functional relationship of decay and interference. *Psychological Science, 13*, 27–33.

Altschul, I., Oyserman, D., & Bybee, D. (2006). Racial-ethnic identity in mid-adolescence: Content and change as predictors of academic achievement. *Child Development, 77*, 1155–1169.

Amabile, T. M., & Hennessey, B. A. (1992). The motivation for creativity in children. In A. K. Boggiano & T. S. Pittman (Eds.), *Achievement and motivation: A social-developmental perspective*. Cambridge, England: Cambridge University Press.

Ambrose, D., Allen, J., & Huntley, S. B. (1994). Mentorship of the highly creative. *Roeper Review, 17*, 131–133.

American Educational Research Association, American Psychological Association, & National Council on Measurement in Education. (1999). *Standards for educational and psychological testing* (2nd ed.). Washington, DC: American Educational Research Association.

American Psychiatric Association. (2000). *Diagnostic and statistical manual of mental disorders* (4th ed.). Washington, DC: Author.

Ames, C. (1984). Competitive, cooperative, and individualistic goal structures: A cognitive-motivational analysis. In R. Ames & C. Ames (Eds.), *Research on motivation in education: Vol. 1. Student motivation*. San Diego, CA: Academic Press.

Ames, C. (1992). Classrooms: Goals, structures, and student motivation. *Journal of Educational Psychology, 84*, 261–271.

Amrein, A. L., & Berliner, D. C. (2002a, December). *An analysis of some unintended and negative consequences of high-stakes testing* (Report EPSL-0211-125-EPRU). Tempe: Educational Policy Study Laboratory, Arizona State University. Retrieved April 28, 2003, from www.asu.edu/educ/epsl/EPRU/epru_2002_Research_Writing.htm

Amrein, A. L., & Berliner, D. C. (2002b, March 28). High-stakes testing, uncertainty, and student learning. *Education Policy Analysis Archives, 10*(18). Retrieved April 9, 2002, from http://epaa.asu.edu/epaa/v10n18

Amsterlaw, J. (2006). Children's beliefs about everyday reasoning. *Child Development, 77*, 443–464.

Anderman, E. M. (2002). School effects on psychological outcomes during adolescence. *Journal of Educational Psychology, 94*, 795–809.

Anderman, E. M., Griesinger, T., & Westerfield, G. (1998). Motivation and cheating during early adolescence. *Journal of Educational Psychology, 90*, 84–93.

Anderman, E. M., & Maehr, M. L. (1994). Motivation and schooling in the middle grades. *Review of Educational Research, 64*, 287–309.

Anderman, E. M., Noar, S., Zimmerman, R. S., & Donohew, L. (2004). The need for sensation as a prerequisite for motivation to engage in academic tasks. In M. L. Maehr & P. Pintrich (Eds.), *Advances in motivation and achievement: Motivating students, improving schools: The legacy of Carol Midgley* (Vol. 13). Greenwich, CT: JAI Press.

Anderman, L. H., Patrick, H., Hruda, L. Z., & Linnenbrink, E. A. (2002). Observing classroom goal structures to clarify and expand goal theory. In C. Midgley (Ed.), *Goals, goal structures, and patterns of adaptive learning* (pp. 243–278). Mahwah, NJ: Erlbaum.

Anderson, C. A., Berkowitz, L., Donnerstein, E., Huesmann, L. R., Johnson, J. D., Linz, D., Malamuth, N. M., & Wartella, E. (2003). The influence of media violence on youth. *Psychological Science in the Public Interest, 4,* 81–110.

Anderson, J. R. (1983). *The architecture of cognition.* Cambridge, MA: Harvard University Press.

Anderson, J. R. (2005). *Cognitive psychology and its implications* (6th ed.). New York: Worth.

Anderson, J. R., Greeno, J. G., Reder, L. M., & Simon, H. A. (2000). Perspectives on learning, thinking, and activity. *Educational Researcher, 29*(4), 11–13.

Anderson, J. R., Reder, L. M., & Simon, H. A. (1996). Situated learning and education. *Educational Researcher, 25*(4), 5–11.

Anderson, L. H. (1999). *Speak.* New York: Puffin Books.

Anderson, L. M. (1993). Auxiliary materials that accompany textbooks: Can they promote "higher-order" learning? In B. K. Britton, A. Woodward, & M. Binkley (Eds.), *Learning from textbooks: Theory and practice.* Mahwah, NJ: Erlbaum.

Anderson, L. W., Krathwohl, D. R., Airasian, P. W., Cruikshank, K. A., Mayer, R. E., Pintrich, P. R., Raths, J., & Wittrock, M. C. (Eds.). (2001). *A taxonomy for learning, teaching, and assessing: A revision of Bloom's taxonomy of educational objectives.* New York: Longman.

Anderson, L. W., & Pellicer, L. O. (1998). Toward an understanding of unusually successful programs for economically disadvantaged students. *Journal of Education for Students Placed at Risk, 3,* 237–263.

Anderson, R. C., Nguyen-Jahiel, K., McNurlen, B., Archodidou, A., Kim, S.-Y., Reznitskaya, A., Tillmanns, M., & Gilbert, L. (2001). The snowball phenomenon: Spread of ways of talking and ways of thinking across groups of children. *Cognition and Instruction, 19,* 1–46.

Anderson, R. C., Reynolds, R. E., Schallert, D. L., & Goetz, E. T. (1977). Frameworks for comprehending discourse. *American Educational Research Journal, 14,* 367–381.

Andre, T., & Windschitl, M. (2003). Interest, epistemological belief, and intentional conceptual change. In G. M. Sinatra & P. R. Pintrich (Eds.), *Intentional conceptual change* (pp. 173–197). Mahwah, NJ: Erlbaum.

Andriessen, J. (2006). Arguing to learn. In R. K. Sawyer (Ed.), *The Cambridge handbook of the learning sciences* (pp. 443–459). Cambridge, England: Cambridge University Press.

Angold, A., Worthman, C., & Costello, E. J. (2003). Puberty and depression. In C. Hayward (Ed.), *Gender differences at puberty* (pp. 137–164). Cambridge, England: Cambridge University Press.

Ansley, T. (1997). The role of standardized achievement tests in grades K–12. In G. D. Phye (Ed.), *Handbook of classroom assessment: Learning, achievement, and adjustment.* San Diego, CA: Academic Press.

Anzai, Y. (1991). Learning and use of representations for physics expertise. In K. A. Ericsson & J. Smith (Eds.), *Toward a general theory of expertise: Prospects and limits.* Cambridge, England: Cambridge University Press.

Appel, J. B., & Peterson, N. J. (1965). Punishment: Effects of shock intensity on response suppression. *Psychological Reports, 16,* 721–730.

Applebee, A. N., Langer, J. A., Nystrand, M., & Gamoran, A. (2003). Discussion-based approaches to developing understanding: Classroom instruction and student performance in middle and high school English. *American Educational Research Journal, 40,* 685–730.

Arbib, M. (Ed.). (2005). *Action to language via the mirror neuron system.* New York: Cambridge University Press.

Archer, S. L. (1982). The lower age boundaries of identity development. *Child Development, 53,* 1551–1556.

Ardoin, S. P., Martens, B. K., & Wolfe, L. A. (1999). Using high-probability instructional sequences with fading to increase student compliance during transitions. *Journal of Applied Behavior Analysis, 32,* 339–351.

Arlin, M. (1984). Time, equality, and mastery learning. *Review of Educational Research, 54,* 65–86.

Arnett, J. J. (1999). Adolescent storm and stress, reconsidered. *American Psychologist, 54,* 317–326.

Arnold, M. L. (2000). Stage, sequence, and sequels: Changing conceptions of morality, post-Kohlberg. *Educational Psychology Review, 12,* 365–383.

Aron, A. R. (2008). Progress in executive-function research: From tasks to functions to regions to networks. *Current Directions in Psychological Science, 17,* 124–129.

Aronson, E., & Patnoe, S. (1997). *The jigsaw classroom: Building cooperation in the classroom* (2nd ed.). New York: Longman.

Aronson, J., Lustina, M. J., Good, C., Keough, K., Steele, C. M., & Brown, J. (1999). When white men can't do math: Necessary and sufficient factors in stereotype threat. *Journal of Experimental Social Psychology, 35,* 29–46.

Aronson, J., & Steele, C. M. (2005). Stereotypes and the fragility of academic competence, motivation, and self-concept. In A. J. Elliot & C. S. Dweck (Eds.), *Handbook of competence and motivation* (pp. 436–456). New York: Guilford Press.

Arter, J. A., & Spandel, V. (1992). Using portfolios of student work in instruction and assessment. *Educational Measurement: Issues and Practice, 11*(1), 36–44.

Artman, L., & Cahan, S. (1993). Schooling and the development of transitive inference. *Developmental Psychology, 29,* 753–759.

Ash, D. (2002). Negotiations of thematic conversations about biology. In G. Leinhardt, K. Crowley, & K. Knutson (Eds.), *Learning conversations in museums* (pp. 357–400). Mahwah, NJ: Erlbaum.

Ashcraft, M. H. (2002). Math anxiety: Personal, educational, and cognitive consequences. *Current Directions in Psychological Science, 11,* 181–184.

Asher, S. R., & Renshaw, P. D. (1981). Children without friends: Social knowledge and social skill training. In S. R. Asher & J. M. Gottman (Eds.), *The development of children's friendships.* New York: Cambridge University Press.

Ashiabi, G. S., & O'Neal, K. K. (2008). A framework for understanding the association between food insecurity and children's developmental outcomes. *Child Development Perspectives, 2,* 71–77.

Ashton, P. (1985). Motivation and the teacher's sense of efficacy. In C. Ames & R. Ames (Eds.), *Research on motivation in education: Vol. 2. The classroom milieu.* San Diego, CA: Academic Press.

Assor, A., & Connell, J. P. (1992). The validity of students' self-reports as measures of performance affecting self-appraisals. In D. H. Schunk & J. L. Meece (Eds.), *Student perceptions in the classroom.* Mahwah, NJ: Erlbaum.

Astington, J. W., & Pelletier, J. (1996). The language of mind: Its role in teaching and learning. In D. R. Olson & N. Torrance (Eds.), *The handbook of education and human development: New models of learning, teaching, and schooling.* Cambridge, MA: Blackwell.

Astor, R. A., Meyer, H. A., & Behre, W. J. (1999). Unowned places and times: Maps and interviews about violence in high schools. *American Educational Research Journal, 36,* 3–42.

Atance, C. M. (2008). Future thinking in young children. *Current Directions in Psychological Science, 17,* 295–298.

Atkinson, R. C., & Shiffrin, R. M. (1968). Human memory: A proposed system and its control processes. In K. W. Spence & J. T. Spence (Eds.), *The psychology of learning and motivation: Advances in research and theory* (Vol. 2). San Diego, CA: Academic Press.

Atkinson, R. K., Derry, S. J., Renkl, A., & Wortham, D. (2000). Learning from examples: Instructional principles from the worked examples research. *Review of Educational Research, 70,* 181–214.

Atkinson, R. K., Levin, J. R., Kiewra, K. A., Meyers, T., Kim, S., Atkinson, L. A., Renandya, W. A., & Hwang, Y. (1999). Matrix and mnemonic text-processing adjuncts: Comparing and combining their components. *Journal of Educational Psychology, 91,* 342–357.

Atran, S., Medin, D. L., & Ross, N. O. (2005). The cultural mind: Environmental decision making and cultural modeling within and across populations. *Psychological Review, 112,* 744–776.

Attie, I., Brooks-Gunn, J., & Petersen, A. (1990). A developmental perspective on eating disorders and eating problems. In M. Lewis & S. M. Miller (Eds.), *Handbook of developmental psychopathology* (pp. 409–420). New York: Plenum Press.

Au, K. H. (1980). Participation structures in a reading lesson with Hawaiian children: Analysis of a culturally appropriate instructional event. *Anthropology and Education Quarterly, 11,* 91–115.

Au, W. (2007). High-stakes testing and curricular control: A qualitative metasynthesis. *Educational Researcher, 36*(5), 258–267.

Aulls, M. W. (1998). Contributions of classroom discourse to what content students learn during curriculum enactment. *Journal of Educational Psychology, 90,* 56–69.

Aunola, K., & Nurmi, J.-E. (2005). The role of parenting style in children's problem behavior. *Child Development, 76,* 1144–1159.

Austin, J. L, & Soeda, J. M. (2008). Fixed-time teacher attention to decrease off-task behaviors of typically developing third graders. *Journal of Applied Behavior Analysis, 41,* 279–283.

Ausubel, D. P., Novak, J. D., & Hanesian, H. (1978). *Educational psychology: A cognitive view* (2nd ed.). New York: Holt, Rinehart & Winston.

Azevedo, R. (2005a). Computer environments as metacognitive tools for enhancing learning. *Educational Psychologist, 40,* 193–197.

Azevedo, R. (2005b). Using hypermedia as a metacognitive tool for enhancing student learning? The role of self-regulated learning. *Educational Psychologist, 40,* 199–209.

Azrin, N. H. (1960). Effects of punishment intensity during variable-interval reinforcement. *Journal of the Experimental Analysis of Behavior, 3,* 123–142.

Azrin, N. H., Vinas, V., & Ehle, C. T. (2007). Physical activity as reinforcement for classroom calmness of ADHD children: A preliminary study. *Child and Family Behavior Therapy, 29,* 1–8.

Babad, E. (1993). Teachers' differential behavior. *Educational Psychology Review, 5,* 347–376.

Babad, E. (1995). The "teacher's pet phenomenon," students' perceptions of teachers' differential behavior, and students' morale. *Journal of Educational Psychology, 87,* 361–374.

Babad, E., Avni-Babad, D., & Rosenthal, R. (2003). Teachers' brief nonverbal behaviors in defined instructional situations can predict students' evaluations. *Journal of Educational Psychology, 95,* 553–562.

Baddeley, A. D. (2001). Is working memory still working? *American Psychologist, 56,* 851–864.

Baek, S. (1994). Implications of cognitive psychology for educational testing. *Educational Psychology Review, 6,* 373–389.

Bagley, C., & Mallick, K. (1998). Field independence, cultural context and academic achievement: A commentary. *British Journal of Educational Psychology, 68,* 581–587.

Baker, J. (1999). Teacher-student interaction in urban at-risk classrooms: Differential behavior, relationship quality, and student satisfaction with school. *Elementary School Journal, 100,* 57–70.

Baker, L. (1989). Metacognition, comprehension monitoring, and the adult reader. *Educational Psychology Review, 1,* 3–38.

Baker, L., & Brown, A. L. (1984). Metacognitive skills of reading. In D. Pearson (Ed.), *Handbook of reading research.* White Plains, NY: Longman.

Balfanz, R., Legters, N., West, T. C., & Weber, L. M. (2007). Are NCLB's measures, incentives, and improvement strategies the right ones for the nation's low-performing high schools? *American Educational Research Journal, 44,* 559–593.

Ballenger, C. (1992). Because you like us: The language of control. *Harvard Educational Review, 62,* 199–208.

Bandura, A. (1965). Influence of models' reinforcement contingencies on the acquisition of imitative responses. *Journal of Personality and Social Psychology, 1,* 589–595.

Bandura, A. (1977). *Social learning theory.* Upper Saddle River, NJ: Prentice Hall.

Bandura, A. (1982). Self-efficacy mechanism in human agency. *American Psychologist, 37,* 122–147.

Bandura, A. (1986). *Social foundations of thought and action: A social cognitive theory.* Upper Saddle River, NJ: Prentice Hall.

Bandura, A. (1989). Human agency in social cognitive theory. *American Psychologist, 44,* 1175–1184.

Bandura, A. (1997). *Self-efficacy: The exercise of control.* New York: Freeman.

Bandura, A. (2000). Exercise of human agency through collective efficacy. *Current Directions in Psychological Science, 9,* 75–78.

Bandura, A. (2006). Toward a psychology of human agency. *Perspectives on Psychological Science, 1,* 164–180.

Bandura, A., Barbaranelli, C., Caprara, G. V., & Pastorelli, C. (2001). Self-efficacy beliefs as shapers of children's aspirations and career trajectories. *Child Development, 72,* 187–206.

Bandura, A., Ross, D., & Ross, S. A. (1961). Transmission of aggression through imitation of aggressive models. *Journal of Abnormal and Social Psychology, 63,* 575–582.

Bandura, A., Ross, D., & Ross, S. A. (1963). Imitation of film-mediated aggressive models. *Journal of Abnormal and Social Psychology, 66,* 3–11.

Bangert-Drowns, R. L., Hurley, M. M., & Wilkinson, B. (2004). The effects of school-based writing-to-learn interventions on academic achievement: A meta-analysis. *Review of Educational Research, 74,* 29–58.

Bangert-Drowns, R. L., Kulik, C. C., Kulik, J. A., & Morgan, M. (1991). The instructional effect of feedback in test-like events. *Review of Educational Research, 61,* 213–238.

Banks, J. A. (1991). Multicultural literacy and curriculum reform. *Educational Horizons, 69*(3), 135–140.

Banks, J. A. (1994). *An introduction to multicultural education.* Boston: Allyn & Bacon.

Banks, J. A., & Banks, C. A. M. (Eds.). (1995). *Handbook of research on multicultural education.* New York: Macmillan.

Banks, J., Cochran-Smith, M., Moll, L., Richert, A., Zeichner, K., LePage, P., Darling-Hammond, L., & Duffy, H. (with McDonald, M.). (2005). Teaching diverse learners. In L. Darling-Hammond & J. Bransford (Eds.), *Preparing teachers for a changing world: What teachers should learn and be able to do* (pp. 232–274). San Francisco: Jossey-Bass/Wiley.

Banta, T. W. (Ed.) (2003). *Portfolio assessment: Uses, cases, scoring, and impact.* San Francisco: Jossey-Bass.

Bao, X., & Lam, S. (2008). Who makes the choice? Rethinking the role of autonomy and relatedness in Chinese children's motivation. *Child Development, 79,* 269–283.

Barab, S. A., & Plucker, J. A. (2002). Smart people or smart contexts? Cognition, ability, and talent development in an age of situated approaches to knowing and learning. *Educational Psychologist, 37,* 165–182.

Barber, B. K., Stolz, H. E., & Olsen, J. A. (2005). Parental support, psychological control, and behavioral control: Assessing relevance across time, culture, and method. *Monographs of the Society for Research in Child Development, 70* (4; Serial No. 282).

Barbetta, P. M. (1990). GOALS: A group-oriented adapted levels system for children with behavior disorders. *Academic Therapy, 25,* 645–656.

Barbetta, P. M., Heward, W. L., Bradley, D. M., & Miller, A. D. (1994). Effects of immediate and delayed error correction on the acquisition and maintenance of sight words by students with developmental disabilities. *Journal of Applied Behavior Analysis, 27,* 177–178.

Barchfeld, P., Sodian, B., Thoermer, C., & Bullock, M. (2005, April). *The development of experiment generation abilities from primary school to late adolescence.* Poster presented at the biennial meeting of the Society for Research in Child Development, Atlanta, GA.

Barkley, R. A. (2006). *Attention-deficit hyperactivity disorder: A handbook for diagnosis and treatment* (3rd ed.). New York: Guilford Press.

Barnett, J. E. (2001, April). *Study strategies and preparing for exams: A survey of middle and high school students.* Paper presented at the annual meeting of the American Educational Research Association, Seattle, WA.

Barnett, J. E., Di Vesta, F. J., & Rogozinski, J. T. (1981). What is learned in note taking? *Journal of Educational Psychology, 73,* 181–192.

Barnett, M. (2005, April). *Engaging inner city students in learning through designing remote operated vehicles.* Paper presented at the annual meeting of the American Educational Research Association, Montreal.

Barnett, S. M., & Ceci, S. J. (2002). When and where do we apply what we learn? A taxonomy of far transfer. *Psychological Bulletin, 128,* 612–637.

Baron, J. B. (1987). Evaluating thinking skills in the classroom. In J. B. Baron & R. J. Sternberg (Eds.), *Teaching thinking skills: Theory and practice.* New York: Freeman.

Barrish, H. H., Saunders, M., & Wolf, M. M. (1969). Good behavior game: Effects of individual contingencies for group consequences on disruptive behavior in a classroom. *Journal of Applied Behavior Analysis, 2,* 119–124.

Barron, B. (2000). Problem solving in video-based microworlds: Collaborative and individual outcomes of high-achieving sixth-grade students. *Journal of Educational Psychology, 92,* 391–398.

Barsalou, L. W., Simmons, W. K., Barbey, A., & Wilson, C. D. (2003). Grounding conceptual knowledge in modality-specific systems. *Trends in Cognitive Sciences, 7,* 84–91.

Bartlett, F. C. (1932). *Remembering: A study in experimental and social psychology.* Cambridge, England: Cambridge University Press.

Bartlett, M., Rudolph, K. D., Flynn, M., Abaied, J., & Koerber, C. (2007, March). *Need for approval as a moderator of children's responses to victimization.* Paper presented at the biennial meeting of the Society for Research in Child Development, Boston.

Barton, A. C., Tan, E., & Rivet, A. (2008). Creating hybrid spaces for engaging school science among urban middle school girls. *American Educational Research Journal, 45,* 68–103.

Basinger, K. S., Gibbs, J. C., & Fuller, D. (1995). Context and the measurement of moral judgment. *International Journal of Behavioral Development, 18,* 537–556.

Bassett, D. S., Jackson, L., Ferrell, K. A., Luckner, J., Hagerty, P. J., Bunsen, T. D., & MacIsaac, D. (1996). Multiple perspectives on inclusive education: Reflections of a university faculty. *Teacher Education and Special Education, 19,* 355–386.

Bassok, M. (2003). Analogical transfer in problem solving. In J. E. Davidson & R. J. Sternberg (Eds.), *The psychology of problem solving* (pp. 343–369). Cambridge, England: Cambridge University Press.

Bates, J. E., & Pettit, G. S. (2007). Temperament, parenting, and socialization. In J. E. Grusec & P. D. Hastings (Eds.), *Handbook of socialization: Theory and research* (pp. 153–177). New York: Guilford Press.

Batson, C. D. (1991). *The altruism question: Toward a social-psychological answer.* Hillsdale, NJ: Erlbaum.

Batson, C. D., & Thompson, E. R. (2001). Why don't moral people act morally? Motivational considerations. *Current Directions in Psychological Science, 10,* 54–57.

Battin-Pearson, S., Newcomb, M. D., Abbott, R. D., Hill, K. G., Catalano, R. F., & Hawkins, J. D. (2000). Predictors of early high school dropout: A test of five theories. *Journal of Educational Psychology, 92,* 568–582.

Battistich, V., Solomon, D., Kim, D., Watson, M., & Schaps, E. (1995). Schools as communities, poverty levels of student populations, and students' attitudes, motives, and performance: A multilevel analysis. *American Educational Research Journal, 32,* 627–658.

Battistich, V., Solomon, D., Watson, M., & Schaps, E. (1997). Caring school communities. *Educational Psychologist, 32,* 137–151.

Bauer, P. J., DeBoer, T., & Lukowski, A. F. (2007). In the language of multiple memory systems: Defining and describing developments in long-term declarative memory. In L. M. Oakes & P. J. Bauer (Eds.), *Short- and long-term memory in infancy and early childhood: Taking the first steps toward remembering* (pp. 240–270). New York: Oxford University Press.

Baumeister, R. F., Campbell, J. D., Krueger, J. I., & Vohs, K. D. (2003). Does high self-esteem cause better performance, interpersonal success, happiness, or healthier lifestyles? *Psychological Science in the Public Interest, 4,* 1–44.

Baumeister, R. F., Smart, L., & Boden, J. M. (1996). Relation of threatened egotism to violence and aggression: The dark side of high self-esteem. *Psychological Review, 103,* 5–33.

Baumrind, D. (1989). Rearing competent children. In W. Damon (Ed.), *Child development today and tomorrow.* San Francisco: Jossey-Bass.

Baumrind, D. (1991). Parenting styles and adolescent development. In R. Lerner, A. C. Petersen, & J. Brooks-Gunn (Eds.), *The encyclopedia of adolescence.* New York: Garland Press.

Baxter, G. P., Elder, A. D., & Glaser, R. (1996). Knowledge-based cognition and performance assessment in the science classroom. *Educational Psychologist, 31,* 133–140.

Bay-Hinitz, A. K., Peterson, R. F., & Quilitch, H. R. (1994). Cooperative games: A way to modify aggressive and cooperative behaviors in young children. *Journal of Applied Behavior Analysis, 27,* 435–446.

Bebko, J. M., Burke, L., Craven, J., & Sarlo, N. (1992). The importance of motor activity in sensorimotor development: A perspective from children with physical handicaps. *Human Development, 35*(4), 226–240.

Beck, I. L., & McKeown, M. G. (1994). Outcomes of history instruction: Paste-up accounts. In M. Carretero & J. F. Voss (Eds.), *Cognitive and instructional processes in history and the social sciences* (pp. 237–256). Mahwah, NJ: Erlbaum.

Beck, I. L., & McKeown, M. G. (2001). Inviting students into the pursuit of meaning. *Educational Psychology Review, 13,* 225–241.

Beck, S. R., Robinson, E. J., Carroll, D. J., & Apperly, I. A. (2006). Children's thinking about counterfactuals and future hypotheticals as possibilities. *Child Development, 77,* 413–426.

Becker, B. E., & Luthar, S. S. (2002). Social-emotional factors affecting achievement outcomes among disadvantaged students: Closing the achievement gap. *Educational Psychologist, 37,* 197–214.

Beckett, C., Maughan, B., Rutter, M., Castle, J., Colvert, E., Groothues, C., Kreppner, J., Stevens, S., O'Connor, T. G., & Sonuga-Barke, E. J. S. (2006). Do the effects of early severe deprivation on cognition persist into early adolescence? Findings from the English and Romanian adoptees study. *Child Development, 77,* 696–711.

Bédard, J., & Chi, M. T. H. (1992). Expertise. *Current Directions in Psychological Science, 1,* 135–139.

Begg, I., Anas, A., & Farinacci, S. (1992). Dissociation of processes in belief: Source recollection, statement familiarity, and the illusion of truth. *Journal of Experimental Psychology: General, 121,* 446–458.

Behr, M., & Harel, G. (1988, April). Cognitive conflict in procedure applications. In D. Tirosh (Chair), *The role of inconsistent ideas in learning mathematics.* Symposium conducted at the annual meeting of the American Educational Research Association, New Orleans, LA.

Behrmann, M. (2000). The mind's eye mapped onto the brain's matter. *Current Directions in Psychological Science, 9,* 50–54.

Beilock, S. L. (2008). Math performance in stressful situations. *Current Directions in Psychological Science, 17,* 339–343.

Beilock, S. L., & Carr, T. H. (2005). When high-powered people fail: Working memory and "choking under pressure" in math. *Psychological Science, 16,* 101–105.

Beirne-Smith, M., Patton, J. R., & Kim, S. H. (2006). *Mental retardation: An introduction to intellectual disabilities* (7th ed.). Upper Saddle River, NJ: Merrill/Prentice Hall.

Belfiore, P. J., & Hornyak, R. S. (1998). Operant theory and application to self-monitoring in adolescents. In D. H. Schunk & B. J. Zimmerman (Eds.), *Self-regulated learning: From teaching to self-reflective practice.* New York: Guilford Press.

Belfiore, P. J., Lee, D. L., Vargas, A. U., & Skinner, C. H. (1997). Effects of high-preference single-digit mathematics problem completion on multiple-digit mathematics problem performance. *Journal of Applied Behavior Analysis, 30,* 327–330.

Bell, N., Grossen, M., & Perret-Clermont, A. (1985). Sociocognitive conflict and intellectual growth. In M. W. Berkowitz (Ed.), *Peer conflict and psychological growth.* San Francisco: Jossey-Bass.

Bell, P., & Linn, M. C. (2002). Beliefs about science: How does science instruction contribute? In B. K. Hofer & P. R. Pintrich (Eds.), *Personal epistemology: The psychology of beliefs about knowledge and knowing* (pp. 321–346). Mahwah, NJ: Erlbaum.

Bellezza, F. S. (1986). Mental cues and verbal reports in learning. In G. H. Bower (Ed.), *The psychology of learning and motivation: Advances in research and theory* (Vol. 20). San Diego, CA: Academic Press.

Belsky, J., Bakermans-Kranenburg, M. J., & van IJzendoorn, M. H. (2007). For better *and* for worse: Differential susceptibility to environmental influences. *Current Directions in Psychological Science, 16,* 300–304.

Bem, S. L. (1981). Gender schema theory: A cognitive account of sex typing. *Psychological Review, 88,* 354–364.

Bem, S. L. (1983). Gender schema theory and its implications for child development: Raising gender-aschematic children in a gender-schematic society. *Signs: Journal of Women in Culture and Society, 8,* 598–616.

Bem, S. L. (1984). Androgyny and gender schema theory: A conceptual and empirical integration. In R. A. Dienstbier & T. B. Sonderegger (Eds.), *Nebraska Symposium on Motivation* (Vol. 34). Lincoln: University of Nebraska Press.

Bembenutty, H., & Karabenick, S. A. (2004). Inherent association between academic delay of gratification, future time perspective, and self-regulated learning. *Educational Psychology Review, 16,* 35–57.

Bender, G. (2001). Resisting dominance? The study of a marginalized masculinity and its construction within high school walls. In J. N. Burstyn, G. Bender, R. Casella, H. W. Gordon, D. P. Guerra, K. V. Luschen, R. Stevens, & K. M. Williams, *Preventing violence in schools: A challenge to American democracy* (pp. 61–77). Mahwah, NJ: Erlbaum.

Bendixen, L. D., & Rule, D. C. (2004). An integrative approach to personal epistemology: A guiding model. *Educational Psychologist, 39,* 69–80.

Benenson, J. F., & Christakos, A. (2003) The greater fragility of females' versus males' closest same-sex friendships. *Child Development, 74,* 1123–1129.

Benenson, J. F., Maiese, R., Dolenszky, E., Dolensky, N., Sinclair, N., & Simpson, A. (2002). Group size regulates self-assertive versus self-deprecating responses to interpersonal competition. *Child Development, 73,* 1818–1829.

Benes, F. M. (2007). Corticolimbic circuitry and psychopathology: Development of the corticolimbic system. In D. Coch, G. Dawson, & K. W. Fischer (Eds.), *Human behavior, learning, and the developing brain: Atypical development* (pp. 331–361). New York: Guilford Press.

Bennett, G. K., Seashore, H. G., & Wesman, A. G. (1982). *Differential Aptitude Tests.* San Antonio, TX: Psychological Corporation.

Benton, S. L. (1997). Psychological foundations of elementary writing instruction. In G. D. Phye (Ed.), *Handbook of academic learning: Construction of knowledge* (pp. 235–264). San Diego, CA: Academic Press.

Benware, C., & Deci, E. L. (1984). Quality of learning with an active versus passive motivational set. *American Educational Research Journal, 21,* 755–765.

Ben-Yehudah, G., & Fiez, J. A. (2007). Development of verbal working memory. In D. Coch, K. W. Fischer, & G. Dawson (Eds.), *Human behavior, learning, and the developing brain: Typical development* (pp. 301–328). New York: Guilford Press.

Ben-Zeev, T., Carrasquillo, C. M., Ching, A. M. L., Kliengklom, T. J., McDonald, K. L., Newhall, D. C., et al. (2005). "Math is hard!" (Barbie™, 1994): Responses of threat vs. challenge-mediated arousal to stereotypes alleging intellectual inferiority. In A. M. Gallagher & J. C. Kaufman (Eds.), *Gender differences in mathematics: An integrative psychological approach* (pp. 189–206). Cambridge, England: Cambridge University Press.

Berardi-Coletta, B., Buyer, L. S., Dominowski, R. L., & Rellinger, E. A. (1995). Metacognition and problem solving: A process-oriented approach. *Journal of Experimental Psychology: Learning, Memory, and Cognition, 21,* 205–223.

Bereiter, C. (1995). A dispositional view of transfer. In A. McKeough, J. Lupart, & A. Marini (Eds.), *Teaching for transfer: Fostering generalization in learning.* Mahwah, NJ: Erlbaum.

Bereiter, C., & Scardamalia, M. (2006). Education for the Knowledge Age: Design-centered models of teaching and instruction. In P. A. Alexander & P. H. Winne (Eds.), *Handbook of educational psychology* (2nd ed., pp. 695–713). Mahwah, NJ: Erlbaum.

Berg, W. K., Wacker, D. P., Cigrand, K., Merkle, S., Wade J., Henry, K., et al. (2007). Comparing functional analysis and paired-choice assessment results in classroom settings. *Journal of Applied Behavior Analysis, 40,* 545–552.

Bergeron, R., & Floyd, R. G. (2006). Broad cognitive abilities of children with mental retardation: An analysis of group and individual profiles. *American Journal of Mental Retardation, 111,* 417–432.

Bergin, D. A., & Cooks, H. C. (2008). High school students of color talk about accusations of "acting White." In J. U. Ogbu (Ed.), *Minority status, oppositional culture, and schooling* (pp. 145–166). New York: Routledge.

Berk, L. E. (1994). Why children talk to themselves. *Scientific American, 271,* 78–83.

Berliner, D. C. (1988, February). *The development of expertise in pedagogy.* Paper presented at the American Association of Colleges for Teacher Education, New Orleans, LA.

Berliner, D. C. (2001). Learning about and learning from expert teachers. *International Journal of Educational Research, 35,* 463–483.

Berliner, D. C. (2005, April). *Ignoring the forest, blaming the trees: Our impoverished view of educational reform.* Paper presented at the annual meeting of the American Educational Research Association, Montreal.

Berlyne, D. E. (1960). *Conflict, arousal, and curiosity.* New York: McGraw-Hill.

Bermejo, V. (1996). Cardinality development and counting. *Developmental Psychology, 32,* 263–268.

Berndt, T. J. (1992). Friendship and friends' influence in adolescence. *Current Directions in Psychological Science, 1,* 156–159.

Berndt, T. J., & Keefe, K. (1996). Friends' influence on school adjustment: A motivational analysis. In J. Juvonen & K. R. Wentzel (Eds.), *Social motivation: Understanding children's school adjustment* (pp. 248–278). Cambridge, England: Cambridge University Press.

Berndt, T. J., Laychak, A. E., & Park, K. (1990). Friends' influence on adolescents' academic achievement motivation: An experimental study. *Journal of Educational Psychology, 82,* 664–670.

Berzonsky, M. D. (1988). Self-theorists, identity status, and social cognition. In D. K. Lapsley & F. C. Power (Eds.), *Self, ego, and identity: Integrative approaches* (pp. 243–261). New York: Springer-Verlag.

Best, R. M., Dockrell, J. E., & Braisby, N. (2006). Lexical acquisition in elementary science classes. *Journal of Educational Psychology, 98,* 824–838.

Beyer, B. K. (1985). Critical thinking: What is it? *Social Education, 49,* 270–276.

Bialystok, E. (1994). Representation and ways of knowing: Three issues in second language acquisition. In N. C. Ellis (Ed.), *Implicit and explicit learning of languages.* London: Academic Press.

Bialystok, E. (2001). *Bilingualism in development: Language, literacy, and cognition.* Cambridge, England: Cambridge University Press.

Bielaczyc, K., & Collins, A. (1999). Learning communities in classrooms: A reconceptualization of educational practice. In C. M. Reigeluth (Ed.), *Instructional-design theories and models: A new paradigm of instructional theory* (pp. 269–292). Mahwah, NJ: Erlbaum

Bielaczyc, K., & Collins, A. (2006). Fostering knowledge-creating communities. In A. M. O'Donnell, C. E. Hmelo-Silver, & G. Erkens (Eds.), *Collaborative learning, reasoning, and technology* (pp. 37–60). Mahwah, NJ: Erlbaum.

Biemiller, A., Shany, M., Inglis, A., & Meichenbaum, D. (1998). Factors influencing children's acquisition and demonstration of self-regulation on academic tasks. In D. H. Schunk & B. J. Zimmerman (Eds.), *Self-regulated learning: From teaching to self-reflective practice* (pp. 203–224). New York: Guilford Press.

Bierman, K. L., Miller, C. L., & Stabb, S. D. (1987). Improving the social behavior and peer acceptance of rejected boys: Effect of social skill training with instructions and prohibitions. *Journal of Consulting and Clinical Psychology, 55,* 194–200.

Bigler, R. S., & Liben, L. S. (2007). Developmental intergroup theory: Explaining and reducing children's social stereotyping and prejudice. *Current Directions in Psychological Science, 16,* 162–166.

Binder, L. M., Dixon, M. R., & Ghezzi, P. M. (2000). A procedure to teach self-control to children with attention deficit hyperactivity disorder. *Journal of Applied Behavior Analysis, 33,* 233–237.

Binns, K., Steinberg, A., Amorosi, S., & Cuevas, A. M. (1997). *The Metropolitan Life survey of the American teacher 1997: Examining gender issues in public schools.* New York: Louis Harris and Associates.

Bishop, D. V. M. (2006). What causes specific language impairment in children? *Current Directions in Psychological Science, 15,* 217–221.

Bivens, J. A., & Berk, L. E. (1990). A longitudinal study of the development of elementary school children's private speech. *Merrill-Palmer Quarterly, 36,* 443–463.

Bjorklund, D. F. (1987). How age changes in knowledge base contribute to the development of children's memory: An interpretive review. *Developmental Review, 7,* 93–130.

Bjorklund, D. F. (1997). In search of a metatheory for cognitive development (or, Piaget is dead and I don't feel so good myself). *Child Development, 68,* 144–148.

Bjorklund, D. F., & Coyle, T. R. (1995). Utilization deficiencies in the development of memory strategies. In F. E. Weinert & W. Schneider (Eds.), *Research on memory development: State of the art and future directions.* Mahwah, NJ: Erlbaum.

Bjorklund, D. F., & Green, B. L. (1992). The adaptive nature of cognitive immaturity. *American Psychologist, 47,* 46–54.

Bjorklund, D. F., & Jacobs, J. W. (1985). Associative and categorical processes in children's memory: The role of automaticity in the development of organization in free recall. *Journal of Experimental Child Psychology, 39,* 599–617.

Bjorklund, D. F., Muir-Broaddus, J. E., & Schneider, W. (1990). The role of knowledge in the development of strategies. In D. F. Bjorklund (Ed.), *Children's strategies: Contemporary views of cognitive development.* Mahwah, NJ: Erlbaum.

Bjorklund, D. F., Schneider, W., Cassel, W. S., & Ashley, E. (1994). Training and extension of a memory strategy: Evidence for utilization deficiencies in high- and low-IQ children. *Child Development, 65,* 951–965.

Blackwell, L. S., Trzesniewski, K. H., & Dweck, C. S. (2007). Implicit theories of intelligence predict achievement across an adolescent transition: A longitudinal study and an intervention. *Child Development, 78,* 246–263.

Blair, C. (2002). School readiness: Integrating cognition and emotion in a neurobiological conceptualization of children's functioning at school entry. *American Psychologist, 57,* 111–127.

Blair, C., & Razza, R. P. (2007). Relating effortful control, executive function, and false belief understanding to emerging math and literacy ability in kindergarten. *Child Development, 78,* 647–663.

Blanchard, F. A., Lilly, T., & Vaughn, L. A. (1991). Reducing the expression of racial prejudice. *Psychological Science, 2,* 101–105.

Blasi, A. (1980). Bridging moral cognition and moral action: A critical review of the literature. *Psychological Bulletin, 88,* 593–637.

Blasi, A. (1995). Moral understanding and the moral personality: The process of moral integration. In W. M. Kurtines & J. L. Gewirtz (Eds.), *Moral development: An introduction.* Boston: Allyn & Bacon.

Bleeker, M. M., & Jacobs, J. E. (2004). Achievement in math and science: Do mothers' beliefs matter 12 years later? *Journal of Educational Psychology, 96,* 97–109.

Bleske-Rechek, A., Lubinski, D., & Benbow, C. P. (2004). Meeting the educational needs of special populations: Advanced Placement's role in developing exceptional human capital. *Psychological Science, 15,* 217–224.

Block, J. H. (1980). Promoting excellence through mastery learning. *Theory into Practice, 19,* 66–74.

Block, J. H. (1983). Differential premises arising from differential socialization of the sexes: Some conjectures. *Child Development, 54,* 1335–1354.

Bloom, B. S. (1981). *All our children learning.* New York: McGraw-Hill.

Blugental, D. B., Lyon, J. E., Lin, E. K., McGrath, E. P., & Bimbela, A. (1999). Children "tune out" to the ambiguous communication style of powerless adults. *Child Development, 70,* 214–230.

Blumenfeld, P. C. (1992). The task and the teacher: Enhancing student thoughtfulness in science. In J. Brophy (Ed.), *Advances in research on teaching: Vol. 3. Planning and managing learning tasks and activities.* Greenwich, CT: JAI Press.

Blumenfeld, P. C., Kempler, T. M., & Krajcik, J. S. (2006). Motivation and cognitive engagement in learning environments. In R. K. Sawyer (Ed.), *The Cambridge handbook of the learning sciences* (pp. 475–488). Cambridge, England: Cambridge University Press.

Blumenfeld, P. C., Marx, R. W., Soloway, E., & Krajcik, J. (1996). Learning with peers: From small group cooperation to collaborative communities. *Educational Researcher, 25*(8), 37–40.

Boggiano, A. K., & Pittman, T. S. (Eds.). (1992). *Achievement and motivation: A social-developmental perspective.* Cambridge, England: Cambridge University Press.

Boling, C. J., & Evans, W. H. (2008). Reading success in the secondary classroom. *Preventing School Failure, 52*(2), 59–66.

Bong, M., & Skaalvik, E. M. (2003). Academic self-concept and self-efficacy: How different are they really? *Educational Psychology Review, 15,* 1–40.

Boom, J., Brugman, D., & van der Heijden, P. G. M. (2001). Hierarchical structure of moral stages assessed by a sorting task. *Child Development, 72,* 535–548.

Borko, H., & Putnam, R. T. (1996). Learning to teach. In D. C. Berliner & R. C. Calfee (Eds.), *Handbook of educational psychology.* New York: Macmillan.

Borkowski, J. G., Carr, M., Rellinger, E., & Pressley, M. (1990). Self-regulated cognition: Interdependence of metacognition, attributions, and self-esteem. In B. F. Jones & L. Idol (Eds.), *Dimensions of thinking and cognitive instruction.* Mahwah, NJ: Erlbaum.

Bornholt, L. J., Goodnow, J. J., & Cooney, G. H. (1994). Influences of gender stereotypes on adolescents' perceptions of their own achievement. *American Educational Research Journal, 31,* 675–692.

Bornstein, M. H., Hahn, C.-S., Bell, C., Haynes, O. M., Slater, A., Golding, J., Wolke, D., & the ALSPAC Study Team (2006). Stability in cognition across early childhood: A developmental cascade. *Psychological Science, 17,* 151–158.

Bortfeld, H., & Whitehurst, G. J. (2001). Sensitive periods in first language acquisition. In D. B. Bailey, Jr., J. T. Bruer, F. J. Symons, & J. W. Lichtman (Eds.), *Critical thinking about critical periods* (pp. 173–192). Baltimore: Brookes.

Bosacki, S. L. (2000). Theory of mind and self-concept in preadolescents: Links with gender and language. *Journal of Educational Psychology, 92,* 709–717.

Boschee, F., & Baron, M. A. (1993). *Outcome-based education: Developing programs through strategic planning.* Lancaster, PA: Technomic.

Bouchard, T. J., Jr. (1997). IQ similarity in twins reared apart: Findings and responses to critics. In R. J. Sternberg & E. L. Grigorenko (Eds.), *Intelligence, heredity, and environment* (pp. 126–160). Cambridge, England: Cambridge University Press.

Bouchey, H. A., & Harter, S. (2005). Reflected appraisals, academic self-perceptions, and math/science performance during early adolescence. *Journal of Educational Psychology, 97,* 673–686.

Boutte, G. S., & McCormick, C. B. (1992). Authentic multicultural activities: Avoiding pseudomulticulturalism. *Childhood Education, 68,* 140–144.

Bower, G. H. (1994). Some relations between emotions and memory. In P. Ekman & R. J. Davidson (Eds.), *The nature of emotion: Fundamental questions.* New York: Oxford University Press.

Bower, G. H., Black, J. B., & Turner, T. J. (1979). Scripts in memory for text. *Cognitive Psychology, 11,* 177–220.

Bower, G. H., Clark, M. C., Lesgold, A. M., & Winzenz, D. (1969). Hierarchical retrieval schemes in recall of categorized word lists. *Journal of Verbal Learning and Verbal Behavior, 8,* 323–343.

Bower, G. H., & Forgas, J. P. (2001). Mood and social memory. In J. P. Forgas (Ed.), *Handbook of affect and social cognition* (pp. 95–120). Mahwah, NJ: Erlbaum.

Bower, G. H., Karlin, M. B., & Dueck, A. (1975). Comprehension and memory for pictures. *Memory and Cognition, 3,* 216–220.

Bowey, J. (1986). Syntactic awareness and verbal performance from preschool to fifth grade. *Journal of Psycholinguistic Research, 15,* 285–308.

Boyatzis, R. E. (1973). Affiliation motivation. In D. C. McClelland & R. S. Steele (Eds.), *Human motivation: A book of readings.* Morristown, NJ: General Learning Press.

Boykin, A. W. (1994). Harvesting talent and culture: African-American children and educational reform. In R. J. Rossi (Ed.), *Schools and students at risk: Context and framework for positive change.* New York: Teachers College Press.

Braaksma, M. A. H., Rijlaarsdam, G., & van den Bergh, H. (2002). Observational learning and the effects of model-observer similarity. *Journal of Educational Psychology, 94,* 405–415.

Bracken, B. A., McCallum, R. S., & Shaughnessy, M. F. (1999). An interview with Bruce A. Bracken and R. Steve McCallum, authors of the Universal Nonverbal Intelligence Test (UNIT). *North American Journal of Psychology, 1,* 277–288.

Bracken, B. A., & Walker, K. C. (1997). The utility of intelligence tests for preschool children. In D. P. Flanagan, J. L. Genshaft, & P. L. Harrison (Eds.), *Contemporary intellectual assessment: Theories, tests, and issues* (pp. 484–502). New York: Guilford Press.

Braden, J. P. (1992). Intellectual assessment of deaf and hard-of-hearing people: A quantitative and qualitative research synthesis. *School Psychology Review, 21,* 82–94.

Bradley, L., & Bryant, P. E. (1991). Phonological skills before and after learning to read. In S. A. Brady & D. P. Shankweiler (Eds.), *Phonological processes in literacy.* Mahwah, NJ: Erlbaum.

Brainerd, C. J. (2003). Jean Piaget, learning research, and American education. In B. J. Zimmerman & D. H. Schunk (Eds.), *Educational psychology: A century of contributions* (pp. 251–287). Mahwah, NJ: Erlbaum.

Brainerd, C. J., & Reyna, V. F. (2005). *The science of false memory.* Oxford, England: Oxford University Press.

Branch, C. (1999). Race and human development. In R. H. Sheets & E. R. Hollins (Eds.), *Racial and ethnic identity in school practices: Aspects of human development* (pp. 7–28). Mahwah, NJ: Erlbaum.

Brand, S., Felner, R., Shim, M., Seitsinger, A., & Duman, T. (2003). Middle school improvement and reform: Development and validation of a school-level assessment of climate, cultural pluralism, and school safety. *Journal of Educational Psychology, 95,* 570–588.

Bransford, J., Darling-Hammond, L., & LePage, P. (2005). Introduction. In L. Darling-Hammond & J. Bransford (Eds.), *Preparing teachers for a changing world: What teachers should learn and be able to do* (pp. 1–39). San Francisco: Jossey-Bass/Wiley.

Bransford, J., Derry, S., Berliner, D., & Hammerness, K. (with Beckett, K. L.). (2005). Theories of learning and their roles in teaching. In L. Darling-Hammond & J. Bransford (Eds.), *Preparing teachers for a changing world: What teachers should learn and be able to do* (pp. 40–87). San Francisco: Jossey-Bass/Wiley.

Bransford, J. D., & Franks, J. J. (1971). The abstraction of linguistic ideas. *Cognitive Psychology, 2,* 331–350.

Bransford, J. D., & Schwartz, D. L. (1999). Rethinking transfer: A simple proposal with multiple implications. *Review of Research in Education* (Vol. 24, pp. 61–100). Washington, DC: American Educational Research Association.

Bransford, J., Stevens, R., Schwartz, D., Meltzoff, A., Pea, R., Reschelle, J., Vye, N., Kuhl, P., Bell, P., Barron, B., Reeves, B., & Sabelli, N. (2006). Learning theories and education: Toward a decade of synergy. In P. A. Alexander & P. H. Winne (Eds.), *Handbook of educational psychology* (2nd ed., pp. 209–244). Mahwah, NJ: Erlbaum.

Braukmann, C. J., Kirigin, K. A., & Wolf, M. M. (1981). Behavioral treatment of juvenile delinquency. In S. W. Bijou & R. Ruiz (Eds.), *Behavior modification: Contributions to education.* Mahwah, NJ: Erlbaum.

Braun, L. J. (1998). *The cat who saw stars.* New York: G. P. Putnam's Sons.

Brayboy, B. M. J., & Searle, K. A. (2007). Thanksgiving and serial killers: Representations of American Indians in schools. In S. Books (Ed.), *Invisible children in the society and its schools* (3rd ed., pp. 173–192). Mahwah, NJ: Erlbaum.

Brendgen, M., Boivin, M., Vitaro, F., Bukowski, W. M., Dionne, G., Tremblay, R. E., et al. (2008). Linkages between children's and their friends' social and physical aggression: Evidence for a gene-environment interaction? *Child Development, 79,* 13–29.

Brendgen, M., Wanner, G., Vitaro, F., Bukowski, W. M., & Tremblay, R. E. (2007). Verbal abuse by the teacher during childhood and academic, behavioral, and emotional adjustment in young adulthood. *Journal of Educational Psychology, 99,* 26–38.

Brenner, M. E., Mayer, R. E., Moseley, B., Brar, T., Durán, R., Reed, B. S., & Webb, D. (1997). Learning by understanding: The role of multiple representations in learning algebra. *American Educational Research Journal, 34,* 663–689.

Bressler, S. L. (2002). Understanding cognition through large-scale cortical networks. *Current Directions in Psychological Science, 11,* 58–61.

Brigham, F. J., & Scruggs, T. E. (1995). Elaborative maps for enhanced learning of historical information: Uniting spatial, verbal, and imaginal information. *Journal of Special Education, 28,* 440.

Brody, G. H., Chen, Y.-F., Murry, V. M., Ge, X.,

Simons, R. L., Gibbons, F. X., Gerrard, M., & Cutrona, C. E. (2006). Perceived discrimination and the adjustment of African American youths: A five-year longitudinal analysis with contextual moderation effects. *Child Development, 77,* 1170–1189.

Brody, G. H., & Shaffer, D. R. (1982). Contributions of parents and peers to children's moral socialization. *Developmental Review, 2,* 31–75.

Brody, N. (1992). *Intelligence* (2nd ed.). San Diego, CA: Academic Press.

Brody, N. (1997). Intelligence, schooling, and society. *American Psychologist, 52,* 1046–1050.

Brody, N. (1999). What is intelligence? *International Review of Psychiatry, 11,* 19–25.

Bronfenbrenner, U. (1989). Ecological systems theory. In R. Vasta (Ed.), *Annals of child development* (Vol. 6, pp. 187–251). Greenwich, CT: JAI Press.

Bronfenbrenner, U. (2005). *Making human beings human: Bioecological perspectives on human development.* Thousand Oaks, CA: Sage.

Bronfenbrenner, U., & Morris, P. A. (1998). The ecology of developmental processes. In W. Damon (Series Ed.) & R. M. Lerner (Vol. Ed.), *Handbook of child psychology: Vol. 1. Theoretical models of human development* (5th ed., pp. 993–1028). New York: Wiley.

Bronson, M. B. (2000). *Self-regulation in early childhood: Nature and nurture.* New York: Guilford Press.

Brooke, R. R., & Ruthren, A. J. (1984). The effects of contingency contracting on student performance in a PSI class. *Teaching of Psychology, 11,* 87–89.

Brookhart, S. M. (2004). *Grading.* Upper Saddle River, NJ: Merrill/Prentice Hall.

Brooks, L. W., & Dansereau, D. F. (1987). Transfer of information: An instructional perspective. In S. M. Cormier & J. D. Hagman (Eds.), *Transfer of learning: Contemporary research and applications.* San Diego, CA: Academic Press.

Brooks-Gunn, J. (2003). Do you believe in magic?: What we can expect from early childhood intervention programs. *Social Policy Report of the Society for Research in Child Development, 17*(1), 3–14.

Brooks-Gunn, J., Klebanov, P. K., & Duncan, G. J. (1996). Ethnic differences in children's intelligence test scores: Role of economic deprivation, home environment, and maternal characteristics. *Child Development, 67,* 396–408.

Brooks-Gunn, J., Linver, M. R., & Fauth, R. C. (2005). Children's competence and socioeconomic status in the family and neighborhood. In A. J. Elliot & C. S. Dweck (Eds.), *Handbook of competence and motivation* (pp. 414–435). New York: Guilford Press.

Brooks-Gunn, J., & Paikoff, R. L. (1993). "Sex is a gamble, kissing is a game": Adolescent sexuality and health promotion. In S. G. Millstein, A. C. Petersen, & E. O. Nightingale (Eds.), *Promoting the health of adolescents: New directions for the twenty-first century* (pp. 180–208). New York: Oxford University Press.

Brophy, J. E. (1986). *On motivating students* (Occasional Paper No. 101). East Lansing: Michigan State University, Institute for Research on Teaching.

Brophy, J. E. (1987). Synthesis of research on strategies for motivating students to learn. *Educational Leadership, 45*(2), 40–48.

Brophy, J. E. (2002). Social promotion. In J. Guthrie (Ed.), *Encyclopedia of education* (2nd ed., Vol. 6, pp. 2262–2265). New York: Macmillan.

Brophy, J. E. (2004). *Motivating students to learn* (2nd ed.). Mahwah, NJ: Erlbaum.

Brophy, J. E. (2006). Observational research on generic aspects of classroom teaching. In P. A. Alexander & P. H. Winne (Eds.), *Handbook of educational psychology* (2nd ed., pp. 755–780). Mahwah, NJ: Erlbaum.

Brophy, J. (2008). Developing students' appreciation for what is taught in school. *Educational Psychologist, 43,* 132–141.

Brophy, J. E., & Alleman, J. (1991). Activities as instructional tools: A framework for analysis and evaluation. *Educational Researcher, 20*(4), 9–23.

Brophy, J. E., & Alleman, J. (1992). Planning and managing learning activities: Basic principles. In J. Brophy (Ed.), *Advances in research on teaching: Vol. 3. Planning and managing learning tasks and activities.* Greenwich, CT: JAI Press.

Brophy, J. E., & Alleman, J. (1996). *Powerful social studies for elementary students.* Fort Worth, TX: Harcourt, Brace.

Brophy, J. E., & Good, T. L. (1986). Teacher effects. In M. C. Wittrock (Ed.), *Handbook of research on teaching* (3rd ed.). New York: Macmillan.

Brophy, J. E., & VanSledright, B. (1997). *Teaching and learning history in elementary schools.* New York: Teachers College Press.

Brouwer, N., & Korthagen, F. (2005). Can teacher education make a difference? *American Educational Research Journal, 42,* 153–224.

Brown, A. L., & Campione, J. C. (1994). Guided discovery in a community of learners. In K. McGilly (Ed.), *Classroom lessons: Integrating cognitive theory and classroom practice.* Cambridge, MA: MIT Press.

Brown, A. L., & Campione, J. C. (1996). Psychological theory and the design of innovative learning environments: On procedures, principles, and systems. In L. Schauble & R. Glaser (Eds.), *Innovations in learning: New environments for education.* Mahwah, NJ: Erlbaum.

Brown, A. L., Campione, J., & Day, J. (1981). Learning to learn: On training students to learn from texts. *Educational Researcher, 10*(2), 14–21.

Brown, A. L., & Palincsar, A. S. (1987). Reciprocal teaching of comprehension strategies: A natural history of one program for enhancing learning. In J. Borkowski & J. D. Day (Eds.), *Cognition in special education: Comparative approaches to retardation, learning disabilities, and giftedness.* Norwood, NJ: Ablex.

Brown, A. L., & Palincsar, A. S. (1989). Guided, cooperative learning and individual knowledge acquisition. In L. B. Resnick (Ed.), *Knowing, learning, and instruction: Essays in honor of Robert Glaser.* Mahwah, NJ: Erlbaum.

Brown, A. L., & Reeve, R. A. (1987). Bandwidths of competence: The role of supportive contexts in learning and development. In L. S. Liben (Ed.), *Development and learning: Conflict or congruence?* Mahwah, NJ: Erlbaum.

Brown, A. L., Smiley, S. S., Day, J. D., Townsend, M. A. R., & Lawton, S. C. (1977). Intrusion of a thematic idea in children's comprehension and retention of stories. *Child Development, 48,* 1454–1466.

Brown, B. B. (1990). Peer groups. In S. Feldman & G. Elliott (Eds.), *At the threshold: The developing adolescent* (pp. 171–196). Cambridge, MA: Harvard University Press.

Brown, B. B. (1993). School culture, social politics, and the academic motivation of U.S. students. In T. M. Tomlinson (Ed.), *Motivating students to learn: Overcoming barriers to high achievement.* Berkeley, CA: McCutchan.

Brown, B. B. (1999). "You're going out with *who?*" Peer group influences on adolescent romantic relationships. In W. Furman, B. B. Brown, & C. Feiring (Eds.), *The development of romantic relationships in adolescence* (pp. 291–329). Cambridge, England: Cambridge University Press.

Brown, B. B., Eicher, S. A., & Petrie, S. (1986). The importance of peer group ("crowd") affiliation in adolescence. *Journal of Adolescence, 9,* 73–96.

Brown, B. B., Feiring, C., & Furman, W. (1999). Missing the love boat: Why researchers have shied away from adolescent romance. In W. Furman, B. B. Brown, & C. Feiring (Eds.), *The development of romantic relationships in adolescence* (pp. 1–16). Cambridge, England: Cambridge University Press.

Brown, B. B., Herman, M., Hamm, J. V., & Heck, D. J. (2008). Ethnicity and image: Correlates of crowd affiliation among ethnic minority youth. *Child Development, 79,* 529–546.

Brown, J. S., Collins, A., & Duguid, P. (1989). Situated cognition and the culture of learning. *Educational Researcher, 18*(1), 32–42.

Brown, L. M., Tappan, M. B., & Gilligan, C. (1995). Listening to different voices. In W. M. Kurtines & J. L. Gewirtz (Eds.), *Moral development: An introduction.* Boston: Allyn & Bacon.

Brown, R. D., & Bjorklund, D. F. (1998). The biologizing of cognition, development, and education: Approach with cautious enthusiasm. *Educational Psychology Review, 10,* 355–373.

Brown, R. T., Reynolds, C. R., & Whitaker, J. S. (1999). Bias in mental testing since *Bias in Mental Testing. School Psychology Quarterly, 14,* 208–238.

Brown, W. H., Fox, J. J., & Brady, M. P. (1987). Effects of spatial density on 3- and 4-year-old children's socially directed behavior during freeplay: An investigation of a setting factor. *Education and Treatment of Children, 10,* 247–258.

Brownell, M. T., Mellard, D. F., & Deshler, D. D. (1993). Differences in the learning and transfer performance between students with learning disabilities and other low-achieving students on problem-solving tasks. *Learning Disabilities Quarterly, 16,* 138–156.

Brown-Mizuno, C. (1990). Success strategies for learners who are learning disabled as well as gifted. *Teaching Exceptional Children, 23*(1), 10–12.

Bruer, J. T. (1999). *The myth of the first three years: A new understanding of early brain development and lifelong learning.* New York: Free Press.

Bruer, J. T., & Greenough, W. T. (2001). The subtle science of how experience affects the brain. In D. B. Bailey, Jr., J. T. Bruer, F. J. Symons, & J. W. Lichtman (Eds.), *Critical thinking about critical periods* (pp. 209–232). Baltimore: Brookes.

Bruner, J. S. (1966). *Toward a theory of instruction.* Cambridge, MA: Harvard University Press.

Bruning, R. H., Schraw, G. J., & Ronning, R. R. (1995). *Cognitive psychology and instruction* (2nd ed.). Upper Saddle River, NJ: Merrill/Prentice Hall.

Bryan, J. H. (1975). Children's cooperation and helping behaviors. In E. M. Hetherington (Ed.), *Review of child development research* (Vol. 5). Chicago: University of Chicago Press.

Bryan, T. (1991). Social problems and learning disabilities. In B. Y. L. Wong (Ed.), *Learning about learning disabilities.* San Diego, CA: Academic Press.

Bryan, T., Burstein, K., & Bryan, J. (2001). Students with learning disabilities: Homework problems and promising practices. *Educational Psychologist, 36,* 167–180.

Buchoff, T. (1990). Attention deficit disorder: Help for the classroom teacher. *Childhood Education, 67,* 86–90.

Buck, G., Kostin, I., & Morgan, R. (2002). *Examining the relationship of content to gender-based performance differences in advanced placement exams* (Research Report No. 2002-12). New York: College Board.

Buehl, M. M., & Alexander, P. A. (2001). Beliefs about academic knowledge. *Educational Psychology Review, 13,* 385–418.

Buehl, M. M., & Alexander, P. A. (2006). Examining the dual nature of epistemological beliefs. *International Journal of Educational Research, 45,* 28–42.

Bugelski, B. R., & Alampay, D. A. (1961). The role of frequency in developing perceptual sets. *Canadian Journal of Psychology, 15,* 205–211.

Buhs, E. S., Ladd, G. W., & Herald, S. L. (2006). Peer exclusion and victimization: Processes that mediate the relation between peer group rejection and children's classroom engagement and achievement? *Journal of Educational Psychology, 98,* 1–13.

Bukowski, W. M., Brendgen, M., & Vitaro, F. (2007). Peers and socialization: Effects on externalizing and internalizing problems. In J. E. Grusec & P. D. Hastings (Eds.), *Handbook of socialization: Theory and research* (pp. 355–381). New York: Guilford Press.

Bulgren, J. A., Deshler, D. D., Schumaker, J. B., & Lenz, B. K. (2000). The use and effectiveness of analogical instruction in diverse secondary content classrooms. *Journal of Educational Psychology, 92,* 426–441.

Bulgren, J. A., Schumaker, J. B., & Deshler, D. D. (1994). The effects of a recall enhancement routine on the test performance of secondary students with and without learning disabilities. *Learning Disabilities Research and Practice, 9,* 2–11.

Bureau of Justice Statistics. (2005). *Sourcebook of criminal justice statistics.* Washington, DC: Author.

Burger, H. G. (1973). Cultural pluralism and the schools. In C. S. Brembeck & W. H. Hill (Eds.), *Cultural challenges to education: The influence of cultural factors in school learning.* Lexington, MA: Heath.

Burger, S., & Burger, D. (1994). Determining the validity of performance-based assessment. *Educational Measurement: Issues and Practice, 13*(1), 9–15.

Burgess, K. B., Wojslawowicz, J. C., Rubin, K. H., Rose-Krasnor, L., & Booth-LaForce, C. (2006). Social information processing and coping strategies of shy/withdrawn and aggressive children: Does friendship matter? *Child Development, 77,* 371–383.

Burhans, K. K., & Dweck, C. S. (1995). Helplessness in early childhood: The role of contingent worth. *Child Development, 66,* 1719–1738.

Burkam, D. T., Lee, V. E., & Smerdon, B. A. (1997). Gender and science learning early in high school: Subject matter and laboratory experiences. *American Educational Research Journal, 34,* 297–331.

Burnett, P. (2001). Elementary students' preferences for teacher praise. *Journal of Classroom Interaction, 36,* 16–23.

Burstyn, J. N., & Stevens, R. (2001). Involving the whole school in violence prevention. In J. N. Burstyn, G. Bender, R. Casella, H. W. Gordon, D. P. Guerra, K. V. Luschen, R. Stevens, & K. M. Williams, *Preventing violence in schools: A challenge to American democracy* (pp. 139–158). Mahwah, NJ: Erlbaum.

Bushman, B. J., & Anderson, C. A. (2001). Media violence and the American public: Scientific facts versus media misinformation. *American Psychologist, 56,* 477–489.

Bussey, K., & Bandura, A. (1992). Self-regulatory mechanisms governing gender development. *Child Development, 63,* 1236–1250.

Butler, D. L., & Winne, P. H. (1995). Feedback and self-regulated learning: A theoretical synthesis. *Review of Educational Research, 65,* 245–281.

Butler, R. (1990). The effects of mastery and competitive conditions on self-assessment at different ages. *Child Development, 61,* 201–210.

Butler, R. (1994). Teacher communication and student interpretations: Effects of teacher responses to failing students on attributional inferences in two age groups. *British Journal of Educational Psychology, 64,* 277–294.

Butler, R. (1998a). Age trends in the use of social and temporal comparison for self-evaluation: Examination of a novel developmental hypothesis. *Child Development, 69,* 1054–1073.

Butler, R. (1998b). Determinants of help seeking: Relations between perceived reasons for classroom help-avoidance and help-seeking behaviors in an experimental context. *Journal of Educational Psychology, 90,* 630–644.

Butler, R. (2005). Competence assessment, competence, and motivation between early and middle childhood. In A. J. Elliot & C. S. Dweck (Eds.), *Handbook of competence and motivation* (pp. 202–221). New York: Guilford Press.

Butterfield, E. C., & Ferretti, R. P. (1987). Toward a theoretical integration of cognitive hypotheses about intellectual differences among children. In J. G. Borkowski & J. D. Day (Eds.), *Cognition in special children: Approaches to retardation, learning disabilities, and giftedness.* Norwood, NJ: Ablex.

Byrne, B. M. (2002). Validating the measurement and structure of self-concept: Snapshots of past, present, and future research. *American Psychologist, 57,* 897–909.

Byrnes, J. P. (2001). *Minds, brains, and learning: Understanding the psychological and educational relevance of neuroscientific research.* New York: Guilford Press.

Byrnes, J. P. (2003). Factors predictive of mathematics achievement in White, Black, and Hispanic 12th graders. *Journal of Educational Psychology, 95,* 316–326.

Byrnes, J. P. (2007). Some ways in which neuroscientific research can be relevant to education. In D. Coch, K. W. Fischer, & G. Dawson (Eds.), *Human behavior, learning, and the developing brain: Typical development* (pp. 30–49). New York: Guilford Press.

Byrnes, J. P., & Fox, N. A. (1998). The educational relevance of research in cognitive neuroscience. *Educational Psychology Review, 10,* 297–342.

Cacioppo, J. T., Petty, R. E., Feinstein, J. A., & Jarvis, W. B. G. (1996). Dispositional differences in cognitive motivation: The life and times of individuals varying in need for cognition. *Psychological Bulletin, 119,* 197–253.

Cairns, H. S. (1996). *The acquisition of language* (2nd ed.). Austin, TX: Pro-Ed.

Calderhead, J. (1996). Teachers: Beliefs and knowledge. In D. C. Berliner & R. C. Calfee (Eds.), *Handbook of educational psychology.* New York: Macmillan.

Caldwell, C. H., Zimmerman, M. A., Bernat, D. H., Sellers, R. M., & Notaro, P. C. (2002). Racial identity, maternal support, and psychological distress among African American adolescents. *Child Development, 73,* 1322–1336.

Caldwell, M. S., Rudolph, K. D., Troop-Gordon, W., & Kim, D. (2004). Reciprocal influences among relational self-views, social disengagement, and peer stress during early adolescence. *Child Development, 75,* 1140–1154.

Calfee, R. (1981). Cognitive psychology and educational practice. In D. C. Berliner (Ed.), *Review of research in education* (Vol. 9). Washington, DC: American Educational Research Association.

Calfee, R., Dunlap, K., & Wat, A. (1994). Authentic discussion of texts in middle grade schooling: An analytic-narrative approach. *Journal of Reading, 37,* 546–556.

Callanan, M. A., & Oakes, L. M. (1992). Preschoolers' questions and parents' explanations: Causal thinking in everyday activity. *Cognitive Development, 7,* 213–233.

Cameron, J. (2001). Negative effects of reward on intrinsic motivation—a limited phenomenon: Comment on Deci, Koestner, and Ryan (2001). *Review of Educational Research, 71,* 29–42.

Cameron, J., & Pierce, W. D. (1994). Reinforcement, reward, and intrinsic motivation: A meta-analysis. *Review of Educational Research, 64,* 363–423.

Cameron, L., Rutland, A., Brown, R., & Douch, R. (2006). Changing children's intergroup attitudes toward refugees: Testing different models of extended contact. *Child Development, 77,* 1208–1219.

Cammilleri, A. P., Tiger, J. H., & Hanley, G. P. (2008). Developing stimulus control of young children's requests to teachers: Classwide applications of multiple schedules. *Journal of Applied Behavior Analysis, 41,* 299–303.

Campbell, D. E. (1996). *Choosing democracy: A practical guide to multicultural education.* Upper Saddle River, NJ: Merrill/Prentice Hall.

Campbell, F. A., & Burchinal, M. R. (2008). Early childhood interventions: The Abecedarian Project. In P. C. Kyllonen, R. D. Roberts, & L. Stankov (Eds.), *Extending intelligence: Enhancement and new constructs* (pp. 61–84). New York: Erlbaum/Taylor & Francis.

Campbell, L., Campbell, B., & Dickinson, D. (1998). *Teaching and learning through multiple intelligences* (2nd ed.). Boston: Allyn & Bacon.

Campione, J. C., Brown, A. L., & Bryant, N. R. (1985). Individual differences in learning and memory. In R. J. Sternberg (Ed.), *Human abilities: An information-processing approach.* New York: Freeman.

Campione, J. C., Shapiro, A. M., & Brown, A. L. (1995). Forms of transfer in a community of learners: Flexible learning and understanding. In A. McKeough, J. Lupart, & A. Marini (Eds.), *Teaching for transfer: Fostering generalization in learning.* Mahwah, NJ: Erlbaum.

Camras, L. A., Chen, Y., Bakeman, R., Norris, K., & Cain, T. R. (2006). Culture, ethnicity, and children's facial expressions: A study of European American, Mainland Chinese, Chinese American, and adopted Chinese girls. *Emotion, 6,* 103–114.

Candler-Lotven, A., Tallent-Runnels, M. K., Olivárez, A., & Hildreth, B. (1994, April). *A comparison of learning and study strategies of gifted, average-ability, and learning-disabled ninth-grade students.* Paper presented at the annual meeting of the American Educational Research Association, New Orleans, LA.

Capelli, C. A., Nakagawa, N., & Madden, C. M. (1990). How children understand sarcasm: The role of context and intonation. *Child Development, 61,* 1824–1841.

Caprara, G. V., Barbaranelli, C., Pastorelli, C., Bandura, A., & Zimbardo, P. G. (2000). Prosocial foundations of children's academic achievement. *Psychological Science, 11,* 302–306.

Caprara, G. V., Dodge, K. A., Pastorelli, C., & Zelli, A. (2007). How marginal deviations sometimes grow into serious aggression. *Child Development Perspectives, 1,* 33–39.

Capron, C., & Duyme, M. (1989). Assessment of effects of socio-economic status on IQ in a full cross-fostering study. *Nature, 340,* 552–554.

Carbrera, N. J., Shannon, J. D., West, J., & Brooks-Gunn, J. (2006). Parental interactions with Latino infants: Variation by country of origin and English proficiency. *Child Development, 77,* 1190–1207.

Card, N. A., & Ramos, J. F. (2005, April). *Friends' similarity on academic characteristics: A meta-analytic review.* Paper presented at the annual meeting of the American Educational Research Association, Montreal.

Card, N. A., Stucky, B. D., Sawalani, G. M., & Little, T. D. (2008). Direct and indirect aggression during childhood and adolescence: A meta-analytic review of gender differences, intercorrelations, and relations to maladjustment. *Child Development, 79,* 1185–1229.

Carey, L. M. (1994). *Measuring and evaluating school learning* (2nd ed.). Boston: Allyn & Bacon.

Carey, R. G., & Bucher, B. (1983). Positive practice overcorrection: The effects of duration of positive practice on acquisition and response reduction. *Journal of Applied Behavior Analysis, 16,* 101–109.

Carey, S. (1978). The child as word learner. In M. Halle, J. Bresnan, & G. A. Miller (Eds.), *Linguistic theory and psychological reality.* Cambridge, MA: MIT Press.

Carey, S. (1985). *Conceptual change in childhood.* Cambridge, MA: MIT Press.

Carhill, A., Suárez-Orozco, C., & Páez, M. (2008). Explaining English language proficiency among adolescent immigrant students. *American Educational Research Journal, 45,* 1045–1079.

Carlin, M. T., Soraci, S. A., Strawbridge, C. P., Dennis, N., Loiselle, R., & Checile, N. A. (2003). Detection of changes in naturalistic scenes: Comparison of individuals with and without mental retardation. *Journal of Mental Retardation, 108,* 181–193.

Carlson, R., Chandler, P., & Sweller, J. (2003). Learning and understanding science instructional material. *Journal of Educational Psychology, 95,* 629–640.

Carlson, S. M., & Moses, L. J. (2001). Individual differences in inhibitory control and children's theory of mind. *Child Development, 72,* 1032–1053.

Carmichael, C. A., & Hayes, B. K. (2001). Prior knowledge and exemplar encoding in children's concept acquisition. *Child Development, 72,* 1071–1090.

Carnagey, N. L., Anderson, C. A., & Bartholow, B. D. (2007). Media violence and social neuroscience: New questions and new opportunities. *Current Directions in Psychological Science, 16,* 178–182.

Carney, R. N., & Levin, J. R. (2002). Pictorial illustrations *still* improve students' learning from text. *Educational Psychology Review, 14,* 5–26.

Carnine, D. (1989). Teaching complex content to learning disabled students: The role of technology. *Exceptional Children, 55,* 524–533.

Carr, A. A. (1997, March). *The participation "race": Kentucky's site based decision teams.* Paper presented at the annual meeting of the American Educational Research Association, Chicago.

Carr, E. G., Levin, L., McConnachie, G., Carlson, J. I., Kemp, D. C., & Smith, C. E. (1994). *Communication-based intervention for problem behavior: A user's guide for producing positive change.* Baltimore: Brookes.

Carr, M., & Biddlecomb, B. (1998). Metacognition in mathematics from a constructivist perspective. In D. J. Hacker, J. Dunlosky, & A. C. Graesser (Eds.), *Metacognition in educational theory and practice* (pp. 69–91). Mahwah, NJ: Erlbaum.

Carr, M., & Borkowski, J. G. (1989). Attributional training and the generalization of reading strategies with underachieving children. *Learning and Individual Differences, 1,* 327–341.

Carrasco, R. L. (1981). Expanded awareness of student performance: A case study in applied ethnographic monitoring in a bilingual classroom. In H. T. Trueba, G. P. Guthrie, & K. H. Au (Eds.), *Culture and the bilingual classroom: Studies in classroom ethnography.* Rowley, MA: Newbury House.

Carroll, J. B. (1993) *Human cognitive abilities: A survey of factor-analytic studies.* New York: Cambridge University Press.

Carroll, J. B. (2003). The higher stratum structure of cognitive abilities: Current evidence supports *g* and about ten broad factors. In H. Nyborg (Ed.), *The scientific study of general intelligence.* New York: Pergamon.

Carter, K., & Doyle, W. (2006). Classroom management in early childhood and elementary classrooms. In C. M. Evertson & C. S. Weinstein (Eds.), *Handbook of classroom management: Research, practice, and contemporary issues* (pp. 373–406). Mahwah, NJ: Erlbaum.

Carter, R., Williams, S., & Silverman, W. K. (2008). Cognitive and emotional facets of test anxiety in African American school children. *Cognition and Emotion, 22,* 539–551.

Carver, C. S., & Scheier, M. F. (1990). Origins and functions of positive and negative affect: A control-process view. *Psychological Review, 97,* 19–35.

Carver, S. M. (2006). Assessing for deep understanding. In R. K. Sawyer (Ed.), *The Cambridge handbook of the learning sciences* (pp. 205–221). Cambridge, England: Cambridge University Press.

Case, R. (1985). *Intellectual development: Birth to adulthood.* Orlando, FL: Academic Press.

Case, R. (1991). *The mind's staircase: Exploring the conceptual underpinnings of children's thought and knowledge.* Hillsdale, NJ: Erlbaum.

Case, R., & Okamoto, Y., in collaboration with Griffin, S., McKeough, A., Bleiker, C., Henderson, B., & Stephenson, K. M. (1996). The role of central conceptual structures in the development of children's thought. *Monographs of the Society for Research in Child Development, 61*(1, Serial No. 246).

Casella, R. (2001a). The cultural foundations of peer mediation: Beyond a behaviorist model of urban school conflict. In J. N. Burstyn, G. Bender, R. Casella, H. W. Gordon, D. P. Guerra, K. V. Luschen, R. Stevens, & K. M. Williams, *Preventing violence in schools: A challenge to American democracy* (pp. 159–179). Mahwah, NJ: Erlbaum.

Casella, R. (2001b). What is violent about "school violence"? The nature of violence in a city high school. In J. N. Burstyn, G. Bender, R. Casella, H. W. Gordon, D. P. Guerra, K. V. Luschen, R. Stevens, & K. M. Williams, *Preventing violence in schools: A challenge to American democracy* (pp. 15–46). Mahwah, NJ: Erlbaum.

Casey, B. J. (2001). Disruption of inhibitory control in developmental disorders: A mechanistic model of implicated frontostriatal circuitry. In J. L. McClelland & R. S. Siegler (Eds.), *Mechanisms of cognitive development: Behavioral and neural perspectives* (pp. 327–349). Mahwah, NJ: Erlbaum.

Casey, B. M., Andrews, N., Schindler, H., Kersh, J. E., Samper, A., & Copley, J. (2008). The development of spatial skills through interventions involving block building activities. *Cognition and Instruction, 26,* 269–309.

Casey, W. M., & Burton, R. V. (1982). Training children to be consistently honest through verbal self-instructions. *Child Development, 53,* 911–919.

Caspi, A. (1998). Personality development across the life course. In W. Damon (Series Ed.) & N. Eisenberg (Vol. Ed.), *Handbook of child psychology: Vol. 3. Social, emotional, and personality development* (5th ed., pp. 311–388). New York: Wiley.

Caspi, A., & Silva, P. A. (1995). Temperamental qualities at age three predict personality traits in young adulthood: Longitudinal evidence from a birth cohort. *Child Development, 66,* 486–498.

Caspi, A., Taylor, A., Moffitt, T. E., & Plomin, R. (2000). Neighborhood deprivation affects children's mental health: Environmental risks identified in a genetic design. *Psychological Science, 11,* 338–342.

Cassady, J. C. (2004). The influence of cognitive test anxiety across the learning-testing cycle. *Learning and Instruction, 14,* 569–592.

Cassady, J. C., & Johnson, R. E. (2002). Cognitive test anxiety and academic performance. *Contemporary Educational Psychology, 27,* 270–295.

Cassidy, J., Ziv, Y., Mehta, T. G., & Feeney, B. C. (2003). Feedback seeking in children and adolescents: Associations with self-perceptions, attachment representations, and depression. *Child Development, 74,* 612–628.

Castagno, A. E., & Brayboy, B. M. J. (2008). Culturally responsive schooling for Indigenous youth: A review of the literature. *Review of Educational Research, 78,* 941–993.

Cattani, A., Clibbens, J., & Perfect, T. J. (2007). Visual memory for shapes in deaf signers and nonsigners and in hearing signers and nonsigners: Atypical lateralization and enhancement. *Neuropsychology, 21,* 114–121.

Cattell, R. B. (1963). Theory of fluid and crystallized intelligence: A critical experiment. *Journal of Educational Psychology, 54,* 1–22.

Cattell, R. B. (1987). *Intelligence: Its structure, growth, and action.* Amsterdam: North-Holland.

Cazden, C. B. (2001). *Classroom discourse: The language of teaching and learning* (2nd ed.). Portsmouth, NH: Heinemann.

Ceci, S. J. (2003). Cast in six ponds and you'll reel in something: Looking back on 25 years of research. *American Psychologist, 58,* 855–864.

Celio, C. I., Durlak, J. A., Pachan, M. K., & Berger, S. R. (2007, March). *Helping others and helping oneself: A meta-analysis of service-learning programs.* Paper presented at the biennial meeting of the Society for Research in Child Development, Boston.

Center for Media Literacy (n.d.). CML's five key questions. In *Five key questions that can change the world: Deconstruction.* Retrieved January 27, 2009, from www.medialit.org/reading_room/article661.html

Certo, J., Cauley, K. M., & Chafin, C. (2002, April). *Students' perspectives on their high school experience.* Paper presented at the annual meeting of the American Educational Research Association, New Orleans, LA.

Certo, J., Miller, J. A., Reffitt, K., Moxley, K., & Sportsman, E. (2008, March). *Social skills and leadership abilities among children in literature circles: A mixed methods study.* Paper presented at the annual meeting of the American Educational Research Association, New York.

Chabrán, M. (2003). Listening to talk from and about students on accountability. In M. Carnoy, R. Elmore, & L. S. Siskin (Eds.), *The new accountability: High schools and high-stakes testing* (pp. 129–145). New York: RoutledgeFalmer.

Chall, J. S. (1996). *Stages of reading development* (2nd ed.). Fort Worth, TX: Harcourt Brace.

Chalmers, J., & Townsend, M. (1990). The effects of training in social perspective taking on socially maladjusted girls. *Child Development, 61,* 178–190.

Chambliss, M. J. (1994). Why do readers fail to change their beliefs after reading persuasive text? In R. Garner & P. A. Alexander (Eds.), *Beliefs about text and instruction with text.* Mahwah, NJ: Erlbaum.

Chambliss, M. J., & Calfee, R. C. (1989). Designing science textbooks to enhance student understanding. *Educational Psychologist, 24,* 307–322.

Champagne, A. B., & Bunce, D. M. (1991). Learning-theory-based science teaching. In S. M. Glynn, R. H. Yeany, & B. K. Britton (Eds.), *The psychology of learning science* (pp. 21–41). Hillsdale, NJ: Erlbaum.

Chan, J. M., & O'Reilly, M. F. (2008). A Social Stories™ intervention package for students with autism in inclusive classroom settings. *Journal of Applied Behavior Analysis, 41,* 405–409.

Chandler, M. (1987). The Othello effect: Essay on the emergence and eclipse of skeptical doubt. *Human Development, 30,* 137–159.

Chandler, M. J., Hallett, D., & Sokol, B. W. (2002). Competing claims about competing knowledge claims. In B. K. Hofer & P. R. Pintrich (Eds.), *Personal epistemology: The psychology of beliefs about knowledge and knowing* (pp. 145–168). Mahwah, NJ: Erlbaum.

Chang, L. (2003) Variable effects of children's aggression, social withdrawal, and prosocial leadership as functions of teacher beliefs and behaviors. *Child Development, 74,* 535–548.

Chang, L., Liu, H., Wen, Z., Fung, K. Y., Wang, Y., & Xu, Y. (2004). Mediating teacher liking and moderating authoritative teachering on Chinese adolescents' perceptions of antisocial and prosocial behaviors. *Journal of Educational Psychology, 96,* 369–380.

Chapman, J. W. (1988). Learning disabled children's self-concepts. *Review of Educational Research, 58,* 347–371.

Chapman, J. W., Tunmer, W. E., & Prochnow, J. E. (2000). Early reading-related skills and performance, reading self-concept, and the development of academic self-concept: A longitudinal study. *Journal of Educational Psychology, 92,* 703–708.

Charity, A. H., Scarborough, H. S., & Griffin, D. M. (2004). Familiarity with school English in African American children and its relation to early reading achievement. *Child Development, 75,* 1340–1356.

Charness, N., Tuffiash, M., & Jastrzembski, T. (2004). Motivation, emotion, and expert skill acquisition. In D. Y. Dai & R. J. Sternberg (Eds.), *Motivation, emotion, and cognition: Integrative perspectives on intellectual functioning and development* (pp. 299–319). Mahwah, NJ: Erlbaum.

Chavous, T. M., Bernat, D. H., Schmeelk-Cone, K., Caldwell, C. H., Kohn-Wood, L., & Zimmerman, M. A. (2003). Racial identity and academic attainment among African American adolescents. *Child Development, 74,* 1076–1090.

Chen, J., & Morris, D. (2008, March). *Sources of science self-efficacy beliefs among high school students in different tracking levels.* Paper presented at the annual meeting of the American Educational Research Association, New York.

Chen, W.-B., & Gregory, A. (2008, March). *Parental involvement in schooling: What types work for low-achieving adolescents and what does this mean for schools?* Paper presented at the annual meeting of the American Educational Research Association, New York.

Chen, X., Anderson, R. C., Li, W., Hao, M., Wu, X., & Shu, H. (2004). Phonological awareness of bilingual and monolingual Chinese children. *Journal of Educational Psychology, 96,* 142–151.

Chen, X., Chang, L., He, Y., & Liu, H. (2005). The peer group as a context: Moderating effects on relations between maternal parenting and social and school adjustment in Chinese children. *Child Development, 76,* 417–434.

Chen, Z. (1999). Schema induction in children's analogical problem solving. *Journal of Educational Psychology, 91,* 703–715.

Cheng, L. R. (1987). *Assessing Asian language performance.* Rockville, MD: Aspen.

Cherry, E. C. (1953). Some experiments on the recognition of speech, with one and with two ears. *Journal of the Acoustical Society of America, 25,* 975–979.

Chester, M. D., & Beaudin, B. Q. (1996). Efficacy beliefs of newly hired teachers in urban schools. *American Educational Research Journal, 33,* 233–257.

Cheyne, J. A., & Walters, R. H. (1970). Punishment and prohibition: Some origins of self-control. In

T. M. Newcomb (Ed.), *New directions in psychology*. New York: Holt, Rinehart & Winston.
Chi, M. T. H. (1978). Knowledge structures and memory development. In R. S. Siegler (Ed.), *Children's thinking: What develops?* Mahwah, NJ: Erlbaum.
Chinn, C. A. (2006). Learning to argue. In A. M. O'Donnell, C. E. Hmelo-Silver, & G. Erkens (Eds.), *Collaborative learning, reasoning, and technology* (pp. 355–383). Mahwah, NJ: Erlbaum.
Chinn, C. A., Anderson, R. C., & Waggoner, M. A. (2001). Patterns of discourse in two kinds of literature discussion. *Reading Research Quarterly, 36,* 378–411.
Chinn, C. A., & Malhotra, B. A. (2002). Children's responses to anomalous scientific data: How is conceptual change impeded? *Journal of Educational Psychology, 94,* 327–343.
Chisholm, J. S. (1996). Learning "respect for everything": Navajo images of development. In C. P. Hwant, M. E. Lamb, & I. E. Sigel (Eds.), *Images of childhood* (pp. 167–183). Mahwah, NJ: Erlbaum.
Chiu, C.-Y., & Hong, Y.-Y. (2005). Cultural competence: Dynamic processes. In A. J. Elliot & C. S. Dweck (Eds.), *Handbook of competence and motivation* (pp. 489–505). New York: Guilford Press.
Chiu, M. M. (2008). Effects of argumentation on group micro-creativity: Statistical discourse analyses of algebra students' collaborative problem solving. *Contemporary Educational Psychology, 33,* 382–402.
Chomsky, N. (1972). *Language and mind* (enlarged ed.). San Diego, CA: Harcourt Brace Jovanovich.
Chomsky, N. (2006). *Language and mind* (3rd ed.). Cambridge, England: Cambridge University Press.
Christenson, S. L. (2004). Families with aggressive children and adolescents. In J. C. Conoley & A. P. Goldstein (Eds.), *School violence intervention* (2nd ed., pp. 359–399). New York: Guilford Press.
Christenson, S. L., & Sheridan, S. M. (2001). *Schools and families: Creating essential connections for learning*. New York: Guilford Press.
Christenson, S. L., & Thurlow, M. L. (2004). School dropouts: Prevention, considerations, interventions, and challenges. *Current Directions in Psychological Science, 13,* 36–39.
Church, M. A., Elliot, A. J., & Gable, S. L. (2001). Perceptions of classroom environment, achievement goals, and achievement outcomes. *Journal of Educational Psychology, 93,* 43–54.
Cillessen, A. H. N., & Mayeux, L. (2007). Variations in the association between aggression and social status: Theoretical and empirical perspectives. In P. H. Hawley, T. D. Little, & P. C. Rodkin (Eds.). *Aggression and adaptation: The bright side to bad behavior* (pp. 135–156). Mahwah, NJ: Erlbaum.
Cillessen, A. H. N., & Rose, A. J. (2005). Understanding popularity in the peer system. *Current Directions in Psychological Science, 14,* 102–105.
Cizek, G. J. (2003). *Detecting and preventing classroom cheating: Promoting integrity in assessment*. Thousand Oaks, CA: Corwin.
Clark, A.-M., Anderson, R. C., Kuo, L., Kim, I., Archodidou, A., & Nguyen-Jahiel, K. (2003). Collaborative reasoning: Expanding ways for children to talk and think in school. *Educational Psychology Review, 15,* 181–198.
Clark, B. (1997). *Growing up gifted* (5th ed.). Upper Saddle River, NJ: Merrill/Prentice Hall.
Clark, C. C. (1992). Deviant adolescent subcultures: Assessment strategies and clinical interventions. *Adolescence, 27*(106), 283–293.
Clark, D. B. (2006). Longitudinal conceptual change in students' understanding of thermal equilibrium: An examination of the process of conceptual restructuring. *Cognition and Instruction, 24,* 467–563.
Clark, J. M., & Paivio, A. (1991). Dual coding theory and education. *Educational Psychology Review, 3,* 149–210.
Clark, R. E., & Blake, S. B. (1997). Designing training for novel problem-solving transfer. In R. D. Tennyson, F. Schott, N. M. Seel, & S. Dijkstra (Eds.), *Instructional design: International perspectives. Vol. 1: Theory, research, and models* (pp. 183–214). Mahwah, NJ: Erlbaum.
Clark, R. M. (1983). *Family life and school achievement: Why poor black children succeed or fail*. Chicago: University of Chicago Press.
Clarke, S., Dunlap, G., Foster-Johnson, L., Childs, K. E., Wilson, D., White, R., & Vera, A. (1995). Improving the conduct of students with behavioral disorders by incorporating student interests into curricular areas. *Behavioral Disorders, 20,* 221–237.
Clement, J. (1991). Non-formal reasoning in science: The use of analogies, extreme cases, and physical intuition. In J. F. Voss, D. N. Perkins, & J. Siegel (Eds.), *Informal reasoning and education*. Hillsdale, NJ: Erlbaum.
Cleveland, M. J., Gibbons, F. X., Gerrard, M., Pomery, E. A., & Brody, G. H. (2005). The impact of parenting on risk cognitions and risk behavior: A study of mediation and moderation in a panel of African American adolescents. *Child Development, 76,* 900–916.
Clifford, M. M. (1990). Students need challenge, not easy success. *Educational Leadership, 48*(1), 22–26.
Cobb, P., Wood, T., Yackel, E., Nicholls, J., Wheatley, G., Trigatti, B., & Perlwitz, M. (1991). Assessment of a problem centered second-grade mathematics project. *Journal for Research in Mathematics Education, 22,* 3–29.
Cobb, P., & Yackel, E. (1996). Constructivist, emergent, and sociocultural perspectives in the context of developmental research. *Educational Psychologist, 31,* 175–190.
Coch, D., Dawson, G., & Fischer, K. W. (Eds.). (2007). *Human behavior, learning, and the developing brain: Atypical development*. New York: Guilford Press.
Cochran, K. F., & Jones, L. L. (1998). The subject matter knowledge of preservice science teachers. In B. J. Fraser & K. G. Tobin (Eds.), *International handbook of science education* (Part II). Dordrecht, Netherlands: Kluwer.
Cochran-Smith, M., & Lytle, S. (1993). *Inside out: Teacher research and knowledge*. New York: Teachers College Press.
Coddington, C. S., & Guthrie, J. T. (2008, March). *Intrinsic and avoidance motivation for school reading*. Paper presented at the annual meeting of the American Educational Research Association, New York.
Coe, J., Salamon, L., & Molnar, J. (1991). *Homeless children and youth*. New Brunswick, NJ: Transaction.
Cognition and Technology Group at Vanderbilt. (1990). Anchored instruction and its relationship to situated cognition. *Educational Researcher, 19*(6), 2–10.
Cognition and Technology Group at Vanderbilt. (1993). Anchored instruction and situated cognition revisited. *Educational Technology, 33*(3), 52–70.
Cognition and Technology Group at Vanderbilt. (1996). Looking at technology in context: A framework for understanding technology and education research. In D. C. Berliner & R. C. Calfee (Eds.), *Handbook of educational psychology* (pp. 807–840). New York: Macmillan.
Cohen, E. G. (1994). Restructuring the classroom: Conditions for productive small groups. *Review of Educational Research, 64,* 1–35.
Cohen, E. G., Lockheed, M. E., & Lohman, M. R. (1976). The center for interracial cooperation: A field experiment. *Sociology of Education, 59,* 47–58.
Cohen, E. G., & Lotan, R. A. (1995). Producing equal-status interaction in the heterogeneous classroom. *American Educational Research Journal, 32,* 99–120.
Cohen, I. L. (2007). A neural network model of autism: Implications for theory and treatment. In D. Mareschal, S. Sirois, G. Westermann, & M. H. Johnson (Eds.), *Neuroconstructivism: Vol. 2. Perspectives and prospects* (pp. 231–264). Oxford, England: Oxford University Press.
Cohen, R. L. (1989). Memory for action events: The power of enactment. *Educational Psychology Review, 1,* 57–80.
Coie, J. D., & Cillessen, A. H. N. (1993). Peer rejection: Origins and effects on children's development. *Current Directions in Psychological Science, 2,* 89–92.
Coie, J. D., & Dodge, K. A. (1998). Aggression and antisocial behavior. In W. Damon (Series Ed.) & N. Eisenberg (Vol. Ed.), *Handbook of child psychology: Vol. 3. Social, emotional, and personality development* (5th ed., pp. 779–862). New York: Wiley.
Colby, A., & Kohlberg, L. (1984). Invariant sequence and internal consistency in moral judgment stages. In W. M. Kurtines & J. L. Gewirtz (Eds.), *Morality, moral behavior, and moral development*. New York: Wiley.
Colby, A., Kohlberg, L., Gibbs, J., & Lieberman, M. (1983). A longitudinal study of moral judgment. *Monographs of the Society for Research in Child Development, 48*(1–2, Serial No. 200).
Cole, A. S., & Ibarra, R. A. (2005). Examining gender-related differential item functioning using insights from psychometric and multicontext theory. In A. M. Gallagher & J. C. Kaufman (Eds.), *Gender differences in mathematics: An integrative psychological approach* (pp. 143–171). Cambridge, England: Cambridge University Press.
Cole, D. A., Martin, J. M., Peeke, L. A., Seroczynski, A. D., & Fier, J. (1999). Children's over- and underestimation of academic competence: A longitudinal study of gender differences, depression, and anxiety. *Child Development, 70,* 459–473.
Cole, D. A., Maxwell, S. E., Martin, J. M., Peeke, L. G., Seroczynski, A. D., Tram, J. M., Hoffman, K. B., Ruiz, M. D., Jacquez, F., & Maschman, T. (2001). The development of multiple domains of child and adolescent self-concept: A cohort sequential longitudinal design. *Child Development, 72,* 1723–1746.
Cole, M. (1990). Cognitive development and formal schooling: The evidence from cross-cultural research. In L. C. Moll (Ed.), *Vygotsky and education* (pp. 89–110). New York: Cambridge University Press.
Cole, M. (2006). Culture and cognitive development in phylogenetic, historical and ontogenetic perspective. In W. Damon & R. M. Lerner (Series Eds.), D. Kuhn, & R. Siegler (Vol. Eds.), *Handbook of child psychology: Vol. 2. Cognition, perception, and language* (6th ed.). New York: Wiley.
Cole, N. S. (1990). Conceptions of educational achievement. *Educational Researcher, 19*(3), 2–7.
Cole, P. M., Bruschi, C. J., & Tamang, B. L. (2002). Cultural differences in children's emotional reactions to difficult situations. *Child Development, 73,* 983–996.
Cole, P. M., Tamang, B. L., & Shrestha, S. (2006). Cultural variations in the socialization of young children's anger and shame. *Child Development, 77,* 1237–1251.
Cole, P. M., & Tan, P. Z. (2007). Emotion socialization from a cultural perspective. In J. E. Grusec & P. D. Hastings (Eds.), *Handbook of socialization: Theory and research* (pp. 516–542). New York: Guilford Press.
Collier, V. P. (1992). The Canadian bilingual immersion debate: A synthesis of research findings. *Studies in Second Language Acquisition, 14,* 87–97.
Collins, A. (2006). Cognitive apprenticeship. In R. K. Sawyer (Ed.), *The Cambridge handbook of the learning sciences* (pp. 47–60). Cambridge, England: Cambridge University Press.
Collins, A., Brown, J. S., & Newman, S. E. (1989). Cognitive apprenticeship: Teaching the crafts of reading, writing, and mathematics. In L. B. Resnick (Ed.), *Knowing, learning, and instruction: Essays in honor of Robert Glaser*. Mahwah, NJ: Erlbaum.
Collins, W. A., Maccoby, E. E., Steinberg, L., Hetherington, E. M., & Bornstein, M. H. (2000). Contemporary research on parenting: The case for nature and nurture. *American Psychologist, 55,* 218–232.
Coltheart, M., Lea, C. D., & Thompson, K. (1974). In defense of iconic memory. *Quarterly Journal of Experimental Psychology, 26,* 633–641.
Colvin, G., Ainge, D., & Nelson, R. (1997). How to defuse defiance, threats, challenges, confrontations. *Teaching Exceptional Children, 29*(6), 47–51.

Combs, A. W., Richards, A. C., & Richards, F. (1976). *Perceptual psychology: A humanistic approach to the study of persons*. New York: Harper & Row.

Comeau, L., Cormier, P., Grandmaison, É., & Lacroix, D. (1999). A longitudinal study of phonological processing skills in children learning to read in a second language. *Journal of Educational Psychology, 91*, 29–43.

Connell, J. P., & Wellborn, J. G. (1991). Competence, autonomy, and relatedness: A motivational analysis of self-system processes. In M. R. Gunnar & L. A. Sroufe (Eds.), *Self processes and development: The Minnesota Symposia on Child Psychology* (Vol. 23). Mahwah, NJ: Erlbaum.

Connolly, F. W., & Eisenberg, T. E. (1990). The feedback classroom: Teaching's silent friend. *T.H.E. Journal, 17*(5), 75–77.

Connolly, J., & Goldberg, A. (1999). Romantic relationships in adolescence: The role of friends and peers in their emergence and development. In W. Furman, B. B. Brown, & C. Feiring (Eds.), *The development of romantic relationships in adolescence* (pp. 266–290). Cambridge, England: Cambridge University Press.

Connor, D. F. (2006). Stimulants. In R. A. Barkley, *Attention-deficit hyperactivity disorder: A handbook for diagnosis and treatment* (3rd ed., pp. 608–647). New York: Guilford Press.

Conte, R. (1991). Attention disorders. In B. Y. L. Wong (Ed.), *Learning about learning disabilities*. San Diego, CA: Academic Press.

Conyers, C., Miltenberger, R., Maki, A., Barenz, R., Jurgens, M., Sailer, A., Haugen, M., & Kopp, B. (2004). A comparison of response cost and differential reinforcement of other behavior to reduce disruptive behavior in a preschool classroom. *Journal of Applied Behavior Analysis, 37*, 411–415.

Cook, P. J., & Ludwig, J. (2008). The burden of "acting White": Do Black adolescents disparage academic achievement? In J. U. Ogbu (Ed.), *Minority status, oppositional culture, and schooling* (pp. 275–297). New York: Routledge.

Cook, R. G., & Smith, J. D. (2006). Stages of abstraction and exemplar memorization in pigeon category learning. *Psychological Science, 17*, 1059–1067.

Cook, T. D., Herman, M. R., Phillips, M., & Settersten, R. A., Jr. (2002). Some ways in which neighborhoods, nuclear families, friendship groups, and schools jointly affect changes in early adolescent development. *Child Development, 73*, 1283–1309.

Cooney, C. (1997). *Wanted*. New York: Scholastic.

Cooper, H. (1989). Synthesis of research on homework. *Educational Leadership, 47*(3), 85–91.

Cooper, H., Lindsay, J. J., Nye, B., & Greathouse, S. (1998). Relationships among attitudes about homework, amount of homework assigned and completed, and student achievement. *Journal of Educational Psychology, 90*, 70–83.

Cooper, H., Robinson, J. C., & Patall, E. A. (2006). Does homework improve academic achievement? A synthesis of research, 1987–2003. *Review of Educational Research, 76*, 1–62.

Cooper, H., & Valentine, J. C. (2001). Using research to answer practical questions about homework. *Educational Psychologist, 36*, 143–153.

Cooper, H. M., & Good, T. (1983). *Pygmalion grows up: Studies in the expectation communication process*. White Plains, NY: Longman.

Corbett, D., Wilson, B., & Williams, B. (2002). *Effort and excellence in urban classrooms*. New York: Teachers College Press.

Corkill, A. J. (1992). Advance organizers: Facilitators of recall. *Educational Psychology Review, 4*, 33–67.

Cornell, D. G., Pelton, G. M., Bassin, L. E., Landrum, M., Ramsay, S. G., Cooley, M. R., Lynch, K. A., & Hamrick, E. (1990). Self-concept and peer status among gifted program youth. *Journal of Educational Psychology, 82*, 456–463.

Corno, L. (1993). The best-laid plans: Modern conceptions of volition and educational research. *Educational Researcher, 22*(2), 14–22.

Corno, L. (1996). Homework is a complicated thing. *Educational Researcher, 25*(8), 27–30.

Corno, L. (2008). On teaching adaptively. *Educational Psychologist, 43*, 161–173.

Corno, L., Cronbach, L. J., Kupermintz, H., Lohman, D. F., Mandinach, E. B., Porteu, A. W., & Talbert, J. E. (2002). *Remaking the concept of aptitude: Extending the legacy of Richard E. Snow*. Mahwah, NJ: Erlbaum.

Corno, L., & Mandinach, E. B. (2004). What we have learned about student engagement in the past twenty years. In D. M. McInerney & S. Van Etten (Eds.), *Big theories revisited* (pp. 299–328). Greenwich, CT: Information Age.

Corno, L., & Snow, R. E. (1986). Adapting teaching to individual differences among learners. In M. C. Wittrock (Ed.), *Handbook of research on teaching* (3rd ed.). New York: Macmillan.

Corpus, J. H., McClintic-Gilberg, M. S., & Hayenga, A. O. (2006, April). *Understanding intrinsic and extrinsic motivation: Age differences and links to children's beliefs and goals*. Paper presented at the annual meeting of the American Educational Research Association, San Francisco.

Corpus, J. H., Tomlinson, T. D., & Stanton, P. R. (April, 2004). Does social-comparison praise undermine children's intrinsic motivation? Paper presented at the American Educational Research Association, San Diego, CA.

Correa-Chávez, M., Rogoff, B., & Mejía Arauz, R. (2005). Cultural patterns in attending to two events at once. *Child Development, 76*, 664–678.

Corriveau, K., Pasquini, E., & Goswami, U. (2007). Basic auditory processing skills and specific language impairment: A new look at an old hypothesis. *Journal of Speech, Language, and Hearing Research, 50*, 647–666.

Cosden, M., Morrison, G., Albanese, A. L., & Macias, S. (2001). When homework is not home work: After-school programs for homework assistance. *Educational Psychologist, 36*, 211–221.

Costa, P. T., Jr., & McCrae, R. R. (1992). Trait psychology comes of age. In T. B. Sondereger (Ed.), *Nebraska Symposium on Motivation: Psychology and aging* (pp. 169–204). Lincoln: University of Nebraska Press.

Cothern, N. B., Konopak, B. C., & Willis, E. L. (1990). Using readers' imagery of literary characters to study text meaning construction. *Reading Research and Instruction, 30*, 15–29.

Courchesne, E., Townsend, J., Akshoomoff, N. A., Saitoh, O., Yeung-Courchesne, R., Lincoln, A. J., James, H. E., Haas, R. H., Schreibman, L., & Lau, L. (1994). Impairment of shifting attention in autistic and cerebellar patients. *Behavioral Neuroscience, 108*, 848–865.

Covington, M. V. (1987). Achievement motivation, self-attributions, and the exceptional learner. In J. D. Day & J. G. Borkowski (Eds.), *Intelligence and exceptionality*. Norwood, NJ: Ablex.

Covington, M. V. (1992). *Making the grade: A self-worth perspective on motivation and school reform*. Cambridge, England: Cambridge University Press.

Covington, M. V. (2000). Intrinsic versus extrinsic motivation in schools: A reconciliation. *Current Directions in Psychological Science, 9*, 22–25.

Covington, M. V., & Müeller, K. J. (2001). Intrinsic versus extrinsic motivation: An approach/avoidance reformulation. *Educational Psychology Review, 13*, 157–176.

Cowan, N. (1995). *Attention and memory: An integrated framework*. New York: Oxford University Press.

Cowan, N. (2007). What infants can tell us about working memory development. In L. M. Oakes & P. J. Bauer (Eds.), *Short- and long-term memory in infancy and early childhood: Taking the first steps toward remembering* (pp. 126–150). New York: Oxford University Press.

Cowan, N., Saults, J. S., & Morey, C. C. (2006). Development of working memory for verbal-spatial associations. *Journal of Memory and Language, 55*, 274–289.

Cox, B. D. (1997). The rediscovery of the active learner in adaptive contexts: A developmental-historical analysis of transfer of training. *Educational Psychologist, 32*, 41–55.

Craft, M. (1984). Education for diversity. In M. Craft (Ed.), *Educational and cultural pluralism*. London: Falmer Press.

Craft, M. A., Alberg, S. R., & Heward, W. L. (1998). Teaching elementary students with developmental disabilities to recruit teacher attention in a general education classroom: Effects on teacher praise and academic productivity. *Journal of Applied Behavior Analysis, 31*, 399–415.

Crago, M. B. (1988). *Cultural context in the communicative interaction of young Inuit children*. Unpublished doctoral dissertation, McGill University.

Crago, M. B., Annahatak, B., & Ningiuruvik, L. (1993). Changing patterns of language socialization in Inuit homes. *Anthropology and Education Quarterly, 24*, 205–223.

Craig, D. V. (2009). *Action research essentials*. San Francisco: Jossey-Bass.

Craik, F. I. M. (2006). Distinctiveness and memory: Comments and a point of view. In R. R. Hunt & J. B. Worthen, J. B. (Eds.) *Distinctiveness and memory* (pp. 425–442). Oxford, England: Oxford University Press.

Craik, F. I. M., & Watkins, M. J. (1973). The role of rehearsal in short-term memory. *Journal of Verbal Learning and Verbal Behavior, 12*, 598–607.

Crain, W. (2005). *Theories of development: Concepts and applications* (5th ed.). Upper Saddle River, NJ: Prentice Hall/Pearson.

Creasey, G. L., Jarvis, P. A., & Berk, L. E. (1998). Play and social competence. In O. N. Saracho & B. Spodek (Eds.), *Multiple perspectives on play in early childhood education*. Albany: State University of New York Press.

Crehan, K. D. (2001). An investigation of the validity of scores on locally developed performance measures in a school assessment program. *Educational and Psychological Measurement, 61*, 841–848.

Crick, N. R., & Dodge, K. A. (1994). A review and reformulation of social information-processing mechanisms in children's social adjustment. *Psychological Bulletin, 115*, 74–101.

Crick, N. R., & Dodge, K. A. (1996). Social information-processing mechanisms in reactive and proactive aggression. *Child Development, 67*, 993–1002.

Crick, N. R., Grotpeter, J. K., & Bigbee, M. A. (2002). Relationally and physically aggressive children's intent attributions and feelings of distress for relational and instrumental peer provocation. *Child Development, 73*, 1134–1142.

Crocker, J., & Knight, K. M. (2005). Contingencies of self-worth. *Current Directions in Psychological Science, 14*, 200–203.

Crockett, L., Losoff, M., & Peterson, A. C. (1984). Perceptions of the peer group and friendship in early adolescence. *Journal of Early Adolescence, 4*, 155–181.

Cromer, R. F. (1993). Language growth with experience without feedback. In P. Bloom (Ed.), *Language acquisition: Core readings*. Cambridge, MA: MIT Press.

Crone, D. A., & Horner, R. H. (2003). *Building positive behavior support systems in schools: Functional behavioral assessment*. New York: Guilford Press.

Crook, C. (1995). On resourcing a concern for collaboration within peer interactions. *Cognition and Instruction, 13*, 541–547.

Crooks, T. J. (1988). The impact of classroom evaluation practices on students. *Review of Educational Research, 58*, 438–481.

Cross, W. E., Jr., Strauss, L., & Fhagen-Smith, P. (1999). African American identity development across the life span: Educational implications. In R. H. Sheets & E. R. Hollins (Eds.), *Racial and ethnic identity in school practices: Aspects of human development* (pp. 29–47). Mahwah, NJ: Erlbaum.

Crouter, A. C., Whiteman, S. D., McHale, S. M., & Osgood, D. W. (2007). Development of gender attitude traditionality across middle childhood and adolescence. *Child Development, 78*, 911–926.

Crowley, K., & Jacobs, M. (2002). Building islands of expertise in everyday family activity. In G. Leinhardt, K. Crowley, & K. Knutson (Eds.), *Learning conversations in museums* (pp. 333–356). Mahwah, NJ: Erlbaum.

Crowley, K., & Siegler, R. S. (1999). Explanation and generalization in young children's strategy learning. *ChildDevelopment, 70,* 304–316.

Csikszentmihalyi, M. (1990). *Flow: The psychology of optimal experience.* New York: HarperPerennial.

Csikszentmihalyi, M. (1996). *Creativity: Flow and the psychology of discovery and invention.* New York: HarperCollins.

Csikszentmihalyi, M., Abuhamdeh, S., & Nakamura, J. (2005). Flow. In A. J. Elliot & C. S. Dweck (Eds.), *Handbook of competence and motivation* (pp. 598–608). New York: Guilford Press.

Csikszentmihalyi, M., & Nakamura, J. (1989). The dynamics of intrinsic motivation: A study of adolescents. In C. Ames & R. Ames (Eds.), *Research on motivation in education: Vol. 3. Goals and cognitions.* San Diego, CA: Academic Press.

Cummins, J. (1981). Age on arrival and immigrant second language learning in Canada: A reassessment. *Applied Linguistics, 2,* 132–149.

Cummins, J. (1984). *Bilingualism and special education: Issues in assessment and pedagogy.* Clevedon, England: Multilingual Matters.

Cummins, J. (2000). *Language, power, and pedagogy: Bilingual children in the crossfire.* Clevedon, England: Multlingual Matters.

Cummins, J. (2008). BICS and CALP: Empirical and theoretical status of the distinction. In B. Street & N. H. Hornberger (Eds.), *Encyclopedia of language and education* (2nd ed., Vol. 2, pp. 71–83). New York: Springer.

Cunningham, C. E., & Cunningham, L. J. (2006). Student-mediated conflict resolution programs. In R. A. Barkley, *Attention-deficit hyperactivity disorder: A handbook for diagnosis and treatment* (3rd ed., pp. 590–607). New York: Guilford Press.

Cunningham, T. H., & Graham, C. R. (2000). Increasing native English vocabulary recognition through Spanish immersion: Cognate transfer from foreign to first language. *Journal of Educational Psychology, 92,* 37–49.

Curry, L. (1990). A critique of the research on learning styles. *Educational Leadership, 47*(2), 50–56.

Curtis, K. A., & Graham, S. (1991, April). *Altering beliefs about the importance of strategy: An attributional intervention.* Paper presented at the annual meeting of the American Educational Research Association, Chicago.

Curtiss, S. (1977). *Genie: A psycholinguistic study of a modern-day "wild child."* New York: Academic Press.

Cushing, L. S., & Kennedy, C. H. (1997). Academic effects of providing peer support in general education classrooms on students without disabilities. *Journal of Applied Behavior Analysis, 30,* 139–151.

Cuskelly, M., Zhang, A., & Hayes, A. (2003). A mental age-matched comparison study of delay of gratification in children with Down syndrome. *International Journal of Disability, Development and Education, 50,* 239–251.

Dahlin, B., & Watkins, D. (2000). The role of repetition in the processes of memorizing and understanding: A comparison of the views of Western and Chinese secondary students in Hong Kong. *British Journal of Educational Psychology, 70,* 65–84.

Dai, D. Y. (2002, April). *Effects of need for cognition and reader beliefs on the comprehension of narrative text.* Paper presented at the annual meeting of the American Educational Research Association, New Orleans.

Dai, D. Y., Gonyea, N., Malkani, J., Zhang, X., & Smith, J. (2005, April). *Educational psychology in action: A qualitative study of students' pedagogical reasoning with classroom cases.* Paper presented at the annual meeting of the American Educational Research Association, Montreal.

Dai, D. Y., & Sternberg, R. J. (2004). Beyond cognitivism: Toward an integrated understanding of intellectual functioning and development. In D. Y. Dai & R. J. Sternberg (Eds.), *Motivation, emotion, and cognition: Integrative perspectives on intellectual functioning and development* (pp. 3–38). Mahwah, NJ: Erlbaum.

d'Ailly, H. (2003). Children's autonomy and perceived control in learning: A model of motivation and achievement in Taiwan. *Journal of Educational Psychology, 95,* 84–96.

Dalrymple, N. J. (1995). Environmental supports to develop flexibility and independence. In K. A. Quill (Ed.), *Teaching children with autism: Strategies to enhance communication and socialization.* New York: Delmar.

Damasio, A. R. (1994). *Descartes' error: Emotion, reason, and the human brain.* New York: Avon Books.

D'Amato, R. C., Chitooran, M. M., & Whitten, J. D. (1992). Neuropsychological consequences of malnutrition. In D. I. Templer, L. C. Hartlage, & W. G. Cannon (Eds.), *Preventable brain damage: Brain vulnerability and brain health.* New York: Springer.

Damon, W. (1984). Peer education: The untapped potential. *Journal of Applied Developmental Psychology, 5,* 331–343.

Damon, W. (1988). *The moral child: Nurturing children's natural moral growth.* New York: Free Press.

Damon, W. (1991). Putting substance into self-esteem: A focus on academic and moral values. *Educational Horizons, 70*(1), 12–18.

Damon, W., & Hart, D. (1988). *Self-understanding from childhood and adolescence.* New York: Cambridge University Press.

Danner, F. (2008, March). *The effects of perceptions of classroom assessment practices and academic press on classroom mastery goals and high school students' self-reported cheating.* Paper presented at the annual meeting of the American Educational Research Association, New York.

Danner, F. W., & Lonky, E. (1981). A cognitive-developmental approach to the effects of rewards on intrinsic motivation. *Child Development, 52,* 1043–1052.

Dansereau, D. F. (1988). Cooperative learning strategies. In C. E. Weinstein, E. T. Goetz, & P. A. Alexander (Eds.), *Learning and study strategies: Issues in assessment, instruction, and evaluation.* San Diego, CA: Academic Press.

Dansereau, D. F. (1995). Derived structural schemas and the transfer of knowledge. In A. McKeough, J. Lupart, & A. Marini (Eds.), *Teaching for transfer: Fostering generalization in learning.* Mahwah, NJ: Erlbaum.

Danthiir, V., Roberts, R. D., Schulze, R., & Wilhelm, O. (2005). Mental speed: On frameworks, paradigms, and a platform for the future. In O. Wilhelm & R. W. Engle (Eds.), *Handbook of understanding and measuring intelligence* (pp. 27–46). Thousand Oaks, CA: Sage.

Dapretto, M., Davies, M. S., Pfeifer, J. H., Scott, A. A., Sigman, M., Bookheimer, S. Y, & Iacoboni, M. (2006). Understanding emotions in others: Mirror neuron dysfunction in children with autism spectrum disorders. *Nature Neuroscience, 9*(1), 28–30.

Darch, C. B., & Kame'enui, E. J. (2004). *Instructional classroom management: A proactive approach to behavior management* (2nd ed.). Upper Saddle River, NJ: Merrill/Prentice Hall.

Darley, J. M., & Gross, P. H. (1983). A hypothesis-confirming bias in labeling effects. *Journal of Personality and Social Psychology, 44,* 20–33.

Darling-Hammond, L., Ancess, J., & Falk, B. (1995). *Authentic assessment in action: Studies of schools and students at work.* New York: Teachers College Press.

Darling-Hammond, L., & Bransford, J. (2005). *Preparing teachers for a changing world: What teachers should learn and be able to do.* San Francisco: Jossey-Bass/Wiley.

Das, J. P., Naglieri, J. A., & Kirby, J. R. (1994). *Assessment of cognitive processes.* Boston: Allyn & Bacon.

Davenport, E. C., Jr., Davison, M. L., Kuang, H., Ding, S., Kim, S., & Kwak, N. (1998). High school mathematics course-taking by gender and ethnicity. *American Educational Research Journal, 35,* 497–514.

Davidson, D. (2006). Memory for bizarre and other unusual events: Evidence from script research. In R. R. Hunt & J. B. Worthen, J. B. (Eds.) *Distinctiveness and memory* (pp. 157–179). Oxford, England: Oxford University Press.

Davidson, J. E. (2003). Insights about insightful problem solving. In J. E. Davidson & R. J. Sternberg (Eds.), *The psychology of problem solving* (pp. 149–175). Cambridge, England: Cambridge University Press.

Davidson, J. E., & Sternberg, R. J. (1998). Smart problem solving: How metacognition helps. In D. J. Hacker, J. Dunlosky, & A. C. Graesser (Eds.), *Metacognition in educational theory and practice* (pp. 47–68). Mahwah, NJ: Erlbaum.

Davidson, J. E., & Sternberg, R. J. (Eds.). (2003). *The psychology of problem solving.* Cambridge, England: Cambridge University Press.

Davies, P. G., & Spencer, S. J. (2005). The gender-gap artifact: Women's underperformance in quantitative domains through the lens of stereotype threat. In A. M. Gallagher & J. C. Kaufman (Eds.), *Gender differences in mathematics: An integrative psychological approach* (pp. 172–188). Cambridge, England: Cambridge University Press.

Davies, P. T., & Woitach, M. J. (2008). Children's emotional security in the interparental relationship. *Current Directions in Psychological Science, 17,* 269–274.

Davila, J. (2008). Depressive symptoms and adolescent romance: Theory, research, and implications. *Child Development Perspectives, 2*(1), 26–31.

Davis, C., & Yang, A. (2005). *Parents and teachers working together.* Turners Falls, MA: Northeast Foundation for Children.

Davis, G. A., & Thomas, M. A. (1989). *Effective schools and effective teachers.* Boston: Allyn & Bacon.

Davis, H. A. (2003). Conceptualizing the role and influence of student-teacher relationships on children's social and cognitive development. *Educational Psychologist, 38,* 207–234.

Davis, H. A., Schutz, P. A., & Chambless, C. B. (2001, April). *Uncovering the impact of social relationships in the classroom: Viewing relationships with teachers from different lenses.* Paper presented at the annual meeting of the American Educational Research Association, Seattle, WA.

Davis, L. E., Ajzen, I., Saunders, J., & Williams, T. (2002). The decision of African American students to complete high school: An application of the theory of planned behavior. *Journal of Educational Psychology, 94,* 810–819.

Davis-Kean, P. E., Huesmann, R., Jager, J., Collins, W. A., Bates, J. E., & Lansford, J. E. (2008). Changes in the relation of self-efficacy beliefs and behaviors across development. *Child Development, 79,* 1257–1269.

Davis-Kean, P. E., & Sandler, H. M. (2001). A meta-analysis of measures of self-esteem for young children: A framework for future measures. *Child Development, 72,* 887–906.

Dawson, G., & Bernier, R. (2007). Development of social brain circuitry in autism. In D. Coch, G. Dawson, & K. W. Fischer (Eds.), *Human behavior, learning, and the developing brain: Atypical development* (pp. 28–55). New York: Guilford Press.

Dawson, M., Soulières, I., Gernsbacher, M. A., & Mottron, L. (2007). The level and nature of autistic intelligence. *Psychological Science, 18,* 657–662.

Deaux, K. (1984). From individual differences to social categories: Analysis of a decade's research on gender. *American Psychologist, 39,* 105–116.

DeBacker, T. K., & Crowson, H. M. (2008). Measuring need for closure in classroom learners. *Contemporary Educational Psychology, 33,* 711–732.

deBettencourt, L. U. (2002). Understanding the differences between IDEA and Section 504. *Teaching Exceptional Children, 34*(3), 16–23.

DeBose, C. E. (2007). The Ebonics phenomenon, language planning, and the hegemony of Standard English. In H. S. Alim & J. Baugh (Eds.), *Talkin black talk: Language, education, and social change* (pp. 30–42). New York: Teachers College Press.

DeCasper, A. J., & Fifer, W. P. (1980). Of human bonding: Newborns prefer their mothers' voices. *Science, 208,* 1174–1176.

deCharms, R. (1972). Personal causation training in the schools. *Journal of Applied Social Psychology, 2,* 95–113.

Deci, E. L. (1992). The relation of interest to the motivation of behavior: A self-determination theory perspective. In K. A. Renninger, S. Hidi, & A. Krapp (Eds.), *The role of interest in learning and development.* Mahwah, NJ: Erlbaum.

Deci, E. L., Koestner, R., & Ryan, R. M. (2001). Extrinsic rewards and intrinsic motivation in education: Reconsidered once again. *Review of Educational Research, 71,* 1–27.

Deci, E. L., & Moller, A. C. (2005). The concept of competence: A starting place for understanding intrinsic motivation and self-determined extrinsic motivation. In A. J. Elliot & C. S. Dweck (Eds.), *Handbook of competence and motivation* (pp. 579–597). New York: Guilford Press.

Deci, E. L., & Ryan, R. M. (1985). *Intrinsic motivation and self-determination in human behavior.* New York: Plenum Press.

Deci, E. L., & Ryan, R. M. (1992). The initiation and regulation of intrinsically motivated learning and achievement. In A. K. Boggiano & T. S. Pittman (Eds.), *Achievement and motivation: A social-developmental perspective.* Cambridge, England: Cambridge University Press.

Deci, E. L., & Ryan, R. M. (1995). Human autonomy: The basis for true self-esteem. In M. H. Kernis (Ed.), *Efficacy, agency, and self-esteem.* New York: Plenum Press.

De Corte, E. (2003). Transfer as the productive use of acquired knowledge, skills, and motivations. *Current Directions in Psychological Science, 12,* 142–146.

De Corte, E., Greer, B., & Verschaffel, L. (1996). Mathematics teaching and learning. In D. C. Berliner & R. C. Calfee (Eds.), *Handbook of educational psychology.* New York: Macmillan.

Dee-Lucas, D., & Larkin, J. H. (1991). Equations in scientific proofs: Effects on comprehension. *American Educational Research Journal, 28,* 661–682.

DeGrandpre, R. J. (2000). A science of meaning: Can behaviorism bring meaning to psychological science? *American Psychologist, 55,* 721–739.

Dehaene, S. (2007). A few steps toward a science of mental life. *Mind, Brain, and Education, 1*(1), 28–47.

de Jong, T., & van Joolingen, W. R. (1998). Scientific discovery learning with computer simulations of conceptual domains. *Review of Educational Research, 68,* 179–201.

Delandshere, G., & Petrosky, A. R. (1998). Assessment of complex performances: Limitations of key measurement assumptions. *Educational Researcher, 27*(2), 14–24

deLeeuw, N., & Chi, M. T. H. (2003). Self-explanation: Enriching a situation model or repairing a domain model? In G. M. Sinatra & P. R. Pintrich (Eds.), *Intentional conceptual change* (pp. 55–78). Mahwah, NJ: Erlbaum.

Delgado-Gaitan, C. (1994). Socializing young children in Mexican-American families: An intergenerational perspective. In P. M. Greenfield & R. R. Cocking (Eds.), *Cross-cultural roots of minority child development.* Mahwah, NJ: Erlbaum.

De Lisi, R., & Golbeck, S. L. (1999). Implications of Piagetian theory for peer learning. In A. M. O'Donnell & A. King (Eds.), *Cognitive perspectives on peer learning* (pp. 3–37). Mahwah, NJ: Erlbaum.

DeLoache, J. S., & Todd, C. M. (1988). Young children's use of spatial categorization as a mnemonic strategy. *Journal of Experimental Child Psychology, 46,* 1–20.

Delval, J. (1994). Stages in the child's construction of social knowledge. In M. Carretero & J. F. Voss (Eds.), *Cognitive and instructional processes in history and the social sciences* (pp. 77–102). Mahwah, NJ: Erlbaum.

Demetriou, A., Christou, C., Spanoudis, G., & Platsidou, M. (2002). The development of mental processing: Efficiency, working memory, and thinking. *Monographs of the Society for Research in Child Development, 67*(1, Serial No. 268).

Dempster, F. N. (1985). Proactive interference in sentence recall: Topic-similarity effects and individual differences. *Memory and Cognition, 13,* 81–89.

Dempster, F. N. (1991). Synthesis of research on reviews and tests. *Educational Leadership, 48*(7), 71–76.

Dempster, F. N., & Corkill, A. J. (1999). Interference and inhibition in cognition and behavior: Unifying themes for educational psychology. *Educational Psychology Review, 11,* 1–88.

Denckla, M. B. (2007). Executive function: Binding together the definitions of attention-deficit/hyperactivity disorder and learning disabilities. In L. Meltzer (Ed.), *Executive function in education: From theory to practice* (pp. 5–18). New York: Guilford Press.

Dennis, T. A., Cole, P. M., Zahn-Waxler, C., & Mizuta, I. (2002). Self in context: Autonomy and relatedness in Japanese and U.S. mother-preschooler dyads. *Child Development, 73,* 1803–1817.

DeRidder, L. M. (1993). Teenage pregnancy: Etiology and educational interventions. *Educational Psychology Review, 5,* 87–107.

Derry, S. J. (1996). Cognitive schema theory in the constructivist debate. *Educational Psychologist, 31,* 163–174.

Derry, S. J., Levin, J. R., Osana, H. P., & Jones, M. S. (1998). Developing middle school students' statistical reasoning abilities through simulation gaming. In S. P. Lajoie (Ed.), *Reflections on statistics: Learning, teaching, and assessment in grades K–12* (pp. 175–195). Mahwah, NJ: Erlbaum.

Desberg, P., & Taylor, J. H. (1986). *Essentials of task analysis.* Lanham, MD: University Press of America.

Deshler, D. D., Schumaker, J. B., Lenz, B. K., Bulgren, J. A., Hock, M. F., Knight, J., et al. (2001). Ensuring content-area learning by secondary students with learning disabilities. *Learning Disabilities Research and Practice, 16,* 96–108.

Desoete, A., Roeyers, H., & De Clercq, A. (2003). Can offline metacognition enhance mathematical problem solving? *Journal of Educational Psychology, 95,* 188–200.

Deutsch, M. (1993). Educating for a peaceful world. *American Psychologist, 48,* 510–517.

DeVault, G., Krug, C., & Fake, S. (1996, September). Why does Samantha act that way: Positive behavioral support leads to successful inclusion. *Exceptional Parent,* 43–47.

DeVoe, J. F., Peter, K., Kaufman, P., Ruddy, S. A., Miller, A. K., Planty, M., Snyder, T. D., & Rand, M. R. (2003). *Indicators of school crime and safety: 2003* (NCES 2004–004/NCJ 201257). Washington, DC: U.S. Departments of Education and Justice. Retrieved February 27, 2004, from http://nces.ed.gov

DeVoe, J. F., Peter, K., Noonan, M., Snyder, T. D., & Baum, K. (2005). *Indicators of school crime and safety: 2005* (NCES 2006–001/NCJ 210697). Washington, DC: U.S. Departments of Education and Justice. Retrieved February 6, 2007, from http://ojp.usdoj.gov/bjs/abstract/iscs05.htm

DeVries, R. (1997). Piaget's social theory. *Educational Researcher, 26*(2), 4–17.

DeVries, R., & Zan, B. (1996). A constructivist perspective on the role of the sociomoral atmosphere in promoting children's development. In C. T. Fosnot (Ed.), *Constructivism: Theory, perspectives, and practice.* New York: Teachers College Press.

Dewhurst, S. A., & Conway, M. A. (1994). Pictures, images, and recollective experience. *Journal of Experimental Psychology: Learning, Memory, and Cognition, 20,* 1088–1098.

Deyhle, D. (2008). Navajo youth and Anglo racism: Cultural integrity and resistance. In J. U. Ogbu (Ed.), *Minority status, oppositional culture, and schooling* (pp. 433–480). New York: Routledge.

Deyhle, D., & LeCompte, M. (1999). Cultural differences in child development: Navajo adolescents in middle schools. In R. H. Sheets & E. R. Hollins (Eds.), *Racial and ethnic identity in school practices: Aspects of human development* (pp. 123–139). Mahwah, NJ: Erlbaum.

Deyhle, D., & Margonis, F. (1995). Navajo mothers and daughters: Schools, jobs, and the family. *Anthropology and Education Quarterly, 26,* 135–167.

Diamond, S. C. (1991). What to do when you can't do anything: Working with disturbed adolescents. *Clearing House, 64,* 232–234.

Diaz, R. M. (1983). Thought and two languages: The impact of bilingualism on cognitive development. In E. W. Gordon (Ed.), *Review of research in education* (Vol. 10). Washington, DC: American Educational Research Association.

Diaz, R. M., & Klingler, C. (1991). Toward an explanatory model of the interaction between bilingualism and cognitive development. In E. Bialystok (Ed.), *Language processing in bilingual children.* Cambridge, England: Cambridge University Press.

Dickens, W. T., & Flynn, J. R. (2006). Black Americans reduce the racial IQ gap: Evidence from standardization samples. *Psychological Science, 17,* 913–920.

Dien, T. (1998). Language and literacy in Vietnamese American communities. In B. Pérez (Ed.), *Sociocultural contexts of language and literacy.* Mahwah, NJ: Erlbaum.

Dijkstra, P., Kuyper, H., van der Werf, G., Buunk, A. P., & van der Zee, Y. G. (2008). Social comparison in the classroom: A review. *Review of Educational Research, 78,* 828–879.

DiMartino, J. (2007, April 25). Accountability, or mastery? *Education Week, 26*(34), 36, 44.

DiMartino, J., & Castaneda, A. (2007). Assessing applied skills. *Educational Leadership, 64,* 38–42.

Dirks, J. (1982). The effect of a commercial game on children's Block Design scores on the WISC-R test. *Intelligence, 6,* 109–123.

diSessa, A. A. (1996). What do "just plain folk" know about physics? In D. R. Olson & N. Torrance (Eds.), *The handbook of education and human development: New models of learning, teaching, and schooling.* Cambridge, MA: Blackwell.

diSessa, A. A. (2006). A history of conceptual change research. In R. K. Sawyer (Ed.), *The Cambridge handbook of the learning sciences* (pp. 265–281). Cambridge, England: Cambridge University Press.

diSessa, A. A. (2007). An interactional analysis of clinical interviewing. *Cognition and Instruction, 25,* 523–565.

diSessa, A. A., & Minstrell, J. (1998). Cultivating conceptual change with benchmark lessons. In J. G. Greeno & S. V. Goldman (Eds.), *Thinking practices in mathematics and science learning* (pp. 155–187). Hillsdale, NJ: Erlbaum.

Di Vesta, F. J., & Gray, S. G. (1972). Listening and notetaking. *Journal of Educational Psychology, 63,* 8–14.

Di Vesta, F. J., & Peverly, S. T. (1984). The effects of encoding variability, processing activity and rule example sequences on the transfer of conceptual rules. *Journal of Educational Psychology, 76,* 108–119.

Division for Learning Disabilities. (2007). *Thinking about response to intervention and learning disabilities: A teacher's guide.* Arlington, VA: Author.

Dixon, J. A., & Kelley, E. (2007). Theory revision and redescription. *Current Directions in Psychological Science, 16,* 111–115.

Dodge, K. A., Asher, S. R., & Parkhurst, J. T. (1989). Social life as a goal-coordination task. In C. Ames & R. Ames (Eds.), *Research on motivation in education: Vol. 3. Goals and cognitions.* San Diego: Academic Press.

Dodge, K. A., Greenberg, M. T., Malone, P. S., & Conduct Problems Prevention Research Group. (2008). Testing an idealized dynamic cascade model of the development of serious violence in adolescence. *Child Development, 79,* 1907–1927.

Dodge, K. A., Lansford, J. E., Burks, V. S., Bates, J. E., Pettit, G. S., Fontaine, R., & Price, J. M. (2003). Peer rejection and social information-processing factors in the development of aggressive behavior problems in children. *Child Development, 74,* 374–393.

Dodge, K. A., Lochman, J. E., Harnish, J. D., Bates, J. E., & Pettit, G. S. (1997). Reactive and proactive aggression in school children and psychiatrically impaired chronically assaultive youth. *Journal of Abnormal Psychology, 106*, 37–51.

Dodge, K. A., Pettit, G. S., Bates, J. E., & Valente, E. (1995). Social information processing patterns partially mediate the effect of early physical abuse on later conduct problems. *Journal of Abnormal Psychology, 104*, 632–643.

Dole, J. A., Duffy, G. G., Roehler, L. R., & Pearson, P. D. (1991). Moving from the old to the new: Research on reading comprehension instruction. *Review of Educational Research, 61*, 239–264.

Dole, S. (2000). The implications of the risk and resilience literature for gifted students with learning disabilities. *Roeper Review, 23*, 91–96.

Doll, B., Song, S., & Siemers, E. (2004). Classroom ecologies that support or discourage bullying. In D. L. Espelage & S. M. Swearer (Eds.), *Bullying in American schools: A social-ecological perspective on prevention and intervention* (pp. 161–183). Mahwah, NJ: Erlbaum.

Dominowski, R. L. (1998). Verbalization and problem solving. In D. J. Hacker, J. Dunlosky, & A. C. Graesser (Eds.), *Metacognition in educational theory and practice* (pp. 25–45). Mahwah, NJ: Erlbaum.

Donaldson, S. K., & Westerman, M. A. (1986). Development of children's understanding of ambivalence and causal theories of emotion. *Developmental Psychology, 22*, 655–662.

Donnelly, C. M., & McDaniel, M. A. (1993). Use of analogy in learning scientific concepts. *Journal of Experimental Psychology: Learning, Memory, and Cognition, 19*, 975–987.

Dovidio, J. F., & Gaertner, S. L. (1999). Reducing prejudice: Combating intergroup biases. *Current Directions in Psychological Science, 8*, 101–105.

Dowson, M., & McInerney, D. M. (2001). Psychological parameters of students' social and work avoidance goals: A qualitative investigation. *Journal of Educational Psychology, 93*, 35–42.

Doyle, A. (1982). Friends, acquaintances, and strangers: The influence of familiarity and ethnolinguistic backgrounds on social interaction. In K. Rubin & H. Ross (Eds.), *Peer relationships and social skills in childhood*. New York: Springer-Verlag.

Doyle, W. (1983). Academic work. *Review of Educational Research, 53*, 159–199.

Doyle, W. (1984). How order is achieved in classrooms: An interim report. *Journal of Curriculum Studies, 16*, 259–277.

Doyle, W. (1986a). Classroom organization and management. In M. C. Wittrock (Ed.), *Handbook of research on teaching* (3rd ed.). New York: Macmillan.

Doyle, W. (1986b). Content representation in teachers' definitions of academic work. *Journal of Curriculum Studies, 18*, 365–379.

Doyle, W. (1990). Classroom management techniques. In O. C. Moles (Ed.), *Student discipline strategies: Research and practice*. Albany: State University of New York Press.

Doyle, W. (2006). Ecological approaches to classroom management. In C. M. Evertson & C. S. Weinstein (Eds.), *Handbook of classroom management: Research, practice, and contemporary issues* (pp. 97–125). Mahwah, NJ: Erlbaum.

Dreikurs, R. (1998). *Maintaining sanity in the classroom: Classroom management techniques* (2nd ed.). Bristol, PA: Hemisphere.

Dreikurs, R., & Cassel, P. (1972). *Discipline without tears* (2nd ed.). New York: Dutton.

Driver, R. (1995). Constructivist approaches to science teaching. In L. P. Steffe & J. Gale (Eds.), *Constructivism in education*. Mahwah, NJ: Erlbaum.

Driver, R., Asoko, H., Leach, J., Mortimer, E., & Scott, P. (1994). Constructing scientific knowledge in the classroom. *Educational Researcher, 23*(7), 5–12.

Dryfoos, J. G. (1997). The prevalence of problem behaviors: Implications for programs. In R. P. Weissberg, T. P. Gullotta, R. L. Hampton, B. A. Ryan, & G. R. Adams (Eds.), *Enhancing children's wellness* (Vol. 8, pp. 17–46). Thousand Oaks, CA: Sage.

DuBois, D. L., Burk-Braxton, C., Swenson, L. P., Tevendale, H. D., & Hardesty, J. L. (2002). Race and gender influences on adjustment in early adolescence: Investigation of an integrative model. *Child Development, 73*, 1573–1592.

Dubow, E. F., Huesmann, L. R., & Greenwood, D. (2007). Media and youth socialization: Underlying processes and moderators of effects. In J. E. Grusec & P. D. Hastings (Eds.), *Handbook of socialization: Theory and research* (pp. 404–430). New York: Guilford Press.

Duchardt, B. A., Deshler, D. D., & Schumaker, J. B. (1995). A strategy intervention for enabling students with learning disabilities to identify and change their ineffective beliefs. *Learning Disability Quarterly, 18*, 186–201.

Duckworth, A. L., & Seligman, M. E. P. (2005). Self-discipline outdoes IQ in predicting academic performance of adolescents. *Psychological Science, 16*, 939–944.

Duckworth, A. L., & Seligman, M. E. P. (2006). Self-discipline gives girls the edge: Gender in self-discipline, grades, and achievement test scores. *Journal of Educational Psychology, 98*, 198–208.

Duff, P. A. (2001). Language, literacy, content, and (pop) culture: Challenges for ESL students in mainstream courses. *Canadian Modern Language Review, 58*(1), 103–132.

Duit, R. (1991). Students' conceptual frameworks: Consequences for learning science. In S. M. Glynn, R. H. Yeany, & B. K. Britton (Eds.), *The psychology of learning science*. Mahwah, NJ: Erlbaum.

Duke, N. K. (2000). For the rich it's richer: Print experiences and environments offered to children in very low- and very high-socioeconomic status first-grade classrooms. *American Educational Research Journal, 37*, 441–478.

DuNann, D. G., & Weber, S. J. (1976). Short- and long-term effects of contingency managed instruction on low, medium, and high GPA students. *Journal of Applied Behavior Analysis, 9*, 375–376.

Duncan, G. J., Dowsett, C. J., Claessens, A., Magnuson, K., Huston, A. C., Klevanov, P., et al. (2007). School readiness and later achievement. *Developmental Psychology, 43*, 1428–1446.

Duncan, G. J., & Magnuson, K. A. (2005). Can family socioeconomic resources account for racial and ethnic test score gaps? *The Future of Children, 15*(1), 35–54.

Duncker, K. (1945). On problem solving. *Psychological Monographs, 58* (Whole No. 270).

Dunlap, G., dePerczel, M., Clarke, S., Wilson, D., Wright, S., White, R., & Gomez, A. (1994). Choice making to promote adaptive behavior for students with emotional and behavioral challenges. *Journal of Applied Behavior Analysis, 27*, 505–518.

Dunlosky, J., Rawson, K. A., & McDonald, S. L. (2002). Influence of practice tests on the accuracy of predicting memory performance for paired associates, sentences, and text material. In T. J. Perfect & B. L. Schwartz (Eds.), *Applied metacognition* (pp. 68–92). Cambridge, England: Cambridge University Press.

Dunning, D., Heath, C., & Suls, J. M. (2004). Flawed self-assessment: Implications for health, education, and the workplace. *Psychological Science in the Public Interest, 5*, 69–106.

DuPaul, G. J., & Eckert, T. L. (1994). The effects of social skills curricula: Now you see them, now you don't. *School Psychology Quarterly, 9*, 113–132.

DuPaul, G. J., Ervin, R. A., Hook, C. L., & McGoey, K. E. (1998). Peer tutoring for children with attention deficit hyperactivity disorder: Effects on classroom behavior and academic performance. *Journal of Applied Behavior Analysis, 31*, 579–592.

DuPaul, G., & Hoff, K. (1998). Reducing disruptive behavior in general education classrooms: The use of self-management strategies. *School Psychology Review, 27*, 290–304.

Durik, A. M., & Harackiewicz, J. M. (2007). Different strokes for different folks: How individual interest moderates the effects of situational factors on task interest. *Journal of Educational Psychology, 99*, 597–610.

Durik, A. M., Vida, M., & Eccles, J. S. (2006). Task values and ability beliefs as predictors of high school literacy choices: A developmental analysis. *Journal of Educational Psychology, 98*, 382–393.

Durkin, K. (1995). *Developmental social psychology: From infancy to old age*. Cambridge, MA: Blackwell.

Durost, W. N. (1961). How to tell parents about standardized test results. *Test Service Notebook* (No. 26). New York: Harcourt, Brace, & World.

Dweck, C. S. (1986). Motivational processes affecting learning. *American Psychologist, 41*, 1040–1048.

Dweck, C. S. (2000). *Self-theories: Their role in motivation, personality, and development*. Philadelphia: Psychology Press.

Dweck, C. S., & Elliott, E. S. (1983). Achievement motivation. In E. M. Hetherington (Ed.), *Handbook of child psychology: Vol. 4. Socialization, personality, and social development* (4th ed., pp. 643–691). New York: Wiley.

Dweck, C. S., & Leggett, E. L. (1988). A social-cognitive approach to motivation and personality. *Psychological Review, 95*, 256–273.

Dweck, C. S., Mangels, J. A., & Good, C. (2004). Motivational effects on attention, cognition, and performance. In D. Y. Dai & R. J. Sternberg (Eds.), *Motivation, emotion, and cognition: Integrative perspectives on intellectual functioning and development* (pp. 41–55). Mahwah, NJ: Erlbaum.

Dweck, C. S., & Molden, D. C. (2005). Self-theories: Their impact on competence motivation and acquisition. In A. J. Elliot & C. S. Dweck (Eds.), *Handbook of competence and motivation* (pp. 122–140). New York: Guilford Press.

Dwyer, K., & Osher, D. (2000). *Safeguarding our children: An action guide*. Washington, DC: U.S. Departments of Education and Justice, American Institutes for Research. Retrieved February 26, 2004, from www.ed.gov/pubs/edpubs.html

Dwyer, K., Osher, D., & Warger, C. (1998). *Early warning, timely response: A guide to safe schools*. Washington, DC: U.S. Department of Education. Retrieved February 26, 2004, from www.ed.gov/offices/OSERS/OSEP/earlywrn.html

D'Ydewalle, G., Swerts, A., & De Corte, E. (1983). Study time and test performance as a function of test expectations. *Contemporary Educational Psychology, 8*(1), 55–67.

Dymond, S. K., Renzaglia, A., & Chun, E. (2007). Elements of effective high school service learning programs that include students with and without disabilities. *Remedial and Special Education, 28*(4), 227–243.

Dyson, A. (2008). Disproportionality in special needs education in England. *Journal of Special Education, 42*(1), 36–46.

Eacott, M. J. (1999). Memory for the events of early childhood. *Current Directions in Psychological Science, 8*, 46–49.

Eaton, J. F., Anderson, C. W., & Smith, E. L. (1984). Students' misconceptions interfere with science learning: Case studies of fifth-grade students. *Elementary School Journal, 84*, 365–379.

Eaton, W. O., & Enns, L. R. (1986). Sex differences in human motor activity level. *Psychological Bulletin, 100*, 19–28.

Ebbinghaus, H. (1913). *Memory: A contribution to experimental psychology* (H. A. Ruger & C. E. Bussenius, Trans.) New York: Teachers College, Columbia University. (Original work published 1885)

Eccles, J. S. (2005). Subjective task value and the Eccles et al. model of achievement-related choices. In A. J. Elliot & C. S. Dweck (Eds.), *Handbook of competence and motivation* (pp. 105–121). New York: Guilford Press.

Eccles, J. S. (2007). Families, schools, and developing achievement-related motivations and engagement. In J. E. Grusec & P. D. Hastings (Eds.), *Handbook of socialization: Theory and research* (pp. 665–691). New York: Guilford Press.

Eccles, J. S. (2009). Who am I and what am I going to do with my life? Personal and collective identities as motivators of action. *Educational Psychology, 44*, 78–89.

Eccles, J. S., & Jacobs, J. E. (1986). Social forces shape

math attitudes and performance. *Signs: Journal of Women in Culture and Society, 11*, 367–380.

Eccles, J. S., Jacobs, J., Harold-Goldsmith, R., Jayaratne, T., & Yee, D. (1989, April). *The relations between parents' category-based and target-based beliefs: Gender roles and biological influences.* Paper presented at the Society for Research in Child Development, Kansas City, MO.

Eccles, J. S., & Midgley, C. (1989). Stage-environment fit: Developmentally appropriate classrooms for young adolescents. In C. Ames & R. Ames (Eds.), *Research on motivation in education: Vol. 3. Goals and cognition.* San Diego, CA: Academic Press.

Eccles, J. S., Wigfield, A., & Flanagan, C., Miller, C., Reuman, D., & Yee, D. (1989). Self-concepts, domain values, and self-esteem: Relations and changes at early adolescence. *Journal of Personality, 57*, 283–310.

Eccles, J. S., Wigfield, A., & Schiefele, U. (1998). Motivation to succeed. In W. Damon (Series Ed.) & N. Eisenberg (Vol. Ed.), *Handbook of child psychology: Vol. 3. Social, emotional, and personality development* (5th ed., pp. 1017–1095). New York: Wiley.

Eccles (Parsons), J. S. (1983). Expectancies, values, and academic behaviors. In J. T. Spence (Ed.), *Achievement and achievement motivation.* San Francisco: Freeman.

Echols, L. D., West, R. F., Stanovich, K. E., & Kehr, K. S. (1996). Using children's literacy activities to predict growth in verbal cognitive skills: A longitudinal investigation. *Journal of Educational Psychology, 88*, 296–304.

Eckert, P. (1989). *Jocks and burnouts: Social categories and identity in the high school.* New York: Teachers College Press.

Edelson, D. C., & Reiser, B. J. (2006). Making authentic practices accessible to learners. In R. K. Sawyer (Ed.), *The Cambridge handbook of the learning sciences* (pp. 335–354). Cambridge, England: Cambridge University Press.

Eden, G. F., Stein, J. F., & Wood, F. B. (1995). Verbal and visual problems in reading disability. *Journal of Learning Disabilities, 28*, 272–290.

Edens, K. M., & Potter, E. F. (2001). Promoting conceptual understanding through pictorial representation. *Studies in Art Education, 42*, 214–233.

Educational Testing Service. (2008). *The Praxis Series™: Official guide.* New York: McGraw Hill.

Eeds, M., & Wells, D. (1989). Grand conversations: An explanation of meaning construction in literature study groups. *Research in the Teaching of English, 23*, 4–29.

Egbert, J. (2009). *Supporting learning with technology: Essentials of classroom practice.* Upper Saddle River, NJ: Pearson/Merrill Prentice Hall.

Eid, M., & Diener, E. (2001). Norms for experiencing emotions in different cultures: Inter- and intranational differences. *Journal of Personality and Social Psychology, 81*, 869–885.

Eigsti, I.-M., Zayas, V., Mischel, W., Shoda, Y., Ayduk, O., Dadlani, M. B., Davidson, M. C., Aber, J. L., & Casey, B. J. (2006). Predicting cognitive control from preschool to late adolescence and young adulthood. *Psychological Science, 17*, 478–484.

Eilam, B. (2001). Primary strategies for promoting homework performance. *American Educational Research Journal, 38*, 691–725.

Eisenberg, N. (1982). The development of reasoning regarding prosocial behavior. In N. Eisenberg (Ed.), *The development of prosocial behavior.* San Diego, CA: Academic Press.

Eisenberg, N. (1995). Prosocial development: A multifaceted model. In W. M. Kurtines & J. L. Gewirtz (Eds.), *Moral development: An introduction.* Boston: Allyn & Bacon.

Eisenberg, N., Carlo, G., Murphy, B., & Van Court, N. (1995). Prosocial development in late adolescence: A longitudinal study. *Child Development, 66*, 1179–1197.

Eisenberg, N., & Fabes, R. A. (1998). Prosocial development. In W. Damon (Series Ed.) & N. Eisenberg (Vol. Ed.), *Handbook of child psychology: Vol. 3. Social, emotional, and personality development* (5th ed., pp. 701–778). New York: Wiley.

Eisenberg, N., Lennon, R., & Pasternack, J. F. (1986). Altruistic values and moral judgment. In N. Eisenberg (Ed.), *Altruistic emotion, cognition, and behavior.* Mahwah, NJ: Erlbaum.

Eisenberg, N., Martin, C. L., & Fabes, R. A. (1996). Gender development and gender effects. In D. C. Berliner & R. C. Calfee (Eds.), *Handbook of educational psychology.* New York: Macmillan.

Eisenberg, N., Zhou, Q., & Koller, S. (2001). Brazilian adolescents' prosocial moral judgment and behavior: Relations to sympathy, perspective taking, gender-role orientation, and demographic characteristics. *Child Development, 72*, 518–534.

Elder, A. D. (2002). Characterizing fifth grade students' epistemological beliefs in science. In B. K. Hofer & P. R. Pintrich (Eds.), *Personal epistemology: The psychology of beliefs about knowledge and knowing* (pp. 347–363). Mahwah, NJ: Erlbaum.

Elia, J. P. (1994). Homophobia in the high school: A problem in need of a resolution. *Journal of Homosexuality, 77*(1), 177–185.

Elkind, D. (1981). *Children and adolescents: Interpretive essays on Jean Piaget* (3rd ed.). New York: Oxford University Press.

Elkind, D. (1987). *Miseducation: Preschoolers at risk.* New York: Alfred A Knopf.

Ellenwood, S., & Ryan, K. (1991). Literature and morality: An experimental curriculum. In W. M. Kurtines & J. L. Gewirtz (Eds.), *Moral behavior and development: Vol. 3. Application.* Mahwah, NJ: Erlbaum.

Elliot, A. J. (2005). A conceptual history of the achievement goal construct. In A. J. Elliot & C. S. Dweck (Eds.), *Handbook of competence and motivation* (pp. 52–72). New York: Guilford Press.

Elliot, A. J., & Dweck, C. S. (Eds.). (2005). *Handbook of competence and motivation.* New York: Guilford Press.

Elliot, A. J., & McGregor, H. A. (2000, April). Approach and avoidance goals and autonomous-controlled regulation: Empirical and conceptual relations. In A. Assor (Chair), *Self-determination theory and achievement goal theory: Convergences, divergences, and educational implications.* Symposium conducted at the annual meeting of the American Educational Research Association, New Orleans, LA.

Elliott, D. J. (1995). *Music matters: A new philosophy of music education.* New York: Oxford University Press.

Elliott, S. N., & Busse, R. T. (1991). Social skills assessment and intervention with children and adolescents. *School Psychology International, 12*, 63–83.

Ellis, E. S., & Friend, P. (1991). Adolescents with learning disabilities. In B. Y. L. Wong (Ed.), *Learning about learning disabilities.* San Diego, CA: Academic Press.

Ellis, N. R. (Ed.). (1979). *Handbook of mental deficiency: Psychological theory and research.* Mahwah, NJ: Erlbaum.

Ellis, W. E., & Zarbatany, L. (2007). Peer group status as a moderator of group influence on children's deviant, aggressive, and prosocial behavior. *Child Development, 78*, 1240–1254.

Ellison, N. B., Steinfield, C., & Lampe, C. (2007). The benefits of *Facebook* "friends": Social capital and college students' use of online social network sites. *Journal of Computer-Mediated Communication, 12*, 1143–1168.

Emmer, E. T. (1987). Classroom management and discipline. In V. Richardson-Koehler (Ed.), *Educators' handbook: A research perspective.* White Plains, NY: Longman.

Emmer, E. T. (1994, April). *Teacher emotions and classroom management.* Paper presented at the annual meeting of the American Educational Research Association, New Orleans, LA.

Emmer, E. T., & Evertson, C. M. (1981). Synthesis of research on classroom management. *Educational Leadership, 38*(4), 342–347.

Emmer, E. T., Evertson, C. M., & Worsham, M. E. (2000). *Classroom management for secondary teachers* (5th ed.). Boston: Allyn & Bacon.

Emmer, E. T., & Gerwels, M. C. (2006). Classroom management in middle and high school classrooms. In C. M. Evertson & C. S. Weinstein (Eds.), *Handbook of classroom management: Research, practice, and contemporary issues* (pp. 407–437). Mahwah, NJ: Erlbaum.

Emmer, E. T., & Stough, L. M. (2001). Classroom management: A critical part of educational psychology, with implications for teacher education. *Educational Psychologist, 36*, 103–112.

Empson, S. B. (1999). Equal sharing and shared meaning: The development of fraction concepts in a first-grade classroom. *Cognition and Instruction, 17*, 283–342.

Engle, R. A. (2006). Framing interactions to foster generative learning: A situative explanation of transfer in a community of learners. *Journal of the Learning Sciences, 15*, 451–498.

Engle, R. A., & Conant, F. R. (2002). Guiding principles for fostering productive disciplinary engagement: Explaining an emergent argument in a community of learners classroom. *Cognition and Instruction, 20*, 399–483.

Engle, R. W. (2002). Working memory capacity as executive attention. *Current Directions in Psychological Science, 11*, 19–23.

Englemann, S., & Carnine, D. (1982). *Theory of instruction: Principles and applications.* New York: Irvington.

Epstein, J. L. (1983). Longitudinal effects of family-school-person interactions on student outcomes. *Research in Sociology of Education and Socialization, 4*, 101–127.

Epstein, J. L. (1986). Friendship selection: Developmental and environmental influences. In E. Mueller & C. Cooper (Eds.), *Process and outcome in peer relationships* (pp. 129–160). New York: Academic Press.

Epstein, J. L. (1989). Family structures and student motivation. In R. E. Ames & C. Ames (Eds.), *Research on motivation in education: Vol. 3. Goals and cognitions* (pp. 259–295). New York: Academic Press.

Epstein, J. L. (1996). Perspectives and previews on research and policy for school, family, and community partnerships. In A. Booth & J. F. Dunn (Eds.), *Family-school links: How do they affect educational outcomes?* Mahwah, NJ: Erlbaum.

Epstein, J. S. (1998). Introduction: Generation X, youth culture, and identity. In J. S. Epstein (Ed.), *Youth culture: Identity in a postmodern world.* Malden, MA: Blackwell.

Erdelyi, M. H. (1985). *Psychoanalysis: Freud's cognitive psychology.* New York: Freeman.

Ericsson, K. A. (1996). *The road to excellence: The acquisition of expert performance in the arts and science, sports, and games.* Mahwah, NJ: Erlbaum.

Ericsson, K. A. (2003). The acquisition of expert performance as problem solving. In J. E. Davidson & R. J. Sternberg (Eds.), *The psychology of problem solving* (pp. 31–83). Cambridge, England: Cambridge University Press.

Eriks-Brophy, A., & Crago, M. B. (1994). Transforming classroom discourse: An Inuit example. *Language and Education, 8*(3), 105–122.

Erikson, E. H. (1963). *Childhood and society* (2nd ed.). New York: Norton.

Erikson, E. H. (1972). *Eight ages of man.* In C. S. Lavatelli & F. Stendler (Eds.), *Readings in child behavior and child development.* San Diego, CA: Harcourt Brace Jovanovich.

Erwin, P. (1993). *Friendship and peer relations in children.* Chichester, England: Wiley.

Espelage, D. L., Holt, M. K., & Henkel, R. R. (2003). Examination of peer-group contextual effects on aggression during early adolescence. *Child Development, 74*, 205–220.

Espelage, D. L., Mebane, S. E., & Adams, R. S. (2004). Empathy, caring, and bullying: Toward an understanding of complex associations. In D. L. Espelage & S. M. Swearer (Eds.), *Bullying in American schools: A social-ecological perspective on prevention and intervention* (pp. 37–61). Mahwah, NJ: Erlbaum.

Espelage, D. L., & Swearer, S. W. (Eds.). (2004). *Bullying in American schools: A social-ecological perspective on prevention and intervention*. Mahwah, NJ: Erlbaum.

Espinosa, L. (2007). English-language learners as they enter school. In R. Pianta, M. Cox, & K. Snow (Eds.), *School readiness and the transition to kindergarten in the era of accountability* (pp. 175–196). Baltimore: Brookes.

Espinosa, L. M. (2008, January). *Challenging common myths about young English language learners* (FCD Policy Brief No. 8). New York: Foundation for Child Development.

Esquivel, G. B. (1995). Teacher behaviors that foster creativity. *Educational Psychology Review, 7,* 185–202.

Evans, E. D., & Craig, D. (1990). Teacher and student perceptions of academic cheating in middle and senior high schools. *Journal of Educational Research, 84*(1), 44–52.

Evans, G. W. (2004). The environment of childhood poverty. *American Psychologist, 59,* 77–92.

Evans, G. W., & English, K. (2002). The environment of poverty: Multiple stressor exposure, psychophysiological stress, and socioemotional adjustment. *Child Development, 73,* 1238–1248.

Evans, G. W., Gonnella, C., Marcynyszyn, L. A., Gentile, L., & Salpekar, N. (2005). The role of chaos in poverty and children's socioemotional adjustment. *Psychological Science, 16,* 560–565.

Evans, G. W., & Kim, P. (2007). Childhood poverty and health: Cumulative risk exposure and stress dysregulation. *Psychological Science, 18,* 953–957.

Evans, J. J., Floyd, R. G., McGrew, K. S., & Leforgee, M. H. (2001). The relations between measures of Cattell-Horn-Carroll (CHC) cognitive abilities and reading achievement during childhood and adolescence. *School Psychology Review, 31,* 246–262.

Evertson, C. M., & Emmer, E. T. (1982). Effective management at the beginning of the year in junior high classes. *Journal of Educational Psychology, 74,* 485–498.

Evertson, C. M., Emmer, E. T., & Worsham, M. E. (2000). *Classroom management for elementary teachers* (5th ed.). Boston: Allyn & Bacon.

Evertson, C. M., & Harris, A. H. (1992). What we know about managing classrooms. *Educational Leadership, 49*(7), 74–78.

Evertson, C. M., & Weinstein, C. S. (Eds.). (2006). *Handbook of classroom management: Research, practice, and contemporary issues*. Mahwah, NJ: Erlbaum.

Eysenck, M. W. (1992). *Anxiety: The cognitive perspective*. Hove, England: Erlbaum.

Eysenck, M. W., & Keane, M. T. (1990). *Cognitive psychology: A student's handbook*. Hove, England: Erlbaum.

Fabes, R. A., Martin, C. L., & Hanish, L. D. (2003). Young children's play qualities in same-, other-, and mixed-sex peer groups. *Child Development, 74,* 921–932.

Fabos, B., & Young, M. D. (1999). Telecommunication in the classroom: Rhetoric versus reality. *Review of Educational Research, 69,* 217–259.

Fagot, B. I., Hagan, R., Leinbach, M. D., & Kronsberg, S. (1985). Differential reactions to assertive and communicative acts of toddler boys and girls. *Child Development, 56,* 1499–1505.

Fahrmeier, E. D. (1978). The development of concrete operations among the Hausa. *Journal of Cross-Cultural Psychology, 9,* 23–44.

Fairchild, H. H., & Edwards-Evans, S. (1990). African American dialects and schooling: A review. In A. M. Padilla, H. H. Fairchild, & C. M. Valadez (Eds.), *Bilingual education: Issues and strategies.* Newbury Park, CA: Sage.

Falco, L. D. (2008, March). *Improving middle school students' self-beliefs for learning mathematics: A Skill Builders intervention follow-up*. Paper presented at the annual meeting of the American Educational Research Association, New York.

Fall, R., Webb, N. M., & Chudowsky, N. (2000). Group discussion and large-scale language arts assessment: Effects on students' comprehension. *American Educational Research Journal, 37,* 911–941.

Fantuzzo, J. W., King, J., & Heller, L. R. (1992). Effects of reciprocal peer tutoring on mathematics and school adjustment: A component analysis. *Journal of Educational Psychology, 84,* 331–339.

Faraone, S. V., & Doyle, A. E. (2001). The nature and heritabilitiy of attention-deficit/hyperactivity disorder. *Child and Adolescent Psychiatrics Clinics of North America, 10,* 299–316.

Farber, B., Mindel, C. H., & Lazerwitz, B. (1988). The Jewish American family. In C. H. Mindel, R. W. Habenstein, & R. Wright (Eds.), *Ethnic families in America: Patterns and variations.* New York: Elsevier.

Farkas, G. (2008). Quantitative studies of oppositional culture: Arguments and evidence. In J. U. Ogbu (Ed.), *Minority status, oppositional culture, and schooling* (pp. 312–347). New York: Routledge.

Farran, D. C. (2001). Critical periods and early intervention. In D. B. Bailey, Jr., J. T. Bruer, F. J. Symons, & J. W. Lichtman (Eds.), *Critical thinking about critical periods* (pp. 233–266). Baltimore: Brookes.

Farrell, E. (1990). *Hanging in and dropping out: Voices of at-risk high school students.* New York: Teachers College Press.

Farver, J. A. M., & Branstetter, W. H. (1994). Preschoolers' prosocial responses to their peers' distress. *Developmental Psychology, 30,* 334–341.

Farwell, L., & Weiner, B. (1996). Self-perception of fairness in individual and group contexts. *Personality and Social Psychology Bulletin, 22,* 867–881.

Feather, N. T. (1982). *Expectations and actions: Expectancy-value models in psychology*. Mahwah, NJ: Erlbaum.

Federal Interagency Forum on Child and Family Statistics. (2007). *America's children in brief: Key national indicators of well-being, 2007.* Washington, DC: U.S. Government Printing Office.

Feldhusen, J. F., & Treffinger, D. J. (1980). *Creative thinking and problem solving in gifted education*. Dubuque, IA: Kendall/Hunt.

Feldhusen, J. F., Van Winkle, L., & Ehle, D. A. (1996). Is it acceleration or simply appropriate instruction for precocious youth? *Teaching Exceptional Children, 28*(3), 48–51.

Feldman, A. F., & Matjasko, J. L. (2005). The role of school-based extracurricular activities in adolescent development: A comprehensive review and future directions. *Review of Educational Research, 75,* 159–210.

Feldon, D. F. (2007). Cognitive load and classroom teaching: The double-edged sword of automaticity. *Educational Psychologist, 42,* 123–137.

Felner, R. D., Seitsinger, A. M., Brand, S., Burns, A., & Bolton, N. (2007). Creating small learning communities: Lessons from the project on high-performing learning communities about "what works" in creating productive, developmentally enhancing, learning contexts. *Educational Psychologist, 42,* 209–221.

Feltz, D. L., Chase, M. A., Moritz, S. E., & Sullivan, P. J. (1999). A conceptual model of coaching efficacy: Preliminary investigation and instrument development. *Journal of Educational Psychology, 91,* 765–776.

Feltz, D. L., Landers, D. M., & Becker, B. J. (1988). A revised meta-analysis of the mental practice literature on motor skill performance. In D. Druckman & J. A. Swets (Eds.), *Enhancing human performance: Issues, theories, and techniques: Background papers.* Washington, DC: National Research Council.

Fennema, E. (1987). Sex-related differences in education: Myths, realities, and interventions. In V. Richardson-Koehler (Ed.), *Educators' handbook: A research perspective.* White Plains, NY: Longman.

Fenning, P. A., & Bohanon, H. (2006). Schoolwide discipline policies: An analysis of discipline codes of conduct. In C. M. Evertson & C. S. Weinstein (Eds.), *Handbook of classroom management: Research, practice, and contemporary issues* (pp. 1021–1039). Mahwah, NJ: Erlbaum.

Ferguson, E. L., & Hegarty, M. (1995). Learning with real machines or diagrams: Application of knowledge to real-world problems. *Cognition and Instruction, 13,* 129–160.

Ferguson, R. (1998). Can schools narrow the Black-White test score gap? In C. Jencks & M. Phillips (Eds.), *The Black-White test score gap* (pp. 318–374). Washington, DC: Brookings Institute.

Ferrari, M., & Elik, N. (2003). Influences on intentional conceptual change. In G. M. Sinatra & P. R. Pintrich (Eds.), *Intentional conceptual change* (pp. 21–54). Mahwah, NJ: Erlbaum.

Ferrell, K. A. (1996). Your child's development. In M. C. Holbrook (Ed.), *Children with visual impairments: A parent's guide* (pp. 73–96). Bethesda, MD: Woodbine House.

Féry, Y.-A., & Morizot, P. (2000). Kinesthetic and visual image in modeling closed motor skills: The example of the tennis serve. *Perceptual and Motor Skills, 90,* 707–722.

Fessler, M. A., Rosenberg, M. S., & Rosenberg, L. A. (1991). Concomitant learning disabilities and learning problems among students with behavioral/emotional disorders. *Behavioral Disorders, 16,* 97–106.

Feuerstein, R. (1979). *The dynamic assessment of retarded performers: The Learning Potential Assessment Device, theory, instruments, and techniques.* Baltimore: University Park Press.

Feuerstein, R. (1980). *Instrumental enrichment: An intervention program for cognitive modifiability*. Baltimore: University Park Press.

Feuerstein, R. (1990). The theory of structural cognitive modifiability. In B. Z. Presseisen (Ed.), *Learning and thinking styles: Classroom interaction.* Washington, DC: National Education Association.

Fey, M. E., Catts, H., & Larrivee, L. (1995). Preparing preschoolers for the academic and social challenges of school. In M. E. Fey, J. Windsor, & S. F. Warren (Eds.), *Language intervention: Preschool through elementary years.* Baltimore: Brookes.

Fidler, D. J., Hepburn, S. L., Mankin, G., & Rogers, S. J. (2005). Praxis skills in young children with Down syndrome, other developmental disabilities, and typically developing children. *American Journal on Occupational Therapy, 59,* 129–138.

Fiedler, E. D., Lange, R. E., & Winebrenner, S. (1993). In search of reality: Unraveling the myths about tracking, ability grouping and the gifted. *Roeper Review, 16*(1), 4–7.

Field, D. (1987). A review of preschool conservation training: An analysis of analyses. *Developmental Review, 7,* 210–251.

Field, T. F., Woodson, R., Greenberg, R., & Cohen, D. (1982). Discrimination and imitation of facial expressions by neonates. *Science, 218*(8), 179–181.

Finders, M., & Lewis, C. (1994). Why some parents don't come to school. *Educational Leadership, 51*(8), 50–54.

Fingerhut, L. A., & Christoffel, K. K. (2002). Firearm-related death and injury among children and adolescents. *The Future of Children, 12*(2), 25–37.

Finke, R. A., & Bettle, J. (1996). *Chaotic cognition: Principles and applications*. Mahwah, NJ: Erlbaum.

Finkelhor, D., & Ormrod, R. (2000, December). *Juvenile victims of property crimes*. Washington, DC: U.S. Department of Justice, Office of Justice Programs, Office of Juvenile Justice and Delinquency Prevention.

Finn, J. D. (1989). Withdrawing from school. *Review of Educational Research, 59,* 117–142.

Finn, J. D., Pannozzo, G. M., & Achilles, C. M. (2003). The "why's" of class size: Student behavior in small classes. *Review of Educational Research, 73,* 321–368.

Finnigan, K. S., & Gross, B. (2007). Do accountability policy sanctions influence teacher motivation? Lessons from Chicago's low-performing schools. *American Educational Research Journal, 44,* 594–629.

Firestone, W. A., & Mayrowetz, D. (2000). Rethinking "high stakes": Lessons from the United States and England and Wales. *Teachers College Record, 102,* 724–749.

Fischer, K. W., & Bidell, T. (1991). Constraining nativist inferences about cognitive capacities. In S. Carey & R. Gelman (Eds.), *The epigenesis of mind: Essays on biology and cognition.* Hillsdale, NJ: Erlbaum.

Fischer, K. W., & Daley, S. G. (2007). Connecting cognitive science and neuroscience to education: Potentials and pitfalls in inferring executive processes. In L. Meltzer (Ed.), *Executive function in education: From theory to practice* (pp. 55–72). New York: Guilford Press.

Fischer, K. W., & Immordino-Yang, M. H. (2006). Cognitive development and education: From dynamic general structure to specific learning and teaching. In W. Damon & R. M. Lerner (Series Eds.), D. Kuhn, & R. Siegler (Vol. Eds.), *Handbook of child psychology: Vol. 2. Cognition, perception, and language* (6th ed.). New York: Wiley.

Fischer, K. W., Knight, C. C., & Van Parys, M. (1993). Analyzing diversity in developmental pathways: Methods and concepts. In R. Case & W. Edelstein (Eds.), *The new structuralism in cognitive development: Theory and research on individual pathways.* Basel, Switzerland: Karger.

Fischer, K. W., & Rose, S. P. (1996). Dynamic growth cycles of brain and cognitive development. In R. Thatcher, G. R. Lyon, J. Rumsey, & N. Krasnegor (Eds.), *Developmental neuroimaging: Mapping the development of brain and behavior.* New York: Academic Press.

Fiske, A. P., & Fiske, S. T. (2007). Social relationships in our species and cultures. In S. Kitayama & D. Cohen (Eds.), *Handbook of cultural psychology* (pp. 283–306). New York: Guilford Press.

Fivush, R., Haden, C., & Adam, S. (1995). Structure and coherence of preschoolers' personal narratives over time: Implications for childhood amnesia. *Journal of Experimental Child Psychology, 60,* 32–56.

Flanagan, C. A., Cumsille, P., Gill, S., & Gallay, L. S. (2007). School and community climates and civic commitments: Patterns for ethnic minority and majority students. *Journal of Educational Psychology, 99,* 421–431.

Flanagan, C. A., & Faison, N. (2001). Youth civic development: Implications of research for social policy and programs. *Social Policy Report of the Society for Research in Child Development, 15*(1), 1–14.

Flanagan, C. A., & Tucker, C. J. (1999). Adolescents' explanations for political issues: Concordance with their views of self and society. *Developmental Psychology, 35,* 1198–1209.

Flanagan, D. P., & Ortiz, S. O. (2001). *Essentials of cross-battery assessment.* New York: Wiley.

Flavell, J. H. (1994). Cognitive development: Past, present, and future. In R. D. Parke, P. A. Ornstein, J. J. Rieser, & C. Zahn-Waxler (Eds.), *A century of developmental psychology.* Washington, DC: American Psychological Association.

Flavell, J. H. (2000). Development of children's knowledge about the mental world. *International Journal of Behavioral Development, 24*(1), 15–23.

Flavell, J. H., Friedrichs, A. G., & Hoyt, J. D. (1970). Developmental changes in memorization processes. *Cognitive Psychology, 1,* 324–340.

Flavell, J. H., Green, F. L., & Flavell, E. R. (1995). Young children's knowledge about thinking. *Monographs of the Society for Research in Child Development, 60*(1, Serial No. 243).

Flavell, J. H., & Miller, P. H. (1998). Social cognition. In W. Damon (Series Ed.), D. Kuhn, & R. S. Siegler (Vol. Eds.), *Handbook of child psychology: Vol. 2. Cognition, perception, and language* (5th ed.). New York: Wiley.

Flavell, J. H., Miller, P. H., & Miller, S. A. (2002). *Cognitive development* (4th ed.). Upper Saddle River, NJ: Prentice Hall.

Fletcher, J. M., Lyon, G. R., Fuchs, L. S., & Barnes, M. A. (2007). *Learning disabilities: From identification to intervention.* New York: Guilford Press.

Flieller, A. (1999). Comparison of the development of formal thought in adolescent cohorts aged 10 to 15 years (1967–1996 and 1972–1993). *Developmental Psychology, 35,* 1048–1058.

Flood, W. A., Wilder, D. A., Flood, A. L., & Masuda, A. (2002). Peer-mediated reinforcement plus prompting as treatment for off-task behavior in children with attention deficit hyperactivity disorder. *Journal of Applied Behavior Analysis, 35,* 199–204.

Florence, B., Gentaz, E., Pascale, C., & Sprenger-Charolles, L. (2004). The visuo-haptic and haptic exploration of letters increases the kindergarten-children's understanding of the alphabetic principle. *Cognitive Development, 19,* 433–449.

Flum, H., & Kaplan, A. (2006). Exploratory orientation as an educational goal. *Educational Psychologist, 41,* 99–110.

Flynn, J. R. (2003). Movies about intelligence: The limitations of *g*. *Current Directions in Psychological Science, 12,* 95–99.

Flynn, J. R. (2007). *What is intelligence? Beyond the Flynn effect.* New York: Cambridge University Press.

Flynn, J. R. (2008). The history of the American mind in the 20th century: A scenario to explain IQ gains over time and a case for the irrelevance of *g*. In P. C. Kyllonen, R. D. Roberts, & L. Stankov (Eds.), *Extending intelligence: Enhancement and new constructs* (pp. 245–264). New York: Erlbaum/Taylor & Francis.

Fontaine, R. G., Yang, C., Dodge, K. A., Bates, J. E., & Pettit, G. S. (2008). Testing an individual systems model of response evaluation and decision (RED) and antisocial behavior across adolescence. *Child Development, 79,* 462–475.

Foos, P. W., & Fisher, R. P. (1988). Using tests as learning opportunities. *Journal of Educational Psychology, 80,* 179–183.

Ford, D. Y., & Harris, J. J. (1992). The American achievement ideology and achievement differentials among preadolescent gifted and nongifted African American males and females. *The Journal of Negro Education, 61*(1), 45–64.

Ford, D. Y., Moore, J. L., III, & Whiting, G. W. (2006). Eliminating deficit orientations: Creating classrooms and curricula for gifted students from diverse cultural backgrounds. In M. G. Constantine & D. W. Sue (Eds.), *Addressing racism: Facilitating cultural competence in mental health and educational settings* (pp. 173–193). New York: Wiley.

Ford, M. E. (1992). *Motivating humans: Goals, emotions, and personal agency beliefs.* Newbury Park, CA: Sage.

Ford, M. E. (1996). Motivational opportunities and obstacles associated with social responsibility and caring behavior in school contexts. In J. Juvonen & K. R. Wentzel (Eds.), *Social motivation: Understanding children's school adjustment* (pp. 126–153). Cambridge, England: Cambridge University Press.

Ford, M. E., & Smith, P. R. (2007). Thriving with social purpose: An integrative approach to the development of optimal human functioning. *Educational Psychologist, 42,* 153–171.

Försterling, F., & Morgenstern, M. (2002). Accuracy of self-assessment and task performance: Does it pay to know the truth? *Journal of Educational Psychology, 94,* 576–585.

Fosnot, C. T. (1996). Constructivism: A psychological theory of learning. In C. T. Fosnot (Ed.), *Constructivism: Theory, perspectives, and practice.* New York: Teachers College Press.

Foster-Johnson, L., Ferro, J., & Dunlap, G. (1994). Preferred curriculum activities and reduced problem behaviors in students with intellectual disabilities. *Journal of Applied Behavior Analysis, 27,* 493–504.

Fowler, S. A., & Baer, D. M. (1981). "Do I have to be good all day?" The timing of delayed reinforcement as a factor in generalization. *Journal of Applied Behavior Analysis, 14,* 13–24.

Fox, N. A., Henderson, H. A., Rubin, K. H., Calkins, S. D., & Schmidt, L. A. (2001). Continuity and discontinuity of behavioral inhibition and exuberance: Psychophysical and behavioral influences across the first four years of life. *Child Development, 72,* 1–21.

Fox, P. W., & LeCount, J. (1991, April). *When more is less: Faculty misestimation of student learning.* Paper presented at the annual meeting of the American Educational Research Association, Chicago.

Frankenberger, K. D. (2000). Adolescent egocentrism: A comparison among adolescents and adults. *Journal of Adolescence, 23,* 343–354.

Frasier, M. M. (1989). Identification of gifted black students: Developing new perspectives. In C. J. Maker & S. W. Schiever (Eds.), *Critical issues in gifted education: Vol. 2. Defensible programs for cultural and ethnic minorities.* Austin, TX: Pro-Ed.

Frederiksen, J. R., & Collins, A. (1989). A systems approach to educational testing. *Educational Researcher, 18*(9), 27–32.

Frederiksen, N. (1984a). Implications of cognitive theory for instruction in problem-solving. *Review of Educational Research, 54,* 363–407.

Frederiksen, N. (1984b). The real test bias: Influences of testing on teaching and learning. *American Psychologist, 39,* 193–202.

Fredricks, J. A., Blumenfeld, P. C., & Paris, A. H. (2004). School engagement: Potential of the concept, state of the evidence. *Review of Educational Research, 74,* 59–109.

Freedman, B. A. (2003, April). *Boys and literacy: Why boys? Which boys? Why now?* Paper presented at the annual meeting of the American Educational Research Association, Chicago.

Freedman, S. G. (1990). *Small victories: The real world of a teacher, her students, and their high school.* New York: Harper & Row.

Freedom Writers, The (with Gruwell, E.). (1999). *The Freedom Writers diary: How a teacher and 150 teens used writing to change themselves and the world around them.* New York: Broadway Books.

Freeland, J. T., & Noell, G. H. (1999). Maintaining accurate math responses in elementary school students: The effects of delayed intermittent reinforcement and programming common stimuli. *Journal of Applied Behavior Analysis, 32,* 211–215.

Freeman, K. E., Gutman, L. M., & Midgley, C. (2002). Can achievement goal theory enhance our understanding of the motivation and performance of African American young adolescents? In C. Midgley (Ed.), *Goals, goal structures, and patterns of adaptive learning* (pp. 175–204). Mahwah, NJ: Erlbaum.

Freiberg, H. J., & Lapointe, J. M. (2006). Research-based programs for preventing and solving discipline problems. In C. M. Evertson & C. S. Weinstein (Eds.), *Handbook of classroom management: Research, practice, and contemporary issues* (pp. 735–786). Mahwah, NJ: Erlbaum.

French, D. C., Jansen, E. A., & Pidada, S. (2002). United States and Indonesian children's and adolescents' reports of relational aggression by disliked peers. *Child Development, 73,* 1143–1150.

Friedel, M. (1993). *Characteristics of gifted/creative children.* Warwick, RI: National Foundation for Gifted and Creative Children.

Fries, S., Dietz, F., & Schmid, S. (2008). Motivational interference in learning: The impact of leisure alternatives on subsequent self-regulation. *Contemporary Educational Psychology, 33,* 119–133.

Frisbie, D. A., & Waltman, K. K. (1992). Developing a personal grading plan. *Educational Measurement: Issues and Practice, 11*(3), 35–42. Reprinted in K. M. Cauley, F. Linder, & J. H. McMillan (Eds.), (1994), *Educational psychology 94/95.* Guilford, CT: Dushkin.

Frost, J. L., Shin, D., & Jacobs, P. J. (1998). Physical environments and children's play. In O. N. Saracho & B. Spodek (Eds.), *Multiple perspectives on play in early childhood education.* Albany: State University of New York Press.

Frydenberg, E., & Lewis, R. (2000). Teaching coping to adolescents: When and to whom? *American Educational Research Journal, 37,* 727–745.

Fuchs, D., Fuchs, L. S., Mathes, P. G., & Simmons, D. C. (1997). Peer-assisted learning strategies: Making classrooms more responsive to diversity. *American Educational Research Journal, 34,* 174–206.

Fuchs, L. S., Compton, D. L., Fuchs, D., Hollenbeck, K. N., Craddock, C. F., & Hamlett, C. L. (2008). Dynamic assessment of algebraic learning in predicting third graders' development of mathematical problem solving. *Journal of Educational Psychology, 100,* 829–850.

Fuchs, L. S., Compton, D. L., Fuchs, D., Paulsen, K., Bryant, J. D., & Hamlett, C. L. (2005). The prevention, identification, and cognitive determinants of math difficulty. *Journal of Educational Psychology, 97,* 493–513.

Fuchs, L. S., & Fuchs, D. (2007). A model for implementing responsiveness to intervention. *Teaching Exceptional Children, 39*(5), 14–20.

Fuchs, L. S., Fuchs, D., Craddock, C., Hollenbeck, K. N., Hamlett, C. L., & Schatschneider, C. (2008). Effects of small-group tutoring with and without validated classroom instruction on at-risk, students' math problem solving: Are two tiers of prevention better than one? *Journal of Educational Psychology, 100,* 491–509.

Fuchs, L. S., Fuchs, D., Karns, K., Hamlett, C. L., Dutka, S., & Katzaroff, M. (1996). The relation between student ability and the quality and effectiveness of explanations. *American Educational Research Journal, 33,* 631–664.

Fuchs, L. S., Fuchs, D., Karns, K., Hamlett, C. L., Katzaroff, M., & Dutka, S. (1997). Effects of task-focused goals on low-achieving students with and without learning disabilities. *American Educational Research Journal, 34,* 513–543.

Fuchs, L. S., Fuchs, D., Prentice, K., Burch, M., Hamlett, C. L., Owen, R., Hosp, M., & Jancek, D. (2003). Explicitly teaching for transfer: Effects on third-grade students' mathematical problem solving. *Journal of Educational Psychology, 95,* 295–305.

Fueyo, V., & Bushell, D., Jr. (1998). Using number line procedures and peer tutoring to improve the mathematics computation of low-performing first graders. *Journal of Applied Behavior Analysis, 31,* 417–430.

Fujimura, N. (2001). Facilitating children's proportional reasoning: A model of reasoning processes and effects of intervention on strategy change. *Journal of Educational Psychology, 93,* 589–603.

Fuligni, A. J. (1998). The adjustment of children from immigrant families. *Current Directions in Psychological Science, 7,* 99–103.

Fuligni, A. J., & Hardway, C. (2004). Preparing diverse adolescents for the transition to adulthood. *The Future of Children, 14*(2), 99–119.

Fuller, M. L. (2001). Multicultural concerns and classroom management. In C. A. Grant & M. L. Gomez, *Campus and classroom: Making schooling multicultural* (2nd ed., pp. 109–134). Upper Saddle River, NJ: Merrill/Prentice Hall.

Funder, D. C. (1991). Global traits: A neo-Allportian approach to personality. *Psychological Science, 2,* 31–39.

Furman, W., Brown, B. B., & Feiring, C. (Eds.). (1999). *The development of romantic relationships in adolescence.* Cambridge, England: Cambridge University Press.

Furman, W., & Simon, V. A. (1999). Cognitive representations of adolescent romantic relationships. In W. Furman, B. B. Brown, & C. Feiring (Eds.), *The development of romantic relationships in adolescence* (pp. 75–98). Cambridge, England: Cambridge University Press.

Furnham, A., & Mak, T. (1999). Sex-role stereotyping in television commercials: A review and comparison of fourteen studies done on five continents over 25 years. *Sex Roles, 41,* 413–437.

Furrer, C., & Skinner, E. (2003). Sense of relatedness as a factor in children's academic engagement and performance. *Journal of Educational Psychology, 95,* 148–162.

Gabriele, A. J. (2007). The influence of achievement goals on the constructive activity of low achievers during collaborative problem solving. *British Journal of Educational Psychology, 77,* 1221–141.

Gabriele, A. J., & Boody, R. M. (2001, April). *The influence of achievement goals on the constructive activity of low achievers during collaborative problem solving.* Paper presented at the annual meeting of the American Educational Research Association, Seattle, WA.

Gage, N. L. (1991). The obviousness of social and educational research results. *Educational Researcher, 20*(1), 10–16.

Gagné, E. D. (1985). *The cognitive psychology of school learning.* Boston: Little, Brown.

Gagné, R. M. (1985). *The conditions of learning and theory of instruction* (4th ed.). New York: Holt, Rinehart & Winston.

Gaines, M. L., & Davis, M. (1990, April). *Accuracy of teacher prediction of elementary student achievement.* Paper presented at the annual meeting of the American Educational Research Association, Boston.

Galambos, N. L., Barker, E. T., & Almeida, D. M. (2003). Parents *do* matter: Trajectories of change in externalizing and internalizing problems in early adolescence. *Child Development, 74,* 578–594.

Gallagher, A. M., & Kaufman, J. C. (Eds.). (2005). *Gender differences in mathematics: An integrative psychological approach.* Cambridge, England: Cambridge University Press.

Gallimore, R., & Goldenberg, C. (2001). Analyzing cultural models and settings to connect minority achievement and school improvement research. *Educational Psychologist, 36,* 45–56.

Gallini, J. (2000, April). *An investigation of self-regulation developments in early adolescence: A comparison between non-at-risk and at-risk students.* Paper presented at the annual meeting of the American Educational Research Association, New Orleans, LA.

Galton, F. (1880). Statistics of mental imagery. *Mind, 5,* 301–318.

Garbarino, J., Bradshaw, C. P., & Vorrasi, J. A. (2002). Mitigating the effects of gun violence on children and youth. *The Future of Children, 12*(2), 73–85.

Garbe, G., & Guy, D. (2006, Summer). No homework left behind. *Educational Leadership* (online issue). Retrieved February 23, 2009, from www.ascd.org/publications/educational_leadership/summer06/vol63/num09/toc.aspx

García, E. E. (1992). "Hispanic" children: Theoretical, empirical, and related policy issues. *Educational Psychology Review, 4,* 69–93.

García, E. E. (1994). *Understanding and meeting the challenge of student cultural diversity.* Boston: Houghton Mifflin.

García, E. E. (1995). Educating Mexican American students: Past treatment and recent developments in theory, research, policy, and practice. In J. A. Banks & C. A. M. Banks (Eds.), *Handbook of research on multicultural education.* New York: Macmillan.

García, E. E. (2005, April). *Any test in English is a test of English: Implications for high stakes testing.* Paper presented at the annual meeting of the American Educational Research Association, Montreal.

Gardiner, H. W., & Kosmitzki, C. (2008). *Lives across cultures: Cross-cultural human development* (4th ed.). Boston: Allyn & Bacon.

Gardner, H. (1983). *Frames of mind: The theory of multiple intelligences.* New York: Basic Books.

Gardner, H. (1998, April). *Where to draw the line: The perils of new paradigms.* Paper presented at the annual meeting of the American Educational Research Association, San Diego, CA.

Gardner, H. (1999). *Intelligence reframed: Multiple intelligences for the 21st century.* New York: Basic Books.

Gardner, H. (2000a). A case against spiritual intelligence. *International Journal of the Psychology of Religion, 10*(1), 27–34.

Gardner, H. (2000b). *The disciplined mind: Beyond facts and standardized tests, the K–12 education that every child deserves.* New York: Penguin Books.

Gardner, H. (2003, April). *Multiple intelligences after twenty years.* Paper presented at the annual meeting of the American Educational Research Association, Chicago.

Gardner, H., & Hatch, T. (1990). Multiple intelligences go to school: Educational implications of the theory of multiple intelligences. *Educational Researcher, 18*(8), 4–10.

Gardner, H., Torff, B., & Hatch, T. (1996). The age of innocence reconsidered: Preserving the best of the progressive traditions in psychology and education. In D. R. Olson & N. Torrance (Eds.), *The handbook of education and human development: New models of learning, teaching, and schooling.* Cambridge, MA: Blackwell.

Garibaldi, A. M. (1992). Educating and motivating African American males to succeed. *The Journal of Negro Education, 61*(1), 4–11.

Garner, R. (1998). Epilogue: Choosing to learn or not-learn in school. *Educational Psychology Review, 10,* 227–237.

Garner, R., Alexander, P. A., Gillingham, M. G., Kulikowich, J. M., & Brown, R. (1991). Interest and learning from text. *American Educational Research Journal, 28,* 643–659.

Garner, R., Brown, R., Sanders, S., & Menke, D. J. (1992). "Seductive details" and learning from text. In K. A. Renninger, S. Hidi, & A. Krapp (Eds.), *The role of interest in learning and development.* Mahwah, NJ: Erlbaum.

Garnier, H. E., Stein, J. A., & Jacobs, J. K. (1997). The process of dropping out of high school: A 19-year perspective. *American Educational Research Journal, 34,* 395–419.

Garrison, L. (1989). Programming for the gifted American Indian student. In C. J. Maker & S. W. Schiever (Eds.), *Critical issues in gifted education: Vol. 2. Defensible programs for cultural and ethnic minorities.* Austin, TX: Pro-Ed.

Gaskill, P. J. (2001, April). *Differential effects of reinforcement feedback and attributional feedback on second-graders' self-efficacy.* Paper presented at the annual meeting of the American Educational Research Association, Seattle, WA.

Gaskins, I. W., & Pressley, M. (2007). Teaching metacognitive strategies that address executive function processes within a schoolwide curriculum. In L. Meltzer (Ed.), *Executive function in education: From theory to practice* (pp. 261–286). New York: Guilford Press.

Gaskins, R. (1999). "Adding legs to a snake": A reanalysis of motivation and the pursuit of happiness from a Zen Buddhist perspective. *Journal of Educational Psychology, 91,* 204–215.

Gathercole, S. E., & Hitch, G. J. (1993). Developmental changes in short-term memory: A revised working memory perspective. In A. F. Collins, S. E. Gathercole, M. A. Conway, & P. E. Morris (Eds.), *Theories of memory.* Hove, England: Erlbaum.

Gatzke-Kopp, L. M., & Beauchaine, T. P. (2007). Central nervous system substrates of impulsivity: Implications for the development of attention-deficit/hyperactivity disorder and conduct disorder. In D. Coch, G. Dawson, & K. W. Fischer (Eds.), *Human behavior, learning, and the developing brain: Atypical development* (pp. 239–263). New York: Guilford Press.

Gaudry, E., & Bradshaw, G. D. (1971). The differential effect of anxiety on performance in progressive and terminal school examinations. In E. Gaudry & C. D. Spielberger (Eds.), *Anxiety and educational achievement.* Sydney, Australia: Wiley.

Gauvain, M. (2001). *The social context of cognitive development.* New York: Guilford Press.

Gavin, L. A., & Fuhrman, W. (1989). Age differences in adolescents' perceptions of their peer groups. *Developmental Psychology, 25,* 827–834.

Gay, G. (2006). Connections between classroom management and culturally responsive teaching. In C. M. Evertson & C. S. Weinstein (Eds.), *Handbook of classroom management: Research, practice, and contemporary issues* (pp. 343–370). Mahwah, NJ: Erlbaum.

Gayford, C. (1992). Patterns of group behavior in open-ended problem solving in science classes of 15-year-old students in England. *International Journal of Science Education, 14,* 41–49.

Gazelle, H., & Ladd, G. W. (2003). Anxious solitude and peer exclusion: A diathesis-stress model of internalizing trajectories in childhood. *Child Development, 74,* 257–278.

Gearheart, B. R., Weishahn, M. W., & Gearheart, C. J. (1992). *The exceptional child in the regular classroom* (5th ed.). Upper Saddle River, NJ: Merrill/Prentice Hall.

Geary, D. C. (1998). What is the function of mind and brain? *Educational Psychology Review, 10,* 377–387.

Geary, D. C. (2005). Folk knowledge and academic learning. In B. J. Ellis & D. F. Bjorklund (Eds.), *Origins of the social mind: Evolutionary psychology and child development* (pp. 493–519). New York: Guilford Press.

Geary, D. C., Hoard, M. K., Byrd-Craven, J., Nugent, L., & Numtee, C. (2007). Cognitive mechanisms underlying achievement deficits in children with mathematical learning disability. *Child Development, 78*, 1343–1359.

Geckeler, A. S., Libby, M. E., Graff, R. B., & Ahearn, W. H. (2000). Effects of reinforcer choice measured in single-operant and concurrent-schedule procedures. *Journal of Applied Behavior Analysis, 33*, 347–351.

Gehlbach, H., Brown, S. W., Ioannou, A., Boyer, M. A., Hudson, N., Niv-Solomon, A., et al. (2008). Increasing interest in social studies: Social perspective taking and self-efficacy in stimulating stimulations. *Contemporary Educational Psychology, 33*, 894–914.

Geiger, M. A. (1997). An examination of the relationship between answer changing, testwiseness and examination performance. *Journal of Experimental Education, 66*, 49–60.

Gelman, R., & Baillargeon, R. (1983). A review of some Piagetian concepts. In J. H. Flavell & E. M. Markman (Eds.), *Handbook of child psychology: Vol. 3. Cognitive development.* New York: Wiley.

Gelman, S. A. (2003). *The essential child: Origins of essentialism in everyday thought.* New York: Oxford University Press.

Gelman, S. A., & Kalish, C. W. (2006). Conceptual development. In W. Damon & R. M. Lerner (Series Eds.), D. Kuhn, & R. Siegler (Vol. Eds.), *Handbook of child psychology: Vol. 2. Cognition, perception, and language* (6th ed.). New York: Wiley.

Genesee, F. (1985). Second language learning through immersion: A review of U.S. programs. *Review of Educational Research, 55*, 541–561.

Genova, W. J., & Walberg, H. J. (1984). Enhancing integration in urban high schools. In D. E. Bartz & M. L. Maehr (Eds.), *Advances in motivation and achievement: Vol 1. The effects of school desegregation on motivation and achievement.* Greenwich, CT: JAI Press.

Gentner, D., & Namy, L. L. (2006). Analogical processes in language learning. *Current Directions in Psychological Science, 15*, 297–301.

Gentry, M., Gable, R. K., & Rizza, M. G. (2002). Students' perceptions of classroom activities: Are there grade-level and gender differences? *Journal of Educational Psychology, 94*, 539–544.

George, T. R., & Feltz, D. L. (1995). Motivation in sport from a collective efficacy perspective. *International Journal of Sport Psychology, 26*(1), 98–116.

Gerard, J. M., & Buehler, C. (2004). Cumulative environmental risk and youth maladjustment: The role of youth attributes. *Child Development, 75*, 1832–1849.

Gernsbacher, M. A., Stevenson, J. L., Khandakar, S., & Goldsmith, H. H. (2008). Why does joint attention look atypical in autism? *Child Development Perspectives, 2*(1), 38–45.

Gershkoff-Stowe, L., & Thelen, E. (2004). U-shaped changes in behavior: A dynamic systems perspective. *Journal of Cognition and Development, 1*(5), 11–36.

Gershoff, E. T., Aber, J. L., Raver, C. C., & Lennon, M. C. (2007). Income is not enough: Incorporating material hardship into models of income associations with parenting and child development. *Child Development, 78*, 70–95.

Gerst, M. S. (1971). Symbolic coding processes in observational learning. *Journal of Personality and Social Psychology, 19*, 7–17.

Gest, S. D., Domitrovich, C. E., & Welsh, J. A. (2005). Peer academic reputation in elementary school: Associations with changes in self-concept and academic skills. *Journal of Educational Psychology, 97*, 337–346.

Gettinger, M. (1988). Methods of proactive classroom management. *School Psychology Review, 17*, 227–242.

Gettinger, M., & Kohler, K. M. (2006). Process-outcome approaches to classroom management and effective teaching. In C. M. Evertson & C. S. Weinstein (Eds.), *Handbook of classroom management: Research, practice, and contemporary issues* (pp. 73–95). Mahwah, NJ: Erlbaum.

Ghetti, S., & Angelini, L. (2008). The development of recollection and familiarity in childhood and adolescence: Evidence from the dual-process signal detection model. *Child Development, 79*, 339–358.

Giaconia, R. M. (1988). Teacher questioning and wait-time (Doctoral dissertation, Stanford University, 1988). *Dissertation Abstracts International, 49*, 462A.

Giaconia, R. M., & Hedges, L. V. (1982). Identifying features of effective open education. *Review of Educational Research, 52*, 579–602.

Gibbs, J. C. (1995). The cognitive developmental perspective. In W. M. Kurtines & J. L. Gewirtz (Eds.), *Moral development: An introduction.* Boston: Allyn & Bacon.

Gillies, R. M. (2003). The behaviors, interactions, and perceptions of junior high school students during small-group learning. *Journal of Educational Psychology, 95*, 137–147.

Gillies, R. M., & Ashman, A. D. (1998). Behavior and interactions of children in cooperative groups in lower and middle elementary grades. *Journal of Educational Psychology, 90*, 746–757.

Gilligan, C. F. (1982). *In a different voice.* Cambridge, MA: Harvard University Press.

Gilligan, C. F. (1985, March). Keynote address. Conference on Women and Moral Theory, Stony Brook, NY.

Gilligan, C. F. (1987). Moral orientation and moral development. In E. F. Kittay & D. T. Meyers (Eds.), *Women and moral theory.* Totowa, NJ: Rowman & Littlefield.

Gilligan, C., & Attanucci, J. (1988). Two moral orientations: Gender differences and similarities. *Merrill-Palmer Quarterly, 34*, 223–237.

Gilliland, H. (1988). Discovering and emphasizing the positive aspects of the culture. In H. Gilliland & J. Reyhner (Eds.), *Teaching the Native American.* Dubuque, IA: Kendall/Hunt.

Gilpin, L. (1968). *The enduring Navaho.* Austin: University of Texas Press.

Ginsburg, H. P., Cannon, J., Eisenband, J., & Pappas, S. (2006). Mathematical thinking and learning. In K. McCartney & D. Phillips (Eds.), *Blackwell handbook of early childhood development* (pp. 208–229). Malden, MA: Blackwell.

Ginsburg-Block, M. D., Rohrbeck, C. A., & Fantuzzo, J. W. (2006). A meta-analytic review of social, self-concept, and behavioral outcomes of peer-assisted learning. *Journal of Educational Psychology, 98*, 732–749.

Girotto, V., & Light, P. (1993). The pragmatic bases of children's reasoning. In P. Light & G. Butterworth (Eds.), *Context and cognition: Ways of learning and knowing.* Mahwah, NJ: Erlbaum.

Gladwell, M. (2006, May). Behavior in the blink of an eye. Presentation at the annual meeting of the Association for Psychological Science, New York.

Glanzer, M., & Nolan, S. D. (1986). Memory mechanisms in text comprehension. In G. H. Bower (Ed.), *The psychology of learning and motivation: Advances in research and theory* (Vol. 20). San Diego, CA: Academic Press.

Glaser, D. (2000). Child abuse and neglect and the brain: A review. *Journal of Child Psychology and Psychiatry and Allied Disciplines, 41*, 97–116.

Glasser, W. (1969). *Schools without failure.* New York: Harper & Row.

Glover, J. A. (1989). The "testing" phenomenon: Not gone but nearly forgotten. *Journal of Educational Psychology, 81*, 392–399.

Glover, J. A., Ronning, R. R., & Reynolds, C. R. (Eds.). (1989). *Handbook of creativity.* New York: Plenum Press.

Glucksberg, S., & Krauss, R. M. (1967). What do people say after they have learned to talk? Studies of the development of referential communication. *Merrill-Palmer Quarterly, 13*, 309–316.

Glynn, S. M., Yeany, R. H., & Britton, B. K. (1991). A constructive view of learning science. In S. M. Glynn, R. H. Yeany, & B. K. Britton (Eds.), *The psychology of learning science.* Mahwah, NJ: Erlbaum.

Gnepp, J. (1989). Children's use of personal information to understand other people's feelings. In C. Saarni & P. L. Harris (Eds.), *Children's understanding of emotion.* Cambridge, England: Cambridge University Press.

Goddard, R. D. (2001). Collective efficacy: A neglected construct in the study of schools and student achievement. *Journal of Educational Psychology, 93*, 467–476.

Goddard, R. D., Hoy, W. K., & Woolfolk Hoy, A. (2000). Collective teacher efficacy: Its meaning, measure, and impact on student achievement. *American Educational Research Journal, 37*, 479–507.

Goetz, T., Frenzel, A. C., Hall, N. C., & Pekrun, R. (2008). Antecedents of academic emotions: Testing the internal/external frame of reference model for academic enjoyment. *Contemporary Educational Psychology, 33*, 9–33.

Goldenberg, C. (1992). The limits of expectations: A case for case knowledge about teacher expectancy effects. *American Educational Research Journal, 29*, 517–544.

Goldenberg, C. (2001). Making schools work for low-income families in the 21st century. In S. B. Neuman & D. K. Dickinson (Eds.), *Handbook of early literacy research* (pp. 211–231). New York: Guilford Press.

Goldenberg, C., Gallimore, R., Reese, L., & Garnier, H. (2001). Cause or effect? A longitudinal study of immigrant Latino parents' aspirations and expectations, and their children's school performance. *American Educational Research Journal, 38*, 547–582.

Goldstein, L. S., & Lake, V. E. (2000). "Love, love, and more love for children": Exploring preservice teachers' understanding of caring. *Teaching and Teacher Education, 16*, 861–872.

Goldstein, N. E., Arnold, D. H., Rosenberg, J. L., Stowe, R. M., & Ortiz, C. (2001). Contagion of aggression in day care classrooms as a function of peer and teacher responses. *Journal of Educational Psychology, 93*, 708–719.

Goldstein, S., & Brooks, R. B. (2006). Why study resilience? In. S. Goldstein & R. B. Brooks (Eds.), *Handbook of resilience in children* (pp. 3–15). New York: Springer.

Goldstein, S., & Rider, R. (2006). Resilience and the disruptive disorders of childhood. In. S. Goldstein & R. B. Brooks (Eds.), *Handbook of resilience in children* (pp. 203–222). New York: Springer.

Goldston, D. B., Molock, S. D., Whitbeck, L. B., Murakami, J. L., Zayas, L. H., & Nagayama Hall, G. C. (2008). Cultural considerations in adolescent suicide prevention and psychosocial treatment. *American Psychologist, 63*, 14–31.

Gollnick, D. M., & Chinn, P. C. (2002). *Multicultural education in a pluralistic society* (6th ed.). Upper Saddle River, NJ: Merrill/Prentice Hall.

Good, C., Aronson, J., & Inzlicht, M. (2003). Improving adolescents' standardized test performance: An intervention to reduce the effects of stereotype threat. *Journal of Applied Developmental Psychology, 24*, 645–662.

Good, T. L., & Brophy, J. E. (1994). *Looking in classrooms* (6th ed.). New York: HarperCollins.

Good, T. L., McCaslin, M. M., & Reys, B. J. (1992). Investigating work groups to promote problem solving in mathematics. In J. Brophy (Ed.), *Advances in research on teaching: Vol. 3. Planning and managing learning tasks and activities.* Greenwich, CT: JAI Press.

Good, T. L., & Nichols, S. L. (2001). Expectancy effects in the classroom: A special focus on improving the reading performance of minority students in first-grade classrooms. *Educational Psychologist, 36*, 113–126.

Goodenow, C. (1993). Classroom belonging among early adolescent students: Relationships to motivation and achievement. *Journal of Early Adolescence, 13*, 21–43.

Goodman, C. S., & Tessier-Lavigne, M. (1997). Molecular mechanisms of axon guidance and target recognition. In W. M. Cowan, T. M. Jessell, & S. L. Zipursky (Eds.), *Molecular and cellular approaches to neural development* (pp. 108–137). New York: Oxford University Press.

Goodnow, J. J. (1992). *Parental belief systems: The psychological consequences for children*. Mahwah, NJ: Erlbaum.

Goodwin, M. H. (2006). *The hidden life of girls: Games of stance, status, and exclusion*. Malden, MA: Blackwell.

Gootman, M. E. (1998). Effective in-house suspension. *Educational Leadership, 56*(1), 39–41.

Gopnik, A., & Meltzoff, A. N. (1997). *Words, thoughts, and theories*. Cambridge, MA: MIT Press.

Gopnik, M. (Ed.). (1997). *The inheritance and innateness of grammars*. New York: Oxford University Press.

Goswami, U. (2007). Typical reading development and developmental dyslexia across languages. In D. Coch, G. Dawson, & K. W. Fischer (Eds.), *Human behavior, learning, and the developing brain: Atypical development* (pp. 145–167). New York: Guilford Press.

Gottfredson, D. C. (2001). *Schools and delinquency*. Cambridge, England: Cambridge University Press.

Gottfredson, G. D., & Gottfredson, D. C. (1985). *Victimization in schools*. New York: Plenum Press.

Gottfried, A. E., Fleming, J. S., & Gottfried, A. W. (1994). Role of parental motivational practices in children's academic intrinsic motivation and achievement. *Journal of Educational Psychology, 86*, 104–113.

Gottfried, A. E., Fleming, J. S., & Gottfried, A. W. (2001). Continuity of academic intrinsic motivation from childhood through late adolescence: A longitudinal study. *Journal of Educational Psychology, 93*, 3–13.

Gottfried, A. W., Gottfried, A. E., Bathurst, K., & Guerin, D. W. (1994). *Gifted IQ: Early developmental aspects*. New York: Plenum Press.

Gottlieb, G. (2000). Environmental and behavioral influences on gene activity. *Current Directions in Psychological Science, 9*, 93–97.

Gottman, J. M. (1986). The world of coordinated play: Same- and cross-sex friendship in young children. In J. M. Gottman & J. G. Parker (Eds.), *Conversations of friends: Speculations on affective development* (pp. 139–191). Cambridge, England: Cambridge University Press.

Gottman, J. M., & Mettetal, G. (1986). Speculations about social and affective development: Friendship and acquaintanceship through adolescence. In J. M. Gottman & J. G. Parker (Eds.), *Conversations of friends: Speculations on affective development* (pp. 192–237). Cambridge, England: Cambridge University Press.

Gould, E., Beylin, A., Tanapat, P., Reeves, A., & Shors, T. J. (1999). Learning enhances adult neurogenesis in the hippocampal formation. *Nature Neuroscience, 2*, 260–265.

Grabe, M. (1986). Attentional processes in education. In G. D. Phye & T. Andre (Eds.), *Cognitive classroom learning: Understanding, thinking, and problem solving*. San Diego, CA: Academic Press.

Grace, D. M., David, B. J., & Ryan, M. K. (2008). Investigating preschoolers' categorical thinking about gender through imitation, attention, and the use of self-categories. *Child Development, 79*, 1928–1941.

Graesser, A. C., McNamara, D. S., & VanLehn, K. (2005). Scaffolding deep comprehension strategies through Point&Query, AutoTutor, and iSTART. *Educational Psychologist, 40*, 225–234.

Graesser, A., & Person, N. K. (1994). Question asking during tutoring. *American Educational Research Journal, 31*, 104–137.

Graham, S. (1989). Motivation in Afro-Americans. In G. L. Berry & J. K. Asamen (Eds.), *Black students: Psychosocial issues and academic achievement*. Newbury Park, CA: Sage.

Graham, S. (1990). Communicating low ability in the classroom: Bad things good teachers sometimes do. In S. Graham & V. S. Folkes (Eds.), *Attribution theory: Applications to achievement, mental health, and interpersonal conflict*. Mahwah, NJ: Erlbaum.

Graham, S. (1991). A review of attribution theory in achievement contexts. *Educational Psychology Review, 3*, 5–39.

Graham, S. (1997). Using attribution theory to understand social and academic motivation in African American youth. *Educational Psychologist, 32*, 21–34.

Graham, S., & Golen, S. (1991). Motivational influences on cognition: Task involvement, ego involvement, and depth of information processing. *Journal of Educational Psychology, 83*, 187–194.

Graham, S., & Harris, K. R. (1996). Addressing problems in attention, memory, and executive functioning. In G. R. Lyon & N. A. Krasnegor (Eds.), *Attention, memory, and executive function* (pp. 349–365). Baltimore: Brookes.

Graham, S., & Hudley, C. (1994). Attributions of aggressive and nonaggressive African-American male early adolescents: A study of construct accessibility. *Developmental Psychology, 30*, 365–373.

Graham, S., & Weiner, B. (1996). Theories and principles of motivation. In D. C. Berliner & R. C. Calfee (Eds.), *Handbook of educational psychology*. New York: Macmillan.

Grandin, T. (1995). *Thinking in pictures and other reports of my life with autism*. New York: Random House.

Grandin, T., & Johnson, C. (2005). *Animals in translation: Using the mysteries of autism to decode animal behavior*. New York: Simon & Schuster.

Granger, D. A., Whalen, C. K., Henker, B., & Cantwell, C. (1996). ADHD boys' behavior during structured classroom social activities: Effects of social demands, teacher proximity, and methylphenidate. *Journal of Attention Disorders, 1*(1), 16–30.

Grant, C. A., & Gomez, M. L. (2001). *Campus and classroom: Making schooling multicultural* (2nd ed.). Upper Saddle River, NJ: Merrill/Prentice Hall.

Grant, H., & Dweck, C. (2001). Cross-cultural response to failure: Considering outcome attributions with different goals. In F. Salili & C. Chiu (Eds.), *Student motivation: The culture and context of learning* (pp. 203–219). Dordrecht, The Netherlands: Kluwer Academic.

Gray, M. R., & Steinberg, L. (1999). Unpacking authoritative parenting: Reassessing a multidimensional concept. *Journal of Marriage and the Family, 61*, 574–587.

Gray, W. D., & Orasanu, J. M. (1987). Transfer of cognitive skills. In S. M. Cormier & J. D. Hagman (Eds.), *Transfer of learning: Contemporary research and applications*. San Diego, CA: Academic Press.

Green, C. L., Walker, J. M. T., Hoover-Dempsey, K. V., & Sandler, H. M. (2007). Parents' motivation for involvement in children's education: An empirical test of a theoretical model of parental involvement. *Journal of Educational Psychology, 99*, 532–544.

Green, L., Fry, A. F., & Myerson, J. (1994). Discounting of delayed rewards: A life-span comparison. *Psychological Science, 5*, 33–36.

Greenberg, M. T., Weissberg, R. P., O'Brien, M. U., Zins, J. E., Fredericks, L., Resnik, H., & Elias, M. J. (2003). Enhancing school-based prevention and youth development through coordinated social, emotional, and academic learning. *American Psychologist, 58*, 466–474.

Greenfield, P. M. (1994). Independence and interdependence as developmental scripts: Implications for theory, research, and practice. In P. M. Greenfield & R. R. Cocking (Eds.), *Cross-cultural roots of minority child development*. Mahwah, NJ: Erlbaum.

Greenfield, P. M. (1998). The cultural evolution of IQ. In U. Neisser (Ed.), *The rising curve: Long-term gains in IQ and related measures* (pp. 81–123). Washington, DC: American Psychological Association.

Greenfield, P. M., Trumbull, E., Keller, H., Rothstein-Fisch, C., Suzuki, L. K., & Quiroz, B. (2006). Cultural conceptions of learning and development. In P. A. Alexander & P. H. Winne (Eds.), *Handbook of educational psychology* (2nd ed., pp. 675–692). Mahwah, NJ: Erlbaum.

Greenhoot, A. F., Tsethlikai, M., & Wagoner, B. J. (2006). The relations between children's past experiences, social knowledge, and memories for social situations. *Journal of Cognition and Development, 7*, 313–340.

Greeno, J. G., Collins, A. M., & Resnick, L. B. (1996). Cognition and learning. In D. C. Berliner & R. C. Calfee (Eds.), *Handbook of educational psychology*. New York: Macmillan.

Greenough, W. T., Black, J. E., & Wallace, C. S. (1987). Experience and brain development. *Child Development, 58*, 539–559.

Greenspan, D. A., Solomon, B., & Gardner, H. (2004). The development of talent in different domains. In L. V. Shavinina & M. Ferrari (Eds.), *Beyond knowledge: Extracognitive aspects of developing high ability* (pp. 119–135). Mahwah, NJ: Erlbaum.

Greenspan, S., & Granfield, J. M. (1992). Reconsidering the construct of mental retardation: Implications of a model of social competence. *American Journal of Mental Retardation, 96*, 442–453.

Greenwood, C. R., Carta, J. J., & Hall, R. V. (1988). The use of peer tutoring strategies in classroom management and educational instruction. *School Psychology Review, 17*, 258–275.

Gregg, M., & Leinhardt, G. (1994, April). *Constructing geography*. Paper presented at the annual meeting of the American Educational Research Association, New Orleans, LA.

Gregoire, M. (2003). Is it a challenge or a threat? A dual-process model of teachers' cognition and appraisal processes during conceptual change. *Educational Psychology Review, 15*, 147–179.

Gresham, F. M., & MacMillan, D. L. (1997). Social competence and affective characteristics of students with mild disabilities. *Review of Educational Research, 67*, 377–415.

Griffin, M. M., & Griffin, B. W. (1994, April). *Some can get there from here: Situated learning, cognitive style, and map skills*. Paper presented at the annual meeting of the American Educational Research Association, New Orleans, LA.

Griffin, S. A., Case, R., & Capodilupo, A. (1995). Teaching for understanding: The importance of the central conceptual structures in the elementary mathematics curriculum. In A. McKeough, J. Lupart, & A. Marini (Eds.), *Teaching for transfer: Fostering generalization in learning*. Mahwah, NJ: Erlbaum.

Grinberg, D., & McLean-Heywood, D. (1999). *Perceptions of behavioural competence in depressed and non-depressed children with behavioural difficulties*. Paper presented at the annual meeting of the American Educational Research Association, Montreal, Canada.

Grissmer, D. W., Williamson, S., Kirby, S. N., & Berends, M. (1998). Exploring the rapid rise in Black achievement scores in the United States (1970–1990). In U. Neisser (Ed.), *The rising curve: Long-term gains in IQ and related measures* (pp. 251–285). Washington, DC: American Psychological Association.

Griswold, K. S., & Pessar, L. F. (2000). Management of bipolar disorder. *American Family Physician, 62*, 1343–1356.

Grodzinsky, G. M., & Diamond, R. (1992). Frontal lobe functioning in boys with attention-deficit hyperactivity disorder. *Developmental Neuropsychology, 8*, 427–445.

Grolnick, W. S., & Ryan, R. M. (1987). Autonomy in children's learning: An experimental and individual difference investigation. *Journal of Personality and Social Psychology, 52*, 890–898.

Gronlund, N. E. (2004). *Writing instructional objectives for teaching and assessment* (7th ed.). Upper Saddle River, NJ: Merrill/Prentice Hall.

Gronlund, N. E., & Brookhart, S. M. (2009). *Writing instructional objectives* (8th ed.). Upper Saddle River, NJ: Merrill/Pearson.

Gronlund, N. E., & Waugh, C. K. (2009). *Assessment of student achievement* (9th ed.). Upper Saddle River, NJ: Merrill/Pearson.

Gross, E. F. (2004). Adolescent Internet use: What we expect, what teens report. *Journal of Applied Developmental Psychology, 25*, 633–649.

Gross, E. F., Juvonen, J., & Gable, S. L. (2002). Internet use and well-being in adolescence. *Journal of Social Issues, 58,* 75–90.

Gruman, D. H., Harachi, T. W., Abbott, R. D., Catalano, R. F., & Fleming, C. B. (2008). Longitudinal effects of student mobility on three dimensions of elementary school engagement. *Child Development, 79,* 1833–1852.

Grusec, J. E., & Hastings, P. D. (Eds.). (2007). *Handbook of socialization: Theory and research.* New York: Guilford Press.

Guay, F., Boivin, M., & Hodges, E. V. E. (1999). Social comparison processes and academic achievement: The dependence of the development of self-evaluations on friends' performance. *Journal of Educational Psychology, 91,* 564–568.

Guerra, N. G., & Slaby, R. G. (1990). Cognitive mediators of aggression in adolescent offenders: 2. Intervention. *Developmental Psychology, 26,* 269–277.

Guerra, N. G., Huesmann, L. R., & Spindler, A. (2003). Community violence exposure, social cognition, and aggression among urban elementary school children. *Child Development, 74,* 1561–1576.

Guinee, K. (2003, April). *Comparison of second-graders' narrative stories written using paper-and-pencil and a multimedia computer-based writing tool.* Paper presented at the annual meeting of the American Educational Research Association, Chicago.

Gulley, V., Northup, J., Hupp, S., Spera, S., LeVelle, J., & Ridgway, A. (2003). Sequential evaluation of behavioral treatments and methylphenidate dosage for children with attention deficit hyperactivity disorder. *Journal of Applied Behavior Analysis, 36,* 375–378.

Gummerum, M., Keller, M., Takezawa, M., & Mata, J. (2008). To give or not to give: Children's and adolescents' sharing and moral negotiations in economic decision situations. *Child Development, 79,* 562–576.

Guskey, T. R. (1985). *Implementing mastery learning.* Belmont, CA: Wadsworth.

Guskey, T. R. (1988). Teacher efficacy, self-concept, and attitudes toward the implementation of instructional innovation. *Teaching and Teacher Education, 4,* 63–69.

Guskey, T. R., & Sparks, D. (2002, April). *Linking professional development to improvements in student learning.* Paper presented at the annual meeting of the American Educational Research Association, New Orleans, LA.

Gustafsson, J., & Undheim, J. O. (1996). Individual differences in cognitive functions. In D. C. Berliner & R. C. Calfee (Eds.), *Handbook of educational psychology.* New York: Macmillan.

Guthrie, P. (2001). "Catching sense" and the meaning of belonging on a South Carolina sea island. In S. S. Walker (Ed.), *African roots/American cultures: Africa in the creation of the Americas* (pp. 275–283). Lanham, MD: Rowman & Littlefield.

Gutiérrez, K. D., & Rogoff, B. (2003). Cultural ways of learning: Individual traits or repertoires of practice. *Educational Researcher, 32*(5), 19–25.

Hacker, D. J. (1998). Self-regulated comprehension during normal reading. In D. J. Hacker, J. Dunlosky, & A. C. Graesser (Eds.), Metacognition in educational theory and practice (pp. 165–191). Mahwah, NJ: Erlbaum.

Hacker, D. J., & Bol, L. (2004). Metacognitive theory: Considering the social-cognitive influences. In D. M. McInerney & S. Van Etten (Eds.), *Big theories revisited* (pp. 275–297). Greenwich, CT: Information Age.

Hacker, D. J., Bol, L., Horgan, D. D., & Rakow, E. A. (2000). Test prediction and performance in a classroom context. *Journal of Educational Psychology, 92,* 160–170.

Hacker, D. J., & Tenent, A. (2002). Implementing reciprocal teaching in the classroom: Overcoming obstacles and making modifications. *Journal of Educational Psychology, 94,* 699–718.

Hadjioannou, X. (2007). Bringing the background to the foreground: What do classroom environments that support authentic discussions look like? *American Educational Research Journal, 44,* 370–399.

Haenan, J. (1996). Piotr Gal'perin's criticism and extension of Lev Vygotsky's work. *Journal of Russian and East European Psychology, 34*(2), 54–60.

Hagtvet, K. A., & Johnsen, T. B. (Eds.). (1992). *Advances in test anxiety research* (Vol. 7). Amsterdam: Swets & Zeitlinger.

Hahn, H. (1989). The politics of special education. In D. K. Lipsky & A. Gartner (Eds.), *Beyond separate education: Quality education for all.* Baltimore: Brookes.

Haier, R. J. (2003). Positron emission tomography studies of intelligence: From psychometrics to neurobiology. In H. Nyborg (Ed.), *The scientific study of general intelligence.* New York: Pergamon.

Hale-Benson, J. E. (1986). *Black children: Their roots, culture, and learning styles.* Baltimore: Johns Hopkins University Press.

Halford, G. S. (1989). Cognitive processing capacity and learning ability: An integration of two areas. *Learning and Individual Differences, 1,* 125–153.

Halford, G. S., & Andrews, G. (2006). Reasoning and problem solving. In W. Damon & R. M. Lerner (Series Eds.), D. Kuhn, & R. Siegler (Vol. Eds.), *Handbook of child psychology: Vol. 2. Cognition, perception, and language* (6th ed.). New York: Wiley.

Halgunseth, L. C., Ispa, J. M., & Rudy, D. (2006). Parental control in Latino families: An integrated review of the literature. *Child Development, 77,* 1282–1297.

Hall, R. V., Axelrod, S., Foundopoulos, M., Shellman, J., Campbell, R. A., & Cranston, S. S. (1971). The effective use of punishment to modify behavior in the classroom. *Educational Technology, 11*(4), 24–26.

Hallahan, D. P., Kauffman, J. M., & Pullen, P. C. (2009). *Exceptional learners: An introduction to special education* (11th ed.). Boston: Allyn & Bacon.

Hallenbeck, M. J. (1996). The cognitive strategy in writing: Welcome relief for adolescents with learning disabilities. *Learning Disabilities Research and Practice, 11,* 107–119.

Haller, E. P., Child, D. A., & Walberg, H. J. (1988). Can comprehension be taught? A quantitative synthesis of "metacognitive" studies. *Educational Researcher, 17*(9), 5–8.

Hallinan, M. T., & Teixeria, R. A. (1987). Opportunities and constraints: Black-white differences in the formation of interracial friendships. *Child Development, 58,* 1358–1371.

Hallowell, E. (1996). *When you worry about the child you love.* New York: Simon & Schuster.

Halpern, D. F. (1997). *Critical thinking across the curriculum: A brief edition of thought and knowledge.* Mahwah, NJ: Erlbaum.

Halpern, D. F. (1998). Teaching critical thinking for transfer across domains. *American Psychologist, 53,* 449–455.

Halpern, D. F. (2004). A cognitive-process taxonomy for sex differences in cognitive abilities. *Current Directions in Psychological Science, 13,* 135–139.

Halpern, D. F. (2006). Assessing gender gaps in learning and academic achievement. In P. A. Alexander & P. H. Winne (Eds.), *Handbook of educational psychology* (2nd ed., pp. 635–653). Mahwah, NJ: Erlbaum.

Halpern, D. F. (2008). Is intelligence critical thinking? Why we need a new definition of intelligence. In P. C. Kyllonen, R. D. Roberts, & L. Stankov (Eds.), *Extending intelligence: Enhancement and new constructs* (pp. 349–370). New York: Erlbaum/ Taylor & Francis.

Halpern, D. F., Benbow, C. P., Geary, D. C., Gur, R. C., Hyde, J. S., & Gernsbacher, M. A. (2007). The science of sex differences in science and mathematics. *Psychological Science in the Public Interest, 8*(1), 1–51.

Halpern, D. F., & LaMay, M. L. (2000). The smarter sex: A critical review of sex differences in intelligence. *Educational Psychology Review, 12,* 229–246.

Halpin, G., & Halpin, G. (1982). Experimental investigations of the effects of study and testing on student learning, retention, and ratings of instruction. *Journal of Educational Psychology, 74,* 32–38.

Halvorsen, A. T., & Sailor, W. (1990). Integration of students with severe and profound disabilities: A review of research. In R. Gaylord-Ross (Ed.), *Issues and research in special education* (Vol. 1, pp. 110–172). New York: Teachers College Press.

Hambleton, R. K. (1996). Advances in assessment models, methods, and practices. In D. C. Berliner & R. C. Calfee (Eds.), *Handbook of educational psychology.* New York: Macmillan.

Hamers, J. H. M., & Ruijssenaars, A. J. J. M. (1997). Assessing classroom learning potential. In G. D. Phye (Ed.), *Handbook of academic learning: Construction of knowledge.* San Diego, CA: Academic Press.

Hamman, D., Berthelot, J., Saia, J., & Crowley, E. (2000). Teachers' coaching of learning and its relation to students' strategic learning. *Journal of Educational Psychology, 92,* 342–348.

Hammerness, K., Darling-Hammond, L., & Bransford, J. (with Berliner, D., Cochran-Smith, M., McDonald, M., & Zeichner, K.). (2005). How teachers learn and develop. In L. Darling-Hammond & J. Bransford (Eds.), *Preparing teachers for a changing world: What teachers should learn and be able to do* (pp. 358–389). San Francisco: Jossey-Bass/Wiley.

Hamovitch, B. (2007). Hoping for the best: "Inclusion" and stigmatization in a middle school. In S. Books (Ed.), *Invisible children in the society and its schools* (3rd ed., pp. 263–281). Mahwah, NJ: Erlbaum.

Hamp-Lyons, L. (1992). Holistic writing assessment for L.E.P. students. In *Focus on evaluation and measurement* (Vol. 2). Washington, DC: U.S. Department of Education.

Hampson, S. E. (2008). Mechanisms by which childhood personality traits influence adult well-being. *Current Directions in Psychological Science, 17,* 264–268.

Hamre, B. K., & Pianta, R. C. (2005). Can instructional and emotional support in the first-grade classroom make a difference for children at risk of school failure? *Child Development, 76,* 949–967.

Hanich, L. B., Jordan, N. C., Kaplan, D., & Dick, J. (2001). Performance across different areas of mathematical cognition in children with learning difficulties. *Journal of Educational Psychology, 93,* 615–626.

Hanish, L. D., Kochenderfer-Ladd, B., Fabes, R. A., Martin, C. L., & Denning, D. (2004). Bullying among young children: The influence of peers and teachers. In D. L. Espelage & S. M. Swearer (Eds.), *Bullying in American schools: A social-ecological perspective on prevention and intervention* (pp. 141–159). Mahwah, NJ: Erlbaum.

Hankin, B. L., Mermelstein, R., & Roesch, L. (2007). Sex differences in adolescent depression: Stress exposure and reactivity models. *Child Development, 78,* 279–295.

Hansen, J., & Pearson, P. D. (1983). An instructional study: Improving the inferential comprehension of good and poor fourth-grade readers. *Journal of Educational Psychology, 75,* 821–829.

Hardré, P. L., Crowson, H. M., DeBacker, T. K., & White, D. (2007). Predicting the motivation of rural high school students. *Journal of Experimental Education, 75,* 247–269.

Hardré, P. L., & Reeve, J. (2003). A motivational model of rural students' intentions to persist in, versus drop out of, high school. *Journal of Educational Psychology, 95,* 347–356.

Hardy, I., Jonen, A., Möller, K., & Stern, E. (2006). Effects of instructional support within constructivist learning environments for elementary school students' understanding of "floating and sinking." *Journal of Educational Psychology, 98,* 307–326.

Hardy, M. S. (2002). Behavior-oriented approaches to reducing youth gun violence. *The Future of Children, 12*(2), 101–117.

Hareli, S., & Weiner, B. (2002). Social emotions and personality inferences: A scaffold for a new direction in the study of achievement motivation. *Educational Psychologist, 37,* 183–193.

Haring, N. G., & Liberty, K. A. (1990). Matching strategies with performance in facilitating generalization. *Focus on Exceptional Children, 22*(8), 1–16.

Harlow, H. F., & Zimmerman, R. R. (1959). Affectional responses in the infant monkey. *Science, 130*, 421–432.

Harmon-Jones, E. (2001). The role of affect in cognitive-dissonance processes. In J. P. Forgas (Ed.), *Handbook of affect and social cognition* (pp. 237–255). Mahwah, NJ: Erlbaum.

Harnishfeger, K. K. (1995). The development of cognitive inhibition: Theories, definitions, and research evidence. In F. N. Dempster & C. J. Brainerd (Eds.), *Interference and inhibition in cognition*. San Diego, CA: Academic Press.

Harris, A. C. (1986). *Child development*. St. Paul, MN: West.

Harris, C. R. (1991). Identifying and serving the gifted new immigrant. *Teaching Exceptional Children, 23*(4), 26–30.

Harris, J. R. (1995). Where is the child's environment? A group socialization theory of development. *Psychological Review, 102*, 458–489.

Harris, J. R. (1998). *The nurture assumption: Why children turn out the way they do*. New York: Free Press.

Harris, K. R. (1982). Cognitive-behavior modification: Application with exceptional students. *Focus on Exceptional Children, 15*, 1–16.

Harris, K. R. (1986). Self-monitoring of attentional behavior versus self-monitoring of productivity: Effects of on-task behavior and academic response rate among learning disabled children. *Journal of Applied Behavior Analysis, 19*, 417–423.

Harris, K. R., & Alexander, P. A. (1998). Integrated, constructivist education: Challenge and reality. *Educational Psychology Review, 10*, 115–127.

Harris, M. (1992). *Language experience and early language development: From input to uptake*. Hove, England: Erlbaum.

Harris, M. B. (1997). Preface: Images of the invisible minority. In M. B. Harris (Ed.), *School experiences of gay and lesbian youth: The invisible minority* (pp. xiv–xxii). Binghamton, NY: Harrington Park Press.

Harris, M. J., & Rosenthal, R. (1985). Mediation of interpersonal expectancy effects: 31 meta-analyses. *Psychological Bulletin, 97*, 363–386.

Harris, N. G. S., Bellugi, U., Bates, E., Jones, W., & Rossen, M. (1997). Contrasting profiles of language development in children with Williams and Down syndromes. *Developmental Neuropsychology, 13*, 345–370.

Harris, P. L. (2006). Social cognition. In W. Damon & R. M. Lerner (Series Eds.), D. Kuhn, & R. Siegler (Vol. Eds.), *Handbook of child psychology: Vol. 2. Cognition, perception, and language* (6th ed.). New York: Wiley.

Harris, R. J. (1977). Comprehension of pragmatic implications in advertising. *Journal of Applied Psychology, 62*, 603–608.

Hart, B., & Risley, T. R. (1995). *Meaningful differences in the everyday experience of young American children*. Baltimore: Brookes.

Hart, D. (1988). The adolescent self-concept in social context. In D. K. Lapsley & F. C. Power (Eds.), *Self, ego, and identity: Integrative approaches* (pp. 71–90). New York: Springer-Verlag.

Hart, D., Atkins, R., & Fegley, S. (2003). Personality and development in childhood: A person-centered approach. *Monographs of the Society for Research in Child Development, 68*(1, Serial No. 272).

Hart, D., Donnelly, T. M., Youniss, J., & Atkins, R. (2007). High school community service as a predictor of adult voting and volunteering. *American Educational Research Journal, 44*, 197–219.

Hart, D., & Fegley, S. (1995). Prosocial behavior and caring in adolescence: Relations to self-understanding and social judgment. *Child Development, 66*, 1346–1359.

Hart, E. L., Lahey, B. B., Loeber, R., Applegate, B., & Frick, P. J. (1995). Developmental changes in attention-deficit hyperactivity disorder in boys: A four-year longitudinal study. *Journal of Abnormal Child Psychology, 23*, 729–750.

Harter, S. (1978). Pleasure derived from challenge and the effects of receiving grades on children's difficulty level choices. *Child Development, 49*, 788–799.

Harter, S. (1983). Children's understanding of multiple emotions: A cognitive-developmental approach. In W. F. Overton (Ed.), *The relationship between social and cognitive development*. Mahwah, NJ: Erlbaum.

Harter, S. (1990). Causes, correlates, and the functional role of global self-worth: A life-span perspective. In R. J. Sternberg & J. Kolligian, Jr. (Eds.), *Competence considered*. New Haven, CT: Yale University Press.

Harter, S. (1992). The relationship between perceived competence, affect, and motivational orientation within the classroom: Processes and patterns of change. In A. K. Boggiano & T. S. Pittman (Eds.), *Achievement and motivation: A social-developmental perspective*. Cambridge, England: Cambridge University Press.

Harter, S. (1996). Teacher and classmate influences on scholastic motivation, self-esteem, and level of voice in adolescents. In J. Juvonen & K. Wentzel (Eds.), *Social motivation: Understanding children's school adjustment*. New York: Cambridge University Press.

Harter, S. (1999). *The construction of the self: A developmental perspective*. New York: Guilford Press.

Harter, S., & Whitesell, N. R. (1989). Developmental changes in children's understanding of single, multiple, and blended emotion concepts. In C. Saarni & P. Harris (Eds.), *Children's understanding of emotion* (pp. 81–116). Cambridge, England: Cambridge University Press.

Harter, S., Whitesell, N. R., & Junkin, L. J. (1998). Similarities and differences in domain-specific and global self-evaluations of learning-disabled, behaviorally disordered, and normally achieving adolescents. *American Educational Research Journal, 35*, 653–680.

Harter, S., Whitesell, N. R., & Kowalski, P. (1992). Individual differences in the effects of educational transitions on young adolescents' perceptions of competence and motivational orientation. *American Educational Research Journal, 29*, 777–807.

Hartley, J., & Trueman, M. (1982). The effects of summaries on the recall of information from prose: Five experimental studies. *Human Learning, 1*, 63–82.

Hartley, K., & Bendixen, L. D. (2001). Educational research in the Internet age: Examining the role of individual characteristics. *Educational Researcher, 30*(9), 22–26.

Hartup, W. W. (1983). Peer relations. In E. M. Hetherington (Ed.), *Handbook of child psychology: Vol. 4. Socialization, personality, and social development* (4th ed., pp. 103–196). New York: Wiley.

Hartup, W. W. (1989). Social relationships and their developmental significance. *American Psychologist, 44*, 120–126.

Hartup, W. W. (1992). Friendships and their developmental significance. In H. McGurk (Ed.), *Contemporary issues in childhood social development*. London: Routledge.

Harwood, R. L., Miller, J. G., & Irizarry, N. L. (1995). *Culture and attachment: Perceptions of the child in context*. New York: Guilford Press.

Haskell, R. E. (2001). *Transfer of learning: Cognition, instruction, and reasoning*. San Diego, CA: Academic Press.

Hastings, P. D., Utendale, W. T., & Sullivan, C. (2007). The socialization of prosocial development. In J. E. Grusec & P. D. Hastings (Eds.), *Handbook of socialization: Theory and research* (pp. 638–664). New York: Guilford Press.

Hatano, G., & Inagaki, K. (1991). Sharing cognition through collective comprehension activity. In L. B. Resnick, J. M. Levine, & S. D. Teasley (Eds.), *Perspectives on socially shared cognition*. Washington, DC: American Psychological Association.

Hatano, G., & Inagaki, K. (1993). Desituating cognition through the construction of conceptual knowledge. In P. Light & G. Butterworth (Eds.), *Context and cognition: Ways of learning and knowing*. Mahwah, NJ: Erlbaum.

Hatano, G., & Inagaki, K. (2003). When is conceptual change intended? A cognitive-sociocultural view. In G. M. Sinatra & P. R. Pintrich (Eds.), *Intentional conceptual change* (pp. 407–427). Mahwah, NJ: Erlbaum.

Hatano, G., & Oura, Y. (2003). Commentary: Reconceptualizing school learning using insight from expertise research. *Educational Researcher, 32*(8), 26–29.

Hathaway, W. L., Dooling-Litfin, J. K., & Edwards, G. (2006). Integrating the results of an evaluation: Ten clinical cases. In R. A. Barkley, *Attention-deficit hyperactivity disorder: A handbook for diagnosis and treatment* (3rd ed., pp. 410–412). New York: Guilford Press.

Hattie, J., Biggs, J., & Purdie, N. (1996). Effects of learning skills interventions on student learning: A meta-analysis. *Review of Educational Research, 66*, 99–136.

Hattie, J., & Timperley, H. (2007). The power of feedback. *Review of Educational Research, 77*, 81–112.

Hauser-Cram, P., Sirin, S. R., & Stipek, D. (2003). When teachers' and parents' values differ: Teachers' ratings of academic competence in children from low-income families. *Journal of Educational Psychology, 95*, 813–820.

Hawkins, F. P. L. (1997). *Journey with children: The autobiography of a teacher*. Niwot: University Press of Colorado.

Hawley, C. A., (2005). Saint or sinner? Teacher perceptions of a child with traumatic brain injury. *Pediatric Rehabilitation, 8*, 117–129.

Haxby, J. V., Gobbini, M. I., Furey, M. L., Ishai, A., Schouten, J. L., & Pietrini, P. (2001). Distributed and overlapping representations of faces and objects in ventral temporal cortex. *Science, 293*, 2425–2430.

Hay, I., Ashman, A. F., van Kraayenoord, C. E., & Stewart, A. L. (1999). Identification of self-verification in the formation of children's academic self-concept. *Journal of Educational Psychology, 91*, 225–229.

Hay, P. J. (2008). (Mis)appropriations of criteria and standards-referenced assessment in a performance-based subject. *Assessment in Education: Principles, Policy, and Practice, 15*, 153–168.

Hayes, S. C., Rosenfarb, I., Wulfert, E., Munt, E. D., Korn, Z., & Zettle, R. D. (1985). Self-reinforcement effects: An artifact of social standard setting? *Journal of Applied Behavior Analysis, 18*, 201–214.

Hayes-Roth, B., & Thorndyke, P. W. (1979). Integration of knowledge from text. *Journal of Verbal Learning and Verbal Behavior, 18*, 91–108.

Hayslip, B., Jr. (1994). Stability of intelligence. In R. J. Sternberg (Ed.), *Encyclopedia of human intelligence* (Vol. 2). New York: Macmillan.

Hayward, C. (Ed.). (2003). *Gender differences at puberty*. Cambridge, England: Cambridge University Press.

Haywood, H. C., & Lidz, C. S. (2007). *Dynamic assessment in practice: Clinical and educational applications*. Cambridge, England: Cambridge University Press.

Hearold, S. (1986). A synthesis of 1,043 effects of television on social behavior. In G. Comstock (Ed.), *Public communication and behavior* (Vol. 1). New York: Academic Press.

Heath, S. B. (1980). Questioning at home and at school: A comparative study. In G. Spindler (Ed.), *The ethnography of schooling: Educational anthropology in action*. New York: Holt, Rinehart & Winston.

Heath, S. B. (1989). Oral and literate traditions among black Americans living in poverty. *American Psychologist, 44*, 367–373.

Heatherton, T. F., Macrae, C. N., & Kelley, W. M. (2004). What the social brain sciences can tell us about the self. *Current Directions in Psychological Science, 13*, 190–193.

Hecht, S. A., Close, L., & Santisi, M. (2003). Sources of individual differences in fraction skills. *Journal of Experimental Child Psychology, 86*, 277–302.

Heck, A., Collins, J., & Peterson, L. (2001). Decreasing

children's risk taking on the playground. *Journal of Applied Behavior Analysis, 34*, 349–352.

Hedges, L. V., & Nowell, A. (1995). Sex differences in mental test scores, variability, and numbers of high-scoring individuals. *Science, 269*, 41–45.

Hegarty, M., & Kozhevnikov, M. (1999). Types of visual-spatial representations and mathematical problem solving. *Journal of Educational Psychology, 91*, 684–689.

Heine, S. J. (2007). Culture and motivation: What motivates people to act in the ways that they do? In S. Kitayama & D. Cohen (Eds.), *Handbook of cultural psychology* (pp. 714–733). New York: Guilford Press.

Helton, G. B., & Oakland, T. D. (1977). Teachers' attitudinal responses to differing characteristics of elementary school students. *Journal of Educational Psychology, 69*, 261–266.

Helwig, C. C., & Jasiobedzka, U. (2001). The relation between law and morality: Children's reasoning about socially beneficial and unjust laws. *Child Development, 72*, 1382–1393.

Helwig, C. C., Zelazo, P. D., & Wilson, M. (2001). Children's judgments of psychological harm in normal and noncanonical situations. *Child Development, 72*, 66–81.

Hembree, R. (1988). Correlates, causes, effects, and treatment of test anxiety. *Review of Educational Research, 58*, 47–77.

Hemmings, A. B. (2004). *Coming of age in U.S. high schools: Economic, kinship, religious, and political crosscurrents.* Mahwah, NJ: Erlbaum.

Hennessey, B. A. (1995). Social, environmental, and developmental issues and creativity. *Educational Psychology Review, 7*, 163–183.

Hennessey, B. A., & Amabile, T. M. (1987). *Creativity and learning.* Washington, DC: National Education Association.

Hennessey, M. G. (2003). Metacognitive aspects of students' reflective discourse: Implications for intentional conceptual change teaching and learning. In G. M. Sinatra & P. R. Pintrich (Eds.), *Intentional conceptual change* (pp. 103–132). Mahwah, NJ: Erlbaum.

Herbert, J., & Stipek, D. (2005). The emergence of gender differences in children's perceptions of their academic competence. *Journal of Applied Developmental Psychology, 26*, 276–295.

Herman, M. (2004). Forced to choose: Some determinants of racial identification in multiracial adolescents. *Child Development, 75*, 730–748.

Hernandez, D. J. (2004). Demographic change and the life circumstances of immigrant families. *The Future of Children, 14*(2), 17–48.

Hernandez, D. J., Denton, N. A., & Macartney, S. E. (2008). Children in immigrant families: Looking to America's future. *Social Policy Report, 22*(3) (Society for Research in Child Development).

Heron, W. (1957). The pathology of boredom. *Scientific American, 196*(1), 52–56.

Herrell, A., & Jordan, M. (2004). *Fifty strategies for teaching English language learners* (2nd ed.). Upper Saddle River, NJ: Merrill/Prentice Hall.

Herrenkohl, L. R., & Guerra, M. R. (1998). Participant structures, scientific discourse, and student engagement in fourth grade. *Cognition and Instruction, 16*, 431–473.

Hess, R. D., & Azuma, M. (1991). Cultural support for learning: Contrasts between Japan and the United States. *Educational Researcher, 29*(9), 2–8.

Hess, R. D., & Holloway, S. D. (1984). Family and school as educational institutions. In R. D. Parke, R. N. Emde, H. P. McAdoo, & G. P. Sackett (Eds.), *Review of child development research* (Vol. 7). Chicago: University of Chicago Press.

Hess, R. D., & McDevitt, T. M. (1989). Family. In E. Barnouw (Ed.), *International encyclopedia of communications.* New York: Oxford University Press.

Hettinger, H. R., & Knapp, N. F. (2001). Potential, performance, and paradox: A case study of J.P., a verbally gifted, struggling reader. *Journal for the Education of the Gifted, 24*, 248–289.

Heuer, F., & Reisberg, D. (1992). Emotion, arousal, and memory for detail. In S. Christianson (Ed.), *Handbook of emotion and memory.* Hillsdale, NJ: Erlbaum.

Heward, W. L. (2009). *Exceptional children: An introduction to special education* (9th ed.). Upper Saddle River, NJ: Merrill/Pearson Education.

Hewitt, J., Brett, C., Scardamalia, M., Frecker, K., & Webb, J. (1995, April). *Schools for thought: Transforming classrooms into learning communities.* Paper presented at the annual meeting of the American Educational Research Association, San Francisco.

Hewitt, J., & Scardamalia, M. (1996, April). *Design principles for the support of distributed processes.* Paper presented at the annual meeting of the American Educational Research Association, New York.

Hewitt, J., & Scardamalia, M. (1998). Design principles for distributed knowledge building processes. *Educational Psychology Review, 10*, 75–96.

Heyman, G. D. (2008). Children's critical thinking when learning from others. *Current Directions in Psychological Science, 17*, 344–347.

Hiaasen, C. (2006). *Hoot.* New York: Random House.

Hickey, D. T. (1997). Motivation and contemporary socio-constructivist instructional perspectives. *Educational Psychologist, 32*, 175–193.

Hicks, L. (1997). Academic motivation and peer relationships—how do they mix in an adolescent world? *Middle School Journal, 28*, 18–22.

Hidalgo, N. M., Siu, S., Bright, J. A., Swap, S. M., & Epstein, J. L. (1995). Research on families, schools, and communities: A multicultural perspective. In J. A. Banks & C. A. M. Banks (Eds.), *Handbook of research on multicultural education.* New York: Macmillan.

Hidi, S. (1990). Interest and its contribution as a mental resource for learning. *Review of Educational Research, 60*, 549–571.

Hidi, S., & Anderson, V. (1986). Producing written summaries: Task demands, cognitive operations, and implications for instruction. *Review of Educational Research, 86*, 473–493.

Hidi, S., & Harackiewicz, J. M. (2000). Motivating the academically unmotivated: A critical issue for the 21st century. *Review of Educational Research, 70*, 151–179.

Hidi, S., & Renninger, K. A. (2006). The four-phase model of interest development. *Educational Psychologist, 41*, 111–127.

Hidi, S., Renninger, K. A., & Krapp, A. (2004). Interest, a motivational variable that combines affecting and cognitive functioning. In D. Y. Dai & R. J. Sternberg (Eds.), *Motivation, emotion, and cognition: Integrative perspectives on intellectual functioning and development* (pp. 89–115). Mahwah, NJ: Erlbaum.

Hidi, S., Weiss, J., Berndorff, D., & Nolan, J. (1998). The role of gender, instruction, and a cooperative learning technique in science education across formal and informal settings. In L. Hoffman, A. Krapp, K. Renninger, & J. Baumert (Eds.), *Interest and learning: Proceedings of the Seeon Conference on Interest and Gender* (pp. 215–227). Kiel, Germany: IPN.

Hiebert, E. H., & Fisher, C. W. (1992). The tasks of school literacy: Trends and issues. In J. Brophy (Ed.), *Advances in research on teaching: Vol. 3. Planning and managing learning tasks and activities.* Greenwich, CT: JAI Press.

Hiebert, E. H., & Raphael, T. E. (1996). Psychological perspectives on literacy and extensions to educational practice. In D. C. Berliner & R. C. Calfee (Eds.), *Handbook of educational psychology.* New York: Macmillan.

Hiebert, E. H., Valencia, S. W., & Afflerbach, P. P. (1994). Definitions and perspectives. In S. W. Valencia, E. H. Hiebert, & P. P. Afflerbach (Eds.), *Authentic reading assessment: Practices and possibilities.* Newark, DE: International Reading Association.

Hiebert, J., Carpenter, T. P., Fennema, E., Fuson, K. C., Wearne, D., Murray, H., Olivier, A., & Human, P. (1997). *Making sense: Teaching and learning mathematics with understanding.* Portsmouth, NH: Heinemann.

Higgins, A. (1995). Educating for justice and community: Lawrence Kohlberg's vision of moral education. In W. M. Kurtines & J. L. Gewirtz (Eds.), *Moral development: An introduction.* Boston: Allyn & Bacon.

Higgins, A. T., & Turnure, J. E. (1984). Distractibility and concentration of attention in children's development. *Child Development, 55*, 1799–1810.

Hill, C. (1994). Testing and assessment: An applied linguistic perspective. *Educational Assessment, 2*(3), 179–212.

Hill, H. C., Blunk, M. L., Charalambous, C. Y., Lewis, J. M., Phelps, G. C., Sleep, L., et al. (2008). Mathematical knowledge for teaching and the mathematical quality of instruction: An exploratory study. *Cognition and Instruction, 26*, 430–511.

Hill, K. T. (1984). Debilitating motivation and testing: A major educational problem, possible solutions, and policy applications. In R. Ames & C. Ames (Eds.), *Research on motivation in education: Vol. 1. Student motivation.* San Diego, CA: Academic Press.

Hill, K. T., & Sarason, S. B. (1966). The relation of test anxiety and defensiveness to test and school performance over the elementary school years: A further longitudinal study. *Monographs for the Society of Research in Child Development, 31*(2, Serial No. 104).

Hill, K. T., & Wigfield, A. (1984). Test anxiety: A major educational problem and what can be done about it. *Elementary School Journal, 85*, 105–126.

Hill, N. E., Bush, K. R., & Roosa, M. W. (2003). Parenting and family socialization strategies and children's mental health: Low-income Mexican-American and Euro-American mothers and children. *Child Development, 74*, 189–204.

Hill, N. E., Castellino, D. R., Lansford, J. E., Nowlin, P., Dodge, K. A., Bates, J. E., & Pettit, G. S. (2004). Parent academic involvement as related to school behavior, achievement, and aspirations: Demographic variations across adolescence. *Child Development, 75*, 1491–1509.

Hill, N. E., & Craft, S. A. (2003). Parent-school involvement and school performance: Mediated pathways among socioeconomically comparable African American and Euro-American families. *Journal of Educational Psychology, 95*, 74–83.

Hill, N. E., & Taylor, L. C. (2004). Parental school involvement and children's academic achievement: Pragmatics and issues. *Current Directions in Psychological Science, 13*, 161–164.

Hill, P. R., Hogben, J. H., & Bishop, D. M. V. (2005). Auditory frequency discrimination in children with specific language impairment: A longitudinal study. *Journal of Speech, Language and Hearing Research, 48*, 1136–1146.

Hine, P., & Fraser, B. J. (2002, April). *Combining qualitative and quantitative methods in a study of Australian students' transition from elementary to high school.* Paper presented at the annual meeting of the American Educational Research Association, New Orleans, LA.

Hines, M., Golombok, S., Rust, J., Johnston, K. J., Golding, J., & the Avon Longitudinal Study of Parents and Children Study Team. (2002). Testosterone during pregnancy and gender role behavior of preschool children: A longitudinal, population study. *Child Development, 73*, 1678–1687.

Hinkley, J. W., McInerney, D. M., & Marsh, H. W. (2001, April). *The multi-faceted structure of school achievement motivation: A case for social goals.* Paper presented at the annual meeting of the American Educational Research Association, Seattle, WA.

Hirsch, E. D., Jr. (1996). *The schools we need and why we don't have them.* New York: Doubleday.

Hitlin, S., Brown, J. S., & Elder, G. H., Jr. (2006). Racial self-categorization in adolescence: Multiracial development and social pathways. *Child Development, 77*, 1298–1308.

Hmelo-Silver, C. E. (2004). Problem-based learning: What and how do students learn? *Educational Psychology Review, 16*, 235–266.

Hmelo-Silver, C. E. (2006). Design principles for scaffolding technology-based inquiry. In A. M. O'Donnell, C. E. Hmelo-Silver, & G. Erkens (Eds.), *Collaborative learning, reasoning, and technology* (pp. 147–170). Mahwah, NJ: Erlbaum.

Hmelo-Silver, C. E., Duncan, R. G., & Chinn, C. A. (2007). Scaffolding and achievement in problem-based and inquiry learning: A response to Kirschner, Sweller, and Clark (2006). *Educational Psychologist, 42,* 99–107.

Ho, A. D. (2008). The problem with "proficiency": Limitations of statistics and policy under No Child Left Behind. *Educational Researcher, 37,* 351–360.

Ho, D. Y. F. (1994). Cognitive socialization in Confucian heritage cultures. In P. M. Greenfield & R. R. Cocking (Eds.), *Cross-cultural roots of minority child development.* Mahwah, NJ: Erlbaum.

Hobson, P. (2004). *The cradle of thought: Exploring the origins of thinking.* Oxford, England: Oxford University Press.

Hoerger, M. L., & Mace, F. C. (2006). A computerized test of self-control predicts classroom behavior. *Journal of Applied Behavior Analysis, 39,* 147–159.

Hofer, B. K. (2004). Epistemological understanding as a metacognitive process: Thinking aloud during online searching. *Educational Psychologist, 39,* 43–55.

Hofer, B. K., & Pintrich, P. R. (1997). The development of epistemological theories: Beliefs about knowledge and knowing and their relation to learning. *Review of Educational Research, 67,* 88–140.

Hofer, B. K., & Pintrich, P. R. (Eds.). (2002). *Personal epistemology: The psychology of beliefs about knowledge and knowing.* Mahwah, NJ: Erlbaum.

Hoff, E. (2003). The specificity of environmental influence: Socioeconomic status affects early vocabulary development via maternal speech. *Child Development, 74,* 1368–1378.

Hofferth, S. L. (1990). Trends in adolescent sexual activity, contraception, and pregnancy in the United States. In J. Bancroft & J. M. Reinisch (Eds.), *Adolescence and puberty* (pp. 217–233). New York: Oxford University Press.

Hoff-Ginsberg, E. (1997). *Language development.* Pacific Grove, CA: Brooks/Cole.

Hoffman, M. L. (1970). Moral development. In P. H. Mussen (Ed.), *Carmichael's manual of child psychology* (Vol. 2). New York: Wiley.

Hoffman, M. L. (1975). Altruistic behavior and the parent-child relationship. *Journal of Personality and Social Psychology, 31,* 937–943.

Hoffman, M. L. (1991). Empathy, social cognition, and moral action. In W. M. Kurtines & J. L. Gewirtz (Eds.), *Moral behavior and development: Vol. 1. Theory* (pp. 275–301). Mahwah, NJ: Erlbaum.

Hogan, D. M., & Tudge, J. R. H. (1999). Implications of Vygotsky's theory for peer learning. In A. M. O'Donnell & A. King (Eds.), *Cognitive perspectives on peer learning* (pp. 39–65). Mahwah, NJ: Erlbaum.

Hogan, K., Nastasi, B. K., & Pressley, M. (2000). Discourse patterns and collaborative scientific reasoning in peer and teacher-guided discussions. *Cognition and Instruction, 17,* 379–432.

Hogan, T., Rabinowitz, M., & Craven, J. A., III. (2003). Representation in teaching: Inferences from research of expert and novice teachers. *Educational Psychologist, 38,* 235–247.

Hoge, R. D., & Coladarci, T. (1989). Teacher-based judgments of academic achievement: A review of literature. *Review of Educational Research, 59,* 297–313.

Hoge, R. D., & Renzulli, J. S. (1993). Exploring the link between giftedness and self-concept. *Review of Educational Research, 63,* 449–465.

Hoglund, W. L. G. (2007). School functioning in early adolescence: Gender-linked responses to peer victimization. *Journal of Educational Psychology, 99,* 683–699.

Holliday, B. G. (1985). Towards a model of teacher-child transactional processes affecting black children's academic achievement. In M. B. Spencer, G. K. Brookins, & W. R. Allen (Eds.), *Beginnings: The social and affective development of black children.* Mahwah, NJ: Erlbaum.

Hollins, E. R. (1996). *Culture in school learning: Revealing the deep meaning.* Mahwah, NJ: Erlbaum.

Hollon, R. E., Roth, K. J., & Anderson, C. W. (1991). Science teachers' conceptions of teaching and learning. In J. Brophy (Ed.), *Advances in research on teaching: Vol. 2. Teachers' knowledge of subject matter as it relates to their teaching practice.* Greenwich, CT: JAI Press.

Holt-Reynolds, D. (1992). Personal history-based beliefs as relevant prior knowledge in course work. *American Educational Research Journal, 29,* 325–349.

Hom, A., & Battistich, V. (1995, April). *Students' sense of school community as a factor in reducing drug use and delinquency.* Paper presented at the annual meeting of the American Educational Research Association, San Francisco.

Homme, L. E., deBaca, P. C., Devine, J. V., Steinhorst, R., & Rickert, E. J. (1963). Use of the Premack principle in controlling the behavior of nursery school children. *Journal of the Experimental Analysis of Behavior, 6,* 544.

Hong, E., O'Neil, H. F., & Feldon, D. (2005). Gender effects on mathematics achievement: Mediating role of state and trait self-regulation. In A. M. Gallagher & J. C. Kaufman (Eds.), *Gender differences in mathematics: An integrative psychological approach* (pp. 264–293). Cambridge, England: Cambridge University Press.

Hong, S., & Ho, H.-Z. (2005). Direct and indirect longitudinal effects of parental involvement on student achievement: Second-order latent growth modeling across ethnic groups. *Journal of Educational Psychology, 97,* 32–42.

Hong, Y., Chiu, C., & Dweck, C. S. (1995). Implicit theories of intelligence: Reconsidering the role of confidence in achievement motivation. In M. H. Kernis (Ed.), *Efficacy, agency, and self-esteem.* New York: Plenum Press.

Hong, Y., Morris, M. W., Chiu, C., & Benet-Martínez, V. (2000). Multicultural minds: A dynamic constructivist approach to culture and cognition. *American Psychologist, 55,* 709–720.

Hong, Y.-Y., Wan, C., No, S., & Chiu, C.-Y. (2007). Multicultural identities. In S. Kitayama & D. Cohen (Eds.), *Handbook of cultural psychology* (pp. 323–345). New York: Guilford Press.

Hoover-Dempsey, K. V., Battiato, A. C., Walker, J. M. T., Reed, R. P., DeJong, J. M., & Jones, K. P. (2001). Parental involvement in homework. *Educational Psychologist, 36,* 195–209.

Horgan, D. D. (1995). *Achieving gender equity: Strategies for the classroom.* Boston: Allyn & Bacon.

Horn, J. L. (2008). Spearman, *g*, expertise, and the nature of human cognitive capability. In P. C. Kyllonen, R. D. Roberts, & L. Stankov (Eds.), *Extending intelligence: Enhancement and new constructs* (pp. 185–230). New York: Erlbaum/Taylor & Francis.

Horne, A. M., Orpinas, P., Newman-Carlson, D., & Bartolomucci, C. L. (2004). Elementary school Bully Busters Program: Understanding why children bully and what to do about it. In D. L. Espelage & S. M. Swearer (Eds.), *Bullying in American schools: A social-ecological perspective on prevention and intervention* (pp. 297–325). Mahwah, NJ: Erlbaum.

Houtz, J. C. (1990). Environments that support creative thinking. In C. Hedley, J. Houtz, & A. Baratta (Eds.), *Cognition, curriculum, and literacy.* Norwood, NJ: Ablex.

Howe, C. K. (1994). Improving the achievement of Hispanic students. *Educational Leadership, 51*(8), 42–44.

Howe, C., Tolmie, A., Greer, K., & Mackenzie, M. (1995). Peer collaboration and conceptual growth in physics: Task influences on children's understanding of heating and cooling. *Cognition and Instruction, 13,* 483–503.

Howell, J. C., & Lynch, J. P. (2000, August). Youth gangs in schools. *Juvenile Justice Bulletin* (OJJDP Publication NCJ-183015). Washington, DC: U.S. Department of Justice, Office of Juvenile Justice and Delinquency Prevention.

Hoy, W. K., Tarter, C. J., & Woolfolk Hoy, A. (2006). Academic optimism of schools: A force for student achievement. *American Educational Research Journal, 43,* 425–446.

Hubbs-Tait, L., Nation, J. R., Krebs, N. F., & Bellinger, D. C. (2005). Neurotoxicants, micronutrients, and social environments: Individual and combined effects on children's development. *Psychological Science in the Public Interest, 6,* 57–121.

Hudley, C., & Graham, S. (1993). An attributional intervention to reduce peer-directed aggression among African American boys. *Child Development, 64,* 124–138.

Huesmann, L. R., Moise-Titus, J., Podolski, C., & Eron, L. (2003). Longitudinal relations between children's exposure to TV violence and their aggressive and violent behavior in young adulthood: 1977–1992. *Developmental Psychology, 39,* 201–221.

Huff, J. A. (1988). Personalized behavior modification: An in-school suspension program that teaches students how to change. *School Counselor, 35,* 210–214.

Hufton, N., Elliott, J., & Illushin, L. (2002). Achievement motivation across cultures: Some puzzles and their implications for future research. *New Directions for Child and Adolescent Development, 96,* 65–85.

Hughes, F. P. (1998). Play in special populations. In O. N. Saracho & B. Spodek (Eds.), *Multiple perspectives on play in early childhood education* (pp. 171–193). Albany: State University of New York Press.

Hughes, J. M., Bigler, R. S., & Levy, S. R. (2007). Consequences of learning about historical racism among European American and African American children. *Child Development, 78,* 1689–1705.

Hughes, J. N. (1988). *Cognitive behavior therapy with children in schools.* New York: Pergamon Press.

Hughes, J. N., & Kwok, O. (2007). Influence of student-teacher and parent-teacher relationships on lower achieving readers' engagement and achievement in the primary grades. *Journal of Educational Psychology, 99,* 39–51.

Hughes, J. N., Luo, W., Kwok, O.-M., & Loyd, L. K. (2008). Teacher-student support, effortful engagement, and achievement: A 3-year longitudinal study. *Journal of Educational Psychology, 100,* 1–14.

Huguet, P., & Régner, I. (2007). Stereotype threat among schoolgirls in quasi-ordinary classroom circumstances. *Journal of Educational Psychology, 99,* 545–560.

Hulit, L. M., & Howard, M. R. (2006). *Born to talk* (4th ed.). Boston: Allyn & Bacon.

Hundert, J. (1976). The effectiveness of reinforcement, response cost, and mixed programs on classroom behaviors. *Journal of Applied Behavior Analysis, 9,* 107.

Hunt, E. (2008). Improving intelligence: What's the difference from education? In P. C. Kyllonen, R. D. Roberts, & L. Stankov (Eds.), *Extending intelligence: Enhancement and new constructs* (pp. 15–35). New York: Erlbaum/Taylor & Francis.

Hunt, P., & Goetz, L. (1997). Research on inclusive educational programs, practices, and outcomes for students with severe disabilities. *Journal of Special Education, 31,* 3–29.

Hunt, R. R., & Worthen, J. B. (Eds.). (2006). *Distinctiveness and memory.* Oxford, England: Oxford University Press.

Huntsinger, C. S., & Jose, P. E. (2006). A longitudinal investigation of personality and social adjustment among Chinese American and European American adolescents. *Child Development, 77,* 1309–1324.

Hursh, D. (2007). Assessing No Child Left Behind and the rise of neoliberal education policies. *American Educational Research Journal, 44,* 493–518.

Hutt, S. J., Tyler, S., Hutt, C., & Christopherson, H. (1989). *Play, exploration, and learning: A natural history of the pre-school.* London: Routledge.

Huttenlocher, P. R., & Dabholkar, A. S. (1997). Regional differences in synaptogenesis in human cerebral cortex. *Journal of Comparative Neurology, 387,* 167–178.

Hyde, J. S. (2005). The gender similarities hypothesis. *American Psychologist, 60,* 581–592.

Hyde, J. S. (2007). New directions in the study of gender similarities and differences. *Current Directions in Psychological Science, 16,* 259–263.

Hyde, J. S., & Durik, A. M. (2005). Gender, competence, and motivation. In A. J. Elliot & C. S. Dweck (Eds.), *Handbook of competence and motivation* (pp. 375–391). New York: Guilford.

Hyde, J. S., Lindberg, S. M., Linn, M. C., Ellis, A. B., & Williams, C. C. (2008). Gender similarities characterize math performance. *Science, 321*(5888), 494–495.

Hyman, I., Kay, B., Tabori, A., Weber, M., Mahon, M., & Cohen, I. (2006). Bullying: Theory, research, and interventions. In C. M. Evertson & C. S. Weinstein (Eds.), *Handbook of classroom management: Research, practice, and contemporary issues* (pp. 855–884). Mahwah, NJ: Erlbaum.

Hyman, I., Mahon, M., Cohen, I., Snook, P., Britton, G., & Lurkis, L. (2004). Student alienation syndrome: The other side of school violence. In J. C. Conoley & A. P. Goldstein (Eds.), *School violence intervention* (2nd ed., pp. 483–506). New York: Guilford Press.

Hymel, S., Comfort, C., Schonert-Reichl, K., & McDougall, P. (1996). Academic failure and school dropout: The influence of peers. In J. Juvonen & K. R. Wentzel (Eds.), *Social motivation: Understanding children's school adjustment* (pp. 313–345). Cambridge, England: Cambridge University Press.

Hynd, C. (1998a). Conceptual change in a high school physics class. In B. Guzzetti & C. Hynd (Eds.), *Perspectives on conceptual change: Multiple ways to understand knowing and learning in a complex world* (pp. 27–36). Mahwah, NJ: Erlbaum.

Hynd, C. (1998b). Observing learning from different perspectives: What does it mean for Barry and his understanding of gravity? In B. Guzzetti & C. Hynd (Eds.), *Perspectives on conceptual change: Multiple ways to understand knowing and learning in a complex world* (pp. 235–244). Mahwah, NJ: Erlbaum.

Hynd, C. (2003). Conceptual change in response to persuasive messages. In G. M. Sinatra & P. R. Pintrich (Eds.), *Intentional conceptual change* (pp. 291–315). Mahwah, NJ: Erlbaum.

Iacoboni, M., & Woods, R. P. (1999). Cortical mechanisms of human imitation. *Science, 286,* 2526–2528.

Igoa, C. (1995). *The inner world of the immigrant child.* Mahwah, NJ: Erlbaum.

Igoa, C. (2007). Immigrant children: Art as a second language. In S. Books (Ed.), *Invisible children in the society and its schools* (3rd ed., pp. 117–140). Mahwah, NJ: Erlbaum.

Imhof, M. (2001, March). *In the eye of the beholder: Children's perception of good and poor listening behavior.* Paper presented at the annual meeting of the International Listening Association, Chicago.

Inagaki, K., & Hatano, G. (2006). Young children's conception of the biological world. *Current Directions in Psychological Science, 15,* 177–181.

Inglehart, M., Brown, D. R., & Vida, M. (1994). Competition, achievement, and gender: A stress theoretical analysis. In P. R. Pintrich, D. R. Brown, & C. E. Weinstein (Eds.), *Student motivation, cognition, and learning: Essays in honor of Wilbert J. McKeachie.* Mahwah, NJ: Erlbaum.

Inglis, A., & Biemiller, A. (1997, March). *Fostering self-direction in mathematics: A cross-age tutoring program that enhances math problem solving.* Paper presented at the annual meeting of the American Educational Research Association, Chicago.

Inhelder, B., & Piaget, J. (1958). *The growth of logical thinking from childhood to adolescence* (A. Parsons & S. Milgram, Trans.). New York: Basic Books.

Irujo, S. (1988). An introduction to intercultural differences and similarities in nonverbal communication. In J. S. Wurzel (Ed.), *Toward multiculturalism: A reader in multicultural education.* Yarmouth, ME: Intercultural Press.

Irvine, J. J., & York, D. E. (1995). Learning styles and culturally diverse students: A literature review. In J. A. Banks & C. A. M. Banks (Eds.), *Handbook of research on multicultural education.* New York: Macmillan.

Irving, M. A., & Hudley, C. (2008). Oppositional identity and academic achievement among African American males. In J. U. Ogbu (Ed.), *Minority status, oppositional culture, and schooling* (pp. 374–394). New York: Routledge.

Iyengar, S. S., & Lepper, M. R. (1999). Rethinking the value of choice: A cultural perspective on intrinsic motivation. *Journal of Personality and Social Psychology, 76,* 349–366.

Izard, C. (2007). Basic emotions, natural kinds, emotion schemas, and a new paradigm. *Perspectives on Psychological Science, 2,* 260–280.

Izard, C., Fine, S., Schultz, D., Mostow, A., Ackerman, B., & Youngstrom, E. (2001). Emotion knowledge as a predictor of social behavior and academic competence in children at risk. *Psychological Science, 12,* 18–23.

Jacob, B. A. (2003). Accountability, incentives, and behavior: The impact of high-stakes testing in the Chicago Public Schools. *Education Next, 3*(1). Retrieved March 10, 2004, from www.educationnext.org/unabridged/20031/jacob.pdf

Jacobs, J. E., Davis-Kean, P., Bleeker, M., Eccles, J. S., & Malanchuk, O. (2005). "I can, but I don't want to": The impact of parents, interests, and activities on gender differences in math. In A. M. Gallagher & J. C. Kaufman (Eds.), *Gender differences in mathematics: An integrative psychological approach* (pp. 246–263). Cambridge, England: Cambridge University Press.

Jacobs, J. E., & Klaczynski, P. A. (2002). The development of judgment and decision making during childhood and adolescence. *Current Directions in Psychological Science, 11,* 145–149.

Jacobs, J. E., Lanza, S., Osgood, D. W., Eccles, J. S., & Wigfield, A. (2002). Changes in children's self-competence and values: Gender and domain differences across grades one through twelve. *Child Development, 73,* 509–527.

Jacobsen, B., Lowery, B., & DuCette, J. (1986). Attributions of learning disabled children. *Journal of Educational Psychology, 78,* 59–64.

Jacoby, R., & Glauberman, N. (Eds.). (1995). *The bell curve debate: History, documents, opinions.* New York: Random House.

Jaffee, S. R., Caspi, A., Moffitt, T. E., Polo-Tomas, M., Price, T. S., & Taylor, A. (2004). The limits of child effects: Evidence for genetically mediated child effects on corporal punishment but not on physical maltreatment. *Developmental Psychology, 40,* 1047–1058.

Jagacinski, C. M., Kumar, S., Lam, H., & Lustenberger, D. E. (2008, March). *An exploratory study of work avoidance in the college classroom.* Paper presented at the annual meeting of the American Educational Research Association, New York.

Jagacinski, C. M., & Nicholls, J. G. (1984). Conceptions of ability and related affects in task involvement and ego involvement. *Journal of Educational Psychology, 76,* 909–919.

Jagacinski, C. M., & Nicholls, J. G. (1987). Competence and affect in task involvement and ego involvement: The impact of social comparison information. *Journal of Educational Psychology, 79,* 107–114.

James, W. (1890). *The principles of psychology.* New York: Holt.

Janos, P. M., & Robinson, N. M. (1985). Psychosocial development in intellectually gifted children. In F. D. Horowitz & M. O'Brien (Eds.), *The gifted and talented: Developmental perspectives.* Washington, DC: American Psychological Association.

Janosz, M., Le Blanc, M., Boulerice, B., & Tremblay, R. E. (2000). Predicting different types of school dropouts: A typological approach with two longitudinal samples. *Journal of Educational Psychology, 92,* 171–190.

Janzen, J. (2008). Teaching English language learners in the content areas. *Review of Educational Research, 78,* 1010–1038.

Jegede, O. J., & Olajide, J. O. (1995). Wait-time, classroom discourse, and the influence of sociocultural factors in science teaching. *Science Education, 79,* 233–249.

Jenlink, C. L. (1994, April). *Music: A lifeline for the self-esteem of at-risk students.* Paper presented at the annual meeting of the American Educational Research Association, New Orleans, LA.

Jimerson, S., Egeland, B., & Teo, A. (1999). A longitudinal study of achievement trajectories: Factors associated with change. *Journal of Educational Psychology, 91,* 116–126.

Johanning, D. I., D'Agostino, J. V., Steele, D. F., & Shumow, L. (1999, April). *Student writing, post-writing group collaboration, and learning in pre-algebra.* Paper presented at the annual meeting of the American Educational Research Association, Montreal, Canada.

Johnson, B. M., Miltenberger, R. G., Knudson, P., Emego-Helm, K., Kelso, P., Jostad, C., & Langley, L. (2006). A preliminary evaluation of two behavioral skills training procedures for teaching abduction-prevention skills to schoolchildren. *Journal of Applied Behavior Analysis, 39,* 25–34.

Johnson, D. W., & Johnson, R. T. (1987). *Learning together and alone: Cooperative, competitive, and individualistic learning* (2nd ed.). Englewood Cliffs, NJ: Prentice Hall.

Johnson, D. W., & Johnson, R. T. (1991). *Learning together and alone: Cooperative, competitive, and individualistic learning* (3rd ed.). Upper Saddle River, NJ: Prentice Hall.

Johnson, D. W., & Johnson, R. T. (1996). Conflict resolution and peer mediation programs in elementary and secondary schools: A review of the research. *Review of Educational Research, 66,* 459–506.

Johnson, D. W., & Johnson, R. T. (2006). Conflict resolution, peer mediation, and peacemaking. In C. M. Evertson & C. S. Weinstein (Eds.), *Handbook of classroom management: Research, practice, and contemporary issues* (pp. 803–832). Mahwah, NJ: Erlbaum.

Johnson, D. W., Johnson, R., Dudley, B., Ward, M., & Magnuson, D. (1995). The impact of peer mediation training on the management of school and home conflicts. *American Educational Research Journal, 32,* 829–844.

Johnson, H. C., & Friesen, B. (1993). Etiologies of mental and emotional disorders in children. In H. Johnson (Ed.), *Child mental health in the 1990s: Curricula for graduate and undergraduate.* Washington, DC: U.S. Department of Health and Human Services.

Johnson, J., Im-Bolter, N., & Pascual-Leone, J. (2003). Development of mental attention in gifted and mainstream children: The role of mental capacity, inhibition, and speed of processing. *Child Development, 74,* 1594–1614.

Johnson, M. H., & de Haan, M. (2001). Developing cortical specialization for visual-cognitive function: The case of face recognition. In J. L. McClelland & R. S. Siegler (Eds.), *Mechanisms of cognitive development: Behavioral and neural perspectives* (pp. 253–270). Mahwah, NJ: Erlbaum.

Johnson, R. S., Mims-Cox, J. S., & Doyle-Nichols, A. (2006). *Developing portfolios in education: A guide to reflection, inquiry, and assessment.* Thousand Oaks, CA: Sage.

Johnson, W., McGue, M., & Iacono, W. G. (2005). Disruptive behavior and school grades: Genetic and environmental relations in 11-year-olds. *Journal of Educational Psychology, 97,* 391–405.

Johnson-Glenberg, M. C. (2000). Training reading comprehension in adequate decoders/poor comprehenders: Verbal versus visual strategies. *Journal of Educational Psychology, 92,* 772–782.

Johnstone, A. H., & El-Banna, H. (1986). Capacities, demands and processes—a predictive model for science education. *Education in Chemistry, 23,* 80–84.

Jonassen, D. H., & Grabowski, B. L. (1993). *Handbook of individual differences: Learning and instruction.* Mahwah, NJ: Erlbaum.

Jonassen, D. H., Hannum, W. H., & Tessmer, M. (1989). *Handbook of task analysis procedures.* New York: Praeger.

Jones, D., & Christensen, C. A. (1999). Relationship between automaticity in handwriting and students' ability to generate written text. *Journal of Educational Psychology, 91,* 44–49.

Jones, E. E., & Berglas, S. (1978). Control of attributions about the self through self-handicapping strategies: The appeal of alcohol and the role of underachievement. *Personality and Social Psychology Bulletin, 4,* 200–206.

Jones, K. M., Drew, H. A., & Weber, N. L. (2000). Noncontingent peer attention as treatment for disruptive classroom behavior. *Journal of Applied Behavior Analysis, 33,* 343–346.

Jones, M. C. (1924). The elimination of children's fears. *Journal of Experimental Psychology, 7,* 382–390.

Jones, M. S., Levin, M. E., Levin, J. R., & Beitzel, B. D. (2000). Can vocabulary-learning strategies and pair-learning formats be profitably combined? *Journal of Educational Psychology, 92,* 256–262.

Jones, S. M., & Dindia, K. (2004). A meta-analytic perspective on sex equity in the classroom. *Review of Educational Research, 74,* 443–471.

Jones, V. (1996). Classroom management. In J. Sikula, T. J. Buttery, & E. Guyton (Eds.), *Handbook of research on teacher education* (2nd ed., pp. 503–521). New York: Macmillan.

Jordan, J. V. (2006). Relational resilience in girls. In. S. Goldstein & R. B. Brooks (Eds.), *Handbook of resilience in children* (pp. 79–90). New York: Springer.

Joshi, M. S., & MacLean, M. (1994). Indian and English children's understanding of the distinction between real and apparent emotion. *Child Development, 65,* 1372–1384.

Josselson, R. (1988). The embedded self: I and Thou revisited. In D. K. Lapsley & F. C. Power (Eds.), *Self, ego, and identity: Integrative approaches* (pp. 91–106). New York: Springer-Verlag.

Joussemet, M., Vitaro, F., Barker, E. D., Côté, S., Nagin, D. S., Zoccolillo, M., et al. (2008). Controlling parenting and physical aggression during elementary school. *Child Development, 79,* 411–425.

Jovanovic, J., & King, S. S. (1998). Boys and girls in the performance-based science classroom: Who's doing the performing? *American Educational Research Journal, 35,* 477–496.

Jozefowicz, D. M., Arbreton, A. J., Eccles, J. S., Barber, B. L., & Colarossi, L. (1994, April). *Seventh grade student, parent, and teacher factors associated with later school dropout or movement into alternative educational settings.* Paper presented at the annual meeting of the American Educational Research Association, New Orleans, LA.

Jusczyk, P. W. (1995). Language acquisition: Speech sounds and phonological development. In J. L. Miller & P. D. Eimas (Eds.), *Handbook of perception and cognition: Vol. 11. Speech, language, and communication.* Orlando, FL: Academic Press.

Jussim, L., Eccles, J., & Madon, S. (1996). Social perception, social stereotypes, and teacher expectations: Accuracy and the quest for the powerful self-fulfilling prophecy. In L. Berkowitz (Ed.), *Advances in experimental social psychology.* New York: Academic Press.

Juvonen, J. (2000). The social functions of attributional face-saving tactics among early adolescents. *Educational Psychology Review, 12,* 15–32.

Juvonen, J. (2006). Sense of belonging, social bonds, and school functioning. In P. A. Alexander & P. H. Winne (Eds.), *Handbook of educational psychology* (2nd ed., pp. 655–674). Mahwah, NJ: Erlbaum.

Juvonen, J., & Cadigan, R. J. (2002). Social determinants of public behavior of middle school youth: Perceived peer norms and need to be accepted. In F. Pajares & T. Urdan (Eds.), *Adolescence and education, Vol. 2: Academic motivation of adolescents* (pp. 277–297). Greenwich, CT: Information Age.

Juvonen, J., & Graham, S. (2004). Research based interventions on bullying. In C. E. Sanders & G. D. Phye (Eds.), *Bullying: Implications for the classroom* (pp. 229–255). San Diego, CA: Academic Press.

Juvonen, J., & Weiner, B. (1993). An attributional analysis of students' interactions: The social consequences of perceived responsibility. *Educational Psychology Review, 5,* 325–345.

Kagan, J., & Snidman, N. (2007). Temperament and biology. In D. Coch, K. W. Fischer, & G. Dawson (Eds.), *Human behavior, learning, and the developing brain: Typical development* (pp. 219–246). New York: Guilford Press.

Kağitçibaşi, Ç. (2007). *Family, self, and human development across cultures: Theory and applications* (2nd ed.). Mahwah, NJ: Erlbaum.

Kahl, B., & Woloshyn, V. E. (1994). Using elaborative interrogation to facilitate acquisition of factual information in cooperative learning settings: One good strategy deserves another. *Applied Cognitive Psychology, 8,* 465–478.

Kahle, J. B., & Lakes, M. K. (1983). The myth of equality in science classrooms. *Journal of Research in Science Teaching, 20,* 131–140.

Kahne, J. E., & Sporte, S. E. (2008). Developing citizens: The impact of civic learning opportunities on students' commitment to civic participation. *American Educational Research Journal, 45,* 738–766.

Kail, R. V. (1990). *The development of memory in children* (3rd ed.). New York: Freeman.

Kail, R. V. (2000). Speed of information processing: Developmental change and links to intelligence. *Journal of School Psychology, 38,* 51–61.

Kail, R. V. (2007). Longitudinal evidence that increases in processing speed and working memory enhance children's reasoning. *Psychological Science, 18,* 312–313.

Kane, M. T. (2008). Terminology, emphasis, and utility in validation. *Educational Researcher, 37,* 76–82.

Kaplan, A., & Midgley, C. (1997). The effect of achievement goals: Does level of perceived academic competence make a difference? *Contemporary Educational Psychology, 22,* 415–435.

Kaplan, A., & Midgley, C. (1999). The relationship between perceptions of the classroom goal structure and early adolescents' affect in school: The mediating role of coping strategies. *Learning and Individual Differences, 11,* 187–212.

Karau, S. J., & Williams, K. D. (1995). Social loafing: Research findings, implications, and future directions. *Current Directions in Psychological Science, 4,* 134–140.

Kardash, C. A. M., & Amlund, J. T. (1991). Self-reported learning strategies and learning from expository text. *Contemporary Educational Psychology, 16,* 117–138.

Kardash, C. A. M., & Howell, K. L. (2000). Effects of epistemological beliefs and topic-specific beliefs on undergraduates' cognitive and strategic processing of dual-positional text. *Journal of Educational Psychology, 92,* 524–535.

Kardash, C. A. M., & Scholes, R. J. (1996). Effects of preexisting beliefs, epistemological beliefs, and need for cognition on interpretation of controversial issues. *Journal of Educational Psychology, 88,* 260–271.

Karmiloff-Smith, A. (1979). Language development after five. In P. Fletcher & M. Garman (Eds.), *Language acquisition: Studies in first language development.* Cambridge, England: Cambridge University Press.

Karmiloff-Smith, A. (1993). Innate constraints and developmental change. In P. Bloom (Ed.), *Language acquisition: Core readings.* Cambridge, MA: MIT Press.

Karpov, Y. V. (2003). Vygotsky's doctrine of scientific concepts: Its role for contemporary education. In A. Kozulin, B. Gindis, V. S. Ageyev, & S. M. Miller (Eds.), *Vygotsky's educational theory in cultural context* (pp. 65–82). Cambridge, England: Cambridge University Press.

Katchadourian, H. (1990). Sexuality. In S. S. Feldman & G. R. Elliott (Eds.), *At the threshold: The developing adolescent* (pp. 330–351). Cambridge, MA: Harvard University Press.

Kavale, K. A., & Forness, S. R. (1987). Substance over style: Assessing the efficacy of modality testing and teaching. *Exceptional Children, 54,* 228–239.

Keele, S. W. (1981). Behavioral analysis of movement. In J. W. Brookhart, V. B. Mountcastle, & V. B. Brooks (Eds.), *Handbook of physiology: Vol. II. Motor control* (pp. 1391–1414). Bethesda, MD: American Physiological Society.

Kehle, T. J., Clark, E., Jenson, W. R., & Wampold, B. (1986). Effectiveness of the self-modeling procedure with behaviorally disturbed elementary age children. *School Psychology Review, 15,* 289–295.

Keil, F. C. (1986). The acquisition of natural kind and artifact terms. In W. Demopolous & A. Marras (Eds.), *Language learning and concept acquisition.* Norwood, NJ: Ablex.

Keil, F. C. (1987). Conceptual development and category structure. In U. Neisser (Ed.), *Concepts and conceptual development: Ecological and intellectual factors in categorization.* Cambridge, England: Cambridge University Press.

Keil, F. C. (1989). *Concepts, kinds, and cognitive development.* Cambridge, MA: MIT Press.

Keil, F. C. (1991). Theories, concepts, and the acquisition of word meaning. In S. A. Gelman & J. P. Byrnes (Eds.), *Perspectives on language and thought: Interrelations in development.* Cambridge, England: Cambridge University Press.

Keil, F. C., & Silberstein, C. S. (1996). Schooling and the acquisition of theoretical knowledge. In D. R. Olson & N. Torrance (Eds.), *The handbook of education and human development: New models of learning, teaching, and schooling.* Cambridge, MA: Blackwell.

Kelemen, D. (1999). Why are rocks pointy? Children's preference for teleological explanations of the natural world. *Developmental Psychology, 35,* 1440–1452.

Kelemen, D. (2004). Are children "intuitive theists"?: Reasoning about purpose and design in nature. *Psychological Science, 15,* 295–301.

Kellam, S. G., Rebok, G. W., Ialongo, N., & Mayer, L. S. (1994). The course and malleability of aggressive behavior from early first grade into middle school: Results of a developmental epidemiology-based preventive trial. *Journal of Child Psychology and Psychiatry and Allied Disciplines, 35,* 259–281.

Keller, H. R., & Tapasak, R. C. (2004). Classroom-based approaches. In J. C. Conoley & A. P. Goldstein (Eds.), *School violence intervention* (2nd ed., pp. 103–130). New York: Guilford Press.

Kelley, M. L., & Carper, L. B. (1988). Home-based reinforcement procedures. In J. C. Witt, S. N. Elliott, & F. M. Gresham (Eds.), *Handbook of behavior therapy in education.* New York: Plenum Press.

Kelly, A., & Smail, B. (1986). Sex stereotypes and attitudes to science among eleven-year-old children. *British Journal of Educational Psychology, 56,* 158–168.

Kemler Nelson, D. G., Egan, L. C., & Holt, M. B. (2004). When children ask, "What is it?" what do they want to know about artifacts? *Psychological Science, 15,* 384–389.

Keogh, B. K. (2003). *Temperament in the classroom.* Baltimore: Brookes.

Kermani, H., & Moallem, M. (1997, March). *Cross-age tutoring: Exploring features and processes of peer-mediated learning.* Paper presented at the annual meeting of the American Educational Research Association, Chicago.

Kern, L., Dunlap, G., Childs, K. E., & Clark, S. (1994). Use of a classwide self-management program to improve the behavior of students with emotional and behavioral disorders. *Education and Treatment of Children, 17,* 445–458.

Kerns, L. L., & Lieberman, A. B. (1993). *Helping your depressed child.* Rocklin, CA: Prima.

Kerr, B. (1991). Educating gifted girls. In N. Coangelo & G. A. Davis (Eds.), *Handbook of gifted education.* Boston: Allyn & Bacon.

Khattri, N., & Sweet, D. (1996). Assessment reform: Promises and challenges. In M. B. Kane & R. Mitchell (Eds.), *Implementing performance assessment: Promises, problems, and challenges* (pp. 1–21). Mahwah, NJ: Erlbaum.

Kieffer, M. J. (2008). Catching up or falling behind? Initial English proficiency, concentrated poverty, and the reading growth of language minority learners in the United States. *Journal of Educational Psychology, 100,* 851–868.

Kiewra, K. A. (1985). Investigating notetaking and review: A depth of processing alternative. *Educational Psychologist, 20,* 23–32.

Kiewra, K. A. (1989). A review of note-taking: The encoding-storage paradigm and beyond. *Educational Psychology Review, 1,* 147–172.

Kiewra, K. A., Benton, S. L., & Lewis, L. B. (1987). Qualitative aspects of notetaking and their relationship with information-processing ability and academic achievement. *Journal of Instructional Psychology, 14*(3), 110–117.

Kiewra, K. A., DuBois, N. F., Christian, D., & McShane, A. (1988). Providing study notes: Comparison of three types of notes for review. *Journal of Educational Psychology, 80,* 595–597.

Killen, M. (2007). Children's social and moral reasoning about exclusion. *Current Directions in Psychological Science, 16,* 32–36.

Killen, M., & Smetana, J. (2008). Moral judgment and moral neuroscience: Intersections, definitions, and issues. *Child Development Perspectives, 2*(1), 1–6.

Kim, D., Solomon, D., & Roberts, W. (1995, April). *Classroom practices that enhance students' sense of community.* Paper presented at the annual meeting of the American Educational Research Association, San Francisco.

Kim, H. S., & Kamil, M. L. (2004). Adolescents, computer technology, and literacy. In T. L. Jetton & J. A. Dole (Eds.), *Adolescent literacy research and practice* (pp. 351–368). New York: Guilford.

Kim, J., & Cicchetti, D. (2006). Longitudinal trajectories of self-system processes and depressive symptoms among maltreated and nonmaltreated children. *Child Development, 77,* 624–639.

Kim, J. M., & Turiel, E. (1996). Korean and American children's concepts of adult and peer authority. *Social Development, 5,* 310–329.

Kindermann, T. A. (2007). Effects of naturally existing peer groups on changes in academic engagement in a cohort of sixth graders. *Child Development, 78,* 1186–1203.

Kindermann, T. A., McCollam, T., & Gibson, E. (1996). Peer networks and students' classroom engagement during childhood and adolescence. In J. Juvonen & K. Wentzel (Eds.), *Social motivation: Understanding children's school adjustment.* Cambridge, England: Cambridge University Press.

King, A. (1992). Comparison of self-questioning, summarizing, and notetaking-review as strategies for learning from lectures. *American Educational Research Journal, 29,* 303–323.

King, A. (1994). Guiding knowledge construction in the classroom: Effects of teaching children how to question and how to explain. *American Educational Research Journal, 31,* 338–368.

King, A. (1997). ASK to THINK—TEL WHY®©: A model of transactive peer tutoring for scaffolding higher level complex learning. *Educational Psychologist, 32,* 221–235.

King, A. (1998). Transactive peer tutoring: Distributing cognition and metacognition. *Educational Psychology Review, 10,* 57–74.

King, A. (1999). Discourse patterns for mediating peer learning. In A. M. O'Donnell & A. King (Eds.), *Cognitive perspectives on peer learning* (pp. 87–115). Mahwah, NJ: Erlbaum.

King, A., Staffieri, A., & Adelgais, A. (1998). Mutual peer tutoring: Effects of structuring tutorial interaction to scaffold peer learning. *Journal of Educational Psychology, 90,* 134–152.

King, N. J., & Ollendick, T. H. (1989). Children's anxiety and phobic disorders in school settings: Classification, assessment, and intervention issues. *Review of Educational Research, 59,* 431–470.

King, P. M., & Kitchener, K. S. (2002). The reflective judgment model: Twenty years of research on epistemic cognition. In B. K. Hofer & P. R. Pintrich (Eds.), *Personal epistemology: The psychology of beliefs about knowledge and knowing* (pp. 37–61). Mahwah, NJ: Erlbaum.

Kirk, S. A. (1972). Ethnic differences in psycholinguistic abilities. *Exceptional Children, 39,* 112–118.

Kirkland, M. C. (1971). The effect of tests on students and schools. *Review of Educational Research, 41,* 303–350.

Kirschner, P. A., Sweller, J., & Clark, R. E. (2006). Why minimal guidance during instruction does not work: An analysis of the failure of constructivist, discovery, problem-based, experiential, and inquiry-based teaching. *Educational Psychologist, 41,* 75–86.

Kitayama, S., & Cohen, D. (Eds.). (2007). *Handbook of cultural psychology.* New York: Guilford Press.

Kitayama, S., Duffy, S., & Uchida, Y. (2007). Self as cultural mode of being. In S. Kitayama & D. Cohen (Eds.), *Handbook of cultural psychology* (pp. 136–174). New York: Guilford Press.

Kitsantas, A., Zimmerman, B. J., & Cleary, T. (2000). The role of observation and emulation in the development of athletic self-regulation. *Journal of Educational Psychology, 92,* 811–817.

Klaczynski, P. A. (2001). Analytic and heuristic processing influences on adolescent reasoning and decision-making. *Child Development, 72,* 844–861.

Klahr, D. (2001). Time matters in cognitive development. In J. L. McClelland & R. S. Siegler (Eds.), *Mechanisms of cognitive development: Behavioral and neural perspectives* (pp. 291–301). Mahwah, NJ: Erlbaum.

Klahr, D., & Nigam, M. (2004). The equivalence of learning paths in early science instruction: Effects of direct instruction and discovery learning. *Psychological Science, 15,* 661–667.

Klassen, R. (2002). Writing in early adolescence: A review of the role of self-efficacy beliefs. *Educational Psychology Review, 14,* 173–203.

Klein, J. D. (1990, April). *The effect of interest, task performance, and reward contingencies on self-efficacy.* Paper presented at the annual meeting of the American Educational Research Association, Boston.

Klein, P. D. (1999). Reopening inquiry into cognitive processes in writing-to-learn. *Educational Psychology Review, 11,* 203–270.

Klein, P. D. (2000). Elementary students' strategies for writing-to-learn in science. *Cognition and Instruction, 18,* 317–348.

Klin, A., Volkmar, F. R., & Sparrow, S. S. (Eds.). (2000). *Asperger syndrome.* New York: Guilford Press.

Knapp, M. S., Turnbull, B. J., & Shields, P. M. (1990). New directions for educating the children of poverty. *Educational Leadership, 48*(1), 4–9.

Knapp, M. S., & Woolverton, S. (1995). Social class and schooling. In J. A. Banks & C. A. M. Banks (Eds.), *Handbook of research on multicultural education.* New York: Macmillan.

Knowlton, D. (1995). Managing children with oppositional behavior. *Beyond Behavior, 6*(3), 5–10.

Kochanska, G., Aksan, N., Knaack, A., & Rhines, H. M. (2004). Maternal parenting and children's conscience: Early security as moderator. *Child Development, 75,* 1229–1242.

Kochanska, G., Gross, J. N., Lin, M.-H., & Nichols, K. E. (2002). Guilt in young children: Development, determinants, and relations with a broader system of standards. *Child Development, 73,* 461–482.

Kodluboy, D. W. (2004). Gang-oriented interventions. In J. C. Conoley & A. P. Goldstein (Eds.), *School violence intervention* (2nd ed., pp. 194–232). New York: Guilford Press.

Koedinger, K. R., & Corbett, A. (2006). Cognitive tutors: Technology bringing learning sciences to the classroom. In R. K. Sawyer (Ed.), *The Cambridge handbook of the learning sciences* (pp. 61–77). Cambridge, England: Cambridge University Press.

Koegel, L. K. (1995). Communication and language intervention. In R. L. Koegel & L. K. Koegel (Eds.), *Strategies for initiating positive interactions and improving learning opportunities.* Baltimore: Brookes.

Koegel, L. K., Koegel, R. L., & Dunlap, G. (Eds.). (1996). *Positive behavioral support: Including people with difficult behavior in the community.* Baltimore: Brookes.

Koeppel, J., & Mulrooney, M. (1992). The Sister Schools Program: A way for children to learn about cultural diversity—when there isn't any in their school. *Young Children, 48*(1), 44–47.

Koestner, R., Ryan, R. M., Bernieri, F., & Holt, K. (1984). Setting limits in children's behavior: The differential effects of controlling versus informational styles on intrinsic motivation and creativity. *Journal of Personality, 52,* 233–248.

Koger, S. M., Schettler, T., & Weiss, B. (2005). Environmental toxins and developmental disabilities: A challenge for psychologists. *American Psychologist, 60,* 243–255.

Kohlberg, L. (1976). Moral stages and moralization: The cognitive-developmental approach. In T. Lickona (Ed.), *Moral development and behavior: Theory, research, and social issues.* New York: Holt, Rinehart & Winston.

Kohlberg, L. (1981). *The philosophy of moral development: Moral stages and the idea of justice.* San Francisco: Harper & Row.

Kohlberg, L. (1984). *The psychology of moral development: The nature and validity of moral stages.* San Francisco: Harper & Row.

Kohlberg, L. (1986). A current statement on some theoretical issues. In S. Modgil & C. Modgil (Eds.), *Lawrence Kohlberg: Consensus and controversy.* Philadelphia: Falmer Press.

Kohlberg, L., & Kramer, R. (1969). Continuities and discontinuities in childhood and adult moral development. *Human Development, 12,* 93–120.

Kohn, A. (1993). Choices for children: Why and how to let students decide. *Phi Delta Kappan, 75*(1), 8–20.

Kolb, B., Gibb, R., & Robinson, T. E. (2003). Brain plasticity and behavior. *Current Directions in Psychological Science, 12,* 1–5.

Kolodner, J. (1985). Memory for experience. In G. H. Bower (Ed.), *The psychology of learning and motivation: Advances in research and theory* (Vol. 19). San Diego, CA: Academic Press.

Koltko-Rivera, M. E. (2004). The psychology of worldviews. *Review of General Psychology, 8,* 3–58.

Koretz, D., Stecher, B., Klein, S., & McCaffrey, D. (1994). The Vermont Portfolio Assessment Program: Findings and implications. *Educational Measurement: Issues and Practice, 13*(3), 5–16.

Kornhaber, M., Fierros, E., & Veenema, S. (2004). *Multiple intelligences: Best ideas from research and practice.* Boston: Allyn & Bacon.

Kosslyn, S. M. (1985). Mental imagery ability. In R. J. Sternberg (Ed.), *Human abilities: An information-processing approach.* New York: Freeman.

Kosslyn, S. M., Margolis, J. A., Barrett, A. M., Goldknopf, E. J., & Daly, P. F. (1990). Age differences in imagery ability. *Child Development, 61,* 995–1010.

Kounin, J. S. (1970). *Discipline and group management in classrooms.* New York: Holt, Rinehart & Winston.

Kovacs, D. M., Parker, J. G., & Hoffman, L. W. (1996). Behavioral, affective, and social correlates of involvement in cross-sex friendship in elementary school. *Child Development, 67,* 2269–2286.

Kovas, Y., & Plomin, R. (2007). Learning abilities and disabilities: Generalist genes, specialist environments. *Current Directions in Psychological Science, 16,* 284–288.

Kozulin, A., & Falik, L. (1995). Dynamic cognitive assessment of the child. *Current Directions in Psychological Science, 4,* 192–196.

Krajcik, J. S. (1991). Developing students' understanding of chemical concepts. In S. M. Glynn, R. H. Yeany, & B. K. Britton (Eds.), *The psychology of learning science.* Mahwah, NJ: Erlbaum.

Krajcik, J. S., & Blumenfeld, P. C. (2006). Project-based learning. In R. K. Sawyer (Ed.), *The Cambridge handbook of the learning sciences* (pp. 317–333). Cambridge, England: Cambridge University Press.

Kramarski, B., & Mevarech, Z. R. (2003). Enhancing mathematical reasoning in the classroom: The effects of cooperative learning and metacognitive training. *American Educational Research Journal, 40,* 281–310.

Krampen, G. (1987). Differential effects of teacher comments. *Journal of Educational Psychology, 79,* 137–146.

Krashen, S. D. (1996). *Under attack: The case against bilingual education.* Culver City, CA: Language Education Associates.

Krätzig, G. P., & Arbuthnott, K. D. (2006). Perceptual learning style and learning proficiency: A test of the hypothesis. *Journal of Educational Psychology, 98*, 238–246.

Krauss, S., Brunner, M., Kunter, M., Baumert, J., Blum, W., Neubrand, M., et al. (2008). Pedagogical content knowledge and content knowledge of secondary mathematics teachers. *Journal of Educational Psychology, 100*, 716–725.

Krebs, D. L. (2008). Morality: An evolutionary account. *Perspectives on Psychological Science, 3*, 149–172.

Krebs, D. L., & Van Hesteren, F. (1994). The development of altruism: Toward an integrative model. *Developmental Review, 14*, 103–158.

Krumboltz, J. D., & Krumboltz, H. B. (1972). *Changing children's behavior.* Upper Saddle River, NJ: Prentice Hall.

Ku, Y.-M., Chan, W.-C., Wu, Y.-C., & Chen, Y.-H. (2008, March). *Improving children's comprehension of science text: Effects of adjunct questions and notetaking*. Paper presented at the annual meeting of the American Educational Research Association, New York.

Kucan, L., & Beck, I. L. (1997). Thinking aloud and reading comprehension research: Inquiry, instruction, and social interaction. *Review of Educational Research, 67*, 271–299.

Kugiumutzakis, G. (1988). Neonatal imitation in the intersubjective companion space. In S. Braten (Ed.), *Intersubjective communication and emotion in early ontogeny* (pp. 63–88). Cambridge, England: Cambridge University Press.

Kuhl, J. (1985). Volitional mediators of cognition-behavior consistency: Self-regulatory processes and actions versus state orientation. In J. Kuhl & J. Beckmann (Eds.), *Action control: From cognition to behavior.* Berlin, Germany: Springer-Verlag.

Kuhl, J., & Kraska, K. (1989). Self-regulation and metamotivation: Computational mechanisms, development, and assessment. In R. Kanfer, P. L. Ackerman, & R. Cudeck (Eds.), *Abilities, motivation, and methodology: The Minnesota Symposium on Learning and Individual Differences* (pp. 343–374). Mahwah, NJ: Erlbaum.

Kuhl, P. K. (2004). Early language acquisition: Cracking the speech code. *Nature Reviews Neuroscience, 5*, 831–843.

Kuhl, P. K., Conboy, B. T., Padden, D., Nelson, T., & Pruitt, J. (2005). Early speech perception and later language development: Implications for the "critical period." *Language Learning and Development, 1*, 237–264.

Kuhn, D. (2001a). How do people know? *Psychological Science, 12*, 1–8.

Kuhn, D. (2001b). Why development does (and does not) occur: Evidence from the domain of inductive reasoning. In J. L. McClelland & R. S. Siegler (Eds.), *Mechanisms of cognitive development: Behavioral and neural perspectives* (pp. 221–249). Mahwah, NJ: Erlbaum.

Kuhn, D. (2006). Do cognitive changes accompany developments in the adolescent brain? *Perspectives on Psychological Science, 1*, 59–67.

Kuhn, D. (2007). Is direct instruction an answer to the right question? *Educational Psychologist, 42*, 109–113.

Kuhn, D., Daniels, S., & Krishnan, A. (2003, April). *Epistemology and intellectual values as core metacognitive constructs*. Paper presented at the annual meeting of the American Educational Research Association, Chicago.

Kuhn, D., & Franklin, S. (2006). The second decade: What develops (and how)? In W. Damon & R. M. Lerner (Series Eds.), D. Kuhn, & R. Siegler (Vol. Eds.), *Handbook of child psychology: Vol. 2. Cognition, perception, and language* (6th ed.). New York: Wiley.

Kuhn, D., Garcia-Mila, M., Zohar, A., & Andersen, C. (1995). Strategies of knowledge acquisition. *Monographs of the Society for Research in Child Development, 60* (Whole No. 245).

Kuhn, D., & Park, S.-H. (2005). Epistemological understanding and the development of intellectual values. *International Journal of Educational Research, 43*, 111–124.

Kuhn, D., & Pease, M. (2008). What needs to develop in the development of inquiry skills? *Cognition and Instruction, 26*, 512–599.

Kuhn, D., & Udell, W. (2003). The development of argument skills. *Child Development, 74*, 1245–1260.

Kuhn, D., & Weinstock, M. (2002). What is epistemological thinking and why does it matter? In B. K. Hofer & P. R. Pintrich (Eds.), *Personal epistemology: The psychology of beliefs about knowledge and knowing* (pp. 121–144). Mahwah, NJ: Erlbaum.

Kuiper, E., Volman, M., & Terwel, J. (2005). The Web as an information resource in K–12 education: Strategies for supporting students in searching and processing information. *Review of Educational Research, 75*, 285–328.

Kuklinski, M. R., & Weinstein, R. S. (2001). Classroom and developmental differences in a path model of teacher expectancy effects. *Child Development, 72*, 1554–1578.

Kulik, C. C., Kulik, J. A., & Bangert-Drowns, R. L. (1990). Effectiveness of mastery learning programs: A meta-analysis. *Review of Educational Research, 60*, 265–299.

Kulik, J. A., & Kulik, C. C. (1988). Timing of feedback and verbal learning. *Review of Educational Research, 58*, 79–97.

Kulik, J. A., & Kulik, C. C. (1997). Ability grouping. In N. Colangelo & G. Davis (Eds.), *Handbook of gifted education* (2nd ed., pp. 230–242). Boston: Allyn & Bacon.

Kumar, R., Gheen, M. H., & Kaplan, A. (2002). Goal structures in the learning environment and students' disaffection from learning and schooling. In C. Midgley (Ed.), *Goals, goal structures, and patterns of adaptive learning* (pp. 143–173). Mahwah, NJ: Erlbaum.

Kunzinger, E. L., III. (1985). A short-term longitudinal study of memorial development during early grade school. *Developmental Psychology, 21*, 642–646.

Kupersmidt, J. B., & Coie, J. D. (1990). Preadolescent peer status, aggression, and school adjustment as predictors of externalizing problems in adolescence. *Child Development, 61*, 1350–1362.

Kurtines, W. M., Berman, S. L., Ittel, A., & Williamson, S. (1995). Moral development: A co-constructivist perspective. In W. M. Kurtines & J. L. Gewirtz (Eds.), *Moral development: An introduction.* Boston: Allyn & Bacon.

Kyllonen, P. C., Stankov, L., & Roberts, R. D. (2008). Enhancement and new constructs: Overview and rationale. In P. C. Kyllonen, R. D. Roberts, & L. Stankov (Eds.), *Extending intelligence: Enhancement and new constructs* (pp. 3–11). New York: Erlbaum/Taylor & Francis.

LaBar, K. S., & Phelps, E. A. (1998). Arousal-mediated memory consolidation: Role of the medial temporal lobe in humans. *Psychological Science, 9*, 490–493.

LaBlance, G. R., Steckol, K. F., & Smith, V. L. (1994). Stuttering: The role of the classroom teacher. *Teaching Exceptional Children, 26*(2), 10–12.

Laboratory of Human Cognition. (1982). Culture and intelligence. In R. J. Sternberg (Ed.), *Handbook of human intelligence.* Cambridge, England: Cambridge University Press.

Labouvie-Vief, G., & González, M. M. (2004). Dynamic integration: Affect optimization and differentiation in development. In D. Y. Dai & R. J. Sternberg (Eds.), *Motivation, emotion, and cognition: Integrative perspectives on intellectual functioning and development* (pp. 237–272). Mahwah, NJ: Erlbaum.

Ladd, G. W. (2006). Peer rejection, aggressive or withdrawn behavior, and psychological madadjustment from ages 5 to 12: An examination of four predictive models. *Child Development, 77*, 822–846.

Ladd, G. W., Herald-Brown, S. L., & Reiser, M. (2008). Does chronic classroom peer rejection predict the development of children's classroom participation during the grade school years? *Child Development, 79*, 1001–1015.

Ladd, G. W., & Troop-Gordon, W. (2003). The role of chronic peer difficulties in the development of children's psychological adjustment problems. *Child Development, 74*, 1344–1367.

Ladson-Billings, G. (1994a). *The dreamkeepers: Successful teachers of African American children.* San Francisco: Jossey-Bass.

Ladson-Billings, G. (1994b). What we can learn from multicultural education research. *Educational Leadership, 51*(8), 22–26.

Ladson-Billings, G. (1995a). But that's just good teaching! The case for culturally relevant pedagogy. *Theory into Practice, 34*, 159–165.

Ladson-Billings, G. (1995b). Toward a theory of culturally relevant pedagogy. *American Educational Research Journal, 32*, 465–491.

LaFromboise, T., Coleman, H. L. K., & Gerton, J. (1993). Psychological impact of biculturalism: Evidence and theory. *Psychological Bulletin, 114*, 395–412.

Laird, J., Kienzl, G., DeBell, M., & Chapman, C. (2007). *Dropout rates in the United States: 2005* (Compendium Report, National Center for Education Statistics 2007-059). Washington: NCES.

Lajoie, S. P., & Derry, S. J. (Eds.). (1993). *Computers as cognitive tools.* Mahwah, NJ: Erlbaum.

Lamborn, S. D., Mounts, N. S., Steinberg, L., & Dornbusch, S. M. (1991). Patterns of competence and adjustment among adolescents from authoritative, authoritarian, indulgent, and neglectful families. *Child Development, 62*, 1049–1065.

Lamon, M., Chan, C., Scardamalia, M., Burtis, P. J., & Brett, C. (1993, April). *Beliefs about learning and constructive processes in reading: Effects of a computer supported intentional learning environment (CSILE).* Paper presented at the annual meeting of the American Educational Research Association, Atlanta, GA.

Lampert, M., Rittenhouse, P., & Crumbaugh, C. (1996). Agreeing to disagree: Developing sociable mathematical discourse. In D. R. Olson & N. Torrance (Eds.), *The handbook of education and human development: New models of learning, teaching, and schooling.* Cambridge, MA: Blackwell.

Lan, W. Y., Repman, J., Bradley, L., & Weller, H. (1994, April). *Immediate and lasting effects of criterion and payoff on academic risk taking.* Paper presented at the annual meeting of the American Educational Research Association, New Orleans, LA.

Landau, S., & McAninch, C. (1993). Young children with attention deficits. *Young Children, 48*(4), 49–58.

Landers, D. M. (2007). The arousal-performance relationship revisited. In D. Smith (Ed.), *Essential readings in sport and exercise psychology* (pp. 211–218). Champaign, IL: Human Kinetics.

Landrum, T. J., & Kauffman, J. M. (2006). Behavioral approaches to classroom management. In C. M. Evertson & C. S. Weinstein (Eds.), *Handbook of classroom management: Research, practice, and contemporary issues* (pp. 47–71). Mahwah, NJ: Erlbaum.

Lane, K., Falk, K., & Wehby, J. (2006). Classroom management in special education classrooms and resource rooms. In C. M. Evertson & C. S. Weinstein (Eds.), *Handbook of classroom management: Research, practice, and contemporary issues* (pp. 439–460). Mahwah, NJ: Erlbaum.

Langer, E. J. (1997). *The power of mindful learning.* Reading, MA: Addison-Wesley.

Langer, E. J. (2000). Mindful learning. *Current Directions in Psychological Science, 9*, 220–223.

Langer, J. A. (2000). Excellence in English in middle and high school: How teachers' professional lives support student achievement. *American Educational Research Journal, 37*, 397–439.

Lannie, A. L., & Martens, B. K. (2004). Effects of task difficulty and type of contingency on students' allocation of responding to math worksheets. *Journal of Applied Behavior Analysis, 37*, 53–65.

Lapan, R. T., Tucker, B., Kim, S.-K., & Kosciulek, J. F. (2003). Preparing rural adolescents for post-high school transitions. *Journal of Counseling and Development, 81*, 329–342.

La Paro, K. M., & Pianta, R. C. (2000). Predicting children's competence in the early school years: A meta-analytic review. *Review of Educational Research, 70*, 443–484.

Lapsley, D. K. (1993). Toward an integrated theory of

adolescent ego development: The "new look" at adolescent egocentrism. *American Journal of Orthopsychiatry, 63,* 562–571.

Larkin, R. W. (1979). *Suburban youth in cultural crisis.* New York: Oxford University Press.

Larrivee, B. (2006). The convergence of reflective practice and effective classroom management. In C. M. Evertson & C. S. Weinstein (Eds.), *Handbook of classroom management: Research, practice, and contemporary issues* (pp. 983–1001). Mahwah, NJ: Erlbaum.

Larson, R. W. (2000). Toward a psychology of positive youth development. *American Psychologist, 55,* 170–183.

Larson, R. W., & Brown, J. R. (2007). Emotional development in adolescence: What can be learned from a high school theater program? *Child Development, 78,* 1083–1099.

Larson, R. W., Clore, G. L., & Wood, G. A. (1999). The emotions of romantic relationships: Do they wreak havoc on adolescents? In W. Furman, B. B. Brown, & C. Feiring (Eds.), *The development of romantic relationships in adolescence* (pp. 19–49). Cambridge, England: Cambridge University Press.

Larson, R. W., Moneta, G., Richards, M. H., & Wilson, S. (2002). Continuity, stability, and change in daily emotional experience across adolescence. *Child Development, 73,* 1151–1165.

Lau, S., & Nie, Y. (2008). Interplay between personal goals and classroom goal structures in predicting student outcomes: A multilevel analysis of person-context interactions. *Journal of Educational Psychology, 100,* 15–29.

Laupa, M., & Turiel, E. (1995). Social domain theory. In W. M. Kurtines & J. L. Gewirtz (Eds.), *Moral development: An introduction.* Boston: Allyn & Bacon.

Laursen, B., Bukowski, W. M., Aunola, K., & Nurmi, J.-E. (2007). Friendship moderates prospective associations between social isolation and adjustment problems in young children. *Child Development, 78,* 1395–1404.

Lautrey, J. (1993). Structure and variability: A plea for a pluralistic approach to cognitive development. In R. Case & W. Edelstein (Eds.), *The new structuralism in cognitive development: Theory and research on individual pathways.* Basel, Switzerland: Karger.

Lave, J., & Wenger, E. (1991). *Situated learning: Legitimate peripheral participation.* Cambridge, England: Cambridge University Press.

Lawlor, M. S., & Schonert-Reichl, L. A. (2008, March). *The benefits of being good during early adolescence: Altruism, happiness, and the mediating role of relatedness.* Paper presented at the annual meeting of the American Educational Research Association, New York.

Lazarus, R. S. (1991). *Emotion and adaptation.* New York: Oxford University Press.

Leaper, C., & Friedman, C. K. (2007). The socialization of gender. In J. E. Grusec & P. D. Hastings (Eds.), *Handbook of socialization: Theory and research* (pp. 561–587). New York: Guilford Press.

Learning First Alliance. (2001). *Every child learning: Safe and supportive schools.* Washington, DC: Association for Supervision and Curriculum Development.

Leary, M. R. (1999). Making sense of self-esteem. *Current Directions in Psychological Science, 8,* 32–35.

Leary, M. R., & Hill, D. A. (1996). Moving on: Autism and movement disturbance. *Mental Retardation, 34,* 39–53.

LeBlanc, L. A., Coates, A. M., Daneshvar, S., Charlop-Christy, M. H., Morris, C., & Lancaster, B. M. (2003). Using video modeling and reinforcement to teach perspective-taking skills to children with autism. *Journal of Applied Behavior Analysis, 36,* 253–257.

Lee, J., & Wong, K. K. (2004). The impact of accountability on racial and socioeconomic equity: Considering both school resources and achievement outcomes. *American Educational Research Journal, 41,* 797–832.

Lee, J.-S., & Bowen, N. K. (2006). Parent involvement, cultural capital, and the achievement gap among elementary school children. *American Educational Research Journal, 43,* 193–218.

Lee, O. (1999). Science knowledge, world views, and information sources in social and cultural contexts: Making sense after a natural disaster. *American Educational Research Journal, 36,* 187–219.

Lee, S. (1985). Children's acquisition of conditional logic structure: Teachable? *Contemporary Educational Psychology, 10,* 14–27.

Lee, V. E., & Burkam, D. T. (2003). Dropping out of high school: The role of school organization and structure. *American Educational Research Journal, 40,* 353–393.

Lee-Pearce, M. L., Plowman, T. S., & Touchstone, D. (1998). Starbase-Atlantis, a school without walls: A comparative study of an innovative science program for at-risk urban elementary students. *Journal of Education for Students Placed at Risk, 3,* 223–235.

Leffert, J. S., Siperstein, G. N., & Millikan, E. (2000). Understanding social adaptation in children with mental retardation: A social-cognitive perspective. *Exceptional Children, 66,* 530–545.

Lehmann, M., & Hasselhorn, M. (2007). Variable memory strategy use in children's adaptive intratask learning behavior: Developmental changes and working memory influences in free recall. *Child Development, 78,* 1068–1082.

Leichtman, M. D., & Ceci, S. J. (1995). The effects of stereotypes and suggestions on preschoolers' reports. *Developmental Psychology, 31,* 568–578.

Leiter, J., & Johnsen, M. C. (1997). Child maltreatment and school performance declines: An event-history analysis. *American Educational Research Journal, 34,* 563–589.

Lejuez, C. W., Schaal, D. W., & O'Donnell, J. (1998). Behavioral pharmacology and the treatment of substance abuse. In J. J. Plaud & G. H. Eifert (Eds.), *From behavior theory to behavior therapy* (pp. 116–135). Boston: Allyn & Bacon.

Lennon, R., Ormrod, J. E., Burger, S., & Warren, E. (1990, October). *Belief systems of teacher education majors and their possible influences on future classroom performance.* Paper presented at the Northern Rocky Mountain Educational Research Association, Greeley, CO.

Lenroot, R. K., & Giedd, J. N. (2007). The structural development of the human brain as measured longitudinally with magnetic resonance imaging. In D. Coch, K. W. Fischer, & G. Dawson (Eds.), *Human behavior, learning, and the developing brain: Typical development* (pp. 50–73). New York: Guilford Press.

Lepper, M. R., Aspinwall, L. G., Mumme, D. L., & Chabay, R. W. (1990). Self-perception and social perception processes in tutoring: Subtle social control strategies of expert tutors. In J. M. Olson & M. P. Zanna (Eds.), *Self-inference processes: The Ontario Symposium.* Mahwah, NJ: Erlbaum.

Lepper, M. R., Corpus, J. H., & Iyengar, S. S. (2005). Intrinsic and extrinsic motivational orientations in the classroom: Age differences and academic correlates. *Journal of Educational Psychology, 97,* 184–196.

Lepper, M. R., & Hodell, M. (1989). Intrinsic motivation in the classroom. In C. Ames & R. Ames (Eds.), *Research on motivation in education: Vol. 3. Goals and cognitions.* San Diego, CA: Academic Press.

Lerman, D. C., & Iwata, B. A. (1995). Prevalence of the extinction burst and its attenuation during treatment. *Journal of Applied Behavior Analysis, 28,* 93–94.

Lerman, D. C., Kelley, M. E., Vorndran, C. M., Kuhn, S. A. C., & LaRue, R. H., Jr. (2002). Reinforcement magnitude and responding during treatment with differential reinforcement. *Journal of Applied Behavior Analysis, 35,* 29–48.

Lerman, D. C., & Vorndran, C. M. (2002). On the status of knowledge for using punishment: Implications for treating behavior disorders. *Journal of Applied Behavior Analysis, 35,* 431–464.

Lerner, J. W. (1985). *Learning disabilities: Theories, diagnosis, and teaching strategies* (4th ed.). Boston: Houghton Mifflin.

Lesgold, A. M. (2001). The nature and methods of learning by doing. *American Psychologist, 56,* 965–973.

Lester, F. K., Jr., Lambdin, D. V., & Preston, R. V. (1997). A new vision of the nature and purposes of assessment in the mathematics classroom. In G. D. Phye (Ed.), *Handbook of classroom assessment: Learning, achievement, and adjustment.* San Diego, CA: Academic Press.

Leung, A. K., Maddux, W. W. Galinsky, A. D., & Chiu, C. (2008). Multicultural experience enhances creativity: The when and how. *American Psychologist, 63,* 169–181.

Leventhal, T., & Brooks-Gunn, J. (2000). The neighborhoods they live in: The effects of neighborhood residence upon child and adolescent outcomes. *Psychological Bulletin, 126,* 309–337.

Levin, J. R., & Mayer, R. E. (1993). Understanding illustrations in text. In B. K. Britton, A. Woodward, & M. Binkley (Eds.), *Learning from textbooks: Theory and practice.* Mahwah, NJ: Erlbaum.

Levine, D. U., & Lezotte, L. W. (1995). Effective schools research. In J. A. Banks & C. A. M. Banks (Eds.), *Handbook of research on multicultural education.* New York: Macmillan.

Levitt, M. J., Guacci-Franco, N., & Levitt, J. L. (1993). Convoys of social support in childhood and early adolescence: Structure and function. *Developmental Psychology, 29,* 811–818.

Levstik, L. S. (1994). Building a sense of history in a first-grade classroom. In J. Brophy (Ed.), *Advances in research on teaching: Vol. 4. Case studies of teaching and learning in social studies.* Greenwich, CT: JAI Press.

Levy, I., Kaplan, A., & Patrick, H. (2000, April). *Early adolescents' achievement goals, intergroup processes, and attitudes towards collaboration.* Paper presented at the annual meeting of the American Educational Research Association, New Orleans, LA.

Levy-Tossman, I., & Kaplan, A. (April, 2004). Goal orientation and intergroup processes in school: A person-centered longitudinal investigation. Paper presented at the American Educational Research Association, San Diego, CA.

Lewis, M., & Sullivan, M. W. (2005). The development of self-conscious emotions. In A. J. Elliot & C. S. Dweck (Eds.), *Handbook of competence and motivation* (pp. 185–201). New York: Guilford Press.

Lewis, M. D., & Stieben, J. (2004). Emotion regulation in the brain: Conceptual issues and directions for developmental research. *Child Development, 75,* 371–376.

Lewis, T. J., Newcomer, L. L., Trussell, R., & Richter, M. (2006). Schoolwide positive behavior support: Building systems to develop and maintain appropriate social behavior. In C. M. Evertson & C. S. Weinstein (Eds.), *Handbook of classroom management: Research, practice, and contemporary issues* (pp. 833–854). Mahwah, NJ: Erlbaum.

Li, J. (2004). High abilities and excellence: A cultural perspective. In L. V. Shavinina & M. Ferrari (Eds.), *Beyond knowledge: Extracognitive aspects of developing high ability* (pp. 187–208). Mahwah, NJ: Erlbaum.

Li, J. (2005). Mind or virtue: Western and Chinese beliefs about learning. *Current Directions in Psychological Science, 14,* 190–194.

Li, J. (2006). Self in learning: Chinese adolescents' goals and sense of agency. *Child Development, 77,* 482–501.

Li, J., & Fischer, K. W. (2004). Thought and affect in American and Chinese learners' beliefs about learning. In D. Y. Dai & R. J. Sternberg (Eds.), *Motivation, emotion, and cognition: Integrative perspectives on intellectual functioning and development* (pp. 385–418). Mahwah, NJ: Erlbaum.

Li, Y., Anderson, R. C., Nguyen-Jahiel, K., Dong, T., Archodidou, A., Kim, I.-H., Kuo, L.-J., Clark, A.-M., Wu, X., Jadallah, M., & Miller, B. (2007). Emergent leadership in children's discussion groups. *Cognition and Instruction, 25,* 75–111.

Liben, L. S., & Bigler, R. S. (2002). The developmental course of gender differentiation: Conceptualizing, measuring, and evaluating constructs and pathways. *Monographs of the Society for Research in Child Development, 67*(2, Serial No. 269).

Liben, L. S., Bigler, R. S., & Krogh, H. R. (2002). Language at work: Children's gendered interpretations of occupational titles. *Child Development, 73,* 810–828.

Liben, L. S., & Downs, R. M. (1989). Understanding maps as symbols: The development of map concepts in children. In H. W. Reese (Ed.), *Advances in child development and behavior* (Vol. 22). San Diego, CA: Harcourt Brace Jovanovich.

Liben, L. S., & Myers, L. J. (2007). Developmental changes in children's understanding of maps: What, when, and how? In J. M. Plumert & J. P. Spencer (Eds.), *The emerging spatial mind* (pp. 193–218). New York: Oxford University Press.

Lichtman, J. W. (2001). Developmental neurobiology overview: Synapses, circuits, and plasticity. In D. B. Bailey, Jr., J. T. Bruer, F. J. Symons, & J. W. Lichtman (Eds.), *Critical thinking about critical periods* (pp. 27–42). Baltimore: Brookes.

Lickona, T. (1991). Moral development in the elementary school classroom. In W. M. Kurtines & J. L. Gewirtz (Eds.), *Moral behavior and development: Vol. 3. Application.* Mahwah, NJ: Erlbaum.

Lidz, C. S. (1991). Issues in the assessment of preschool children. In B. A. Bracken (Ed.), *The psychoeducational assessment of preschool children* (2nd ed., pp. 18–31). Boston: Allyn & Bacon.

Lidz, C. S., & Gindis, B. (2003). Dynamic assessment of the evolving cognitive functions in children. In A. Kozulin, B. Gindis, V. S. Ageyev, & S. M. Miller (Eds.), *Vygotsky's educational theory in cultural context* (pp. 99–116). Cambridge, England: Cambridge University Press.

Liem, A. D., Lau, S., & Nie, Y. (2008). The role of self-efficacy, task value, and achievement goals in predicting learning strategies, task disengagement, peer relationship, and achievement outcome. *Contemporary Educational Psychology, 33,* 486–512.

Liew, J., McTigue, E., Barrois, L., & Hughes, J. N. (2008, March). *I am, therefore I think: Effortful control, academic self-efficacy, and achievement in early grade school.* Paper presented at the annual meeting of the American Educational Research Association, New York.

Lillard, A. S. (1997). Other folks' theories of mind and behavior. *Psychological Science, 8,* 268–274.

Lind, G. (1994, April). *Why do juvenile delinquents gain little from moral discussion programs?* Paper presented at the annual meeting of the American Educational Research Association, New Orleans, LA.

Linn, M. C., Clement, C., Pulos, S., & Sullivan, P. (1989). Scientific reasoning during adolescence: The influence of instruction in science knowledge and reasoning strategies. *Journal of Research in Science Teaching, 26,* 171–187.

Linn, M. C., & Muilenburg, L. (1996). Creating lifelong science learners: What models form a firm foundation? *Educational Researcher, 25*(5), 18–24.

Linn, M. C., Songer, N. B., & Eylon, B. (1996). Shifts and convergences in science learning and instruction. In D. C. Berliner & R. C. Calfee (Eds.), *Handbook of educational psychology.* New York: Macmillan.

Linn, R. L. (1994). Performance assessment: Policy promises and technical measurement standards. *Educational Researcher, 23*(9), 4–14.

Linn, R. L. (2000). Assessments and accountability. *Educational Researcher, 29*(2), 4–16.

Linn, R. L., & Miller, M.D. (2005). *Measurement and assessment in teaching* (9th ed.). Upper Saddle River, NJ: Merrill/Prentice Hall.

Linnenbrink, E. A. (2005). The dilemma of performance-approach goals: The use of multiple goal contexts to promote students' motivation and learning. *Journal of Educational Psychology, 97,* 197–213.

Linnenbrink, E. A., & Pintrich, P. R. (2002). Achievement goal theory and affect: An asymmetrical bidirectional model. *Educational Psychologist, 37,* 69–78.

Linnenbrink, E. A., & Pintrich, P. R. (2003). Achievement goals and intentional conceptual change. In G. M. Sinatra & P. R. Pintrich (Eds.), *Intentional conceptual change* (pp. 347–374). Mahwah, NJ: Erlbaum.

Linnenbrink, E. A., & Pintrich, P. R. (2004). Role of affect in cognitive processing in academic contexts. In D. Y. Dai & R. J. Sternberg (Eds.), *Motivation, emotion, and cognition: Integrative perspectives on intellectual functioning and development* (pp. 57–87). Mahwah, NJ: Erlbaum.

Lipka, J. (1994). Schools failing minority teachers. *Educational Foundations, 8,* 57–80.

Lipka, J., with Mohatt, G. V., & the Ciulistet Group. (1998). *Transforming the culture of schools: Yup'ik Eskimo examples.* Mahwah, NJ: Erlbaum.

Lipman, P. (1995). "Bringing out the best in them": The contribution of culturally relevant teachers to educational reform. *Theory into Practice, 34,* 202–208.

Lippa, R. A. (2002). *Gender, nature, and nurture.* Mahwah, NJ: Erlbaum.

Lipson, M. Y. (1983). The influence of religious affiliation on children's memory for text information. *Reading Research Quarterly, 18,* 448–457.

Liss, M. B. (1983). Learning gender-related skills through play. In M. B. Liss (Ed.), *Social and cognitive skills: Sex roles and children's play.* San Diego, CA: Academic Press.

Little, L. (2002). Middle class mothers' perceptions of peer and sibling victimization among children with Asperger's syndrome and nonverbal learning disorders. *Comprehensive Pediatric Nursing, 25,* 43–57.

Liu, J., Golinkoff, R. M., & Sak, K. (2001). One cow does not an animal make: Young children can extend novel words at the superordinate level. *Child Development, 72,* 1674–1694.

Liu, L. G. (1990, April). *The use of causal questioning to promote narrative comprehension and memory.* Paper presented at the annual meeting of the American Educational Research Association, Boston.

Lochman, J. E., & Dodge, K. A. (1994). Social-cognitive processes of severely violent, moderately aggressive, and nonaggressive boys. *Journal of Consulting and Clinical Psychology, 62,* 366–374.

Locke, E. A., & Latham, G. P. (1990). *A theory of goal setting and task performance.* Upper Saddle River, NJ: Prentice Hall.

Locke, E. A., & Latham, G. P. (2006). New directions in goal-setting theory. *Current Directions in Psychological Science, 15,* 265–268.

Locke, J. L. (1993). *The child's path to spoken language.* Cambridge, MA: Harvard University Press.

Lockhart, K. L., Chang, B., & Story, T. (2002). Young children's beliefs about the stability of traits: Protective optimism? *Child Development, 73,* 1408–1430.

Lodewyk, K. R., & Winne, P. H. (2005). Relations among the structure of learning tasks, achievement, and changes in self-efficacy in secondary students. *Journal of Educational Psychology, 97,* 3–12.

Lodico, M. G., Ghatala, E. S., Levin, J. R., Pressley, M., & Bell, J. A. (1983). The effects of strategy monitoring training on children's selection of effective memory strategies. *Journal of Experimental Child Psychology, 35,* 273–277.

Loftus, E. F., & Loftus, G. R. (1980). On the permanence of stored information in the human brain. *American Psychologist, 35,* 409–420.

Lomawaima, K. T. (1995). Educating Native Americans. In J. A. Banks & C. A. M. Banks (Eds.), *Handbook of research on multicultural education.* New York: Macmillan.

Lopez, A. M. (2003). Mixed-race school-age children: A summary of census 2000 data. *Educational Researcher, 32*(6), 25–37.

López, G. R. (2001). Redefining parental involvement: Lessons from high-performing migrant-impacted schools. *American Educational Research Journal, 38,* 253–288.

Loranger, A. L. (1994). The study strategies of successful and unsuccessful high school students. *Journal of Reading Behavior, 26,* 347–360.

Lorch, E. P., Diener, M. B., Sanchez, R. P., Milich, R., Welsh, R., & van den Broek, P. (1999). The effects of story structure on the recall of stories in children with attention deficit hyperactivity disorder. *Journal of Educational Psychology, 91,* 273–283.

Lorch, R. F., Jr., Calderhead, W. J., Dunlap, E. E., Hodell, E. C., Freer, B. D., & Lorch, E. P. (2008, March). *Teaching the control of variables strategy in fourth grade classrooms.* Paper presented at the annual meeting of the American Educational Research Association, New York.

Lorch, R. F., Jr., Lorch, E. P., & Inman, W. E. (1993). Effects of signaling topic structure on text recall. *Journal of Educational Psychology, 85,* 281–290.

Losey, K. M. (1995). Mexican American students and classroom interaction: An overview and critique. *Review of Educational Research, 65,* 283–318.

Losh, S. C. (2003). On the application of social cognition and social location to creating causal explanatory structures. *Educational Research Quarterly, 26*(3), 17–33.

Lotan, R. A. (2006). Managing groupwork in heterogeneous classrooms. In C. M. Evertson & C. S. Weinstein (Eds.), *Handbook of classroom management: Research, practice, and contemporary issues* (pp. 525–539). Mahwah, NJ: Erlbaum.

Lou, Y., Abrami, P. C., & d'Apollonia, S. (2001). Small group and individual learning with technology: A meta-analysis. *Review of Educational Research, 71,* 449–521.

Lou, Y., Abrami, P. C., Spence, J. C., Poulsen, C., Chambers, B., & d'Apollonia, S. (1996). Within-class grouping: A meta-analysis. *Review of Educational Research, 66,* 423–458.

Lovell, K. (1979). Intellectual growth and the school curriculum. In F. B. Murray (Ed.), *The impact of Piagetian theory: On education, philosophy, psychiatry, and psychology.* Baltimore: University Park Press.

Lovett, S. B., & Flavell, J. H. (1990). Understanding and remembering: Children's knowledge about the differential effects of strategy and task variables on comprehension and memorization. *Child Development, 61,* 1842–1858.

Lovitt, T. C., Guppy, T. E., & Blattner, J. E. (1969). The use of free-time contingency with fourth graders to increase spelling accuracy. *Behaviour Research and Therapy, 7,* 151–156.

Lowry, R., Sleet, D., Duncan, C., Powell, K., & Kolbe, L. (1995). Adolescents at risk for violence. *Educational Psychology Review, 7,* 7–39.

Lubart, T. I., & Mouchiroud, C. (2003). Creativity: A source of difficulty in problem solving. In J. E. Davidson & R. J. Sternberg (Eds.), *The psychology of problem solving* (pp. 127–148). Cambridge, England: Cambridge University Press.

Lubinski, D., & Bleske-Rechek, A. (2008). Enhancing development in intellectually talented populations. In P. C. Kyllonen, R. D. Roberts, & L. Stankov (Eds.), *Extending intelligence: Enhancement and new constructs* (pp. 109–132). New York: Erlbaum/Taylor & Francis.

Lucariello, J., Kyratzis, A., & Nelson, K. (1992). Taxonomic knowledge: What kind and when? *Child Development, 63,* 978–998.

Luchins, A. S. (1942). Mechanization in problem solving: The effect of Einstellung. *Psychological Monographs, 54* (Whole No. 248).

Luchins, A. S., & Luchins, E. H. (1950). New experimental attempts at preventing mechanization in problem solving. *Journal of General Psychology, 42,* 279–297.

Luckasson, R., Borthwick-Duffy, S., Buntinx, W. H. E., Coulter, D. L., Craig, E. M., Reeve, A., Schalock, R. L., Snell, M. E., Spitalnik, D. M., Spreat, S., & Tassé, M. J. (Eds.). (2002). *Mental retardation: Definition, classification, and systems of supports* (10th ed.). Washington, DC: American Association on Mental Retardation.

Lueptow, L. B. (1984). *Adolescent sex roles and social change.* New York: Columbia University Press.

Luna, B., Garver, K. E., Urban, T. A., Lazar, N. A., & Sweeney, J. A. (2004). Maturation of cognitive processes from late childhood to adulthood. *Child Development, 75,* 1357–1372.

Lundeberg, M. A., & Fox, P. W. (1991). Do laboratory findings on test expectancy generalize to classroom outcomes? *Review of Educational Research, 61,* 94–106.

Lupart, J. L. (1995). Exceptional learners and teaching

for transfer. In A. McKeough, J. Lupart, & A. Marini (Eds.), *Teaching for transfer: Fostering generalization in learning.* Mahwah, NJ: Erlbaum.

Lustig, C., & Hasher, L. (2001). Implicit memory is vulnerable to proactive interference. *Psychological Science, 12,* 408–412.

Lustig, C., Konkel, A., & Jacoby, L. L. (2004). Which route to recovery? Controlled retrieval and accessibility bias in retroactive interference. *Psychological Science, 15,* 729–735.

Luthar, S. S. (2006). Over-scheduling versus other stressors: Challenges of high socioeconomic status families. *Social Policy Report, 20*(4), 16–17. Ann Arbor, MI: Society for Research in Child Development.

Luthar, S. S., & Latendresse, S. J. (2005). Children of the affluent: Challenges to well-being. *Current Directions in Psychological Science, 14,* 49–53.

Lykken, D. T. (1997). The American crime factory. *Psychological Inquiry, 8,* 261–270.

Lyon, G. R., & Krasnegor, N. A. (Eds.). (1996). *Attention, memory, and executive function.* Baltimore: Brookes.

Lytton, H., & Romney, D. M. (1991). Parents' differential socialization of boys and girls: A meta-analysis. *Psychological Bulletin, 109,* 267–296.

Maccoby, E. E. (2002). Gender and group process: A developmental perspective. *Current Directions in Psychological Science, 11,* 54–58.

MacDonald, S., Uesiliana, K., & Hayne, H. (2000). Cross-cultural and gender differences in childhood amnesia. *Memory, 8,* 365–376.

Mace, F. C., Belfiore, P. J., & Shea, M. C. (1989). Operant theory and research on self-regulation. In B. J. Zimmerman & D. H. Schunk (Eds.), *Self-regulated learning and academic achievement: Theory, research, and practice.* New York: Springer-Verlag.

Mace, F. C., Hock, M. L., Lalli, J. S., West, B. J., Belfiore, P., Pinter, E., & Brown, D. K. (1988). Behavioral momentum in the treatment of noncompliance. *Journal of Applied Behavior Analysis, 21,* 123–141.

Mace, F. C., & Kratochwill, T. R. (1988). Self-monitoring. In J. C. Witt, S. N. Elliott, & F. M. Gresham (Eds.), *Handbook of behavior therapy in education.* New York: Plenum Press.

Machiels-Bongaerts, M., Schmidt, H. G., & Boshuizen, H. P. (1993). Effects of mobilizing prior knowledge on information processing: Studies of free recall and allocation of study time. *British Journal of Psychology, 84,* 481–498.

Mac Iver, D. J., Reuman, D. A., & Main, S. R. (1995). Social structuring of the school: Studying what is, illuminating what could be. In J. T. Spence, J. M. Darley, & D. J. Foss (Eds.), *Annual review of psychology* (Vol. 46, pp. 375–400). Palo Alto, CA: Annual Review, Inc.

Mac Iver, D. J., Stipek, D. J., & Daniels, D. H. (1991). Explaining within-semester changes in student effort in junior high school and senior high school courses. *Journal of Educational Psychology, 83,* 201–211.

MacLean, D. J., Sasse, D. K., Keating, D. P., Stewart, B. E., & Miller, F. K. (1995, April). *All-girls' mathematics and science instruction in early adolescence: Longitudinal effects.* Paper presented at the annual meeting of the American Educational Research Association, San Francisco.

MacMaster, K., Donovan, L. A., & MacIntyre, P. D. (2002). The effects of being diagnosed with a learning disability on children's self-esteem. *Child Study Journal, 32,* 101–108.

Madden, N. A., & Slavin, R. E. (1983). Mainstreaming students with mild handicaps: Academic and social outcomes. *Review of Educational Research, 53,* 519–569.

Maehr, M. L. (1984). Meaning and motivation: Toward a theory of personal investment. In R. Ames & C. Ames (Eds.), *Research on motivation in education: Vol. 1. Student motivation.* San Diego, CA: Academic Press.

Maehr, M. L., & Anderman, E. M. (1993). Reinventing schools for early adolescents: Emphasizing task goals. *Elementary School Journal, 93,* 593–610.

Maehr, M. L., & McInerney, D. M. (2004). Motivation as personal investment. In D. M. McInerney & S. Van Etten (Eds.), *Big theories revisited* (pp. 61–90). Greenwich, CT: Information Age.

Maehr, M. L., & Meyer, H. A. (1997). Understanding motivation and schooling: Where we've been, where we are, and where we need to go. *Educational Psychology Review, 9,* 371–409.

Magill, R. A. (1993). Modeling and verbal feedback influences on skill learning. *International Journal of Sport Psychology, 24,* 358–369.

Magnusson, S. J., Boyle, R. A., & Templin, M. (1994, April). *Conceptual development: Re-examining knowledge construction in science.* Paper presented at the annual meeting of the American Educational Research Association, New Orleans, LA.

Mahoney, J. L., Cairns, B. D., & Farmer, T. W. (2003). Promoting interpersonal competence and educational success through extracurricular activity participation. *Journal of Educational Psychology, 95,* 409–418.

Maikovich, A. K., Jaffee, S. R., Odgers, C. L., & Gallop, R. (2008). Effects of family violence on psychopathology symptoms in children previously exposed to maltreatment. *Child Development, 79,* 1498–1512.

Maker, C. J. (1993). Creativity, intelligence, and problem solving: A definition and design for cross-cultural research and measurement related to giftedness. *Gifted Education International, 9*(2), 68–77.

Maker, C. J., & Schiever, S. W. (Eds.). (1989). *Critical issues in gifted education: Vol. 2. Defensible programs for cultural and ethnic minorities.* Austin, TX: Pro-Ed.

Mangels, J. (2004, May). *The influence of intelligence beliefs on attention and learning: A neurophysiological approach.* Invited address presented at the annual meeting of the American Psychological Society, Chicago.

Manset, G., & Semmel, M. I. (1997). Are inclusive programs for students with mild disabilities effective? A comparative review of model programs. *Journal of Special Education, 31,* 155–180.

Mantzicopoulos, P. Y., Knutson, D. J. (2000). Head Start children: School mobility and achievement in the early grades. *Journal of Educational Research, 93,* 305–311.

Mar, R. A., & Oatley, K. (2008). The function of fiction is the abstraction and simulation of social experience. *Perspectives on Psychological Science, 3,* 173–192.

Marachi, R., Friedel, J., & Midgley, C. (2001, April). *"I sometimes annoy my teacher during math": Relations between student perceptions of the teacher and disruptive behavior in the classroom.* Paper presented at the annual meeting of the American Educational Research Association, Seattle, WA.

Maratsos, M. (1998). Some problems in grammatical acquisition. In W. Damon (Series Ed.), D. Kuhn, & R. S. Siegler (Vol. Eds.), *Handbook of child psychology: Vol. 2. Cognition, perception, and language* (5th ed.). New York: Wiley.

Marcia, J. E. (1980). Identity in adolescence. In J. Adelson (Ed.), *Handbook of adolescent psychology.* New York: Wiley.

Marcia, J. E. (1988). Common processes underlying ego identity, cognitive/moral development, and individuation. In D. K. Lapsley & F. C. Power (Eds.), *Self, ego, and identity: Integrative approaches* (pp. 211–225). New York: Springer-Verlag.

Marcia, J. E. (1991). Identity and self-development. In R. M. Lerner, A. C. Petersen, & J. Brooks-Gunn (Eds.), *Encyclopedia of adolescence* (Vol. 1, pp. 529–533). New York: Garland.

Marcus, R. F. (1980). Empathy and popularity of preschool children. *Child Study Journal, 10,* 133–145.

Mareschal, D., Johnson, M. H., Sirois, S., Spratling, M. W., Thomas, M. S. C., & Westermann, G. (2007). *Neuroconstructivism: Vol. 1. How the brain constructs cognition.* Oxford, England: Oxford University Press.

Margolin, G., & Gordis, E. B. (2004). Children's exposure to violence in the family and community. *Current Directions in Psychological Science, 13,* 152–155.

Maria, K. (1998). Self-confidence and the process of conceptual change. In B. Guzzetti & C. Hynd (Eds.), *Perspectives on conceptual change: Multiple ways to understand knowing and learning in a complex world* (pp. 7–16). Mahwah, NJ: Erlbaum.

Markman, E. M. (1977). Realizing that you don't understand: A preliminary investigation. *Child Development, 48,* 986–992.

Marks, H. M. (2000). Student engagement in instructional activity: Patterns in the elementary, middle, and high school years. *American Educational Research Journal, 37,* 153–184.

Markus, H. R., & Hamedani, M. G. (2007). Sociocultural psychology: The dynamic interdependence among self systems and social systems. In S. Kitayama & D. Cohen (Eds.), *Handbook of cultural psychology* (pp. 3–39). New York: Guilford Press.

Markus, H. R., & Kitayama, S. (1991). Culture and the self: Implications for cognition, emotion, and motivation. *Psychological Review, 98,* 224–253.

Marley, S. C., Szabo, Z., Levin, J. R., & Glenberg, A. M. (2008, March). *Activity, observed activity, and children's recall of orally presented narrative passages.* Paper presented at the annual meeting of the American Educational Research Association, New York.

Marsh, H. W. (1990). Causal ordering of academic self-concept and academic achievement: A multiwave, longitudinal panel analysis. *Journal of Educational Psychology, 82,* 646–656.

Marsh, H. W., & Craven, R. (1997). Academic self-concept: Beyond the dustbowl. In G. D. Phye (Ed.), *Handbook of classroom assessment: Learning, achievement, and adjustment.* San Diego, CA: Academic Press.

Marsh, H. W., & Craven, R. G. (2006). Reciprocal effects of self-concept and performance from a multidimensional perspective: Beyond seductive pleasure and unidimensional perspectives. *Perspectives on Psychological Science, 1,* 133–163.

Marsh, H. W., Gerlach, E., Trautwein, U., Lüdtke, O., & Brettschneider, W.-D. (2007). Longitudinal study of preadolescent sport self-concept and performance reciprocal effects and causal ordering. *Child Development, 78,* 1640–1656.

Marsh, H. W., Hau, K.-T., & Kong, C.-K. (2002). Multilevel causal ordering of academic self-concept and achievement: Influence of language of instruction (English compared with Chinese) for Hong Kong students. *American Educational Research Journal, 39,* 727–763.

Marsh, H. W., Martin, A. J., & Cheng, J. H. S. (2008). A multilevel perspective on gender in classroom motivation and climate: Potential benefits of male teachers for boys? *Journal of Educational Psychology, 100,* 78–95.

Marshall, H. H. (1981). Open classrooms: Has the term outlived its usefulness? *Review of Educational Research, 51,* 181–192.

Martin, A. J., Marsh, H. W., Williamson, A., & Debus, R. L. (2003). Self-handicapping, defensive pessimism, and goal orientation: A qualitative study of university students. *Journal of Educational Psychology, 95,* 617–628.

Martin, C. L., & Ruble, D. (2004). Children's search for gender cues: Cognitive perspectives on gender development. *Current Directions in Psychological Science, 13,* 67–70.

Martin, S. S., Brady, M. P., & Williams, R. E. (1991). Effects of toys on the social behavior of preschool children in integrated and nonintegrated groups: Investigation of a setting event. *Journal of Early Intervention, 15,* 153–161.

Martínez, P., Bannan-Ritland, B., Kitsantas, A., & Baek, J. Y. (2008, March). *The impact of an integrated science reading intervention on elementary children's misconceptions regarding slow geomorphological changes caused by water.* Paper presented at the annual meeting of the American Educational Research Association, New York.

Marzano, R. J., with Marzano, J. S., & Pickering, D. J. (2003). *Classroom management that works: Research-based strategies for every teacher.* Alexandria, VA: Association for Supervision and Curriculum Development.

Mason, L. (2003). Personal epistemologies and intentional conceptual change. In G. M. Sinatra & P. R. Pintrich (Eds.), *Intentional conceptual change* (pp. 199–236). Mahwah, NJ: Erlbaum.

Mason, L., Gava, M., & Boldrin, A. (2008). On warm conceptual change: The interplay of text, epistemological beliefs, and topic interest. *Journal of Educational Psychology, 100,* 291–309.

Massialas, B. G., & Zevin, J. (1983). *Teaching creatively: Learning through discovery.* Malabar, FL: Krieger.

Masten, A. S. (2001). Ordinary magic: Resilience processes in development. *American Psychologist, 56,* 227–238.

Masten, A. S., & Coatsworth, J. D. (1998). The development of competence in favorable and unfavorable environments. *American Psychologist, 53,* 205–220.

Mastropieri, M. A., & Scruggs, T. E. (1992). Science for students with disabilities. *Review of Educational Research, 62,* 377–411.

Mastropieri, M. A., & Scruggs, T. E. (2007). *The inclusive classroom: Strategies for effective instruction* (3rd ed.). Upper Saddle River, NJ: Merrill/Prentice Hall.

Masur, E. F., McIntyre, C. W., & Flavell, J. H. (1973). Developmental changes in apportionment of study time among items in a multitrial free recall task. *Journal of Experimental Child Psychology, 15,* 237–246.

Mathan, S. A., & Koedinger, K. R. (2005). Fostering the intelligent novice: Learning from errors with metacognitive tutoring. *Educational Psychologist, 40,* 257–265.

Mathes, P. G., Torgesen, J. K., & Allor, J. H. (2001). The effects of peer-assisted literacy strategies for first-grade readers with and without additional computer-assisted instruction. *American Educational Research Journal, 38,* 371–410.

Mathews, J. (1988). *Escalante: The best teacher in America.* New York: Henry Holt.

Matthews, G., Zeidner, M., & Roberts, R. D. (2006). Models of personality and affect for education: A review and synthesis. In P. A. Alexander & P. H. Winne (Eds.), *Handbook of educational psychology* (2nd ed., pp. 163–186). Mahwah, NJ: Erlbaum.

Mattingly, D. J., Prislin, R., McKenzie, T. L., Rodrigues, J. L., & Kayzar, B. (2002). Evaluating evaluations: The case of parent involvement programs. *Review of Educational Research, 72,* 549–576.

Matute-Bianchi, M. E. (2008). Situational ethnicity and patterns of school performance among immigrant and nonimmigrant Mexican-descent students. In J. U. Ogbu (Ed.), *Minority status, oppositional culture, and schooling* (pp. 398–432). New York: Routledge.

Maughan, A., & Cicchetti, D. (2002). Impact of child maltreatment and interadult violence on children's emotion regulation abilities and socioemotional adjustment. *Child Development, 73,* 1525–1542.

Maxmell, D., Jarrett, O. S., & Dickerson, C. (1998, April). *Are we forgetting the children's needs? Recess through the children's eyes.* Paper presented at the annual meeting of the American Educational Research Association, San Diego, CA.

Mayer, R. E. (1974). Acquisition processes and resilience under varying testing conditions for structurally different problem-solving procedures. *Journal of Educational Psychology, 66,* 644–656.

Mayer, R. E. (1984). Aids to text comprehension. *Educational Psychologist, 19,* 30–42.

Mayer, R. E. (1985). Implications of cognitive psychology for instruction in mathematical problem solving. In E. A. Silver (Ed.), *Teaching and learning mathematical problem solving: Multiple research perspectives.* Mahwah, NJ: Erlbaum.

Mayer, R. E. (1989). Models for understanding. *Review of Educational Research, 59,* 43–64.

Mayer, R. E. (1992). *Thinking, problem solving, cognition* (2nd ed.). New York: Freeman.

Mayer, R. E. (1996). Learning strategies for making sense out of expository text: The SOI model for guiding three cognitive processes in knowledge construction. *Educational Psychology Review, 8,* 357–371.

Mayer, R. E. (1998). Does the brain have a place in educational psychology? *Educational Psychology Review, 10,* 389–396.

Mayer, R. E. (1999). *The promise of educational psychology: Learning in the content areas.* Upper Saddle River, NJ: Merrill/Prentice Hall.

Mayer, R. E. (2003). The promise of multimedia learning: Using the same instructional design methods across different media. *Learning and Instruction, 13,* 125–139.

Mayer, R. E. (2004). Should there be a three-strikes rule against pure discovery learning? *American Psychologist, 59,* 14–19.

Mayer, R. E., & Gallini, J. (1990). When is an illustration worth ten thousand words? *Journal of Educational Psychology, 82,* 715–726.

Mayer, R. E., & Massa, L. J. (2003). Three facets of visual and verbal learners: Cognitive ability, cognitive style, and learning preference. *Journal of Educational Psychology, 95,* 833–846.

Mayer, R. E., & Wittrock, M. C. (1996). Problem-solving transfer. In D. C. Berliner & R. C. Calfee (Eds.), *Handbook of educational psychology.* New York: Macmillan.

Mayfield, K. H., & Chase, P. N. (2002). The effects of cumulative practice on mathematics problem solving. *Journal of Applied Behavior Analysis, 35,* 105–123.

McAlpine, L. (1992). Language, literacy and education: Case studies of Cree, Inuit and Mohawk communities. *Canadian Children, 17*(1), 17–30.

McAlpine, L., & Taylor, D. M. (1993). Instructional preferences of Cree, Inuit, and Mohawk teachers. *Journal of American Indian Education, 33*(1), 1–20.

McAshan, H. H. (1979). *Competency-based education and behavioral objectives.* Englewood Cliffs, NJ: Educational Technology.

McBrien, J. L. (2005a). *Discrimination and academic motivation in adolescent refugee girls.* Unpublished doctoral dissertation. Emory University, Atlanta, GA.

McBrien, J. L. (2005b). Educational needs and barriers for refugee students in the United States: A review of the literature. *Review of Educational Research, 75,* 329–364.

McCall, R. B. (1994). Academic underachievers. *Current Directions in Psychological Science, 3,* 15–19.

McCall, R. B., & Plemons, B. W. (2001). The concept of critical periods and their implications for early childhood services. In D. B. Bailey, Jr., J. T. Bruer, F. J. Symons, & J. W. Lichtman (Eds.), *Critical thinking about critical periods* (pp. 267–287). Baltimore: Brookes.

McCallum, R. S., & Bracken, B. A. (1993). Interpersonal relations between school children and their peers, parents, and teachers. *Educational Psychology Review, 5,* 155–176.

McCarty, T. L., & Watahomigie, L. J. (1998). Language and literacy in American Indian and Alaska Native communities. In B. Pérez (Ed.), *Sociocultural contexts of language and literacy.* Mahwah, NJ: Erlbaum.

McCaslin, M., & Good, T. L. (1996). The informal curriculum. In D. C. Berliner & R. C. Calfee (Eds.), *Handbook of educational psychology.* New York: Macmillan.

McClelland, J. L. (2001). Failures to learn and their remediation: A Hebbian account. In J. L. McClelland & R. S. Siegler (Eds.), *Mechanisms of cognitive development: Behavioral and neural perspectives* (pp. 97–121). Mahwah, NJ: Erlbaum.

McClelland, J. L., Fiez, J. A., & McCandliss, B. D. (2002). Teaching the /r/–/l/ discrimination to Japanese adults: Behavioral and neural aspects. *Physiology and Behavior, 77,* 657–662.

McClowry, S. G. (1998). The science and art of using temperament as the basis for intervention. *School Psychology Review, 27,* 551–563.

McComas, J. J., Thompson, A., & Johnson, L. (2003). The effects of presession attention on problem behavior maintained by different reinforcers. *Journal of Applied Behavior Analysis, 36,* 297–307.

McCombs, B. L. (1996). Alternative perspectives for motivation. In L. Baker, P. Afflerbach, & D. Reinking (Eds.), *Developing engaged readers in school and home communities.* Hillsdale, NJ: Erlbaum.

McCoy, L. P. (1990, April). *Correlates of mathematics anxiety.* Paper presented at the annual meeting of the American Educational Research Association, Boston.

McCrudden, M. T., & Schraw, G. (2007). Relevance and goal-focusing in text processing. *Educational Psychology Review, 19,* 113–139.

McDaniel, L. (1997). *For better, for worse, forever.* New York: Bantam.

McDaniel, M. A., & Einstein, G. O. (1989). Material-appropriate processing: A contextualist approach to reading and studying strategies. *Educational Psychology Review, 1,* 113–145.

McDaniel, M. A., & Schlager, M. S. (1990). Discovery learning and transfer of problem-solving skills. *Cognition and Instruction, 7,* 129–159.

McDaniel, M. A., Waddill, P. J., Finstad, K., & Bourg, T. (2000). The effects of text-based interest on attention and recall. *Journal of Educational Psychology, 92,* 492–502.

McDevitt, M., & Chaffee, S. H. (1998). Second chance political socialization: "Trickle-up" effects of children on parents. In T. J. Johnson, C. E. Hays, & S. P. Hays (Eds.), *Engaging the public: How government and the media can reinvigorate American democracy* (pp. 57–66). Lanhan, MD: Rowman & Littlefield.

McDevitt, T. M. (1990). Encouraging young children's listening skills. *Academic Therapy, 25,* 569–577.

McDevitt, T. M., & Ford, M. E. (1987). Processes in young children's communicative functioning and development. In M. E. Ford & D. H. Ford (Eds.), *Humans as self-constructing living systems: Putting the framework to work.* Mahwah, NJ: Erlbaum.

McDevitt, T. M., & Ormrod, J. E. (2010). *Child development and education* (4th ed.). Upper Saddle River, NJ: Merrill/Prentice Hall.

McDevitt, T. M., Spivey, N., Sheehan, E. P., Lennon, R., & Story, R. (1990). Children's beliefs about listening: Is it enough to be still and quiet? *Child Development, 61,* 713–721.

McElhaney, K. B., Antonishak, J., & Allen, J. P. (2008). "They like me, they like me not": Popularity and adolescents' perceptions of acceptance predicting social functioning over time. *Child Development, 79,* 720–731.

McGee, K. D., Knight, S. L., & Boudah, D. J. (2001, April). *Using reciprocal teaching in secondary inclusive English classroom instruction.* Paper presented at the annual meeting of the American Educational Research Association, Seattle, WA.

McGee, L. M. (1992). An exploration of meaning construction in first graders' grand conversations. In C. K. Kinzer & D. J. Leu (Eds.), *Literacy research, theory, and practice: Views from many perspectives.* Chicago: National Reading Conference.

McGill, P. (1999). Establishing operations: Implications for the assessment, treatment, and prevention of problem behavior. *Journal of Applied Behavior Analysis, 32,* 393–418.

McGinn, P. V., Viernstein, M. C., & Hogan, R. (1980). Fostering the intellectual development of verbally gifted adolescents. *Journal of Educational Psychology, 72,* 494–498.

McGlothlin, H., & Killen, M. (2006). Intergroup attitudes of European American children attending ethnically homogeneous schools. *Child Development, 77,* 1375–1386.

McGlynn, S. M. (1998). Impaired awareness of deficits in a psychiatric context: Implications for rehabilitation. In D. J. Hacker, J. Dunlosky, & A. C. Graesser (Eds.), *Metacognition in educational theory and practice* (pp. 221–248). Mahwah, NJ: Erlbaum.

McGovern, M. L., Davis, A., & Ogbu, J. U. (2008). The Minority Achievement Committee: Students leading students to greater success in school. In J. U. Ogbu (Ed.), *Minority status, oppositional culture, and schooling* (pp. 560–573). New York: Routledge.

McGregor, H. A., & Elliot, A. J. (2002). Achievement goals as predictors of achievement-relevant processes prior to task engagement. *Journal of Educational Psychology, 94,* 381–395.

McGrew, K. S., Flanagan, D. P., Zeith, T. Z., & Vanderwood, M. (1997). Beyond *g*: The impact of *Gf-Gc* specific cognitive abilities research on the future use and interpretation of intelligence tests in the schools. *School Psychology Review, 26,* 189–210.

McKeachie, W. J. (1987). Cognitive skills and their transfer: Discussion. *International Journal of Educational Research, 11,* 707–712.

McKown, C., & Weinstein, R. S. (2003). The development and consequences of stereotype consciousness in middle childhood. *Child Development, 74,* 498–515.

McLoyd, V. C. (1998). Socioeconomic disadvantage and child development. *American Psychologist, 53,* 185–204.

McMillan, J. H., & Reed, D. F. (1994). At-risk students and resiliency: Factors contributing to academic success. *Clearing House, 67*(3), 137–140.

McMillan, J. H., Singh, J., & Simonetta, L. G. (1994). The tyranny of self-oriented self-esteem. *Educational Horizons, 72*(3), 141–145.

McNamara, D. S., & Healy, A. F. (1995). A generation advantage for multiplication skill training and nonword vocabulary acquisition. In A. F. Healy & L. E. Bourne, Jr. (Eds.), *Learning and memory of knowledge and skills: Durability and specificity.* Thousand Oaks, CA: Sage.

McNamara, E. (1987). Behavioural approaches in the secondary school. In K. Wheldall (Ed.), *The behaviourist in the classroom.* London: Allen & Unwin.

Mechelli, A., Crinion, J. T., Noppeney, U., O'Doherty, J., Ashburner, J., Frackowiak, R., & Price, C. J. (2004). Structural plasticity in the bilingual brain. *Nature, 431,* 757.

Medin, D. L. (2005, August). *Role of culture and expertise in cognition.* Invited address presented at the annual meeting of the American Psychological Association, Washington, DC.

Medin, D. L., Unsworth, S. J., & Hirschfeld, L. (2007). Culture, categorization, and reasoning. In S. Kitayama & D. Cohen (Eds.), *Handbook of cultural psychology* (pp. 615–644). New York: Guilford Press.

Meece, J. L. (1994). The role of motivation in self-regulated learning. In D. H. Schunk & B. J. Zimmerman (Eds.), *Self-regulation of learning and performance: Issues and educational applications.* Mahwah, NJ: Erlbaum.

Meece, J. L., & Holt, K. (1993). A pattern analysis of students' achievement goals. *Journal of Educational Psychology, 85,* 582–590.

Meehan, B. T., Hughes, J. N., & Cavell, T. A. (2003). Teacher-student relationships as compensatory resources for aggressive children. *Child Development, 74,* 1145–1157.

Mehan, H. (1979). *Social organization in the classroom.* Cambridge, MA: Harvard University Press.

Meichenbaum, D. (1977). *Cognitive-behavior modification: An integrative approach.* New York: Plenum Press.

Meichenbaum, D. (1985). Teaching thinking: A cognitive-behavioral perspective. In S. F. Chipman, J. W. Segal, & R. Glaser (Eds.), *Thinking and learning skills: Vol. 2. Research and open questions.* Mahwah, NJ: Erlbaum.

Meichenbaum, D., & Goodman, J. (1971). Training impulsive children to talk to themselves: A means of developing self-control. *Journal of Abnormal Psychology, 77,* 115–126.

Mejía-Arauz, R., Rogoff, B., Dexter, A., & Najafi, B. (2007). Cultural variation in children's social organization. *Child Development, 78,* 1001–1014.

Mellard, D. F., & Johnson, E. (2008). *RTI: A practitioner's guide to implementing response to intervention.* Thousand Oaks, CA: Corwin.

Mellers, B. A., & McGraw, A. P. (2001). Anticipated emotions as guides to choice. *Current Directions in Psychological Science, 10,* 210–214.

Meloth, M. S., & Deering, P. D. (1999). The role of the teacher in promoting cognitive processing during collaborative learning. In A. M. O'Donnell & A. King (Eds.), *Cognitive perspectives on peer learning* (pp. 235–255). Mahwah, NJ: Erlbaum.

Meltzer, L. (Ed.). (2007). *Executive function in education: From theory to practice.* New York: Guilford Press.

Meltzer, L., & Krishnan, K. (2007). Executive function difficulties and learning disabilities: Understandings and misunderstandings. In L. Meltzer (Ed.), *Executive function in education: From theory to practice* (pp. 77–105). New York: Guilford Press.

Meltzer, L., Pollica, L. S., & Barzillai, M. (2007). Executive function in the classroom: Embedding strategy instruction into daily teaching practices. In L. Meltzer (Ed.), *Executive function in education: From theory to practice* (pp. 165–193). New York: Guilford Press.

Meltzoff, A. N. (2005). Imitation and other minds: The "like me" hypothesis. In S. Hurley & N. Chater (Eds.), *Perspectives on imitation: From neuroscience to social science* (pp. 55–77). Cambridge, MA: MIT Press.

Mendoza-Denton, R., & Mischel, W. (2007). Integrating system approaches to culture and personality: The cultural cognitive-affective processing system. In S. Kitayama & D. Cohen (Eds.), *Handbook of cultural psychology* (pp. 175–195). New York: Guilford Press.

Menéndez, R. (Director). (1988). *Stand and deliver* [Motion picture]. United States: Warner Studios.

Menon, M., Tobin, D. D., Corby, B. C., Menon, M., Hodges, E. V. E., & Perry, D. G. (2007). The developmental costs of high self-esteem for antisocial children. *Child Development, 78,* 1627–1639.

Mercer, C. D., & Pullen, P. C. (2005). *Students with learning disabilities* (6th ed.). Upper Saddle River, NJ: Merrill/Prentice Hall.

Mergendoller, J. R., Markham, T., Ravitz, J., & Larmer, J. (2006). Pervasive management of project based learning: Teachers as guides and facilitators. In C. M. Evertson & C. S. Weinstein (Eds.), *Handbook of classroom management: Research, practice, and contemporary issues* (pp. 583–615). Mahwah, NJ: Erlbaum.

Merrill, P. F., Hammons, K., Vincent, B. R., Reynolds, P. L., Christensen, L., & Tolman, M. N. (1996). *Computers in education* (3rd ed.). Boston: Allyn & Bacon.

Merzenich, M. M. (2001). Cortical plasticity contributing to child development. In J. L. McClelland & R. S. Siegler (Eds.), *Mechanisms of cognitive development: Behavioral and neural perspectives* (pp. 67–95). Mahwah, NJ: Erlbaum.

Mesquita, B., & Leu, J. (2007). The cultural psychology of emotion. In S. Kitayama & D. Cohen (Eds.), *Handbook of cultural psychology* (pp. 734–759). New York: Guilford Press.

Messer, S. B. (1976). Reflection-impulsivity: A review. *Psychological Bulletin, 83,* 1026–1052.

Messick, S. (1983). Assessment of children. In W. Kessen (Ed.), *Handbook of child psychology* (Vol. 1). New York: Wiley.

Messick, S. (1994a). The interplay of evidence and consequences in the validation of performance assessments. *Educational Researcher, 23*(2), 13–23.

Messick, S. (1994b). The matter of style: Manifestations of personality in cognition, learning, and testing. *Educational Psychologist, 29,* 121–136.

Metz, K. E. (1995). Reassessment of developmental constraints on children's science instruction. *Review of Educational Research, 65,* 93–127.

Metz, K. E. (2004). Children's understanding of scientific inquiry: Their conceptualizations of uncertainty in investigations of their own design. *Cognition and Instruction, 22,* 219–290.

Meyer, D., Madden, D., & McGrath, D. J. (2005). English language learner students in U.S. public schools: 1994 and 2000. *Education Statistics Quarterly, 6*(3). Retrieved April 7, 2008, from http://nces.ed.gov/programs/quarterly/vol_6/6_3/3_4.asp

Meyer, D. K., & Turner, J. C. (2002). Discovering emotion in classroom motivation research. *Educational Psychologist, 37,* 107–114.

Meyer, D. K., & Turner, J. C. (2006). Re-conceptualizing emotion and motivation to learn in classroom contexts. *Educational Psychology Review, 18,* 377–390.

Meyer, K. A. (1999). Functional analysis and treatment of problem behavior exhibited by elementary school children. *Journal of Applied Behavior Analysis, 32,* 229–232.

Meyer, L. H., Weir, K. F., McClure, J., & Walkey, F. (2008, March). *The relationship of motivation orientations to future achievement in secondary school.* Paper presented at the annual meeting of the American Educational Research Association, New York.

Meyer, M. S. (2000). The ability-achievement discrepancy: Does it contribute to an understanding of learning disabilities? *Educational Psychology Review, 12,* 315–337.

Meyers, D. T. (1987). The socialized individual and individual autonomy: An intersection between philosophy and psychology. In E. F. Kittay & D. T. Meyers (Eds.), *Women and moral theory.* Totowa, NJ: Rowman & Littlefield.

Michael, J. (2000). Implications and refinements of the establishing operation concept. *Journal of Applied Behavior Analysis, 33,* 401–410.

Middleton, M., & Abrams, E. (2004, April). *The effect of pre-service teachers' sense of efficacy on their self-reflective practice.* Paper presented at the Annual Meeting of the American Educational Research Association, San Diego, CA.

Middleton, M. J., & Midgley, C. (1997). Avoiding the demonstration of lack of ability: An under-explored aspect of goal theory. *Journal of Educational Psychology, 89,* 710–718.

Middleton, M. J., & Midgley, C. (2002). Beyond motivation: Middle school students' perceptions of press for understanding in math. *Contemporary Educational Psychology, 27,* 373–391.

Midgley, C. (1993). Motivation and middle level schools. In M. Maehr & P. R. Pintrich (Eds.), *Advances in motivation and achievement* (Vol. 8, pp. 217–274). Greenwich, CT: JAI Press.

Midgley, C. (Ed.). (2002). *Goals, goal structures, and patterns of adaptive learning.* Mahwah, NJ: Erlbaum.

Midgley, C., Kaplan, A., & Middleton, M. (2001). Performance-approach goals: Good for what, for whom, under what circumstances, and at what cost? *Journal of Educational Psychology, 93,* 77–86.

Midgley, C., Kaplan, A., Middleton, M., Maehr, M., Urdan, T., Anderman, L., et al. (1998). The development and validation of scales assessing students' achievement goal orientations. *Contemporary Educational Psychology, 23,* 113–131.

Midgley, C., Middleton, M. J., Gheen, M. H., & Kumar, R. (2002). Stage-environment fit revisited: A goal theory approach to examining school transitions. In C. Midgley (Ed.), *Goals, goal structures, and patterns of adaptive learning* (pp. 109–142). Mahwah, NJ: Erlbaum.

Mikaelsen, B. (1996). *Countdown.* New York: Hyperion Books for Children.

Mikulincer, M., & Shaver, P. R. (2005). Attachment security, compassion, and altruism. *Current Directions in Psychological Science, 14,* 34–38.

Miles, S. B., & Stipek, D. (2006). Contemporaneous and longitudinal associations between social behavior and literacy achievement in a sample of low-income elementary school children. *Child Development, 77,* 103–117.

Miller, A. (1987). Cognitive styles: An integrated model. *Educational Psychology, 7,* 251–268.

Miller, A. (2006). Contexts and attributions for difficult behavior in English classrooms. In C. M. Evertson & C. S. Weinstein (Eds.), *Handbook of classroom management: Research, practice, and contemporary issues* (pp. 1093–1120). Mahwah, NJ: Erlbaum.

Miller, B. C., & Benson, B. (1999). Romantic and sexual relationship development during adolescence. In W. Furman, B. B. Brown, & C. Feiring (Eds.), *The development of romantic relationships in adolescence* (pp. 99–121). Cambridge, England: Cambridge University Press.

Miller, D. L., & Kelley, M. L. (1994). The use of goal setting and contingency contracting for improving children's homework performance. *Journal of Applied Behavior Analysis, 27,* 73–84.

Miller, G. A. (1956). The magical number seven, plus or minus two: Some limits on our capacity for processing information. *Psychological Review, 63,* 81–97.

Miller, J. G. (1997). A cultural-psychology perspective on intelligence. In R. J. Sternberg & E. L. Grigorenko (Eds.), *Intelligence, heredity, and environment* (pp. 269–302). Cambridge, England: Cambridge University Press.

Miller, J. G. (2007). Cultural psychology of moral development. In S. Kitayama & D. Cohen (Eds.), *Handbook of cultural psychology* (pp. 477–499). New York: Guilford Press.

Miller, L. S. (1995). *An American imperative: Accelerating minority educational advancement.* New Haven, CT: Yale University Press.

Miller, M. D., Linn, R. L., & Gronlund, N. E. (2009). *Measurement and assessment in teaching* (10th ed.). Upper Saddle River, NJ: Merrill/Pearson.

Miller, P. A., Eisenberg, N., Fabes, R. A., & Shell, R. (1996). Relations of moral reasoning and vicarious emotion to young children's prosocial behavior toward peers and adults. *Developmental Psychology, 32,* 210–219.

Miller, R. B., & Brickman, S. J. (2004). A model of future-oriented motivation and self-regulation. *Educational Psychology Review, 16,* 9–33.

Miller, R. R., & Barnet, R. C. (1993). The role of time in elementary associations. *Current Directions in Psychological Science, 2,* 106–111.

Miller, S. D., Heafner, T., Massey, D., & Strahan, D. B. (2003, April). *Students' reactions to teachers' attempts to create the necessary conditions to promote the acquisition of self-regulation skills.* Paper presented at the annual meeting of the American Educational Research Association, Chicago.

Miller, S. D., & Meece, J. L. (1997). Enhancing elementary students' motivation to read and write: A classroom intervention study. *Journal of Educational Research, 90,* 286–300.

Miller, S. M. (2003). How literature discussion shapes thinking: ZPDs for teaching/learning habits of the heart and mind. In A. Kozulin, B. Gindis, V. S. Ageyev, & S. M. Miller (Eds.), *Vygotsky's educational theory in cultural context* (pp. 289–316). Cambridge, England: Cambridge University Press.

Millman, J., Bishop, C. H., & Ebel, R. (1965). An analysis of test-wiseness. *Educational and Psychological Measurement, 25,* 707–726.

Mills, G. E. (2007). *Action research: A guide for the teacher researcher* (3rd ed.). Upper Saddle River, NJ: Merrill/Prentice Hall.

Milner, H. R. (2006). Classroom management in urban classrooms. In C. M. Evertson & C. S. Weinstein (Eds.), *Handbook of classroom management: Research, practice, and contemporary issues* (pp. 491–522). Mahwah, NJ: Erlbaum.

Minami, M., & McCabe, A. (1996). Compressed collections of experiences: Some Asian American traditions. In A. McCabe (Ed.), *Chameleon readers: Some problems cultural differences in narrative structure pose for multicultural literacy programs* (pp. 72–97). New York: McGraw-Hill.

Minami, M., & Ovando, C. J. (1995). Language issues in multicultural contexts. In J. A. Banks & C. A. M. Banks (Eds.), *Handbook of research on multicultural education.* New York: Macmillan.

Mineka, S., & Zinbarg, R. (2006). A contemporary learning theory perspective on the etiology of anxiety disorders: It's not what you thought it was. *American Psychologist, 61,* 10–26.

Minogue, J., & Jones, M. G. (2006). Haptics in education: Exploring an untapped sensory modality. *Review of Educational Research, 76,* 317–348.

Minsky, M. (2006). *The emotion machine: Commonsense thinking, artificial intelligence, and the future of the human mind.* New York: Simon & Schuster.

Minstrell, J., & Stimpson, V. (1996). A classroom environment for learning: Guiding students' reconstruction of understanding and reasoning. In L. Schauble & R. Glaser (Eds.), *Innovations in learning: New environments for education.* Mahwah, NJ: Erlbaum.

Mintzes, J. J., Trowbridge, J. E., Arnaudin, M. W., & Wandersee, J. H. (1991). Children's biology: Studies on conceptual development in the life sciences. In S. M. Glynn, R. H. Yeany, & B. K. Britton (Eds.), *The psychology of learning science.* Mahwah, NJ: Erlbaum.

Mintzes, J. J., Wandersee, J. H., & Novak, J. D. (1997). Meaningful learning in science: The human constructivist perspective. In G. D. Phye (Ed.), *Handbook of academic learning: Construction of knowledge.* San Diego, CA: Academic Press.

Mischel, W., & Grusec, J. E. (1966). Determinants of the rehearsal and transmission of neutral and aversive behaviors. *Journal of Personality and Social Psychology, 3,* 197–205.

Mitchell, K. J., Wolak, J., & Finkelhor, D. (2005). Internet sex crimes against minors. In K. A. Kendall-Tackett & S. M. Giacomoni (Eds.), *Child Victimization: Maltreatment, bulling and dating violence, prevention and intervention.* Kingston, NJ: Civic Research Institute.

Mitchell, M. (1993). Situational interest: Its multifaceted structure in the secondary school mathematics classroom. *Journal of Educational Psychology, 85,* 424–436.

Mitchem, K. J., & Young, K. R. (2001). Adapting self-management programs for classwide use. *Remedial and Special Education, 22*(2), 75–88.

Mithaug, D. K., & Mithaug, D. E. (2003). Effects of teacher-directed versus student-directed instruction on self-management of young children with disabilities. *Journal of Applied Behavior Analysis, 36,* 133–136.

Mohatt, G., & Erickson, F. (1981). Cultural differences in teaching styles in an Odawa school: A sociolinguistic approach. In H. T. Trueba, G. P. Guthrie, & K. H. Au (Eds.), *Culture and the bilingual classroom: Studies in classroom ethnography.* Rowley, MA: Newbury House.

Moje, E. B., & Hinchman, K. (2004). Culturally responsive practices for youth literacy learning. In T. L. Jetton & J. A. Dole (Eds.), *Adolescent literacy research and practice* (pp. 321–350). New York: Guilford.

Moje, E. B., & Shepardson, D. P. (1998). Social interactions and children's changing understanding of electric circuits: Exploring unequal power relations in "peer"-learning groups. In B. Guzzetti & C. Hynd (Eds.), *Perspectives on conceptual change: Multiple ways to understand knowing and learning in a complex world* (pp. 225–234). Mahwah, NJ: Erlbaum.

Moles, O. C. (Ed.). (1990). *Student discipline strategies: Research and practice.* Albany: State University of New York Press.

Monte-Sano, C. (2008). Qualities of historical writing instruction: A comparative case study of two teachers' practices. *American Educational Research Journal, 45,* 1045–1079.

Montgomery, J. W., & Windsor, J. (2007). Examining the language performances of children with and without specific language impairment: Contributions of phonological short-term memory and speed of processing. *Journal of Speech, Language, and Hearing Research, 50,* 778–797.

Moon, S. M., Feldhusen, J. F., & Dillon, D. R. (1994). Long-term effects of an enrichment program based on the Purdue Three-Stage Model. *Gifted Child Quarterly, 38,* 38–48.

Mooney, C. M. (1957). Age in the development of closure ability in children. *Canadian Journal of Psychology, 11,* 219–226.

Moore, D. S., & Erickson, P. I. (1985). Age, gender, and ethnic differences in sexual and contraceptive knowledge, attitudes, and behavior. *Family and Community Health, 8,* 38–51.

Moore, J. W., & Edwards, R. P. (2003). An analysis of aversive stimuli in classroom demand contexts. *Journal of Applied Behavior Analysis, 36,* 339–348.

Morales, J. R., & Guerra, N. G. (2006). Effects of multiple context and cumulative stress on urban children's adjustment in elementary school. *Child Development, 77,* 907–923.

Moran, C. E., & Hakuta, K. (1995). Bilingual education: Broadening research perspectives. In J. A. Banks & C. A. M. Banks (Eds.), *Handbook of research on multicultural education.* New York: Macmillan.

Moran, S., & Gardner, H. (2006). Extraordinary achievements: A developmental and systems analysis. In W. Damon & R. M. Lerner (Series Eds.), D. Kuhn, & R. Siegler (Vol. Eds.), *Handbook of child psychology: Vol. 2. Cognition, perception, and language* (6th ed.). New York: Wiley.

Morelli, G. A., & Rothbaum, F. (2007). Situating the child in context: Attachment relationships and self-regulation in different cultures. In S. Kitayama & D. Cohen (Eds.), *Handbook of cultural psychology* (pp. 500–527). New York: Guilford Press.

Moreno, R. (2006). Learning in high-tech and multimedia environments. *Current Directions in Psychological Science, 15,* 63–67.

Moreno, R., Mayer, R. E., Spires, H. A., & Lester, J. C. (2001). The case for social agency in computer-based teaching: Do students learn more deeply when they interact with animated pedagogical agents? *Cognition and Instruction, 19,* 177–213.

Morgan, D. P., & Jenson, W. R. (1988). *Teaching behaviorally disordered students: Preferred practices.* Upper Saddle River, NJ: Merrill/Prentice Hall.

Morris, C. D., Bransford, J. D., & Franks, J. J. (1977). Levels of processing versus transfer appropriate processing. *Journal of Verbal Learning and Verbal Behavior, 16,* 519–533.

Morrison, G. M., Furlong, M. J., D'Incau, B., & Morrison, R. L. (2004). The safe school: Integrating the school reform agenda to prevent disruption and violence at school. In J. C. Conoley & A. P. Goldstein (Eds.), *School violence intervention* (2nd ed., pp. 256–296). New York: Guilford Press.

Morrow, S. L. (1997). Career development of lesbian and gay youth: Effects of sexual orientation, coming out, and homophobia. In M. B. Harris (Ed.), *School experiences of gay and lesbian youth: The invisible minority* (pp. 1–15). Binghamton, NY: Harrington Park Press.

Mosborg, S. (2002). Speaking of history: How adolescents use their knowledge of history in reading the daily news. *Cognition and Instruction, 20,* 323–358.

Mostow, A. J., Izard, C. E., Fine, S., & Trantacosta, C. J. (2002). Modeling emotional, cognitive, and behavioral predictors. *Child Development, 73,* 1775–1787.

Mueller, M. M., Edwards, R. P., & Trahant, D. (2003). Translating multiple assessment techniques into an intervention selection model for classrooms. *Journal of Applied Behavior Analysis, 36,* 563–573.

Muis, K. R. (2007). The role of epistemic beliefs in self-regulated learning. *Educational Psychologist, 42,* 173–190.

Muis, K. R., Bendixen, L. D., & Haerle, F. C. (2006). Domain-generality and domain-specificity in personal epistemology research: Philosophical and empirical reflections in the development of a theoretical framework. *Educational Psychology Review, 18,* 3–54.

Munakata, Y. (2006). Information processing approaches to development. In W. Damon & R. M. Lerner (Series Eds.), D. Kuhn, & R. Siegler (Vol. Eds.), *Handbook of child psychology: Vol. 2. Cognition, perception, and language* (6th ed.). New York: Wiley.

Munn, P., Johnstone, M., & Chalmers, V. (1990, April). *How do teachers talk about maintaining effective discipline in their classrooms?* Paper presented at the annual meeting of the American Educational Research Association, Boston.

Murata, A., Fadiga, L., Fogassi, L., Gallese, V., Raos, V., & Rizzolatti, G. (1997). Object representation in the ventral premotor cortex (area F5) of the monkey. *Journal of Neurophysiology, 78,* 2226–2230.

Murdock, T. B. (1999). The social context of risk: Status and motivational predictors of alienation in middle school. *Journal of Educational Psychology, 91,* 62–75.

Murdock, T. B. (2000). Incorporating economic context into educational psychology: Methodological and conceptual challenges. *Educational Psychologist, 35,* 113–124.

Murdock, T. B., & Anderman, E. M. (2006). Motivational perspectives on student cheating: Toward an integrated model of academic dishonesty. *Educational Psychologist, 41,* 129–145.

Murdock, T. B., Hale, N. M., & Weber, M. J. (2001). Predictors of cheating among early adolescents: Academic and social motivations. *Contemporary Educational Psychology, 26,* 96–115.

Murphy, E. S., McSweeney, F. K., Smith, R. G., & McComas, J. J. (2003). Dynamic changes in reinforcer effectiveness: Theoretical, methodological, and practical implications for applied research. *Journal of Applied Behavior Analysis, 36,* 421–438.

Murphy, P. K. (2007). The eye of the beholder: The interplay of social and cognitive components in change. *Educational Psychologist, 42,* 41–53.

Murphy, P. K., & Alexander, P. A. (2000). A motivated exploration of motivation terminology. *Contemporary Educational Psychology, 25,* 3–53.

Murphy, P. K., & Alexander, P. A. (2004). Persuasion as a dynamic, multidimensional process: An investigation of individual and intraindividual differences. *American Educational Research Journal, 41,* 337–363.

Murphy, P. K., & Alexander, P. A. (2008). Examining the influence of knowledge, beliefs, and motivation in conceptual change. In S. Vosniadou (Ed.), *Handbook of research on conceptual change* (pp. 583–616). New York: Taylor and Francis.

Murphy, P. K., & Mason, L. (2006). Changing knowledge and beliefs. In P. A. Alexander & P. H. Winne (Eds.), *Handbook of educational psychology* (2nd ed., pp. 305–324). Mahwah, NJ: Erlbaum.

Myles, B. S., & Simpson, R. L. (2001). Understanding the hidden curriculum: An essential social skill for children and youth with Asperger syndrome. *Intervention in School and Clinic, 36,* 279–286.

Narváez, D., & Rest, J. (1995). The four components of acting morally. In W. M. Kurtines & J. L. Gewirtz (Eds.), *Moral development: An introduction.* Boston: Allyn & Bacon.

National Association of Bilingual Education. (1993). Census reports sharp increase in number of non-English-speaking Americans. *NABE News, 16*(6), 1, 25.

National Association of Secondary School Principals (NASSP). (2004). *Breaking ranks II: Strategies for leading high school reform.* Reston, VA: Author.

National Center for Education Statistics. (2007, September). *Crime, violence, discipline, and safety in U.S. public schools: Findings from the School Survey on Crime and Safety, 2005–06.* Washington: U.S. Department of Education.

National Commission on Excellence in Education. (1983). *A nation at risk: The imperative for educational reform.* Washington, DC: U.S. Government Printing Office.

National Research Council. (2000). *How people learn: Brain, mind, experience, and school* (expanded ed.). Washington, DC: National Academy Press.

National Research Council. (2004). *Engaging schools: Fostering high school students' motivation to learn.* Washington, DC: National Academies Press.

National Science Foundation. (2007). *Women, minorities, and persons with disabilities in science and engineering: 2007.* Arlington, VA: Author. Retrieved July 12, 2007, from www.nsf.gov/statistics/wmpd

Naveh-Benjamin, M. (1991). A comparison of training programs intended for different types of text-anxious students: Further support for an information-processing model. *Journal of Educational Psychology, 83,* 134–139.

NCSS Task Force on Ethnic Studies Curriculum Guidelines. (1992). Curriculum guidelines for multicultural education. *Social Education, 56,* 274–294.

Nee, D. E., Berman, M. G., Moore, K. S., & Jonides, J. (2008). Neuroscientific evidence about the distinction between short- and long-term memory. *Current Directions in Psychological Science, 17,* 102–106.

Neef, N. A., Marckel, J., Ferreri, S. J., Bicard, D. F., Endo, S., Aman, M. G., et al. (2005). Behavioral assessment of impulsivity: A comparison of children with and without attention deficit hyperactivity disorder. *Journal of Applied Behavior Analysis, 38,* 23–37.

Neel, R. S., Jenkins, Z. N., & Meadows, N. (1990). Social problem-solving behaviors and aggression in young children: A descriptive observational study. *Behavioral Disorders, 16,* 39–51.

Neisser, U. (1967). *Cognitive psychology.* New York: Appleton-Century-Crofts.

Neisser, U. (1998a). Introduction: Rising test scores and what they mean. In U. Neisser (Ed.), *The rising curve: Long-term gains in IQ and related measures* (pp. 3–22). Washington, DC: American Psychological Association.

Neisser, U. (Ed.). (1998b). *The rising curve: Long-term gains in IQ and related measures.* Washington, DC: American Psychological Association.

Neisser, U., Boodoo, G., Bouchard, T. J., Boykin, A. W., Brody, N., Ceci, S. J., Halpern, D. F., Loehlen, J. C., Perloff, R., Sternberg, R. J., & Urbina, S. (1996). Intelligence: Knowns and unknowns. *American Psychologist, 51,* 77–101.

Nell, V. (2002). Why young men drive dangerously: Implications for injury prevention. *Current Directions in Psychological Science, 11,* 75–79.

Nelson, C. A., III, Thomas, K. M., & de Haan, M. (2006). Neural bases of cognitive development. In D. Kuhn, R. Siegler (Vol. Eds.), W. Damon, & R. M. Lerner (Series Eds.), *Handbook of child psychology. Vol. 2: Cognition, perception, and language* (6th ed., pp. 3–57).

Nelson, J. R., Smith, D. J., Young, R. K., & Dodd, J. M. (1991). A review of self-management outcome research conducted with students who exhibit behavioral disorders. *Behavioral Disorders, 16,* 169–179.

Nelson, K. (1996). *Language in cognitive development: The emergence of the mediated mind.* Cambridge, England: Cambridge University Press.

Nelson-Barber, S., & Estrin, E. T. (1995). Bringing Native American perspectives to mathematics and science teaching. *Theory into Practice, 34,* 174–185.

Nesbit, J. C., & Adesope, O. O. (2006). Learning with concept and knowledge maps: A meta-analysis. *Review of Educational Research, 76,* 413–448.

Nesdale, D., Maass, A., Durkin, K., & Griffiths, J. (2005). Group norms, threat, and children's racial prejudice. *Child Development, 76,* 652–663.

Nettles, S. M., Caughy, M. O., & O'Campo, P. J. (2008). School adjustment in the early grades: Toward an integrated model of neighborhood, parental, and child processes. *Review of Educational Research, 78,* 3–32.

Newby, T. J., Ertmer, P. A., & Stepich, D. A. (1994, April). *Instructional analogies and the learning of concepts.* Paper presented at the annual meeting of the American Educational Research Association, New Orleans, LA.

Newcomb, A. F., & Bagwell, C. L. (1995). Children's friendship relations: A meta-analysis review. *Psychological Bulletin, 117,* 306–347.

Newcomb, A. F., Bukowski, W. M., & Pattee, L. (1993). Children's peer relations: A meta-analytic review of popular, rejected, neglected, controversial, and average sociometric status. *Psychological Bulletin, 113,* 99–128.

Newkirk, T. (2002). *Misreading masculinity: Boys, literacy, and popular culture.* Portsmouth, NH: Heinemann.

Newman, L. S. (1990). Intentional and unintentional memory in young children: Remembering vs. playing. *Journal of Experimental Child Psychology, 50,* 243–258.

Newman, R. S. (2008). Adaptive and nonadaptive help seeking with peer harassment: An integrative perspective of coping and self-regulation. *Educational Psychologist, 43,* 1–15.

Newman, R. S., & Murray, B. J. (2005). How students and teachers view the seriousness of peer harassment: When is it appropriate to seek help? *Journal of Educational Psychology, 97,* 347–365.

Newman, R. S., & Schwager, M. T. (1995). Students' help seeking during problem solving: Effects of grade, goal, and prior achievement. *American Educational Research Journal, 32,* 352–376.

Newmann, F. M. (1981). Reducing student alienation in high schools: Implications of theory. *Harvard Educational Review, 51,* 546–564.

Newmann, F. M. (1997). Authentic assessment in social studies: Standards and examples. In G. D. Phye (Ed.), *Handbook of classroom assessment: Learning, achievement, and adjustment.* San Diego, CA: Academic Press.

Newmann, F. M., & Wehlage, G. G. (1993). Five standards of authentic instruction. *Educational Leadership, 50*(7), 8–12.

Newport, E. L. (1990). Maturational constraints on language learning. *Cognitive Science, 14,* 11–28.

Ni, Y., & Zhou, Y.-D. (2005). Teaching and learning fraction and rational numbers: The origins and implications of whole number bias. *Educational Psychologist, 40,* 27–52.

Nicholls, J. G. (1990). What is ability and why are we mindful of it? A developmental perspective. In R. J. Sternberg & J. Kolligian (Eds.), *Competence considered.* New Haven, CT: Yale University Press.

Nicholls, J. G., Cobb, P., Yackel, E., Wood, T., & Wheatley, G. (1990). Students' theories of mathematics and their mathematical knowledge: Multiple dimensions of assessment. In G. Kulm (Ed.), *Assessing higher order thinking in mathematics.* Washington, DC: American Association for the Advancement of Science.

Nichols, J. D. (1996). The effects of cooperative learning on student achievement and motivation in a high school geometry class. *Contemporary Educational Psychology, 21,* 467–476.

Nichols, J. D. (April, 2004). *Empowerment and relationships: A classroom model to enhance student motivation.* Paper presented at the American Educational Research Association, San Diego, CA.

Nichols, J. D., Ludwin, W. G., & Iadicola, P. (1999). A darker shade of gray: A year-end analysis of discipline and suspension data. *Equity and Excellence in Education, 32*(1), 43–55.

Nichols, P. D., & Mittelholtz, D. J. (1997). Constructing the concept of aptitude: Implications for the assessment of analogical reasoning. In G. D. Phye (Ed.), *Handbook of academic learning: Construction of knowledge.* San Diego, CA: Academic Press.

Nichols, S. L. (1999). Gay, lesbian, and bisexual youth: Understanding diversity and promoting tolerance in schools. *Elementary School Journal, 99,* 505–519.

Nickerson, R. S., & Adams, M. J. (1979). Long-term memory for a common object. *Cognitive Psychology, 1,* 287–307.

Nieto, S. (1995). *Affirming diversity* (2nd ed.). White Plains, NY: Longman.

Nikopoulos, C. K., & Keenan, M. (2004). Effects of video modeling on social initiations by children with autism. *Journal of Applied Behavior Analysis, 37,* 93–96.

Nippold, M. A. (1988). The literate lexicon. In M. A. Nippold (Ed.), *Later language development: Ages nine through nineteen.* Boston: Little, Brown.

Nix, R. L., Pinderhughes, E. E., Dodge, K. A., Bates, J. E., Pettit, G. S., & McFadyen-Ketchum, S. A. (1999). The relation between mothers' hostile attribution tendencies and children's externalizing behavior problems: The mediating role of mothers' harsh discipline practices. *Child Development, 70,* 896–909.

Nixon, A. S. (2005, April). *Moral reasoning in the digital age: How students, teachers, and parents judge appropriate computer uses.* Paper presented at the annual meeting of the American Educational Research Association, Montreal.

Noble, K. G., Tottenham, N., & Casey, B. J. (2005). Neuroscience perspectives on disparities in school readiness and cognitive achievement. *The Future of Children, 15*(1), 71–89.

Nokes, J. D., & Dole, J. A. (2004). Helping adolescent readers through explicit strategy instruction. In T. L. Jetton & J. A. Dole (Eds.), *Adolescent literacy research and practice* (pp. 162–182). New York: Guilford.

Nolen, S. B. (1996). Why study? How reasons for learning influence strategy selection. *Educational Psychology Review, 8,* 335–355.

Nolen, S. B. (2007). Young children's motivation to read and write: Development in social contexts. *Cognition and Instruction, 25,* 219–270.

Norenzayan, A., Choi, I., & Peng, K. (2007). Perception and cognition. In S. Kitayama & D. Cohen (Eds.), *Handbook of cultural psychology* (pp. 569–594). New York: Guilford Press.

Northup, J., Broussard, C., Jones, K., George, T., Vollmer, T. R., & Herring, M. (1995). The differential effects of teachers and peer attention on the disruptive classroom behavior of three children with a diagnosis of attention deficit hyperactivity disorder. *Journal of Applied Behavior Analysis, 28,* 227–228.

Noss, R., & Hoyles, C. (2006). Exploring mathematics through construction and collaboration. In R. K. Sawyer (Ed.), *The Cambridge handbook of the learning sciences* (pp. 389–405). Cambridge, England: Cambridge University Press.

Novak, J. D. (1998). *Learning, creating, and using knowledge: Concept maps as facilitative tools in schools and corporations.* Mahwah, NJ: Erlbaum.

Novak, J. D., & Gowin, D. B. (1984). *Learning how to learn.* Cambridge, England: Cambridge University Press.

Nucci, L. P. (2001). *Education in the moral domain.* Cambridge, England: Cambridge University Press.

Nucci, L. P. (2006). Classroom management for moral and social development. In C. M. Evertson & C. S. Weinstein (Eds.), *Handbook of classroom management: Research, practice, and contemporary issues* (pp. 711–731). Mahwah, NJ: Erlbaum.

Nucci, L. (2009). *Nice is not enough: Facilitating moral development.* Upper Saddle River, NJ: Merrill/Pearson.

Nucci, L. P., & Nucci, M. S. (1982). Children's social interactions in the context of moral and conventional transgressions. *Child Development, 53,* 403–412.

Nucci, L. P., & Weber, E. K. (1995). Social interactions in the home and the development of young children's conceptions of the personal. *Child Development, 66,* 1438–1452.

Nunner-Winkler, G. (1984). Two moralities? A critical discussion of an ethic of care and responsibility versus an ethic of rights and justice. In W. M. Kurtines & J. L. Gewirtz (Eds.), *Morality, moral behavior, and moral development.* New York: Wiley.

Nussbaum, E. M. (2008). Collaborative discourse, argumentation, and learning: Preface and literature review. *Contemporary Educational Psychology, 33,* 345–359.

Nuthall, G. (1996). Commentary: Of learning and language and understanding the complexity of the classroom. *Educational Psychologist, 31,* 207–214.

Nuttall, R. L., Casey, M. B., & Pezaris, E. (2005). Spatial ability as mediator of gender differences on mathematics tests. In A. M. Gallagher & J. C. Kaufman (Eds.), *Gender differences in mathematics: An integrative psychological approach* (pp. 121–142). Cambridge, England: Cambridge University Press.

Oakes, J., & Guiton, G. (1995). Matchmaking: The dynamics of high school tracking decisions. *American Educational Research Journal, 32,* 3–33.

Oakes, L. M., & Rakison, D. H. (2003). Issues in the early development of concepts and categories: An introduction. In D. H. Rakison & L. M. Oakes (Eds.), *Early category and concept development: Making sense of the blooming, buzzing confusion* (pp. 3–23). Oxford, England: Oxford University Press.

Obama, B. H. (2004). *Dreams from my father: A story of race and inheritance* (rev. ed.) New York: Three Rivers Press.

O'Boyle, M. W., & Gill, H. S. (1998). On the relevance of research findings in cognitive neuroscience to educational practice. *Educational Psychology Review, 10,* 397–409.

Ochs, E. (1982). Talking to children in western Samoa. *Language and Society, 11,* 77–104.

Ochsner, K. N., & Lieberman, M. D. (2001). The emergence of social cognitive neuroscience. *American Psychologist, 56,* 717–734.

O'Connor, E., & McCartney, K. (2007). Examining teacher-child relationships and achievement as part of an ecological model of development. *American Educational Research Journal, 44,* 340–369.

O'Donnell, A. M. (1999). Structuring dyadic interaction through scripted cooperation. In A. M. O'Donnell & A. King (Eds.), *Cognitive perspectives on peer learning* (pp. 179–196). Mahwah, NJ: Erlbaum.

O'Donnell, A. M. (2006). The role of peers and group learning. In P. A. Alexander & P. H. Winne (Eds.), *Handbook of educational psychology* (2nd ed., pp. 781–802). Mahwah, NJ: Erlbaum.

O'Donnell, A. M., & O'Kelly, J. (1994). Learning from peers: Beyond the rhetoric of positive results. *Educational Psychology Review, 6,* 321–349.

O'Donnell, D. A., Schwab-Stone, M. E., & Muyeed, A. Z. (2002). Multidimensional resilience in urban children exposed to community violence. *Child Development, 73,* 1265–1282.

Ogbu, J. U. (1999). Beyond language: Ebonics, proper English, and identity in a Black-American speech community. *American Educational Research Journal, 36,* 147–184.

Ogbu, J. U. (2003). *Black American students in an affluent suburb: A study of academic disengagement.* Mahwah, NJ: Erlbaum.

Ogbu, J. U. (2008a). Collective identity and the burden of "acting White" in Black history, community, and education. In J. U. Ogbu (Ed.), *Minority status, oppositional culture, and schooling* (pp. 29–63). New York: Routledge.

Ogbu, J. U. (2008b). Multiple sources of peer pressures among African American students. In J. U. Ogbu (Ed.), *Minority status, oppositional culture, and schooling* (pp. 89–111). New York: Routledge.

Ogden, E. H., & Germinario, V. (1988). *The at-risk student: Answers for educators.* Lancaster, PA: Technomic.

O'Grady, W. (1997). *Syntactic development.* Chicago: University of Chicago.

Öhman, A., & Mineka, S. (2003). The malicious serpent: Snakes as a prototypical stimulus for an evolved module of fear. *Current Directions in Psychological Science, 12,* 5–9.

Okagaki, L. (2001). Triarchic model of minority children's school achievement. *Educational Psychologist, 36,* 9–20.

O'Leary, K. D., & O'Leary, S. G. (Eds.). (1972). *Classroom management: The successful use of behavior modification.* New York: Pergamon Press.

Olneck, M. R. (1995). Immigrants and education. In J. A. Banks & C. A. M. Banks (Eds.), *Handbook of research on multicultural education.* New York: Macmillan.

O'Mara, A. J., Marsh, H. W., Craven, R. G., & Debus, R. L. (2006). Do self-concept interventions make a difference? A synergistic blend of construct validation and meta-analysis. *Educational Psychologist, 41,* 181–206.

Onosko, J. J. (1989). Comparing teachers' thinking about promoting students' thinking. *Theory and Research in Social Education, 17,* 174–195.

Onosko, J. J. (1996). Exploring issues with students despite the barriers. *Social Education, 60*(1), 22–27.

Onosko, J. J., & Newmann, F. M. (1994). Creating more thoughtful learning environments. In J. N. Mangieri & C. C. Block (Eds.), *Advanced educational psychology: Enhancing mindfulness.* Fort Worth, TX: Harcourt Brace Jovanovich.

Oppenheimer, L. (1986). Development of recursive thinking: Procedural variations. *International Journal of Behavioral Development, 9,* 401–411.

O'Reilly, T., & McNamara, D. S. (2007). The impact of science knowledge, reading skill, and reading strategy knowledge on more traditional "high-stakes" measures of high school students' science achievement. *American Educational Research Journal, 44,* 161–196.

Orenstein, P. (1994). *Schoolgirls: Young women, self-esteem, and the confidence gap.* New York: Doubleday.

Ormrod, J. E. (2008). *Human learning* (5th ed.). Upper Saddle River, NJ: Merrill/Prentice Hall.

Ormrod, J. E., & McGuire, D. J. (2007). *Case studies: Applying educational psychology* (2nd ed.). Upper Saddle River, NJ: Merrill/Prentice Hall.

Ornstein, R. (1997). *The right mind: Making sense of the hemispheres.* San Diego, CA: Harcourt Brace.

Ortony, A., Turner, T. J., & Larson-Shapiro, N. (1985). Cultural and instructional influences on figurative comprehension by inner city children. *Research in the Teaching of English, 1*(1), 25–36.

Osborne, J. W., & Simmons, C. M. (2002, April). *Girls, math, stereotype threat, and anxiety: Physiological evidence.* Paper presented at the annual meeting of the American Educational Research Association, New Orleans, LA.

Oskamp, S. (Ed.). (2000). *Reducing prejudice and discrimination.* Mahwah, NJ: Erlbaum.

Osterman, K. F. (2000). Students' need for belonging in the school community. *Review of Educational Research, 70,* 323–367.

O'Sullivan, J. T., & Joy, R. M. (1994). If at first you don't succeed: Children's metacognition about reading problems. *Contemporary Educational Psychology, 19,* 118–127.

Otero, J., & Kintsch, W. (1992). Failures to detect contradictions in a text: What readers believe versus what they read. *Psychological Science, 3,* 229–235.

Otis, N., Grouzet, F. M. E., & Pelletier, L. G. (2005). Latent motivational change in an academic setting: A 3-year longitudinal study. *Journal of Educational Psychology, 97,* 170–183.

O'Toole, M. E. (2000). *The school shooter: A threat assessment perspective.* Quantico, VA: Federal Bureau of Investigation. Retrieved February 26, 2004, from www.fbi.gov/publications/school/school2.pdf

Owens, R. E., Jr. (2008). *Language development* (7th ed.). Boston: Allyn & Bacon.

Ozonoff, S., & Schetter, P. L. (2007). Executive dysfunction in autism spectrum disorders: From research to practice. In L. Meltzer (Ed.), *Executive function in education: From theory to practice* (pp. 133–160). New York: Guilford Press.

Paciello, M., Fida, R., Tramontano, C., Lupinetti, C., & Caprara, G. V. (2008). Stability and change of moral disengagement and its impact on aggression and violence in late adolescence. *Child Development, 79,* 1288–1309.

Padilla, A. M. (1994). Bicultural development: A theoretical and empirical examination. In R. G. Malgady & O. Rodriguez (Eds.), *Theoretical and conceptual issues in Hispanic mental health* (pp. 20–51). Malabar, FL: Krieger.

Padilla, A. M. (2006). Second language learning: Issues in research and teaching. In P. A. Alexander & P. H. Winne (Eds.), *Handbook of educational psychology* (2nd ed., pp. 571–591). Mahwah, NJ: Erlbaum.

Padilla-Walker, L. M. (2006). The impact of daily extra credit quizzes on exam performance. *Teaching of Psychology, 33,* 236–239.

Paget, K. F., Kritt, D., & Bergemann, L. (1984). Understanding strategic interactions in television commercials: A developmental study. *Journal of Applied Developmental Psychology, 5,* 145–161.

Page-Voth, V., & Graham, S. (1999). Effects of goal setting and strategy use on the writing performance and self-efficacy of students with writing and learning problems. *Journal of Educational Psychology, 91,* 230–240.

Pajares, F. (2005). Gender differences in mathematics self-efficacy beliefs. In A. M. Gallagher & J. C. Kaufman (Eds.), *Gender differences in mathematics: An integrative psychological approach* (pp. 294–315). Cambridge, England: Cambridge University Press.

Pajares, F., & Valiante, G. (1999). *Writing self-efficacy of middle school students: Relation to motivation constructs, achievement, gender, and gender orientation.* Paper presented at the annual meeting of the American Educational Research Association, Montreal, Canada.

Paley, V. G. (1984). *Boys and girls: Superheroes in the doll corner.* Chicago: University of Chicago Press.

Palincsar, A. S., & Brown, A. L. (1984). Reciprocal teaching of comprehension-fostering and comprehension-monitoring activities. *Cognition and Instruction, 1,* 117–175.

Palincsar, A. S., & Brown, A. L. (1989). Classroom dialogues to promote self-regulated comprehension. In J. Brophy (Ed.), *Advances in research on teaching* (Vol. 1). Greenwich, CT: JAI Press.

Palincsar, A. S., & Herrenkohl, L. R. (1999). Designing collaborative contexts: Lessons from three research programs. In A. M. O'Donnell & A. King (Eds.), *Cognitive perspectives on peer learning* (pp. 151–177). Mahwah, NJ: Erlbaum.

Palmer, D. J., & Goetz, E. T. (1988). Selection and use of study strategies: The role of the studier's beliefs about self and strategies. In C. E. Weinstein, E. T. Goetz, & P. A. Alexander (Eds.), *Learning and study strategies: Issues in assessment, instruction, and evaluation.* San Diego: Academic Press.

Palmer, E. L. (1965). Accelerating the child's cognitive attainments through the inducement of cognitive conflict: An interpretation of the Piagetian position. *Journal of Research in Science Teaching, 3,* 324.

Pan, B. A., Rowe, M. L., Singer, J. D., & Snow, C. E. (2005). Maternal correlates of growth in toddler vocabulary production in low-income families. *Child Development, 76,* 763–782.

Pang, V. O. (1995). Asian Pacific American students: A diverse and complex population. In J. A. Banks & C. A. M. Banks (Eds.), *Handbook of research on multicultural education.* New York: Macmillan.

Paris, S. G., & Ayres, L. R. (1994). *Becoming reflective students and teachers with portfolios and authentic assessment.* Washington, DC: American Psychological Association.

Paris, S. G., & Cunningham, A. E. (1996). Children becoming students. In D. C. Berliner & R. C. Calfee (Eds.), *Handbook of educational psychology.* New York: Macmillan.

Paris, S. G., Lawton, T. A., Turner, J. C., & Roth, J. L. (1991). A developmental perspective on standardized achievement testing. *Educational Researcher, 20*(5), 12–20, 40.

Paris, S. G., & Paris, A. H. (2001). Classroom applications of research on self-regulated learning. *Educational Psychologist, 36,* 89–101.

Paris, S. G., & Turner, J. C. (1994). Situated motivation. In P. R. Pintrich, D. R. Brown, & C. E. Weinstein (Eds.), *Student motivation, cognition, and learning: Essays in honor of Wilbert J. McKeachie.* Mahwah, NJ: Erlbaum.

Paris, S. G., & Winograd, P. (1990). How metacognition can promote academic learning and instruction. In B. F. Jones & L. Idol (Eds.), *Dimensions of thinking and cognitive instruction.* Mahwah, NJ: Erlbaum.

Parke, R. D. (1974). Rules, roles, and resistance to deviation: Explorations in punishment, discipline, and self-control. In A. Pick (Ed.), *Minnesota Symposia on Child Psychology* (Vol. 8). Minneapolis: University of Minnesota Press.

Parke, R. D., Coltrane, S., Duffy, S., Buriel, R., Dennis, J., Powers, J., French, S., & Widaman, K. F. (2004). Economic stress, parenting, and child adjustment in Mexican American and European American families. *Child Development, 75,* 1632–1656.

Parker, W. D. (1997). An empirical typology of perfectionism in academically talented children. *American Educational Research Journal, 34,* 545–562.

Parkes, J. (2001). The role of transfer in the variability of performance assessment scores. *Educational Assessment, 7,* 143–164.

Parkhurst, J. T., & Hopmeyer, A. (1998). Sociometric popularity and peer-perceived popularity: Two distinct dimensions of peer status. *Journal of Early Adolescence, 18,* 125–144.

Parks, C. P. (1995). Gang behavior in the schools: Reality or myth? *Educational Psychology Review, 7,* 41–68.

Parsons, J. E., Kaczala, C. M., & Meece, J. L. (1982). Socialization of achievement attitudes and beliefs: Classroom influences. *Child Development, 53,* 322–339.

Pashler, H., Rohrer, D., Cepeda, N. J., & Carpenter, S. K. (2007). Enhancing learning and retarding forgetting: Choices and consequences. *Psychonomic Bulletin & Review, 14,* 187–193.

Patall, E. A., Cooper, H., & Robinson, J. C. (2008). Parent involvement in homework: A research synthesis. *Review of Educational Research, 78,* 1039–1101.

Patall, E. A., Cooper, H., & Wynn, S. (2008, March). *The importance of providing choices in the classroom.* Paper presented at the annual meeting of the American Educational Research Association, New York.

Patrick, H. (1997). Social self-regulation: Exploring the relations between children's social relationships, academic self-regulation, and school performance. *Educational Psychologist, 32,* 209–220.

Patrick, H., Anderman, L. H., & Ryan, A. M. (2002). Social motivation and the classroom social environment. In C. Midgley (Ed.), *Goals, goal structures, and patterns of adaptive learning* (pp. 85–108). Mahwah, NJ: Erlbaum.

Patrick, H., Mantzicopoulos, Y., & Samarapungavan, A. (2009). Motivation for learning science in kindergarten: Is there a gender gap and does integrated inquiry and literacy instruction make a difference? *Journal of Research in Science Teaching, 46,* 166–191.

Patrick, H., & Pintrich, P. R. (2001). Conceptual change in teachers' intuitive conceptions of learning, motivation, and instruction: The role of motivational and epistemological beliefs. In B. Torff & R. J. Sternberg (Eds.), *Understanding and teaching the intuitive mind: Student and teacher learning* (pp. 117–143). Mahwah, NJ: Erlbaum.

Patrick, H., Ryan, A. M., & Kaplan, A. M. (2007). Early adolescents' perceptions of the classroom social environment, motivational beliefs, and engagement. *Journal of Educational Psychology, 99,* 83–98.

Patterson, C. J. (1995). Sexual orientation and human development: An overview. *Developmental Psychology, 31,* 3–11.

Patton, J. R., Blackbourn, J. M., & Fad, K. S. (1996). *Exceptional individuals in focus* (6th ed.). Upper Saddle River, NJ: Merrill/Prentice Hall.

Paulson, F. L., Paulson, P. R., & Meyer, C. A. (1991). What makes a portfolio a portfolio? *Educational Leadership, 49*(5), 60–63.

Paus, T., Zijdenbos, A., Worsley, K., Collins, D. L., Blumenthal, J., Giedd, J. N., Rapoport, J. L., & Evans, A. C. (1999). Structural maturation of neural pathways in children and adolescents: In vivo study. *Science, 283,* 1908–1911.

Pavlov, I. P. (1927). *Conditioned reflexes* (G. V. Anrep, Trans.). London: Oxford University Press.

Pawlas, G. E. (1994). Homeless students at the school door. *Educational Leadership, 51*(8), 79–82.

Paxton, R. J. (1999). A deafening silence: History textbooks and the students who read them. *Review of Educational Research, 69,* 315–339.

Payne, R. K. (2005). *A framework for understanding poverty* (4th rev. ed.). Highlands, TX: aha! Process, Inc.

Pea, R. D. (1987). Socializing the knowledge transfer problem. *International Journal of Educational Research, 11,* 639–663.

Pea, R. D. (1993). Practices of distributed intelligence and designs for education. In G. Salomon (Ed.), *Distributed cognitions: Psychological and educational considerations.* Cambridge, England: Cambridge University Press.

Pea, R. D., & Maldonado, H. (2006). WILD for learning: Interacting through new computing devices anytime, anywhere. In R. K. Sawyer (Ed.), *The Cambridge handbook of the learning sciences* (pp. 427–441). Cambridge, England: Cambridge University Press.

Pearce, M. J., Jones, S. M, Schwab-Stone, M. E., & Ruchkin, V. (2003). The protective effects of religiousness and parent involvement on the development of conduct problems among youth exposed to violence. *Child Development, 74,* 1682–1696.

Pearce, R. R. (2006). Effects of cultural and social structural factors on the achievement of White and Chinese American students at school transition points. *American Educational Research Journal, 43,* 75–101.

Pedersen, E., Faucher, T. A., & Eaton, W. W. (1978). A new perspective on the effects of first-grade teachers on children's subsequent adult status. *Harvard Educational Review, 48*(1), 1–31.

Pedersen, S., Vitaro, F., Barker, E. D., & Borge, A. I. H. (2007). The timing of middle-childhood peer rejection and friendship: Linking early behavior to early-adolescent adjustment. *Child Development, 78,* 1037–1051.

Pekrun, R. (2006). The control-value theory of achievement emotions: Assumptions, corrolaries, and implications for educational research and practice. *Educational Psychology Review, 18,* 315–341.

Pekrun, R., Goetz, T., Titz, W., & Perry, R. P. (2002). Academic emotions in students' self-regulated learning and achievement: A program of qualitative and quantitative research. *Educational Psychologist, 37,* 91–105.

Pellegrini, A. D. (2002). Bullying, victimization, and sexual harassment during the transition to middle school. *Educational Psychologist, 37,* 151–163.

Pellegrini, A. D., & Archer, J. (2005). Sex differences in competitive and aggressive behavior. In B. J. Ellis & D. F. Bjorklund (Eds.), *Origins of the social mind: Evolutionary psychology and child development* (pp. 219–244). New York: Guilford Press.

Pellegrini, A. D., & Bartini, M. (2000). A longitudinal study of bullying, victimization, and peer affiliation during the transition from primary school to middle school. *American Educational Research Journal, 37,* 699–725.

Pellegrini, A. D., Bartini, M., & Brooks, F. (1999). School bullies, victims, and aggressive victims: Factors relating to group affiliation and victimization in early adolescence. *Journal of Educational Psychology, 91,* 216–224.

Pellegrini, A. D., & Bjorklund, D. F. (1997). The role of recess in children's cognitive performance. *Educational Psychologist, 32,* 35–40.

Pellegrini, A. D., & Bohn, C. M. (2005). The role of recess in children's cognitive performance and school adjustment. *Educational Researcher, 34*(1), 13–19.

Pellegrini, A. D., & Horvat, M. (1995). A developmental contextualist critique of attention deficit hyperactivity disorder. *Educational Researcher, 24*(1), 13–19.

Pellegrini, A. D., Huberty, P. D., & Jones, I. (1995). The effects of recess timing on children's playground and classroom behaviors. *American Educational Research Journal, 32,* 845–864.

Pellegrini, A. D., Kato, K., Blatchford, P., & Baines, E. (2002). A short-term longitudinal study of children's playground games across the first year of school: Implications for social competence and adjustment to school. *American Educational Research Journal, 39,* 991–1015.

Pellegrini, A. D., & Long, J. D. (2004). Part of the solution and part of the problem: The role of peers in bullying, dominance, and victimization during the transition from primary school through secondary school. In D. L. Espelage & S. M. Swearer (Eds.), *Bullying in American schools: A social-ecological perspective on prevention and intervention* (pp. 107–117). Mahwah, NJ: Erlbaum.

Pelphrey, K. A., & Carter, E. J. (2007). Brain mechanisms underlying social perception deficits in autism. In D. Coch, G. Dawson, & K. W. Fischer (Eds.), *Human behavior, learning, and the developing brain: Atypical development* (pp. 56–86). New York: Guilford Press.

Penner, A. M. (2003). International gender X item difficulty interactions in mathematics and science achievement tests. *Journal of Educational Psychology, 95,* 650–655.

Peretz, I. (2008). Musical disorders: From behavior to genes. *Current Directions in Psychological Science, 17,* 329–333.

Pérez, B. (1998). *Sociocultural contexts of language and literacy.* Mahwah, NJ: Erlbaum.

Perkins, D. N. (1990). The nature and nurture of creativity. In B. F. Jones & L. Idol (Eds.), *Dimensions of thinking and cognitive instruction.* Mahwah, NJ: Erlbaum.

Perkins, D. N. (1992). *Smart schools: From training memories to educating minds.* New York: Free Press/Macmillan.

Perkins, D. N. (1995). *Outsmarting IQ: The emerging science of learnable intelligence.* New York: Free Press.

Perkins, D. N., & Ritchhart, R. (2004). When is good

thinking? In D. Y. Dai & R. J. Sternberg (Eds.), *Motivation, emotion, and cognition: Integrative perspectives on intellectual functioning and development* (pp. 351–384). Mahwah, NJ: Erlbaum.

Perkins, D. N., & Salomon, G. (1987). Transfer and teaching thinking. In D. N. Perkins, J. Lochhead, & J. Bishop (Eds.), *Thinking: The second international conference.* Mahwah, NJ: Erlbaum.

Perkins, D. N., & Salomon, G. (1989). Are cognitive skills context-bound? *Educational Researcher, 18*(1), 16–25.

Perkins, D. N., & Simmons, R. (1988). Patterns of misunderstanding: An integrative model for science, math, and programming. *Review of Educational Research, 58,* 303–326.

Perkins, D. N., Tishman, S., Ritchhart, R., Donis, K., & Andrade, A. (2000). Intelligence in the wild: A dispositional view of intellectual traits. *Educational Psychology Review, 12,* 269–293.

Perner, J., & Wimmer, H. (1985). "John *thinks* that Mary *thinks* that . . ." Attribution of second-order beliefs by 5- to 10-year-old children. *Journal of Experimental Child Psychology, 39,* 437–471.

Perry, D. G., & Perry, L. C. (1983). Social learning, causal attribution, and moral internalization. In J. Bisanz, G. L. Bisanz, & R. Kail (Eds.), *Learning in children: Progress in cognitive development research.* New York: Springer-Verlag.

Perry, M. (1991). Learning and transfer: Instructional conditions and conceptual change. *Cognitive Development, 6,* 449–468.

Perry, N. E. (1998). Young children's self-regulated learning and contexts that support it. *Journal of Educational Psychology, 90,* 715–729.

Perry, N. E., Turner, J. C., & Meyer, D. K. (2006). Classrooms as contexts for motivating learning. In P. A. Alexander & P. H. Winne (Eds.), *Handbook of educational psychology* (2nd ed., pp. 327–348). Mahwah, NJ: Erlbaum.

Perry, N. E., VandeKamp, K. O., Mercer, L. K., & Nordby, C. J. (2002). Investigating teacher-student interactions that foster self-regulated learning. *Educational Psychologist, 37,* 5–15.

Perry, N. E., & Winne, P. H. (2004). Motivational messages from home and school: How do they influence young children's engagement in learning? In D. M. McInerney & S. Van Etten (Eds.), *Big theories revisited* (pp. 199–222). Greenwich, CT: Information Age.

Perry, R. P. (1985). Instructor expressiveness: Implications for improving teaching. In J. G. Donald & A. M. Sullivan (Eds.), *Using research to improve teaching* (pp. 35–49). San Francisco: Jossey-Bass.

Petersen, G. A., Sudweeks, R. R., & Baird, J. H. (1990, April). *Test-wise responses of third-, fifth-, and sixth-grade students to clued and unclued multiple-choice science items.* Paper presented at the annual meeting of the American Educational Research Association, Boston.

Peterson, C. (1990). Explanatory style in the classroom and on the playing field. In S. Graham & V. S. Folkes (Eds.), *Attribution theory: Applications to achievement, mental health, and interpersonal conflict.* Mahwah, NJ: Erlbaum.

Peterson, C. (2006). *A primer in positive psychology.* New York: Oxford University Press.

Peterson, C., Maier, S., & Seligman, M. (1993). *Learned helplessness: A theory for the age of personal control.* New York: Oxford University Press.

Peterson, C. C. (2002). Drawing insight from pictures: The development of concepts of false drawing and false belief in children with deafness, normal hearing, and autism. *Child Development, 73,* 1442–1459.

Peterson, L. R., & Peterson, M. J. (1959). Short-term retention of individual items. *Journal of Experimental Psychology, 58,* 193–198.

Peterson, P. L. (1979). Direct instruction reconsidered. In P. L. Peterson & H. L. Walberg (Eds.), *Research on teaching: Concepts, findings and implications.* Berkeley, CA: McCutchan.

Peterson, S. E. (1993). The effects of prior achievement and group outcome on attributions and affect in cooperative tasks. *Contemporary Educational Psychology, 18,* 479–485.

Petterson, S. M., & Albers, A. B. (2001). Effects of poverty and maternal depression on early child development. *Child Development, 72,* 1794–1813.

Pettit, G. S. (2004). Violent children in developmental perspective: Risk and protective factors and the mechanisms through which they (may) operate. *Current Directions in Psychological Science, 13,* 194–197.

Pettito, A. L. (1985). Division of labor: Procedural learning in teacher-led small groups. *Cognition and Instruction, 2,* 233–270.

Peverly, S. T., Brobst, K. E., Graham, M., & Shaw, R. (2003). College adults are not good at self-regulation: A study on the relationship of self-regulation, note taking, and test taking. *Journal of Educational Psychology, 95,* 335–346.

Pexman, P. M. (2008). It's fascinating research: The cognition of verbal irony. *Current Directions in Psychological Science, 17,* 286–290.

Pezdek, K., & Banks, W. P. (Eds.). (1996). *The recovered memory/false memory debate.* San Diego: Academic Press.

Pfeifer, J. H., Brown, C. S., & Juvonen, J. (2007). Teaching tolerance in schools: Lessons learned since Brown v. Board of Education about the development and reduction of children's prejudice. *Social Policy Report, 21*(2), 3–13, 16–17, 20–23. Ann Arbor, MI: Society for Research in Child Development.

Pfiffner, L. J., Barkley, R. A., & DuPaul, G. J. (2006). Treatment of ADHD in school settings. In R. A. Barkley, *Attention-deficit hyperactivity disorder: A handbook for diagnosis and treatment* (3rd ed., pp. 547–589). New York: Guilford Press.

Pfiffner, L. J., & O'Leary, S. G. (1993). School-based psychological treatments. In J. L. Matson (Ed.), *Handbook of hyperactivity in children* (pp. 234–255). Boston: Allyn & Bacon.

Pfiffner, L. J., Rosen, L. A., & O'Leary, S. G. (1985). The efficacy of an all-positive approach to classroom management. *Journal of Applied Behavior Analysis, 18,* 257–261.

Phalet, K., Andriessen, I., & Lens, W. (2004). How future goals enhance motivation and learning in multicultural classrooms. *Educational Psychology Review, 16,* 59–89.

Phelan, P., Davidson, A. L., & Cao, H. T. (1991). Students' multiple worlds: Negotiating the boundaries of family, peer, and school cultures. *Anthropology and Education Quarterly, 22,* 224–250.

Phelan, P., Yu, H. C., & Davidson, A. L. (1994). Navigating the psychosocial pressures of adolescence: The voices and experiences of high school youth. *American Educational Research Journal, 31,* 415–447.

Phelps, E. A., & Sharot, T. (2008). How (and why) emotion enhances the subjective sense of recollection. *Current Directions in Psychological Science, 17,* 147–152.

Phelps, L., McGrew, K. S., Knopik, S. N., & Ford, L. (2005). The general (g), broad, and narrow CHC stratum characteristics of the WJ III and WISC-III tests: A confirmatory cross-battery investigation. *School Psychology Quarterly, 20,* 66–88.

Phillips, B. N., Pitcher, G. D., Worsham, M. E., & Miller, S. C. (1980). Test anxiety and the school environment. In I. G. Sarason (Ed.), *Test anxiety: Theory, research, and applications.* Mahwah, NJ: Erlbaum.

Phillips, E. L., Phillips, E. A., Fixsen, D. L., & Wolf, M. M. (1971). Achievement place: Modification of the behaviors of predelinquent boys within a token economy. *Journal of Applied Behavior Analysis, 4,* 45–59.

Phillips, G., McNaughton, S., & MacDonald, S. (2004). Managing the mismatch: Enhancing early literacy progress for children with diverse language and cultural identities in mainstream urban schools in New Zealand. *Journal of Educational Psychology, 96,* 309–323.

Phinney, J. (1990). Ethnic identity in adolescents and adults: Review of research. *Psychological Bulletin, 108,* 499–514.

Phinney, J. (1993). A three-stage model of ethnic identity development in adolescence. In M. E. Bernal & G. P. Knight (Eds.), *Ethnic identity: Formation and transmission among Hispanics and other minorities* (pp. 61–79). Albany: State University of New York Press.

Phye, G. D. (1997). Classroom assessment: A multidimensional perspective. In G. D. Phye (Ed.), *Handbook of classroom assessment: Learning, achievement, and adjustment.* San Diego, CA: Academic Press.

Piaget, J. (1928). *Judgment and reasoning in the child* (M. Warden, Trans.). New York: Harcourt, Brace.

Piaget, J. (1929). *The child's conception of the world.* New York: Harcourt, Brace.

Piaget, J. (1952a). *The child's conception of number* (C. Gattegno & F. M. Hodgson, Trans.). London: Routledge & Kegan Paul.

Piaget, J. (1952b). *The origins of intelligence in children* (M. Cook, Trans.). New York: Norton.

Piaget, J. (1959). *The language and thought of the child* (3rd ed.; M. Gabain, Trans.). London: Routledge & Kegan Paul.

Piaget, J. (1970). Piaget's theory. In P. H. Mussen (Ed.), *Carmichael's manual of psychology.* New York: Wiley.

Piaget, J. (1971). The theory of stages in cognitive development. In D. R. Green (Ed.), *Measurement and Piaget* (pp. 1–11). New York: McGraw-Hill.

Piaget, J. (1980). *Adaptation and intelligence: Organic selection and phenocopy* (S. Eames, Trans.). Chicago: University of Chicago Press.

Pianta, R. C. (1999). *Enhancing relationships between children and teachers.* Washington, DC: American Psychological Association.

Pianta, R. C. (2006). Classroom management and relationships between children and teachers: Implications for research and practice. In C. M. Evertson & C. S. Weinstein (Eds.), *Handbook of classroom management: Research, practice, and contemporary issues* (pp. 685–709). Mahwah, NJ: Erlbaum.

Pianta, R. C., Belsky, J., Vandergrift, N., Houts, R., & Morrison, F. J. (2008). Classroom effects on children's achievement trajectories in elementary school. *American Educational Research Journal, 45,* 365–397.

Pickens, J. (2006, Winter). "Poop study" engages primary students. *Volunteer Monitor* (National Newsletter of Volunteer Watershed Monitoring), *18*(1), 13, 21.

Piersel, W. C. (1987). Basic skills education. In C. A. Maher & S. G. Forman (Eds.), *A behavioral approach to education of children and youth.* Mahwah, NJ: Erlbaum.

Pietsch, J., Walker, R., & Chapman, E. (2003). The relationship among self-concept, self-efficacy, and performance in mathematics during secondary school. *Journal of Educational Psychology, 95,* 589–603.

Pigott, H. E., Fantuzzo, J. W., & Clement, P. W. (1986). The effects of reciprocal peer tutoring and group contingencies on the academic performance of elementary school children. *Journal of Applied Behavior Analysis, 19,* 93–98.

Piirto, J. (1999). *Talented children and adults: Their development and education* (2nd ed.). Upper Saddle River, NJ: Merrill/Prentice Hall.

Pillow, B. H. (2002). Children's and adults' evaluation of the certainty of deductive inferences, inductive inferences, and guesses. *Child Development, 73,* 779–792.

Pine, K. J., & Messer, D. J. (2000). The effect of explaining another's actions on children's implicit theories of balance. *Cognition and Instruction, 18,* 35–51.

Pinker, S. (1987). The bootstrapping problem in language acquisition. In B. MacWhinney (Ed.), *Mechanisms of language acquisition.* Mahwah, NJ: Erlbaum.

Pintrich, P. R. (2003). Motivation and classroom learning. In W. M. Reynolds, G. E. Miller (Vol. Eds.), & I. B. Weiner (Editor-in-Chief), *Handbook of psychology: Vol. 7. Educational psychology* (pp. 103–122). New York: Wiley.

Pintrich, P. R., & De Groot, E. V. (1990). Motivational and self-regulated learning components of classroom academic performance. *Journal of Educational Psychology, 82,* 33–40.

Pintrich, P. R., Marx, R. W., & Boyle, R. A. (1993). Beyond cold conceptual change: The role of motivational beliefs and classroom contextual factors in the process of conceptual change. *Review of Educational Research, 63,* 167–199.

Pintrich, P. R., & Schrauben, B. (1992). Students' motivational beliefs and their cognitive engagement in academic tasks. In D. Schunk & J. Meece (Eds.), *Students' perceptions in the classroom: Causes and consequences.* Mahwah, NJ: Erlbaum.

Pintrich, P. R., & Schunk, D. H. (2002). *Motivation in education: Theory, research, and applications* (2nd ed.). Upper Saddle River, NJ: Merrill/Prentice Hall.

Piontkowski, D., & Calfee, R. (1979). Attention in the classroom. In G. A. Hale & M. Lewis (Eds.), *Attention and cognitive development.* New York: Plenum Press.

Pipher, M. (1994). *Reviving Ophelia: Saving the selves of adolescent girls.* New York: Putnam.

Pitner, R. O., Astor, R. A., Benbenishty, R., Haj-Yahia, M. M., & Zeira, A. (2003). The effects of group stereotypes on adolescents' reasoning about peer retribution. *Child Development, 74,* 413–425.

Pitoniak, M. J., & Royer, J. M. (2001). Testing accommodations for examinees with disabilities: A review of psychometric, legal, and social policy issues. *Review of Educational Research, 71,* 53–104.

Pittman, K., & Beth-Halachmy, S. (1997, March). *The role of prior knowledge in analogy use.* Paper presented at the annual meeting of the American Educational Research Association, Chicago.

Plomin, R. (1994). *Genetics and experience: The interplay between nature and nurture.* Thousand Oaks, CA: Sage.

Plucker, J. A., Beghetto, R. A., & Dow, G. T. (2004). Why isn't creativity more important to educational psychologists? Potentials, pitfalls, and future directions in creativity research. *Educational Psychologist, 39,* 83–96.

Plumert, J. M. (1994). Flexibility in children's use of spatial and categorical organizational strategies in recall. *Developmental Psychology, 30,* 738–747.

Poche, C., McCubbrey, H., & Munn, T. (1982). The development of correct toothbrushing technique in preschool children. *Journal of Applied Behavior Analysis, 15,* 315–320.

Poche, C., Yoder, P., & Miltenberger, R. (1988). Teaching self-protection to children using television techniques. *Journal of Applied Behavior Analysis, 21,* 253–261.

Pogrow, S., & Londer, G. (1994). The effects of an intensive general thinking program on the motivation and cognitive development of at-risk students: Findings from the HOTS program. In H. F. O'Neil, Jr., & M. Drillings (Eds.), *Motivation: Theory and research.* Mahwah, NJ: Erlbaum.

Polakow, V. (2007). In the shadows of the ownership society: Homeless children and their families. In S. Books (Ed.), *Invisible children in the society and its schools* (3rd ed., pp. 39–62). Mahwah, NJ: Erlbaum.

Pollack, W. S. (2006). Sustaining and reframing vulnerability and connection: Creating genuine resilience in boys and young males. In S. Goldstein & R. B. Brooks (Eds.), *Handbook of resilience in children* (pp. 65–77). New York: Springer.

Polloway, E. A., & Patton, J. R. (1993). *Strategies for teaching learners with special needs* (5th ed.). Upper Saddle River, NJ: Merrill/Prentice Hall.

Polman, J. L. (2004). Dialogic activity structures for project-based learning environments. *Cognition and Instruction, 22,* 431–466.

Pomerantz, E. M., Altermatt, E. R., & Saxon, J. L. (2002). Making the grade but feeling distressed: Gender differences in academic performance and internal distress. *Journal of Educational Psychology, 94,* 396–404.

Pomerantz, E. M., & Saxon, J. L. (2001). Conceptions of ability as stable and self-evaluative processes: A longitudinal examination. *Child Development, 72,* 152–173.

Pool, J., Dittrich, C., & Pool, K. (2008, October). *Arts integration in teacher preparation: Teaching the teachers.* Paper presented at the annual meeting of the National Social Science Association, Albuquerque, NM.

Popham, W. J. (1990). *Modern educational measurement: A practitioner's perspective* (2nd ed.). Upper Saddle River, NJ: Prentice Hall.

Popham, W. J. (1995). *Classroom assessment: What teachers need to know.* Boston: Allyn & Bacon.

Porat, D. A. (2004). *It's not written here, but this is what happened:* Students' cultural comprehension of textbook narratives on the Israeli-Arab conflict. *American Educational Research Journal, 41,* 963–996.

Porath, M. (1988, April). *Cognitive development of gifted children: A neo-Piagetian perspective.* Paper presented at the annual meeting of the American Educational Research Association, New Orleans, LA.

Porter, A. C., & Polikoff, M. S. (2007). NCLB: State interpretations, early effects, and suggestions for reauthorization. *Social Policy Report, 21*(4) (Society for Research in Child Development).

Portes, P. R. (1996). Ethnicity and culture in educational psychology. In D. C. Berliner & R. C. Calfee (Eds.), *Handbook of educational psychology.* New York: Macmillan.

Posner, G. J., Strike, K. A., Hewson, P. W., & Gertzog, W. A. (1982). Accommodation of a scientific conception: Toward a theory of conceptual change. *Science Education, 66,* 211–227.

Posner, M. I., & Rothbart, M. K. (2007). *Educating the human brain.* Washington, DC: American Psychological Association.

Potoczak, K., Carr, J. E., & Michael, J. (2007). The effects of consequence manipulation during functional analysis of problem behavior maintained by negative reinforcement. *Journal of Applied Behavior Analysis, 40,* 719–724.

Poulin, F., & Boivin, M. (1999). Proactive and reactive aggression and boys' friendship quality in mainstream classrooms. *Journal of Emotional and Behavioral Disorders, 7,* 168–177.

Powell, G. J. (1983). *The psychosocial development of minority children.* New York: Brunner/Mazel.

Powell, S., & Nelson, B. (1997). Effects of choosing academic assignments on a student with attention deficit hyperactivity disorder. *Journal of Applied Behavior Analysis, 30,* 181–183.

Power, F. C., Higgins, A., & Kohlberg, L. (1989). *Lawrence Kohlberg's approach to moral education.* New York: Columbia University Press.

Powers, L. E., Sowers, J. A., & Stevens, T. (1995). An exploratory, randomized study of the impact of mentoring on the self-efficacy and community-based knowledge of adolescents with severe physical challenges. *Journal of Rehabilitation, 61*(1), 33–41.

Powers, M. D., & Crowel, R. L. (1985). The educative effects of positive practice overcorrection: Acquisition, generalization, and maintenance. *School Psychology Review, 14,* 360–372.

Powers, S. I., Hauser, S. T., & Kilner, L. A. (1989). Adolescent mental health. *American Psychologist, 44,* 200–208.

Prawat, R. S. (1989). Promoting access to knowledge, strategy, and disposition in students: A research synthesis. *Review of Educational Research, 59,* 1–41.

Prawat, R. S. (1993). The value of ideas: Problems versus possibilities in learning. *Educational Researcher, 22*(6), 5–16.

Premack, D. (1959). Toward empirical behavior laws: I. Positive reinforcement. *Psychological Review, 66,* 219–233.

Premack, D. (1963). Rate differential reinforcement in monkey manipulation. *Journal of Experimental Analysis of Behavior, 6,* 81–89.

Premack, D. (2004). Is language the key to human intelligence? *Science, 303,* 318–320.

Pressley, M. (1977). Imagery and children's learning: Putting the picture in developmental perspective. *Review of Educational Research, 47,* 586–622.

Pressley, M. (1982). Elaboration and memory development. *Child Development, 53,* 296–309.

Pressley, M., with McCormick, C. B. (1995). *Advanced educational psychology for educators, researchers, and policymakers.* New York: HarperCollins.

Pressley, M., Borkowski, J. G., & Schneider, W. (1987). Cognitive strategies: Good strategy users coordinate metacognition and knowledge. In R. Vasta (Ed.), *Annals of child development* (Vol. 4). Greenwich, CT: JAI Press.

Pressley, M., El-Dinary, P. B., Marks, M. B., Brown, R., & Stein, S. (1992). Good strategy instruction is motivating and interesting. In K. A. Renninger, S. Hidi, & A. Krapp (Eds.), *The role of interest in learning and development.* Mahwah, NJ: Erlbaum.

Pressley, M., Harris, K. R., & Marks, M. B. (1992). But good strategy instructors are constructivists! *Educational Psychology Review, 4,* 3–31.

Pressley, M., & Hilden, K. (2006). Cognitive strategies: Production deficiencies and successful strategy instruction everywhere. In W. Damon & R. M. Lerner (Series Eds.), D. Kuhn, & R. Siegler (Vol. Eds.), *Handbook of child psychology: Vol. 2. Cognition, perception, and language* (6th ed.). New York: Wiley.

Pressley, M., Levin, J. R., & Delaney, H. D. (1982). The mnemonic keyword method. *Review of Educational Research, 52,* 61–91.

Pressley, M., Woloshyn, V., Lysynchuk, L. M., Martin, V., Wood, E., & Willoughby, T. (1990). A primer of research on cognitive strategy instruction: The important issues and how to address them. *Educational Psychology Review, 2,* 1–58.

Pressley, M., Yokoi, L., van Meter, P., Van Etten, S., & Freebern, G. (1997). Some of the reasons why preparing for exams is so hard: What can be done to make it easier? *Educational Psychology Review, 9,* 1–38.

Price-Williams, D. R., Gordon, W., & Ramirez, M. (1969). Skill and conservation: A study of pottery-making children. *Developmental Psychology, 1,* 769.

Proctor, B. E., Floyd, R. G., & Shaver, R. B. (2005). Cattell-Horn-Carroll broad cognitive ability profiles of low math achievers. *Psychology in the Schools, 42*(1), 1–12.

Proctor, R. W., & Dutta, A. (1995). *Skill acquisition and human performance.* Thousand Oaks, CA: Sage.

Pruitt, R. P. (1989). Fostering creativity: The innovative classroom environment. *Educational Horizons, 68*(1), 51–54.

Pugh, K. J., & Bergin, D. A. (2005). The effect of schooling on students' out-of-school experience. *Educational Researcher, 34*(9), 15–23.

Pugh, K. J., & Bergin, D. A. (2006). Motivational influences on transfer. *Educational Psychologist, 41,* 147–160.

Pugh, K. J., Linnenbrink, E. A., Kelly, K. L., Manzey, C., & Stewart, V. C. (2006, April). *Motivation, learning, and transformative experience: A study of deep engagement in science.* Paper presented at the annual meeting of the American Educational Research Association, San Francisco, CA.

Pulos, S., & Linn, M. C. (1981). Generality of the controlling variables scheme in early adolescence. *Journal of Early Adolescence, 1,* 26–37.

Puntambekar, S., & Hübscher, R. (2005). Tools for scaffolding students in a complex learning environment: What have we gained and what have we missed? *Educational Psychologist, 40,* 1–12.

Purcell-Gates, V. (1995). *Other people's words: The cycle of low literacy.* Cambridge, MA: Harvard University Press.

Purdie, N., & Hattie, J. (1996). Cultural differences in the use of strategies for self-regulated learning. *American Educational Research Journal, 33,* 845–871.

Purdie, N., Hattie, J., & Carroll, A. (2002). A review of the research on interventions for attention deficit hyperactivity disorder: What works best? *Review of Educational Research, 72,* 61–99.

Purdie, N., Hattie, J., & Douglas, G. (1996). Student conceptions of learning and their use of self-regulated learning strategies: A cross-cultural comparison. *Journal of Educational Psychology, 88,* 87–100.

Putnam, R. T. (1992). Thinking and authority in elementary-school mathematics tasks. In J. Brophy

(Ed.), *Advances in research on teaching: Vol. 3. Planning and managing learning tasks and activities.* Greenwich, CT: JAI Press.

Putwain, D. W. (2007). Test anxiety in UK schoolchildren: Prevalence and demographic patterns. *British Journal of Educational Psychology, 77,* 579–593.

Qian, G., & Pan, J. (2002). A comparison of epistemological beliefs and learning from science text between American and Chinese high school students. In B. K. Hofer & P. R. Pintrich (Eds.), *Personal epistemology: The psychology of beliefs about knowledge and knowing* (pp. 365–385). Mahwah, NJ: Erlbaum.

Qin, Z., Johnson, D. W., & Johnson, R. T. (1995). Cooperative versus competitive efforts and problem solving. *Review of Educational Research, 65,* 129–143.

Quellmalz, E., & Hoskyn, J. (1997). Classroom assessment of reading strategies. In G. D. Phye (Ed.), *Handbook of classroom assessment: Learning, achievement, and adjustment.* San Diego, CA: Academic Press.

Quill, K. A. (1995). Visually cued instruction for children with autism and pervasive developmental disorders. *Focus on Autistic Behavior, 10*(3), 10–20.

Quintana, C., Zhang, M., & Krajcik, J. (2005). A framework for supporting metacognitive aspects of online inquiry through software-based scaffolding. *Educational Psychologist, 40,* 235–244.

Raber, S. M. (1990, April). *A school system's look at its dropouts: Why they left school and what has happened to them.* Paper presented at the annual meeting of the American Educational Research Association, Boston.

Rabinowitz, M., & Glaser, R. (1985). Cognitive structure and process in highly competent performance. In F. D. Horowitz & M. O'Brien (Eds.), *The gifted and the talented: Developmental perspectives.* Washington, DC: American Psychological Association.

Rachlin, H. (1991). *Introduction to modern behaviorism* (3rd ed.). New York: Freeman.

Radziszewska, B., & Rogoff, B. (1988). Influence of adult and peer collaborators on children's planning skills. *Developmental Psychology, 24,* 840–848.

Raikes, H., Pan, B. A., Luze, G., Tamis-LeMonda, C. S., Brooks-Gunn, J., Constantine, J., Tarullo, L. B., Raikes, H. A., & Rodriguez, E. T. (2006). Mother-child bookreading in low-income families: Correlates and outcomes during the first three years of life. *Child Development, 77,* 924–953.

Raine, A. (2008). From genes to brain to antisocial behavior. *Current Directions in Psychological Science, 17,* 323–328.

Raine, A., Reynolds, C., & Venables, P. H. (2002). Stimulation seeking and intelligence: A prospective longitudinal study. *Journal of Personality and Social Psychology, 82,* 663–674.

Ramey, C. T. (1992). High-risk children and IQ: Altering intergenerational patterns. *Intelligence, 16,* 239–256.

Ramey, C. T., & Ramey, S. L. (1998). Early intervention and early experience. *American Psychologist, 53,* 109–120.

Ramsey, P. G. (1987). *Teaching and learning in a diverse world: Multicultural education for young children.* New York: Teachers College Press.

Ramsey, P. G. (1995). Growing up with the contradictions of race and class. *Young Children, 50,* 18–22.

Ratelle, C. F., Guay, F., Vallerand, R. J., Larose, S., & Senécal, C. (2007). Autonomous, controlled, and amotivated types of academic motivation: A person-oriented analysis. *Journal of Educational Psychology, 99,* 734–746.

Raudenbush, S. W. (1984). Magnitude of teacher expectancy effects on pupil IQ as a function of credibility induction: A synthesis of findings from 18 experiments. *Journal of Educational Psychology, 76,* 85–97.

Rawsthorne, L. J., & Elliot, A. J. (1999). Achievement goals and intrinsic motivation: A meta-analytic review. *Personality and Social Psychology Review, 3,* 326–344.

Rayner, K., Foorman, B. R., Perfetti, C. A., Pesetsky, D., & Seidenberg, M. S. (2001). How psychological science informs the teaching of reading. *Psychological Science in the Public Interest, 2,* 31–74.

Redfield, D. L., & Rousseau, E. W. (1981). A meta-analysis of experimental research on teacher questioning behavior. *Review of Educational Research, 51,* 237–245.

Reed, J. H., Schallert, D. L., Beth, A. D., & Woodruff, A. L. (2004). Motivated reader, engaged writer: The role of motivation in the literate acts of adolescents. In T. L. Jetton & J. A. Dole (Eds.), *Adolescent literacy research and practice* (pp. 251–282). New York: Guilford.

Reeve, J. (2006). Extrinsic rewards and inner motivation. In C. M. Evertson & C. S. Weinstein (Eds.), *Handbook of classroom management: Research, practice, and contemporary issues* (pp. 645–664.). Mahwah, NJ: Erlbaum.

Reeve, J., Bolt, E., & Cai, Y. (1999). Autonomy-supportive teachers: How they teach and motivate students. *Journal of Educational Psychology, 91,* 537–548.

Reeve, J., Deci, E. L., & Ryan, R. M. (2004). Self-determination theory: A dialectical framework for understanding sociocultural influences on student motivation. In D. M. McInerney & S. Van Etten (Eds.), *Big theories revisited* (pp. 31–60). Greenwich, CT: Information Age.

Régner, I., Escribe, C., & Dupeyrat, C. (2007). Evidence of social comparison in mastery goals in natural academic settings. *Journal of Educational Psychology, 99,* 575–583.

Reich, P. A. (1986). *Language development.* Upper Saddle River, NJ: Prentice Hall.

Reid, R., Trout, A. L., & Schartz, M. (2005). Self-regulation interventions for children with attention deficit/hyperactivity disorder. *Exceptional Children, 71,* 361–377.

Reimann, P., & Schult, T. J. (1996). Turning examples into cases: Acquiring knowledge structures for analogical problem solving. *Educational Psychologist, 31,* 123–132.

Reimer, J., Paolitto, D. P., & Hersh, R. H. (1983). *Promoting moral growth: From Piaget to Kohlberg* (2nd ed.). White Plains, NY: Longman.

Reiner, M., Slotta, J. D., Chi, M. T. H., & Resnick, L. B. (2000). Naive physics reasoning: A commitment to substance-based conceptions. *Cognition and Instruction, 18,* 1–34.

Reinking, D., & Leu, D. J. (Chairs). (2008, March). *Understanding Internet reading comprehension and its development among adolescents at risk of dropping out of school.* Poster session presented at the annual meeting of the American Educational Research Association, New York.

Reisberg, D. (1997). *Cognition: Exploring the science of the mind.* New York: Norton.

Reisberg, D., & Heuer, F. (1992). Remembering the details of emotional events. In E. Winograd & U. Neisser (Eds.), *Affect and accuracy in recall: Studies of "flashbulb" memories.* Cambridge, England: Cambridge University Press.

Reiter, S. N. (1994). Teaching dialogically: Its relationship to critical thinking in college students. In P. R. Pintrich, D. R. Brown, & C. E. Weinstein (Eds.), *Student motivation, cognition, and learning: Essays in honor of Wilbert J. McKeachie.* Mahwah, NJ: Erlbaum.

Renkl, A., & Atkinson, R. K. (2003). Structuring the transition from example study to problem solving in cognitive skill acquisition: A cognitive load perspective. *Educational Psychologist, 38,* 15–22.

Renkl, A., Mandl, H., & Gruber, H. (1996). Inert knowledge: Analyses and remedies. *Educational Psychologist, 31,* 115–121.

Renninger, K. A., Hidi, S., & Krapp, A. (Eds.). (1992). *The role of interest in learning and development.* Mahwah, NJ: Erlbaum.

Rescorla, R. A. (1967). Pavlovian conditioning and its proper control procedures. *Psychological Review, 74,* 71–80.

Rescorla, R. A. (1988). Pavlovian conditioning: It's not what you think it is. *American Psychologist, 43,* 151–160.

Resnick, L. B. (1988). Treating mathematics as an ill-structured discipline. In R. I. Charles & E. A. Silver (Eds.), *The teaching and assessing of mathematical problem solving* (pp. 32–60). Mahwah, NJ: Erlbaum.

Resnick, L. B. (1989). Developing mathematical knowledge. *American Psychologist, 44,* 162–169.

Resnick, L. B., & Resnick, D. P. (1992). Assessing the thinking curriculum: New tools for educational reform. In B. G. Gifford & M. C. O'Connor (Eds.), *Changing assessments: Alternative views of aptitude, achievement and instruction* (pp. 37–75). Boston: Kluwer Academic.

Rest, J., Narvaez, D., Bebeau, M., & Thoma, S. (1999). A neo-Kohlbergian approach: The DIT and schema theory. *Educational Psychology Review, 11,* 291–324.

Reusser, K. (1990, April). *Understanding word arithmetic problems: Linguistic and situational factors.* Paper presented at the annual meeting of the American Educational Research Association, Boston.

Reyna, C. (2000). Lazy, dumb, or industrious: When stereotypes convey attribution information in the classroom. *Educational Psychology Review, 12,* 85–110.

Reyna, C., & Weiner, B. (2001). Justice and utility in the classroom: An attributional analysis of the goals of teachers' punishment and intervention strategies. *Journal of Educational Psychology, 93,* 309–319.

Reyna, V. F., & Farley, F. (2006). Risk and rationality in adolescent decision making: Implications for theory, practice, and public policy. *Psychological Science in the Public Interest, 7*(1), 1–44.

Reynolds, M. C., & Birch, J. W. (1988). *Adaptive mainstreaming: A primer for teachers and principals* (3rd ed.). White Plains, NY: Longman.

Reynolds, R. E., & Shirey, L. L. (1988). The role of attention in studying and learning. In C. E. Weinstein, E. T. Goetz, & P. A. Alexander (Eds.), *Learning and study strategies: Issues in assessment, instruction, and evaluation.* San Diego, CA: Academic Press.

Reynolds, R. E., Taylor, M. A., Steffensen, M. S., Shirey, L. L., & Anderson, R. C. (1982). Cultural schemata and reading comprehension. *Reading Research Quarterly, 17,* 353–366.

Rhodes, B. (2008). Challenges and opportunities for intelligence augmentation. In P. C. Kyllonen, R. D. Roberts, & L. Stankov (Eds.), *Extending intelligence: Enhancement and new constructs* (pp. 395–405). New York: Erlbaum/Taylor & Francis.

Rhodes, M., & Gelman, S. A. (2008). Categories influence predictions about individual consistency. *Child Development, 79,* 1270–1287.

Rhodewalt, F., & Vohs, K. D. (2005). Defensive strategies, motivation, and the self: A self-regulatory process view. In A. J. Elliot & C. S. Dweck (Eds.), *Handbook of competence and motivation* (pp. 548–565). New York: Guilford Press.

Ricciardi, J. N., Luiselli, J. K., & Camare, M. (2006). Shaping approach responses as intervention for specific phobia in a child with autism. *Journal of Applied Behavior Analysis, 39,* 445–448.

Ricciuti, H. N. (1993). Nutrition and mental development. *Current Directions in Psychological Science, 2,* 43–46.

Rice, M., Hadley, P. A., & Alexander, A. L. (1993). Social biases toward children with speech and language impairments: A correlative causal model of language limitations. *Applied Psycholinguistics, 14,* 445–471.

Richards, C. M., Symons, D. K., Greene, C. A., & Szuszkiewicz, T. A. (1995). The bidirectional relationship between achievement and externalizing behavior disorders. *Journal of Learning Disabilities, 28,* 8–17.

Richards, J. M. (2004). The cognitive consequences of concealing feelings. *Current Directions in Psychological Science, 13,* 131–134.

Ricks, J. H. (1959). On telling parents about test results. *Test Service Bulletin* (No. 59). New York: Psychological Corporation.

Riding, R. J., & Cheema, I. (1991). Cognitive styles—

an overview and integration. *Educational Psychology, 11,* 193–215.

Riggs, J. M. (1992). Self-handicapping and achievement. In A. K. Boggiano & T. S. Pittman (Eds.), *Achievement and motivation: A social-developmental perspective.* Cambridge, England: Cambridge University Press.

Rimm, D. C., & Masters, J. C. (1974). *Behavior therapy: Techniques and empirical findings.* San Diego, CA: Academic Press.

Ripple, R. E. (1989). Ordinary creativity. *Contemporary Educational Psychology, 14,* 189–202.

Rittle-Johnson, B. (2006). Promoting transfer: Effects of self-explanation and direct instruction. *Child Development, 77,* 1–15.

Rittle-Johnson, B., & Koedinger, K. R. (2005). Designing knowledge scaffolds to support mathematical problem solving. *Cognition and Instruction, 23,* 313–349.

Ritts, V., Patterson, M. L., & Tubbs, M. E. (1992). Expectations, impressions, and judgments of physically attractive students: A review. *Review of Educational Research, 62,* 413–426.

Roberts, G. C., Treasure, D. C., & Kavussanu, M. (1997). Motivation in physical activity contexts: An achievement goal perspective. *Advances in Motivation and Achievement, 10,* 413–447.

Roberts, T. A. (2005). Articulation accuracy and vocabulary size contributions to phonemic awareness and word reading in English language learners. *Journal of Educational Psychology, 97,* 601–616.

Robertson, J. S. (2000). Is attribution training a worthwhile classroom intervention for K–12 students with learning difficulties? *Educational Psychology Review, 12,* 111–134.

Robins, R. W., & Trzesniewski, K. H. (2005). Self-esteem development across the lifespan. *Current Directions in Psychological Science, 14,* 158–162.

Robinson, A. (1991). Cooperation or exploitation? The argument against cooperative learning for talented students. *Journal for the Education of the Gifted, 14,* 9–27.

Robinson, D. H., & Kiewra, K. A. (1995). Visual argument: Graphic organizers are superior to outlines in improving learning from text. *Journal of Educational Psychology, 87,* 455–467.

Robinson, D. R., Schofield, J. W., & Steers-Wentzell, K. L. (2005). Peer and cross-age tutoring in math: Outcomes and their design implications. *Educational Psychology Review, 17,* 327–362.

Robinson, S. L., & Griesemer, S. M. R. (2006). Helping individual students with problem behavior. In C. M. Evertson & C. S. Weinstein (Eds.), *Handbook of classroom management: Research, practice, and contemporary issues* (pp. 787–802). Mahwah, NJ: Erlbaum.

Robinson, T. R., Smith, S. W., Miller, M. D., & Brownell, M. T. (1999). Cognitive behavior modification of hyperactivity-impulsivity and aggression: A meta-analysis of school-based studies. *Journal of Educational Psychology, 91,* 195–203.

Roderick, M., & Camburn, E. (1999). Risk and recovery from course failure in the early years of high school. *American Educational Research Journal, 36,* 303–343.

Roditi, B. N., & Steinberg, J. (2007). The strategy math classroom: Executive function processes and mathematics learning. In L. Meltzer (Ed.), *Executive function in education: From theory to practice* (pp. 237–260). New York: Guilford Press.

Roediger, H. L., III, & Karpicke, J. D. (2006). The power of testing memory: Basic research and implications for educational practice. *Perspectives on Psychological Science, 1,* 181–210.

Roediger, H. L., III, & McDermott, K. B. (2000). Tricks of memory. *Current Directions in Psychological Science, 9,* 123–127.

Roeser, R. W., Eccles, J. S., & Sameroff, A. J. (2000). School as a context of early adolescents' academic social-emotional development: A summary of research findings. *The Elementary School Journal, 100,* 443–471.

Roeser, R. W., Marachi, R., & Gehlbach, H. (2002). A goal theory perspective on teachers' professional identities and the contexts of teaching. In C. Midgley (Ed.), *Goals, goal structures, and patterns of adaptive learning* (pp. 205–241). Mahwah, NJ: Erlbaum.

Rogers, C. R. (1983). *Freedom to learn for the 80's.* Upper Saddle River, NJ: Merrill/Prentice Hall.

Rogers, T. B., Kuiper, N. A., & Kirker, W. S. (1977). Self-reference and the encoding of personal information. *Journal of Personality and Social Psychology, 35,* 677–688.

Rogoff, B. (1990). *Apprenticeship in thinking: Cognitive development in social context.* New York: Oxford University Press.

Rogoff, B. (1991). Social interaction as apprenticeship in thinking: Guidance and participation in spatial planning. In L. B. Resnick, J. M. Levine, & S. D. Teasley (Eds.), *Perspectives on socially shared cognition.* Washington, DC: American Psychological Association.

Rogoff, B. (1994, April). *Developing understanding of the idea of communities of learners.* Paper presented at the annual meeting of the American Educational Research Association, New Orleans, LA.

Rogoff, B. (2001). *Everyday cognition: Its development in social context.* New York: Replica Books.

Rogoff, B. (2003). *The cultural nature of human development.* Oxford, England: Oxford University Press.

Rogoff, B. (2007, March). Cultural perspectives help us see developmental processes. In M. Gauvain & R. L. Munroe (Chairs), *Contributions of socio-historical theory and cross-cultural research to the study of child development.* Symposium conducted at the biennial meeting of the Society for Research in Child Development, Boston.

Rogoff, B., Matusov, E., & White, C. (1996). Models of teaching and learning: Participation in a community of learners. In D. R. Olson & N. Torrance (Eds.), *The handbook of education and human development: New models of learning, teaching, and schooling.* Cambridge, MA: Blackwell.

Rogoff, B., Moore, L., Najafi, B., Dexter, A., Correa-Chávez, M., & Solís, J. (2007). Children's development of cultural repertoires through participation in everyday routines and practices. In J. E. Grusec & P. D. Hastings (Eds.), *Handbook of socialization: Theory and research* (pp. 490–515). New York: Guilford Press.

Rohrbeck, C. A., Ginsburg-Block, M. D., Fantuzzo, J. W., & Miller, T. R. (2003). Peer-assisted learning interventions with elementary school students: A meta-analytic review. *Journal of Educational Psychology, 95,* 240–257.

Rohrer, D., & Pashler, H. (2007). Increasing retention without increasing study time. *Current Directions in Psychological Science, 16,* 183–186.

Roopnarine, J. L., Lasker, J., Sacks, M., & Stores, M. (1998). The cultural contexts of children's play. In O. N. Saracho & B. Spodek (Eds.), *Multiple perspectives on play in early childhood education.* Albany: State University of New York Press.

Root, M. P. P. (1999). The biracial baby boom: Understanding ecological constructions of racial identity in the 21st century. In R. H. Sheets & E. R. Hollins (Eds.), *Racial and ethnic identity in school practices: Aspects of human development* (pp. 67–89). Mahwah, NJ: Erlbaum.

Rortvedt, A. K., & Miltenberger, R. G. (1994). Analysis of a high-probability instructional sequence and time-out in the treatment of child noncompliance. *Journal of Applied Behavior Analysis, 27,* 327–330.

Rosch, E. H. (1977). Human categorization. In N. Warren (Ed.), *Advances in cross-cultural psychology* (Vol. 1). San Diego, CA: Academic Press.

Rosch, E. H., Mervis, C. B., Gray, W. D., Johnson, D. M., & Boyes-Braem, P. (1976). Basic objects in natural categories. *Cognitive Psychology, 8,* 382–439.

Roscoe, R. D., & Chi, M. T. H. (2007). Understanding tutor learning: Knowledge-building and knowledge-telling in peer tutors' explanations and questions. *Review of Educational Research, 77,* 534–574.

Rose, A. J. (2002). Co-rumination in the friendship of girls and boys. *Child Development, 73,* 1830–1843.

Rose, A. J., & Asher, S. R. (2004). Children's strategies and goals in response to help-giving and help-seeking tasks within a friendship. *Child Development, 75,* 749–763.

Rose, S. C., & Thornburg, K. R. (1984). Mastery motivation and need for approval in young children: Effects of age, sex, and reinforcement condition. *Educational Research Quarterly, 9*(1), 34–42.

Rosen, P. J., Milich, R., & Harris, M. J. (2007). Victims of their own cognitions: Implicit social cognitions, emotional distress, and peer victimization. *Journal of Applied Developmental Psychology, 28,* 211–226.

Rosenshine, B., & Meister, C. (1992). The use of scaffolds for teaching higher-level cognitive strategies. *Educational Leadership, 49*(7), 26–33.

Rosenshine, B., & Meister, C. (1994). Reciprocal teaching: A review of the research. *Review of Educational Research, 64,* 479–530.

Rosenshine, B., Meister, C., & Chapman, S. (1996). Teaching students to generate questions: A review of the intervention studies. *Review of Educational Research, 66,* 181–221.

Rosenshine, B., & Stevens, R. (1986). Teaching functions. In M. C. Wittrock (Ed.), *Handbook of research on teaching* (3rd ed.). New York: Macmillan.

Rosenthal, R. (1994). Interpersonal expectancy effects: A 30-year perspective. *Current Directions in Psychological Science, 3,* 176–179.

Rosenthal, R. (2002). Covert communication in classrooms, clinics, courtrooms, and cubicles. *American Psychologist, 57,* 839–849.

Rosenthal, R., & Jacobson, L. (1968). *Pygmalion in the classroom: Teacher expectation and pupils' intellectual development.* New York: Holt, Rinehart & Winston.

Rosenthal, T. L., Alford, G. S., & Rasp, L. M. (1972). Concept attainment, generalization, and retention through observation and verbal coding. *Journal of Experimental Child Psychology, 13,* 183–194.

Rosenthal, T. L., & Bandura, A. (1978). Psychological modeling: Theory and practice. In S. L. Garfield & A. E. Begia (Eds.), *Handbook of psychotherapy and behavior change: An empirical analysis* (2nd ed.). New York: Wiley.

Rosenthal, T. L., & Zimmerman, B. J. (1978). *Social learning and cognition.* San Diego, CA: Academic Press.

Ross, B. H., & Spalding, T. L. (1994). Concepts and categories. In R. J. Sternberg (Ed.), *Handbook of perception and cognition* (Vol. 12). New York: Academic Press.

Rosser, R. (1994). *Cognitive development: Psychological and biological perspectives.* Boston: Allyn & Bacon.

Rotenberg, K. J., & Mayer, E. V. (1990). Delay of gratification in Native and White children: A cross-cultural comparison. *International Journal of Behavioral Development, 13,* 23–30.

Roth, K. J. (1990). Developing meaningful conceptual understanding in science. In B. F. Jones & L. Idol (Eds.), *Dimensions of thinking and cognitive instruction.* Mahwah, NJ: Erlbaum.

Roth, K. J. (2002). Talking to understand science. In J. Brophy (Ed.), *Social constructivist teaching: Affordances and constraints* (pp. 197–262). New York: Elsevier.

Roth, K. J., & Anderson, C. (1988). Promoting conceptual change learning from science textbooks. In P. Ramsden (Ed.), *Improving learning: New perspectives.* London: Kogan Page.

Roth, W., & Bowen, G. M. (1995). Knowing and interacting: A study of culture, practices, and resources in a grade 8 open-inquiry science classroom guided by a cognitive apprenticeship metaphor. *Cognition and Instruction, 13,* 73–128.

Rothbart, M. K. (2007). Temperament, development, and personality. *Current Directions in Psychological Science, 16,* 207–212.

Rothbart, M. K., Sheese, B. E., & Posner, M. I. (2007). Executive attention and effortful control: Linking temperament, brain networks, and genes. *Child Development Perspectives, 1,* 2–7.

Rothbaum, F., & Trommsdorff, G. (2007). Do roots and wings complement or oppose one another?

The socialization of relatedness and autonomy in cultural context. In J. E. Grusec & P. D. Hastings (Eds.), *Handbook of socialization: Theory and research* (pp. 461–489). New York: Guilford Press.

Rothbaum, F., Weisz, J., Pott, M., Miyake, K., & Morelli, G. (2000). Attachment and culture: Security in the United States and Japan. *American Psychologist, 55,* 1093–1104.

Rothstein-Fisch, C. & Trumbull, E. (2008). *Managing diverse classrooms: How to build on students' strengths.* Alexandria, VA: Association for Supervision and Curriculum Development.

Roughead, W. G., & Scandura, J. M. (1968). What is learned in mathematical discovery. *Journal of Educational Psychology, 59,* 283–289.

Rowe, D. C., Jacobson, K. C., & Van den Oord, E. J. C. G. (1999). Genetic and environmental influences on Vocabulary IQ: Parental education level as moderator. *Child Development, 70,* 1151–1162.

Rowe, M. B. (1974). Wait-time and rewards as instructional variables, their influence on language, logic, and fate control: Part one—wait time. *Journal of Research in Science Teaching, 11,* 81–94.

Rowe, M. B. (1978). *Teaching science as continuous inquiry.* New York: McGraw-Hill.

Rowe, M. B. (1987). Wait-time: Slowing down may be a way of speeding up. *American Educator, 11,* 38–43, 47.

Rozalski, M. E., & Yell, M. L. (2004). Law and school safety. In J. C. Conoley & A. P. Goldstein (Eds.), *School violence intervention* (2nd ed., pp. 507–523). New York: Guilford Press.

Rubin, D. C. (2006). The basic-systems model of episodic memory. *Perspectives on Psychological Science, 1,* 277–311.

Rubin, K. H. (1982). Nonsocial play in preschoolers: Necessarily evil? *Child Development, 53,* 651–657.

Rudman, M. K. (1993). Multicultural children's literature: The search for universals. In M. K. Rudman (Ed.), *Children's literature: Resource for the classroom* (2nd ed.). Norwood, MA: Christopher-Gordon.

Rudolph, K. D., Caldwell, M. S., & Conley, C. S. (2005). Need for approval and children's well-being. *Child Development, 76,* 309–323.

Rudolph, K. D., Lambert, S. F., Clark, A. G., & Kurlakowsky, K. D. (2001). Negotiating the transition to middle school: The role of self-regulatory processes. *Child Development, 72,* 929–946.

Rueda, R., & Moll, L. C. (1994). A sociocultural perspective on motivation. In H. F. O'Neil, Jr., & M. Drillings (Eds.), *Motivation: Theory and research.* Mahwah, NJ: Erlbaum.

Ruef, M. B., Higgins, C., Glaeser, B., & Patnode, M. (1998). Positive behavioral support: Strategies for teachers. *Intervention in School and Clinic, 34*(1), 21–32.

Rueger, D. B., & Liberman, R. P. (1984). Behavioral family therapy for delinquent substance-abusing adolescents. *Journal of Drug Abuse, 14,* 403–418.

Ruffman, T., Perner, J., Olson, D. R., & Doherty, M. (1993). Reflecting on scientific thinking: Children's understanding of the hypothesis-evidence relation. *Child Development, 64,* 1617–1636.

Ruffman, T., Slade, L., & Crowe, E. (2002). The relation between children's and mothers' mental state language and theory-of-mind understanding. *Child Development, 73,* 734–751.

Rumberger, R. W. (1995). Dropping out of middle school: A multilevel analysis of students and schools. *American Educational Research Journal, 32,* 583–625.

Rumelhart, D. E., & Ortony, A. (1977). The representation of knowledge in memory. In R. C. Anderson, R. J. Spiro, & W. E. Montague (Eds.), *Schooling and the acquisition of knowledge.* Mahwah, NJ: Erlbaum.

Runco, M. A. (2004). Creativity as an extracognitive phenomenon. In L. V. Shavinina & M. Ferrari (Eds.), *Beyond knowledge: Extracognitive aspects of developing high ability* (pp. 17–25). Mahwah, NJ: Erlbaum.

Runco, M. A., & Chand, I. (1995). Cognition and creativity. *Educational Psychology Review, 7,* 243–267.

Rushton, J. P. (1980). *Altruism, socialization, and society.* Upper Saddle River, NJ: Prentice Hall.

Russ, S. W. (1993). *Affect and creativity: The role of affect and play in the creative process.* Mahwah, NJ: Erlbaum.

Rutter, M. L. (1997). Nature-nurture integration: The example of antisocial behavior. *American Psychologist, 52,* 390–398.

Ryan, A. M. (2000). Peer groups as a context for the socialization of adolescents' motivation, engagement, and achievement in school. *Educational Psychologist, 35,* 101–111.

Ryan, A. M. (2001). The peer group as a context for the development of young adolescent motivation and achievement. *Child Development, 72,* 1135–1150.

Ryan, A. M., & Patrick, H. (2001). The classroom social environment and changes in adolescents' motivation and engagement during middle school. *American Educational Research Journal, 38,* 437–460.

Ryan, A. M., Pintrich, P. R., & Midgley, C. (2001). Avoiding seeking help in the classroom: Who and why? *Educational Psychology Review, 13,* 93–114.

Ryan, K. E., & Ryan, A. M. (2005). Psychological processes underlying stereotype threat and standardized math test performance. *Educational Psychologist, 40,* 53–63.

Ryan, K. E., Ryan, A. M., Arbuthnot, K., & Samuels, M. (2007). Students' motivation for standardized math exams: Insights from students. *Educational Researcher, 36*(1), 5–13.

Ryan, R. M., & Brown, K. W. (2005). Legislating competence: High-stakes testing policies and their relations with psychological theories and research. In A. J. Elliot & C. S. Dweck (Eds.), *Handbook of competence and motivation* (pp. 354–372). New York: Guilford Press.

Ryan, R. M., Connell, J. P., & Grolnick, W. S. (1992). When achievement is *not* intrinsically motivated: A theory of internalization and self-regulation in school. In A. K. Boggiano & T. S. Pittman (Eds.), *Achievement and motivation: A social-developmental perspective.* Cambridge, England: Cambridge University Press.

Ryan, R. M., & Deci, E. L. (2000). Self-determination theory and the facilitation of intrinsic motivation, social development, and well-being. *American Psychologist, 55,* 68–78.

Ryan, R. M., & Kuczkowski, R. (1994). The imaginary audience, self-consciousness, and public individuation in adolescence. *Journal of Personality, 62,* 219–237.

Ryan, R. M., Mims, V., & Koestner, R. (1983). Relation of reward contingency and interpersonal context to intrinsic motivation: A review and test using cognitive evaluation theory. *Journal of Personality and Social Psychology, 45,* 736–750.

Saarni, C., Campos, J. J., Camras, L. A., & Witherington, D. (2006). Emotional development: Action, communication, and understanding. In W. Damon & R. M. Lerner (Eds. in Chief) & N. Eisenberg (Vol. Ed.), *Handbook of child psychology, Vol. 3. Social, emotional, and personality development* (6th ed., pp. 226–299). Hoboken, NJ: Wiley.

Sabers, D. S., Cushing, K. S., & Berliner, D. C. (1991). Differences among teachers in a task characterized by simultaneity, multidimensionality, and immediacy. *American Educational Research Journal, 28,* 63–88.

Sadker, M. P., & Miller, D. (1982). *Sex equity handbook for schools.* White Plains, NY: Longman.

Sadker, M. P., & Sadker, D. (1994). *Failing at fairness: How our schools cheat girls.* New York: Touchstone.

Sadoski, M., & Paivio, A. (2001). *Imagery and text: A dual coding theory of reading and writing.* Mahwah, NJ: Erlbaum.

Saffran, J. R. (2003). Statistical language learning: Mechanisms and constraints. *Current Directions in Psychological Science, 12,* 110–114.

Saffran, J. R., Aslin, R. N., & Newport, E. L. (1996). Statistical learning by 8-month-old infants. *Science, 274,* 1926–1928.

Salend, S. J., & Taylor, L. (1993). Working with families: A cross-cultural perspective. *Remedial and Special Education, 14*(5), 25–32, 39.

Saljo, R., & Wyndhamn, J. (1992). Solving everyday problems in the formal setting: An empirical study of the school as context for thought. In S. Chaiklin & J. Lave (Eds.), *Understanding practice.* New York: Cambridge University Press.

Salomon, G. (1993). No distribution without individuals' cognition: A dynamic interactional view. In G. Salomon (Ed.), *Distributed cognitions: Psychological and educational considerations* (pp. 111–138). Cambridge, England: Cambridge University Press.

Saltz, E. (1971). *The cognitive bases of human learning.* Homewood, IL: Dorsey.

Sameroff, A. J., Seifer, R., Baldwin, A., & Baldwin, C. (1993). Stability of intelligence from preschool to adolescence: The influence of social and family risk factors. *Child Development, 64,* 80–97.

Sanborn, M. P. (1979). Counseling and guidance needs of the gifted and talented. In A. H. Passow (Ed.), *The gifted and the talented: Their education and development. The seventy-eighth yearbook of the National Society for the Study of Education.* Chicago: University of Chicago Press.

Sanchez, F., & Anderson, M. L. (1990). Gang mediation: A process that works. *Principal, 69*(4), 54–56.

Sanders, C. E. (1997). Assessment during the preschool years. In G. D. Phye (Ed.), *Handbook of classroom assessment: Learning, achievement, and adjustment.* San Diego, CA: Academic Press.

Sanders, M. G. (1996). Action teams in action: Interviews and observations in three schools in the Baltimore School-Family-Community Partnership Program. *Journal of Education for Students Placed at Risk, 1,* 249–262.

Sands, D. J., & Wehmeyer, M. L. (Eds.). (1996). *Self-determination across the life span: Independence and choice for people with disabilities.* Baltimore: Brookes.

Sapon-Shevin, M., Dobbelaere, A., Corrigan, C., Goodman, K. & Mastin, M. (1998). Everyone here can play. *Educational Leadership, 56*(1), 42–45.

Sarason, I. G. (Ed.). (1980). *Test anxiety: Theory, research, and applications.* Mahwah, NJ: Erlbaum.

Sasso, G. M., & Rude, H. A. (1987). Unprogrammed effects of training high-status peers to interact with severely handicapped children. *Journal of Applied Behavior Analysis, 20,* 35–44.

Sattler, J. M. (2001). *Assessment of children: Cognitive applications* (4th ed.). San Diego, CA: Author.

Saudino, K. J., & Plomin, R. (2007). Why are hyperactivity and academic achievement related? *Child Development, 78,* 972–986.

Sawyer, R. J., Graham, S., & Harris, K. R. (1992). Direct teaching, strategy instruction, and strategy instruction with explicit self-regulation: Effects on the composition skills and self-efficacy of students with learning disabilities. *Journal of Educational Psychology, 84,* 340–352.

Sawyer, R. K. (2003). Emergence in creativity and development. In R. K. Sawyer, V. John-Steiner, S. Moran, R. J. Sternberg, D. H. Feldman, J. Nakamura, & M. Csikszentmihalyi, *Creativity and development* (pp. 12–60). Oxford, England: Oxford University Press.

Sawyer, R. K. (2006). Introduction: The new science of learning. In R. K. Sawyer (Ed.), *The Cambridge handbook of the learning sciences* (pp. 1–16). Cambridge, England: Cambridge University Press.

Sax, G. (1989). *Principles of educational and psychological measurement and evaluation* (3rd ed.). Belmont, CA: Wadsworth.

Scarcella, R. (1990). *Teaching language-minority students in the multicultural classroom.* Upper Saddle River, NJ: Prentice Hall.

Scardamalia, M., & Bereiter, C. (1985). Fostering the development of self-regulation in children's knowledge processing. In S. F. Chipman, J. W. Segal, & R. Glaser (Eds.), *Thinking and learning skills: Vol. 2. Research and open questions.* Mahwah, NJ: Erlbaum.

Scardamalia, M., & Bereiter, C. (2006). Knowledge building: Theory, pedagogy, and technology. In R. K. Sawyer (Ed.), *The Cambridge handbook of the learning sciences* (pp. 97–115). Cambridge, England: Cambridge University Press.

Scarr, S. (1992). Developmental theories for the 1990s: Development and individual differences. *Child Development, 63,* 1–19.

Scarr, S., & McCartney, K. (1983). How people make their own environments: A theory of genotype environment effects. *Child Development, 54,* 424–435.

Scevak, J. J., Moore, P. J., & Kirby, J. R. (1993). Training students to use maps to increase text recall. *Contemporary Educational Psychology, 18,* 401–413.

Schacter, D. L. (1999). The seven sins of memory: Insights from psychology and neuroscience. *American Psychologist, 54,* 182–203.

Schank, R. C. (1979). Interestingness: Controlling inferences. *Artificial Intelligence, 12,* 273–297.

Schank, R. C., & Abelson, R. P. (1995). Knowledge and memory: The real story. In R. S. Wyer, Jr. (Ed.), *Advances in social cognition: Vol. 8. Knowledge and memory: The real story.* Mahwah, NJ: Erlbaum.

Schauble, L. (1990). Belief revision in children: The role of prior knowledge and strategies for generating evidence. *Journal of Experimental Child Psychology, 49,* 31–57.

Schauble, L. (1996). The development of scientific reasoning in knowledge-rich contexts. *Developmental Psychology, 32,* 102–119.

Schick, B., de Villiers, P., de Villiers, J., & Hoffmeister, R. (2007). Language and theory of mind: A study of deaf children. *Child Development, 78,* 376–396.

Schiefele, U. (1991). Interest, learning, and motivation. *Educational Psychologist, 26,* 299–323.

Schiffman, G., Tobin, D., & Buchanan, B. (1984). Microcomputer instruction for the learning disabled. *Annual Review of Learning Disabilities, 2,* 134–136.

Schimmoeller, M. A. (1998, April). *Influence of private speech on the writing behaviors of young children: Four case studies.* Paper presented at the annual meeting of the American Educational Research Association, San Diego, CA.

Schirmer, B. R. (1994). *Language and literacy development in children who are deaf.* Boston: Allyn & Bacon.

Schlaefli, A., Rest, J. R., & Thoma, S. J. (1985). Does moral education improve moral judgment? A meta-analysis of intervention studies using the defining issues test. *Review of Educational Research, 55,* 319–352.

Schliemann, A. D., & Carraher, D. W. (1993). Proportional reasoning in and out of school. In P. Light & G. Butterworth (Eds.), *Context and cognition: Ways of learning and knowing.* Mahwah, NJ: Erlbaum.

Schmidt, R. A., & Bjork, R. A. (1992). New conceptualizations of practice: Common principles in three paradigms suggest new concepts for training. *Psychological Science, 3,* 207–217.

Schmidt, W. H. (2008, Spring). What's missing from math standards? *American Educator.* Retrieved March 3, 2008, from www.aft.org/pubs-reports/american_educator/issues/spring2008/schmidt.htm

Schneider, W. (1993). Domain-specific knowledge and memory performance in children. *Educational Psychology Review, 5,* 257–273.

Schneider, W., & Lockl, K. (2002). The development of metacognitive knowledge in children and adolescents. In T. J. Perfect & B. L. Schwartz (Eds.), *Applied metacognition* (pp. 224–257). Cambridge, England: Cambridge University Press.

Schneider, W., & Pressley, M. (1989). *Memory development between 2 and 20.* New York: Springer-Verlag.

Schoenfeld, A. H., & Hermann, D. J. (1982). Problem perception and knowledge structure in expert and novice mathematical problem solvers. *Journal of Experimental Psychology: Learning, Memory, and Cognition, 8,* 484–494.

Schofield, J. W. (1995). Improving intergroup relations among students. In J. A. Banks & C. A. M. Banks (Eds.), *Handbook of research on multicultural education.* New York: Macmillan.

Schofield, J. W. (2006). Internet use in schools: Promise and problems. In R. K. Sawyer (Ed.), *The Cambridge handbook of the learning sciences* (pp. 521–534). Cambridge, England: Cambridge University Press.

Schommer, M. (1990). Effects of beliefs about the nature of knowledge on comprehension. *Journal of Educational Psychology, 82,* 498–504.

Schommer, M. (1994a). An emerging conceptualization of epistemological beliefs and their role in learning. In R. Garner & P. A. Alexander (Eds.), *Beliefs about text and instruction with text.* Mahwah, NJ: Erlbaum.

Schommer, M. (1994b). Synthesizing epistemological belief research: Tentative understandings and provocative confusions. *Educational Psychology Review, 6,* 293–319.

Schommer, M. (1997). The development of epistemological beliefs among secondary students: A longitudinal study. *Journal of Educational Psychology, 89,* 37–40.

Schommer, M., Calvert, C., Gariglietti, G., & Bajaj, A. (1997). The development of epistemological beliefs among secondary students: A longitudinal study. *Journal of Educational Psychology, 89,* 37–40.

Schommer-Aikins, M. (2001). An evolving theoretical framework for an epistemological belief system. In B. K. Hofer & P. R. Pintrich (Eds.), *Personal epistemology: The psychology of beliefs about knowledge and knowing.* Mahwah, NJ: Erlbaum.

Schommer-Aikins, M., & Easter, M. (2008). Epistemological beliefs' contributions to study strategies of Asian Americans and European Americans. *Journal of Educational Psychology, 100,* 920–929.

Schoon, I. (2006). *Risk and resilience: Adaptations in changing times.* Cambridge, England: Cambridge University Press.

Schraw, G. (2006). Knowledge: Structures and processes. In P. A. Alexander & P. H. Winne (Eds.), *Handbook of educational psychology* (2nd ed., pp. 245–263). Mahwah, NJ: Erlbaum.

Schraw, G., Flowerday, T., & Lehman, S. (2001). Increasing situational interest in the classroom. *Educational Psychology Review, 13,* 211–224.

Schraw, G., & Lehman, S. (2001). Situational interest: A review of the literature and directions for future research. *Educational Psychology Review, 13,* 23–52.

Schraw, G., & Moshman, D. (1995). Metacognitive theories. *Educational Psychology Review, 7,* 351–371.

Schraw, G., Wade, S. E., & Kardash, C. A. M. (1993). Interactive effects of text-based and task-based importance on learning from text. *Journal of Educational Psychology, 85,* 652–661.

Schult, C. A. (2002). Children's understanding of the distinction between intentions and desires. *Child Development, 73,* 1727–1747.

Schultz, G. F., & Switzky, H. N. (1990). The development of intrinsic motivation in students with learning problems: Suggestions for more effective instructional practice. *Preventing School Failure, 34*(2), 14–20.

Schultz, K., Buck, P., & Niesz, T. (2000). Democratizing conversations: Racialized talk in a post-desegregated middle school. *American Educational Research Journal, 37,* 33–65.

Schumaker, J. B., & Hazel, J. S. (1984). Social skill assessment and training for the learning disabled: Who's on first and what's on second? (Pt. 1). *Journal of Learning Disabilities, 17,* 422–431.

Schunk, D. H. (1981). Modeling and attributional effects on children's achievement: A self-efficacy analysis. *Journal of Educational Psychology, 73,* 93–105.

Schunk, D. H. (1983). Developing children's self-efficacy and skills: The roles of social comparative information and goal setting. *Contemporary Educational Psychology, 8,* 76–86.

Schunk, D. H. (1987). Peer models and children's behavioral change. *Review of Educational Research, 57,* 149–174.

Schunk, D. H. (1989a). Self-efficacy and achievement behaviors. *Educational Psychology Review, 1,* 173–208.

Schunk, D. H. (1989b). Self-efficacy and cognitive skill learning. In C. Ames & R. Ames (Eds.), *Research on motivation in education: Vol. 3. Goals and cognitions.* San Diego, CA: Academic Press.

Schunk, D. H. (1989c). Social cognitive theory and self-regulated learning. In B. J. Zimmerman & D. H. Schunk (Eds.), *Self-regulated learning and academic achievement: Theory, research, and practice.* New York: Springer-Verlag.

Schunk, D. H. (1990, April). *Socialization and the development of self-regulated learning: The role of attributions.* Paper presented at the annual meeting of the American Educational Research Association, Boston.

Schunk, D. H. (1998). Teaching elementary students to self-regulate practice of mathematical skills with modeling. In D. H. Schunk & B. J. Zimmerman (Eds.), *Self-regulated learning: From teaching to self-reflective practice* (pp. 137–159). New York: Guilford Press.

Schunk, D. H., & Hanson, A. R. (1985). Peer models: Influence on children's self-efficacy and achievement. *Journal of Educational Psychology, 77,* 313–322.

Schunk, D. H., Hanson, A. R., & Cox, P. D. (1987). Peer-model attributes and children's achievement behaviors. *Journal of Educational Psychology, 79,* 54–61.

Schunk, D. H., & Pajares, F. (2004). Self-efficacy in education revisited: Empirical and applied evidence. In D. M. McInerney & S. Van Etten (Eds.), *Big theories revisited* (pp. 115–138). Greenwich, CT: Information Age.

Schunk, D. H., & Pajares, F. (2005). Competence perceptions and academic functioning. In A. J. Elliot & C. S. Dweck (Eds.), *Handbook of competence and motivation* (pp. 85–104). New York: Guilford Press.

Schunk, D. H., & Swartz, C. W. (1993). Goals and progress feedback: Effects on self-efficacy and writing achievement. *Contemporary Educational Psychology, 18,* 337–354.

Schunk, D. H., & Zimmerman, B. J. (1997). Social origins of self-regulatory competence. *Educational Psychologist, 32,* 195–208.

Schutz, P. A. (1994). Goals as the transactive point between motivation and cognition. In P. R. Pintrich, D. R. Brown, & C. E. Weinstein (Eds.), *Student motivation, cognition, and learning: Essays in honor of Wilbert J. McKeachie.* Mahwah, NJ: Erlbaum.

Schwartz, D., Dodge, K. A., Coie, J. D., Hubbard, J. A., Cillessen, A. H., Lemerise, E. A., & Bateman, H. (1998). Social-cognitive and behavioral correlates of aggression and victimization in boys' play groups. *Journal of Abnormal Child Psychology, 26,* 431–440.

Schwartz, D., Gorman, A. H., Nakamoto, J., & Toblin, R. L. (2005). Victimization in the peer group and children's academic functioning. *Journal of Educational Psychology, 97,* 425–435.

Schwartz, D. L., & Heiser, J. (2006). Spatial representations and imagery in learning. In R. K. Sawyer (Ed.), *The Cambridge handbook of the learning sciences* (pp. 283–298). Cambridge, England: Cambridge University Press.

Schwartz, D. L., & Martin, T. (2004). Inventing to prepare for future learning: The hidden efficiency of encouraging original student production in statistics instruction. *Cognition and Instruction, 22,* 129–184.

Schwarz, B. B., Neuman, Y., & Biezuner, S. (2000). Two wrongs may make a right . . . if they argue together! *Cognition and Instruction, 18,* 461–494.

Schwarz, C. V., & White, B. Y. (2005). Metamodeling knowledge: Developing students' understanding of scientific modeling. *Cognition and Instruction, 23,* 165–205.

Scott, J., & Bushell, D. (1974). The length of teacher contacts and students' off-task behavior. *Journal of Applied Behavior Analysis, 7,* 39–44.

Scruggs, T. E., & Lifson, S. A. (1985). Current conceptions of test-wiseness: Myths and realities. *School Psychology Review, 14,* 339–350.

Scruggs, T. E., & Mastropieri, M. A. (1992). Classroom

applications of mnemonic instruction: Acquisition, maintenance, and generalization. *Exceptional Children, 58,* 219–229.

Scruggs, T. E., & Mastropieri, M. A. (1994). Successful mainstreaming in elementary science classes: A qualitative study of three reputational cases. *American Educational Research Journal, 31,* 785–811.

Seaton, E. K., Scottham, K. M., & Sellers, R. M. (2006). The status model of racial identity development in African American adolescents: Evidence of structure, trajectories, and well-being. *Child Development, 77,* 1416–1426.

Sedikides, C., & Gregg, A. P. (2008). Self-enhancement: Food for thought. *Perspectives on Psychological Science, 3,* 102–116.

Seeley, K. (1989). Facilitators for the gifted. In J. Feldhusen, J. VanTassel-Baska, & K. Seeley, *Excellence in educating the gifted.* Denver, CO: Love.

Seligman, M. E. P. (1975). *Helplessness: On depression, development, and death.* San Francisco: Freeman.

Seligman, M. E. P. (1991). *Learned optimism.* New York: Knopf.

Selman, R. L. (1980). *The growth of interpersonal understanding.* San Diego, CA: Academic Press.

Semb, G. B., Ellis, J. A., & Araujo, J. (1993). Long-term memory for knowledge learned in school. *Journal of Educational Psychology, 85,* 305–316.

Sergeant, J. (1996). A theory of attention: An information processing perspective. In G. R. Lyon & N. A. Krasnegor (Eds.), *Attention, memory, and executive function* (pp. 57–69). Baltimore: Brookes.

Serpell, R., Baker, L., & Sonnenschein, S. (2005). *Becoming literate in the city: The Baltimore Early Childhood Project.* Cambridge, England: Cambridge University Press.

Sfard, A. (1998). On two metaphors for learning and the dangers of choosing just one. *Educational Researcher, 27*(2), 4–13.

Shabani, D. B., Katz, R. C., Wilder, D. A., Beauchamp, K., Taylor, C. R., & Fischer, K. J. (2002). Increasing social initiations in children with autism: Effects of a tactile prompt. *Journal of Applied Behavior Analysis, 35,* 79–83.

Shanahan, C. (2004). Teaching science through literacy. In T. L. Jetton & J. A. Dole (Eds.), *Adolescent literacy research and practice* (pp. 75–93). New York: Guilford.

Shanahan, T. (2004). Overcoming the dominance of communication: Writing to think and to learn. In T. L. Jetton & J. A. Dole (Eds.), *Adolescent literacy research and practice* (pp. 59–74). New York: Guilford.

Shapiro, A. M. (2004). How including prior knowledge as a subject variable may change outcomes of learning research. *American Educational Research Journal, 41,* 159–189.

Shavelson, R. J., Baxter, G. P., & Pine, J. (1992). Performance assessments: Political rhetoric and measurement reality. *Educational Researcher, 21*(4), 22–27.

Shavinina, L. V., & Ferrari, M. (2004). Extracognitive facets of developing high ability: Introduction to some important issues. In L. V. Shavinina & M. Ferrari (Eds.), *Beyond knowledge: Extracognitive aspects of developing high ability* (pp. 3–13). Mahwah, NJ: Erlbaum.

Shaw, P., Eckstrand, K., Sharp, W., Blumenthal, J., Lerch, J. P., Greenstein, D., et al. (2007). Attention-deficit/hyperactivity disorder is characterized by a delay in cortical maturation. *Proceedings of the National Academy of Sciences, 104*(49), 19,649–19,654.

Sheets, R. H. (1999). Human development and ethnic identity. In R. H. Sheets & E. R. Hollins (Eds.), *Racial and ethnic identity in school practices: Aspects of human development* (pp. 91–101). Mahwah, NJ: Erlbaum.

Sheets, R. H., & Hollins, E. R. (Eds.). (1999). *Racial and ethnic identity in school practices: Aspects of human development.* Mahwah, NJ: Erlbaum.

Sheldon, A. (1974). The role of parallel function in the acquisition of relative clauses in English. *Journal of Verbal Learning and Verbal Behavior, 13,* 272–281.

Shepard, L. (2000). The role of assessment in a learning culture. *Educational Researcher, 29*(7), 4–14.

Shepard, L., Hammerness, K., Darling-Hammond, L., & Rust, F. (with Snowden, J. B., Gordon, E., Gutierrez, C., & Pacheco, A.). (2005). Assessment. In L. Darling-Hammond & J. Bransford (Eds.), *Preparing teachers for a changing world: What teachers should learn and be able to do* (pp. 275–326). San Francisco: Jossey-Bass/Wiley.

Shepard, R. N., & Metzler, J. (1971). Mental rotation of three-dimensional objects. *Science, 171,* 701–703.

Shepperd, J. A., & McNulty, J. K. (2002). The affective consequences of expected and unexpected outcomes. *Psychological Science, 13,* 85–88.

Sherman, D. K., & Cohen, G. L. (2002). Accepting threatening information: Self-affirmation and the reduction of defensive biases. *Current Directions in Psychological Science, 11,* 119–123.

Shernoff, D. J., & Hoogstra, L. A. (2001). Continuing motivation beyond the high school classroom. In M. Michaelson & J. Nakamura (Eds.), *Supportive frameworks for youth engagement* (pp. 73–87). San Francisco: Jossey-Bass.

Shernoff, D. J., Knauth, S., & Makris, E. (2000). The quality of classroom experiences. In M. Csikszentmihalyi & B. Schneider, *Becoming adult: How teenagers prepare for the world of work.* New York: Basic Books.

Shernoff, D. J., Schneider, B., & Csikszentmihalyi, M. (2001, April). *An assessment of multiple influences on student engagement in high school classrooms.* Paper presented at the annual meeting of the American Educational Research Association, Seattle, WA.

Shih, S.-S., & Alexander, J. M. (2000). Interacting effects of goal setting and self- or other-referenced feedback on children's development of self-efficacy and cognitive skill within the Taiwanese classroom. *Journal of Educational Psychology, 92,* 536–543.

Shim, S. S., & Ryan, A. M. (2006, April). *The nature and the consequences of changes in achievement goals during early adolescence.* Paper presented at the annual meeting of the American Educational Research Association, San Francisco, CA.

Shim, S. S., Ryan, A. M., & Anderson, C. J. (2008). Achievement goals and achievement during early adolescence: Examining time-varying predictor and outcome variables in growth-curve analysis. *Journal of Educational Psychology, 100,* 655–671.

Shipman, S., & Shipman, V. C. (1985). Cognitive styles: Some conceptual, methodological, and applied issues. In E. W. Gordon (Ed.), *Review of research in education* (Vol. 12). Washington, DC: American Educational Research Association.

Shoda, Y., Mischel, W., & Peake, P. K. (1990). Predicting adolescent cognitive and self-regulatory competencies from preschool delay of gratification: Identifying diagnostic conditions. *Developmental Psychology, 26,* 978–986.

Short, E. J., Schatschneider, C. W., & Friebert, S. E. (1993). Relationship between memory and metamemory performance: A comparison of specific and general strategy knowledge. *Journal of Educational Psychology, 85,* 412–423.

Shrum, W., & Cheek, N. H. (1987). Social structure during the school years: Onset of the degrouping process. *American Sociological Review, 52,* 218–223.

Shuell, T. J. (1996). Teaching and learning in a classroom context. In D. C. Berliner & R. C. Calfee (Eds.), *Handbook of educational psychology.* New York: Macmillan.

Shulman, L. S. (1986). Those who understand: Knowledge growth in teaching. *Educational Researcher, 15*(2), 4–14.

Shulman, S., Elicker, J., & Sroufe, L. A. (1994). Stages of friendship growth in preadolescence as related to attachment history. *Journal of Social and Personal Relationships, 11,* 341–361.

Shute, V. J. (2008). Focus on formative feedback. *Review of Educational Research, 78,* 153–189.

Shweder, R. A., Goodnow, J., Hatano, G., Levine, R. A., Marcus, H., & Miller, P. (1998). The cultural psychology of development: One mind, many mentalities. In W. Damon (Editor-in-Chief) & R. M. Lerner (Vol. Ed.), *Handbook of child psychology: Vol. 1. Theoretical models of human development* (5th ed., pp. 865–937). New York: Wiley.

Shymansky, J. A., Hedges, L. V., & Woodworth, G. (1990). A reassessment of the effects of inquiry-based science curricula of the 60s on student performance. *Journal of Research in Science Teaching, 27,* 127–144.

Sieber, J. E., Kameya, L. I., & Paulson, F. L. (1970). Effect of memory support on the problem-solving ability of test-anxious children. *Journal of Educational Psychology, 61,* 159–168.

Sidel, R. (1996). *Keeping women and children last: America's war on the poor.* New York: Penguin Books.

Sideridis, G. D. (2005). Goal orientation, academic achievement, and depression: Evidence in favor of a revised goal theory framework. *Journal of Educational Psychology, 97,* 366–375.

Siegel, D. J. (1999). *The developing mind: How relationships and the brain interact to shape who we are.* New York: Guilford.

Siegler, R. S., & Alibali, M. W. (2005). *Children's thinking* (4th ed.). Upper Saddle River, NJ: Prentice Hall.

Siegler, R. S., & Jenkins, E. (1989). *How children discover new strategies.* Hillsdale, NJ: Erlbaum.

Sigman, M., & Whaley, S. E. (1998). The role of nutrition in the development of intelligence. In U. Neisser (Ed.), *The rising curve: Long-term gains in IQ and related measures* (pp. 155–182). Washington, DC: American Psychological Association.

Silberman, M. L., & Wheelan, S. A. (1980). *How to discipline without feeling guilty: Assertive relationships with children.* Champaign, IL: Research Press.

Silk, J. S., Steinberg, L., & Morris, A. S. (2003). Adolescents' emotion regulation in daily life: Links to depressive symptoms and problem behavior. *Child Development, 74,* 1869–1880.

Silverberg, R. P. (2003, April). *Developing relational space: Teachers who came to understand themselves and their students as learners.* Paper presented at the annual meeting of the American Educational Research Association, Chicago.

Silveri, M. M., Rohan, M. L., Pimentel, P. J., Gruber, S. A., Rosso, I. M., & Yurgelun-Todd, D. A. (2006). Sex differences in the relationship between white matter microstructure and impulsivity in adolescents. *Magnetic Resonance Imaging, 24,* 833–841.

Silverman, L. K. (1994). The moral sensitivity of gifted children and the evolution of society. *Roeper Review, 17*(2), 110–116.

Silvia, P. J. (2008). Interest—the curious emotion. *Current Directions in Psychological Science, 17,* 57–60.

Simon, H. A. (1974). How big is a chunk? *Science, 183,* 482–488.

Simons, R. L., Whitbeck, L. B., Conger, R. D., & Conger, K. J. (1991). Parenting factors, social skills, and value commitments as precursors to school failure, involvement with deviant peers, and delinquent behavior. *Journal of Youth and Adolescence, 20,* 645–664.

Simonton, D. K. (2000). Creativity: Cognitive, personal, developmental, and social aspects. *American Psychologist, 55,* 151–158.

Simonton, D. K. (2001). Talent development as a multidimensional, multiplicative, and dynamic process. *Current Directions in Psychological Science, 10,* 39–42.

Simonton, D. K. (2004). Exceptional creativity and chance: Creative thought as a stochastic combinatorial process. In L. V. Shavinina & M. Ferrari (Eds.), *Beyond knowledge: Extracognitive aspects of developing high ability* (pp. 39–72). Mahwah, NJ: Erlbaum.

Sinatra, G. M., & Pintrich, P. R. (Eds.). (2003). *Intentional conceptual change.* Mahwah, NJ: Erlbaum.

Sinatra, G. M., Southerland, S. A., McConaughy, F., & Demastes, J. (2003). Intentions and beliefs in students' understanding and acceptance of biological evolution. *Journal of Research on Science Teaching, 40,* 510–528.

Singer, D. G., & Singer, J. L. (1994). *Barney & Friends*

as education and entertainment: Phase 3. A national study: Can preschoolers learn through exposure to Barney & Friends? New Haven, CT: Yale University Family Television Research and Consultation Center.

Sins, P. H. M., van Joolingen, W. R., Savelsbergh, E. R., & van Hout-Wolters, B. (2008). Motivation and performance within a collaborative computer-based modeling task: Relations between students' achievement goal orientation, self-efficacy, cognitive processing, and achievement. *Contemporary Educational Psychology, 33,* 58–77.

Sireci, S. G., Scarpati, S. E., & Li, S. (2005). Test accommodations for students with disabilities: An analysis of the interaction hypothesis. *Review of Educational Research, 75,* 457–490.

Sirin, S. R. (2005). Socioeconomic status and academic achievement: A meta-analytic review of research. *Review of Educational Research, 75,* 417–453.

Siskin, L. S. (2003a). Outside the core: Accountability in tested and untested subjects. In M. Carnoy, R. Elmore, & L. S. Siskin (Eds.), *The new accountability: High schools and high-stakes testing* (pp. 87–98). New York: RoutledgeFalmer.

Siskin, L. S. (2003b). When an irresistable force meets an immovable object: Core lessons about high schools and accountability. In M. Carnoy, R. Elmore, & L. S. Siskin (Eds.), *The new accountability: High schools and high-stakes testing* (pp. 175–194). New York: RoutledgeFalmer.

Sitko, B. M. (1998). Knowing how to write: Metacognition and writing instruction. In D. J. Hacker, J. Dunlosky, & A. C. Graesser (Eds.), *Metacognition in educational theory and practice* (pp. 93–115). Mahwah, NJ: Erlbaum.

Sizer, T. R. (1992). *Horace's school: Redesigning the American high school.* Boston: Houghton Mifflin.

Sizer, T. R. (2004). *Horace's compromise: The dilemma of the American high school.* Boston: Houghton Mifflin.

Skaalvik, E. (1997). Self-enhancing and self-defeating ego orientation: Relations with task avoidance orientation, achievement, self-perceptions, and anxiety. *Journal of Educational Psychology, 89,* 71–81.

Skiba, R. J., & Knesting, K. (2001). Zero tolerance, zero evidence: An analysis of school disciplinary practice. In R. J. Skiba & G. G. Noam (Eds.), *New directions for youth development: Theory, practice, research* (pp. 11–43). San Francisco: Jossey-Bass.

Skiba, R. J., & Rausch, M. K. (2006). Zero tolerance, suspension, and expulsion: Questions of equity and effectiveness. In C. M. Evertson & C. S. Weinstein (Eds.), *Handbook of classroom management: Research, practice, and contemporary issues* (pp. 1063–1089). Mahwah, NJ: Erlbaum.

Skinner, B. F. (1954). The science of learning and the art of teaching. *Harvard Educational Review, 24,* 86–97.

Skinner, B. F. (1968). *The technology of teaching.* New York: Appleton-Century-Crofts.

Skinner, B. F., & Epstein, R. (1982). *Skinner for the classroom.* Champaign, IL: Research Press.

Skinner, E., Furrer, C., Marchand, G., & Kindermann, T. (2008). Engagement and disaffection in the classroom: Part of a larger motivational dynamic? *Journal of Educational Psychology, 100,* 765–781.

Skowronek, J. S., Leichtman, M. D., & Pillemer, D. B. (2008). Long-term episodic memory in children with attention-deficit/hyperactivity disorder. *Learning Disabilities Research and Practice, 23*(1), 25–35.

Slater, W. H. (2004). Teaching English from a literacy perspective: The goal of high literacy for all students. In T. L. Jetton & J. A. Dole (Eds.), *Adolescent literacy research and practice* (pp. 40–58). New York: Guilford.

Slavin, R. E. (1983). When does cooperative learning increase student achievement? *Psychological Bulletin, 94,* 429–445.

Slavin, R. E. (1987). Ability grouping and student achievement in elementary schools: A best-evidence synthesis. *Review of Educational Research, 57,* 293–336.

Slavin, R. E. (1990). *Cooperative learning: Theory, research, and practice.* Upper Saddle River, NJ: Prentice Hall.

Slavin, R. E., & Cheung, A. (2005). A synthesis of research on language of reading instruction for English language learners. *Review of Educational Research, 75,* 247–284.

Slavin, R. E., Karweit, N. L., & Madden, N. A. (Eds.). (1989). *Effective programs for students at risk.* Boston: Allyn & Bacon.

Slavin, R. E., & Lake, C. (2008). Effective programs in elementary mathematics: A best-evidence synthesis. *Review of Educational Research, 78,* 427–515.

Sleeter, C. E., & Grant, C. A. (1999). *Making choices for multicultural education: Five approaches to race, class, and gender* (3rd ed.). Upper Saddle River, NJ: Merrill/Prentice Hall.

Slife, B. R., Weiss, J., & Bell, T. (1985). Separability of metacognition and cognition: Problem solving in learning disabled and regular students. *Journal of Educational Psychology, 77,* 437–445.

Slonim, M. B. (1991). *Children, culture, ethnicity: Evaluating and understanding the impact.* New York: Garland.

Slusher, M. P., & Anderson, C. A. (1996). Using causal persuasive arguments to change beliefs and teach new information: The mediating role of explanation availability and evaluation bias in the acceptance of knowledge. *Journal of Educational Psychology, 88,* 110–122.

Small, M. Y., Lovett, S. B., & Scher, M. S. (1993). Pictures facilitate children's recall of unillustrated expository prose. *Journal of Educational Psychology, 85,* 520–528.

Smetana, J. G. (1981). Preschool children's conceptions of moral and social rules. *Child Development, 52,* 1333–1336.

Smetana, J. G. (2005). Adolescent-parent conflict: Resistance and subversion as developmental process. In L. Nucci (Ed.), *Conflict, contradiction, and contrarian elements in moral development and education* (pp. 69–91). Mahwah, NJ: Erlbaum.

Smetana, J. G. (2006). Social cognitive domain theory: Consistencies and variations in children's moral and social judgments. In M. Killen & J. Smetana (Eds.), *Handbook of moral development* (pp. 119–154). Mahwah, NJ: Erlbaum.

Smetana, J. G., & Braeges, J. L. (1990). The development of toddlers' moral and conventional judgments. *Merrill-Palmer Quarterly, 36,* 329–346.

Smith, C. L. (2007). Bootstrapping processes in the development of students' commonsense matter theories: Using analogical mappings, thought experiments, and learning to measure to promote conceptual restructuring. *Cognition and Instruction, 25,* 337–398.

Smith, C. L., Maclin, D., Grosslight, L., & Davis, H. (1997). Teaching for understanding: A study of students' preinstruction theories of matter and a comparison of the effectiveness of two approaches to teaching about matter and density. *Cognition and Instruction, 15,* 317–393.

Smith, D. C., & Neale, D. C. (1991). The construction of subject-matter knowledge in primary science teaching. In J. Brophy (Ed.), *Advances in research on teaching: Vol. 2. Teachers' knowledge of subject matter as it relates to their teaching practice.* Greenwich, CT: JAI Press.

Smith, D. J., Young, K. R., West, R. P., Morgan, R. P., & Rhode, G. (1988). Reducing the disruptive behavior of junior high school students: A classroom self-management procedure. *Behavioral Disorders, 13,* 231–239.

Smith, E. E. (2000). Neural bases of human working memory. *Current Directions in Psychological Science, 9,* 45–49.

Smith, E. R., & Semin, G. R. (2007). Situated social cognition. *Current Directions in Psychological Science, 16,* 132–135.

Smith, H. L. (1998). Literacy and instruction in African American communities: Shall we overcome? In B. Pérez (Ed.), *Sociocultural contexts of language and literacy.* Mahwah, NJ: Erlbaum.

Smith, J. L. (2004). Understanding the process of stereotype threat: A review of mediational variables and new performance goal directions. *Educational Psychology Review, 16,* 177–206.

Smith, K., Johnson, D. W., & Johnson, R. T. (1981). Can conflict be constructive? Controversy versus concurrence seeking in learning groups. *Journal of Educational Psychology, 73,* 651–663.

Smith, R. E., & Smoll, F. L. (1997). Coaching the coaches: Youth sports as a scientific and applied behavioral setting. *Current Directions in Psychological Science, 6*(1), 16–21.

Smitherman, G. (1994). "The blacker the berry the sweeter the juice": African American student writers. In A. H. Dyson & C. Genishi (Eds.), *The need for story: Cultural diversity in classroom and community.* Urbana, IL: National Council of Teachers of English.

Smitherman, G. (2007). The power of the rap: The Black idiom and the new Black poetry. In H. S. Alim & J. Baugh (Eds.), *Talkin black talk: Language, education, and social change* (pp. 77–91). New York: Teachers College Press.

Snarey, J. (1995). In a communitarian voice: The sociological expansion of Kohlbergian theory, research, and practice. In W. M. Kurtines & J. L. Gewirtz (Eds.), *Moral development: An introduction.* Boston: Allyn & Bacon.

Sneider, C., & Pulos, S. (1983). Children's cosmographies: Understanding the earth's shape and gravity. *Science Education, 67,* 205–221.

Snider, V. E. (1990). What we know about learning styles from research in special education. *Educational Leadership, 48*(2), 53.

Snir, J., Smith, C. L., & Raz, G. (2003). Linking phenomena with competing underlying models: A software tool for introducing students to the particulate model of matter. *Science Education, 87,* 794–830.

Snow, C. E. (1990). Rationales for native language instruction: Evidence from research. In A. M. Padilla, H. H. Fairchild, & C. M. Valadez (Eds.), *Bilingual education: Issues and strategies.* Newbury Park, CA: Sage.

Snow, R. E., Corno, L., & Jackson, D., III (1996). Individual differences in affective and conative functions. In D. C. Berliner & R. C. Calfee (Eds.), *Handbook of educational psychology.* New York: Macmillan.

Snyder, J., Schrepferman, L., McEachern, A., Barner, S., Johnson, K., & Provines, J. (2008). Peer deviancy training and peer coercion: Dual processes associated with early-onset conduct problems. *Child Development, 79,* 252–268.

Solomon, R. C. (1984). Getting angry: The Jamesian theory of emotion in anthropology. In R. Shweder & R. A. Levine (Eds.), *Culture theory: Essays on mind, self, and emotion* (pp. 238–256). Cambridge, England: Cambridge University Press.

Solórzano, R. W. (2008). High stakes testing: Issues, implications, and remedies for English language learners. *Educational Researcher, 78,* 260–329.

Son, L. K., & Schwartz, B. L. (2002). The relation between metacognitive monitoring and control. In T. J. Perfect & B. L. Schwartz (Eds.), *Applied metacognition* (pp. 15–38). Cambridge, England: Cambridge University Press.

Soodak, L. C., & McCarthy, M. R. (2006). Classroom management in inclusive settings. In C. M. Evertson & C. S. Weinstein (Eds.), *Handbook of classroom management: Research, practice, and contemporary issues* (pp. 461–489). Mahwah, NJ: Erlbaum.

Southerland, S. A., & Sinatra, G. M. (2003). Learning about biological evolution: A special case of intentional conceptual change. In G. M. Sinatra & P. R. Pintrich (Eds.), *Intentional conceptual change* (pp. 317–345). Mahwah, NJ: Erlbaum.

Spandel, V. (1997). Reflections on portfolios. In G. D. Phye (Ed.), *Handbook of academic learning: Construction of knowledge.* San Diego, CA: Academic Press.

Spaulding, C. L. (1992). *Motivation in the classroom.* New York: McGraw-Hill.

Spear, L. P. (2000). Neurobehavioral changes in adolescence. *Current Directions in Psychological Science, 9,* 111–114.

Spear, L. P. (2007). Brain development and adolescent behavior. In D. Coch, K. W. Fischer, & G. Dawson (Eds.), *Human behavior, learning, and the developing brain: Typical development* (pp. 362–396). New York: Guilford Press.

Spearman, C. (1904). General intelligence, objectively determined and measured. *American Journal of Psychology, 15*, 201–293.

Spearman, C. (1927). *The abilities of man: Their nature and measurement*. New York: Macmillan.

Spelke, E. S. (2003). What makes humans smart? In D. Gentner & S. Goldin-Meadow (Eds.), *Advances in the investigation of language and thought*. Cambridge, MA: MIT Press.

Spelke, E. S. (2005). Sex differences in intrinsic aptitude for mathematics and science? A critical review. *American Psychologist, 60*, 950–958.

Spencer, J. P., Simmering, V. R., Schutte, A. R., & Schöner, G. (2007). What does theoretical neuroscience have to offer the study of behavioral development? Insights from a dynamic field theory of spatial cognition. In J. M. Plumert & J. P. Spencer (Eds.), *The emerging spatial mind* (pp. 320–361). New York: Oxford University Press.

Spencer, M. B., Noll, E., Stoltzfus, J., & Harpalani, V. (2001). Identity and school adjustment: Revisiting the "acting White" phenomenon. *Educational Psychologist, 36*, 21–30.

Spera, C. (2005). A review of the relationship among parenting practices, parenting styles, and adolescent school achievement. *Educational Psychology Review, 17*, 125–146.

Spicker, H. H. (1992). Identifying and enriching: Rural gifted children. *Educational Horizons, 70*(2), 60–65.

Spinath, F. M., Price, T. S., Dale, P. S., & Plomin, R. (2004). The genetic and environmental origins of language disability and ability. *Child Development, 75*, 445–454.

Spinelli, C. G. (2008). Addressing the issue of cultural and linguistic diversity and assessment: Informal evaluation measures for English language learners. *Reading and Writing Quarterly, 24*, 101–118.

Spires, H. A., & Donley, J. (1998). Prior knowledge activation: Inducing engagement with informational texts. *Journal of Educational Psychology, 90*, 249–260.

Sroufe, L. A., Carlson, E., & Shulman, S. (1993). Individuals in relationships: Development from infancy through adolescence. In D. C. Funder, R. D. Parke, C. Tomlinson-Keasey, & K. Widaman (Eds.), *Studying lives through time: Personality and development* (pp. 315–342). Washington, DC: American Psychological Association.

Sroufe, L. A., Cooper, R. G., DeHart, G., & Bronfenbrenner, U. (1992). *Child development: Its nature and course* (2nd ed.). New York: McGraw-Hill.

Stacey, K. (1992). Mathematical problem solving in groups: Are two heads better than one? *Journal of Mathematical Behavior, 11*, 261–275.

Stack, C. B., & Burton, L. M. (1993). Kinscripts. *Journal of Comparative Family Studies, 24*, 157–170.

Stahl, G., Koschmann, T., & Suthers, D. D. (2006). Computer-supported collaborative learning. In R. K. Sawyer (Ed.), *The Cambridge handbook of the learning sciences* (pp. 409–425). Cambridge, England: Cambridge University Press.

Stahl, S. A., & Shanahan, C. (2004). Learning to think like a historian: Disciplinary knowledge through critical analysis of multiple documents. In T. L. Jetton & J. A. Dole (Eds.), *Adolescent literacy research and practice* (pp. 94–115). New York: Guilford.

Stainback, S., & Stainback, W. (1992). Schools as inclusive communities. In W. Stainback & S. Stainback (Eds.), *Controversial issues confronting special education: Divergent perspectives*. Boston: Allyn & Bacon.

Stanley, J. C. (1980). On educating the gifted. *Educational Researcher, 9*(3), 8–12.

Stanovich, K. E. (1999). *Who is rational? Studies of individual differences in reasoning*. Mahwah, NJ: Erlbaum.

Stanovich, K. E. (2000). *Progress in understanding reading: Scientific foundations and new frontiers*. New York: Guilford Press.

Stanovich, K. E., West, R. F., & Harrison, M. R. (1995). Knowledge growth and maintenance across the life span: The role of print exposure. *Developmental Psychology, 31*, 811–826.

Staples, M. (2007). Supporting whole-class collaborative inquiry in a secondary mathematics classroom. *Cognition and Instruction, 25*, 161–217.

Starr, E. J., & Lovett, S. B. (2000). The ability to distinguish between comprehension and memory: Failing to succeed. *Journal of Educational Psychology, 92*, 761–771.

Staub, D. (1998). *Delicate threads: Friendships between children with and without special needs in inclusive settings*. Bethesda, MD: Woodbine House.

Stefanou, C. R., Perencevich, K. C., DiCintio, M., & Turner, J. C. (2004). Supporting autonomy in the classroom: Ways teachers encourage student decision making and ownership. *Educational Psychologist, 39*, 97–110.

Steffensen, M. S., Joag-Dev, C., & Anderson, R. C. (1979). A cross-cultural perspective on reading comprehension. *Reading Research Quarterly, 15*, 10–29.

Stein, B. S. (1989). Memory and creativity. In J. A. Glover, R. R. Ronning, & C. R. Reynolds (Eds.), *Handbook of creativity*. New York: Plenum Press.

Stein, D. M., & Reichert, P. (1990). Extreme dieting behaviors in early adolescence. *Journal of Early Adolescence, 10*, 108–121.

Stein, J. A., & Krishnan, K. (2007). Nonverbal learning disabilities and executive function: The challenges of effective assessment and teaching. In L. Meltzer (Ed.), *Executive function in education: From theory to practice* (pp. 106–132). New York: Guilford Press.

Steinberg, L. (1996). *Beyond the classroom: Why school reform has failed and what parents need to do*. New York: Touchstone.

Steinberg, L. (2007). Risk taking in adolescence. *Current Directions in Psychological Science, 16*, 55–59.

Steinberg, L., Blinde, P. L., & Chan, K. S. (1984). Dropping out among language minority youth. *Review of Educational Research, 54*, 113–132.

Steiner, H. H., & Carr, M. (2003). Cognitive development in gifted children: Toward a more precise understanding of emerging differences in intelligence. *Educational Psychology Review, 15*, 215–246.

Stepans, J. (1991). Developmental patterns in students' understanding of physics concepts. In S. M. Glynn, R. H. Yeany, & B. K. Britton (Eds.), *The psychology of learning science*. Mahwah, NJ: Erlbaum.

Sternberg, R. J. (1985). *Beyond IQ: A triarchic theory of human intelligence*. Cambridge, England: Cambridge University Press.

Sternberg, R. J. (1997). The concept of intelligence and its role in lifelong learning and success. *American Psychologist, 52*, 1030–1037.

Sternberg, R. J. (1998). Teaching triarchically improves school achievement. *Journal of Educational Psychology, 90*, 374–384.

Sternberg, R. J. (2002). Raising the achievement of all students: Teaching for successful intelligence. *Educational Psychology Review, 14*, 383–393.

Sternberg, R. J. (2003). *Wisdom, intelligence, and creativity synthesized*. Cambridge, England: Cambridge University Press.

Sternberg, R. J. (2004). Culture and intelligence. *American Psychologist, 59*, 325–338.

Sternberg, R. J. (2005). Intelligence, competence, and expertise. In A. J. Elliot & C. S. Dweck (Eds.), *Handbook of competence and motivation* (pp. 15–30). New York: Guilford Press.

Sternberg, R. J. (2007). Intelligence and culture. In S. Kitayama & D. Cohen (Eds.), *Handbook of cultural psychology* (pp. 547–568). New York: Guilford Press.

Sternberg, R. J., & Detterman, D. K. (Eds.). (1986). *What is intelligence? Contemporary views on its nature and definition*. Norwood, NJ: Ablex.

Sternberg, R. J., Forsythe, G. B., Hedlund, J., Horvath, J. A., Wagner, R. K., Williams, W. M., Snook, S. A., & Grigorenko, E. L. (2000). *Practical intelligence in everyday life*. Cambridge, England: Cambridge University Press.

Sternberg, R. J., & Frensch, P. A. (1993). Mechanisms of transfer. In D. K. Detterman & R. J. Sternberg (Eds.), *Transfer on trial: Intelligence, cognition, and instruction*. Norwood, NJ: Ablex.

Sternberg, R. J., Grigorenko, E. L., & Kidd, K. K. (2005). Intelligence, race, and genetics. *American Psychologist, 60*, 46–59.

Sternberg, R. J., & Horvath, J. A. (1995). A prototype view of expert teaching. *Educational Researcher, 24*(6), 9–17.

Stevahn, L., Johnson, D. W., Johnson, R. T., Oberle, K., & Wahl, L. (2000). Effects of conflict resolution training integrated into a kindergarten curriculum. *Child Development, 71*, 772–784.

Stevens, G. (2004). Using census data to test critical-period hypothesis for second-language acquisition. *Psychological Science, 15*, 215–216.

Stevens, R. J., & Slavin, R. E. (1995). The cooperative elementary school: Effects of students' achievement, attitudes, and social relations. *American Educational Research Journal, 32*, 321–351.

Stevenson, H. C., & Fantuzzo, J. W. (1986). The generality and social validity of a competency-based self-control training intervention for underachieving students. *Journal of Applied Behavior Analysis, 19*, 269–272.

Stevenson, H. W., Chen, C., & Uttal, D. H. (1990). Beliefs and achievement: A study of black, white, and Hispanic children. *Child Development, 61*, 508–523.

Stewart, L., & Pascual-Leone, J. (1992). Mental capacity constraints and the development of moral reasoning. *Journal of Experimental Child Psychology, 54*, 251–287.

Stice, E. (2003). Puberty and body image. In C. Hayward (Ed.), *Gender differences at puberty* (pp. 61–76). Cambridge, England: Cambridge University Press.

Stice, E., & Barrera, M., Jr. (1995). A longitudinal examination of the reciprocal relations between perceived parenting and adolescents' substance use and externalizing behaviors. *Developmental Psychology, 31*, 322–334.

Stiggins, R. (2008). *An introduction to student-involved assessment for learning* (5th ed.). Upper Saddle River, NJ: Merrill/Pearson.

Stipek, D. J. (1984). Sex differences in children's attributions for success and failure on math and spelling tests. *Sex Roles, 11*, 969–981.

Stipek, D. J. (1993). *Motivation to learn: From theory to practice* (2nd ed.). Boston: Allyn & Bacon.

Stipek, D. J. (1996). Motivation and instruction. In D. C. Berliner & R. C. Calfee (Eds.), *Handbook of educational psychology*. New York: Macmillan.

Stipek, D. J. (2002). At what age should children enter kindergarten? A question for policy makers and parents. *Social Policy Report of the Society for Research in Child Development, 16*(2), 3–16.

Stipek, D. J., & Miles, S. (2008). Effects of aggression on achievement: Does conflict with the teacher make it worse? *Child Development, 79*, 1721–1735.

Stodolsky, S. S., Salk, S., & Glaessner, B. (1991). Student views about learning math and social studies. *American Educational Research Journal, 28*, 89–116.

Stokes, T. F., & Baer, D. M. (1977). An implicit technology of generalization. *Journal of Applied Behavior Analysis, 10*, 349–367.

Stone, N. J. (2000). Exploring the relationship between calibration and self-regulated learning. *Educational Psychology Review, 12*, 437–475.

Striepling-Goldstein, S. H. (2004). The low-aggression classroom: A teacher's view. In J. C. Conoley & A. P. Goldstein (Eds.), *School violence intervention* (2nd ed., pp. 23–53). New York: Guilford Press.

Stright, A. D., Gallagher, K. C., & Kelley, K. (2008). Infant temperament moderates relations between maternal parenting in early childhood and children's adjustment in first grade. *Child Development, 79*, 186–200.

Stright, A. D., Neitzel, C., Sears, K. G., & Hoke-Sinex, L. (2001). Instruction begins in the home: Relations between parental instruction and children's self-regulation in the classroom. *Journal of Educational Psychology, 93,* 456–466.

Strike, K. A., & Posner, G. J. (1992). A revisionist theory of conceptual change. In R. A. Duschl & R. J. Hamilton (Eds.), *Philosophy of science, cognitive psychology, and educational theory and practice.* New York: State University of New York Press.

Stringer, E. (2008). *Action research in education* (2nd ed.). Upper Saddle River, NJ: Merrill/Pearson Education.

Stringfield, S. C., & Yakimowski-Srebnick, M. E. (2005). Promise, progress, problems, and paradoxes of three phases of accountability: A longitudinal case study of the Baltimore City Public Schools. *American Educational Research Journal, 42,* 43–75.

Strozer, J. R. (1994). *Language acquisition after puberty.* Washington, DC: Georgetown University Press.

Sue, D. W. (1990). Culture-specific strategies in counseling: A conceptual framework. *Professional Psychology: Research and Practice, 21,* 424–433.

Sue, S., & Chin, R. (1983). The mental health of Chinese-American children: Stressors and resources. In G. J. Powell (Ed.), *The psychosocial development of minority children.* New York: Brunner/Mazel.

Suh, S., Suh, J., & Houston, I. (2007). Predictors of categorical at-risk high school dropouts. *Journal of Counseling & Development, 85,* 196–203.

Suina, J. H., & Smolkin, L. B. (1994). From natal culture to school culture to dominant society culture: Supporting transitions for Pueblo Indian students. In P. M. Greenfield & R. R. Cocking (Eds.), *Cross-cultural roots of minority child development.* Mahwah, NJ: Erlbaum.

Sullivan, A. L. (2008, March). *Examining the local context of English language learner representation in special education.* Poster presented at the annual meeting of the American Educational Research Association, New York.

Sullivan, J. R., & Conoley, J. C. (2004). Academic and instructional interventions with aggressive students. In J. C. Conoley & A. P. Goldstein (Eds.), *School violence intervention* (2nd ed., pp. 235–255). New York: Guilford Press.

Sullivan, J. S. (1989). Planning, implementing, and maintaining an effective in-school suspension program. *Clearing House, 62,* 409–410.

Sullivan, R. C. (1994). Autism: Definitions past and present. *Journal of Vocational Rehabilitation, 4,* 4–9.

Sullivan-DeCarlo, C., DeFalco, K., & Roberts, V. (1998). Helping students avoid risky behavior. *Educational Leadership, 56*(1), 80–82.

Sun-Alperin, M. K., & Wang, M. (2008). Spanish-speaking children's spelling errors with English vowel sounds that are represented by different graphemes in English and Spanish words. *Contemporary Educational Psychology, 33,* 932–948.

Sund, R. B. (1976). *Piaget for educators.* Upper Saddle River, NJ: Merrill/Prentice Hall.

Suskind, R. (1998). *A hope in the unseen: An American odyssey from the inner city to the Ivy League.* New York: Broadway Books.

Sutherland, K. S., & Morgan, P. L. (2003). Implications of transactional processes in classrooms for students with emotional/behavioral disorders. *Preventing School Failure, 48*(6), 32–45.

Suttles, G. D. (1970). Friendship as a social institution. In G. J. McCall, M. McCall, N. K. Denzin, G. D. Scuttles, & S. Kurth (Eds.), *Social relationships* (pp. 95–135). Chicago: Aldine de Gruyter.

Sutton, R. E., & Wheatley, K. F. (2003). Teachers' emotions and teaching: A review of the literature and directions for future research. *Educational Psychology Review, 15,* 327–358.

Swan, K., Mitrani, M., Guerrero, F., Cheung, M., & Schoener, J. (1990, April). *Perceived locus of control and computer-based instruction.* Paper presented at the annual meeting of the American Educational Research Association, Boston.

Swanborn, M. S. L., & de Glopper, K. (1999). Incidental word learning while reading: A meta-analysis. *Review of Educational Research, 69,* 261–285.

Swann, W. B., Jr., Chang-Schneider, C., & McClarty, K. L. (2007). Do people's self-views matter? Self-concept and self-esteem in everyday life. *American Psychologist, 62,* 84–94.

Swanson, D. B., Norman, G. R., & Linn, R. L. (1995). Performance-based assessment: Lessons from the health professions. *Educational Researcher, 24*(5), 5–11, 35.

Swanson, H. L. (1993). An information processing analysis of learning disabled children's problem solving. *American Educational Research Journal, 30,* 861–893.

Swanson, H. L., Cooney, J. B., & O'Shaughnessy, T. E. (1998). Learning disabilities and memory. In B. Y. L. Wong (Ed.), *Learning about learning disabilities* (2nd ed.). San Diego, CA: Academic Press.

Swanson, H. L., & Jerman, O. (2006). Math disabilities: A selective meta-analysis of the literature. *Review of Educational Research, 76,* 249–274.

Swanson, H. L., Jerman, O., & Zheng, X. (2008). Growth in working memory and mathematical problem solving in children at risk and not at risk for serious math difficulties. *Journal of Educational Psychology, 100,* 343–379.

Swanson, H. L., & Lussier, C. M. (2001). A selective synthesis of the experimental literature on dynamic assessment. *Review of Educational Research, 71,* 321–363.

Swanson, H. L., Mink, J., & Bocian, K. M. (1999). Cognitive processing deficits in poor readers with symptoms of reading disabilities and ADHD: More alike than different? *Journal of Educational Psychology, 91,* 321–333.

Swanson, H. L., O'Connor, J. E., & Cooney, J. B. (1990). An information processing analysis of expert and novice teachers' problem solving. *American Educational Research Journal, 27,* 533–556.

Sweeny, K., Carroll, P. J., & Shepperd, J. A. (2006). Is optimism always best? Future outlooks and preparedness. *Current Directions in Psychological Science, 15,* 302–306.

Sweller, J., Kirschner, P. A., & Clark, R. E. (2007). Why minimally guided teaching techniques do not work: A reply to commentaries. *Educational Psychologist, 42,* 115–121.

Tager-Flusberg, H. (2007). Evaluating the theory-of-mind hypothesis of autism. *Current Directions in Psychological Science, 16,* 311–315.

Tager-Flusberg, H., & Skwerer, D. P. (2007). Williams syndrome: A model developmental syndrome for exploring brain-behavior relationships. In D. Coch, G. Dawson, & K. W. Fischer (Eds.), *Human behavior, learning, and the developing brain: Atypical development* (pp. 87–116). New York: Guilford Press.

Tamburrini, J. (1982). Some educational implications of Piaget's theory. In S. Modgil & C. Modgil (Eds.), *Jean Piaget: Consensus and controversy.* New York: Praeger.

Tanner, J. M., & Inhelder, B. (Eds.). (1960). *Discussions of child development: A consideration of the biological, psychological, and cultural approaches to the understanding of human development and behavior: Vol. 4. The proceedings of the fourth meeting of the World Health Organization Study Group on the Psychobiological Development of the Child, Geneva, 1956.* New York: International Universities Press.

Tarver, S. G. (1992). Direct Instruction. In W. Stainback & S. Stainback (Eds.), *Controversial issues confronting special education.* Boston: Allyn & Bacon.

Tate, W. F. (1995). Returning to the root: A culturally relevant approach to mathematics pedagogy. *Theory into Practice, 34,* 166–173.

Tatum, B. D. (1997). *"Why are all the black kids sitting together in the cafeteria?" and other conversations about race.* New York: Basic Books.

Taub, J., & Pearrow, M. (2006). Resilience through violence prevention in schools. In. S. Goldstein & R. B. Brooks (Eds.), *Handbook of resilience in children* (pp. 357–371). New York: Springer.

Taylor, J. C., & Romanczyk, R. G. (1994). Generating hypotheses about the function of student problem behavior by observing teacher behavior. *Journal of Applied Behavior Analysis, 27,* 251–265.

Taylor, S. M. (1994, April). *Staying in school against the odds: Voices of minority adolescent girls.* Paper presented at the annual meeting of the American Educational Research Association, New Orleans, LA.

Tenenbaum, H. R., & Ruck, M. D. (2007). Are teachers' expectations different for racial minority than for European American students? A meta-analysis. *Journal of Educational Psychology, 99,* 253–273.

Tennyson, R. D., & Cocchiarella, M. J. (1986). An empirically based instructional design theory for teaching concepts. *Review of Educational Research, 56,* 40–71.

Terry, A. W. (2008). Student voices, global echoes: Service-learning and the gifted. *Roeper Review, 30,* 45–51.

Tessler, M., & Nelson, K. (1994). Making memories: The influence of joint encoding on later recall by young children. *Consciousness and Cognition, 3,* 307–326.

Tharp, R. G. (1989). Psychocultural variables and constants: Effects on teaching and learning in schools. *American Psychologist, 44,* 349–359.

Tharp, R. G. (1994). Intergroup differences among Native Americans in socialization and child cognition: An ethnogenetic analysis. In P. M. Greenfield & R. R. Cocking (Eds.), *Cross-cultural roots of minority child development.* Mahwah, NJ: Erlbaum.

Théberge, C. L. (1994, April). *Small-group vs. whole-class discussion: Gaining the floor in science lessons.* Paper presented at the annual meeting of the American Educational Research Association, New Orleans, LA.

Thelen, E., & Smith, L. B. (1998). Dynamic systems theories. In W. Damon (Series Ed.) & R. M. Lerner (Vol. Ed.), *Handbook of child psychology: Vol. 1. Theoretical models of human development* (5th ed.). New York: Wiley.

Themann, K. S., & Goldstein, H. (2001). Social stories, written text cues, and video feedback: Effects on social communication of children with autism. *Journal of Applied Behavior Analysis, 34,* 425–446.

Théoret, H., Halligan, E., Kobayashi, M., Fregni, F., Tager-Flusberg, H., & Pascual-Leone, A. (2005). Impaired motor facilitation during action observation in individuals with autism spectrum disorder. *Current Biology, 15,* 84–85.

Thomas, A., & Chess, S. (1977). *Temperament and development.* New York: Brunner/Mazel.

Thomas, J. R., & French, K. E. (1985). Gender differences across age in motor performance: A meta-analysis. *Psychological Bulletin, 98,* 260–282.

Thomas, J. W. (1993a). Expectations and effort: Course demands, students' study practices, and academic achievement. In T. M. Tomlinson (Ed.), *Motivating students to learn: Overcoming barriers to high achievement.* Berkeley, CA: McCutchan.

Thomas, J. W. (1993b). Promoting independent learning in the middle grades: The role of instructional support practices. *Elementary School Journal, 93,* 575–591.

Thomas, M. S. C., & Johnson, M. H. (2008). New advances in understanding sensitive periods in brain development. *Current Directions in Psychological Science, 17,* 1–5.

Thomas, R. M. (2005). *High-stakes testing: Coping with collateral damage.* Mahwah, NJ: Erlbaum.

Thomas, S., & Oldfather, P. (1997). Intrinsic motivations, literacy, and assessment practices: "That's my grade. That's me." *Educational Psychologist, 32,* 107–123.

Thomas, S. P., Groër, M., & Droppleman, P. (1993). Physical health of today's school children. *Educational Psychology Review, 5,* 5–33.

Thompson, H., & Carr, M. (1995, April). *Brief metacognitive intervention and interest as predictors of memory for text.* Paper presented at the annual meeting of the American Educational Research Association, San Francisco.

Thompson, M., & Grace, C. O. (with Cohen, L. J.).

(2001). *Best friends, worst enemies: Understanding the social lives of children*. New York: Ballantine.

Thompson, R. A. (1998). Early sociopersonality development. In W. Damon (Series Ed.) & N. Eisenberg (Vol. Ed.), *Handbook of child psychology: Vol. 3: Social, emotional, and personality development* (5th ed.). New York: Wiley.

Thompson, R. A., & Nelson, C. A. (2001). Developmental science and the media: Early brain development. *American Psychologist, 56*, 5–15.

Thompson, R. A., & Wyatt, J. M. (1999). Current research on child maltreatment: Implications for educators. *Educational Psychology Review, 11*, 173–201.

Thompson, T. L., & Zerbinos, E. (1995). Gender roles in animated cartoons: Has the picture changed in 20 years? *Sex Roles, 32*, 651–673.

Thorndike, E. L. (1924). Mental discipline in high school studies. *Journal of Educational Psychology, 15*, 1–22, 83–98.

Thorndike, R. M. (1997). *Measurement and evaluation in psychology and education* (6th ed.). Upper Saddle River, NJ: Merrill/Prentice Hall.

Tiedemann, J. (2000). Parents' gender stereotypes and teachers' beliefs as predictors of children's concept of their mathematical ability in elementary school. *Journal of Educational Psychology, 92*, 144–151.

Tiger, J. H., Hanley, G. P., & Hernandez, E. (2006). An evaluation of the value of choice with preschool children. *Journal of Applied Behavior Analysis, 39*, 1–16.

Timm, P., & Borman, K. (1997). The soup pot don't stretch that far no more: Intergenerational patterns of school leaving in an urban Appalachian neighborhood. In M. Sellter & L. Weis (Eds.), *Beyond black and white: New faces and voices in U.S. schools*. Albany: State University of New York Press.

Tirosh, D., & Graeber, A. O. (1990). Evoking cognitive conflict to explore preservice teachers' thinking about division. *Journal for Research in Mathematics Education, 21*, 98–108.

Tisak, M. (1993). Preschool children's judgments of moral and personal events involving physical harm and property damage. *Merrill-Palmer Quarterly, 39*, 375–390.

Tobias, S. (1994). Interest, prior knowledge, and learning. *Review of Educational Research, 64*, 37–54.

Tobin, K. (1987). The role of wait time in higher cognitive level learning. *Review of Educational Research, 57*, 69–95.

Tomasello, M. (2000). Culture and cognitive development. *Current Directions in Psychological Science, 9*, 37–40.

Tomback, R. M., Williams, A. Y., & Wentzel, K. R. (2005, April). *Young adolescents' concerns about the transition to high school*. Poster presented at the annual meeting of the American Educational Research Association, Montreal.

Tompkins, G. E., & McGee, L. M. (1986). Visually impaired and sighted children's emerging concepts about written language. In D. B. Yaden, Jr., & S. Templeton (Eds.), *Metalinguistic awareness and beginning literacy: Conceptualizing what it means to read and write*. Portsmouth, NH: Heinemann.

Tong, F., Lara-Alecio, R., Irby, B., Mathes, P., & Kwok, O.-M. (2008). *American Educational Research Journal, 45*, 1011–1044.

Torrance, E. P. (1970). *Encouraging creativity in the classroom*. Dubuque, IA: Wm. C. Brown.

Torrance, E. P. (1989). A reaction to "Gifted black students: Curriculum and teaching strategies." In C. J. Maker & S. W. Schiever (Eds.), *Critical issues in gifted education: Vol. 2. Defensible programs for cultural and ethnic minorities*. Austin, TX: Pro-Ed.

Torrance, E. P. (1995). Insights about creativity: Questioned, rejected, ridiculed, ignored. *Educational Psychology Review, 7*, 313–322.

Torrance, E. P., & Myers, R. E. (1970). *Creative learning and teaching*. New York: Dodd, Mead.

Torres-Guzmán, M. E. (1998). Language, culture, and literacy in Puerto Rican communities. In B. Pérez (Ed.), *Sociocultural contexts of language and literacy*. Mahwah, NJ: Erlbaum.

Tourniaire, F., & Pulos, S. (1985). Proportional reasoning: A review of the literature. *Educational Studies in Mathematics, 16*, 181–204.

Townsend, T. (2008, March). *Supporting students who struggle to learn: A community approach to development*. Paper presented at the annual meeting of the American Educational Research Association, New York.

Traub, R. E. (1993). On the equivalence of the traits assessed by multiple-choice and constructed-response tests. In R. E. Bennett & W. C. Ward (Eds.), *Construction versus choice in cognitive measurement: Issues in constructed response, performance testing, and portfolio assessment* (pp. 29–44). Mahwah, NJ: Erlbaum.

Trautner, H. M. (1992). The development of sex-typing in children: A longitudinal analysis. *German Journal of Psychology, 16*, 183–199.

Trautwein, U., Gerlach, E., & Lüdtke, O. (2008). Athletic classmates, physical self-concept, and free-time physical activity: A longitudinal study of frame of reference effects. *Journal of Educational Psychology, 100*, 988–1001.

Trautwein, U., & Köller, O. (2003). The relationship between homework and achievement—still much of a mystery. *Educational Psychology Review, 15*, 115–145.

Trautwein, U., & Lüdtke, O. (2007). Students' self-reported effort and time on homework in six school subjects: Between-student differences and within-student variation. *Journal of Educational Psychology, 99*, 432–444.

Trautwein, U., Lüdtke, O., Kastens, C., & Köller, O. (2006). Effort on homework in grades 5–9: Development, motivational antecedents, and the association with effort on classwork. *Child Development, 77*, 1094–1111.

Trawick-Smith, J. (2003). *Early childhood development: A multicultural perspective* (3rd ed.). Upper Saddle River, NJ: Merrill/Prentice Hall.

Treffert, D. A., & Wallace, G. L. (2002). Islands of genius. *Scientific American, 286*(6), 76–85.

Triandis, H. C. (1995). *Individualism and collectivism*. Boulder, CO: Westview Press.

Troop-Gordon, W., & Asher, S. R. (2005). Modification in children's goals when encountering obstacles in conflict resolution. *Child Development, 76*, 568–582.

Troop-Gordon, W., & Ladd, G. W. (2005). Trajectories of peer victimization and perceptions of the self and schoolmates: Precursors to internalizing and externalizing problems. *Child Development, 76*, 1072–1091.

Trout, J. D. (2003). Biological specializations for speech: What can the animals tell us? *Current Directions in Psychological Science, 12*, 155–159.

Tryon, G. S. (1980). The measurement and treatment of anxiety. *Review of Educational Research, 50*, 343–372.

Tsai, J. L. (2007). Ideal affect: Cultural causes and behavioral consequences. *Perspectives on Psychological Science, 2*, 242–259.

Tsai, J. L., & Chentsova-Dutton, Y. (2003). Variation among European Americans in emotional facial expression. *Journal of Cross Cultural Psychology, 34*, 650–657.

Tsai, Y.-M., Kunter, M., Lüdtke, O., Trautwein, U., & Ryan, R. M. (2008). What makes lessons interesting? The role of situational and individual factors in three school subjects. *Journal of Educational Psychology, 100*, 460–472.

Tschannen-Moran, M., Woolfolk Hoy, A., & Hoy, W. K. (1998). Teacher efficacy: Its meaning and measure. *Review of Educational Research, 68*, 202–248.

Tse, L. (2001). *Why don't they learn English: Separating fact from fallacy in the U.S. language debate*. New York: Teachers College Press.

Tsethlikai, M., & Greenhoot, A. F. (2006). The influence of another's perspective on children's recall of previously misconstrued events. *Developmental Psychology, 42*, 732–745.

Tsethlikai, M., Guthrie-Fulbright, Y., & Loera, S. (2007, March). *Social perspective coordination ability and children's recall of mutual conflict*. Paper presented at the biennial meeting of the Society for Research in Child Development, Boston.

Tucker, V. G., & Anderman, L. H. (1999, April). *Cycles of learning: Demonstrating the interplay between motivation, self-regulation, and cognition*. Paper presented at the annual meeting of the American Educational Research Association, Montreal, Canada.

Tudge, J., Hogan, D., Lee, S., Tammeveski, P., Meltsas, M., Kulakova, N., Snezhkova, I., & Putnam, S. (1999). Cultural heterogeneity: Parental values and beliefs and their preschoolers' activities in the United States, South Korea, Russia, and Estonia. In A. Göncü (Ed.), *Children's engagement in the world: Sociocultural perspectives* (pp. 62–96). Cambridge, England: Cambridge University Press.

Tuerk, P. W. (2005). Research in the high-stakes era: Achievement, resources, and No Child Left Behind. *Psychological Science, 16*, 419–425.

Tulving, E. (1983). *Elements of episodic memory*. Oxford, England: Oxford University Press.

Tulving, E., & Thomson, D. M. (1973). Encoding specificity and retrieval processes in episodic memory. *Psychological Review, 80*, 352–373.

Tunstall, P., & Gipps, C. (1996). Teacher feedback to young children in formative assessment: A typology. *British Educational Research Journal, 22*, 389–404.

Turiel, E. (1983). *The development of social knowledge: Morality and convention*. Cambridge, England: Cambridge University Press.

Turiel, E. (1998). The development of morality. In W. Damon (Series Ed.) & N. Eisenberg (Vol. Ed.), *Handbook of child psychology: Vol. 3. Social, emotional, and personality development* (5th ed., pp. 863–932). New York: Wiley.

Turiel, E. (2002). *The culture of morality: Social development, context, and conflict*. Cambridge, England: Cambridge University Press.

Turkanis, C. G. (2001). Creating curriculum with children. In B. Rogoff, C. G. Turkanis, & L. Bartlett (Eds.), *Learning together: Children and adults in a school community* (pp. 91–102). New York: Oxford University Press.

Turkheimer, E. (2000). Three laws of behavior genetics and what they mean. *Current Directions in Psychological Science, 9*, 160–164.

Turkheimer, E., Haley, A., Waldron, M., D'Onofrio, B., & Gottesman, I. I. (2003). Socioeconomic status modifies heritability of IQ in young children. *Psychological Science, 14*, 623–628.

Turnbull, A. P., Pereira, L., & Blue-Banning, M. (2000). Teachers as friendship facilitators. *Teaching Exceptional Children, 32*(5), 66–70.

Turnbull, A. P., Turnbull, R., & Wehmeyer, M. L. (2007). *Exceptional lives: Special education in today's schools* (5th ed.). Upper Saddle River, NJ: Merrill/Prentice Hall.

Turner, J. C. (1995). The influence of classroom contexts on young children's motivation for literacy. *Reading Research Quarterly, 30*, 410–441.

Turner, J. C., Meyer, D. K., Cox, K. E., Logan, C., DiCintio, M., & Thomas, C. T. (1998). Creating contexts for involvement in mathematics. *Journal of Educational Psychology, 90*, 730–745.

Turner, J. C., & Patrick, H. (2008). How does motivation develop and why does it change? Reframing motivation research. *Educational Psychologist, 43*, 119–131.

Turner, J. C., Thorpe, P. K., & Meyer, D. K. (1998). Students' reports of motivation and negative affect: A theoretical and empirical analysis. *Journal of Educational Psychology, 90*, 758–771.

Tuttle, D. W., & Tuttle, N. R. (1996). *Self-esteem and adjusting with blindness: The process of responding to life's demands* (2nd ed.). Springfield, IL: Charles C Thomas.

Tutwiler, S. W. (2007). How schools fail African American boys. In S. Books (Ed.), *Invisible children in the society and its schools* (3rd ed., pp. 141–156). Mahwah, NJ: Erlbaum.

Tyler, K. M., Uqdah, A. L., Dillihunt, M. L., Beatty-Hazelbaker, R., Connor, T., Gadson, N., et al. (2008). Cultural discontinuity: Toward a quantitative investigation of a major hypothesis in education. *Educational Researcher, 37,* 280–297.

Tzuriel, D. (2000). Dynamic assessment of young children: Educational and intervention perspectives. *Educational Psychology Review, 12,* 385–435.

Udall, A. J. (1989). Curriculum for gifted Hispanic students. In C. J. Maker & S. W. Schiever (Eds.), *Critical issues in gifted education: Vol. 2. Defensible programs for cultural and ethnic minorities.* Austin, TX: Pro-Ed.

Ulichny, P. (1996). Cultures in conflict. *Anthropology and Education Quarterly, 27,* 331–364.

Urdan, T. (2004). Predictors of academic self-handicapping and achievement: Examining achievement goals, classroom goal structures, and culture. *Journal of Educational Psychology, 96,* 251–264.

Urdan, T. C., & Maehr, M. L. (1995). Beyond a two-goal theory of motivation and achievement: A case for social goals. *Review of Educational Research, 65,* 213–243.

Urdan, T. C., & Midgley, C. (2001). Academic self-handicapping: What we know, what more there is to learn. *Educational Psychology Review, 13,* 115–138.

Urdan, T. C., Midgley, C., & Anderman, E. M. (1998). The role of classroom goal structure in students' use of self-handicapping strategies. *American Educational Research Journal, 35,* 101–122.

Urdan, T. C., Ryan, A. M., Anderman, E. M., & Gheen, M. H. (2002). Goals, goal structures, and avoidance behaviors. In C. Midgley (Ed.), *Goals, goal structures, and patterns of adaptive learning* (pp. 55–83). Mahwah, NJ: Erlbaum.

U.S. Census Bureau. (2008). *Income, poverty, and health insurance coverage in the United States: 2007.* Washington, DC: U.S. Author.

U.S. Department of Education. (1992). *To assure the free appropriate public education of all children with disabilities: Fourteenth annual report to Congress on the implementation of the Individuals with Disabilities Education Act.* Washington, DC: Author.

U.S. Department of Education. (1993). *National excellence: A case for developing America's talent.* Washington, DC: Office of Educational Research and Improvement.

U.S. Department of Education. (1997). *To assure the free appropriate public education of all children with disabilities: Nineteenth annual report to Congress on the implementation of the Individuals with Disabilities Education Act.* Washington, DC: Author.

U.S. Department of Education. (2006). *26th annual report to Congress on the implementation of the Individuals with Disabilities Education Act, 2004.* Washington, DC: Author.

U.S. Department of Education, National Center for Education Statistics. (2007). *The Condition of Education 2007* (NCES 2007-064). Washington, DC: Author.

Usher, E. L., & Pajares, F. (2008). Sources of self-efficacy in school: Critical review of the literature and future directions. *Review of Educational Research, 78,* 751–796.

U.S. Secret Service National Threat Assessment Center, in collaboration with the U.S. Department of Education. (2000, October). *Safe school initiative: An interim report on the prevention of targeted violence in schools. Washington, DC: Author.*

Valdés, G., Bunch, G., Snow, C., & Lee, C. (with Matos, L.). (2005). Enhancing the development of students' language(s). In L. Darling-Hammond & J. Bransford (Eds.), *Preparing teachers for a changing world: What teachers should learn and be able to do* (pp. 126–168). San Francisco: Jossey-Bass/Wiley.

Valencia, S. W., Hiebert, E. H., & Afflerbach, P. P. (1994). Realizing the possibilities of authentic assessment: Current trends and future issues. In S. W. Valencia, E. H. Hiebert, & P. P. Afflerbach (Eds.), *Authentic reading assessment: Practices and possibilities.* Newark, DE: International Reading Association.

Valente, N. (2001). *"Who cares about school?" A student responds to learning.* Unpublished paper, University of New Hampshire, Durham.

Valentine, J. C., DuBois, D. L., & Cooper, H. (2004). The relation between self-beliefs and academic achievement: A meta-analytic review. *Educational Psychologist, 39,* 111–133.

Valiente, C., Lemery-Calfant, K., Swanson, J., & Reiser, M. (2008). Prediction of children's academic competence from their effortful control, relationships, and classroom participation. *Journal of Educational Psychology, 100,* 67–77.

Valkenburg, P. M., & Peter, J. (2007). Preadolescents' and adolescents' online communication and their closeness to friends. *Developmental Psychology, 43,* 267–277.

Valkenburg, P. M., Peter, J., & Schouten, A. P. (2006). Friend networking sites and their relationship to adolescents' well-being and social self-esteem. *CyberPsychology and Behavior, 9,* 584–590.

Valli, L., & Buese, D. (2007). The changing roles of teachers in an era of high-stakes accountability. *American Educational Research Journal, 44,* 519–558.

Van Camp, C. M., Lerman, D. C., Kelley, M. E., Roane, H. S., Contrucci, S. A., & Vorndran, C. M. (2000). Further analysis of idiosyncratic antecedent influences during the assessment and treatment of problem behavior. *Journal of Applied Behavior Analysis, 33,* 207–221.

van den Broek, P., Lorch, R. F., Jr., Linderholm, T., & Gustafson, M. (2001). The effects of readers' goals on inference generation and memory for texts. *Memory and Cognition, 29,* 1081–1087.

Van Dooren, W., De Bock, D., Hessels, A., Janssens, D., & Verschaffel, L. (2005). Not everything is proportional: Effects of age and problem type on propensities for overgeneralization. *Cognition and Instruction, 23,* 57–86.

van Drie, J., van Boxtel, C., & van der Linden, J. (2006). Historical reasoning in a computer-supported collaborative learning environment. In A. M. O'Donnell, C. E. Hmelo-SIlver, & G. Erkens (Eds.), *Collaborative learning, reasoning, and technology* (pp. 265–296). Mahwah, NJ: Erlbaum.

van Garderen, D. (2004). Reciprocal teaching as a comprehension strategy for understanding mathematical word problems. *Reading and Writing Quarterly, 20,* 225–229.

van Goozen, S. H. M., Fairchild, G., & Harold, G. T. (2008). The role of neurobiological deficits in childhood antisocial behavior. *Current Directions in Psychological Science, 17,* 224–228.

Van Houten, R., Nau, P., MacKenzie-Keating, S., Sameoto, D., & Colavecchia, B. (1982). An analysis of some variables influencing the effectiveness of reprimands. *Journal of Applied Behavior Analysis, 15,* 65–83.

van IJzendoorn, M. H., & Juffer, F. (2005). Adoption is a successful natural intervention enhancing adopted children's IQ and school performance. *Current Directions in Psychological Science, 14,* 326–330.

van Kraayenoord, C. E., & Paris, S. G. (1997). Australian students' self-appraisal of their work samples and academic progress. *Elementary School Journal, 97,* 523–537.

van Laar, C. (2000). The paradox of low academic achievement but high self-esteem in African American students: An attributional account. *Educational Psychology Review, 12,* 33–61.

van Merriënboer, J. J. G., Kirschner, P. A., & Kester, L. (2003). Taking the load off a learner's mind: Instructional design for complex learning. *Educational Psychologist, 38,* 5–13.

Van Meter, P. (2001). Drawing construction as a strategy for learning from text. *Journal of Educational Psychology, 93,* 129–140.

Van Meter, P., & Garner, J. (2005). The promise and practice of learner-generated drawing: Literature review and synthesis. *Educational Psychology Review, 17,* 285–325.

Van Meter, P., Yokoi, L., & Pressley, M. (1994). College students' theory of notetaking derived from their perceptions of notetaking. *Journal of Educational Psychology, 86,* 323–338.

VanSledright, B., & Brophy, J. (1992). Storytelling, imagination, and fanciful elaboration in children's historical reconstructions. *American Educational Research Journal, 29,* 837–859.

vanSledright, B., & Limón, M. (2006). Learning and teaching social studies: A review of cognitive research in history and geography. In P. A. Alexander & P. H. Winne (Eds.), *Handbook of educational psychology* (2nd ed., pp. 545–570). Mahwah, NJ: Erlbaum.

Vansteenkiste, M., Lens, W., & Deci, E. L. (2006). Intrinsic versus extrinsic goal contents in self-determination theory: Another look at the quality of academic motivation. *Educational Psychologist, 41,* 19–31.

Vansteenkiste, M., Zhou, M., Lens, W., & Soenens, B. (2005). Experiences of autonomy and control among Chinese learners: Vitalizing or immobilizing? *Journal of Educational Psychology, 97,* 468–483.

VanTassel-Baska, J. L. (Ed.). (2008). *Alternative assessments with gifted and talented students.* Waco, TX: Prufrock Press.

Varelas, M., & Pappas, C. C. (2006). Intertextuality in read-alouds of integrated science-literacy units in urban primary classrooms: Opportunities for the development of thought and language. *Cognition and Instruction, 24,* 211–259.

Varma, S., McCandliss, B. D., & Schwartz, D. L. (2008). Scientific and pragmatic challenges for bridging education and neuroscience. *Educational Researcher, 37*(3), 140–152.

Vaughn, B. J., & Horner, R. H. (1997). Identifying instructional tasks that occasion problem behaviors and assessing the effects of student versus teacher choice among these tasks. *Journal of Applied Behavior Analysis, 30,* 299–312.

Vaughn, S. (1991). Social skills enhancement in students with learning disabilities. In B. Y. L. Wong (Ed.), *Learning about learning disabilities.* San Diego, CA: Academic Press.

Veenman, S. (1984). Perceived problems of beginning teachers. *Review of Educational Research, 54,* 143–178.

Venn, J. J. (2000). *Assessing students with special needs* (2nd ed.). Upper Saddle River, NJ: Merrill/Prentice Hall.

Verdi, M. P., & Kulhavy, R. W. (2002). Learning with maps and texts: An overview. *Educational Psychology Review, 14,* 27–46.

Verdi, M. P., Kulhavy, R. W., Stock, W. A., Rittschof, K. A., & Johnson, J. T. (1996). Text learning using scientific diagrams: Implications for classroom use. *Contemporary Educational Psychology, 21,* 487–499.

Vermeer, H. J., Boekaerts, M., & Seegers, G. (2000). Motivational and gender differences: Sixth-grade students' mathematical problem-solving behavior. *Journal of Educational Psychology, 92,* 308–315.

Vintere, P., Hemmes, N. S., Brown, B. L., & Poulson, C. L. (2004). Gross-motor skill acquisition by preschool dance students under self-instruction procedures. *Journal of Applied Behavior Analysis, 37,* 305–322.

Vitaro, F., Brendgen, M., Larose, S., & Tremblay, R. E. (2005). Kindergarten disruptive behaviors, protective factors, and educational achievement by early adulthood. *Journal of Educational Psychology, 97,* 617–629.

Vitaro, F., Gendreau, P. L., Tremblay, R. E., & Oligny, P. (1998). Reactive and proactive aggression differentially predict later conduct problems. *Journal of Child Psychology and Psychiatry and Allied Disciplines, 39,* 377–385.

Volet, S. (1999). Learning across cultures: Appropriateness of knowledge transfer. *International Journal of Educational Research, 31,* 625–643.

Vollmer, T. R., & Hackenberg, T. D. (2001). Reinforcement contingencies and social reinforcement: Some reciprocal relations between basic and applied research. *Journal of Applied Behavior Analysis, 34,* 241–253.

Vosniadou, S. (1994). Universal and culture-specific properties of children's mental models of the earth. In L. A. Hirschfeld & S. A. Gelman (Eds.), *Mapping the mind: Domain specificity in cognition and culture.* Cambridge, England: Cambridge University Press.

Vosniadou, S. (2003). Exploring the relationships between conceptual change and intentional learning. In G. M. Sinatra & P. R. Pintrich (Eds.), *Intentional conceptual change* (pp. 377–406). Mahwah, NJ: Erlbaum.

Voss, J. F. (1987). Learning and transfer in subject-matter learning: A problem-solving model. *International Journal of Educational Research, 11,* 607–622.

Vucko, S., & Hadwin, A. (2004, April). *Going beyond* I like it *in a portfolio context: Scaffolding the development of six grade-two students' reflections.* Paper presented at the American Educational Research Association, San Diego, CA.

Vye, N. J., Schwartz, D. L., Bransford, J. D., Barron, B. J., Zech, L., & The Cognition and Technology Group at Vanderbilt. (1998). SMART environments that support monitoring, reflection, and revision. In D. J. Hacker, J. Dunlosky, & A. C. Graesser (Eds.), *Metacognition in educational theory and practice* (pp. 305–346). Mahwah, NJ: Erlbaum.

Vygotsky, L. S. (1978). *Mind in society: The development of higher psychological processes.* Cambridge, MA: Harvard University Press.

Vygotsky, L. S. (1986). *Thought and language* (rev. ed; A. Kozulin, Ed. and Trans.). Cambridge, MA: MIT Press. (Original work published 1934)

Vygotsky, L. S. (1987). *The collected works of L. S. Vygotsky* (Vol. 3; R. W. Rieber & A. S. Carton, Eds.). New York: Plenum Press.

Vygotsky, L. S. (1997). *Educational psychology* (R. Silverman, Trans.). Boca Raton, FL: St. Lucie Press.

Wade, S. E. (1992). How interest affects learning from text. In K. A. Renninger, S. Hidi, & A. Krapp (Eds.), *The role of interest in learning and development.* Mahwah, NJ: Erlbaum.

Wade-Stein, D., & Kintsch, E. (2004). Summary Street: Interactive computer support for writing. *Cognition and Instruction, 22,* 333–362.

Wagner, R. K. (1996). From simple structure to complex function: Major trends in the development of theories, models, and measurements of memory. In G. R. Lyon & N. A. Krasnegor (Eds.), *Attention, memory, and executive function* (pp. 139–156). Baltimore: Brookes.

Wainryb, C., Brehl, B. A., & Matwin, S. (2005). Being hurt and hurting others: Children's narrative accounts and moral judgments of their own interpersonal conflicts. *Monographs of the Society for Research in Child Development, 70* (3; Serial No. 281).

Walker, E. F. (2002). Adolescent neurodevelopment and psychopathology. *Current Directions in Psychological Science, 11,* 24–28.

Walker, E. N. (2006). Urban high school students' academic communities and their effects on mathematics success. *American Educational Research Journal, 43,* 43–73.

Walker, H. M., Horner, R. H., Sugai, G., Bullis, M., Sprague, J. R., Bricker, D., & Kaufman, M. J. (1996). Integrated approaches to preventing antisocial behavior patterns among school-age children and youth. *Journal of Emotional and Behavioral Disorders, 4,* 194–209.

Walker, J. M. T. (2001, April). *A cross-sectional study of student motivation, strategy knowledge and strategy use during homework: Implications for research on self-regulated learning.* Paper presented at the annual meeting of the American Educational Research Association, Seattle, WA.

Walker, J. M. T., & Hoover-Dempsey, K. V. (2006). Why research on parental involvement is important to classroom management. In C. M. Evertson & C. S. Weinstein (Eds.), *Handbook of classroom management: Research, practice, and contemporary issues* (pp. 665–684). Mahwah, NJ: Erlbaum.

Walker, L. J. (1991). Sex differences in moral reasoning. In W. M. Kurtines & J. L. Gewirtz (Eds.), *Handbook of moral behavior and development: Vol. 2. Research* (pp. 333–364). Mahwah, NJ: Erlbaum.

Walker, L. J. (1995). Sexism in Kohlberg's moral psychology? In W. M. Kurtines & J. L. Gewirtz (Eds.), *Moral development: An introduction.* Boston: Allyn & Bacon.

Walls, T. A., & Little, T. D. (2005). Relations among personal agency, motivation, and school adjustment in early adolescence. *Journal of Educational Psychology, 97,* 23–31.

Walshaw, M., & Anthony, G. (2008). The teacher's role in classroom discourse: A review of recent research into mathematics classrooms. *Review of Educational Research, 78,* 516–551.

Wang, J., & Lin, E. (2005). Comparative studies on U.S. and Chinese mathematics learning and the implications for standards-based mathematics teaching reform. *Educational Researcher, 34*(5), 3–13.

Wang, Q. (2006). Culture and the development of self-knowledge. *Current Directions in Psychological Science, 15,* 182–187.

Wang, Q., & Ross, M. (2007). Culture and memory. In S. Kitayama & D. Cohen (Eds.), *Handbook of cultural psychology* (pp. 645–667). New York: Guilford Press.

Want, S. C., & Harris, P. L. (2001). Learning from other people's mistakes: Causal understanding in learning to use a tool. *Child Development, 72,* 431–443.

Warren, G. (1979). Essay versus multiple-choice tests. *Journal of Research in Science Teaching, 16,* 563–567.

Warren, J. R., & Halpern-Manners, A. (2007). Is the glass emptying or filling up? Reconciling divergent trends in high school completion and dropout. *Educational Researcher, 36,* 335–343.

Warren, J. S., Bohanon-Edmonson, H. M., Turnbull, A. P., Sailor, W., Wickham, D., Griggs, P., et al. (2006). School-wide positive behavior support: Addressing behavior problems that impeded student learning. *Educational Psychology Review, 18,* 187–198.

Warren, R. L. (1988). Cooperation and conflict between parents and teachers: A comparative study of three elementary schools. In H. T. Trueba & C. Delgado-Gaitan (Eds.), *School and society: Learning content through culture.* New York: Praeger.

Wasik, B. A., Karweit, N., Burns, L., & Brodsky, E. (1998, April). *Once upon a time: The role of rereading and retelling in storybook reading.* Paper presented at the annual meeting of the American Educational Research Association, San Diego, CA.

Wasley, P. A., Hampel, R. L., & Clark, R. W. (1997). *Kids and school reform.* San Francisco: Jossey-Bass.

Waterhouse, L. (2006). Multiple intelligences, the Mozart effect, and emotional intelligence: A critical review. *Educational Psychologist, 41,* 207–225.

Waters, H. S. (1982). Memory development in adolescence: Relationships between metamemory, strategy use, and performance. *Journal of Experimental Child Psychology, 33,* 183–195.

Watson, J. B., & Rayner, R. (1920). Conditioned emotional reactions. *Journal of Experimental Psychology, 3,* 1–14.

Watson, M. (2008). Developmental discipline and moral education. In L. Nucci & D. Narvaez (Eds.), *Handbook of moral and character education* (pp. 175–203). New York: Routledge.

Watson, M., & Battistich, V. (2006). Building and sustaining caring communities. In C. M. Evertson & C. S. Weinstein (Eds.), *Handbook of classroom management: Research, practice, and contemporary issues* (pp. 253–279). Mahwah, NJ: Erlbaum.

Watson, M. W., Andreas, J. B., Fischer, K. W., & Smith, K. (2005). Patterns of risk factors leading to victimization and aggression in children and adolescents. In K. A. Kendall-Tackett & S. M. Giacomoni (Eds.), *Child Victimization: Maltreatment, bulling and dating violence, prevention and intervention.* Kingston, NJ: Civic Research Institute.

Way, N. (1998). *Everyday courage: The lives and stories of urban teenagers.* New York: New York University Press.

Weatherford, J. (1988). *Indian givers: How the Indians of the Americas transformed the world.* New York: Crown.

Weaver, C. A., III, & Kelemen, W. L. (1997). Judgments of learning at delays: Shifts in response patterns or increased metamemory accuracy? *Psychological Science, 8,* 318–321.

Webb, N. M. (1989). Peer interaction and learning in small groups. *International Journal of Educational Research, 13,* 21–39.

Webb, N. M., & Farivar, S. (1994). Promoting helping behavior in cooperative small groups in middle school mathematics. *American Educational Research Journal, 31,* 369–395.

Webb, N. M., & Farivar, S. (1999). Developing productive group interaction in middle school mathematics. In A. M. O'Donnell & A. King (Eds.), *Cognitive perspectives on peer learning* (pp. 117–149). Mahwah, NJ: Erlbaum.

Webb, N. M., Franke, M. L., Ing, M., Chan, A., De, T., Freund, D., et al. (2008). The role of teacher instructional practices in student collaboration. *Contemporary Educational Psychology, 33,* 360–381.

Webb, N. M., & Mastergeorge, A. M. (2003). The development of students' helping behavior and learning in peer-directed small groups. *Cognition and Instruction, 21,* 361–428.

Webb, N. M., Nemer, K. M., Chizhik, A. W., & Sugrue, B. (1998). Equity issues in collaborative group assessment: Group composition and performance. *American Educational Research Journal, 35,* 607–651.

Webb, N. M., Nemer, K. M., & Zuniga, S. (2002). Short circuits or superconductors? Effects of group composition on high-achieving students' science assessment performance. *American Educational Research Journal, 39,* 943–989.

Webb, N. M., & Palincsar, A. S. (1996). Group processes in the classroom. In D. C. Berliner & R. C. Calfee (Eds.), *Handbook of educational psychology.* New York: Macmillan.

Webber, J., & Plotts, C. A. (2008). *Emotional and behavioral disorders: Theory and practice* (5th ed.). Boston: Allyn & Bacon.

Webber, J., Scheuermann, B., McCall, C., & Coleman, M. (1993). Research on self-monitoring as a behavior management technique in special education classrooms: A descriptive review. *Remedial and Special Education, 14*(2), 38–56.

Wehmeyer, M. L., Agran, M., Hughes, C., Martin, J., Mithaug, D. E., & Palmer, S. (2007). *Promoting self-determination in students with intellectual and developmental disabilities.* New York: Guilford.

Weichold, K., Silbereisen, R. K., & Schmitt-Rodermund, E. (2003). Short-term and long-term consequences of early versus late physical maturation in adolescents. In C. Hayward (Ed.), *Gender differences at puberty* (pp. 241–276). Cambridge, England: Cambridge University Press.

Weiner, B. (1984). Principles for a theory of student motivation and their application within an attributional framework. In R. Ames & C. Ames (Eds.), *Research on motivation in education: Vol. 1. Student motivation.* San Diego, CA: Academic Press.

Weiner, B. (1986). *An attributional theory of motivation and emotion.* New York: Springer-Verlag.

Weiner, B. (2000). Intrapersonal and interpersonal theories of motivation from an attributional perspective. *Educational Psychology Review, 12,* 1–14.

Weiner, B. (2004). Attribution theory revisited: Transforming cultural plurality into theoretical unity. In D. M. McInerney & S. Van Etten (Eds.), *Big theories revisited* (pp. 13–29). Greenwich, CT: Information Age.

Weiner, B. (2005). Motivation from an attribution perspective and the social psychology of perceived competence. In A. J. Elliot & C. S. Dweck (Eds.), *Handbook of competence and motivation* (pp. 73–84). New York: Guilford Press.

Weinert, F. E., & Helmke, A. (1995). Learning from wise Mother Nature or Big Brother Instructor: The wrong choice as seen from an educational perspective. *Educational Psychologist, 30,* 135–142.

Weinstein, C. E., Goetz, E. T., & Alexander, P. A. (Eds.). (1988). *Learning and study strategies: Issues in assessment, instruction, and evaluation.* San Diego, CA: Academic Press.

Weinstein, C. E., Hagen, A. S., & Meyer, D. K. (1991, April). *Work smart . . . not hard: The effects of combining instruction in using strategies, goal using, and executive control on attributions and academic performance*. Paper presented at the annual meeting of the American Educational Research Association, Chicago.

Weinstein, C. E., & Hume, L. M. (1998). *Study strategies for lifelong learning*. Washington, DC: American Psychological Association.

Weinstein, R. S. (1993). Children's knowledge of differential treatment in school: Implications for motivation. In T. M. Tomlinson (Ed.), *Motivating students to learn: Overcoming barriers to high achievement*. Berkeley, CA: McCutchan.

Weinstein, R. S., Madison, S. M., & Kuklinski, M. R. (1995). Raising expectations in schooling: Obstacles and opportunities for change. *American Educational Research Journal, 32*, 121–159.

Weisberg, R. W. (1993). *Creativity: Beyond the myth of genius*. New York: Freeman.

Weisgram, E. S., & Bigler, R. S. (2007). Effects of learning about gender discrimination on adolescents girls' attitudes toward and interest in science. *Psychology of Women Quarterly, 31*, 262–269.

Weiss, L. H., & Schwarz, J. C. (1996). The relationship between parenting types and older adolescents' personality, academic achievement, adjustment, and substance use. *Child Development, 67*, 2101–2114.

Weiss, M. R., & Klint, K. A. (1987). "Show and tell" in the gymnasium: An investigation of developmental differences in modeling and verbal rehearsal of motor skills. *Research Quarterly for Exercise and Sport, 58*, 234–241.

Weissberg, R. P. (1985). Designing effective social problem-solving programs for the classroom. In B. H. Schneider, K. H. Rubin, & J. E. Ledingham (Eds.), *Children's peer relations: Issues in assessment and intervention*. New York: Springer-Verlag.

Welch, G. J. (1985). Contingency contracting with a delinquent and his family. *Journal of Behavior Therapy and Experimental Psychiatry, 16*, 253–259.

Wellman, H. M. (1985). The child's theory of mind: The development of conceptions of cognition. In S. R. Yussen (Ed.), *The growth of reflection in children*. San Diego, CA: Academic Press.

Wellman, H. M. (1990). *The child's theory of mind*. Cambridge, MA: MIT Press.

Wellman, H. M., Cross, D., & Watson, J. (2001). Meta-analysis of theory-of-mind development: The truth about false belief. *Child Development, 72*, 655–684.

Wellman, H. M., & Gelman, S. A. (1998). Acquisition of knowledge. In W. Damon (Series Ed.), D. Kuhn, & R. S. Siegler (Vol. Eds.), *Handbook of child psychology: Vol. 2. Cognition, perception, and language* (5th ed.). New York: Wiley.

Wellman, H. M., Phillips, A. T., & Rodriguez, T. (2000). Young children's understanding of perception, desire, and emotion. *Child Development, 71*, 895–912.

Wenke, D., & Frensch, P. A. (2003). Is success or failure at solving complex problems related to intellectual ability? In J. E. Davidson & R. J. Sternberg (Eds.), *The psychology of problem solving* (pp. 87–126). Cambridge, England: Cambridge University Press.

Wentzel, K. R. (1999). Social-motivational processes and interpersonal relationships: Implications for understanding motivation at school. *Journal of Educational Psychology, 91*, 76–97.

Wentzel, K. R., & Asher, S. R. (1995). The academic lives of neglected, rejected, popular, and controversial children. *Child Development, 66*, 754–763.

Wentzel, K. R., Barry, C. M., & Caldwell, K. A. (2004). Friendships in middle school: Influences on motivation and school adjustment. *Journal of Educational Psychology, 96*, 195–203.

Wentzel, K. R., Filisetti, L., & Looney, L. (2007). Adolescent prosocial behavior: The role of self-processes and contextual cues. *Child Development, 78*, 895–910.

Wentzel, K. R., & Looney, L. (2007). Socialization in school settings. In J. E. Grusec & P. D. Hastings (Eds.), *Handbook of socialization: Theory and research* (pp. 382–403). New York: Guilford Press.

Wentzel, K. R., & Wigfield, A. (1998). Academic and social motivational influences on students' academic performance. *Educational Psychology Review, 10*, 155–175.

Werner, E. E. (1995). Resilience in development. *Current Directions in Psychological Science, 4*, 81–85.

Werner, E. E. (2006). What can we learn about resilience from large-scale longitudinal studies? In S. Goldstein & R. B. Brooks (Eds.), *Handbook of resilience in children* (pp. 91–105). New York: Springer.

Werner, E. E., & Smith, R. S. (2001). *Journeys from childhood to midlife: Risk, resilience, and recovery*. Ithaca, NY: Cornell University Press.

Wertsch, J. V. (1984). The zone of proximal development: Some conceptual issues. *Children's learning in the zone of proximal development: New directions for child development* (No. 23). San Francisco: Jossey-Bass.

West, R. F., Toplak, M. E., & Stanovich, K. E. (2008). Heuristics and biases as measures of critical thinking: Associations with cognitive ability and thinking dispositions. *Journal of Educational Psychology, 100*, 930–941.

Wheeler, L., & Suls, J. (2005). Social comparison and self-evaluations of competence. In A. J. Elliot & C. S. Dweck (Eds.), *Handbook of competence and motivation* (pp. 566–578). New York: Guilford Press.

Whitaker Sena, J. D., Lowe, P. A., & Lee, S. W. (2007). Significant predictors of test anxiety among students with and without learning disabilities. *Journal of Learning Disabilities, 40*, 360–376.

White, A. G., & Bailey, J. S. (1990). Reducing disruptive behaviors of elementary physical education students with sit and watch. *Journal of Applied Behavior Analysis, 23*, 353–359.

White, B. Y., & Frederiksen, J. R. (1998). Inquiry, modeling, and metacognition: Making science accessible to all students. *Cognition and Instruction, 16*, 3–118.

White, B. Y., & Frederiksen, J. R. (2005). A theoretical framework and approach for fostering metacognitive development. *Educational Psychologist, 40*, 211–223.

White, J. J., & Rumsey, S. (1994). Teaching for understanding in a third-grade geography lesson. In J. Brophy (Ed.), *Advances in research on teaching: Vol. 4. Case studies of teaching and learning in social studies*. Greenwich, CT: JAI Press.

White, R. (1959). Motivation reconsidered: The concept of competence. *Psychological Review, 66*, 297–333.

White, R., & Cunningham, A. M. (1991). *Ryan White: My own story*. New York: Signet.

Whitesell, N. R., Mitchell, C. M., Kaufman, C. E., Spicer, P., & the Voices of Indian Teens Project Team. (2006). Developmental trajectories of personal and collective self-concept among American Indian adolescents. *Child Development, 77*, 1487–1503.

Whitley, B. E., Jr., & Frieze, I. H. (1985). Children's causal attributions for success and failure in achievement settings: A meta-analysis. *Journal of Educational Psychology, 77*, 608–616.

Wideen, M., Mayer-Smith, J., & Moon, B. (1998). A critical analysis of the research on learning to teach: Making the case for an ecological perspective on inquiry. *Review of Educational Research, 68*, 130–178.

Wigfield, A. (1994). Expectancy-value theory of achievement motivation: A developmental perspective. *Educational Psychology Review, 6*, 49–78.

Wigfield, A., Byrnes, J. P., & Eccles, J. S. (2006). Development during early and middle adolescence. In P. A. Alexander & P. H. Winne (Eds.), *Handbook of educational psychology* (2nd ed., pp. 87–113). Mahwah, NJ: Erlbaum.

Wigfield, A., & Eccles, J. (1992). The development of achievement task values: A theoretical analysis. *Developmental Review, 12*, 265–310.

Wigfield, A., & Eccles, J. (2000). Expectancy-value theory of achievement motivation. *Contemporary Educational Psychology, 25*, 68–81.

Wigfield, A., Eccles, J. S., Mac Iver, D., Reuman, D., & Midgley, C. (1991). Transitions at early adolescence: Changes in children's domain-specific self-perceptions and general self-esteem across the transition to junior high school. *Developmental Psychology, 27*, 552–565.

Wigfield, A., Eccles, J. S., & Pintrich, P. R. (1996). Development between the ages of 11 and 25. In D. C. Berliner & R. C. Calfee (Eds.), *Handbook of educational psychology*. New York: Macmillan.

Wigfield, A., & Meece, J. L. (1988). Math anxiety in elementary and secondary school students. *Journal of Educational Psychology, 80*, 210–216.

Wigfield, A., Tonks, S., & Eccles, J. S. (2004). Expectancy value theory in cross-cultural perspective. In D. M. McInerney & S. Van Etten (Eds.), *Big theories revisited* (pp. 165–198). Greenwich, CT: Information Age.

Wigfield, A., & Wagner, A. L. (2005). Competence, motivation, and identity development during adolescence. In A. J. Elliot & C. S. Dweck (Eds.), *Handbook of competence and motivation* (pp. 222–239). New York: Guilford Press.

Wiggins, G. (1992). Creating tests worth taking. *Educational Leadership, 49*(8), 26–33.

Wiggins, G., & McTighe, J. (2005). *Understanding by Design* (2nd ed.). Alexandria, VA: Association for Supervision and Curriculum Development.

Wilder, A. A., & Williams, J. P. (2001). Students with severe learning disabilities can learn higher order comprehension skills. *Journal of Educational Psychology, 93*, 268–278.

Wiles, J., & Bondi, J. (2001). *The new American middle school: Educating preadolescents in an era of change*. Upper Saddle River, NJ: Merrill/Prentice Hall.

Wiley, D. E., & Haertel, E. H. (1996). Extended assessment tasks: Purposes, definitions, scoring, and accuracy. In M. B. Kane & R. Mitchell (Eds.), *Implementing performance assessment: Promises, problems, and challenges* (pp. 61–89). Mahwah, NJ: Erlbaum.

Wiley, J., & Bailey, J. (2006). Effects of collaboration and argumentation on learning from Web pages. In A. M. O'Donnell, C. E. Hmelo-Silver, & G. Erkens (Eds.), *Collaborative learning, reasoning, and technology* (pp. 297–321). Mahwah, NJ: Erlbaum.

Will, M. C. (1986). Educating children with learning problems: A shared responsibility. *Exceptional Children, 52*, 411–415.

Willard, N. E. (2007). *Cyberbullying and cyberthreats: Responding to the challenge of online social aggression, threats, and distress*. Champaign, IL: Research Press.

Williams, B., & Woods, M. (1997). Building on urban learners' experiences. *Educational Leadership, 51*(8), 29–32.

Williams, D. (1996). *Autism: An inside-outside approach*. London: Jessica Kingsley.

Williams, J. P. (1991). Comprehension by learning-disabled and nondisabled adolescents of personal/social problems presented in text. *American Journal of Psychology, 104*, 563–586.

Williams, K. M. (2001a). "Frontin' it": Schooling, violence, and relationships in the 'hood. In J. N. Burstyn, G. Bender, R. Casella, H. W. Gordon, D. P. Guerra, K. V. Luschen, R. Stevens, & K. M. Williams, *Preventing violence in schools: A challenge to American democracy* (pp. 95–108). Mahwah, NJ: Erlbaum.

Williams, K. M. (2001b). What derails peer mediation?. In J. N. Burstyn, G. Bender, R. Casella, H. W. Gordon, D. P. Guerra, K. V. Luschen, R. Stevens, & K. M. Williams, *Preventing violence in schools: A challenge to American democracy* (pp. 199–208). Mahwah, NJ: Erlbaum.

Willingham, D. B. (1999). The neural basis of motor-skill learning. *Current Directions in Psychological Science, 8*, 178–182.

Willingham, D. B., & Goedert-Eschmann, K. (1999). The relation between implicit and explicit learning: Evidence for parallel development. *Psychological Science, 10*, 531–534.

Willingham, D. T. (2004). *Cognition: The thinking animal* (2nd ed.). Upper Saddle River, NJ: Prentice Hall.

Wilson, B. L., & Corbett, H. D. (2001). *Listening to urban kids: School reform and the teachers they want*. Albany: State University of New York Press.

Wilson, C. C., Piazza, C. C., & Nagle, R. (1990). Investigation of the effect of consistent and inconsistent behavioral examples upon children's donation behaviors. *Journal of Genetic Psychology, 151*, 361–376.

Wilson, M. (1989). Child development in the context of the black extended family. *American Psychologist, 44*, 380–383.

Wilson, P. T., & Anderson, R. C. (1986). What they don't know will hurt them: The role of prior knowledge in comprehension. In J. Orasanu (Ed.), *Reading comprehension: From research to practice*. Mahwah, NJ: Erlbaum.

Wilson, T. D., & Gilbert, D. T. (2008). Explaining away: A model of affective adaptation. *Perspectives on Psychological Science, 3*, 370–386.

Wimmer, H., & Perner, J. (1983). Beliefs about beliefs: Representation and constraining function of wrong beliefs in young children's understanding of deception. *Cognition, 13*, 103–128.

Windschitl, M. (2002). Framing constructivism in practice as the negotiation of dilemmas: An analysis of the conceptual, pedagogical, cultural, and political challenges facing teachers. *Review of Educational Research, 72*, 131–175.

Wine, J. D. (1980). Cognitive-attentional theory of test anxiety. In I. G. Sarason (Ed.), *Test anxiety: Theory, research, and applications*. Mahwah, NJ: Erlbaum.

Wingfield, A., & Byrnes, D. L. (1981). *The psychology of human memory*. San Diego, CA: Academic Press.

Winn, W. (1991). Learning from maps and diagrams. *Educational Psychology Review, 3*, 211–247.

Winn, W. (2002). Current trends in educational technology research: The study of learning environments. *Educational Psychology Review, 14*, 331–351.

Winne, P. H. (1995). Inherent details in self-regulated learning. *Educational Psychologist, 30*, 173–187.

Winne, P. H., & Hadwin, A. F. (1998). Studying as self-regulated learning. In D. J. Hacker, J. Dunlosky, & A. C. Graesser (Eds.), *Metacognition in educational theory and practice* (pp. 277–304). Mahwah, NJ: Erlbaum.

Winne, P. H., & Marx, R. W. (1989). A cognitive-processing analysis of motivation with classroom tasks. In C. Ames & R. Ames (Eds.), *Research on motivation in education* (Vol. 3). San Diego, CA: Academic Press.

Winner, E. (1988). *The point of words*. Cambridge, MA: Harvard University Press.

Winner, E. (1996). The rage to master: The decisive role of talent in the visual arts. In K. A. Ericsson (Ed.), *The road to excellence: The acquisition of expert performance in the arts and sciences, sports, and games* (pp. 271–302). Mahwah, NJ: Erlbaum.

Winner, E. (1997). Exceptionally high intelligence and schooling. *American Psychologist, 52*, 1070–1081.

Winner, E. (2000a). Giftedness: Current theory and research. *Current Directions in Psychological Science, 9*, 153–156.

Winner, E. (2000b). The origins and ends of giftedness. *American Psychologist, 55*, 159–169.

Winsler, A., Díaz, R. M., Espinosa, L., & Rodriguez, J. L. (1999). When learning a second language does not mean losing the first: Bilingual language development in low-income, Spanish-speaking children attending bilingual preschool. *Child Development, 70*, 349–362.

Winsler, A., & Naglieri, J. (2003). Overt and covert verbal problem-solving strategies: Developmental trends in use, awareness, and relations with task performance in children aged 5 to 17. *Child Development, 74*, 659–678.

Wise, B. W., & Olson, R. K. (1998). Studies of computer-aided remediation for reading disabilities. In C. Hulme & R. M. Joshi (Eds.), *Reading and spelling: Development and disorders*. Mahwah, NJ: Erlbaum.

Wisner Fries, A. B., & Pollak, S. D. (2007). Emotion processing and the developing brain. In D. Coch, K. W. Fischer, & G. Dawson (Eds.), *Human behavior, learning, and the developing brain: Typical development* (pp. 329–361). New York: Guilford Press.

Witmer, S. (1996). Making peace, the Navajo way. *Tribal College Journal, 8*, 24–27.

Wittmer, D. S., & Honig, A. S. (1994). Encouraging positive social development in young children. *Young Children, 49*(5), 4–12.

Wittwer, J., & Renkl, A. (2008). Why instructional explanations often do not work: A framework for understanding the effectiveness of instructional explanations. *Educational Psychologist, 43*, 49–64.

Wixson, K. K. (1984). Level of importance of post-questions and children's learning from text. *American Educational Research Journal, 21*, 419–433.

Wixted, J. T. (2005). A theory about why we forget what we once knew. *Current Directions in Psychological Science, 14*, 6–9.

Wlodkowski, R. J. (1978). *Motivation and teaching: A practical guide*. Washington, DC: National Education Association.

Wlodkowski, R. J., & Ginsberg, M. B. (1995). *Diversity and motivation: Culturally responsive teaching*. San Francisco: Jossey-Bass.

Wodtke, K. H., Harper, F., & Schommer, M. (1989). How standardized is school testing? An exploratory observational study of standardized group testing in kindergarten. *Educational Evaluation and Policy Analysis, 11*, 223–235.

Wolfram, W., & Schilling-Estes, N. (2006). *American English: Dialects and variation* (2nd ed.). Malden, MA: Blackwell.

Wolpe, J., & Plaud, J. J. (1997). Pavlov's contributions to behavior therapy: The obvious and the not so obvious. *American Psychologist, 52*, 966–972.

Wolters, C. A. (1998). Self-regulated learning and college students' regulation of motivation. *Journal of Educational Psychology, 90*, 224–235.

Wolters, C. A. (2003). Regulation of motivation: Evaluating an underemphasized aspect of self-regulated learning. *Educational Psychologist, 38*, 189–205.

Wolters, C. A. (2004). Advancing achievement goal theory: Using goal structures and goal orientations to predict students' motivation, cognition, and achievement. *Journal of Educational Psychology, 96*, 236–250.

Wolters, C. A., & Rosenthal, H. (2000). The relation between students' motivational beliefs and their use of motivational regulation strategies. *International Journal of Educational Research, 33*, 801–820.

Wong, B. Y. L. (1985). Self-questioning instructional research: A review. *Review of Educational Research, 55*, 227–268.

Wong, B. Y. L. (Ed.). (1991a). *Learning about learning disabilities*. San Diego, CA: Academic Press.

Wong, B. Y. L. (1991b). The relevance of metacognition to learning disabilities. In B. Y. L. Wong (Ed.), *Learning about learning disabilities*. San Diego, CA: Academic Press.

Wong, B. Y. L., Hoskyn, M., Jai, D., Ellis, P., & Watson, K. (2008). The comparative efficacy of two approaches to teaching sixth graders opinion essay writing. *Contemporary Educational Psychology, 33*, 757–784.

Wood, D., Bruner, J. S., & Ross, G. (1976). The role of tutoring in problem-solving. *Journal of Child Psychology and Psychiatry, 17*, 89–100.

Wood, D., Wood, H., Ainsworth, S., & O'Malley, C. (1995). On becoming a tutor: Toward an ontogenetic model. *Cognition and Instruction, 13*, 565–581.

Wood, E., Willoughby, T., Bolger, A., & Younger, J. (1993). Effectiveness of elaboration strategies for grade school children as a function of academic achievement. *Journal of Experimental Child Psychology, 56*, 240–253.

Wood, E., Willoughby, T., McDermott, C., Motz, M., Kaspar, V., & Ducharme, M. J. (1999). Developmental differences in study behavior. *Journal of Educational Psychology, 91*, 527–536.

Wood, J. W. (1998). *Adapting instruction to accommodate students in inclusive settings* (3rd ed.). Upper Saddle River, NJ: Merrill/Prentice Hall.

Wood, J. W., & Rosbe, M. (1985). Adapting the classroom lecture for the mainstreamed student in the secondary schools. *Clearing House, 58*, 354–358.

Woolfe, T., Want, S. C., & Siegal, M. (2002). Signposts to development: Theory of mind in deaf children. *Child Development, 73*, 768–778.

Woolfolk, A. E., & Brooks, D. M. (1985). The influence of teachers' nonverbal behaviors on students' perceptions and performances. *Elementary School Journal, 85*, 513–528.

Woolfolk Hoy, A., Davis, H., & Pape, S. J. (2006). Teacher knowledge and beliefs. In P. A. Alexander & P. H. Winne (Eds.), *Handbook of educational psychology* (2nd ed., pp. 715–737). Mahwah, NJ: Erlbaum.

Woolfolk Hoy, A., & Weinstein, C. S. (2006). Student and teacher perspectives on classroom management. In C. M. Evertson & C. S. Weinstein (Eds.), *Handbook of classroom management: Research, practice, and contemporary issues* (pp. 181–219). Mahwah, NJ: Erlbaum.

Woolley, J. D. (1995). The fictional mind: Young children's understanding of pretense, imagination, and dreams. *Developmental Review, 15*, 172–211.

Worthen, B. R., & Leopold, G. D. (1992). Impediments to implementing alternative assessment: Some emerging issues. *New Directions for Education Reform, 1*(2), 1–20.

Wright, M. O., & Masten, A. S. (2006). Resilience processes in development: Fostering positive adaptation in the context of adversity. In. S. Goldstein & R. B. Brooks (Eds.), *Handbook of resilience in children* (pp. 17–37). New York: Springer.

Wright, S. C., Taylor, D. M., & Macarthur, J. (2000). Subtractive bilingualism and the survival of the Inuit language: Heritage- versus second-language education. *Journal of Educational Psychology, 92*, 63–84.

Wright, W. E. (2006). A Catch-22 for language learners. *Educational Leadership, 64*(3), 22–27.

Wynne, E. A. (1990). Improving pupil discipline and character. In O. C. Moles (Ed.), *Student discipline strategies: Research and practice*. Albany: State University of New York Press.

Xu, J. (2008). Models of secondary school students' interest in homework: A multilevel analysis. *American Educational Research Journal, 45*, 1180–1205.

Yaden, D. B., Jr., & Templeton, S. (Eds.). (1986). *Metalinguistic awareness and beginning literacy: Conceptualizing what it means to read and write*. Portsmouth, NH: Heinemann.

Yates, M., & Youniss, J. (1996). A developmental perspective on community service in adolescence. *Social Development, 5*, 85–111.

Yau, J., & Smetana, J. G. (2003). Conceptions of moral, social-conventional, and personal events among Chinese preschoolers in Hong Kong. *Child Development, 74*, 647–658.

Yell, M. L., Robinson, T. R., & Drasgow, E. (2001). Cognitive behavior modification. In T. J. Zirpoli & K. J. Melloy, *Behavior management: Applications for teachers* (3rd ed., pp. 200–246). Upper Saddle River, NJ: Merrill/Prentice Hall.

Yeo, R. A., Gangestad, S. W., & Thoma, R. J. (2007). Developmental instability and individual variation in brain development: Implications for the origin of neurodevelopmental disorders. *Current Directions in Psychological Science, 16*, 245–249.

Yerkes, R. M., & Dodson, J. D. (1908). The relation of strength of stimulus to rapidity of habit-formation. *Journal of Comparative Neurology of Psychology, 18*, 459–482.

Yeung, R. S., & Leadbeater, B. J. (2007, March). *Peer victimization and emotional and behavioral problems in adolescence: The moderating effect of adult emotional support*. Paper presented at the biennial meeting of the Society for Research in Child Development, Boston.

Yip, T., & Fuligni, A. J. (2002). Daily variation in ethnic identity, ethnic behaviors, and psychological well-being among American adolescents of Chinese descent. *Child Development, 73*, 1557–1572.

Youniss, J., & Yates, M. (1999). Youth service and

moral-civic identity: A case for everyday morality. *Educational Psychology Review, 11*, 361–376.

Yu, S. L., Elder, A. D., & Urdan, T. C. (1995, April). *Motivation and cognitive strategies in students with a "good student" or "poor student" self-schema*. Paper presented at the annual meeting of the American Educational Research Association, San Francisco.

Yuker, H. E. (Ed.). (1988). *Attitudes toward persons with disabilities*. New York: Springer.

Zahn-Waxler, C., Friedman, R. J., Cole, P. M., Mizuta, I., & Hiruma, N. (1996). Japanese and United States preschool children's responses to conflict and distress. *Child Development, 67*, 2462–2477.

Zahn-Waxler, C., Radke-Yarrow, M., Wagner, E., & Chapman, M. (1992). Development of concern for others. *Developmental Psychology, 28*, 126–136.

Zahn-Waxler, C., & Robinson, J. (1995). Empathy and guilt: Early origins of feelings of responsibility. In J. P. Tangney & K. W. Fischer (Eds.), *Self-conscious emotions: The psychology of shame, guilt, embarrassment, and pride* (pp. 143–173). New York: Guilford Press.

Zahorik, J. A. (1994, April). *Making things interesting*. Paper presented at the annual meeting of the American Educational Research Association, New Orleans, LA.

Zajonc, R. B. (1980). Feeling and thinking: Preferences need no inferences. *American Psychologist, 35*, 151–175.

Zambo, D., & Brem, S. K. (2004). Emotion and cognition in students who struggle to read: New insights and ideas. *Reading Psychology, 25*, 1–16.

Zambo, D., & Brozo, W. G. (2009). *Bright beginnings for boys: Engaging young boys in active literacy*. Newark, DE: International Reading Association.

Zaragoza, J. M., & Fraser, B. J. (2008, March). Learning environments and attitudes among elementary-school students in traditional environmental science and field-study classrooms. Paper presented at the annual meeting of the American Educational Research Association, New York.

Zeelenberg, R., Wagenmakers, E.-J., & Rotteveel, M. (2006). The impact of emotion on perception: Bias or enhanced processing? *Psychological Science, 17*, 287–291.

Zeidner, M. (1998). *Test anxiety: The state of the art*. New York: Plenum Press.

Zeidner, M., & Matthews, G. (2005). Evaluation anxiety: Current theory and research. In A. J. Elliot & C. S. Dweck (Eds.), *Handbook of competence and motivation* (pp. 141–163). New York: Guilford Press.

Zeldin, A. L., & Pajares, F. (2000). Against the odds: Self-efficacy beliefs of women in mathematical, scientific, and technological careers. *American Educational Research Journal, 37*, 215–246.

Zelli, A., Dodge, K. A., Lochman, J. E., & Laird, R. D. (1999). The distinction between beliefs legitimizing aggression and deviant processing of social cues: Testing measurement validity and the hypothesis that biassed processing mediates the effects of beliefs on aggression. *Journal of Personality and Social Psychology, 77*, 150–166.

Zhang, L.-F., & Sternberg, R. J. (2006). *The nature of intellectual styles*. Mahwah, NJ: Erlbaum.

Ziegert, D. I., Kistner, J. A., Castro, R., & Robertson, B. (2001). Longitudinal study of young children's responses to challenging achievement situations. *Child Development, 72*, 609–624.

Ziegler, S. G. (1987). Effects of stimulus cueing on the acquisition of groundstrokes by beginning tennis players. *Journal of Applied Behavior Analysis, 20*, 405–411.

Zigler, E. F., & Finn-Stevenson, M. (1992). Applied developmental psychology. In M. H. Bornstein & M. E. Lamb (Eds.), *Developmental psychology: An advanced textbook*. Mahwah, NJ: Erlbaum.

Zigmond, N., Jenkins, J., Fuchs, L. S., Deno, S., Fuchs, D., Baker, J. N., Jenkins, L., & Couthino, M. (1995, March). Special education in restructured schools: Findings from three multi-year studies. *Phi Delta Kappan*, 531–540.

Zimmerman, B. J. (1998). Developing self-fulfilling cycles of academic regulation: An analysis of exemplary instructional models. In D. H. Schunk & B. J. Zimmerman (Eds.), *Self-regulated learning: From teaching to self-reflective practice* (pp. 1–19). New York: Guilford Press.

Zimmerman, B. J. (2004). Sociocultural influence and students' development of academic self-regulation: A social-cognitive perspective. In D. M. McInerney & S. Van Etten (Eds.), *Big theories revisited* (pp. 139–164). Greenwich, CT: Information Age.

Zimmerman, B. J., Bandura, A., & Martinez-Pons, M. (1992). Self-motivation for academic attainment: The role of self-efficacy beliefs and personal goal setting. *American Educational Research Journal, 29*, 663–676.

Zimmerman, B. J., & Campillo, M. (2003). Motivating self-regulated problem solvers. In J. E. Davidson & R. J. Sternberg (Eds.), *The psychology of problem solving* (pp. 233–262). Cambridge, England: Cambridge University Press.

Zimmerman, B. J., & Didenedetto, M. K. (2008). Mastery learning and assessment: Implications for students and teachers in an era of high-stakes testing. *Psychology in the Schools, 45*, 206–216.

Zimmerman, B. J., & Kitsantas, A. (1999). Acquiring writing revision skill: Shifting from process to outcome self-regulatory goals. *Journal of Educational Psychology, 91*, 241–250.

Zimmerman, B. J., & Kitsantas, A. (2005). The hidden dimension of personal competence: Self-regulated learning and practice. In A. J. Elliot & C. S. Dweck (Eds.), *Handbook of competence and motivation* (pp. 509–526). New York: Guilford Press.

Zimmerman, B. J., & Risemberg, R. (1997). Self-regulatory dimensions of academic learning and motivation. In G. D. Phye (Ed.), *Handbook of academic learning: Construction of knowledge*. San Diego, CA: Academic Press.

Zimmerman, B. J., & Schunk, D. H. (2003). Albert Bandura: The scholar and his contributions to educational psychology. In B. J. Zimmerman & D. H. Schunk (Eds.), *Educational psychology: A century of contributions* (pp. 431–457). Mahwah, NJ: Erlbaum.

Zimmerman, B. J., & Schunk, D. H. (2004). Self-regulating intellectual processes and outcomes; A social cognitive perspective. In D. Y. Dai & R. J. Sternberg (Eds.), *Motivation, emotion, and cognition: Integrative perspectives on intellectual functioning and development* (pp. 323–349). Mahwah, NJ: Erlbaum.

Zirpoli, T. J., & Melloy, K. J. (2001). *Behavior management: Applications for teachers*. Upper Saddle River, NJ: Merrill/Prentice Hall.

Zohar, A., & Aharon-Kraversky, S. (2005). Exploring the effects of cognitive conflict and direct teaching for students of different academic levels. *Journal of Research in Science Teaching, 42*, 829–855.

Zook, K. B. (1991). Effects of analogical processes on learning and misrepresentation. *Educational Psychology Review, 3*, 41–72.

Zook, K. B., & Di Vesta, F. J. (1991). Instructional analogies and conceptual misrepresentations. *Journal of Educational Psychology, 83*, 246–252.

Zwick, R., & Sklar, J. C. (2005). Predicting college grades and degree completion using high school grades and SAT scores: The role of student ethnicity and first language. *American Educational Research Journal, 42*, 439–464.

Name Index

Subject Index

Photo Credits

p. xxiv, istockphoto.com; p. 3, Frank Siteman; p. 9, Anthony Magnacca/Merrill Education; p. 18, istockphoto.com; p. 21, Jeff Greenberg/PhotoEdit; p. 49, Comstock RF; p. 54, The Gazette Laura Schmitt/AP Images; p. 60, istockphoto.com; p. 62, Lori Whitley/Merrill Education; p. 65, Anthony Magnacca/Merrill Education; p. 88, Susan Burger p. 99, Jeff Greenberg/PhotoEdit Inc.; p. 102, Bob Daemmrich Photography; p. 109, Jim Carter/Photo Researchers; p. 111, Michael Newman/PhotoEdit; p. 123, Lon C. Diehl/PhotoEdit; p. 129, Gregory G. Dimijian/Photo Researchers; p. 131, Susan Burger; p. 132, Bob Daemmrich/The Image Works; p. 136, Patrick White/Merrill Education; p. 138, David Young-Wolff/PhotoEdit ; p. 142, Mary Kate Denny/Stone/Getty Images; p. 156, Richard Hutchings/PhotoEdit ; p. 163, Bob Daemmrich Photography; p. 168, Richard Hutchings/PhotoEdit; p. 170, Susan Burger; p. 173, Russell Curtis/Photo Researchers; p. 178, Lindfors Photography; p. 208, Susan Burger; p. 209, Jeff Greenberg/PhotoEdit; p. 216, Photos To Go; p. 221, Bob Daemmrich/The Image Works; p. 229, Comstock RF; p. 241, Bob Daemmrich Photography; p. 248, Elizabeth Crews/The Image Works; p. 255, Patrick White/Merrill Education; p. 256, Bob Daemmrich Photography; p. 265, Susan Burger; p. 277, Stockbyte/Getty Images RF; p. 284, Bob Daemmrich Photography; p. 291, Susan Burger; p. 304, Susan Burger; p. 310, Ellen Senisi; p. 310, Tom Watson/Merrill Education; p. 313, Ellen Senisi; p. 322, Frank Siteman; p. 324, David Mager/Pearson Learning Photo Studio; p. 327, Scott Cunningham/Merrill Education; p. 336, Ellen Senisi; p. 339, Jupiter Images RF; p. 349, Anthony Magnacca/Merrill Education; p. 360, Bill Aron/PhotoEdit; p. 369, Bob Daemmrich Photography; p. 373, Photos To Go; p. 382, Ellen Senisi; p. 388, Will Hart/PhotoEdit; p. 393, Ellen Senisi/The Image Works; p. 405, Bob Daemmrich Photography; p. 412, Bob Daemmrich Photography; p. 428, Elizabeth Crews Photography; p. 439, Frank Siteman; p. 444, Will Hart/PhotoEdit; p. 447, Scott Cunningham/Merrill Education; p. 458, David Young-Wolff/PhotoEdit; p. 461, Will Hart/PhotoEdit; p. 466, Scott Cunningham/Merrill Education; p. 471, Scott Cunningham/Merrill Education; p. 476, Susan Burger; p. 482, Nancy Sheehan; p. 488, Frank Siteman; p. 502, Bob Daemmrich Photography; p. 506 (l), Bob Daemmrich Photography; p. 506 (r), Bob Daemmrich/PhotoEdit; p. 513, Bob Daemmrich Photography; p. 520, Will & Deni McIntyre/Photo Researchers; p. 527, Anthony Magnacca/Merrill Education; p. 531, Scott Cunningham/Merrill Education; p. 535, Gabe Palmer/Corbis; p. 545, Will Hart/PhotoEdit; p. 466, Scott Cunningham/Merrill Education; p. 552, Bob Daemmrich Photography; p. 571, Scott Cunningham/Merrill Education; p. 578, Bob Daemmrich Photography; p. 580, Rex Interstock/Stock Connection.